DESTINATION FLORIDA

The beaches that outline the Florida peninsula are legendary the world over. Long, wide, straight, and surf-pounded on the east coast, they're powder-soft, pure-white, and gently washed by often-azure waters of the Gulf of Mexico on the west. Resorts come in all shapes and sizes—tall and glitzy, green and sprawling. Golf courses splash the flat landscape with acres of green. And theme parks thrive, complete with some of the highest, wildest, and fastest roller coasters around. In other words, fun in the sun is high art in Florida. But stray a few miles from your air-conditioned hotel room and you might glimpse the land that welcomed sponge divers from Greece, cigar makers from Cuba, and boat people from Haiti. Cattle ranches and horse farms reach north and east long, empty miles from the border of Walt Disney World. And as glittering, high-energy Miami anchors the south with a Latin beat, rockets tower over the east coast, and red-soil hills and sleepy Southern villages crowd the Georgia border to the north. Every corner of Florida richly rewards those who take the time to get to know it better. Have a fabulous trip!

Karen Cure, Editorial Director

CONTENTS

Fodor's 04

FLORIDA

Where to Stay and Eat
for All Budgets

Must-See Sights
and Local Secrets

Ratings You Can Trust

Fodor's Travel Publications
www.fodors.com

...kland

FODOR'S FLORIDA 2004
Editor: Paul Eisenberg

Editorial Production: David Downing
Editorial Contributors: Nancy Orr Athnos, David Downing, Kathy Foster, Lynne Helm, Jennie Hess, Satu Hummasti, Diane Marshall, Karen Schlesinger, Chelle Koster Walton
Maps: David Lindroth *cartographer;* Bob Blake and Rebecca Baer, *map editors*
Design: Fabrizio La Rocca, *creative director;* Guido Caroti, *art director;* Melanie Marin, *senior picture editor*
Production/Manufacturing: Robert B. Shields
Cover Photo: Len Kaufman

COPYRIGHT

SPECIAL SALES

Fodor's Travel Publications are available at special discounts for bulk purchases for sales promotions or premiums. Special editions, including personalized covers, excerpts of existing guides, and corporate imprints, can be created in large quantities for special needs. For more information, contact your local bookseller or write to Special Markets, Fodor's Travel Publications, 1745 Broadway, New York, NY 10019. Inquiries from Canada should be directed to your local Canadian bookseller or sent to Random House of Canada, Ltd., Marketing Department, 2775 Matheson Boulevard East, Mississauga, Ontario L4W 4P7. Inquiries from the United Kingdom s ould be sent to Fodor's Travel Publications, 20 Vauxhall Bridge Road, London SW1V 2SA, England.

AN IMPORTANT TIP & AN INVITATION

Although all prices, opening times, and other details in this book are based on information supplied to us at press time, changes occur all the time in the travel world, and Fodor's cannot accept responsibility for facts that become outdated or for inadvertent errors or omissions. So **always confirm information when it matters,** especially if you're making a detour to visit a specific place. Your experiences—positive and negative—matter to us. If we have missed or misstated something, **please write to us.** We follow up on all suggestions. Contact the Florida editor at editors@fodors.com or c/o Fodor's at 1745 Broadway, New York, NY 10019.

ON THE ROAD WITH FODOR'S

A trip takes you out of yourself. Concerns of life at home completely disappear, driven away by more immediate thoughts—about, say, what marvels will beguile the next day, or where you'll have dinner. That's where Fodor's comes in. We make sure that you know all your options, so that you don't miss something that's around the next bend just because you didn't know it was there. Because the best memories of your trip might well have nothing to do with what you came to Florida to see, we guide you to sights large and small all over the region. You might set out to laze on the beach, but back at home you find yourself unable to forget exploring the historic Spanish fort in St. Augustine or celebrating the sunset in Key West. With Fodor's at your side, serendipitous discoveries are never far away.

Our success in showing you every corner of the Sunshine State is a credit to our extraordinary writers. Although there's no substitute for travel advice from a good friend who knows your style, our contributors are the next best thing—the kind of people you would poll for travel advice if you knew them.

Nancy Orr Athnos has more than 20 years experience in the publishing industry and spent 12 years at *Southern Living* magazine before starting her own freelance business in 1996. She lives in Northeast Florida and stays busy writing for local and regional publications, as well as designing Web sites for small businesses.

Florida-raised **David Downing,** a full-time Fodor's staffer, is convinced that the Panhandle is the most wonderfully enigmatic region in the Sunshine State. The editor of Fodor's/Compass American *Florida,* Downing has been featured on The Travel Channel, and his writing appears on fodors.com and on *New York Times* on the Web.

Travel writer **Kathy Foster** has explored almost every spot from Miami to the Keys via bicycle. When not biking, she's at work as an editor for the *Miami Herald*'s feature section.

After being hired sight unseen by a South Florida newspaper, Fort Lauderdale–based freelance travel writer **Lynne Helm** arrived from the Midwest anticipating a couple years of palm-fringed fun. More than a quarter century later, she's still enamored by South Florida's sun-drenched charms.

Jennie Hess is a travel and feature writer based in Orlando and is the author of Fodor's *Around Orlando with Kids.* A former newspaper journalist, Hess was a publicist for Walt Disney World Resort from 1988 through 1999. Today, she enjoys sharing the "inside scoop" on Orlando with visitors—including insights gleaned from her husband and two sons.

Intrepid traveler and intrepid shopper **Diane Marshall** was formerly editor of Travel Holiday magazine and the newsletter "The Savvy Shopper: The Traveler's Guide to Shopping Around the World." From her home in the Keys, she has written for numerous travel guides, newspapers, magazines, and on-line services.

Freelance writer **Karen Schlesinger** has been exploring Florida for more than a decade and currently resides in the sleepy seaside town of Ocean Ridge. She enjoys writing about what's hip and haute in South Florida, contributing frequently to local newspapers and magazines, Web sites, and books. For this edition of Fodor's *Florida,* she updated the Miami shopping section as well as the Palm Beach chapter.

From her home of more than 20 years on Sanibel Island, **Chelle Koster Walton** has written and contributed to ten guidebooks—two of which won Lowell Thomas Awards—and written magazine articles for *FamilyFun, Caribbean Travel & Life, National Geographic Traveler, Arthur Frommer's Budget Travel, Endless Vacation,* the *New York Post,* and other print and electronic media. Walton is cofounder of www.guidebookwriters.com and a member of the Society of American Travel Writers.

You can rest assured that you're in good hands—and that no property mentioned in the book has paid to be included. Each has been selected strictly on its merits, as the best of its type in its price range.

ABOUT THIS BOOK

There's no doubt that the best source for travel advice is a like-minded friend who's just been where you're headed. But with or without that friend, you'll have a better trip with a Fodor's guide in hand. Once you've learned to find your way around its pages, you'll be in great shape to find your way around your destination.

SELECTION

Our goal is to cover the best properties, sights, and activities in their category, as well as the most interesting communities to visit. We make a point of including local food-lovers' hot spots as well as neighborhood options, and we avoid all that's touristy unless it's really worth your time. You can go on the assumption that everything you read about in this book is recommended wholeheartedly by our writers and editors. Flip to On the Road with Fodor's to learn more about who they are. It goes without saying that no property mentioned in the book has paid to be included.

RATINGS

Fodor's Choice denote sights and properties that our editors and writers consider the very best in the area covered by the entire book. These, the best of the best, are listed in the Fodor's Choice section in the front of the book. Black stars ★ highlight the sights and properties we deem Highly Recommended, the don't-miss sights within any region. Fodor's Choice and Highly Recommended options in each region are usually listed on the title page of the chapter covering that region. Use the index to find complete descriptions. In cities, sights pinpointed with numbered map bullets ❶ in the margins tend to be more important than those without bullets.

SPECIAL SPOTS

Pleasures & Pastimes focuses on types of experiences that reveal the spirit of the destination. Watch for Off the Beaten Path sights. Some are out of the way, some are quirky, and all are worth your while. If the munchies hit while you're exploring, look for Need a Break? suggestions.

TIME IT RIGHT

Wondering when to go? Check On the Calendar up front and chapters' Timing sections for weather and crowd overviews and best days and times to visit.

SEE IT ALL

Use Fodor's exclusive Great Itineraries as a model for your trip. (For a good overview of the entire destination, follow those that begin the book, or mix regional itineraries from several chapters.) In cities, Good Walks guide you to important sights in each neighborhood; ☞ indicates the starting points of walks and itineraries in the text and on the map.

BUDGET WELL

Hotel and restaurant price categories from ¢ to $$$$ are defined in the opening pages of each chapter—expect to find a balanced selection for every budget. For attractions, we always give standard adult admission fees; reductions are usually available for children, students, and senior citizens. Look in Discounts & Deals in Smart Travel Tips for information on destination-wide ticket schemes.

BASIC INFO

Smart Travel Tips lists travel essentials for the entire area covered by the book; city- and region-specific basics end each chapter. To find the best way to get around, see the transportation section; see individual modes of travel ("By Car," "By Train") for details. We assume you'll check Web sites or call for particulars.

ON THE MAPS	Maps throughout the book show you what's where and help you find your way around. Black and orange numbered bullets ❶❶ in the text correlate to bullets on maps.
BACKGROUND	In general, we give background information within the chapters in the course of explaining sights as well as in CloseUp boxes and in Understanding Florida at the end of the book. To get in the mood, review the suggestions in Books & Movies. The glossary can be invaluable.
FIND IT FAST	Within the book, chapters are arranged regionally. Chapters are divided into smaller regions, within which towns are covered in logical geographical order; attractive routes and interesting places between towns are flagged as En Route. Heads at the top of each page help you find what you need within a chapter.
DON'T FORGET	Restaurants are open for lunch and dinner daily unless we state otherwise; we mention dress only when there's a specific requirement and reservations only when they're essential or not accepted—it's always best to book ahead. Hotels have private baths, phone, TVs, and air-conditioning and operate on the European Plan (a.k.a. EP, meaning without meals). We always list facilities but not whether you'll be charged extra to use them, so when pricing accommodations, find out what's included.
SYMBOLS	

Many Listings
- ★ Fodor's Choice
- ★ Highly recommended
- ✉ Physical address
- ✛ Directions
- ✍ Mailing address
- ☎ Telephone
- 🖷 Fax
- ⊕ On the Web
- ✎ E-mail
- 🎟 Admission fee
- ◷ Open/closed times
- ⚑ Start of walk/itinerary
- Ⓜ Metro stations
- ▭ Credit cards

Outdoors
- ⛳ Golf
- ⛺ Camping

Hotels & Restaurants
- 🏨 Hotel
- 🛏 Number of rooms
- ⚘ Facilities
- �𝄇 Meal plans
- ✕ Restaurant
- ⚘ Reservations
- 🏛 Dress code
- ⊠ Smoking
- ⚐ BYOB
- ✕🏨 Hotel with restaurant that warrants a visit

Other
- ☺ Family-friendly
- 🛈 Contact information
- ⇨ See also
- ✉ Branch address
- ☞ Take note

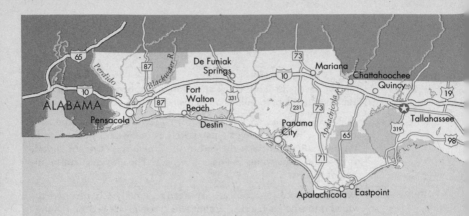

Gulf of Mexico

Florida

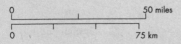

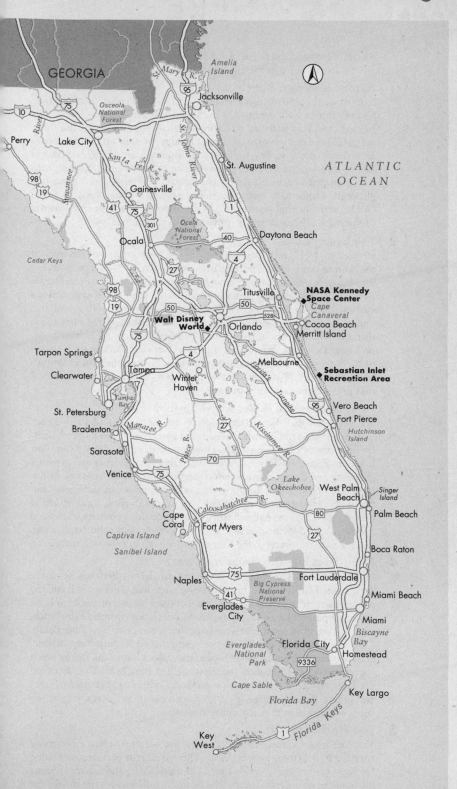

WHAT'S WHERE

These thumbnail sketches of various regions and metro areas should help you find your place in the Sunshine State:

(1) Miami & Miami Beach

Almost at the end of the line on Florida's east coast, Miami-Dade County throbs with energy. On the mainland is Miami itself, Florida's biggest city. This gateway to Latin America overflows with the food, language, and culture of many ethnic groups, most notably Cuban emigrés. Across Biscayne Bay, to the east, is Miami's island neighbor, Miami Beach. Its boutique Art Deco hotels and giant luxury resorts, along with a rejuvenated beach and café scene, attract wanna-bes and bona fide glitterati. Other tony and chic towns around Miami, such as Coral Gables and Coconut Grove, add to the allure of this happening corner of the state, while suburban sprawl fills in relentlessly.

(2) The Everglades

Created in 1947, this national park in the southernmost extremity of the peninsula preserves a portion of the slow-moving "River of Grass"— a 50-mi-wide stream flowing through marshy grassland en route to Florida Bay. The Everglades are actually much larger than the area contained within the national park. Nevertheless, most people who visit this unique ecosystem will do so within park boundaries via only a few roads that access its western, northern, and southeastern sections. Not far away, on Florida's southeastern tip, is Biscayne National Park, a park that is 96% underwater and that contains the northern extremities of Florida's living coral reefs. Between the two parks is a corridor of "civilization" that provides motels and fast food.

(3) Fort Lauderdale & Broward County

Wedged between Miami-Dade County to the south and Palm Beach County to the north, Broward County has as its hub the canal-laced, boat-friendly city of Fort Lauderdale. Downtown along the New River, Fort Lauderdale has forged a new arts and entertainment district as well as trendy shopping and dining districts, which are matched on the coast by its unobstructed beachfront. To the north and south lie ocean-side communities with varying amounts of view-blocking high-rises, modest family motels, fishing piers, natural areas, and beach-side promenades. Inland are the Western-style town of Davie, that ever-present suburban sprawl, and the eastern fringes of the Everglades (though not the national park).

(4) Palm Beach & the Treasure Coast

North of Broward, in Palm Beach County, are the northern reaches of the aptly named Gold Coast—noted for its golden sun, golden sand, and the golden bank accounts of many of the people who live or vacation here. The centerpiece of tourism is oh-so-ritzy Mediterranean-inspired Palm Beach, while the center of commerce is the larger but lower-crust West Palm Beach. This mainland stepsister has of late strengthened its corporate, artistic, and entertainment life, however. Sophisticated Boca Raton and Delray Beach round out county highlights. The coast north of Palm Beach County, called the Treasure Coast, is also worth exploring. Comprising Martin, St. Lucie, and Indian River counties, it's dotted with nature preserves, fishing villages, and towns with active cultural scenes.

(5) The Florida Keys

This slender necklace of landfalls off the southern tip of Florida is strung together by a 110-mi-long highway. Though all part of Monroe County, the Keys are generally divided into Upper, Middle, and Lower sections for the sake of differentiation. The further south you go, the slower the pace of life seems to flow. The Keys are at once a huge traffic jam, a rowdy honky-tonk, an angler's and diver's paradise (there are many living coral reefs offshore), and a hideaway for those eager to "get away from it all"—temporarily or permanently. The Keys' main city, Key West, is a funky town that embraces its old-time multicultural and countercultural charm while opening itself to an onslaught of newer, more commercial tourism.

⑥ Walt Disney World® & the Orlando Area

When Walt Disney chose 28,000 acres in Central Florida as the site of his eastern Disneyland, he forever changed the face of a cattle-and-citrus town called Orlando. Today Disney isn't the only show in town: Universal Orlando, SeaWorld, and various smaller attractions give Mickey a run for his money. It's easy to spend weeks—and lots of cash—in these artificial worlds.

⑦ The Tampa Bay Area

As on the Atlantic, much of the Gulf Coast is known for its barrier-island beaches, and this central section is no exception. At its heart is Tampa Bay itself, with the cities of Tampa and St. Petersburg staring eyeball to eyeball at each other across the water. Tampa is a bustling commercial city with a significant Cuban district, while St. Pete, a peninsula between bay and gulf, is known for its string of beach communities. Following the coast north on its way to its westward bend, you'll find a much less developed area, dotted with fishing towns and natural areas renowned for manatees and other wildlife. South of the bay, the barrier-island-flanked resorts continue, including the culturally vibrant city of Sarasota.

⑧ Southwest Florida

Between the southern end of Tampa Bay and the northern reaches of the Everglades, the lower gulf coast is another region that serves up what Florida is famous for: a subtropical climate; soft, sandy beaches (some a treasure trove of shells); golf and tennis; and pockets of little-touched Florida beauty—from cypress swamps to mangrove islets. Development is much more recent here than on the east coast, making some of it more informed—there's generally better beach access, for example—and some of it just newer. Resort communities include upscale Naples, often considered the Palm Beach of the gulf coast, and Fort Myers and its nearby barrier islands, Sanibel and Captiva.

⑨ The Panhandle

With its magnolias, live oaks, and loblolly pines, northwest Florida has more in common with the Deep South than with the Florida of the Everglades. Even the high season is different: by May, when activities are winding down south of Tampa, the Panhandle is just gearing up. The fabulous beaches, however, are a constant. Perdido Key State Recreation Area, St. Joseph Peninsula State Park, and St. George Island State Park are considered by many to be some of the best beaches in the country. Tallahassee is flavored by the state government, Pensacola has the feel of the historic old port town that it is, and the Air Force maintains a significant presence around Fort Walton Beach.

⑩ Northeast Florida

The northeast corner of the state is an area of remarkable diversity. Only a short drive separates the more than 400-year-old town of St. Augustine from the spring-break and auto-racing mecca of Daytona Beach. Along the entire northeast coast are slender barrier islands—some relatively pristine, all with fabulous beaches. Inland is the university town of Gainesville, Ocala horse country, and the backwoods scrub made famous by Marjorie Kinnan Rawlings.

GREAT ITINERARIES

Florida is far more diverse than you might realize. Sure there are the world-class theme parks, with the biggest, most sparkling rides on the globe. And if you're the average visitor, that's one of the things you come for. But if you've got time to stop and smell the orange blossoms, there's a lot more here. The state is full of natural wonders and cultural experiences from Latin-American rhythms to hip, movie-star chic. If you have at least a week, plan on flying to Orlando—an ideal gateway because of its central location (which is why Walt Disney chose it) and its abundance of direct flights.

Highlights of Florida
11 to 15 days

ORLANDO

3 or 4 days. You'll want to budget at least two days for Disney offerings, including the newest of the parks, Disney's Animal Kingdom. If you've got youngsters, a day at the Magic Kingdom, including a character breakfast, is a must. If you love thrill rides, have teenagers in tow, or are a Dr. Seuss fan, Universal's Islands of Adventure is worth at least a day as is movie-theme Universal Studios. The charming, water-based SeaWorld Orlando—with Discovery Cove—and dozens of other, smaller amusements could easily take up a week; pick the attractions most interesting to you and then hit the road. ⇨ Disney Theme Parks and Other Theme Parks *in* Chapter 6.

TAMPA & ST. PETERSBURG

1 day. There are two must-dos when you visit these Gulf Coast cities on a 5-mi-wide bay: get a taste of Latin culture in Tampa's Ybor City (originally a Cuban cigar-manufacturing district and now a neighborhood abounding in culinary spots and hot nightclubs), and watch a clas-

sic Florida sunset at St. Pete Beach. ⇨ Tampa and St. Petersburg *in* Chapter 7.

SANIBEL & CAPTIVA

1 day. Lee County has wonderful barrier islands, including charming Sanibel, home of the J. N. "Ding" Darling National Wildlife Refuge, where you can canoe through a rich mangrove swamp. The beaches of Sanibel and its neighbor, Captiva, have exceptional shelling, and you may see loggerhead turtles and other extraordinary wildlife. ⇨ The Coastal Islands *in* Chapter 8.

NAPLES & MARCO ISLAND

1 day. Naples, a sophisticated town 40 minutes south of Sanibel, backs up to the western Everglades. If you don't have time to access the Glades from the east, you may want to take a swamp buggy or airboat tour from Naples or Marco Island. Marco, which has great beaches and beachfront hotels, makes a good overnight stop because of a "shortcut" to Key West—a three-hour ferry as opposed to a six-hour drive. ⇨ Naples Area *in* Chapter 8.

THE FLORIDA KEYS

2 or 3 days. Key West, 100 mi by boat or bridge-laden highway from the mainland, has a classic island feel, with a laid-back culture and a quaint downtown dotted with famous watering holes. Clear waters make a snorkel or dive trip a must. It's also great fun to tour the island by moped, which you can rent at numerous spots downtown. On your way to Miami through the Middle and Upper Keys, make sure to leave time for a stop at Bahia Honda State Park, one of the loveliest spots in Florida. ⇨ The Florida Keys *in* Chapter 5.

MIAMI & MIAMI BEACH

2 or 3 days. Miami has its own spin on the urban experience, a cultural confluence of Latin vibes and subtropical hedonism mixed with an eco-

nomic vibrancy based on its status as the U.S. gateway to Latin America; to envelop yourself in Latin culture, stop in the Calle Ocho district of Little Havana. Miami is considered hot by most anyone in this hemisphere who is chic or wants to be. In Miami Beach's South Beach you're as likely to see Madonna or Elton John as you are in Hollywood. The protected natural areas of Everglades and Biscayne National Park are only 45 mi southwest. ⇨ Exploring Miami and Miami Beach *in* Chapter 1 and Everglades National Park *in* Chapter 2.

PALM BEACH

1 or 2 days. If you feel at home at a polo match and don't shop at anyplace less upscale than Neiman-Marcus, Palm Beach is for you. It's the richest town, per capita, in Florida and one of the world's playgrounds for the extremely wealthy. And the rich don't choose shabby places. The sun-drenched beaches here are as impressive as the shopping and dining along Worth Avenue and the luxurious hotels, including the famous Breakers. ⇨ Palm Beach *in* Chapter 4.

Natural Wonders
5 to 8 days

Having no appreciable winter has done more for Florida than make it a good place for theme parks and golf courses. The constant spring-summer seasonal mix that has prevailed for 100 millennia or so has created beautiful forests and wetlands. If you have a map, a car, and several days you can see a side of nature here you won't see elsewhere.

BISCAYNE NATIONAL PARK & KEY LARGO

1 or 2 days. At Biscayne National Park, 30 minutes south of Miami, you can see living coral reefs by snorkeling, scuba diving, or taking a glass-bottom boat. Perhaps the best snorkeling and scuba

Jacksonville

Gainesville

250 mi

75

Wekiva Springs SP

Orlando

Walt Disney World

FLORIDA'S TNPK.

4

80 mi

Tampa

15 mi

St. Petersburg

275

75

Sarasota

Port Charlotte

120 mi

75

Gulf of Mexico

Fort Myers

Captiva Island

867

Sanibel Island

16 mi

46 mi

75

Naples

951

15 mi

Marco Island

80 mi

Fort Pierce

FLORIDA'S TNPK.

110 mi

ATLANTIC OCEAN

Lake Okeechobee

Palm Beach

95

50 mi

41

95

Miami Beach

Miami

1

Everglades NP

50 mi

Biscayne NP

905

John Pennekamp Coral Reef SP

Key Largo

Key West

90 mi

1

Bahia Honda SP

diving, however, is another hour south at magnificent John Pennekamp Coral Reef State Park, near Key Largo, the northernmost of the Florida Keys. ⇨ Biscayne National Park *in* Chapter 2 and the Upper Keys *in* Chapter 5.

THE EVERGLADES
1 or 2 days. For nature lovers, going to Florida and not seeing the Everglades would be like going to Arizona and not seeing the Grand Canyon. Miami is a great gateway to America's biggest protected wetland, and you can try anything from self-guided canoe tours (probably not a good idea for first-timers) to swamp buggy, airboat, and even airplane tours, offered by several parks and commercial operators on U.S. 41 west of Miami. ⇨ Ev-

erglades National Park *in* Chapter 2.

ORLANDO AREA
1 or 2 days. Wekiva Springs State Park is 45 minutes from Disney but may as well be on another planet. Here you'll

find the still unspoiled, undeveloped, and un-neoned Florida, the way it was before the civilized world laid a hand on it. ⇨ Exploring Walt Disney World and the Orlando Area A to Z *in* Chapter 6.

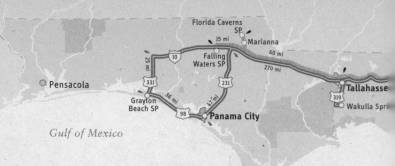

TALLAHASSEE AREA

2 days. Within an hour of Florida's capital you'll find a variety of natural treasures. Florida Caverns State Park, near Marianna, offers guided tours of a huge underground cave, where you can see Carlsbad-like formations, including stalactites and stalagmites, along with thousands of critters that live in the dark. A short drive west, near Chipley, Falling Waters State Park contains Florida's largest, and perhaps only, waterfall. The falls alone wouldn't warrant a trip to the Panhandle, but they make a nice side trip from Florida Caverns. Wild and exotic Wakulla Springs State Park, 15 mi south of Tallahassee, has glass-bottom boat tours of impressive junglelike waterways. You'll see incredible wildlife, including the ubiquitous and much-loved alligator. ⇨ Inland and Across the Panhandle and Tallahassee *in* Chapter 9.

Great Beaches
6 to 10 days

With more than 1,200 mi of coastline, it's obvious that Florida has many beaches; and the variety of beaches—secluded beaches, people-watcher beaches, family beaches—is equaled only by the variety of reasons to visit them. You can marvel at amazing sand or fabulous sunsets, undertake countless waterborne activities, or reenergize after more tiring pursuits, since many Florida beaches are close to other popular attractions.

MIAMI AREA

1 or 2 days. Beaches in the Miami area are not unlike some Los Angeles–area beaches, with lots of male and female model would-bes rollerblading along walkways adjacent to the strand. In South Beach, a vibrant café and nightclub district faces the sand. Ten miles north at Haulover Beach you'll find Florida's only legal nude beach. (Signs mark the area.) Or try the sands at Key Biscayne's Bill Baggs Cape Florida State Recreation Area, a lovely park with a lighthouse and a great view of the Miami skyline. Along with their particular "scene," Miami's beaches offer surprisingly clear aqua water. ⇨ South Beach–Miami Beach and Virginia Key and Key Biscayne *in* Chapter 1.

DAYTONA BEACH & THE SPACE COAST

1 or 2 days. A sand pail's throw from one another sit one of America's most famous beaches, Daytona Beach, and one of its least spoiled, Canaveral National Seashore. Daytona is one of the few places in the nation where you can drive on the sand, which backs up right on a hotel and nightlife strip that keeps hopping after sundown. Canaveral closes after dark, but by day you can gaze at windswept dunes and the blue Atlantic along 24 mi of beachfront and then visit the adjacent Kennedy Space Center or Merritt Island National Wildlife Refuge. ⇨ Along the Coast *in* Chapter 10.

ST. AUGUSTINE & AMELIA ISLAND

2 days. Heading north, you can relax on St. Augustine Beach or Vilano Beach on Anastasia Island, near historic St. Augustine. North of Jacksonville, Amelia Island has great beaches and the historic town of Fernandina Beach, which is loaded with B&Bs. Sample the wonderful beaches, dunes and facilities at Hannah Park in Jacksonville Beach, or take some time out to explore the St. Augustine Lighthouse, near the beach and with great views of the entire St. Augustine area. ⇨ St. Augustine and Jacksonville to Amelia Island *in* Chapter 10.

THE PANHANDLE

1 or 2 days. The beaches of northwest Florida are justifiably renowned, routinely making the annual best-beaches list of the University of Maryland's Laboratory for Coastal Research. In fact scenic Grayton Beach State Park, one of Florida's prettiest beaches, made the list so consistently that it has essentially been retired from contention. Halfway between Panama City and Pensacola, Grayton Beach has sugar-white sands and aqua waters as clear as you'd find in the Keys or the Bahamas. And that's just one of many fine Panhandle beaches. If you like hotels, nightclubs, and arcades near your beach blanket, visit Panama City Beach, which actively courts spring-break revelers. ⇨ Around Pensacola Bay and the Gulf Coast *in* Chapter 9.

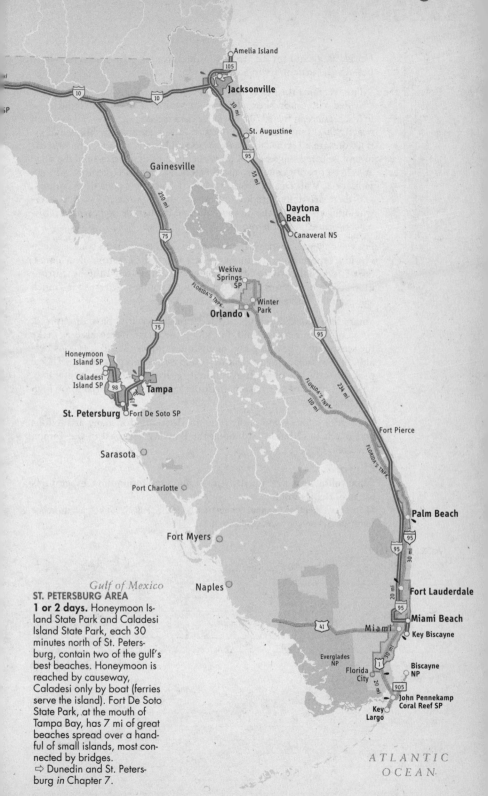

Amelia Island

105

Jacksonville

30 mi

St. Augustine

95

Gainesville

55 mi

250 mi

Daytona
Beach

Canaveral NS

75

Wekiva
Springs
SP

Winter
Park

Orlando

FLORIDA'S TNPK

95

75

Honeymoon
Island SP

Caladesi
Island SP

98

Tampa

St. Petersburg   Fort De Soto SP

234 mi

FLORIDA'S TNPK

110 mi

Sarasota

Fort Pierce

Port Charlotte

FLORIDA'S TNPK

Palm Beach

Fort Myers

95

95

30 mi

20 mi

Fort Lauderdale

Gulf of Mexico

Naples

95

Miami Beach

ST. PETERSBURG AREA

1 or 2 days. Honeymoon Island State Park and Caladesi
Island State Park, each 30
minutes north of St. Petersburg, contain two of the gulf's
best beaches. Honeymoon is
reached by causeway,
Caladesi only by boat (ferries
serve the island). Fort De Soto
State Park, at the mouth of
Tampa Bay, has 7 mi of great
beaches spread over a handful of small islands, most connected by bridges.
⇨ Dunedin and St. Peters-
burg *in Chapter 7.*

41

Miami

Key Biscayne

Everglades
NP

Florida
City

Biscayne
NP

1

20 mi

905

John Pennekamp
Coral Reef SP

Key
Largo

*ATLANTIC
OCEAN*

WHEN TO GO

Florida is a state for all seasons, although most visitors prefer October–April, particularly in South Florida.

Winter remains the height of the tourist season, when South Florida is crowded with "snowbirds" fleeing cold weather in the north. (It did snow in Miami once in the 1970s, but since then the average snowfall has been exactly 00.00 inches.) Hotels, bars, discos, restaurants, shops, and attractions are all crowded. Hollywood and Broadway celebrities appear in sophisticated supper clubs, and other performing artists hold the stage at ballets, operas, concerts, and theaters. From mid-December through January 2, Walt Disney World's Magic Kingdom is lavishly decorated, and there are daily parades and other extravaganzas, as well as overwhelming crowds. In the Jacksonville and Panhandle area, winter is off-season—an excellent bargain.

For the college crowd, spring vacation is still the time to congregate in Florida, especially in Panama City Beach and the Daytona Beach area; Fort Lauderdale, where city officials have refashioned the beachfront more as a family resort, no longer indulges young revelers, so it's much less popular with college students than it once was.

Summer in Florida, as smart budget-minded visitors have discovered, is often hot and very humid, but along the coast, ocean breezes make the season quite bearable and many hotels lower their prices considerably. In the Panhandle and Central Florida, summer is peak season. Theme park lines shrink only after children return to school in September. Large numbers of international visitors keep year-round visitation high at theme parks.

For senior citizens, fall is the time for discounts for many attractions and hotels in Orlando and along the Pinellas Suncoast in the Tampa Bay area.

Climate

What follows are average daily maximum and minimum temperatures for major cities in Florida.

🚩 Forecasts **Weather Channel Connection** ☎ 900/932-8437, 95¢ per minute from a Touch-Tone phone ⊕ www.weather.com.

JACKSONVILLE

Jan.	64F	18C	May	84F	29C	Sept.	86F	30C
	42	6		63	17		69	21
Feb.	67F	19C	June	89F	32C	Oct.	79F	26C
	44	7		69	21		60	16
Mar.	73F	23C	July	91F	33C	Nov.	73F	23C
	50	10		72	22		51	11
Apr.	79F	26C	Aug.	89F	32C	Dec.	66F	19C
	55	13		72	22		44	7

KEY WEST (THE KEYS)

Jan.	76F	24C	May	85F	29C	Sept.	90F	32C
	65	18		74	23		77	25
Feb.	76F	24C	June	88F	31C	Oct.	83F	28C
	67	19		77	25		76	24
Mar.	79F	26C	July	90F	32C	Nov.	79F	26C
	68	20		79	26		70	21
Apr.	81F	27C	Aug.	90F	32C	Dec.	76F	24C
	72	22		79	26		67	19

MIAMI

Jan.	74F	23C	May	83F	28C	Sept.	86F	30C
	63	17		72	22		76	24
Feb.	76F	24C	June	85F	29C	Oct.	83F	28C
	63	17		76	24		72	22
Mar.	77F	25C	July	88F	31C	Nov.	79F	26C
	65	18		76	24		67	19
Apr.	79F	26C	Aug.	88F	31C	Dec.	76F	26C
	68	20		77	25		63	17

ORLANDO

Jan.	70F	21C	May	88F	31C	Sept.	88F	31C
	49	9		67	19		74	23
Feb.	72F	22C	June	90F	32C	Oct.	83F	28C
	54	12		72	22		67	19
Mar.	76F	24C	July	90F	32C	Nov.	76F	24C
	56	13		74	23		58	14
Apr.	81F	27C	Aug.	90F	32C	Dec.	70F	21C
	63	17		74	23		52	11

PANAMA CITY

Jan.	62F	17C	May	83F	28C	Sept.	87F	31C
	39	4		61	16		69	21
Feb.	65F	18C	June	88F	31C	Oct.	80F	27C
	41	5		68	20		55	13
Mar.	71F	22C	July	89F	32C	Nov.	71F	22C
	47	8		71	22		48	9
Apr.	77F	25C	Aug.	89F	32C	Dec.	64F	18C
	53	12		71	22		40	4

TAMPA

Jan.	70F	21C	May	86F	30C	Sept.	89F	32C
	52	11		69	21		74	23
Feb.	72F	22C	June	89F	32C	Oct.	84F	29C
	54	12		74	23		68	20
Mar.	76F	24C	July	90F	32C	Nov.	78F	26C
	59	15		75	24		61	16
Apr.	81F	27C	Aug.	90F	32C	Dec.	72F	22C
	62	17		75	24		55	13

ON THE CALENDAR

Florida really does have seasons, and with them come festivals and events that capture special moments throughout the state. Plan well in advance if you hope to be in town for any of these celebrations.

WINTER	
Dec.	**Monthlong Victorian Seaside Christmas** (☎ 904/277–0717) takes place oceanside on Amelia Island.
	Walt Disney World's Very Merry Christmas Parade in the Magic Kingdom (☎ 407/824–4321) celebrates the season at the Magic Kingdom.
	In mid-December, the **Winterfest Boat Parade** (☎ 954/767–0686 ⊕ www.winterfestparade.com) lights up the Intracoastal Waterway in Fort Lauderdale.
Late Dec.– early Jan.	The **Orange Bowl and Junior Orange Bowl Festival** (☎ 305/371–4600), in the Miami area, are best known for the downtown King Orange Jamboree Parade on December 31 and the Orange Bowl Football Classic at Pro Player Stadium but also include more than 20 youth-oriented events.
	On December 31 in Tampa's Ybor City is the **Outback Bowl Blast** (☎ 813/874–2695), a street festival with live music; the next day some of the nation's best college football teams meet in the Outback Bowl. Also on New Year's Day are the **Florida Citrus Bowl** (☎ 407/423–2476) in Orlando, and the **Gator Bowl** (☎ 904/798–1700) in Jacksonville.
Jan.	Mid-month, **Art Deco Weekend** (☎ 305/672–2014) spotlights Miami Beach's historic district with an art deco street fair along Ocean Drive, a 1930s-style Moon Over Miami Ball, and live entertainment.
	Easterlin Park in Oakland is the setting for the mid-month **South Florida Folk Festival** (☎ 800/785–8924 ⊕ www.southfloridafolkfest.com) with national touring companies, dance and music.
	The **Florida Citrus Festival and Polk County Fair** (☎ 863/292–9810 ⊕ www.citrusfestival.com) in Winter Haven the second half of the month, showcases the citrus harvest with displays and entertainment.
	The **Miami Jazz Festival** (☎ 305/858–8545 ⊕ www.miamijazzfestival.com) usually falls on the third weekend and takes place beneath the stars at the Bayfront Park Amphitheater.
	Martin Luther King Jr. Festivals (☎ 407/246–2221) are celebrated throughout the state.
	The **Everglades Seafood Festival** (☎ 941/695–4100), a month-long celebration of the ocean's bounty, features free entertainment with music, crafts, and seafood each weekend.
	Early in the month, **Polo Season** (☎ 561/793–1440) opens at the Palm Beach Polo and Country Club in West Palm Beach.
	The **Winter Equestrian Festival at International Stadium** (☎ 561/793–5867) begins jumping in Wellington later in the month and continues through mid-March. The festival, which includes 3,500 horses and seven major grand-prix equestrian events, then moves to the **Bob Thomas Equestrian Center** (☎ 813/740–3500) in Tampa through April.

Feb.

More than 300,000 visitors head to Mount Dora the first full weekend in February for the Mount Dora Arts Festival (☎ 352/383–0880 ⊕ www.mountdoracenterforthearts.com), the city's signature event, spotlighting more than 300 artists.

The Florida Strawberry Festival (☎ 813/752–9194 ⊕ www.flstrawberryfestival.com), in Plant City, has celebrated the town's winter harvest for more than six decades with two weeks of country-music stars, rides, exhibits, and strawberry delicacies.

Irish and Scottish crafts, food and beverages, bagpipes and Highland games are the main attractions at the mid-February Celtic Festival (☎ 941/774–3267) at Celebration Gardens–Florida Sports Park in Naples.

The Gasparilla Festival (☎ 813/223–2752 or 888/224–1733 ⊕ www.gasparillapiratefest.com) on the first Saturday of the month, celebrates the legendary pirate's invasion of Tampa with street parades, an art festival, and music.

The Olustee Battle Festival (☎ 396/752–9150 ⊕ www.olusteefestival.com) in Lake City, is the second-largest (Gettysburg has the largest) Civil War reenactment in the nation.

Speed Weeks (☎ 356/254–2700 or 800/854–1234) is a three-week celebration of auto racing that culminates in the famous Daytona 500, at the Daytona International Speedway in Daytona Beach.

The Coconut Grove Art Festival (☎ 305/447–0401) mid-month, is the state's largest.

The Miami Film Festival (☎ 305/348–5555 ⊕ www.miamifilmfestival.com), sponsored by the Film Society of America, is 10 days of international, domestic, and local films.

SPRING

Mar.

Early March brings the Peace River Seafood Festival & Boat Show in Punta Gorda where folks gather along the town's waterfront for arts and crafts, fresh seafood, and a water ski show.

The Sanibel Shell Fair (☎ 941/472–2155), which runs for four days starting the first Thursday of the month, is the largest event of the year on Sanibel Island.

The Azalea Festival (☎ 396/326–4001 ⊕ www.flazaleafest.com) is a beauty pageant, arts-and-crafts show, and parade held in downtown Palatka and Riverfront Park.

Bike Week (☎ 356/255–0981), one of Daytona's biggest annual events, draws 400,000 riders from across the United States for 10 days of races, plus parades and even coleslaw wrestling.

The self-proclaimed world's largest street party, Calle Ocho (☎ 305/644–8888 ⊕ www.carnaval-miami.org) packs 1 million people onto Miami's Southwest Eighth Street for a frenetic day of live Latin music, ethnic food, and massive corporate product giveaways.

	St. Augustine's Rhythm and Ribs Festival (☎ 904/829–5565) spotlights the country's championship barbecuers with cook-offs, special recipes and plenty of southern barbecue.
	SeaFest (☎ 321/459–2200 ⊕ www.seafest.com) in Port Canaveral has loads of fun, sun, and scrumptious seafood.
	Mount Dora's Antique Boat Festival (☎ 352/742–8038), held the fourth weekend in March, is one of the largest in the Southeast, highlighting more than 150 antique, classic, and historic boats.
	Winter Park Sidewalk Arts Festival (☎ 407/672–6390 ⊕ www.wpsaf.org) is one of the Southeast's most prestigious outdoor fine arts festivals and spotlights internationally known artists.
	The Sarasota Jazz Festival (☎ 941/336–1552) is a showcase for well-known musicians from around the world.
	The Lauderdale-by-the-Sea Craft Festival (☎ 954/472–3755) features crafts vendors and live entertainment on the beachfront along Commercial Boulevard and A1A; there's a second festival held in October.
Late Mar.–early Apr.	Springtime Tallahassee (☎ 850/224–5012 ⊕ www.springtimetallahassee.com) is a major cultural, sporting, and culinary event in the capital.
	The Florida Renaissance Festival North (☎ 386/364–4590 or 800/373–6337 ⊕ www.ren-fest.com) fills the Spirit of Suwannee Music Park in Live Oak with hundreds of authentic-looking costumed festival goers each year.
	Nationally recognized performers and local talent entertain flocks of blues lovers during the two day Springing the Blues Festival (☎ 904/249–3972 ⊕ www.springingtheblues.com) at the Jacksonville Beach pavilion in early April.
	A case of the blues also hits Tampa around this time each year. The Tampa Bay Blues Festival (☎ 727/824–6163 ⊕ www.tampabaybluesfest.com), along the city's waterfront, donates all proceeds to three local charity organizations.
	Pensacola gyrates to the sounds of jazz during its annual Pensacola Jazz Fest (☎ 850/433–8382 ⊕ jazzpensacola.com), now in its 20th year.
	Fort Myers adds a touch of Latin to its jazz festival. Latin Jazz Fest IV, Salsa on the River (☎ 941/541–7218 ⊕ www.latinjazzfest.com), celebrates the city's growing Hispanic community with exotic foods, music, and Grammy-award-winning artists.
Apr.	The Delray Affair (☎ 561/278–0424, www.delrayaffair.com), held the weekend following Easter, is Delray Beach's biggest event and includes arts, crafts, and food.
	The Florida Heritage Seafood Festival (☎ 941/747–1998) takes place in Bradenton in early April.
Late Apr.–early May	The Conch Republic Celebration (☎ 305/296–0123 ⊕ www.conchrepublic.com) honors the founding fathers of the Conch Republic, "the small island nation of Key West."

The Sun 'n' Fun Festival (☎ 727/562–4800), held throughout Clearwater, includes an illuminated parade, a "disc golf" tournament, day and nighttime concerts, and kids events.

| May | The Air & Sea Show (☎ 954/527–5600 Ext. 4 ⊕ www.airseashow.com) draws more than 2 million people to the Fort Lauderdale beachfront for performances by big names in aviation, such as the navy's Blue Angels and the air force's Thunderbirds. |

Historic downtown Fernandina Beach, chock-full of Victorian architecture, is the setting for Amelia Island's Isle of Eight Flags Seafood Festival (☎ 904/261–3248 ⊕ www.shrimpfestival.com). Held in early May, the entire historical area is filled with arts and crafts and plenty of seafood.

Nationally recognized Cajun and zydeco performers, the state's largest outdoor dance floor, and 25,000 pounds of crawfish attract both young and old to Fort Lauderdale's stadium for the Cajun Zydeco Crawfish Festival (☎ 954/828–5934) in mid-May.

West Palm Beach celebrates everything under the sun during Sunfest (☎ 407/659–5992 or 800/786–3378 ⊕ www.sunfest.org).

Top-name recording artists draw crowds to Jacksonville's Metro Park for an evening of free entertainment during the Spring Music Fest (☎ 904/630–3690).

Stephen Foster State Park, near the Suwannee River in White Springs, is the gathering spot for the 51st annual Florida Folk Festival (☎ 850/245–6400) in late May, an event featuring nationally recognized performers.

SUMMER

| June | The Miami-Bahamas Goombay Festival (☎ 305/567-1399 ⊕ www.miamigoombay.com), in Miami's Coconut Grove, celebrates the city's Bahamian heritage the first weekend of the month with food, crafts, and street music all day. |

The Billy Bowlegs Pirate Festival (☎ 850/244–8191 or 800/322–3319), in downtown Fort Walton Beach, is a week of activities in memory of a pirate who ruled the area in the late 1700s.

Pensacola celebrates its heritage with Fiesta of Five Flags (☎ 904/433–6512 ⊕ www.fiestaoffiveflags.org), a week-long event featuring treasure hunts, parades, a coronation ball, and concerts.

The Panhandle city of Chipley celebrates its Watermelon Festival (☎ 850/638–6180) the last Saturday of the month; Washington County's largest event features eating and seed-spitting contests and a watermelon auction.

| June–July | Beethoven by the Beach (☎ 954/561–2997), in Fort Lauderdale, features Beethoven's symphonies, chamber pieces, and piano concertos performed by the Florida Philharmonic. |

| July | Cities all over the state celebrate Independence Day with outdoor events and spectacular fireworks displays. Titusville celebrates the |

4th at Sand Point Park with Hometown USA (☎ 321/383–8962), which includes patriotic concerts and a grand fireworks display.

Fort Lauderdale gathers at the beach and Alexander Park for Fourth Along the Coast (☎ 954/761–5813) and Jacksonville's two venues include the beach and downtown's Metro Park where the city gathers for Freedom, Fanfare and Fireworks (☎ 904/630–3690).

Aug.

The Annual Wausau Possum Funday & Parade (☎ 850/638–7888) is held in the Possum Palace, Wausau, the first Saturday in the month in homage to the critter that once sustained the diets of the town's populace.

Cocoa Beach celebrates Cajun culture with food, music, arts, and dance in mid-August with the 7th Annual Fais-Dais-Dos Cajun Festival (☎ 321/632–7445).

FALL

Sept.

The Anniversary of the Founding of St. Augustine (☎ 904/825–1010), also called Days in Spain, commemorates the landing of Pedro Menendez in St. Augustine in 1565. It is held on the seaside grounds of the Mission of Nombre de Dios.

Oct.

The Destin Seafood Festival (☎ 850/837–6241), held the first full weekend in the month, gives you three days to sample smoked amberjack, fried mullet, and shark kebabs.

The Fort Lauderdale International Boat Show (☎ 954/764–7642), the world's largest show based on exhibit size, displays boats of every size, price, and description at the Bahia Mar marina and four other venues.

The Florida Manatee Festival (☎ 352/795–3149), in Crystal River, focuses on both the river and the endangered manatee.

Biketoberfest (☎ 800/854–1234) is highlighted by championship racing at the Daytona International Speedway, the Main Street Rally, concerts, and swap meets that last four days.

The second week of the month Panama City Beach celebrates the Indian Summer Seafood Festival (☎ 800/553–1300 ⊕ www.pcbseafoodfestival.org) with country music and fresh seafood in Aaron Bessant Park.

Boggy Bayou Mullet Festival (☎ 904/678–1615) is a three-day hoedown held the third full weekend in October in celebration of the "Twin Cities," Valparaiso and Niceville, and the famed scavenger fish, the mullet.

The Cedar Key Seafood Festival (☎ 352/543–5600) is held on Main Street in Cedar Key.

The Fall RiverFest Arts Festival (☎ 904/328–8998) takes place downtown along the St. Johns River in Palatka.

Fantasy Fest (☎ 305/296–1817 ⊕ www.fantasyfest.net), in Key West, is a no-holds-barred Halloween costume party, parade, and town fair.

Oct.–Nov.	The Jacksonville Jazz Festival (☎ 904/353–7770 ⊕ www.jaxjazzfest. com) is three days of jazz performances, arts and crafts, and food, plus the Great American Jazz Piano Competition.
	The Fort Lauderdale International Film Festival (☎ 954/760–9898 ⊕ www.fliff.com) showcases three weeks of independent cinema from around the world beginning in late October.
Nov.	The Florida Seafood Festival (☎ 850/653–8011 ⊕ www. floridaseafoodfestival.com) in Apalachicola's Battery Park celebrates the famous oyster harvest, with oyster-shucking-and-consumption contests and parades.
	All eyes look skyward during the Spacecoast Birding & Wildlife Festival (☎ 321/268–5224), formerly Flyway Fest, in Titusville.
	The Miami Book Fair International (☎ 305/237–3032 ⊕ www.mdcc. edu/bookfair), the largest book fair in the United States, is held on the Wolfson campus of Miami-Dade Community College.
	St. Augustine unwraps Christmas a bit early with the Nights of Lights (☎ 904/829–1711). More than 1 million tiny white lights illuminate the historic city beginning in mid-November for 75 days, during which time the city celebrates with historical Christmas events.

PLEASURES & PASTIMES

Beaches
No point in the state is more than 60 miles from salt water. The long, lean peninsula is bordered by a 526-mi Atlantic coast from Fernandina Beach to Key West and a 792-mi coast along the Gulf of Mexico and Florida Bay from Pensacola to Key West. If you were to stretch Florida's convoluted coast in a straight line, it would extend for about 1,800 mi. What's more, if you add in the perimeter of every island surrounded by saltwater, Florida has about 8,500 mi of tidal shoreline—more than any other state except Alaska. Florida's coastline comprises more than 1,000 mi of sand beaches.

Canoeing
The Everglades has areas suitable for flat-water wilderness canoeing. Other popular canoeing rivers include the Blackwater, Econlokahatchee, Juniper, Loxahatchee, Peace, Oklawaha, Suwannee, St. Marys, and Santa Fe. The Florida Department of Environmental Protection provides maps and brochures on 1,550 mi of canoe trails in various parts of the state. Also contact individual national forests, parks, monuments, reserves, and seashores for information on their canoe trails. Local chambers of commerce have information on trails in county parks. The best time to canoe in Florida is winter—the dry season—when you're less likely to get caught in a torrential downpour or become a snack for mosquitoes.

Fishing
Saltwater fishing is plentiful from the Keys all the way up the Atlantic coast to Georgia and up the Gulf Coast to Alabama. Many seaside communities have fishing piers that charge admission to anglers (and usually a lower rate to spectators). These piers generally have a bait-and-tackle shop. It's easy to find a boat-charter service that will take you out into deep water. Some of the best are in the Panhandle, where Destin and Fort Walton Beach have huge fleets. The Keys, too, are dotted with charter services, and Key West has a big sportfishing fleet. Depending on your taste, budget, and needs, you can charter anything from an old wooden craft to a luxurious waterborne palace with state-of-the-art amenities.

Inland there are more than 7,000 fresh-water lakes. The largest—448,000-acre Lake Okeechobee, the third-largest natural lake in the United States—is home to bass, bluegill, speckled perch, and succulent catfish (which the locals call "sharpies"). In addition to the state's many natural fresh-water rivers, South Florida also has an extensive system of flood-control canals. In 1989 scientists found high mercury levels in largemouth bass and warmouth caught in parts of the Everglades and in Palm Beach, Broward, and Dade counties and warned against eating fish from those areas. Those warnings remain in effect, and warnings have been extended to parts of northern Florida.

Golf
Except in the heart of the Everglades, you'll never be far from one of Florida's more than 1,100 golf courses. Palm Beach County and Naples are the state's leading golf locales, and the PGA, LPGA, and National Golf Foundation all have headquarters in the state. And just north of St. Augustine are World Golf Village and the World Golf Hall of Fame. Many of the best golf courses in Florida allow you to play without being members or hotel guests. You should reserve tee times in advance, especially in winter. Ask about golf reservations when you make your lodging reservations.

Key Lime Time

Almost every Florida restaurant claims to make the best key lime pie. Traditional key lime pie is yellow, not green, with an old-fashioned graham cracker crust and meringue top. Some restaurants serve their key lime pie with a pastry crust; most substitute whipped cream for the more temperamental meringue. Each pie will be a little different. Try several.

Even if you eat dessert first—this is, after all, your vacation—save room for a meal. Florida's cuisine changes as you move across the state, depending upon on who settled the area and who now operates the restaurants. You can expect seafood to be a staple on nearly every menu, however, with greater variety on the coasts, and catfish, frogs' legs, and gator tail to be popular around inland lakes and at Miccosukee restaurants along the Tamiami Trail. South Florida has a diverse assortment of Latin American restaurants and it's also easy to find island specialties born of the Bahamas, Haiti, and Jamaica. A fusion of tropical, Continental, and nouvelle cuisine—some call it Floribbean—has gained widespread popularity. It draws on exotic fruits, spices, and fresh seafood. The influence of earlier Hispanic settlements remains in Key West and Tampa's Ybor City.

Natural Areas

Although Florida is the fourth-most-populous state in the nation, more than 10 million acres of public and private recreation facilities are set aside in national forests, parks, monuments, reserves, and seashores; state forests and parks; county parks; and nature preserves owned and managed by private conservation groups. All told, Florida now has some 3,500 mi of trails, encompassing 1,550 mi of canoe and kayak trails, about 670 mi for bicycling and other uses, 900 mi exclusively for hiking, about 350 exclusively for equestrian use, plus some 30 mi of purely interpretive trails, chiefly in state parks. An active greenways development plan seeks to protect wildlife habitat as much as foster recreation.

Scuba Diving & Snorkeling

South Florida and the Keys attract most of the divers and snorkelers, but the more than 300 statewide dive shops schedule drift-, reef-, and wreck-diving trips for scuba divers all along Florida's Atlantic and Gulf coasts. The low-tech pleasures of snorkeling can be enjoyed throughout the Keys and elsewhere where shallow reefs hug the shore. Inland in northern and central Florida, you can explore more than 100 grottoes, rivers, sinkholes, and springs. In some locations you can swim near endangered manatees ("sea cows"), which migrate in from the sea to congregate around comparatively warm springs during the cool winter months.

FODOR'S CHOICE

The sights, restaurants, hotels, and other travel experiences on these pages are our editors' top picks—our Fodor's Choices. They're the best of their type in the area covered by the book—not to be missed and always worth your time. In the destination chapters that follow, you will find all the details.

LODGING

$$$$ **The Breakers, Palm Beach.** The building, an opulent Italian Renaissance palace, is amazing as is the resort's ability to balance old-world luxury with modern conveniences.

$$$$ **Delano Hotel, Miami Beach.** An air of surrealism surrounds this much-talked-about SoBe hotel, the hot spot for celebrities and other well-to-do visitors.

$$$$ **Don CeSar Beach Resort, St. Pete Beach** A delicious checkered past and stunning sands are among the treats at this cotton-candy "Pink Palace."

$$$$ **Little Palm Island, Florida Keys.** On its own palm-fringed island 3 mi off the shores of Little Torch Key, this dazzling resort of thatch-roof villas on stilts provides a secluded, one-of-a-kind experience.

$$$$ **Mandarin Oriental, Miami.** Attention to detail, proximity to downtown and the beaches, and a stellar restaurant, Azul, add up to a singular experience.

$$$$ **Renaissance Vinoy Resort, St. Petersburg.** Historic preservation makes you feel the grandeur of St. Petersburg's early heyday and the Gatsby era.

$$$$ **Ritz-Carlton Amelia Island.** Ritz-Carltons are known for stylish elegance, superb comfort, and excellent service. This one also comes with a pristine beach, its own golf course, and the outstanding and unusual Grill restaurant.

$$$ **Marriott's Bay Point Resort Village, Panama City Beach.** The tropical-chic guest rooms, private patios, and myriad amenities of this bayfront property are pleasant surprises.

$$$ **SanDestin Golf and Beach Resort.** Whether you've come to Sandestin for golfing, fishing, boating, dining, or just relaxing on the beach, this classy, 2,500-acre resort situated between the Intracoastal and the Gulf of Mexico is bound to please.

BUDGET LODGING

Banyan Marina Resort, Fort Lauderdale. Try these waterfront apartments at half the price of a first-class hotel but with comparable amenities.

Big Pine Key Fishing Lodge. Find family activities and nice sea breezes (the non-alcoholic kind) at this lodge-campground combo.

Ocean Surf, Miami. If you like deco, small but impeccable rooms, and a view of the beach, look into this money-saver north of SoBe.

Parmer's Place, Little Torch Key. Repeat guests, including many families, dig the water sports, aviaries, and friendly service.

Travelodge Orlando Convention Center. A motel with amenities that lets kids under 17 stay free is tough to find—especially ¼ mi from SeaWorld.

RESTAURANTS

$$$$	Norman's, Coral Gables. Chef Norman Van Aken turns out artful masterpieces of New World cuisine, combining bold tastes from Latin, American, Caribbean, and Asian traditions.
$$$–$$$$	Café des Artistes, Key West. A tropical version of French cuisine is served here in a series of intimate dining rooms filled with tropical art and on an outdoor patio.
$$–$$$$	Bern's Steak House, Tampa. Tour the kitchen and wine cellar after dinner to understand just how much love and care go into the finest meal you can have in the Tampa Bay area.
$$–$$$$	Mark's Las Olas, Fort Lauderdale. South Florida culinary star Mark Militello blends Caribbean, southwestern, and Mediterranean flavors.
$$–$$$	Armadillo Café, Davie. The atmosphere is as creative and fun as the crowd-pleasing southwestern-style South Florida seafood.
$$–$$$	Columbia Restaurant, Tampa. Flamenco dancing and paella set the scene at this Ybor City institution.
$$–$$$	Le Coq au Vin, Orlando. The traditional French cuisine is expertly prepared, and the setting is delightfully unstuffy.
$$–$$$	Tamara's Cafe Floridita, Apalachicola. This newcomer adds a uniquely South American flair to Apalachicola's up-and-coming dining scene.

BUDGET RESTAURANTS

$	Leo's Pizza, Tarpon Springs. Wonderful pies, parmigiana, and, because it's Florida, grouper, keep this joint ahead of the pack.
¢–$	Backwaters, Weeki Wachee. Discover tasty grouper 10 different ways and get a taste of Old Florida, too.
¢–$	Mel's Diner, Fort Myers. Neon and blue-plates and pies that have zing—these are a few of our favorite things.
¢–$	Pit Bar-B-Q, Tamiami Trail. The service is simple, the food delicious. It feels like a summer backyard barbecue.
¢–$	7 Mile Grill, Marathon Creamy shrimp bisque and a celebrated slice of key lime pie keep bringing the faithful back to this 50-year-old eatery.
¢–$	Ted Peters Famous Smoked Fish, St. Petersburg Mackerel, mullet, and salmon—oh, my! Devour smoked fish with flip-flop–wearing fishermen at this Pasadena favorite.
¢–$	Toni and Joe's, New Smyrna Beach. Righteous hoagies and no shoes required: two welcome bits of news as you quit the beach for lunch.

BEACHES

Bill Baggs Cape Florida State Recreation Area, Key Biscayne. Consistently voted one of South Florida's best beaches, this 414-acre park has a plethora of facilities, a historic lighthouse, and great views of the Miami skyline.

Broadwalk, Hollywood. While it's technically a walkway along the beach, this 27-ft-wide thoroughfare is ideal for strolling or biking.

Caladesi Island, Dunedin. Seclusion and soft, luxurious sand make this beach a standout.

Canaveral National Seashore. With its 24 mi of undeveloped coastline backed by windswept dunes stretching from New Smyrna Beach to Titusville, this 57,000-acre park is remarkable.

Clearwater Beach. Try this happening beach, with nonstop volleyball and a nightly sunset celebration at the pier.

Delnor-Wiggins Pass State Recreation Area, Naples. Loggerhead turtles, anglers, and sun worshipers love this quiet, natural beach.

Fort Clinch State Park, Amelia Island. A beach runs the entire length of Amelia Island's east coast. Its northernmost section is an almost empty expanse of white sand, part of a park with a well-preserved brick fort.

Grayton Beach State Park, Panhandle The beach here is constantly ranked among the finest in the nation, but this quiet spot gets extra points for its beautifully kept campground and its brand-new cabins, which are downright stylish.

Ocean Drive, Miami. A 10-block stretch from 5th to 15th Street, with a wide beach on one side and bustling art deco hotels, cafés, and boutiques on the other, is the perpetually "it" beachfront in America.

St. Andrews State Park, Panhandle Families with youngsters will love the shallow, protected swimming areas and facilities galore; nature enthusiasts will be stunned by the natural beauty of Panama City Beach.

St. George Island State Park, Panhandle. Nine miles of fantastic beachfront with sand as white and fine as biscuit flour make this a must-see—and must-swim—Panhandle favorite. Florida beaches don't get any better than this.

HISTORY

Castillo de San Marcos National Monument, St. Augustine. The 300-year-old Spanish fort comes complete with moat, turrets, and 16-ft-thick walls.

Edison's winter home and museum, Fort Myers. Everything is just as the inventor left it; you can imagine him tinkering with the first phonograph in the laboratory.

Henry Morrison Flagler Museum, Palm Beach. Whitehall, Flagler's mansion, is the backdrop for art and railway memorabilia.

Morikami Museum and Japanese Gardens, Delray Beach. The leading U.S. center for Japanese and American cultural exchange is in a model of a Japanese imperial villa.

Vizcaya Museum and Gardens, Coconut Grove. The Italian Renaissance–style villa anchoring the estate of industrialist James Deering contains Renaissance, baroque, rococo, and neoclassical art and furniture.

Ybor City, Tampa. As in the days of yore, Ybor City's National Historic Landmark District in Tampa brings together diverse people to celebrate life like they did in the old social clubs of the cigar-making era.

THEME PARKS & ATTRACTIONS

Busch Gardens, Tampa. Two of the world's largest roller coasters, good shows, and live animals are loosely brought together under a turn-of-the-last-century Africa theme on 335 acres.

Kennedy Space Center Visitor Complex, Cocoa Beach. The home of the real *Apollo 13* illuminates the romance of the early space program. It's also one of Florida's best bargains.

SeaWorld Orlando. Weaving learning and laughter, this water-centered mega-zoo lets you get up close to all sorts of ocean life.

Universal Orlando. The saucy, sassy, and hip movie-theme Universal Studios is joined by the ultracool Universal Islands of Adventure in a Universal empire.

Walt Disney World, Orlando. Don't miss a visit here: it's everything it's cracked up to be—and there's more of it every year.

VIEWS

A1A from Delray Beach. Head north through Manalapan for one of this highway's most breathtaking vistas.

Everglades National Park from the tower on Shark Valley Loop. This 50-ft observation tower yields a splendid panorama of the so-called River of Grass.

Inland Waterway, Sanibel. Scattered here are dozens and dozens of tiny mangrove islets, a lovely sight.

Ocean Drive in the Art Deco District, Miami Beach. This palm-lined beachfront is hopping around the clock.

Seven Mile Bridge, Keys. Find out for yourself why this expanse—actually 6.79 mi long—is one of the most-photographed images in the Keys.

Sunshine Skyway across Tampa Bay. One of the world's great monumental sculptures carries six lanes of traffic soaring across the mouth of Florida's largest estuary.

SMART TRAVEL TIPS

Finding out about your destination before you leave home means you won't squander time organizing everyday minutiae once you've arrived. You'll be more streetwise when you hit the ground as well, better prepared to explore the aspects of Florida that drew you here in the first place. The organizations in this section can provide information to supplement this guide; contact them for up-to-the-minute details, and consult the A to Z sections that end each chapter for facts on the various topics as they relate to the Florida's many regions. Happy landings!

AIR TRAVEL

BOOKING

When you book, **look for nonstop flights** and **remember that "direct" flights stop at least once.** Try to avoid connecting flights, which require a change of plane. Two airlines may operate a connecting flight jointly, so ask whether your airline operates every segment of the trip; you may find that the carrier you prefer flies you only part of the way. To find more booking tips and to check prices and make online flight reservations, log on to www.fodors.com.

CARRIERS

🛪 Major Airlines **Air Canada** ☎ 888/247-2262 ⊕ www.aircanada.ca**com. American** ☎ 800/433-7300 ⊕ www.aa.com. **Continental** ☎ 800/525-0280 ⊕ www.continental.com. **Delta** ☎ 800/221-1212 ⊕ www.delta.com. **Northwest** ☎ 800/225-2525 ⊕ www.nwa.com. **Spirit** ☎ 800/772-7117 ⊕ www.spiritair.com. **TWA** ☎ 800/221-2000 ⊕ www.twa.com. **United** ☎ 800/241-6522 ⊕ www.ual.com. **US Airways** ☎ 800/428-4322 ⊕ www.usair.com.

🛪 Regional Airlines **AirTran** ☎ 800/247-8726 ⊕ www.airtran.com to Miami, Pensacola, Tallahassee, Fort Lauderdale, Fort Myers, Jacksonville, Orlando, and Tampa. **Jet Blue** ☎ 800/538-2583 ⊕ www.jetblue.com to Tampa, Fort Lauderdale, Fort Myers, West Palm Beach, and Orlando. **Midwest Express** ☎ 800/452-2022 ⊕ www.midwestexpress.com to Fort Lauderdale, Fort Myers, Orlando, and Tampa. **Southwest** ☎ 800/435-9792 ⊕ www.southwesst.com to Jacksonville, Tampa, Fort Lauderdale, West Palm Beach, and Orlando.

🛪 From the U.K. **American** ☎ 0845/601-0619. **British Airways** ☎ 0845/773-3377. **Continental** ☎ 0800/776-464 via Newark. **Delta** ☎ 0800/414-767. **Northwest** ☎ 0990/561-000 via Detroit or Minneapolis. **TWA** ☎ 0800/222-222 via St. Louis.

United ☎ 0800/888-555. Virgin Atlantic ☎ 01293/747-747.

CHECK-IN & BOARDING

Always **ask your carrier about its check-in policy.** Plan to arrive at the airport about two hours before your scheduled departure time for domestic flights and 2½ to 3 hours before international flights. You may need to arrive earlier if you're flying from one of the busier airports or during peak air-traffic times. To avoid delays at airport-security checkpoints, try not to wear any metal. Jewelry, belt and other buckles, steel-toe shoes, barrettes, and underwire bras are among the items that can set off detectors.

Assuming that not everyone with a ticket will show up, airlines routinely overbook planes. When everyone does, airlines ask for volunteers to give up their seats. In return, these volunteers usually get a several-hundred-dollar flight voucher, which can be used toward the purchase of another ticket, and are rebooked on the next flight out. If there are not enough volunteers, the airline must choose who will be denied boarding. The first to get bumped are passengers who checked in late and those flying on discounted tickets, so **get to the gate and check in as early as possible,** especially during peak periods.

Always **bring a government-issued photo I.D. to the airport;** even when it's not required, a passport is best.

CUTTING COSTS

The least expensive airfares to Florida are priced for round-trip travel and must usually be purchased in advance. Airlines generally allow you to change your return date for a fee; most low-fare tickets, however, are nonrefundable. It's smart to **call a number of airlines and check the Internet;** when you are quoted a good price, **book it on the spot**—the same fare may not be available the next day, or even the next hour. Always **check different routings** and look into using alternate airports. Also, price off-peak flights, which may be significantly less expensive than others. Travel agents, especially low-fare specialists (⇨ Discounts and Deals), are helpful.

Consolidators are another good source. They buy tickets for scheduled flights at reduced rates from the airlines, then sell them at prices that beat the best fare available directly from the airlines. Sometimes you can even get your money back if you need to return the ticket. Carefully read the fine print detailing penalties for changes and cancellations, purchase the ticket with a credit card, and **confirm your consolidator reservation with the airline.**

When you **fly as a courier,** you trade your checked-luggage space for a ticket deeply subsidized by a courier service. There are restrictions on when you can book and how long you can stay. Some courier companies list with membership organizations, such as the Air Courier Association and the International Association of Air Travel Couriers; these require you to become a member before you can book a flight.

Many airlines, singly or in collaboration, offer discount air passes that allow foreigners to travel economically in a particular country or region. These visitor passes usually must be reserved and purchased before you leave home. Information about passes often can be found on most airlines' international Web pages, which tend to be aimed at travelers from outside the carrier's home country. Also, try typing the name of the pass into a search engine, or search for "pass" within the carrier's Web site.

⁊ Consolidators AirlineConsolidator.com ☎ 888/468-5385 ⊕ www.airlineconsolidator.com; for international tickets. **Best Fares** ☎ 800/576-8255 or 800/576-1600 ⊕ www.bestfares.com; $59.90 annual membership. **Cheap Tickets** ☎ 800/377-1000 or 888/922-8849 ⊕ www. cheaptickets.com. **Expedia** ☎ 800/397-3342 or 404/728-8787 ⊕ www.expedia.com. **Hotwire** ☎ 866/468-9473 or 920/330-9418 ⊕ www. hotwire.com. **Now Voyager Travel** ✉ 45 W. 21st St., 5th floor, New York, NY 10010 ☎ 212/459-1616 ⊟ 212/243-2711 ⊕ www.nowvoyagertravel.com. **Onetravel.com** ⊕ www.onetravel.com. **Orbitz** ☎ 888/656-4546 ⊕ www.orbitz.com. **Priceline. com** ⊕ www.priceline.com. **Travelocity** ☎ 888/709-5983; 877/282-2925 in Canada; 0870/876-3876 in U.K. ⊕ www.travelocity.com.
⁊ Cheap Rates from the U.K. Flight Express Travel ✉ 77 New Bond St., London W1Y 9DB, U.K. ☎ 0171/409-3311. **Trailfinders** ✉ 42-50 Earls Court Rd., London W8 6FT, U.K. ☎ 0171/937-5400. **Travel Cuts** ✉ 295A Regent St., London W1R 7YA, U.K. ☎ 0171/637-3161.
⁊ Courier Resources Air Courier Association/ Cheaptrips.com ☎ 800/282-1202 ⊕ www. aircourier.org or www.cheaptrips.com. **International Association of Air Travel Couriers** ☎ 308/632-3273 ⊕ www.courier.org. **Now Voyager Travel**

✉ 315 W. 49th St. Plaza Arcade, New York, NY 10019 ☎ 212/459-1616 🖷 212/262-7407 ⊕ www. nowvoyagertravel.com.

ENJOYING THE FLIGHT

State your seat preference when purchasing your ticket, and then repeat it when you confirm and when you check in. For more legroom, you can request one of the few emergency-aisle seats at check-in, if you are capable of lifting at least 50 pounds—a Federal Aviation Administration requirement of passengers in these seats. Seats behind a bulkhead also offer more legroom, but they don't have underseat storage. Don't sit in the row in front of the emergency aisle or in front of a bulkhead, where seats may not recline.

Ask the airline whether a snack or meal is served on the flight. If you have dietary concerns, **request special meals when booking.** These can be vegetarian, low-cholesterol, or kosher, for example. It's a good idea to pack some healthful snacks and a small (plastic) bottle of water in your carry-on bag. On long flights, try to maintain a normal routine, to help fight jet lag. At night, **get some sleep.** By day, **eat light meals, drink water** (not alcohol), and **move around the cabin** to stretch your legs. For additional jet-lag tips consult *Fodor's FYI: Travel Fit & Healthy* (available at bookstores everywhere).

Domestic American carriers prohibit smoking on all of their flights, and most every major international airline has followed suit; ask your carrier about its policy.

FLYING TIMES

Flying times to Florida vary based on the city you're flying to, but typical times are 3 hours from New York, 4 hours from Chicago, 2¾ hours from Dallas, 4½–5½ hours from Los Angeles, and 8–8½ hours from London.

HOW TO COMPLAIN

If your baggage goes astray or your flight goes awry, complain right away. Most carriers require that you **file a claim immediately.** The Aviation Consumer Protection Division of the Department of Transportation publishes *Fly-Rights,* which discusses airlines and consumer issues and is available on-line.

🚩 Airline Complaints **Aviation Consumer Protection Division** ✉ U.S. Department of Transportation, C-75, Room 4107, 400 7th St. NW, Washington, DC 20590 ☎ 202/366-2220 ⊕ www.dot.gov/airconsumer. **Federal Aviation Administration Consumer Hotline** ✉ For inquiries: FAA, 800 Independence Ave. SW, Room 810, Washington, DC 20591 ☎ 800/322-7873 ⊕ www.faa.gov.

RECONFIRMING

Check the status of your flight before you leave for the airport. You can do this on your carrier's Web site, by linking to a flight-status checker (many Web booking services offer these), or by calling your carrier or travel agent.

AIRPORTS

Because Florida is dotted with both major and regional airports, you can usually pick one quite close to your destination and often choose from a couple of nearby options. If you're destined for the north side of Miami-Dade County (metro Miami), or are renting a car at the airport, **consider flying into Fort Lauderdale–Hollywood International**; it's much easier to use than Miami International, and often—if not always—cheaper. The airports are only 40 minutes apart by car.

🚩 Airport Information **Daytona Beach International Airport (DAB)** ☎ 904/248-8069 ⊕ www.volusia.org/airport. **Fort Lauderdale–Hollywood International (FLL)** ☎ 954/359-6100 ⊕ www.broward.org/airport. **Jacksonville International (JAX)** ☎ 904/741-4902 ⊕ www.jaxairports.org. **Miami International Airport (MIA)** ☎ 305/876-7000 ⊕ www.miami-airport.com. **Orlando International (MCO)** ☎ 407/825-2001 ⊕ www.orlandoairports.net. **Palm Beach International (PBI)** ☎ 561/471-7420 ⊕ www.pbia.org. **St. Petersburg–Clearwater International Airport (PIE)** ☎ 727/453-7800 ⊕ www.stpete-clwairport.com. **Tampa International (TPA)** ☎ 813/870-8700 ⊕ www.tampaairport.com.

BIKE TRAVEL

Many cities throughout Florida do not offer safe biking paths such as sidewalks and specially marked bike lanes. However, you will find plenty of wide open space and scenic trails twisting through the state's various national and state parks.

Florida statutes require that bikers under 16 wear a helmet. Bicycle passengers under 4 years old must be in a sling or child seat. All bikes must have lamps or re-flectors—white in the front, and red in the back, visible from 500 ft—between sunset and sunrise. *See* Outdoor Activities and Sports for more biking information.

BIKES IN FLIGHT

Most airlines accommodate bikes as lug-gage; check with individual airlines about packing requirements. Some airlines sell bike boxes, which are often free at bike shops, for about $15 (bike bags can be considerably more expensive). Interna-tional travelers often can substitute a bike for a piece of checked luggage at no charge; otherwise, the cost is about $100. U.S. and Canadian airlines charge $40–$80 each way.

BUSINESS HOURS

MUSEUMS & SIGHTS

Many museums in Florida are closed Mondays, but offer extended hours on an-other weekday and are usually open on weekends. Popular visitor attractions are usually open daily with the exception of Thanksgiving and Christmas Day.

PHARMACIES

Most pharmacies are open seven days a week, but some may close early on week-ends. Many Wal-Mart stores and Wal-greens pharmacies offer 24-hour pharmacy services.

BUS TRAVEL

Greyhound passes through practically every major city in Florida. For schedules and fares, **contact your local Greyhound Information Center.**

PAYING

Using a major credit card you can pur-chase Greyhound tickets on-line or from the designated 800 number. You can also purchase tickets using cash, travelers checks, or major credit cards at any Grey-hound terminal where tickets are sold or through one of the many independent agents representing Greyhound. A com-plete state-by-state list of agents is avail-able at the Greyhound Web site.
🚌 Bus Information **Greyhound Lines** ☎ 800/231-2222; 800/229-9424 credit card sales ⊕ www.greyhound.com.

CAMERAS & PHOTOGRAPHY

The *Kodak Guide to Shooting Great Travel Pictures* (available at bookstores everywhere) is loaded with tips.
🚌 Photo Help **Kodak Information Center** ☎ 800/242-2424 ⊕ www.kodak.com.

EQUIPMENT PRECAUTIONS

Don't pack film and equipment in checked luggage, where it is much more suscepti-ble to damage. X-ray machines used to view checked luggage are extremely pow-erful and therefore are likely to ruin your film. Try to **ask for hand inspection of film,** which becomes clouded after re-peated exposure to airport X-ray ma-chines, and **keep videotapes and computer disks away from metal detectors.** Always keep film, tape, and computer disks out of the sun. Carry an extra supply of batteries, and be prepared to turn on your camera, camcorder, or laptop to prove to airport security personnel that the device is real.

CAR RENTAL

In-season rates in Miami begin at $36 a day and $170 a week for an economy car with air-conditioning, an automatic trans-mission, and unlimited mileage. Rates in Orlando begin at $35 a day and $149 a week. Rates in Fort Lauderdale begin at $36 a day and $159 a week. Rates in Tampa begin at $34 a day and $149 a week. This does not include tax on car rentals, which is 7%. Bear in mind that rates fluctuate tremendously—both above and below these quoted figures—depend-ing on demand and the season. Rental cars are more expensive (and harder to find) during peak holidays and in season.

In the past, major rental agencies were lo-cated at the airport whereas cheaper firms weren't. Now, however, all over Florida, even the majors might be off airport prop-erty. Speedy check-in and frequent shuttle buses make off-airport rentals almost as convenient as on-site service. However, it's wise to allow a little extra time for bus travel between the rental agency and the airport.
🚌 Major Agencies **Alamo** ☎ 800/327-9633 ⊕ www.alamo.com. **Avis** ☎ 800/331-1212 or 800/879-2847; 800/272-5871 in Canada; 0870/606-0100 in U.K.; 02/9353-9000 in Australia; 09/526-2847 in New Zealand ⊕ www.avis.com. **Budget** ☎ 800/527-0700; 0870/156-5656 in U.K. ⊕ www.budget.

com. **Dollar** ☎ 800/800-4000; 0124/622-0111 in U. K., where it's affiliated with Sixt; 02/9223-1444 in Australia ⊕ www.dollar.com. **Hertz** ☎ 800/654-3131; 800/263-0600 in Canada; 0870/844-8844 in U. K.; 02/9669-2444 in Australia; 09/256-8690 in New Zealand ⊕ www.hertz.com. **National Car Rental** ☎ 800/227-7368; 0870/600-6666 in U.K. ⊕ www. nationalcar.com.

CUTTING COSTS

For a good deal, **book through a travel agent who will shop around.** Also, **price local car-rental companies**—whose prices may be lower still, although their service and maintenance may not be as good as those of major rental agencies—and **research rates on the Internet.** Remember to ask about required deposits, cancellation penalties, and drop-off charges if you're planning to pick up the car in one city and leave it in another. If you're traveling during a holiday period, also make sure that a confirmed reservation guarantees you a car.

📁 Local Agencies **Sunshine Rent A Car** ☎ 954/467-8100 in Fort Lauderdale. **Continental Florida Auto Rental** ☎ 954/764-1008 or 800/327-3791 in Fort Lauderdale. **InterAmerican Car Rental** ☎ 305/871-3030 or 800/327-1278 in Clearwater, Fort Lauderdale, Kissimmee, Miami, Miami Beach, Orlando, and Tampa. **U-Save Auto Rental** ☎ 813/287-1872 or 800/526-5499 in Clearwater, New Port Richey, Orlando, Palm Harbor, and Tampa-St. Petersburg. **Tropical Rent-A-Car** ☎ 305/294-8136 in Key West.

INSURANCE

When driving a rented car you are generally responsible for any damage to or loss of the vehicle. You also may be liable for any property damage or personal injury that you may cause while driving. Before you rent, see what coverage you already have under the terms of your personal auto-insurance policy and credit cards.

For about $10 to $25 a day, rental companies sell protection, known as a collision- or loss-damage waiver (CDW or LDW), that eliminates your liability for damage to the car; it's always optional and should never be automatically added to your bill. In most states you don't need a CDW if you have personal auto insurance or other liability insurance. However, **make sure you have enough coverage to pay for the car.** If you do not have auto insurance or an umbrella policy that covers damage to third parties, purchasing liability insurance

and a CDW or LDW is highly recommended.

REQUIREMENTS & RESTRICTIONS

In Florida you must be 21 to rent a car, and rates may be higher if you're under 25. Non-U.S. residents need a reservation voucher (for prepaid reservations that were made in the traveler's home country), a passport, a driver's license, and a travel policy that covers each driver, when picking up a car.

SURCHARGES

Before you pick up a car in one city and leave it in another, **ask about drop-off charges or one-way service fees,** which can be substantial. Note, too, that some rental agencies charge extra if you return the car before the time specified in your contract. To avoid a hefty refueling fee, **fill the tank just before you turn in the car,** but be aware that gas stations near the rental outlet may overcharge. It's almost never a deal to buy the tank of gas that's in the car when you rent it; the understanding is that you'll return it empty, but some fuel usually remains. Surcharges may apply if you're under 25 or if you take the car outside the area approved by the rental agency. You'll pay extra for child seats (about $6 a day), which are compulsory for children under five, and usually for additional drivers (about $10 per day).

CAR TRAVEL

Three major interstates lead to Florida. Interstate 95 begins in Maine, runs south through the Mid-Atlantic states, and enters Florida just north of Jacksonville. It continues south past Daytona Beach, the Space Coast, Vero Beach, Palm Beach, and Fort Lauderdale, eventually ending in Miami.

Interstate 75 begins in Michigan at the Canadian border and runs south through Ohio, Kentucky, Tennessee, and Georgia, then moves south through the center of the state before veering west into Tampa. It follows the west coast south to Naples, then crosses the state through the northern section of the Everglades, and ends in Fort Lauderdale.

California and most southern states are connected to Florida by Interstate 10, which moves east from Los Angeles through Arizona, New Mexico, Texas,

Louisiana, Mississippi, and Alabama; it enters Florida at Pensacola and runs straight across the northern part of the state, ending in Jacksonville.

ROAD CONDITIONS

Florida has its share of traffic problems. Downtown areas of such major cities as Miami, Orlando, and Tampa can be extremely congested during rush hours, usually 7 to 9 AM and 4 to 6 PM on weekdays. When you drive the interstate system in Florida, try to **plan your trip so that you are not entering, leaving, or passing through a large city during rush hour,** when traffic can slow to 10 mph for 10 mi or more. In addition, snowbirds usually rent in Florida for a month at a time, which means they all arrive on the first of the month and leave on the 31st. Believe it or not, from November to March, when the end and beginning of a month occur on a weekend, north–south routes like Interstate 75 and Interstate 95 almost come to a standstill during daylight hours. It's best to avoid traveling on these days if possible.

RULES OF THE ROAD

Speed limits are 55 mph on state highways, 30 mph within city limits and residential areas, and 55–70 mph on interstates and Florida's Turnpike. Be alert for signs announcing exceptions.

Always **strap children under age three into approved child-safety seats.** All passengers are required to wear seat belts. The driver will be held responsible for passengers under the age of 16 who are not wearing a seatbelt. Florida's Alcohol/Controlled Substance DUI Law is one of the toughest in the United States. A blood alcohol level of .08 or higher can have serious repercussions even for the first-time offender.

Always **secure children under age five into an approved child-restraint device.**

SAFETY

Before setting off on any drive, make sure you know where you're going and carry a map. At the car-rental agency or at your hotel ask if there are any areas that you should avoid. Always **keep your doors locked,** and ask questions only at toll booths, gas stations, or other obviously safe locations. Also, **don't stop if your car is bumped from behind** or if you're asked

for directions. One hesitates to foster rude behavior, but at least for now the roads are too risky to stop any place you're not familiar with (other than as traffic laws require). If you'll be renting a car and won't have a cellular phone with you, **ask the car-rental agency for a cellular phone.** Alamo, Avis, and Hertz are among the companies with in-car phones.

CHILDREN IN FLORIDA

Fodor's Around Miami with Kids and *Fodor's Around Orlando with Kids,* available in bookstores everywhere, can help you plan your days together.

If you are renting a car, don't forget to **arrange for a car seat** when you reserve. For general advice about traveling with children, consult *Fodor's FYI: Travel with Your Baby* (available in bookstores everywhere).

FLYING

If your children are two or older, **ask about children's airfares.** As a general rule, infants under two not occupying a seat fly at greatly reduced fares or even for free. But if you want to guarantee a seat for an infant, you have to pay full fare. Consider flying during off-peak days and times; most airlines will grant an infant a seat without a ticket if there are available seats. Experts agree that it's a good idea to use safety seats aloft for children weighing less than 40 pounds. Airlines set their own policies: If you use a safety seat, U.S. carriers usually require that the child be ticketed, even if he or she is young enough to ride free, because the seats must be strapped into regular seats. And even if you pay the full adult fare for the seat, it may be worth it, especially on longer trips. Do **check your airline's policy about using safety seats during takeoff and landing.** Safety seats are not allowed everywhere in the plane, so get your seat assignments as early as possible.

When reserving, **request children's meals or a freestanding bassinet** (not available at all airlines) if you need them. But note that bulkhead seats, where you must sit to use the bassinet, may lack an overhead bin or storage space on the floor.

WHERE TO STAY

Florida may have the highest concentration of hotels with organized children's programs in the United States. Activities range from simple fun and recreation to shell-hunting at Marriott's Marco Island Resort and learning about the Keys' environment from marine-science counselors at Cheeca Lodge. Sometimes kids' programs are complimentary; sometimes there's a charge. Not all accept children in diapers, and some offer programs when their central reservations services say they don't. Some programs are only offered during peak seasons or restrict hours in less-busy times. It always pays to **confirm details with the hotel in advance.** And re-**serve space as soon as possible**; programs are often full by the morning or evening you need them.

Most hotels in Florida allow children under a certain age to stay in their parents' room at no extra charge, but others charge for them as extra adults. Many bed-and-breakfasts and inns do not welcome young children; be sure to **find out the cutoff age for any applicable discounts or age restrictions.** In Orlando, in addition to the properties listed below, most properties on the Walt Disney World grounds have children's programs.

🎏 Fort Lauderdale **Marriott's Harbor Beach Resort's Beachside Buddies** ✉ 3030 Holiday Dr., Fort Lauderdale, FL 33316 ☎ 954/525-4000; 800/228-9290, ages 5-12.

🎏 The Keys **Cheeca Lodge's Camp Cheeca** ✉ MM 82, OS, Box 527, Islamorada, FL 33036 ☎ 800/327-2888, ages 6-12. **Hawks Cay Resort's Island Adventure Club** ✉ MM 61, Duck Key, FL 33050 ☎ 800/432-2242, ages 3-12.

🎏 Miami Area **Sonesta Beach Resort's Just Us Kids** ✉ 350 Ocean Dr., Key Biscayne, FL 33149 ☎ 305/361-2021 or 800/766-3782, ages 5-13.

🎏 Northeast Florida **Amelia Island Plantation's Kid's Camp Amelia** ✉ 3000 First Coast Hwy., Amelia Island, FL 32034 ☎ 904/261-6161, ages 3-11.

🎏 Orlando Area **Holiday Inn SunSpree Resort Lake Buena Vista's Camp Holiday** ✉ 13351 State Rd. 535, Orlando, FL 32821 ☎ 407/239-4500 or 800/366-6299, ages 4-12. **Hyatt Regency Grand Cypress Resort's Camp Hyatt** ✉ 1 Grand Cypress Blvd., Orlando, FL 32836 ☎ 407/239-1234 or 800/228-9000, ages 5-12.

🎏 Palm Beach & the Treasure Coast **Club Med's Sandpiper** ✉ 3500 S.E. Morningside Blvd., Port St. Lucie, FL 34952 ☎ 772/398-5100 or 800/258-2633, Baby Club ages 4-24 months, Mini Club ages 2-11. **Hutchinson Island Marriott Resort's Castaway Summer** ✉ 555 N.E. Ocean Blvd., Hutchinson Island, Stuart, FL 34996 ☎ 772/225-3700, ages 4-12, plus a teen program.

🎏 Southwest Florida **Marriott's Marco Island Resort's Kids Klub** ✉ 400 S. Collier Blvd., Marco Island, FL 33937 ☎ 941/394-2511 or 800/228-9290, ages 5-12. **Radisson Suite Beach Resort's Fun Factory** ✉ 600 S. Collier Blvd., Marco Island, FL 33937 ☎ 941/394-4100 or 800/333-3333, ages 4-12. **Sanibel Harbour Resort & Spa's Kids Klub** ✉ 17260 Harbour Pointe Dr., Fort Myers, FL 33908 ☎ 941/466-4000 or 800/767-7777, ages 5-12. **South Seas Plantation's Explorer Fun Factory** ✉ 5400 Captiva Rd., Captiva Island, FL 33924 ☎ 941/472-5111 or 800/227-8482, ages 4-12, plus activities for teens.

SIGHTS & ATTRACTIONS

Places that are especially appealing to children are indicated by a rubber-duckie icon (🐤) in the margin.

TRANSPORTATION

Florida law requires that all children three years old or younger ride in a federally approved child safety seat when in any motor vehicle, regardless of the vehicle's registration state. Children four and five years of age must be restrained in either a child safety seat, booster seat, or safety belt.

CONSUMER PROTECTION

Whether you're shopping for gifts or purchasing travel services, **pay with a major credit card** whenever possible, so you can cancel payment or get reimbursed if there's a problem (and you can provide documentation). If you're doing business with a particular company for the first time, **contact your local Better Business Bureau and the attorney general's offices** in your state and (for U.S. businesses) the company's home state as well. Have any complaints been filed? Finally, if you're buying a package or tour, always **consider travel insurance** that includes default coverage (⇨ Insurance).

🎏 BBBs **Council of Better Business Bureaus** ✉ 4200 Wilson Blvd., Suite 800, Arlington, VA 22203 ☎ 703/276-0100 🖷 703/525-8277 ⊕ www.bbb.org.

CRUISE TRAVEL

The port of Miami is the cruise capital of the world, with the world's largest year-round fleet. It also handles more megaships—vessels capable of transporting more than 2,000 people at a time—than any other port in the world. Port Everglades, located 23 mi north of Miami, is the world's second-busiest cruise ship terminal. Seven-day eastern and western Caribbean cruises are the most popular type of cruise leaving from Miami-area ports. To learn how to plan, choose, and book a cruise, check out Cruise How-To's on www.fodors.com or consult *Fodor's FYI: Plan & Enjoy Your Cruise* (available in bookstores everywhere).

🛂 Cruise Lines **Royal Caribbean** ☎ 800/398-9819, **Celebrity Cruises** ☎ 800/437-3111, **Costa Cruises Lines** ☎ 800/462-6782, **Crystal Cruises** ☎ 800/446-6620, **Cunard Cruise Line** ☎ 800/728-6273, **Discovery Cruises** ☎ 800/866-8687, **Holland America Cruises** ☎ 877/932-4259, **Imperial Majesty Cruise Lines** ☎ 800/511-5737, **Norwegian Cruises** ☎ 800/327-7030 Ext. 211, **Princess** ☎ 800/774-6237, **Sea Escape Cruises** ☎ 800/327-2005, **SilverSea Cruises** ☎ 800/722-9955, **Windjammer** ☎ 800/327-2601.

DINING

An anti-smoking amendment endorsed by Florida voters in 2002 bans smoking statewide in most enclosed indoor workplaces, including restaurants. Exemptions are permitted for stand-alone bars where food takes a back seat to the libations. If smoking matters to you one way or the other, phone the property before you go to find out how they're complying with the new regulations.

A cautionary word: Raw oysters have been identified as a potential problem for people with chronic illness of the liver, stomach, or blood, or who have immune disorders. Since 1993, all Florida restaurants serving raw oysters are required to post a notice in plain view of all patrons warning of the risks associated with consuming them.

The restaurants we list are the cream of the crop in each price category. Properties indicated by ✕⌂ are lodging establishments whose restaurant warrants a special trip.

CATEGORY	COST*
$$$$	over $30
$$$	$20–$30
$$	$15–$20
$	$10–$15
¢	under $10

*per person for a main course at dinner

CUTTING COSTS

Coupons are a good way to cut dining costs. You'll find coupon booklets outside supermarkets, restaurants, and shopping malls. A particularly worthy booklet is "The Best Read Guide," filled with discount coupons for dining and shopping. Many Florida restaurants have the famed "early bird" specials and offer reduced prices if you dine early, and many restaurants allow plate sharing for a nominal fee. You'll also find senior citizens discounts. If discount policies aren't posted, it never hurts to ask.

RESERVATIONS & DRESS

Reservations are always a good idea; we mention them only when they're essential or not accepted. Book as far ahead as you can, and reconfirm as soon as you arrive. (Large parties should always call ahead to check the reservations policy.) We mention dress only when men are required to wear a jacket or a jacket and tie.

SPECIALTIES

A trip to the Tampa area or South Florida is incomplete without a taste of Cuban food. The cuisine is heavy, with pork dishes like *lechon asado,* served in garlic-based sauces. The two most typical dishes are *arroz con frijoles* (the staple side dish of rice and black beans) and *arroz con pollo* (chicken in a sticky yellow rice). Key West is a mecca for lovers of key lime pie (the best is found here) and conch fritters, another local favorite. Stone crab claws, another South Florida delicacy, can be savored November through May.

WINE, BEER & SPIRITS

Beer and wine is usually available in Florida's restaurants, whether you're dining first class or at a beachside bistro. A few chain restaurants in the major cities are microbreweries and have a variety of premise-made beers that change with the season. Liquor is generally available at fine-dining establishments only.

DISABILITIES & ACCESSIBILITY

Although there's no single organization that offers a completely comprehensive list of motels or inns that are equipped for travelers with disabilities, you'll find helpful information and links at Florida Disabled Outdoor Association (FDOA) and Disability Travel and Recreation Resources. The Society for Accessible Travel and Hospitality is another good source.

Metro-Dade Disability Services publishes a free guidebook on the accessibility of Florida's hotels and motels, entitled *Directory of Services for the Physically Disabled in Dade County.*

Local Resources Florida Disabled Outdoor Association (FDOA) ☎ 850/668-7323 ⊕ www.nettally.com/fdoa. **Disability Travel and Recreation Resources** ⊕ www.makoa.org/travel.htm. **Society for Accessible Travel and Hospitality** ☎ 212/447-7284 ⊕ www.sath.org. **Metro-Dade Disability Services** ✉ 1335 N.W. 14th St., Miami, FL 33125 ☎ 305/547-5445; 305/545-3575 TDD publishes a free guidebook on the accessibility of Florida's hotels and motels, entitled *Directory of Services for the Physically Disabled in Dade County.*

Deaf Services Center ✉ 2182 McGreggor Blvd., Fort Myers, FL 33901 ☎ 941/461-0334; 813/939-9977 TDD. **Florida Relay Service** ☎ 800/955-8770.

LODGING

Despite the Americans with Disabilities Act, the definition of accessibility seems to differ from hotel to hotel. Some properties may be accessible by ADA standards for people with mobility problems but not for people with hearing or vision impairments, for example.

If you have mobility problems, ask for the lowest floor on which accessible services are offered. If you have a hearing impairment, check whether the hotel has devices to alert you visually to the ring of the telephone, a knock at the door, and a fire–emergency alarm. Some hotels provide these devices without charge. Discuss your needs with hotel personnel if this equipment isn't available, so that a staff member can personally alert you in the event of an emergency.

If you're bringing a guide dog, get authorization ahead of time and write down the name of the person with whom you spoke.

RESERVATIONS

When discussing accessibility with an operator or reservations agent, **ask hard questions.** Are there any stairs, inside *or* out? Are there grab bars next to the toilet *and* in the shower/tub? How wide is the doorway to the room? To the bathroom? For the most extensive facilities meeting the latest legal specifications, **opt for newer accommodations.** If you reserve through a toll-free number, consider also calling the hotel's local number to confirm the information from the central reservations office. Get confirmation in writing when you can.

TRANSPORTATION

Complaints Aviation Consumer Protection Division (⇨ Air Travel) for airline-related problems. **Departmental Office of Civil Rights** ✉ For general inquiries, U.S. Department of Transportation, S-30, 400 7th St. SW, Room 10215, Washington, DC 20590 ☎ 202/366-4648 ☐ 202/366-9371 ⊕ www.dot.gov/ost/docr/index.htm. **Disability Rights Section** ✉ NYAV, U.S. Department of Justice, Civil Rights Division, 950 Pennsylvania Ave. NW, Washington, DC 20530 ☐ ADA information line 202/514-0301; 800/514-0301; 202/514-0383 TTY; 800/514-0383 TTY ⊕ www.ada.gov. **U.S. Department of Transportation Hotline** ☎ For disability-related air-travel problems, 800/778-4838; 800/455-9880 TTY.

TRAVEL AGENCIES

In the United States, the Americans with Disabilities Act requires that travel firms serve the needs of all travelers. Some agencies specialize in working with people with disabilities.

Travelers with Mobility Problems Access Adventures ✉ 206 Chestnut Ridge Rd., Scottsville, NY 14624 ☎ 585/889-9096 ✍ dltravel@prodigy.net, run by a former physical-rehabilitation counselor. **Accessible Vans of America** ✉ 9 Spielman Rd., Fairfield, NJ 07004 ☎ 877/282-8267, 973/808-9709 reservations ☐ 973/808-9713 ⊕ www.accessiblevans.com. **CareVacations** ✉ No. 5, 5110-50 Ave., Leduc, Alberta, Canada, T9E 6V4 ☎ 780/986-6404 or 877/478-7827 ☐ 780/986-8332 ⊕ www.carevacations.com, for group tours and cruise vacations. **Flying Wheels Travel** ✉ 143 W. Bridge St., Box 382, Owatonna, MN 55060 ☎ 507/451-5005 ☐ 507/451-1685 ⊕ www.flyingwheelstravel.com.

Travelers with Developmental Disabilities New Directions ✉ 5276 Hollister Ave., Suite 207, Santa Barbara, CA 93111 ☎ 805/967-2841 or 888/967-2841 ☐ 805/964-7344 ⊕ www.newdirectionstravel.com. **Sprout** ✉ 893 Amsterdam Ave., New York, NY 10025 ☎ 212/222-9575 or 888/222-9575 ☐ 212/222-9768 ⊕ www.gosprout.org.

DISCOUNTS & DEALS

Be a smart shopper and **compare all your options** before making decisions. A plane ticket bought with a promotional coupon from travel clubs, coupon books, and direct-mail offers or purchased on the Internet may not be cheaper than the least expensive fare from a discount ticket agency. And always keep in mind that what you get is just as important as what you save.

Theme park savvy: If visiting the Orlando theme parks, consider purchasing a multi-day "Park Hopper" pass before leaving home. You'll save money by purchasing your advance tickets online at ⊕ www. disneyworld.com. You can also save by getting your tickets at a local ticket booth prior to arriving at the theme park. If you leave the park and plan to return the same day, remember to get your hand stamped for re-admission. Also, you can save as much as $10 a day by bringing your own stroller. And it's always a good idea to have lots of water on hand; refillable water bottles are quick and easy and will save you several dollars a day.

DISCOUNT RESERVATIONS

To save money, **look into discount reservations services** with Web sites and toll-free numbers, which use their buying power to get a better price on hotels, airline tickets (⇨ Air Travel), even car rentals. When booking a room, always **call the hotel's local toll-free number** (if one is available) rather than the central reservations number—you'll often get a better price. Always ask about special packages or corporate rates.

🔁 Airline Tickets **Air 4 Less** ☎ 800/AIR4LESS; low-fare specialist.

🔁 Hotel Rooms **Accommodations Express** ☎ 800/444-7666 or 800/277-1064 ⊕ www. accommodationsexpress.com. **Central Reservation Service (CRS)** ☎ 800/555-7555 or 800/548-3311 ⊕ www.roomconnection.net. **Quikbook** ☎ 800/789-9887 ⊕ www.quikbook.com. **RMC Travel** ☎ 800/245-5738 ⊕ www.rmcwebtravel.com. **Steigenberger Reservation Service** ☎ 800/223-5652 ⊕ www.srs-worldhotels.com. **Travel Interlink** ☎ 800/888-5898 ⊕ www.travelinterlink.com. **Turbotrip.com** ☎ 800/473-7829 ⊕ www. turbotrip.com.

PACKAGE DEALS

Don't confuse packages and guided tours. When you buy a package, you travel on your own, just as though you had planned the trip yourself. Fly/drive packages, which combine airfare and car rental, are often a good deal. In cities, ask the local visitor's bureau about hotel packages that include tickets to major museum exhibits or other special events.

ECOTOURISM

Florida's varied environment is one of its chief draws; it's also very fragile. If you're out in nature, follow the basic rules of environmental responsibility: **take nothing but pictures; leave nothing but footprints.** Most important, **be extremely careful around the tenuous dunes.** Picking the sea grasses that hold the dunes in place can carry stiff fines, as can walking or playing or digging in the dunes. An afternoon of roughhousing can completely destroy a dune that could take years for nature to rebuild. Ecotours (⇨ Tours *in* each chapter's A to Z section) operate throughout the state and can help you see some of what makes Florida so distinct, usually in a way that makes the least impact possible.

GAY & LESBIAN TRAVEL

Destinations within Florida that have a reputation for being especially gay and lesbian friendly include South Beach and Key West.

For details about the gay and lesbian scene, consult *Fodor's Gay Guide to the USA* (available in bookstores everywhere). 🔁 Gay- & Lesbian-Friendly Travel Agencies **Different Roads Travel** ✉ 8383 Wilshire Blvd., Suite 520, Beverly Hills, CA 90211 ☎ 323/651-5557 or 800/429-8747 (Ext. 14 for both) 🖷 323/651-3678 ✉ lgernert@tzell.com. **Kennedy Travel** ✉ 130 W. 42nd St., Suite 401, New York, NY 10036 ☎ 212/840-8659 or 800/237-7433 🖷 212/730-2269 ⊕ www. kennedytravel.com. **Now, Voyager** ✉ 4406 18th St., San Francisco, CA 94114 ☎ 415/626-1169 or 800/255-6951 🖷 415/626-8626 ⊕ www.nowvoyager. com. **Skylink Travel and Tour** ✉ 1455 N. Dutton Ave., Suite A, Santa Rosa, CA 95401 ☎ 707/546-9888 or 800/225-5759 🖷 707/636-0951; serving lesbian travelers.

GUIDEBOOKS

Plan well and you won't be sorry. Guidebooks are excellent tools—and you can take them with you. You may want to check out Fodor's Florida regional gold guides: *Fodor's Walt Disney World Resort, Universal Orlando Resort, and Central Florida* and *Fodor's Miami.* Or study color-photo-illustrated *Fodor's Exploring Florida* and *Compass American Guide: Florida,* thorough on culture and history; or *Fodor's Road Guide USA: Florida* for comprehensive restaurant, hotel, and attractions listings. *Fodor's Around Miami with Kids* and *Fodor's Around Orlando with Kids* can help you plan your family days together. All are available at on-line retailers and bookstores everywhere.

HEALTH

If you are unaccustomed to strong sub-tropical sun, you run a risk of sunburn and heat prostration, even in winter. So hit the beach or play tennis, golf, or another outdoor sport before 10 or after 3. If you must be out **at midday, limit strenuous exercise, drink plenty of liquids, and wear a hat.** If you begin to feel faint, get out of the sun immediately and sip water slowly. Even on overcast days, ultraviolet rays shine through the haze, so **use a sunscreen with an SPF of at least 15,** and have children wear a waterproof SPF 30 or better.

While you're frolicking on the beach, **steer clear of what look like blue bubbles on the sand.** These are Portuguese man-of-wars, and their tentacles can cause an allergic reaction. Also be careful of other large jellyfish, some of which can sting.

If you walk across a grassy area on the way to the beach, you'll probably encounter sand spurs. They are quite tiny, light brown, and remarkably prickly. You'll feel them before you see them; if you get stuck with one, just pull it out.

DIVERS' ALERT

Do not fly within 24 hours of scuba diving.

HOLIDAYS

Major national holidays are New Year's Day (Jan. 1); Martin Luther King Day (3rd Mon. in Jan.); Presidents' Day (3rd Mon. in Feb.); Memorial Day (last Mon. in May); Independence Day (July 4); Labor Day (1st Mon. in Sept.); Columbus Day (2nd Mon. in Oct.); Thanksgiving Day (4th Thurs. in Nov.); Christmas Eve and Christmas Day (Dec. 24 and 25); and New Year's Eve (Dec. 31).

INSURANCE

The most useful travel-insurance plan is a comprehensive policy that includes coverage for trip cancellation and interruption, default, trip delay, and medical expenses (with a waiver for preexisting conditions).

Without insurance you'll lose all or most of your money if you cancel your trip, regardless of the reason. Default insurance covers you if your tour operator, airline, or cruise line goes out of business. Trip-delay covers expenses that arise because of bad weather or mechanical delays. Study the fine print when comparing policies.

U.K. residents can buy a travel-insurance policy valid for most vacations taken during the year in which it's purchased (but check preexisting-condition coverage).

Always **buy travel policies directly from the insurance company;** if you buy them from a cruise line, airline, or tour operator that goes out of business you probably won't be covered for the agency or operator's default, a major risk. Before making any purchase, **review your existing health and home-owner's policies** to find what they cover away from home.

Travel Insurers In the U.S.: **Access America** ⌂ 6600 W. Broad St., Richmond, VA 23230 ☎ 800/284-8300 🖷 804/673-1491 or 800/346-9265 ⊕ www.accessamerica.com. **Travel Guard International** ⌂ 1145 Clark St., Stevens Point, WI 54481 ☎ 715/345-0505 or 800/826-1300 🖷 800/955-8785 ⊕ www.travelguard.com.

FOR INTERNATIONAL TRAVELERS

CAR RENTAL

When picking up a rental car, non-U.S. residents need a reservation voucher for any prepaid reservations that were made in the traveler's home country, a passport, a driver's license, and a travel policy that covers each driver.

CAR TRAVEL

In Florida gasoline costs $1.39–$1.69 a gallon at press time. Stations are plentiful. Most stay open late (24 hours along large highways and in big cities), except in rural areas, where Sunday hours are limited and where you may drive long stretches without a refueling opportunity. Highways are well paved. Interstate highways—limited-access, multilane highways whose numbers are prefixed by "I–"—are the fastest routes. Interstates with three-digit numbers encircle urban areas, which may have other limited-access expressways, freeways, and parkways as well. Tolls may be levied on limited-access highways. So-called U.S. highways and state highways are not necessarily limited-access but may have several lanes.

Along larger highways, roadside stops with rest rooms, fast food restaurants, and sundries stores are well spaced. State police and tow trucks patrol major highways and lend assistance. If your car breaks down on an interstate, pull onto the shoulder and wait for help, or have your passengers wait while you walk to an emergency phone. If you carry a cell phone, dial *55, noting your location on the small green roadside mileage markers.

Driving in the United States is on the right. Do **obey speed limits** posted along roads and highways. Watch for lower limits in small towns and on back roads. On weekdays between 6 and 10 AM and again between 4 and 7 PM **expect heavy traffic.** To encourage carpooling, some freeways have special lanes for so-called high-occupancy vehicles (HOV)—cars carrying more than one passenger.

Bookstores, gas stations, convenience stores, and rest stops sell maps (about $3) and multiregion road atlases (about $10).

CURRENCY

The dollar is the basic unit of U.S. currency. It has 100 cents. Coins include the copper penny (1¢); the silvery nickel (5¢), dime (10¢), quarter (25¢), and half-dollar (50¢); and the golden $1 coin, replacing a now-rare silver dollar. Bills are denominated $1, $5, $10, $20, $50, and $100, all green and identical in size; designs vary. The exchange rate at press time was U.S.$1.59 per British pound, $.64 per Canadian dollar, $.56 per Australian dollar, and $.51 per New Zealand dollar.

ELECTRICITY

The U.S. standard is AC, 110 volts/60 cycles. Plugs have two flat pins set parallel to each other.

EMERGENCIES

For police, fire, or ambulance, **dial 911** (0 in rural areas).

INSURANCE

Britons and Australians need extra medical coverage when traveling overseas. ✈ Insurance Information In the U.K.: **Association of British Insurers** ✉ 51 Gresham St., London EC2V 7HQ ☎ 020/7600-3333 📠 020/7696-8999 ⊕ www.abi.org.uk. In Australia: **Insurance Council of Australia** ✉ Insurance Enquiries and Complaints, Level 3, 56 Pitt St., Sydney, NSW 2000 ☎ 1300/363683 or

02/9251-4456 📠 02/9251-4453 ⊕ www.iecltd.com.au. In Canada: **RBC Insurance** ✉ 6880 Financial Dr., Mississauga, Ontario L5N 7Y5 ☎ 800/565-3129 📠 905/813-4704 ⊕ www.rbcinsurance.com. In New Zealand: **Insurance Council of New Zealand** ✉ Level 7, 111-115 Customhouse Quay, Box 474, Wellington ☎ 04/472-5230 📠 04/473-3011 ⊕ www.icnz.org.nz.

MAIL & SHIPPING

You can buy stamps and aerograms and send letters and parcels in post offices. Stamp-dispensing machines can occasionally be found in airports, bus and train stations, office buildings, drugstores, and the like. You can also deposit mail in the stout, dark blue, steel bins at strategic locations everywhere and in the mail chutes of large buildings; pickup schedules are posted.

For mail sent within the United States, you need a 37¢ stamp for first-class letters weighing up to 1 ounce (23¢ for each additional ounce) and 23¢ for postcards. You pay 80¢ for 1-ounce airmail letters and 70¢ for airmail postcards to most other countries; to Canada and Mexico, you need a 60¢ stamp for a 1-ounce letter and 50¢ for a postcard. An aerogram—a single sheet of lightweight blue paper that folds into its own envelope, stamped for overseas airmail—costs 70¢.

To receive mail on the road, have it sent c/o General Delivery at your destination's main post office (use the correct five-digit ZIP code). You must pick up mail in person within 30 days and show a driver's license or passport.

PASSPORTS & VISAS

When traveling internationally, **carry your passport** even if you don't need one (it's always the best form of I.D.) and **make two photocopies of the data page** (one for someone at home and another for you, carried separately from your passport). If you lose your passport, promptly call the nearest embassy or consulate and the local police.

Visitor visas aren't necessary for Canadian or European Union citizens, or for citizens of Australia who are staying fewer than 90 days. ✈ Australian Citizens **Passports Australia** ☎ 131-232 ⊕ www.passports.gov.au. **United States Consulate General** ✉ MLC Centre, Level 59, 19-29

Martin Pl., Sydney, NSW 2000 ☎ 02/9373-9200; 1902/941-641 fee-based visa-inquiry line ⊕ usembassy-australia.state.gov/sydney.

🛂 **Canadian Citizens Passport Office** ✉ To mail in applications: 200 Promenade du Portage, Hull, Québec J8X 4B7 ☎ 819/994-3500 or 800/567-6868 ⊕ www.ppt.gc.ca.

🛂 **New Zealand Citizens New Zealand Passports Office** ✉ For applications and information, Level 3, Boulcott House, 47 Boulcott St., Wellington ☎ 0800/22-5050 or 04/474-8100 ⊕ www. passports.govt.nz. **Embassy of the United States** ✉ 29 Fitzherbert Terr., Thorndon, Wellington ☎ 04/462-6000 ⊕ usembassy.org.nz. **U.S. Consulate General** ✉ Citibank Bldg., 3rd fl., 23 Customs St. E, Auckland ☎ 09/303-2724 ⊕ usembassy. org.nz.

🛂 **U.K. Citizens U.K. Passport Service** ☎ 0870/ 521-0410 ⊕ www.passport.gov.uk. **American Consulate General** ✉ Queen's House, 14 Queen St., Belfast, Northern Ireland BT1 6EQ ☎ 028/ 9032-8239 🖷 028/9024-8482 ⊕ www.usembassy. org.uk. **American Embassy** ✉ For visa and immigration information (enclose an SASE), Consular Information Unit, 24 Grosvenor Sq., London W1 1AE ✉ To submit an application via mail, Visa Branch, 5 Upper Grosvenor St., London W1A 2JB ☎ 09068/ 200-290 recorded visa information; 09055/444-546 operator service, both with per-minute charges; 0207/499-9000 main switchboard ⊕ www. usembassy.org.uk.

TELEPHONES

All U.S. telephone numbers consist of a three-digit area code and a seven-digit local number. Within many local calling areas, you dial only the seven-digit number. Within some area codes, you must dial 1 first for calls outside the local area. To call between area-code regions, dial 1 then all 10 digits; the same goes for calls to numbers prefixed by 800, 888, 866, and 877—all toll free. For calls to numbers preceded by 900 you must pay—usually dearly.

For international calls, dial 011 followed by the country code and the local number. For help, dial 0 and ask for an overseas operator. The country code is 61 for Australia, 64 for New Zealand, 44 for the United Kingdom. Calling Canada is the same as calling within the United States. Most local phone books list country codes and U.S. area codes. The country code for the United States is 1.

For operator assistance, dial 0. To obtain someone's phone number, call directory assistance at 555-1212 or occasionally

411 (free at public phones). To have the person you're calling foot the bill, phone collect; dial 0 instead of 1 before the 10-digit number.

At pay phones, instructions often are posted. Usually you insert coins in a slot (usually 25¢–50¢ for local calls) and wait for a steady tone before dialing. When you call long-distance, the operator tells you how much to insert; prepaid phone cards, widely available in various denominations, are easier. Call the number on the back, punch in the card's personal identification number when prompted, then dial your number.

LANGUAGE

While English is spoken everywhere in Florida, Spanish can be quite useful to know in South Florida, especially in Miami-Dade county, where Hispanics make up more than half the population. A good percentage of Miami tourism comes from Latin America, so Spanish can be heard quite frequently in hotels, stores, and restaurants. In general, when you order a regular coffee, you get coffee with milk and sugar.

LODGING

Florida has every conceivable type of lodging—from tree houses to penthouses, mansions for hire to hostels. Even with occupancy rates inching above 70%, there are almost always rooms available, except maybe at Christmas and other holidays.

Children are welcome generally everywhere in Florida. Pets are another matter, so **inquire ahead of time if you're bringing an animal with you.**

In the busy seasons—over Christmas and from late January through Easter in the southern half of the state, during the summer along the Panhandle and around Jacksonville, and all over Florida during holiday weekends in summer—always **reserve ahead for the top properties.** Fall is the slowest season: rates are low and availability is high, but this is also the prime time for hurricanes. St. Augustine stays busy all summer because of its historic flavor. Key West is jam-packed for Fantasy Fest at Halloween. If you're not booking through a travel agent, call the visitors bureau or the chamber of commerce in the area where you're going to check whether any special event is scheduled for when you plan to arrive.

The lodgings we list are the cream of the crop in each price category. We always list the facilities that are available—but we don't specify whether they cost extra: when pricing accommodations, always ask what's included and what costs extra.

CATEGORY	COST*
$$$$	over $220
$$$	$140–$220
$$	$100–$140
$	$80–$100
¢	under $80

All prices are for a standard double room, excluding 6% sales tax (more in some counties) and 1%–4% tourist tax.

Assume that hotels operate on the **European Plan** (EP, with no meals), unless we specify that they use the **Continental Plan** (CP, with a Continental breakfast), **Breakfast Plan** (BP, with a full breakfast), **Modified American Plan** (MAP, with breakfast and dinner), or the **Full American Plan** (FAP, with all meals).

Properties are assigned price categories based on the range from their least-expensive standard double room at high season (excluding holidays) to the most expensive. Properties marked ✕🖾 are lodging establishments whose restaurants warrant a special trip.

APARTMENT & VILLA RENTALS

If you want a home base that's roomy enough for a family and comes with cooking facilities, **consider a furnished rental.** These can save you money, especially if you're traveling with a group. Home-exchange directories sometimes list rentals as well as exchanges.

🖪 International Agents **Hideaways International** ✉ 767 Islington St., Portsmouth, NH 03802 ☎ 603/430-4433 or 800/843-4433 🖶 603/430-4444 ⊕ www.hideaways.com, membership $129. **Hometours International** ✉ 1108 Scottie La., Knoxville, TN 37919 ☎ 865/690-8484 or 866/367-4668 ⊕ http://thor.he.net/~hometour/. **Interhome** ✉ 1990 N.E. 163rd St., Suite 110, North Miami Beach, FL 33162 ☎ 305/940-2299 or 800/882-6864 🖶 305/940-2911 ⊕ www.interhome.us. **Vacation Home Rentals Worldwide** ✉ 235 Kensington Ave., Norwood, NJ 07648 ☎ 201/767-9393 or 800/633-3284 🖶 201/767-5510 ⊕ www.vhrww.com.
🖪 Local Agents **American Realty** ✉ Box 1133, Captiva, FL 33924 ☎ 800/547-0127 ⊕ www.captivaisland.com/amrc. **Fairfield Resorts** ✉ 5259 Coconut Creek Pkwy., Margate, FL 33063 ☎ 800/251-8736

⊕ www.efairfield.com. **Florida Sunbreak** ✉ 828 Washington Ave., Miami Beach, FL 33139 ☎ 800/786-2732 or 305/532-1516 ⊕ www.floridasunbreak.com. **Freewheeler Vacations** ✉ Box 1634 [MM 86], Islamorada, FL 33036 ☎ 305/664-2075 ⊕ www.freewheeler-realty.com. **Marr Properties** ✉ 101925 Overseas Hwy., Key Largo, FL 33037 ☎ 800/277-3728 or 305/451-4078. **Resort Quest International** ✉ 530 Oak Court., Memphis, TN 38117 ☎ 877/588-5800 ⊕ www.resortquest.com. **Sand Key Realty** ✉ 2701 Gulf Blvd., Clearwater, FL 33785 ☎ 800/257-7332 or 727/595-5441. **Abbott Resorts** ✉ 35000 Emerald Coast Pkwy., Destin, FL 32541 ☎ 800/336-4853. **Coldwell Banker Suncoast Realty** ✉ 224 Franklin Blvd., St. George Island, FL 32328 ☎ 800/341-2021.

BED-AND-BREAKFASTS

Small inns and guest houses are increasingly numerous in Florida, but they vary tremendously, ranging from economical places that are plain but serve a good home-style breakfast to elegantly furnished Victorian houses with four-course gourmet morning meals and rates to match. Many offer a homelike setting. In fact, many are in private homes with owners who treat you almost like family, while others are more businesslike. It's a good idea to **make specific inquiries of B&Bs you're interested in.** The association listed below offers descriptions and suggestions for B&Bs throughout Florida. *Superior Small Lodging, a Guide to Fine Small Hotels,* is available through the Daytona Beach Convention and Visitors Bureau.

🖪 Bed & Breakfast Association **Florida Bed and Breakfast Inn** ✉ Box 6187, Palm Harbor, FL 34684 ☎ 281/499-1374 or 800/524-1880 ⊕ www.florida-inns.com. *Superior Small Lodging, a Guide to Fine Small Hotels* ✉ 126 E. Orange Ave., Daytona Beach, FL 32114 ☎ 356/255-0415 or 800/854-1234.

CAMPING

Camping is popular throughout the state, especially in central Florida near the major Orlando attractions, and on the mellower west coast. Camping on nondesignated beach sites is not allowed. For information on camping facilities, contact the national and state parks and forests you plan to visit and the Florida Department of Environmental Protection (⇨ National Parks).

To find a commercial campground, **pick up a copy of the free annual "Official Florida Camping Directory,"** which lists 305 campgrounds, with more than 55,000 sites. It's available at Florida welcome centers, from the Florida Tourism Industry Marketing Corporation (⇨ Visitor Information), and from the Florida Association of RV Parks & Campgrounds.

▪ Camping Association **Florida Association of RV Parks & Campgrounds** ⊠ 1340 Vickers Dr., Tallahassee, FL 32303-3041 ☎ 850/562-7151 🖷 850/562-7179 ⊕ www.gocampingamerica.com.

CONDOS

▪ Condo Guide *The Condo Lux Vacationer's Guide to Condominium Rentals in the Southeast* (Vintage Books/Random House, New York; $9.95), by Jill Little.

CUTTING COSTS

Affordable lodgings can be found in even the most glittery resort towns, typically motel rooms that may cost as little as $50–$60 a night; they may not be in the best part of town, mind you, but they won't be in the worst, either (perhaps along busy highways where you'll need the roar of the air-conditioning to drown out the traffic). Since beachfront properties tend to be more expensive, **look for properties a little off the beach.** Still, many beachfront properties are surprisingly affordable, too, as in places like St. Petersburg Beach, on the west coast, and Cocoa Beach, on the east coast.

If demand isn't especially high for the time you have in mind to visit, you can often **save by showing up at a lodging in mid-to late afternoon**—desk clerks are typically willing to negotiate with travelers in order to fill those rooms late in the day. In addition, **check with chambers of commerce for discount coupons for selected properties.**

HOME EXCHANGES

If you would like to exchange your home for someone else's, **join a home-exchange organization,** which will send you its updated listings of available exchanges for a year and will include your own listing in at least one of them. It's up to you to make specific arrangements.

▪ Exchange Clubs **HomeLink International** 🖅 Box 47747, Tampa, FL 33647 ☎ 813/975-9825 or 800/638-3841 🖷 813/910-8144 ⊕ www.homelink. org; $110 yearly for a listing, on-line access, and catalog; $40 without catalog. **Intervac U.S.** ⊠ 30 Corte San Fernando, Tiburon, CA 94920 ☎ 800/756-4663 🖷 415/435-7440 ⊕ www.intervacus.com; $105 yearly for a listing, on-line access, and a catalog; $50 without catalog.

HOSTELS

No matter what your age, you can **save on lodging costs by staying at hostels.** In some 4,500 locations in more than 70 countries around the world, Hostelling International (HI), the umbrella group for a number of national youth-hostel associations, offers single-sex, dorm-style beds and, at many hostels, rooms for couples and family accommodations. Membership in any HI national hostel association, open to travelers of all ages, allows you to stay in HI-affiliated hostels at member rates; one-year membership is about $28 for adults (C$35 for a two-year minimum membership in Canada, £13.50 in the U. K., A$52 in Australia, and NZ$40 in New Zealand); hostels charge about $10–$30 per night. Members have priority if the hostel is full; they're also eligible for discounts around the world, even on rail and bus travel in some countries.

▪ Organizations **Hostelling International–USA** ⊠ 8401 Colesville Rd., Suite 600, Silver Spring, MD 20910 ☎ 301/495-1240 🖷 301/495-6697 ⊕ www. hiayh.org. **Hostelling International–Canada** ⊠ 400–205 Catherine St., Ottawa, Ontario K2P 1C3 ☎ 613/237-7884 or 800/663-5777 🖷 613/237-7868 ⊕ www.hihostels.ca. **YHA England and Wales** ⊠ Trevelyan House, Dimple Rd., Matlock, Derbyshire DE4 3YH, U.K. ☎ 0870/870-8808 🖷 0870/770-6127 ⊕ www.yha.org.uk. **YHA Australia** ⊠ 422 Kent St., Sydney, NSW 2001 ☎ 02/9261-1111 🖷 02/9261-1969 ⊕ www.yha.com.au. **YHA New Zealand** ⊠ Level 3, 193 Cashel St., Box 436, Christchurch ☎ 03/379-9970 or 0800/278-299 🖷 03/365-4476 ⊕ www.yha.org.nz.

HOTELS

Wherever you look in Florida, it seems, you'll find lots of plain, inexpensive motels and luxurious resorts, independents alongside national chains, and an ever-growing number of modern properties as well as quite a few timeless classics. In fact, since Florida has been a favored travel destination for some time, vintage hotels are everywhere, both grand edifices like the Breakers in Palm Beach, the Boca Raton Resort & Club in Boca Raton, the Biltmore in Coral Gables, and the Casa Marina in Key West as well as smaller, historic places, like the Governors Inn in Tallahassee and the New World Inn in Pensacola.

All hotels listed have private bath unless otherwise noted.

7 Toll-Free Numbers **Adam's Mark** ☎ 800/444-2326 ⊕ www.adamsmark.com. **Baymont Inns** ☎ 800/428-3438 ⊕ www.baymontinns.com. **Best Western** ☎ 800/528-1234 ⊕ www.bestwestern.com. **Choice** ☎ 800/424-6423 ⊕ www.choicehotels.com. **Clarion** ☎ 800/424-6423 ⊕ www.choicehotels.com. **Comfort Inn** ☎ 800/424-6423 ⊕ www.choicehotels.com.**Days Inn** ☎ 800/325-2525 ⊕ www.daysinn.com. **Doubletree Hotels** ☎ 800/222-8733 ⊕ www.doubletree.com. **Embassy Suites** ☎ 800/362-2779 ⊕ www.embassysuites.com. **Fairfield Inn** ☎ 800/228-2800 ⊕ www.marriott.com. **Four Seasons** ☎ 800/332-3442 ⊕ www.fourseasons.com. **Hilton** ☎ 800/445-8667 ⊕ www.hilton.com. **Holiday Inn** ☎ 800/465-4329 ⊕ www.sixcontinentshotels.com. **Howard Johnson** ☎ 800/446-4656 ⊕ www.hojo.com. **Hyatt Hotels & Resorts** ☎ 800/233-1234 ⊕ www.hyatt.com. **Inter-Continental** ☎ 800/327-0200 ⊕ www.intercontinental.com. **La Quinta** ☎ 800/531-5900 ⊕ www.laquinta.com. **Marriott** ☎ 800/228-9290 ⊕ www.marriott.com.**Omni** ☎ 800/843-6664 ⊕ www.omnihotels.com. **Quality Inn** ☎ 800/424-6423 ⊕ www.choicehotels.com. **Radisson** ☎ 800/333-3333 ⊕ www.radisson.com. **Ramada** ☎ 800/228-2828; 800/854-7854 international reservations ⊕ www.ramada.com or www.ramadahotels.com. **Renaissance Hotels & Resorts** ☎ 800/468-3571 ⊕ www.renaissancehotels.com/. **Ritz-Carlton** ☎ 800/241-3333 ⊕ www.ritzcarlton.com. **Sheraton** ☎ 800/325-3535 ⊕ www.starwood.com/sheraton. **Sleep Inn** ☎ 800/424-6423 ⊕ www.choicehotels.com. **Westin Hotels & Resorts** ☎ 800/228-3000 ⊕ www.starwood.com/westin.**Wyndham Hotels & Resorts** ☎ 800/822-4200 ⊕ www.wyndham.com.

VACATION OWNERSHIP RESORTS

Vacation ownership resorts sell hotel rooms, condominium apartments, and villas in weekly, monthly, or quarterly increments. The weekly arrangement is most popular; it's often referred to as "interval ownership" or "time sharing." Of more than 3,000 vacation ownership resorts around the world, some 500 are in Florida, with the heaviest concentration in the Walt Disney World–Orlando area. Nonowners can rent at many of these resorts by contacting the individual property or a real-estate broker in the area.

MONEY MATTERS

Prices throughout this guide are given for adults. Substantially reduced fees are almost always available for children, students, and senior citizens. For information on taxes, *see* Taxes.

ATMS

Automatic Teller Machines (ATMs) are ubiquitous in Florida. In addition to banks, you will find them at grocery store chains like Publix and Winn-Dixie, in shopping malls big and small, and, increasingly, at gas stations.

CREDIT CARDS

Throughout this guide, the following abbreviations are used: **AE**, American Express; **D**, Discover; **DC**, Diners Club; **MC**, MasterCard; and **V**, Visa.

7 Reporting Lost Cards **American Express** ☎ 800/441-0519. **Diners Club** ☎ 800/234-6377. **Discover** ☎ 800/347-2683. **MasterCard** ☎ 800/622-7747. **Visa** ☎ 800/ 847-2911.

NATIONAL PARKS

Look into discount passes to save money on park entrance fees. For $50, the National Parks Pass admits you (and any passengers in your private vehicle) to all national parks, monuments, and recreation areas, as well as other sites run by the National Park Service, for a year. (In parks that charge per person, the pass admits you, your spouse and children, and your parents, when you arrive together.) Camping and parking are extra. The $15 Golden Eagle Pass, a hologram you affix to your National Parks Pass, functions as an upgrade, granting entry to all sites run by the NPS, the U.S. Fish and Wildlife Service, the U.S. Forest Service, and the Bureau of Land Management. The upgrade, which expires with the parks pass, is sold by most national-park, Fish-and-Wildlife, and BLM fee stations. A percentage of the proceeds from pass sales funds National Parks projects.

Both the Golden Age Passport ($10), for U.S. citizens or permanent residents who are 62 and older, and the Golden Access Passport (free), for those with disabilities, entitle holders (and any passengers in their private vehicles) to lifetime free entry to all national parks, plus 50% off fees for the use of many park facilities and services. (The discount doesn't always apply to companions.) To obtain them, you must show proof of age and of U.S. citizenship or permanent residency—such as a U.S. passport, driver's license, or birth certificate—and, if requesting Golden Access, proof of disability. The Golden Age and

Golden Access passes are available only at NPS-run sites that charge an entrance fee. The National Parks Pass is also available by mail and via the Internet.

📶 **National Park Foundation** ⊠ 11 Dupont Circle NW, 6th fl., Washington, DC 20036 ☎ 202/238-4200 ⊕ www.nationalparks.org. **National Park Service** ⊠ National Park Service/Department of Interior, 1849 C St. NW, Washington, DC 20240 ☎ 202/208-6843 ⊕ www.nps.gov. **National Parks Conservation Association** ⊠ 1300 19th St. NW, Suite 300, Washington, DC 20036 ☎ 202/223-6722 ⊕ www.npca.org.

📶 **Passes by Mail & On-Line National Park Foundation** ⊕ www.nationalparks.org. **National Parks Pass** ⌗ Box 34108, Washington, DC 20043 ☎ 888/467-2757 ⊕ www.nationalparks.org; include a check or money order payable to the National Park Service, plus $3.95 for shipping and handling, or call for passes by phone.

PRIVATE PRESERVES

📶 **Florida Sanctuary Information Audubon Florida** ⊠ 444 Birckell Ave., Suite 850, Miami, FL 33131 ☎ 305/371-6399 ⊕ www.audubonofflorida.org. **Nature Conservancy** ⊠ Blowing Rocks Preserve 574 South Beach Rd., Hobe Sound, FL 33455 ☎ 561/744-6668 ⊠ Disney Wilderness Preserve 2700 Scrub Jay Trail, Kissimmee, FL 34759 ☎ 407/935-0002 ⊠ Apalachicola Bluffs and Ravines Preserve, NW Florida Program County Road 270, Bristol, FL 32321 ☎ 850/643-2756 ⊠ SE Division 222 S. Westmonte Dr., Suite 300, Altamonte Springs, FL 32714 ☎ 407/682-3664 ⊠ 333 Fleming St., Key West, FL 33040 ☎ 305/745-8402 ⊠ 225 E. Stuart Ave., Lake Wales, FL 33853 ☎ 863/635-7506 ⊠ 625 N. Adams St., Tallahassee, FL 32301 ☎ 850/222-0199 ⊠ Comeau Bldg., 319 Clematis St., Suite 611, West Palm Beach, FL 33401 ☎ 954/564-6144.

STATE PARKS

Florida's Department of Environmental Protection (DEP) is responsible for hundreds of historic buildings, landmarks, nature preserves, and parks. When requesting a free *Florida State Park Guide*, mention which parts of the state you plan to visit. For information on camping facilities at the state parks, ask for the free "Florida State Parks, Fees and Facilities" and "Florida State Parks Camping Reservation Procedures" brochures. Responding to cutbacks in its budget, the DEP established Friends of Florida State Parks, a citizen support organization open to all.

📶 **State Parks Information Florida Department of Environmental Protection** ⊠ Marjory Stoneman Douglas Bldg., MS 536, 3900 Commonwealth Blvd., Tallahassee, FL 32399-3000 ☎ 850/488-9872; **Friends of Florida State Parks** ☎ 850/488-8243.

OUTDOORS & SPORTS

Recreational opportunities abound throughout Florida. The Governor's Council on Physical Fitness and Sports puts on the Sunshine State Games each July in a different part of the state.

📶 **General Information Florida Department of Environmental Protection** ⊠ Office of Greenways and Trails, MS 795, 3900 Commonwealth Blvd., Tallahassee, FL 32399-3000 ☎ 850/245-2052 or 877/822-5208 ⊕ www.dep.state.fl.us for information on bicycling, canoeing, kayaking, and hiking trails.

📶 **Marine Charts Teall's Guides** ⊠ 111 Saguaro La., Marathon, FL 33050 ☎ 305/743-3942 ⊠ 305/743-3943, $7.95 set, $3.60 each individual chart.

BIKING

Biking is a popular Florida sport. Rails to Trails, a nationwide group that turns unused railroad rights-of-way into bicycle and walking paths, has made great inroads in Florida, particularly around the Tampa–St. Pete area. In addition, just about every town in Florida has its own set of bike paths and a bike rental outfit. For bike information, **check with Florida's Department of Transportation (DOT),** which publishes free bicycle trail guides, dispenses free touring information packets, and provides names of bike coordinators around the state.

📶 **Bicycle Information Rails to Trails** ☎ 850/942-2379. **DOT state bicycle-pedestrian coordinator** ⊠ 605 Suwannee St., MS 82, Tallahassee, FL 32399-0450 ☎ 850/487-1200.

CANOEING & KAYAKING

You can canoe or kayak along 1,550 mi of trails encompassing creeks, rivers, and springs. Both the DEP (⇨ General Information) and outfitter associations provide information on trails and their conditions, events, and contacts for trips and equipment rental.

📶 **Outfitters & Outfitting Associations Canoe Outpost System** ⊠ 2816 N.W. Rte. 661, Arcadia, FL 33821 ☎ 863/494-1215 or 800/268-0083, comprising five outfitters. **Florida Professional Paddlesports Association** ⊠ Box 1764, Arcadia, FL 34265 ☎ No phone ⊕ www.paddleflausa.com has a state map available on-line and a directory of local resources.

FISHING

In Atlantic and gulf waters, fishing seasons and other regulations vary by location and species. You will need to **buy one license for freshwater fishing and another license for saltwater fishing.** Nonresident fees for a saltwater license are $31.50. Nonresidents can purchase freshwater licenses good for three days ($6.50), seven days ($16.50), or for one year ($31.50). Typically, you'll pay a $1.50 surcharge at most any marina, bait shop, Kmart, Wal-Mart, or other license vendor.
⚡ Fishing Information Florida Fish and Wildlife Conservation Commission ✉ 620 S. Meridian St., Tallahassee, FL 32399-1600 ☎ 850/488-1960 for the free *Florida Fishing Handbook* with license vendors, regional fishing guides, and educational bulletins.

HORSEBACK RIDING

Horseback riding is a popular sport outside of Florida's metropolitan areas. There are trails around the state and even beaches on which you can ride. Please refer to outdoor activities listed in individual chapters.

JOGGING, RUNNING & WALKING

Many towns have walking and running trails, and most of Florida's beaches stretch on for miles, testing the limits of even the most stalwart runners and walkers. Local running clubs all over the state sponsor weekly public events. The Miami Runners Club has information about South Florida events. The Road Runners Club of America has chapters throughout the state.
⚡ Clubs & Events Miami Runners Club ✉ 8720 N. Kendall Dr., Suite 206, Miami, FL 33176 ⊕ www.miamirunnersclub.com. **Road Runners Club of America** northern state info ✉ 65 Winterbourne St. N, Orange Park, FL 32073 ☎ 904/278-2926 ✉ Southern state info: 23059 Redfish La., Cudjoe Key, FL 33042 ☎ 305/745-3027.

PARI-MUTUEL SPORTS

Jai-alai frontons and greyhound-racing tracks are in most major Florida cities. Patrons can bet on the teams or dogs or on televised horse races.
⚡ Schedules Department of Business & Professional Regulations **Division of Pari-Mutuel Wagering** ✉ 1940 N. Monroe St., Tallahassee, FL 32399 ☎ 850/488-9130 ☎ 850/488-0550.

TENNIS

Tennis is extremely popular in Florida, and virtually every town has well-maintained public courts. In addition, many tennis tournaments are held in the state.
⚡ Tournament & Event Schedules USA Tennis Florida ✉ 1 Deuce Court, Suite 100, Daytona Beach, FL 32124 ☎ 386/671-8949 ☎ 386/671-8948 ⊕ www.usta-fl.com.

WILDERNESS & RECREATION AREAS

Florida is studded with trails, rivers, and parks that are ideal for hiking, bird-watching, canoeing, bicycling, and horseback riding. *Florida Trails: A Guide to Florida's Natural Habitats,* available from Florida Tourism Industry Marketing Corporation (⇨ Visitor Information), has information for bicycling, canoeing, horseback riding, and walking trails; camping; snorkeling and scuba diving; and Florida ecosystems.
⚡ Publications *Florida Wildlife Viewing Guide* 📀 available from Falcon Press Box 1718, Helena, MT 59624 ☎ 800/582-2665; $10.95 plus $4 shipping, by Susan Cerulean and Ann Morrow, for marked wildlife-watching sites. *Recreation Guide to District Lands* 📀 Available from St. Johns River Water Management District Box 1429, Palatka, FL 32178-1429 ☎ 386/329-4111; free for marine, wetland, and upland recreational areas.

PACKING

The northern part of the state is much cooler in winter than the southern part, and you'll want to take a heavy sweater if you plan on traveling there in the winter months. Even in the summer ocean breezes can be cool, so always **take a sweater or jacket** just in case.

The Miami area and the Naples–Fort Myers area are warm year-round and often extremely humid in summer months. Be prepared for sudden summer storms all over Florida in the summer months, but keep in mind that plastic raincoats are uncomfortable in the high humidity.

Dress is casual throughout the state, with sundresses, jeans, or walking shorts appropriate during the day; **bring comfortable walking shoes or sneakers** for theme parks. A few restaurants request that men wear jackets and ties, but most do not. Be prepared for air-conditioning working in overdrive.

You can generally swim year-round in peninsular Florida from about New

Smyrna Beach south on the Atlantic coast and from Tarpon Springs south on the Gulf Coast. Be sure to **take a sun hat and sunscreen** because the sun can be fierce, even in winter and even if it is chilly or overcast.

In your carry-on luggage, **pack an extra pair of eyeglasses or contact lenses and enough of any medication** you take to last a few days longer than the entire trip. You may also ask your doctor to write a spare prescription using the drug's generic name, as brand names may vary from country to country. In luggage to be checked, **never pack prescription drugs, valuables, or undeveloped film.** And don't forget to carry with you the addresses of offices that handle refunds of lost traveler's checks. Check *Fodor's How to Pack* (available at on-line retailers and bookstores everywhere) for more tips.

To avoid customs and security delays, carry medications in their original packaging. Don't pack any sharp objects in your carry-on luggage, including knives of any size or material, scissors, and corkscrews, or anything else that might arouse suspicion.

To avoid having your checked luggage chosen for hand inspection, don't cram bags full. The U.S. Transportation Security Administration suggests packing shoes on top and placing personal items you don't want touched in clear plastic bags.

CHECKING LUGGAGE

You're allowed to carry aboard one bag and one personal article, such as a purse or a laptop computer. Make sure what you carry on fits under your seat or in the overhead bin. Get to the gate early, so you can board as soon as possible, before the overhead bins fill up.

Baggage allowances vary by carrier, destination, and ticket class. On international flights, you're usually allowed to check two bags weighing up to 70 pounds (32 kilograms) each, although a few airlines allow checked bags of up to 88 pounds (40 kilograms) in first class. Some international carriers don't allow more than 66 pounds (30 kilograms) per bag in business class and 44 pounds (20 kilograms) in economy. On domestic flights, the limit may be 50 pounds (23 kilograms) per bag. Most airlines won't accept bags that weigh more than 100 pounds (45 kilograms) on domestic or international flights. Check baggage restrictions with your carrier before you pack.

Airline liability for baggage is limited to $2,500 per person on flights within the United States. On international flights it amounts to $9.07 per pound or $20 per kilogram for checked baggage (roughly $640 per 70-pound bag) and $400 per passenger for unchecked baggage. You can buy additional coverage at check-in for about $10 per $1,000 of coverage, but it often excludes a rather extensive list of items, shown on your airline ticket.

Before departure, **itemize your bags' contents** and their worth, and label the bags with your name, address, and phone number. (If you use your home address, cover it so potential thieves can't see it readily.) Include a label inside each bag and **pack a copy of your itinerary.** At check-in, **make sure each bag is correctly tagged** with the destination airport's three-letter code. Because some checked bags will be opened for hand inspection, the U.S. Transportation Security Administration recommends that you leave luggage unlocked or use the plastic locks offered at check-in. TSA screeners place an inspection notice inside searched bags, which are re-sealed with a special lock.

If your bag has been searched and contents are missing or damaged, file a claim with the TSA Consumer Response Center as soon as possible. If your bags arrive damaged or fail to arrive at all, file a written report with the airline before leaving the airport.

Complaints U.S. Transportation Security Administration Consumer Response Center ☎ 866/289-9673 ⊕ www.tsa.gov.

SAFETY

Stepped-up policing of thieves who prey on tourists in rental cars has helped address what was a serious issue in the early '90s. Still, visitors should be especially wary when driving in strange neighborhoods and leaving the airport, especially in the Miami area. Don't assume that valuables are safe in your hotel room; use in-room safes or the hotel's safety deposit boxes. Try to use ATMs only during the day or in brightly lit, well-traveled locales.

BEACH SAFETY

Before swimming, **make sure there's no undertow.** Rip currents, caused when the tide rushes out through a narrow break in the water, can overpower even the strongest swimmer. If you do get caught in one, resist the urge to swim straight back to shore—you'll tire before you make it. Instead, stay calm. Swim parallel to the shore line until you are outside the current's pull, then work your way in to shore.

SENIOR-CITIZEN TRAVEL

Since Florida has a significant retired population, senior-citizen discounts are ubiquitous throughout the state. To qualify for age-related discounts, **mention your senior-citizen status up front** when booking hotel reservations (not when checking out) and before you're seated in restaurants (not when paying the bill). Be sure to have identification on hand. When renting a car, ask about promotional car-rental discounts, which can be cheaper than senior-citizen rates.

🛈 Educational Programs **Elderhostel** ✉ 11 Ave. de Lafayette, Boston, MA 02111-1746 ☎ 877/426-8056; 978/323-4141 international callers; 877/426-2167 TTY 🖷 877/426-2166 ⊕ www.elderhostel.org. **Interhostel** ✉ University of New Hampshire, 6 Garrison Ave., Durham, NH 03824 ☎ 603/862-1147 or 800/733-9753 🖷 603/862-1113 ⊕ www.learn.unh.edu.

STUDENTS IN FLORIDA

Students flock to the beaches of Florida during spring break, but there are also special tours for students year-round. Students presenting identification qualify for discounts at most movie theaters and art museums.

🛈 I.D.s & Services **STA Travel** ✉ 10 Downing St., New York, NY 10014 ☎ 212/627-3111 or 800/777-0112 🖷 212/627-3387 ⊕ www.sta.com. **Travel Cuts** ✉ 187 College St., Toronto, Ontario M5T 1P7, Canada ☎ 416/979-2406 or 800/592-2887; 866/246-9762 in Canada 🖷 416/979-8167 ⊕ www.travelcuts.com.

TAXES

SALES TAX

Florida's sales tax is currently 7%, but local sales and tourist taxes can raise that number considerably, especially for certain items, such as lodging. Miami hoteliers, for example, collect roughly 12.5% for city and resort taxes. It's best to **ask about additional costs up front,** to avoid a rude awakening.

TELEPHONES

To make local calls within the 305 (Miami area) and 407 (Orlando area) calling areas, **begin calls with the local area code,** dialing a total of 10 digits.

TIME

The western portion of the Panhandle is in the Central Time Zone, but the rest of Florida is in the Eastern Time Zone.

TIPPING

Whether they carry bags, open doors, deliver food, or clean rooms, hospitality employees work to receive a portion of your travel budget. In deciding how much to give, **base your tip on what the service is and how well it's performed.**

In transit, tip an airport valet $1–$3 per bag, a taxi driver 15%–20% of the fare.

For hotel staff, recommended amounts are $1–$3 per bag for a bellhop, $1–$2 per night per guest for chambermaids, $5–$10 for special concierge service, $1–$3 for a doorman who hails a cab or parks a car, 15% of the greens fee for a caddy, 15%–20% of the bill for a massage, and 15% of a room service bill (bear in mind that sometimes 15%–18% is automatically added to room service bills, so don't add it twice).

In a restaurant, give 15%–20% of your bill before tax to the server, 5%–10% to the maître d', 15% to a bartender, and 15% of the wine bill for a wine steward who makes a special effort in selecting and serving wine.

TOURS & PACKAGES

Because everything is prearranged on a prepackaged tour or independent vacation, you spend less time planning—and often get it all at a good price.

BOOKING WITH AN AGENT

Travel agents are excellent resources. But it's a good idea to collect brochures from several agencies, as some agents' suggestions may be influenced by relationships with tour and package firms that reward them for volume sales. If you have a special interest, **find an agent with expertise**

in that area; the American Society of Travel Agents (ASTA; ⇨ Travel Agencies) has a database of specialists worldwide.

Make sure your travel agent knows the accommodations and other services of the place being recommended. Ask about the hotel's location, room size, beds, and whether it has a pool, room service, or programs for children, if you care about these. Has your agent been there in person or sent others whom you can contact?

Do some homework on your own, too: local tourism boards can provide information about lesser-known and small-niche operators, some of which may sell only direct.

BUYER BEWARE

Each year consumers are stranded or lose their money when tour operators—even large ones with excellent reputations—go out of business. So **check out the operator.** Ask several travel agents about its reputation, and try to **book with a company that has a consumer-protection program.** (Look for information in the company's brochure.) In the United States, members of the National Tour Association and the United States Tour Operators Association are required to set aside funds to cover payments and travel arrangements in the event that the company defaults. It's also a good idea to choose a company that participates in the American Society of Travel Agents' Tour Operator Program; ASTA will act as mediator in any disputes between you and your tour operator.

Remember that the more your package or tour includes, the better you can predict the ultimate cost of your vacation. Make sure you know exactly what is covered, and **beware of hidden costs.** Are taxes, tips, and transfers included? Entertainment and excursions? These can add up.

⚡ Tour-Operator Recommendations American Society of Travel Agents (⇨ Travel Agencies). **National Tour Association (NTA)** ✉ 546 E. Main St., Lexington, KY 40508 ☎ 859/226-4444 or 800/682-8886 🖷 859/226-4404 ⊕ www.ntaonline.com. **United States Tour Operators Association (USTOA)** ✉ 275 Madison Ave., Suite 2014, New York, NY 10016 ☎ 212/599-6599 or 800/468-7862 🖷 212/599-6744 ⊕ www.ustoa.com.

TRAIN TRAVEL

Amtrak provides north–south service on two routes to the major cities of Jack-

sonville, Orlando, Tampa, West Palm Beach, Fort Lauderdale, and Miami, and east–west service through Jacksonville, Tallahassee, and Pensacola, with many stops in between on all routes.

🚆 Train Information Amtrak ☎ 800/872-7245 ⊕ www.amtrak.com.

TRAVEL AGENCIES

A good travel agent puts your needs first. Look for an agency that has been in business at least five years, emphasizes customer service, and has someone on staff who specializes in your destination. In addition, **make sure the agency belongs to a professional trade organization.** The American Society of Travel Agents (ASTA)—the largest and most influential in the field with more than 20,000 members in some 140 countries—maintains and enforces a strict code of ethics and will step in to help mediate any agent-client disputes involving ASTA members if necessary. ASTA (whose motto is "Without a travel agent, you're on your own") also maintains a Web site that includes a directory of agents. (If a travel agency is also acting as your tour operator, *see* Buyer Beware *in* Tours and Packages.)

🚆 Local Agent Referrals American Society of Travel Agents (ASTA) ✉ 1101 King St., Suite 200, Alexandria, VA 22314 ☎ 703/739-2782; 800/965-2782 24-hr hot line 🖷 703/739-3268 ⊕ www.astanet.com. **Association of British Travel Agents** ✉ 68-71 Newman St., London W1T 3AH ☎ 020/7637-2444 🖷 020/7637-0713 ⊕ www.abtanet.com. **Association of Canadian Travel Agents** ✉ 130 Albert St., Suite 1705, Ottawa, Ontario K1P 5G4 ☎ 613/237-3657 🖷 613/237-7052 ⊕ www.acta.ca. **Australian Federation of Travel Agents** ✉ Level 3, 309 Pitt St., Sydney, NSW 2000 ☎ 02/9264-3299 🖷 02/9264-1085 ⊕ www.afta.com.au. **Travel Agents' Association of New Zealand** ✉ Level 5, Tourism and Travel House, 79 Boulcott St., Box 1888, Wellington 6001 ☎ 04/499-0104 🖷 04/499-0786 ⊕ www.taanz.org.nz.

VISITOR INFORMATION

For general information about Florida's attractions, contact the office below; welcome centers are located on Interstate 10, Interstate 75, Interstate 95, and U.S. 231 (near Graceville), and in the lobby of the New Capitol in Tallahassee. For regional tourist bureaus and chambers of commerce see individual chapters.

CONVERSIONS

DISTANCE

KILOMETERS/MILES

To change kilometers (km) to miles (mi), multiply km by .621. To change mi to km, multiply mi by 1.61.

km to mi	mi to km
1 = .62	1 = 1.6
2 = 1.2	2 = 3.2
3 = 1.9	3 = 4.8
4 = 2.5	4 = 6.4
5 = 3.1	5 = 8.1
6 = 3.7	6 = 9.7
7 = 4.3	7 = 11.3
8 = 5.0	8 = 12.9

METERS/FEET

To change meters (m) to feet (ft), multiply m by 3.28. To change ft to m, multiply ft by .305.

m to ft	ft to m
1 = 3.3	1 = .30
2 = 6.6	2 = .61
3 = 9.8	3 = .92
4 = 13.1	4 = 1.2
5 = 16.4	5 = 1.5
6 = 19.7	6 = 1.8
7 = 23.0	7 = 2.1
8 = 26.2	8 = 2.4

WEIGHT

KILOGRAMS/POUNDS

To change kilograms (kg) to pounds (lb), multiply kg by 2.20. To change lb to kg, multiply lb by .455.

kg to lb	lb to kg
1 = 2.2	1 = .45
2 = 4.4	2 = .91
3 = 6.6	3 = 1.4
4 = 8.8	4 = 1.8
5 = 11.0	5 = 2.3
6 = 13.2	6 = 2.7
7 = 15.4	7 = 3.2
8 = 17.6	8 = 3.6

GRAMS/OUNCES

To change grams (g) to ounces (oz), multiply g by .035. To change oz to g, multiply oz by 28.4.

g to oz	oz to g
1 = .04	1 = 28
2 = .07	2 = 57
3 = .11	3 = 85
4 = .14	4 = 114
5 = .18	5 = 142
6 = .21	6 = 170
7 = .25	7 = 199
8 = .28	8 = 227

CLOTHING SIZE

WOMEN'S CLOTHING

US	UK	EUR
4	6	34
6	8	36
8	10	38
10	12	40
12	14	42

WOMEN'S SHOES

US	UK	EUR
5	3	36
6	4	37
7	5	38
8	6	39
9	7	40

MEN'S SUITS

US	UK	EUR
34	34	44
36	36	46
38	38	48
40	40	50
42	42	52
44	44	54
46	46	56

MEN'S SHIRTS

US	UK	EUR
14½	14½	37
15	15	38
15½	15½	39
16	16	41
16½	16½	42
17	17	43
17½	17½	44

MEN'S SHOES

US	UK	EUR
7	6	39½
8	7	41
9	8	42
10	9	43
11	10	44½
12	11	46

TEMPERATURE

METRIC CONVERSIONS

To change centigrade or Celsius (C) to Fahrenheit (F), multiply C by 1.8 and add 32. To change F to C, subtract 32 from F and multiply by .555.

°F	°C
0	-17.8
10	-12.2
20	-6.7
30	-1.1
32	0
40	+4.4
50	10.0
60	15.5
70	21.1
80	26.6
90	32.2
98.6	37.0
100	37.7

LIQUID VOLUME

LITERS/U.S. GALLONS

To change liters (L) to U.S. gallons (gal), multiply L by .264. To change U.S. gal to L, multiply gal by 3.79.

L to gal	gal to L
1 = .26	1 = 3.8
2 = .53	2 = 7.6
3 = .79	3 = 11.4
4 = 1.1	4 = 15.2
5 = 1.3	5 = 19.0
6 = 1.6	6 = 22.7
7 = 1.8	7 = 26.5
8 = 2.1	8 = 30.3

Learn more about foreign destinations by checking government-issued travel advisories and country information. For a broader picture, consider information from more than one country.

🚩 State **Florida Tourism Industry Marketing Corporation** ✉ Box 1100, 661 E. Jefferson St., Suite 300, Tallahassee, FL 32302 ☎ 850/488-5607 📠 850/224-2938 ⊕ www.flausa.com.

🚩 In the U.K. **ABC Florida** ✉ Box 35, Abingdon, Oxon OX14 4TB, U.K. ☎ 0891/600-555, 50p per minute; send £2 for vacation pack.

🚩 Government Advisories **Consular Affairs Bureau of Canada** ☎ 800/267-6788 or 613/944-6788 ⊕ www.voyage.gc.ca. U.K. **Foreign and Commonwealth Office** ✉ Travel Advice Unit, Consular Division, Old Admiralty Building, London SW1A 2PA ☎ 020/7008-0232 or 020/7008-0233 ⊕ www.fco.gov.uk/travel. **Australian Department of Foreign Affairs and Trade** ☎ 02/6261-1299 Consular Travel Advice Faxback Service ⊕ www.dfat.gov.au. **New Zealand Ministry of Foreign Affairs and Trade** ☎ 04/439-8000 ⊕ www.mft.govt.nz.

WEB SITES

Do check out the World Wide Web when planning your trip. You'll find everything from weather forecasts to virtual tours of famous cities. Be sure to **visit Fodors.com** (⊕ www.fodors.com), a complete travel-planning site. You can research prices and book plane tickets, hotel rooms, rental cars, vacation packages, and more. In addition, you can post your pressing questions in the Travel Talk section. Other planning tools include a currency converter and weather reports, and there are loads of links to travel resources.

The state of Florida is very visitor-oriented and has a terrific Web site— ⊕ www.flausa.com—with superb links to help you find out all you want to know. It's a wonderful place to learn about everything from fancy resorts to camping trips to car routes to beach towns.

MIAMI AND
MIAMI BEACH

FODOR'S CHOICE

Bill Baggs Cape Florida State Recreation Area, Key Biscayne

Delano Hotel, SoBe surrealism, South Beach

Mandarin Oriental Miami, downtown hotel, Brickell Key

Norman's, contemporary cuisine, Coral Gables

Ocean Drive, the "it" strip, South Beach

Ocean Surf, budget lodging, South Beach

HIGHLY RECOMMENDED

WHAT TO SEE   Espanola Way, South Beach

Fairchild Tropical Garden, Coral Gables

Fontainebleau Hilton Resort and Towers, South Beach

Gusman Center for the Performing Arts, Downtown

Miami City Ballet, South Beach

Miami-Dade Cultural Center, Downtown

Venetian Pool, Coral Gables

Wolfsonian–Florida International University, South Beach

Many other great hotels and restaurants enliven this area. For other favorites, look for the black stars as you read this chapter.

Updated by
Kathy Foster

MIAMI IS DIFFERENT from any other city in America—or any city in Latin America for that matter, even though it has a distinctly Latin flavor. Both logically and geologically, Miami shouldn't even be here. Resting on a paved swamp between the Everglades and the Atlantic Ocean, the city is subject to periodic flooding, hurricanes, and the onslaught of swallow-size mosquitoes. Despite the downsides, however, Miami is a vibrant city. The Tequesta Indians called this area home long before Spain's gold-laden treasure ships sailed along the Gulf Stream a few miles offshore. Foreshadowing 20th-century corporations, the Tequesta traded with mainland neighbors to the north and island brethren to the south. Today their descendants are the 150-plus U.S. and multinational companies whose Latin American headquarters are based in Greater Miami. For fans of international business and random statistics, Greater Miami has more than 40 foreign bank agencies, 11 Edge Act banks, 23 foreign trade offices, 31 binational chambers of commerce, and 53 foreign consulates.

The city has seen a decade of big changes. In the late 1980s Miami Beach was an oceanside geriatric ward. Today's South Beach residents have the kind of hip that doesn't break. The average age dropped from the mid-sixties in 1980 to a youthful early forties today. Toned young men outnumber svelte young women two to one, and hormones are as plentiful as pierced tongues. At night the revitalized Lincoln Road Mall is in full swing with cafés, galleries, and theaters, but it is also suffering vacancies due to rapidly rising rents. The bloom may not be off the rose, but cash-crazy entrepreneurs hoping to strike it rich on Miami's popularity are finding the pie isn't large enough to feed their financial fantasies. Those who have seen how high rents can crush a dream are heading to North Beach and the southern neighborhoods of South Beach, whose few remaining derelict buildings are a flashback to the pre-renaissance days of the 1980s. If the many high-rises under construction are any indication, this is where the next revival is taking place.

As you plan your trip, know that winter *is* the best time to visit, but if money is an issue, come in the off-season—after Easter and before October. You'll find plenty to do, and room rates are considerably lower. Summer brings many European and Latin American vacationers, who find Miami congenial despite the heat, humidity, and intense afternoon thunderstorms. Regardless of when you arrive, once you're here, you'll suspect that you've entered Cuban air space. No matter where you spin your radio dial, virtually every announcer punctuates each sentence with an emphatic "COO-BAH!" Look around, and you'll see Spanish on billboards, hear it on elevators, and pick it up on the streets. But Miami sways to more than just a Latin beat. In addition to populations from Brazil, Colombia, Argentina, El Salvador, Haiti, Jamaica, Nicaragua, Panama, Puerto Rico, Venezuela, and, of course, Cuba, there are also representatives from China, Germany, Greece, Iran, Israel, Italy, Lebanon, Malaysia, Russia, and Sweden. Miami has accepted its montage of nationalities, and it now celebrates this cultural diversity through languages, festivals, world-beat music, and a wealth of exotic restaurants.

If you're concerned about Miami crime, you'll be glad to know that criminals are off the street—and seem to be running for public office. Forget about D.C. If you want weird politics, spread out a blanket and enjoy the show. Miamians still talk about Mayor Xavier Suarez's being removed from office after a judge threw out absentee ballots that included votes from dead people. That pales in comparison to the Miami foul-ups in the 2002 gubernatorial primary: in the wake of complaints about hanging chads in the 2000 presidential election, the state had switched to computerized voting. However, bugs in the computer system caused even

Numbers in the text correspond to numbers in the margin and on the Miami Beach; Downtown Miami; Miami, Coral Gables, Coconut Grove, and Key Biscayne; and South Dade maps.

If you have 3 days

Grab your lotion and head to the ocean, more specifically **Ocean Drive** on **South Beach,** and catch some rays while relaxing on the white sands. Afterward, take a guided or self-guided tour of the **Art Deco District** to see what all the fuss is about. Keep the evening free to socialize at Ocean Drive cafés. The following day drive through **Little Havana** to witness the heartbeat of Miami's Cuban culture on your way south to Coconut Grove's Vizcaya. Wrap up the evening a few blocks away in downtown **Coconut Grove,** enjoying its party-like mood and many nightspots. On the last day head over to **Coral Gables** to take in the eye-popping display of 1920s Mediterranean revival architecture in the neighborhoods surrounding the city center and the majestic **Biltmore Hotel** 25; then take a dip in the fantastic thematic **Venetian Pool** 23. That night indulge in an evening of fine dining in Coral Gables.

If you have 5 days

Follow the suggested three-day itinerary, and on day four add a visit to the beaches of **Virginia Key** and **Key Biscayne.** Take a diving trip or fishing excursion, learn to wind surf, or do absolutely nothing but watch the water. On day five step back to the 1950s with a cruise up **Collins Avenue** to some of the monolithic hotels, such as the **Fontainebleau Hilton** and **Eden Roc**; continue north to the elegant shops of **Bal Harbour**; and return to **South Beach** for an evening of shopping, drinking, and outdoor dining at **Lincoln Road Mall.**

If you have 7 days

A week gives you just enough time to experience fully the multicultural, cosmopolitan, tropical mélange that is Greater Miami and its beaches. On day six see where it all began. Use the Miami Metromover to ride above downtown Miami before touring the streets (if possible, on a tour with historian Dr. Paul George). Take time to visit the **Miami-Dade Cultural Center** 14, home of art and history museums. In the evening check out the shops and clubs at **Bayside Marketplace.** The final day can be used to visit **South Miami,** site of **Fairchild Tropical Garden** 30 and the **Shops at Sunset Place.** Keep the evening free to revisit your favorite nightspots.

---

candidate Janet Reno, a Miami native, to be turned away on her first attempt to vote. Three hours after the election began, 1 out of 10 polling places was still closed. While most of the state was using the new touch-screen machines, only the counties of Miami-Dade and Broward, just to the north, had problems. As for human error, the Miami City Commission chairman was removed following a voter fraud conviction, a county commissioner was arrested and removed from office for using campaign money for her own personal use, and a state senator was re-elected despite being under indictment for pocketing profits from sham home-health-care companies.

Corrupt politicians aside, Miami has its share of the same crimes that plague any other major city. However, the widely publicized crimes against tourists a decade ago led to the creation of effective visitor-safety programs and neighborhood police stations in high-crime areas. Patrol cars driven by TOP (Tourist Oriented Police) Cops cruise heavily visited areas. Identification that made rental cars conspicuous to would-be criminals has been removed, and multilingual pamphlets on avoiding crime are widely distributed. The precautions have had a positive impact. In the last decade the number of tourist robberies has decreased by more than 80%. While it's still prudent to avoid crime-ridden areas, the incidents of lost tourists' being robbed are so rare now that special direction signs—with red-sunburst logos placed at ¼-mi intervals on major roads to guide tourists from the airport to major destinations such as Key Biscayne and Miami Beach—have been taken down.

What *is* on the rise is Miami's film profile. Arnold Schwarzenegger and Jamie Lee Curtis filmed *True Lies* here, Al Pacino and Johnny Depp shot scenes for *Donnie Brasco,* Jim Carrey rose to stardom through the Miami-based *Ace Ventura: Pet Detective,* Robin Williams and Nathan Lane used two deco buildings on Ocean Drive as their nightclub in *The Birdcage,* and traffic on MacArthur Causeway ceased for several days to film an incredible car-carrier wreck scene for *Bad Boys II*. It's a far cry from when Esther Williams used to perform water ballet in Coral Gables' Venetian Pool. Daily fashion-magazine and TV shoots add to the frenetic mix.

Fun here can easily drain your wallet, but look for less flashy ways to explore Miami, too. Skip the chichi restaurant and go for an ethnic eatery. Tour Lincoln Road Mall, downtown Coral Gables, or Coconut Grove on foot. Or take South Beach's colorful Electrowave shuttle, Florida's first electric transportation system, which really works for getting around traffic-clogged SoBe. Nearly 10 million tourists flock annually to Miami-Dade County and discover a multicultural metropolis that invites the world to celebrate its diversity.

EXPLORING MIAMI & MIAMI BEACH

If you had arrived here 40 years ago with Fodor's guide in hand, chances are you'd be thumbing through listings looking for alligator wrestlers and you-pick strawberry fields or citrus groves. Well, things have changed. While Disney sidetracked families in Orlando, Miami was developing a grown-up attitude courtesy of *Miami Vice,* European fashion photographers, and historic preservationists. Nowadays the wildest ride is the city itself. Climb aboard and check out the different sides of Greater Miami. Miami on the mainland is South Florida's commercial hub, while its sultry sister, Miami Beach (America's Riviera), encompasses 17 islands in Biscayne Bay. Seducing winter refugees with its sunshine, beaches, palms, and nightlife, this is what most people envision when planning a trip to what they think of as Miami. These same visitors fail to realize that there's more to Miami Beach than the bustle of South Beach and its Deco District. Indeed there are quieter areas to the north like Sunny Isles Beach, Surfside, and Bal Harbour.

During the day downtown Miami has become the lively hub of the mainland city, now more accessible thanks to the Metromover extension, a supplementary rail system linking many downtown sights that conveniently connects Metrorail's Government Center and Brickell stations. Other major attractions include Coconut Grove, Coral Gables, Little Havana, and, of course, the South Beach/Art Deco District; but since these areas are spread out beyond the reach of public transportation, you'll have to drive. Rent a convertible if you can. There's nothing quite

1

Surf

Greater Miami has numerous free beaches to fit every style. A sandy, 300-ft-wide beach with several distinct sections extends for 10 mi from the foot of Miami Beach north to Haulover Beach Park. Between 23rd and 44th streets, Miami Beach built boardwalks and protective walkways atop a dune landscaped with sea oats, sea grapes, and other native plants whose roots keep the sand from blowing away. Farther north there's even a nude beach, and Key Biscayne adds more great strands to Miami's collection.

If you can sail in Miami, do. Blue skies, calm seas, and a view of the city skyline make for a pleasurable outing—especially at twilight, when the fabled "moon over Miami" casts a soft glow on the water. Key Biscayne's calm waves and strong breezes are perfect for sailing and windsurfing, and although Dinner Key and the Coconut Grove waterfront remain the center of sailing in Greater Miami, sailboat moorings and rentals sit along other parts of the bay and up the Miami River. Greater Miami has numerous marinas, and dockmasters can provide information on any marine services you may need. Ask for *Teall's Tides and Guides, Miami-Dade County,* and other nautical publications.

Nightlife

Fast, hot, and as transient as the crowds who pass through their doors, Miami's nightspots sizzle, keeping pace with their New York and L.A. counterparts. The densest concentration of clubs is on South Beach along Washington Avenue, Lincoln Road Mall, and Ocean Drive. Other nightlife centers on Little Havana and Coconut Grove, and on the fringes of downtown Miami. Miami's nightspots offer jazz, reggae, salsa, various forms of rock, disco, and Top 40 sounds, most played at a body-thumping, ear-throbbing volume. Some clubs refuse entrance to anyone under 21, others to those under 25, so if that is a concern, call ahead. If you prefer to hear what people are saying, try the many lobby bars at South Beach's art deco hotels. Throughout Greater Miami, bars and cocktail lounges in larger, newer hotels operate nightly discos with live weekend entertainment.

Food

Miami cuisine is what mouths were made for. The city serves up a veritable United Nations of dining experiences, including dishes native to Spain, Cuba, and Nicaragua as well as China, India, Thailand, Vietnam, and other Asian cultures. Chefs from the tropics combine fresh, natural foods—especially seafood—with classic island-style dishes, creating a new American cuisine that is sometimes called Floribbean. Another style finding its way around U.S. restaurants is the Miami-born New World cuisine. The title comes from chefs who realized their latest creations were based on ingredients found along the trade routes discovered by early explorers of the "New World."

Spectator Sports

Greater Miami has franchises in basketball, football, and baseball. Fans still turn out en masse for the Dolphins, and—in the best fair-weather-fan tradition—show up for basketball's Heat and baseball's Marlins, who are fighting to regain fans with yet another new owner after the hard-to-forget sell-off of players who won the 1997 World Series. Miami also hosts top-rated events in golf, tennis, boat racing, auto racing, and jai alai. Each winter, the FedEx Orange Bowl Football Classic highlights two of the top teams in college football.

like wearing cool shades and feeling the wind in your hair as you drive across one of the causeways en route to Miami Beach.

To find your way around Greater Miami, learn how the numbering system works. Miami is laid out on a grid with four quadrants—northeast, northwest, southeast, and southwest—which meet at Miami Avenue and Flagler Street. Miami Avenue separates east from west, and Flagler Street separates north from south. Avenues and courts run north–south; streets, terraces, and ways run east–west. Roads run diagonally, northwest–southeast. But other districts—Miami Beach, Coral Gables, and Hialeah—may or may not follow this system, and along the curve of Biscayne Bay, the symmetrical grid may shift diagonally. It's best to buy a detailed map, stick to the major roads, and ask directions early and often. However, make sure you're in a safe neighborhood or public place when you seek guidance; cabbies and cops are good resources.

South Beach/Miami Beach

The hub of Miami Beach is South Beach (SoBe, to anyone but locals), and the hub of South Beach is the 1-square-mi Art Deco District, fronted on the east by Ocean Drive and on the west by Alton Road. The story of South Beach has become the story of Miami. In the early 1980s South Beach's vintage hotels were badly run down, catering mostly to infirm retirees. But a group of visionaries led by the late Barbara Baer Capitman, a spirited New York transplant, saw this collection of buildings as an architectural treasure to be salvaged from a sea of mindless urban renewal. It was, and is, a peerless grouping of art deco architecture from the 1920s to 1950s, whose forms and decorative details are drawn from nature, the streamlined shapes of modern transportation and industrial machinery, and human extravagance.

Investors started fixing up the interiors of these hotels and repainting their exteriors with a vibrant pastel palette—a look that *Miami Vice* made famous and that TV shows such as MTV's *Real World* and *CSI: Miami* continue to keep on the pop-culture radar screen. Fashion photographers and the media took note, and celebrities like singer Gloria Estefan; the late designer Gianni Versace, whose fashions captured the feel of the awakening city; and record executive Chris Blackwell bought a piece of the action. As a result, South Beach now holds the distinction of being the nation's first 20th-century district on the National Register of Historic Places, with more than 800 significant buildings making the roll. New high-rises and hotels spring up, areas like SoFi (south of Fifth) blossom, and clubs open (and close) with dizzying speed.

Yet Miami Beach is more than just SoBe. (The northern edge of South Beach is generally considered to be around 24th–28th streets, while Miami Beach itself extends well north.) It also consists of a collection of quiet neighborhoods where Little Leaguers play ball, senior citizens stand at bus stops, and locals do their shopping away from the prying eyes of visitors. Surprisingly, Miami Beach is a great walking town in the middle of a great city. Several things are plentiful in SoBe: pierced body parts, cell phones, and meter maids. Tickets are given freely when meters expire, and towing charges are high. Check the meter to see when parking fees are required; times vary by district. From mid-morning on, parking is scarce along Ocean Drive. You'll do better on Collins or Washington Avenue, the next two streets to the west. Fortunately, there are several surface parking lots south and west of the Jackie Gleason Theater, on 17th Street, and parking garages on Collins Avenue at 7th and 13th streets, on Washington Avenue at 12th Street, and west of Washington at 17th Street. Keep these sites in mind, especially at night, when cruising traf-

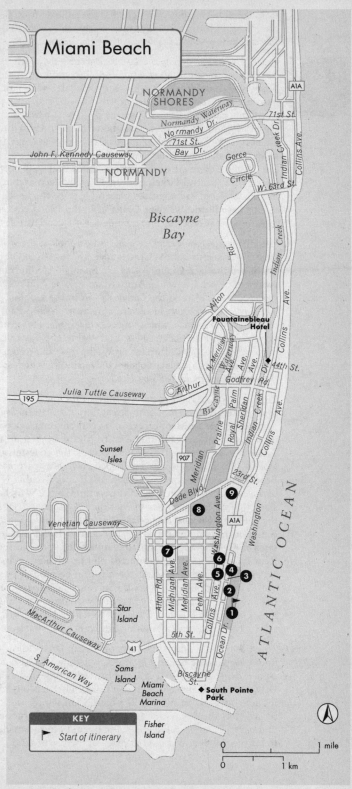

fic makes it best to park your car and see SoBe on foot. Better yet, catch the colorful Electrowave shuttle buses that cover South Beach well into the wee hours—for 25¢, they're the best deal in town.

Ocean Drive—primarily the 10-block stretch from 5th to 15th Street—has become the most talked-about beachfront in America. A bevy of art deco jewels hugs the drive, while across the street lies palm-fringed **Lummus Park ❶** ▶, the south end of which is a good starting point for a walk. Beginning early (at 8) gives you the pleasure of watching the awakening city without distraction. Sanitation men hose down dirty streets, merchants prepare window displays, bakers bake, and construction workers change the skyline one brick at a time. Cross to the west side of Ocean Drive, where there are many sidewalk cafés, and walk north, taking note of the Park Central Hotel, built in 1937 by deco architect Henry Hohauser. At 10th Street recross Ocean Drive to the beach side and visit the **Art Deco District Welcome Center ❷** in the 1950s-era Oceanfront Auditorium. Rent tapes or hire a guide for a Deco District tour.

Look back across Ocean Drive and take a look at the wonderful flying-saucer architecture of the Clevelander, at No. 1020. On the next block you'll see the late Gianni Versace's Spanish Mediterranean **Casa Casuarina ❸**, once known as Amsterdam Palace. You may recognize the Leslie (No. 1244) and the **Carlyle ❹**, from the Robin Williams movie *The Birdcage*. Walk two blocks west (away from the ocean) on 13th Street to Washington Avenue, where a mix of chic restaurants, avant-garde shops, delicatessens, produce markets, and nightclubs has spiced up a once-derelict neighborhood. Turn left on Washington and walk 2½ blocks south to **Wolfsonian–Florida International University ❺**, which showcases artistic movements from 1885 to 1945.

Provided you haven't spent too long in the museum, return north on Washington Avenue past 14th Street, and turn left on **Espanola Way ❻**, a narrow street of Mediterranean revival buildings, eclectic shops, and a weekend market. Continue west to Meridian Avenue and turn right. Three blocks north of Espanola Way is the redesigned **Lincoln Road Mall ❼**, which is often paired with Ocean Drive as part of must-see South Beach. The next main street north of Lincoln Road is 17th Street, and to the east is the Miami Beach Convention Center. Walk behind the massive building to the corner of Meridian Avenue and 19th Street to see the chilling **Holocaust Memorial ❽**, a monumental record honoring the 6 million Jewish victims of the Holocaust. Head east to the **Bass Museum of Art ❾**, a Maya-inspired temple filled with European splendors. Return to Ocean Drive in time to pull up a chair at an outdoor café, order an espresso, and settle down for an evening of people-watching, SoBe's most popular pastime. If you've seen enough people, grab some late rays at one of the area's beaches, with different sands for different tans. Go back to Lummus Park (*the* beach) or head north, where there's a boardwalk for walking but no allowance for skates and bicycles.

TIMING To see only the art deco buildings on Ocean Drive, allow one hour minimum. Depending on your interests, schedule at least five hours and include a drink or meal at a café and browsing time in the shops on Ocean Drive, along Espanola Way, and at Lincoln Road Mall. Start your walking tour as early in the day as possible. In winter the street becomes crowded as the day wears on, and in summer, afternoon heat and humidity can be unbearable. Finishing by mid-afternoon also enables you to hit the beach and cool your heels in the warm sand.

What to See

2 Art Deco District Welcome Center. Run by the Miami Design Preservation League, the center provides information about the buildings in the District. A gift shop sells 1930s–1950s art deco memorabilia, posters, and books on Miami's history. Several tours—covering Lincoln Road, Espanola Way, North Beach, the entire Art Deco District—start here. Rent audiotapes for a self-guided tour, join the regular Saturday-morning or Thursday-evening walking tours, or take a bicycle tour. Don't miss the special boat tours during Art Deco Weekend in early January. ✉ *1001 Ocean Dr., at Barbara Capitman Way (10th St.), South Beach* ☏ *305/531–3484 or 305/672–2014* ✆ *Tours $10–$15* ☉ *Sun.–Thurs. 10–10, Fri.–Sat. 10 AM–midnight.*

Bal Harbour. Known for its upscale shops, this affluent community has a stretch of prime beach real estate where wealthy condominium owners cluster in winter. Look close and you may spy Bob Dole sunning himself outside his condo. ✉ *Collins Ave. between 96th and 103rd Sts., Bal Harbour.*

9 Bass Museum of Art. European art is the focus of this impressive museum in historic Collins Park, a short drive north of SoBe's key sights. Works on display include *The Holy Family,* a painting by Peter Paul Rubens; *The Tournament,* one of several 16th-century Flemish tapestries; and works by Albrecht Dürer and Henri de Toulouse-Lautrec. An $8 million, three-phase expansion by architect Arata Isozaki added another wing, cafeteria, and theater, doubling the museum's size to nearly 40,000 square ft. ✉ *2121 Park Ave., South Beach* ☏ *305/673–7530* ⊕ *www. bassmuseum.org* ✆ *$5* ☉ *Tues.–Sat. 10–5, Thurs. 10–9, Sun. 11–5.*

4 The Carlyle. Built in 1941 this deco gem was one of the first hotels to be restored and is now shuttered for a second redo. Fans will recognize it and its neighbor, the Leslie, as the nightclub from *The Birdcage.* ✉ *1250 Ocean Dr., South Beach.*

3 Casa Casuarina. In the early 1980s before South Beach became a hotbed of chicness the late Italian designer Gianni Versace purchased this run-down Spanish Mediterranean residence, built before the arrival of deco. Today the home is an ornate three-story palazzo with a guest house and a copper-dome rooftop observatory and pool that were added at the expense of a 1950s hotel, the Revere. Its loss and the razing of the fabled deco Senator became a rallying point for preservationists. Although the Casuarina is now owned by a private investor, picture-taking tourists still flock to see the villa and its broad front stairs where Versace was tragically gunned down by a stalker in 1997 as he returned home from breakfast at the nearby News Café. ✉ *1114 Ocean Dr., South Beach.*

★ 6 Espanola Way. The Mediterranean revival buildings along this road were constructed in 1925 and frequented through the years by artists and writers. In the 1930s future bandleader Desi Arnaz strapped on a conga drum and started beating out a rumba rhythm at a nightclub that is now the Clay Hotel, a youth hostel that covers most of a block. The best time to visit is on a Sunday afternoon, when itinerant dealers and craftspeople set up shop to sell everything from garage-sale items to handcrafted bongo drums. Between Washington and Drexel avenues, the road has been narrowed to a single lane, and Miami Beach's trademark pink sidewalks have been widened to accommodate sidewalk cafés and shops selling imaginative clothing, jewelry, and art. ✉ *Espanola Way between 14th and 15th Sts. from Washington to Jefferson Ave., South Beach.*

★ Fontainebleau Hilton Resort and Towers. For a sense of what Miami was like during the Fabulous '50s, take a drive north to see the finest example of Miami Beach's grandiose architecture. By the 1950s smaller deco-era hotels were passé, and architects like Morris Lapidus got busy designing free-flowing hotels that affirmed the American attitude of "bigger is better." Even if you're not a guest, wander through the lobby and spectacular pool area just to feel the energy generated by an army of bellhops, clerks, concierges, and travelers. ⊠ *4441 Collins Ave., between 44th and 45th Sts., South Beach* ☎*305/538–2000* ⊕*www.fontainebleau. hilton.com.*

🔄 **Haulover Beach Park.** At this county park, far from the action of SoBe, see the Miami of 30 years ago. Pack a picnic, use the barbecue grills, or grab a snack at the concession stand. There are tennis and volleyball courts and paths designed for walking and bicycling. The beach is nice if you want water without long marches across hot sand, and a popular clothing-optional section at the north end of the beach lures people who want to tan every nook and cranny. Other offerings are kite rentals, kayak rentals, charter-fishing excursions, and a par-3, 9-hole golf course. ⊠ *10800 Collins Ave., Sunny Isles Beach* ☎ *305/947–3525* ⊕ *www. miami-dade.fl.us/parks.com* ⊠ *$4 per vehicle* ☉ *Daily dawn–dusk.*

8 Holocaust Memorial. The focus of the memorial is a 42-ft-high bronze arm rising from the ground, with sculptured people climbing the arm seeking escape. Don't stare from the street; enter the courtyard to see the chilling memorial wall and hear the eerie songs that seem to give voice to the victims. ⊠ *1933–1945 Meridian Ave., South Beach* ☎ *305/ 538–1663* ⊕ *www.holocaustmmb.org* ⊠ *Free* ☉ *Daily 9–9.*

> **need a break?** If your feet are still holding up, head to the **Delano Hotel** (⊠ 1685 Collins Ave., South Beach ☎ 305/674–6400) for a drink. This surrealistic hotel, like a Calvin Klein ad come to life, delivers fabulousness every step of the way. It's popular among SoBe's fashion models and hepcats.

★ 🔄 **7 Lincoln Road Mall.** The Morris Lapidus–renovated Lincoln Road is fun, lively, and friendly for people old, young, gay, and straight—and their dogs. Folks skate, scoot, bike, or jog here past the electronics stores at the Collins Avenue end toward the chichi boutiques and outdoor cafés heading west. The best times to hit the road are during Sunday-morning farmers markets and on weekend evenings when cafés are bustling; art galleries, like Romero Britto's Britto Central, schedule openings; street performers take the stage; and bookstores, import shops, and clothing stores are open for late-night purchases. ⊠ *Lincoln Rd. between Collins Ave. and Alton Rd., South Beach.*

🔄 ▶ **1 Lummus Park.** Once part of a turn-of-the-last-century plantation owned by brothers John and James Lummus, this palm-shaded oasis on the beach side of Ocean Drive attracts beach-going families with its children's play area. Senior citizens and health-conscious locals predominate early in the day. Volleyball playing, in-line skating along the wide and winding sidewalk, and a lot of posing go on here. Gays like the beach between 11th and 13th streets. The lush foliage is a pleasing, natural counterpoint to the ultrachic activity across the street, where endless sidewalk cafés make it easy to come ashore for everything from burgers to quiche. Like New York's Central Park, this is a natural venue for big-name public concerts by such performers as Luciano Pavarotti and past Art Deco Weekend stars Cab Calloway and Lionel Hampton. ⊠ *East of Ocean Dr. between 5th and 15th Sts., South Beach.*

North Beach. Families and those who like things quiet prefer this section of beach. Metered parking is ample right behind the dune and a block behind Collins Avenue along a pleasant, old shopping street. With high prices discouraging developers from SoBe, this area will no doubt see some redevelopment in years to come. However, without the cafés or 300-ft-wide beach to lure tourists, it may never match SoBe's appeal. ⊠ *Ocean Terr. between 73rd and 75th Sts., North Beach.*

off the beaten path

Oleta River State Recreation Area. At nearly 1,000 acres, this is the largest urban park in Florida. It's backed by lush tropical growth rather than hotels and offers group and youth camping, 14 log cabins, kayak and canoe rentals, mountain-bike trails, and a fishing pier. Popular with outdoors enthusiasts, it also attracts dolphins, ospreys, and manatees, who arrive for the winter. ⊠ *3400 N.E. 163rd St., North Miami Beach* ☎ *305/919–1846* ⊕ *www.dep.state. fl.us/parks/district5/oletariver* ☞ *$4 per vehicle with up to 8 people, pedestrians $1* ☉ *Daily 8–sunset.*

Sanford L. Ziff Jewish Museum of Florida. A permanent exhibit, *MOSAIC: Jewish Life in Florida* depicts more than 235 years of the Florida Jewish experience through lectures, films, storytelling, walking tours, and special events. If you've never seen a crate of kosher citrus or ark ornaments from a Florida synagogue, drop in. And for a flashback to what Miss Florida looked like in the '80s—the 1880s, that is—look for the snapshot of Mena Williams. The building is the former Congregation Beth Jacob Synagogue. ⊠ *301 Washington Ave., South Beach* ☎ *305/672– 5044* ⊕ *www.jewishmuseum.com* ☞ *$5* ☉ *Tues.–Sun. 10–5.*

South Pointe Park. From the 50-yard Sunshine Pier, which adjoins the 1-mi-long jetty at the mouth of Government Cut, fish while watching huge ships pass. No bait or tackle is available in the park. Facilities include two observation towers, rest rooms, and volleyball courts. ⊠ *1 Washington Ave., South Beach.*

Surfside. *Parlez-vous français?* If you do, you'll feel quite comfortable in and around this French Canadian enclave. It's one of the few spots on the beach yet to be reinvented, making it (and down the island to 72nd Street) an affordable place for many folks to spend the winter. ⊠ *Collins Ave. between 88th and 96th Sts., Surfside.*

★ ❺ **Wolfsonian–Florida International University.** An elegantly renovated 1927 storage facility is now both a research center and the site of the 80,000-plus-item collection of modern design and "propaganda arts" amassed by Miami native Mitchell Wolfson, Jr., a world traveler and connoisseur. Included in the museum's eclectic holdings, representing art moderne, art nouveau, arts and crafts, and other artistic movements, is a 1930s braille edition of Hitler's *Mein Kampf*. Exhibitions such as World's Fair designs and the architectural heritage of S. H. Kress add to the appeal. ⊠ *1001 Washington Ave., South Beach* ☎ *305/531–1001* ⊕ *www.wolfsonian. fiu.edu* ☞ *$5* ☉ *Mon.–Tues. and Fri.–Sat. 11–6, Thurs. 11–9, Sun. noon–5.*

Downtown Miami

Although steel-and-glass buildings have sprung up around downtown, the heart of the city hasn't changed much since the 1960s—except that it's a little seedier. By day there's plenty of activity downtown, as office workers and motorists crowd the area. Staid, suited lawyers and bankers share the sidewalks with Latino merchants wearing open-neck, intricately embroidered shirts called guayaberas. Fruit merchants sell their wares from pushcarts, young European travelers with backpacks stroll the streets, and foreign businesspeople haggle over prices in import-export shops, including more electronics and camera shops than you'd see in Tokyo. You'll hear Arabic, Chinese, Creole, French, German, Hebrew, Hindi, Japanese, Portuguese, Spanish, Yiddish, and even some English. But what's best in the heart of downtown Miami is its Latinization and the sheer energy of Latino shoppers. At night, however, downtown is sorely neglected. Except for Bayside Marketplace, the AmericanAirlines Arena, and a few ever-changing clubs in warehouses, the area is deserted, and arena patrons rarely linger. Travelers spend little time here, since most tourist attractions are in other neighborhoods, but there is a movement afoot to bring a renaissance to downtown. A huge new performing-arts center is scheduled to open in late 2004 and, with it, new cafés and nightspots. Thanks to the Metromover, which has inner and outer loops through downtown plus north and south extensions, this is an excellent tour to take by rail, and it's free. Attractions are conveniently located within about two blocks of the nearest station. Parking downtown is no less convenient or more expensive than in any other city, but the best idea is to park near Bayside Marketplace or leave your car at an outlying Metrorail station and take the train downtown.

a good tour

Start at the Bayfront Park Metromover stop. There's plenty of parking in lots in the median of Biscayne Boulevard and slightly more expensive covered parking at the Bayfront Marketplace. If you want, wait until you return to walk through the **Mildred and Claude Pepper Bayfront Park** ⑩ ▶, but look south of the park and you'll see the Hotel Inter-Continental Miami, which displays *The Spindle,* a huge sculpture by Henry Moore, in its lobby. A trip to **Brickell Village** ⑪ on the south side of the Brickell Avenue Bridge makes a good detour. Next, board the Metromover northbound and take in the fine view of Bayfront Park's greenery, the bay beyond, the stunning AmericanAirlines Arena, the Port of Miami in the bay, and Miami Beach across the water. The next stop, College/Bayside, serves the downtown campus of **Miami-Dade Community College** ⑫, which has two fine galleries. As the Metromover rounds the curve after the College/Bayside station, look northeast for a view of the vacant **Freedom Tower** ⑬, an important milepost in the history of Cuban immigration now being renovated as a Cuban museum. You'll also see the *Miami Herald* building and the rapidly rising performing-arts center. Survey the city as the train works its way toward Government Center station. Look off to your right (north) as you round the northwest corner of the loop to see the round, windowless, pink Miami Arena.

It's time to hoof it, so get off the train at Government Center, a large station with small shops, restaurants, and a hair salon, in case you're looking shaggy. It's also where the 21-mi elevated Metrorail commuter system connects with the Metromover, so this is a good place to start your tour if you're coming downtown by train. Walk out the east doors to Northwest 1st Street and head a block south to the **Miami-Dade Cultural Center** ⑭, which contains the city's main art museum, historical museum, and library and made an appearance in the movie *There's Something About Mary.* After sopping up some culture, walk east down Flagler Street. On the corner is the **Dade County Courthouse** ⑮, whose pinnacle is accented by circling vultures. Now you're in the heart of downtown, where the smells range from pleasant (hot-dog carts) to rancid (hot-dog carts). If you cleaned up the streets and put a shine on them, you'd see Miami circa 1950. Still thriving today, the downtown area is a far cry from what it was in 1896, when it was being carved out of pine woods and palmetto scrub to make room for Flagler's railroad. If you're in the market for jewelry, avoid the street peddlers and duck into the Seybold Building, at 36 Northeast 1st Street; it comprises 10 stories with 250 jewelers hawking watches, rings, bracelets, etc. Just a few blocks from your starting point at the Bayfront Park Metromover station, stop in at the **Gusman Center for the Performing Arts** ⑯, a beautiful movie palace that now serves as downtown Miami's concert hall. If there's a show on—even a bad one—get tickets. It's worth it just to sit in here. When you get back to your car and the entrance to the Bayfront Marketplace, opt to hit the road, go shopping, or grab a brew at a bay-front bar.

TIMING To walk and ride to the various points of interest, allow two hours. If you want to spend additional time eating and shopping at Bayside, allow at least four hours. To include museum visits, allow six hours.

What to See

AmericanAirlines Arena. The stylish bay-front home of the NBA's Miami Heat includes Gloria Estefan's Bongos restaurant and shops. ⊠ *Biscayne Blvd. between N.E. 8th and 9th Sts., Downtown* ☎ *305/577–4328* ⊕ *www.aaarena.com.*

⑪ **Brickell Village.** Brickell (rhymes with fickle) is an up-and-coming downtown area with new low- and high-rise condos, a shopping area, Brickell Park, and plenty of popular restaurants. **Hardaway's Firehouse Four** (⊠ 1000 S. Miami Ave., Brickell Village), underwritten by—you guessed it—NBA star Tim Hardaway, has a legendary happy hour and good burgers (including a tuna burger) in an old firehouse. **Perricone's Marketplace and Café** (⊠ 15 S.E. 10th St., Brickell Village) is the biggest and most popular of the area's many Italian restaurants, in a 120-year-old Vermont barn. The cooking is simple and good. Buy your wine from the on-premises deli and bring it to your table for a small corking fee. ⊠ *Between Miami River and S.W. 15 St., Brickell Village.*

⑮ **Dade County Courthouse.** Built in 1928, this was once the tallest building south of Washington, D.C. Unlike at Capistrano, turkey vultures— not swallows—return to roost here in winter. ⊠ *73 W. Flagler St., Downtown* ☎ *305/349–7000.*

⑬ **Freedom Tower.** In the 1960s this imposing Spanish baroque structure was the Cuban Refugee Center, processing more than 500,000 Cubans who entered the United States after fleeing Fidel Castro's regime. Built in 1925 for the *Miami Daily News,* it was inspired by the Giralda, an 800-year-old bell tower in Seville, Spain. The tower's exterior was restored in 1988 and restoration of the interior is ongoing. ⊠ *600 Biscayne Blvd., at N.E. 7th St., Downtown.*

★ ⑯ **Gusman Center for the Performing Arts.** Carry an extra pair of socks when you come here; the beauty of this former movie palace will knock yours clean off. Reopened in the '70s as a concert hall and given an additional $2.1 million restoration in 2002, it resembles an ornate Moorish courtyard on the inside, with twinkling stars in the sky. You can catch performances by the Florida Philharmonic and movies of the Miami Film Festival. If the hall is closed, call the office and they may let you in. ⊠ *174 E. Flagler St., Downtown* ☎ *305/372–0925.*

⑫ **Miami-Dade Community College.** The campus has two fine galleries: the larger, third-floor **Centre Gallery** hosts photography, painting, and sculpture exhibitions, and the fifth-floor **Frances Wolfson Art Gallery** has smaller photo exhibits. ⊠ *300 N.E. 2nd Ave., Downtown* ☎ *305/ 237–3278* 🎫 *Free* ☉ *Mon.–Wed. and Fri. 10–4, Thurs. noon–6.*

★ ☺ ⑭ **Miami-Dade Cultural Center.** Containing three important cultural resources, this 3-acre complex is one of the focal points of downtown. The **Miami Art Museum** (☎ 305/375–3000 ⊕ www.miamiartmuseum. org) has a permanent collection and major touring exhibitions of work

Downtown
Miami

TO AIRPORT
395

Venetian
Causeway

MacArthur

41

Causeway

TO MIAMI
BEACH

Dolphin

Expressway

N. E. 15th St.

SCHOOL
BOARD

OMNI

Biscayne Blvd.

Bayshore Dr.

N. E. 14th St.

N. E. 13th St.

N. W. 12th St.

CULMER

BICENTENNIAL
PARK

Bicentennial
Park

95

N. W. 11th St.

N. E. 11th St.

ELEVENTH
STREET

N. W. 10th St.

N. E. 10th St.

N. W. 9th St.

N. E. 9th St.

OMNI
EXTENSION

American Airlines
Arena

South

TO PORT OF
MIAMI

N. W. 8th St.

N. E. 8th St.

PARK
WEST

American

Way

N. W. 7th St.

N. E. 7th St.

OVERTOWN/
ARENA

FREEDOM
TOWER

13

N. W. 6th St.

STATE PLAZA/
ARENA

N. E. 6th St.

N. W. 5th St.

METROMOVER

COLLEGE
NORTH

Biscayne Blvd.

Bayside
Marketplace

METRORAIL

N. Miami Ave.

N. E. 4th St.

12

N. W. 4th St.

N. E. 3rd St.

COLLEGE
BAYSIDE

N. W. 2nd Ave.

N. W. 1st Ave.

GOVERNMENT
CENTER

N. E. 2nd St.

N. E. 2nd Ave.

FIRST STREET

N. W. 5th Ave.

N. W. 4th Ave.

N. W. 3rd Ave.

N. E. 1st St.

10

W. Flagler St.

14

15

N. E. 1st Ave.

E. Flagler St.

BAYFRONT
PARK

S. W. 1st St.

S. E. 1st St.

MIAMI
AVE.

16

S. W. 2nd St.

KNIGHT
CENTER

S. E. 2nd St.

S. W. 3rd St.

THIRD STREET

Miami

S. W. 4th St.

S. W. 14th St.

S.E. 4th St.

Biscayne Blvd. Way

S. W. 5th St.

River

S. E. 5th St.

BRICKELL
EXTENSION

Brickell
Key

95

S. W. 6th St.

S. E. 6th St.

FIFTH STREET

S. W. 7th Ave.

S. W. 4th Ave.

S. W. 3rd Ave.

S. W. 2nd Ave.

S. W. 7th St.

S. E. 7th St.

11

Brickell
Park

METRORAIL

Miami Ave.

S. W. 8th St.

S. E. 8th St.

S. W. 8th St.

EIGHTH STREET

0   1/4 mile

0   1/4 km

KEY

Ⓜ   Metro stops

  Metromover

▶   Start of walk

by international artists, focusing on work completed since 1945. Open Tuesday–Friday 10–5 and weekends noon–5, the museum charges $5 admission ($6 including the Historical Museum). At the **Historical Museum of Southern Florida** (☎ 305/375–1492 ⊕ www.historical-museum. org) you'll be treated to pure Floridiana, including an old Miami streetcar, cigar labels, and a railroad exhibit as well as a display on prehistoric Miami. Admission is $5 ($6 including the Miami Art Museum), and hours are Monday–Wednesday and Friday–Saturday 10–5, Thursday 10–9, and Sunday noon–5. The **Main Public Library** (☎ 305/375–2665), which is open Monday–Wednesday and Friday–Saturday 9–6, Thursday 9–9, and, some Sundays 1–5 (call for hours), has nearly 4 million holdings and offers art exhibits in the auditorium and second-floor lobby. ✉ *101 W. Flagler St., Downtown.*

▶ ⑩ **Mildred and Claude Pepper Bayfront Park.** This oasis among the skyscrapers borders the Bayfront Marketplace, making it a natural place for a pre- or post-shopping walk. An urban landfill in the 1920s, it became the site of a World War II memorial in 1943, which was revised in 1980 to include the names of victims of later wars. Japanese sculptor Isamu Noguchi redesigned the park before his death in 1989 to include two amphitheaters, a memorial to the *Challenger* astronauts, and a fountain honoring the late Florida congressman Claude Pepper and his wife. At the park's north end the Friendship Torch was erected to honor JFK during his presidency and was dedicated in 1964. ✉ *Biscayne Blvd. between 2nd and 3rd Sts., Downtown.*

Little Havana

More than 40 years ago, Cubans fleeing the Castro regime flooded into an older neighborhood west of downtown Miami. Don't expect a sparkling and lively reflection of 1950s Havana, however. What you will find are ramshackle motels and cluttered storefronts. With a million Cubans and other Latinos—who make up more than half the metropolitan population—dispersed throughout Greater Miami, Little Havana and neighboring East Little Havana remain magnets for Hispanics and Anglos alike. That culture, of course, functions in Spanish. Many Little Havana residents and shopkeepers speak little or no English.

a good tour

From downtown go west on Flagler Street across the Miami River to Teddy Roosevelt Avenue (Southwest 17th Avenue) and pause at **Plaza de la Cubanidad** ⑰ ▶, on the southwest corner. The plaza's monument is indicative of the prominent role of Cuban history and culture here. Turn left at Douglas Road (Southwest 37th Avenue), drive south to **Calle Ocho** ⑱ (Southwest 8th Street), and turn left again. You are now on the main commercial thoroughfare of Little Havana. After you cross Unity Boulevard (Southwest 27th Avenue), Calle Ocho becomes a one-way street eastbound through the heart of Little Havana. At Avenida Luis Muñoz Marín (Southwest 15th Avenue), stop at **Domino Park** ⑲, where elderly Cuban men pass the day with their black-and-white tiles. The **Brigade 2506 Memorial** ⑳, commemorating the victims of the unsuccessful 1961 Bay of Pigs invasion, stands at Memorial Boulevard (Southwest 13th Avenue). A block south are several other monuments relevant to Cuban history, including a bas-relief of and quotations by José Martí.

TIMING If the history hidden in the monuments is your only interest, set aside one hour. Allow more time to stop along Calle Ocho for a strong cup of Cuban coffee or to shop for a cigar made of Honduran tobacco handrolled in the United States by Cubans.

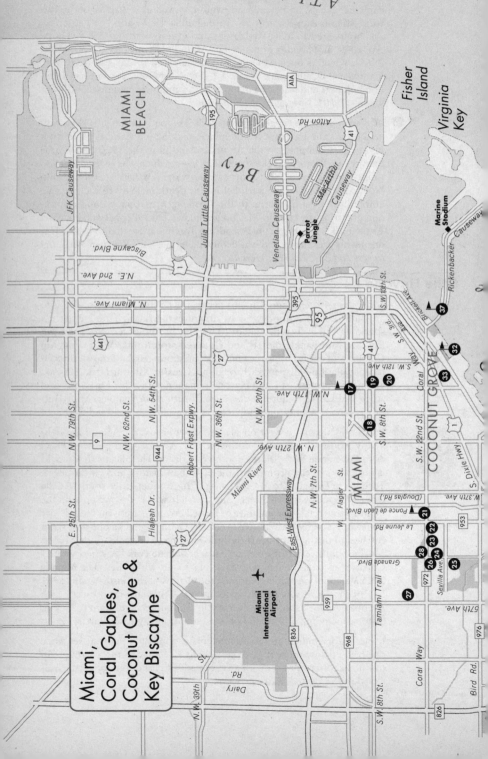

Miami,
Coral Gables,
Coconut Grove &
Key Biscayne

ATLANTIC OCEAN

MIAMI BEACH

Bay

Fisher Island

Virginia Key

Marine Stadium

Parrot Jungle

JFK Causeway

Julia Tuttle Causeway

Venetian Causeway

MacArthur Causeway

Rickenbacker Causeway

Biscayne Blvd.

N.E. 2nd Ave.

N. Miami Ave.

Brickell Ave.

S.W. 13th St.

COCONUT GROVE

N.W. 79th St.

N.W. 62nd St.

N.W. 54th St.

N.W. 36th St.

N.W. 20th St.

Robert Frost Expwy.

Hialeah Dr.

E. 25th St.

Miami River

N.W. 27th Ave.

N.W. 17th Ave.

N.W. 7th St.

W. Flagler St.

MIAMI

Ponce de León Blvd.

Le Jeune Rd.

(Douglas Rd.)

Granada Blvd.

Sevilla Ave.

Tamiami Trail

57th Ave.

Coral Way

S.W. 8th St.

Dairy Rd.

Bird Rd.

S. Dixie Hwy.

S.W. 37th Ave.

S.W. 22nd St.

Coral Way

S.W. 3rd Ave.

S.W. 12th Ave.

S.W. 8th St.

Miami International Airport

Alton Rd.

17 18 19 20 21 22 23 24 25 26 27 28 32 33 37

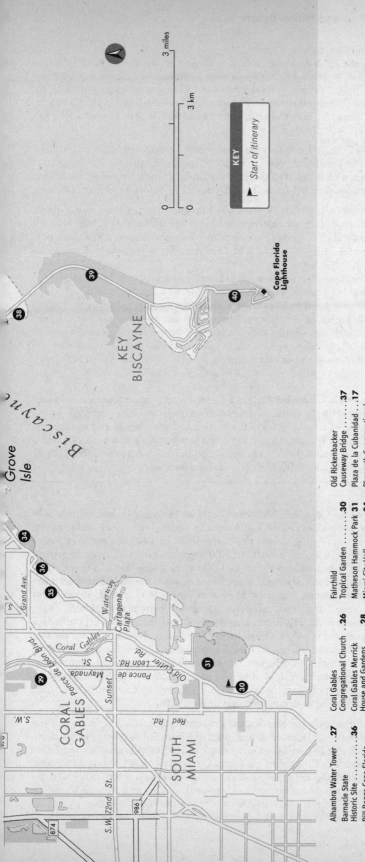

What to See

㉔ Brigade 2506 Memorial. To honor those who died in the Bay of Pigs invasion, an eternal flame burns atop a simple stone monument with the inscription CUBA—A LOS MÁRTIRES DE LA BRIGADA DE ASALTO ABRIL 17 DE 1961. The monument also bears a shield with the Brigade 2506 emblem, a Cuban flag superimposed on a cross. ⊠ *S.W. 8th St. and S.W. 13th Ave., Little Havana.*

⑱ Calle Ocho. In Little Havana's commercial heart, experience such Cuban customs as hand-rolled cigars or sandwiches piled with meats and cheeses. Although it all deserves exploring, if time is limited try the stretch from Southwest 14th to 11th Avenue. ⊠ *S.W. 8th St., Little Havana.*

⑲ Domino Park. Officially known as Maximo Gomez Park, this is a major gathering place for elderly, guayabera-clad Cuban males, who after 40 years still pass the day playing dominoes while arguing anti-Castro politics. ⊠ *S.W. 8th St. and S.W. 15th Ave., Little Havana* ⊙ *Daily 9–6.*

off the beaten path

Elián González's House. This humble two-bedroom home was where six-year-old González stayed for nearly six months after surviving a raft journey from Cuba that killed his mother. From this same house, he was removed by federal agents in a predawn raid that ultimately united him with his father, who took him home to Cuba. The Miami relatives have since moved but bought the property to turn it into a shrine and museum. ⊠ *2319 N.W. 2nd St., at N.W. 23rd Ave., Little Havana* ⊠ *Free* ⊙ *Sun. 10–6.*

▶ **⑰ Plaza de la Cubanidad.** Redbrick sidewalks surround a fountain and monument with the words of José Martí, a leader in Cuba's struggle for independence from Spain and a hero to Cuban refugees and immigrants in Miami. The quotation, LAS PALMAS SON NOVIAS QUE ESPERAN (The palm trees are waiting brides), counsels hope and fortitude to the Cubans. ⊠ *W. Flagler St. and S.W. 17th Ave., Little Havana.*

Coral Gables

If not for George E. Merrick, Coral Gables would be just another suburb. Merrick envisioned an American Venice, with canals and gracious homes spreading across the community. In 1911 his minister father died, and Merrick inherited 1,600 acres of citrus and avocado groves; by 1921 he had upped that to 3,000 acres. Using this as a foundation, Merrick began designing a city based on centuries-old prototypes from Mediterranean countries. He planned lush landscaping, magnificent entrances, and broad boulevards named for Spanish explorers, cities, and provinces. His uncle, Denman Fink, helped Merrick crystallize his artistic vision, and he hired architects trained abroad to create themed neighborhood villages, such as Florida pioneer, Chinese, French city, Dutch South African, and French Normandy. The result was a planned community with Spanish Mediterranean architecture that justifiably calls itself the City Beautiful—a moniker it acquired by following the Garden City method of urban planning in the 1920s.

Unfortunately for Merrick the devastating no-name hurricane of 1926 and the Great Depression prevented him from fulfilling many of his plans. He died at 54, working for the post office. His city languished until after World War II but then grew rapidly. Today Coral Gables has a population of about 43,000. In its bustling downtown more than 150 companies have headquarters or regional offices, and the University of Miami campus in the southern part of Coral Gables brings a youthful vibrancy: the median age of residents is 38. Like much of Miami, Coral

ART DECO HOTELS: MIAMI NICE

WITH APOLOGIES TO the flamingo, Miami's most recognizable icons are now the art deco hotels of South Beach. Their story begins in the 1920s, when Miami Beach was a winter playground of the rich, and grand themed hotels ruled. By the late '20s, however, shipping problems and a hurricane had turned the boom to bust, and another approach to attract vacationers was needed.

In the early 1930s it was the turn of the middle class, which was drawn south by a more affordable version of paradise. New hotels were needed, and the architectural motif of choice became what is called deco (for purists, moderne), based on a sleek and cheerful look with geometric designs and creative colors. It was introduced in Paris in the '20s and later crossed the Atlantic.

In South Beach, architects added other shapes brought to America by industrial designers: streamlined, aerodynamic forms based on trains, ocean liners, and automobiles. Using a steel-and-concrete box as a foundation, architects dipped into this new grab bag of styles to accessorize their hotels. Pylons, spheres, cylinders, and cubes thrust out from facades and roofs. "Eyebrows," small ledges topping window frames, popped out of buildings like concrete caps. To soften sharp edges, designers added wraparound windows and curved corners, many ornamented with racing stripes. To reflect the beach locale, nautical elements were added: portholes appeared in sets of three. Small images of seaweed, starfish, and rolling waves were plastered, painted, or etched on walls. Buildings looked ready to go to sea. Also taking advantage of the environment, sunlight, an abundant commodity, was brought indoors through glass blocks. But because there was no air-conditioning, coolness was achieved by planting shady palms and laying terrazzo tile.

Of course, everything has a life span, and the deco hotels were no exception. Eventually, bold colors and creative accents became cliché, and ensuing decades saw owners hide their hotels beneath coats of plain white or beige paint. Deco still had its proponents, inspiring later architects, most notably Morris Lapidus, to create larger-than-life 1950s deco hotels, such as the Fontainebleau and Eden Roc. But the days of small deco hotels had passed. By the 1970s they were no longer welcoming tourists . . . or welcoming to look at. Most had matured into flophouses or dirt-cheap homes for retirees. Various plans ranging from leveling the buildings to legalizing gambling were proposed—and defeated.

Then in the 1980s an unusual confluence of people and events proved the area's salvation. The hyperactive cop show Miami Vice, set against the newly painted pastel facades of Ocean Drive, portrayed an exotic tropical appeal. European fashion photographers, restaurateurs, and entrepreneurs started using the area as a backdrop for models, cafés, and resurrected hotels. Above all, there was Barbara Baer Capitman, a senior citizen who reviewed South Beach's buildings and proposed them for the National Register of Historic Places. Thanks to her efforts and the ongoing drive of others to rescue, maintain, and improve these historic jewels, a new generation (you included) can experience the same tropical pleasures enjoyed by travelers of the 1930s.

Gables has realized the aesthetic and economic importance of historic preservation and has passed a design ordinance, rewarding businesses for maintaining their building's architectural style. Even the street signs (ground-level markers that are hard to see in daylight, impossible at night) are preserved due to their historical value. They're worth the inconvenience, if only to honor the memory of Merrick.

a good tour

This tour contains some backtracking. Unfortunately, no matter how you navigate Coral Gables, directions get confusing. This plan takes in the highlights first and lets you fill out the balance of your day as you see fit. Heading south on downtown's Brickell Avenue, turn right onto Coral Way—also marked as Southwest 13th Street—and stay on Coral Way even as it turns into Southwest 3rd Avenue and Southwest 22nd Street. An arch of banyan trees prepares you for the grand entrance onto **Miracle Mile** ㉑ ➤, the heart of downtown Coral Gables. Park your car and take time to explore on foot. When you've seen enough, continue driving west, passing the 1930s Miracle Theater on your left, which now serves as home of the Actors' Playhouse. Keep heading west, cross LeJeune Road, and bear right onto Coral Way, catching an eyeful of the ornate Spanish Renaissance **Coral Gables City Hall** ㉒. Continue a few blocks until you see Toledo Street and make a left. A few blocks up on your left, you'll see the gates surrounding the exotic and unusual Merrick-designed **Venetian Pool** ㉓, created from an old coral quarry. There's parking on your right. Immediately ahead of you is the Merrick-designed **De Soto Plaza and Fountain** ㉔.

As in many areas of Coral Gables, there's a traffic circle surrounding the fountain. Head to 12 o'clock (the opposite side of the fountain) and stay on De Soto for a magnificent vista and entrance to the, yes, Merrick-designed and reborn **Biltmore Hotel** ㉕. On your right, before you reach the hotel, you'll see the **Coral Gables Congregational Church** ㉖, one of the first churches in this planned community. After visiting the hotel, double back to the fountain, this time circling to 9 o'clock and Granada Boulevard. Several blocks away you'll arrive at the Granada Golf Course, where you turn left onto North Greenway. As you cruise up the street, notice the stand of banyan trees that separates the fairways. At the end of the course the road makes a horseshoe bend, but instead cross Alhambra to loop around the restored **Alhambra Water Tower** ㉗, a city landmark dating from 1924. By the way, it's Merrick designed.

Return to Alhambra and follow it straight to the next light (Coral Way); turn left and ogle beautifully maintained Spanish homes from the 1920s. Although there's only a small sign to announce it, the **Coral Gables Merrick House and Gardens** ㉘, Merrick's boyhood home, is at Coral Way and Toledo Street. It's a charming glimpse into old-time Florida. Parking is behind the house. Afterward, take a right on Coral Way, followed by a left on Granada, which winds south past Bird Road and eventually to Ponce de León Boulevard. Turn right and follow it to the entrance of the main campus of the **University of Miami** ㉙. Turn right at the first stoplight (Stanford Drive) to enter the campus; park in the lot on your right designated for visitors to the Lowe Art Museum.

TIMING Strolling Miracle Mile should take slightly more than an hour—unless you plan to shop. In that case, allow four hours. Save time for a dip at the Venetian Pool, and plan to spend at least an hour getting acquainted with the Biltmore—longer if you'd like to order a drink and linger poolside. If you can pull yourself away from the lap of luxury, allow an hour to visit the University of Miami campus (if you're into college campuses).

What to See

㉗ Alhambra Water Tower. In 1924 this city landmark stored water and was clad in a decorative Moresque lighthouselike exterior. It was restored a decade ago after more than 50 years of neglect and now delights viewers with its copper-rib dome and multicolor frescoes—pretty impressive when you consider its peers are merely steel containers. ⊠ *Alhambra Circle, Greenway Ct., and Ferdinand St., Coral Gables.*

㉕ Biltmore Hotel. Bouncing back from dark days as an army hospital, this 1926 hotel is now the jewel of Coral Gables. Reopened a decade ago after extensive renovations, the opulent landmark played host to President Clinton and regularly books visiting heads of state in its presidential suite. Tucked away on the easternmost side of the ground floor is performance space for one of Miami's top theater companies, GablesStage. The pink hotel was recently designated a National Historic Landmark. Its 16-story tower, like the Freedom Tower in downtown Miami, is a replica of Seville's Giralda tower. To the west is the Biltmore Country Club, a richly ornamented beaux arts–style structure with a superb colonnade and courtyard; it was reincorporated into the hotel in 1989. Free tours are offered. ⊠ *1200 Anastasia Ave., Coral Gables* ☎ *305/445–1926* ⊕ *www.biltmorehotel.com* ☉ *Tours Sun. at 1:30, 2:30, and 3:30.*

㉒ Coral Gables City Hall. Far more attractive than today's modular city halls, this 1928 building has a three-tier tower topped with a clock and a 500-pound bell. A mural by Denman Fink (George Merrick's uncle and artistic adviser), inside the dome ceiling on the second floor, depicts the four seasons. (Although not as well known as Maxfield Parrish, Fink demonstrated a similar utopian vision.) Also on display are paintings, photos, and ads touting 1920s Coral Gables. ⊠ *405 Biltmore Way, Coral Gables* ☎ *305/446–6800* ☉ *Weekdays 8–5.*

> **need a break?** Whether you want to relax or try Miami's "in" snack, you can't miss with **Sushi Maki** (⊠ 2334 Ponce de León Blvd., Coral Gables ☎ 305/443–1884). In the center of the action in the Gables, this corner hangout is a remarkably inexpensive spot to rest your soles while sinking into dark red cushions and chowing down on a few California rolls or savoring a slice of key lime pie.

㉖ Coral Gables Congregational Church. The parish was organized in 1923, and with George Merrick as a charter member (and donor of the land), this small church became the first in the city. Rumor has it Merrick built it in honor of his father, a Congregational minister. The original interiors are still intact. ⊠ *3010 De Soto Blvd., Coral Gables* ☎ *305/448–7421* ☉ *Weekdays 8:30–7; Sun. services at 9:15 and 10:45 AM.*

㉘ Coral Gables Merrick House and Gardens. In 1976 the city of Coral Gables acquired George Merrick's boyhood home. Restored to its 1920s appearance, it contains Merrick family furnishings and artwork. The lush and lazy tropical feel suggests the inspiration for George's masterpiece: Coral Gables. ⊠ *907 Coral Way, Coral Gables* ☎ *305/460–5361* 🎫 *House $5, grounds free* ☉ *House Wed. and Sun. 1–4, grounds daily 8–sunset and by appointment.*

㉔ De Soto Plaza and Fountain. Water flows from the mouths of four sculpted faces on a classical column on a pedestal in this Denman Fink–designed fountain from the early 1920s. The closed eyes of the face looking west symbolize the day's end. ⊠ *Granada Blvd. and Sevilla Ave., Coral Gables.*

▶ **㉑ Miracle Mile.** This upscale yet neighborly stretch of retail stores is actually only ½ mi long. After years of neglect, it's been updated and upgraded and now offers a delightful mix of owner-operated shops and chain stores, bridal shops, art galleries and bistros, and enough late-night hot spots to keep things hopping. ✉ *Coral Way between S.W. 37th Ave. (Douglas Rd.) and S.W. 42nd Ave. (LeJeune Rd.), Coral Gables.*

㉙ **University of Miami.** With almost 14,000 full-time, part-time, and non-credit students, UM is the largest private research university in the Southeast. Visit the **Lowe Art Museum,** which has a permanent collection of 8,000 works that include Renaissance and baroque art, American paintings, Latin American art, and Navajo and Pueblo Indian textiles and baskets. The museum also hosts traveling exhibitions and the popular Beaux Arts Festival in January. ✉ *1301 Stanford Dr., Coral Gables* 🕾 *305/284–3535 or 305/284–3536* ⊕ *www.miami.edu* 🎫 *$5* ☉ *Tues.–Wed. and Fri.–Sat. 10–5, Thurs. noon–7, Sun. noon–5.*

★ ♻ ㉓ **Venetian Pool.** Sculpted from a rock quarry in 1923 and fed by artesian wells, this 825,000-gallon municipal pool remains quite popular due to its themed architecture—a fantasized version of a waterfront Italian village—created by Denman Fink. The pool has earned a place on the National Register of Historic Places and displays vintage photos depicting 1920s beauty pageants and swank soirees held long ago. Paul Whiteman played here, Johnny Weissmuller and Esther Williams swam here, and you should, too (but no kids under three). A snack bar, lockers, and showers make this must-see user-friendly as well. ✉ *2701 De Soto Blvd., Coral Gables* 🕾 *305/460–5356* ⊕ *www.venetianpool.com* 🎫 *$9, free parking across De Soto Blvd.* ☉ *June–Aug., weekdays 11–7:30, weekends 10–4:30; Sept.–Oct. and Apr.–May, Tues.–Fri. 11–5:30, weekends 10–4:30; Nov.–Mar., Tues.–Fri. 10–4:30, weekends 10–4:30.*

South Miami

South of Miami and Coral Gables is a city called South Miami, which is not to be confused with the region known as South Dade. A pioneer farm community, it grew into a suburb but retains its small-town charm. Fine old homes and stately trees line Sunset Drive, a city-designated Historic and Scenic Road to and through the town. The pace in this friendly community has picked up steam since the arrival of the Shops at Sunset Place, a retail complex larger than Coconut Grove's CocoWalk.

a good tour

Drive south from Sunset Drive on Red Road (watching for the plentiful orchid merchants) and turn left on Old Cutler Road, which curves north along the uplands of southern Florida's coastal ridge toward the 83-acre **Fairchild Tropical Garden** ㉚ ⌐. Just north of the gardens Old Cutler Road traverses Dade County's **Matheson Hammock Park** ㉛. From here follow the road back to U.S. 1, heading north to Miami.

TIMING Allow half a day for these three natural attractions, a full day if ornithology and botany are your thing. Driving from SoBe should take only 25 minutes—longer during afternoon rush hour.

What to See

★ ♻ ⌐ ㉚ **Fairchild Tropical Garden.** Comprising 83 acres, this is the largest tropical botanical garden in the continental United States. Eleven lakes, a rain forest, and lots of palm trees, cycads, and flowers, including orchids, mountain roses, bellflowers, coral trees, and bougainvillea make it a garden for the senses—and there's special assistance for the hearing impaired. Take the free guided tram tour, which leaves on the hour. Spicing up the social calendar are garden sales (don't miss the Ramble in November or the International Mango Festival in July), moonlight strolls, and symphony concerts. A gift shop in the visitor center is a popular source for books on gardening and horticulture, ordered by botanists the world over. ✉ *10901 Old Cutler Rd., Coral Gables* ☎ *305/667–1651* ⊕ *www. fairchildgarden.org* ✉ *$8* ⊙ *Daily 9:30–4:30.*

☺ ㉛ **Matheson Hammock Park.** In the 1930s the Civilian Conservation Corps developed this 100-acre tract of upland and mangrove swamp on land donated by a local pioneer, Commodore J. W. Matheson. The park, Miami-Dade County's oldest and most scenic, has a bathing beach and changing facilities and a popular restaurant housed in a historic coral rock building that overlooks the swimming lagoon. The marina has slips for 243 boats, 71 dry-storage spaces, and a bait-and-tackle shop. Noticeably absent are fishing and diving charters, although there is a sailing school. ✉ *9610 Old Cutler Rd., Coral Gables* ☎ *305/665–5475* ⊕ *www.co.miami-dade.fl.us/parks* ✉ *Parking for beach and marina $3.50 per car, $8 per car with trailer, $6 per bus and RV; limited free upland parking* ⊙ *Daily 6–sunset. Pool lifeguards winter, daily 8:30–5; summer, weekends 8:30–6.*

off the beaten path

☺ **Parrot Jungle.** One of South Florida's original tourist attractions, Parrot Jungle opened in 1936 and has now relocated to Watson Island, linked by the MacArthur Causeway (Interstate 395) to Miami and Miami Beach. In addition to a thousand exotic birds, the attraction will include a 17-ft Asian crocodile, 9-ft albino alligators, a serpentarium filled with venomous snakes, a petting zoo, and a two-story-high aviary with more than 100 free-flying macaws. A restaurant with indoor and outdoor seating will overlook a lake where 60 postcard-perfect Caribbean flamingos hang out. Orchids and ferns and even trees from the original site are being transplanted along a Disneyesque jungle river that will meander through the park. The original site on Southwest 57th Avenue has been purchased by the Village of Pinecrest, which promises to preserve its popular trails, massive oaks, and bald cypress and add a Vita-course, a public library, and snack bar. ✉ *1111 Parrot Jungle Trail, Watson Island* ☎ *305/666–7834* ⊕ *www.parrotjungle.com* ✉ *$23.95* ⊙ *Daily 10–6 (last admission at 4:30; later in season).*

Coconut Grove

South Florida's oldest settlement, "The Grove" was inhabited as early as 1834 and established by 1873, two decades before Miami. Its early settlers included Bahamian blacks, "Conchs" (white Key Westers, many originally from the Bahamas), and New England intellectuals, who built a community that attracted artists, writers, and scientists to establish winter homes. To this day Coconut Grove reflects its pioneers' eclectic origins. Posh estates mingle with rustic cottages, modest frame homes, and stark modern dwellings, often on the same block. To keep Coconut Grove a village in a jungle, residents lavish affection on exotic plantings while battling to protect remaining native vegetation. The historic center of the Village of Coconut Grove went through a hippie period in the 1960s, a laid-back funkiness in the 1970s, and a teenybopper invasion in the early 1980s. Today the tone is upscale and urban. On weekends the Grove is jam-packed with both locals and tourists—especially teenagers—shopping at the Streets of Mayfair, CocoWalk, and small boutiques. Parking can be a problem, especially on weekend evenings, when police direct traffic and prohibit turns at some intersections to prevent gridlock. Be prepared to walk several blocks from the periphery into the heart of the Grove.

From downtown Miami take Brickell Avenue south and follow the signs pointing to Vizcaya and Coconut Grove. If you're interested in seeing celeb estates, turn left at Southeast 32nd Road and follow the loop—Sylvester Stallone's former estate is the one with the huge gates on the right at the turn, and Madonna's past abode is the one at 3029 Brickell. Turn left back on South Miami Avenue. Immediately on your left you'll see the entrance to the **Vizcaya Museum and Gardens** ㉜ ⌐. Less than 100 yards down the road on your right is the **Miami Museum of Science and Space Transit Planetarium** ㉝. The road switches from four lanes to two and back again as you approach downtown Coconut Grove. With 28 waterfront acres of Australian pine, lush lawns, and walking and jogging paths, the bayside David T. Kennedy Park makes a pleasant stop. If you're interested in the history of air travel, take a quick detour down Pan American Drive to see the 1930s art deco Pan Am terminal, which has been horribly renovated inside to become **Miami City Hall** ㉞. You'll also see the Coconut Grove Convention Center, where antiques, boat, and home shows are held, and Dinner Key Marina, where seabirds soar and sailboats ride at anchor. South Miami Avenue, now known as South Bayshore Drive, heads directly into McFarlane Road, which takes a sharp right into the center of the action. If you can forsake instant gratification, turn left on Main Highway and drive less than ½ mi to Devon Road and the interesting **Plymouth Congregational Church** ㉟ and its gardens. Return to Main Highway and travel northeast toward the historic Village of Coconut Grove. As you reenter the village center, note on your left the Coconut Grove Playhouse. On your right, beyond the benches and shelter, is the entrance to the **Barnacle State Historic Site** ㊱. After getting your fill of history, relax and spend the evening mingling with Coconut Grove's eccentrics.

TIMING Plan on devoting from six to eight hours to enjoy Vizcaya, other bayfront sights, and the village's shops, restaurants, and nightlife.

What to See

㊱ **Barnacle State Historic Site.** The oldest Miami home still on its original foundation rests in the middle of 5 acres of native hardwood and landscaped lawns surrounded by flashy Coconut Grove. Built by Florida's first snowbird—New Yorker Commodore Ralph Munroe—the home has many original furnishings, a broad sloping roof, and deeply recessed verandas that channel sea breezes into the house. If your timing is right, you may catch one of the monthly Moonlight Concerts. ✉ *3485 Main Hwy., Coconut Grove* ☎ *305/448–9445* ⊕ *www.dep.state.fl.us/parks* ▨ *$1, concerts $5* ⊙ *Fri.–Sun. 9–4; tours at 10, 11:30, 1, and 2:30 (call ahead); group tours for 10 or more Tues.–Thurs. by reservation; concerts on evenings near the full moon 6–9 (call ahead for exact dates).*

㉞ **Miami City Hall.** Built in 1934 as the terminal for the Pan American Airways seaplane base at Dinner Key, the building retains its nautical-style art deco trim. Sadly, the interior is generic government, but a 1938 Pan Am menu on display (with filet mignon, *petit pois au beurre,* and Jenny Lind pudding) lets you know Miami officials appreciate from whence they came. ✉ *3500 Pan American Dr., Coconut Grove* ☎ *305/250–5400* ⊙ *Weekdays 8–5.*

㉝ **Miami Museum of Science and Space Transit Planetarium.** This museum is chock-full of hands-on sound, gravity, and electricity displays for children and adults alike. A wildlife center has native Florida snakes, turtles, tortoises, and birds of prey. Traveling exhibits appear throughout the year, and virtual-reality and life-science demonstrations are on hand every day. Stick around after dark on Friday and Saturday nights for the laser-light rock-and-roll shows presented in the planetarium. ✉ *3280 S. Miami Ave., Coconut Grove* ☎ *305/854–4247 for museum; 305/854– 2222 for planetarium information* ⊕ *www.miamisci.org* ✉ *Museum exhibits, planetarium shows, and wildlife center $8–$10; laser show $6* ☉ *Daily 10–6.*

③⑤ **Plymouth Congregational Church.** Opened in 1917, this handsome coral-rock structure resembles a Mexican mission church. The front door, made of hand-carved walnut and oak with original wrought-iron fittings, came from an early 17th-century monastery in the Pyrenees. Also on the 11-acre grounds are the first schoolhouse in Miami-Dade County (one room), moved to this property, and the site of the original Coconut Grove water and electric works. ✉ *3400 Devon Rd., Coconut Grove* ☎ *305/444–6521* ☉ *Weekdays 9–4:30, Sun. service at 10* AM.

★ ▶ ③② **Vizcaya Museum and Gardens.** Of the 10,000 people living in Miami between 1912 and 1916, about 1,000 of them were gainfully employed by Chicago industrialist James Deering to build this $20 million Italian Renaissance–style winter residence. Once comprising 180 acres, the grounds now cover a still-substantial 30-acre tract, including a native hammock and more than 10 acres of formal gardens and fountains overlooking Biscayne Bay. The house, open to the public, has 70 rooms, 34 of which are filled with paintings, sculpture, and antique furniture dating from the 15th through the 19th centuries and representing the Renaissance, baroque, rococo, and neoclassical styles. Vizcaya's guest list has included Ronald Reagan, Pope John Paul II, Queen Elizabeth II, Bill Clinton, and Boris Yeltsin. It's a shame the guided tour can be far less impressive than the home's guest list and surroundings. ✉ *3251 S. Miami Ave., Coconut Grove* ☎ *305/250–9133* ⊕ *www.vizcayamuseum. com* ✉ *$10* ☉ *Daily 9:30–4:30, garden 9:30–5:30.*

Virginia Key & Key Biscayne

Government Cut and the Port of Miami separate the city's dense urban fabric from two of its playground islands, Virginia Key and Key Biscayne. Parks occupy much of both keys, providing facilities for golf, tennis, softball, picnicking, and sunbathing, plus uninviting but ecologically valuable stretches of dense mangrove swamp. Key Biscayne's long and winding roads are great for rollerblading and bicycling, and its lush laziness provides a respite from the buzz-saw tempo of SoBe.

a good tour

To reach Virginia Key and Key Biscayne take the Rickenbacker Causeway ($1 per car) across Biscayne Bay from the mainland at Brickell Avenue and Southwest 26th Road, about 2 mi south of downtown Miami. The causeway links several islands in the bay. The William M. Powell Bridge rises 75 ft above the water to eliminate the need for a draw span. The view from the top includes the bay, keys, port, and downtown skyscrapers, with Miami Beach and the Atlantic Ocean in the distance. Just south of the Powell Bridge a stub of the **Old Rickenbacker Causeway Bridge** ③⑦ ▶, built in 1947, is now a fishing pier. Immediately after crossing the Rickenbacker Causeway onto Virginia Key, you'll see a long strip of bay front popular with windsurfers and jet skiers. Nearby rest rooms and a great view of the curving shoreline make this an ideal place to park and have your own tailgate party. Look for the gold dome of the **Miami Seaquarium** ③⑧, one of the country's first marine attractions. Opposite the causeway from the Seaquarium, a road leads north to Virginia Key Beach and the adjacent Virginia Key Critical Wildlife Area, which is often closed to the public to protect nesting birds. From Virginia Key the causeway crosses Bear Cut to the north end of Key Biscayne and becomes Crandon Boulevard. The boulevard bisects 1,211-acre **Crandon Park** ③, with a popular Atlantic Ocean beach and nature center. On your right are entrances to the Crandon Park Golf Course and the Tennis Center at Crandon Park, home of the Nasdaq 100 Open. Keep your eyes open for pure Miami icons: coconut palms and iguana-crossing signs. From the traffic circle at the south end of Crandon Park, Crandon Boulevard continues to the **Bill Baggs Cape Florida State Recreation Area** ④, a 460-acre park with the brick Cape Florida Lighthouse and light keeper's cottage. Follow Crandon Boulevard back to Crandon Park through Key Biscayne's downtown village, where shops and a 10-acre village green cater mainly to local residents. On your way back to the mainland, pause as you approach the Powell Bridge to admire the Miami skyline. At night the brightly lighted Bank of America building looks like a clipper ship running under full sail before the breeze.

TIMING   Set aside the better part of a day for this tour, and double that if you're into beaches, fishing, and water sports.

What to See

👆 ④   **Bill Baggs Cape Florida State Recreation Area.** Thanks to its beaches, blue-
Fodor'sChoice   green waters, amenities, sunsets, and a lighthouse, this park at Key Bis-
★   cayne's southern tip is well worth the drive. Since Hurricane Andrew, it has returned better than ever, with native trees replacing the once-ubiquitous Australian pines, an additional 54 acres of wetlands, new boardwalks over sea grass–studded dunes, 18 picnic shelters, and two rustic waterfront cafés. A stroll or bike ride along paths and boardwalks provides wonderful views of Miami's skyline. Also on-site are bicycle and skate rentals, a playground, fishing piers, and kayak rental. Guided tours of the cultural complex and the **Cape Florida Lighthouse,** South Florida's oldest structure, are offered, but call for availability. The lighthouse was built in 1845 to replace an earlier one destroyed in an 1836 Seminole attack, in which the keeper's helper was killed. ✉ *1200 S. Crandon Blvd., Key Biscayne* ☎ *305/361–5811 or 305/361–8779* ⊕ *www.dep.state.fl. us/parks* ✆ *$4 per vehicle with up to 8 people; $1 per person on bicycle, bus, motorcycle, or foot* ⊙ *Daily 8–sunset, tours Thurs.–Mon. 10 and 1 (sign up ½ hr beforehand).*

③   **Crandon Park.** This laid-back park in northern Key Biscayne is popular with families, and many educated beach enthusiasts rate the 3½-mi county beach here among the top 10 beaches in North America. The sand is soft, and parking is both inexpensive and plentiful. So large is this park that it includes a marina, a golf course, a tennis center, and ball fields. There are also a kids' section with a playground and a splash pool. At the north end of the beach is the free **Marjory Stoneman Douglas Biscayne Nature Center** (☎ 305/361–6767). Explore natural habitats by taking a tour that includes dragging nets through sea-grass beds to catch, study, and release such marine creatures as sea cucumbers, sea horses, crabs, and shrimp. Nature center hours vary, so call ahead. ✉ *4000 Crandon Blvd., Key Biscayne* ☎ *305/361–5421* ⊕ *www.co. miami-dade.fl.us/parks* ✆ *Free; $4 per vehicle* ⊙ *Daily 8–sunset.*

👆 ㊳   **Miami Seaquarium.** This old-fashioned attraction has six daily shows with sea lions, dolphins, and Lolita, a killer whale. (Lolita's tank is small for seaquariums—just three times her length—and so some wildlife advocates are trying to get her back to sea.) Exhibits include a shark pool, a 235,000-gallon tropical-reef aquarium, and manatees. Glass-bottom boats take tours of Biscayne Bay. Want to get your feet (and everything else) wet? The Water and Dolphin Exploration (WADE) program enables you to swim with dolphins during a two-hour session. Reservations are required. ✉ *4400 Rickenbacker Causeway, Virginia Key*

☎ *305/361–5705* ⊕ *www.miamiseaquarium.com* ▣ *$24.45, WADE $140, parking $4* ⊙ *Daily 9:30–6 (last admission at 4:30); WADE Wed.–Sun. at noon and 3:30.*

▶ ③ **Old Rickenbacker Causeway Bridge.** Watch boat traffic pass through the channel, pelicans and other seabirds soar and dive, and dolphins cavort in the bay. Park at its entrance, about a mile from the tollgate, and walk past anglers tending their lines to the gap where the center draw span across Biscayne Bay was removed. ⊠ *Rickenbacker Causeway south of Powell Bridge, east of Coconut Grove.*

WHERE TO EAT

Restaurants listed here have passed the test of time, but you might double-check by phone before you set out for the evening. At many of the hottest spots, you'll need a reservation to avoid a long wait for a table. And when you get your check, note whether a gratuity is already included; most restaurants add 15% (ostensibly for the convenience of, and protection from, the many Latin-American and European tourists who are used to this practice in their homelands), but reduce or supplement it depending on your opinion of the service.

WHAT IT COSTS				
$$$$	**$$$**	**$$**	**$**	**¢**
RESTAURANTS over $30	$20–$30	$15–$20	$10–$15	under $10

Restaurant prices are per person for a main course at dinner.

Coconut Grove

Contemporary

$$–$$$$ ✕ **Baleen.** The new culinary director of this resort restaurant, Arturo Paz, studied under popular chef Robbin Haas, named the Best New Chef by *Food & Wine* magazine a few years ago for his New World cuisine. Paz smartly lets the Haas influence linger in such popular dishes as tangy Caesar salad and wood-roasted shrimp; Roquefort-crusted filet mignon with red wine sauce; and Chinese whole fried snapper with coconut rice, julienne vegetables, and black-bean vinaigrette. Main plates are à la carte, with steak house–type side dishes padding the bill. ⊠ *Grove Isle Hotel, 4 Grove Isle Dr., Coconut Grove,* ☎ *305/858–8300* ⌂ *Reservations essential* ▭ *AE, D, DC, MC, V.*

$$–$$$$ ✕ **Mayfair Grill and Orchids Champagne and Wine Bar.** This long-running dining room in the Mayfair House Hotel may have a muffled and carpeted elegance, but the cooking is more innovative than the interior would suggest: Thai crab cakes with *panko* crumbs and a sesame-chili glaze; Colorado buffalo-loin carpaccio splashed with white truffle oil; roulade of free-range chicken stuffed with spinach and goat cheese; and rack of lamb barbecued with notes of apple and ancho chile. There's also the outdoor courtyard at Orchids, the only champagne bar in town, where bubbly personalities can feel free to be themselves. ⊠ *3000 Florida Ave., Coconut Grove* ☎ *305/441–0000* ▭ *AE, D, DC, MC, V* ⊙ *No lunch.*

$$$ ✕ **Aria.** As pretty as an operatic melody, this dining room in the Ritz-Carlton resort provides a high-end, global experience. Choose your view: the 126-seat restaurant has an exhibition kitchen, although an alfresco area offers views of landscaped gardens or breeze-brushed beaches. Then select your food, which may be even more difficult, given chef Jeff Vigila's artistry—items range from asparagus cappuccino with crab frittata and nutmeg foam to braised veal cheeks with langoustines, lentil

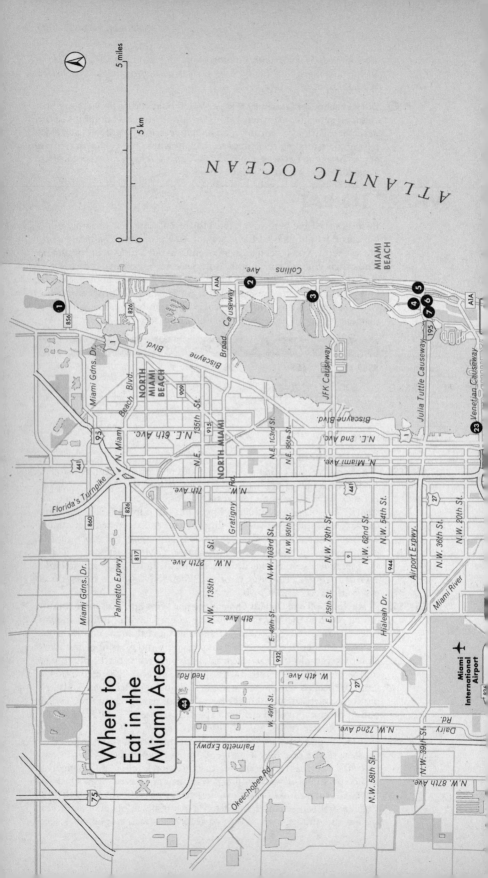

ragout, and summer truffles. ⊠ *455 Grand Bay Dr., Key Biscayne* ☎ *305/365–4500* ⌖ *Reservations essential* ▤ *AE, D, DC, MC, V.*

Indian

$–$$$ ✕ **Anokha.** "There is no doubt that all Indians love food," the menu says at Anokha, and there's also no doubt that all Miamians love *this* Indian food. Standouts are mahimahi steamed with green chiles and cilantro and wrapped in a banana leaf, and chicken with an almond-cream curry and chicken marinaded in a puree of spinach, cilantro, and yogurt. The wait between courses can seem as long as a cab ride in Manhattan during rush hour, but don't fret—there's only one cook in the kitchen, and she's worth the wait. ⊠ *3195 Commodore Plaza, Coconut Grove* ☎ *786/552–1030* ▤ *AE, MC, V* ⊘ *Closed Mon.*

Coral Gables

Caribbean

$$–$$$$ ✕ **Ortanique on the Mile.** Named after an exotic citrus fruit, this restaurant screams "island"—or, more accurately, island resort—from the breezy interior decorated like a Jamaican terraced garden to the exquisite pan-Caribbean cuisine. Proprietor Delius Shirley and chef-proprietor Cindy Hutson offer such favorites as pumpkin soup; fried calamari salad; escovitched whole yellowtail snapper; or jerk pork loin. Dessert doesn't get better than drunken banana fritters, unless you accompany them with a press pot of Blue Mountain coffee, direct from Jamaica and practically vibrating with caffeine. ⊠ *278 Miracle Mile, Miracle Mile* ☎ *305/446–7710* ▤ *AE, DC, MC, V* ⊘ *No lunch weekends.*

Contemporary

$$$–$$$$ ✕ **Norman's.** This destination restaurant, which has won as many awards
Fodor'sChoice   as it has customers, turns out some of Miami's most imaginative cui-
★   sine. Chef Norman Van Aken created an international buzz by perfecting New World cuisine—a combination rooted in Latin, North American, Caribbean, and Asian influences. Bold tastes pervade the changing selections, which might include rum-and-pepper-painted grouper on a mango-*habañero* sauce. The ultragracious staff never seems harried, even when all seats are filled (usually every minute between opening and closing). ⊠ *21 Almeria Ave., Coral Gables* ☎ *305/446–6767* ⌖ *Reservations suggested* ▤ *AE, DC, MC, V* ⊘ *Closed Sun. No lunch.*

$–$$$$ ✕ **Restaurant St. Michel.** While this spot is utterly French, the hotel it's in evokes the Mediterranean, and the food is new American. Stuart Bornstein's window on Coral Gables is a lace-curtained café with sidewalk tables that would be at home across from a railroad station in Avignon or Bordeaux. Lighter dishes include angel hair pasta in garlic, basil, and tomato sauce topped with grilled jumbo shrimp. Among the heartier entrées are a grilled fillet of salmon atop asparagus-crab risotto; sesame-seared loin of tuna; and local yellowtail snapper with a fruit salsa. ⊠ *162 Alcazar Ave., Coral Gables* ☎ *305/444–1666* ▤ *AE, DC, MC, V.*

French

$$–$$$ ✕ **Pascal's on Ponce.** Chef-proprietor Pascal Oudin has been cooking here since the 1980s, when he opened Dominique's in the Alexander Hotel. His stream-lined French cuisine disdains trends and discounts flash. Instead, you're supplied with substantive delicacies such as sautéed Australian sea bass with Mediterranean vegetables en croute or tenderloin of beef sautéed with snails and wild mushrooms. Service is proper, textures perfect, and wines ideally complementary. The only dilemma is deciding between Oudin's own tart Tatin or a cheese course for dessert. ⊠ *2611 Ponce de León Blvd., Coral Gables* ☎ *305/444–2024* ▤ *AE, D, DC, MC, V* ⊘ *No lunch weekends.*

Italian

$$–$$$ ✕ **Caffè Abbracci.** Much-beloved, this Italian restaurant is more like a club than an eatery. Start with some cold and hot antipasti, various carpaccios, porcini mushrooms, calamari, grilled goat cheese, shrimp, and mussels. Most pasta is made fresh, so consider sampling two or three, maybe with pesto sauce, Gorgonzola sauce and fresh tomatoes. Patrons tend to fare better when they're recognized, so go with a local if you can. ⊠ *318 Aragon Ave., Coral Gables* ☎ *305/441–0700* ⌂ *Reservations essential* ⊟ *AE, DC, MC, V* ⊘ *No lunch weekends.*

Japanese

¢–$ ✕ **Sushi Maki.** At night, the twentysomething set seems to gravitate to this Gables restaurant for the current "in" nibble—sushi, washed down with Japanese beer, saki, or green tea. But if sushi and sashimi make you squeamish, there are cooked rolls and hot dishes such as teriyaki, tempura, and noodle bowls. Diehards dig the Volcano, a roll of smoked salmon, crab, cream cheese, and rice topped with a spicy burnt orange "lava" of conch-spiked mayonnaise. Entrées come with miso soup or a simple salad. ⊠ *2334 Ponce de León Blvd., Coral Gables* ☎ *305/443– 1884* ⊠ *5818 Sunset Dr., South Miami* ☎ *305/667–7677* ⊟ *AE, MC, V* ⊘ *No lunch Sun.*

Downtown Miami

Chinese

$–$$$$ ✕ **Tony Chan's Water Club.** Off the lobby of the Doubletree Grand Hotel, this spot overlooks a bayside marina. On the menu of more than 200 appetizers and entrées are minced quail tossed with bamboo shoots and mushrooms wrapped in lettuce leaves. Indulge in a seafood spectacular of shrimp, conch, scallops, fish cakes, and crabmeat tossed with broccoli in a bird's nest, or go for pork chops sprinkled with green pepper in a black bean–garlic sauce. A lighter favorite is steamed sea bass with ginger and garlic. ⊠ *1717 N. Bayshore Dr., Downtown* ☎ *305/374– 8888* ⊟ *AE, D, DC, MC, V* ⊘ *No lunch weekends.*

Contemporary

★ $$–$$$$ ✕ **Azul.** This sumptuous eatery has truly conquered the devil in the details. In addition to chef Michelle Bernstein's exquisite French-Caribbean cuisine, the thoughtful touches in service graciously anticipate your needs. Does your sleeveless top mean your shoulders are too cold to properly appreciate the poached eggs with lobster-knuckle hollandaise? Ask for one of the house pashminas. Forgot your reading glasses and can't decipher the hanger steak with foie gras sauce? Request a pair from the host. Want to see how the other half lives? Descend the staircase to Cafe Sambal, the all-day casual restaurant. ⊠ *Mandarin Oriental Hotel, 500 Brickell Key Dr., Brickell Key* ☎ *305/913–8288* ⌂ *Reservations essential* ⊟ *AE, MC, V* ⊘ *Closed Sun. No lunch Sat.*

Italian

$–$$$ ✕ **Perricone's Marketplace and Café.** Brickell Avenue south of the Miami River is burgeoning with Italian restaurants. This is the biggest and most popular among them, in a 120-year-old barn from Vermont. The recipes were handed down from grandmother to mother to daughter, and the cooking is simple and good. Buy your wine from the on-premises deli and bring it to your table for a small corkage fee. Enjoy a glass with homemade minestrone; a generous antipasto; linguine with a sauté of jumbo shrimp, fresh asparagus, and chopped tomatoes; or gnocchi with four cheeses. The homemade tiramisu and fruit tart are top-notch. ⊠ *15 S.E. 10th St., Brickell Village* ☎ *305/374–9449* ⊟ *AE, MC, V.*

Latin

¢–$$$ ✕ **Los Ranchos.** This steak-house chain sustains the tradition of Managua's original Los Ranchos by serving Argentine-style beef—lean, grass-fed tenderloin served with three Nicaraguan sauces. There are *chimichurri* (a thick sauce of olive oil, vinegar, cayenne, and herbs), a tomato-based marinara, and a fiery *cebollitas encurtidas* (with jalapeño and pickled onion). In addition to churrasco steak, specialties include spicy chorizo and an appetizer of fried cheese and plantain chips with a spicy dipping sauce. There's live entertainment. ✉ *Bayside Marketplace, 401 Biscayne Blvd., Downtown* ☎ *305/375–8188 or 305/375–0666* ✉ *CocoWalk, 3015 Grand Ave., Coconut Grove* ☎ *305/461–8222* ✉ *125 S.W. 107th Ave., Sweetwater* ☎ *305/221–9367* ✉ *2728 Ponce de León Blvd., Coral Gables* ☎ *305/446–0050* ✉ *The Falls, 8888 S.W. 136th St., Suite 303, Kendall, Miami* ☎ *305/238–6867* ⊟ *AE, DC, MC, V.*

Middle Eastern

¢   ✕ **The Original Daily Bread Marketplace.** At this pan–Middle Eastern marketplace, run by an Israeli family, falafel and gyro pita pockets—some of the most tempting in the county—share the bill with Arabic meat pies and Greek spinach pies. Desserts are uniformly sticky with honey, drenched with butter, and encrusted with nuts—a good bet, whether you eat in at the self-service tables or take out. ✉ *2400 S.W. 27th St., Downtown* ☎ *305/856–5893* ⊟ *AE, D, MC, V.*

Seafood

¢–$$ ✕ **Fishbone Grill.** The campy furnishings here are artsy, the fish artful: have it grilled, blackened, sautéed, baked, Française-style, or Asian. Pizzas are available, too, as is a mean cioppino, the San Francisco–style tomato-based fish stew. Consider opening your meal with the cakelike jalapeño corn bread served with a small salad. Fishbone serves beer and wine only and justifiably prides itself on a reasonably priced, varied selection. Watch for wine makers' dinners when superb vintages are paired with the chef's whims. ✉ *650 S. Miami Ave., Downtown* ☎ *305/530–1915* ⊟ *AE, MC, V* ☉ *No dinner Sun.*

Mexican

¢–$ ✕ **Taquerias el Mexicano.** This modest storefront on the edge of Little Havana is a find for authentic Mexican fare such as enchiladas, chicken *mole* (chocolate sauce), and fajitas. Dinner begins with a basket of chips to dip in a salsa brimming with fresh cilantro. Not a lot of English is spoken here, but the waitstaff is eager to help. ✉ *521 SW 8th St., Downtown* ☎ *305/858–1160* ⊟ *AE, MC, V.*

Little Havana

Cuban

¢–$$$ ✕ **Versailles.** Cubans meet to dine on Calle Ocho in what is quite possibly the most ornate budget restaurant you'll ever see, all mirrors and candelabras. And the royal treatment is not limited to the furnishings. The food is terrific, especially such classics as *ropa vieja* (a saucy shredded beef served over rice), *arroz con pollo* (chicken and rice), *palomilla* (thin, boneless) steak, *sopa de platanos* (plantain soup), ham shank, and roast pork. To complete the experience, have the town's strongest Cuban coffee and terrific flan or sweet *tres leches* (literally, "three milks," a creamy Latin dessert) to finish. ✉ *3555 S.W. 8th St., Little Havana* ☎ *305/444–0240* ⊟ *AE, D, DC, MC, V.*

Spanish

¢–$$$ ✕ **Las Neuvas Culebrinas.** A Spanish *tapacería* (literally, "house of little plates") is a place to live each meal as if it were your last, though you

FLORIBBEAN CUISINE

NEW FLORIDA," OR "FLORIBBEAN," cuisine, a unique collection of flavors at once light and hearty, has elevated a handful of Miami chefs to stardom in recent years. The fusion of American cooking traditions with Caribbean and Latin American ingredients makes for exceptional, eye-opening eating.

From Cuba and other islands comes the platano, or plantain, a green banana that is usually fried as a side dish. In Miami, chefs use the plantain in ways that Cuban home cooks might never have imagined: most famous might be lush dolphin coated in mashed plantain and then gently fried, a dish that's become one of the signature tastes here.

The mango, which crowds gigantic backyard trees in late summer, is a luscious, sweet, and juicy inspiration for inventive cooking. You'll see it pureed into sauces for fish and chicken, frozen into homemade sorbet (it's wonderful with lemon sorbet), and sliced into a bracing salad with watercress, red onion, and vinaigrette. You've not had a proper cheesecake until you've sampled mango cheesecake with strawberry puree.

Bored with mashed potato? Try mashed boniato, a faintly sweet, faintly coconutty root vegetable that has so much more character than the lowly spud. Another tuber, yuca (or cassava) might be the blandest taste you've encountered, until you drizzle it with a mojo sauce made of garlic, oil, and sometimes onion or lime.

A menu standard here is ceviche, fish and seafood "cooked" (actually, marinated without heat) in lime juice and flavored with onion, cilantro, garlic, vinegar, and other seasonings, depending on the country of origin. Puerto Rico is noted for a ceviche of octopus, and you'll find it prevalent in Miami.

One of the world's spiciest cuisines is that of Haiti, fired by the bright yellow Scotch bonnet pepper. The pepper has a fierce burn, but get beyond that and you'll experience a wonderfully complex flavor that mixes well with tomato, citrus, and anything tangy in complex chowders made of pumpkin, fish, and other ingredients.

What's the Caribbean's most universal influence on Miami's dining habits? Hands down, it's coffee. On almost any street corner here, try un cafecito, a tiny plastic thimble of oil-slick black espresso, super-sweetened as it's made and downed in one shot. Some say it fuels Miami's commerce; no doubt it's crucial to the nonstop nightlife of the insomniac city.

may wait for it as long as some inmates do for an appeal. Tapas are not small at all; some are entrée size, such as a succulent mix of garbanzos with ham, sausage, red peppers, and oil, or the Spanish tortilla, a giant Frisbee-shape omelet. Indulge in a tender fillet of crocodile, fresh fish, grilled pork, or the kicker, goat in Coca-Cola sauce. For dessert there's *crema Catalana*, caramelized tableside with a blowtorch. ⊠ *4700 W. Flagler St., Little Havana* ☎ *305/445–2337* ⊟ *AE, MC, V.*

Vietnamese

★ ¢–$$ ✕ **Hy-Vong Vietnamese Cuisine.** This plain little restaurant is an anomaly on Calle Ocho, and also a novelty—come before 7 PM to avoid a wait. Spring springs forth in spring rolls of ground pork, cellophane noodles, and black mushrooms wrapped in homemade rice paper. Folks will mill about on the sidewalk for hours to sample the whole fish panfried with *nuoc man* (a garlic-lime fish sauce), not to mention the thinly sliced pork barbecued with sesame seeds, almonds, and peanuts. Beer-savvy proprietor Kathy Manning serves a half-dozen top brews (Singha, Sapporo, and Spaten, among them) to further inoculate the experience from the ordinary. ⊠ *3458 S.W. 8th St., Little Havana* ☎ *305/446–3674* ⊟ *AE, D, MC, V* ⊘ *Closed Mon. No lunch.*

Miami Beach North of South Beach

Contemporary

$–$$$ ✕ **Crystal Café.** As cozy as Grandma's dining room, this new Continental restaurant takes the classics and lightens them up. Beef Stroganoff and chicken *paprikash* are two such updated stars; and osso buco falls off the bone. More contemporary items include chicken Kiev, stuffed with goat cheese and topped with a tricolor salad, and pan-seared duck breast with raspberry sauce. Multiple Golden Spoon award–winning Macedonian chef-proprietor Klime Kovaceski takes pride in serving more food than you can possibly manage, including home-baked rhubarb pie. ⊠ *726 41st St., Miami Beach* ☎ *305/673–8266* ⊟ *AE, D, DC, MC, V* ⊘ *Closed Mon. No lunch.*

Continental

$$$–$$$$ ✕ **The Forge.** This landmark bills itself as the Versailles of steak. Each intimate dining salon has historical artifacts, including a chandelier that hung in James Madison's White House. The wine cellar contains 380,000 bottles—including more than 500 dating from 1822. In addition to steak, specialties include Norwegian salmon with spinach vinaigrette and free-range duck roasted with black currants. For dessert try the blacksmith pie. ⊠ *432 Arthur Godfrey Rd., Miami Beach* ☎ *305/ 538–8533* ⌖ *Reservations essential* ⊟ *AE, DC, MC, V* ⊘ *No lunch.*

Delicatessens

¢–$ ✕ **Arnie and Richie's.** Take a deep whiff when you walk in and you'll know what you're in for: onion rolls, smoked whitefish salad, half-sour pickles, herring in sour cream sauce, chopped liver, corned beef, and pastrami. At this casual-to-the extreme, family-run operation, most customers are regulars and seat themselves at tables that have baskets of plastic knives and forks; if you request a menu, it's a clear sign you're a newcomer. Service can be brusque, but it sure is quick. ⊠ *525 41st St., Miami Beach* ☎ *305/531–7691* ⊟ *AE, MC, V.*

Italian

★ ¢–$$ ✕ **Café Prima Pasta.** One of Miami's many signatures is this exemplary Argentine-Italian spot, which rules the emerging North Beach neighborhood. Service can be erratic, but you forget it all on delivery of fresh-made bread with a bowl of spiced olive oil. Tender carpaccio and plentiful antipasti are a delight to share, but the real treat here is the hand-rolled pasta, which can range from crab-stuffed ravioli to simple fettuccine with seafood. If overexposed tiramisu hasn't made an enemy of you yet, try this legendary one in order to add espresso notes to your unavoidable garlic breath. ⊠ *414 71st St., North Beach, Miami Beach* ☎ *305/867–0106* ⊟ *MC, V.*

Japanese

¢–$$ ✕ **Sushi Republic.** A long and narrow storefront with sponge-painted walls, this eatery prides itself on welcoming customers, so don't be surprised when the sushi chefs say "Hi!" when you walk in. Nor should you expect anything but the freshest sashimi, which is elegantly presented and perfectly succulent. As far as cooked fare goes, the Republic is more like a democracy—everything is even and consistent. *Shumai*, soft shrimp dumplings with *ponzu* (soy, rice vinegar, sake, seaweed, and dried bonito flakes) dipping sauce; whole fried soft-shell crab; and salmon teriyaki are particularly noteworthy. ⊠ *9583 Harding Ave., Surfside* ☎ *305/867–8036* ⊟ *AE, D, DC, MC, V* ⊙ *Closed Mon. No lunch weekends.*

Mediterranean

¢–$$ ✕ **Oasis Café.** The emphasis in Mediterranean fare is on health, and Oasis, a coolly tiled spot, makes sure you don't keel over at the tables—the chefs here stuff grape leaves, not arteries. Starters include eggplant salads, hummus, grilled sesame tofu, and sautéed garlic spinach. Roasted vegetable lasagna, grilled fresh salmon on focaccia, and penne with turkey, tomato, saffron, and pine nuts are worthy entrées. The homemade rum cake is a superb way to drink dessert. ⊠ *976 41st St., Miami Beach* ☎ *305/674–7676* ⊟ *AE, D, DC, MC, V* ⊙ *Closed Sun.*

North Miami Beach & North Dade

Contemporary

★ $$$–$$$$ ✕ **Chef Allen's.** Chef Allen Susser presents his global fare in this art gallery of a dining room. At the 25-ft-wide picture window, watch him create masterpieces from a menu that changes nightly. After a salad of baby greens and warm wild mushrooms or a rock-shrimp hash with roasted corn, consider swordfish with conch-citrus couscous, macadamia nuts, and lemon or grilled lamb chops with eggplant timbale and a three-nut salsa. It's hard to resist finishing off your meal with a soufflé; order it early to eliminate a wait at the end of your meal. ⊠ *19088 N.E. 29th Ave., Aventura, North Miami Beach* ☎ *305/935–2900* ⌕ *Reservations essential* ⊟ *AE, DC, MC, V.*

Steak

$$$–$$$$ ✕ **Shula's Steak House.** Prime rib, fish, steaks, and 3-pound lobsters are almost an afterthought to the *objets de sport* in this NFL shrine in the Don Shula's Hotel. Dine in a manly wood-lined room with a fireplace, surrounded by memorabilia of retired coach Don Shula's perfect 1972 season with the Miami Dolphins. Polish off the 48-ounce porterhouse steak and achieve a sort of immortality—your name posted on Shula's Web site and an autographed picture of Shula to take home. There's also Shula's Steak 2, a sports-celebrity hangout in the resort's hotel section, as well as a branch at the Alexander Hotel in Miami Beach. ⊠ *7601 N.W. 154th St., Miami Lakes* ☎ *305/820–8102* ⊟ *AE, DC, MC, V.*

South Beach

American

$$–$$$ ✕ **Joe Allen.** In a neighborhood of condos, town houses, and stores, this casual upscale eatery is a hangout for locals who crave a good martini

along with a terrific burger. The eclectic crowd includes kids and grand-
parents, and the menu, printed daily, has everything from pizzas to calves'
liver to steaks. Start with a salad, such as arugula with pear, prosciutto,
and Parmesan with a lemon-shallot dressing. Desserts include banana
cream pie and ice cream and cookie sandwiches. ⊠ *1787 Purdy Ave.,
South Beach* ☎ *305/531–7007* ▭ *MC, V.*

Cafés

★ ¢–$$ ✕ **News Café.** An Ocean Drive landmark, this 24-hour café attracts a
crowd with snacks, light meals, and drinks, and the people parade on
the sidewalk out front. Most prefer sitting outside, where they can feel
the salt breeze and gawk at the human scenery. Offering a little of this
and a little of that—bagels, eggs, stuffed grape leaves, chocolate fon-
due, sandwiches, and a terrific wine list—this joint has something for
all appetites. Although service can be indifferent to the point of laissez-
faire, the café remains a scene. ⊠ *800 Ocean Dr., South Beach* ☎ *305/
538–6397* ⌕ *Reservations not accepted* ▭ *AE, DC, MC, V.*

¢–$$ ✕ **Van Dyke Café.** Just as its parent, News Café, draws the fashion
crowd, this offshoot attracts the artsy crowd. Indeed this place seems
even livelier than its Ocean Drive counterpart, with pedestrians passing by on the Lincoln Road Mall and live jazz playing upstairs every
evening—or, technically, every early morning. The kitchen serves dishes
from mammoth omelets with home fries to soups and grilled dolphin
sandwiches to basil-grilled lamb and pasta dishes, though it's best to
stick to basics. ⊠ *846 Lincoln Rd., South Beach* ☎ *305/534–3600*
▭ *AE, DC, MC, V.*

Contemporary

★ $$$–$$$$ ✕ **Blue Door at the Delano.** In a hotel where style reigns supreme, this restau-
rant provides both glamour and tantalizing food. Acclaimed consulting
chef Claude Troisgros and executive chef Elizabeth Barlow combine the
flavors of classic French fare with South American influences to create
dishes such as the Big Ravioli, filled with crab-and-scallop mousseline,
and osso buco in Thai curry sauce with caramelized pineapple and ba-
nanas. Equally pleasing is dining with the crème de la crème of Miami
(and New York, and Paris) society. ⊠ *1685 Collins Ave., South Beach*
☎ *305/674–6400* ⌕ *Reservations essential* ▭ *AE, D, DC, MC, V.*

★ $$$–$$$$ ✕ **Nemo.** The open-air, bright colors, copper fixtures, and tree-shaded
courtyard lend Nemo casual comfort, but it's the menu that earns raves.
Caribbean, Asian, Mediterranean, and Middle Eastern influences blend
boldly, and succeed. Appetizers include garlic-cured salmon rolls with
Tabiko caviar and wasabi mayo, and crispy prawns with spicy salsa *cruda.*
Main courses might include wok-charred salmon or Indian-spice pork
chop. Hedy Goldsmith's funky pastries are exquisite. ⊠ *100 Collins Ave.,
South Beach* ☎ *305/532–4550* ▭ *AE, DC, MC, V.*

$$$–$$$$ ✕ **Wish.** If what you wish for is stupendous food served in a designer-
deco environment, consider your wish granted. Fashion designer Todd
Oldham redid the former Tiffany Hotel, the art deco gem that houses
this fresh, youthful restaurant. His whimsy and use of color (you'll
marvel at the creative use of dozens of hanging light fixtures) provide
an apt backdrop for chef E. Michael Redit's French-Brazilian cuisine.
Dishes like seared scallops over parsnip puree with a drizzle of foie gras
or rare tuna with charred watermelon and avocado Hollandaise make
as much of a statement as the room. ⊠ *801 Collins Ave., South Beach*
☎ *305/674–9474* ▭ *AE, D, DC, MC, V.*

$$–$$$ ✕ **Rumi.** Rumi is what happens when club kids and party organizers like
Alan Roth and Sean Saladino grow up: they open a dinner lounge
named for a mystical poet. Co-chefs J. D. Harris and Scott Fredel con-
tribute to the sensual, heavy-lidded environment with culinary delights

such as Florida pompano with truffled Peruvian potatoes or Sonoma duck breast with orange crepes. After 11 or so, the two-story storefront turns into a club, complete with velvet rope and mandatory champagne purchases if you sit at a table. ✉ *330 Lincoln Rd., South Beach* ☎ *305/ 672–4353* ⌕ *Reservations essential* ▤ *AE, MC, V* ☉ *No lunch.*

Italian

$$–$$$$ ✕ **Escopazzo.** A romantic storefront takes you away, like Calgon, from the din of bustling Washington Avenue. The Roman menu offers some of the area's best—and most expensive—Italian food. Indulge in sea bass with Grand Marnier, golden raisins and pine nuts, risottos with such combinations as goat cheese and arugula, and various soufflés with the freshest produce and seafood. Service can be slow as a speedboat in a manatee zone; pass the time by taking a tour of the 1,000-bottle wine cellar. ✉ *1311 Washington Ave., South Beach* ☎ *305/674–9450* ▤ *AE, DC, MC, V* ☉ *No lunch.*

★ **$$–$$$$** ✕ **Tuscan Steak.** Dark wood and mirrors define this masculine, chic, expensive place, where food is served family style. Tuscan can be busy as a subway stop, and still the staff will be gracious and giving. The chefs take their cues from the Tuscan countryside, where pasta is rich with truffles and main plates are simply but deliciously grilled. Sip a deep red Barolo with any of the house specialties: three-mushroom risotto with white truffle oil, gnocchi with Gorgonzola cream, Florentine T-bone with roasted garlic puree, whole yellowtail snapper with braised garlic, or the filet mignon with a Gorgonzola crust. ✉ *431 Washington Ave., South Beach* ☎ *305/534–2233* ▤ *AE, DC, MC, V.*

$–$$ ✕ **Spiga.** When you need a break from Miami's abundant exotic fare, savor the modestly priced Italian standards at this neighborhood favorite. Homemade pastas and breads are fresh daily. Carpaccio *di tonno* (thinly sliced tuna with avocado and onion) is a typical appetizer, and the *zuppa di pesce* (fish stew) is unparalleled. Entrées include ravioli *di vitello ai funghi shitaki* (homemade ravioli stuffed with veal and sautéed with shiitake mushrooms). Customers sometimes bring in CDs for personalized enjoyment. ✉ *1228 Collins Ave., South Beach* ☎ *305/534–0079* ▤ *AE, D, DC, MC, V* ☉ *No lunch.*

Pan-Asian

★ **$$$–$$$$** ✕ **Pacific Time.** Packed nearly every night, chef-proprietor Jonathan Eismann's superb eatery has a high blue ceiling, banquettes, plank floors, and an open kitchen. The brilliant American-Asian food includes such masterpieces as Sizzling Local Yellowtail Hot & Sour Tempura, a crisp, ginger-stuffed whole fish served filleted over ribbon vegetables with herbs and a dipping sauce, or dry-aged Colorado beef grilled with shiitake mushrooms and bok choy. Diners can start with a spicy coconut curry of local pink shrimp and end with a soothing tropical sorbet. ✉ *915 Lincoln Rd., South Beach* ☎ *305/534–5979* ⌕ *Reservations essential* ▤ *AE, DC, MC, V.*

$–$$$$ ✕ **China Grill.** This crowded, noisy celebrity haunt turns out not Chinese food but rather "world cuisine" in large portions meant for sharing. Crispy duck with scallion pancakes and caramelized black-vinegar sauce is a nice surprise, as is the flash-fried crispy spinach that shatters like a good martini glass thrown into a fireplace. Unless you're frequent diner Boris Becker or George Clooney, don't expect your drinks to arrive before your food. ✉ *404 Washington Ave., South Beach* ☎ *305/534–2211* ⌕ *Reservations essential* ▤ *AE, DC, MC, V* ☉ *No lunch Sat.*

Seafood

¢–$$$$ ✕ **Joe's Stone Crab Restaurant.** Joe's stubbornly operates by its own rules: be prepared to wait up to an hour just to register your name for a table, and resign yourself to waiting up to another *two* hours before you finally sit down. The centerpiece of the ample à la carte menu is, of course, stone crab, with a piquant mustard sauce. Side orders include creamed garlic spinach, fried sweet potatoes, fried green tomatoes, and hash browns. Desserts include a justifiably famous key lime pie. If you can't stand loitering hungrily, come for lunch or go next door for Joe's takeout. ⊠ *11 Washington Ave., South Beach* ☎ *305/673–0365; 305/ 673–4611 for takeout; 800/780–2722 for overnight shipping* ⌂ *Reservations not accepted* ▤ *AE, D, DC, MC, V* ☉ *Closed May–mid-Oct. No lunch Sun.–Mon.*

Steak

$$$–$$$$ ✕ **Gaucho Room.** Granted, you may never bite down on a more succulent steak than in this Argentine cowboy–theme room, but don't you dare call this a steak house. The chef cut his culinary teeth on fusion cuisine, and the results are seen in pancetta-wrapped rabbit loin with crimson lentil and duck-confit cassoulet or a coriander-crusted Chilean sea bass, which is not to say that you shouldn't order the supple *churrasco* (a whole skirt steak that is marinated, grilled, and then sliced tableside). Service may be the finest and most solicitous in South Beach. ⊠ *Loews Hotel, 1601 Collins Ave., South Beach* ☎ *305/604–5290* ⌂ *Reservations essential* ▤ *AE, D, DC, MC, V* ☉ *No lunch. Closed Mon.*

South Miami

Barbecue

¢–$$ ✕ **Shorty's.** When "Shorty" opened his barbecue spot in 1951, some folks would ride in on horseback. Now the rustic outpost sits in the shadow of "Downtown Dadeland," and plate glass and air-conditioning have replaced screens, but it still serves up the best barbecue in these parts. You sit at long picnic tables; chow down on pork barbecue sandwiches, baby backs, or a combo plate of chicken and ribs; order a side of corn on the cob drenched in butter; and slake your thirst with a glass of iced tea (sweetened or not) while recalling the simpler days before high-rises and Metrorail. Clean off the addictive barbecue sauce with rolls of paper towels and throw the bones into individual brown paper bags. If there's room, key lime pie or a soft-serve ice cream cone makes a great ending. ⊠ *9200 S. Dixie Hwy., Miami* ☎ *305/670–7732* ⊠ *11575 S. W. 40th St. (Bird Rd.), West Dade* ☎ *305/227–3196* ⊠ *2255 N.W. 87th Ave. (Bird Rd.), Miami* ☎ *305/471–5554* ▤ *AE, MC, V.*

Contemporary

$$–$$$ ✕ **Two Chefs.** Meet the two chefs—Jan Jorgensen and Soren Bredahl—both Danes, who've been cooking together for decades. This restaurant, decorated like a Williams-Sonoma catalog, has an ever-changing menu, but scan for oak-baked Portobello with Gruyère cheese and sourdough toast or New York strip with lobster potato galette and escargots. The chefs pride themselves on the unexpected and think nothing of pairing grilled salmon with a Jerusalem artichoke hash or creating a calzone with lobster, mozzarella, and asparagus. ⊠ *8287 S. Dixie Hwy., South Miami* ☎ *305/663–2100* ▤ *AE, D, DC, MC, V* ☉ *Closed Sun.*

¢–$$ ✕ **Sunset Tavern.** Innovative food, such as a seafood enchilada topped with fried flat noodles, comes with a relatively low price tag in this preppie tavern near Sunset Place. The open-faced steak sandwich is loaded with sautéed mushrooms and onions, and the burger is a half pound of sirloin. Among many tasty bangs for the buck include handmade Hawaiian pizza, roasted duck and lentil salad, and maple-glazed meat loaf served with potato cake and spring vegetables. ⊠ *5818 Sunset Dr., South Miami* ☎ *305/665–9996* ▤ *AE, MC, V.*

Seafood

$–$$$ ✕ **Captain's Tavern.** This beloved family fish house has an unusually interesting menu fortified with Caribbean and South American influences. The paneled walls and padded captain's chairs may be dated, but the fabulous food and impressive wine list make up for it. Beyond good versions of the typical fare—seafood platters and conch fritters—you'll find Portuguese fish stew (Cataplana), a hearty conch chowder served with a shot of sherry, fish with various tropical fruits, and oysters in cream sauce with fresh rosemary, not to mention decadent desserts. ✉ *7495 S.E. 98th St., South Miami* ☎ *305/661–4237* ▤ *AE, MC, V.*

West Miami

Chinese

¢–$$$$ ✕ **Tropical Chinese Restaurant.** This big, lacquer-free room feels and sounds as open and busy as a railway station. The extensive menu is filled with tofu combinations, poultry, beef, and pork, as well as tender seafood. An exuberant dim sum lunch—brunch on the weekends—allows you to choose an assortment of small dishes from wheeled carts. In the open kitchen 10 chefs prepare everything as if for dignitaries. ✉ *7991 S.W. 40th St. (Bird Rd.), Westchester, West Miami* ☎ *305/262–7576 or 305/262–1552* ▤ *AE, DC, MC, V.*

Spanish

¢–$ ✕ **Latin American Cafeteria.** A visit to this tiny eatery, part of a local chain, gives you a taste of quintessential Miami. A seat at a horseshoe bar provides a first-hand look at the creation of Cuban-style sandwiches. The only Spanish one needs to know is *medianoche, por favor*; this "midnight" sandwich is a luscious layering of ham, cheese, and pork in a sweet Cuban bun toasted on the grill. The brightly lighted Sunset Drive restaurant is more spacious and modern, with comfortable booths as well as a counter and a walk-up window for Café Cubano. Just point to the bilingual menu to order chicken strips, steak fajitas, or one of the daily specials: *arroz con pollo* (chicken with rice), *ropa vieja*, or *caldo gallego* (Spanish bean soup). Kids eat American-style—spaghetti or a hot dog and fries. ✉ *9608 72nd St. (Sunset Dr.), West Miami* ☎ *305/279–4353* ✉ *2940 Coral Way, north of Miracle Mile Miami* ☎ *305/446–5622* ✉ *2740 S.W. 27th Ave., Coconut Grove* ☎ *305/445–9339* ✉ *401 Biscayne Blvd., Bayside* ☎ *305/381–7774* ▤ *MC, V.*

WHERE TO STAY

Although some hotels (especially on the mainland) have adopted steady year-round rates, many adjust their rates to reflect seasonal demand. The peak occurs in winter, with a dip in summer (prices are often more negotiable than rate cards let on). You'll find the best values between Easter and Memorial Day (which is actually a delightful time in Miami but a difficult time for many people to travel) and in September and October (the height of hurricane season). Keep in mind that Miami hoteliers collect roughly 12.5%—ouch—for city and resort taxes; parking fees can run up to $16 per evening; and tips for bellhops, valet parkers, concierges, and housekeepers add to the expense. Some hotels actually tack on an automatic 15% gratuity. All told, you can easily spend 25% more than your room rate to sleep in Miami.

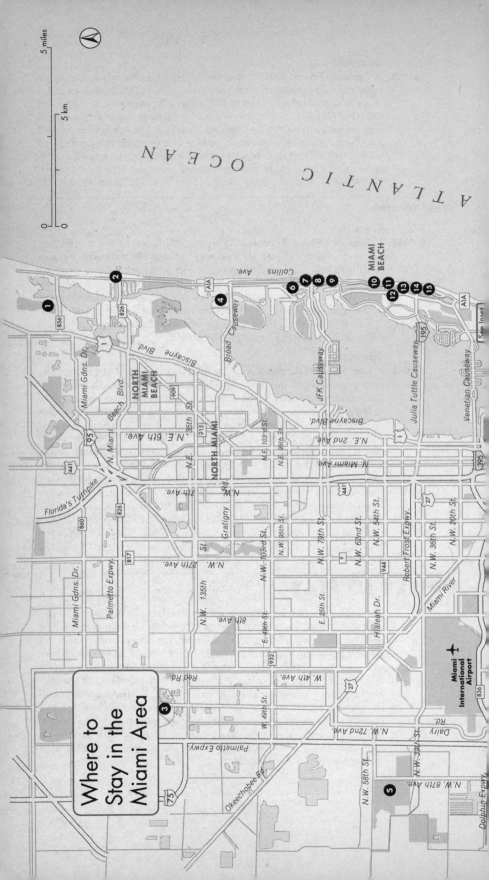

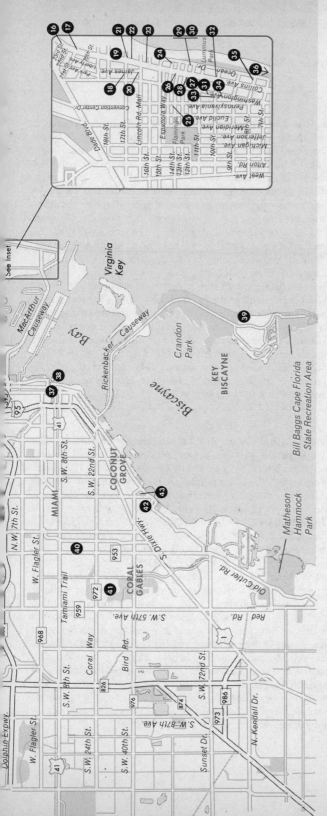

The Albion **20**
Bay Harbor Inn **4**
Bayliss Guest House ...**25**
Best Western
South Beach **31**
Biltmore Hotel **41**
Cadet Hotel **18**
Casa Grande **35**
Claridge Hotel **15**
The Creek **16**

Crystal Beach Suites **9**
Days Inn Convention
Center **17**
Day's Inn North Beach ...**7**
Days Inn Oceanside **14**
Delano Hotel **41**
Don Shula's Hotel
& Golf Club **3**
Doral Golf
Resort and Spa **5**

Eden Roc **11**
Essex House **32**
Fontainebleau **13**
Hilton Resort **33**
Hotel Astor **33**
Hotel Impala **28**
Hotel Ocean **29**
Hotel Place St. Michel ..**40**
Hyatt Regency Miami ...**37**
Indian Creek Hotel **12**

Kent **27**
Loews Miami
Beach Hotel **23**
Mayfair House **42**
Mandarin Oriental Miami **38**
Miami Beach Marriott at
South Beach **36**
Nassau Suite Hotel **26**
National Hotel **22**

Newport
Beachside Resort **2**
Ocean Surf **8**
Paradise Inn **6**
Raleigh Hotel **19**
Sonesta Beach Resort Key
Biscayne **39**
Royal Hotel **34**
The Tides **30**

Turnberry Isle
Resort & Club **1**
WinterHaven **24**
Wyndham Bay **43**
Wyndham Miami
Beach Resort **10**

WHAT IT COSTS				
$$$$	$$$	$$	$	¢
HOTELS	over $220	$140–$220	$100–$140	$80–$100	under $80

Hotel prices are for a standard double room, excluding 6% sales tax (more in some counties) and 1%–4% tourist tax.

Coconut Grove

★ $$$–$$$$ ▥ **Wyndham Grand Bay.** Combining the classical elegance of Greece, a stepped facade that looks vaguely Aztec, a hint of the South, and a brush of the tropical, the Grand Bay is like no other in South Florida. Guest rooms are filled with superb touches, such as antique sideboards that store away house phones and televisions. But what sets the hotel apart are the atypically spacious suite terraces—perfect for private dinners— with sweeping views of Biscayne Bay. Bice, a trendy Italian restaurant on the premises, is extremely popular. ⊠ 2669 S. Bayshore Dr., Coconut Grove, 33133 ☎ 305/858–9600 or 800/327–2788 ⊟ 305/859–2026 ⊕ www.wyndham.com/coconutgrove ⇋ 125 rooms, 52 suites ⌕ Restaurant, pool, hair salon, health club, hot tub, massage, sauna, bar, concierge, parking (fee) ☰ AE, DC, MC, V.

$$–$$$$ ▥ **Mayfair House.** This European-style luxury hotel sits within the Streets of Mayfair, an upscale mall in the heart of the Grove. That feel is mirrored in the Tiffany windows, imported ceramics, polished mahogany, and impressive glass elevator. The individually furnished suites have a Roman tub inside or a Japanese hot tub on a private terrace or balcony. ⊠ 3000 Florida Ave., Coconut Grove, 33133 ☎ 305/441–0000 or 800/433–4555 ⊟ 305/447–9173 ⊕ www.mayfairhousehotel.com ⇋ 179 suites ⌕ Restaurant, snack bar, pool, hot tub, bar, laundry service, concierge, business services, parking (fee) ☰ AE, D, DC, MC, V.

Coral Gables

★ $$$$ ▥ **Biltmore Hotel.** Miami's boom-time hotel recaptures the Roaring '20s with its artwork, period furnishings, vast lawns, and huge pool flanked by a colonnaded walkway. Now owned by Coral Gables, the 1926 hotel rises like an ornate wedding cake in the heart of a residential area. Large rooms are done in a restrained Moorish style. For $2,750, you can book the Everglades Suite—Bill Clinton's favorite. ⊠ 1200 Anastasia Ave., Coral Gables 33134 ☎ 305/445–1926 or 800/727–1926 ⊟ 305/913–3159 ⊕ www.biltmorehotel.com ⇋ 237 rooms, 38 suites ⌕ Restaurant, café, 18-hole golf course, 10 tennis courts, pool, health club, sauna, spa, bar, lobby lounge, meeting room ☰ AE, D, DC, MC, V.

★ $$$ ▥ **Hotel Place St. Michel.** Art nouveau chandeliers suspended from vaulted ceilings light the public areas of this intimate hotel within easy walking distance of Miracle Mile. Built in 1926, the historic inn is kept filled with the scent of fresh flowers, circulated by paddle fans. Each room has its own dimensions, personality, and antiques imported from England, Scotland, and France, although plusher beds would be welcome. Dinner at the superb Restaurant St. Michel is a must, but there is also a more casual bar-dining area behind the lobby, best suited for quiet breakfasts or late-night aperitifs. ⊠ 162 Alcazar Ave., Coral Gables 33134 ☎ 305/444–1666 or 800/848–4683 ⊟ 305/529–0074 ⊕ www. hotelplacestmichel.com ⇋ 24 rooms, 3 suites ⌕ Restaurant, bar, laundry service, parking (fee) ☰ AE, DC, MC, V ❢⊙❢ CP.

Downtown Miami

$$$$ ⊞ **Mandarin Oriental Miami.** Though it's a favorite of Wall Street tycoons
Fodor'sChoice and Latin American CEOs doing business with the Brickell Avenue
★ banks, anyone who can afford to stay here won't regret it. The location
is excellent, at the tip of Brickell Key in Biscayne Bay; rooms facing west
have a dazzling view of the downtown skyline, while those facing east
overlook Miami Beach and the blue Atlantic beyond. The Mandarin is
fanatically picky about details, from the Bulova alarm clocks and hand-
painted room numbers on rice paper to the recessed data ports on room
desks that eliminate laptop cord clutter. ⊠ *500 Brickell Key Dr., Brickell Key, 33131* ☎ *305/913–8288 or 866/888–6780* 🖷 *305/913–8300*
⊕ *www.mandarinoriental.com* ↩ *329 rooms* ⟁ *Restaurant, in-room
data ports, in-room safes, pool, spa, 2 bars, dry cleaning, laundry service, concierge, business services, meeting rooms, parking (fee)* ☰ *AE,
D, DC, MC, V.*

$$$$ ⊞ **Hyatt Regency Miami.** The Hyatt is well positioned to enjoy the fruits
of Miami's late '90s renaissance—the Miami Avenue Bridge, the Port
of Miami, and AmericanAirlines Arena seemed to sprout up around it—
if your vacation is based on boats, basketball, or business, you can't do
much better. The distinctive public spaces are more colorful than businesslike, and guest rooms are done in an unusual combination of avocado, beige, and blond. Rooms also yield views of the river or port. The
James L. Knight International Center is accessible without stepping
outside, as are the downtown Metromover and its Metrorail connection. ⊠ *400 S.E. 2nd Ave., Downtown, 33131* ☎ *305/358–1234 or 800/
233–1234* 🖷 *305/358–0529* ⊕ *www.miami.hyatt.com* ↩ *612 rooms,
51 suites* ⟁ *Restaurant, pool, health club, 2 bars, laundry service, concierge, business services, parking (fee)* ☰ *AE, D, DC, MC, V.*

Key Biscayne

$$$$ ⊞ **Sonesta Beach Resort Key Biscayne.** Architecturally dull but still one
of Miami's best, this beautifully located resort has stunning sea views
from east-facing units. Rooms are done in sand tones with fabrics in
emerald, purple, gold, and ruby. The villa is actually a three-bedroom
home with a full kitchen and screened pool. The 750-ft beach, one of
Florida's most gorgeous, its Olympic pool, activities, and kids' program
make the resort a good family getaway. Museum-quality modern art by
prominent painters and sculptors graces public areas. ⊠ *350 Ocean Dr.,
Key Biscayne, 33149* ☎ *305/361–2021 or 800/766–3782* 🖷 *305/361–
3096* ⊕ *www.sonesta.com* ↩ *284 rooms, 15 suites, 1 villa* ⟁ *3 restaurants, snack bar, some kitchens, 9 tennis courts, pool, fitness classes, health
club, massage, steam room, beach, windsurfing, parasailing, 3 bars, children's programs (ages 5–13)* ☰ *AE, D, DC, MC, V.*

Miami Beach North of South Beach

$$$–$$$$ ⊞ **Claridge Hotel.** A cool Mediterranean breeze in a somewhat stagnant
corner of Miami Beach, the Claridge is the city's most impressive hotel
renovation. All accomodations are suites, a mix of Asian and European
influences, with straw mats laid over wood floors, and ornate wood fur-
niture. The exterior has been restored to the canary-yellow glory of the
1928 original; inside, rich Venetian frescoed walls are hung with Peru-
vian oil paintings, the floors are fashioned from volcanic ash, and the
whole is supported by majestic volcanic stone columns. A Moroccan ter-
race overlooks the soaring inner atrium, which has a splash Jacuzzi at
the far end. ⊠ *3500 Collins Ave., Mid-Beach, 33140* ☎ *305/604–8485
or 888/422–9111* 🖷 *305/674–0881* ⊕ *www.claridgefl.com* ↩ *50 suites*

  ♻ *Restaurant, in-room data ports, in-room safes, hot tub, concierge, business services, parking (fee)* = *AE, D, DC, MC, V.*

$$$-$$$$ ▣ **Eden Roc Renaissance Resort & Spa.** This grand 1950s hotel designed by Morris Lapidus, with its free-flowing lines of deco architecture, has a hip lobby bar with low-slung meandering couches, an indoor rock-climbing wall at its 55,000-square-ft spa, and a beachside sports bar. Rooms blend a touch of the '50s with informal elegance. ⊢ *4525 Collins Ave., Mid-Beach, 33140* ☎ *305/531–0000 or 800/327–8337* 🖷 *305/674–5555* ♿ *www.renaissancehotels.com* ⇭ *349 rooms* ♻ *2 restaurants, 2 pools, gym, spa, basketball, racquetball, squash, sports bar, meeting rooms* = *AE, MC, V.*

★ $$$-$$$$ ▣ **Fontainebleau Hilton Resort.** This big, busy, and ornate grande dame has completed an overhaul of its original building, but even more grandiose plans are in the works, with the ongoing construction of a new hotel-condominium complex that will remove several tennis courts but add a spa. All public areas and guest rooms have been renovated, but rooms still vary wildly, ranging from 1950s to very contemporary furnishings. Adults enjoy free admission to the hotel's *Club Tropigala* Vegas-style floor show. The most popular spot for kids is Cookie's World, a water playground with multiple slides and jets emerging from a giant purple octopus. ⊢ *4441 Collins Ave., Mid-Beach, 33140* ☎ *305/538–2000 or 800/548–8886* 🖷 *305/673–5351* ♿ *www.hilton.com* ⇭ *1,146 rooms, 60 suites* ♻ *12 restaurants, 4 tennis courts, 3 pools, health club, sauna, spa, beach, windsurfing, boating, jet skiing, parasailing, volleyball, 4 bars, nightclub, children's programs (ages 5–14), playground, convention center, some pets allowed (fee)* = *AE, D, DC, MC, V.*

★ $$$-$$$$ ▣ **Wyndham Miami Beach Resort.** Of the great Miami Beach hotels, this 18-story modern glass tower is a standout, as is its polished staff offering exceptional service, from helping you find the best shopping to bringing you an icy drink on the beach. The bright rooms have a tropical blue color scheme and wonderful details including mini-refrigerators, three layers of drapes (including blackout curtains), big closets, and bathrooms with high-end toiletries and a magnifying mirror. Two presidential suites were designed in consultation with the Secret Service, and a rooftop meeting room offers views of bay and ocean. ⊢ *4833 Collins Ave., Mid-Beach, 33140* ☎ *305/532–3600 or 800/203–8368* 🖷 *305/534–7409* ♿ *www.wyndham.com* ⇭ *378 rooms, 46 suites* ♻ *2 restaurants, tennis court, pool, gym, massage, beach, 2 bars, meeting room* = *AE, D, DC, MC, V.*

★ $$-$$$$ ▣ **Indian Creek Hotel.** Not as grand as the North Beach behemoths or as hectic as the Ocean Drive offerings, this 1936 Pueblo deco jewel may just be Miami's most charming and sincere lodge. Owner Marc Levin rescued the inn and filled its rooms with art deco furniture. Suites have VCR/CD players and modem capabilities. The dining room has an eclectic menu that you can also enjoy outdoors by the lush pool and garden. Stay a while, and the staff will have you feeling like family. ⊢ *2727 Indian Creek Dr., Mid-Beach, 33140* ☎ *305/531–2727 or 800/491–2772* 🖷 *305/531–5651* ♿ *www.indiancreekhotelmb.com* ⇭ *55 rooms, 6 suites* ♻ *Restaurant, some in-room data ports, some in-room VCRs, refrigerators, pool, meeting room* = *AE, D, DC, MC, V.*

¢-$$$ ▣ **Days Inn Oceanside/Beach Front.** Pets are allowed at this eight-story budget hotel not far from the renowned and much more expensive Eden Roc and Fontainebleau resorts. North of the protected Art Deco District, this eight-story lodging survives in an area where older hotels are fast giving way to the wrecking ball and high-rise resorts. Expect to pay top price for rooms with an ocean view, but all rooms are just steps from the beach and a Tiki bar, where you can conjure up dreams of margaritaville. The rooms, however, are no-nonsense, with two double beds or one king and a color TV. ✉ *4299 Collins Ave., Mid-Beach, 33141* ☎ *305/673–1513 or 800/825–6800* 🖨 *305/538–0727* ⊕ *www.daysinn. com* ➲ *143 rooms* ♨ *2 restaurants, in-room safes, pool, bar, dry cleaning, laundry facilities, parking (fee)* ⊟ *AE, DC, MC, V.*

¢–$$ 🏨 **Crystal Beach Suites.** This updated beachfront hotel is easy to miss, as the entrance and sign are on 71st Street, not Collins. But for those who prefer modern comforts, it's worth seeking. A large marble-floor lobby leads to a huge fitness center and a beautiful outdoor pool and hot tub surrounded by palm trees. Even the hallways are attractive, with new carpeting, chair railings, and colorful framed paintings. All of the rooms are actually suites, tastefully done in dark green and pink with floral drapes and upholstery. The bathroom and living areas are spacious, with a sleeper couch and a compact, fully outfitted kitchenette cleverly placed in a corner set off by a bar. ✉ *6985 Collins Ave., Mid-Beach, 33140* ☎ *305/865–9555 or 800/435–0766* 🖨 *305/866–3514* ⊕ *www.crystalbeachsuites.com* ➲ *84 suites* ♨ *Microwaves, refrigerators, pool, gym, hot tub, massage, steam room, beach, parking (fee)* ⊟ *AE, MC, V.*

¢–$$ 🏨 **Days Inn North Beach.** If you're looking for a bargain and don't care about a pool or restaurant, this seven-story hotel, built in 1932 and updated in 2001, might be the place for you. It's on Ocean Terrace, across from the beach. The porch and lobby still have the original terrazzo floors, and the interior is newly painted sea-foam green with a light pink trim. The rooms are standard issue, though some have an ocean view. For a few dollars more, a family can book one of three suites with two bedrooms connected by a bath or one of two junior suites with a bedroom, bath, and living room with a sleeper couch. ✉ *7450 Ocean Terr., 1 block east of Collins Ave., Mid-Beach, 33141* ☎ *305/866–1631 or 800/825–6800* 🖨 *305/868–4617* ⊕ *www.daysinn.com* ➲ *92 rooms* ♨ *Pool, game room, laundry facilities* ⊟ *AE, DC, MC, V* ⧖ *CP.*

¢–$ 🏨 **Ocean Surf.** For those who dig deco, this is a gem. Built in 1940 at
Fodor'sChoice   the height of the art deco era, this three-story hotel looks like it's straight
★   out of South Beach, with large porthole windows, ship-style railings, and wide ribbons of pink-and-white terrazzo swirling through the lobby. If one of the four oceanfront rooms is available, spend the extra $15, as the view through the large porthole over the bed is remarkable. Rooms are smallish but impeccably clean. The tables on the front porch, with a great view of the beach across a quiet street, are a perfect spot for enjoying the complimentary Continental breakfast. ✉ *7436 Ocean Terr., 1 block east of Collins Ave., Mid-Beach, 33141* ☎ *305/866–1648 or 800/555–0411* 🖨 *305/* ⊕ *www.oceansurf.com* ➲ *49 rooms* ♨ *In-room safes, parking (fee)* ⊟ *AE, MC, V* ⧖ *CP.*

¢   🏨 **Paradise Inn.** The price is the primary reason to stay at this older, two-story motor court, which spans half a block. Continental breakfast is complimentary, and parking, just outside your room, is also free, but the view is of other older hotels and apartments, and one of the three bordering streets is a busy thoroughfare. If noise is a problem ask for a room near the back. The beach is 1½ blocks away, and a bus stop out front offers an inexpensive way to visit South Beach. Expect older appliances and fixtures in the bathrooms and the efficiencies, which cost $5 more. Standard rooms have jalousie windows and one queen or two single beds. ✉ *8520 Harding, Mid-Beach, 33141* ☎ *305/865–6216,* 🖨 *305/865–9028* ⊕ *www.paradiseinnmiamibeach.com* ➲ *93 rooms* ♨ *Pool, laundry facilities, free parking* ⊟ *MC, V.*

North Miami, North Miami Beach & North Dade

★ $$$$ 🏨 **Turnberry Isle Resort & Club.** Finest of the grand resorts, even more so with the addition of a stellar spa, Turnberry is a tapestry of islands and waterways on 300 superbly landscaped acres by the bay. You'll stay at the 1920s Addison Mizner–designed Country Club Hotel on the Intracoastal Waterway, where oversize rooms in light woods and earth tones have large curving terraces and hot tubs. The marina has moorings for 117 boats, and there are not one but two Robert Trent Jones golf courses. The oceanfront Ocean Club has a playground for kids but no longer offers accommodations. ⊠ *19999 W. Country Club Dr., Aventura, North Miami Beach 33180* ☎ *305/932–6200 or 800/327–7028* 🖷 *305/933–6560* ⊕ *www.turnberryisle.com* ⮐ *354 rooms, 41 suites* ♿ *4 restaurants, in-room safes, minibars, 2 18-hole golf courses, 19 tennis courts, 2 pools, health club, spa, steam room, beach, docks, windsurfing, boating, racquetball, 5 bars, helipad* 🖃 *AE, D, DC, MC, V.*

$$$–$$$$ 🏨 **Don Shula's Hotel & Golf Club.** This low-rise resort is part of Miami Lakes, a planned town about 14 mi northwest of downtown. The well-maintained golf club, opened in 1962, has a championship course, a lighted executive course, and a golf school. All club rooms are English traditional in style, rich in leather and dark wood, and have balconies. The hotel, on the other hand, has a typical Florida-tropics look—light pastels and furniture of wicker and light wood. In both locations the best rooms are near the lobby for convenient access. Sixteen two-bedroom suites are geared for extended stays, with refrigerator, microwave, and VCR. ⊠ *6842 Main St., Miami Lakes 33014* ☎ *305/821–1150 or 800/ 247–4852* 🖷 *305/820–8071* ⊕ *www.donshula.com* ⮐ *205 rooms, 16 suites* ♿ *2 restaurants, some microwaves, some refrigerators, some in-room VCRs, 2 18-hole golf courses, 9 tennis courts, 2 pools, fitness classes, health club, sauna, steam room, basketball, racquetball, volleyball, 2 bars* 🖃 *AE, DC, MC, V.*

$$–$$$$ 🏨 **Bay Harbor Inn.** The inn's not on the ocean, but the tranquil Indian Creek flowing outside is sure to soothe. One of the most pleasing touches is your own front porch; sit with a book or a drink and enjoy a view of Bal Harbour a five-minute walk away. Rooms have queen- and king-size beds, and baths are large. The hotel staff is composed largely of hotel students from Johnson & Wales University, so the service is enthusiastic but not flawlessly professional. ⊠ *9660 E. Bay Harbor Dr., Bal Harbour, Miami Beach 33154* ☎ *305/868–4141* 🖷 *305/867–9094* ⊕ *www.bayharborinn.com* ⮐ *22 rooms, 23 suites* ♿ *Restaurant, pool, gym, bar, meeting room* 🖃 *AE, MC, V* ⦾ *CP.*

★ $$–$$$$ 🏨 **Newport Beachside Resort.** Built before the present crop of luxury towers sprang up, Newport is still one of the nicest hotels in Sunny Isles Beach. The combination time-share and hotel is a good place to enjoy the beach and outdoor activities. There's a wading pool and a standard pool, not to mention the ocean and fishing pier—the only remaining hotel fishing pier in Miami. Back inside, the lobby is large and bright, and so are the rooms, after a remodeling that replaced all remaining standard rooms with one-bedroom suites. ⊠ *16701 Collins Ave., Sunny Isles, Miami Beach 33160* ☎ *305/949–1300 or 800/327–5476* 🖷 *305/947–5873* ⊕ *www. newportbeachsideresort.com* ⮐ *290 suites* ♿ *4 restaurants, microwaves, refrigerators, pool, wading pool, gym, beach, bar, nightclub, shops, concierge, meeting rooms, parking (fee)* 🖃 *AE, D, DC, MC, V.*

South Beach

★ $$$$ 🏨 **Casa Grande.** A luxe and spicy Eastern-tinged flavor sets this hotel apart from the typical icy-cool minimalism found on Ocean Drive. Luxurious Balinese-inspired suites are done in teak and mahogany, with dhurrie rugs, Indonesian fabrics and artifacts, two-poster beds with ziggurat turns, full electric kitchens with utensils, and large baths—practically unheard of in the Art Deco District. Insulated windows keep the noise of Ocean Drive revelers at bay. ⊠ *834 Ocean Dr., South Beach, 33139* ☎ *305/672–7003* ⌂ *305/673–3669* ⊕ *www.casagrandehotel.com* ➳ *34 suites* ♢ *Café, in-room safes, kitchenettes, refrigerators, in-room VCRs, beach, shops, laundry service, concierge, business services, travel services* ▤ *AE, D, DC, MC, V.*

$$$$ ▦ **Delano Hotel.** You'll marvel at the lobby hung with massive white,
Fodor'sChoice billowing drapes and yet try to act casual while watching for celebrities
★ such as Ben Affleck, George Clooney, and Spike Lee, all of whom stop by when in town. Fashion models and men of independent means gather beneath cabanas, pose by the infinity pool, and sniff the heady aromas from the Blue Door restaurant. There are comprehensive business services and a rooftop bathhouse and solarium. Although the standard rooms are of average size, their stark whiteness makes them appear larger. The real appeal here is the *Alice in Wonderland*–like surrealism. ⊠ *1685 Collins Ave., South Beach, 33139* ☎ *305/672–2000 or 800/555–5001* ⌂ *305/532–0099* ➳ *184 rooms, 24 suites* ♢ *Restaurant, pool, health club, spa, beach, bar, lobby lounge, laundry service, concierge, business services* ▤ *AE, D, DC, MC, V.*

$$$$ ▦ **National Hotel.** The most spectacular part of this resurrected 1939 hotel is its tropical pool—Miami Beach's longest, at 205 ft. It's a perfect backdrop for the film crews that often work here. But poolside rooms display little of the creativity of other restored hotels. Rooms in the main building are far more appealing. A notable highlight is the clubby 1930s-style Press Room cigar bar and meeting room, off the lobby. ⊠ *1677 Collins Ave., South Beach, 33139* ☎ *305/532–2311 or 800/327–8370* ⌂ *305/534–1426* ⊕ *www.nationalhotel.com* ➳ *115 rooms, 5 suites* ♢ *Restaurant, in-room data ports, in-room safes, minibars, pool, gym, beach, bar, laundry service, concierge, meeting room, parking (fee); no-smoking floor* ▤ *AE, DC, MC, V.*

$$$$ ▦ **Raleigh Hotel.** Hidden behind a thick veil of greenery, this hotel was among the first Art Deco District hotels to be renovated, and it has retained Victorian accents (hallway chandeliers and in-room oil paintings) to soften the 20th-century edges. Standard rooms are spacious, and the suites more so. The fleur-de-lis pool is the focal point year-round, especially on December 31, when synchronized swimmers dive in at the stroke of midnight. Other pluses: the lobby coffee bar, a romantic restaurant (Tiger Oak Room), and the old-fashioned Martini Bar. ⊠ *1775 Collins Ave., South Beach, 33139* ☎ *305/534–6300 or 800/848–1775* ⌂ *305/538–8140* ⊕ *www.raleighhotel.com* ➳ *111 rooms, 18 suites* ♢ *Restaurant, in-room data ports, in-room safes, refrigerators, in-room VCRs, pool, gym, massage, beach, bar, laundry service, concierge, business services, meeting room, parking (fee)* ▤ *AE, D, DC, MC, V.*

★ **$$$$** ▦ **The Tides.** Miami hotels like white, and this one is no exception. However, hotelier and music magnate Chris Blackwell has put a creative twist on what can often be a sterile design motif by introducing hospitality-inspiring elements, from the small (telescopes in each room, since they all have big windows and face the ocean; a blackboard for messages for housekeeping; newspapers on request) to the large (a king-size bed in every room, capacious closets, and generous baths, the result of turning 115 rooms into 45 suites). At the 50-ft-long mezzanine pool, women can go topless. ⊠ *1220 Ocean Dr., South Beach, 33139* ☎ *305/604–5000 or 800/688–7678* ⌂ *305/604–5180* ⊕ *www.islandoutpost.com* ➳ *45 suites* ♢ *2 restaurants, in-room data ports, in-room safes, mini-*

bars, pool, gym, beach, baby-sitting, dry cleaning, concierge, business services, meeting room, travel services = AE, D, DC, MC, V.

$$$–$$$$ ⊡ **The Albion.** Avant-garde Boston architect Carlos Zapata updated this stylish 1939 nautical-deco building by Igor Polevitzky. The two-story lobby sweeps into a secluded courtyard and is framed by an indoor waterfall. A crowd of hip but friendly types makes up the clientele; they like to gather at the mezzanine-level pool, which has portholes that allow courtyard strollers an underwater view of the swimmers. As with other Rubell properties (the Beach House and the Greenview), guest rooms are minimalist in design, though filled with upscale touches. ✉ *1650 James Ave., South Beach, 33139* ☎ *305/913–1000 or 888/665–0008* 🖷 *305/674–0507* ⊕ *www.rubellhotels.com* ↪ *85 rooms, 9 suites* ♻ *2 restaurants, in-room data ports, minibars, pool, gym, bar, laundry service, concierge, meeting room* = AE, D, DC, MC, V.

$$$–$$$$ ⊡ **Essex House.** A favorite with Europeans, Essex House moved into the upscale category over the past few years with a major renovation and amenities like the Il Paradiso day spa. Reverse the damage of a day at the beach with a combination of massages, facials, and peeling treatments. The large suites are well worth the price: each has a wet bar, king-size bed, pullout sofa, 100-square-ft bathroom, refrigerator, and hot tub. Rooms are no slouches, either: club chairs, custom carpet and lighting, mahogany entertainment units and matching desks, and marble tubs. ✉ *1001 Collins Ave., South Beach, 33139* ☎ *305/534–2700 or 800/ 553–7739* 🖷 *305/532–3827* ⊕ *www.essexhotel.com* ↪ *59 rooms, 20 suites* ♻ *In-room data ports, in-room safes, some in-room hot tubs, some minibars, some refrigerators, in-room VCRs, pool, spa, bar, dry cleaning, laundry service, parking (fee)* = AE, D, MC, V.

★ $$$–$$$$ ⊡ **Hotel Astor.** The Astor stands apart from the crowd by double-insulating walls against noise and offering such quiet luxuries as thick towels, down pillows, paddle fans, and a seductive pool. Rooms are built to recall deco ocean-liner staterooms, with faux-portholes, custom-milled French furniture, Roman shades, and sleek sound and video systems. A tasteful, muted color scheme and the most comfortable king beds imaginable make for eminently restful nights, and excellent service eliminates any worries about practical matters. The Astor Place restaurant has exceptional fare and service. ✉ *956 Washington Ave., South Beach, 33139* ☎ *305/531–8081 or 800/270–4981* 🖷 *305/531–3193* ⊕ *www. hotelastor.com* ↪ *40 rooms* ♻ *Restaurant, room service, in-room data ports, in-room safes, minibars, massage, bar, laundry service, concierge, business services, parking (fee)* = AE, DC, MC, V.

★ $$$–$$$$ ⊡ **Hotel Impala.** It's all very European here at the Impala, from the mineral water and orchids to the Mediterranean-style armoires, Italian fixtures, and Eastlake sleigh beds. Everything from wastebaskets to towels to toilet paper is of extraordinary quality. The building, a stunning tropical Mediterranean Revival, is a block from the beach. Iron, mahogany, and stone on the inside are in sync with the sporty white-trim ocher exterior and quiet courtyard. Rooms come with a TV/VCR/stereo and a stock of CDs and videos. The hotel does not admit children under 16. ✉ *1228 Collins Ave., South Beach, 33139* ☎ *305/673–2021 or 800/ 646–7252* 🖷 *305/673–5984* ⊕ *www.hotelimpalamiamibeach.com* ↪ *14 rooms, 3 suites* ♻ *Restaurant, in-room data ports, in-room VCRs, bar, laundry service, concierge* = AE, D, DC, MC, V ⦿ CP.

$$$–$$$$ ⊡ **Hotel Ocean.** If the street signs didn't read Ocean Drive, you might suspect you were whiling away the day on the Riviera at this property formerly known as the Ocean Front Hotel. The tropical French feel is evident when you enter the shaded, bougainvillea-draped courtyard and see diners enjoying a complimentary breakfast in the hotel's brasserie. The two buildings connected by this courtyard contain a few surprises:

soft beds; authentic 1930s art deco pieces; large foldout couches; clean, spacious baths; and soundproof windows, which ensure that rooms are comfortable and quiet. ☒ *1230–38 Ocean Dr., South Beach, 33139* ☎*305/672–2579 or 800/783–1725* ☐*305/672–7665* ⊕*www.hotelocean. com* ♺ *4 rooms, 23 suites* ☖ *Restaurant, in-room data ports, in-room safes, minibars, in-room VCRs, bar, concierge* ⊟ *AE, D, DC, MC, V.*

★ **$$$–$$$$** ☒ **Loews Miami Beach Hotel.** Unlike other neighborhood properties, this 18-story, 800-room gem was built from the blueprints up. Not only did Loews manage to snag 99 ft of beach, it also took over the vacant St. Moritz next door and restored it to its original 1939 art deco splendor, adding another 100 rooms to the complex. The resort has kids' programs, a health spa, 85,000 square ft of meeting space, and an enormous ocean-view grand ballroom. Dining, too, is a pleasure, courtesy of the Argentine-inspired Gaucho Room, Preston's South Beach Coffee Bar, and Hemisphere Lounge. ☒ *1601 Collins Ave., South Beach, 33139* ☎ *305/604–1601* ☐ *305/531–8677* ⊕ *www.loewshotels.com* ♺ *740 rooms, 50 suites* ☖ *4 restaurants, pool, spa, beach, 2 bars, lobby lounge, children's programs (ages 4–12), meeting room* ⊟ *AE, D, DC, MC, V.*

$$$–$$$$ ☒ **Miami Beach Marriott at South Beach.** Continuing the trend started by Loews, Marriott's move into South Beach was late and big, with nouveau art deco flourishes meant to conceal a pragmatic beach resort. The rooms are larger than most on the beach, with a liberal helping of very un-Marriott-like tropical color that proves the mega-brand really is trying to fit in. A mini spa, quiet beach, and reliable service make this a safe bet for business types or families who want to experience South Beach while keeping the wildest partying at a distance. ☒ *161 Ocean Dr., South Beach, 33139* ☎ *305/536–7700 or 800/228–9290* ☐ *305/536–9900* ⊕ *www.miamibeachmarriott.com* ♺ *236 rooms, 7 suites* ☖ *Restaurant, in-room data ports, in-room safes, pool, spa, beach, 2 bars, laundry service, concierge, business services, meeting rooms, parking (fee)* ⊟ *AE, D, DC, MC, V.*

$$$–$$$$ ☒ **Nassau Suite Hotel.** For a boutique hotel one block from the beach, this airy retreat almost qualifies as a steal (by South Beach standards). The original 1937 floor plan of 50 rooms gave way to 22 spacious and smart-looking suites with king beds, hardwood floors, white wood blinds, and free local calls. The Nassau is in the heart of the action yet quiet enough to give you the rest you need. Note: this three-floor hotel has an old elevator and no bellhop. There's also very limited parking. ☒ *1414 Collins Ave., South Beach, 33139* ☎ *305/534–2354 or 866/ 859–4177* ☐ *305/534–3133* ⊕ *www.nassausuite.com* ♺ *22 suites* ☖ *In-room data ports, kitchens, concierge* ⊟ *AE, D, DC, MC, V.*

★ **$$$–$$$$** ☒ **WinterHaven.** "Bright" and "airy" are not words usually associated with South Beach hotels, but this artfully restored classic is both—in spades. WinterHaven is a riot of color, from the garnet-and-aquamarine lobby to the ginger-and-cream upholstery in guest rooms. The two-story lobby and split-level mezzanine regularly play host to parties and fashion shoots, but if you take your complimentary breakfast up to the rooftop sundeck, you'll have a bird's-eye view of South Beach at dawn. ☒ *1400 Ocean Dr., South Beach, 33139* ☎ *305/531–5571 or 800/ 395–2322* ☐ *305/538–6387* ⊕ *www.winterhavenhotelsobe.com* ♺ *71 rooms* ☖ *In-room data ports, in-room safes, bar, concierge, parking (fee)* ⊟ *AE, D, DC, MC, V* ⦿ *CP.*

$$$ ☒ **Kent.** There are toys in the Day-Glo–colored lobby, beanbag chairs in the rooms, and chrome ceiling fans throughout at this wackiest of the South Beach Island Outpost offerings (the Tides and the Marlin are the others). Sure, the rooms are on the small side, and there isn't much of a view, but the vibe, the pumped-up staff, and those great prices make the Kent hard to beat if you're in the mood for a good time. ☒ *1131*

Collins Ave., South Beach, 33139 ☎ 305/604–5000 or 800/688–7678 ⓐ 305/531–0720 ⊕ www.islandoutpost.com ➴ 52 rooms, 2 suites ⚲ In-room safes, minibars, in-room VCRs, business services, meeting room, travel services ⊟ AE, D, DC, MC, V.

$$-$$$ ▦ **Cadet Hotel.** Clark Gable stayed in Room 225 when he came to Miami for Army Air Corps training in the 1940s. Although this Lincoln Road district lodging doesn't have the glamour to attract stars today, it's still a clean, friendly, and perfectly placed little hotel. Just a few minutes' walk from the convention center and two blocks from the ocean, it's about half the cost of an Ocean Drive hotel. Bright without glitz, rooms have ordinary furniture, which is mixed but not necessarily matched—nor is it crummy. A complimentary breakfast is served in the lobby or on the terrace. ⊠ 1701 James Ave., South Beach, 33139 ☎305/672–6688 or 800/432–2338 ⓐ305/532–1676 ⊕www.cadethotel. com ➴ 44 rooms ⚲ Refrigerators ⊟ AE, D, DC, MC, V ⦿ CP.

$-$$$ ▦ **Best Western South Beach.** Utilitarian comfort is the theme at this recently renovated spot, now under chain ownership. The glass-block facade of the lobby invites you to a no-nonsense lodging experience, extending to clean but smallish rooms with twin or king-size beds. A strong selling point here is the surprising amount of privacy, on what's a very active street; a quiet pool (and bar) hidden behind a low wall allows you to tan without being the subject of voyeurs. You're only a short walk from the clubs and shops of South Beach—and you get a free breakfast, to boot. ⊠ 1020–1050 Washington Ave., South Beach, 33139 ☎ 305/ 532–1930 or 888/424–1930 ⓐ 305/972–4666 ⊕ www.bestwestern. com ➴ 132 rooms ⚲ Refrigerators, pool, bar ⊟ AE, MC, V ⦿ CP.

★ $-$$$ ▦ **Royal Hotel.** Austin Powers meets 2001: A Space Odyssey in this avant-garde hotel, which doesn't take itself too seriously. Each room really only has two pieces of furniture: a "digital chaise lounge" and a bed, both molded white plastic contortions from designer Jordan Mozer. The bed's projecting wings hold a phone and alarm clock. The headboard arcs back like a car spoiler and doubles as a minibar. The chaise lounge holds a TV/Web TV and keyboard for surfing the Net. A wild shag carpet and rainbow-paisley bathrobes remind you you're here to have fun—Yeah, baby. ⊠ 758 Washington Ave., South Beach, 33139 ☎ 305/673–9009 or 888/394–6835 ⓐ 305/673–9244 ⊕ www.royalhotelsouthbeach.com ➴ 38 rooms, 4 suites ⚲ In-room data ports, laundry service, business services, meeting room ⊟ AE, D, DC, MC, V.

$-$$ ▦ **Days Inn Convention Center.** Nothing flashy and nothing trashy, this link in a well-known chain is a fairly decent one. The lobby is bright and floral, with a fountain and gift shop. Rooms include in-room safes and cable TV; deluxe rooms throw in impressive views of the ocean. If you're more concerned about your wallet than your image, this is a good bet. Keep in mind that if you want something with character, you can find that elsewhere at these rates. Here you'll find the basic franchise dependables literally seconds from the beach and the Miami Beach Cultural Center. ⊠ 100 21st St., South Beach, 33139 ☎ 305/538–6631 or 800/451–3345 ⓐ 305/674–0954 ⊕ www.daysinnsouthbeach.com ➴ 172 rooms ⚲ Restaurant, in-room safes, refrigerators, pool, beach, bar, laundry service, parking (fee) ⊟ AE, D, DC, MC, V.

¢-$$$ ▦ **The Creek.** This may seem like a university dormitory—indeed, some rooms have dorm-style bunk beds for about $17 a night—but all have baths—and the cleanliness, friendliness, and abundance of activities make this spot worth checking into, especially for hard-core student travelers. The Bungalow's social center is the large pool area, which has outdoor grills and is surrounded by a patio bar, game room, and café. Some may be put off by the smell of the brackish canal nearby, but for others it's a small price to pay. ⊠2360 Collins Ave., South Beach, 33139 ☎305/

538–1951 or 800/746–7835 🖷 *305/531–3217* 📞 *62 private rooms, 23 dorm-style rooms* ⚐ *Café, pool, billiards, bar, recreation room, video game room, laundry service* 🗐 *MC, V* 🍽 *CP.*

¢–$$ 🖼 **Bayliss Guest House.** At the Bayliss, rooms are abnormally large and surprisingly inexpensive. Not only are the bedrooms large, so are the kitchen, the sitting room, and bath. There are also kitchenless standard rooms available. An easy three blocks west of the ocean, the Bayliss is in a residential neighborhood that's comfortably close to—but far enough away from—the din of the Art Deco District. You can't do much better than this, if you don't mind carrying your own bags. There's very limited parking. ✉ *500–504 14th St., South Beach, 33139* 🕾 *305/ 531–3488* 🖷 *305/531–4440* 📞 *12 rooms, 7 suites* ⚐ *Some kitchens, refrigerators, laundry facilities* 🗐 *AE, D, DC, MC, V.*

West Dade

$$$–$$$$ 🖼 **Doral Golf Resort and Spa.** This 650-acre golf-and-tennis resort has five beautifully renovated, low-slung lodges nestled alongside its golf courses. Rooms, done in understated tropical hues, open onto the green or a garden and have private balconies and terraces. Plantation shutters keep out the strong sun but invite in the Caribbean breezes. An expansive spa, with head-to-foot massages, European facials, and dozens of other indulgences, rejuvenates the adults while the Blue Lagoon, an extravagant water park, and friendly golf instruction, entertains the kids. ✉ *4400 N.W. 87th Ave., West Miami, 33178* 🕾 *305/592–2000 or 800/713–6725* 🖷 *305/591–4682* 🌐 *www.doralresort.com* 📞 *693 rooms, 48 suites* ⚐ *5 restaurants, 5 18-hole golf courses, 11 tennis courts, pro shop, pool, health club, spa, fishing, basketball, volleyball, 3 bars, concierge, business services* 🗐 *AE, D, DC, MC, V.*

NIGHTLIFE & THE ARTS

Greater Miami's English-language daily newspaper, the **Miami Herald,** publishes reliable reviews and comprehensive listings in its "Weekend" section on Friday and in the "IN South Florida" section on Sunday. It also publishes a free tabloid, **Street,** with entertainment listings. Call ahead to confirm details. **El Nuevo Herald** is the paper's Spanish version. If you read Spanish, check **Diario Las Américas,** the area's largest independent Spanish-language paper, for information on the Spanish theater and a smattering of general performing-arts news. The best, most complete source is the **New Times,** a free weekly distributed throughout Miami-Dade County each Thursday. A good source of information on the performing arts and nightspots is the calendar in **Miami Today,** a free weekly newspaper available each Thursday in downtown Miami, Coconut Grove, and Coral Gables. Various tabloids reporting on Deco District entertainment and the Miami social scene come and go. **Wire** reports on the gay community. The free **Greater Miami Calendar of Events** is published twice a year by the Miami-Dade **County Cultural Affairs Council** (✉ 111 N.W. 1st St., Suite 625, Downtown, 33128 🕾305/375–4634). The **Greater Miami Convention & Visitors Bureau** (🕾 305/539–3000 or 800/283–2707 🌐 www. tropiculture.com) publishes a comprehensive list of dance venues, theaters, and museums, as well as a seasonal guide to cultural events.

The Arts

Greater Miami's cultural renaissance is a work in progress. The basics are in place: solid cultural institutions such as the Florida Grand Opera, the New World Symphony, the Miami City Ballet, the Concert Association of South Florida, the Fort Lauderdale–based Florida Philharmonic; a plethora of multicultural arts groups and festivals year-round; and burgeoning arts districts in South Beach, Coral Gables, the Design District north of downtown, to name a few. The massive performing-arts center downtown, which spans both sides of Biscayne Boulevard, is sparking a neighborhood revival even before it opens its doors in the fall of 2004. In addition to established music groups, several churches and synagogues run classical-music series with international performers. In theater, Miami offers English-speaking audiences an assortment of professional, collegiate, and amateur productions of musicals, comedy, and drama. Spanish theater also is active.

The not-for-profit **Concert Association of Florida** (⊠ 555 17th St., South Beach, Miami Beach ☎ 305/808–7446), led by Judith Drucker, presents classical arts, music, and dance in venues throughout Miami-Dade and Broward counties. On its roster have been some of the greatest names in the worlds of music and dance—Itzhak Perlman, Isaac Stern, Baryshnikov, Pavarotti, and the Russian National Ballet.

To order tickets for performing-arts events by telephone, call **TicketMaster** (☎ 305/358–5885).

Arts Venues

What was once a 1920s movie theater has become the 465-seat **Colony Theater** (⊠ 1040 Lincoln Rd., South Beach, Miami Beach ☎ 305/674–1040). Undergoing a second renovation, the city-owned performing-arts center, which spotlights dance, drama, music, and experimental cinema, is expected to reopen in winter 2004.

If you have the opportunity to attend a concert, ballet, or touring stage production at the **Gusman Center for the Performing Arts** (⊠ 174 E. Flagler St., Downtown, Miami 33131 ☎ 305/374–2444 for administration; 305/372–0925 for box office), do so. Originally a movie palace, this 1,700-plus-seat theater is as far from a mall multiplex as you can get. The stunningly beautiful hall resembles a Moorish courtyard, with twinkling stars and rolling clouds skirting across the ceiling and freshly restored Roman statues guarding the wings.

Not to be confused with the ornate Gusman theater, **Gusman Concert Hall** (⊠ 1314 Miller Dr., Coral Gables ☎ 305/284–2438) is a 600-seat facility on the University of Miami campus. Presenting primarily recitals and concerts by students, it has good acoustics and plenty of room, but parking is a problem when school is in session.

Acoustics and visibility are perfect for all 2,700 seats in the **Jackie Gleason Theater of the Performing Arts** (TOPA; ⊠ 1700 Washington Ave., South Beach, Miami Beach ☎ 305/673–7300). A pleasant walk from the heart of SoBe, TOPA hosts the Broadway Series, with five or six major productions annually; guest artists, such as David Copperfield, Stomp, and Shirley MacLaine; and classical-music concerts.

Midway between Coral Gables and downtown Miami, the **Miami-Dade County Auditorium** (⊠ 2901 W. Flagler St., Little Havana, Miami 33135 ☎ 305/545–3395) satisfies patrons with nearly 2,500 comfortable seats, good sight lines, and acceptable acoustics. Opera, concerts, and touring musicals are usually on the schedule, and past performers have included David Helfgott and Celia Cruz.

Dance

★ The **Miami City Ballet** (⊠ 2200 Liberty Ave., South Beach, Miami Beach ☎ 305/929–7000) has risen rapidly to international prominence since its arrival in 1985. Under the direction of Edward Villella (a principal dancer with the New York City Ballet under George Balanchine),

Florida's first major, fully professional resident ballet company has become a world-class ensemble. The company re-creates the Balanchine repertoire and introduces works of its own during its September–March season. Villella also hosts children's works-in-progress programs. Performances are held at the Jackie Gleason Theater of the Performing Arts; the Broward Center for the Performing Arts; Bailey Concert Hall, also in Broward County; the Raymond F. Kravis Center for the Performing Arts; and the Naples Philharmonic Center for the Arts.

Film

Several theaters and events cater specifically to fans of fine film. In December, Florida International University sponsors the **Jewish Film Festival** (☎ 305/576–4030 Ext. 14), which presents screenings of new work as well as workshops and panel discussions with filmmakers in several Miami Beach locations. Screenings of new films from all over the world—including some made here—are part of the **FIU–Miami Film Festival** (✉ 444 Brickell Ave., Suite 229, Miami ☎ 305/377–3456 ⊕ www. miamifilmfestival.com). Each year more than 45,000 people descend on the eye-popping Gusman Center for the Performing Arts to watch about 25 movies over 10 days in February. Two more venues—South Beach's Colony Theater and Regal Cinema—have been added, and the number of movies is expected to double.

In April the **Miami Gay and Lesbian Film Festival** (☎ 305/534–9924) presents screenings at various Miami Beach venues. In March the **Miami Latin Film Festival** (☎ 305/279–1809 ⊕ www.hispanicfilm.com) actually presents French, Italian, and Portuguese movies along with exhibitions of Spanish and Latin American movies. Each May, South Beach hosts the **Brazilian Film Festival** (☎ 305/899–8998 ⊕ www. brazilianfilmfestival.com), which unveils on a huge outdoor movie screen built on the beach especially for the occasion.

Music

From October to May, **Friends of Chamber Music** (✉ 169 E. Flagler St., Suite 1619, Downtown ☎ 305/372–2975) presents a series of chamber concerts by internationally known guest ensembles, such as the Emerson and Guarneri quartets. Concerts are held at the Gusman Concert Hall at the University of Miami, with tickets averaging about $20.

Although Greater Miami has no resident symphony orchestra, the **New World Symphony** (✉ 555 Lincoln Rd., South Beach, Miami Beach ☎ 305/ 673–3331 or 305/673–3330), known as "America's training orchestra" because its musicians are recent graduates of the best music schools, helps fill the void. Under the direction of conductor Michael Tilson Thomas, the New World has become an artistically dazzling group that tours extensively. In a season that runs October–May, performances take place in its home venue, the Lincoln Theater on Lincoln Road Mall. The symphony's concerts are broadcast live via speaker (and sometimes video) over the Lincoln Road Mall. Guest conductors have included Leonard Bernstein and Georg Solti.

Opera

South Florida's leading company, the **Florida Grand Opera** (✉ 1200 Coral Way, Miami ☎ 305/854–1643), presents five operas each year in the Miami-Dade County Auditorium, featuring the Florida Philharmonic Orchestra (Stewart Robinson, musical director) from Fort Lauderdale. The series brings such luminaries as Placido Domingo and Luciano Pavarotti (Pavarotti made his American debut with the company in 1965 in *Lucia di Lammermoor*). Operas are sung in the original language, with English subtitles projected above the stage.

Theater

Actor's Playhouse at the Miracle Theater (✉ 280 Miracle Mile, Coral Gables ☎ 305/444–9293 ⊕ www.actorsplayhouse.org), a professional Equity company, presents musicals, comedies, and dramas year-round in Coral Gables' very hip, newly renovated 600-seat Miracle Theater. Performances of musical theater for younger audiences take place in the 300-seat Children's Balcony Theatre.

Built in 1926 as a movie theater, the **Coconut Grove Playhouse** (✉ 3500 Main Hwy., Coconut Grove ☎ 305/442–4000 or 305/442–2662) is now a serious regional theater owned by the state of Florida. The Spanish rococo Grove stages tried-and-true Broadway plays and musicals, many with Broadway actors, as well as experimental productions in its main theater and cabaret-style/black box Encore Room.

The critically acclaimed **GableStage** (✉ 1200 Anastasia Ave., Coral Gables ☎ 305/446–1119) presents classic and contemporary theater in an intimate space on the first floor of the Biltmore Hotel. Call to verify location for the 2004–2005 season.

Productions at the University of Miami's **Jerry Herman Ring Theater** (✉ 1380 Miller Dr., Coral Gables ☎ 305/284–3355 ⊕ www.miami.edu/tha/ring) are often as ambitious as those by its professional counterparts (Broadway legend Jerry Herman is the drama school's most successful alumnus).

Lyric Theater. Once one of the major centers of entertainment for the African-American community, the Lyric showcased more than 150 performers, including Aretha Franklin, Count Basie, Sam Cooke, B. B. King, Ella Fitzgerald, and the Ink Spots. This newly restored theater is now the anchor site of the Historic Overtown Folklife Village. ✉ *819 N.W. 2 Ave., Overtown* ☎ *305/358–1146.*

New Theatre. In an intimate 104-seat theater, the company mounts contemporary and classical plays, with an emphasis on new works and imaginative staging. ✉ *4120 Laguna St., Coral Gables* ☎ *305/443–5909* ⊕ *www.new-theatre.org.*

SPANISH THEATER — Spanish theater prospers, although many companies have short lives. About 20 Spanish companies perform light comedy, puppetry, vaudeville, and political satire. To find them, read the Spanish newspapers. When you call, be prepared for a conversation in Spanish—few box office personnel speak English. **Teatro Avante.** This is the city's most successful crossover theater, programming works that cater to the tastes of its middle-aged Cuban-American audiences and providing subtitles on an overhead screen for the benefit of non-Spanish-speakers. Each summer Teatro Avante sponsors the Hispanic Theatre Festival, during which international theater artists converge on Miami, often presenting the most provocative stagings around, all in Spanish, English, and Portuguese and attracting a multicultural audience to various venues in the Greater Miami area. ✉ *235 Alcazar Ave., Coral Gables* ☎ *305/445–8877* ⊕ *www.teatroavante.com.*

The 255-seat **Teatro de Bellas Artes** (✉ 2173 S.W. 8th St., Little Havana ☎ 305/325–0515), on Calle Ocho, presents plays, musicals, and other acts.

Nightlife

Bars & Lounges

COCONUT GROVE — Drinking cold beer and gorilla-size margaritas in the middle of the Grove at CocoWalk is part of the fun at touristy **Fat Tuesday** (✉ 3015

Grand Ave., Coconut Grove ☎ 305/441–2992). The bar offers up drinks called 190 Octane (190-proof alcohol), Swampwater (also 190 proof), and Grapeshot (a meager 151-proof rum and bourbon concoction). At the Streets of Mayfair, the **Iguana Cantina and Babalu Bar** (✉ 3390 Mary St., Coconut Grove ☎ 305/443–3300) serves up salsa, merengue, and Latin music on weekends. The waterfront **Monty's in the Grove** (✉ 2550 S. Bayshore Dr., at Aviation Ave., Coconut Grove ☎ 305/858–1431) has lots of Caribbean flair, thanks to live calypso and island music. It's very kid-friendly on weekends days, when Mom and Dad can kick back and enjoy a beer and the raw bar while the youngsters dance to live music. Evenings bring a DJ and reggae music.

CORAL GABLES What fueled the Gables' nightlife renaissance? Some think it was the **Globe** (✉ 377 Alhambra Circle ☎ 305/445–3555). Crowds of twentysomethings spill out onto the street for live jazz on Saturday. Two Irishmen missed the Emerald Isle, so they opened **John Martin's Restaurant and Irish Pub** (✉ 253 Miracle Mile ☎ 305/445–3777). It serves up fish-and-chips, bangers and mash, and shepherd's pie—plus the requisite pints of Guinness, Harp, Bass, and other ales. In a building that dates from 1926, **Stuart's Bar-Lounge** (✉ 162 Alcazar Ave. ☎ 305/444–1666), inside the charming Hotel Place St. Michel, is favored by locals. The style is created by beveled mirrors, mahogany paneling, French posters, pictures of old Coral Gables, and art nouveau lighting.

MIAMI **Tobacco Road** (✉ 626 S. Miami Ave. ☎ 305/374–1198), opened in 1912, holds Miami's oldest liquor license: Number 0001! Upstairs in space occupied by a speakeasy during Prohibition, blues bands perform nightly, accompanied by single-malt Scotch and bourbon.

MIAMI BEACH At the **Clevelander** (✉ 1020 Ocean Dr. ☎ 305/531–3485), a giant pool-bar area attracts a young crowd of revelers for happy-hour drink specials and live music. The Rose Bar at the **Delano** (✉ 1685 Collins Ave. ☎ 305/672–2000) is dramatic and chic, with long gauzy curtains and huge pillars creating private conversation nooks around the outdoor infinity pool. Inside, the cool, chic lounge area creates a glamorous space for the modelesque crowd. **Lola** (✉ 247 23rd St. ☎ 305/695–8697) attracts savvy locals and celebs who want to keep a low profile. Offering more character than chic, the **Marlin** (✉ 1200 Collins Ave. ☎ 305/673–8770) gleams with the high-tech look of stainless steel. DJs spin different music every night for the 25-to-40 crowd. At the upscale **Mynt Ultra Lounge** (✉ 1921 Collins Ave., South Beach ☎ 786/276–6132), the name is meant to be taken literally—not only are the walls bathed in soft green shades, but an aromatherapy system pumps out different fresh scents, including mint. The glass-topped bar at the **Tides** (✉ 1220 Ocean Dr. ☎ 305/604–5000) is the place to go for martinis and piano jazz. At the long-awaited Shore Club, the **Sky Bar** (✉ 1901 Collins Ave., South Beach ☎ 305/695–3100), is a hip open air garden/poolside spot.

Dance Clubs

MIAMI Want 24-hour partying? **Club Space** (✉ 142 N.E. 11th St., Downtown ☎ 305/375–0001), created from four warehouses downtown, has three dance rooms, an outdoor patio, a New York industrial look, and a 24-hour liquor license. It's open on weekends only, and you'll need to look good to be allowed past the velvet ropes.

KEY BISCAYNE **Madfish House** (✉ 3301 Rickenbacker Causeway, Key Biscayne ☎ 305/365–9391) has reggae 'til the wee hours on Friday and salsa on Saturday. The view of the skyline along the waterfront is spectacular.

MIAMI BEACH South Beach is headquarters for nightclubs that start late and stay open until the early morning. The clientele includes freak-show rejects, sullen male models, and sultry women.

The **Bermuda Bar & Grille** (✉ 3509 N.E. 163rd St. ☎ 305/945–0196) is way north of SoBe but worth the drive if you want to hang with the locals. Rock radio stations do remote broadcasts, and hard liquor and bottled beer are favored over silly drinks with umbrellas. The music is as loud as the space is large—two floors and seven bars—and hours run 4 PM–6 AM. Male bartenders wear knee-length kilts, while female bartenders are in matching minis. The vibe and crowd, though, are stylish, and there's a big tropical-forest scene, booths to hide in, and pool tables to dive into. The joint is closed from Sunday through Tuesday.

One of several high-profile venues to hit South Beach, **Billboardlive** (✉ 1501 Collins Ave., South Beach ☎ 305/538–2251) is four dazzling floors of fun with a performance stage, restaurants, bars, dance floors, private rooms, and a skybox. Expect to find world-class DJs here, too. **crobar** (✉ 1445 Washington Ave. ☎ 305/531–5027), an import from Chicago, is the latest hot spot—the exterior is the historic Cameo Theater, while the interior is a *Blade Runner*–esque blend of high-tech marvels with some performance art thrown in. It's dazzling and lots of fun. **Honey** (✉ 645 Washington Ave. ☎ 305/604–8222) has soft lighting, cozy couches, and chaise longues, and vibey music that goes down as smoothly as their trademark honey-dipped apples. **Level** (✉ 1235 Washington Ave. ☎ 305/532–1525) has an impressive four dance floors, and—as its name suggests—lots of levels to search out fun.

Nikki Beach Club and Barefoot Beach Club (✉ 1 Ocean Dr. ☎ 305/538–1231) has seven bars in a beautiful beachfront location—complete with tepee cabanas—and includes Pearl Restaurant and Champagne Bar, fast becoming a celeb hangout. Popular with casually chic twenty- and thirtysomethings, **Opium Garden** (✉ 136 Collins Ave., at 1st St., South Beach ☎ 305/674–8360) has a lush waterfall, Asian temple motif with lots of candles, dragons and tapestries, and restaurant next door.

Gay Nightlife

Aside from a few bars and lounges on the mainland, Greater Miami's gay action centers on the dance clubs in South Beach. That tiny strip of sand rivals New York and San Francisco as a hub of gay nightlife, if not in the number of clubs then in the intensity of the partying. The neighborhood's large gay population, plus the generally tolerant attitudes of the hip straights who live and visit here, encourages gay-friendliness at most South Beach venues that are not specifically gay, such that you'll have many options from which to choose. In fact many mixed clubs, like crobar, have one or two gay nights. Laundry Bar has a mixed scene, which also hosts a gay night, including one for the ladies. Generally gay life in Miami is overwhelmingly male-oriented, and lesbians, although welcome everywhere, will find themselves in the minority. To find out what's going on, pick up the South Beach club rags *Outlook* and *Hotspots,* widely available as the weekend approaches, or the alternative weekly *Wire* (⊕ www.thewireonline).

MIAMI **Cactus Nightclub.** In the northern reaches of downtown, this is the place to head if you don't want to stay up 'til 4 AM to get some nightlife in. Special events include drag nights, male strippers, and a very popular Noche Latina on Saturday. ✉ 2041 Biscayne Blvd., at 20th St., Downtown, ☎ 305/138 0662.

SOUTH BEACH **crobar.** Steamy club windows on Monday nights are due to the fantastically popular Back Door Bamby night, with go-go girls and boys. Keep in mind the carpeted dance floor—your lug soles will resist movement. ✉ *1445 Washington Ave., at 14th St.* ☎ *305/531–5027.*

Pump. This afterhours club gets going at 3 AM, so party through breakfast. ✉ *841 Washington Ave., at 8th St.* ☎ *305/538–7867.*

Score. This popular Lincoln Road hangout draws a good-looking, largely younger crowd. There's loud dance music and an outdoor patio perfect for people-watching. The Sunday tea dance is packed, with a DJ spinning old disco tunes and progressive music. ✉ *727 Lincoln Rd., at Euclid Ave.* ☎ *305/535–1111.*

Twist. This longtime hot spot and local favorite with two levels, an outdoor patio, and a game room is crowded from 8 PM on, especially on Monday, Thursday (2-for-1), and Friday nights. ✉ *1057 Washington Ave., at 10th St.* ☎ *305/538–9478.*

SOUTH MIAMI **Ozone.** One of the most popular men's dance clubs on the mainland, this South Miami multilevel dance complex attracts Latin and Anglo patrons in their 20s and 30s. Pool tables and other games offer an alternative to elbow bending. ✉ *6620 Red Rd., 1 block off U.S. 1* ☎ *305/667–2888.*

Jazz

MIAMI BEACH **Jazid** (✉ 1342 Washington Ave., at 13th St., South Beach ☎ 305/673–9372), a stylishly redecorated standout on the strip, is sultry and candlelighted; the music is jazz, with blues and R&B. More restaurant than jazz club, **Van Dyke Café** (✉ 846 Lincoln Rd. ☎ 305/534–3600) serves music on the second floor seven nights a week. Its location on the Lincoln Road Mall makes it a great spot to take a break during an evening shopping excursion.

Nightclub

MIAMI BEACH Dine as you watch the show at the Fontainebleau Hilton's **Club Tropigala** (✉ 4441 Collins Ave. ☎ 305/672–7469), which tries to blend modern Vegas with 1950s Havana. The four-tier round room is decorated with orchids, banana leaves, and philodendrons. Some of the performances are stellar, with a Latin flavor—Ricky Martin, Julio Iglesias, and Jose Feliciano have made appearances here. Hotel guests are comped, but others pay a $20 cover. Reservations are suggested.

SPORTS & THE OUTDOORS

In addition to contacting the addresses below directly, get tickets to major events from **TicketMaster** (☎ 305/358–5885).

Auto Racing

Hialeah Speedway holds stock-car races on a ⅓-mi asphalt oval in a 5,000-seat stadium. Don't be fooled: the enthusiasm of the local drivers makes this as exciting as Winston Cup races. Five divisions of cars run weekly. The Marion Edwards, Jr., Memorial Race for late-model cars is held in December. The speedway is on U.S. 27, ¼ mi east of the Palmetto Expressway (Route 826). ✉ *3300 W. Okeechobee Rd., Hialeah* ☎ *305/821–6644* ⊕ *www.hialeahspeedway.net* ✍ *$10, special events $15* ◷ *Sat., gates open at 5:30 PM, races 7–11* ◷ *Closed mid-Dec.–late Jan.*

For Winston Cup events, head south to the **Homestead-Miami Speedway.** The Winston Cup race highlights the annual speedway schedule and is held on the second Sunday in November in conjunction with the Miami 300, part of the NASCAR Busch series. The racing facility, visible for miles in the flat, rural landscape, also holds the Infiniti Grand Prix of Miami (usually in the spring) and Indy car racing. Other major races include the Grand Am Sports Car Event in spring and a NASCAR

Craftsmen Truck Series in fall. From Miami take Florida's Turnpike (Route 821) south to Exit 6, at Southwest 137th Avenue. ⊠ *1 Speedway Blvd., Homestead* ☎ *305/230–7223* ⊕ *www.homesteadmiamispeedway.com* ☉ *Weekdays 9–5* ☑ *Varies according to event.*

Baseball

A new owner is keeping ticket prices low to woo back fans of the **Florida Marlins,** whose 1997 World Series win was tarred with the subsequent sell-off of popular players. It's not hard to buy a last-minute ticket, and special promotions offer all kinds of goodies to the first few thousands through the turnstiles. Home games are played at Pro Player Stadium, which is 16 mi northwest of downtown. ⊠ *2267 N.W. 199th St., Lake Lucerne* ☎ *305/626–7400 or 305/626–7426* ⊕ *www.marlins.mlb.com* ☑ *$4–$55, parking $9.*

Basketball

The **Miami Heat,** coached by four-time NBA champion Pat Riley, play their games at the 19,600-seat waterfront AmericanAirlines Arena, which has restaurants. Home games are held November–April. ⊠ *AmericanAirlines Arena, 601 Biscayne Blvd., Downtown, Miami* ☎ *786/777–4328; 800/462–2849 for ticket hot line* ⊕ *www.nba.com/heat* ☑ *$10–$180.*

Biking

Perfect weather and flat terrain make Miami-Dade County a popular place for cyclists. A free map that points out streets best suited for bicycles, as well as information about bike rack–equipped buses, is available from bike shops and also from the **Miami-Dade County Bicycle Coordinator** (⊠ Metropolitan Planning Organization, 111 N.W. 1st St., Suite 910, Miami 33128 ☎ 305/375–1647), whose purpose is to share with you the glories of bicycling in South Florida. Information on dozens of monthly group rides is available from the **Everglades Bicycle Club** (☎ 305/255–0452). On Key Biscayne, **Mangrove Cycles** (⊠ 260 Crandon Blvd., Key Biscayne ☎ 305/361–5555) rents bikes for $9 for two hours or $12 per day. On Miami Beach, the proximity of the **Miami Beach Bicycle Center** (MBBC; ⊠ 601 5th St., South Beach, Miami Beach ☎ 305/674–0150) to Ocean Drive and the ocean itself makes it worth the $20 per day (or $5 per hour). Tours of the Deco District are held monthly.

Boating

The popular full-service **Crandon Park Marina** (⊠ 4000 Crandon Blvd., Key Biscayne ☎ 305/361–1281) is a one-stop shop for all things oceany. The office is open daily 8–6. Embark on deep-sea-fishing or scuba-diving excursions, dine at a marina restaurant, or rent powerboats through **Club Nautico** (⊠ 5420 Crandon Blvd., Key Biscayne ☎ 305/361–9217 ⊠ 2560 Bayshore Dr., Coconut Grove ☎ 305/858–6258), a national powerboat rental company. Do half- to full-day rentals from $229 to $699 or buy a membership, which costs a bundle at first but cuts the cost of future rentals by 40% to 60%. Whether you're looking to be on the water for a few hours or a few days, **Cruzan Yacht Charters** is a good choice for renting manned or unmanned sailboats and motor yachts. If you plan to captain the boat yourself, expect a three- to four-hour checkout cruise and at least a $425 daily rate (three-day minimum). ⊠ *3375 Pan American Dr., Coconut Grove* ☎ *305/858–2822 or 800/628–0785.*

Named for an island where early settlers had picnics, **Dinner Key Marina** is Greater Miami's largest, with nearly 600 moorings at nine piers. There is space for transients and a boat ramp. ⊠ *3400 Pan American Dr., Coconut Grove* ☎ *305/579–6980* ☉ *Daily 7 AM–11 PM.*

Haulover Marine Center is low on glamour but high on service. It has a bait-and-tackle shop, marine gas station, and boat launch. ✉ *15000 Collins Ave., Sunny Isles, Miami Beach* ☎ *305/945-3934* ⊘ *Bait shop and gas station 24 hrs.*

Although **Matheson Hammock Park** has no charter services, it does have 252 slips and boat ramps. It also has **Castle Harbor** (☎ 305/665-4994), which rents sailboats for those with U.S. Sailing certification and holds classes for those without. When you're ready to rent, take your pick of boats, ranging from 20 ft to 41 ft. ✉ *9610 Old Cutler Rd., Coral Gables* ☎ *305/665-5475* ⊕ *www.castleharbor.com* ⊘ *Weekdays 9–4, weekends 9–5.*

Near the Art Deco District, **Miami Beach Marina** has about every marine facility imaginable—restaurants, charters, boat and vehicle rentals, a complete marine-hardware store, a dive shop, excursion vendors, a large grocery store, a fuel dock, concierge services, and 400 slips accommodating vessels of up to 190 ft. There's also a U.S. Customs clearing station. One charter outfit here is the family-owned **Florida Yacht Charters** (☎ 305/532–8600 or 800/537–0050). After completing the requisite checkout cruise and paperwork, take off for the Keys or the Bahamas on a catamaran, sailboat, or motor yacht. Charts, lessons, and captains are available if needed. ✉ *300 Alton Rd., South Beach, Miami Beach* ☎ *305/673–6000 for marina* ⊘ *Daily 7–6.*

Dog Racing

Flagler Greyhound Track has dog races during its June–November season and a poker room that's open when the track is running. Closed-circuit TV brings harness-racing action here as well. The track is five minutes east of Miami International Airport, off Dolphin Expressway (Route 836) and Douglas Road (N.W. 37th Avenue). ✉ *401 N.W. 38th Ct., Little Havana, Miami* ☎ *305/649–3000* ▣ *Grandstand and clubhouse free; parking free–$3* ⊘ *Daily at 8:05 PM and also on Tues., Thurs., and Sat. at 1:05 PM.*

Fishing

Before there was fashion, there was fishing. Deep-sea fishing is still a major draw in Miami, and anglers drop a line for sailfish, kingfish, dolphin, snapper, wahoo, grouper, and tuna. Small charter boats cost $450–$500 for a half day and provide everything but food and drinks. If you're on a budget, you might be better off paying around $30 for passage on a larger fishing boat—rarely are they filled to capacity. Most charters have a 50/50 plan, which allows you to take (or sell) half your catch while they do the same. Just don't let anyone sell you an individual fishing license; a blanket license for the boat should cover all passengers.

Crandon Park Marina has earned an international reputation for its knowledgeable charter-boat captains and good catches. Heading out to the edge of the Gulf Stream (about 3 to 4 mi), you're sure to wind up with something on your line (sailfish are catch-and-release). ✉ *4000 Crandon Blvd., Key Biscayne* ☎ *305/361–1281* ▣ *6-passenger boats $699 full day, $499 half day (5 hrs).*

Haulover Beach Park. Plenty of ocean-fishing charters depart from Haulover Beach Park, including **Blue Waters Sportfishing Charters,** (☎ 305/944–4531) where a six-passenger boat is $750 for a full day, $450 for a half day., the **Kelley Fleet** (☎ 305/945–3801), which charges $29 per person for 65- or 85-ft party boats, *Therapy IV* (☎ 305/945–1578), where a six-passenger boat is $90 per person, and about 10 others. ✉ *Haulover Beach Park, 10800 Collins Ave., Sunny Isles, Miami Beach* ☎ *305/947–3525* ▣ *$4 per vehicle* ⊘ *Daily sunrise–sunset.*

Among the charter services at **Miami Beach Marina** is the two-boat **Reward Fleet** (☎ 305/372–9470). Rates run $30 per person including bait, rod, reel, and tackle. ✉ *MacArthur Causeway, 300 Alton Rd., South Beach, Miami Beach* ☎ *305/673–6000.*

Football

Consistently ranked as one of the top teams in the NFL, the **Miami Dolphins** (☎ 305/620–2578) have one of the largest average attendance figures in the league. Fans may be secretly hoping to see a repeat of the 1972 perfect season, when the team, led by legendary coach Don Shula, compiled a 17–0 record (a record that has yet to be broken by another team). From September through January, on home-game days, the Metro Miami-Dade Transit Agency runs buses to **Pro Player Stadium**, 16 mi northwest of downtown. ✉ *2267 N.W. 199th St., Downtown, Miami* ☎ *305/626–7426* ⊕ *www.miamidolphins.com* ✎ *Tickets $29–$165, parking $20.*

Also worth checking out is the **University of Miami Hurricanes** (☎ 305/ 284–2263 or 800/462–2637) football team. A powerhouse within the Big East Conference, the team is regularly a top-10 contender, with five national football championships since 1983. During the September–November season, the home-team advantage is measured in decibels, as some 70,000 fans literally rock the stadium when the team is on a roll. They play their home games at downtown's aging but beloved **Orange Bowl Stadium.** ✉ *1145 N.W. 11th St., Downtown* ☎ *305/643–7100* ✎ *Tickets $20–$50, parking $20–$30.*

Golf

Greater Miami has more than 30 private and public courses. Fees at most courses are higher on weekends and in season, but save money by playing weekdays and after 1 PM or 3 PM (call to find out when afternoon or twilight rates go into effect). That said, costs are reasonable. The **"Golfer's Guide for South Florida"** (☎ 800/864–6101 to order) includes information on most courses in Miami and surrounding areas. The cost is $3.

The 18-hole, par-71 championship **Biltmore Golf Course,** known for its scenic layout, has been restored to its original Donald Ross design, circa 1925. Greens fees range from $29 to $55 in season, and the gorgeous hotel makes a great backdrop. Optional cart rental is $21. ✉ *1210 Anastasia Ave., Coral Gables* ☎ *305/460–5364.*

The **California Golf Club** has an 18-hole, par-72 course, with a tight front nine and three of the area's toughest finishing holes. A round of 18 holes will set you back between $30 and $40, cart included. ✉ *20898 San Simeon Way, North Miami Beach* ☎ *305/651–3590.*

Overlooking the bay, the **Crandon Golf Course,** formerly the Links at Key Biscayne, is a top-rated 18-hole, par-72 public course in a beautiful tropical locale. Expect to pay around $131 for a round in winter, $53 in summer, cart included. After 3, the winter rate drops to $36, cart included. The Royal Caribbean Classic and the Senior PGA are held here. ✉ *6700 Crandon Blvd., Key Biscayne* ☎ *305/361–9129.*

Don Shula's Hotel & Golf Club has one of the longest championship courses in Miami (7,055 yards, par 72), a lighted par-3 course, and a golf school, and it hosts more than 100 tournaments a year. Weekdays, play the championship course for $99, $139 on weekends; golf carts are included. The lighted par-3 course is $12 weekdays, $15 weekends, and $15 for an optional cart. ✉ *7601 Miami Lakes Dr., Miami Lakes* ☎ *305/820–8106.*

Among its six courses and many annual tournaments, the **Doral Golf Resort and Spa** is best known for the par-72 Blue Monster course and the annual Ford Championship, with $2 million in prize money. Fees range from $190 to $275, cart included. ⊠ *4400 N.W. 87th Ave., West Miami* ☎ *305/592–2000 or 800/713–6725.*

For a casual family outing or for beginners, the 9-hole, par-3 **Haulover Golf Course** is right on the Intracoastal Waterway at the north end of Miami Beach. The longest hole on this walking course is 120 yards; greens fees are only $6, less weekdays for senior citizens. ⊠ *10800 Collins Ave., Sunny Isles, Miami Beach* ☎ *305/940–6719.*

Normandy Shores Golf Course is good for senior citizens, with some modest slopes and average distances; greens fees are $60 in season, including cart. ⊠ *2401 Biarritz Dr., Miami Beach* ☎ *305/868–6502.*

The **Turnberry Isle Resort & Club** has 36 holes designed by Robert Trent Jones. The South Course's 18th hole is a killer, and greens fees range from $100 to $154, but since it's private, you won't be able to play unless you're a hotel guest. ⊠ *19999 W. Country Club Dr., Aventura, North Miami Beach* ☎ *305/933–6929.*

Horse Racing

The **Calder Race Course,** opened in 1971, is Florida's largest glass-enclosed, air-conditioned sports facility. Its season runs from late April to early January. The high point of the season, the Tropical Park Derby for three-year-olds, comes in the final week. The track is on the Miami-Dade–Broward county line near Interstate 95 and the Hallandale Beach Boulevard exit, ¾ mi from Pro Player Stadium. ⊠ *21001 N.W. 27th Ave., Lake Lucerne* ☎ *305/625–1311* ☒ *Grandstand $2, clubhouse $4, parking $1–$5* ☉ *Gates open at 11, racing 12:25–5.*

Gulfstream Park, north of the Miami-Dade county line, is open from mid-January through late March. The track's premier race is the Florida Derby. ⊠ *21301 Biscayne Blvd. (U.S. 1), between Ives Dairy Rd. and Hallandale Beach Blvd., Hallandale* ☎ *954/454–7000* ☒ *Grandstand $3, clubhouse $5, parking free* ☉ *Wed.–Mon. post time 1* PM.

Jai Alai

Built in 1926, the **Miami Jai Alai Fronton,** a mile east of the airport, is America's oldest fronton. It presents 13 games (14 on Friday and Saturday) daily except Tuesday—some singles, some doubles. This game, invented in the Basque region of northern Spain, is the world's fastest. Jai alai balls, called pelotas, have been clocked at speeds exceeding 170 mph. The game is played in a 176-ft-long court, and players literally climb the walls to catch the ball in a cesta (a woven basket), which has an attached glove. Either place your wager on the team you think will win or on the order in which you think the teams will finish. ⊠ *3500 N.W. 37th Ave., Downtown, Miami* ☎ *305/633–6400* ☒ *General admission $1, reserved seats $2, Courtview Club $5* ☉ *Wed.–Thurs. noon–5; Mon. and Fri.–Sat. noon–5 and 7–midnight; Sun. 1–6.*

Jogging

There are numerous places to run in Miami, but these recommended jogging routes are considered among the most scenic and the safest: in Coconut Grove, along the pedestrian-bicycle path on South Bayshore Drive, cutting over the causeway to Key Biscayne for a longer run; from the south shore of the Miami River, downtown, south along the sidewalks of Brickell Avenue to Bayshore Drive, where you can run alongside the bay; in Miami Beach, along Bay Road (parallel to Alton Road) or on the sidewalk skirting the Atlantic Ocean, opposite the cafés of Ocean Drive; and in Coral Gables, around the Riviera Country Club golf course, south of the Biltmore Country Club. **Foot Works** (⊠ 5724 Sunset Dr., South Miami ☎ 305/667–9322), a running-shoe store that sponsors races and organizes marathon training, is a great source of information. The **Miami Runners Club** (⊠ 8720 N. Kendall Dr., Suite 206, Miami ☎ 305/227–1500) has information on routes and races.

Scuba Diving & Snorkeling

Diving and snorkeling on the offshore coral wrecks and reefs can be comparable to the Caribbean, especially on a calm day. Chances are excellent you'll come face to face with a flood of tropical fish. One option is to find Fowey, Triumph, Long, and Emerald reefs in 10- to 15-ft dives that are perfect for snorkelers and beginning divers. On the edge of the continental shelf a little more than 3 mi out, these reefs are just ¼ mi away from depths greater than 100 ft. Another option is to paddle around the tangled prop roots of the mangrove trees that line the coast, peering at the fish, crabs, and other creatures hiding there. Perhaps the most unusual diving options in Greater Miami are the artificial reefs. Since 1981 **Miami-Dade County's Department of Environmental Resources Management (DERM)** (⊠ 1920 Meridian Ave., South Beach, Miami Beach ☎ 305/672–1270) has sunk tons of limestone boulders and a water tower, army tanks, a 727 jet, and almost 200 boats of all descriptions to create a "wreckreational" habitat where you can swim with yellow tang, barracudas, nurse sharks, snapper, eels, and grouper. Most dive shops sell a book listing the location of these wrecks.

H20 Scuba (⊠ 160 Sunny Isles Blvd., Sunny Isles, Miami Beach ☎ 305/956–3483 or 888/389–DIVE), is the place many local divers recommend for buying or renting your scuba or snorkel equipment. It's an all-purpose dive shop with PADI affiliation and runs night and wreck dives from its Coast Guard–certified charter boat docked right behind the store. **Divers Paradise of Key Biscayne** (⊠ 4000 Crandon Blvd., Key Biscayne ☎ 305/361–3483), next to the full-service Crandon Park Marina, has a complete dive shop and diving-charter service. On offer are equipment rental and scuba instruction with PADI affiliation. The PADI-affiliated **Diving Locker** (⊠ 223 Sunny Isles Blvd., Sunny Isles, North Miami Beach ☎ 305/947–6025) sells, services, and repairs scuba equipment, plus it has three-day and three-week international certification courses as well as more advanced certifications. The three-day accelerated course for beginners is $350. Wreck and reef sites are reached aboard fast and comfortable six-passenger dive boats.

Tennis

Greater Miami has more than a dozen tennis centers open to the public, and county-wide nearly 500 public courts are open to visitors. Nonresidents are charged an hourly fee. If you're on a tight schedule, try calling in advance, as some courts take reservations on weekdays. **Biltmore Tennis Center** has 10 hard courts and a view of the beautiful Biltmore Hotel. ⊠ *1150 Anastasia Ave., Coral Gables* ☎ *305/460–5360* 🎫 *Day rate $4.75 per person per hr, night rate $6.25* ⊘ *Weekdays 7* AM–*10* PM, *weekends 7* AM–*8* PM.

Very popular with locals, **Flamingo Tennis Center** has 19 clay courts smack dab in the middle of Miami Beach. You can't get much closer to the action. ⊠ *1000 12th St., South Beach, Miami Beach* ☎ *305/673–7761* 🎫 *Day rate $2.66 per person per hr, night rate $3.20* ⊘ *Weekdays 8* AM–*9* PM, *weekends 8–8.*

The 30-acre **Tennis Center at Crandon Park** is one of America's best. Included are 2 grass, 8 clay, and 17 hard courts. Reservations are required for night play. The clay and grass courts are closed at night. The courts are open to the public except during the **Nasdaq 100 Open** (formerly the Ericsson Open; ☎ 305/442–3367), held for 11 days each spring. Top players such as Pete Sampras, Andre Agassi, Gustavo Kuerten, Venus and Sabrina Williams, and Jennifer Capriati compete in a 14,000-seat stadium for more than $6 million in prize money. ✉ *7300 Crandon Blvd., Key Biscayne* ☎ *305/365–2300* ✑ *Laykold courts day rate $3 per person per hr, night rate $5; clay and grass courts $6 per person per hr day rate* ☉ *Daily 8 AM–9 PM.*

Windsurfing

Windsurfing is more popular than ever in Miami. The safest and most popular windsurfing area is at **Hobie Beach,** sometimes called Windsurfer Beach, just off the Rickenbacker Causeway on your way to Key Biscayne. In Miami Beach the best spots are at **1st Street** (north of the Government Cut jetty) and at **21st Street**; also windsurf on the beach at 3rd, 10th, and 14th streets. **Sailboards Miami** (✉ 1 Rickenbacker Causeway, Key Biscayne ☎ 305/361–7245), ⅓ mi past the causeway tollbooth, rents equipment and claims to teach more windsurfers each year than anyone else in the United States. Rentals average $20 for 1 hour, $38 for 2 hours, and $150 for 10 hours. The outfit promises to teach anyone to windsurf within two hours.

SHOPPING

Revised by
Karen
Schlesinger

In Greater Miami you're never more than 15 minutes from a major shopping area that serves as both a shopping and entertainment venue for tourists and locals. Miami-Dade County has more than a dozen major malls and hundreds of miles of commercial streets lined with stores and small shopping centers. Latin neighborhoods contain a wealth of Latin merchants and merchandise, including children's *vestidos de fiesta* (party dresses) and men's guayaberas (a pleated, embroidered tropical shirt), conveying the feel of a South American *mercado* (market).

Malls

Aventura Mall (✉ 19501 Biscayne Blvd., Aventura, North Miami Beach) has more than 250 upscale shops anchored by Macy's, Lord & Taylor, JCPenney, Sears Roebuck, Burdines, and Bloomingdale's, along with a 24-screen theater with stadium seating and a Cheesecake Factory. In a tropical garden, **Bal Harbour Shops** (✉ 9700 Collins Ave., Bal Harbour, Miami Beach) is a swank collection of 100 shops, boutiques, and department stores, such as Chanel, Gucci, Cartier, Gianfranco Ferre, Hermès, Neiman Marcus, and Saks Fifth Avenue. **Bayside Marketplace** (✉ 401 Biscayne Blvd., Downtown), the 16-acre shopping complex on Biscayne Bay, has more than 150 specialty shops, live entertainment, tourboat docks, and a food court. It's open late (until 10 during the week, 11 on Friday and Saturday), but its restaurants stay open even later. Browse, buy, or simply relax by the bay with a tropical drink.

The heartbeat of Coconut Grove, **CocoWalk** (✉ 3015 Grand Ave., Coconut Grove) has three floors of nearly 40 specialty shops (Victoria's Secret, Gap, among others) that stay open almost as late as the popular restaurants and clubs. Kiosks with cigars, beads, incense, herbs, and other small items are scattered around the ground level, while the restaurants and nightlife (e.g., Hooters, Fat Tuesday, an AMC theater) are upstairs. If you're ready for an evening of people-watching, this is the place.

The oldest retail mall in the county, **Dadeland Mall** (✉ 7535 N. Kendall Dr., Kendall, Miami Beach) is always upgrading. It sits at the south side of town close to the Dadeland North and Dadeland South Metrorail stations. Retailers include Saks Fifth Avenue, JCPenney, Lord & Taylor, more than 185 specialty stores, 12 restaurants, and the largest Burdines and The Limited/Express in Florida. The $250 million **Dolphin Mall** (✉ 11401 N.W. 12th St., at State Rd. 836 and Florida's Turnpike, West Dade Miami), 5 mi west of the airport, has a Marshall's Megastore, Oshman's Super Sports USA, and Off 5th Saks Fifth Avenue Outlet, plus a 28-screen cinemaplex and 850-seat food court. The **Falls** (✉ 8888 S.W. 136th St., at U.S. 1, South Miami), which derives its name from the waterfalls and lagoons inside, is the most upscale mall on the south side of the city. It has a Macy's and Bloomingdale's as well as another 100 specialty stores, restaurants, and a 12-theater multiplex.

As its name suggests, **Loehmann's Fashion Island** (✉ 18701 Biscayne Blvd., Aventura, North Miami Beach) is dominated by Loehmann's, the nationwide retailer of off-price designer fashions for women and men. Fashion-conscious shoppers can also visit other specialty boutiques and browse in a Barnes & Noble bookstore.

With a huge banyan tree to welcome visitors, **Shops at Sunset Place** (✉ 5701 Sunset Dr., at U.S. 1 and Red Rd., South Miami) is even larger than CocoWalk. The three-story, family-oriented center has upped the ante for shopping-entertainment complexes with a 24-screen cinemaplex, IMAX theater, Virgin Megastore, NikeTown, A/X Armani Exchange, Dan Marino's Town Tavern, and GameWorks. **Streets of Mayfair** (✉ 2911 Grand Ave., Coconut Grove) is an open-air promenade of shops that bustles both day and night. Thanks to its Coconut Grove locale, along with the News Café, the Limited, Borders Books Music Cafe, and a few dozen other shops and restaurants, this is a safe bet. Entertainment is provided by an improv comedy club and nightclubs.

At the Mediterranean-style shopping and dining venue **Village of Merrick Park** (✉ 358 San Lorenzo Ave., Coral Gables), anchors Neiman Marcus and Nordstrom and 115 specialty shops (Burberry, Jimmy Choo, and Boucheron) fulfill most high-fashion and haute-decor shopping fantasies, while 10 international food venues and a day spa round out the indulgent options.

Outdoor Markets

Coconut Grove Farmers Market (✉ Grand Ave., 1 block west of MacDonald Ave. [S.W. 32nd Ave.], Coconut Grove), open Saturday 8–2, originated in 1977 and still specializes in organically grown local produce. The **Española Way Market** (✉ Española Way, Miami Beach) happens Sunday noon–9 along a two-block stretch of quaint storefronts and cafés. Scattered among the handcrafted items and flea-market merchandise, musicians beat out Latin rhythms on bongos, conga drums, steel drums, and guitars. Food vendors sell inexpensive Latin snacks and drinks. Each Saturday morning from 8 to 1, mid-January to late March, some 25 produce and plant vendors sell herbs, fruits, fresh-squeezed juices, chutneys, cakes, and muffins at the **Farmers Market at Merrick Park** (✉ LeJeune Rd. [S.W. 42nd Ave.] and Biltmore Way, Coral Gables). Gardening workshops, children's activities, and cooking demonstrations are offered by Coral Gables' master chefs. More than 500 vendors sell a range of goods at the **Flagler Dog Track** (✉ 401 N.W. 38th Ct., Miami), every weekend 9–4. The **Lincoln Road Farmers Market** (✉ Lincoln Rd. between Meridian and Euclid Aves., Miami Beach), open Sunday 9–6, brings about 20 local produce and bakery vendors. The market is good for people-watching and picking up local plants, especially orchids. From 8 to 5 on the second and fourth Sundays of each month, locals set up the **Outdoor Antique and Collectibles Market** (⊠ Lincoln and Alton Rds., Miami Beach). The eclectic goods should satisfy postimpressionists, deco-holics, Edwardians, Bauhausers, and Gothic, atomic, and '50s junkies.

Shopping Districts

The shopping is great on a two-block stretch of **Collins Avenue** (⊠ between 6th and 8th Aves., Miami Beach). Club Monaco, Polo Sport, Intermix, Nike, Kenneth Cole, Sephora, Armani Exchange, and Banana Republic are among the high-profile tenants, and a parking garage is just a block away on 7th. The busy **Lincoln Road Mall** is just a few blocks from the beach and convention center, making it popular with locals and tourists. There's an energy to shopping here, especially on weekends when the pedestrian mall is filled with locals. You'll find a Victoria's Secret, Pottery Barn, Gap, and a Williams-Sonoma as well as many smaller emporiums. Creative merchandise, galleries, and a Sunday-morning antiques market can be found among the art galleries and cool cafés. An 18-screen movie theater anchors the west end of the street.

The **Miami Design District** (⊠ between N.E. 36th and N.E. 41st Sts. and between N.E. 2nd Ave. and N. Miami Ave., Design District) has some 225 designer showrooms and galleries specializing in interior furnishings, decorative arts, antiques, and a rich mix of exclusive and unusual merchandise. The surrounding area is still rough around the edges, but the Design District is an important and visitor-friendly place to view high-quality and cutting-edge interior design. **Miracle Mile** (⊠ Coral Way between 37th and 42nd Aves., Coral Gables) consists of some 160 shops, galleries, and restaurants along a wide, tree-lined boulevard. Shops range from posh bridal boutiques to bargain basements, from beauty salons to chain restaurants. As you go west, the quality improves.

Specialty Stores

ANTIQUES **Alhambra Antiques Center** (⊠ 2850 Salzedo, Coral Gables ☎ 305/446–1688) is a collection of four antiques dealers that sell high-quality decorative pieces from Europe. **Architectural Antiques** (⊠ 2500 S.W. 28th La., Coconut Grove ☎ 305/285–1330) carries large and eclectic items—railroad crossing signs, statues, English roadsters—in a store so cluttered that shopping here becomes an adventure promising hidden treasures for the determined. **Senzatempo** (⊠ 1655 Meridian Ave., Miami Beach ☎ 305/534–5588) has a unique collection of vintage home accessories by European and American designers of the 1930s through the 1970s, including electric fans, klieg lights, and chrome furniture. **Valerio Antiques** (⊠ 250 Valencia Ave., Coral Gables ☎ 305/448–6779) is a fine collection of French art deco furniture, bronze sculptures, and original art glass by Gallé and Loetz, among others.

BOOKS Like others in the superstore chain, **Barnes & Noble** (⊠ 152 Miracle Mile, Coral Gables ☎ 305/446–4152) manages to preserve the essence of a neighborhood bookstore by encouraging customers to pick a book off the shelf and lounge on a couch without being hassled. A well-stocked magazine and national/international news rack and an espresso bar–café complete the effect. Greater Miami's best English-language bookstore, **Books & Books, Inc.** (⊠ 265 Aragon Ave., Coral Gables ☎ 305/442–4408 ⊠ 933 Lincoln Rd., Miami Beach ☎ 305/532–3222) specializes in books on the arts, architecture, Florida, and contemporary and classical literature. At the newer Coral Gables location, lounge at the café, browse through the photography gallery, or sit in the courtyard and flip through magazines. Both locations host poetry readings, book signings and author readings. **Kafka's** (⊠ 1464 Washington Ave., Miami Beach ☎ 305/673–9669), a bookstore and café, sells previously owned books and has a good selection of art books and literature. In addition, the shop carries obscure and familiar periodicals and has computers for word processing and Internet access for a fee. **Super Heroes Unlimited** (✉ 1788 N.E. 163rd St., N. Miami Beach ☎ 305/940–9539) beckons comic-book readers looking for monthly refills of *Spawn* and *X-Men* and tempts with an enviable selection of Japanese *animé*.

CHILDREN'S
BOOKS & TOYS

Afro-In Books and Things (✉ 5575 N.W. 7th Ave., Miami ☎ 305/756–6107) presents books by African-American writers for children and teen readers—it also has an impressive section of books for adults. The ultimate toy store, **F.A.O. Schwarz** (✉ 9700 Collins Ave., Bal Harbour Shops, Bal Harbour, Miami Beach ☎ 305/865–2361 ✉ 19501 Biscayne Blvd., Aventura Mall, Aventura, North Miami Beach ☎ 305/692–9200), has a gigantic store in Aventura and a boutique in Bal Harbour. **Peekaboo** (✉ 6807 Main St., Miami Lakes ☎ 305/556–6910) carries educational toys and exceptional European clothing for kids.

CIGARS

Smoking anything even remotely affiliated with a legendary Cuban has boosted the popularity of Miami cigar stores and the small shops where you can buy cigars straight from the press. **Bill's Pipe & Tobacco** (✉ 2309 Ponce de León Blvd., Coral Gables ☎ 305/444–1764) has everything for the pipe and cigar smoker, including a wide selection of pipes and pipe tobacco, cigars, accessories, and gifts. **El Credito Cigars** (✉ 1100 S. W. 8th St., Little Havana ☎ 305/858–4162) seems to have been transported from the Cuban capital lock, stock, and stogie. Rows of workers at wooden benches rip through giant tobacco leaves, cut them with rounded blades, wrap them tightly, and press them in vises. Dedicated smokers find their way here to pick up a $90 bundle or peruse the *gigantes, supremos,* panatelas, and Churchills available in natural or maduro wrappers. **Macabi Cigars** (✉ 3475 S.W. 8th St., Miami ☎ 305/446–2606) carries cigars, cigars, and more cigars, including premium and house brands. Humidors and other accessories make great gifts.

CLOTHING FOR
MEN & WOMEN

Base (✉ 939 Lincoln Rd., Miami Beach ☎ 305/531–4982) has good karma and great eclectic island wear for men and women. For women's fashions by Barbara Bui, Catherine Malandrino, and Mint mixed in with up-and-coming designer clothing and accessories, **Chroma** (✉ 920 Lincoln Rd., Miami Beach ☎ 305/695–8808) is where local fashionistas go. **Koko & Palenki** (✉ 3015 Grand Ave., Coconut Grove ☎ 305/444–1772), in CocoWalk, is where Grovers go for a well-edited selection of shoes and accessories by Casadei, Charles David, Stuart Weitzman, Via Spiga, and others.

Orlo (✉ 1665 Michigan Ave., Miami Beach ☎ 305/531–5338) is known for its gorgeous custom-tailored and ready-to-wear men's clothes. The house specialty is the modern dress shirt, made from your choice of exquisite Egyptian cotton patterns. In the Shore Club Hotel, **Scoop** (✉ 1901 Collins Ave., Miami Beach ☎ 305/695–3297) is a small but spaciously arranged store carrying all the latest fashion requirements by Helmut Lang, Marc Jacobs, Earl, and Seven.

Vintage Soul (✉ 1235 Alton Rd., Miami Beach ☎ 305/538–2644) is a shabby-chic style house filled with rooms of vintage clothing and charming home furnishings.

ESSENTIALS

Wall-to-wall merchandise is found at the **Compass Market** (✉ 860 Ocean Dr., Miami Beach ☎ 305/673–2906), a cute and cozy basement shop that carries all the staples you'll need, especially if you're staying in an efficiency. The market stocks sandals, souvenirs, cigars, deli items, umbrellas, newspapers, and produce. If the heat of Miami gets you hot and bothered, try **Condom USA** (✉ 3066 Grand Ave., Coconut Grove ☎ 305/445–7729). Sexually oriented games and condoms are sold by the gross.

JEWELRY **Beverlee Kagan** (✉ 5831 Sunset Dr., South Miami ☎ 305/663–1937) specializes in vintage and antique jewelry, including art deco–era bangles, bracelets, and cuff links. Easily overlooked in the quick pace of downtown, the 10-story **Seybold Building** (✉ 36 N.E. 1st St., Downtown ☎ 305/374–7922) is filled from bottom to top with more than 250 independent jewelry companies. Diamonds, bracelets, necklaces, and rings are sold in a crowded, lively spot. Word is that competition makes prices flexible; it's closed Sunday.

SOUVENIRS & GIFT ITEMS **Art Deco District Welcome Center** (✉ 1001 Ocean Dr., South Beach, Miami Beach ☎ 305/531–3484) hawks the finest in Miami-inspired kitsch, from flamingo salt-and-pepper shakers to alligator-shape ashtrays, along with books and posters celebrating the Art Deco District. **Gotta Have It! Collectibles** (✉ 4231 S.W. 71st Ave., South Miami ☎ 305/446–5757) will make fans of any kind break out in a cold sweat. Autographed sports jerseys, canceled checks from the estate of Marilyn Monroe, fabulously framed album jackets signed by all four Beatles, and an elaborate autographed montage of all the *Wizard of Oz* stars are among this intriguing shop's museum-quality collectibles. The **Indies Company** (✉ 101 W. Flagler St., Downtown ☎ 305/375–1492), the Historical Museum of Southern Florida's gift shop, offers interesting artifacts reflecting Miami's history, including some inexpensive reproductions. The collection of books on Miami and South Florida is impressive.

SIDE TRIP, SOUTH DADE

Hurricane Andrew forever changed the face of these scattered suburbs southwest of Miami-Dade County's urban core, with many residents moving out and millions of dollars of aid pouring in, evident today in the charmingly rebuilt Deering Estate, Metrozoo, and Fruit and Spice Park. The Redland, the southernmost area also known as America's winter vegetable basket, offers a welcome change from urbane Miami. A complete exploration of all the attractions would probably take two days. Keep an eye open for hand-painted signs announcing orchid farms, fruit stands, you-pick farms, and horseback riding.

🐾 ㊼ **Coral Castle of Florida.** The castle was born when 26-year-old Edward Leedskalnin, a Latvian immigrant, was left at the altar by his 16-year-old fiancée. She went on with her life, while he went off the deep end and began carving a castle out of coral rock. It's hard to believe that Eddie, only 5-ft tall and 100 pounds, could maneuver tons of coral rock single-handedly. Built between 1920 and 1940, the 3-acre castle is one of South Florida's original tourist attractions. There's a 9-ton gate a child could open, an accurate working sundial, and a telescope of coral rock aimed at the North Star. ✉ *28655 S. Dixie Hwy.* ☎ *305/248–6345* ⊕ *www.coralcastle.com* ▦ *$9.75* ☉ *Daily 7 AM–8 PM.*

㊶ **Deering Estate at Cutler.** In 1913 Charles Deering, brother of James Deering, who built Vizcaya in Coconut Grove, bought this property for a winter residence. Nine years later he built the Mediterranean revival stone house that stands here today. Far more austere than its ornate cousin Vizcaya, the stone house, with a magnificent view of Biscayne Bay, has wrought-iron gates, copper doors, and a unique stone ceiling. Next door, the fully restored Richmond Cottage, the first inn to be built between Coconut Grove and Key West (1900), is a fine example of South Florida frame vernacular architecture. Take a naturalist-guided tour to learn more about the area's archaeology: scientists discovered human remains here and carbon-dated them to 10,000 years ago; they may belong to Paleo-Indians. A fossil pit contains the bones of dog-size horses, tapirs, jaguars, peccaries, sloths, and bison. Coastal tropical hardwood hammocks, rare orchids and trees, and wildlife, such as gray foxes, bobcats, limpkins, peregrine falcons, and cormorants, populate the property. A huge environmental education and visitor center, with wide viewing porches, presents programs for children and adults. Nature tours and canoe trips to nearby Chicken Key are available. ⊠ *16701 S.W. 72nd Ave.* ☎ *305/235–1668* ⊕ *www.co.miami-dade.fl.us/parks* ⊠ *$6* ☉ *Daily 10–5.*

🐣 ❹❸ **Gold Coast Railroad Museum.** Historic railroad cars on display here include a 1949 *Silver Crescent* dome car and the *Ferdinand Magellan,* the only Pullman car constructed specifically for U.S. presidents. It was used by Franklin Delano Roosevelt, Harry Truman, Dwight Eisenhower, and Ronald Reagan. On weekends, a $5 train ride is offered at the museum. ⊠ *12450 S.W. 152nd St. (S.W. 152nd St.)* ☎ *305/253–0063* ⊕ *www.goldcoast-railroad.org* ⊠ *$5* ☉ *Weekdays 11–3, weekends 11–4.*

🐣 ❹❹ **Metrozoo.** One of the few zoos in the United States in a subtropical environment, the first-class, 290-acre Metrozoo is state of the art. Inside the cageless zoo, some 800 animals roam on islands surrounded by moats. Take the monorail to see major attractions including the Tiger Temple, where white tigers roam, and the African Plains exhibit, where giraffes, ostriches, and zebras graze in a simulated habitat. There are also koalas, Komodo dragons, and other animals whose names begin with a *K*. The free-flight aviary, demolished in Hurricane Andrew, reopened in 2003 with 300 birds, waterfalls, and lush tropical foliage. The children's petting zoo has a meerkat exhibit, and Dr. Wilde's World is an interactive facility with changing exhibits. Kids can touch Florida animals such as alligators and possum at the Ecology Theater. ⊠ *12400 S.W. 152nd St.* ☎ *305/251–0400* ⊕ *www.miamimetrozoo.com* ⊠ *$8.95, 45-min tram tour $2* ☉ *Daily 9:30–5:30 (last admission at 4).*

🐣 ❹❺ **Monkey Jungle.** Still a kitschy attraction for adults, more than 300 monkeys representing 25 species—including orangutans from Borneo and Sumatra and golden lion tamarins from Brazil—roam free here. Exhibits include Lemurs of Madagascar, Parrots of the Amazon, and the Cameroon Jungle. Perhaps the most fun is feeding monkeys who scurry across the fences overhead, hauling up peanuts you place in a metal cup. ⊠ *14805 216th St.* ☎ *305/235–1611* ⊕ *www.monkeyjungle.com* ⊠ *$15.95* ☉ *Daily 9:30–5 (last admission at 4).*

❹❻ **Redland Fruit & Spice Park.** The 35 acres here have been a Dade County treasure since 1944, when it was opened as a 20-acre showcase of tropical fruits and vegetables. Plants are grouped by country of origin and include more than 500 varieties of exotic fruits, herbs, spices, nuts, and poisonous plants from around the world. A sampling reveals 90 types of bananas, 40 varieties of grapes, and dozens of citrus fruits. The park store offers many varieties of tropical-fruit products, jellies, seeds, aromatic teas, and reference books. ⊠ *24801 S.W. 187th Ave.* ☎ *305/247–5727* ⊠ *$4* ☉ *Daily 10–5; tours daily at 11, 1:15, and 2:30.*

🐣 ❹❷ Aviation enthusiasts touch down at **Wings over Miami** to see planes from World War II and the Korean War and earlier vintage bi-planes in a still-evolving museum filling the space that once housed Weeks Air Museum, which moved to the Sun and Fun complex in Lakeland. The museum is inside Tamiami Airport. ⊠ *14710 S.W. 128th St.* ☎ *305/233–5197* ⊕ *www.wingsovermiami.com* ⊠ *$9.95* ☉ *Thurs.–Sun. 10–5.*

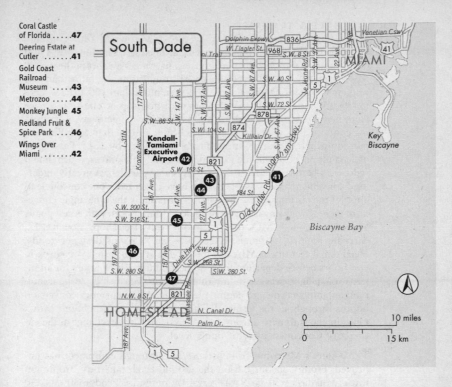

MIAMI & MIAMI BEACH A TO Z

To research prices, get advice from other travelers, and book travel arrangements, visit www.fodors.com.

ADDRESSES

Greater Miami is made up of more than 30 municipalities, and tourist favorites Miami and Miami Beach are only two of the cities that make up what is actually Miami-Dade County. Within Greater Miami, addresses fall into four quadrants: NW, NE, SW, and SE. The north–south dividing line is Flagler Street, and the east–west dividing line is Miami Avenue. Numbering starts from these axes and gets higher the farther away an address is from them. Avenues run north–south and streets east–west. Some municipalities have their own street naming and numbering systems, including Miami Beach, Coral Gables, Coconut Grove, and Key Biscayne, so a map is a good idea. In South Beach, all north–south roads are named, and the main drags are Ocean Drive, Collins, and Washington avenues, and Alton Road. Streets are numbered and run east–west; 1st Street is at the beach's southernmost point, and numbers get higher as you head north.

AIR TRAVEL TO & FROM MIAMI

CARRIERS In addition to the multitude of airlines that fly into Miami International Airport (MIA; *see* Air Travel *in* Smart Travel Tips A to Z), there's also Pan Am Air Bridge—starting over where the original Pan Am began—with seaplane flights. Departing from Watson Island, the 30- to 60-minute rides to Bimini and Paradise Island in the Bahamas are exciting, anachronistic, and somewhat cramped. Still, if you've got an extra $200–$300, a round-trip could be quite fun. Chalk's Ocean Airways offers daily seaplane service from Watson Island in Miami and Fort Lauderdale International Airport to Bimini and Paradise Island.

AIRPORTS & TRANSFERS

Miami International Airport, 6 mi west of downtown Miami, is the only airport in Greater Miami that provides scheduled service. More than 1,400 daily flights make MIA the ninth-busiest passenger airport in the world. Approximately 34 million people pass through annually, more than half of them international travelers. Altogether, more than 100 airlines serve nearly 150 cities and five continents with nonstop or one-stop service from here, making it the nation's top international gateway. Anticipating continued growth, the airport has begun a more than $5 billion expansion program that is expected to be completed by 2015. Passengers will mainly notice rebuilt and expanded gate and public areas, which should reduce congestion. A link to Metrorail is also planned. A greatly underused convenience for passengers who have to get from one concourse to another in this long, horseshoe-shape terminal is the amazingly convenient moving walkway on the skywalk level (third floor), with access points at every concourse. MIA, the first to offer duty-free shops, now has 12, carrying liquors, perfumes, electronics, and various designer goods. Heightened security at MIA has meant that it's suggested you check in two hours before departure for a domestic flight, three hours for an international flight. Services for international travelers include 24-hour multilingual information and paging phones as well as currency conversion booths throughout the terminal. There is an information booth with a multilingual staff across from the 24-hour currency exchange at the entrance of Concourse E on the upper level.

The county's Metrobus still costs $1.25, although equipment has improved. From Concourse E on the ground level, take Bus 7 to downtown (weekdays 5:30 AM–9 PM every 40 minutes, weekends 6:30 AM–7:30 PM every 40 minutes); Bus 37 south to Coral Gables and South Miami (6 AM–10 PM every 30 minutes) or north to Hialeah (5:30 AM–11:30 PM every 30 minutes); Bus J south to Coral Gables (6 AM–12:30 AM every 30 minutes) or east to Miami Beach (4:30 AM–11:30 PM every 30 minutes); and Bus 42 to Coconut Grove (5:30 AM–7:20 PM hourly). Some routes change to 60-minute schedules after 7 PM and on weekends, so be prepared to wait or call the information line for exact times. Miami has more than 100 limousine services, although they're frequently in and out of business. If you rely on the Yellow Pages, look for a company with a street address, not just a phone number. Offering 24-hour service, Club Limousine Service has shuttle vans and minibuses as well as limos. One of the oldest companies in town is Vintage Rolls Royce Limousines of Coral Gables, which operates a 24-hour reservation service and provides chauffeurs for privately owned, collectible Rolls-Royces from the 1940s.

Except for the flat-fare trips described below, cabs cost $3.25 for the first mile, $2 a mile after that, plus a $1 toll for trips originating at MIA or the Port of Miami. Approximate fares from MIA include $11 to Coral Gables or downtown Miami, $31 to Key Biscayne. In addition, Miami's regulatory commission has established flat rates for five zones of the city, four of which are listed here: $24 to between 63rd Street and the foot of Miami Beach (including South Beach); $41 to Golden Beach and Sunny Isles, north of Haulover Beach Park; $34 to between Surfside and Haulover Beach Park; and $29 to between 63rd and 87th streets. These fares are per trip, not per passenger, and include tolls and $1 airport surcharge but not tip. The fare between MIA and the Port of Miami is a flat fare of $18. For taxi service to destinations in the immediate vicinity, ask a uniformed county taxi dispatcher to call an ARTS (Airport Region Taxi Service) cab for you. These special blue cabs offer a short-haul flat fare in two zones. An inner-zone ride is $7; the outer-zone fare is $10. The area of service is north to 36th Street, west to the Palmetto Expressway (77th Avenue), south to Northwest 7th Street, and east to Douglas Road (37th Avenue). Maps are posted in cab windows.

SuperShuttle vans transport passengers between MIA and local hotels, the Port of Miami, and even individual residences on a 24-hour basis. At MIA the vans pick up at the ground level of each concourse (look for clerks with yellow shirts, who will flag one down). The company's service area extends from Palm Beach to Monroe County (including the Lower Keys). Drivers provide narration en route. Service from MIA is available around the clock on demand; for the return it's best to make reservations 24 hours in advance, although the firm will try to arrange pickups within Miami-Dade County on as little as four hours' notice. The cost from MIA to downtown hotels runs $9–$13; to the beaches it can be $13–$17 per passenger, depending on how far north you go. Additional members of a party pay a lower rate for many destinations, and children under three ride free with their parents. There's a pet transport fee of $5 for a cat, $8 for a dog under 50 pounds in kennels.

🛈 Airport Information **Miami International Airport (MIA)** ☎ 305/876-7000 ⊕ www.
miami-airport.com. **Miami International Airport Hotel** ⊠ Concourse E, upper level
☎ 305/871-4100.

🛈 Taxis & Shuttles **Carey South Florida limousines** ⊠ 12050 N.E. 14th Ave., Miami
33161 ☎ 305/892-5800 or 800/824-4820; 800/325-9834 in Florida. **Metrobus** ☎ 305/
770-3131. **SuperShuttle** ☎ 305/871-2000 from MIA; 954/764-1700 from Broward [Fort
Lauderdale]; 800/874-8885 from elsewhere. **Vintage Rolls Royce Limousines** ⊠ 7242
S.W. 42nd Terr., South Miami 33155 ☎ 305/662-5763 or 800/888-7657.

BIKE TRAVEL

Cruise America offers Hondas and Suzukis with daily rentals starting at $109, weekly at $545. You must be 21 with a credit card, valid driver's license, and motorcycle endorsement. Great weather and flat terrain make Miami perfect for cycling enthusiasts, but as a general method of transportation, it shouldn't be your first choice given traffic and limited bike paths. Consider Miami-Dade Transit's "Bike and Ride" program, which lets permitted cyclists take single-seat two-wheelers on Metrorail and select bus routes. **Miami-Dade Bicycle/Pedestrian Coordinator** has details on permits, bike maps, and lockers and is open weekdays 8–5.

🛈 Bike Rentals **Cruise America** ⊠ 5801 N.W. 151st St., Miami Lakes, Miami ☎ 800/
327-7799 or 305/828-1198. **Miami-Dade Bicycle/Pedestrian Coordinator** ☎ 305/
375-4507.

BOAT & FERRY TRAVEL

If you enter the United States in a private vessel along the Atlantic Coast south of Sebastian Inlet, you must call the U.S. **Customs Service.** Customs clears most boats of less than 5 tons by phone, but you may be directed to a marina for inspection. The Port of Miami, in downtown Miami near Bayside Marketplace and the MacArthur Causeway, justifiably bills itself as the Cruise Capital of the World. With 18 ships and the largest year-round cruise fleet in the world, the port accommodates more than 3 million passengers a year. It has 12 air-conditioned terminals, duty-free shopping, and limousine service. Taxicabs are available at all terminals, and Avis is located at the port, although other rental companies offer shuttle service to off-site locations. Parking is $10 per day, and short-term parking is a flat rate of $4. From here, short cruises depart for the Bahamas and Eastern and Western Caribbean, with longer sailings to the Far East, Europe, and South America.

🛈 Cruise Lines **Port of Miami** ⊠ 1015 North American Way, Miami ☎ 305/371-7678
or 305/347-4860. **U.S. Customs Service** ☎ 800/432-1216 for small-vessel arrival near
Miami; 305/536-5263 for Port of Miami office.

Carnival Cruise Lines ☎ 800/327-9501. Celebrity Cruises ☎ 800/437-3111. Norwegian Cruise Lines ☎ 800/327-7030. Royal Caribbean International ☎ 800/255-4373.

BUS TRAVEL TO & FROM MIAMI & MIAMI BEACH

Regularly scheduled, interstate **Greyhound** buses stop at five terminals in Greater Miami; the airport terminal is 24-hour.

🚌 Bus Information Greyhound ☎ 800/231-2222 ✉ Homestead ✉ 5 N.E. 3rd Rd., ☎ 305/247-2040 ✉ Miami Bayside/Downtown ✉ 100 N.W. 6th St., Overtown ☎ 305/374-6160 ✉ Miami South ✉ 20505 S. Dixie Hwy., Cutler Ridge ☎ 305/296-9072 ✉ Miami West/Airport ✉ 4111 N.W. 27th St. ☎ 305/871-1810 ✉ North Miami ✉ 16560 N.E. 6th Ave. ☎ 305/945-0801.

BUS TRAVEL WITHIN MIAMI & MIAMI BEACH

Metrobus stops are marked by blue-and-green signs with a bus logo and route information. The frequency of service varies widely, so call in advance to obtain specific schedules. The fare is $1.25 (exact change), transfers 25¢; 60¢ with 10¢ transfers for people with disabilities, senior citizens (65 and older), and students. Some express routes carry surcharges of $1.50. Reduced-fare tokens, sold 10 for $10, are available from Metropass outlets. All trains and stations are accessible to persons with disabilities; lift-equipped buses for people with disabilities are available on more than 50 routes, including one from the airport that links up with many routes in Miami Beach as well as Coconut Grove, Coral Gables, Hialeah, and Kendall. Miami Beach has a tourism hot line with information on accessibility, sign language interpreters, rental cars, and area recreational activities for the disabled. The best thing to arrive in Miami Beach since sand, the Electrowave is a fleet of electric trolleys running every few minutes up and down Washington Avenue between 5th and 17th streets. Fare is 25¢. New service continues south of 5th Street, west to Alton Road, and over by the Miami Beach Marina. Considering the great lengths between South Beach attractions, it'll save a lot of shoe leather. Trolleys operate Monday–Wednesday 8 AM–2 AM, Thursday–Saturday 8 AM–4 AM, and Sunday and holidays 10 AM–2 AM.

FARES & SCHEDULES

🚌 Bus Information Electrowave ☎ 305/843-9283. Special Transportation Services ☎ 305/263-5400.

CAR RENTAL

The following agencies have booths near the baggage-claim area on MIA's lower level: Avis, Budget, Dollar, Globetrotters, Hertz, National, and Royal. Avis and Budget also have offices at the Port of Miami. If money is no object, check out Excellence Luxury Car Rental. As the name implies, rent some wheels (a Ferrari, perhaps?) to cruise SoBe and pretend you're Don Johnson. If you can't find the excellent car you want, rent a Dodge Viper, BMW, Hummer, Jag, Porsche, or Rolls from Exotic Toys. Airport pickup is provided.

🚗 Local Agencies Alamo ☎ 800/468-2583. Avis ☎ 800/331-1212. Budget ☎ 800/527-0700. Dollar ☎ 800/800-4000. Excellence Luxury Car Rental ☎ 305/526-0000. Exotic Toys Car Rental ☎ 305/888-8448. Hertz ☎ 800/654-3131. National ☎ 800/227-7368. Royal ☎ 800/314-8616.

CAR TRAVEL

The main highways into Greater Miami from the north are Florida's Turnpike (a toll road) and Interstate 95. From the northwest take Interstate 75 or U.S. 27 into town. From the Everglades, to the west, use the Tamiami Trail (U.S. 41), and from the south use U.S. 1 and the Homestead Extension of Florida's Turnpike. In general, Miami traffic is the same as in any other big city, with the same rush hours and the same likelihood that parking garages will be full at peak times. Many drivers who aren't locals and don't know their way around might turn and stop suddenly, or drop off passengers where they shouldn't. Some drivers are short-tempered and will assault those who cut them off or honk their horn. Motorists need to be careful, even when their driving behavior is beyond censure, however, especially in rental cars. Despite the removal of identifying marks, cars piled with luggage or otherwise showing signs that a tourist is at the wheel remain prime targets for thieves. The city has also initiated a TOP (Tourist Oriented Police) Cops program to assist tourists with directions and safety. For more safety advice on driving in Miami, *see* Car Travel *in* Smart Travel Tips A to Z.

EMERGENCIES

Dial 911 for police or ambulance. Dial free from pay phones. Randle Eastern Ambulance Service Inc. operates at all hours, although in an emergency it'll direct you to call 911. Dade County Medical Association is open weekdays 9–5 for medical referral. East Coast District Dental Society is open weekdays 9–4:30 for dental referral. After hours stay on the line and a recording will direct you to a dentist. Services include general dentistry, endodontics, periodontics, and oral surgery.

7 Doctors & Dentists Dade County Medical Association ⊠ 1501 N.W. North River Dr., Miami ☎ 305/324–8717. **South Florida District Dental Society** ⊠ 420 S. Dixie Hwy., Suite 2E, Coral Gables ☎ 305/667–3647.

7 Hot Lines Randle Eastern Ambulance Service Inc. ⊠ 7255 N.W. 19th St., Suite C, Miami 33126 ☎ 305/718–6400.

7 Late-Night Pharmacies Eckerd Drug ⊠ 9031 S.W. 107th Ave., Kendall ☎ 305/274–6776. **Walgreens** ⊠ 4895 E. Palm Ave., Hialeah ☎ 305/231–7454 ⊠ 2750 W. 68th St., Hialeah ☎ 305/828–0268 ⊠ 12295 Biscayne Blvd., North Miami ☎ 305/893–6860 ⊠ 5731 Bird Rd., Miami ☎ 305/666–0757 ⊠ 1845 Alton Rd., South Beach, Miami Beach ☎ 305/531–8868 ⊠ 791 N.E. 167th St., North Miami Beach ☎ 305/652–7332.

MEDIA

Greater Miami is a media hub, offering access to information from around the world in many languages. For international and foreign language papers, check one of the larger hotels or bookstore chains, or try the popular News Café in Coconut Grove or South Beach. The main Coral Gables branch of Books & Books, Inc. (⊠ 265 Aragon Ave.) is a terrific independent bookstore that's worth a trip for magazines and books.

NEWSPAPERS & MAGAZINES
Greater Miami's major newspaper is the *Miami Herald*. Your best bet for weekend happenings is the free alternative weekly, *New Times*, or *Street*, a free weekly with entertainment news, local art and film reviews, events, and nightlife. For Spanish-language news, turn to *El Nuevo Herald*. Regional editions of the *Wall Street Journal* and the *New York Times* can be found just about everywhere—including vending machines—and many of Europe's and Latin America's major dailies and fashion glossies are available at newsstands.

RADIO
Greater Miami is served by all the major cable networks. Major broadcast television stations include WAMI (Telefutur, Spanish-international), WBFS (UPN), WBZL (WB), WFOR (CBS), WLTV (Univision, Spanish-international), WPBT (PBS), WPLG (ABC), WSCV (Telemundo, Spanish-international), WSVN (Fox), and WTVJ (NBC).

Radio stations in Greater Miami include WDNA/88.9 (jazz), WEDR/99.1 (urban), WHYI/100.7 (Top 40), WIOD/610 AM (news), WKIS/99.9 (country), WLRN 91.3 (National Public Radio), WQAM/560 AM (sports), WZTA/94.9 (hard rock), and WBGG/105.9 (classic rock). Near the airport, find basic tourist information, broadcast successively in English, French, German, Portuguese, and Spanish, on the low-wattage WAEM/102.3.

TAXIS

One cab "company" stands out above the rest. It's actually a consortium of drivers who have banded together to provide good service, in marked contrast to some Miami cabbies, who are rude, unhelpful, unfamiliar with the city, or dishonest, taking advantage of those who don't know the area. To plug into this consortium—they don't have a name, simply a number—call the dispatch service, although they can be hard to understand over the phone. If you have to use another company, try to be familiar with your route and destination. For information call the Metro-Dade Passenger Transportation Regulatory Service, also known as the Hack Bureau. It takes complaints and monitors all for-hire vehicles. Fares are set at $3.25 per first mile and $2 every mile thereafter, with no additional charge for up to five passengers, luggage, and tolls. Taxis can be hailed on the street if you can find them—it's better to call for a dispatch taxi or have a hotel doorman hail one for you. Some companies with dispatch service are Central Taxicab Service, Diamond Cab Company, Metro Taxicab Company, Miami-Dade Yellow Cab, Society Cab Company, Super Yellow Cab Company, Tropical Taxicab Company, and Yellow Cab Company. Many now accept credit cards; inquire when you call.

🚖 Taxi Companies **Dispatch service** ☎ 305/888-4444. **Central Taxicab Service** ☎ 305/532-5555. **Diamond Cab Company** ☎ 305/545-5555. **Metro-Dade Passenger Transportation Regulatory Service** ☎ 305/375-2460. **Metro Taxicab Company** ☎ 305/888-8888. **Miami-Dade Yellow Cab** ☎ 305/633-0503. **Society Cab Company** ☎ 305/757-5523. **Super Yellow Cab Company** ☎ 305/888-7777. **Tropical Taxicab Company** ☎ 305/945-1025. **Yellow Cab Company** ☎ 305/444-4444.

TOURS

Coconut Grove Rickshaw centers its operations at CocoWalk. Two-person rickshaws scurry along Main Highway in Coconut Grove's Village Center, nightly 7 PM–midnight. Take a 10-minute ride through Coconut Grove or a 20-minute lovers' moonlight ride to Biscayne Bay; prices start at $5 per person, and you can pick them up curbside.

BOAT TOURS *Island Queen, Island Lady,* and *Pink Lady* are 150-passenger double-decker tour boats docked at Bayside Marketplace. They go on daily 90-minute narrated tours of the Port of Miami and Millionaires' Row, costing $15. Refreshments are available. For something a little more private and luxe, *RA Charters* sails out of the Dinner Key Marina in Coconut Grove. Full- and half-day charters include snorkeling and even sailing lessons on the 40-ft ketch, with extended trips to the Florida Keys and Bahamas. For a romantic night, have Captain Masoud pack some delicious fare and sail sunset to moonlight while you enjoy Biscayne Bay's spectacular skyline view of Miami. Prices range from $300 to $400 for a half day to $600–$700 for a full day, depending on the number of people aboard and refreshments provided.

🚢 Fees & Schedules *Island Queen, Island Lady,* and *Pink Lady* ✉ 401 Biscayne Blvd., Bayside Marketplace ☎ 305/379-5119. *RA Charters* ☎ 305/854-7341 or 305/666-7979.

PRIVATE GUIDES Professor Paul George, a history professor at Miami-Dade Community College and past president of the Florida Historical Society, leads walking tours as well as boat tours and tours that make use of the Metrorail and Metromover. Choose from tours covering downtown, historic neighborhoods, cemeteries, Coconut Grove, and the Miami River. They start Saturday at 10 and Sunday at 11 at various locations, depending on the tour, and generally last about 2½ hours. Call for each weekend's schedule and for additional tours by appointment. The fee is $17.

🚶 Professor Paul George ✉ 1345 S.W. 14th St., Little Havana ☎ 305/858-6021.

WALKING TOURS The Art Deco District Tour, operated by the Miami Design Preservation League, is a 90-minute guided walking tour that departs from the league's welcome center at the Oceanfront Auditorium. It costs $15 (tax-deductible) and starts at 10:30 AM Saturday and 6:30 PM Thursday. Private group tours can be arranged with advance notice. The league's self-guided $10 audio tour takes roughly an hour and a half and is available in English, Spanish, French, and German.

🔒 Fees & Schedules **Art Deco District Tour** ✉ 1001 Ocean Dr., Bin L, South Beach, Miami Beach 33139 ☎ 305/672-2014.

TRAIN TRAVEL

Amtrak provides service from 500 destinations to the Greater Miami area, including three trains daily from New York City. North–south service stops in the major Florida cities of Jacksonville, Orlando, Tampa, West Palm Beach, and Fort Lauderdale. For extended trips, or if you're visiting other areas in Florida, come via Auto Train from Lorton, Virginia, just outside of Washington, D.C., to Sanford, Florida, just outside of Orlando. Tri-Rail, South Florida's commuter train system, offers daily service connecting Miami-Dade with Broward and Palm Beach counties via Metrorail (transfer at the TriRail/Metrorail Station at the Hialeah station, at 79th Street and East 11th Avenue). It also offers shuttle service to and from MIA from its airport station at 3797 Northwest 21st Street. Tri-Rail stops at 18 stations along a 71-mi route. Fares are established by zones, with prices ranging from $3.50 to $9.25 for a round-trip ticket.

Elevated Metrorail trains run from downtown Miami north to Hialeah and south along U.S. 1 to Dadeland, daily 5:30 AM–midnight. Trains run every six minutes during peak hours, every 15 minutes during weekday mid-hours, every 20 minutes on weekends, every 30 minutes after 8 PM. The fare is $1.25. Transfers, which cost 25¢, must be bought at the first station entered. Parking at train stations costs $2. Metromover has two loops that circle downtown Miami, linking major hotels, office buildings, and shopping areas. The system spans 4½ mi, including the 1½-mi Omni Extension, with six stations to the north, and the 1-mi Brickell Extension, with six stations to the south. Quite convenient, and free, thanks to a recently approved half-penny sales tax, it beats walking all around downtown. Service runs daily, every 90 seconds during rush hour and every three minutes off-peak, 6 AM–midnight along the inner loop and 6 AM–10:30 PM on the Omni and Brickell extensions. Transfers to Metrorail are $1.25

🔒 Train Information **Amtrak** ✉ 8303 N.W. 37th Ave., Hialeah ☎ 800/872-7245. **Metromover** ☎ 305/770-3131. **Metrorail** ☎ 305/770-3131. **Tri-Rail** ✉ 1 River Plaza, 305 S. Andrews Ave., Suite 200, Fort Lauderdale ☎ 800/874-7245.

TRANSPORTATION AROUND MIAMI & MIAMI BEACH

Greater Miami resembles Los Angeles in its urban sprawl and traffic. You'll need a car to visit many attractions and points of interest. Some are accessible via the public transportation system, run by a department of the county government—the Metro-Dade Transit Agency, which consists of 650 Metrobuses on 70 routes, the 21-mi Metrorail elevated rapid-transit system, and the Metromover, an elevated light-rail system. Free maps and schedules are available.

🔒 **Miami-Dade Transit** ✉ Government Center Station, 111 N.W. 1st St., Downtown, 33128 ☎ 305/654-6586 for Maps by Mail; 305/770-3131 for route information weekdays 6 AM–10 PM and weekends 9–5.

VISITOR INFORMATION

Florida Gold Coast Chamber of Commerce serves the beach communities of Bal Harbour, Bay Harbor Islands, Golden Beach, North Bay Village, Sunny Isles Beach, and Surfside.

🖪 Tourist Information **Greater Miami Convention & Visitors Bureau** ✉ 701 Brickell Ave., Suite 2700, Downtown, 33131 ☎ 305/539-3063 or 800/283-2707 ⊕ www. miamiandbeaches.com ✉ Bayside Marketplace tourist information center ✉ 401 Biscayne Blvd., Bayside Marketplace, Miami 33132 ☎ 305/539-2980 ✉ Tropical Everglades Visitor Information Center ✉ 160 U.S. 1, Florida City 33034 ☎ 305/245-9180 or 800/388-9669 🖨 305/247-4335. **Coconut Grove Chamber of Commerce** ✉ 2820 McFarlane Rd., Coconut Grove, 33133 ☎ 305/444-7270 🖨 305/444-2498. **Coral Gables Chamber of Commerce** ✉ 50 Aragon Ave., Coral Gables 33134 ☎ 305/446-1657 🖨 305/446-9900. **Florida Gold Coast Chamber of Commerce** ✉ 1100 Kane Concourse, Suite 210, Bay Harbor Islands 33154 ☎ 305/866-6020. **Greater Miami Chamber of Commerce** ✉ 1601 Biscayne Blvd., Miami 33132 ☎ 305/350-7700 🖨 305/374-6902. **Greater North Miami Chamber of Commerce** ✉ 13100 W. Dixie Hwy., North Miami 33181 ☎ 305/891-7811 🖨 305/893-8522. **Greater South Dade/South Miami Chamber of Commerce** ✉ 6410 S.W. 80th St., South Miami 33143-4602 ☎ 305/661-1621 🖨 305/666-0508. **Key Biscayne Chamber of Commerce** ✉ Key Biscayne Village Hall, 88 W. McIntyre St., Key Biscayne, Miami 33149 ☎ 305/361-5207. **Miami Beach Chamber of Commerce** ✉ 1920 Meridian Ave., South Beach, Miami Beach 33139 ☎ 305/672-1270 🖨 305/538-4336. **Surfside Tourist Board** ✉ 9301 Collins Ave., Surfside, Miami Beach 33154 ☎ 305/864-0722 or 800/327-4557 🖨 305/861-1302.

THE EVERGLADES

2

FODOR'S CHOICE

Big Cypress Gallery, Tamiami Trail

Ernest F. Coe Visitor Center, Main Park Road

Ivey House, Everglades City

Ivey House Restaurant, Everglades City

Pit Bar-B-Q, Tamiami Trail

HIGHLY RECOMMENDED

RESTAURANTS   El Toro Taco, Homestead

Richard Accursio's Capri Restaurant and King Richard's Room, Florida City

Robert Is Here, Florida City

Updated by
Diane P.
Marshall

THE ONLY METROPOLITAN AREA in the United States with two national parks and a national preserve in its backyard is Miami. Everglades National Park, created in 1947, was meant to preserve the slow-moving "River of Grass"—a freshwater river 50 mi wide but only 6 inches deep, flowing from Lake Okeechobee through marshy grassland into Florida Bay. Along the Tamiami Trail (U.S. 41), marshes of cattails extend as far as the eye can see, interspersed only with hammocks or tree islands of bald cypress and mahogany, while overhead southern bald eagles make circles in the sky. An assembly of trees and flowers, including ferns, orchids, and bromeliads, shares the brackish waters with otters, turtles, marsh rabbits, and occasionally that gentle giant, the West Indian manatee. Not so gentle, though, is the saw grass. Deceptively graceful, these tall, willowy sedges have small sharp teeth on the edges of their leaves.

Biscayne National Park, established as a national monument in 1968 and 12 years later expanded and designated a national park, is the nation's largest marine park and the largest national park within the continental United States with living coral reefs. A small portion of the park's almost 274 square mi consists of mainland coast and outlying islands, but 96% is underwater, much of it in Biscayne Bay. The islands contain lush, heavily wooded forests with an abundance of ferns and native palm trees. Of particular interest are the mangroves and their tangled masses of stiltlike roots and stems that thicken the shorelines. These "walking trees," as locals sometimes call them, have striking curved prop roots, which arch down from the trunk, while aerial roots drop from branches. These trees draw fresh water from saltwater and create a coastal nursery capable of sustaining all types of marine life. Congress established Big Cypress National Preserve in 1974 after buying up one of the least-developed watershed areas in South Florida to protect the watershed of Everglades National Park. The preserve, on the northern edge of Everglades National Park, entails extensive tracts of prairie, marsh, pinelands, forested swamps, and sloughs. While preservation and recreation are the preserve's mainstay, hunting, off-road vehicle use, oil and gas exploration, and grazing are allowed.

Unfortunately, Miami's backyard is threatened by suburban sprawl, agriculture, and business development. What results is competition among environmental, agricultural, and developmental interests. The biggest issue is water. Originally, alternating floods and dry periods maintained a wildlife habitat and regulated the water flowing into Florida Bay. The brackish seasonal flux sustained a remarkably vigorous bay, including the most productive shrimp beds in American waters, with thriving mangrove thickets and coral reefs at its Atlantic edge. The system nurtured sea life and attracted anglers and divers. Starting in the 1930s, however, a giant flood-control system began diverting water to canals running to the gulf and the ocean. As you travel Florida's north–south routes, you cross this network of canals symbolized by a smiling alligator representing the South Florida Water Management District, ironically known as "Protector of the Everglades" (ironic because most people feel it's done more for the developers than the environment). The unfortunate side effect of flood control has been devastation of the wilderness. Park visitors decry diminished bird counts (a 90% reduction over 50 years); the black bear population has been nearly eliminated; and the Florida panther is nearing extinction. Meanwhile, the loss of fresh water has made Florida Bay saltier, devastating breeding grounds and creating dead zones where pea-green algae has replaced sea grasses and sponges.

The nearly $8 billion, 10-year Comprehensive Plan worked out between government agencies and a host of conservation groups and industries to restore, protect, and preserve the ecosystem is under way. More than 200 projects will tear down levees, fill canals, construct new

2

**If you have
1 day**

You'll have to make a choice—the Everglades, Big Cypress, or Biscayne. If you want interpretive trails and lots of exhibits, go with the Everglades. If you're interested in boating or seeing underwater flora and fauna, Biscayne is your best bet. For quiet, wilderness canoeing, and nature, don't miss Big Cypress. Whichever you choose, you'll experience a little of what's left of the "real" Florida.

Numbers, in the text correspond to numbers in the margin and on the Everglades and Biscayne National Parks map.

For a day in Everglades National Park, begin in **Florida City** ⑭ ➤, the southern–eastern gateway to the park. Head to the **Ernest F. Coe Visitor Center** ① for an overview of the park and its ecosystems, and continue to the **Royal Palm Visitor Center** ② for a boardwalk trail through sloughs populated by alligators and a look at several unique plant systems. Then go to **Flamingo** ③ and rent a boat or take a tour of Florida Bay. If Biscayne is your preference, begin at **Convoy Point** ⑮ for an orientation before forsaking dry land. Sign up for a snorkel or dive trip or an outing on a glass-bottom boat, kayak, or canoe. To spend a day in Big Cypress National Preserve, begin at the **Oasis Visitor Center** ⑨ to pick up information about canoe and walking trails and learn about the park's ecosystem. Then head to **Everglades City** ⑫ and rent a canoe for a tour of the Turner River.

**If you have
3 days**

With three days, explore both the northern and southern Everglades as well as Biscayne National Park. Start in the north by driving west along the Tamiami Trail, stopping at **Everglades Safari Park** ④ ➤ for an airboat ride; at **Shark Valley** ⑥ for a tram tour, walk, or bicycle trip; at the **Miccosukee Indian Village** ⑦ for lunch; at the **Big Cypress Gallery** ⑧ to see Clyde Butcher's photographs; and then at the **Ochopee Post Office** ⑩, before ending in 🚗 **Everglades City** ⑫, home of Everglades National Park's Gulf Coast Visitor Center. From here visit historic Smallwood's Store on Chokoloskee Island and watch the sunset. Day two is for exploring the south. Return east on the Tamiami Trail to **Homestead** ⑬, pausing at Everglades Air Tours to take a sightseeing trip before following the one-day Everglades itinerary above and overnighting in 🚗 **Florida City** ⑭. Biscayne National Park is the subject of day three. If you plan to scuba or take the glass-bottom boat, get an early start. Explore the visitor center at **Convoy Point** ⑮ when you return and finish your day checking out sights in Florida City and Homestead. Snorkel trips leave later, giving you time to see Florida City and Homestead, have lunch, and learn about the park's ecosystem at the visitor center first. Be warned that, although you can fly and then scuba dive, you *can't* dive and then fly within 24 hours. So if you're flying out, reverse the days' sequence accordingly.

**If you have
5 days**

Follow day one above, spending the night in 🚗 **Everglades City** ⑫. Begin the second day with a canoe, kayak, or boat tour of the 10,000 Islands; then make arrangements to rent a canoe for the next day's trip to Big Cypress National Preserve's Turner River. In the late afternoon take a walk on the ½-mi boardwalk at **Fakahatchee Strand Preserve State Park** ⑪ to see rare epiphytic orchids or on a 2½-mi trail at the Big Cypress National Preserve. On day three, drive to the Big Cypress Oasis Visitor Center to put in for the canoe tour. If it's December through April, join a ranger-led canoe tour. Drive east to Coopertown and take a nighttime ride with Ray Cramer's Everglades Airboat Tours. Spend the night in 🎫 **Florida City** ⑭. Spend day four at Biscayne National Park, then sightseeing in **Homestead** ⑬ and Florida City as suggested above. On day five, head to the southern portion of Everglades National Park.

---

water storage areas on land formerly preserved for agriculture or new development, channel water to estuaries and Everglades National Park, and provide flood protection and a reliable water supply. The expectation is that new policies and projects implemented over the next decade will go a long way toward reviving the natural system.

Exploring the Everglades

The southern tip of the Florida peninsula is largely taken up by Everglades National Park, but land access to it is primarily by two roads. The main park road traverses the southern Everglades from the gateway towns of Homestead and Florida City to the outpost of Flamingo, on Florida Bay. In the northern Everglades, take the Tamiami Trail (U. S. 41) from the Greater Miami area in the east to the western park entrance in Everglades City. In far southeastern Florida, Biscayne National Park lies almost completely offshore. As a result, most sports and activities in both national parks are based on water, the study of nature, or both, so even on land, be prepared to get a bit damp on the region's marshy trails. Although relatively compact compared to the national parks of the West, these parks still require a bit of time to see. The narrow, two-lane roads through the Everglades make for long travel, whereas it's the necessity of sightseeing by boat that takes time at Biscayne.

About the Restaurants

With a few exceptions, dining centers on low-key mom-and-pop places that serve hearty home-style food and small eateries that specialize in local fare: seafood, conch, alligator, turtle, and frogs' legs. Native American restaurants add another dimension, serving local favorites as well as catfish, Indian fry bread (a flour-and-water dough), pumpkin bread, Indian burgers (ground beef browned, rolled in fry-bread dough, and deep-fried), and tacos (fry bread with chili, lettuce, tomato, and shredded cheddar cheese on top). Restaurants in Everglades City appear to operate with a "captive audience" philosophy: prices run high, service is mediocre, and food preparation is uninspired. The closest good restaurants are in Naples, 35 mi northwest. Although both Everglades and Biscayne national parks and Big Cypress National Preserve are wilderness areas, there are restaurants within a short drive. Most are between Miami and Shark Valley along the Tamiami Trail (U.S. 41), in the Homestead–Florida City area, in Everglades City, and in the Florida Keys along the Overseas Highway (U.S. 1). The only food service in the preserve or in either of the parks is at Flamingo, in the Everglades, but many independent restaurants will pack picnics. Also find fast-food establishments on the Tamiami Trail east of Krome Avenue and west of Everglades City in Naples, and along U.S. 1 in Homestead–Florida City.

About the Hotels

If spending several days exploring the Everglades, stay either in the park itself (at the Flamingo Resort or one of the campgrounds) or 11 mi away in Homestead–Florida City, where there are reasonably priced motels and RV parks. If you plan to spend only a day in the Everglades, you may prefer staying in the Florida Keys or the Greater Miami–Fort Lauderdale area. Lodgings and campgrounds are also available on the Gulf Coast in Everglades City and Naples. Accommodations near the parks range from inexpensive to moderate and offer off-season rates during the summer months. For those who crave luxury and lots of extras, head for Miami or Naples—where you'll pay more.

	WHAT IT COSTS				
	$$$$	$$$	$$	$	¢
RESTAURANTS	over $30	$20–$30	$15–$20	$10–$15	under $10
HOTELS	over $220	$140–$220	$100–$140	$80–$100	under $80

Restaurant prices are per person for a main course at dinner. Hotel prices are for a standard double room, excluding 6% sales tax (more in some counties) and 1%–4% tourist tax.

Timing

Winter is the best time to visit Everglades National Park and Big Cypress National Preserve. Temperatures and mosquito activity are low to moderate, low water levels concentrate the resident wildlife around sloughs that retain water all year, and migratory birds swell the avian population. Winter is also the busiest time in the park. Make reservations and expect crowds at Flamingo, the main visitor center (known officially as the Ernest F. Coe Visitor Center), and Royal Palm. Be careful with campfires and matches; this is when the wildfire-prone sawgrass prairies and pinelands are most vulnerable. In late spring the weather turns hot and rainy, and tours and facilities are less crowded. Migratory birds depart, and you must look harder to see wildlife. Even if you're not lodging in Everglades National Park, try to stay until dusk, when dozens of bird species feed around the ponds and trails. While shining a flashlight over the water in marshy areas, look for two yellowish-red reflections above the surface—telltale signs of alligators.

Summer brings intense sun and billowing clouds unleashing torrents of rain almost every afternoon. Start your outdoor activities early to avoid the rain and the sun's strongest rays, and use sunscreen. Water levels rise and wildlife disperses. Mosquitoes hatch, swarm, and descend on you in voracious clouds. Carrying mosquito repellent is a good idea at any time of year, but it's a necessity in summer.

EVERGLADES NATIONAL PARK

11 mi southwest of Homestead, 45 mi southwest of Miami International Airport.

The best way to experience the real Everglades is to get your feet wet either by taking a walk in the muck, affectionately called a "slough slog," or by paddling a canoe into the River of Grass to stay in a backcountry campsite. Most day-trippers don't want to do that, however. Luckily, there are several ways to see the wonders of the park with dry feet. Take a boat tour in Everglades City or Flamingo, ride the tram at Shark Valley, or walk the boardwalks along the main park road. And there's more to see than natural beauty. Miccosukee Indians operate a scope of attractions and restaurants worthy of a stop. Admission to Everglades National Park is valid at all entrances for seven days. Coverage below begins in the southern/eastern Everglades, followed by the northern Everglades, starting in the east and ending in Everglades City.

The Main Park Road

The main park road (Route 9336) travels from the main visitor center to Flamingo, across a section of the park's eight distinct ecosystems: hardwood hammock, fresh-water prairie, pinelands, freshwater slough, cypress, coastal prairie, mangrove, and marine-estuarine. Highlights of the trip include a dwarf cypress forest, the ecotone (transition zone) between saw grass and mangrove forest, and a wealth of wading birds at Mrazek and Coot Bay ponds. Boardwalks, looped trails, several short spurs, and observation platforms allow you to stay dry.

Fodor'sChoice
★

❶ Numerous interactive exhibits and films make the **Ernest F. Coe Visitor Center** a worthy and important stop during your tour of the region. Stand in a simulated blind and peer through a spyglass to watch birds in the wild; although it's actually a film, the quality is so good you'll think you're outside. Move on to a bank of telephones to hear differing viewpoints on the Great Water Debate. There's a 15-minute film on the park, two movies on hurricanes, and a 45-minute wildlife film for children. Computer monitors present a schedule of daily ranger-led activities park-wide as well as information on canoe rentals and boat tours. In the Everglades Discovery Shop, browse through a lot of neat nature, science, and kids' stuff and pick up extra insect repellent. The center provides information on the entire park. ⊠ *11 mi southwest of Homestead on Rte. 9336* ☎ *305/242–7700* ⊕ *www.nps.gov/ever* 🕿 *Park $10 per vehicle, $5 per pedestrian or bicyclist, $5 per motorcycle* ☉ *Daily 8–5.*

❷ A must for anyone who wants to experience the real Everglades, the **Royal Palm Visitor Center** permits access to the Anhinga Trail boardwalk, where in winter spying alligators congregating in watering holes is almost guaranteed. Or follow the neighboring Gumbo Limbo Trail through a hardwood hammock. Do both strolls, as they're short (½ mi) and expose you to two of the Everglades' ecosystems. The visitor center has an interpretive display, a bookstore, and vending machines. ⊠ *4 mi west of Ernest F. Coe Visitor Center on Rte. 9336* ☎ *305/242–7700* ☉ *Daily 8–4.*

Flamingo

❸ *38 mi southwest of Ernest F. Coe Visitor Center.*

Here at the far end of the main road, you'll find a cluster of buildings where a former town of the same name was established in 1893. Today, it contains a visitor center, lodge, restaurant and lounge, gift shop, marina, and bicycle rentals, plus an adjacent campground. Tour boats narrated by interpretive guides, fishing expeditions of Florida Bay, and canoe and kayak trips all leave from here. Nearby is Eco Pond, one of the most popular wildlife observation areas. Some facilities, like the restaurant, have abbreviated seasonal hours.

The **Flamingo Visitor Center** provides an interactive display and has natural-history exhibits in the small Florida Bay Flamingo Museum. Check the schedule for ranger-led activities, such as naturalist discussions, evening programs in the campground amphitheater, and hikes along area trails. ☎ *239/695–2945* ☉ *Dec.–Apr., daily 7:30–5; May–Nov., hrs vary.*

Where to Stay & Eat

¢–$$ ✕ **Flamingo Restaurant and Buttonwood Patio Cafe.** The grand view, convivial lounge, and casual style are great reasons to visit here. Big picture windows on the visitor center's second floor overlook Florida Bay, revealing eagles, gulls, pelicans, and vultures. Dine at low tide to see birds flock to the sandbar just offshore. The restaurant menu has seafood and local dishes such as coconut fried shrimp and chicken breast with a mango salsa. Downstairs, the Buttonwood Patio Cafe has pizza, sandwiches, and salads. ⊠ *Flamingo Lodge, 1 Flamingo Lodge Hwy.* ☎ *239/695–3101* ▤ *AE, D, DC, MC, V* ☉ *Restaurant closed May–Oct. Café closed Apr. and Oct.*

2

Biking & Hiking

In the Everglades there are several scenic places to ride and hike. The Shark Valley Loop Road (15 mi round-trip) makes a good bike trip. Lists at the visitor centers describe others. Inquire about insect and weather conditions before you go and plan accordingly, stocking up on insect repellent, sunscreen, and water, as necessary.

Boating & Canoeing

One of the best ways to experience the Everglades is by boat, and almost all of Biscayne National Park is accessible only by water. Boat rentals are available in both parks. Rentals are generally for half day (four hours) and full day (eight hours). In the Everglades the 99-mi inland Wilderness Trail between Flamingo and Everglades City is open to motorboats as well as canoes, although powerboats may have trouble navigating the route above Whitewater Bay. Flat-water canoeing and kayaking are best in winter, when temperatures are moderate, rainfall is minimal, and mosquitoes are tolerable. You don't need a permit for day trips, but tell someone where you're going and when you expect to return. Getting lost is easy, and spending the night without proper gear can be unpleasant, if not dangerous. On the Gulf Coast explore the nooks, crannies, and mangrove islands of Chokoloskee Bay, as well as many rivers near Everglades City. The Turner River Canoe Trail, a pleasant day trip with a guarantee of bird and alligator sightings, passes through mangrove, dwarf cypress, coastal prairie, and fresh-water slough ecosystems of Everglades National Park and Big Cypress National Preserve.

Fishing

Largemouth bass are plentiful in fresh-water ponds, while snapper, redfish, and sea trout are caught in Florida Bay. The mangrove shallows of the 10,000 Islands, along the gulf, yield tarpon and snook. Whitewater Bay is also a favorite spot. **Note:** the state has issued health advisories for sea bass, largemouth bass, and other fresh-water fish, especially those caught in the canals along the Tamiami Trail, due to their high mercury content. Signs are posted throughout the park, and consumption should be limited.

$ **Flamingo Lodge, Marina & Outpost Resort.** This simple low-rise motel is the only lodging inside the park. Accommodations are basic but well kept, and an amiable staff helps you adjust to bellowing alligators, roaming raccoons, and ibis grazing on the lawn. Rooms have contemporary furniture, floral bedspreads, and art prints of birds. They face Florida Bay, but don't necessarily look out over it. Bathrooms are small. Cottages, in a wooded area on the margin of a coastal prairie, can accommodate up to six people. Reservations are essential in winter; Continental breakfast is included from May to October. ⊠ *1 Flamingo Lodge Hwy., Flamingo 33034* ☎ *239/695–3101 or 800/600–3813* ☒ *239/695–3921* ⊕ *www.flamingolodge.com* ⇔ *102 rooms, 24 cottages, 1 suite* ⚭ *Restaurant, snack bar, fans, in-room data ports, some kitchens, some cable TV, pool, beach, boating, fishing, bicycles, hiking, bar, shops, laundry facilities, business services, meeting rooms, some pets allowed; no-smoking rooms* ⊟ *AE, D, DC, MC, V.*

About 12 mi southwest of Florida City, ⚘ **Everglades National Park** has two developed campsites available through a reservation system from late November through April; the rest of the year they're first-come, first-serve. Six miles west of the park's main entrance, ⚠ **Long Pine Key** has no-permit hiking, though you will need separate permits for fresh-water and saltwater fishing. ♿ *Flush toilets, dump station, drinking water, showers (cold), fire pit, grills, picnic tables, public telephones. No hookups* ⌕ *108 drive-up sites* ☎ *301/722–1257; 800/365–2267 for campsite reservations* ⊕ *reservations.nps.gov* ✉ *June–Aug. free; Sept.–May $14 per night, groups $28* ⊟ *D, MC, V.*

Thirty-eight miles southwest of the park's main entrance, ⚠ **Flamingo** has a visitor center and hiking and nature trails. ♿ *Flush toilets, dump station, drinking water, showers (cold), grill, general store. No hookups* ⌕ *234 drive-up sites, 44 walk-in sites, 20 on the water* ☎ *301/722–1257; 800/365–2267 for campsite reservations* ⊕ *reservations.nps.gov* ✉ *June–Aug. free; May–Sept. $14 per night, groups $28* ⊟ *D, MC, V.*

For an intense stay in the "real" Florida, consider one of the 48 backcountry sites deep in the park, many inland, with some on the beach. You'll need to carry your food, water, and supplies in; take care to carry out all your trash. You'll also need a site-specific permit, available on a first-come, first-served basis from the Flamingo or Gulf Coast Visitor Center. These sites cost $10 or more depending on group size.

The Outdoors

BIKING   **Flamingo Lodge, Marina & Outpost Resort** (☎ 239/695–3101) rents bikes for $14 a day, $8 per half day. Snake Bight Trail and the park's main road are good places to ride to see wildlife.

BOATING   The marina at **Flamingo Lodge, Marina & Outpost Resort** (☎ 239/695–3101) rents 16-ft power skiffs for $90 per day, $65 per half day, and $22 per hour; four Carolina skiffs for $155 per day and $100 per half day; as well as fully furnished and outfitted houseboats that sleep up to eight. From November to April, rates (two-day minimum) run $475 without air-conditioning for two days. Off-season (summer) rates are lower. Several private boats are also available for charter. There are two ramps, one for Florida Bay, the other for Whitewater Bay and the backcountry. The hoist across the plug dam separating Florida Bay from the Buttonwood Canal can take boats from 16 ft to 26 ft long. A small store sells food, camping supplies, bait and tackle, propane, and fuel. A concessionaire rents rods, reels, binoculars, and coolers by the half and full day.

CANOEING &   The Everglades has six well-marked canoe trails in the Flamingo area, in-
KAYAKING   cluding the south end of the 99-mi Wilderness Trail from Everglades City to Flamingo. **Flamingo Lodge, Marina & Outpost Resort** (☎ 239/695–3101) rents canoes in two sizes: small (up to two paddlers) and family size (up to four). Small canoes rent for $32 per day, $22 per half day, and $8 per hour; family-size run $40, $30, and $12, respectively. Single-person kayaks cost $43 per day, $27 per half day, and $11 per hour; doubles rent for $54, $38, and $16, respectively. Overnight rentals are also available.

FISHING   **Flamingo Lodge, Marina & Outpost Resort** (☎ 239/695–3101) helps arrange charter fishing trips for two to four persons. The cost is $350 a day for up to two people, $25 each additional person.

Tamiami Trail

141 mi from Miami to Fort Myers.

In 1915 when officials decided to build an east–west highway linking Miami to Fort Myers and continuing north to Tampa, someone suggested calling it the Tamiami Trail. In 1928 the road became a reality, cutting through the Everglades and altering the natural flow of water and the

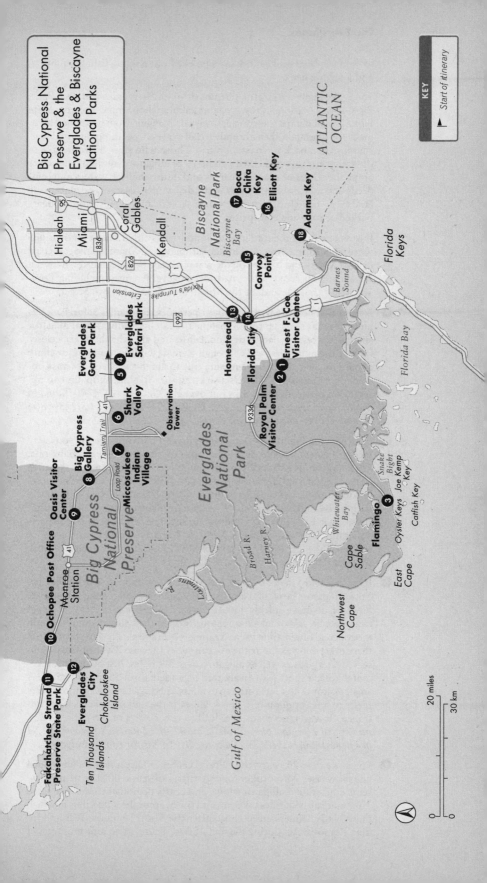

Big Cypress National
Preserve & the
Everglades & Biscayne
National Parks

KEY

▲ Start of itinerary

ATLANTIC OCEAN

Hialeah

Miami

836

Coral Gables

Kendall

826

Florida's Turnpike
Extension

Biscayne National Park

Biscayne Bay

17 Boca Chita Key

16 Elliott Key

18 Adams Key

15 Convoy Point

13 Homestead

14 Florida City

997

Everglades Gator Park

4 Everglades Safari Park

5

6 Shark Valley

Observation Tower

Tamiami Trail 41

Big Cypress Gallery **8**

7 Miccosukee Indian Village

Loop Road

Oasis Visitor Center **9**

Big Cypress National Preserve

Monroe Station

41

Ochopee Post Office **10**

Fakahatchee Strand Preserve State Park **11**

Everglades City **12**

Ten Thousand Islands

Chokoloskee Island

Lostmans R.

Broad R.

Harney R.

Everglades National Park

Whitewater Bay

Cape Sable

Northwest Cape

East Cape

3 Flamingo

Snake Bight

Oyster Keys Joe Kemp Key

Catfish Key

9336

Royal Palm Visitor Center **2 1** Ernest F. Coe Visitor Center

Florida Bay

Barnes Sound

Florida Keys

1

Gulf of Mexico

0   20 miles

0   30 km

ATLANTIC OCEAN

lives of the Miccosukee Indians who eked out a living fishing, hunting, and frogging here.

Today the highway's traffic screams through Everglades National Park, Big Cypress National Preserve, and Fakahatchee Strand Preserve State Park. The landscape is surprisingly varied, changing from hardwood hammocks to pinelands, then abruptly to tall cypress trees dripping with Spanish moss and back to coastal prairie. Those who slow down to take in the scenery are rewarded with glimpses of alligators sunning themselves along the banks of roadside canals and in the shallow waters and hundreds of waterbirds, especially in the dry winter season. The man-made landscape has chickee huts, Native American villages, and airboats parked at roadside enterprises.

Businesses along the trail give their addresses either based on their distance from Krome Avenue, Florida Turnpike, and Miami on the east coast or Fort Myers and Naples on the west coast or by mile marker. Between Miami and Fort Myers, the road goes by several names, including Tamiami Trail, U.S. 41, and, at the Miami end, Southwest 8th Street.

▶ ❹ A perennial favorite with tour-bus operators, **Everglades Safari Park** has an arena that seats up to 300 people to watch an educational alligator show and wrestling demonstration. Before and after the show, get a closer look at the alligators, walk through a small wildlife museum, or climb aboard an airboat for a 30-minute ride through the River of Grass (included in admission). There's also a restaurant, a gift shop, and an observation platform that looks out over the Glades. ✉ *26700 Tamiami Trail, 16 mi west of Krome Ave.* ☎ *305/226–6923 or 305/223–3804* ⊕ *www.evergladessafaripark.com* 🖅 *$15* ☉ *Daily 8:30–5.*

🖰 ❺ After visiting **Everglades Gator Park** you can tell your friends you came face-to-face with—and even touched—an alligator, albeit a baby one. Then squirm in a "reptilium" of venomous and nonpoisonous native snakes or learn about Native Americans of the Everglades through a reproduction of a Miccosukee village. The park also has wildlife shows with native and exotic animals, 45-minute airboat tours, and RV campsites, as well as a gift shop and restaurant. The last airboat ride departs 45 minutes before sunset. ✉ *24050 Tamiami Trail, 12 mi west of Florida Tpke.* ☎ *305/559–2255 or 800/559–2205* ⊕ *www.gatorpark. com* 🖅 *Park $5, tours and park $15* ☉ *Daily 9–sunset.*

❻ It takes a bit of nerve to walk the paved 15-mi loop in **Shark Valley** because alligators lie on and alongside the road, basking in the sun—most, however, do move quickly out of the way. Less fearless, or energetic, types can ride a bicycle or take a tram tour. Stop at the halfway point to climb the concrete observation tower's ramp, which spirals skyward 50 ft. From there everything as far as the eye can see is the vast River of Grass. Observe waterbirds as well as alligators at water holes. Just behind the bike-rental area, a short boardwalk trail meanders through the saw grass. A small visitor center has rotating exhibits, a bookstore, and park rangers ready to answer questions. Shark Valley is the national park's north entrance; however, no roads here lead to other parts of the park. ✉ *23½ mi west of Florida Tpke.* ☎ *305/221–8776* 🖅 *Park $8 per vehicle; $4 per pedestrian, bicyclist, or motorcyclist* ☉ *Visitor center daily 9–5.*

❼ For more than 25 years, the cultural center at **Miccosukee Indian Village** has showcased Miccosukee foods, crafts, skills, and lifestyle. It also presents educational alligator shows and crafts demonstrations. Narrated 30-minute airboat rides take you into the heart of the wilderness in which these Native Americans escaped after the Third Seminole War and Indian Removal Act during the mid-1800s. There's also a restaurant and gift shop. The Everglades Music & Craft Festival falls on a July weekend, and the weeklong Indian Arts Festival is in late December. ✉ *Just west of Shark Valley entrance, 25 mi west of Florida Tpke.* ☎ *305/223–8380* ⊕ *www.miccosukee.com/mivillage.html* 🎟 *Village $5, rides $10* ☉ *Daily 9–5.*

8

Fodor'sChoice

★

Clyde Butcher does for the River of Grass and Big Cypress Swamp what Ansel Adams did for the West; check out his stunning photographs at his **Big Cypress Gallery** in the Big Cypress National Preserve. Working with large-format black-and-white film, Butcher captures every blade of grass, barb of feather, and flicker of light. If you're lucky, Butcher will be on hand to sign your prints. He's always there on Thanksgiving and Labor Day weekends. Special exhibits, lectures, tours, photo expeditions, and slide presentations are given throughout the year, especially Labor Day weekend. ✉ *52388 Tamiami Trail, 45 mi west of Florida Tpke., Ochopee* ☎ *239/695–2428* ⊕ *www.clydebutcher.com* 🎟 *Free* ☉ *Fri.–Mon. 10–5.*

9 Slow down—the **Oasis Visitor Center** is a welcome respite along the Tamiami Trail. If you blow by here as you speed between Miami and Naples you'll miss out on an opportunity to learn about the surrounding Big Cypress National Preserve. Inside the center are a small exhibit area, an information center, a bookshop, a theater that shows a 15-minute film on the preserve and Big Cypress Swamp, and rest rooms. It also has myriad seasonal ranger-led and self-guided activities, such as campfire talks, bike hikes, slough slogs, and canoe excursions. The 8-mi Turner River Canoe Trail begins nearby and crosses through Everglades National Park before ending in Chokoloskee Bay, near Everglades City. Hikers can join the Florida National Scenic Trail, which runs north–south through the preserve for 31 mi. Two 5-mi trails, Concho Billy and Fire Prairie, can be accessed a few miles east off Turner River Road. Turner River Road and Birdon Road form a 17-mi gravel loop drive that is excellent for birding. Bear Island has about 32 mi of scenic, flat, looped trails that are ideal for bicycling. Most trails are hard-packed lime rock, but a few miles are gravel. Cyclists share the road with off-road vehicles, which are most plentiful during General Gun Hunting season, from mid-November through December. The best biking time is January–March, when rangers lead bike tours (239/695–1201). Access is from Turner River Road and State Road 29. All of the trails can be very wet and possibly impassable during the summer rainy season. Rangers at the visitor center provide road-condition information. Five primitive campsites are available on a first-come, first-served basis. ✉ *24 mi east of Everglades City, 50 mi west of Miami, 20 mi west of Shark Valley* ☎ *239/695–4111* 🎟 *Free* ☉ *Daily 8:30–4:30.*

10 The tiny **Ochopee Post Office** is the smallest in North America. Buy a picture postcard of the little one-room shack and mail it to a friend, thereby helping to keep this picturesque spot in business. ✉ *75 mi west of Miami, Ochopee* ☎ *239/695–4131* ☉ *Weekdays 9:30–noon and 1–4:30, Sat. 9:30–11:30.*

11 The ½-mi boardwalk at **Fakahatchee Strand Preserve State Park** gives you an opportunity to see rare plants, bald cypress, and North America's largest stand of native royal palms and largest concentration and variety of epiphytic orchids. It's the main park featured in Susan Orlean's *The Orchid Thief.* From November to April the park's rookery, accessed down a short road 2 mi east of the boardwalk, is a birder's paradise beginning an hour before sunset. The sight of 5,000 to 7,000 wading birds returning to roost for the night is spectacular. Launch a kayak or watch from the shore. Ranger-led swamp walks are given November–February. ✉ *Boardwalk on north side of Tamiami Trail 7 mi west of Rte. 29; rookery on* *south side of Tamiami Trail 5 mi west of Rte. 29; ranger station ¼ mi north of Tamiami Trail on Rte. 29, Box 548, Copeland 34137* ☎ *239/ 695–4593* ⊕ *www.dep.state.fl.us/parks* ☒ *Free* ⊙ *Daily 8–sunset.*

Where to Stay & Eat

¢–$$$ ✕ **Coopertown Restaurant.** For more than a half century this rustic eatery just into the Everglades west of Miami has been full of Old Florida style— not to mention alligator skulls, stuffed alligator heads, and gator accessories. House specialties are frogs' legs and alligator tail prepared breaded or deep-fried, and they're available for breakfast, lunch, or dinner. Also order more conventional selections, such as catfish, shrimp, or sandwiches. ☒ *22700 S.W. 8th St., 11 mi west of Florida Tpke., Miami* ☎ *305/226–6048* ▤ *AE, D, MC, V.*

¢–$ ✕ **Joanie's Blue Crab Café.** Movie-set designers could not have created a more quintessential 1950s-style swamp café than this landmark restaurant near the Ochopee Post Office. Drink in the wood-plank floors, open rafters—recently cleaned of cobwebs but still hung with stuffed owls— postcards from around the globe, and kitschy gator art. Joanie, the chief cook and bottle washer, set up shop here in 1987. The fresh blue crabs used in the sandwiches and soups are caught by staff members, who haul in close to 400 pounds of the critters in a single weekend. Chill out with a beer, glass of wine, or chilly strawberry shake on the screened deck. It's open daily 9 AM to 5 PM. ☒ *39395 Tamiami Trail, 50 mi west of Florida Tpke., Ochopee* ☎ *239/695–2682* ▤ *AE, D, MC, V.*

¢–$ ✕ **Pit Bar-B-Q.** On a day with a breeze, you'll smell this rustic roadside
Fodor'sChoice eatery's barbecue and blackjack-oak smoke long before you can see it.
★ Order at the counter, pick up your food, and eat at one of the indoor or outdoor picnic tables. Specialties include barbecued chicken and ribs with a tangy sauce, french fries, coleslaw, and a fried biscuit as well as catfish and frogs' legs deep-fried in vegetable oil. Popular with families on weekends, it's reminiscent of a summer backyard barbecue. ☒ *16400 Tamiami Trail, 5 mi west of Florida Tpke., Miami* ☎ *305/226–2272* ▤ *AE, D, MC, V.*

¢ ✕ **Miccosukee Restaurant.** Murals depict Native American women cooking and men engaged in a powwow in this Native American restaurant at the Miccosukee Indian Village. Favorites are catfish and frogs' legs breaded and deep-fried, Indian fry bread, pumpkin bread, and Indian burgers and tacos. Breakfast and lunch are served daily. ☒ *25 mi west of Florida Tpke.* ☎ *305/223–8380 Ext. 2374* ▤ *AE, D, MC, V.*

$$–$$$ ▥ **Miccosukee Resort & Convention Center.** Big-name entertainers and major sporting events draw crowds to this resort at the crossroads of Tamiami Trail and Krome Avenue. Like an oasis on the horizon, it's the only facility for miles and it's situated to attract the attention of travelers going to the Everglades, driving across the state, or looking for casino action. Most units have a view of Everglades saw grass and wildlife. In addition to an enormous children's play area and a teen center, there are tours to Everglades National Park and the Miccosukee Indian Village, shuttles to area malls, and a gaming complex. ☒ *500 S.W. 177th Ave., 6 mi west of Florida Tpke., Miami 33194* ☎ *305/925–2555 or 877/242–6464* ⊕ *www.miccosukee.com* ⇄ *256 rooms, 46 suites* ⚄ *3 restaurants, snack bar, in-room data ports, in-room safes, some in-room hot tubs, minibars, cable TV with movies and video games, indoor pool, hair salon, health club, hot tub, sauna, spa, lounge, showroom, video game room, shops, playground, laundry service, Internet, business services, convention center, meeting rooms, airport shuttle, travel services; no-smoking rooms* ▤ *AE, D, DC, MC, V.*

⚠ **Big Cypress National Preserve.** There are four no-fee primitive campgrounds within the preserve along the Tamiami Trail and Loop Road.

A fifth site, Monument Lake Campground, has rest rooms, an amphitheater, and activities and seasonal programs (December–mid-April). Dona Drive Campground has a dump station ($4) and potable water. ⚲ *Flush toilets, dump station, showers (cold)* ⚑ *10 tent, 26 RV or tent sites* ⊠ *Tamiami Trail (Hwy. 41), between Miami and Naples* ⚐ *HCR 61, Box 110, Ochopee 34141* ☎ *239/695–4111* ⊕ *www.nps.gov/bicy* ⊠ *$14* ⊟ *No credit cards.*

⚠ **Everglades Gator Park.** At an airboat tour facility in the heart of the Everglades, this RV park is especially popular with snowbirds, as it's the closest campground to the Port of Miami and Miami airport, and it offers short-term RV storage. Campers store their RVs, then take a cruise or fly to another destination. Campers are surrounded by the sounds of alligators, birds, and frogs by night, departing and arriving air boats by day. ⚲ *Flush toilets, full hookups, drinking water, restaurant, electricity, public phone, general store, lake.* ⚑ *80 partial hookups* ⊠ *24050 S.W. 8th St., Miami* ⚐ *Box 787, Miami 33194* ☎ *305/559–2255 or 800/559–2205* 📠 *305/559–2844* ⊕ *www.gatorpark.com* ⊠ *Partial hookup $25 per night, $100 per week, or $350 per month* ⊟ *AE, D, DC, MC, V.*

The Outdoors
Shark Valley Tram Tours (⊠ Shark Valley ☎ 305/221–8455) rents bikes daily 8:30–4 (last rental at 3) for $5.25 per hour.

Shopping
The shopping alone should lure you to the **Miccosukee Indian Village** (⊠ 25 mi west of Florida Tpke., just west of Shark Valley entrance ☎ 305/223–8380). Wares include well-made Native American crafts including beadwork, moccasins, dolls, pottery, baskets, and patchwork fabric and clothes. There are also some fun, kitschy Florida souvenirs.

Everglades City

⑫ *35 mi southeast of Naples, 83 mi west of Miami.*

Ignore the Circle K and BNP gas stations on the main road into town, and this is perfect Old Florida. No high-rises mar the landscape at this western gateway to Everglades National Park, just off the Tamiami Trail. It was developed in the late 19th century by Barron Collier, a wealthy advertising man. When Collier built a company town to house workers for his numerous projects, including construction of the Tamiami Trail, the town grew and prospered until the Depression and World War II, and in 1953 it changed its name to Everglades City. Today it draws people to the park for canoeing, fishing, and bird-watching excursions. (Airboat tours, though popular with visitors, are banned within the preserve and park because of the environmental damage they cause to the mangroves. They are not recommended even outside the park in this area because operators feed wildlife dog biscuits and marshmallows to attract the alligators to the boats.) The annual Seafood Festival, held the first weekend of February, draws 60,000–75,000 visitors to eat seafood, hear nonstop music, and buy crafts. Dining choices are limited to a few basic eateries. For fine food drive west to Naples. In the past year, several dockside fish markets opened small restaurants inside and outside along the docks. It's best to avoid most of these due to poor food-handling practices. The town is small and unhurried, making it excellent for bicycling. Pedal along the waterfront or take the 2-mi ride along the strand out to Chokoloskee Island.

There's no better place to find information about the park's watery western side than at the **Gulf Coast Visitor Center.** Except during the off-season, it's filled with canoeists checking in for trips to the 10,000 Islands and 99-mi Wilderness Waterway Trail, visitors viewing interpretive exhibits about local flora and fauna while they wait for the departure of a naturalist-led boat trip, rangers answering questions, and backcountry campers purchasing permits. There are no roads from here to other sections of the park. ⊠ *Rte. 29* ☎ *239/695–4731* ✉ *Park free* ⊙ *Mid-Nov.–mid-Apr., daily 7:30–5; mid-Apr.–mid-Nov., daily 8:30–4:30.*

Through artifacts and photographs at the **Museum of the Everglades,** meet the Native Americans, pioneers, businesspeople, and fishermen who played a role in the development of southwest Florida. The museum chronicles the 2,000-year history of human habitation in the southwestern Everglades. It's in the only remaining unaltered structure original to the town of Everglades, where it opened in 1927 as the town's laundry; the building is on the National Register of Historic Places. In addition to the permanent displays, there are traveling exhibits, lectures, and works by local artists. Pick up a free walking guide of the town's historic sites. ⊠ *105 W. Broadway* ☎ *239/695–0008* ✉ *$2* ⊙ *Tues.–Sat. 10–4.*

<table><tr><td>

off the
beaten
path

</td><td>

Smallwood's Store. Ted Smallwood pioneered this last American frontier in 1906 and built a 3,000-square-ft pine trading post raised on pilings in Chokoloskee Bay. Smallwood's granddaughter Lynn McMillin reopened it in 1989, after it had been closed several years, and installed a small gift shop and museum chock-full of original goods from the store; historic photographs; Native American clothing, furs, and hides; and area memorabilia. In March an annual festival celebrates the nearly 100-year relationship the store has had with local Native Americans. ⊠ *360 Mamie St., Chokoloskee Island* ☎ *239/695–2989* ✉ *$2.50* ⊙ *Dec.–Apr., daily 10–5; May–Nov., daily 11–5.*

</td></tr></table>

Where to Stay & Eat

¢–$$$
FodorśChoice
★

✕ **Ivey House Restaurant.** This new eatery is a strong contender for the best restaurant in Everglades City. It combines city savvy with local flavor to yield such dishes as frogs'-legs Provençale sautéed in white wine with onions, mushrooms, tomatoes, and black olives, and Everglades City tournedos in demiglace with mushrooms and artichoke hearts topped with béarnaise sauce. The dining room is brightly lighted, casual, and decorated with plants and high-quality Everglades photographs. There's a Sunday brunch and a "Wednesday Night Gathering" with a prix-fixe menu and a guest lecturer. The clientele is a mix of hotel guests, locals, and day visitors catching a bite after a day on the water or in the swamps. ⊠ *107 Camellia St.* ☎ *239/695–4666 or 239/695–3299* ▭ *MC, V.*

¢–$$$
✕ **JT's Island Grill & Gallery.** In the manner of C. G. McKinney's General Store, which was established here in 1890, the restaurant offers a little of this and a little of that. The emphasis is on local, from the short seafood-dominated menu with seasonal stone crab claws and crab cakes with mango salsa to the walls with artwork depicting Everglades wildlife and landscapes. There's also a sweet and spicy Jamaican jerk with tenderly cooked shrimp and scallops, several tofu dishes, and steak. The more extensive daily lunch fare includes hot and cold sandwiches, wraps, burgers, soups, and salads. ⊠ *238 Mamie St., Chokoloskee Island* ☎ *239/695–3633* ▭ *MC, V* ⊙ *No dinner Sun.–Mon. or Wed.– Thurs.*

¢–$$$
✕ **Rod and Gun Club.** The striking polished woodwork in this historic building dates from the 1920s, when wealthy hunters, anglers, and yachting parties from around the world came for the winter season. The main dining room primarily holds the overflow from the popular enormous

screened porch that overlooks the river. Slow service is a problem; the quality of food is not. Fresh seafood dominates a menu that includes stone crab claws in season, a turf-and-surf combo of steak and shrimp, a swamp-and-turf combo of frogs' legs and steak, and several seafood and pasta pairings. Come by boat or land. ⊠ *200 Riverside Dr.* ☎ *239/ 695–2101* ▭ *No credit cards.*

$–$$ ✕ **Everglades Fish Company.** Every day during stone crab season (October–May) locals, and a growing number of visitors, stop by this fish market to buy the fresh, succulent claws. Pick up a hammer for an extra dollar and take them to your hotel room or the nearby city park for a picnic. There's no debate that these are the best in town. The company ships them, but the cost is outrageous; it's much more affordable to have them pack some in a travel cooler for you to take home. When crab season is over, the inventory leans toward raw fish and raw and cooked shrimp. ⊠ *208 Camellia St.* ☎ *239/695–3241 or 888/695–2208* ▭ *MC, V.*

¢–$$ ✕ **Oar House Restaurant.** Locals line up outside on Friday nights for $12.95 prime rib in this wood-paneled eatery whose picnic table–style booths and mishmash of kitschy fishing implements give it the look of a diner. The menu has a blend of simple seafood and such local specialties as frogs' legs, conch, and gator. To its credit, the service is friendly, prices are reasonable, food is fried in canola and corn oils, and most dishes can be grilled or broiled, if you prefer. It's popular for its country-style breakfasts. ⊠ *305 Collier Ave.* ☎ *239/695–3535* ▭ *AE, D, MC, V.*

¢–$ ✕ **Everglades Seafood Depot.** This 1928 Spanish-style stucco structure on Lake Placid has had many lives. It began as the old Everglades depot, was part of the University of Miami, appeared in the film *Winds across the Everglades,* and has housed several restaurants. Today's menu has well-prepared seafood—from shrimp and grouper to frogs' legs and alligator. The staff is slow but eager to please. For big appetites there are generously portioned entrées of steak and fish specials that include soup or salad, potato or rice, and warm, fresh-baked biscuits. ⊠ *102 Collier Ave.* ☎ *239/695–0075* ▭ *AE, D, MC, V.*

$$ ▦ **Ivey House.** A remodeled 1928 boardinghouse originally for workers
Fodor's Choice building the Tamiami Trail, the Ivey House today fits many budgets. One
★ part is a friendly B&B bargain with shared baths that's open only November–April. The year-round inn, connected by a ramp, has spacious modern rooms with private baths. Most inn rooms surround the screen-enclosed pool and courtyard. Display cases of local flora and fauna decorate the inn, as do photographs of the Everglades and 10,000 Islands taken by photographers who present weekend photo-shoot workshops. The layout is designed to promote camaraderie, but there are secluded patios with chairs and tables for private moments. Rates include a full breakfast. The Ivey House is run by the owners of NACT-Everglades Rentals & Eco Adventures, so stay here before or after the ecotours and save 20% on canoe and kayak rentals. ⊠ *107 Camellia St., 34139* ☎ *239/695– 3299* ▭ *239/695–4155* ⊕ *www.iveyhouse.com* ⇆ *27 rooms, 17 with bath; 1 2-bedroom cottage* ♨ *Restaurant, room service, in-room data ports, some refrigerators, some cable TV, wading pool, boating, bicycles, library, shop, laundry facilities; no smoking* ▭ *MC, V.*

$ ▦ **Bank of the Everglades Inn.** Formerly a bank dating from 1923, this pleasant B&B lodge has spacious rooms, suites, and efficiencies with queen- or king-size beds, stylish coordinating linens, wall coverings, and draperies. Suites and efficiencies have private baths and kitchens. A licensed massage therapist and medical aesthetician operates a new day spa with services ranging from massages and peels to facials and colon hydrotherapy. A complimentary breakfast, including freshly baked breads and muffins, is served in the bank's vault and on the outside deck. Free tennis rackets are provided for use on the public courts next door.

✉ 201 W. Broadway ☎ Box 570, 34139 ☎ 239/695–3151 or 888/431– 1977 🖷 239/695–3335 ⊕ www.banksoftheeverglades.com ⟿ 6 units ♿ Some kitchens, some kitchenettes, cable TV, bicycles, shop; no room phones, no smoking ▤ AE, D, MC, V.

¢ ⚠ **Outdoor Resorts.** This clean, amenity-rich RV resort, set on the water's edge of secluded Chokoloskee Island, has sunny sites with concrete pads. Tropical vegetation adds shade and color. All sites have a view. The property has boat rentals, tennis and shuffleboard, a marina, and a bait shop. A TV hookup and use of a recreation hall and health club are included in the rates and help while the hours away on rainy days. There are rental trailers and a motel for those who come without an RV. *♿ Flush toilets, full hookups, drinking water, laundry facilities, showers, electricity, public telephone, general store, playground, 3 pools ⟿ 283 sites; 8 efficiencies with kitchens, 2 rental trailers ✉ Rte. 29, 6 mi south of Tamiami Trail ☎ Box 39, Chokoloskee Island, 34138 ☎ 239/695–3788 🖷 239/695–3338 ⊕ www.outdoor-resorts.com ▨ Full hookups $40–$55; efficiencies and RV rental trailers $75 ▤ MC, V.*

The Outdoors

BIKING **NACT-Everglades Rentals & Eco Adventures** (✉ Ivey House, 107 Camellia St. ☎ 239/695–4666), the Florida arm of North American Canoe Tours (NACT), rents bikes for $5 per hour, $20 per day (free for Ivey House guests).

BOATING **Glades Haven Marina** (✉ 801 S. Copeland Ave. ☎ 239/695–2579 ⊕ www. gladeshaven.com) Capt. Joe and his wife, Susie, can put you on the water to explore the 10,000 Islands in everything from 16-ft Carolina skiffs and 24-ft pontoon boats to 19-ft sailfish. Rates start at $110 a day, with multiday discounts, a half-day option, and special rates for families. This is one of the few companies that allow overnight boat rentals. It also rent kayaks, canoes, and fishing tackle and has a 24-hour boat ramp and dockage for vessels up to 24 ft.

CANOEING & **Everglades National Park Boat Tours** (✉ Gulf Coast Visitor Center ☎ 239/
KAYAKING 695–4731; 800/445–7724 in Florida) rents 17-ft Grumman canoes for day and overnight use. Rates are $25 per day. Car-shuttle service is provided for canoeists paddling the Wilderness Trail, and travelers with disabilities can be accommodated. **NACT-Everglades Rentals & Eco Adventures** (✉ Ivey House, 107 Camellia St. ☎ 239/695–4666) is an established source for canoes, sea kayaks, and guided Everglades trips (November–April). Canoes cost from $35 the first day, $25 for each day thereafter, and kayaks are from $45 per day. Half-day rentals are available.

GATEWAY TOWNS

The farm towns of Homestead and Florida City, flanked by Everglades National Park on the west and Biscayne National Park on the east, provide the closest visitor facilities to the parks. (The area's better restaurants are in Homestead, but the best lodgings are in Florida City.) The towns date from early in the 20th century, when Henry Flagler extended his railroad to Key West but soon decided that farming would do more for rail revenues than ferrying passengers.

Homestead

❸ *30 mi southwest of Miami.*

After Hurricane Andrew, Homestead rebuilt and redefined itself as the "Gateway to the Keys" and attracted a shopping center, residential development, hotel chains, and a sports center, the Miami-Dade Homestead Motorsports Complex—when car races are scheduled there, hotel rates increase and have minimums. The historic downtown area has become a preservation-driven Main Street city. Krome Avenue (Route 997), which cuts through the city's heart, is lined with restaurants, an arts complex, and antiques shops. West of north–south Krome Avenue, miles of fields grow fresh fruits and vegetables. Some are harvested commercially, while others have U-PICK signs, inviting you to harvest your own. Stands that sell farm-fresh produce and nurseries that grow and sell orchids and tropical plants abound. In addition to its agricultural legacy, the town has an eclectic flavor, attributable to its population mix: descendants of pioneer Crackers, Hispanic growers and farm workers, professionals escaping Miami's hustle and bustle, and latter-day northern retirees. Until Hurricane Andrew, the military had a huge presence at Homestead Air Force Base; the local economy still suffers from the base's closing.

With a saltwater atoll pool that's flushed by tidal action, **Homestead Bayfront Park**, adjacent to Biscayne National Park, is popular among local families as well as anglers and boaters. Highlights include a playground, ramps for people with disabilities (including a ramp that leads into the swimming area), and a picnic pavilion with grills, showers, and rest rooms. ⊠ *9698 S.W. 328th St.* ☎ *305/230–3034* 🖅 *$4 per passenger vehicle, $10 per vehicle with boat, $8 per RV* ☉ *Daily sunrise–sunset.*

I. Stanley Levine and Ellie Schneiderman, founders of the South Florida Art Center in South Beach, are at the forefront of a cultural revival in Homestead. Their fledgling project centers on a 3½-acre complex, **ArtSouth**, which includes the historic First Baptist Church, 28 artists and their studios, galleries, workshops, a gift shop, sculpture garden, and stage. Watch artists at work, take classes, and enjoy performances. Second Saturdays include live entertainment, hands-on art demonstrations, self-guided tours, refreshments, and an antique and collectible car show. ⊠ *240 N. Krome Ave.* ☎ *305/247–9406* 🖅 *Free* ☉ *Tues.–Fri. 9–6, weekends noon–6.*

Where to Stay & Eat

¢–$$ ✕ **Flagler Station Restaurant and Lounge.** Italian, French, and Costa Rican specialties lure the hungry, especially travelers to and from the Keys. You'll find steak, poultry, fish, and lots of pastas, including a scrumptious spinach-stuffed ravioli and a lobster-stuffed cannelloni. Many dishes cost less than $10. High ceilings, subdued lighting, tablecloths, and black-and-white photographs accent the dining room. The patio garden area is casual, but you get the same fresh, uncomplicated fare. Live blues and jazz liven up most weekend nights. Don't just stop here for dinner; the lunch menu satisfies at a bargain price. ⊠ *28 S. Krome Ave.* ☎ *305/ 246–8088* ▤ *AE, D, MC, V.*

★ ¢ ✕ **El Toro Taco.** This rustic, family-run favorite gets high marks for its generous portions, homemade tortilla chips (sometimes a little greasy), and friendly service. Selections range from tasty fajitas, enchiladas, and burritos to more traditional Mexican dishes like *mole de pollo,* which combines unsweetened chocolate and Mexican spices with chicken. Order spicing from mild to tongue-challenging. And if you're tired of the same-old morning fare, consider stopping in here for breakfast. ⊠ *1 S. Krome Ave.* ☎ *305/245–8182* ▤ *D, MC, V* 🍽 *BYOB.*

¢ ✕ **El NicaMex.** More and more gringos are discovering this "plain-Juanita" restaurant frequented primarily by Latin American immigrant farm workers and their families. The food is not Americanized. You get thick, richly flavored corn tortillas in the *gorditas* (tortilla pockets with beef, chicken, or other fillings) and Salvadoran *pupusas* (cornmeal cakes filled with port, cheese, or beans); carrot and cabbage slaw tangy with lime juice instead of vinegar; and roughly chopped jalapeños, tomatoes, and onions in the salsa. Seafood and beef soups are best-sellers and have generous amounts of vegetables and seafood or meat. Choose a domestic or imported beer, pop a coin into the Wurlitzer jukebox, and escape to a foreign land. ⊠ *32 N.W. 1st St., behind the Krome Ave. bandstand,* ☎ *305/246–8300* ⊟ *AE, D, MC, V.*

¢ ✕ **Tiffany's.** A large banyan tree shades this casual restaurant done in a frilly nouveau Victorian style. The room is quaint but noisy. The lunch menu includes crabmeat au gratin, asparagus rolled in ham with hollandaise sauce, shrimp- and egg-salad sandwiches on fresh-baked croissants, and the most popular dish, the daily quiche. Among the homemade desserts, choose from a very tall carrot cake and a harvest pie that has layers of fruits, walnuts, and a caramel topping. Sunday brunch is served, too. ⊠ *22 N.E. 15th St.* ☎ *305/246–0022* ⊟ *MC, V* ⊘ *Closed Mon. No dinner.*

$ 🏨 **Redland Hotel.** When it opened in 1904, the inn was the town's first hotel. It later became the first mercantile store, the first U.S. Post Office, the first library, and the first boarding house. Today, each room has a different layout and furnishings, and some have access to a shared balcony, perfect for gatherings. The style is Victorian, with lots of pastels and reproduction antique furniture. The pub and dining room are fast becoming popular with locals, and there are good restaurants and antiques shops nearby. ⊠ *5 S. Flagler Ave., 33030* ☎ *305/246–1904 or 800/595–1904* ⊕ *www.redlandhotel.com* ⇌ *13 units* ⟁ *Restaurant, room service, fans, in-room data ports, cable TV, in-room VCRs, pub, meeting rooms; no-smoking rooms* ⊟ *AE, D, DC, MC, V.*

¢ 🏨 **Greenstone Motel.** For years this was a ho-hum motel. Now it's part of ArtSouth, an art complex in historic downtown Homestead. Renovations are beginning with signature rooms designed and executed by emerging, resident, and renowned artists such as Romero Britto and Marco. Furnishings are basic throughout and worn in older units. Rooms toward the back are quieter. The staff is friendly and enthusiastic. Free Continental breakfast is set out in the small lobby. ⊠ *304 N. Krome Ave., 33030* ☎ *305/247–8334* ⊕ *www.thegreenstonemotel. com* ⇌ *24 units* ⟁ *Some microwaves, some refrigerators, cable TV with movies, laundry facilities* ⊟ *AE, D, MC, V.*

¢ 🏨 **Grove Inn Country Guesthouse.** It's hard to believe that a few years ago this pleasant, historic, ground-level inn was an ugly duckling. Today, the garden is lush with fruit trees and native plants and the rooms are individually decorated with antiques and period furnishings. Paul, Craig, and Kim, the owners, go out of their way to pamper guests, starting with a country breakfast using local produce, served family-style in a dining room done in Victorian-print pastels. They offer behind-the-scenes tours of orchid nurseries and farms not otherwise open to the public. A vending machine dispenses complimentary cold drinks. ⊠ *22540 S.W. Krome Ave., 6 mi north of downtown, 33170* ☎ *305/247–6572* ⊕ *www.groveinn. com* ⇌ *14 units, 13 doubles, 1 cottage* ⟁ *Dining room, fans, in-room data ports, some kitchens, microwaves, refrigerators, cable TV, pool, piano, laundry facilities, some pets allowed; no-smoking rooms* ⊟ *AE, MC, V.*

Sports & the Outdoors

AUTO RACING The **Miami-Dade Homestead Motorsports Complex** (⊠ 1 Speedway Blvd., 33035 ☎ 305/230–7223 ⊕ www.racemiami.com) is a state-of-the-art facility with two tracks: a 2.21-mi continuous road course and a 1.5-mi oval. There's a schedule of year-round manufacturer and race-team testing, club racing, and other national events.

BOATING Boaters give high ratings to the facilities at **Homestead Bayfront Park.** The 174-slip marina has a ramp, dock, bait-and-tackle shop, fuel station, ice, dry storage, and boat hoist, which can handle vessels up to 25 ft long with lifting rings. The park also has a tidal swimming area. ✉ *9698 S.W. 328th St.* ☎ *305/230–3033* 💲 *$4 per passenger vehicle, $8 per vehicle with boat, $8 per RV, $10 hoist* ☉ *Daily, sunrise–sunset.*

Shopping

In addition to Homestead Boulevard (U.S. 1) and Campbell Drive (Southwest 312th Street and Northeast 8th Street), **Krome Avenue** is popular for shopping. In the heart of old Homestead, it has a brick sidewalk and many antiques stores.

Florida City

⚑ ⑭ *2 mi southwest of Homestead.*

The Florida Turnpike ends in this southernmost town on the peninsula, spilling thousands onto U.S. 1 and eventually west to Everglades National Park, east to Biscayne National Park, or south to the Florida Keys. As the last civilization before 18 mi of mangroves and water, this stretch of U.S. 1 is lined with fast-food eateries, service stations, hotels, bars, dive shops, and restaurants. Hotel rates increase significantly during such special events as the NASCAR races at the nearby Miami-Dade Homestead Motorsports Complex. Like Homestead, Florida City is rooted in agriculture, with hundreds of acres of farmland west of Krome Avenue and a huge farmers market that processes produce shipped nationwide.

Where to Stay & Eat

¢–$$ ✕ **Mutineer Restaurant.** This roadside steak and seafood restaurant with an indoor-outdoor fish and duck pond was built in 1980, back when Florida City was barely on the map. Etched glass divides the bilevel dining rooms, where striped-velvet chairs, stained glass, and a few portholes set the scene; in the lounge are an aquarium and nautical antiques. The big menu offers 18 seafood entrées plus another half dozen daily seafood specials, as well as game, ribs, and steaks. There's an $8.95 hot buffet and salad bar Monday–Saturday 11 AM to 3 PM and live music and dancing Friday and Saturday evenings. ✉ *11 S.E. 1st Ave. (U.S. 1), at Palm Dr.* ☎ *305/245–3377* 🍴 *AE, D, DC, MC, V.*

★ ¢–$$ ✕ **Richard Accursio's Capri Restaurant and King Richard's Room.** Locals have been dining here—one of the oldest family-run restaurants in Miami-Dade County—since 1958. Outside it's a nondescript building with a big parking lot. The interior has dark-wood paneling and heavy wooden furniture. The tasty fare ranges from pizza with light, crunchy crusts and ample toppings to mild, meaty conch chowder. Mussels come in garlic or marinara sauce, and the yellowtail snapper *française* is a worthy selection. Bargain hunters have two choices: the daily early-bird entrées, 4:30–6:30 for $10.50, include soup or salad and potato or spaghetti, and the Monday–Thursday family nights after 4 PM include all-you-can-eat spaghetti, shells, or ziti with salad or soup for $6.95. ✉ *935 N. Krome Ave.* ☎ *305/247–1544* 🍴 *AE, MC, V* ☉ *Closed Sun.*

¢–$ ✕ **Farmers' Market Restaurant.** Although it's in the farmers market and serves fresh vegetables, this restaurant's specialty is seafood. A family of fishermen runs the place, so fish and shellfish are only hours from the sea. Catering to the fishing and farming crowd, it opens at 5:30 AM, serving pancakes, jumbo eggs, and fluffy omelets with home fries or grits. The lunch and dinner menus have shrimp, fish, steaks, and conch baskets, as well as burgers, salads, and sandwiches. Normally the fish comes fried, but you can get it broiled or grilled. ✉ *300 N. Krome Ave.* ☎ *305/242–0008* 🍴 *No credit cards.*

¢ ✗ **Main St. Café.** The café bills itself as "The Music Café" for its Thursday- through Saturday-night dinners with local and national folk, country, and acoustic rock entertainment. The multipage menu of generously sized sandwiches, wraps, wings, chicken tenders, soups, salads, subs, and vegetarian and soy burgers is the same for lunch and dinner. A particularly good deal is the "bottomless" (all you can eat) soup and sandwich specials. Beverage choices include coffee, beer, wine, juice, shakes, smoothies, floats, and sodas. The cobbler is divine, as is the brownie, a thick double-fudge-walnut confection. ✉ *128 N. Krome Ave.* ☎ *305/ 245–7575* ⊟ *AE, D, MC, V* ⊘ *No dinner Sun.–Wed.*

¢ ✗ **Sonny's Real Pit Bar-B-Q.** Sonny Tillman started smoking barbecue in 1968. Though the company now has more than 145 restaurants throughout the South and is the largest barbecue chain in the country, its eateries are still rustic, down-home, family-friendly and bargain-priced for the quality. The menu has wood-fired beef, pork, chicken, and smoked turkey sandwiches and dinners, which include slaw, potato, and garlic bread. Ribs and pulled pork are popular items, as are the all-you-can-eat chicken and ribs specials. Choose veggies, fruits, salad, baked sweet potatoes, and brunswick stew from the 40-item salad bar. ✉ *33505 U. S. 1 (S. Dixie Hwy.)* ☎ *305/245–8585* ⊟ *AE, D, DC, MC, V.*

$$ ⌨ **Hampton Inn.** Racing fans can hear the engines roar from this two-story motel next to an outlet mall and within 15 minutes of the raceway and Everglades and Biscayne national parks. Carpeted rooms are bright and clean and have upholstered chairs, coffee maker, and an iron and ironing board. Included are a Continental breakfast and local calls. ✉ *124 E. Palm Dr., 33034* ☎ *305/247–8833 or 800/426–7866* ⊟ *305/ 247–6456* ⊕ *www.hamptoninnfloridacity.com* ⊅ *123 units* ⟁ *Some refrigerators, cable TV with movies, pool, laundry service; no-smoking rooms* ⊟ *AE, D, DC, MC, V.*

$ ⌨ **Best Western Gateway to the Keys.** If you want easy access to Everglades and Biscayne national parks as well as the Florida Keys, you'll be well situated at this newly renovated two-story motel two blocks off the Florida Turnpike. All rooms are done in tropical colors and have a coffeemaker, hair dryer, and iron. Standard rooms have two queen-size beds or one king-size bed and include a free newspaper. Rooms around the lushly landscaped pool cost slightly more. ✉ *411 S. Krome Ave., 33034* ☎ *305/246–5100* ⊟ *305/242–0056* ⊕ *www.bestwestern.com* ⊅ *114 units* ⟁ *In-room data ports, microwaves, refrigerators, cable TV with movies, pool, hot tub, laundry facilities, meeting rooms; no smoking* ⊟ *AE, D, DC, MC, V* �🍴 *CP.*

¢–$ ⌨ **Comfort Inn.** This is the best buy of the chain motels in town. A third of the rooms are new; the others are recently renovated. Rooms are large, have contemporary tropical furnishings, and are on two floors (there is no elevator). They're outfitted with irons, hair dryers, and coffeemakers. Continental breakfast and newspapers are free. Room Internet connections are high speed. It's just off U.S. 1, where restaurants and fast-food eateries abound. ✉ *333 S.E. 1st Ave., 33034* ☎ *305/248–4009* ⊟ *305/248–7935* ⊕ *www.comfortinn.com* ⊅ *124 units* ⟁ *Dining room, in-room data ports, in-room safes (fee), microwaves, refrigerators, cable TV with movies, pool, laundry facilities, business services, meeting rooms; no smoking* ⊟ *AE, D, V.*

¢ ⌨ **Everglades Hostel.** This HI-AYH hostel is in a minimally restored art deco building on a lush, private acre between Everglades and Biscayne national parks, 20 mi north of Key Largo. Stay in clean, spacious private and dorm style rooms; relax in indoor and outdoor quiet areas; watch videos or TV on a big-screen TV; and take boating, airboat, diving, snorkeling, and sightseeing tours. At mealtime, cook in the communal kitchen, pitch in for a communal dinner ($3), or walk to a nearby restaurant.

Pets are welcome. There's local transportation, and the staff picks up guests from the nearby Greyhound station. ✉ *20 S.W. 2nd Ave., 33034* ☎ *305/248-1122 or 800/372-3874* 🖷 *305/245-7622* ⊕ *www. evergladeshostel.com* ⇔ *46 beds in dorm-style rooms with shared bath, 2 private rooms with shared bath* △ *Dining room, picnic area, fans, dive shop, snorkeling, boating, bicycles, hiking, bicycles, recreation room, laundry facilities, Internet, some pets allowed; no room phones, no room TVs, no smoking* ▭ *MC, V.*

¢ 📺 **Travelodge.** This bargain motor lodge is close to the Florida Turnpike, Everglades and Biscayne national parks, the Florida Keys, and the Miami-Dade Homestead Motorsports Complex. While rooms are clean and colorful but smallish, they have more amenities than usually found in this price range, including complimentary breakfast and newspaper, coffeemaker, hair dryer, iron with ironing board, and voice mail. Fast-food and chain eateries, gas stations, and a visitor's bureau are within walking distance. ✉ *409 S.E. 1st Ave., 33034* ☎ *305/248-9777 or 800/758-0618* 🖷 *305/248-9750* ⊕ *www.travelodgefloridacity.com* ⇔ *88 units* △ *Dining room, in-room safes, microwaves, refrigerators, cable TV with movies, pool, dry cleaning, laundry facilities* ▭ *AE, D, MC, V.*

Shopping
Prime Outlets at Florida City (✉ 250 E. Palm Dr.) has more than 40 dis-
★ count stores plus a small food court. **Robert Is Here** (✉ 19200 Palm Dr. [S.W. 344th St.] ☎ 305/246-1592), a remarkable fruit stand, sells vegetables, fresh-fruit milk shakes, 10 flavors of honey, more than 100 flavors of jams and jellies, fresh juices, salad dressings, and some 40 kinds of tropical fruits, including carambola, litchi, egg fruit, monstera, sapodilla, soursop, sugar apple, and tamarind. The stand started in 1960, when six-year-old Robert sat at this spot selling his father's bumper crop of cucumbers. Now Robert ships around the world, and everything is first quality. Seconds are given to needy area families. The stand opens at 8 and never closes earlier than 7. Despite a recent renovation, it retains its rustic charm.

BISCAYNE NATIONAL PARK

Occupying 180,000 acres along the southern portion of Biscayne Bay, south of Miami and north of the Florida Keys, this national park is 96% underwater, and its altitude ranges from 4 ft above sea level to 10 fathoms, or 60 ft, below. Contained within it are four distinct zones, which from shore to sea are mangrove forest along the coast, Biscayne Bay, the undeveloped upper Florida Keys, and coral reefs. Mangroves line the mainland shore much as they do elsewhere in South Florida. Biscayne Bay functions as a lobster sanctuary and a nursery for fish, sponges, and crabs. Manatees and sea turtles frequent its warm, shallow waters. Lamentably, the bay is under assault from forces similar to those in Florida Bay. To the east, about 8 mi off the coast, lie 44 tiny keys, stretching 18 nautical mi north–south and accessible only by boat. There is no commercial transportation between the mainland and the islands, and only a handful can be visited: Elliott, Boca Chita, Adams, and Sands keys. The rest are either wildlife refuges or too small, or have rocky shores or waters too shallow for boats. It's best to explore the Keys between December and April, when the mosquito population is relatively quiescent. Bring repellent just in case. Diving is best in summer, when calmer wind and smaller seas result in clearer waters. Another 3 mi east of the Keys, in the ocean, lies the park's main attraction—the northernmost section of Florida's living tropical coral reefs. Some are the size of a student's desk, others as large as a football field. Take a glass-bottom boat ride to see this underwater wonderland, but you really have to snorkel or scuba dive to appreciate it fully. A diverse population of colorful fish—angelfish, gobies, grunts, parrot fish, pork fish, wrasses, and many more—flits through the reefs. Shipwrecks from the 18th century are evidence of the area's international maritime heritage. A Native American midden (shell mound) dating from AD 1000, and Boca Chita Key, listed on the National Register of Historic Places for its 10 historic structures, illustrate the park's rich cultural heritage. More than 170 species of birds have been seen around the park. Although all the Keys are excellent for birding, Jones Lagoon, south of Adams Key, between Old Rhodes Key and Totten Key, is one of the best. It's approachable only by nonmotorized craft.

Convoy Point

⓯ *9 mi east of Florida City, 30 mi south of downtown Miami.*

Reminiscent of area pioneer homes, with wooden walks and a metal roof, the **Dante Fascell Visitor Center** has a wide veranda with views across mangroves and Biscayne Bay. Inside is a museum, where hands-on and historical exhibits and videos explore the park's four ecosystems. Among the facilities are a 50-seat auditorium, the park's canoe and tour concessionaire, rest rooms with showers, a ranger information area, and gift shop. The last also sells packaged sandwiches and snacks. A short trail and boardwalk lead to a jetty and launch ramp. This is the only area of the park accessible without a boat. ⊠ *9700 S.W. 328th St., Homestead* ☎ *305/230–7275* ⊕ *www.nps.gov/bisc* ⊠ *Free* ☉ *Daily 8:30–5.*

The Outdoors

CANOEING **Biscayne National Underwater Park, Inc.** (⊠ Convoy Point Visitor Center, Box 1270, Homestead 33090 ☎ 305/230–1100), the park's official concessionaire, has half a dozen canoes and kayaks for rent on a first-come, first-served basis. Canoe prices are $9 an hour, kayaks $16 an hour. It's open daily 9–3.

SCUBA DIVING & **Biscayne National Underwater Park, Inc.** (⊠ Convoy Point Visitor Center,
SNORKELING Box 1270, Homestead 33090 ☎305/230–1100) rents equipment and conducts snorkel and dive trips aboard the 45-ft *Boca Chita.* Three-hour snorkel trips ($32.95) leave twice a day on weekdays, once a day on weekends, and include mask, fins, snorkel, vest, and instruction. About half the time is spent on the reef and wrecks. Two-tank scuba trips to shallow reefs depart at 8:30 AM Saturday–Sunday, with a wall dive for advanced divers on Sunday at the same times, costing $47.95, tanks and weights included. Additional trips are offered in winter. Complete gear rental ($42 extra) and instruction are available. Even with a reservation (recommended), you should arrive one hour before departure to sign up for gear.

Elliott Key

⓰ *9 mi east of Convoy Point.*

This key, accessible only by boat (on your own or from the concessionaire for $25.95 round-trip or $15.95 if you take a snorkel trip), has a rebuilt boardwalk made from recycled plastic and two nature trails with tropical plant life. Take an informal, ranger-led nature walk or walk its 7-mi length on your own along a rough path through a hammock. Videos shown at the ranger station describe the island. Facilities include rest rooms, picnic tables, fresh drinking water, showers (cold), grills, and a campground. Pets are allowed on the island but not on trails. A 30-ft-wide sandy beach about a mile north of the harbor on the west (bay) side of the key is the only one in the national park. Boaters like to anchor off it to swim. For day use only, it has picnic areas and a short trail that follows the shore and cuts through the hammock.

Where to Stay

⚠ **Elliott Key Campground.** The grassy, beachfront tent sites are populated with plenty of native hardwood trees, and there's no light pollution here, so the night sky is brilliant with stars. Spend the day swimming, snorkeling, hiking trails, and fishing. Parties of up to 25 people can share the group campsite, and leashed pets are welcome. Regular ferry service and boat rental are nonexistent, but the park concessionaire's snorkel boat provides drop-off and pickup service to campers ($25.95 round-trip). Reservations are required. If you bring a boat, dock in the marina overnight for $5. Bring plenty of insect repellent. ⚘ *Flush toilets, drinking water, showers (cold), grills, picnic tables, swimming* ⤴ *40 sites* ✉ *9700 S.W. 328th St., Homestead 33090* ☎ *305/230–7275* ⊕ *www.nps.gov/bisc* ✉ *$10* ▭ *No credit cards.*

Boca Chita Key

⑰ *10 mi northeast of Convoy Point.*

This island was once owned by Mark C. Honeywell, former president of Minneapolis's Honeywell Company. A ½-mi hiking trail curves around the south side of the island. Climb the 65-ft ornamental lighthouse for a panoramic view of Miami and surrounding waters. There is no fresh water, access is by private boat only, and no pets are allowed.

Where to Stay

⚠ **Boca Chita Campground.** This small, flat island has a grassy, waterside campground shaded by palm trees that whisper in the breeze. The views are awesome. Check with the park concessionaire for drop-off and pickup service ($25.95 round-trip). Reservations are required. There is no running fresh water. ⚘ *Flush toilets, grills, picnic tables* ⤴ *39 sites* ✉ *9700 S.W. 328th St., Homestead 33090* ☎ *305/230–7275* ⊕ *www.nps.gov/bisc* ▭ *No credit cards.*

Adams Key

⑱ *9 mi southeast of Convoy Point.*

This small key, a stone's throw off the western tip of Elliott Key, is open for day use and has picnic areas, rest rooms, dockage, and a short trail that runs along the shore and through a hardwood hammock. Access is by private boat.

BIG CYPRESS NATIONAL PRESERVE

Through the 1950s and early 1960s, the world's largest cypress-logging industry prospered in the Big Cypress Swamp. The industry died out in the 1960s, and the government began buying parcels. Today, 729,000 acres, or nearly half of the swamp, have become this national preserve. The word "big" in its name refers not to the size of the trees but to the swamp, which juts down into the north side of Everglades National Park like a piece in a jigsaw puzzle. Its size and strategic location make it an important link in the region's hydrological system, in which rainwater first flows through the preserve, then south into the park, and eventually into Florida Bay. Its variegated pattern of wet prairies, ponds, marshes, sloughs, and strands provides a wildlife sanctuary, and due to a politically dictated policy of balanced land use—"use without abuse"—the watery wilderness is devoted to research and recreation as well as preservation. The preserve allows—in limited areas—hunting, off-road vehicle (airboat, swamp buggy) use by permit, and cattle grazing. Compared to Everglades National Park, the preserve is less developed and has fewer visitors. That makes it ideal for naturalists, birders, and hikers who prefer to see more wildlife than humans. Roadside picnic areas are located off the Tamiami Trail. There are three types of trails—walking, canoeing, and bicycling; none are interpretive (though interpretive trails and several boardwalks are in the works). All three existing trail types are easily accessed from the Tamiami Trail near the preserve's visitor center. Equipment can be rented from outfitters in Everglades City, 24 mi west, and Naples, 40 mi west.

THE EVERGLADES A TO Z

To research prices, get advice from other travelers, and book travel arrangements, visit www.fodors.com.

AIRPORTS

Miami International Airport (MIA) is 34 mi from Homestead and 83 mi from Flamingo in Everglades National Park. Airporter runs shuttle buses three times daily that stop at the Hampton Inn in Florida City on their way between MIA and the Florida Keys. Shuttle service, which takes about an hour, runs 6:10–5:20 from Florida City, 7:30–6 from the airport. Reserve in advance. Pickups can be arranged for all baggage-claim areas. The cost is $25 one-way. Greyhound Lines buses from MIA to the Keys make a stop in Homestead four times a day. Buses leave from Concourse E, lower level, and cost from $9.25 one-way, from $18.25 round-trip. SuperShuttle operates 11-passenger air-conditioned vans to Homestead. Service from MIA is available around the clock; booths are outside most luggage areas on the lower level. For the return to MIA, reserve 24 hours in advance. The one-way cost is $43 per person for the first person, $14 for each additional person at the same address.
🚹 Airport Information **Miami International Airport (MIA)** ☎ 305/876-7000 ⊕ www. miami-airport.com. **Airporter** ☎ 800/830-3413. **Greyhound Lines** ☎ 800/231-2222 ✉ 5 N.E. 3rd Rd., Homestead ☎ 305/247-2040. **SuperShuttle** ☎ 305/871-2000 or 800/ 874-8885.

BOAT TRAVEL

If you're entering the United States by pleasure boat, you must phone U.S. Customs either from a marine phone or upon first arriving ashore. Bring aboard the proper *NOAA Nautical Charts* before you cast off to explore park waters. The charts run $17 at many marine stores in South Florida, at the Convoy Point Visitor Center in Biscayne National Park, and at Flamingo Marina in the Everglades. The annual *Waterway Guide* (southern regional edition) is widely used by boaters. Bookstores all over South Florida sell it, or order it directly from the publisher for $39 plus $8 shipping and handling.
🚹 Boat Information **U.S. Customs** ☎ 800/432-1216. *Waterway Guide* ⑤ 326 1st St., Suite 400, Annapolis, MD 21403 ☎ 800/233-3359.

BUS TRAVEL

The Dade-Monroe Express provides daily bus service from the Florida City Wal-Mart Supercenter to Mile Marker 50 in Marathon. The bus makes several stops in Florida City, then heads for the islands for daily round-trips on the hour from 6 AM to 10 PM. The cost is $1.50 each way.
🚹 Bus Information **Dade-Monroe Express** ☎ 305/770-3131.

CAR RENTAL

Agencies in the area include A&A Auto Rental, Budget, and Enterprise Rent-a-Car.
🚹 Local Agencies **A&A Auto Rental** ✉ 30005 S. Dixie Hwy., Homestead 33030 ☎ 305/ 246-0974. **Budget** ✉ 29949 S. Dixie Hwy., Homestead 33030 ☎ 305/248-4524 or 800/

527-0700. **Enterprise Rent-a-Car** ✉ 29130 S. Dixie Hwy., Homestead 33030 ☎ 305/246-2056 or 800/736-8222.

CAR TRAVEL

From Miami the main highways to the area are U.S. 1, the Homestead Extension of Florida Turnpike, and Krome Avenue (Route 997 [old U.S. 27]). To reach Everglades National Park's Ernest F. Coe Visitor Center and Flamingo, head west on Route 9336 (Palm Drive) in Florida City and follow signs. From Florida City the Ernest F. Coe Visitor Center is 11 mi; Flamingo is 49 mi. The north entrance of Everglades National Park at Shark Valley is reached by taking the Tamiami Trail about 20 mi west of Krome Avenue. To reach the west entrance of Everglades National Park at the Gulf Coast Visitor Center in Everglades City, take Route 29 south from the Tamiami Trail. To reach Biscayne National Park from Homestead, take U.S. 1 or Krome Avenue to Lucy Street (Southeast 8th Street) and turn east. Lucy Street becomes North Canal Drive (Southwest 328th Street). Follow signs for about 8 mi to the park headquarters.

EMERGENCIES

Dial 911 for police, fire, or ambulance. In the national parks, rangers answer police, fire, and medical emergencies. The Florida Fish and Wildlife Conservation Commission, a division of the Florida Department of Natural Resources, maintains a 24-hour telephone service for reporting boating emergencies and natural-resource violations. The Miami Beach Coast Guard Base responds to local marine emergencies and reports of navigation hazards. The base broadcasts on VHF-FM Channel 16. The National Weather Service supplies local forecasts.
🖪 **Hospital emergency line** ☎ 305/596-6556. **Homestead Hospital** ✉ 160 N.W. 13th St., Homestead ☎ 305/248-3232; 305/596-6557 physician referral. **Florida Fish and Wildlife Conservation Commission** ☎ 305/956-2500. **Miami Beach Coast Guard Base** ✉ 100 MacArthur Causeway, Miami Beach ☎ 305/535-4300 or 305/535-4314. **National Parks-Biscayne unit** ☎ 305/247-7272. **National Parks-Everglades unit** ☎ 305/247-7272. **National Weather Service** ☎ 305/229-4522.

ENGLISH-LANGUAGE MEDIA

NEWSPAPERS & MAGAZINES   The *South Dade News Leader* is published thrice weekly and covers Homestead, Florida City, and the Redland areas. *Everglades Echo* comes out on Tuesday in Everglades City.

TELEVISION & RADIO   WLRN is National Public Radio, on 91.3, 92.1, or 93.5, depending on your location. WLVE 93.9 plays easy listening; WFLC 97.3, pop.

TAXIS

South Dade Taxi covers the Everglades.
🖪 **Taxi Information** **South Dade Taxi** ☎ 305/256-4444.

TOURS

The National Park Service has free programs, typically focusing on native wildlife, plants, and park history. At Biscayne National Park, for example, rangers give informal tours of Elliott and Boca Chita keys, which you can arrange in advance, depending on ranger availability. Contact the respective visitor center for details. Wings 10,000 Islands Aero-Tours operates scenic, low-level flight tours of the 10,000 Islands, Big Cypress National Preserve, Everglades National Park, and the Gulf of Mexico in a Cessna 185 floatplane. On the 20- to 90-minute flights, see saw-grass prairies, Native American shell mounds, alligators, and wading birds. Prices start at $30 per person. For an all- or multiday outing, opt for flights across the gulf to the Florida Keys or Dry Tortugas in a floatplane. The outfit sells postcards and prints of local scenery shot from the air. Tour season is November–May 20. Wooten's Everglades Airboat

Tours runs airboat and swamp-buggy tours ($17) through the Everglades. (Swamp buggies are giant tractorlike vehicles with oversize rubber wheels.) Tours last approximately 30 minutes. Southwest of Florida City near the entrance to Everglades National Park, Everglades Alligator Farm runs a 4-mi, 30-minute tour of the River of Grass with departures 20 minutes after the hour. The tour ($14.50) includes a free hourly alligator, snake, or wildlife show, or take in the show only ($9).

From the Shark Valley area, Buffalo Tiger's Florida Everglades Airboat Ride is operated by a former chairman of the Miccosukee tribe. Miccosukee Indian guides narrate the 35- to 40-minute trip from the perspective of the Native Americans, who have eked out a living there since the 1800s. Trips run on the north side of Tamiami Trail, where there is more water and wildlife, and includes a stop at an old Native American camp. Tours cost $10 and operate 10–5 daily, except Friday. Reservations are not required. Coopertown Airboat Ride operates the oldest airboat rides in the Everglades (since 1945). The 30- to 40-minute tour ($14) visits two hammocks and alligator holes. Everglades Gator Park offers 45-minute narrated airboat tours ($15). Everglades Safari Park runs 40-minute airboat rides for $15. The price includes a show and gator tour. The Miccosukee Indian Village 30-minute narrated airboat ride stops off at a 100-year-old family camp in the Everglades to hear tales and allow passengers to walk around and explore ($10) in addition to its other attractions.

When the namesake owner sold Ray Cramer's Everglades Airboat Tours, Inc. to longtime friend Bill Barlow, with whom he had fished, frogged, and hunted in the Everglades since 1949, Bill didn't change anything but the number of trips he offered a day. His two-hour personalized excursions, on airboats accommodating only 6 to 12 passengers, venture 40 mi into the River of Grass. Daytime trips are exciting, but the tour that departs an hour before sundown lets you see birds and fish in daylight and alligators, raccoons, and other nocturnal animals when night falls. The two-hour tour costs $40 per person. Half-day trips for two to four people cost $275 for the group. Tours at Biscayne National Park are run by people-friendly Biscayne National Underwater Park, Inc. Daily trips (at 10, with a second trip at 1 during high season, depending on demand) explore the park's living coral reefs 10 mi offshore on *Reef Rover IV*, a 53-ft glass-bottom boat that carries up to 48 passengers. On days when the weather is unsuitable for reef viewing, an alternative three-hour, ranger-led interpretive tour visits Boca Chita Key. Reservations are recommended. The cost is $22.95, and you should arrive at least one hour before departure.

If you're in Everglades National Park, climb aboard a six-passenger boat for the four-hour narrated Dolphin Cruise ($39) through the shallow waters of the backcountry. Flamingo Lodge, Marina & Outpost Resort Boat Tours is the official concession authorized to operate sightseeing tours through Everglades National Park. The two-hour backcountry cruise ($18) is the most popular. The boat winds under a heavy canopy of mangroves, revealing abundant wildlife—from alligators, crocodiles, and turtles to herons, hawks, and egrets. A quieter option is the Sailboat Cruise ($18) into Florida Bay that runs mid-December to spring. The 90-minute Florida Bay cruise ($12) ventures into the bay to explore shallow nursery areas and encounter plentiful bird life and often dolphins, sea turtles, and sharks. Sunset cruises run $20. On the west side, Everglades National Park Boat Tours is the official park concession authorized to operate 1½-hour tours ($16) through the 10,000 Islands region and mangrove wilderness. Boats can accommodate large numbers and wheelchairs (not electric), and one large boat has drink concessions. The 2½-hour Mangrove Wilderness tour ($25) ventures into the shallow waters of the mangrove community, where birds nest and fish have their nurseries, but only when the tide is high enough.

Everglades Rentals & Eco Adventures leads one-day to nine-night Everglades tours November–April. Highlights include bird and gator sightings, mangrove forests, no-man's-land beaches, relics of the hideouts of infamous and just plain reclusive characters, and spectacular sunsets. Included in the cost of extended tours ($450–$1,225) are canoes or kayaks, all necessary equipment, a guide, meals, and lodging for the first night at the Ivey House. There is a four-person minimum. Day trips with a naturalist by van, kayak, canoe, or powerboat cost $50–$125. Starting at the Shark Valley visitor center, Shark Valley Tram Tours follows a 15-mi loop road into the interior, stopping at a 50-ft observation tower especially good for viewing gators. Two-hour narrated tours cost $11 and depart hourly 9–4 December–April; the rest of the year they run from 9:30 to 3. Reservations are recommended December–April.

🔁 Tour Information Biscayne National Underwater Park, Inc. ✉ Convoy Point, east end of North Canal Dr. [9700 S.W. 328th St.] ☎ Box 1270, Homestead 33090 ☎ 305/230-7275 ⊕ www.nps.gov/bisc. **Buffalo Tiger's Florida Everglades Airboat Ride** ✉ 30 mi west of Florida Tpke. on Tamiami Trail ☎ 305/559-5250 or 305/382-0719. **Coopertown Airboat Ride** ✉ 5 mi west of Krome Ave. on Tamiami Trail ☎ 305/226-6048 ⊕ www.coopertownairboats.com. **Everglades Alligator Farm** ✉ 40351 S.W. 192nd Ave. ☎ 305/247-2628 ⊕ www.everglades.com. **Everglades Gator Park** ✉ 12 mi west of Florida Tpke. on Tamiami Trail ☎ 305/559-2255 or 800/559-2205 ⊕ www.gatorpark. com. **Everglades National Park Boat Tours** ✉ Gulf Coast Visitor Center, Everglades City ☎ 239/695-2591; 800/445-7724 in Florida ⊕ www.nps.gov/ever. **Everglades Rentals & Eco Adventures** ✉ Ivey House, 107 Camellia St. ☎ Box 5038, Everglades City 34139 ☎ 239/695-3299 ⊕ www.iveyhouse.com. **Everglades Safari Park** ✉ 26700 Tamiami Trail, 9 mi west of Krome Ave. ☎ 305/226-6923 or 305/223-3804 ⊕ www. evergladessafaripark.com. **Flamingo Lodge, Marina & Outpost Resort Boat Tours** ✉ 1 Flamingo Lodge Hwy., Flamingo ☎ 239/695-3101 Ext. 286 or 180 ⊕ www.flamingolodge. com. **Miccosukee Indian Village** ✉ 25 mi west of Florida Tpke. on Tamiami Trail ☎ 305/223-8380 ⊕ www.miccosukee.com/mivillage.html. **Ray Cramer's Everglades Airboat Tours, Inc.** ✉ Coopertown ☎ Box 940082, Miami 33194 ☎ 305/852-5339 or 305/221-9888. **Shark Valley Tram Tours** ☎ Box 1739, Tamiami Station, Miami 33144 ☎ 305/221-8455 ⊕ www.nps.gov/ever/visit/tours.htm. **Wings Ten Thousand Islands Aero-Tours** ✉ Everglades Airport, 650 Everglades City Airpark Rd. ☎ Box 482, Everglades City 34139 ☎ 239/695-3296. **Wooten's Everglades Airboat Tours** ✉ Wooten's Alligator Farm, 1½ mi east of Rte. 29 on Tamiami Trail ☎ 239/695-2781 or 800/282-2781 ⊕ www.wootens.com.

VISITOR INFORMATION

🔁 Tourist Information Big Cypress National Preserve ☎ HCR 61, Box 11, Ochopee 34141 ☎ 239/695-4111 ⊕ www.nps.gov/bicy. **Biscayne National Park** Dante Fascell Visitor Center, ✉ 9700 S.W. 328th St. ☎ Box 1369, Homestead 33090-1369 ☎ 305/230-7275 ⊕ www.nps.gov/bisc. **Everglades City Chamber of Commerce** ✉ Rte. 29 and Tamiami Trail ☎ Box 130, Everglades City 34139 ☎ 239/695-3941 ⊕ www.florida-everglades. com/chamber/home.htm. **Everglades National Park** Ernest F. Coe Visitor Center ✉ 40001 Rte. 9336, Homestead 33034-6733 ☎ 305/242-7700 ⊕ www.nps.gov/ever. **Flamingo Visitor Center** ✉ 1 Flamingo Lodge Hwy., Flamingo 33034-6798 ☎ 239/695-2945. **Gulf Coast Visitor Center** ✉ Rte. 29, Everglades City 34139 ☎ 239/695-3311 ⊕ www.nps. gov/ever. **Greater Homestead-Florida City Chamber of Commerce** ✉ 43 N. Krome Ave., Homestead 33030 ☎ 305/247-2332 ⊕ www.chamberinaction.com. **Tropical Everglades Visitor Association** ✉ 160 U.S. 1, Florida City 33034 ☎ 305/245-9180 or 800/388-9669 ⊕ www.tropicaleverglades.com.

FORT LAUDERDALE AND BROWARD COUNTY

3

FODOR'S CHOICE

Banyan Marina Resort, Downtown and Beach Causeways
Broadwalk, classic promenade, Hollywood
Fort Lauderdale Beachfront, Along the Beach
Hyatt Regency Pier Sixty-Six, Downtown and Beach Causeways
Mark's Las Olas, contemporary food, Along the Beach
Marriott's Harbor Beach Resort, On the Beach
Shula's on the Beach, hearty American fare Along the Beach

HIGHLY RECOMMENDED

RESTAURANTS Armadillo Cafe, Davie
Blue Moon Fish Company, Along the Beach
Brooks, Deerfield Beach
By Word of Mouth, Along the Beach
Cafe Maxx, Pompano Beach
Canyon Southwest Cafe, Along the Beach
Cap's Place, Lighthouse Point
Whale's Rib, Deerfield Beach

HOTELS Best Western Pelican Beach, On the Beach
Lago Mar Resort & Club, On the Beach
The Westin Diplomat Resort & Spa, Hollywood
Manta Ray Inn, Hollywood

WHAT TO SEE Bonnet House, Along the Beach
Graves Museum of Archaeology, Dania Beach
Museum of Art, Downtown
IGFA Fishing Hall of Fame and Museum, Dania Beach
Museum of Discovery and Science/Blockbuster IMAX Theater, Downtown
Riverwalk, Downtown

Updated by
Lynne Helm

COLLEGE STUDENTS FROM THE 1960S returning to Fort Lauderdale for vacations today would be hard pressed to recognize the onetime Sun and Suds Spring Break Capital of the Universe. Back then, Fort Lauderdale's beachfront was lined with T-shirt shops interspersed with quickie food outlets, and downtown consisted of a lone office tower, some dilapidated government buildings, and motley other structures waiting to be razed. Today, the beach has upscale shops and restaurants, while downtown growth of recent years has exploded with new office and luxury residential development.

The 1960 the film *Where the Boys Are* changed everything for the city. The movie depicted how college students—upward of 20,000—were swarming to the city for the spring break phenomenon. By 1985 the 20,000 had mushroomed to 350,000. Hotel owners complained of a dozen or more students cramming into a room, with civility hitting new lows. Drug trafficking and petty theft proliferated along with downscale bars staging wet T-shirt and banana-eating contests. Fed up, city leaders adopted policies and restrictions designed to encourage spring breakers to go elsewhere. They did, and the complaints of lost business are few—given a new era attracting a far more sophisticated, affluent crowd.

A major beneficiary is Las Olas Boulevard, a shopping street once moribund after 5 PM, which has reinvented itself as a hot venue, with a new mix of trendy shops. Ever more restaurants have sprung up, and both visitors and locals often make an evening of strolling the boulevard. On-street parking on weekends has slowed traffic, providing more of a village feel. Farther west, along New River, is evidence of Fort Lauderdale's cultural renaissance: the Arts and Entertainment District and its crown jewel, the Broward Center for the Performing Arts. Still farther west, in the community of Sunrise, is the Office Depot Center (formerly the National Car Rental Center), serving as the county's major-league sports and concert venue and as home arena for the National Hockey League's Florida Panthers. Of course, a captivating shoreline with wide ribbons of sand for beachcombing and sunbathing is what continues to make Fort Lauderdale and Broward County a major draw.

Tying this all together is a transportation system that, while becoming more crowded, is relatively hassle free compared to elsewhere in congested South Florida. An expressway connects the city and suburbs and provides a direct route to the Fort Lauderdale–Hollywood International Airport and Port Everglades. For a slower, more scenic way to really see this canal-laced city, simply hop a water taxi. None of this was envisioned by Napoleon Bonaparte Broward, Florida's governor from 1905 to 1909, for whom the county was named. His drainage schemes opened much of the marshy Everglades region for farming, ranching, and settling (in retrospect, an environmental disaster). But it was for Major William Lauderdale, who built a fort at the river's mouth in 1838 during the Seminole Indian wars, that the city was named.

Incorporated in 1911 with just 175 residents, Fort Lauderdale grew rapidly during the Florida boom of the 1920s. Today its population is 150,000, and suburbs keep growing—1.6 million live in the county's 30 municipalities and unincorporated areas. Once oriented toward retirees, Broward now attracts younger, working-age families, many living in such newer communities as Weston, southwest of Fort Lauderdale. With a revitalized downtown that now includes multiuse complexes mixing retail and loft housing, the city's many young professionals also are buying and revamping aging beachside condominiums. Long a sane, pleasant place to live, Greater Fort Lauderdale is now one of Florida's most diverse, dynamic places to vacation.

Exploring Fort Lauderdale & Broward County

The Fort Lauderdale metro area is laid out in a basic grid system, and only myriad canals and waterways interrupt the straight-line path of streets and roads. Nomenclature is important here. Streets, roads, courts, and drives run east–west. Avenues, terraces, and ways run north–south. Boulevards can (and do) run any which way. For visitors, Las Olas Boulevard is one of the most important east–west thoroughfares from the beach to downtown, whereas Route A1A—referred to as Atlantic Boulevard and Ocean Boulevard along some stretches—runs along the north–south oceanfront. These names can confuse visitors, since there are separate streets called Atlantic and Ocean in Hollywood and Pompano Beach. Boulevards, composed of either pavement or water, give Fort Lauderdale its distinct character. Honeycombed with more than 260 mi of navigable waterways, the city is home port for about 44,000 privately owned boats. An easy way to tour the canals is via the city's water-taxi system, made up of small motor launches, carrying anywhere from 27 to 70 or so passengers, that provide transportation and quick, narrated tours. Larger, multiple deck touring vessels and motorboat rentals for self-guided tours are other options. The massive Intracoastal Waterway, paralleling Route A1A, is the nautical equivalent of an interstate highway. It runs north–south between downtown Fort Lauderdale and the beach and provides easy access to neighboring beach communities—Deerfield Beach and Pompano Beach lie to the north while Dania Beach and Hollywood lie to the south.

About the Restaurants

Greater Fort Lauderdale offers some of the finest, most varied dining of any U.S. city its size. From among more than 3,500 wining and dining establishments in Broward, choose from basic Americana or the cuisines of Asia, Europe, or Central and South America and enjoy more than just food.

About the Hotels

Though not as posh as Palm Beach or as popular as Miami Beach, Fort Lauderdale has respectable lodging choices, from beachfront luxury suites to intimate B&Bs to chain hotels along the Intracoastal Waterway. If you want to be on the beach, be sure and ask specifically when booking your room, since many hotels advertise "waterfront" accommodations that are actually on the bay, not the beach.

WHAT IT COSTS				
$$$$	**$$$**	**$$**	**$**	**¢**
RESTAURANTS over $30	$20–$30	$15–$20	$10–$15	under $10
HOTELS over $220	$140–$220	$100–$140	$80–$100	under $80

Restaurant prices are per person for a main course at dinner. Hotel prices are for a standard double room, excluding 6% sales tax (more in some counties) and 1%–4% tourist tax.

Timing

Tourists visit all year long, choosing to arrive in winter or summer depending on budget, interests, hobbies, and the climate where they live. The winter season, roughly Thanksgiving through March, attracts the biggest crowds and "snowbirds"—seasonal residents showing up when snow starts up north. Concert, art, and entertainment seasons are at their height then, and restaurants and roadways are packed. In summer waits at even the top restaurants are likely to be shorter, although some venues curtail hours from peak season. Summer is the rainy season, with rain arriving about mid-afternoon and typically soon gone, but heat and humidity do not quickly subside and summer seems to linger at a slow, sticky pace.

Since most Broward County sights are close together, it's easy to pack a lot into a day if you have a vehicle. Catch the history, museums, and shops and bistros in Fort Lauderdale's downtown area and along Las Olas Boulevard. Then if you feel like hitting the beach, just take a 10-minute drive east to the intersection of Las Olas and A1A and you're there. Many neighboring communities, with attractions of their own, are just north or south of Fort Lauderdale. As a result, you'll be able to cover most of the high points in 3 days, and with 7 to 10 days, you can experience virtually all of Broward's mainstream charms.

Numbers in the text correspond to numbers in the margin and on the Broward County and Fort Lauderdale maps.

If you have 3 days

With a bigger concentration of hotels, restaurants, and attractions than its suburbs, ⊡ **Fort Lauderdale** ❶ ▶–❸ makes a logical base of operations for any visit. On your first day, see the downtown area, especially Las Olas Boulevard between Southeast 3rd and Southeast 15th avenues. After lunch at a sidewalk café, head for the nearby Arts and Science District and the downtown **Riverwalk** ❻; enjoy it at a leisurely pace in half a day. On your second day, spend some time at the **Fort Lauderdale beachfront** ❶, shopping or having a cooling libation at an oceanfront lounge if heat drives you off the sand. Tour the waterways on the third day, either on a rented boat from one of the various marinas along Route A1A, or via a sightseeing vessel or water taxi. The latter can be boarded at various points along the Intracoastal Waterway. Reachable by water taxi are attractions such as Beach Place, Broward Center for the Performing Arts, Galleria Mall, Las Olas Boulevard shops, Las Olas Riverfront, and the **Museum of Art** ❸ and **Museum of Discovery and Science** ❼; restaurants such as 15th Street Fisheries, Grill Room at Riverside Hotel, Shula's on the Beach, and dozens of others; and hotels such as the Hyatt Regency Pier Sixty-Six, Radisson Bahia Mar, Riverside Hotel, and Pillars Waterfront.

If you have 5 days

With additional time, see more of the beach and the arts district and still work in some outdoor sports—and you'll be more able to rearrange your plans depending on weather. On the first day, visit the Arts and Science District and the downtown **Riverwalk** ❻ ▶. Set aside the next day for an offshore adventure, perhaps a deep-sea fishing charter, a reef diving trip, or some kitesurfing or parasailing along the beach. Landlubbers might go for hiking at Markham Park or at Tradewinds Park (home of **Butterfly World** ❹). On the third day, shop, dine, and relax along the **Fort Lauderdale beachfront** ❶, and at the end of the day, sneak a peak at the Hillsboro Light, at **Lighthouse Point** ❷⁰. Another good day can be spent at the **Hugh Taylor Birch State Recreation Area** ❷. Enjoy your fifth day in ⊡ **Hollywood** ❷²⁾, perhaps combining time on the Broadwalk with a visit to the Anne Kolb Nature Center, at West Lake Park.

If you have 7 days

With a full week, you have time for more attractions, fitting in beach time around other activities. In fact, enjoy any of the county's public beach areas on your first day. The second day can be spent in another favorite pastime—shopping, either at chic boutiques or at one of the malls. On the next day, tour the waterways on a sightseeing boat or water taxi. Then shop and dine along Las Olas Boulevard. The fourth day might be devoted to the many museums in downtown Fort Lauderdale and/or the African-American Cultural Center on

3

Sistrunk Boulevard west of downtown. The fifth day could be prime for an airboat ride at **Sawgrass Recreation Park** ⓰, at the edge of the Everglades. Since Fort Lauderdale offers plenty of facilities for outdoor recreation, spend the sixth day fishing and picnicking on one of the area's many piers or playing at a top golf course. Set aside the seventh day for 🎦 **Hollywood** ㉒, to stroll the scenic Broadwalk or walk through the aviary at Flamingo Gardens, in **Davie** ㉔, before relaxing in peaceful Hollywood North Beach Park.

For golfers, almost any time is great for play. As they are everywhere, waits for tee times are longer on weekends year-round. Remember that sun can burn all year long, especially at midday. If you jump in the water to cool off when the sun is strongest, rays reflecting off the water can substantially increase your chance of burning. Try planning beach time for early morning and late afternoon, with sightseeing or shopping in between.

FORT LAUDERDALE

Like other southeast Florida neighbors, Fort Lauderdale has been busily revitalizing for several years. In a state where gaudy tourist zones often stand aloof from workaday downtowns, Fort Lauderdale is unusual in that the city exhibits consistency at both ends of the 2-mi Las Olas corridor. The sparkling look results from moves to thoroughly improve both beachfront and downtown, without letting either languish. Matching the downtown's innovative arts district, cafés, and boutiques is an equally inventive beach area with its own share of cafés and shops facing an undeveloped shoreline.

Downtown

The jewel of the downtown area along New River is the Arts and Entertainment District, with Broadway shows, the Florida Philharmonic, the Florida Grand Opera, and the Miami City Ballet at the riverfront Broward Center for the Performing Arts. Clustered within a five-minute walk are the Museum of Discovery and Science, the expanding Fort Lauderdale Historical Museum, and the Museum of Art. Restaurants, sidewalk cafés, bars, and blues, folk, jazz, reggae, and rock clubs flourish. Las Olas Riverfront is a multistory entertainment, dining, and retail complex along several waterfront blocks once owned by pioneers William and Mary Brickell. Tying this district together is the Riverwalk, extending 2 mi along the New River's north and south banks. Tropical gardens with benches and interpretive displays fringe the walk on the north, boat landings on the south. East along Riverwalk's north side is the pioneer Stranahan House, and Las Olas shopping and dining begins a block east. Tropical landscaping and trees separate the traffic lanes in some blocks, setting off fine shops, restaurants, and popular nightspots. From here, depending on traffic, it's 5 or 10 minutes by car or 20 minutes to a half hour by water taxi back to the beach.

a good tour

Start on Southeast 6th Avenue at Las Olas Boulevard, where you'll find **Stranahan House** ❶ ▶, a turn-of-the-last-century structure that's now a museum. Between Southeast 6th and 15th avenues, Las Olas has Spanish colonial buildings with fashion boutiques, jewelry shops, and art galleries. Driving east, you'll cross into the Isles, among Fort Lauderdale's most prestigious neighborhoods, where homes line waterways with seawalls embellished by yachts. Return west on Las Olas to Andrews Avenue, turn right, park in one of the municipal garages, and walk around downtown Fort Lauderdale. First stop is the **Museum of Art** ❸, which has works from the CoBrA (Copenhagen, Brussels, and Amsterdam) movement. Walk one block north to the **Broward County Main Library** ❹ to see works from Broward County's Public Art and Design Program.

Go west on Southeast 2nd Street to Southwest 2nd Avenue, turn left, and stop at the **Old Fort Lauderdale Museum of History** ❺, surveying the city's beginnings. Just to the south is the palm-lined **Riverwalk** ❻, a good place for leisurely strolling. Head north toward a cluster of facilities collectively known as the Arts and Science District. The district contains the outdoor Esplanade, whose exhibits include a hands-on display of the science and history of navigation, the **Museum of Discovery and Science/Blockbuster IMAX Theater** ❼. The adjacent Broward Center for the Performing Arts, a massive glass-and-concrete structure by the river, has Broadway touring shows, Florida Grand Opera, Florida Philharmonic, and Miami City Ballet. Finally, for a glimpse of one of the city's oldest neighborhoods, go west along Las Olas Boulevard to Southwest 7th Avenue and the entrance to **Sailboat Bend** ❽. Return to the start of the tour by traveling east along Las Olas Boulevard.

TIMING Depending on how long you like to linger in museums and how many hours you want to spend in the shops on Las Olas Boulevard, you can devote anywhere from half a day to an entire day on this tour.

What to See

❾ **African-American Research Library and Cultural Center.** A two-story, $14 million gem, this resource provides locals and researchers from around the world with more than 75,000 books, documents, and artifacts centering on the experiences of people of African descent. There's a gift shop and a small café, and parking is free. ✉ *2650 Sistrunk Blvd.* ☏ *954/625–2800* ⊕ *www.broward.org/aarlcc.htm* ✐ *Free* ☉ *Mon. noon–8, Tues.–Thurs. 10–8, Sat. 9–5.*

❹ **Broward County Main Library.** One of the more than 30 libraries in the Broward County system, this eight-story building of Florida limestone with a terraced glass facade was designed by Marcel Breuer to complement the environment. Works are on display here from Broward County's Public Art and Design Program, including paintings, sculpture, photographs, and weavings by nationally renowned and Florida artists. A community technology center has personal computers for public use and assistant/adaptive devices for patrons with special learning and physical disabilities. Productions from theater to poetry readings are presented in a 300-seat auditorium. ✉ *100 S. Andrews Ave.* ☏ *954/357–7444; 954/357–7457 for self-guided Art in Public Places walking tour brochure* ⊕ *www.broward.org/library* ✐ *Free* ☉ *Mon.–Thurs. 9–9, Fri.–Sat. 9–5, Sun. noon–5:30.*

need a break? Don't miss **Charcuterie Too** (✉ 100 S. Andrews Ave. ☏ 954/463–9578), a cozy cafeteria on the second floor of the Broward County Main Library. Breakfast treats include muffins, scones, and coffee cakes, and there is an extensive lunch menu with soups, salads, and entrées. Open weekdays from 8 to 2:30, it caters to library bookworms and downtown worker bees.

❷ **Fort Lauderdale Antique Car Museum.** Retired floral company owner Arthur O. Stone established a foundation to preserve this trove of eyepoppers. Here you'll find nearly two dozen Packards from 1900 to the 1940s, along with auto memorabilia and a gallery saluting FDR. ✉ *1527 S.W. 1st Ave.* ☏ *954/779–7300* ⊕ *www.antiquecarmuseum.org* ✐ *$8* ☉ *Weekdays 10–4.*

★ ❸ **Museum of Art.** In an Edward Larrabee Barnes–designed building that's considered an architectural masterpiece, this museum's impressive permanent collection has 20th-century European and American art, including works by Picasso, Calder, Dalí, Mapplethorpe, Warhol, and Stella, as well as a notable collection of works by celebrated Ashcan School artist William Glackens. When opening in 1986, the museum helped launch revitalization of the downtown district and nearby Riverwalk area. ⊠ *1 E. Las Olas Blvd.* ☎ *954/763–6464* ⊕ *www.museumofart.org* ⊡ *$7* ☉ *Tues.–Sat. 10–5, Sun. noon–5.*

★ ℭ ❼ **Museum of Discovery and Science/Blockbuster IMAX Theater.** The aim here is to show children—*and* adults—the wonders of science in an entertaining fashion. The 52-ft-tall Great Gravity Clock in the courtyard entrance lets arrivals know a cool experience awaits. Inside, exhibits include Choose Health, about healthy lifestyle choices; Kidscience, encouraging youngsters to explore the world around them; and Gizmo City, a look at how gadgets work. Florida Ecoscapes has a living coral reef as well as live bees, bats, frogs, turtles, and alligators. An IMAX theater, part of the complex, shows films (some 3-D) on a five-story screen. ⊠ *401 S.W. 2nd St.* ☎ *954/467–6637 for museum; 954/463–4629 for IMAX* ⊕ *www.mods.org* ⊡ *Museum $14, includes one IMAX show* ☉ *Mon.–Sat. 10–5, Sun. noon–6.*

❺ **Old Fort Lauderdale Museum of History.** Surveying city history from the Seminole era to more recent times, the museum has expanded into several adjacent historic buildings, including the King-Cromartie House, the Historical Society's Hoch Heritage Center archives building, and the New River Inn. The research facility archives original manuscripts, maps, and more than 250,000 photos. ⊠ *231 S.W. 2nd Ave.* ☎ *954/463–4431* ⊕ *www.oldfortlauderdale.org* ⊡ *$5* ☉ *Tues.–Sun. noon–5.*

★ ⌐ ❻ **Riverwalk.** Fantastic views and entertainment prevail on this lovely, paved promenade on the New River's north bank. On the first Sunday of every month a jazz brunch attracts visitors. The walk has been extended 2 mi on both sides of the beautiful urban stream, connecting the facilities of the Arts and Science District.

❽ **Sailboat Bend.** Between Las Olas and the river, as well as just across the river, lies a neighborhood with much of the character of Old Town in Key West and historic Coconut Grove in Miami. There are no shops or services here.

⌐ ❶ **Stranahan House.** The oldest residence in the city was once the home of businessman Frank Stranahan, who arrived in 1892. With his wife, Ivy, the city's first school teacher, he befriended the Seminole Indians, traded with them, and taught them "new ways." In 1901 he built a store and later made it his home. Now it's a museum with many Stranahan original furnishings on display. ⊠ *335 S.E. 6th Ave., at Las Olas Blvd.* ☎ *954/524–4736* ⊕ *www.stranahanhouse.com* ⊡ *$5* ☉ *Wed.–Sat. 10–3, Sun. 1–3.*

Along the Beach

Fort Lauderdale's beachfront offers the best of all possible worlds, with easy access not only to a wide band of beige sand but also to restaurants and shops. For 2 mi heading north, beginning at the Bahia Mar yacht basin along Route A1A you'll have clear views typically across rows of colorful beach umbrellas, to the ocean and ships passing in and out of nearby Port Everglades. If you're on the beach, gaze back on an exceptionally graceful promenade. Pedestrians rank ahead of cars in Fort Lauderdale. Broad walkways line both sides of the beach road, and traffic has been trimmed to two gently curving northbound lanes, where in-line skaters skim past slow-moving cars. On the beach side, a low masonry wall doubles as an extended bench, separating sand from the

Beaches Broward County's beachfront extends for miles without interruption, although the character of communities along the shoreline changes. In Hallandale, the beach is backed by towering condominiums, whereas in Hollywood, you'll find motels and the Broadwalk. Just north of there—blessedly—there's virtually nothing at all.

Fishing Greater Fort Lauderdale has both freshwater and saltwater fishing. Go bottom or drift-boat fishing from party boats, deep-sea fishing for large sport fish on charters, angling for freshwater game fish, or drop a line off a pier. For bottom fishing, party boats typically charge between $20 and $25 per person for up to four hours, including rod, reel, and bait. For charters, a half day for as many as six people runs about $325, six-hour charters at around $495, and full-day charters (eight hours) at just under $600. Captain and crew, plus bait and tackle, are included. Split parties can be arranged for about $85–$90 per person for a full day. Several Broward municipalities—Dania Beach, Lauderdale-by-the-Sea, Pompano Beach, and Deerfield Beach—have fishing piers that draw anglers for pompano, amberjack, bluefish, snapper, blue runners, snook, mackerel, and Florida lobster.

Golf Nearly 60 courses, including famous championship links, green up Greater Fort Lauderdale. Most area courses are inland, and with sometimes great bargains. Off-season (May–October) greens fees start at $20; peak-season (November–April) charges run from $35 to more than $100. Fees can be trimmed by reserving tee times through a local service, Next Day Golf, and many hotels offer golf packages.

Scuba Diving There's good diving within 20 minutes of shore. Among the most popular of the county's 80 dive sites is the 2-mi-wide, 23-mi-long Fort Lauderdale Reef, the product of Florida's most successful artificial reef-building program. More than a dozen houseboats, ships, and oil platforms have been sunk from 10- to 150-ft depths to provide a habitat for fish and other marine life, as well as to help stabilize beaches. The most famous sunken ship is the 198-ft German freighter *Mercedes*, blown onto the pool terrace of the late Palm Beach socialite Mollie Wilmot during a violent Thanksgiving storm in 1984; the vessel is now submerged a mile off Fort Lauderdale beach.

---

promenade. At night the wall is accented with ribbons of fiber-optic color. The most crowded portion of beach is between Las Olas and Sunrise boulevards. Tackier aspects of this onetime strip are now but a fading memory. North of the redesigned beachfront is another 2 mi of open and natural coastal landscape. Much of the way parallels the Hugh Taylor Birch State Recreation Area, preserving a patch of primeval Florida.

a good tour Go east on Southeast 17th Street across the newly improved (higher and wider) bridge over the Intracoastal Waterway and bear left onto Seabreeze Boulevard (Route A1A). You will pass through a neighborhood of older homes set in lush vegetation before emerging at the south end of Fort Lauderdale's beachfront strip. On your left is the Radisson Bahia Mar Beach Resort, where novelist John McDonald's fictional hero, Travis

McGee, is honored with a plaque at marina slip F-18; it's here that McGee docked his houseboat, the *Busted Flush*. Three blocks north, visit the **International Swimming Hall of Fame Museum and Aquatic Complex** ⑩ ☞. As you approach Las Olas Boulevard, you will see the lyrical styling that has given a distinctly European flavor to the **Fort Lauderdale beachfront** ⑪. Plan to break for lunch and perhaps some shopping at Beach Place, the entertainment, retail, and dining complex just north of Las Olas. Turn left off Route A1A at Sunrise Boulevard, then right into **Hugh Taylor Birch State Recreation Area** ⑫, where outdoor activities can be enjoyed amid vivid flora and fauna. Cross Sunrise Boulevard and visit the **Bonnet House** ⑬ to marvel at both the whimsical home and the surrounding subtropical 35-acre estate.

TIMING   The beach is all about recreation and leisure. To enjoy it as it's meant to be, allow at least a day to loll about. For shade you'll find a stand of trees at the southern portion near the Yankee Clipper hotel.

What to See

★ ⑬ **Bonnet House.** A 35-acre oasis in the heart of the beach area, this subtropical estate is a tribute to the history of Old South Florida. The charming home was the winter residence of the late Frederic and Evelyn Bartlett, artists whose personal touches and small surprises are evident throughout. Whether you're interested in architecture, artwork, or the natural environment, this is a special place. Be on the lookout for playful monkeys swinging from trees, a source of amusement at even some of the most solemn outdoor weddings on the grounds. ✉ *900 N. Birch Rd.* ☎ *954/563–5393* ⊕ *www.bonnethouse.org* ☞ *$9* ☉ *Wed.–Fri. 10–3, weekends noon–4.*

⑪ **Fort Lauderdale Beachfront.** A wave theme unifies the setting—from the
FodorsChoice   low, white wave-shape wall between the beach and beachfront promenade to the widened and bricked inner promenade in front of shops, restaurants, and hotels. Alone among Florida's major beachfront communities, Fort Lauderdale's beach remains open and uncluttered. More than ever, the boulevard is worth promenading.

⑫ **Hugh Taylor Birch State Recreation Area.** Amid the tropical greenery of this 180-acre park, stroll along a nature trail, visit the Birch House Museum, picnic, play volleyball, pitch horseshoes, and paddle a rented canoe. Since parking is limited on A1A, park here and take a walkway underpass to the beach (between 9 and 5). ✉ *3109 E. Sunrise Blvd.* ☎ *954/564–4521* ⊕ *www.abfla.com/parks* ☞ *$3.25 per vehicle with up to 8 people* ☉ *Daily 8–sunset; ranger-guided nature walks Fri. at 10:30.*

☞ ⑩ **International Swimming Hall of Fame Museum and Aquatic Complex.** This monument to underwater accomplishments has two 10-lane, 50-meter pools that are open daily to the public, when not hosting international aquatic competitions. The exhibition building has photos, medals, and other souvenirs from major swimming events worldwide, as well as a theater that shows vintage Tarzan–Esther Williams films. ✉ *1 Hall of Fame Dr., 1 block south of Las Olas at A1A* ☎ *954/462–6536 for museum; 954/468–1580 for pool* ⊕ *www.ishof.org* ☞ *Museum $3, pool $3* ☉ *Museum and pro shop mid-Jan.–late Dec., daily 9–7; pool mid-Jan.–late Dec., weekdays 8–4 and 6–8, weekends 8–4.*

Where to Eat

American

$$$–$$$$ ✗ **Shula's on the Beach.** It's only fitting that Don Shula, coaching the Miami
FodorsChoice   Dolphins to that Perfect Season in 1972 and the "winningest" coach in
★   NFL history, should have a winning South Florida steak house. The good

Broward
County

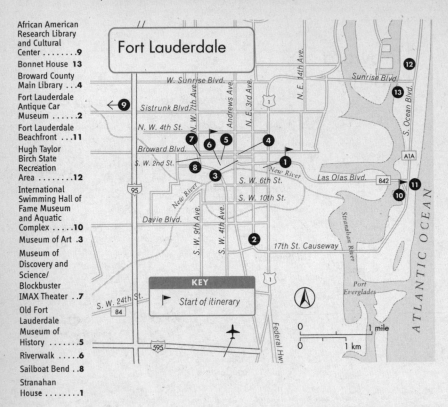

news for steak—and sports—fans is that the staff here turns out winners. Certified Angus beef is cut thick and grilled over a superhot fire
for quick charring. Try Steak Mary Anne, named for Shula's wife, con-
sisting of two sliced filets covered in a savory sauce. Seafood is available, too. Outside tables provide views of sand and ocean; inside seating
provides access to sports memorabilia and large-screen TVs. ✉ *Sheraton Yankee Trader, 321 N. Fort Lauderdale Beach Blvd.* ☎ *954/355–
4000* ▱ *AE, D, DC, MC, V.*

$$–$$$ ✕ **Casablanca Cafe.** You'll get a fabulous view of the ocean and a good
meal to boot at this historic two-story Moroccan-style villa, designed
decades ago by local architect Francis Abreu. The menu is an American potpourri with both tropical and Asian influence (try the mussels
in Thai curry sauce) along with North African specialties like lamb shank
and couscous. There's a piano bar downstairs, and a deck for outside
dining. Service is friendly and attentive. ✉ *A1A and Alhambra St.*
☎ *954/764–3500* ▱ *AE, D, MC, V.*

$$–$$$ ✕ **Tropical Acres.** This popular family-owned restaurant has served up
sizzling steaks from a fireplace grill since 1949—a millennium by South
Florida standards. Choose from more than 40 other entrées, including
excellent seafood dishes. Choose the salmon or take recommendations
from the friendly, seasoned waitstaff. You'll find some of the best early-
bird specials around here, and there's a short wine list with moderate
prices. ✉ *2500 Griffin Rd.* ☎ *954/989–2500* ▱ *AE, DC, MC, V.*

¢–$ ✕ **Floridian.** This Las Olas landmark has been around for as long as any-
one can remember and serves up one of the best breakfasts around. Locals flock here for oversize omelets, sausage, bacon, and biscuits. Servers
can be brisk, bordering on brusque, but chalk it up as part of the experience. It's open 24 hours every day of the year—even during hurricanes;

count on savory sandwiches and hot platters for lunch and dinner. ✉ *1410 E. Las Olas Blvd.* ☎ *954/463–4041* ▤ *No credit cards.*

¢–$ ✕**Southport Raw Bar.** You can't go wrong at this unpretentious spot where the motto, seen on bumper stickers for miles around, proclaims "Eat fish, live longer, eat oysters, love longer, eat clams, last longer." Raw or steamed clams, raw oysters, and combos, along with peel-and-eat shrimp, are market-priced. Hoagies, subs, and burgers are the ticket for under $5. Side orders range from Bimini bread mini-loafs to key lime pie, with conch fritters, beer-battered onions rings, and corn-on-the-cob in between. Order wine by the bottle or glass and beer by the pitcher, bottle, or can. Eat outside overlooking a canal, or inside at booths, tables, or the bars, in front and back. Limited parking is free, and a shopping-center parking lot is within walking distance. ✉ *1536 Cordova Road.* ☎ *954/525–2526* ▤ *MC, V.*

¢–$ ✕**Tom Jenkins.** Big portions of drippingly delicious barbecue are dispensed at this handy spot for eat-in or takeout, south of the New River Tunnel and north of the 17th Street Causeway. Furnishings include an old Singer sewing machine and a wringer washer, and diners partake at a half dozen or so picnic-style tables. Side dishes with dinners under $10 include baked beans, collards, and a mighty tasty macaroni and cheese. For lunch, Tom's pork, beef, and catfish sandwiches are a surefire shortcut to appetite satisfaction. Leave room for sweet-potato pie or apple cobbler. ✉ *1236 S. Federal Hwy.* ☎ *954/522–5046* ▤ *No credit cards* ⊗ *Closed Sun.–Mon.*

¢ ✕**Georgia Pig.** When you're heading out to the area's western reaches, this postage-stamp-size outpost can add some down-home zing to your day. Breakfast, including sausage gravy and biscuits, is served from 6 to 11 AM. But the big attraction is barbecue, beef, pork, or chicken, on platters or in sandwiches. Alternatives include a spicy Brunswick stew and fried jumbo shrimp. There's apple, peach, cherry, and pecan pie, and also a small-fry menu. Order takeout (25¢ extra) or eat at the counter, at wooden tables, or at a half dozen or so booths. ✉ *1285 S. W. 40 Ave. (State Rd. 7/U.S. 441, just south of Davie Blvd.)* ☎ *954/ 587–4420* ▤ *No credit cards.*

¢ ✕**Lester's Diner.** Home of the 14-ounce cup of coffee, Lester's has served as a 24-hour haven for the hungry along State Road 84 since 1967. Truckers head in here on their way to Port Everglades, as do workers from the area's thriving marine industry, suits from downtown toting briefcases, and tourists packing beach bags. Clientele gets even more eclectic in the wee hours. A stick-to-the-ribs menu includes breakfast any time along with homemade soups, sandwiches, salads, and dinners of generous portions. If your cholesterol count can take the hit, try the chicken-fried steak. Lester's has two other locations in western Broward, in Margate and Sunrise, although they close at midnight on weeknights. ✉ *250 State Rd. 84* ☎ *954/525–5641* ✉ *Margate* ✉ *4701 Coconut Creek Pkwy.* ☎ *954/979–4722* ✉ *Sunrise* ✉ *1399 N.W. 136th Ave.* ☎ *954/838–7473* ▤ *D, MC, V.*

¢ ✕**Skyline Chili.** Cincinnati's famed brand has made a name for itself among locals fond of debating the merits of coneys or three-, four, or five-way chili, each making for a meal well under $10. There's also a chili sandwich, made just like the coneys but without the wiener. Eat inside or at a couple of tables out front. ✉ *2590 N. Federal Hwy.* ☎ *954/566–1541* ▤ *D, MC, V.*

Asian

$$$–$$$$ ✕**Mai-Kai.** You'll think you've tripped off to the South Seas rather than South Florida upon arrival at this landmark, operating with lighted torches along Federal Highway since this particular stretch was a two-laner. It's a trifle touristy yet somehow magnetic. Specialties include Lobster Bora

Bora and Peking duck—exotic tropical drinks, and an exciting Polynesian dance review with a flaming finale. Kids' shows are hosted on Sunday evening through the summer, and there's an intriguing gift shop. ⊠ *3599 N. Federal Hwy.* ☎ *954/563–3272* ⊟ *AE, D, MC, V.*

$-$$ ✕ **Siam Cuisine.** Some locals say this restaurant, tucked away in a small storefront in Wilton Manors, serves up the best Thai in the Fort Lauderdale area, and they may be right. The family-run kitchen turns out appealing, flavorful delights. Thai curry dishes with chicken or shrimp are favorites, along with steamed dumplings and roast duck. ⊠ *2010 Wilton Dr.* ☎ *954/564–3411* ⊟ *AE, MC, V.*

Contemporary

★ $$$-$$$$ ✕ **By Word of Mouth.** Unassuming but outstanding, this restaurant never advertises, hence its name. But word suffices because locals consistently put it at the top of "reader's choice" restaurant polls. There is no menu. Patrons are shown the day's specials to make their choice. Count on a solid lineup of fish, fowl, beef, pasta, and vegetarian entrées. A salad is served with each dinner entrée. ⊠ *3200 N.E. 12th Ave.* ☎ *954/564–3663* ⊟ *AE, MC, V.*

$$$-$$$$ ✕ **Creolina's.** As it has moved to more upscale environs within the Himmarshee Village area from its modest storefront birthplace not far away, it's not uncommon to see chef-owner Mark Sulzinski cooking up Cajun-creole delights for city power brokers, including the mayor. Try the Gumbo Ya Ya, crawfish rémoulade or Alligator Piquant (tender strips fried crisp) for starters. Also consider the catfish with pecans or plain old red beans and rice. Warm bread pudding with bourbon sauce is a worthy finale. Despite the fancier digs, prices have remained down to earth. ⊠ *209 S.W. 2nd St.* ☎ *954/524–2003* ⊟ *AE, D, DC, MC, V* ☼ *Closed Sun.–Mon.*

$$-$$$$ ✕ **Mark's Las Olas.** Mark Militello, a star among South Florida chefs, is
Fodor'sChoice in command at this popular restaurant, where he often replicates dishes
★ from the now closed Mark's Place in North Miami. Militello's loyal following is enchanted with his Florida-style preparation, which blends flavors from Caribbean, southwestern, and Mediterranean traditions. Entrées change daily but might include brilliantly prepared gulf shrimp and yellowtail snapper, often paired with combinations of callaloo (a West Indian spinach), chayote, ginger, jícama, and plantain. The charcoal veal flank steak is also worthy. To start, the adventurous might try pancetta-wrapped rabbit loin or lobster with truffle mash. ⊠ *1032 E. Las Olas Blvd.* ☎ *954/463–1000* ⚑ *Reservations essential* ⊟ *AE, D, DC, MC, V* ☼ *No lunch weekends.*

$ ✕ **Maguire's Hill 16.** This comfortable Irish pub has the requisite lineup of libations and sandwiches, a very tasty potato soup, shepherd's pie, Irish stew, bangers and mash, and corned beef and cabbage. ⊠ *535 N Andrews Ave.* ☎ *954/764–4453* ⊟ *AE, D, DC, MC, V.*

Continental

$$$-$$$$ ✕ **Grill Room on Las Olas.** After sampling the area's trendier eateries, you may be ready to opt for the fare at the historic Riverside Hotel. The room is accented in the grand style of a colonial British officers' club, and the menu has grilled steaks, or chateaubriand and rack of lamb—both prepared for two. Many dishes are prepared tableside, including a grand Caesar salad. Choose from an extensive wine list. The adjacent Golden Lyon Bar has the feeling of a pub somewhere in India. ⊠ *Riverside Hotel, 620 E. Las Olas Blvd.* ☎ *954/467–2555* ⊟ *AE, MC, V.*

French

$$-$$$ ✕ **French Quarter.** This 1920 building, formerly a Red Cross headquarters, sits on a quiet street just off bustling Las Olas Boulevard. French-style architecture has a touch of New Orleans, and the food captures

both creole and traditional French elements. Among favorites are shrimp *maison* (large shrimp sautéed with carrots and mushrooms in beurre blanc), bouillabaisse, crab cakes, and escargot appetizers. French baking, including aromatic bread, is done on site, and a prix-fixe three-course pre-theater dinner is served until 6:30. ✉ *215 S.E. 8th Ave.* ☎ *954/463–8000* ⊟ *AE, D, DC, MC, V* ⊙ *Closed Sun. No lunch Sat.*

Italian

$$–$$$$ ✕ **Primavera.** Tucked inside an ordinary shopping plaza is this extraordinary find. Apart from fresh pasta with rich sauces and risotto entrées, choose from creative fish, poultry, veal, and beef dinners. One of chef-owner Giacomo Dresseno's favorites is veal chop Boscaiola (with shallots, wild mushrooms, and bordelaise sauce). If you're in town for a few nights, check out the chef's day or evening cooking classes or wine appreciation dinners. There's live entertainment nightly. ✉ *830 E. Oakland Park Blvd.* ☎ *954/564–6363* ⊕ *www.trueitalian.com* ⊟ *AE, D, DC, MC, V* ⊙ *Closed Mon. No lunch.*

$–$$$$ ✕ **Casa D'Angelo.** Owner-chef Angelo Elia has re-created his former Café D'Angelo into a gem of a Tuscan-style restaurant. Almost everything is made from scratch, and the oak oven turns out some marvelous seafood and beef dishes. The pappardelle with porcini mushrooms takes pasta to pleasant heights. Another favorite from the pasta menu is linguine with arugula, shrimp, and scallops. Be sure to ask about the oven-roasted fish of the day. ✉ *1201 N. Federal Hwy.* ☎ *954/564–1234* ⊟ *AE, D, DC, MC, V* ⊙ *No lunch.*

¢–$$$ ✕ **Louie, Louie Bistro.** Some of the best pasta dishes on Las Olas are served at this friendly, tavern-style establishment. Try individual thin-crust pizzas, sandwiches, or complete dinners. Fresh fish specials are offered daily. The grouper is excellent. Prices are reasonable, and while waiting for a table, graze the large selection of beers on tap. ✉ *1404 E. Las Olas Blvd.* ☎ *954/524–5200* ⊟ *AE, MC, V.*

Mexican

$$–$$$ ✕ **Eduardo de San Angel.** Authentic chiles, spices, and herbs enhance classic seafood, meat, and poultry dishes here. Specialties are beef tenderloin tips sautéed with Portobello mushrooms and onions in a chipotle chili sauce, and a marvelous mesquite-grilled red snapper flavored with jalapeños and mango salsa. ✉ *2822 E. Commercial Blvd.* ☎ *954/772–4731* ⊟ *AE, D, DC, MC, V* ⊙ *Closed Sun.*

Seafood

★ **$$$–$$$$** ✕ **Blue Moon Fish Company.** Virtually every table has an enchanting view of the Intracoastal Waterway, but the real magic is in the kitchen, where chefs Baron Skorish and Bryce Statham create some of the region's best seafood dishes. Favorites include pan-seared snapper with asparagus, sea bass fillet crusted with macadamia nuts, and rare-charred tuna. Appetizers include choices from the raw bar, a sushi sampler, tasty crab and crawfish cakes, and charred Portobello mushrooms. ✉ *4405 W. Tradewinds Ave.* ☎ *954/267–9888* ⊟ *AE, D, DC, MC, V.*

$$–$$$$ ✕ **15th Street Fisheries.** An impressive view of the Intracoastal Waterway is only the beginning at this two-story seafood landmark. Satisfying dishes include a cold seafood salad and a spicy conch chowder for starters. Homemade breads, a specialty, are accompanied by a cheese and chive spread. More than 50 entrées range from the traditional, such as grilled mahimahi, to the exotic, such as alligator. Try the fresh key lime pie, with an Oreo crust. Downstairs seating is more casual. ✉ *1900 S.E. 15th St.* ☎ *954/763–2777* ⊟ *AE, D, DC, MC, V.*

$$–$$$ ✕ **Rustic Inn Crabhouse.** Wayne McDonald started with a cozy one-room roadhouse in 1955, when this stretch was a remote service road just west of the little airport. Now, the plain, rustic place is huge. The ample menu includes steamed crabs seasoned with garlic and herbs, spices, and oil, opened with mallets on tables covered with newspapers, and peel-and-eat shrimp, served either with garlic and butter or spiced and steamed with Old Bay seasoning. A slice of pie or cheesecake is a nice finisher. ⊠ *4331 Ravenswood Rd.* ☎ *954/584–1637* ▤ *AE, D, DC, MC, V.*

Southwestern

★ **$$–$$$** ✕ **Canyon Southwest Cafe.** Adventurous southwestern food helps you escape the ordinary at this small but popular spot next to a movie theater. Take, for example, the ostrich skewers, smoked salmon tostada, Brie and wild-mushroom quesadilla, and marvelous Chilean sea bass. Brook trout is served with a tempting crabmeat salsa. Start off with Canyon's famous prickly-pear margaritas, or choose from a well-rounded wine list or beer selection. ⊠ *1818 E. Sunrise Blvd.* ☎ *954/ 765–1950* ▤ *AE, MC, V* ☺ *No lunch.*

Where to Stay

On the Beach

$$$–$$$$ ▥ **Marriott's Harbor Beach Resort.** Look down from the upper stories (14
FodorsChoice in all) at night, and this 16-acre property south of the big public beach
★ shimmers like a jewel. Spacious guest rooms have rich tropical colors, lively floral art prints, and warm woods. Part of the hotel's big-budget renovation is the addition of a European spa. No other hotel on the beach gives you so many activity options. ⊠ *3030 Holiday Dr., 33316* ☎ *954/525–4000 or 800/222–6543* ☐ *954/766–6152* ⊕ *www.marriottharborbeach. com* ⇨ *602 rooms, 35 suites* ♦ *3 restaurants, in-room data ports, room TVs with movies and video games, 5 tennis courts, 2 pools, gym, spa, beach, snorkeling, boating, parasailing, volleyball, 2 bars, children's programs (ages 5–12)* ▤ *AE, D, DC, MC, V.*

★ **$$–$$$** ▥ **Best Western Pelican Beach.** Directly on the beach and owned-managed by the hospitable Kruse family, this already lovely property has undergone a major transformation and now tries harder than ever to keep you on the premises with a new restaurant and lounge and a totally revamped pool area. ⊠ *2000 N. Atlantic Blvd., 33305* ☎ *954/568–9431 or 800/525–6232* ☐ *954/565–2622* ⊕ *www.pelicanbeach.com* ⇨ *10 rooms, 14 suites* ♦ *Restaurant, lounge, 2 pools* ▤ *AE, DC, MC, V.*

★ **$$–$$$** ▥ **Lago Mar Resort & Club.** The sprawling Lago Mar has been owned by the Banks family since the early 1950s and, after renovations, it's again a premiere oceanfront resort. Most accommodations are suites, ideal for families. Suite highlights include a king-size bed, pull-out sofa, and full kitchens. Allamanda trellises and bougainvillea plantings edge the swimming lagoon, and guests have direct access to a large private beach in an exclusive neighborhood. ⊠ *1700 S. Ocean La., 33316* ☎ *954/523–6511 or 800/524–6627* ☐ *954/524–6627* ⊕ *www.lagomar.com* ⇨ *52 rooms, 160 suites* ♦ *4 restaurants, miniature golf, tennis court, 2 pools, shuffleboard, volleyball, playground* ▤ *AE, DC, MC, V.*

$$–$$$ ▥ **The Pillars Hotel at New River Sound.** Described as Fort Lauderdale's "small secret" by locals in the know, this property is one block in from the beach on the Intracoastal. Its design recalls the colorful architecture of British colonial plantations found in the Caribbean in the 18th century. Most rooms have views of the Intracoastal Waterway or poolside, with French doors opening to individual patios or balconies. Rooms have rattan and mahogany headboards, antique reproduction desks and nightstands, and lush draperies. Suites include wet bars with refrigerators and microwaves. ⊠ *111 N. Birch Rd., 33304* ☎ *954/467–9639* ☐ *954/763–2845* ⊕ *www.pillarshotel.com* ⇨ *19 rooms, 4 suites* ♦ *Room service, in-room data ports, minibars, some microwaves, some* *refrigerators, in-room VCRs, pool, concierge; no kids under 12, no-smoking rooms* ☐ *AE, D, DC, MC, V.*

¢ ☐ **Sea Chateau Resort.** A cozy two-story enclave about a block from the beach, this property has more going for it than affordability. Each room is done differently; many have canopy beds draped with gossamer fabric, and all have spacious closets and tub-showers. Efficiencies with kitchenettes anchor the corners. Rooms face the pool next to a quiet, shaded courtyard. Should you fall in love with the area, the owner is a licensed real estate agent. ⊠ *555 N. Birch Rd., 33304* ☎ *954/566–8331* 🖷 *954/564–8411* ⌁ *17 units* ⚘ *Pool, some kitchenettes, refrigerators* ☐ *No credit cards.*

Downtown & Beach Causeways

$$$–$$$$
Fodor'sChoice
★
☐ **Hyatt Regency Pier Sixty-Six.** The trademark of this high-rise resort on the Intracoastal Waterway is its rooftop Pier Top Lounge, making one 360-degree revolution every 66 minutes. The 17-story tower dominates a 22-acre spread that includes the Spa 66, a full-service European-style spa. Each room has a balcony with views of the 142-slip marina, pool, ocean, or Intracoastal. Some guests prefer the ground-level lanai rooms. Lush landscaping and convenience to the beach, shopping, and restaurants add to the overall allure. Hail the water bus at the resort's dock for a three-minute trip to the beach. ⊠ *2301 S.E. 17th St. Causeway, 33316* ☎ *954/525–6666 or 800/327–3796* 🖷 *954/728–3551* ⊕ *www.pier66.com* ⌁ *380 rooms, 8 suites* ⚘ *6 restaurants, 2 tennis courts, 2 pools, gym, hot tub, spa, snorkeling, boating, marina, parasailing, waterskiing, fishing, 3 bars* ☐ *AE, D, DC, MC, V.*

$$–$$$
☐ **Schubert Hotel.** In the Victoria Park neighborhood, this restored 1950s art deco property is a luxury boutique hotel tucked into a tropical landscape. Rooms are oversize with marble and granite baths; most have either a king-size bed or two double-size beds. A café serves breakfast and lunch overlooking the pool and has a wine bar—a perfect place to unwind. The property feels secluded yet is a short walk from the beach, shopping, and restaurants. ⊠ *855 N.E. 20th Ave., 33304* ☎ *954/763–7434 or 866/338–7666* 🖷 *954/763–4132* ⊕ *www.schuberthotel.com* ⌁ *30 rooms* ⚘ *Café, grill, some kitchenettes, room service, pool, spa, shuffleboard, bar, business services* ☐ *AE, DC, MC, V.*

$–$$$
☐ **Riverside Hotel.** On Las Olas Boulevard, just steps from boutiques, restaurants, and art galleries, this charming hotel was built in 1936 and has taken on unprecedented luster with a $25 million renovation and expansion. The penthouse suites in the new 12-story executive tower have balconies offering sweeping views of Las Olas, New River, and the downtown skyline. Old Fort Lauderdale photos grace the hallways, and rooms are outfitted with antique oak furnishings and framed French prints. Enjoy afternoon tea in the lobby, and dine at Indigo, with Southeast Asian cooking, or the elegant Grill Room. ⊠ *620 E. Las Olas Blvd., 33301* ☎ *954/467–0671 or 800/325–3280* 🖷 *954/462–2148* ⊕ *www.riversidehotel.com* ⌁ *206 rooms, 11 suites* ⚘ *2 restaurants, pool, dock, 2 bars; no-smoking rooms* ☐ *AE, DC, MC, V.*

¢–$
Fodor'sChoice
★
☐ **Banyan Marina Resort.** These outstanding waterfront apartments on a residential isle just off Las Olas Boulevard are set amid imaginative landscaping that includes a walkway through the upper branches of a banyan tree. With leather sofas, comfortable carpets, high-quality art, French doors, and jalousies to court sweeping breezes, the luxurious units are competitive with any first-class hotel—for half the price. Apartments and efficiencies include a full kitchen and dining area. All units enjoy the property's beautiful gardens, dockage for eight yachts, and exemplary housekeeping. ⊠ *111 Isle of Venice, 33301* ☎ *954/524–4430 or 800/524–4431* 🖷 *954/764–4870* ⊕ *www.banyanmarina.com*

↪ *3 rooms, 1 efficiency, 4 1-bedroom apartments, 2 2-bedroom apartments* ⚓ *Pool, dock* ▭ *MC, V.*

Camping

Greater Fort Lauderdale

⚠ **Kozy Kampers RV Park.** This quiet, shaded park with a restaurant next door serves as a central point for exploring Greater Fort Lauderdale or relaxing with such activities as horseshoes and shuffleboard. Leashed dogs up to 35 pounds are allowed, as are big rigs and slide-outs. There are 13 pull-through sights. Just stay the night, or pay a weekly ($225) or monthly ($685) rate in winter; rates are lower in summer. Reservations are advised in winter. ⚓ *Full hookups, dump station, parking, laundry facilities, recreation hall, rest rooms, public telephone, ice* ↪ *104* ✉ *3631 W. Commercial Blvd., Fort Lauderdale* ☎ *954/731–8570* 🖷 *954/731–3140* ⊕ *www.kozykampers.com* ▨ *$35 daily* ▭ *MC, V* ⊙ *Year-round.*

⚠ **Paradise Island RV Resort.** You'll find this long-established park, formerly known as Buglewood, well situated for heading east to the beach or west to attractions. Relax in a large heated pool surrounded by umbrellaed tables or chaise lounges. Or, head for the resource room with modem hook-up, big-screen TV, and a library. Planned group activities including cookouts, and ice cream socials unfold November through April. There's fax service at the front office, and daily trash pickup at no extra cost. Rates for two people November–April range from $36 daily to $216 weekly and $697 monthly, with lower rates available in summer ⚓ *Full hookups, electricity* ↪ *232 paved, level sites* ✉ *2121 N.W. 29th Ct., Fort Lauderdale* ☎ *800/487–7395* 🖷 *954/485–5701* ⊕ *www.paradiseislandrvresort.com* ⚘ *Reservations advised, especially in winter* ▭ *AE, D, MC, V* ⊙ *Year-round.*

⚠ **Twin Lakes Travel Park.** Unwind here in the clubhouse or in the adjacent heated pool overlooking the lake. The park offers free daily trash removal. Rates for two people range from $35 daily to $225 weekly to $695 monthly. ⚓ *Full hookups, electricity* ↪ *232 paved, level sites* ✉ *3055 Burris Rd., Fort Lauderdale* ☎ *954/587–0101* 🖷 *954/587–9512* ⚘ *Reservations advised, especially in winter* ▭ *AE, D, MC, V* ⊙ *Year-round.*

⚠ **Yacht Haven Park and Marina.** Along the New River, this park is pet-friendly for animals up to 40 pounds. There are scheduled activities in the recreation hall during the winter season. A heated pool and spa and fishing are available on the property. Depending on location, daily rates for two range from $33 to $46 in winter, $25 to $33 in summer, with $5 for each extra person, plus tax. Weekly, monthly rates are also available. Reservations are recommended. ⚓ *Laundry facilities, showers, dump station* ↪ *250 paved RV sites, some waterfront* ✉ *2323 State Rd. 84* ☎ *954/583–2322, 800–581–2322* ⊕ *www.yachthavenpark.com* ▭ *AE, D, MC, V* ⊙ *Year-round.*

Nightlife & the Arts

For the most complete weekly listing of events, read the Showtime! entertainment insert and events calendar in the Friday *South Florida Sun-Sentinel.* Weekend, in the Friday Broward edition of the *Miami Herald,* also lists area happenings. The weekly *City Link* is principally an entertainment and dining paper with an "underground" look. *New Times* is a free alternative-news weekly circulating a Broward–Palm Beach County edition. *East Sider* is another free weekly entertainment guide. A 24-hour **Arts & Entertainment Hotline** (☎ 954/357–5700) provides

AN AFRICAN-AMERICAN GEM

WEST OF DOWNTOWN Fort Lauderdale's Arts & Sciences District, in the heart of the African-American community along Sistrunk Boulevard, lies a gem once discounted as a grand idea unlikely to get off the ground.

Yet in late 2002, Fort Lauderdale's African-American Research Library and Cultural Center soared into reality as a sparkling two-story, $14 million repository of history and heritage of African, African-American, and Caribbean cultures, with historic books, papers, and art, much of it pertaining to the African Diaspora. There's a 300-seat auditorium, a story-time area, and 5,000 square ft of gallery space for permanent and traveling exhibits. African symbols, similar to ones on the historic Adinkra cloth, appear as part of the decor. Adinkra, an Akan word that means "to say good-bye," is mostly associated with Asante people of Ghana who developed the art of Adinkra printing around the 19th century.

For Samuel F. Morrison, who retired in 2003 as Broward County Library Director, the center's opening has represented a culmination of his dream, a bold vision to create a worthy showcase reflecting African-American heritage. Broward County government agreed to ante up $5 million for the 60,000-square-ft center, and Morrison raised the rest. "The special collections offer historical lessons through tangible materials to everyone who visits," Morrison says.

Of the three African-American public research facilities in country, Fort Lauderdale's is the only one that includes a focus on the Caribbean. (The other two are New York's Schomburg Center for Research in Black Culture and Atlanta's Auburn Avenue Research Library.) Among the center's offerings is the Alex Haley Collection, including eight of the author's unfinished manuscripts. Other components range from Fisk University research of slave narratives to the Frederic Gomes Cassidy assortment of books on Jamaica and the Caribbean. You'll also find the Kitty Oliver Oral Histories Collection on Broward and Okeechobee and the Niara Sudarkasa Collection of papers, artwork, and other materials of the former president of Lincoln University.

And there's the collection of Dorothy Porter Wesley—in some observers' eyes the greatest of the black bibliophiles. Her collection includes about 500 inscribed and autographed books—some date to 1836—with personal narratives, biographies, histories, fiction, bibliographies, and reference works. Wesley's daughter, Constance Porter Uzelac, refers to "Mama's stuff," noting that "it's not just books and manuscripts . . . what's interesting is the associations she had with the authors and the people." Wesley was known for going to auctions or the homes of the recently deceased to make sure nothing of value was thrown away. Her daughter recalls "she'd get to the house before the body was cold," heading straight to attics and basements to retrieve bits and scraps of history.

Passionate about his dream, Morrison is also adamant about the library's widespread appeal, noting that "these pieces provide glimpses [into] the hearts and minds of people who have made a difference in the lives of not only people of color and African culture, but people of many colors and cultures."

— Lynne Helm

updates on art, attractions, children's events, dance, festivals, films, literature, museums, music, opera, and theater. Tickets are sold at individual box offices and through **Ticketmaster** (☎ 954/523–3309); there's a service charge.

The Arts

Broward Center for the Performing Arts (✉ 201 S.W. 5th Ave. ☎ 954/462–0222) is the waterfront centerpiece of Fort Lauderdale's arts district. There are more than 500 events a year at the 2,700-seat architectural masterpiece, including Broadway musicals, plays, dance, symphony and opera, rock, film, lectures, comedy, and children's theater.

Nightlife

BARS & LOUNGES   **Café Iguana** (✉ Beach Place, 17 S. Fort Lauderdale Beach Blvd. ☎ 954/763–7222) has a nightly DJ to keep the dance floor hopping; dance all night long every night of the week. **Chili Pepper** (✉ 200 W. Broward Blvd. ☎ 954/525–0094) brings hot current rock bands to the stage of this warehouse-size open-air venue. **Howl at the Moon Saloon** (✉ Beach Place, 17 S. Fort Lauderdale Beach Blvd. ☎ 954/522–5054) has dueling piano players and sing-alongs nightly. **Maguire's Hill 16** (✉ 535 N. Andrews Ave. ☎ 954/764–4453) highlights excellent bands in classic Irish-pub surroundings. **O'Hara's Jazz Café** (✉ 722 E. Las Olas Blvd. ☎ 954/524–1764) belts out the live jazz, blues, R&B, and funk nightly. Its packed crowd spills onto this prettiest of downtown streets. **Rush Street** (✉ 220 S.W. 2nd St. ☎ 954/522–6900) is where hipsters line up around the corner to gain access to one of the best martini bars in Broward County. **Side Bar** (✉ 210 S.W. 2nd St. ☎ 954/524–1818) has a contemporary industrial feel with a polished professional crowd. **Tarpon Bend** (✉ 200 S. W. 2nd St. ☎ 954/523–3233) specialties—food, fishing gear and bait, and live bands playing current covers—draw a casual, beer-drinking crowd. **Tavern 213** (✉ 213 S.W. 2nd St. ☎ 954/463–6213) is a small, no-frills club where cover bands do classic rock nightly. **Voodoo Lounge** (✉ 111 S.W. 2nd Ave. ☎ 954/522–0733) plays the latest in club music inside the nightclub and high hip-hop on the elegant outside deck. The scene here doesn't start until close to midnight.

Sports & the Outdoors

Baseball

From mid-February to the end of March the **Baltimore Orioles** (✉ Fort Lauderdale Stadium, 1301 N.W. 55th St. ☎ 954/776–1921) are in spring training.

Biking

Among the most popular routes are Route A1A and Bayview Drive, especially in early morning before traffic builds, and a 7-mi bike path that parallels State Road 84 and the New River and leads to Markham Park, which has mountain-bike trails.

Fishing

If you're interested in a saltwater charter, check out the **Radisson Bahia Mar Beach Resort** (✉ 801 Seabreeze Blvd. ☎ 954/627–6357). Both sport-fishing and drift-fishing bookings can be arranged.

Scuba Diving & Snorkeling

Lauderdale Diver (✉ 1334 S.E. 17th St. Causeway ☎ 954/467–2822 or 800/654–2073), which is PADI affiliated, arranges dive charters throughout the county. Dive trips typically last four hours. Nonpackage reef trips are open to divers for $42; scuba gear is extra.

CRUISING FOR A TAXI

SHOUT "TAXI! TAXI!" IN FORT LAUDERDALE, and look for your ship to come in.

Actually, it's a water bus or water taxi, a floating "cab" that you can hail from the many docks along the Intracoastal Waterway.

The venture was started by longtime resident Bob Bekoff, who decided to combine the need for transportation with one of the area's most appealing features: miles of waterways that make the city known as the Venice of America.

For a day of sightseeing, the taxi will pick you up at any of several hotels along the waterway, and you can stop off at attractions like the Performing Arts Center or Beach Place. For lunch, enjoy a restaurant on Las Olas Boulevard or Las Olas Riverfront. In the evening, water taxis are a great way to go out to dinner or bar-hop.

Water Taxi and Broward County Mass Transit have partnered to create Water Buses. These environmentally friendly electric ferries can carry up to 70 passengers. Ride either the water taxi or water bus unlimited from 6:30 AM to 12:30 AM for $5 (one-way adult fare is $4). For family reunions, special group tours such as the Great River Safari and the History Tours are on tap. And if you're oriented toward the arts, consider the seven-day Arts and Entertainment Passport, for which one price provides unlimited water-taxi use along with discounts at the Broward Center for the Performing Arts and free admission to several museums and attractions, including Bonnet House. The best way to use the water taxi or bus is by calling 954/467–6677 about 20 minutes ahead of your desired pick-up, or check out the schedule at ⊕ www.watertaxi.com.

Alan Macher, updated by Lynne Helm

Pro Dive (⊠ 515 Seabreeze Blvd. ☎ 954/761–3413 or 800/776–3483), a PADI five-star facility, is the area's oldest diving operation and offers packages with Radisson Bahia Mar Beach Resort, from where its 60-ft boat departs. Snorkelers can go out for $27 on a two-hour snorkeling trip, which includes equipment. Scuba divers pay $39 using their own gear or $79 with all rentals included.

Tennis

With 21 courts, 18 of them lighted clay courts, the **Jimmy Evert Tennis Center at Holiday Park** is Fort Lauderdale's largest public tennis facility. Chris Evert learned the sport here under the watchful eye of her father, Jimmy, who retired after 37 years as the center's tennis professional. ⊠ 701 N.E. 12th Ave. ☎ 954/828–5378 ☞ $4.50 per person per hr ⊙ Weekdays 8 AM–9 PM, weekends 8–6.

Shopping

Malls

Just north of Las Olas Boulevard on Route A1A is the happening **Beach Place** (⊠ 17 S. Fort Lauderdale Beach Blvd. [A1A]). Browse through shops, have lunch or dinner at restaurants ranging from casual Caribbean to elegant American, or carouse at a selection of nightspots—all open late. Eateries on the lower level tend toward the more upscale, whereas on the upper level prices are lower, with a superior ocean view. Just west of the Intracoastal Waterway, the split-level **Galleria Mall** (⊠ 2414 E. Sunrise Blvd.) has more than 1 million square ft of retail space, anchored by Neiman-Marcus, Dillard's, Burdines, and Saks Fifth Avenue, with 150 specialty shops for anything from cookware to sportswear and fine jewelry. The **Swap Shop** (⊠ 3291 W. Sunrise Blvd.) is the South's largest flea market, with 2,000 vendors open daily. While exploring this 80-acre indoor-outdoor entertainment and shopping complex, enjoy the giant carousel or the free daily circus, or stick around for evening fun at the adjacent drive-in movies.

Shopping Districts

When you're downtown, check out the **Las Olas Riverfront** (⊠ 1 block west of Andrews Ave. on the New River), a shopping, dining, and entertainment complex. **Vogue Italia** (⊠ Las Olas Riverfront, 300 S.W. 1st Ave. ☎ 954/527–4568) is packed with trendy fashions by D&G, Ferre, Versus, Moschino, Iceberg, and more at wholesale prices. If only for a stroll and some window-shopping, don't miss **Las Olas Boulevard** (⊠ 1 block off New River east of Andrews Ave.). The city's best boutiques plus top restaurants and art galleries line a beautifully landscaped street. **Atlantic Yard** (⊠ 2424 E. Las Olas Blvd. ☎ 954/779–1191) has everything for the avant gardener from unique and unusual gardening goods to stylish teak furniture collections. **Casa Chameleon** (⊠ 619 E. Las Olas Blvd. ☎ 954/763–2543) carries a romantic selection of decorative items including fine gifts, antiques, linens, and beautiful things to top your table. **Kilwin's of Las Olas** (⊠ 809 E. Las Olas Blvd. ☎ 954/523–8338) lures pedestrians with the sweet smell of waffle cones to this old-fashioned confectionery with hand-paddled fudge and scoops of homemade ice cream. **Lily Pulitzer by Lauderdale Lifestyle** (⊠ 819 E. Las Olas Blvd. ☎ 954/524–5459) specializes in the South Florida dress requisite—clothing and accessories in Lily Pulitzer's signature tropical colors and prints. **Pino Formica** (⊠ 825 E. Las Olas Blvd. ☎ 954/522–2479) focuses on sleek shoes, handbags, and belts by Furla, Fendi, Prada, and other Italian labels. **Seldom Seen** (⊠ 817 E. Las Olas Blvd. ☎ 954/764–5590) is a gallery of contemporary and folk art including furniture, jewelry, ceramics, sculpture, and blown glass. **Zola Keller** (⊠ 818 E. Las Olas Blvd. ☎ 954/462–3222) caters to those looking for special-occasion dresses—cocktail dresses, evening gowns, and even Miss Florida and Mrs. America pageant dresses.

Side Trips

The Western Suburbs & Beyond

West of Fort Lauderdale is an ever-growing mass of suburbia, with most of the city's golf courses as well as attractions and malls. As you head west, the terrain takes on more characteristics of the Everglades, and you'll occasionally see an alligator sunning on a canal bank. No matter how dedicated developers are to building over this area, the Everglades keeps asserting itself. Waterbirds, fish, and other creatures populate canals and lakes throughout the western areas.

14 As many as 80 butterfly species from South and Central America, the Philippines, Malaysia, Taiwan, and other Asian nations are typically found within **Butterfly World**, a 3-acre site inside Tradewinds Park. A screened aviary called North American Butterflies is reserved for native species. The Tropical Rain Forest Aviary is a 30-ft-high construction, with observation decks, waterfalls, ponds, and tunnels where thousands of colorful butterflies flutter about. ⊠ 3600 W. Sample Rd., Coconut Creek ☎ 954/977–4400 ⊕ www.butterflyworld.com ☎ $13.95 ☉ Mon.–Sat. 9–5, Sun. 1–5.

15 The 30-acre **Everglades Holiday Park** provides an excellent glimpse of the Everglades. Take an airboat tour, look at an 18th-century-style Native American village, or watch an alligator-wrestling show. A souvenir shop, TJ's Grill, a convenience store, and a campground with RV hookups and tent sites are all here as well. ⊠ 21940 Griffin Rd. ☎ 954/

434–8111 ⊕ *www.evergladesholidaypark.com* ⊠ *Free, airboat tour $15.50* ⊙ *Daily 9–5.*

16 To understand and enjoy the Everglades, take an airboat ride at **Sawgrass Recreation Park.** You'll see all sorts of plants and wildlife from birds and alligators to turtles, snakes, and fish. Included in the entrance fee along with the airboat ride is admission to an Everglades nature exhibit, a native Seminole village, and exhibits about alligators, other reptiles, and birds of prey. A souvenir and gift shop, food service, and an RV park with hook-ups are also at the park. ⊠ *U.S. 27 north of I–595* ☎ *954/ 426–2474* ⊕ *www.evergladestours.com* ⊠ *$15.65* ⊙ *Weekdays 7–6, weekends 6–6; airboat rides daily 9–5.*

17 Some distance from Fort Lauderdale's tranquil beaches, but worth the one-hour drive, is the **Big Cypress Seminole Reservation** and its two very different attractions. At the **Billie Swamp Safari,** experience the majesty of the Everglades firsthand. Daily tours of the wetlands and hammocks, where wildlife abound, yield sightings of deer, water buffalo, bison, wild hogs, hawks, eagles, alligators, and occasionally the rare Florida panther. Tours are provided aboard motorized swamp buggies. ⊠ *19 mi north of I–75 Exit 14* ☎ *863/983–6101 or 800/949–6101* ⊕ *www. seminoletribe.com* ⊠ *Free; combined ecotour, show, airboat ride $38* ⊙ *Daily 8–5.*

Not far away from the Billie Swamp Safari is the **Ah-Tha-Thi-Ki Museum,** whose name means "a place to learn, a place to remember." It is just that. The museum honors the culture and tradition of the Seminoles through artifacts and reenactments of rituals and ceremonies. The site includes a living-history Seminole village, nature trails, and a boardwalk through a cypress swamp. ⊠ *17 mi north of I–75 Exit 14* ☎ *863/902– 1113* ⊕ *www.seminoletribe.com* ⊠ *$6* ⊙ *Tues.–Sun. 9–5.*

WHERE TO ✗ **Wolfgang Puck Café.** Just in case you lack an excuse, here's another
STAY & EAT reason to go to the mall. Amid your shopping bags, you'll be treated to
$–$$$ excellent service and quality dishes. Wolfgang Puck's crispy, plate-size pizzas have such tasty toppings as spicy shrimp with peppers, vegetable combinations, and smoked salmon. Also worthy are the roasted pumpkin ravioli, rosemary chicken, and meat loaf with garlic mashed potatoes. ⊠ *Sawgrass Mills, 2610 Sawgrass Mills Circle, Sunrise* ☎ *954/846– 8668* ⊟ *AE, D, MC, V.*

$$–$$$ ⊞ **Coral Springs Marriott Hotel, Golf Club and Convention Center.** Formerly a Radisson property, this resort is adjacent to the Tournament Players Club golf course in Heron Bay. Its perch near the Sawgrass Expressway also makes it convenient to area attractions. Spacious, updated rooms are furnished with oak and cherry wood. The property also has an outdoor terrace and a game room. ⊠ *11775 Heron Bay Blvd., Coral Springs 33076* ☎ *954/753–5598* ⊟ *954/753–2888* ⊕ *www.marriott. com* ⊅*224 rooms, 7 suites* ⚬ *Restaurant, in-room data ports, golf course, pool, gym, sauna, bar* ⊟ *AE, D, MC, V.*

SPORTS & THE **Fishing.** The marina at **Everglades Holiday Park** (⊠ 21940 Griffin Rd.
OUTDOORS ☎ 954/434–8111) caters to freshwater fishing. For $72.50 for five hours, rent a 14-ft johnboat (with a 9.9-horsepower Yamaha outboard) that carries up to four people. A rod and reel rent for $9 a day with a refundable $20 deposit; bait is extra. For two people, a fishing guide for a half day (four hours) is $170; for a full day (eight hours), $220. A third person adds $35 for a half day, $70 for a full day. Also buy a freshwater fishing license (mandatory) here; a seven-day nonresident license is $17. Out of **Sawgrass Recreation Park** (⊠ U.S. 27 and I–75 ☎ 954/426–2474) rent boats, get fishing licenses, and buy live bait.

Golf. Functioning like a golf concierge, **Next Day Golf** (☎ 954/772–2582) provides no-fee tee-time booking at both public courses and private ones normally limited to members—a big advantage for golfers in summer. Bookings are limited at private courses during the busy winter months. Also offered are last-minute discount tee times (call 12 hours in advance).

Bonaventure Country Club (✉ 200 Bonaventure Blvd. ☎ 954/389–2100) has 36 holes. **Broken Woods Country Club** (✉ 9001 W. Sample Rd., Coral Springs ☎ 954/752–2140) has 18 holes. **Colony West Country Club** (✉ 6800 N.W. 88th Ave. [Pine Island Rd.], Tamarac ☎ 954/726–8430) offers play on 36 holes. **Ft. Lauderdale Country Club** (✉ 418 E. Country Club Cir., Fort Lauderdale ☎ 954/587–4700) is a premier green in Fort Lauderdale. Just west of Florida's Turnpike, the **Inverrary Country Club** (✉ 3840 Inverrary Blvd., Lauderhill ☎ 954/733–7550) has two 18-hole championship courses and an 18-hole executive course. **Jacaranda Golf Club** (✉ 9200 W. Broward Blvd., Plantation ☎ 954/472–5836) has 36 holes to play.

Ice Hockey. Office Depot Center (formerly the National Car Rental Center) is the home of the National Hockey League's **Florida Panthers** (✉ 2555 N.W. 137th Way [Panther Pkwy.], Sunrise ☎ 954/835–8326).

SHOPPING   Broward's shopping extravaganza, **Fashion Mall at Plantation** (✉ 321 N. University Dr., north of Broward Blvd., Plantation), is a jewel of a mall. The three-level complex includes Macy's and Lord & Taylor; a Sheraton Suites Hotel; and more than 100 specialty shops. Apart from a diverse food court, there's Brasserie Max for fine dining. Travel industry surveys reveal that shopping is vacationers' number one activity. With 26 million visitors annually, **Sawgrass Mills** (✉ 12801 W. Sunrise Blvd., at Flamingo Rd., Sunrise), 10 mi west of downtown Fort Lauderdale, proves the point, ranking as the second-biggest tourist attraction in Florida, behind Disney. The complex itself is alligator shape, and walking every nook and cranny is about 2 mi. There are 11,000 self-parking spaces, valet parking, and two information centers. More than 400 shops—many of them manufacturer's outlets, retail outlets, and name-brand discounters—include Last Call from Neiman Marcus, Nautica, Hugo Boss, Puma, Donna Karan, Liz Claiborne, Off 5th Saks Fifth Avenue, Kenneth Cole, and Ron Jon Surf Shop. At the Oasis, restaurants such as Hard Rock Cafe, Legal Sea Foods, Wolfgang Puck Cafe, Rainforest Cafe, and others are joined by entertainment venues Regal 23 Cinemas and GameWorks.

NORTH ON SCENIC A1A

North of Fort Lauderdale's Birch Recreation Area, Route A1A edges back from the beach through the section known as the Galt Ocean Mile, and a succession of ocean-side communities lines up against the sea. Traffic can line up, too, as it passes through a changing pattern of beach-blocking high-rises and modest family vacation towns and back again. Here and there a scenic lighthouse or park dots the landscape, while other attractions and recreational activities are found inland.

Lauderdale-by-the-Sea

⑱ *5 mi north of Fort Lauderdale.*

Tucked just north of Fort Lauderdale's northern boundary, this low-rise family resort town has a tradition of digging in its heels at the thought of multiple-story high-rises. Drive along lawn-divided El Mar Drive, lined with garden-style motels a block east of Route A1A. Getting along without a car in Lauderdale-by-the-Sea is easy—it's only 3 mi long, and restaurants and shops are near hotels and the beach. Where Commercial Boulevard meets the ocean, walk out onto **Anglin's Fishing Pier**, stretching 875 ft into the Atlantic. Fish, stop in at any of the popular restaurants clustered around the seafront plaza, or just soak up the scene.

Where to Stay & Eat

$–$$$$ ✕ **Sea Watch.** After more than 25 years this nautical-theme restaurant right on the beach stays packed during lunch and dinner. The menu has appetizers from oysters Rockefeller to gulf shrimp, clams casino, and Bahamian conch fritters, plus daily entrée specials such as oat-crusted sautéed yellowtail snapper with roasted red bell pepper sauce and basil or a charbroiled dolphin fillet marinated with soy sauce, garlic, black pepper, and lemon juice. Desserts include a cappuccino brownie and strawberries Romanoff. ✉ *6002 N. Ocean Blvd. (Rte. A1A), Fort Lauderdale* ☎ *954/781–2200* ▭ *AE, MC, V.*

$–$$$ ✕ **Aruba Beach Café.** This is your best bet at the pier. A big beachside barn of a place—very casual, always crowded, always fun—it serves big portions of Caribbean conch chowder and a Key West soup loaded with shrimp, calamari, and oysters, plus fresh tropical salads, burgers, sandwiches, and seafood. A band performs Friday and Sunday 2 to 7. ✉ *1 E. Commercial Blvd.* ☎ *954/776–0001* ▭ *AE, D, DC, MC, V.*

$$ ▥ **A Little Inn by the Sea.** Innkeeper Uli Brandt and his family maintain tropical charm at this B&B-style inn, which caters to an international clientele—French, German, and English are spoken here. All rooms have bamboo and rattan furniture and nice views from private balconies, many of which face the beach. A complimentary breakfast is set up each morning in the lobby. ✉ *4546 El Mar Dr., 33308* ☎ *954/772–2450 or 800/492–0311* 🖷 *954/938–9354* ⊕ *www.alittleinn.com* ⌨ *10 rooms, 7 suites, 12 efficiencies* ⟁ *Pool, beach, bicycles* ▭ *AE, D, DC, MC, V.*

¢–$$ ▥ **Blue Seas Courtyard.** Innkeeper Cristie Furth, with her husband, Marc, runs this small one- and two-story motel in a quiet resort area across from the beach. Lattice fencing, fountains, and gardens of cactus and impatiens provide privacy around the brick patio and pool. Guest quarters have a Mexican hacienda look with hand-painted and stenciled furnishings and terra-cotta tiles. ✉ *4525 El Mar Dr., 33308* ☎ *954/ 772–3336* 🖷 *954/772–6337* ⊕ *www.blueseascourtyard.com* ⌨ *12 units* ⟁ *Kitchens, pool, laundry facilities* ▭ *MC, V.*

¢ ▥ **Great Escape Motel.** For comfortable accommodations amid palms and other tropical plants in a poolside courtyard, this could be your great—and economical—escape. Among 12 units are four hotel rooms, five efficiencies, and two one-bedroom apartments. ✉ *4620 North Ocean Dr., 33308* ☎ *954/772–1002* 🖷 *954/772–6488* ⊕ *www.greatescapemotel. com* ⌨ *12 units* ⟁ *Pool, laundry facilities* ▭ *AE, MC, V.*

¢ ▥ **Mardi Gras Motel.** You'll find renovated rooms, a new pool, new kitchens, and new owner-management, but what remains steadfast is a place within the area's affordable small property line-up. The owner's wife speaks Spanish. ✉ *4312 Ocean Dr., 33308* ☎ *954/776–4566* 🖷 *954/772–8929* ⊕ *www.mardigrasmotel.com* ⌨ *16 units* ⟁ *Pool, laundry facilities, phones, Internet* ▭ *AE, D, MC, V.*

¢ ▥ **Rainbow by the Sea Resort.** This family-oriented, owner-managed property has all no-smoking rooms. A carpeted sundeck equipped with loungers faces the ocean on top of the main building. ✉ *4553 El Mar Dr., 33308* ☎ *954/772–0514* 🖷 *954/772–6569* ⌨ *30 units* ⟁ *Pool, laundry facilities; no smoking* ▭ *AE, MC, V.*

¢ ▥ **Villa Orleans.** With just a touch of New Orleans architecture, this little beach-area property rests behind an inviting pool and well-groomed grounds. Spacious rooms provide old-Florida comfort. ⊠ *4513 N. Ocean Dr., 33308* ☎ *888/301–2363* 🖷 *954/491–2363* ⊕ *www. villaorleans.com* ⟿ *12 units* ♻ *Pool, laundry facilities* ⊟ *AE, MC, V.*

The Outdoors

Anglin's Fishing Pier (☎ 954/491–9403) is open for fishing 24 hours a day. Fishing costs $4, tackle rental is an additional $5 (plus $10 deposit), and bait averages $2.

Pompano Beach

⑲ *3 mi north of Lauderdale-by-the-Sea.*

As Route A1A enters this town directly north of Lauderdale-by-the-Sea, the high-rise scene resumes. Sportfishing is big in Pompano Beach, as its name implies, but there's more to beachside attractions than the popular Fisherman's Wharf. Behind a low coral-rock wall, Alsdorf Park extends north and south of the wharf along the road and beach.

Where to Stay & Eat

★ **$$$–$$$$** ✕ **Cafe Maxx.** New-wave epicurean dining had its South Florida start here in the early 1980s, and Cafe Maxx remains popular. Chef Oliver Saucy's menu changes nightly, showcasing tropical appeal with jumbo stone-crab claws with honey-lime mustard sauce and black-bean and banana-pepper chili with Florida avocado. Appetizers include duck and smoked mozzarella ravioli with brown butter, basil, and sun-dried tomatoes. Desserts such as praline macadamia mousse over chocolate cake with butterscotch sauce stay the tropical course. Select from 200 wines offered by the bottle, another 20 by the glass. ⊠ *2601 E. Atlantic Blvd.* ☎ *954/782–0606* ⊟ *AE, D, DC, MC, V* ☉ *No lunch.*

$–$$$ 🏨 **Best Western Beachcomber.** This property's beach location is central to most Broward County attractions and a mile from the Pompano Pier. Ocean views are everywhere, from the oversize guest-room balconies to dining rooms. Although there are also villas and penthouse suites atop the eight-story structure, standard rooms are spacious. The multilingual staff is attentive to guest requests. ⊠ *1200 S. Ocean Blvd., 33062* ☎ *954/941–7830 or 800/231–2423* 🖷 *954/942–7680* ⊕ *www. beachcomberhotel.com* ⟿ *134 rooms, 9 villas, 4 suites* ♻ *Restaurant, 2 pools, beach, shuffleboard, volleyball, bar* ⊟ *AE, D, DC, MC, V.*

Sports & the Outdoors

FISHING **Pompano Pier** (☎ 954/943–1488) extends 1,080 ft into the Atlantic. Admission is $2.65; rod-and-reel rental is $5, plus $5 deposit.

For drift-fishing try *Fish City Pride* (⊠ Fish City Marina, 2621 N. Riverside Dr. ☎ 954/781–1211). Morning, afternoon, and evening trips cost $28 and include fishing gear and bait. Arrange for a saltwater charter boat through the **Hillsboro Inlet Marina** (⊠ 2629 N. Riverside Dr. ☎ 954/ 943–8222). The 10-boat fleet offers half-day charters for $395, including gear for up to six people.

GOLF **Crystal Lake South Course** (⊠ 3800 Crystal Lake Dr. ☎ 954/943–2902) has 36 holes. **Palm-Aire Country Club** (⊠ 3701 Oaks Clubhouse Dr. ☎ 954/978–1737; 954/975–6244 for tee line) has five golf courses, including an executive course with four extra practice holes.

HORSE RACING **Pompano Harness Track,** Florida's only harness track, has world-class trotters and pacers during its October–August meet. The Top o' the Park restaurant overlooks the finish line. The track also has a poker room and afternoon and evening simulcast betting. ⊠ *1800 S.W. 3rd St.* ☎ *954/972–2000* 🎫 *Grandstand free, clubhouse $2* ☉ *Racing Mon., Wed., and Fri.–Sat. at 7:30.*

Shopping

Bargain hunters head to the **Festival Flea Market Mall** (⌧ 2900 W. Sample Rd.), where more than 800 stores, booths, and kiosks sell new brand-name merchandise at a discount. For shopping diversions, there is also an arcade, beauty salon, farmers' market, and food court. The **Pompano Square Mall** (⌧ 2001 N. Federal Hwy., at Copans Rd.) has 60 shops, three department stores, and a few places for food.

Lighthouse Point

20 *2 mi north of Pompano Beach.*

The big attraction here is the view across Hillsboro Inlet to **Hillsboro Light**, the brightest lighthouse in the Southeast. Mariners have used this landmark for decades. When at sea you can see the light almost halfway to the Bahamas. Although the lighthouse is on private property and is inaccessible to the public, it's well worth a peek.

Where to Eat

★ **$–$$$** ✕ **Cap's Place.** On an island that was once a bootlegger's haunt, this seafood restaurant is reached by launch and has served such luminaries as Winston Churchill, FDR, and John F. Kennedy. Cap was Captain Theodore Knight, born in 1871, who, with partner-in-crime Al Hasis, floated a derelict barge to the area in the 1920s. Today the rustic restaurant, built on the barge, is run by descendants of Hasis. Baked wahoo steaks are lightly glazed and meaty, hot and flaky rolls are baked fresh several times a night, and tangy lime pie is a great finishing touch. ⌧ *Cap's Dock, 2765 N.E. 28th Ct.* ☎ *954/941–0418* ▭ *AE, MC, V* ✆ *No lunch.*

en route   To the north, Route A1A traverses the so-called Hillsboro Mile (actually more than 2 mi), a millionaire's row of some of the most beautiful and expensive homes in Broward County. The road runs along a narrow strip of land between the Intracoastal Waterway and the ocean, with bougainvillea and oleander edging the way and yachts docked along both banks. In winter the traffic often creeps at a snail's pace as vacationers and retirees gawk at the views.

Deerfield Beach

21 *3½ mi north of Lighthouse Point.*

☺ The name **Quiet Waters Park** belies what's in store for kids here. Splash Adventure is a high-tech water-play system with slides and tunnels, among other activities. There's also cable waterskiing and boat rental on the park's lake. ⌧ *401 S. Powerline Rd.* ☎ *954/360–1315* ⌧ *Park $1 weekends, free weekdays; Splash Adventure $3* ✆ *Park daily 8–6; Splash Adventure mid-Feb.–Oct., daily 8–6.*

Deerfield Island Park, reached only by boat, is a group of coastal hammock islands. Officially designated an Urban Wilderness Area along the Intracoastal Waterway, it contains a mangrove swamp that provides a critical habitat for gopher tortoises, gray foxes, raccoons, and armadillos. Boat shuttles run on the hour Wednesday 10–noon and Sunday 10–3; space is limited, so call for reservations. Call also for special events. ⌧ *1720 Deerfield Island Park* ☎ *954/360–1320* ⌧ *Free.*

Where to Stay & Eat

★ **$–$$$** ✕ **Brooks.** This is one of the area's better restaurants, thanks to a French perfectionist at the helm, Bernard Perron. Meals are served in a series of rooms filled with replicas of old masters, cut glass, antiques, and floral wallpaper. Fresh ingredients go into distinctly Floridian dishes. Main courses include red snapper in papillote, broiled fillet of pompano with seasoned root vegetables, and a sweet lemongrass linguine with bok choy and julienned crisp vegetables. For dessert, put in your order early in the meal for the chocolate soufflé. ⊠ *500 S. Federal Hwy.* ☎ *954/427–9302* ▤ *AE, D, MC, V.*

★ ¢–$$$ ✕ **Whale's Rib.** For a casual, almost funky nautical experience near the beach, look no further. For more than 20 years the Williams family has served up fish specials along with whale fries—thinly sliced potatoes that look like hot potato chips. Lesser appetites can choose from a good selection of salads and fish sandwiches. Other favorites are specials from the raw bar, Ipswich clams, and a popular fish dip for starters. ⊠ *2031 N.E. 2nd St.* ☎ *954/421–8880* ▤ *AE, MC, V.*

$$–$$$$ ▦ **Ocean Terrace Suites.** This four-story motel is in one of the quieter sections of North Broward, just south of the Palm Beach county line, across the narrow shore road from the beach. Large units—efficiencies and one- and three-bedroom apartments—all have big balconies overlooking the sea. The updated furniture is rattan, and colors vary from shore-washed to bright; pink and green pastels tint the rooms. ⊠ *2080 E. Hillsboro Blvd., 33441* ☎ *954/427–8400* ⊟ *954/427–0555* ⊕ *www.ocean-terracesuites.com* ⤳ *32 units* ⚐ *Kitchens, pool, laundry facilities* ▤ *AE, D, DC, MC, V.*

$–$$$ ▦ **Royal Flamingo Villas.** A small community of houselike villas built in the 1970s reaches from the Intracoastal Waterway to the ocean. The roomy and comfortable one- and two-bedroom villas are condominiums. All are so quiet that you hear only the soft click of the ceiling fans. If you don't need lavish public facilities, this is your upscale choice at a reasonable price. ⊠ *1225 Hillsboro Mile (Rte. A1A), Hillsboro Beach 33062* ☎ *954/427–0660 or 800/241–2477* ⊟ *954/427–6110* ⊕ *www.royalflamingovillas.com* ⤳ *40 villas* ⚐ *Pool, beach, dock, boating, shuffleboard, laundry facilities* ▤ *D, MC, V.*

¢–$ ▦ **Carriage House Resort Motel.** This tidy motel sits one block from the ocean. The white, two-story colonial-style property with black shutters is actually two buildings connected by a second-story sundeck. Steady improvements have been made to the facility, including the addition of Bahama beds that feel and look like sofas. Kitchenettes are equipped with good-quality utensils. Rooms are self-contained and quiet and have walk-in closets and room safes. ⊠ *250 S. Ocean Blvd., 33441* ☎ *954/427–7670* ⊟ *954/428–4790* ⊕ *www.carriagehouseresort.com* ⤳ *6 rooms, 14 efficiencies, 10 1-bedroom apartments* ⚐ *Pool, shuffleboard, laundry facilities* ▤ *AE, D, DC, MC, V.*

Sports & the Outdoors

FISHING The **Cove Marina** (⊠ Hillsboro Blvd. and the Intracoastal Waterway ☎ 954/360–9343) has a deep-sea charter fleet. In the winter season there are excellent runs of sailfish, kingfish, dolphinfish, and tuna. A half-day charter costs about $425 for six people. Enter the marina through the Cove Shopping Center.

GOLF Off Hillsboro Boulevard west of Interstate 95, **Deer Creek Golf Club** (⊠ 2801 Country Club Blvd. ☎ 954/421–5550) has 18 holes.

SCUBA DIVING One of the area's most popular dive boats, the 48-ft *Lady Go-Diver* (⊠ Cove Marina, Hillsboro Blvd. and the Intracoastal Waterway ☎ 954/260–7856) has morning and afternoon dives, plus evening dives on weekends. Snorkelers and certified divers can explore the marine life of nearby reefs and shipwrecks. The cost is $42.50; riders are welcome for $25.

SOUTH BROWARD

From Hollywood's Broadwalk, a 27-ft-wide thoroughfare paralleling 2 mi of palm-fringed beach, to the western reaches of Old West–flavored Davie, this region has a personality all its own. South Broward's roots are in early Florida settlements. Thus far it has avoided some of the glitz and glamour of its neighbors to the north and south, and folks here like it that way. Still, there's plenty to see and do—excellent restaurants in every price range, world-class pari-mutuels, and a new focus on the arts.

Hollywood

22 *7 mi south of Fort Lauderdale.*

Hollywood is a city undergoing a revival. New shops, restaurants, and art galleries open at a persistent clip. The city spiffed up its Broadwalk, a wide pedestrian walkway along the beach, where Rollerbladers are as common as visitors from the North. Trendy sidewalk cafés have opened, vying for space with mom-and-pop T-shirt shops. Downtown, along Harrison Street and Hollywood Boulevard, jazz clubs and still more fashionable restaurants draw young professionals to the scene. Design studios and art galleries are also abundant along these two streets. In 1921 Joseph W. Young, a California real-estate entrepreneur, began developing the community of Hollywood from the woody flatlands. It quickly became a major tourist magnet, with casino gambling and whatever else that made Florida hot. Reminders of the glory days of the Young era remain in places like Young Circle (the junction of U.S. 1 and Hollywood Boulevard) and the stately old homes on east Hollywood streets.

The **Art and Culture Center of Hollywood** is a visual and performing-arts center with an art reference library, outdoor sculpture garden, arts school, and museum store. It's just east of Young Circle. ✉ *1650 Harrison St.* ☎ *954/921–3274* 💲 *$5* ☉ *Tues.–Wed. and Fri.–Sat. 10–4, Thurs. 10–8, and Sun. 1–4.*

Fodor's Choice ★ With the Intracoastal Waterway to its west and the beach and ocean to the east, the 2.2-mi paved promenade known as the **Broadwalk** has been popular with pedestrians and cyclists since 1924. Expect to hear French spoken along this scenic stretch, especially in winter, since Hollywood Beach has been a favorite winter getaway for Québecois ever since Joseph Young hired French-Canadians to work here in the 1920s.

Hollywood North Beach Park is at the north end of the Broadwalk. No high-rises overpower the scene, nothing hip or chic, just a laid-back, old-fashioned place for enjoying the sun, sand, and sea. ✉ *Rte. A1A and Sheridan St.* ☎ *954/926–2444* 💲 *Free; parking $4 until 2, $2 thereafter* ☉ *Daily 8–6.*

☺ Comprising 1,500 acres at the Intracoastal Waterway, **West Lake Park** is one of Florida's largest urban nature facilities. Rent a canoe, kayak, or boat with an electric motor (no fossil fuels are allowed in the park) or take the 40-minute environmental boat tour. Extensive boardwalks traverse a mangrove community, where endangered and threatened species abound. A 65-ft observation tower allows views of the entire park. More than $1 million in exhibits are on display at the **Anne Kolb Nature Center,** named after the late county commissioner who was a leading environmental advocate. The center's exhibit hall has 27 interactive displays, an ecology room, and a trilevel aquarium. ✉ *1200 Sheridan St.* ☎ *954/926–2410* 💲 *Weekends $1, weekdays free; exhibit hall $2* ☉ *Daily 8–6.*

☺ At the edge of Hollywood lies **Seminole Native Village,** a reservation where you can pet a cougar, hold a baby alligator, and watch other wildlife demonstrations. The Seminole also sell their arts and crafts here. Across the street from the Seminole Native Village, **Hollywood Seminole Gaming** (✉ 4150 N. State Rd. 7 ☎ 954/961–3220) is open 24/7 and has high-stakes bingo, low-stakes poker, and more than 1,000 gaming machines. ✉ *3551 N. State Rd. 7* ☎ *954/961–4519* ✆ *Self-guided tour $5, guided tour including alligator wrestling and snake demonstrations $10* ☉ *Daily 9–5.*

Where to Stay & Eat

$$–$$$$ ✕ **Martha's.** You have two choices of dining locations here, both with impressive views of the Intracoastal Waterway. Martha's Tropical Grille, on the upper deck, is more informal. Martha's Supper Club, on the lower level, is dressier, and piano music accompanies dinner. Both floors offer similar menus, chiefly Florida seafood: flaky dolphinfish in a court bouillon; shrimp dipped in a piña colada batter, rolled in coconut, and panfried with orange mustard sauce; and snapper prepared 17 ways. Complimentary dock space is provided if you arrive by boat. ✉ *6024 N. Ocean Dr.* ☎ *954/923–5444* ▤ *AE, D, DC, MC, V.*

$–$$$$ ✕ **Giorgio's Grill.** Good food and service are hallmarks of this 400-seat restaurant overlooking the Intracoastal Waterway. Seafood is a specialty, but you'll also find pasta and meat dishes. A great water view and friendly staff add to the experience. A surprisingly extensive wine list is reasonably priced. ✉ *606 N. Ocean Dr.* ☎ *954/929–7030* ▤ *AE, D, DC, MC, V.*

$$–$$$ ✕ **Las Brisas.** Right next to the beach, this cozy bistro offers seating inside or out, and the food is Argentine with an Italian flair. A small pot sits on each table filled with *chimichurri*—a paste made of oregano, parsley, olive oil, salt, garlic, and crushed pepper—for spreading on steaks. Grilled fish is a favorite, as are pork chops, chicken, and pasta entrées. Desserts include a rum cake, a flan like *mamacita* used to make, and a *dulce con leche* (a sweet milk pudding). ✉ *600 N. Surf Rd.* ☎ *954/923–1500* ▤ *AE, D, DC, MC, V* ☉ *No lunch.*

$–$$ ✕ **Sushi Blues Café.** First-class Japanese food is served up in a cubicle setting that's so jammed you'll wonder where this hip group disappears to by day. Japanese chefs prepare conventional and macrobiotic-influenced dishes that range from sushi and rolls (California, tuna, and the Yozo roll, with snapper, flying-fish eggs, asparagus, and Japanese mayonnaise) to steamed veggies with tofu and steamed snapper with miso sauce. The Sushi Blues Band performs on Friday and Saturday. ✉ *1836 S. Young Circle* ☎ *954/929–9560* ▤ *AE, MC, V* ☉ *No lunch.*

¢–$$ ✕ **Le Tub.** Formerly a Sunoco gas station, this place is now a quirky waterside saloon with a seeming affection for claw-foot bathtubs. Hand-painted tubs are everywhere—under ficus, sea grape, and palm trees. The eatery is favored by locals for affordable food: mostly shrimp, burgers, and barbecue. ✉ *1100 N. Ocean Dr.* ☎ *954/921–9425* ▤ *No credit cards.*

★ $$–$$$$ 🏨 **The Westin Diplomat Resort & Spa.** Opened in 2002 on the site of the original 1950s hotel of the same name, the Diplomat is a grand 39-story, dual-tower property. The hotel has a lobby-atrium area with ceilings soaring to 60 ft in height. A signature of the resort is its 120-ft bridged pool, extending from the lobby to the beachfront. A Mediterranean-inspired spa offers fitness facilities and more than 20 luxury treatments. The Diplomat's country club, across the Intracoastal, has 60 rooms, golf, tennis, and spa. You'll have use of facilities at both properties; shuttle service is provided. ✉ *1995 E. Hallandale Beach Blvd., 33309* ☎ *954/457–2000 or 800/327–1212* ⊕ *www.diplomatresort.com* ⇨ *900 rooms,*

100 suites ♿ 3 restaurants, in-room data ports, minibars, 18-hole golf course, 10 tennis courts, 3 pools, health club, 2 spas, marina, 2 bars, business services, convention center ▭ AE, DC, MC, V.

$–$$$ ▦ **Greenbriar Beach Club.** In a neighborhood of Hollywood Beach known for its flowered streets, this oceanfront all-suite hotel retains its 1950s style outside, but inside the rooms have been renovated and include full kitchens. The staff is multilingual, and TVs have four Spanish and two French channels. On a 200-ft stretch of beach, the hotel bills itself as Florida's best-kept secret, and it just could be. ✉ 1900 S. Surf Rd., 33019 ☎ 954/922–2606 or 800/861–4873 ⊟ 954/923–0897 ⊕ www. greenbriarbc.com ➳ 47 suites ♿ Pool, beach, volleyball, laundry facilities ▭ AE, D, MC, V.

★ ¢–$$ ▦ **Manta Ray Inn.** Canadians Donna and Dwayne Boucher run this immaculate, affordable two-story inn on a beach, perfect for a low-key getaway. Dating from the 1940s, the inn offers casual, comfortable beachfront accommodations with amenities such as cable TV with VCR. Kitchens are equipped with pots, pans, and mini-appliances that make housekeeping convenient. One-bedroom apartments have marble shower stalls, and two-bedroom units also have tubs. ✉ 1715 S. Surf Rd., 33019 ☎ 954/921–9666 or 800/255–0595 ⊟ 954/929–8220 ⊕ www.mantarayinn.com ➳ 12 units ♿ Beach ▭ AE, D, MC, V.

¢–$$ ▦ **Sea Downs.** Directly on the Broadwalk, this three-story lodging is a good choice for efficiency or apartment living (one-bedroom units can be joined to make two-bedroom apartments). All but two units have ocean views. Kitchens are fully equipped, and most units have tub-showers and closets. Housekeeping is provided once a week. In between, fresh towels are provided daily and sheets upon request, but you must make your own bed. ✉ 2900 N. Surf Rd., 33019-3704 ☎ 954/923–4968 ⊟ 954/923–8747 ⊕ www.seadowns.com ➳ 6 efficiencies, 8 1-bedroom apartments ♿ In-room data ports, pool, laundry facilities ▭ No credit cards.

¢–$ ▦ **Driftwood on the Ocean.** Facing the beach at the secluded south end of Surf Road is this attractive late-1950s-era resort motel. The setting is what draws guests, but attention to maintenance and frequent refurbishing are what make it a value. Accommodations range from a studio to a deluxe two-bedroom, two-bath suite. Most units have a kitchen; all have balconies or terraces. ✉ 2101 S. Surf Rd., 33019 ☎ 954/923–9528 or 800/944–3148 ⊟ 954/922–1062 ⊕ www.driftwoodontheocean. com ➳ 7 rooms, 9 2-bedroom apartments, 13 1-bedroom apartments, 20 efficiencies ♿ Some kitchens, pool, beach, bicycles, shuffleboard, laundry facilities ▭ AE, D, MC, V.

Nightlife & the Arts

THE ARTS **Harrison Street Art and Design District** in downtown Hollywood has galleries that carry original artwork (eclectic paintings, sculpture, photography, and mixed media), Costa Rican collectibles, and African artifacts. Friday night the artists' studios, galleries, and shops stay open late while crowds meander along Hollywood Boulevard and Harrison Street. **Indaba** (✉ 2029 Harrison St. ☎ 954/920–2029) celebrates African art with an extensive collection of masks, statues, cloth, baskets, and furniture. **Mosaica** (✉ 2020 Hollywood Blvd. ☎ 954/923–7006) design studio with unique mosaic tile tables, mirrors, and art. The colorful home furnishings gallery, **Alliage** (✉ 2035 Harrison St. ☎ 954/922–7017), has tables, wall consoles, and sculptures handcrafted from brushed aluminum and sand-blasted glass.

NIGHTLIFE Although downtown Hollywood has a small-town feel, it has an assortment of coffee bars, Internet cafés, sports bars, martini lounges, and dance clubs. The downtown area is known for its live jazz and blues venues. **O'Hara's Hollywood** (⊠ 1903 Hollywood Blvd. ☎ 954/925–2555) highlights top local talents with live jazz and blues six nights a week. For New Orleans–style jazz, head to **Ellington's** (⊠ 2009 Harrison St. ☎ 954/920–9322). Sushi café and wine bar **Sushi Blues** (⊠ 1836 Young Circle ☎ 954/929–9560) serves up live blues Friday and Saturday nights starting at 9. **Warehaus 57** (⊠ 1904 Hollywood Blvd. ☎ 954/926–6633) is where aspiring novelists and poets share their words with the café crowd. The late-night coffee bar **Now Art Café** (⊠ 1820 Young Circle ☎ 954/922–0506) hosts art exhibits and live one-man bands.

Sports & the Outdoors

BIKING   The 2-mi **Broadwalk,** which has its own bike path, is popular with cyclists.

DOG RACING   **Hollywood Greyhound Track** has live dog-racing action during its December–May season and simulcasting every day. Relax at the Dog House sports bar and grill. ⊠ *831 N. Federal Hwy., Hallandale* ☎ *954/924–3200* 🎟 *Grandstand $1, clubhouse $2, parking free* ⊙ *Racing nightly at 7:30 and Tues., Thurs., and Sat. at 12:30 PM.*

GOLF   The **Diplomat Country Club & Spa** (⊠ 501 Diplomat Pkwy., Hallandale ☎ 954/457–2000) has 18 holes and a spa. The course at **Emerald Hills** (⊠ 4100 N. Hills Dr. ☎ 954/961–4000) has 18 holes.

HORSE RACING   **Gulfstream Park Race Track** is the winter home of some of the nation's top Thoroughbreds, trainers, and jockeys. In addition to races, there are family days with attractions for kids and scheduled concerts with name performers. The season is capped by the $1 million Florida Derby, with Kentucky Derby hopefuls. Racing unfolds January through April. ⊠ *901 S. Federal Hwy., Hallandale* ☎ *954/454–7000 or 800/771–8873* 🎟 *Grandstand $3, clubhouse $5* ⊙ *Racing Wed.–Mon. at 1 and nightly simulcasting.*

Dania Beach

❷❸ *3 mi north of Hollywood, 4 mi south of Fort Lauderdale.*

This town at the south edge of Fort Lauderdale is probably best known for its antiques dealers, but there are other attractions as well.

★ ℭ   The **Graves Museum of Archaeology and Natural History,** formerly the South Florida Museum of Natural History, has an extensive prehistoric collection including the Bambiraptor feinbergi, better known as "Bambi"—the missing link in the dinosaur–bird evolution. This hidden treasure of a museum also has a permanent collection with pre-Columbian art, Greco-Roman materials, and artifacts from early Florida. Also on display are shipwreck artifacts, dioramas on Tequesta life, and a 3-ton quartz crystal. Lectures, conferences, field trips, and a summer archaeological camp are offered. ⊠ *481 S. Federal Hwy.* ☎ *954/925–7770* ⊕ *www.gravesmuseum.org* 🎟 *$6* ⊙ *Tues.–Fri. 10–4, Sat. 10–6, Sun. noon–6.*

The **John U. Lloyd Beach State Recreation Area** has a pine-shaded beach, a jetty pier where you can fish, a marina, nature trails, and canoeing on Whiskey Creek. This is a fabulous spot to watch cruise ships entering and departing Port Everglades. ⊠ *6503 N. Ocean Dr.* ☎ *954/923–2833* 🎟 *$4 per vehicle with up to 8 people* ⊙ *Daily 8–sunset.*

★   **IGFA Fishing Hall of Fame and Museum** is a shrine to the sport of fishing. Near the Fort Lauderdale airport at Interstate 95 and Griffin Road, the center is the creation of the International Game Fishing Association. In addition to checking out the World Fishing Hall of Fame, a marina, and an extensive museum and research library, visit seven galleries with virtual-reality fishing and other interactive displays. And in the Catch Gallery, cast off via virtual reality and try to reel in a marlin, sailfish, trout, tarpon, or bass. ⊠ *300 Gulfstream Way, Dania Beach* ☎ *954/ 922–4212* ⊕ *www.igfa.org* ⊠ *$4.99* ☉ *Daily 10–6.*

Sports & the Outdoors

FISHING The 920-ft **Dania Pier** (☎ 954/927–0640) is open around the clock. Fishing is $3 (including parking), tackle rental is $6, bait is about $3, and spectators pay $1.

JAI ALAI **Dania Jai-Alai Palace** has one of the fastest ball games on the planet, scheduled year-round. Simulcast wagering from other tracks and a poker room are also available. ⊠ *301 E. Dania Beach Blvd.* ☎ *954/920–1511* ⊠ *$1.50, reserved seats $2–$7* ☉ *Games Tues. and Sat. at noon, Sun. at 1, nightly Tues.–Sat. at 7:15.*

MINIATURE GOLF **Boomers!** has action games for kids of all ages—go-kart and naskart racing, miniature golf, batting cages, bumper boats, lasertron, and a skycoaster. ⊠ *1801 N.W. 1st St.* ☎ *954/921–1411* ☉ *Sun.–Thurs. 10 AM–2 AM, Fri.–Sat. 10 AM–6 AM.*

ROLLER COASTER **Dania Beach Hurricane** roller coaster isn't the highest, fastest, or longest coaster in the world, but it's near the top in all those categories and it is the tallest wooden roller coaster south of Atlanta. This is a retro-feeling ride—a wooden coaster that creaks like an old staircase while you race along its 3,200 ft of track and plummet from a height of 100 ft at speeds of up to 55 mph. ⊠ *1760 N.W. 1st St.* ☎ *954/921–7433* ⊠ *$5.89* ☉ *Sun.–Thurs. 10 AM–11:30 PM, Fri.–Sat. 10 AM–2 AM.*

Shopping

More than 250 antiques dealers in **Dania Antique Row** buy and sell items from antique furniture to vintage knickknacks. This two-square-block area is on Federal Highway (U.S. 1), ½ mi south of the Fort Lauderdale airport and ½ mi north of Hollywood. Take the Stirling Road or Griffin Road East exit off Interstate 95.

Davie

24 *4 mi west of Dania.*

This town's horse farms and estates are the closest thing to the Old West in South Florida. Folks in western wear ride their fine steeds through downtown—where they have the same right of way as motorists—and order up takeout at "ride-through" windows. With 70,000 residents, the town has doubled in size in 15 years, and gated communities are popping up alongside ranches. A monthly rodeo is Davie's most famous activity.

☪ Gators, crocodiles, river otters, and birds of prey can be seen at **Flamingo Gardens and Wray Botanical Collection**, as can a 25,000-square-ft walkthrough aviary, a plant house, and an Everglades museum in the pioneer Wray Home. A half-hour guided tram ride winds through a citrus grove and wetlands area. ⊠ *3750 S. Flamingo Rd.* ☎ *954/473–2955* ⊕ *www.flamingogardens.org* ⊠ *$12, tram ride $3* ☉ *Daily 9:30–5:30; closed Mon. June–Sept.*

☪ At the **Young at Art Children's Museum**, kids can work with paint, graphics, sculpture, and crafts according to themes that change three times a year. Then they take their masterpieces home with them. ⊠ *11584 W. State Rd. 84, in the Plaza* ☎ *954/424–0085* ⊕ *www.youngatartmuseum. org* ⊠ *$5* ☉ *Mon.–Sat. 10–5, Sun. noon–5.*

Where to Eat

★ $$–$$$ ✕ **Armadillo Cafe.** Chefs Eve Montella and Kevin McCarthy have created a restaurant whose southwestern theme and inspired food have made it a favored destination for visitors from around the world for more than a decade. Seafood looms large here, but other specialties include grilled tenderloin of ostrich with sun-dried cherry sauce and steaks with pasilla chili sauce. An extensive wine list offers cult and niche vintages. ✉ *3400 S. University* ☎ *954/423–9954* ▭ *AE, D, DC, MC, V.*

Nightlife & the Arts

THE ARTS   **Bailey Concert Hall** (✉ Central Campus of Broward Community College, 3501 S.W. Davie Rd. ☎ 954/201–6884) is a popular place for classical music concerts, dance, drama, and other performing-arts activities, especially October–April.

NIGHTLIFE   **Davie Junction** (✉ 6311 S.W. 45th St. ☎ 954/581–1132), South Florida's hot venue for country music, is in the heart of Broward's horse country, with dance lessons available. It's open for dinner and dancing until 4 AM Tuesday through Saturday.

Uncle Funny's Comedy Club (✉ 9160 State Rd. 84, Pine Island Plaza ☎ 954/474–5653) showcases national and local comics Wednesday through Friday and Sunday at 8:30, Friday and Saturday at 11, plus Saturday at 7 and 9.

The Outdoors

BIKING   Bicycle and in-line skating enthusiasts can ride at the **Brian Piccolo Skate Park and Velodrome** (✉ 9501 Sheridan St., Cooper City ☎ 954/437–2626), south of Davie. Hours are geared to after-school and weekend skating.

RODEO   The local **Davie Rodeo** (✉ 4271 Davie Rd. ☎ 954/384–7075) is held on the Bergeron Rodeo Grounds the fourth weekend of every month. Saturday-night bull riding starts at 8 PM. Special national rodeos come to town some weekends.

FORT LAUDERDALE & BROWARD COUNTY A TO Z

To research prices, get advice from other travelers, and book travel arrangements, visit www.fodors.com.

AIR TRAVEL

CARRIERS   More than 40 scheduled airlines, commuters and charters serve Fort Lauderdale–Hollywood International Airport.

🛈 Major Airline Contacts **Air Canada** ☎ 800/689-2247. **Air Jamaica** ☎ 800/523-5585. **Air Tran** ☎ 800/247-8726. **America West** ☎ 800/235-9292. **American** ☎ 800/433-7300. **Continental** ☎ 800/525-0280. **Delta** ☎ 800/221-1212. **JetBlue** ☎ 800/538-2583. **MetroJet** ☎ 888/638-7653. **Midway** ☎ 800/446-4392. **Northwest** ☎ 800/225-2525. **Southwest** ☎ 800/435-9792. **Spirit** ☎ 800/772-7117. **TWA** ☎ 800/221-2000. **United** ☎ 800/241-6522. **US Airways** ☎ 800/428-4322.

AIRPORTS

Fort Lauderdale–Hollywood International Airport, 4 mi south of downtown Fort Lauderdale and just off U.S. 1, is one of Florida's busiest, serving more than 16 million passengers a year. Ongoing expansion has added a terminal, parking, and access roads. Broward County Mass Transit operates bus route No. 1 between the airport and its main terminal at Broward Boulevard and Northwest 1st Avenue, in the center of Fort Lauderdale. Service from the airport is every 20 minutes and begins daily at 5:40 AM; the last bus leaves the airport at 11:15 PM. The fare is $1 (50¢ for senior citizens). Airport Express provides limousine service to all parts of Broward County. Fares to most Fort Lauderdale beach hotels are in the $10–$14 range.

🛈 Airport Information **Fort Lauderdale–Hollywood International Airport** ☎ 954/359-6100. **Airport Express** ☎ 954/561-8888. **Broward County Mass Transit** ☎ 954/357-8400.

BOAT & FERRY TRAVEL

Water Taxi provides service along the Intracoastal Waterway in Fort Lauderdale between the 17th Street Causeway and Oakland Park Boulevard daily from 6 AM until midnight.

⛵ Boat & Ferry Information Water Bus, Water Taxi ☎ 954/467-6677.

BUS TRAVEL

Greyhound Lines buses stop in Fort Lauderdale. Broward County Mass Transit bus service covers the entire county and ventures into Dade and Palm Beach counties. The fare is $1; unlimited daily, weekly, and monthly passes are available. Route service starts at 5 AM and continues to 11:30 PM, except on Sunday. Call for route information. City Cruiser is free and covers both the downtown loop and the beach area. The Courthouse Route runs every 10 minutes weekdays from 7:30 until 6. The Las Olas & Beach Route runs on the half hour 5:45 PM–1:45 AM.

CUTTING COSTS Broward County Mass Transit offers special seven-day tourist passes that cost $9 and are good for unlimited use on all county buses. These are available at some hotels, at Broward County libraries, and at the main bus terminal.

⛵ Bus Information Broward County Mass Transit Main Bus Terminal ✉ Broward Blvd. at N.W. 1st Ave., Fort Lauderdale ☎ 954/357-8400. **Greyhound Lines** ✉ 515 N.E. 3rd St., Fort Lauderdale ☎ 800/231-2222 or 954/764-6551. **TMAX** ☎ 954/761-3543.

CAR RENTAL

Agencies in the airport include Avis, Budget, Dollar, and National. Other car rental companies offer shuttle services to nearby rental centers.

⛵ Local Agencies Alamo ☎ 954/525-4713. **Avis** ☎ 954/359-3255. **Budget** ☎ 954/359-4700. **Dollar** ☎ 954/359-7800. **Enterprise** ☎ 954/760-9888. **Hertz** ☎ 954/764-1199. **National** ☎ 954/359-8303.

CAR TRAVEL

Access to Broward County from north or south is via Florida's Turnpike, Interstate 95, U.S. 1, or U.S. 441. Interstate 75 (Alligator Alley) connects Broward with Florida's west coast and runs parallel to State Road 84 within the county. Except during rush hour, Broward County is a fairly easy place in which to drive. East–west Interstate 595 runs from westernmost Broward County and links Interstate 75 with Interstate 95 and U.S. 1, providing handy access to the airport. The scenic but slow Route A1A generally parallels the beach. The Sawgrass Expressway (also known as State Road 869 north of I–595 and I–75 south), is a toll road that links to Sawgrass Mills shopping and the ice-hockey arena, both in Sunrise.

EMERGENCIES

Dial 911 for police or ambulance.

⛵ 24-Hour Pharmacies Eckerd Drug ✉ 1701 E. Commercial Blvd., Fort Lauderdale ☎ 954/771-0660. **Walgreens** ✉ 2855 Stirling Rd., Fort Lauderdale ☎ 954/981-1104 ✉ 601 E. Commercial Blvd., Oakland Park ☎ 954/772-4206 ✉ 289 S. Federal Hwy., Deerfield Beach ☎ 954/481-2993 ✉ 4003 S. University Dr., Davie ☎ 954/475-9375 ✉ 9005 Pines Blvd., Hollywood ☎ 954/392-4749.

MEDIA

NEWSPAPERS & MAGAZINES The *South Florida Sun-Sentinel* and affiliated magazine *City & Shore* cover South Florida news and events.

RADIO On the FM band: 97.3 WFLC and 101.5 WLIF play adult contemporary; 98.7 WKGR plays rock, 105.9 WBGG, classic rock; try 100.7 WHYI for Top 40; 102.7 WMXJ for oldies; 93.9 WLVE for jazz; 99.9 WKIS for country; and 91.3 WLRN for public radio. AM stations include 560

WQAM for sports; 610 WIOD for news; 1360 WKAT for classical; and 1580 WSRF for reggae-Caribbean.

TAXIS

It's difficult to hail a cab on the street. Sometimes you can pick one up at a major hotel. Otherwise, phone ahead. Fares are not cheap; meters run at a rate of $2.75 for the first mile and $2 for each additional mile; waiting time is 25¢ per minute. The major company serving the area is Yellow Cab.

🛈 Taxi Information **Yellow Cab** 🕾 954/565-5400.

TOURS

Carrie B., a 300-passenger day cruiser, gives 90-minute tours up the New River and Intracoastal Waterway. Cruises depart at 11, 1, and 3 each day and cost $11.95. *Jungle Queen III* and *Jungle Queen IV* are 175-passenger and 527-passenger tour boats taking day and night cruises up the New River through the heart of Fort Lauderdale. Sightseeing cruises at 10 and 2 cost $12.95, while the evening dinner cruise costs $27.95. You can also take a daylong trip to Miami's Bayside Marketplace ($15.95), on Biscayne Bay, for shopping and sightseeing on Wednesday and Saturday, departing at 9:15. Call in advance for availability. Professional Diving Charters operates the 60-ft glass-bottom boat *Pro Diver II*. On Tuesday through Saturday mornings and Sunday afternoon, two-hour sightseeing trips costing $22 take in offshore reefs; snorkeling can be arranged at $29 per person.

🛈 Tours Information *Carrie B.* ⊠ Riverwalk at S.E. 5th Ave., Fort Lauderdale 🕾 954/768-9920. *Jungle Queen III* and *Jungle Queen IV* ⊠ Radisson Bahia Mar Beach Resort, 801 Seabreeze Blvd., Fort Lauderdale 🕾 954/462-5596. **Professional Diving Charters** ⊠ 515 Seabreeze Blvd., Fort Lauderdale 🕾 954/761-3413.

TRAIN TRAVEL

Amtrak provides daily service to the Fort Lauderdale station as well as other Broward County stops at Hollywood and Deerfield Beach. Tri-Rail operates train service daily 4 AM–11 PM (more limited on weekends) through Broward, Miami-Dade, and Palm Beach counties. There are six Broward stations west of Interstate 95: Hillsboro Boulevard in Deerfield Beach, Pompano Beach, Cypress Creek, Fort Lauderdale, Fort Lauderdale Airport, Sheridan Street in Hollywood, and Hollywood Boulevard.

🛈 Train Information **Amtrak** ⊠ 200 S.W. 21st Terr., Fort Lauderdale 🕾 800/872-7245 or 954/587-1287. **Tri-Rail** 🕾 800/874-7245.

VISITOR INFORMATION

🛈 Tourist Information **Chamber of Commerce of Greater Fort Lauderdale** ⊠ 512 N. E. 3rd Ave., Fort Lauderdale 33301 🕾 954/462-6000 ⊕ www.ftlchamber.com. **Davie/ Cooper City Chamber of Commerce** ⊠ 4185 S.W. 64th Ave., Davie 33314 🕾 954/581-0790 ⊕ www.davie-coopercity.org. **Greater Deerfield Beach Chamber of Commerce** ⊠ 1601 E. Hillsboro Blvd., Deerfield Beach 33441 🕾 954/427-1050 ⊕ www. deerfieldchamber.com. **Greater Fort Lauderdale Convention & Visitors Bureau** ⊠ 1850 Eller Dr., Suite 303, Fort Lauderdale 33316 🕾 954/765-4466 ⊕ www.broward.org. **Hollywood Chamber of Commerce** ⊠ 330 N. Federal Hwy., Hollywood 33020 🕾 954/923-4000 ⊕ www.hollywoodchamber.org. **Lauderdale-by-the-Sea Chamber of Commerce** ⊠ 4201 N. Ocean Dr., Lauderdale-by-the-Sea 33308 🕾 954/776-1000 ⊕ www.lbts.com. **Pompano Beach Chamber of Commerce** ⊠ 2200 E. Atlantic Blvd., Pompano Beach 33062 🕾 954/941-2940 ⊕ www.pompanobeachchamber.com.

PALM BEACH AND THE TREASURE COAST

4

FODOR'S CHOICE

Bice Ristorante, Palm Beach

The Breakers, Palm Beach

Café Boulud, Palm Beach

Henry Morrison Flagler Museum, Palm Beach

Drive along A1A from Delray Beach north through Manalapan

Four Seasons Resort Palm Beach, Palm Beach

Morikami Museum and Japanese Gardens, Delray Beach

Seagate Beach, Delray Beach

HIGHLY RECOMMENDED

WHAT TO SEE Boca Raton Museum of Art, Boca Raton

Historic downtown Stuart, Stuart

National Croquet Center, West Palm Beach

Norton Museum of Art, West Palm Beach

Society of the Four Arts, Palm Beach

UDT Navy Seals Museum, Fort Pierce

Worth Avenue, Palm Beach

Many other great hotels and restaurants enliven this area. For other favorites, look for the black stars as you read this chapter.

Revised by
Karen
Schlesinger

MUCH LIKE A KALEIDOSCOPE, this multifaceted section of Atlantic coast resists categorization for good reason. The territory from Palm Beach south to Boca Raton glitters as the northern portion of the Gold Coast. North of Palm Beach you'll uncover the comparatively undeveloped Treasure Coast—liberally sprinkled with coastal gems—where towns and wide spots in the road await your discovery. Altogether, you'll find delightful disparity, from Palm Beach, pulsing fast with plenty of surviving old-money wealth, to low-key Hutchinson Island, Manalapan, or Briny Breezes. Seductive as the beach scene interspersed by eclectic dining options can be, you should also take advantage of flourishing commitments to historic preservation and the arts, with town after town yielding intriguing museums, galleries, theaters, and gardens.

Long reigning as the epicenter of where the crème de la crème go to shake off winter's chill, Palm Beach continues to be a seasonal hotbed of platinum-grade consumption. Rare is the visitor to this region who can resist popping over for a peek. Yes, other Florida favorites such as Jupiter Island consistently rank higher on per capita wealth meters of financial intelligence sources such as *Worth* magazine. But there's no competing with the historic social supremacy of Palm Beach, long a winter address for heirs of icons named Rockefeller, Vanderbilt, Colgate, Post, Kellogg, and Kennedy. Yet even newer power brokers with names like Kravis, Peltz, and Trump are made to understand that strict laws govern everything from building to landscaping, and not so much as a pool awning gets added without a town council nod. If Palm Beach were to fly a flag, it's been observed there might be three interlocking Cs, standing not only for Cartier, Chanel, and Charles Jourdan but also for clean, civil, and capricious. Only three bridges allow access to the island, and huge tour buses are a no-no. Yet when a freighter once ran aground near a Palm Beach socialite's pool, she was quick to lament not having "enough Bloody Mary mix for all these sailors."

To learn who's who in Palm Beach, it helps to pick up a copy of the *Palm Beach Daily News*—locals call it the Shiny Sheet because its high-quality paper avoids smudging society hands or the Pratesi linens—for, as it is said, to be mentioned in the Shiny Sheet is to be Palm Beach. All this fabled ambience started with Henry Morrison Flagler, Florida's premier developer and cofounder, along with John D. Rockefeller of Standard Oil. No sooner did Flagler bring the railroad to Florida in the 1890s, than he erected the famed Royal Poinciana and Breakers hotels. Rail access sent real estate prices soaring, and ever since princely sums have been forked over for personal stationery engraved with the 33480 zip code of Palm Beach. To service Palm Beach with servants and other workers, Flagler also developed an off-island community a mile or so west. West Palm Beach now bustles with its own affluent identity even if there's still no competing with one of the world's toniest island resorts.

With Palm Beach proper representing only 1% of Palm Beach County's land, remaining territory is given over to West Palm and other classic Florida coastal towns, along with—to the west—citrus farms, the Arthur R. Marshall–Loxahatchee National Wildlife Refuge, and Lake Okeechobee, a world-class bass-fishing hot spot and Florida's largest lake. Well worth exploring are the Treasure Coast territory, covering northernmost Palm Beach County, plus Martin, St. Lucie, and Indian River counties. Despite a growing number of malls and beachfront condominiums, much shoreline remains blissfully undeveloped. Inland you'll find cattle ranching in tracts of pine and palmetto scrub along with sugar and citrus production. Shrimp farming utilizes techniques for acclimatizing shrimp from saltwater—land near seawater is costly—to fresh water, all the better to serve demand from restaurants popping up all over the

4

Tucked into an island 14 mi long and about ½ mi wide, Palm Beach can be covered in a day or two. In several days, explore everything from galleries to subtropical wildlife preserves, and with a week on tap, it's possible to expand horizons from Sebastian all the way south to Boca Raton. Or you could do as so many others do—laze around, soak up sunshine, and venture out mostly for mealtime pleasures.

Numbers in the text correspond to numbers in the margin and on the Gold Coast and Treasure Coast and the Palm Beach and West Palm Beach maps.

If you have
3 days

When time is tight, make 🏨 **Palm Beach** ❶ ⟊–⓫ your base. On the first day, start downtown on **Worth Avenue** ❼ to window-shop and gallery-browse. After a *très* chic bistro lunch, head for that other must-see on even the shortest itinerary, the **Henry Morrison Flagler Museum** ❷. Your second day is for the beach. Consider either Lantana Public Beach or Oceanfront Park in **Boynton Beach** ㉕. Budget your last day for exploring attractions that pique your interest such as the Morikami Museum and Japanese Gardens in nearby **Delray Beach** ㉗, tantamount to day-tripping to Japan, or Lion Country Safari in 🏨 **West Palm Beach** ⓬–㉒, yielding tastes of Africa.

If you have
5 days

Five days allow you more contemplation at the galleries and museums, more leisure at the beaches, with time for more serendipitous exploring. Stay in 🏨 **Palm Beach** ❶ ⟊–⓫ for two nights. The first day visit the **Henry Morrison Flagler Museum** ❷ and the luxury hotel known as the **Breakers** ❹, another Flagler legacy. Then head to **Worth Avenue** ❼ for lunch and afternoon shopping, even if it's only the window variety. On the second day, drive over to 🏨 **West Palm Beach** ⓬–㉒ and the **Norton Museum of Art** ⓭, with many 19th- and 20th-century paintings and sculptures. On day three, choose between an overnight visit to 🏨 **Lake Okeechobee**, the world's bass-fishing capital, or Palm Beach for another night and a drive of a half hour or so to explore the Arthur R. Marshall–Loxahatchee National Wildlife Refuge. Or head for the **National Croquet Center** ⓲. Bring your own mallets or rent from the pro shop. Head south to 🏨 **Boca Raton** ㉘ on the fourth day, and check into a hotel near the beach before spending the afternoon wandering through Mizner Park's shops. On your fifth day, meander through Mizner Park's Boca Raton Museum of Art in the morning and get some sun at South Beach Park after lunch.

If you have
7 days

With an entire week, get a more comprehensive look at the Gold and Treasure coasts, with time to fit in sailing, taking in a polo match, deep-sea fishing, or jet skiing. Stay two nights in 🏨 **Palm Beach** ❶ ⟊–⓫, spending your first day enjoying stellar sights, mentioned above. On day two, rent a bicycle and follow the bike path along Lake Worth, providing great glimpses at backyards of many Palm Beach mansions. In fall you'll encounter gardeners busy clipping hedges and trimming palm fronds in preparation for the winter social season. Drive north on day three, going first to the mainland and then across Jerry Thomas Bridge to Singer Island and John D. MacArthur Beach State Park. Spend the third night farther north, on 🏨 **Hutchinson Island** ㉞, and relax the next morning on the beach at your hotel. On your way back south, explore **Stuart** ㉝ and its intriguing historic downtown area, and pause at the Arthur R. Marshall–Loxahatchee National Wildlife

Refuge before ending up in ⊠ **Boca Raton** ㉘, for three nights at a hotel near the beach. Split day five between shopping at Mizner Park and sunning at South Beach Park. Day six is for cultural attractions: the Boca Raton Museum of Art followed by the Atlantic Avenue galleries and the Morikami in **Delray Beach** ㉗. With time to spare on your last day, check out one of Boca Raton's other two beaches, Spanish River and Red Reef parks.

---

region. Along the coast, the broad tidal lagoon called the Indian River separates barrier islands from the mainland. Sea turtles come ashore at night from late April to the end of September to lay eggs on its beaches.

Exploring Palm Beach & the Treasure Coast

Palm Beach, with Gatsby-era architecture, stone and stucco estates, extravagant landscaping, and highbrow shops, can reign as the focal point for your sojourn any time of year. From Palm Beach, head off in any of three directions: south along the scenic Gold Coast toward Boca Raton along an especially scenic route known as A1A, back to the mainland and north to the barrier-island treasures of the Treasure Coast, or west for more rustic inland delights.

About the Restaurants

Not surprisingly, numerous elegant establishments offer upscale Continental and contemporary fare, but the area also teems with casual waterfront spots serving up affordable burgers and fresh seafood feasts. Grouper, fried or blackened, is especially big here, along with the ubiquitous shrimp. An hour west from the coast, around Lake Okeechobee, dine on catfish, panfried to perfection and so fresh it seems barely out of the water. Early-bird menus, a Florida hallmark, typically entice the budget-minded with several dinner entrées at reduced prices when ordered during certain hours, usually before 5 or 6 PM.

About the Hotels

Palm Beach has a number of smaller hotels in addition to the famous Breakers. Lower-priced hotels and motels can be found in West Palm Beach and Lake Worth. To the south, the coastal town of Manalapan has the Ritz-Carlton, Palm Beach; and the posh Boca Raton Resort & Club is on the beach in Boca Raton. To the north in suburban Palm Beach Gardens is the PGA National Resort & Spa. To the west, small towns near Lake Okeechobee offer country-inn accommodations.

WHAT IT COSTS				
$$$$	**$$$**	**$$**	**$**	**¢**
RESTAURANTS over $30	$20–$30	$15–$20	$10–$15	under $10
HOTELS over $220	$140–$220	$100–$140	$80–$100	under $80

Restaurant prices are per person for a main course at dinner. Hotel prices are for a standard double room, excluding 6% sales tax (more in some counties) and 1%–4% tourist tax.

Timing

You'll find the weather optimum November through May, but the trade-off is that roadways and facilities are more crowded and prices higher. From May through November, which is the off-season, many stores and restaurants temporarily close. In summer, to spend much time outside, it helps to have a tolerance for heat, humidity, and afternoon downpours. No matter when you visit, bring insect repellent for outdoor activities.

PALM BEACH

78 mi north of Miami.

Setting the tone in this town of unparalleled Florida opulence is the ornate architectural work of Addison Mizner, who began designing homes and public buildings here in the 1920s and whose Moorish-Gothic style has influenced virtually all community landmarks. Thanks to Mizner and his lasting influence, Palm Beach remains a magnetic backdrop for the playground of the rich, famous, and discerning.

Exploring Palm Beach

For a taste of what it's like to jockey for position in this status-conscious town, stake out a parking place on Worth Avenue, and squeeze in among the Mercedes and Bentleys. Actually, the easiest, most affordable way to reach Worth Avenue is by foot, since there's little on-street parking and space is at a premium at nearby lots. Away from downtown, along County Road and Ocean Boulevard (the shore road, also designated as Route A1A), are Palm Beach's other defining landmarks: residences that are nothing short of palatial, topped by the seemingly de rigueur barrel-tile roofs and often fronted by 20-ft thick hedgerows. The low wall that separates the dune-top shore road from the sea hides shoreline that varies in many places from expansive to eroded. Here and there, where the strand deepens, homes are built directly on the beach.

a good tour

Start on the island's north end with a quick drive through the bit of sandstone and limestone intrigue called the **Canyon of Palm Beach** ❶ ▶ on Lake Way Road. Drive south, across Royal Poinciana Way, to the **Henry Morrison Flagler Museum** ❷, a 73-room palace Flagler built for his third wife. From here, backtrack to Royal Poinciana Way, turn right, and follow the road until it ends at North County Road and the Spanish-style **Palm Beach Post Office** ❸. Here County Road changes from north to south designations. Head southbound and look for the long, stately driveway on the left that leads to the **Breakers** ❹, built by Flagler in the style of an Italian Renaissance palace. There's limited free parking out front and ample valets under the porte-cochere. Continue south on South County Road about ¼ mi farther to **Bethesda-by-the-Sea** ❺, a Spanish Gothic Episcopal church. Keep driving south on South County Road until you reach Royal Palm Way; turn right, then right again on Cocoanut Row. Within a few blocks you'll see the gardens of the **Society of the Four Arts** ❻. Head south on Cocoanut Row until you reach famed **Worth Avenue** ❼. Park, stroll, and ogle designer goods. Then drive south on South County Road to peek at magnificent estates, including **El Solano** ❽, designed by Addison Mizner, and the fabled **Mar-a-Lago** ❾, now owned by Donald Trump and operating as a private club. At this point, if you want some sun and fresh air, continue south on South County Road until you reach **Phipps Ocean Park** ❿ and its stretch of beach, or head back toward town along South Ocean Boulevard to the popular **Mid-Town Beach** ⓫.

TIMING   You'll need half a day, minimum, for these sights. A few destinations are closed Sunday, Monday, or during the summer. In winter, often-heavy traffic gets worse as the day wears on, so plan most exploring for the morning.

What to See

❺ **Bethesda-by-the-Sea.** This Spanish Gothic Episcopal church with stained-glass windows was built in 1925 by the first Protestant congregation in southeast Florida. Guided tours follow some services, and there's a book shop. Adjacent are the formal, ornamental **Cluett Memorial Gardens**.

✉ *141 S. County Rd.* ☎ *561/655–4554* ⊕ *www.bbts.org* ☉ *Church and gardens daily 8–5. Services Sept.–May, Sun. at 8, 9, and 11; Tues. at 8; Wed. and Fri. at 12:05; June–Aug., Sun. at 8 and 10. Call to confirm.*

★ ❹ **The Breakers.** Originally built by Henry Flagler in 1895 and rebuilt by his descendants after a 1925 fire, this luxury hotel resembling an Italian Renaissance palace helped launch Florida tourism with its gilded-age opulence, attracting influential, wealthy northerners. Head for the lobby to gaze at painted arched ceilings hung with crystal chandeliers, the ornate Florentine Dining Room with its 15th-century Flemish tapestries, and other museum-quality public spaces. ✉ *1 S. County Rd.* ☎ *561/655–6611* ⊕ *www.thebreakers.com.*

▶ ❶ **Canyon of Palm Beach.** A road runs through a ridge of reddish-brown sandstone and oolite limestone, providing a brief sense of the desert Southwest. It's the remains of an ancient coral reef, and 15-ft-high canyon walls line both sides of the road. ✉ *Lake Way Rd.*

❽ **El Solano.** No Palm Beach mansion better represents the town's luminous legacy than the Spanish-style home built by Addison Mizner as his personal residence in 1925. Mizner then sold El Solano to Harold Vanderbilt, and the property was long a favorite among socialites for parties and photo shoots. Vanderbilt, like many of the other socially attuned, would open his home to social peers to accommodate good, often charitable causes. Beatle John Lennon and Yoko Ono bought it less than a year before Lennon's death, and it's now privately owned and not open to the public. ✉ *721 S. County Rd.*

❷ **Henry Morrison Flagler Museum.** The opulence of Florida's gilded age lives on at Whitehall, the palatial 73-room mansion Henry Flagler commissioned in 1901 for his third wife, Mary Lily Kenan. Architects John Carrère and Thomas Hastings were instructed to create the finest home imaginable, and they outdid themselves. Whitehall rivals the grandeur of European palaces and has an entrance hall with baroque ceiling similar to Louis XIV's Versailles. To create the museum, Flagler's granddaughter, Jean Flagler Matthews, in 1960 bought back the property, which had been operating as the Whitehall Hotel from 1929 to 1959. You'll see original furnishings, an art collection, a 1,200-pipe organ, and Florida East Coast Railway exhibits, along with Flagler's personal rail car, the *Rambler,* awaiting behind the building. Tours take about an hour and are offered at frequent intervals. ✉ *1 Whitehall Way* ☎ *561/655–2833* ⊕ *www.flagler.org* ✉ *$8* ☉ *Tues.–Sat. 10–5, Sun. noon–5.*

FodorsChoice
★

❾ **Mar-a-Lago.** Breakfast-food heiress Marjorie Meriweather Post commissioned a Hollywood set designer to create Ocean Boulevard's famed Mar-a-Lago, with Italianate towers silhouetted against the sky. Owner Donald Trump has turned it into a private membership club. ✉ *1100 S. Ocean Blvd.*

⑪ **Mid-Town Beach.** Just east of Worth Avenue, this small beach is convenient, but be warned that parking is scarce, with the only meters along Ocean Boulevard—ergo, the only easy public parking access—between Worth Avenue and Royal Palm Way. ✉ *400 S. Ocean Blvd.* ☎ *no phone* ✉ *Parking 25¢ for 15 mins* ☉ *Daily 8–8.*

❸ **Palm Beach Post Office.** Spanish-style architecture defines the exterior of this 1932 National Historic Site building. Inside, murals depict Seminole Indians in the Everglades and stately royal and coconut palms. ✉ *95 N. County Rd.* ☎ *800/275–8777.*

⑩ **Phipps Ocean Park.** In addition to the shoreline, picnic tables, and grills, this park has a Palm Beach County landmark in the **Little Red School-**

4

Beaches

Logically from a tourism marketing standpoint, many towns along this idyllic stretch officially embrace the word *beach,* and why not? Here you'll find miles of golden strands—some relatively quiet, others buzzing—blessed with shades of blue-green waters you won't encounter farther north. Among the least crowded are those at Hobe Sound National Wildlife Refuge and Fort Pierce Inlet State Recreation Area. To see and be seen, head for Boca Raton's three beaches or Delray Beach's broad stretch of sand.

Fishing

Except for ice fishing, you'll find within a 50-mi radius of Palm Beach virtually every form of hook-and-line activity going on any season you please. Charter boats for deep-sea fishing abound from Boca Raton to Sebastian Inlet. West of Vero Beach, there's great marsh fishing for catfish and perch. Lake Okeechobee is the place for bass fishing.

Golf

Golfers love this region, starting with the Professional Golfing Association (PGA) headquarters at the PGA National Resort & Spa in Palm Beach Gardens, with five courses. If you're not yet ready to go pro, the Academy at PGA National Resort & Spa can help you improve with its golf school packages. In all, more than 150 public, private, and semiprivate golf courses dot Palm Beach County, and challenging courses also await along the Treasure Coast.

Shopping

There's no shortage of baubles to ogle on Palm Beach's Worth Avenue, known locally as the Avenue and often compared to Beverly Hills' Rodeo Drive, even though such California comparisons displease many old-line Palm Beachers. There's also plenty of reasonably priced shopping at the Mall at Wellington Green, Town Center, and the Gardens. For open-air shopping, dining, and entertainment, CityPlace and Mizner Park are great choices. Both have upscale national retailers mixed with unique independent boutiques and art galleries. Browse through more art galleries and antiques shops all along this stretch, especially in Vero Beach and Delray Beach.

---

house. Dating from 1886, it served as the first schoolhouse in what was then Dade County. No alcoholic beverages are permitted in the park. ⊠ *2185 S. Ocean Blvd.* ☎ *561/832–0731* ☜ *Free* ☉ *Daily dawn–dusk.*

★ ❻ **Society of the Four Arts.** Feel like unwinding amid Blackberry Lilies and Japanese Sago Palms, Confederate Jasmine, Weeping Juniper, and Fairy Carpet Begonias? Despite widespread misconceptions of members-only exclusivity, this privately endowed institution—founded in 1936 to encourage appreciation of art, music, drama, and literature—is funded for public enjoyment. A gallery building—designed by Addison Mizner, of course—artfully melds an exhibition hall, library, 13 distinct gardens, and the Philip Hulitar Sculpture Garden. Open from about Thanksgiving to Easter, programs are extensive and there's ample free parking. ⊠ *2 Four Arts Plaza* ☎ *561/655–7226* ⊕ *www.fourarts.org* ☜ *$4* ☉ *Galleries Dec.–mid-Apr., Mon.–Sat. 10–5, Sun. 2–5. Library, children's library, and gardens Nov.–May, weekdays 10–5, Sat. 9–1.*

★ ❼ **Worth Avenue.** Called the Avenue by Palm Beachers, this ¼-mi-long street is synonymous with exclusive shopping. Nostalgia lovers recall an era when faces or names served as charge cards, purchases were delivered home before customers returned from lunch, and bills were sent directly to private accountants. Times have changed, but a stroll amid the Moorish architecture of its shops offers a tantalizing taste of the island's ongoing commitment to elegant consumerism. ⊠ *Between Cocoanut Row and S. Ocean Blvd.*

Where to Stay & Eat

$$$$ ✕ **Leopard Supper Club and Lounge.** In the Chesterfield hotel, this enclave feels like an exclusive club. Choose a cozy banquette set off by black and red lacquer trim or a table near the open kitchen. Start with sweet corn and crab chowder with Peruvian purple potato or a jumbo crab cake, moving on to an arugula or spinach salad followed by a prime strip steak or a glazed rack of lamb. As the night progresses, the Leopard turns into a popular nightclub for Palm Beach's old guard. ⊠ *363 Cocoanut Row* ☎ *561/659–5800* ▤ *AE, DC, MC, V.*

$$$–$$$$ ✕ **Bice Ristorante.** A favorite of Palm Beach society, this historic Addison Mizner spot has such a thoroughly Italian feel that you may be surprised when you're greeted in English. The villa's bougainvillea-laden trellises set the scene at the main entrance on Peruvian Way. Weather permitting, many patrons prefer the outside patio dining. The aroma of basil, chives, and oregano fills the air as waiters bring out home-baked focaccia to accompany delectable pastas, veal chops, and a duck breast sautéed in mushroom sauce with venison truffle ravioli, among other dishes. ⊠ *313½ Worth Ave.* ☎ *561/835–1600* ▤ *AE, DC, MC, V.*

Fodor'sChoice
★

$$$–$$$$ ✕ **Café Boulud.** Celebrated chef Daniel Boulud opened his outpost of New York's Café Boulud in the Brazilian Court hotel. The warm and welcoming French American venue is casual, yet elegant, with a pallet of honey, gold and citron and natural light spilling through arched glass doors. Lunch and dinner entrées on Boulud's signature four-muse menu reflect classic French, seasonal, vegetarian, and a rotating selection of international dishes. The lounge with its backlit amber glass bar is the perfect perch to take in the jet-set crowd that comes for a hint of the South of France in South Florida. ⊠ *Brazilian Court, 301 Australian Ave.* ☎ *561/655–6060* ⌖ *Reservations essential* ▤ *AE, DC, MC, V.*

Fodor'sChoice
★

$$$–$$$$ ✕ **Café L'Europe.** One of the most enduring, elegant Palm Beach enclaves, this classy restaurant is consistently ranked as one of the best by dining critics. To remain at the pinnacle, management pays close attention to service and consistency of excellence here. Best-sellers include rack of lamb and Dover sole, along with creations such as crispy sweetbreads with poached pear and mustard sauce. Depending on how you look at it, the champagne-caviar bar can work as an appetizer or dessert. ⊠ *331 S. County Rd.* ☎ *561/655–4020* ⌖ *Reservations essential* ⌂ *Jacket required* ▤ *AE, DC, MC, V* ☉ *No lunch.*

★ $$$–$$$$ ✕ **Chez Jean-Pierre.** With walls adorned with Dalí- and Picasso-like art, this is where the Palm Beach old guard likes to let down its guard, all the while partaking of sumptuous French cuisine and an impressive wine list. Forget calorie or cholesterol concerns and indulge in scrambled eggs with caviar or homemade duck foie gras, along with desserts like hazelnut soufflé or profiteroles au chocolat. Waiters are friendly and very attentive. ⊠ *132 N. County Rd.* ☎ *561/833–1171* ⌖ *Reservations essential* ▤ *AE, MC, V* ☉ *Closed Sun. No lunch.*

★ $$–$$$ ✕ **Amici.** A celebrity-magnet bistro feel with an open view to the kitchen in back has proved a crowd-pleaser with the Palm Beach crowd. The northern Italian menu highlights house specialties such as rigatoni with spicy tomato sauce and roasted eggplant, potato gnocchi, grilled veal chops, risottos, and pizzas from a wood-burning oven. There are nightly

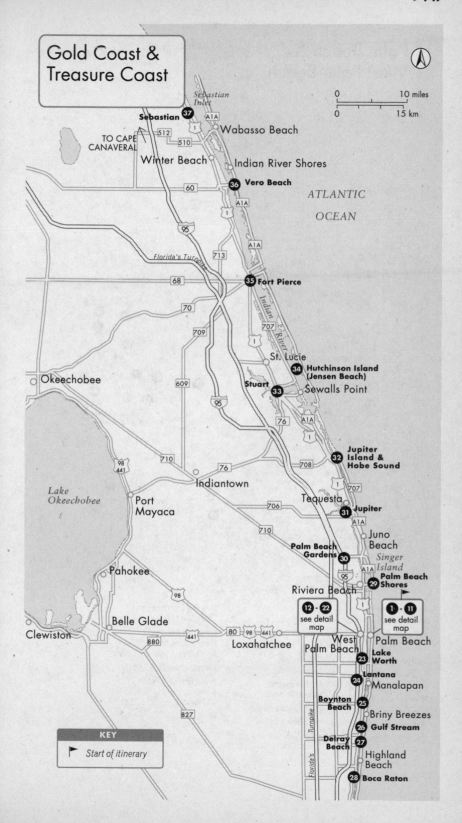

Gold Coast & Treasure Coast

KEY

⚑ Start of itinerary

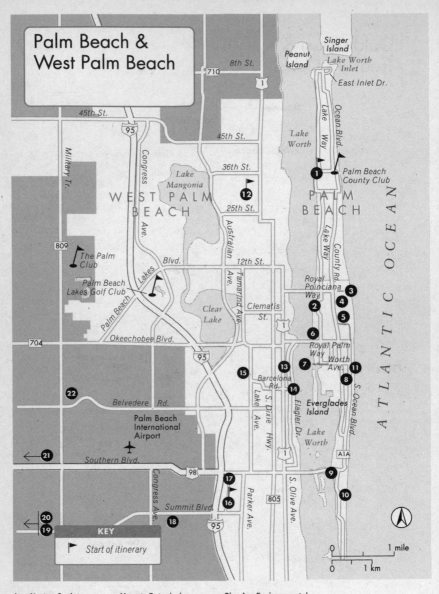

Palm Beach &
West Palm Beach

pasta and fresh-fish specials as well. To avoid the crowds, stop by for a late lunch or early dinner. ✉ *288 S. County Rd.* ☎ *561/832–0201* ⬧ *Reservations essential* ⊟ *AE, DC, MC, V* ⊘ *No lunch Sun.*

$$–$$$ ✕ **Chuck & Harold's.** Locals and tourists eager to people-watch flock to this combo power-lunch bar, sidewalk café, and nocturnal jazz hot spot for breakfast, lunch, and dinner. For optimum viewing, take a seat in the outdoor café next to begonia pots mounted on the sidewalk rail. Worthy are local clams from Sebastian, conch chowder, terrific hamburgers, grilled steaks, and key lime pie. ✉ *207 Royal Poinciana Way* ☎ *561/659–1440* ⊟ *AE, DC, MC, V.*

$$–$$$ ✕ **Echo.** Palm Beach's window on Asia has a sleek sushi bar and floor-to-ceiling glass doors separating the interior from a popular terrace dining. Chinese, Japanese, Thai, and Vietnamese selections are neatly categorized: Wind (small plates starting your journey), Water (beverages, sushi), Fire (from grill, wok, fry pan), and Earth (land and sea) to Flavor (desserts, sweets). Pick from dim sum to sashimi, pad Thai to Peking duck, steamed sea bass to lobster lo mein. ✉ *230-A Sunrise Ave.* ☎ *561/802–4222* ⬧ *Reservations essential* ⊟ *AE, D, MC, V* ⊘ *Closed Mon. No lunch.*

★ **$$–$$$** ✕ **Ta-boó.** This peach stucco landmark with green shutters has ruled on Worth Avenue for more than 60 years. Table seating counts here, with the best by the windows at the front or near the bar or fireplace. Entrées include Black Angus dry-aged beef or roast duck, along with main-course salads, pizzas, and burgers, plus coconut lust, a signature dessert. Drop in late night during the winter season when the nightly music is playing and you'll probably spot a celebrity or two. ✉ *221 Worth Ave.* ☎ *561/835–3500* ⊟ *AE, DC, MC, V.*

¢–$ ✕ **Hamburger Heaven.** A local favorite on Palm Beach since 1945, this spot is loud and casual and has some of the best burgers on the island. Vegetarian meals, fresh salads, sandwiches, homemade pastries, and daily soup and hot-plate specials are also available. During the week, it is a typical lunch stop for working locals. ✉ *314 S. County Rd.* ☎ *561/655–5277* ⊟ *No credit cards* ⊘ *Closed Sun.*

¢ ✕ **Pastry Heaven.** Head to the counter of this bakery and sandwich shop to place your breakfast or lunch order. Choose from the daily selection of fresh quiche, pastries, sandwiches (fresh turkey on a baked-that-morning croissant) and salads (chicken with grapes and walnuts); eye a chocolate chip cookie; and help yourself to a beverage. If you are lucky to secure one of the few tight tables inside or out on the patio, grab one of the complimentary local papers and magazines to read up on the town's happenings while you eat. ✉ *375 S. County Rd.* ☎ *561/655–0610* ⊟ *No credit cards* ⊘ *Closed Sun. No dinner.*

¢ ✕ **Pizza Al Fresco.** Off of Worth Avenue's beaten path, this European pizzeria (beer and wine only) provides outdoor dining under a canopy of century-old banyans in a charming courtyard. Specialties are 12″ hand-tossed brick-oven pizzas; calzones, salads, and sandwiches round out the selection. Slices are available with such interesting toppings as prosciutto, arugula, and caviar; there's even a dessert pizza topped with Nutella. Delivery is available, by limo, of course. ✉ *14 Via Mizner, at Worth Ave.* ☎ *561/832–0032* ⊟ *AE, MC, V* ⊘ *No lunch Sun.*

★ **$$$$** ▦ **Brazilian Court.** A short stroll from Worth Avenue shopping, the yellow stucco Spanish-style facade and red-tile roof here underscore this boutique hotel's Roaring '20s origins. Renovated as a luxury condo-hotel, all of the studio and one- and two-bedroom suites are appointed with rich limestone baths and showers, Sub-Zero wine refrigerators, and personal butler service. Bay windows look out into the impeccably maintained gardens and enchanting flower-filled courtyards. Amenities include video-conference capabilities in a state-of-the-art business center, a Frederic Fekkai hair salon and spa, and Café Boulud, a New York outpost from famed restaurateur Daniel Boulud; hotel guests reportedly have a better shot than outsiders at procuring a table. ✉ *301 Australian Ave., 33480* ☎ *561/655–7740* 📠 *561/655–0801* 🌐 *www.braziliancourt.com* *80 rooms* *Restaurant, room service, in-room data ports, refrigerators, some in-room VCRs, pool, gym, hair salon, spa, bicycles, bar, library, laundry facilities, concierge, meeting rooms, some pets allowed (fee); no-smoking rooms* ▭ *AE, D, DC, MC, V.*

$$$$ Fodor'sChoice ★ **The Breakers.** Dating from 1896 and on the National Register of Historic Places, this opulent Italian Renaissance–style resort sprawls over 140 ocean-front acres. Cupids frolic at the main Florentine fountain, while majestic frescoes grace ceilings leading to restaurants. More than an opulent hotel, the Breakers is a modern resort lacking few amenities, from a 20,000-square-ft luxury spa and beach club to golf and tennis clubhouses that support the 10 tennis courts and 2 18-hole golf courses. Jackets and ties are no longer *required* after 7 PM. ✉ *1 S. County Rd., 33480* ☎ *561/655–6611 or 888/273–2537* 📠 *561/659–8403* 🌐 *www.thebreakers.com* *569 rooms, 57 suites* *5 restaurants, room service, in-room data ports, room TVs with movies and video games, 2 18-hole golf courses, putting green, 10 tennis courts, 5 pools, health club, sauna, spa, beach, boating, croquet, shuffleboard, 4 bars, shops, baby-sitting, children's programs (ages 3–12), concierge, business services* ▭ *AE, D, DC, MC, V.*

$$$$ Fodor'sChoice ★ **Four Seasons Resort Palm Beach.** Relaxed elegance are the watchwords at this four-story resort on 6 acres with a delightful beach at the south end of town. Fanlight windows, marble, chintz, and palms are serene and inviting. Rooms are spacious, with a separate seating area and private balcony, many with ocean views. On weekends, piano music accompanies cocktails in the Living Room lounge. Jazz groups perform on some weekends in season. The in-house restaurants are worth sampling, and all three have children's menus. ✉ *2800 S. Ocean Blvd., 33480* ☎ *561/582–2800 or 800/432–2335* 📠 *561/547–1557* 🌐 *www.fourseasons.com* *200 rooms, 10 suites* *3 restaurants, room service, in-room data ports, in-room safes, minibars, golf privileges, 3 tennis courts, pool, hair salon, health club, hot tub, sauna, spa, steam room, beach, boating, fishing, bicycles, 2 bars, shop, baby-sitting, children's programs (ages 3–12), dry cleaning, concierge, business services, meeting rooms; no-smoking rooms* ▭ *AE, D, DC, MC, V.*

$$$–$$$$ **The Colony.** What distinguishes this legendary pale yellow British colonial–style hotel is that it is only steps from Worth Avenue and a beautiful beach on the Atlantic Ocean. An attentive staff, youthful yet experienced, is buzzing with competence and a desire to please. Cool and classical guest rooms, with small baths, have fluted blond cabinetry and matching curtains and bedcovers in floral pastels. In addition to the rooms and suites, there are ample penthouses with refigerators as well as seven 2-bedroom villas (rentable by the week or month) with full kitchens and laundry facilities. For convenient in-house fare and fun, check out the nightly dinner cabaret show. ✉ *155 Hammon Ave., 33480* ☎ *561/655–5430 or 800/521–5525* 📠 *561/659–8104* 🌐 *www.thecolonypalmbeach.com* *68 rooms, 14 suites* *Restaurant, pool, spa, bicycles, bar, concierge, meeting rooms* ▭ *AE, DC, MC, V.*

$–$$$$ **The Chesterfield.** Two blocks north of Worth Avenue is find this elegant four-story, white stucco, European-style luxury hotel with inviting rooms ranging from small to spacious. All are richly decorated with plush upholstered chairs, antique desks, paintings, and marble baths. Settle on a leather couch near the cozy library's fireplace with an international newspaper or a book selected from floor-to-ceiling shelves. A quiet courtyard surrounds a large pool. Ongoing but unobtrusive renovation and redecoration keep this hotel in tip-top shape. ✉ *363 Cocoanut Row, 33480* ☎ *561/659–5800 or 800/243–7871* 📠 *561/659–6707* 🌐 *www.*

chesterfieldpb.com ⬡ *44 rooms, 11 suites ⚥ Restaurant, room service, some refrigerators, some in-room VCRs, pool, bar, library, concierge, Internet, business services, meeting rooms ⊟ AE, D, DC, MC, V.*

$–$$$ ⊞ **Palm Beach Historic Inn.** Downtown, tucked between Town Hall and a seaside residential block, this B&B has touches that include a deluxe Continental breakfast served in bed or in the courtyard and tea and cookies delivered to your room upon your arrival. Guest rooms tend toward the frilly with lace, ribbons, and scalloped edges. Most are furnished with Victorian antiques and reproductions and chiffon draped above the bed. ⊠ *365 S. County Rd., 33480* ☎ *561/832–4009* ⎙ *561/832–6255* ⊕ *www.palmbeachbandb.com* ⬡ *9 rooms, 4 suites ⚥ Refrigerators, some in-room VCRs, library ⊟ AE, D, DC, MC, V* �| *CP.*

$–$$$ ⊞ **Palm Beach Oceanfront Inn.** Families seeking closer-to-earth prices gravitate to this casual two-story resort on the beach. Don't count on anything fancy, but large, adequately furnished rooms and suites face tropical gardens. Beach frontage is the draw here. A wide wooden sundeck surrounds the free-form pool, and both look to the ocean. The informal restaurant and outdoor bar also overlook the water. ⊠ *3550 S. Ocean Blvd., 33480* ☎ *561/582–5631 or 800/457–5631* ⎙ *561/588–4563* ⊕ *www.palmbeachhawaiian.com* ⬡ *50 rooms, 8 suites ⚥ Restaurant, room service, refrigerators, pool, beach, bar ⊟ D, MC, V.*

$–$$$ ⊞ **Plaza Inn.** This three-story hotel, deco-designed from the 1930s with a vibrant pink exterior, operates B&B style. Its Stray Fox Pub Piano Bar, palm- and ficus-lined pool, and courtyard gardens have the intimate charm of a trysting place. Courteous staff and a location in the heart of Palm Beach are pluses. Uncluttered rooms are individually decorated and have phones and refrigerators, a welcome change from other B&Bs. ⊠ *215 Brazilian Ave., 33480* ☎ *561/832–8666 or 800/233–2632* ⎙ *561/835–8776* ⊕ *www.plazainnpalmbeach.com* ⬡ *48 rooms, 5 suites ⚥ In-room data ports, refrigerators, pool, hot tub, bar, concierge, some pets allowed ⊟ AE, MC, V* O| *BP.*

Nightlife & the Arts

The Arts

The **Royal Poinciana Playhouse** (⊠ 70 Royal Poinciana Plaza ☎ 561/659–3310) presents more than a half dozen productions each year between December and April. **Society of the Four Arts** (⊠ 2 Four Arts Plaza ☎ 561/655–7226) has concerts, lectures, and films December–March. Movie tickets can be purchased at time of showing; other tickets may be obtained a week in advance.

Nightlife

Although Palm Beach is teeming with restaurants that turn into late-night scenes and hotel lobby bars perfect for tête-à-têtes, the only true nightclub in town is **251** (⊠ 251 Sunrise Ave. ☎ 561/820–9777). Known for its live music and late-night partying, 251 is a locals hot spot. The old guard gathers at the **Leopard Lounge** (⊠ 363 Cocoanut Row ☎ 561/659–5800) in the Chesterfield Hotel for piano music during cocktail hour and later to dance until the wee hours. As the weekend dinner crowd thins out, late-night revelers fill up **Ta-boó** (⊠ 221 Worth Ave. ☎ 561/835–3500), where a DJ keeps everyone moving.

Sports & the Outdoors

Biking

Bicycling is a pivotal way for getting a closer look at Palm Beach. Only 14 mi long, ½ mi wide, flat as the top of a billiard table, and just as green, it's a perfect biking locale. The palm-fringed **Palm Beach Bicycle**

Trail (⊠ parallel to Lake Way) skirts the backyards of many palatial mansions and the edge of Lake Worth. The trail starts at the Society of the Four Arts, heading north—just follow the signs. A block from the bike trail, the **Palm Beach Bicycle Trail Shop** (⊠ 223 Sunrise Ave. ☎ 561/659–4583) rents by the hour or day.

Dog Racing

Since 1932 the hounds have raced year-round at the 4,300-seat **Palm Beach Kennel Club.** Enjoy simulcasts of jai alai and horse racing, and wager on live and televised sports; there is also a 30-table card room. ⊠ 1111 N. Congress Ave. ☎ 561/683–2222 ☜ 50¢, terrace level $1, parking free ⊙ Racing Mon., Wed., and Fri.–Sat. at 12:40, Wed.–Sat. also at 7:30, Sun. at 1. Simulcasts Thurs.–Tues. at 12:30; Mon., Wed., and Fri. at 7:35.

Golf

Breakers Hotel Golf Club (⊠ 1 S. County Rd. ☎ 561/659–8407) has the historic Ocean Course. The **Town of Palm Beach Golf Club** (⊠ 2345 S. Ocean Blvd. ☎ 561/547–0598) has 18 holes, including 4 on the Atlantic and 3 on the inland waterway.

Shopping

One of the world's showcases for high-quality shopping, **Worth Avenue** runs ¼ mi east–west across Palm Beach, from the beach to Lake Worth. The street has more than 250 shops, and many upscale stores (Gucci, Hermès, Pucci, Saks Fifth Avenue, and Tourneau) are represented, their merchandise appealing to the discerning tastes of the Palm Beach clientele. The six blocks of **South County Road** north of Worth Avenue have interesting (and somewhat less expensive) stores. For specialty items (out-of-town newspapers, health foods, and books), try the shops along the north side of **Royal Poinciana Way.** Most stores are closed on the weekend, and many go on hiatus during the summer months.

Visit **At Home . . . with Nancy and Beth** (⊠ Paramount, 139 N. County Rd. ☎ 561/659–0550) for a hand-picked selection of vintage housewares, decorative items, memorabilia, and original retro fashions. **Calypso** (⊠ 247-B Worth Ave. ☎ 561/832–5006), tucked into Via Encantada, is where owner Christiane Celle—known for handcrafted fragrances—has curated a lively collection of resortwear for the whole family. **Chris Kellogg** (⊠ Gucci Courtyard, 256 Worth Ave. ☎ 561/820–2407) stocks the Palm Beach uniform of linen button-down shirts and cotton toile print pants. An institution on the island, the thrift store **Church Mouse** (⊠ 374 S. County Rd. ☎ 561/659–2154) is where many high-end resale boutique owners first grab their merchandise. **Déjà Vu** (⊠ Via Testa, 219 Royal Poinciana Way ☎ 561/833–6624) could be the resale house of Chanel, as it has so many gently used, top-quality pieces. There is no digging through piles here; clothes are in impeccable condition and very organized. **Designers to You** (⊠ 307 Royal Poinciana Way ☎ 561/833–3363) has discount special-occasion clothing by Carolina Herrera, Cerruti, Halston, and other couture designers. Skirt suits and dresses are organized by price on racks. **Giorgio's** (⊠ 230 Worth Ave. ☎ 561/655–2446) is over-the-top indulgence, with 50 colors of silk and cashmere sweaters and 22 colors of ostrich and alligator adorning everything from bags to bicycles. Giorgio's also has men's and women's boutiques in the Breakers. Collector and trader **Otten von Emmerich** (⊠ Via Flora, 240 Worth Ave. ☎ 561/659–0071) offers a museumlike historical presentation of antique and pre-owned Louis Vuitton and Hermès and maritime art. **Tracey Tooker Hats** (⊠ Via Bice, 313½ Worth Ave. ☎ 561/835–1663) custom-made creations are appointed with bone buttons, real and faux fur, double grosgrain silk bows, satin linings, ostrich feathers, and silk flowers.

Holding court for more than 60 years, **Van Cleef** Arpels (⊠ 249 Worth Ave. ☏ 561/655–6767) is where legendary members of Palm Beach society shop for tiaras and formal jewels.

WEST PALM BEACH

2 mi west of Palm Beach.

Long considered Palm Beach's less-privileged relative, sprawling West Palm has evolved into an economically vibrant destination of its own, ranking as the cultural, entertainment, and business center of the entire county and territory to the north. Sparkling buildings like the mammoth Palm Beach County Judicial Center and Courthouse and the State Administrative Building underscore the breadth of the city's governmental and corporate activity, and facilities such as the glittering Kravis Center for the Performing Arts attest to the strength of the arts and entertainment community. Kravis Center officials, intent on driving home commitment to quality, created quite a stir by declaring an unprecedented ticket refund to the tune of $60,000 for a sold-out performance that it categorized as substandard.

Downtown

The heart of revived West Palm Beach is a small, attractive downtown area, spurred on by active historic preservation. Along beautifully landscaped Clematis Street, you'll find boutiques and restaurants in charmingly restored buildings and an increasingly exuberant nightlife. In fact, downtown rocks on Thursdays from 5:30 PM on with Clematis by Night, a celebration of music, dance, art, and food at Centennial Square. Even on downtown's fringes, you'll find sights of cultural interest.

a good tour

From a geographical perspective, the best place to start is at the north end of the city with a walk through the **Old Northwood Historic District** ⑫ ⌐, on the National Register of Historic Places. Drive south on U.S. 1, take a left onto 12th Street, and then a right onto South Olive Avenue to view the exceptional art collection at the **Norton Museum of Art** ⑬. From here, it is just a few blocks south to the peaceful **Ann Norton Sculpture Gardens** ⑭. Finally, drive west across Barcelona Road to the **Robert and Mary Montgomery Armory Arts Center** ⑮ to check out the current exhibit.

TIMING Late morning is ideal for starting this tour. Walk through the historic neighborhood before having lunch on Clematis Street. In the afternoon you'll need about three hours at the various arts-oriented sights. Being out during daytime business hours is pivotal for this tour.

What to See

⑭ **Ann Norton Sculpture Gardens.** This monument to the late American sculptor Ann Weaver Norton, second wife of Norton Museum founder Ralph H. Norton, consists of charming 3-acre grounds displaying seven granite figures and six brick megaliths. The plantings were designed by Norton, an environmentalist, to attract native bird life. ⊠ 253 Barcelona Rd. ☏ 561/832–5328 ⊡ $5 ☉ Wed.–Sun. 11–4 (call ahead; schedule is not always observed) or by appointment.

★ ⑬ **Norton Museum of Art.** Constructed in 1941 by steel magnate Ralph H. Norton, this museum has an extensive permanent collection of 19th- and 20th-century American and European paintings, including works by Picasso, Monet, Matisse, Pollack, and O'Keeffe, and Chinese, contemporary, and photographic art. There's a sublime outdoor covered loggia, Chinese bronze and jade sculptures, and a library. Galleries, including the Great Hall of the Museum, also showcase traveling exhibits. ⊠ *1451 S. Olive Ave.* ☎ *561/832–5196* ⊕ *www.norton.org* ☎ *$8* ☉ *Tues.–Sat. 10–5, Sun. 1–5.*

⯈ ⑫ **Old Northwood Historic District.** This 1920s-era neighborhood, on the National Register of Historic Places, hosts special events, Saturday green markets, and free Sunday walking tours. ⊠ *West of Flagler Dr. between 26th and 35th Sts.*

⑮ **Robert and Mary Montgomery Armory Arts Center.** Built by the WPA in 1939, the facility is now a visual-arts center hosting rotating exhibitions and art classes throughout the year. ⊠ *1703 Lake Ave.* ☎ *561/832–1776* ☎ *Free* ☉ *Weekdays 9–5:30, Sat. 9:30–2:30.*

Away from Downtown

West Palm Beach's outskirts, flat stretches lined with fast-food outlets and car dealerships, may not inspire but are worth driving through to reach attractions scattered around the city's southern and western reaches. Several are especially rewarding for children and other animal and nature lovers.

a good tour

Head south from downtown and turn right on Southern Boulevard, left onto Parker Avenue, and right onto Summit Boulevard to reach the **Palm Beach Zoo at Dreher Park** ⑯ ⯈. In the same area (just turn right onto Dreher Trail) and also appealing to kids, the **South Florida Science Museum** ⑰, with its Aldrin Aquarium and McGinty Aquarium, is full of hands-on exhibits. If a quick game of croquet intrigues you, head to **National Croquet Center** ⑱, less than 2 mi from the museum by turning right onto Summit Boulevard from Dreher Trail North and proceeding to Florida Mango Road, where you will again turn right. Backtrack to Summit Boulevard and go west to the 150-acre **Pine Jog Environmental Education Center** ⑲. For more natural adventure, head farther west on Summit until you reach Forest Hills Boulevard, where you turn right to reach the **Okeeheelee Nature Center** ⑳ and its miles of wooded trails. Now retrace your route to Summit Boulevard, drive east until you reach Military Trail, and take a left. Drive north to Southern Boulevard and turn west to reach **Lion Country Safari** ㉑, a 500-acre cageless zoo. For the last stop on this tour, backtrack to Military Trail and travel north to the gardens of the **Mounts Botanical Gardens** ㉒.

TIMING Tailor your time based on specific interests, since you could easily spend most of a day at any of these attractions. Gird yourself for heavy rush-hour traffic, and remember that sightseeing in the morning (not *too* early, to avoid rush hour) will be less congested.

What to See

☝ ㉑ **Lion Country Safari.** Drive your own vehicle (with windows closed) on 8 mi of paved roads through a 500-acre cageless zoo with 1,000 free-roaming animals. Lions, elephants, white rhinos, giraffes, zebras, antelopes, chimpanzees, and ostriches are among the wild things in residence. Exhibits include the Kalahari, designed after a South African bush plateau and containing water buffalo and Nilgai (the largest type of Asian antelope), and the Gir Forest, modeled after a game forest in India and showcasing a pride of lions. A walk-through park area has bird feeding and a petting zoo, or take a pontoon boat tour. There's also paddleboating, miniature golf, and picnic tables. No convertibles or pets are allowed. ⊠ *2003 Lion Country Safari Rd., at Southern Blvd.* ⓦ ☎ *561/793–1084* ⊕ *www.lioncountrysafari.com* ☎ *$16.95, van rental $8 per 1½ hrs* ☉ *Daily 9:30–5:30 (last vehicle in by 4:30).*

㉒ **Mounts Botanical Gardens.** Take advantage of balmy weather by walking among the tropical and subtropical plants here. Join a free tour or explore the 13 acres of exotic trees, rain-forest area, and butterfly and water gardens on your own. ⊠ *531 N. Military Trail* ☎ *561/233–1749* ⊕ *www.mounts.org* ⊠ *Free; tours $2* ⊗ *Mon.–Sat. 8:30–4:30, Sun. 1–5; tours Sat. at 11, Sun. at 2, and by appointment.*

★ ⑱ **National Croquet Center.** The world's largest croquet complex, the 10-acre center is also the headquarters for the U.S. Croquet Association. Vast expanses of manicured lawn are the stage for fierce competitions—in no way resembling the casual backyard games where kids play with wide wire wickets. There's also a clubhouse with a pro shop and Café Croquet, with verandas for dining and viewing, and a museum hall. Half-day and full-day reservations for play on a dozen lawns can be booked. From January through April, get a court for two hours including 30 minutes with a pro to teach you golf croquet at $50 for two, $80 for four. Courts can be reserved up to seven days in advance. ⊠ *700 Florida Mango Rd., at Summit Blvd.* ☎ *561/478–2300* ⊕ *www.croquetnational.com* ⊗ *Court times daily 9–5* ⊠ *$15 per player per 2-hr period.*

⑳ **Okeeheelee Nature Center.** Explore 5 mi of trails through 90 acres of pine-flat woods and wetlands. A visitor center–gift shop has hands-on exhibits. ⊠ *7715 Forest Hill Blvd.* ☎ *561/233–1400* ⊠ *Free* ⊗ *Visitor center Tues.–Fri. 1–4:45, Sat. 8:15–4:45; trails daily dawn–dusk.*

⊙ ▶ ⑯ **Palm Beach Zoo at Dreher Park.** This wild kingdom is a 23-acre complex with more than 400 animals representing more than 125 species, from Florida panthers to the giant Aldabra tortoise and the first outdoor exhibit of Goeldi's monkeys in the nation. The Tropics of America exhibit has 6 acres of rain forest plus Maya ruins, an Amazon river village, and an aviary. Also notable are a nature trail, the otter exhibit, and a children's petting zoo. ⊠ *1301 Summit Blvd.* ☎ *561/533–0887* ⊕ *www. palmbeachzoo.com* ⊠ *$7.50* ⊗ *Daily 9–5.*

⊙ ⑲ **Pine Jog Environmental Education Center.** The draw here is 150 acres of mostly undisturbed Florida pine-flat woods with one self-guided ½-mi trail. Formal landscaping around five one-story buildings includes native plants, while dioramas and displays illustrate ecosystems. School groups use the trails during the week, but the public is also welcome. Call for an event schedule. ⊠ *6301 Summit Blvd.* ☎ *561/686–6600* ⊠ *Free* ⊗ *Weekdays 9–5.*

⊙ ⑰ **South Florida Science Museum.** Here at the museum, which includes the Aldrin Planetarium and McGinty Aquarium, you'll find hands-on exhibits with touch tanks, laser shows with the likes of Pink Floyd and Led Zeppelin, and a chance to observe the heavens Friday nights through the most powerful telescope in South Florida (weather permitting). ⊠ *4801 Dreher Trail N* ☎ *561/832–1988* ⊕ *www.sfsm.org* ⊠ *$6.50, planetarium $2 extra, laser show $4 extra for matinee, $6.50 for evening* ⊗ *Mon.–Thurs. 10–5, Fri. 10–10, Sat. 10–6, Sun. noon–6.*

Where to Stay & Eat

$$–$$$$ ✕**Raindancer Steak House.** Since 1975, steak lovers have headed for this dark, cozy establishment to indulge in thick and juicy filet mignons, 24-ounce porterhouse cuts, sizzling sirloins for two, New York strips prepared au poivre, and grilled lean flanks. If beef isn't your choice, there are also lamb chops, chicken, and seafood available. ⊠ *2300 Palm Beach Lakes Blvd.* ☎ *561/684–2811* ⊟ *AE, MC, V* ⊗ *No lunch.*

$–$$$ ✕**Café Protégé.** At this 150-seat restaurant of the Florida Culinary Institute, sample superb Continental fare at less than astronomical prices.

Menus change frequently, and there's a $12 chef's buffet lunch. Watch students slicing, dicing, and sautéing in the observation kitchen. ⊠ 2400 *Metrocentre Blvd.* ☎ 561/687–2433 ☰ AE, MC, V ☉ *No lunch weekends, no dinner Sun.–Mon.*

$–$$ ✕ **Pescatore Seafood and Oyster Bar.** After wandering around Clematis Street, slip through the French doors of this trendy spot for a light lunch, afternoon snack, or leisurely dinner. Fresh oysters and clams star, but you'll also find grilled fish and shrimp, steamed Maine lobster, assorted pasta dishes; and a grilled Black Angus burger. ⊠ *200 Clematis St.* ☎ 561/837–6633 ☰ AE, DC, MC, V.

¢–$$ ✕ **Aleyda's Tex-Mex Restaurant.** This casual, family-friendly eatery consistently scores high on local popularity polls. Fajitas, the house specialty, are brought to the table sizzling in the pan, along with such classic Mexican offerings as enchiladas, chili con queso, and quesadillas. The bartenders claim to make the best margaritas in town. ⊠ *1890 Okeechobee Blvd.* ☎ 561/688–9033 ☰ AE, MC, V ☉ *No lunch weekends.*

¢ ✕ **Manzo's Italian Deli.** Slightly off the West Okeechobee Boulevard main drag and tucked inside a shopping center is a fine sandwich shop. Favorite sandwiches include the #8 (homemade mozzarella and tomato with basil) and the #22 (eggplant parmigiana on warm Italian bread). Sides include tricolor tortellini, macaroni, potato, and mushroom salads. ⊠ *400 Village Blvd.* ☎ 561/697–9411 ☰ *No credit cards* ☉ *Closed Sun.*

¢ ✕ **Middle East Bakery.** This hole-in-the-wall Middle Eastern bakery, deli, and market fills at lunchtime with regulars who are on a first-name basis with the gang behind the counter. From the nondescript parking lot, the place doesn't look like much, but inside, delicious hot and cold Mediterranean treats await. Choose from traditional gyro sandwiches and lamb salads with sides of grapes leaves, tabbouleh, and couscous. ⊠ *327 5th St., at Olive Ave.* ☎ 561/659–7322 ☰ AE, MC, V ☉ *Closed Sun.*

★ $–$$$ ▥ **Hibiscus House.** Hosts Raleigh Hill and Colin Rayner work diligently to promote not only their delightful B&B but also their neighborhood, Old Northwood, which is now listed on the National Register of Historic Places thanks to their efforts. Filling their Cape Cod–style property are antiques Hill has collected, including a 150-year-old four-square piano, a green cane planter chair, and Louis XV pieces in the living room. Individually decorated guest rooms are done in a mix of antiques and reproductions, and the tropical pool-patio area is delightful. ⊠ *501 30th St., 33407* ☎ 561/863–5633 or 800/203–4927 ☒ 561/863–5633 ⊕ *www.hibiscushouse.com* ⬠ *8 rooms* ♨ *Pool* ☰ AE, DC, MC, V ⊨ BP.

★ ¢–$$$ ▥ **Hotel Biba.** In the El Cid historic district, this 1940s motel has gotten a fun, stylish revamp from Barbara Hulanicki, designer of the 1960s Biba fashion line. Each guest room has a vibrant mélange of colors along with handcrafted mirrors, mosaic bathroom floors, and custom mahogany furnishings. Luxury touches include Egyptian cotton sheets, down pillows and duvets, and lavender-scented closets. The hotel is about a mile from Clematis Street nightlife. ⊠ *320 Belvedere Rd., 33405* ☎ 561/832–0094 ☒ 561/833–7848 ⊕ *www.hotelbiba.com* ⬠ *43 rooms* ♨ *In-room data ports, pool, bar* ☰ AE, DC, MC, V.

¢–$ ▥ **Tropical Gardens Bed & Breakfast.** In the historic Old Northwood area, this cozy, informal cottage house painted in a sunny yellow with white trim has room options ranging from the twin-bedded Canary Room to the deluxe Carriage House, in a separate building with French doors leading out to the pool. With its tropical colors and a laid-back approach, this B&B feels very Key West. Included in the complimentary Continental breakfast are tasty homemade bread and scones. ⊠ *419 32nd St., 33407* ☎ 561/848–4064 or 800/736–4064 ☒ 561/848–2422 ⊕ *www.tropicalgardensbandb.com* ⬠ *4 rooms* ♨ *Pool, bicycles; no smoking* ☰ AE, D, MC, V ⊨ CP.

Nightlife & the Arts

The Arts

Starring amid the treasury of local arts attractions is the **Raymond F. Kravis Center for the Performing Arts** (⊠701 Okeechobee Blvd. ☎561/832–7469), a 2,200-seat glass, copper, and marble showcase perched on what passes for high ground near the railroad tracks in West Palm Beach. Its 250-seat Rinker Playhouse has children's programming, family productions, and other events. A packed year-round schedule unfolds here with drama, dance, and music—from gospel and bluegrass to jazz and classical, including performances of the Palm Beach Pops, New World Symphony, and Miami City Ballet.

Palm Beach Opera (⊠ 415 S. Olive Ave. ☎ 561/833–7888) stages four productions each winter at the Kravis Center with English translations projected above the stage and tickets from $18 to $225. The **Carefree Theatre** (⊠2000 S. Dixie Hwy. ☎561/833–7305) is Palm Beach County's premier showcase of foreign and art films.

Nightlife

Palm Beach Casino Line. Take to the high seas on a five-hour getaway aboard the *Palm Beach Princess,* sailing twice daily from the Port of Palm Beach. You'll find a 15,000-square-ft casino, assorted lounges, a sports booking bar with nine televisions, a gift shop, and entertainment, along with a prime rib buffet in the evening. Sailings are at 11:30 AM and 6:30 PM daily, and you'll need to allow time for pre-boarding procedures. Fares are $30 per person weekdays, $35 weekends. ⊠ *777 E. Port Rd.* ☎ *561/845–2101 or 800/841–7447.*

CityPlace comes alive at **Blue Martini** (⊠ 550 S. Rosemary Ave. ☎ 561/835–8601), a bar with eclectic music that attracts a diverse crowd. At **Level 2** (⊠313 Clematis St. ☎561/833–1444), DJs spin high energy dance tunes for an energetic young crowd. Thursday is college night.

You'll find full-size palm trees and trellises bright with bougainvillea blooms plus a light-and-laser sound system and a 7,500-square-ft dance floor at the Caribbean-theme **Monkeyclub** (⊠ 219 Clematis St. ☎ 561/833–6500) where the music is 1970s, '80s, and '90s. The **Respectable Street Café** (⊠ 518 Clematis St. ☎ 561/832–9999) explodes in high energy like an indoor Woodstock. This hip, dimly lit alterna-lounge has underground sound, new wave, and retro. **Underground Coffeeworks** (⊠ 105 Narcissus Ave. ☎ 561/835–4792), a retro '60s spot, has mellow live music and a good selection of coffees Tuesday–Saturday. Cover charges vary, depending on performers.

Sports & the Outdoors

If you yearn for drag racing action, the **Moroso Motorsports Park** (⊠17047 Beeline Hwy., Palm Beach Gardens ☎ 561/622–1400) awaits with swap meets and diversified events all year long on a 2¼-mi-long strip. Spectator admission is $12 on Saturday, $15 on Sunday, and there's a $20 two-day pass. Picturesque **Binks Forest Golf Club** (⊠400 Binks Forest Dr., Wellington ☎ 561/795–0595) has an 18-hole layout. The plush **Emerald Dunes** (⊠2100 Emerald Dunes Dr. ☎ 561/687–1700) has 18 holes of golf designed by Tom Fazio. The semi-private **Palm Beach Polo and Country Club** (⊠ 13198 Forest Hill Blvd., Wellington ☎561/798–7000) has 45 holes. The **Palm Beach National Golf & Country Club** (⊠ 7500 St. Andrews Rd., Lake Worth ☎ 561/965–3381) classic course is a Joe Lee championship layout and home of the Joanne Carner Golf Academy.

Shopping

If you are looking for a mix of food, art, performance, landscaping, and retailing, then head to renewed downtown West Palm around **Clematis Street.** Water-view parks with attractive plantings and lighting—including fountains where kids can cool off—add to the pleasure of browsing, window-shopping, and resting at an outdoor café. Hip national retailers such as Gap, Banana Republic, Ann Taylor Loft, and Chico's blend in with stores that carry the gamut from fabric to tattoos. The 55-acre, $550 million **CityPlace** (⌂ 700 S. Rosemary Ave. ☎ 561/366–1000) attracts people of all ages to enjoy the restaurants, cafés, and outdoor bars; a 20-screen Muvico; the Harriet Himmel Gilman Theater; and a 36,000-gallon dance, water, and light show. This family-friendly dining, shopping, and entertainment complex has plenty to see and do. Among CityPlace's 78 stores are popular national retailers Macy's, FAO Schwarz, and Restoration Hardware and several boutiques unique to Florida. Inside **Reading Etc.** (☎ 561/514–0991), spaciously organized books and creative items for the family and home line the walls of this Egyptian-inspired room. It's a perfect place for lovers of art, music, reading, and writing to browse in. Behind the punchy, brightly colored clothing in the front window of **C. Orrico** (☎ 561/832–9203) are family fashions and accessories by Lily Pulitzer and girlie casual gear by Three Dots and Trina Turk. **Rhythm Clothiers** (☎ 561/833–7677) attracts fashion-forward types with a stock of men's and women's clothing by Dolce & Gabbana, Beth Bowley, Diesel, Miss Sixty, and Samsonite. With shelves piled high with men's shirts and armoires overflowing with ladies' knits, **Stuart Norman** (☎ 561/835–9335) shows how dressed-up casual is done in South Florida. The free downtown trolley runs a continuous loop linking Clematis Street and CityPlace, so you won't miss a shop.

Lake Okeechobee

40 mi west of West Palm Beach.

Rimming the western edges of Palm Beach and Martin counties, the United States' second-largest fresh-water lake is girdled by 120 mi of road yet remains shielded from sight for almost its entire circumference. Lake Okeechobee—the Seminole's Big Water and the heart of the great Everglades watershed—measures 730 square mi, roughly 33 mi north–south, and 30 mi east–west, with an average natural depth of only 10 ft (flood control brings the figure up to 12 ft and deeper). Six major lock systems and 32 separate water-control structures manage the water. Encircling the lake is a 30-ft-high grassy levee—locals call it "the wall"—and the Lake Okeechobee Scenic Trail, a segment of the Florida National Scenic Trail, challenging for even the most experienced hikers and mountain bicyclists. This primitive and intriguing 110-mi trail encircles the lake atop the 35-ft Herbert Hoover Dike. Inside the wall, on the lake itself, you'll spot happy anglers from all over, hooked themselves on some of the best bass fishing in North America.

Small towns dot the lakeshore in this still largely agricultural area. To the southeast is Belle Glade—motto: HER SOIL IS HER FORTUNE—playing a role as the eastern hub of the 700,000-acre Everglades Agricultural Area, the crescent of farmlands south and east of the lake. To the southwest lies Clewiston, billing itself as "the sweetest town in America" thanks to the presence of "Big Sugar," more formally known as the United States Sugar Corporation. At the lake's north end, around Okeechobee, citrus production has outgrown cattle ranching as the principal economy, and still-important dairying diminishes as the state acquires more acreage in efforts to reduce water pollution. Set back from the lake, Indiantown is the western hub of Martin County, noteworthy for citrus production, cattle ranching, and timbering. The town reached its apex in 1927, when the Seaboard Airline Railroad briefly established its southern head-quarters and a model town here.

Detailing city history, the **Clewiston Museum** tells stories not only of Big Sugar and the Herbert Hoover Dike construction but also of a ramie crop grown here to make rayon, of World War II RAF pilots training at the Clewiston airfield, and of a German POW camp. ⊠ *114 S. Commercio St., Clewiston* ☎ *863/983–2870* ☞ *Free* ☉ *Mon.–Sat. 1–5.*

In the **Municipal Complex.** are the public library and the **Lawrence E. Will Museum,** both with materials on town history. On the front lawn is a Ferenc Verga sculpture of a family fleeing a wall of water rising from the lake during the catastrophic hurricane of 1928. More than 2,000 people perished and 15,000 families were left homeless by torrential flooding. ⊠ *530 Main St., Belle Glade* ☎ *561/996–3453* ☞ *Free* ☉ *Mon.–Wed. 10–8, Thurs.–Sat. 10–5.*

Where to Stay & Eat

¢–$$ ✕ **Colonial Dining Room.** The Clewiston Inn's restaurant has ladder-back chairs, chandeliers, fanlight windows, and an attitude that's anything but fancy. The southern regional and Continental dishes—chicken, pork, steak, and the ubiquitous catfish—are mighty tasty. ⊠ *108 Royal Palm Ave., at U.S. 27, Clewiston* ☎ *863/983–8151* ▤ *MC, V.*

¢–$ ✕ **Lightsey's.** The pick of the lake, this lodgelike restaurant at the Okee-Tantie Recreation Area started closer to town as a fish company with four tables in a corner. Now folks gladly trek out here. Get most items fried, steamed, broiled, or grilled. The freshest are the catfish, cooter (freshwater turtle), frogs' legs, and gator. ⊠ *10430 Rte. 78 W, Okeechobee* ☎ *863/763–4276* ▤ *D, MC, V.*

$–$$ ▦ **Clewiston Inn.** A classic antebellum-style country hotel in the heart of town, this inn was built in 1938. The cypress-panel lobby, wood-burning fireplace, colonial dining room, and Everglades lounge with a wraparound Everglades mural are standouts. Pleasant rooms with reproduction furniture are an excellent value, and rates include a full breakfast cooked to order. There's a pool across the street in the park. ⊠ *108 Royal Palm Ave., at U.S. 27, Clewiston 33440* ☎ *863/983–8151 or 800/ 749–4466* 🖷 *863/983–4602* ⊕ *www.clewistoninn.com* ➷ *48 rooms, 5 suites* ⚘ *Restaurant, 6 tennis courts, bar* ▤ *AE, MC, V* ☉⎮ *BP.*

★ ¢–$$ ▦ **Seminole Country Inn.** Once the Seaboard Airline Railroad's southern headquarters, this two-story, Mediterranean revival inn with its cypress ceilings and pine hardwood floors was restored by Holman Wall. It's now run by the late Indiantown patriarch's daughter, Jonnie Wall Williams, a fifth-generation native. Carpeted rooms are done in country ruffles and prints, with comfy beds. Rocking chairs await on the porch, and there's Indiantown memorabilia in the lobby, a sitting area on the second floor, and good local art throughout. ⊠ *15885 S.W. Warfield Blvd., Indiantown 34956* ☎ *772/597–3777 or 888/394–3777* 🖷 *772/ 597–2883* ⊕ *www.seminoleinn.com* ➷ *22 rooms* ⚘ *2 restaurants, pool, horseback riding* ▤ *AE, D, MC, V* ☉⎮ *CP.*

¢–$ ▦ **Pier II Resort.** This two-story motel on the rim canal has a five-story observation tower for peeking over the lake's levee. Large, motel-plain rooms are nicely maintained. Out back are a 650-ft fishing pier and the Oyster Bar, one of the lake area's best hangouts for shooting pool or watching TV, attracting a mix of locals and out-of-towners. ⊠ *2200 S.*

E. *U.S. 441, Okeechobee 34974* ☎ *863/763–8003 or 800/874–3744* ⊟ *863/763–2245* ⊕ *www.pier2resort.com* ⪢ *83 rooms, 6 suites* ⚐ *Refrigerators, fishing, bar* ⊟ *AE, D, DC, MC, V* ⦿ *CP.*

¢ ⊞ **Okeechobee Inn.** Rooms in this simple, two-story L-shape motel, 2 mi west of Belle Glade, are done in green floral prints. Large windows let in plenty of light, and balconies overlook the pool. Fishing and boat ramps are a mile away. ⊠ *265 N. U.S. 27, South Bay 33493* ☎ *561/ 996–6517* ⪢ *115 rooms* ⚐ *Pool, playground* ⊟ *MC, V.*

¢ ⚠ **Belle Glade Marina Campground.** A few miles north of downtown Belle Glade, just offshore in Lake Okeechobee, is Torry Island. Campsites have horseshoes, shuffleboard, boating, fishing, and docks. ⚐ *Full hookups, partial hookups (electric and water), picnic tables, playground.* ⪢ *370 campsites.* ⊠ *Torry Island* ☎ *561/996–6322* ⬚ *$15* ⊟ *MC, V.*

¢ ⚠ **Okee-Tantie Recreation Area.** The park has RV sites, tent sites, boating, fishing, and a dock. Lightsey's restaurant overlooks the marina. ⚐ *Flush toilets, showers, picnic tables, restaurant, general store, playground.* ⪢ *215 RV sites, 38 tent sites.* ⊠ *10430 Rte. 78 W, Okeechobee* ☎ *863/763–2622* ⬚ *$25–$28* ⊟ *MC, V.*

Sports & the Outdoors

Fishing. J-Mark Fish Camp (⊠ Torry Island ☎ 561/996–5357) has fully equipped bass boats, airboat rides, fishing guides, tackle, bait, and licenses. Since the **Okee-Tantie Recreation Area** (⊠ 10430 Rte. 78 W, Okeechobee ☎ 863/763–2622) has direct lake access, it's a popular fishing outpost. There are two public boat ramps, fish-cleaning stations, a marina, picnic areas and a restaurant, a playground, rest rooms, showers, and a **bait shop** (☎ 863/763–9645) that stocks groceries. In addition to operating the bridge to Torry Island (among Florida's last remaining swing bridges—it's cranked open and closed by hand, swinging at right angles to the road), brothers Charles and Gordon Corbin run **Slim's Fish Camp** (⊠ Torry Island ☎ 561/996–3844). Here you'll find a complete tackle shop, guides, camping facilities, bass boats, and even the name of a taxidermist to mount your trophy. **Golf. Belle Glade Municipal Country Club** (⊠ Torry Island Rd., Belle Glade ☎ 561/996–6605) has an 18-hole golf course and restaurant open to the public.

SOUTH TO BOCA RATON

Strung together by Route A1A, the towns between Palm Beach and Boca Raton are notable for their variety. Although the aura of Palm Beach has rubbed off here and there, you'll also find pockets of modesty such as Briny Breezes with its oceanside trailers. In one town you'll find a cluster of art galleries and fancy dining, while the very next town will yield mostly hamburger joints and mom-and-pop stores.

Lake Worth

㉓ *2 mi south of West Palm Beach.*

For years, tourists looked here mainly for inexpensive lodging and easy access to Palm Beach, since a bridge leads from the mainland to a barrier island with Lake Worth's beach. Now Lake Worth has several blocks of restaurants and art galleries, making this a worthy destination on its own. Also known as Casino Park, **Lake Worth Municipal Park** has a beach, Olympic-size swimming pool, fishing pier, picnic areas, shuffleboard, restaurants, and shops. ⊠ *Rte. A1A at end of Lake Worth Bridge* ☎ *561/533–7367* ⬚ *Pool $3, parking 25¢ for 15 mins* ◔ *Daily 9–5.*

Where to Stay & Eat

$$$–$$$$ ✕ **Paradiso.** The aroma of garlic prevails as you step into this noisy, popular Italian eatery with a mural depicting the Italian countryside. Numerous pastas are served as appetizers or entrées. Other delicious options include veal scallopini with prosciutto, chicken breast stuffed with goat cheese, and risotto specials. ✉ *625 Lucerne Ave.* ☎ *561/547–2500* ⊟ *AE, MC, V* ⊘ *No lunch Sun.*

¢–$ ✕ **John G's.** Count on a line here until closing at 3 PM. The menu is as big as the crowd: grand fruit platters, sandwich-board superstars, grilled burgers, seafood, eggs every which way, and the house specialty, French toast. Breakfast is served until 11. ✉ *10 S. Ocean Blvd. (Lake Worth Casino)* ☎ *561/585–9860* ⌲ *Reservations not accepted* ⊟ *No credit cards* ⊘ *No dinner.*

¢ ✕ **Benny's on the Beach.** Perched on the Lake Worth Pier, Benny's has diner-style food that's cheap and nothing fancy, but the spectacular view of the sun (or moon) glistening on the water and the waves crashing directly below is what dining here is all about. Reservations and credit cards are only permitted at dinner. ✉ *10 Ocean Ave.* ☎ *561/582–9001* ⊟ *V, MC* ⊘ *No dinner Fri.–Sun.*

¢–$$ ▣ **Mango Inn.** It's only a 10-minute walk to the beach from this white frame B&B built as a private house in 1915. The two first-floor rooms have French doors opening out onto a patio and overlooking the pool. A poolside cottage has two bedrooms, two bathrooms, and houselike amenities. Have your complimentary breakfast in the dining room, on the veranda overlooking the heated pool, or in the courtyard. ✉ *128 N. Lakeside Dr., 33460* ☎ *561/533–6900 or 888/626–4619* ▤ *561/533–6992* ⊕ *www.mangoinn.com* ⇨ *7 rooms, 1 cottage* ♨ *Some refrigerators, pool; no kids, no room phones in some rooms, no smoking, no TV in some rooms* ⊟ *AE, MC, V* ⋈ *BP.*

★ ¢–$$ ▣ **Sabal Palm House.** Built in 1936, this historic two-story frame enclave is a short walk from the Intracoastal Waterway and a golf course. Three rooms and a suite are in the main house with three more rooms across a brick courtyard in the carriage house. Each room is inspired by a different artist—including Renoir, Dalí, Norman Rockwell, and Chagall—and all have oak floors, antique furnishings, and private balconies. Two units have Jacuzzis. There's an inviting parlor, and breakfast is served indoors or in the courtyard, under the palms. ✉ *109 N. Golfview Rd., 33460* ☎ *561/582–1090 or 888/722–2572* ▤ *561/582–0933* ⊕ *www. sabalpalmhouse.com* ⇨ *6 rooms, 1 suite* ♨ *Some in-room hot tubs; no kids under 14* ⊟ *AE, D, MC, V* ⋈ *BP.*

¢ ▣ **Hummingbird Hotel.** This historic but no-frills B&B offers a comfortable room and personable staff. In the heart of downtown Lake Worth, Hummingbird Hotel is very close to art galleries, antiques shops, and eclectic restaurants. Most rooms have semiprivate baths, and a few rooms have a private bath. Efficiencies have kitchenettes, but full kitchen and laundry facilities are available to guests. ✉ *631 Lucerne Ave., 33460* ☎ *561/582–3224* ▤ *561/540–8817* ⊕ *www.hummingbirdhotel. com* ⇨ *25 rooms, 6 with bath* ⊟ *AE, D, MC, V* ⋈ *CP.*

Nightlife & the Arts

NIGHTLIFE Some nights you'll encounter free concerts by local and regional artists, and other nights the headliners are nationally known professionals. But every night, Tuesday through Saturday, there's traditional blues at the **Bamboo Room** (✉ 25 S. J St. ☎ 561/585–2583).

THE ARTS **Lake Worth Playhouse** (✉ 713 Lake Ave., 33461 ☎ 561/586–6410) presents drama and popular musicals on its main stage including works by Andrew Lloyd Webber and Tim Rice. Regular season runs from September through June with two adjacent venues each showing six shows. Tickets range from $12 to $22.

The **Palm Beach Institute of Contemporary Art** (⊠ 601 Lake Ave., 33460 ☎ 561/582–0006), in a former art deco movie theater, is a 6,400-square-ft rotating exhibition space with a new media lounge, family art workshops, contemporary art lectures, and gallery tours. PBICA is open Tuesday through Sunday from noon to 6 PM.

Sports & the Outdoors

The **Gulfstream Polo Club,** the oldest such club along the Palm Beaches, began in the 1920s and plays medium-goal polo (for teams with handicaps of 8–16 goals). There are six polo fields. ⊠ *4550 Polo Rd.* ☎ *561/965–2057* ⊠ *Free* ⊙ *Games Dec.–Apr.*

Lantana

24   *2 mi south of Lake Worth.*

Lantana—just a bit farther south from Palm Beach than Lake Worth—also has inexpensive lodging and a bridge connecting the town to its own beach on Palm Beach's barrier island. Tucked between Lantana and Boynton Beach is **Manalapan,** a tiny but posh residential community crowned by a luxury Ritz-Carlton beach resort. Ideal for sprawling, beach-combing, or power-walking, **Lantana Public Beach** is also worthy for its proximity to one of the most popular food concessions in town, the **Dune Deck Cafe.** You'll find fresh fish on weekends and breakfast and lunch specials every day outdoors under beach umbrellas. ⊠ *100 N. Ocean Ave.* ☎ *No phone* ⊠ *Parking 25¢ for 15 mins* ⊙ *Daily 9–4:45.*

Where to Stay & Eat

★ $$$ ✕ **I&J's Station House Restaurant.** The best Maine lobster in South Florida reportedly resides at this delicious dive, where all the seafood is cooked to perfection. Sticky seats and tablecloths are an accepted part of the scene, so wear jeans and a T-shirt. Although it's casual and family-oriented here, reservations are recommended, since it's a local favorite. ⊠ *233 W. Lantana Rd.* ☎ *561/547–9487* ⊟ *AE, MC, V.*

$–$$$ ✕ **Old Key Lime House.** Overlooking the Intracoastal Waterway, the 1889 Lyman House has grown in spurts over the years and is now a patchwork of shedlike spaces, an informal Old Florida seafood house that serves local seafood and key lime pie—the house specialty. Although there's air-conditioning, dining is open-air most evenings and in cooler weather. ⊠ *300 E. Ocean Ave.* ☎ *561/533–5220* ⊟ *AE, MC, V.*

★ $$$$ ▦ **Ritz-Carlton, Palm Beach.** Despite its name, this bisque-color, triple-tower landmark is actually in Manalapan, halfway between Palm Beach and Delray Beach. A huge double-sided marble fireplace dominates the elegant lobby and foreshadows the luxury of the guest rooms, which have rich upholstered furnishings and marble tubs. Most rooms have ocean views, and all have balconies. Apart from a fabulous beach, there's a large pool and courtyard shaded by coconut palms—all of which are served by attendants who can fulfill whims from iced drinks to cool face towels. ⊠ *100 S. Ocean Blvd., Manalapan 33462* ☎ *561/533–6000 or 800/241–3333* 🖷 *561/588–4555* ⊕ *www.ritz-carlton.com* ⌨ *257 rooms, 13 suites* ♿ *4 restaurants, room service, in-room data ports, mini-bars, 5 tennis courts, pool, hair salon, massage, sauna, spa, steam room, beach, snorkeling, bicycles, basketball, 2 bars, baby-sitting, children's programs (ages 5–12), laundry service, concierge, business services; no-smoking rooms* ⊟ *AE, D, DC, MC, V.*

¢ ▦ **Super 8 Motel.** What's special about this sprawling one-story motel is the price—a bargain, considering its proximity to Palm Beach. Efficiencies and rooms (some with refrigerator and microwave) are clean but basic. ⊠ *12.5.5 Hypoluxo Rd., 33462* ☎ *561/585-3970* ⚏ *561/586-3028* ➭ *129 rooms, 8 efficiencies* ⚭ *Some microwaves, some refrigerators, pool, laundry facilities* ⊟ *AE, DC, MC, V.*

Sports & the Outdoors
B-Love Fleet (⊠ 314 E. Ocean Ave. ☎ 561/588-7612) offers three deep-sea fishing excursions daily: 8–noon, 1–5, and 7–11. No reservations are needed; just show up 30 minutes before the boat is scheduled to leave. The cost is $27 per person and includes fishing license, bait, and tackle.

Boynton Beach
㉕ *3 mi south of Lantana.*

In 1884, when fewer than 50 settlers lived in the area, Nathan Boynton, a Civil War veteran from Michigan, paid $25 for 500 acres with a mile-long stretch of beachfront thrown in. How things have changed, with today's population at about 118,000 and property values still on an upswing. Far enough from Palm Beach to remain low-key, Boynton Beach has two parts, the mainland and the barrier island, the town of Ocean Ridge, connected by a causeway.

An inviting beach, boardwalk, concessions, grills, a jogging trail, and playground await at **Boyton Beach Oceanfront Park.** Parking costs more if you're not a Boynton resident. ⊠ *6415 Ocean Blvd. (Rte. A1A)* ☎ *no phone* ⌦ *Parking $10 per day in winter, $5 per day rest of yr* ⊙ *Daily 9 AM–midnight.*

Dating from the 1930s, when the trees were planted by the partners of the *Amos & Andy* radio show, **Knollwood Groves** offers a 30-minute, 30-acre tram tour through the orange groves and a processing plant. Also visit the **Hallpatee Seminole Indian Village,** with an alligator exhibit and crafts shop. During the high season, Native American educator Martin Twofeathers conducts a weekly one-hour alligator-handling show. ⊠ *8053 Lawrence Rd.* ☎ *561/734-4800* ⊕ *www.knollwoodgroves.com* ⌦ *Tour $1, show $6* ⊙ *Daily 9–5:30, show Sat. at 2* ⊙ *Closed Sun. June–Oct.*

off the beaten path

Arthur R. Marshall–Loxahatchee National Wildlife Refuge. The most robust part of the Everglades, this 221-square-mi refuge is one of three huge water-retention areas accounting for much of the Everglades outside the national park. These areas are managed less to protect natural resources, however, than to prevent flooding to the south. Start from the visitor center, where there are two walking trails: a boardwalk through a dense cypress swamp and a marsh trail to a 20-ft-high observation tower overlooking a pond. There is also a 5½-mi canoe trail, best for more experienced canoeists, since it's overgrown. Wildlife viewing is good year-round, and you can fish for bass and panfish. ⊠ *10119 Lee Rd., off U.S. 441 between Boynton Beach Blvd. (Rte. 804) and Atlantic Ave. (Rte. 806), west of Boynton Beach* ☎ *561/734-8303* ⌦ *$5 per vehicle, pedestrians $1* ⊙ *Daily 6 AM–sunset; visitor center weekdays 9–4, weekends 9–4:30.*

Where to Stay & Eat
¢-$$ ✕ **Mama Jennie's.** Tucked in a strip mall, this Italian restaurant attracts families hungry for big pizzas. Spaghetti with meatballs, eggplant parmigiana, and stuffed shells are also fine choices, and all dishes are homemade. ⊠ *706 W. Boynton Beach Blvd.* ☎ *561/737-2407* ⊟ *AE, MC, V* ⊙ *No lunch.*

$–$$ ⊞ **Emerald Shores Resort.** Tidy and quaint, this green and white two-story motel has one- and two-bedroom apartments with full kitchens. A large sundeck surrounds the heated pool. The property is well situated—just across Route A1A from the beach—tucked into a quite residential area with a mix of single and multifamily properties in Ocean Ridge, the barrier island of Boynton Beach. ⊠ *6600 N. Ocean Blvd., 33435* ☎ *561/738–2063 or 800/433–0786* ➪ *16 rooms, 2 suites* ⚘ *Kitchens, pool, laundry facilities* ☰ *AE, D, DC, MC, V.*

¢–$ ⊞ **Holiday Inn Express.** Conveniently perched right off Interstate 95, this four-story hotel has large rooms with purple and green fabrics, blond-wood furniture, and a small sitting area. A large sundeck surrounds the heated pool. Complimentary breakfast is served, and complimentary beverages are on tap at the end of the day. ⊠ *480 W. Boynton Beach Blvd., 33435* ☎ *561/734–9100* 🖶 *561/738–7193* ➪ *105 rooms, 6 suites* ⚘ *Pool, laundry facilities* ☰ *AE, DC, MC, V* ⑩ *BP.*

Sports & the Outdoors

FISHING Fish the canal at the **Arthur R. Marshall–Loxahatchee National Wildlife Refuge** (☎ 561/734–8303). There's a boat ramp, and the waters are decently productive, but bring your own equipment.

GOLF **Links at Boynton Beach** (⊠ 8020 Jog Rd. ☎ 561/742–6500) has 18-hole and 9-hole executive courses.

Gulf Stream

㉖ *2 mi south of Boynton Beach.*

Quiet money, and quite a lot of it, resides in this small beachfront community, whose architecture reflects Mizner's influence. As you pass the bougainvillea-topped walls of the Gulf Stream Club, don't be surprised if a private security officer stops traffic for a golfer to cross.

Delray Beach

㉗ *2 mi south of Gulf Stream.*

A onetime artists' retreat with a small settlement of Japanese farmers, Delray has grown into a sophisticated beach town. Atlantic Avenue, the once dilapidated main drag, has evolved into a 1-mi stretch of palm-dotted brick sidewalks, almost entirely lined with stores, art galleries, and dining establishments. Running east–west and ending at the beach, it's a pleasant place for a stroll, day or night. Another active pedestrian way begins at the edge of town, across Northeast 8th Street (George Bush Boulevard), along the big, broad swimming beach that extends north and south of Atlantic Avenue.

Just off Atlantic Avenue, the **Old School Square Cultural Arts Center** has several museums in restored school buildings dating 1913 and 1926. The **Cornell Museum of Art & History** offers ever-changing art exhibits. During its season, the **Crest Theatre** showcases local and national live performances. ⊠ *51 N. Swinton Ave.* ☎ *561/243–7922* ⊕ *www.oldschool. org* 🎟 *$6* ⊘ *Tues.–Sat. 11–4, Sun. 1–4.*

A restored Victorian-style home that dates from about 1915, **Cason Cottage** now serves as the Delray Beach Historical Society's offices. It's filled with Victorian-era relics, including a pipe organ donated by descendants of a Delray Beach pioneer family. Periodic displays celebrate the town's architectural evolution. The cottage is a block north of the cultural center. ⊠ *5 N.E. 1st St.* ☎ *561/243–0223* 🎟 *Free* ⊘ *Tues.–Fri. 11–4.*

THE MORIKAMI: ESSENCE OF JAPAN IN FLORIDA

A MAGICAL 200-ACRE GARDEN where the Far East meets the South lies just beyond Palm Beach's allure of sun and sea and glittering resorts. It's called the Morikami Museum and Japanese Gardens, and it's a testament to one man's perseverance against agricultural angst. The largest Japanese garden outside of Japan, it's also a soothing destination for reflection, an oasis of culture, pine forest, trails, and lakes.

In 1904, Jo Sakai, a New York University graduate, returned to his homeland of Miyazu, Japan, to recruit hands for farming what is now northern Boca Raton. With help from Henry Flagler's East Coast Railroad subsidiary they colonized as Yamato, an ancient name for Japan. When crops fell short, everyone left except for George Sukeji Morikami, who carried on cultivating local crops, eventually donating his land to memorialize the Yamato Colony. His dream took on new dimension with the 1977 opening of the Morikami, a living monument bridging cultural understanding between Morikami's two homelands.

The original Yamato-Kan building chronicles the Yamato Colony, and a main museum has rotating exhibits along with 5,000 art objects and artifacts including a 500-piece collection of tea-ceremony items. Enjoy a demonstration of sado, the Japanese tea ceremony, in the Seishin-an tea house, or learn about Japanese history in the 5,000-book library. There are also expansive Japanese gardens with strolling paths, a tropical bonsai collection, small lakes teeming with koi, plus picnic areas, a shop, and a café.

— Lynne Helm

The chief landmark along Atlantic Avenue is the Mediterranean revival–style **Colony Hotel,** still open only for the winter season as it has been almost every year since 1926. ⊠ 525 E. Atlantic Ave. ☎ 561/276–4123.

Fodor'sChoice ★ Out in the boonies west of Delray Beach seems an odd place to encounter the inscrutable East, but there awaits **Morikami Museum and Japanese Gardens,** a cultural and recreational facility heralding the Yamato Colony of Japanese farmers. The on-site Cornell Café serves light Asian fare. ⊠ 4000 Morikami Park Rd. ☎ 561/495–0233 ⊕ www.morikami.org ☞ Park and museum $8, free Sun. 10–noon ☉ Park daily dawn–dusk, museum and café Tues.–Sun. 10–5.

Fodor'sChoice ★ Enjoy many types of water-sport rentals—sailing, kayaking, windsurfing, boogie boarding, surfing, snorkeling—or scuba diving at a sunken Spanish galleon less than ½ mi offshore at **Seagate Beach.** ⊠ ½ mi south of Atlantic Ave. at Rte. A1A.

Volleyball courts dot the main stretch of the public **Delray Beach Municipal Beach.** ⊠ Atlantic Ave. at Rte. A1A.

Where to Stay & Eat

★ $$–$$$$ ✕ **32 East.** While restaurants come and go on a trendy street like Atlantic Avenue, 32 East is a consistent staple, if not the best restaurant on any given night in Delray Beach. A daily menu of wood-oven pizzas, salads, soups, seafood, meat, and desserts is all based on what is fresh and plentiful; then the kitchen does its magic by using extraordinary ingredients in what normally would be ordinary dishes. ⊠ 32 E. Atlantic Ave. ☎ 561/276–7868 ☴ AE, D, DC, MC, V ☉ No lunch.

$–$$$ ✕ **Splendid Blendeds Café.** Dine on the sidewalk or in the dining room decorated with original primitive art. The café is popular day and night, and food is a blend of savory Italian, Mexican, Asian, and contemporary. Tasty starters include roasted corn chowder and grilled Thai duck satay. Entrées range from pasta dishes to grilled yellowfin tuna, filet mignon stuffed with roasted garlic, or jerk chicken. ⊠ *432 E. Atlantic Ave.* ☎ *561/265–1035* ▤ *AE, MC, V* ☉ *Closed Sun.*

$$ ✕ **Peter's Stone Crabs.** There's no mystery to the main attraction here, but apart from stone crabs at market price served for dinner every day, order from a diverse menu with pastas, several kinds of fish, veal, beef, and, sometimes, Alaskan king crab. ⊠ *411 E. Atlantic Ave.* ☎ *561/278– 0036* ☉ *No lunch* ▤ *AE, DC, MC, V.*

¢–$$$ ✕ **Pineapple Grille.** A magnet for regulars, this informal tropical enclave serves up dependable Caribbean fare. An extensive menu includes macadamia nut–crusted crab cakes and mango goat-cheese chicken, along with imaginative pizzas. There's also a good and affordable wine list and live music on weekends. ⊠ *800 Palm Trail, in Palm Trail Plaza* ☎ *561/ 265–1368* ▤ *AE, MC, V.*

★ ¢–$$ ✕ **Blue Anchor.** Yes, this pub was actually shipped from England, where it stood for 150 years as the Blue Anchor Pub in London's historic Chancery Lane. There it was a watering hole for famed Englishmen, including Winston Churchill. The Delray Beach incarnation has stuck to authentic British pub fare. Chow down on a ploughman's lunch (a chunk of Stilton cheese, a hunk of bread, and pickled onions), shepherd's pie, fish-and-chips, and bangers and mash (sausages with mashed potatoes). English beers and ales are on tap and by the bottle. ⊠ *804 E. Atlantic Ave.* ☎ *561/272–7272* ▤ *AE, MC, V.*

¢–$$ ✕ **Boston's on the Beach.** Restaurants overlooking a beach often rely on location alone to keep tables filled. Such is true at Boston's, where you'll find beer flowing and the ocean breeze blowing. Decent bar fare includes New England clam chowder, several lobster dishes, and fresh fish. The walls are laden with paraphernalia from the Boston Bruins, New England Patriots, and Boston Red Sox, including a veritable shrine to Ted Williams. Catch ocean breezes from an outdoor deck upstairs. ⊠ *40 S. Ocean Blvd. (Rte. A1A)* ☎ *561/278–3364* ▤ *AE, MC, V.*

★ ¢ ✕ **Señor Torito.** Home-style Mexican favorites abound here. The homemade salsa and chips can fill you up, so save room for the spinach and cheese enchiladas, tacos asada, or mole verde burritos. Someone always orders the sizzling fajitas, which fill the rooms with the aroma of onions and peppers. Señor Torito has a brother restaurant, Señor Burrito, in Boca Raton; both are delicious, casual dining. ⊠ *142 S.E. 6th Ave. (Federal Hwy.)* ☎ *561/278–5757* ▤ *AE, MC, V* ☉ *No lunch weekends.*

$$–$$$$ ▦ **Delray Beach Marriott.** A bright pink five-story hotel, it's by far the largest property in Delray, with a stellar location at Atlantic Avenue's east end, across the road from the beach and within walking distance of restaurants, shops, and galleries. Rooms and suites are spacious, and many have stunning ocean views. The giant, free-form pool is surrounded by a comfortable deck. ⊠ *10 N. Ocean Blvd., 33483* ☎ *561/ 274–3200* 🖷 *561/274–3202* ⊕ *www.marriott.com* ↳ *268 rooms, 88 suites* ☒ *3 restaurants, room service, in-room data ports, in-room safes, minibars, pool, health club, hot tub, beach, 2 bars, laundry facilities, business services* ▤ *AE, DC, MC, V.*

★ $–$$$$ ▦ **Seagate Hotel & Beach Club.** At this lovely garden enclave, all units have at least kitchenettes; less expensive studios have compact facilities behind foldaway doors, while others have a separate living room and larger kitchen. The one- and two-bedroom suites are chintz and rattan, with many upholstered pieces. Dress up and dine in a smart little mahogany- and lattice-trimmed beachfront salon or have the same Continental fare in casual attire in the equally stylish bar. As a guest, you'll have access to the private beach club. ⊠ *400 S. Ocean Blvd., 33483*

☎ *561/276–2421 or 800/233–3581* 🖷 *561/243–4714* ⊕ *www. hudsonhotels.com* ➥ *70 suites* ♿ *Restaurant, in-room data ports, kitchenettes, 2 pools, beach, bar* ▤ *AE, DC, MC, V.*

¢–$$$ 🏨 **Colony Hotel & Cabana Club.** In the heart of downtown Delray, this lovely and charming historic building underwent an exterior renovation that luckily did not do away with stables in the back, which date back to 1926 when the hotel was built. Today it's listed on Delray's local Register of Historic Places and maintains an air of the 1920s with its Mediterranean revival architecture. The cabana club is a separate property on the ocean about a mile away, with a private beach, club, and heated saltwater pool. A convivial bar and live music weekend nights make the lobby area a great place to wind down. Fine shops selling leather goods, body products, and stationery fill the lower-level storefronts. ✉ *525 E. Atlantic Ave., 33483* ☎ *561/276–4123 or 800/552–2363* 🖷 *561/276–0123* ⊕ *www.thecolonyhotel.com* ➥ *70 rooms* ♿ *In-room data ports, pool, beach, bar, shops* ▤ *AE, DC, MC, V* ⎰⎱ *CP.*

Nightlife & the Arts

THE ARTS The **Crest Theater** (✉ 51 N. Swinton Ave. ☎ 561/243–7922), in the Old School Square Cultural Arts Center, presents productions in dance, music, and theater.

NIGHTLIFE **Sopra's** (✉ 110 E. Atlantic Ave. ☎ 561/274–7077) bar is packed with local society, which means a celebrity or two. The drinks flow and so does the food, but there's no dancing, only posing. **Dada** (✉ 52 N. Swinton Ave. ☎ 561/330–3232) presents live music in the living room of a historic house, while movies play on the wall. It is a place where those who don't drink will also feel comfortable. **Delux** (✉ 16 E. Atlantic Ave. ☎ 561/279–4792) is where the young South Beach wanna-be crowd goes to dance all night long.

Sports & the Outdoors

BIKING There is a bicycle path in Barwick Park and a special oceanfront lane along Route A1A. **Richwagen's Cycles** (✉ 32 S.E. 2nd Ave. ☎ 561/276–4234) rents bikes by the hour or day and provides maps.

SCUBA DIVING & Scuba and snorkeling equipment can be rented from longtime family-
SNORKELING owned **Force E** (✉ 660 Linton Blvd. ☎ 561/276–0666). It has PADI affiliation, provides instruction at all levels, and offers charters.

TENNIS Each winter the **Delray Beach Tennis Center** (✉ 201 W. Atlantic Ave. ☎ 561/243–7360) hosts professional tournaments and trains top-ranked players such as Andy Roddick. It offers individual lessons and clinics and is a great place year-round to practice or learn on 14 clay courts and 5 hard courts.

WATERSKIING **Lake Ida Park** (✉ 2929 Lake Ida Rd. ☎ 561/964–4420) is a great place to waterski, whether you're a beginner or a veteran. The park has a boat ramp, a slalom course, and a trick ski course.

Shopping

Street-scaped **Atlantic Avenue** is a showcase for art galleries, shops, and restaurants. This charming area, from Swinton Avenue east to the ocean, has maintained much of its small-town integrity. **Snappy Turtle** (✉ 1038 Atlantic Ave. ☎ 561/276–8088) is a multiroom extravaganza where Mackenzie Childs and Lily Pulitzer mingle with other fun fashions for the home and family. A store in the historic Colony Hotel, **Escentials Apothecaries** (✉ 533 Atlantic Ave. ☎ 561/276–7070) is packed with all things good-smelling for your bath, body, and home. Just off Atlantic is **Mermaid's Purse** (✉ 6 S.E. 5th Ave. ☎ 561/276–5937), where vintage bags, hand-picked from local estate sales and European flea markets, are tucked into every corner and hanging from the ceiling.

Boca Raton

28 *6 mi south of Delray Beach.*

Less than an hour south of Palm Beach and anchoring the county's south end, upscale Boca Raton has much in common with its fabled cousin. Both reflect the unmistakable architectural influence of Addison Mizner, their principal developer in the mid-1920s. The meaning of the name Boca Raton (pronounced boca rah-*tone*) often arouses curiosity, with many folks mistakenly assuming it means "rat's mouth." Historians say the probable origin is Boca Ratones, an ancient Spanish geographical term for an inlet filled with jagged rocks or coral. Miami's Biscayne Bay had such an inlet, and in 1823, a mapmaker copying Miami terrain confused the more northern inlet, thus mistakenly labeling this area Boca Ratones. No matter what, you'll know you've arrived in the heart of downtown when spotting the town hall's gold dome on the main drag, Federal Highway.

★ ☾ In a spectacular building in Mizner Park, the **Boca Raton Museum of Art** has an interactive children's gallery and changing exhibition galleries showcasing internationally known artists. Upstairs galleries house a permanent collection including works by Picasso, Degas, Matisse, Klee, and Modigliani as well as notable pre-Columbian art. ⊠ *501 Plaza Real* ☎ *561/392–2500* ⊕ *www.bocamuseum.org* ⊠ *$8* ☉ *Tues., Thurs., and Sat., 10–5; Wed. and Fri. 10–9; Sun. noon–5.*

☾ A big draw for kids, **Gumbo Limbo Nature Center** has four huge saltwater tanks brimming with sea life—from coral to stingrays—and a boardwalk through dense forest with a 50-ft tower you can climb to overlook the tree canopy. In spring and early summer, staffers lead nocturnal turtle walks for watching nesting females come ashore and lay eggs. ⊠ *1801 N. Ocean Blvd.* ☎ *561/338–1473* ⊕ *www.fau.edu/gumbo* ⊠ *Free; turtle tours $5 (tickets must be obtained in advance)* ☉ *Mon.–Sat. 9–4, Sun. noon–4; turtle tours May–Aug., Mon.–Thurs. 9 PM–midnight.*

Built in 1925 as the headquarters of the Mizner Development Corporation, **2 East El Camino Real** is an example of Mizner's characteristic Spanish revival architectural style, with its wrought-iron grilles and handmade tiles. As for Mizner's grandiose vision of El Camino Real, the architect-promoter once prepared brochures promising a sweeping wide boulevard with Venetian canals and arching bridges. Camino Real is pretty, heading east to the Boca Raton Resort & Club, but don't count on feeling you're in Venice.

With a shimmering golden dome, **Town Hall Museum** has a vital repository of archival material and special exhibits on the area's development. Tours and the gift shop are hosted by the Boca Raton Historical Society. ⊠ *71 N. Federal Hwy.* ☎ *561/395–6766* ⊕ *www.bocahistory.org* ⊠ *Free* ☉ *Weekdays 10–4.*

A residential area behind the Boca Raton Art School on Palmetto Park Road, **Old Floresta** was developed by Addison Mizner starting in 1925 and landscaped with varieties of palms and cycads. It includes houses that are mainly in a Mediterranean style, many with upper balconies supported by exposed wood columns. Home tours are held twice a year.

☾ Hands-on interactive exhibits make the **Children's Science Explorium**, at Sugar Sands Park, a kid pleaser. Children can create their own laser-light shows, explore a 3-D kiosk that illustrates wave motion, and try assorted electrifying experiments. There are also wind tunnels, microscopes, and microwave and radiation experiment stations. ⊠ *300 S. Military Trail* ☎ *561/347–3913* 🖃 *Free* ☉ *Weekdays 9–6, weekends 10–5.*

Where to Stay & Eat

★ **$$$–$$$$** ✕**La Vieille Maison.** One of the Gold Coast's temples of haute cuisine, this restaurant set in a 1920s-era dwelling is pricey, and worth it. Intimate private dining rooms set the stage for seasonal prix-fixe and à la carte menus showcasing Provençale dishes with tropical overtones. Don't miss the *soupe au pistou* (vegetable soup with basil and Parmesan), venison chop with red currant–pepper sauce and roasted chestnuts, and French apple tart, if they're available. The wine list is one of Florida's most extensive, and service is impeccable. ⊠ *770 E. Palmetto Park Rd.* ☎ *561/391–6701* 🖃 *AE, D, DC, MC, V.*

★ **$$$–$$$$** ✕**Mark's at the Park.** Exotic cars pour into valet parking at this Mark Militello property, where a whimsical interpretation of retro and art deco design competes with a masterful seasonal menu for your attention. The dazzling food includes starters of scallops with foie gras–infused mashed potatoes and spicy steamed mussels; main courses range from crab-crusted mahimahi to roast duck with sweet potatoes. Desserts are deliciously old-fashioned. You'll need to make reservations for weekend nights. ⊠*344 Plaza Real, Mizner Park* ☎ *561/395–0770* 🖃 *AE, D, MC, V.*

$$–$$$$ ✕**Tiramisu.** The food is an extravaganza of taste treats; veal chops, tuna, and anything with mushrooms draw raves, but count on hearty fare rather than a light touch. Start with the Portobello mushroom with garlic or the Corsican baby sardines in olive oil. For a main course, try the ricotta ravioli; scallopini of veal stuffed with crabmeat, lobster, and Gorgonzola; or the Tuscan fish stew. ⊠ *855 S. Federal Hwy.* ☎ *561/ 392–1838* 🖃 *AE, DC, MC, V* ☉ *Closed Sun. No lunch Sat.*

$$–$$$ ✕**Crab House Seafood Restaurant.** Crowds come here day and night for fresh Florida seafood and the restaurant's well-known crab specials along with chicken, steaks, and salads. There's a nautical theme and a wide deck for outside dining, a raw bar, and a cocktail lounge. ⊠ *6909 S.W. 18th St.* ☎ *561/750–0498* 🖃 *AE, D, MC, V.*

★ **$$–$$$** ✕**Uncle Tai's.** The draw at Boca's most upscale Chinese restaurant is some of the best Szechuan food on Florida's east coast. House specialties include sliced duck with snow peas and water chestnuts in a tangy plum sauce and Orange Beef Delight—flank steak stir-fried until crispy and then sautéed with pepper sauce, garlic, and orange peel. Uncle Tai's will go easy on the heat on request. Service is quietly efficient. ⊠ *5250 Town Center Circle* ☎ *561/368–8806* 🖃 *AE, MC, V.*

¢–$$ ✕**Tom's Place.** "This place is a blessing from God," says the sign over the fireplace, and after sampling Tom's sauce-slathered ribs, you may add, "Amen!" Baby-backs or St. Louis–style ribs can be ordered in half or full racks. Also rating raves are fried catfish, collard greens, and corn bread. Pick up a bottle of Tom's barbecue sauce to go, just as have a rush of entertainers and NFL players, and other happy patrons. ⊠ *7251 N. Federal Hwy.* ☎ *561/997–0920* 🖃 *AE, MC, V* ☉ *Closed Sun.–Mon.*

¢–$ ✕**Draft House.** Sports aficionados love this place. It's decorated with sports equipment, memorabilia, and photos of famed coaches, players, and moments in sports, plus a dozen televisions for can't-miss events. Apart from inexpensive draft beer, regulars favor homemade chili wings, fried chicken tenders, and juicy burgers. For the more ravenous, there are char-grilled New York strips or racks of baby-back ribs. ⊠ *22191 Powerline Rd.* ☎ *561/394–6699* 🖃 *AE, MC, V.*

¢–$ ✕**TooJay's.** TooJay's has several branches in Florida, and it's definitely the place for huge sandwiches piled high, from corned beef on rye and roast beef and onion on pumpernickel to tuna melts. While here you might also want to give in to your urge for chicken soup, meat loaf, lox and bagels, or killer desserts; they also serve beer and wine. Aside from the Boca locations there are others in Lake Worth, Vero Beach, Palm Beach, and Wellington. All menus are identical, although daily specials and soups of the day may vary. ⊠ *5030 Champion Blvd.* ☎ *561/241–5903* ⊠ *3013 Yamato Rd.* ☎ *561/997–9911* ▤ *AE, DC, MC, V.*

★ **$$$–$$$$** ▥ **Boca Raton Resort & Club.** Addison Mizner built the Mediterranean-stye Cloister Inn here in 1926, and additions over time have created this sparkling; sprawling resort with a beach accessible by shuttle. There are recreational activities here and many lodging options: traditional Cloister rooms are small but warmly decorated; accommodations in the 27-story Tower are more spacious; Beach Club rooms are light, airy, and contemporary; golf villas are large and attractive. In addition to a re-designed golf course, there's a two-story golf clubhouse, and a deluxe Tennis & Fitness Center. ⊠ *501 E. Camino Real, 33432* ☎ *561/447–3000 or 800/327–0101* ⎙ *561/447–3183* ⊕ *www.bocaresort.com* ⇄ *840 rooms, 63 suites, 60 golf villas* ♨ *11 restaurants, room service, in-room safes, some kitchens, 36-hole golf course, 40 tennis courts, 5 pools, hair salon, 3 health clubs, beach, snorkeling, windsurfing, boating, marina, fishing, basketball, racquetball, 3 bars, nightclub, shops, children's programs (ages 2–17), laundry service, concierge, business services, convention center, meeting rooms* ▤ *AE, DC, MC, V.*

$–$$$ ▥ **Ocean Breeze Inn.** If golf is your game, this is an excellent choice. Inn guests can play the outstanding course at the adjoining Ocean Breeze Golf & Country Club, otherwise available only to club members. Rooms are in a three-story building, and most have a patio or balcony. Although the inn is nearly 30 years old, refurbished small rooms are comfortable and contemporary. ⊠ *5800 N.W. 2nd Ave., 33487* ☎ *561/994–0400* ⎙ *561/998–8279* ⇄ *46 rooms* ♨ *Restaurant, 27-hole golf course, 6 tennis courts* ▤ *AE, DC, MC, V.*

¢–$ ▥ **Ocean Lodge.** Since its across the street from rather than on the beach, this small hotel has a nice price. Rooms are in a simple two-story building, and all have refrigerators. Eleven rooms also have small kitchenettes with a two-burner stove top. Restaurants are within walking distance. ⊠ *531 N. Ocean Blvd., 33432* ☎ *561/395–7772 or 800/782–9262* ⎙ *561/395–0554* ⇄ *18 rooms* ♨ *Some kitchenettes, refrigerators, pool, laundry facilities* ▤ *AE, DC, MC, V.*

Nightlife & the Arts

THE ARTS **Caldwell Theatre Company** (⊠ 7873 N. Federal Hwy. ☎ 561/241–7432) hosts the multimedia Mizner Festival each April and May and stages four productions each season from October through May.

NIGHTLIFE Drop by **Gatsby's Boca** (⊠ 5970 S.W. 18th St., Shoppes at Village Point ☎ 561/393–3900) any night of the week for a lively crowd shooting pool on the 18 pool tables or watching sporting events on the six giant screens. **Hush Lounge** (⊠ 99 S.E. 1st Ave. ☎ 561/361–7244) is happening late night Tuesday–Saturday, when DJs spin the latest house, dance, and trance music. VIP rooms are available.

Sports & the Outdoors

BEACHES **Red Reef Park** (⊠ 1400 N. Rte. A1A) has a beach and playground plus picnic tables and grills. Popular **South Beach Park** (⊠ 400 N. Rte. A1A) has a concession stand. In addition to its beach, **Spanish River Park** (⊠ 3001 N. Rte. A1A) has picnic tables, grills, and a large playground.

BIKING Plenty of bike trails and quiet streets make for pleasant pedaling. Rent all styles and speeds of bikes at **International Bicycle** (⊠ 1013 N. Federal Hwy. ☎ 561/394–0404) by the hour or the day. Free bike maps show off the trails in the area.

BOATING   For the thrill of blasting across the water at up to 80 mph, try **Air and Sea Charters** (✉ 107 E. Palmetto Park Rd., Suite 330 ☎ 561/368–3566). For $80 per person (three-person minimum), spend a wild-eyed half hour gripping your life vest aboard a 1,000-horsepower offshore racing boat. More leisurely are the two 55-ft catamarans or 45-ft sailboat; rates start at $35 per person for 2½ hours.

GOLF   Two championship courses and golf programs run by Dave Pelz and Nick-laus/Flick are available at **Boca Raton Resort & Club** (✉ 501 E. Camino Real ☎ 561/447–3078).

POLO   **Royal Palm Polo Sports Club** (✉ 18000 Jog Rd., at Old Clint Moore Rd. ☎ 561/994–1876), founded in 1959 by Oklahoma oilman John T. Oxley and now home to the $100,000 International Gold Cup Tournament, has seven polo fields within two stadiums. Games take place January through April, Sunday at 1 and 3. Admission is $8 to $15 for seats, $15 per car.

SCUBA DIVING &   **Force E** (✉ 877 E. Palmetto Park Rd. ☎ 561/368–0555) has informa-
SNORKELING   tion on dive trips and also rents scuba and snorkeling equipment.

Shopping

Locals know that Boca "strip malls" contain great shops. While stopping by for essentials at Publix, be sure to check out that unassuming consignment, shoe, or fashion boutique next door and you may discover one of Boca's better finds.

Mizner Park (✉ Federal Hwy., one block north of Palmetto Park Rd. ☎ 561/447–8105) is a distinctive 30-acre shopping center with apartments and town houses among its gardenlike retail and restaurant spaces. Some three dozen stores, including national and local retailers, mingle with fine restaurants, sidewalk cafés, galleries, a movie theater, museum, and amphitheater. **Town Center Mall** (✉ 6000 W. Glades Rd. ☎ 561/368–6000) is an upscale shopping mall. Major retailers include Nordstrom, Bloomingdale's, Burdines, Lord & Taylor, Saks Fifth Avenue, and Sears. The mall's specialty may be women's fashion, but there are more than 200 stores and restaurants.

THE TREASURE COAST

From south to north, the Treasure Coast encompasses the top of Palm Beach County plus Martin, St. Lucie, and Indian River counties. Although dotted with destinations, this coastal section is one of Florida's quietest. Most towns are small with a lot of undeveloped land in between. Vero Beach, the region's most sophisticated area, is the one place you'll find fine-dining establishments and upscale shops. Beaches along here are sought out by nesting sea turtles; join locally organized watches to view the turtles laying their eggs in the sand between late April and August. It's illegal to touch or disturb turtles or their nests.

Palm Beach Shores

❷❾ *7 mi north of Palm Beach.*

Rimmed by mom-and-pop motels, this residential town is at the southern tip of Singer Island, across Lake Worth Inlet from Palm Beach. To travel between the two, however, you must cross over to the mainland before returning to the beach. This unpretentious community has affordable beachfront lodging and is near several nature parks.

Peanut Island. In the Intracoastal Waterway between Palm Beach Shores and Riviera Beach, this 79-acre island was opened in 1999 as a recre-

CloseUp

FLORIDA'S SEA TURTLES: THE NESTING SEASON

FROM MAY TO OCTOBER it's turtle nesting season all along the Florida coast. Female loggerhead, Kemp's ridley, and other species living in the Atlantic Ocean or Gulf of Mexico swim up to 2,000 mi to the Florida shore. By night, they drag their 100- to 400-pound bodies onto the beach to the dune line. Then each digs a hole with her flippers, drops in 100 or so eggs, covers them up, and returns to sea.

The babies hatch about 60 days later, typically at night, sometimes taking days to surface. Once they burst out of the sand, the hatchlings must get to sea rapidly or risk becoming dehydrated from the sun or being caught by crabs, birds, or other predators.

Instinctively baby turtles head toward bright light, probably because for millions of years starlight or moonlight reflected on the waves was the brightest light around, serving to guide hatchlings to water. But now light from beach development can lead the babies in the wrong direction, and many hatchings are crushed by vehicles after running to the street rather than the water. To help, many coastal towns enforce light restrictions during nesting months, and more than one Florida homeowner has been surprised by a police officer at the door requesting that lights be dimmed on behalf of baby sea turtles.

At night, volunteers walk the beaches, searching for signs of turtle nests. Upon finding telltale scratches in the sand, they cordon off the sites, so beachgoers will leave the spots undisturbed. Volunteers also keep watch over nests when babies are about to hatch and assist if the hatchlings do get disoriented.

It's a hazardous world for baby turtles. They can die after eating tar balls or plastic debris, or they can be gobbled by sharks or circling birds. Only about 1 in 1,000 survives to adulthood. Once reaching the water, the babies make their way to warm currents. East coast hatchlings drift into the Gulf Stream, spending years floating around the Atlantic.

Males never, ever return to land, but when females attain maturity, taking 15–20 years, they return to shore to lay eggs. Remarkably, even though migrating hundreds and even thousands of miles out at sea, most return to the very beach where they were born to deposit their eggs. Sea turtles nest at least twice a season— sometimes as many as 10 times—and then skip a year or two. Each time they nest, they come back to the same stretch of beach. In fact, the more they nest, the more accurate they get, until eventually they return time and again to within a few feet of where they last laid their eggs. These incredible navigation skills remain for the most part a mystery despite intense scientific study. To learn more, check out the Sea Turtle Survival League's and Caribbean Conservation Corporation's Web site at www.cccturtle.org.

— Pam Acheson

ational park. There is a 20-ft-wide walking path surrounding the entire island, a 19-slip boat dock, a 170-ft T-shape fishing pier, six picnic pavilions, a visitor center, and 20 overnight campsites. The small **Palm Beach Maritime Museum** (☎ 561/842–8202) is open Wednesday through Sunday and showcases the "Kennedy Bunker," a bomb shelter prepared for President John F. Kennedy (call for tour hours.) To get to the island, you'll need your own boat or a water taxi (call for schedules and pickup locations). ⊠ *6500 Peanut Island Rd., Riviera Beach* ☎ *561/845–4445* ⊕ *www.pbmm.org* ☒ *Free* ☉ *Daily dawn–dusk for noncampers.*

off the
beaten
path

John D. MacArthur Beach State Park. Almost 2 mi of beach, good fishing and shelling, and one of the finest examples of subtropical coastal habitat remaining in southeast Florida are among treasures here. To learn about what you see, take an interpretive walk to a mangrove estuary along the upper reaches of Lake Worth. Or visit the William T. Kirby Nature Center (☎ 561/624–6952), open Wednesday to Monday from 9 to 5, which has exhibits on the coastal environment. ⊠ *10900 Rte. A1A, North Palm Beach* ☎ *561/624–6950* ☒ *$3.25 per vehicle (up to 8 people)* ☉ *Daily 8–5:30.*

Loggerhead Park Marine Life Center of Juno Beach. Established by Eleanor N. Fletcher, the "turtle lady of Juno Beach," the center focuses on sea turtle history, including loggerheads and leatherbacks, with displays of coastal natural history, sharks, whales, and shells. ⊠ *14200 U.S. Hwy. 1, Juno Beach* ☎ *561/627–8280* ⊕ *www. marinelife.org* ☒ *Free* ☉ *Tues.–Sat. 10–4, Sun. noon–3.*

Where to Stay & Eat

$–$$$ ✗ **Sailfish Marina Restaurant.** Once known as the Galley, this waterfront restaurant looking out to Peanut Island remains a great place to chill out after a hot day of mansion gawking or beach bumming. Sit inside or outdoors to order tropical drinks or mainstays like conch chowder, grouper, or meat loaf. More upscale entrées—this, after all, is still Palm Beach County—include lobster tail or baby sea scallops sautéed in garlic and lemon butter. Breakfast is a winner here, too. ⊠ *98 Lake Dr.* ☎ *561/842–8449* ☰ *MC, V.*

$$–$$$$ 🏨 **Palm Beach Shores Resort.** At the edge of a long stretch of golden beach is this pink, six-story resort with a red tile roof that's a superb family destination. All rooms are suites with a separate bedroom, living room with a sofa bed, plus refrigerator, microwave, and dining area. Suites are furnished in natural rattan and tropical prints. The oceanfront pool is surrounded by a brick courtyard. The Beach Buddies Kids Club has many programs including field trips, arts and crafts, seashell hunts, and water sports. ⊠ *181 Ocean Ave., 33404* ☎ *561/863–4000* 🖷 *561/ 863–9502* ⊕ *www.pbsr.net* ⇋ *257 suites* ⚭ *Restaurant, microwaves, refrigerators, pool, health club, spa, beach, bar, children's programs (ages 2–12)* ☰ *AE, D, DC, MC, V.*

★ $–$$ 🏨 **Sailfish Marina and Sportfishing Resort.** This one-story motel has a marina with 94 deep-water slips and 30 rooms and efficiencies that open to landscaped grounds. None are directly on the water, but Units 9–11 have ocean views across the blacktop drive. Rooms have peaked ceilings, carpeting, king-size or twin beds, and stall showers; all have ceiling fans. From the seawall, you'll see fish through the clear inlet water. The motel allows pets for a fee of $10 per night. ⊠ *98 Lake Dr., 33404* ☎ *561/844–1724 or 800/446–4577* 🖷 *561/848–9684* ⊕ *www. sailfishmarina.com* ⇋ *30 units* ⚭ *Restaurant, grocery, pool, dock, bar* ☰ *AE, MC, V.*

Sports & the Outdoors

BIKING   To rent bikes by the hour, half day, or full day, head for the **Sailfish Marina and Resort** (⊠ 98 Lake Dr. ☎ 561/844–1724). Ask for a free map of the bike trails.

FISHING   The **Sailfish Marina and Resort** (⊠ 98 Lake Dr. ☎ 561/844–1724) has a large sportfishing fleet, with 28-ft to 60-ft boats and seasoned captains. Book a full- or half-day of deep-sea fishing for up to six people.

Palm Beach Gardens

30 *5 mi north of West Palm Beach.*

About 15 minutes northwest of Palm Beach is this relaxed, upscale residential community known for its high-profile golf complex, the PGA National Resort & Spa. Although not on the beach, the town is less than a 30-minute drive away from the ocean.

Where to Stay & Eat

$–$$$ ✕ **Arezzo.** The aroma of fresh garlic will draw you into this outstanding Tuscan grill at the PGA National Resort & Spa. Families are attracted by affordable prices (as well as the food), so romantics might be tempted to pass on by, but that would be a mistake. Dishes include chicken, veal, fish, steaks, a dozen pastas, and almost as many pizzas. Thanks to the unusually relaxed attitude of the resort itself, you'll be equally comfortable in shorts or in jacket and tie. ⊠ *400 Ave. of the Champions* ☎ *561/627–2000* ▭ *AE, MC, V* ☉ *No lunch.*

★ **$–$$**   ✕ **River House.** Patrons keep returning to this waterfront restaurant for large portions of straightforward American fare; the large salad bar and fresh, slice-it-yourself breads; and the competent service. Choices include seafood (with a daily catch), steaks, chops, and seafood-steak combo platters. Booths and freestanding tables are surrounded by light wood, high ceilings, and nautical art. Expect a wait on Saturday night in season; however, you can make reservations for the 20 upstairs tables, available weekends only, where it's slightly more formal and there's no salad bar. ⊠ *2373 PGA Blvd.* ☎ *561/694–1188* ▭ *AE, MC, V* ☉ *No lunch.*

¢–$ ✕ **No Anchovies.** Sharing is half the fun here, so don't be shy about it at this casual and generous neighborhood trattoria. Sandwiches come on your choice of Italian loaf, semolina, whole wheat, or a spinach tortilla wrap with fillings such as oven-roasted turkey breast with sun-dried tomatoes or chicken salad. Entrées range from pastas to chicken or shrimp. Consider making your own pizza, perhaps with fresh goat cheese from the Turtle Creek dairy. There is another No Anchovies in West Palm Beach. ⊠ *2650 PGA Blvd.* ☎ *561/622–7855* ▭ *AE, MC, V.*

★ **$$$–$$$$**   ▥ **PGA National Resort & Spa.** The entire resort is richly detailed, from the outstanding mission-style rooms done in deep-toned florals to the lavish landscaping to the extensive sports facilities to the excellent dining. The spa is in a building styled after a Mediterranean fishing village, and six outdoor therapy pools, dubbed Waters of the World, are joined by a collection of imported mineral salt pools. Flowering plants adorn golf courses and croquet courts amid a 240-acre nature preserve. Lodgings include two-bedroom, two-bath cottages with kitchens. Among the restaurants is a Don Shula's Steakhouse. ⊠ *400 Ave. of the Champions, 33418* ☎ *561/627–2000 or 800/633–9150* ⊜ *561/622–0261* ⊕ *www.pga-resorts.com* ⇱ *279 rooms, 60 suites, 80 cottages* ♿ *5 restaurants, room service, in-room safes, some kitchens, some refrigerators, 90-hole golf course, 19 tennis courts, 9 pools, lake, health club, hot tub, massage, sauna, spa, boating, croquet, 4 bars, baby-sitting, children's programs (ages 3–12), business services, meeting rooms* ▭ *AE, D, DC, MC, V.*

Nightlife

For DJ'd Top 40s, try the **Club Safari** (✉ Palm Beach Gardens Marriott, 4000 RCA Blvd. ☎ 561/622–7024), except on Thursday, when the focus is on oldies.

Sports & the Outdoors

AUTO RACING Weekly ¼-mi drag racing; monthly 2¼-mi, 10-turn road racing; and monthly AMA motorcycle road racing take place year-round at the **Moroso Motorsports Park** (✉ 17047 Beeline Hwy. ☎ 561/622–1400).

GOLF **PGA National Resort & Spa** (✉ 1000 Ave. of the Champions ☎ 561/627–1800) has a reputedly tough 90 holes and lessons available at the Academy of Golf.

Shopping

The **Gardens Mall** (✉ 3101 PGA Blvd. ☎ 561/775–7750) could be the most civilized mall in South Florida. It offers an above-par shopping-mall experience—a calm, spacious, airy, and well-lit environment. Anchors Bloomingdale's, Burdines, Macy's, Saks Fifth Avenue, and Sears Roebuck support more than 160 specialty retailers including Swarovski, Godiva, Tommy Hilfiger, Laura Ashley, and Charles David.

Jupiter

③ *12 mi north of Palm Beach Shores.*

Jupiter is one of the few little towns in the region not fronted by an island. Beaches here are part of the mainland, and Route A1A runs for almost 4 mi along the beachfront dunes.

A beach is just one of the draws of **Carlin Park,** which has picnic pavilions, hiking trails, a baseball diamond, playground, six tennis courts, and fishing sites. The Park Galley, serving snacks and burgers, is open daily 9–5. ✉ *400 Rte. A1A* ☎ *no phone* ☉ *Daily dawn–dusk.*

Take a look at how life once was at the **Dubois Home,** a modest pioneer outpost dating from 1898. Sitting atop an ancient Jeaga Indian mound 20 ft high and looking onto Jupiter Inlet, it has Cape Cod as well as Cracker (old Florida) design. Even if you arrive when the house is closed, surrounding **Dubois Park** is worth the visit for its lovely beaches and swimming lagoons. ✉ *Dubois Rd.* ☎ *561/747–6639* 🎫 *Free* ☉ *Wed. and Sun. 1–4; park daily dawn–dusk.*

Permanent exhibits at the **Florida History Center and Museum** review not only modern-day development along the Loxahatchee River but also shipwrecks, railroads, and steamboat-era, Seminole, and pioneer history. ✉ *805 N. U.S. 1, Burt Reynolds Park* ☎ *561/747–6639* 🎫 *$5* ☉ *Tues.–Fri. 10–5, weekends 1–5.*

Designed by Civil War hero General George Meade, the redbrick Coast Guard **Jupiter Inlet Lighthouse** has operated here since 1860. Tours of the 105-ft-tall landmark unfold every half hour, and there is a small museum. The lighthouse has undergone significant change, courtesy of an $858,000 federal grant, transforming it from bright red to natural brick, the way it looked from 1860 to 1918. ✉ *Capt. Armour's Way (U.S. 1 and Beach Rd.)* ☎ *561/747–8380* ⊕ *www.jupiterinletlighthouse.com* 🎫 *Tour $6* ☉ *Sun.–Wed. 10–4 (last tour at 3:15).*

Where to Stay & Eat

★ $$$–$$$$ ✗ **Charley's Crab.** The grand view across the Jupiter River complements the soaring ceilings and striking interior architecture of this marine-side restaurant. Come here for expertly prepared seafood, such as grouper, pompano, red snapper, or yellowfin tuna. There are also great pasta choices such as the *pagliara* with scallops, fish, shrimp, mussels, spinach, garlic, and olive oil. Other Charley's Crab branches are in Deerfield Beach, Fort Lauderdale, and Palm Beach. ⊠ *1000 N. U.S. 1* ☎ *561/744–4710* ⊟ *AE, D, DC, MC, V.*

$–$$$ ✕ **Sinclairs Ocean Grill & Rotisserie.** This popular spot in the Jupiter Beach Resort has French doors looking out to the pool, and a menu with a daily selection of fresh fish, such as cashew-encrusted grouper, Cajun-spiced tuna, and mahimahi with pistachio sauce. There are also thick juicy steaks—filet mignon is the house specialty—or chicken and veal dishes. Sunday brunch is a big draw. ⊠ *5 N. Rte. A1A* ☎ *561/745–7120* ⊟ *AE, MC, V.*

¢–$ ✕ **Lighthouse Restaurant.** Low prices match the plain look in this coffee shop–style building, but the food is a tasty surprise. Order chicken breast stuffed with sausage and fresh vegetables, burgundy beef stew, king-crab cakes, and great pastries. The same people-pleasing formula has been employed since 1936: round-the-clock service (except 10 PM Sunday–6 AM Monday) and a menu that changes daily to take advantage of best seasonal market buys. ⊠ *1510 U.S. 1* ☎ *561/746–4811* ⊟ *D, DC, MC, V.*

$$–$$$$ ▥ **Jupiter Beach Resort.** While unpretentious, this resort has undergone a multimillion-dollar makeover, and it shows. Rooms, in pastels with floral prints and rattan, are within an eight-story tower, most with balconies. Those on higher floors have great ocean views. Plentiful activities and a casual approach draw families here, and the resort offers turtle watches in season, May through October. Snorkeling and scuba equipment and Jet Skis are for rent. ⊠ *5 N. Rte. A1A, 33475* ☎ *561/746–2511 or 800/228–8810* 🖷 *561/747–3304* ⊕ *www.jupiterbeachresort. com* ⇆ *125 rooms, 28 suites* ₺ *2 restaurants, tennis court, pool, beach, dive shop, 2 bars, recreation room, laundry facilities, business services* ⊟ *AE, D, MC, V.*

Sports & the Outdoors

BASEBALL   Both the **St. Louis Cardinals and Montreal Expos** (⊠ 4751 Main St. ☎ 561/775–1818) train at the $28 million Roger Dean Stadium, which seats 7,000 and has 12 practice fields.

CANOEING   **Canoe Outfitters of Florida** (⊠ 9060 W. Indiantown Rd. ☎ 561/746–7053) runs trips along 8 mi of the Loxahatchee River, Florida's only government-designated Wild and Scenic River. Canoe rental for two, with drop-off and pickup, costs $35 for the first two hours (two-hour minimum) and then $4 per additional hour plus tax.

GOLF   The **Golf Club of Jupiter** (⊠ 1800 Central Blvd. ☎ 561/747–6262) has 18 holes of varying difficulty. **Jupiter Dunes Golf Club** (⊠ 401 Rte. A1A ☎ 561/746–6654) has 18 holes and a putting green.

Jupiter Island & Hobe Sound

㉜ *5 mi north of Jupiter.*

Northeast across the Jupiter Inlet from Jupiter is the southern tip of Jupiter Island, including a planned community of the same name. Here expansive and expensive estates often retreat from the road behind screens of vegetation, while at the north end of the island, turtles come to nest in a wildlife refuge. To the west, on the mainland, is the little community of Hobe Sound.

In **Blowing Rocks Preserve,** within the 73-acre Nature Conservancy holding, you'll find plant communities native to beachfront dune, coastal strand (the landward side of the dunes), mangrove, and hammock (tropical hardwood forests). The best time to visit is when high tides and strong offshore winds coincide, causing the sea to blow spectacularly through holes in the eroded outcropping. Park in the lot; police ticket cars parked along the road. ⊠ *574 South Beach Rd. (Rte. 707), Jupiter Island* ☎ *561/744–6668* 🖅 *$3* ☉ *Daily 9–4:30.*

Two tracts comprise **Hobe Sound National Wildlife Refuge:** 232 acres of sand-pine and scrub-oak forest in Hobe Sound and 735 acres of coastal sand dune and mangrove swamp on Jupiter Island. Trails are open to the public in both places. Turtles nest and shells wash ashore on the 3½-mi beach, which has been severely eroded by winter high tides and strong winds. ⊠ *13640 S.E. Federal Hwy., Hobe Sound* ☎ *561/546–6141* ⊠ *Beach Rd. off Rte. 707, Jupiter Island* 🖅 *$5 per vehicle* ☉ *Daily dawn–dusk.*

Ⓒ Although on the Hobe Sound National Wildlife Refuge, **Hobe Sound Nature Center** is an independent organization. Its museum, which has baby alligators and crocodiles, and a scary-looking tarantula, is a child's delight. Interpretive exhibits focus on the environment, and a ½-mi trail winds through a forest of sand pine and scrub oak—one of Florida's most unusual and endangered plant communities. A classroom program on environmental issues is for preschool-age children to adults. ⊠ *13640 S.E. Federal Hwy., Hobe Sound* ☎ *561/546–2067* 🖅 *Free* ☉ *Trail daily dawn–dusk; nature center weekdays 9–3 (call for Sat. hrs).*

Once you've gotten to **Jonathan Dickinson State Park,** follow signs to **Hobe Mountain.** An ancient dune topped with a tower, it yields a panoramic view across the park's 10,285 acres of varied terrain, as well as the Intracoastal Waterway. The Loxahatchee River, part of the federal government's Wild and Scenic Rivers program, cuts through the park and harbors manatees in winter and alligators year-round. Two-hour boat tours of the river leave four times daily. Among amenities here are bicycle and hiking trails, a campground, and a snack bar. ⊠ *16450 S.E. Federal Hwy., Hobe Sound* ☎ *561/546–2771* 🖅 *$3.25 per vehicle (up to 8 people), boat tours $12* ☉ *Daily 8–dusk.*

Sports & the Outdoors

Jonathan Dickinson's River Tours (⊠ Jonathan Dickinson State Park ☎ 561/ 746–1466) rents canoes for use around the park.

Stuart

③③ *7 mi north of Hobe Sound.*

This compact little town on a peninsula that juts out into the St. Lucie River has a remarkable amount of river shoreline for its size as well as a charming historic district. The ocean is about 5 mi east.

★ Strict architectural and zoning standards guide civic renewal projects in **historic downtown Stuart,** which has antiques shops, restaurants, and more than 50 specialty shops within a two-block area. A self-guided walking-tour pamphlet is available at assorted locations downtown to clue you in on this once small fishing village's early days. On the National Register of Historic Places, the **Lyric Theatre** (⊠ 59 S.W. Flagler Ave. ☎ 772/ 286–7827) has been revived for performing and community events; a gazebo has free music performances. The old courthouse has become the **Cultural Court House Center** (⊠ 80 E. Ocean Blvd. ☎ 772/288–2542) and presents art exhibits. The George W. Parks General Store is now the **Stuart Heritage Museum** (⊠ 161 S.W. Flagler Ave. ☎ 772/220–4600). For information on the historic downtown, contact the **Stuart Main Street** (⊠ 201 S.W. Flagler Ave., 34994 ☎ 772/286–2848).

Where to Stay & Eat

★ $–$$$ ✕ **Jolly Sailor Pub.** In an old historic-district bank building, this eatery is owned by a British Merchant Navy veteran, which accounts for all the ship paraphernalia. A veritable Cunard museum, it has a model of the *Britannia,* prints of 19th-century side-wheelers, and a big bar painting of the *QE2.* There is a wonderful brass-rail wood bar and fitting pub grub such as fish-and-chips, cottage pie, and bangers and mash, with Guinness and Double Diamond ales on tap. You also can get steaks and seafood. ✉ *1 S.W. Osceola St.* ☎ *772/221–1111* ▭ *AE, MC, V.*

¢–$$ ✕ **The Ashley.** Despite the hanging plants and artwork, this restaurant still has elements of the old bank that was robbed three times early in the 20th century by the Ashley Gang (hence the name). The big outdoor mural in the French Impressionist style was paid for by downtown revivalists, whose names are duly inscribed on wall plaques inside. The Continental menu has lots of salads, fresh fish, and pastas. Crowds head to the lounge for a popular happy hour. Brunch is the only meal served on Sunday. ✉ *61 S.W. Osceola St.* ☎ *772/221–9476* ▭ *AE, MC, V.*

$$–$$$ ▣ **Pirates Cove Resort and Marina.** On the banks of the St. Lucie River and in the heart of Sailfish Alley, this cozy enclave provides the perfect place to recoup after a day at sea. This mid-size resort is relaxing and casual but packed with recreational activities for the day and nightly live music and dancing at the Pirates Loft Restaurant and Lounge. The tropically furnished rooms are large, with balconies to enjoy the waterfront views. ✉ *4307 S.E. Bayview St., 34997* ☎ *772/287–2500 or 800/332–1414* ✉ *772/220–2704* ⊕ *www.piratescoveresortandmarina. com* ⇢ *50 rooms* ♿ *Restaurant, room service, pool, boating, bar, shop* ▭ *AE, D, DC, MC, V.*

Sports & the Outdoors

Deep-sea charters are available at the **Sailfish Marina** (✉ 3565 S.E. St. Lucie Blvd. ☎ 772/283–1122).

Shopping

More than 60 restaurants and shops with antiques, art, and fashions have opened along **Osceola Street** in the restored downtown area. Operating for more than two decades, the **B&A Flea Market,** the oldest and largest such enterprise on the Treasure Coast, has a street-bazaar feel with shoppers happily scouting for the practical and unusual. ✉ *2885 S.E. Federal Hwy.* ☎ *772/288–4915* ▱ *Free* ☉ *Weekends 8–3.*

Hutchinson Island (Jensen Beach)

㉞ *5 mi northeast of Stuart.*

Area residents have payed unusual care here to curb the runaway development that has created the commercial crowding found to the north and south, although some high-rises have popped up along the shore. The small town of Jensen Beach, occupying the core of the island, actually stretches across both sides of the Indian River. Citrus farmers and fishermen still play a big community role, anchoring the area's down-to-earth feel. Between late April and August more than 600 turtles come here to nest along the town's Atlantic beach.

Run by the Florida Oceanographic Society, the **Coastal Science Center** consists of a coastal hardwood hammock and mangrove forest. Expansion has yielded a visitor center, a science center with interpretive exhibits on coastal science and environmental issues, and a ½-mi interpretive boardwalk. Guided nature walks and stingray feedings are offered at various times during the day. ✉ *890 N.E. Ocean Blvd.* ☎ *772/225–0505* ⊕ *www.fosusa.org* ▱ *$6* ☉ *Mon.–Sat. 10–5, Sun. noon–4.*

The pastel-pink **Elliott Museum** was erected in 1961 in honor of Sterling Elliott, inventor of an early automated addressing machine and a four-wheel cycle. The museum has antique cars, dolls and toys, and fixtures from an early general store, blacksmith shop, and apothecary shop. ✉ *825 N.E. Ocean Blvd.* ☎ *772/225–1961* 💲 *$6* ☉ *Daily 10–4.*

Built in 1875, **Gilbert's House of Refuge Museum** is the only remaining building of nine such structures built by the U.S. Life Saving Service (a predecessor of the Coast Guard) to aid stranded sailors. Exhibits include antique lifesaving equipment, maps, artifacts from nearby wrecks, and boat-making tools. ✉ *301 S.E. MacArthur Blvd.* ☎ *772/225–1875* 💲 *$4* ☉ *Daily 10–4.*

🖰 Linking the watery past with a permanent record of maritime and yachting events contributing to Treasure Coast lore, the **Maritime & Yachting Museum** has programs for children, historic exhibits, restoration of vessels, and ship modelers. Call for an events and activities schedule. ✉ *3250 S. Kanner Hwy.* ☎ *772/692–1234* 💲 *Free* ☉ *Mon.–Sat. 11–4, Sun. 1–5.*

Where to Stay & Eat

★ $$–$$$ ✕ **11 Maple Street.** With a mere 16 tables, this spot is as good as it gets on the Treasure Coast, with a Continental menu that changes nightly. Soft recorded jazz and friendly staff satisfy along with food served in ample portions. Appetizers run from panfried conch and crispy calamari to spinach salad, and entrées include pan-seared rainbow trout, wood-grilled venison with onion potato hash, and beef tenderloin with white truffle and chive butter. Desserts such as a white-chocolate custard with blackberry sauce are seductive, too. ✉ *3224 Maple Ave.* ☎ *772/334– 7714* 🍴 *Reservations essential* 🖃 *MC, V* ☉ *Closed Mon.–Tues. No lunch.*

$$–$$$ ✕ **Scalawags.** The look is plantation tropical—coach lanterns, gingerbread molding, wicker, slow-motion paddle fans—but the top-notch buffets are aimed at today's resort guests. Standouts are the prime-rib buffet on Friday night and the all-you-can-eat Wednesday-evening seafood extravaganza with jumbo shrimp, Alaskan crab legs, clams on the half shell, marinated salmon, and fresh catch. There's also a regular menu with a big selection of fish. The main dining room in this second-floor restaurant overlooks the Indian River. ✉ *Marriott Beach Resort, 555 N.E. Ocean Blvd.* ☎ *772/225–6818* 🖃 *AE, D, DC, MC, V.*

$$ ✕ **Conchy Joe's.** This classic Florida stilt house full of antique fish mounts, gator hides, and snakeskins dates from the 1920s, although Conchy Joe's, like a hermit crab sliding into a new shell, moved up from West Palm Beach in 1983. Under a huge Seminole-built *chickee* platform with a palm through the roof, you'll find a supercasual attitude and seafood from a menu changing daily. Staples are grouper marsala, broiled sea scallops, and fried cracked conch. There's live music Thursday, Friday, and Saturday nights; heady rum drinks; and a happy hour daily 3 to 6 and during NFL games. ✉ *3945 N.E. Indian River Dr.* ☎ *772/ 334–1130* 🖃 *AE, D, MC, V.*

¢–$ ✕ **The Emporium.** Hutchinson Island Beach Resort Resort & Marina's coffee shop is an old-fashioned soda fountain and grill that also serves hearty breakfasts. Specialties include eggs Benedict, omelets, deli sandwiches, and salads. ✉ *555 N.E. Ocean Blvd.* ☎ *772/225–3700* 🖃 *AE, D, DC, MC, V.*

$$–$$$$ 🏨 **Hutchinson Island Marriott Beach Resort & Marina.** With golf, tennis, a 77-slip marina, and a full water-sports program, plus many restaurants and bars, this 200-acre self-contained resort is excellent for families. Reception, some restaurants, and many rooms are in a trio of yellow four-story buildings that form an open courtyard with a large pool. Additional rooms and apartments with kitchens are spread over the property, some

overlooking the Intracoastal Waterway and marina, others looking onto the ocean or tropical gardens. ⊠ *555 N.E. Ocean Blvd., Hutchinson Island, Stuart 34996* ☎ *772/225–3700 or 800/775–5936* 🖷 *772/225–0033* ⊕ *www.marriotthotels.com* 🖙 *290 rooms, 27 suites, 150 condominiums* ♿ *5 restaurants, some kitchens, golf privileges, 13 tennis courts, 4 pools, spa, beach, dock, boating, 4 bars, business services, meeting rooms* ▭ *AE, D, DC, MC, V.*

$$–$$$ 🏨 **Hutchinson Inn.** Sandwiched among the high-rises, this modest two-story motel from the mid-1970s has the feel of a B&B thanks to the management's friendly attitude. An expanded Continental breakfast is served in the lobby or on tables outside. Borrow books or magazines to take to your room, where homemade cookies are delivered nightly. On Saturday there's a noon barbecue. Motel-style rooms range from small but comfortable to fully equipped efficiencies and two seafront suites with private balconies. ⊠ *9750 S. Ocean Dr., 34957* ☎ *772/229–2000* 🖷 *772/229–8875* ⊕ *www.hutchinsoninn.com* 🖙 *21 rooms, 2 suites* ♿ *Pool, beach* ▭ *MC, V* ⊦◉⊦ *CP.*

Sports & the Outdoors

BASEBALL The **New York Mets** (⊠ 525 N.W. Peacock Blvd., Port St. Lucie ☎ 772/871–2100) train at the St. Lucie County Sport Complex.

BEACHES **Bathtub Reef Park** (⊠ MacArthur Blvd. off Rte. A1A), at the north end of the Indian River Plantation, is ideal for children because the waters are shallow for about 300 ft offshore and usually calm. At low tide bathers can walk to the reef. Facilities include rest rooms and showers.

GOLF **Hutchinson Island Marriott Golf Club** (⊠ 555 N.E. Ocean Blvd. ☎ 772/225–6819) has 18 holes. The PGA-operated **PGA Golf Club at the PGA Villages** (⊠ 1916 Perfect Dr., Port St. Lucie ☎ 772/467–1300 or 800/800–4653) is a public facility with three courses.

Fort Pierce

❸❺ *11 mi north of Stuart.*

About an hour north of Palm Beach, this community has a distinctive rural feel, focusing on ranching and citrus farming. There are several worthwhile stops, including those easily seen while following Route 707.

♿ Once a reservoir, the 550-acre **Savannahs Recreation Area** has been returned to its natural state. Today the semi-wilderness area has campsites, boat ramps, and trails. ⊠ *1400 E. Midway Rd.* ☎ *772/464–7855* 🎫 *$1 per vehicle* ☉ *Daily 8–6.*

A self-guided tour of the **Heathcote Botanical Gardens** takes in a palm walk, a Japanese garden, and subtropical foliage. ⊠ *210 Savannah Rd.* ☎ *772/464–4672* 🎫 *$4* ☉ *Mar.–Oct., Tues.–Sat. 9–5; Nov.–Apr., Tues.–Sat. 9–5, Sun. 1–5.*

As the home of the Treasure Coast Art Association, the **A. E. "Bean" Backus Gallery** displays works of one of Florida's foremost landscape artists. The gallery mounts changing exhibits and offers exceptional buys on work by local artists. ⊠ *500 N. Indian River Dr.* ☎ *772/465–0630* 🎫 *Donation welcome* ☉ *Tues.–Sat. 10–4, Sun. noon–4.*

Accessible only by footbridge, the **Jack Island Wildlife Refuge** has 4⅓ mi of trails. The 1½-mi Marsh Rabbit Trail across the island traverses a mangrove swamp to a 30-ft observation tower overlooking the Indian River. ⊠ *Rte. A1A* ☎ *772/468–3985* 🎫 *Free* ☉ *Daily 8–dusk.*

★ Commemorating more than 3,000 navy frogmen training along Treasure Coast shoreline during World War II, the **UDT Navy Seals Museum** has weapons and equipment on view and exhibits depicting the history of the UDTs (Underwater Demolition Teams). Patrol boats and vehicles are displayed outdoors. ✉ *3300 N. Rte. A1A* ☎ *772/595–5845* 🔖 *$4* ◷ *Tues.–Sat. 10–4, Sun. noon–4.*

Highlights of the **St. Lucie County Historical Museum** include early 20th-century memorabilia, photos, vintage farm tools, a restored 1919 American La France fire engine, replicas of a general store and the old Fort Pierce railroad station, and the restored 1905 Gardner House. ✉ *414 Seaway Dr.* ☎ *772/462–1795* 🔖 *$3* ◷ *Tues.–Sat. 10–4, Sun. noon–4.*

The 340-acres at the **Fort Pierce Inlet State Recreation Area** contain sand dunes and a coastal hammock. The park has swimming, surfing, picnic facilities, hiking, and a self-guided nature trail. ✉ *905 Shorewinds Dr.* ☎ *772/468–3985* 🔖 *$3.25 per vehicle (up to 8 people)* ◷ *Daily 8–dusk.*

Explore the world of underwater science at the **Harbor Branch Oceanographic Institution,** a research and teaching facility. Its research fleet—particularly two submersibles—operates globally for NASA and NATO, among other contractors. A 90-minute tour of the 500-acre facility includes aquariums of sea life indigenous to the Indian River Lagoon and marine technology exhibits. Look for lifelike, whimsical bronze sculptures created by founder J. Seward Johnson, Jr., and a gift shop with imaginative sea-related items. ✉ *5600 Old Dixie Hwy.* ☎ *772/465–2400* ⊕ *www.hboi.edu* 🔖 *$12; lagoon boat tours $17* ◷ *Boat tours Mon.–Sat. at 10, 1, and 3.*

Where to Stay & Eat

$$–$$$ ✗ **Mangrove Mattie's.** Since opening in the 1980s, this upscale but rustic spot on Fort Pierce Inlet has provided dazzling waterfront views with delicious seafood. Dine on the terrace or within the dining room, and try the coconut-fried shrimp or the chicken and scampi. Or come by during happy hour (weekdays 5–8) for a free buffet of snacks. ✉ *1640 Seaway Dr.* ☎ *772/466–1044* 🖃 *AE, D, DC, MC, V.*

$–$$ ✗ **Theo Thudpucker's Raw Bar.** People dressed for work mingle here with folks in shorts fresh from the beach. On squally days everyone piles in off the jetty. Specialties include oyster stew, smoked fish spread, conch salad and conch fritters, fresh catfish, and alligator tail. ✉ *2025 Seaway Dr. (South Jetty)* ☎ *772/465–1078* 🖃 *MC, V.*

$–$$ 🏨 **Mellon Patch Inn.** Across the shore road from a beach park and at the end of a canal leading to the Indian River Lagoon, this property is in a prime spot. One side of the canal has attractive homes; the other has the Jack Island Wildlife Refuge. Andrea and Arthur Mellon built this B&B, and images of split-open melons permeate the house—on pillows, crafts, and candies on night tables. All guest rooms face the finger canal behind the inn, and each themed room has imaginative accessories. The cathedral-ceiling living room has a fireplace. ✉ *3601 N. Rte. A1A, North Hutchinson Island 34949* ☎ *772/461–5231 or 800/656–7824* 🖶 *772/464–6463* ⊕ *www.mellonpatchinn.com* 🛏 *4 rooms* ⚷ *Hot tub, dock, boating, fishing* 🖃 *AE, MC, V* ⎩ *BP.*

¢ 🏨 **Dockside Harbor Light Resort.** Formerly two adjacent motels, this expanded resort is the pick of the pack of lodgings lining the Fort Pierce Inlet along Seaway Drive. Spacious units on two floors have a kitchen or wet bar and routine but well-cared-for furnishings. Some rooms have a waterfront porch or balcony. In addition to the motel units a set of four apartments is across the street (off the water), where in-season weekly rates are $360. ✉ *1160 Seaway Dr., 34949* ☎ *772/468–3555* *or 800/286–1745* ☎ *772/489–9848* ⊕ *www.docksideinn.com* ↘ *60 rooms, 4 apartments* ⚘ *2 pools, spa, fishing, laundry facilities* ☰ *AE, D, DC, MC, V* ⦿⎮ *CP.*

Sports & the Outdoors

FISHING For charter boats and fishing guides, try the **Dockside Harbor Light Resort** (⊠ 1152 Seaway Dr. ☎ 561/461–4824).

JAI ALAI **Fort Pierce Jai Alai** (⊠ 1750 S. Kings Hwy., off Okeechobee Rd. ☎ 772/464–7500 or 800/524–2524) operates seasonally for live jai alai and year-round for off-track betting on horse-racing simulcasts. Admission is $1, with live games January through April, Wednesday and Saturday at noon and 7, Friday at 7, and Sunday at 1. Call to confirm the schedule.

SCUBA DIVING Some 200 yards from shore and ¼ mi north of the UDT-Seal Museum on North Hutchinson Island, the **Urca de Lima Underwater Archaeological Preserve** contains remains of a flat-bottom, round-bellied store ship. Once part of a treasure fleet bound for Spain, it was destroyed by a hurricane. Dive boats can be chartered through the **Dockside Harbor Light Resort** (⊠ 1152 Seaway Dr. ☎ 561/461–4824).

⬭ **en route** To reach Vero Beach, you have two options—Route A1A, along the coast, or Route 605 (also called Old Dixie Highway), on the mainland. As you approach Vero on the latter, you'll pass through an ungussied landscape of small farms and residential areas. On the beach route, part of the drive is through an unusually undeveloped section of the Florida coast. Both trips are relaxing.

Vero Beach

③⑥ *12 mi north of Fort Pierce.*

Tranquil and charming, this Indian River County town has a strong commitment to the environment and the arts. You'll find plenty of outdoor activities here, even though many visitors gravitating to this training ground for the L.A. Dodgers opt to do little at all. In the town's exclusive Riomar Bay area, roads are shaded by massive live oaks, and a popular cluster of restaurants and shops is just off the beach.

On the National Register of Historic Places, the 18-acre **McKee Botanical Garden** has a hammock supporting a diverse collection and several restored architectural treasures. There's a gift shop, library, and café. ⊠ *350 U.S. Hwy. 1* ☎ *772/794–0601* ⊕ *www.mckeegarden.org* ⊡ *$6* ⊙ *Tues.–Sat. 10–5, Sun. noon–5.*

More grapefruit is shipped from the Indian River area than anywhere else in the world, as you'll learn at the **Indian River Citrus Museum,** where memorabilia harks back to when families washed and wrapped the luscious fruit to sell at roadside stands, and oxen hauled citrus-filled crates with distinctive Indian River labels to the rail station. A video shows current harvesting and shipping methods. Book free guided grove tours. ⊠ *2140 14th Ave.* ☎ *772/770–2263* ⊡ *Free* ⊙ *Tues.–Fri. 10–4, Sun. 1–4.*

Environmental Learning Center. In addition to aquariums filled with Indian River Lagoon life, the outstanding 51-acres here have a 600-ft boardwalk through mangrove shoreline and a 1-mi canoe trail. The center is on the north edge of Vero Beach, on Wabasso Island, and the pretty drive is worth the trip. ⊠ *255 Live Oak Dr.* ☎ *772/589–5050* ⊕ *www.elcweb.org* ⊡ *Free* ⊙ *Tues.–Fri. 10–4, Sat. 9–noon, Sun. 1–4.*

Where to Stay & Eat

$$$ ✕ **Black Pearl Riverfront.** One of Vero's trendiest dining options, this intimate, sophisticated restaurant has a stunning riverfront location accompanying superb international food. Fish is a specialty and there's a martini bar. Choose from appetizers such as the house specialty, fish chowder, or chilled leek-and-asparagus soup. Entrées might include onion-crusted grouper and beef Wellington. For dessert, try the hot chocolate lava cake, similar to a chocolate soufflé. You'll need reservations from October through April. ⊠ *4455 N. Rte. A1A* ☎ *772/234–4426* ⊟ *AE, MC, V* ⊘ *No lunch weekends.*

★ **$$–$$$** ✕ **Ocean Grill.** Opened by Waldo Sexton as a hamburger shack in 1938, the Ocean Grill with its ocean view now has Tiffany-style lamps, wrought-iron chandeliers, and paintings of pirates and Seminoles. Count on at least three kinds of seafood any day on the menu, along with pork chops, tasty soups, and salads. The house drink, the Leaping Limey, a curious blend of vodka, blue curaçao, and lemon, commemorates the 1894 wreck of the *Breconshire,* which occurred just offshore and from which 34 British sailors escaped. ⊠ *1050 Sexton Plaza (Beachland Blvd. east of Ocean Dr.)* ☎ *772/231–5409* ⊟ *AE, D, DC, MC, V* ⊘ *Closed 2 wks following Labor Day. No lunch weekends.*

$–$$ ✕ **Pearl's Bistro.** Caribbean-style cuisine is the draw at this island-style restaurant. For starters try the Bahamian conch fritters or the Jamaican jerk shrimp, and consider moving on to the baby-back barbecued pork ribs, grouper pepper pot, or blackened New York strip with peppery rum sauce. ⊠ *56 Royal Palm Blvd.* ☎ *772/778–2950* ⊟ *AE, MC, V* ⊘ *No lunch weekends.*

★ **$$$–$$$$** ▥ **Disney's Vero Beach Resort.** On 71 pristine oceanfront acres, this sprawling family-oriented retreat, operating both as a time-share and a hotel, is Vero's top resort. The main four-story building, three freestanding villas, and six beach cottages, all painted in pastels with gabled roofing in an approximation of turn-of-the-19th-century old Florida style, are nestled among tropical greenery. Units, some with kitchens and many with balconies, have bright interiors with rattan furniture and tile floors. Shutters, one of two restaurants, has American food. ⊠ *9250 Island Grove Terr., 32963* ☎ *772/234–2000 or 800/359–8000* ☎ *772/234–2030* ⊕ *www.dvc.disney.go.com* ➷ *161 rooms, 14 suites, 6 cottages* ☊ *2 restaurants, room service, in-room safes, some kitchens, some refrigerators, in-room VCRs, miniature golf, 6 tennis courts, pool, wading pool, hot tub, massage, sauna, beach, boating, bicycles, basketball, bar, video game room, baby-sitting, children's programs (ages 4–12), laundry facilities; no-smoking rooms* ⊟ *AE, D, DC, MC, V.*

$$$ ▥ **The Vero Beach Hotel & Club.** A five-story rose-color stucco hotel, formerly flagged as a DoubleTree property, is right on the beach and near restaurants, specialty shops, and boutiques. One- and two-bedroom suites have patios opening onto a pool, or balconies, and excellent ocean views. ⊠ *3500 Ocean Dr., 32963* ☎ *772/231–5666 or 800/841–5666* ☎ *772/234–4866* ⊕ *www.oceanguestsuites.com* ➷ *54 suites* ☊ *Restaurant, room service, in-room data ports, refrigerators, pool, wading pool, hot tub, bar* ⊟ *AE, D, DC, MC, V.*

$$ ▥ **Palm Court Resort.** Tucked among palm trees on the beach is this white, five-story building with outstanding views. Oceanfront units look out to the water across private balconies. Most other units have partial ocean views. Rattan furnishings and pastels provide a comfortable, tropical sense of well-being. The rectangular pool looks out over the water, and pink shade umbrellas and blue-and-white-striped cabanas line the beach. ⊠ *3244 Ocean Dr., 32963* ☎ *772/231–2800 or 800/245–3297* ☎ *772/231–3446* ⊕ *www.palmcourtvero.com* ➷ *110 rooms, 4 effi-*

ciencies, 2 suites ⚘ *Restaurant, some kitchens,pool, exercise equipment, beach, room service, cable TV, meeting rooms; no-smoking rooms* ▤ *AE, D, DC, MC, V.*

$–$$ ▦ **Vero Beach Inn Resort.** After undergoing a million-dollar renovation, this intimate beachfront resort shines. Each room has an ocean view and is freshly decorated with tropical furnishings. One- and two-bedroom suites are available with a microwave, refrigerator, and wet bar. ⊠ *4700 N. Rte. A1A, 32963* ☎ *772/231–1600 or 800/227–8615* ▤ *772/231–9547* ⊕ *verobeachinn.com* ▨ *104 rooms* ⚘ *Restaurant, room service, in-room data port, some microwaves, some minibars, some refrigerators, pool, hot tub, lounge, beach, meeting room, laundry facilities, shop* ▤ *AE, D, DC, MC, V.*

The Arts

The **Civic Arts Center** (⊠ Riverside Park), a cluster of cultural facilities, includes the **Riverside Theatre** (⊠ 3250 Riverside Park Dr. ☎ 772/231–6990), staging six productions each season in its 633-seat performance hall; the **Agnes Wahlstrom Youth Playhouse** (⊠ 3280 Riverside Park Dr. ☎ 772/234–8052), mounting children's productions; and the **Center for the Arts** (⊠ 3001 Riverside Park Dr. ☎ 772/231–0700), which presents exhibitions, art movies, lectures, workshops, and other events, with a focus on Florida artists.

Riverside Children's Theatre (⊠ 3280 Riverside Park Dr. ☎ 772/234–8052) offers a series of professional touring and local productions, as well as acting workshops at the Agnes Wahlstrom Youth Playhouse.

Sports & the Outdoors

BASEBALL The **Los Angeles Dodgers** (⊠ 4101 26th St. ☎ 772/569–4900) train at Holman Stadium in Vero Beach's Dodgertown.

BEACHES **Humiston Park** is one of the beach-access parks along the east edge of town that have boardwalks and steps bridging the foredune. There are picnic tables and a children's play area. ⊠ *Ocean Dr. below Beachland Blvd.* ☎ *772/231–5790* ▨ *Free* ⊙ *Daily 7 AM–10 PM.*

Full-service **Round Island Park** (⊠ A1A near the Indian River–St. Lucie county line ☎ 772/234–2604) is a good bet for relaxation. There are many services at **Treasure Shores Park** (⊠ A1A, 3 mi north of County Rd. 510 at the Wabasso Bridge ☎ 772/581–4997). **Wabasso Beach Park** (⊠ County Rd. 510, east of A1A intersection, north of Disney Resort ☎ 772/581–4998) is a good option for a day in the sun.

Shopping

Along **Ocean Drive** near Beachland Boulevard, a specialty shopping area includes art galleries, antiques shops, and upscale clothing stores. The eight-block area of Oceanside has an interesting mix of boutiques, specialty shops, and eateries. Just west of Interstate 95, **Prime Outlets at Vero Beach** (⊠ 1824 94th Dr. ☎ 772/770–6171) is a discount shopping destination with brand-name stores including Anne Klein, Bose, Levi's, Lenox, Reebok, and Versace.

Sebastian

㊲ *14 mi north of Vero Beach.*

One of few sparsely populated areas on Florida's east coast, this fishing village has as remote a feeling as you're likely to find between Jacksonville and Miami Beach. That adds to the appeal of the recreation area around Sebastian Inlet, where you can walk for miles along quiet beaches and catch some of Florida's best waves for surfing.

You'll really come upon hidden loot when entering **Mel Fisher's Treasure Museum.** See some of what was recovered in 1985 from the Spanish treasure ship *Atocha* and its sister ships of the 1715 fleet. A similar museum in Key West is also operated by the late Mel Fisher's family. ⊠ *1322 U. S. 1* ☎ *772/589–9875* ⊕ *www.melfisher.com* ⊠ *$5* ☉ *Mon.–Sat. 10–5, Sun. noon–5.*

Founded in 1903 by President Theodore Roosevelt as the nation's first national wildlife refuge, **Pelican Island National Wildlife Refuge** is in the Indian River Lagoon between Sebastian and Wabasso. The island is only accessible by boat or kayak. Public facilities—a boardwalk and observation tower, built for the refuge's centennial—enable visitors to see various birds, endangered species, and habitats.

Because of the highly productive fishing waters of Sebastian Inlet, at the north end of Orchid Island, the 578-acre **Sebastian Inlet State Recreation Area** is one of the Florida park system's biggest draws. Both sides of the high bridge spanning the inlet—views are spectacular—attract plenty of anglers as well as those eager to enjoy the fine sandy shores, known for having some of the best waves in the state. A concession stand on the inlet's north side sells short-order food, rents various craft, and has an apparel and surf shop. There's a boat ramp, and not far away is a dune area that's part of the **Archie Carr National Wildlife Refuge,** a haven for sea turtles and other protected Florida wildlife. ⊠ *9700 S. Rte. A1A, Melbourne Beach* ☎ *321/984–4852* ⊠ *1300 Rte. A1A* ☎ *772/ 562–3909* ⊕ *www.dep.state.fl.us/parks* ⊠ *$3.25* ☉ *Daily; bait and tackle shop daily 7:30–6, concession stand daily 8–5.*

A National Historical Landmark, the **McLarty Treasure Museum** underscores the credo "Wherever gold glitters or silver beckons, man will move mountains." It has displays of coins, weapons, and tools salvaged from the 1715 storm sinking a fleet of Spanish treasure ships, leaving some 1,500 survivors struggling to shore between Sebastian and Fort Pierce. ⊠ *13180 N. Rte. A1A* ☎ *772/589–2147* ⊠ *$1* ☉ *Daily 10–4:30.*

Where to Stay & Eat

$$–$$$ ✕ **Hurricane Harbor.** Built in 1927 as a garage and used during Prohibition as a smugglers' den, this restaurant draws a year-round crowd for lunch and dinner. Waterfront window seats are especially coveted on stormy nights, when waves break outside in the Indian River Lagoon. Count on seafood, steaks, and grills, along with lighter fare. There's live music nightly, and on-premises docking. Peek into the Antique Dining Room, with a huge breakfront, used for special occasions. ⊠ *1540 Indian River Dr.* ☎ *772/589–1773* ⊟ *AE, D, MC, V* ☉ *Closed Mon.*

$–$$ ✕ **Capt. Hiram's Restaurant.** This family-friendly outpost on the Indian River Lagoon is easygoing, fanciful, and fun—as the sign says, NECKTIES ARE PROHIBITED. Don't miss Capt. Hiram's Sandbar, where kids can play while parents enjoy drinks at stools set in an outdoor shower or a beached boat. Order the fresh catch, crab cakes, stuffed shrimp, rawbar items, or a juicy steak. There's a weekday happy hour and nightly entertainment in season. ⊠ *1606 N. Indian River Dr.* ☎ *772/589– 4345* ⊟ *AE, D, MC, V.*

$–$$ 🛏 **Capt. Hiram's Key West Inn.** A pale-aqua inn trimmed in white with a lobby embellished with a classic surfboard collection brings a Key West look to Sebastian's Riverfront, about 17 mi north of Vero at Marker 66 on the Intracoastal. All rooms have a private balcony and most have oak furnishings. Minisuites include microwave, refrigerator, and wet bar; deluxe suites also include dishwasher and stove. A heated pool has a tropical sun deck, shaded by tables with umbrellas. A complimentary deluxe Continental breakfast is included. ⊠ *1580 U.S. 1, 32958* ☎ *772/*

388–8588 ᗧ 772/589–4346 ⊕ *www.hirams.com* ⟿ *56 rooms* ⚼ *Restaurant, in-room data ports, some microwaves, some minibars, some refrigerators, pool, dock, lounge* ⊟ *AE, D, MC, V* ⵙ *CP.*

¢–$ ▥ **The Angler Inn.** Perched on the shores of the Indian River, this 1936 grove house with two floors of wraparound verandas caters to guests who love to fish. Rooms are furnished with antiques, and all have private entry and bath. Rates include expanded Continental breakfast, but early morning anglers can receive a discounted rate that does not include breakfast. ⊠ *805 Indian River Dr., 32958* ☎ *772/589–1150* ⊕ *www.anglerinn.net* ⟿ *3 suites* ⚼ *Kitchenettes, hot tub, fishing, boating, some pets allowed* ⊟ *AE, DC, MC, V* ⵙ *CP.*

¢ ▥ **Davis House Inn.** Owner Steve Wild, a Vero native, modeled his two-story inn after the clubhouse at Augusta National, yet it fits right in with Sebastian's fishing-town look. Overhung roofs shade wraparound porches. In a companion house that Steve calls the Gathering Room, a complimentary expanded Continental breakfast is served. Rooms are expansive—virtual suites, with large sitting areas—although sparsely furnished. Grill or chill out at the self-serve Tiki Bar. Overall, it's a terrific value. ⊠ *607 Davis St., 32958* ☎ *772/589–4114* ᗧ *772/589–1722* ⊕ *www.davishouseinn.com* ⟿ *12 rooms* ⚼ *Kitchenettes, microwaves, bicycles, laundry facilities* ⊟ *AE, D, MC, V.*

Sports & the Outdoors

CANOEING & The concession stand at **Sebastian Inlet State Recreation Area** (⊠ 9700 S.
KAYAKING Rte. A1A, Melbourne Beach ☎ 321/984–4852) rents canoes, kayaks, and paddleboats.

FISHING The region's best inlet fishing is at **Sebastian Inlet State Recreation Area** (⊠ 9700 S. Rte. A1A, Melbourne Beach), where the catch includes bluefish, flounder, jack, redfish, sea trout, snapper, snook, and Spanish mackerel. For single, double, or triple days of onshore and offshore fishing, try **Saltwater Adventures** (⊠ Dock at Capt. Hiram's Restaurant ☎ 772/581–9080); there are even two levels of fishing training camp. **Sebastian Inlet Marina at Capt. Hiram's** (⊠ 1606 Indian River Dr. ☎ 772/589–4345) offers half- and full-day fishing charters.

PALM BEACH & THE TREASURE COAST A TO Z

To research prices, get advice from other travelers, and book travel arrangements, visit www.fodors.com.

AIR TRAVEL

CARRIERS Palm Beach International Airport (PBIA) is served by Air Canada, American/American Eagle, Bahamasair, Comair, Continental, Delta, JetBlue, Northwest, Southwest Airlines, Spirit Airlines, United, and US Airways/ US Airways Express.

🖪 Airlines & Contacts **Air Canada** ☎ 800/776-3000. **American/American Eagle** ☎ 800/ 433-7300. **Bahamasair** ☎ 800/222-4262. **Comair** ☎ 800/354-9822. **Continental** ☎ 800/525-0280. **Delta** ☎ 800/221-1212. **JetBlue** ☎ 800/538-2583. **Northwest** ☎ 800/225-2525. **Southwest Airlines** ☎ 800/435-9792. **Spirit Airlines** ☎ 800/772-7117. **United** ☎ 800/241-6522. **US Airways/US Airways Express** ☎ 800/428-4322.

AIRPORT INFORMATION

Palm Tran Routes 44 and 50 run from the airport to Tri-Rail's nearby Palm Beach airport station daily. Palm Beach Transportation provides taxi and limousine service from PBIA. Reserve at least a day in advance for a limo. The lowest fares are $1.75 per mile, with the meter starting at $1.25. Depending on your destination, a flat rate (from PBIA only) may save money. Wheelchair-accessible vehicles are available.

🛈 Airport Information **Palm Beach International Airport (PBIA)** ⊠ Congress Ave. and Belvedere Rd., West Palm Beach ☎561/471-7420. **Palm Beach Transportation** ☎561/689-4222. **Tri-Rail Commuter Bus Service** ☎ 800/874-7245.

BUS TRAVEL

Greyhound Lines buses arrive at the station in West Palm Beach. Palmtran buses, running between Worth Avenue and Royal Palm Way in Palm Beach and major areas of West Palm Beach, require exact change. Fares are $1.25, or 60¢ for students, senior citizens, and people with disabilities (with reduced-fare I.D.). Service operates seven days a week. Call for schedules, routes, and rates for multiple-ride punch cards.

🛈 Bus Information **Greyhound Lines** ☎ 800/229-9424 ⊠ 205 S. Tamarind Ave., West Palm Beach ☎ 561/833-8536. **Palmtran** ☎ 561/841-4200.

CAR TRAVEL

Interstate 95 runs north–south, linking West Palm Beach with Fort Lauderdale and Miami to the south and with Daytona, Jacksonville, and the rest of the Atlantic coast to the north. To access Palm Beach, exit east at Belvedere Road or Okeechobee Boulevard. Florida's Turnpike runs from Miami north through West Palm Beach before angling northwest to reach Orlando. U.S. 1 threads north–south along the coast, connecting most coastal communities, while the more scenic Route A1A ventures out onto the barrier islands. Interstate 95 runs parallel to U.S. 1 but a few miles inland. A nonstop four-lane route, Okeechobee Boulevard carries traffic from west of downtown West Palm Beach, near the Amtrak station in the airport district, directly to the Flagler Memorial Bridge and into Palm Beach. The best way to access Lake Okeechobee from West Palm is to drive west on Southern Boulevard from Interstate 95 past the cutoff road to Lion Country Safari. From there, the boulevard is designated U.S. 98/441.

EMERGENCIES

Dial 911 for police or ambulance.

🛈 Late-Night Pharmacies **Eckerd Drug** ⊠ 3187 S. Congress Ave., Palm Springs ☎ 561/965-3367. **Walgreens** ⊠ 3184 S. Congress Ave., Palm Springs ☎ 561/968-8211 ⊠ 3900 N. Federal Hwy., Boca Raton ☎ 561/338-6130 ⊠ 1634 S. Federal Hwy., Boynton Beach ☎ 561/737-1160 ⊠ 1208 Royal Palm Beach Blvd., Royal Palm Beach ☎ 561/798-9048 ⊠ 1800 W. Indiantown Rd., Jupiter ☎ 561/744-6822 ⊠ 2501 Broadway, Riviera Beach ☎ 561/848-6464.

ENGLISH-LANGUAGE MEDIA

NEWSPAPERS & MAGAZINES To keep abreast of local issues and find what's new in entertainment options, pick up copies of the *Sun-Sentinel, Palm Beach Post, Palm Beach Daily News, Vero Press Journal,* or *Boca Magazine, Vive, Via, Palm Beach Illustrated,* and *Palm Beach Society* magazines.

RADIO WLRN 91.3 FM is a public radio station. Tune into WLVE 93.9 FM and WDBF 1420 AM for jazz; WZTA 94.9 for rock; WRMF 97.9 for adult contemporary; WHYI 100.7 for top 40; WMXJ 102.7 for oldies; WPBZ 103.1 for alternative; WMGE 103.5 for disco; and WBGG for 105.9 classic rock.

TAXIS

Palm Beach Transportation has a single number serving several cab companies. Meters start at $1.25, and the charge is $1.75 per mile within West Palm Beach city limits; if the trip at any point leaves the city limits, the fare is $2 per mile. Some cabs may charge more. Waiting time is 50¢ per minute.

🛈 Taxi Information **Palm Beach Transportation** ☎ 561/689-2222.

TOURS

Capt. Doug's offers three-hour lunch and dinner cruises along the Indian River on a 35-ft sloop. The cost is $100 per couple, including meal, beer, wine, and tips. J-Mark Fish Camp has 45- to 60-minute airboat rides for $30 per person, with a minimum of two people and a maximum of six. Jonathan Dickinson's River Tours runs two-hour guided riverboat cruises daily at 9, 11, 1, and 3. The cost is $12. Loxahatchee Everglades Tours operates airboat tours year-round from west of Boca Raton through the marshes between the built-up coast and Lake Okeechobee. The *Manatee Queen,* a 49-passenger catamaran, offers day and evening cruises November–May on the Intracoastal Waterway and into the park's cypress swamps. *River Rose Riverboat* operates luncheon and sight-seeing cruises along the Intracoastal Waterway. Water Taxi Scenic Cruises has several different daily sightseeing tours in a 16-person launch. Two are designed to let you get a close-up look at the mansions of the rich and famous. The southern tour passes Peanut, Singer, and Munyan islands, and Palm Beach mansions. A second tour runs solely along the shore of Palm Beach mansions. A third tour passes the Craig Norman estate and goes into Lake Worth and Sawgrass Creek.

The Boca Raton Historical Society offers tours of the Boca Raton Resort & Club on Tuesday and trolley tours of city sites on Thursday during season. Main Street Fort Pierce gives walking tours of the town's historic section, past buildings erected by early settlers, the second Wednesday of each month. The Indian River County Historical Society conducts walking tours of downtown Vero on Wednesday at 11 and 1 (by reservation). Old Northwood Historic District Tours leads two-hour walking tours that include visits to historic home interiors. They leave typically during season Sunday at 2, and a $5 donation is requested. Tours for groups of six or more can be scheduled almost any day.

🛈 Tours Information **Audubon Society of the Everglades** ✉ Box 16914, West Palm Beach 33461 ☎ 561/588-6908. **Boca Raton Historical Society** ✉ 71 N. Federal Hwy., Boca Raton ☎ 561/395-6766. **Capt. Doug's** ✉ Sebastian Marina, Sebastian ☎ 772/589-2329. **Indian River County Historical Society** ✉ 2336 14th Ave., Vero Beach ☎ 772/778-3435. **J-Mark Fish Camp** ✉ Torry Island ☎ 561/996-5357. **Jonathan Dickinson's River Tours** ✉ Jonathan Dickinson State Park, 16450 S.E. Federal Hwy., Hobe Sound ☎ 561/746-1466. **Loxahatchee Everglades Tours** ✉ 10400 Loxahatchee Rd. ☎ 561/482-6107. **Main Street Fort Pierce** ✉ 210 S. Depot St., Fort Pierce ☎ 772/466-3880. *Manatee Queen* ✉ Jonathan Dickinson State Park, 1065 N. Hwy. A1A, Hobe Sound ☎ 561/744-2191. **Old Northwood Historic District Tours** ✉ 501 30th St., West Palm Beach ☎ 561/863-5633. *River Rose Riverboat* ✉ 1 N.E. 1st St., Delray Beach ☎ 561/243-0686. **Water Taxi Scenic Cruises** ✉ Panama Hatties Restaurant, 11511 Ellison Wilson Rd. North Palm Beach ☎ 561/775-2628.

TRAIN TRAVEL

Amtrak connects West Palm Beach with cities along Florida's east coast and the Northeast daily and via the *Sunset Limited* to New Orleans and Los Angeles three times weekly. Included in Amtrak's service is transport from West Palm Beach to Okeechobee; the station is unmanned. Tri-Rail, the commuter rail system, has 13 stops altogether between West Palm Beach and Miami, where tickets can be purchased. The one-way round-trip fare is $5.50, $2.75 for students and senior citizens.

🛈 Train Information **Amtrak** ☎ 800/872-7245 ✉ 201 S. Tamarind Ave., West Palm Beach ☎ 561/832-6169 ✉ 801 N. Parrott Ave., Okeechobee. **Tri-Rail** ☎ 800/874-7245.

VISITOR INFORMATION

🛈 Tourist Information **Belle Glade Chamber of Commerce** ✉ 540 S. Main St., Belle Glade 33430 ☎ 561/996-2745. **Chamber of Commerce of the Palm Beaches** ✉ 401 N. Flagler Dr., West Palm Beach 33401 ☎ 561/833-3711. **Clewiston Chamber of Com-**

merce ⊠ 544 W. Sugarland Hwy., Clewiston 33440 ☎ 863/983-7979. **Delray Beach Chamber of Commerce** ⊠ 64-A S.E. 5th Ave., Delray Beach 33483 ☎ 561/278-0424. **Glades County Chamber of Commerce** ⊠ 998 U.S. 27 SE, Moore Haven 33471 ☎ 863/946-0440. **Indian River County Tourist Council** ⊠1216 21st St., Vero Beach 32960 ☎772/567-3491. **Indiantown and Western Martin County Chamber of Commerce** ⊠ Box 602, Indiantown 34956 ☎ 772/597-2184. **Okeechobee County Chamber of Commerce** ⊠ 55 S. Parrott Ave., Okeechobee 34974 ☎ 863/763-6464. **Pahokee Chamber of Commerce** ⊠ 115 E. Main St., Pahokee 33476 ☎ 561/924-5579. **Palm Beach County Convention & Visitors Bureau** ⊠1555 Palm Beach Lakes Blvd., Suite 204, West Palm Beach 33401 ☎ 561/471-3995. **St. Lucie County Tourist Development Council** ⊠ 2300 Virginia Ave., Fort Pierce 34982 ☎ 772/462-1535. **Stuart/Martin County Chamber of Commerce** ⊠1650 S. Kanner Hwy., Stuart 34994 ☎ 772/287-1088. **Town of Palm Beach Chamber of Commerce** ⊠ 45 Cocoanut Row, Palm Beach 33480 ☎ 561/655-3282. **U.S. Army Corps of Engineers (Okeechobee area information)** ⊠ South Florida Operations Office, 525 Ridgelawn Rd., Clewiston 33440-5399 ☎ 863/983-8101.

THE FLORIDA KEYS

5

FODOR'S CHOICE

Bahia Honda State Park, Bahia Honda Key

Barracuda Grill, Marathon

Big Pine Key Fishing Lodge

Café Marquesa, Key West

Casa Morada, hotel, Islamorada

John Pennekamp Coral Reef State Park, Key Largo

Key West Museum of Art and History, Key West

Little Palm Island, Little Torch Key

Marquesa Hotel, Key West

Parmer's Place, Little Torch Key

Pierre's, French fare, Islamorada

Seven Mile Bridge, Marathon

7 Mile Grill, Marathon

HIGHLY RECOMMENDED

WHAT TO SEE City Cemetery, Key West

East Martello Tower, Key West

Fort Zachary Taylor State Historic Site, Key West

Hemingway Home and Museum, Key West

Many other great hotels and restaurants enliven this area. For other favorites, look for the black stars as you read this chapter.

Revised by
Diane P.
Marshall

A WILDERNESS OF FLOWERING JUNGLES and shimmering seas, a jade necklace of mangrove-fringed islands dangling toward the tropics, the Florida Keys are also, at the same time and in direct contrast to this, a string of narrow islands overburdened by a growing population and booming tourism that have created sewage contamination at beaches and a 110-mi traffic jam lined with garish billboards, hamburger stands, shopping centers, motels, and trailer courts. Unfortunately, in the Keys you can't have one without the other. The river of visitor traffic gushes along U.S. 1 (also called the Overseas Highway), the main artery linking the inhabited islands. Residents of Monroe County live by diverting the river's flow of green dollars to their own pockets. In the process, the fragile beauty of the Keys—or at least the 45 that are inhabited and linked to the mainland by 43 bridges—is paying an environmental price. At the top, nearest the mainland, is Key Largo, becoming more and more congested as it evolves into a bedroom community and weekend hideaway for escaping residents of Miami and Fort Lauderdale. At the bottom, 106 mi southwest, is Key West, where for several years now the effluent of the overburdened island has washed into the near-shore waters and closed the island's major beaches for months.

Despite designation as "an area of critical state concern" in 1975 and a subsequent state-mandated development slowdown, growth has continued, and the Keys' natural resources remain imperiled. Congress established the Florida Keys National Marine Sanctuary, covering 2,800 square nautical mi of coastal waters. Adjacent to the Keys landmass are spectacular, unique, and nationally significant marine environments, including sea-grass meadows, mangrove islands, and extensive living coral reefs. These fragile environments support rich and diverse biological communities possessing extensive conservation, recreational, commercial, ecological, historical, research, educational, and aesthetic values. The sanctuary protects the coral reefs and water quality, but problems continue. Increased salinity in Florida Bay causes large areas of sea grass to die and drift in mats out of the bay. These mats then block sunlight from reaching the reefs, stifling their growth and threatening both the Keys' recreational diving economy and tourism in general.

Other threats to the Keys' charm also loom. Debate continues on the expansion of U.S. 1 to the mainland to four lanes, opening the floodgates to increased traffic, population, and tourism. Observers wonder if the four-laning of the rest of U.S. 1 throughout the Keys can be far away. For now, however, take pleasure as you drive down U.S. 1 along the islands. Gaze over the silvery blue and green Atlantic and its still-living reef, with Florida Bay, the Gulf of Mexico, and the backcountry on your right (the Keys extend east–west from the mainland). At a few points the ocean and gulf are as much as 10 mi apart. In most places, however, they are from 1 to 4 mi apart, and on the narrowest landfill islands, they are separated only by the road. First, remind yourself to get off the highway. Once you do, rent a boat, anchor, and then fish, swim, or marvel at the sun, sea, and sky. In the Atlantic, dive spectacular coral reefs or pursue grouper, blue marlin, and other deep-water game fish. Along Florida Bay's coastline, kayak and canoe to secluded islands and bays or seek out the bonefish, snapper, snook, and tarpon that lurk in the grass flats and in the shallow, winding channels of the backcountry.

More than 600 kinds of fish populate the reefs and islands. Diminutive deer and pale raccoons, related to but distinct from their mainland cousins, inhabit the Lower Keys. And throughout the islands you'll find such exotic West Indian plants as Jamaican dogwood, pigeon plum, poisonwood, satin leaf, and silver and thatch palms, as well as tropical birds, including the great white heron, mangrove cuckoo, roseate spoonbill, and white-crowned pigeon. Mangroves, with their gracefully bowed prop roots, appear to march out to sea. Day by day they busily add more keys to the archipelago. With virtually no distracting air pollution or obstructive high-rises, sunsets are a pure, unadulterated spectacle that each evening attracts thousands to waterfront parks, piers, restaurants, bars, and resorts throughout the Keys. Weather is another attraction: winter is typically 10°F warmer than on the mainland; summer is usually 10°F cooler. The Keys also get substantially less rain, around 30 inches annually, compared to an average 55–60 inches in Miami and the Everglades. Most rain falls in quick downpours on summer afternoons, except in June, September, and October, when tropical storms can dump rain for two to four days. Winter continental cold fronts occasionally stall over the Keys, dragging overnight temperatures down to the high 40s.

The Keys were only sparsely populated until the early 20th century. In 1905, however, railroad magnate Henry Flagler began building the extension of his Florida railroad south from Homestead to Key West. His goal was to establish a Miami to Key West rail link to his steamships that sailed between Key West and Havana, just 90 mi across the Straits of Florida. The railroad arrived at Key West in 1912 and remained a lifeline of commerce until the Labor Day hurricane of 1935 washed out much of its roadbed. The Overseas Highway, built over the railroad's old roadbeds and bridges, was completed in 1938.

Exploring the Florida Keys

Finding your way around the Keys isn't hard once you understand the unique address system. Many addresses are simply given as a mile marker (MM) number. The markers themselves are small, green rectangular signs along the side of the Overseas Highway (U.S. 1). They begin with MM 126, a mile south of Florida City, and end with MM 0, in Key West. Keys residents use the abbreviation BS for the bay side of U.S. 1 and OS for the ocean side. From Marathon to Key West, residents may refer to the bay side as the gulf side. The Keys are divided into four areas: the Upper Keys, from Key Largo to the Long Key Channel (MM 106–65) and Ocean Reef and North Key Largo, off Card Sound Road and Route 905, respectively; the Middle Keys, from Conch (pronounced *konk*) Key through Marathon to the south side of the Seven Mile Bridge, including Pigeon Key (MM 65–40); the Lower Keys, from Little Duck Key south through Big Coppitt Key (MM 40–9); and Key West, from Stock Island through Key West (MM 9–0). The Keys don't end with the highway, however; they stretch another 70 mi west of Key West to the Dry Tortugas.

About the Restaurants

A number of talented young chefs have settled in the Keys—especially Key West—contributing to the area's image as one of the nation's points of culinary interest. Restaurants' menus, rum-based fruit beverages, and music reflect the Keys' tropical climate and their proximity to Cuba and other Caribbean islands. Better restaurants serve imaginative and tantalizing fusion cuisine that draws on traditions from all over the world. Florida citrus, seafood, and tropical fruits figure prominently, and Florida lobster and stone crab should be local and fresh from August to March. Also keep an eye out for authentic key lime pie. The real McCoy has a yellow custard in a graham-cracker crust and tastes like nothing else. Restaurants may close for a two- to four-week vacation during the slow season—between mid-September and mid-November. Check local newspapers or call ahead, especially if driving any distance.

5

Numbers in the text correspond to numbers in the margin and on the Florida Keys and Key West maps.

If you have 3 days

You can fly and then dive; but if you dive, you can't fly for 24 hours, so spend your first morning diving or snorkeling at John Pennekamp Coral Reef State Park in 🔲 **Key Largo** ➋ ▶. If you aren't certified, take a resort course, and you'll be exploring the reefs by afternoon. Afterward, breeze through the park's visitor center. The rest of the afternoon can be whiled away either lounging around a pool or beach or visiting the Maritime Museum of the Florida Keys. Dinner or cocktails at a bayside restaurant or bar will give you your first look at a fabulous Keys sunset. On day two, get an early start to savor the breathtaking views on the two-hour drive to Key West. Along the way make stops at the natural-history museum that's part of the Museums and Nature Center of Crane Point Hammock, in **Marathon** ➑, and Bahia Honda State Park, on **Bahia Honda Key** ➒; stretch your legs on a forest trail or snorkel on an offshore reef. Once in 🔲 **Key West** ⓲–㉞, watch the sunset before dining at one of the island's first-class restaurants. Spend the next morning exploring beaches, visiting any of the myriad museums, or taking a walking or trolley tour of Old Town before driving back to the mainland.

If you have 4 days

Spend the first day as you would above, overnighting in 🔲 **Key Largo** ➋ ▶. Start the second day by renting a kayak and exploring the mangroves and small islands of Florida Bay or take an ecotour of the islands in Everglades National Park. In the afternoon stop by the Florida Keys Wild Bird Rehabilitation Center before driving down to 🔲 **Islamorada** ➍. Pause to read the inscription on the Hurricane Monument, and before day's end, make plans for the next day's fishing. After a late lunch on day three—perhaps at one of the many restaurants that will prepare your catch for you—set off for 🔲 **Key West** ⓲–㉞. Enjoy the sunset celebration at Mallory Square, and spend the last day as you would above.

If you have 7 days

Spend your first three days as you would in the four-day itinerary, but stay the third night in 🔲 **Islamorada** ➍. In the morning catch a boat, or rent a kayak to paddle, to Lignumvitae Key State Botanical Site, before making the one-hour drive to 🔲 **Marathon** ➑. Visit the natural-history museum that's part of the Museums and Nature Center of Crane Point Hammock and walk or take a train across the Old Seven Mile Bridge to Pigeon Key. The next stop is just 10 mi away at Bahia Honda State Park, on 🔲 **Bahia Honda Key** ➒. Take a walk on a wilderness trail, go snorkeling on an offshore reef, wriggle your toes in the beach's soft sand, and spend the night in a waterfront cabin, letting the waves lull you to sleep. Your sixth day starts with either a half day of fabulous snorkeling or diving at Looe Key Reef or a visit to the National Key Deer Refuge, on **Big Pine Key** ➓. Then continue on to 🔲 **Key West** ⓲–㉞, and get in a little sightseeing before watching the sunset. The next morning take a walking, bicycling, or trolley tour of town or catch a ferry or seaplane to Dry Tortugas National Park before heading home.

About the Hotels

Resorts and water sports marry throughout the Keys, giving couples and families, novices and veterans, chances to snorkel and dive. Some properties do charge an additional required $15 daily resort fee for equipment rental, which can cover spa use and other services. Key West's lodging portfolio includes historic cottages, restored Conch houses, and large resorts. A few rooms cost as little as $65 a night, but most range from $100 to $300. Some guest houses and inns do not welcome children under 16, and some do not permit smoking.

	WHAT IT COSTS				
	$$$$	$$$	$$	$	¢
RESTAURANTS	over $30	$20–$30	$15–$20	$10–$15	under $10
HOTELS	over $220	$140–$220	$100–$140	$80–$100	under $80

Restaurant prices are per person for a main course at dinner. Hotel prices are for a standard double room, excluding 6% sales tax (more in some counties) and 1%–4% tourist tax.

Timing

High season in the Keys is mid-December through March, and traffic on the Overseas Highway is inevitably heavy. From November to the middle of December, crowds are thinner, the weather is superlative, and hotels and shops drastically reduce their prices. Summer, which is hot and humid, is becoming a second high season, especially among families and Europeans. Key West's annual Fantasy Fest is the last week in October; if you plan to attend this popular event, reserve at least six months in advance. Rooms are also scarce the first few weekends of lobster season, which starts in August.

THE UPPER KEYS

The tropical coral-reef tract that runs a few miles off the seaward coast accounts for most of the Upper Keys' reputation. Divers benefit from accessible islands and dive sites and an established tourism infrastructure. Yet although diving is king here, fishing, kayaking, and nature touring draw an enviable number of people. Within 1½ mi of the bay coast lie the islands of Everglades National Park; here naturalists lead eco-tours to see one of the world's few saltwater forests, endangered manatees, dolphins, roseate spoonbills, and tropical-bird rookeries. Although the number of birds has dwindled since John James Audubon captured their beauty on a visit to the Keys, bird-watchers won't be disappointed. At sunset flocks take to the skies, and in spring and autumn migrating birds add their numbers. Tarpon and bonefish teem in the shallow waters surrounding the islands, providing food for birds and a challenge to light-tackle anglers. These same crystal-clear waters attract windsurfers, sailors, and powerboaters. Wherever you go, you'll find a pleasant mix of locals, visitors, snowbirds (in season), and South Floridian weekenders.

With few exceptions, dining in the Upper Keys tends toward the casual in food, service, and dress. Accommodations are as varied as they are plentiful. The majority are in small waterfront resorts, whose efficiency and one- or two-bedroom units are decorated in tropical colors. They offer dockage and either provide or will arrange boating, diving, and fishing excursions. Depending on which way the wind blows and how close the property is to the highway, noise from U.S. 1 can be bothersome. In high season, expect to pay $85–$165 for an efficiency (in low season, $65–$145). Campground and RV park rates with electricity and water run $25–$55.

Biking

Cyclists are able to ride all but a tiny portion of the Florida Keys Overseas Heritage Trail bike path, which runs along the Overseas Highway from MM 106 south to the Seven Mile Bridge. The state plans to extend the route throughout the Keys. Some areas have lots of cross traffic, however, so ride with care.

Boating

5

If it floats, local marinas rent it. For up-close exploration of the mangroves and near-shore islands in Florida Bay, nothing beats a kayak or canoe. Paddle within a few feet of a flock of birds without disturbing them, and on days when the ocean is too rough for diving or fishing, the rivers that course through the bayside mangroves are tranquil. Visiting the backcountry islands and inlets of Everglades National Park requires a shallow-draft boat: a 14- to 17-ft skiff with a 40- to 50-horsepower outboard is sufficient. Rental companies prohibit smaller boats from going on the ocean side. For diving the reef or fishing on the open ocean, you'll need a larger boat with greater horsepower. Houseboats are ideal for cruising the Keys. Only experienced sailors should attempt to navigate the shallow waters surrounding the Keys with deep-keeled sailboats. On the other hand, small shallow-draft, single-hull sailboats and catamarans are ideal. Personal water vehicles, such as Wave Runners and Jet Skis, can be rented by the half hour or hour but are banned in many areas. Flat, stable pontoon boats are a good choice for anyone with seasickness. Those interested in experiencing the reef without getting wet can take a glass-bottom boat trip.

Fishing

These sun-bathed waters have many species of game fish as well as lobster, shrimp, and crabs. Flats fishing and backcountry fishing are Keys specialties. In flats fishing, a guide poles a shallow-draft outboard boat through the shallow, sandy-bottom waters while sighting for bonefish and snook to be caught on light tackle, spin, and fly. Backcountry fishing may include flats fishing or fishing in the channels and basins around islands in Florida Bay. Charter boats fish the reef and Gulf Stream for deep-sea fish. Party boats, which can be crowded, carry up to 50 people to fish the reefs for grouper, kingfish, and snapper. Some operators have a guarantee, or "no fish, no pay" policy. It's customary to tip the crew 15%–20% of the trip price if they were helpful.

Scuba Diving & Snorkeling

Diving in the Keys is spectacular. In shallow and deep water with visibility up to 120 ft, explore sea canyons and mountains covered with waving sea plumes, brain and star coral, historic shipwrecks, and sunken submarines. The colors of the coral are surpassed only by the brilliance of the fish that live around it. There's no best season for diving, but occasional storms in June, September, and October cloud the waters and make seas rough. Dive the reefs with scuba, snuba (a cross between scuba and snorkeling), or snorkeling gear, using your own boat or a rented boat or by booking a tour with a dive shop. Tours depart two or three times a day, stopping at two sites on each trip. The first trip of the day is usually the best. It's less crowded—vacationers like to sleep in—and visibility is better before the wind picks up in the afternoon. There's also night diving. If you want to scuba dive but are not certified, take an introductory resort course. Although it doesn't result in certification, it allows you to dive with an instructor in the afternoon following morning classroom and pool instruction. Nearly all the waters surrounding the Keys are part of the Florida Keys National Marine Sanctuary and thus are protected. Signs, brochures, tour guides, and marine enforcement agents remind visitors that the reef is fragile and shouldn't be touched.

Some properties require two- or three-day minimum stays during holidays and on weekends in high season. Conversely, discounts are given for midweek, weekly, and monthly stays, and rates can drop 20%–40% April–June and October–mid-December. Keep in mind that salty winds and soil play havoc with anything man-made, and constant maintenance is a must; inspect your accommodations before checking in.

Key Largo

56 mi south of Miami International Airport.

The first Key reachable by car, 30-mi-long Key Largo—named Cayo Largo ("long key") by the Spanish—is also the largest island in the chain. Comprising three areas—North Key Largo, Key Largo, and Tavernier—it runs northeast–southwest between Lake Surprise and Tavernier Creek, at MM 95. Most businesses are on the four-lane divided highway (U.S. 1) that runs down the middle, but away from the overdevelopment and generally suburban landscape are many areas of wilderness. One such area **1** is **North Key Largo,** which still has a wide tract of virgin hardwood hammock and mangroves as well as a crocodile sanctuary (not open to the public). To reach North Key Largo, take Card Sound Road just south of Florida City, or from within the Keys, take Route 905 north.

Rest rooms, information kiosks, and picnic tables make 2,400-acre **Dagny Johnson Key Largo Hammocks State Botanical Site** a user-friendly place to explore the largest remaining stand of the vast West Indian tropical hardwood hammock and mangrove wetland that once covered most of the Keys' upland areas. Nearly 100 species of protected plants and animals coexist here, including the endangered American crocodile, Key Largo wood rat, Key Largo cotton mouse, and Schaus swallowtail butterfly. Interpretive signs describe many of the tropical tree species along a 1¼-mi paved road (2½ mi round-trip) that invites walking, rollerblading, and biking. Rangers give guided tours and encourage you to taste the fruits of native plants. Pets are welcome if on a 6-ft leash. ⊠ *1 mi north of U.S. 1 on Rte. 905, OS, North Key Largo* ☎ *305/451–1202* ☜ *Free* ☉ *Daily 8–5. Tours Thurs. and Sun. at 10.*

Taking the Overseas Highway from the mainland lands you closer to ▶ **2** **Key Largo** proper, abounding with shopping centers, chain restaurants, and, of course, dive shops.

Fodor's Choice ★ Whenever people talk about the best diving sites in the world, **John Pennekamp Coral Reef State Park** is on the short list. The park encompasses 78 square mi of coral reefs, sea-grass beds, and mangrove swamps. Its reefs contain 40 of the 52 species of coral in the Atlantic Reef System and more than 650 varieties of fish. Its revamped visitor center–aquarium has a large center floor-to-ceiling aquarium surrounded by numerous smaller tanks, a video room, and exhibits. A concessionaire rents canoes and powerboats and offers snorkel, dive, and glass-bottom boat trips to the reef. The park also has short nature trails, two man-made beaches, picnic shelters, a snack bar, and a campground. No pets are allowed for visitors who are camping or going out on a boat trip.

⊠ *MM 102.5, OS* ⊕ *Box 487, 33037* ☎ *305/451–1202* ⊕ *www.dep. state.fl.us/parks* ⊠ *$2.50 for 1 person, $5 per vehicle for 2 people, plus 50¢ per each additional person; $1.50 per pedestrian or bicyclist* ☉ *Daily 8–sunset.*

❸ The southernmost part of Key Largo is **Tavernier.** Here at the **Florida Keys Wild Bird Rehabilitation Center,** injured and recovering ospreys, hawks, pelicans, cormorants, terns, and herons of various types rest undisturbed in large, screened enclosures lining a winding boardwalk on some of the best waterfront real estate in the Keys. The center is especially popular among photographers, who arrive at 3:30 PM, when hundreds of wild waterbirds fly in and feed within arm's distance. Woodcarver and teacher Laura Quinn founded and operates the center. Rehabilitated birds are set free, while others become permanent residents. A short nature trail runs into the mangrove forest (bring bug spray May–October), and a video explains the center's mission. ⊠ *MM 93.6, BS, Tavernier* ☎ *305/852–4486* ⊠ *Free* ☉ *Daily sunrise–sunset.*

Weekends are crowded at **Harry Harris County Park,** which has play equipment, a small swimming lagoon, a boat ramp, ball fields, barbecue grills, and rest rooms. Although the turnoff is clearly marked on the Overseas Highway, the road to the ocean is circuitous. ⊠ *MM 93, OS, at Burton Dr., Tavernier* ☎ *305/852–7161 or 888/227–8136* ⊠ *Weekdays free, weekends $5* ☉ *Daily 7:30 AM–sunset.*

Jenifer and Leon Dermer opened the not-for-profit **World Parrot Mission** as a sanctuary for neglected and abandoned parrots. Parrots perform at free shows throughout the day to educate the public on the birds' special needs as pets. There's a shop with bird-related gifts, from crystal jewelry to works by local artists. The mission is serving as a temporary home while the Dermers raise money for a large, permanent aviary. ⊠ *MM 99.1, BS, Key Largo* ☎ *305/453–1800* ⊕ *www.worldparrotmission.org* ⊠ *Free* ☉ *Tues.–Sat. 10–6, Sun. 11–6.*

Where to Stay & Eat

★ $–$$$ ✕ **The Fish House.** A nautical, Keys-y casualness and friendly, diligent servers create the feeling of dining in the home of a friend, albeit a friend who knows how to prepare fresh seafood like a superchef. Fish is prepared any way you like—from charbroiled or fried to Jamaican jerked or pan-sautéed. Nightly specials like shrimp and lobster creole in a spicy tomato sauce keep happy diners coming back. The key lime pie is homemade. To ease the long waiting lines, they added outdoor seating and opened Encore next door. It has many of the same dishes, but with slightly higher prices and a more formal dining room, including a piano bar. ⊠ *MM 102.4, OS* ☎ *305/451–4665 or 305/451–0650* ⊕ *www.fishhouse. com* ⊟ *AE, D, MC, V* ☉ *Closed early Sept.–early Oct.*

★ $–$$$ ✕ **Frank Keys Café.** Hundreds of little white twinkling lights visible from the porch and windows of the wooden Victorian-style house add a little romance to dinner. Equally enticing is the skillfully prepared cuisine, which includes fresh-fish dishes like yellowtail *tropicale* (a pan-sautéed yellowtail snapper topped with fresh tropical fruit in a Malibu rum sauce). There's a different dessert soufflé each night. A Fish n' Franks lunch menu includes hot dogs, sandwiches, and daily specials. ⊠ *MM 100, OS* ☎ *305/453–0310* ⊟ *AE, MC, V* ☉ *Closed Mon.–Tues.*

★ ¢–$$$ ✕ **Café Largo.** You're on vacation and someone in your group wants Italian while someone else craves seafood. This bistro-style eatery prepares both quite well. The penne with shrimp and broccoli has tender shrimp, al dente broccoli, and a hint of garlic. There's lobster and shrimp scampi, too. A more than ample wine list, international beers, Italian bottled waters, focaccia, garlic rolls, and, of course, espresso and cappuccino are offered, and the dessert list is short but sweet. For lunch with a view, try the sister restaurant, the Bayside Grille, behind the café. ⊠ *MM 99.5, BS* ☎ *305/451–4885* ⊟ *AE, MC, V* ☉ *No lunch.*

¢–$$ ✕ **Mrs. Mac's Kitchen.** Fortunately, some things never change. The architecture and feel of this rustic wood-paneled, screened, open-air restaurant hark back to the 1950s, when the Keys had more fishermen than well-heeled visitors. The cooks still serve up traditional American sandwiches, burgers, barbecue, and seafood, like the popular TJ Dolphin, a mahimahi fillet with a spicy tomato salsa served with black beans and rice. At breakfast and lunch, the counter and booths fill up early with locals. The chili is always good, and regular nightly specials are also worth the stop. ⊠ *MM 99.4, BS* ☎ *305/451-3722* ⊟ *No credit cards* ☉ *Closed Sun.*

¢–$ ✕ **Alabama Jack's.** Floating on two roadside barges in an old fishing community 13 mi southeast of Homestead is this weathered open-air seafood restaurant. Regular customers include Keys characters, Sunday cyclists, local retirees, and boaters, who come to admire tropical birds in the nearby mangroves, the occasional crocodile in the canal, or the live band on weekends. The menu has traditional Keys dishes like cracked and fried conch, fish sandwiches, burgers, fries, salads, and lots of beer. The crab-cakes, made from local blue crabs, are exceptional. Jack's closes by 7 or 7:30, when the skeeters come out. ⊠ *58000 Card Sound Rd., Card Sound* ☎ *305/248-8741* ⊟ *MC, V.*

¢–$ ✕ **Cafe Las Brisas.** Joe and Celia Pineda opened one of the smallest restaurants in town, but it's among the busiest thanks to the generously sized Latin and American dishes grilled and richly flavored with garlic and spices. Sandwiches are quite tasty, especially the Texas sandwich, made with Cuban bread and layered with chicken or pork, cheese, hot sauce, more cheese, and then pressed. The restaurant sits right on Tavernier Creek, next to Tavernier Creek Marina, affording diners at the half dozen tables a waterfront view through picture windows. On nice days sit outside on picnic benches. ⊠ *MM 90.8, BS* ☎ *305/853–0042* ⊟ *No credit cards* ☉ *Closed Tues.–Wed. No lunch Sun.–Thurs.*

¢–$ ✕ **Chad's Deli & Bakery.** After years of customer requests for dinner service, Chad expanded into the space next door, where he still serves his legendary sandwiches in pita wraps or on one of eight fresh-baked breads. He also turns out white-chocolate macadamia nut and chocolate chip cookies that are a whopping 8 inches around. For dinner he's added pastas with freshly made sauces, pizzas on wheat and whole wheat crusts, and large salads. ⊠ *MM 92.3, BS* ☎ *305/853-5566* ⊟ *No credit cards.*

¢–$ ✕ **Harriette's Restaurant.** If you're looking for comfort food, try this refreshing throwback. Little has changed over the years in this bright-yellow-and-turquoise roadside eatery. Owner Harriette Mattson still personally welcomes her guests, and the regulars—many of whom have been coming here since it opened—still come for breakfast: steak and eggs with hash browns or grits and toast and jelly for $7.95 or old-fashioned hot cakes with butter and syrup and sausage or bacon for $4.75. ⊠ *MM 95.7, BS* ☎ *305/852-8689* ⊟ *No credit cards* ☉ *No dinner.*

$$$$ ▣ **Jules' Undersea Lodge.** Had he been a time traveler to this century, 19th-century namesake French writer Jules Verne might have enjoyed staying in this hotel, a former underwater research lab, at 5 fathoms (30 ft) below the surface with a 42-inch round window for viewing sea life. The only way to gain access to the lodge is by diving, and guests must either be certified divers or take the hotel's three-hour introductory course (an additional $75). Rates include breakfast, dinner, snacks, beverages, and unlimited dives and diving gear. Because of the length of stay underwater, once back on terra firma, you can't fly for 24 hours. ⊠ *MM 103.2, OS, 51 Shoreland Dr., 33037* ☎ *305/451-2353* ⯗ *305/451-4789*

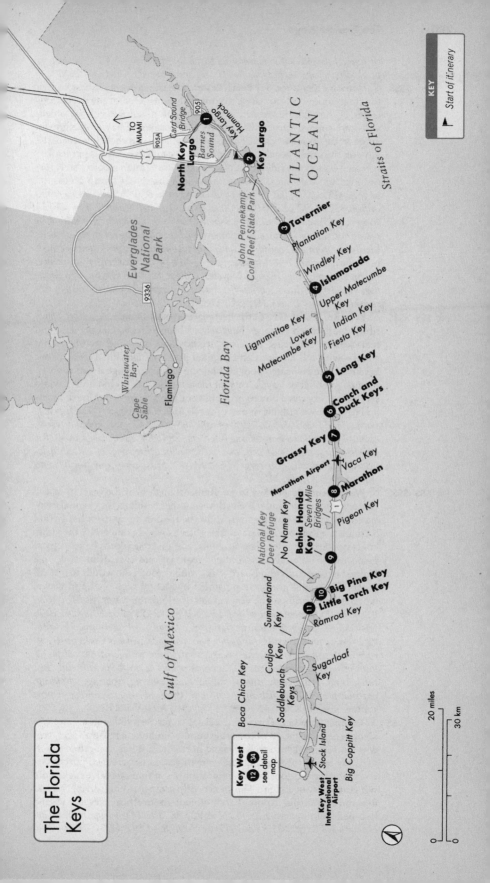

The Florida Keys

KEY

▲ Start of itinerary

TO MIAMI

Card Sound Bridge

North Key Largo

Barnes Sound

❶ Key Largo Hammock

905

905A

1

Everglades National Park

9336

Whitewater Bay

Cape Sable

Flamingo

Florida Bay

John Pennekamp Coral Reef State Park

❷ **Key Largo**

❸ **Tavernier**

Plantation Key

Windley Key

❹ **Islamorada**

Upper Matecumbe Key

Lignumvitae Key

Lower Matecumbe Key

Indian Key

Fiesta Key

❺ **Long Key**

❻ **Conch and Duck Keys**

❼ Grassy Key

Marathon Airport

Vaca Key

❽ **Marathon**

Pigeon Key

ATLANTIC OCEAN

Straits of Florida

Gulf of Mexico

National Key Deer Refuge

No Name Key

Bahia Honda Key

Seven Mile Bridges

❾

❿ ⓫ **Big Pine Key**

Little Torch Key

Ramrod Key

Summerland Key

Cudjoe Key

Saddlebunch Keys

Sugarloaf Key

Boca Chica Key

Stock Island

Big Coppitt Key

Key West International Airport

Key West
⓬ - ㉚
see detail map

20 miles

30 km

⊕ *www.jul.com* 🗪 *2 rooms* ⚒ *Kitchens, in-room VCRs, saltwater pool, dive shop; no kids under 10, no smoking* ⊟ *AE, D, MC, V.*

$$$$ ⊞ **Marriott's Key Largo Bay Beach Resort.** The Upper Keys are best known for small mom-and-pop-style accommodations. One of the exceptions is this 17-acre bayside resort, whose five lemon-yellow, grill-balconied, and spire-topped stories slice between highway and bay and exude an air of warm, indolent days. There are diversions galore. While away the days on the sandy beach or poolside or take an adventurous parasail or personal-watercraft ride. Rooms and suites have rattan tropical-style furnishings and balconies. From some, watch the sunset sweep across the bay. ⊠ *MM 103.8, BS, 103800 Overseas Hwy., 33037* ☎ *305/453–0000 or 800/932–9332* 🖷 *305/453–0093* ⊕ *www.marriotthotels.com* 🗪 *153 rooms, 20 3-bedroom suites, 6 3-bedroom suites, 1 penthouse suite* ⚒ *3 restaurants, room service, fans, in-room data ports, in-room safes, some kitchens, minibars, cable TV with movies, miniature golf, tennis court, pool, health club, hot tub, spa, beach, dive shop, snorkeling, jet skiing, marina, parasailing, fishing, bicycles, volleyball, 3 bars, shop, dry cleaning, laundry facilities, concierge, business services, meeting rooms; no-smoking rooms* ⊟ *AE, D, DC, MC, V.*

★ $$$–$$$$ ⊞ **Kona Kai Resort.** One of the best places to stay in the Keys, these beautifully landscaped cottages have tropical furnishings, CD players, and fruit-scented toiletries. Spacious studios and one- and two-bedroom suites—with full kitchens and original art—are light filled. Beachfront hammocks and a heated pool beckon you to relax, though if you're ansty, try a paddleboat or kayak, or visit the art gallery or orchid house. Maid service is every third day to prolong your privacy; however, fresh linens and towels are available at any time. ⊠ *MM 97.8, BS, 97802 Overseas Hwy., 33037* ☎ *305/852–7200 or 800/365–7829* ⊕ *www.konakairesort.com* 🗪 *11 units* ⚒ *Fans, some kitchens, cable TV, some in-room VCRs, tennis court, pool, hot tub, beach, dock, boating, basketball, shuffleboard, volleyball, concierge, Internet; no kids, no room phones, no smoking* ⊟ *AE, D, MC, V.*

★ $$$–$$$$ ⊞ **Westin Beach Resort, Key Largo.** Rather than destroy the vegetation and clutter the roadside landscape with yet another building, the original owners ensconced this compact resort off the road in a bay-front hardwood hammock. Most rooms overlook the water or woods; others face the lushly landscaped parking lot. The spacious, comfortable rooms have tropical furnishings. Rates include buffet breakfast and two drink coupons. Lighted nature trails and boardwalks wind through the woods to a small beach. Two small pools are separated by a coral rock wall and waterfall. Both restaurants, one very casual, overlook the water. ⊠ *MM 96.9, BS, 97000 Overseas Hwy., 33037* ☎ *305/852–5553 or 800/826–1006* 🖷 *305/852–8669* ⊕ *www.keylargoresort.com* 🗪 *190 rooms, 10 suites* ⚒ *2 restaurants, 2 grills, tapas bar, room service, in-room data ports, in-room safes, minibars, some microwaves, some refrigerators, cable TV with movies and video games, 2 tennis courts, 2 pools, health club, hot tub, sauna, spa, beach, dive shop, dock, snorkeling, boating, jet skiing, marina, parasailing, fishing, piano bar, shop, business services, airport shuttle; no-smoking rooms* ⊟ *AE, D, DC, MC, V* ⦿ *BP.*

$$ ⊞ **Coconut Palm Inn.** This small, casual waterfront lodge in a quiet residential neighborhood of towering gumbo-limbo and buttonwood trees was built in the 1930s to withstand hurricanes. It has more than 400 ft of sandy beach for relaxing and watching sunsets. Screened porches let you enjoy the outdoors without mosquitoes in summer. Dive racks hold wet gear to dry overnight. The owners help arrange fishing, diving, kayaking, and ecotouring. Rooms vary from one-room efficiencies to one- and two-bedroom apartments. ⊠ *MM 92, BS, 198 Harborview Dr., Tavernier 33070* ☎ *305/852–3017 or 800/765–5397* 🖷 *305/852–3880*

⊕ *www.fkeyhaven.com* ↩ *16 units ⛄ Grill, fans, some kitchens, refrigerators, cable TV, pool, beach, dock, snorkeling, boating, fishing, laundry facilities; no smoking* ▤ *MC, V.*

★ $$ 🔲 **Largo Lodge.** A palpable calm hangs over the 1950s-vintage adults-only one-bedroom guest cottages hidden in a tropical garden of palms, sea grapes, and orchids. Accommodations are cozy and equipped with small kitchens, rattan furniture, and screened porches. There's 200 ft of bay frontage for swimming, sitting, or contemplating. Late in the day, wild ducks, pelicans, herons, and other birds come looking for a handout from longtime owner Harriet "Hat" Stokes, who sets the tone at this laid-back, top-value tropical hideaway not too far down the Keys. ✉ *MM 101.7, BS, 101740 Overseas Hwy., 33037* ☎ *305/451–0424 or 800/468–4378* ⊕ *www.largolodge.com* ↩ *6 apartments, 1 efficiency ⛄ Fans, kitchenettes, cable TV, beach, dock; no kids under 16, no room phones.* ▤ *MC, V.*

$ 🔲 **Popp's Motel.** A high wall with stylized metal white herons marks the entrance to this 50-year-old family-run motel. It's roomy, homey, breezy, and ideal for families, whose kids can safely play on swings and a sandy beach just yards from their rooms. Clean, well-maintained bedroom units and efficiencies have a kitchen, dark wood paneling, and terrazzo floors. It's simple but a gem of a resort. A weekly stay is required during busy periods. ✉ *MM 95.5, BS, 95500 Overseas Hwy., 33037* ☎ *305/852–5201* 🖷 *305/852–5200* ⊕ *www.popps.com* ↩ *10 units ⛄ Picnic area, fans, kitchens, cable TV, beach, dock, snorkeling, boating, water-skiing, fishing, shuffleboard, playground* ▤ *AE, MC, V.*

¢–$ 🔲 **Seafarer Fish and Dive Resort.** While the Seafarer bills itself as a fish and dive resort, it's very popular with families, whose young children busy themselves building sand castles on the beach and feeding resident squirrels. Rooms, apartments, and cottages are basic and clean, with a hodgepodge of furnishings. Some have private patio seating areas. Guests like to gather at the beachfront picnic table for al fresco dining and on the dock and lounge chairs for sunset watching. ✉ *MM 97.8, BS, 97870 Overseas Hwy., 33037* ☎ *305/852–5349 or 800/599–7712* 🖷 *305/852–2265* ⊕ *www.keylargoparadise.com* ↩ *6 units ⛄ Grill, picnic area, fans, in-room data ports, some kitchens, refrigerators, cable TV, beach, dive shop, dock, snorkeling, boating, laundry facilities.* ▤ *MC, V.*

¢ 🔲 **Coconut Bay Resort.** The value at this small waterfront resort is as refreshing as the simply furnished pretty rooms, efficiencies, and cottages. There's lots of sandy beach for lounging under palm trees and launching kayaks. A covered sundeck at the shore is perfect for watching watery sunsets. Restaurants are within walking distance. ✉ *MM 97.7, BS, 97770 Overseas Hwy., 33037* ☎ *305/852–1625 or 800/385–0986* ⊕ *www.thefloridakeys.com/coconutbay.com* ↩ *6 units ⛄ Picnic area, fans, some kitchens, microwaves, refrigerators, cable TV, pool, beach, dock, boating, some pets allowed (fee).* ▤ *AE, D, MC, V.*

🔺 **America Outdoors.** Nestled in a heavily wooded 2 ½-acre strip along Florida Bay, this friendly waterfront campground fills up with repeat campers, especially snowbirds from January to mid-March, and South Floridians, who crowd the place on weekends and holidays. Security is tight, and it has the Keys' best camping amenities, including satellite TV, a recreation center, shuffleboard, horseshoes, two tidy air-conditioned bathhouses, a marina, fishing pier, bait shop, boat ramp and rentals, windsurfing, and Internet access. It's family oriented, pet friendly, clean, orderly, and well managed. Some sites are on the beach. Weekly RV rentals are available. ⛄ *Flush toilets, full hookups, dump station, drinking water, laundry facilities, showers, grills, picnic tables, restaurant, snack bar, electricity, public telephone, general store, swimming (ocean)* ↩ *151*

full hookups, 3 tent sites ⊠ *MM 97.5, BS, 97450 Overseas Hwy.,
33037* ☎ *305/852–8054* ⊕ *www.aokl.com* ⊠ *Full hookups $55–$90,
tent sites $35–$40* ⊟ *AE, D, MC, V.*

⚠ **John Pennekamp Coral Reef State Park.** Campsites are carved out of
hardwood hammock, providing shade and privacy away from the heavy
day-use areas. Nearby water laps the shore, lulling you to sleep. Groups
have numerous facilities for spreading out. There's a campground host,
campfire programs, and vending machines for late-night snack attacks.
Day-use activities and facilities include boating, fishing, hiking, boat-
slip rentals, dock, boat tours, nature center, marina, scuba and snorkel,
and volleyball. ♿ *Flush toilets, partial hookups (electric and water), dump
station, drinking water, showers, fire pits, grills, picnic tables, snack bar,
electricity, public telephone, general store, ranger station, playground,
swimming (ocean)* ⟿ *47 partial hookups for RVs and tents* ⊠ *MM 102.5,
OS* ☎ *305/451–1202* ⊕ *www.reserveamerica.com* ⊠ *All sites $19*
⊟ *AE, D, MC, V.*

Nightlife

The semiweekly *Keynoter* (Wednesday and Saturday), weekly *Reporter*
(Thursday), and Friday through Sunday editions of the *Miami Herald*
are the best sources of information on entertainment and nightlife.

Local movers and shakers mingle with visitors over cocktails and sunsets at **Breezers Tiki Bar** (⊠ MM 103.8, BS ☎ 305/453–0000), in Marriott's Key Largo Bay Beach Resort. Walls plastered with Bogart
memorabilia remind customers that the classic 1948 Bogart-Bacall flick
Key Largo was shot in the **Caribbean Club** (⊠ MM 104, BS ☎ 305/451–
9970). An archetype of a laid-back Keys bar, it draws a hairy-faced, down-
home group to shoot the breeze while shooting pool but is friendlier than
you might imagine. It also has postcard-perfect sunsets and live entertainment that's good enough to draw late-night crowds on Friday and
Saturday and at 6 on Sunday evening. **Coconuts** (⊠ MM 100, OS, 528
Caribbean Dr. ☎ 305/453–9794), in Marina Del Mar Resort, has
nightly entertainment year-round, except Sunday for karaoke and Monday during football season. The crowd is primarily thirty- and fortysome-
thing, sprinkled with a few grizzled locals.

The Outdoors

BIKING **Tavernier Bicycle & Hobbies** (⊠ MM 91.9, BS, 91958 Overseas Hwy., Tavernier ☎ 305/852–2859) rents single-speed adult and children's bikes.
Cruisers go for $8 a day, $40 a week. Helmets and locks are free with
rental. It's closed on Sunday.

FISHING **Sailors Choice** (⊠ MM 99.7, OS ☎ 305/451–1802 or 305/451–0041)
runs a party boat twice daily plus a night trip on Friday and Saturday.
The ultramodern 60-ft, 49-passenger boat with air-conditioned cabin
costs $33 and leaves from the Holiday Inn docks.

SCUBA DIVING & Diving fans of American Diving Headquarters will find a new sign on
SNORKELING the building. **Ocean Divers** (⊠ MM 105.5, BS and 522 Caribbean Dr.,
MM 100, OS ☎ 305/451–0037 or 877/451–0037; 305/451–1113 or
800/451–1113 ⊕ www.oceandiver.com) purchased the outfit and now
operates two shops under the Ocean Divers name. Both are PADI five-
star CDC facilities and offer day and night dives, fully stocked stores,
instruction, and dive-lodging packages. The cost is $65 for a two-tank
reef dive with tank and weight rental, $100 if you need everything;
$106–$112 includes a wet suit, suggested in winter.

Amy Slate's Amoray Dive Resort (⊠ MM 104.2, BS ☎ 305/451–3595 or
800/426–6729 ⊕ www.amoray.com) makes diving easy. You get out of

bed, walk out of your room and into a full-service dive shop (NAUI, PADI, TDI, and British BSAC certified), then onto a 45-ft catamaran. They provide multidive discounts and accommodations packages and perform underwater weddings.

Coral Reef Park Co. (✉ John Pennekamp Coral Reef State Park, MM 102.5, OS ☎ 305/451–6322) gives scuba and snorkeling tours of the park aboard sailing and motorized boats.

Divers City, USA (✉ MM 107.9, BS ☎ 305/451–4554 or 800/649–4659) moved to Gilbert's Resort to offer full resort-dive packages starting at $348 per person for five nights and 10 dives. Three and seven-day packages are also available. It also has some of the best prices on equipment in town and runs two-tank, two-location dives for $49.95, tanks and weights included.

Quiescence Diving Service, Inc. (✉ MM 103.5, BS ☎ 305/451–2440) sets itself apart in two ways: it limits groups to six to ensure personal attention and offers day, night, and twilight (in summer) dives an hour before sundown, the time when sea creatures are most active.

WATER SPORTS   **Coral Reef Park Co.** (✉ John Pennekamp Coral Reef State Park, MM 102.5, OS ☎ 305/451–1621) frequently renews its fleet of canoes and kayaks for scooting around the mangrove trails or the sea. Rent a canoe, a one- or two-person sea kayak, or even camping equipment from **Florida Bay Outfitters** (✉ MM 104, BS ☎ 305/451–3018). Real pros, they help with trip planning and match the equipment to the skill level, so even novices feel confident paddling off. Rentals are by the half day or full day. They also run myriad tours and sell camping and outdoor accessories, kayaks, and canoes.

Shopping

Original works by major international artists—including American photographer Clyde Butcher, French painter Jalinepol W, and French sculptor Polles—are shown at the **Gallery at Kona Kai** (✉ MM 97.8, BS, 97802 Overseas Hwy. ☎ 305/852–7200), in the Kona Kai Resort. There are lots of shops in the Keys that carry fun souvenirs. **Shellworld** (✉ MM 97.5, center median ☎ 305/852–8245) is one of the largest. Inside the long Keys-style building are two floors crowded with high-quality home furnishings, CDs of local music, shells, cards, resort clothing, jewelry, and, yes, tacky souvenirs. There is a supersale the weekend after Thanksgiving.

Islamorada

❹ *MM 90.5–70.*

Early settlers named Islamorada after their schooner, the *Island Home,* but to make the name more romantic, they translated it into Spanish— *isla morada* (while the translation endured, the local pronunciation is now the non-Spanish EYE-la-mor-AH-da). The local chamber of commerce prefers to say it means "the purple isles." Early maps show Islamorada as only Upper Matecumbe Key, but the incorporated "Village of Islands" comprises the islands between Tavernier Creek at MM 90 and Fiesta Key at MM 70, including Plantation Key, Windley Key, Upper Matecumbe Key, Lower Matecumbe Key, Craig Key, and Fiesta Key. In addition, two islands—Indian Key, in the Atlantic Ocean, and Lignumvitae Key, in Florida Bay—belong to the group. Islamorada is one of the world's most renowned sportfishing areas. For nearly 100 years, seasoned anglers have recognized these clear, warm waters, with game fish as well as lobster, shrimp, and crabs. The rich, the famous, and the powerful have all fished here, including Lou Gehrig, Ted Williams, Zane Grey, and presidents Hoover, Truman, Carter, and Bush Sr. More than 150 backcountry guides and 400 offshore captains operate out of this 20-mi stretch. Activities range from fishing tournaments to historic reenactments. During September and October, Heritage Days highlights include free lectures on Islamorada history, a golf tournament, and the Indian Key Festival. Holiday Isle Resort sponsors boating, fishing, car, and golf tournaments as well as bikini and body-building contests.

Between 1885 and 1915, settlers earned good livings growing pineapples at **Plantation Key,** using black Bahamian workers to plant and harvest their crops. The plantations are gone, replaced by a dense concentration of homes, businesses, and a public park. ⊠ *MM 90.5–86.*

At 16 ft above sea level, **Windley Key** is the highest point in the Keys. Originally two islets, the area was first inhabited by Native Americans, who left middens and other remains, and then by settlers, who farmed and fished in the mid-1800s and called the islets the Umbrella Keys. The Florida East Coast Railway bought the land from homesteaders in 1908, filled in the inlet between the two islands, and changed the name. They quarried rock for the rail bed and bridge approaches in the Keys—the same rock used in many historic South Florida structures, including Miami's Vizcaya and the Hurricane Monument on Upper Matecumbe. Although the Quarry Station stop was destroyed by the 1935 hurricane, quarrying continued until the 1960s. Today a few resorts and attractions occupy the island. ⊠ *MM 86–84.*

Islamorada Founder's Park. Formerly part of a commercial resort, this is now a public village park with a beach, marina, dog park, skate park, water-sports equipment rentals, an Olympic-size pool, and clean restroom and shower facilities. If you're staying in Islamorada hotels, enter the park free and pay the village rate of $2–$3 weekdays/weekends for the pool. Guests of other Keys hotels pay $4–$6 to enter the park and $4–$6 to use the pool. ⊠ *MM 87, BS* ☎ *305/853–1685.*

The once-living fossilized coral reef at **Windley Key Fossil Reef State Geologic Park,** laid down about 125,000 years ago, shows that the Florida Keys were at some time underwater. Excavation of Windley Key's limestone bed by the Florida East Coast Railway exposed the petrified reef. The park contains the **Alison Fahrer Environmental Education Center,** with historic, biological, and geological displays about the area. There also are guided and self-guided tours along trails that lead to the railway's old quarrying equipment and cutting pits, where you can take rubbings of beautifully fossilized brain coral and sea ferns from the quarry walls. There's an annual festival in February. ⊠ *MM 85.5, BS* ☎ *305/ 664–2540* ⊕ *www.dep.state.fl.us/parks* ✎ *Education center free, quarry trails $1.50, ranger-guided tours $2.50* ☉ *Education center Thurs.–Mon. 8–5; inquire about quarry tour schedule.*

The lush, tropical 17-acre **Theater of the Sea** is the second-oldest marine mammal center in the world. Entertaining and educational shows provide insight into conservation issues, natural history, and mammal anatomy, physiology, and husbandry. Shows run continuously. Ride a glass-bottom boat and take a four-hour Dolphin Adventure Snorkel Cruise or guided tours to view marine life, raptors, and reptiles. Visit dolphins and sea lions and participate in animal interaction programs such as Swim with the Dolphins ($140), Swim with Sea Lions ($95), Stingray Reef Swim ($45), and Trainer for a Day ($85). Reservations are recommended for interaction programs. Program fees include general admission. Try lunch at the grill, shop, and sunbathe at a lagoonside beach. ⊠ *MM 84.5, OS,*

84721 Overseas Hwy., 33036 ☎ *305/664–2431* ⊕ *www.theaterofthesea.com* 🖃 *$18* ⊘ *Daily 9:30–4.*

Early homesteaders were so successful at growing pineapples in the rocky soil of **Upper Matecumbe Key** that at one time the island had the largest U.S. pineapple crop. However, Cuban pineapples and the hurricane of 1935 killed the industry. Today life centers on fishing and tourism, and the island is lively with homes, charter-fishing boats, bait shops, restaurants, stores, nightclubs, marinas, nurseries, and offices. It's one of the earliest of the Upper Keys to be permanently settled. ✉ *MM 84–79.*

Home to the local chamber of commerce, a **red train caboose** sits at the site where the Florida East Coast Railway had a station and living quarters, before they washed away with the hurricane of 1935. ✉ *MM 82.5, BS* 🖃 *Free* ⊘ *Weekdays 9–5, Sat. 9–4, Sun. 9–3.*

While the possibility of a hurricane is something Keys residents live with, few hurricanes actually make landfall here. One major exception was the 1935 Labor Day hurricane, in which 423 people died. Beside the highway, the 65-ft by 20-ft art deco–style **Hurricane Monument** commemorates their deaths. Many of those who perished were World War I veterans who had been working on the Overseas Highway. The monument, built of Keys coral limestone with a ceramic map of the Keys, depicts wind-driven waves and palms bowing before the storm's fury. ✉ *MM 81.6, OS.*

Tucked away behind the Islamorada library is **Islamorada County Park**, with a small beach on a creek. The water isn't very deep, but it is crystal clear. Currents are swift, making swimming unsuitable for young children, but kids can enjoy the playground as well as picnic tables, grassy areas, and rest rooms. ✉ *MM 81.5, BS.*

off the beaten path

Indian Key State Historic Site. Murder, mystery, and misfortune surround 10½-acre Indian Key on the ocean side of the Matecumbe islands. Before it became one of the first European settlements outside of Key West, it was inhabited by Native Americans for several thousand years. The islet served as a county seat and base for 19th-century shipwreck salvagers until an Indian attack wiped out the settlement in 1840. Dr. Henry Perrine, a noted botanist, was killed in the raid. Today his plants overgrow the town's ruins. In October the Indian Key Festival celebrates the key's heritage. Take a guided tour, Thursday–Monday at 9 and 1, or roam among the marked trails and sites. The island is reachable by boat—your own, a rental, or a ferry. Robbie's Marina, the official concessionaire, rents kayaks and boats and operates twice-daily ferry service daily except Tuesday and Wednesday. For information, contact Long Key State Recreation Area. Locals kayak out from Indian Key Fill (✉ *MM 78.5, BS*). Rentals are available from Florida Keys Kayak and Sail. ✉ *MM 78.5, OS* ☎ *305/664–9814 ferry service; 305/664–4815 Long Key State Recreation Area* 🖃 *Ferry (includes tour) $15, $25 with Lignumvitae Key* ⊘ *Daily sunrise–sunset.*

Lignumvitae Key State Botanical Site. On the National Register of Historic Places, this 280-acre bayside island is the site of a virgin hardwood forest and home and gardens that chemical magnate William Matheson built as a private retreat in 1919. Access is by boat—your own, a rental, or a ferry operated by the official concessionaire, Robbie's Marina, which also rents kayaks and boats. (Kayaking out from Indian Key Fill, at MM 78.5, is a popular pastime.) On the key, take a tour with the resident ranger and request a list of native and well-naturalized plants. As a courtesy, you should arrange for a tour in advance with Long Key State Recreation Area if you're using your own or a rental boat. On the first weekend in December, the park service holds an annual Lignumvitae Christmas Celebration. ⊠ *MM 78.5, BS* ☎ *305/664–9814 ferry service; 305/664–4815 Long Key State Recreation Area* ☒ *Free; tour $1; ferry (includes tour) $15, $25 with Indian Key* ☉ *Tours Thurs.–Mon. at 10 and 2.*

Tarpon, large prehistoric-looking denizens of the not-so-deep, congregate around the docks at **Robbie's Marina** on Lower Matecumbe Key, where children—and lots of adults—buy a $2 bucket of bait fish to feed them. ⊠ *MM 77.5, BS* ☎ *305/664–9814 or 877/664–8498* ☒ *Dock access $1* ☉ *Daily 8–5.*

On Lower Matecumbe Key, **Anne's Beach** is a popular village park whose beach is best enjoyed at low tide. It also has a ½-mi elevated wooden boardwalk that meanders through a natural wetland hammock. Covered picnic areas along the boardwalk provide a place to rest and enjoy the view. Rest rooms are at the north end. Weekends are packed with Miami day-trippers. ⊠ *MM 73.5, OS* ☎ *305/853–1685.*

Where to Stay & Eat

$$–$$$$
Fodor's Choice
★

✕ **Pierre's.** A two-story sister to the Morada Bay restaurant, this spot marries British colonial decadence with South Florida trendiness. It oozes style with dark wood, rattan, French doors, Indian and Asian architectural artifacts, and a wicker chair–strewn veranda that overlooks the bay. The food, inspired by those same Asian, Indian, and Floridian accents, is complex: layered, colorful, and beautifully presented. Weather permitting, dine outside. The sophisticated downstairs bar provides a perfect vantage point for sunset watching. Reservations are recommended. ⊠ *MM 81.5, BS* ☎ *305/664–3225* ▭ *AE, MC, V.*

★ **$–$$$**
✕ **Morada Bay.** Wildly popular, this bay-front restaurant has a spectacular water view and traditional wooden Conch architecture, decorated with Clyde Butcher's black-and-white Everglades photos. Best of all is the contemporary menu, including tapas, mostly from the sea. Meals start with a basket of fresh rolls and a plate of tapenade, white-bean dip, and garlic-infused olive oil. Dine indoors (noisy) or outdoors overlooking a beach dotted with Adirondack chairs. There's frequently live entertainment, especially on weekends, and a monthly full-moon party. ⊠ *MM 81, BS* ☎ *305/664–0604* ▭ *AE, MC, V.*

$–$$
✕ **Manny & Isa's.** Here's a Keys institution with no frills or pretense but with friendly waitresses who serve consistently delicious Cuban and Spanish dishes and local seafood in a simple, crowded room. There are daily fish, chicken, and pork-chop specials and a paella loaded with seafood. Order it the day before for at least two people ($20.95 each). Manny's sweet-tart key lime pies are legendary. Order them by the slice or by the pie. There's always a wait for dinner on weekends and during the winter high season. Avoid the line by calling for takeout. ⊠ *MM 81.6, OS, 81610 Old Hwy.* ☎ *305/664–5019* ☒ *Reservations not accepted* ▭ *AE, D, MC, V* ☉ *Closed Tues. and mid-Oct.–mid-Nov.*

★ **¢–$$$**
✕ **Squid Row.** The food is so fresh and good at this seafood eatery that no gimmicks are needed to lure customers. That doesn't prevent the affable staff from offering a playful challenge: if you eat the nightly special seafood bouillabaisse ($28.95)—thick with stone crab claws and other savories—all by yourself, you'll get a free slice of key lime pie. Other fish choices are grilled to divinely flaky perfection or breaded and sautéed. Meals begin with a slice of warm banana bread, also nice with your coffee. ⊠ *MM 81.9, OS* ☎ *305/664–9865* ▭ *AE, D, DC, MC, V.*

$$$$ 🏨 **Casa Morada.** Three women hoteliers brought their cumulative 50 years
Fodor'sChoice of New York and Miami Beach experience to the Keys. Using their trans-
   ★   formative magic, they're turning this waterfront resort into a showcase
befitting the French Riviera, with a Caribbean accent, of course. New
landscaping, a renovated pool surrounded by a sandy "beach," artwork,
minibars, CD players, and outdoor lounges are just the start. Clean, cool
tile and renovated terrazzo floors invite you to kick off your shoes and
step out to your private patio overlooking the gardens and bay. Breakfast is included. ⊠ *MM 82, BS, 136 Madeira Rd., 33036* ☎ *305/664–
0044 or 888/881–3030* 🖷 *305/664–0674* ∰ *www.casamorada.com*
🛏 *16 suites* ♻ *Room service, fans, in-room data ports, in-room safes,
minibars, cable TV, pool, some in-room hot tubs, dock, boating, marina, boccie, lounge, concierge; no smoking* ⊟ *AE, MC, V.*

$$$–$$$$ 🏨 **Cheeca Lodge.** This classy, classic resort combines a sense of luxury
with a sense of familiarity. A complex of buildings, gardens, beach, and
fish-filled lagoons stretches across 27 oceanfront acres. Tropically dec-
orated units and screened balconies (on suites) encourage you to linger,
but the beach, sports, and massages, facials, and body treatments at the
Avanyu Spa beckon. Suites have kitchens; fourth-floor rooms in the main
lodge have ocean or bay views. The resort is the local leader in green
activism with everything from recycling programs to ecotours. Camp
Cheeca for kids is both fun and educational. ⊠ *MM 82, OS* ⌖ *Box
527, 33036* ☎ *305/664–4651 or 800/327–2888* 🖷 *305/664–2893*
∰ *www.cheeca.com* 🛏 *139 rooms, 64 suites* ♻ *2 restaurants, room ser-
vice, in-room data ports, some minibars, some refrigerators, cable TV
with movies, in-room VCRs, 9-hole golf course, 6 tennis courts, 2 pools,
saltwater pool, health club, 5 outdoor hot tubs, spa, beach, dive shop,
dock, snorkeling, boating, parasailing, fishing, bicycles, bar, lobby
lounge, shops, baby-sitting, children's programs (ages 6–12), play-
ground, laundry service, business services, meeting rooms; no-smoking
rooms* ⊟ *AE, D, DC, MC, V.*

★ **$$$–$$$$**   🏨 **The Moorings.** When you think of a tropical retreat, visions of palm
trees, beaches, and wooden houses with porches and wicker furniture
may spring to mind. That's what you'll find here at one of the Keys' finest
hostelries. Tucked in a beachfront tropical forest are one-, two-, and three-
bedroom cottages and two-story houses outfitted with wicker and artis-
tic African fabrics and pristine kitchens. There are exquisite touches, from
thick towels to cushy bedcovers. The beach has Adirondack chairs and
hammocks and a swimming dock. There's a two-night minimum on one-
bedrooms and a one-week minimum on other lodgings. ⊠ *MM 81.6, OS,
123 Beach Rd., 33036* ☎ *305/664–4708* 🖷 *305/664–4242* ∰ *www.
themooringsvillage.com* 🛏 *5 cottages, 13 houses* ♻ *Fans, in-room data
ports, some kitchens, some kitchenettes, cable TV, tennis court, pool, beach,
windsurfing, boating, laundry facilities* ⊟ *MC, V.*

★ **$$–$$$$**   🏨 **The Caribbean Resort and Marina.** On 8½ acres, this picturesque resort has a beautiful sandy beach, two docks, and two types of accom-
modations. Old concrete duplex "villas" were modernized with very
tasteful island furnishings, tile floors, and a private deck or patio.
You'll smell the sea from all of them. Next door are the gilded lilies:
Caribbean-style one- and two-bedroom houses with open-beam ceilings,
wraparound porches, and light, breezy, oh-so-tropical furnishings. Public areas are equally appealing. The large walk-in, beach-entry-style pool
is surrounded by palm trees and lounge chairs. ⊠ *MM 82, OS, 109 E.
Carroll St.* ⌖ *Box 1298, 33036* ☎ *305/664–2235 or 800/799–9175*
🖷 *305/664–2093* ∰ *www.thecaribbeanresort.com* 🛏 *21 units, 9 villas, 12 houses* ♻ *Grill, fans, some kitchens, cable TV, some in-room
VCRs, pool, outdoor hot tub, beach, dock, snorkeling, marina, fishing*
⊟ *AE, MC, V.*

$$$ ⌷ **White Gate Court.** On the edge of Florida Bay, this well-run inn includes five restored wooden 1940s cottages laid out on three pretty landscaped acres along 200 ft of white-sand beach. Resident owner Susanne Orias de Cargnelli created this intimate escape, where everyone in the family, including the dog, is welcome. All the units, which sleep either two or four, are as well equipped as your own home, except your backyard probably doesn't have the barbecue grill and umbrella-shaded table under big old palm trees swaying with the sea breeze. Rates include use of water toys. ⌧ *MM 76, BS, 76010 Overseas Hwy., 33036* ☎ *305/664–4136 or 800/645–4283* ⊕ *www.whitegatecourt.com* ⤴ *7 units* ⌕ *Grill, picnic area, fans, in-room data ports, kitchens, cable TV, beach, dock, snorkeling, boating, bicycle, laundry facilities, some pets allowed (fee)* ▭ *MC, V.*

¢ ⌷ **Key Lantern Motel and Blue Fin Inn.** This pair of side-by-side no-frills motels are on the highway in the heart of Islamorada within walking distance of restaurants and shops. Terrazzo floors and brick walls reveal their age, but they're spacious and have well-maintained tile bathrooms with some new fixtures. The staff is helpful and friendly. It's a bargain if you just need a place to rest your body after a long day on the water. ⌧ *MM 82.1, BS, 33036* ☎ *305/664–4572* ⊕ *www.keylantern. com* ⤴ *24 units* ⌕ *Grills, fans, some kitchenettes, refrigerators, cable TV, laundry facilities* ▭ *MC, V.*

¢ ⌷ **Ragged Edge Resort.** Smack on the water's edge, this laid-back getaway has simple rooms with pine paneling, chintz, and a tile bath suite. Many downstairs units have screened porches, although upper units have large decks, more windows, and beam ceilings. Congregate under the thatch-roof observation tower by day and at the barbecue pits by night to grill up your catch. Minimal staffing and no in-room phones are among the measures that make this place affordable. There's not much of a beach, but you can swim off the dock. ⌧ *MM 86.5, OS, 243 Treasure Harbor Rd., 33036* ☎ *305/852–5389 or 800/436–2023* ⊕ *www.ragged-edge. com* ⤴ *10 units* ⌕ *Picnic area, fans, some kitchens, some kitchenettes, some refrigerators, pool, dock, marina, fishing, bicycles, shuffleboard; no room phones, no TV in some rooms* ▭ *MC, V.*

Nightlife

Holiday Isle Beach Resorts & Marina (⌧ MM 84, OS ☎ 305/664–2321) is the liveliest spot in the Upper Keys. On weekends, especially during spring break and holidays, the resort's three entertainment areas are mobbed, primarily with the under-30 set. Live bands play everything from reggae to heavy metal nightly. Behind the larger-than-life mermaid is the Keys-easy, over-the-water cabana bar the **Lorelei** (⌧ MM 82, BS ☎ 305/664–4656). Live nightly sounds are mostly reggae and light rock. **Zane Grey Long Key Lounge** (⌧ MM 81.5, BS ☎ 305/664–4244), above the World Wide Sportsman, was created to honor Zane Grey, one of South Florida's greatest legends in fishing and writing and one of the most famous members of the Long Key Fishing Club. The lounge displays the author's photographs, books, and memorabilia and has live blues, jazz, and Motown Thursday–Saturday and a wide veranda that invites sunset watching.

Sports & the Outdoors

BOATING Wildlife in the Keys is most active at sunrise and sunset. Be there comfortably at both times with **Houseboat Vacations of the Florida Keys** (⌧ MM 85.9, BS, 85944 Overseas Hwy., 33036 ☎ 305/664–4009 ⊕ www. thefloridakeys.com/houseboats), which rents a fleet of 42- to 44-ft boats that accommodate from six to eight people and come fully outfitted with safety equipment and necessities—except food. The three-day minimum starts at $847; a week costs $1,408. Kayaks, canoes, and 17- to 27-ft skiffs suitable for the ocean are also for hire.

Robbie's Boat Rentals & Charters (⊠ MM 77.5, BS, 77520 Overseas Hwy., 33036 ☎ 305/664–9814) prides itself on service. It delivers boats to hotels, provides orientation and instruction to new users, and rents fishing gear as well as boats starting from a 16-ft skiff with a 25-horse-power outboard (the smallest available) for $25 an hour, $70 for four hours, and $90 for the day. Boats up to 27 ft are also available, but there's a two-hour minimum; pontoon boats have a half-day minimum.

When you're in the Keys, do as the locals do. Get out on the water, prefer-ably for a few days. Captains Pam and Pete Anderson of **Treasure Harbor Marine** (⊠ MM 86.5, OS, 200 Treasure Harbor Dr., 33036 ☎ 305/852–2458 or 800/352–2628 ⊕ www.treasureharbor.com) provide every-thing you'll need for a vacation at sea: linens, safety gear, and, best of all, advice on where to find the best beaches, marinas, and lobster sites. Rent a vessel bareboat or crewed, with sail or with power. Boats range from a 19-ft Cape Dory to a 41-ft Morgan Out Island. Rates start at $110 a day, $450 a week. Captains start at $125 a day. Marina facili-ties are basic—water, electric, ice machine, laundry, picnic tables, and shower/rest rooms—and dockage is only $1.25 a foot.

FISHING Long before fly-fishing became a trendy sport, Sandy Moret was fishing the Keys for bonefish, tarpon, and redfish. Now he operates **Florida Keys Outfitters** (⊠ MM 82, BS ☎ 305/664–5423 ⊕ www.floridakeysoutfitters.com), with a store and the Florida Keys Fly Fishing School, which attracts anglers from around the world. Two-day weekend fly-fishing classes, which include classroom instruction, equipment, arrival cocktails, and daily breakfast and lunch, cost $895. Add another $900 for two days of fish-ing. Guided fishing trips cost $310 for a half day, $450 for a full day. Fish-ing and accommodations packages (at Cheeca Lodge) are available.

The 65-ft party boat *Miss Islamorada* (⊠ Bud n' Mary's Marina, MM 79.8, OS ☎ 305/664–2461) has full-day ($55 includes everything) and night trips. Bring your lunch or buy one from the dockside deli.

Captain Ken Knudsen of the *Hubba Hubba* (⊠ MM 79.8, OS ☎ 305/664–9281) quietly poles his flats boat through the shallow water, barely making a ripple. Then he points and his clients cast. Five seconds later there's a zing, and the excitement of bringing in a snook, redfish, trout, or tarpon begins. Knudsen has fished Keys waters since he was 12. That's more than 40 years. Now a licensed backcountry guide, he's ranked among the top 10 guides in Florida by national fishing magazines. He offers four-hour sunset trips for tarpon ($330) and two-hour sunset trips for bonefish ($175), as well as half- (300) and full-day ($400) outings. Prices are for one or two anglers. Tackle and bait are included.

Like other top fly-fishing and light-tackle guides, Captain Geoff Colmes of **Fishabout Charters** (⌂ 105 Palm La., Islamorada, 33036 ☎ 305/853–0741 or 800/741–5955 ⎙ 305/852–3085 ⊕ www.floridakeysflyfish.com) helps his clients land double-figure fish in the waters around the Florida Keys ($300–$400). But unlike the others, he also heads across Florida Bay to fish the coastal Everglades on three- and five-day trips (from $3,595 for two anglers) off the 60-ft mother ship, the *Fishabout*. It has three staterooms, private baths, living room, kitchen, satellite TV, phone, and separate crew quarters. It's especially ideal when cold, windy weather shuts out fishing around the Keys. Rates include captain, crew, guide fees, lodging, all meals, tackle, and use of canoes for getting deep into shallow inlets of the Everglades.

SCUBA DIVING &
SNORKELING

Florida Keys Dive Center (✉ MM 90.5, OS ☎ 305/852–4599 or 800/433–8946 ⊕ www.floridakeysdivectr.com) organizes dives from John Pennekamp Coral Reef State Park to Alligator Light. The center has two Coast Guard–approved dive boats, offers scuba training, and is one of the few Keys dive centers to offer Nitrox (mixed gas) diving. Since 1980, **Lady Cyana Divers** (✉ MM 85.9, BS ☎ 305/664–8717 or 800/221–8717 ⊕ www.ladycyana.com), a PADI five-star training resort, has operated dives on deep and shallow wrecks and reefs between Molasses and Alligator reefs. The 40- and 55-ft boats provide everything a diver needs, including full bathrooms.

TENNIS

Not all Keys' recreation is on the water. Play tennis year-round at the **Islamorada Tennis Club** (✉ MM 76.8, BS ☎ 305/664–5340). It's a well-run facility with four clay and two hard courts (five lighted), same-day racket stringing, ball machines, private lessons, a full-service pro shop, night games, and partner pairing. Rates are from $12 an hour.

WATER SPORTS

Florida Keys Kayak and Sail (✉ MM 77.5, BS, 77522 Overseas Hwy. ☎ 305/664–4878) rents kayaks within a 20- to 30-minute paddle of Indian and Lignumvitae keys, two favorite destinations for kayakers. Rates are $15 per hour, $30 per half day.

Shopping

Whether you're looking to learn more about Keys history, flora and fauna, or fishing, you'll find it in a large selection of books, cards, and maps on Florida and the region at **Cover to Cover Books** (✉ Tavernier Towne Shopping Center, MM 91.2, BS, 91272 Overseas Hwy. ☎305/852–1415). At **Down to Earth** (✉ MM 82.2, OS, 82229 Overseas Hwy. ☎ 305/664–9828), indulge your passion for *objets* that are at once practical and fanciful such as salad tongs carved from polished coconut shells or Italian dishes painted with palm trees. Prices are reasonable, too. When locals need a one-of-a-kind gift, they head for the **Gallery at Morada Bay** (✉ MM 81.6, BS ☎ 305/664–3650), stocked with blown glass and glassware, and home furnishings, original paintings and lithographs, sculptures, and hand-painted scarves and earrings by top South Florida artists. Among the best buys in town are the used best-sellers and hardbacks that sell for less than $5 after locals trade them in for store credit at **Hooked on Books** (✉ MM 82.6, OS, 82681 Overseas Hwy. ☎ 305/517–2602). There are also new titles, audio books, cards, and CDs. **Island Silver & Spice** (✉ MM 82, OS ☎ 305/664–2714) bills itself as a "tropical department store." To that end, it sells women's and men's resort wear, a large jewelry selection with high-end Swiss watches and marine-theme pieces, tropical housewares, cards, toys and games, bedding, and bath goods.

Former U.S. presidents, celebs, and record holders beam alongside their catches in black-and-white photos on the walls at **World Wide Sportsman** (✉ MM 81.5, BS ☎ 305/664–4615), a two-level attraction and retail center that sells upscale fishing equipment, art, resort clothing, and gifts. There's also a marina and the Zane Grey Long Key Lounge.

ART GALLERIES

Art Lovers Gallery (✉ MM 82.2, OS ☎ 305/664–3675) showcases the work of almost 100 primarily South Florida artists, including Kendall Van Sant (bronze sculptures) and Jim Lewk (copper creations). It's an unlikely spot for an art gallery. That said, the **Carpet Gallery** (✉ MM 88.6, OS, 88665 Overseas Hwy. ☎ 305/852–6101), which derives its name from the carved carpets created by resident rug artisan Thomas Gallagher as well as the carpets, tiles, and wood flooring that it sells, is attracting crowds to its one-artist exhibitions. A new show opens with a meet-the-artist reception on the first Friday of each month. The **Rain**

Barrel (✉ MM 86.7, BS ☎ 305/852–3084) is a natural and unhurried shopping showplace. Set in a tropical garden of shady trees, native shrubs, and orchids, the 1977 crafts village has shops with works by local and national artists and eight resident artists in studios, including John Hawver, noted for Florida landscapes and seascapes. In March it hosts the largest arts show in the Keys, with some 20,000 visitors, 100 artists, and live jazz. The **Garden Café** (☎ 305/852–6499)is a beautiful respite and has a primarily vegetarian menu of sandwiches and salads. The **Redbone Gallery** (✉ MM 81, OS, 200 Industrial Dr. ☎ 305/664–2002), the largest sporting-art gallery in Florida, has hand-stitched clothing and giftware in addition to wood and bronze sculptors such as Kendall Van Sant; watercolorists Chet Reneson, Jeanne Dobie, and Kathleen Denis; and painters C. D. Clarke and Tim Borski. One of the most-photographed subjects in the Upper Keys is the enormous fabricated lobster by artist Richard Blaes that stands in front of **Treasure Village** (✉ MM 86.7, OS, 86729 Old Hwy. ☎ 305/852–0511), a former 1950s treasure museum that has a dozen crafts and specialty shops and a small restaurant.

Long Key

⑤ *MM 70–65.5.*

Long Key is steeped in cultural and ecological history. Among its attributes is **Long Key State Recreation Area.** On the ocean side, the Golden Orb Trail leads onto a boardwalk through a mangrove swamp alongside a lagoon, where waterbirds congregate. The park has a campground, picnic area, rest rooms and showers, a canoe trail through a tidal lagoon, and a not-very-sandy beach fronting a broad expanse of shallow grass flats. Bring a mask and snorkel to observe the marine life in this rich nursery area. Repairs and replantings following hurricanes have left the park with improved facilities, but with a lot less shade. Replanting efforts continue. Across the road, near a historical marker partially obscured by foliage, is the **Layton Nature Trail** (✉ MM 67.7, BS), which takes 20–30 minutes to walk and leads through tropical hardwood forest to a rocky Florida Bay shoreline overlooking shallow grass flats. A marker relates the history of the Long Key Viaduct, the first major bridge on the rail line, and the exclusive Long Key Fishing Camp, which Henry Flagler established nearby in 1906 and which attracted sportsman Zane Grey, the noted western novelist and conservationist, who served as its first president. The camp was washed away in the 1935 hurricane and never rebuilt. For Grey's efforts, the creek running near the recreation area was named for him. ✉ *MM 67.5, OS* ⌂ *Box 776, 33001* ☎ *305/664–4815* ⊕ *www.dep.state.fl.us/parks* 🖂 *$3.75 per 1 person, plus 50¢* each additional person; canoe rental $4 per hr, $10 per day; Layton Nature Trail free ☉ Daily 8–sunset.

Where to Stay & Eat

¢–$$ ✕ **Little Italy.** Good food, good value. It doesn't say it on the menu, but ask locals about this traditional family-style Italian and seafood restaurant and that is often the answer. Lunch favorites include Caesar salad, chicken marsala, stone crabs, and stuffed snapper for $4.95–$8.95. Dinner selections are equally tasty and well priced—pasta, chicken, seafood, veal, and steak. Don't miss the rich, dreamy hot chocolate-pecan pie. Breakfast, too, is served, and a light-bites menu has smaller portions for kids and calorie-watchers. ✉ *MM 68.5, BS* ☎ *305/664–4472* ▭ *AE, MC, V.*

$$ ▤ **Lime Tree Bay Resort.** This popular 2½-acre resort is on Florida Bay and far from the hubbub of other hotels and businesses. An on-site water-

sports concession encourages activity. However, if you would rather do nothing more energetic than turn the pages of a book, head for the beach or settle into a hammock in the pleasantly landscaped garden. Newly renovated rooms have breezy wicker- and rattan-furnishings. The best units are the cottages out back (no bay views) and four deluxe rooms upstairs that have cathedral ceilings and skylights. The best bet for two couples traveling together is the upstairs Tree House. ⊠ *MM 68.5, BS* ⊕ *Box 839, Layton 33001* ☎ *305/664–4740 or 800/723–4519* 🖷 *305/664–0750* ⊕ *www.limetreebayresort.com* ⟋ *29 rooms* ⚄ *Grills, picnic area, fans, some kitchens, cable TV with movies, tennis court, pool, outdoor hot tub, beach, dive shop, dock, snorkeling, windsurfing, boating, jet skiing, fishing, bicycles, horseshoes, shuffleboard; no-smoking rooms* ⊟ *AE, D, DC, MC, V.*

⚠ **Long Key State Recreation Area.** Trees and shrubs border all of these oceanfront tent and RV sites. By day there is biking, hiking 10 mi of trail, boating, and fishing for bonefish, permit (bigger than bonefish), and tarpon in the near-shore flats. By night there are seasonal campfire programs. All sites have water and electricity, and campground hostesses are available to help out. Reserve up to 11 months in advance by phone or in person. Sites cost $19, plus $2 for electricity. ⚄ *Flush toilets, partial hookups (electric and water), dump station, drinking water, showers, grills, picnic tables, electricity, public telephone, ranger station, swimming (ocean)* ⟋ *60 partial hookups, 50 RV sites, 10 tent sites* ⊠ *MM 67.5, OS* ⊕ *Box 776, 33001* ☎ *305/664–4815* ⊕ *www.reserveamerica. com* 🖾 *All sites $19* ⊟ *AE, D, MC, V.*

The Outdoors

At **Lime Tree Water Sports** (⊠ MM 68.5, BS, Lime Tree Bay Resort Motel ☎ 305/664–0052) sign up for backcountry fishing trips and snorkeling or rent a powerboat, kayak, sailboard, or Wave Runner.

en route   As you cross Long Key Channel, look beside you at the old **Long Key Viaduct.** The second-longest bridge on the former rail line, this 2-mi-long structure has 222 reinforced-concrete arches.

THE MIDDLE KEYS

Stretching from Conch Key to the far side of the Seven Mile Bridge, the Middle Keys contain U.S. 1's most impressive stretch, MM 65–40, bracketed by the Keys' two longest bridges—Long Key Viaduct and Seven Mile Bridge, both historic landmarks. Activity centers on the town of Marathon, the Keys' third-largest metropolitan area. Fishing and diving are the main attractions. In both bay and ocean, the deep-water fishing is superb at places like the Marathon West Hump, whose depth ranges from 500 to more than 1,000 ft. Anglers successfully fish from a half dozen bridges, including Long Key Bridge, the Old Seven Mile Bridge, and both ends of Toms Harbor. There are also many beaches and natural areas to enjoy in the Middle Keys.

Conch & Duck Keys

❻ *MM 63–61.*

This stretch of islands is rustic. Fishing dominates the economy, and many residents are descendants of immigrants from the mainland South. Across a causeway from Conch Key, a tiny fishing and retirement village, lies Duck Key, an upscale community and resort.

Where to Stay & Eat

$$$–$$$$ ✕ **Waters Edge.** At the Hawk's Cay Resort, this plush yet relaxed restaurant gathers flavors and techniques from the Caribbean, Florida, and Europe. Favorites include St. Thomas, a land-and-sea combo of jumbo shrimp and tournedos of beef; chicken Key West, stuffed with crab, shrimp, and scallops; and Florida stone crab claws (in season); for dessert there is mud pie and coconut ice cream. Soup and a 40-item salad bar are included with dinners. Dine indoors or out. A collection of historic photos on the walls recalls the regional history and the notable visitors. ✉ *MM 61, OS, Duck Key* ☎ *305/743–7000* ▬ *AE, D, DC, MC, V* ⊘ *No lunch mid-Dec.–mid-Apr.*

★ $$$$ ▥ **Hawk's Cay Resort.** Popular with vacationing families is this rambling Caribbean-style retreat, which opened in 1959. Two-bedroom villas and upgrades have improved the tony resort, which has spacious rooms with wicker and earthy colors. Sports and recreational facilities are extensive, as are supervised programs for kids and teens. The Dolphin Connection provides three educational experiences with dolphins, including the in-the-water Dolphin Discovery program, which lets you get up-close and personal with the intelligent mammals. Rate does not include the $10–$20 daily resort fee. ✉ *MM 61, OS* ☎ *305/743–7000 or 888/443–6393* 🖷 *305/743–5215* ⊕ *www.hawkscay.com* ↯ *177 rooms, 16 suites, 269 2-bedroom villas ⅄ 4 restaurants, room service, fans, in-room data ports, some kitchens, refrigerators, cable TV with movies, golf privileges, 8 tennis courts, 5 pools, health club, outdoor hot tub, dive shop, snorkeling, boating, jet skiing, parasailing, water-skiing, fishing, basketball, volleyball, 2 bars, shop, children's programs (ages 5–12), laundry facilities, laundry service, concierge, business services, meeting rooms, airport shuttle, car rental; no-smoking rooms* ▬ *AE, D, DC, MC, V.*

$$ ▥ **Conch Key Cottages.** Flowering shrubs, palm trees, hammocks, a beach, and ocean breezes evoke the spirit of the tropics at this small, secluded resort composed of a four-plex motel efficiency and lattice-trimmed pastel-color cottages furnished in reed, rattan, and wicker. One- and two-bedroom cottages have kitchens. Three cottages face the beach. Although not on the water, the small honeymoon cottage is very charming. On rare days when the wind shifts, highway noise can be distracting. Complimentary use of a double kayak is included. There's a three-night minimum and check-in or check-out on Wednesday and Saturday only from mid-December through April. ✉ *MM 62.3, OS* ⌖ *R. R. 1, Box 424, Marathon 33050* ☎ *305/289–1377 or 800/330–1577* 🖷 *305/743–8207* ⊕ *www.conchkeycottages.com* ↯ *12 units ⅄ Grill, fans, some kitchens, some kitchenettes, cable TV, some in-room VCRs, pool, hot tub, beach, dock, snorkeling, laundry facilities; no room phones, no-smoking rooms* ▬ *D, MC, V.*

Grassy Key

❼ *MM 60–57.*

Local lore has it that this sleepy little key was named not for its vegetation—mostly native trees and shrubs—but for an early settler with the name Grassy. It's primarily inhabited by a few families who operate small fishing camps and motels.

The original *Flipper* movie popularized the notion of dolphins interacting with humans. The film's creator, Milton Santini, also created this facility, the **Dolphin Research Center,** now home to a colony of dolphins and sea lions. The not-for-profit organization has tours, narrated programs every 30 minutes, and several programs that allow interaction with dolphins in the water (Dolphin Encounter) or from a submerged platform

CloseUp

CLOSE ENCOUNTERS
OF THE FLIPPER KIND

HERE IN THE FLORIDA KEYS, *where Milton Santini created the original 1963 Flipper movie, close encounters of the Flipper kind are an everyday occurrence at a handful of facilities that allow you to commune with trained dolphins. There are in-water and waterside programs. The former are the most sought-after and require advance reservations. All of the programs emphasize education and consist of three parts: first, you learn about dolphin physiology and behavior from a marine biologist or researcher; then you go waterside for an orientation on dos and don'ts (for example, don't talk with your hands—you might, literally, send the wrong signal); finally, you interact with the dolphins—into the water you go.*

For the in-water programs, the dolphins swim around you and cuddle up next to you. If you lie on your back with your feet out, they use their snouts to push you around; or grab onto a dorsal fin and hang on for an exciting ride. The in-water encounter lasts about 10 to 25 minutes, depending on the program. On waterside-interaction programs, participants feed, shake hands, kiss, and do tricks with the dolphins from a submerged platform. The programs vary from facility to facility but share a few rules, and the entire program, from registration to departure, takes about two hours. The best time to go is when it's warm, from March through December. You spend a lot of time near or in and out of the water, and even with a wetsuit on you can get cold on a chilly day.

Call ahead to get information on restrictions (there are often age or height requirements) and other relevant details. Also, be wary of programs not listed below. Some industrious types have made a business of chartering boats, chumming the waters, and then letting wild dolphins swim with you—this is very dangerous and can lead to serious injury.

Dolphin Connection at Hawk's Cay Resort. *Marine biologists at the Dolphin Connection inspire awareness and promote conservation through programs at this stylish mid-Keys resort. Dolphin Discovery is an in-water, nonswim program that lasts about 45 minutes and lets you kiss, touch, and feed the dolphins.* ⊠ MM 61 OS, 61 Hawks Cay Blvd., Duck Key ☎ 888/814–9174 ⊠ Cost: $100 resort guests, $110 nonguests.

Dolphin Cove. *The educational part of the Dolphin Encounter program takes place on a 30-minute boat ride on adjoining Florida Bay. Then it's back to the facilities lagoon for a get-acquainted session from a platform. Then you slip into the water for the program's highlight: swimming and playing with your new dolphin pals.* ⊠ MM 101.9, BS, 101900 Overseas Hwy., Key Largo ☎ 305/451–4060 ⊠ $160.

Dolphin Research Center. *This not-for-profit organization has a colony of Atlantic bottlenose dolphins and California sea lions. Dolphin Encounter is a swim-interaction program, and in Dolphin Splash you stand on a submerged platform rather than swim.* ⊠ MM 59, Marathon Shores ☎ 305/289–1121 or 305/289–0002 ⊠ Dolphin Encounter $155, Dolphin Splash $75.

Dolphins Plus, Inc. *Programs here emphasize education and therapy. Natural Swim begins with a one-hour briefing; then you don snorkel gear and enter the water to become totally immersed in the dolphins' world.* ⊠ MM 99, 31 Corrine Pl., Key Largo ☎ 305/ 451–1993 or 866/860–7946 ⊠ $125.

Theater of the Sea. *The Dolphin Swim program at this marine park starts with a 30-minute classroom session and orientation. Then, through trained behaviors, including kisses, dorsal tows, and jumps, dolphins interact with swimmers in a 15-ft-deep saltwater lagoon.* ⊠ MM 84.7, 84721 Overseas Hwy., Islamorada ☎ 305/664–2431 ⊠ $140.

— Diane Marshall

(Dolphin Splash). Some programs have age or height restrictions, and some require 30-day advance reservations. ⊠ *MM 59, BS* ⌖ *Box 522875, Marathon Shores 33052* ☎ *305/289–1121 general information; 305/289–0002 interactive program information* ⊕ *www.dolphins. org* ⊠ *Tours $17.50, Dolphin Splash $75, Dolphin Encounter $155* ⊙ *Daily 9–4; walking tours daily at 10, 11, 12:30, 2, and 3:30.*

off the beaten path

Curry Hammock State Park. On the ocean and bay sides of U.S. 1, this littoral park covers 260 acres of upland hammock, wetlands, and mangroves. On the bay side, there's a trail through thick hardwoods to a rocky shoreline. The ocean side is more developed, with a sandy beach, a clean bathhouse, picnic tables, playground, grills, and a parking lot. Brown park signs mark the entrance. Plans for a campground and entrance fees are still undecided. Locals consider the trails that meander under canopies of arching mangroves one of the best areas for kayaking in the Keys. Manatees frequent the area, and it's a rich repository for birders. Information is provided by Long Key State Recreation Area. ⊠ *MM 57, OS, Crawl Key* ☎ *305/664–4815* ⊠ *Free* ⊙ *Daily 8–sunset.*

Where to Stay

¢ ▦ **Bonefish Resort.** Tucked among palms, banana leaves, and hibiscus flowers, this hideaway sits along a row of small, unfussy beachfront resorts on Grassy Key. Rooms, efficiencies, and suites are simply decorated with floral linens, wicker, tile floors, and tropical motifs, painted by a local artist, on entrance doors and some interior walls. The resort has a small beach, and guests have privileges at the nearby Cabana Club, which has a larger beach and pool. Hammocks, chaises, and a covered waterfront deck invite relaxation, and kayaks and paddleboats encourage exploration. ⊠ *MM 58 OS, 58070 Overseas Hwy., 33050* ☎ *305/743–7107 or 800/274–9949* ✂ *305/743–0449* ⊕ *www. bonefishresort.com* ⊠ *13 units* ⌖ *Grill, fans, some kitchens, microwaves, refrigerators, cable TV, hot tub, beach, boating, fishing, some pets allowed ($10)* ⊟ *D, MC, V.*

¢ ▦ **Gulf View Waterfront Resort.** With just 11 guest rooms and one- and two-bedroom apartments, this cozy resort feels more like a large private home than a hotel. Other than the talking, squawking, and singing of exotic birds in large cages, about the only sounds you'll hear while putting on the small green, dozing in a hammock, or floating in the pool are the rustling of palm leaves, the lapping of waves, and the splashing of canoe and kayak paddles. ⊠ *MM 58.5 BS, 58743 Overseas Hwy., 33050* ☎ *305/289–1414* ✂ *305/743–8629* ⊕ *www.gulfviewwaterfrontresort.com* ⊠ *11 units* ⌖ *Grill, picnic area, fans, in-room data ports, some kitchens, microwaves, refrigerators, cable TV, putting green, pool, beach, dock, boating, fishing, laundry facilities, some pets allowed ($10)* ⊟ *D, MC, V.*

¢ ▦ **Valhalla Beach Motel.** Just steps from the water, this simple motel has rooms, efficiencies, and a suite. Lounge on the beach or read in the Adirondack chairs, grill dinner on a barbecue, or paddle a canoe through mangrove trails in the neighboring state park. It's quiet here, and the views of the undisturbed outdoors are awesome. ⊠ *MM 56.3, OS, 56243 Ocean Dr., Crawl Key 33050* ☎ *305/289–0616* ⊠ *4 rooms, 1 suite, 5 efficiencies* ⌖ *Fans, some kitchens, some refrigerators, cable TV, beach, dock, boating; no room phones* ⊟ *No credit cards.*

¢ ▦ **Valhalla Point.** This unpretentious Crawl Key motel with a to-die-for waterfront location has the feel of a friend's simple beach house. There are hammocks and chaises on a very good beach, a dock from which manatees are frequently sighted, picnic tables, barbecue grills, and kayaks and canoes, a nice touch, since the property borders Curry

Hammock State Park. Family-oriented snorkeling trips to the reefs are offered. ⊠ *MM 56.2, OS, 56223 Ocean Dr., Crawl Key 33050* ☎ *305/ 289–0614* ⊕ *www.keysresort.com* ⤴ *1 room, 3 efficiencies, 1 suite* ♿ *Picnic area, some kitchens, cable TV, beach, dock, snorkeling, boating; no room phones* ⊟ *MC, V.*

Marathon

❽ *MM 53–47.5.*

Marathon, an independent municipality in the Middle Keys, began as a commercial fishing village in the early 1800s. Pirates, salvagers, fishermen, spongers, and, later, farmers eked out a living, traveling by boat between islands. About half the population were blacks who stoked charcoal furnaces for a living. According to local lore, Marathon was renamed when a worker commented that it was a marathon task to rebuild the railway across the 6-mi island after a 1906 hurricane. The railroad brought businesses and a hotel, and today Marathon is a bustling town by Keys standards. Fishing, diving, and boating are the primary attractions.

🐚 Tucked away from the highway behind a stand of trees, Crane Point— part of a 63-acre tract that includes the last-known undisturbed thatch-palm hammock—is an undeveloped oasis of greenery. It's the site of the **Museums and Nature Center of Crane Point Hammock,** which includes the **Museum of Natural History of the Florida Keys,** with a few dioramas, a shell exhibit, and displays on Keys geology, wildlife, and cultural history. Also here is the **Florida Keys Children's Museum,** with iguanas, fish, and a replica of a 17th-century Spanish galleon and pirate dress-up room where children can play as swashbucklers. Outside, on the 1-mi indigenous loop trail, visit the remnants of a Bahamian village, site of the restored **George Adderly House,** the oldest surviving example of Bahamian tabby (a cement-type material created from sand and seashells) construction outside of Key West. A boardwalk crosses wetlands, a river, and mangroves before ending at Adderly Village. From November to Easter, docent-led tours, included in the price, are available; bring good walking shoes and bug repellent during warm weather months. ⊠ *MM 50.5, BS, 5550 Overseas Hwy.* ⬡ *Box 536, 33050* ☎ *305/743– 9100* 💲*$7.50* ⊗ *Mon.–Sat. 9–5, Sun. noon–5; call to arrange trail tours.*

Pleasant, shaded picnic kiosks overlook a grassy stretch and the Atlantic Ocean at **Sombrero Beach.** Separate areas allow swimmers, jet boats, and windsurfers to share the beach. There are lots of facilities, as well as a grassy park with barbecue grills, picnic kiosks, showers, rest rooms, plus a baseball diamond, a large playground, and a volleyball court. The park is accessible for travelers with disabilities and allows leashed pets. Turn left at the traffic light in Marathon and follow signs to the end. ⊠ *MM 50, OS, Sombrero Rd.* ☎ *305/743–0033* 💲 *Free* ⊗ *Daily 8–sunset.*

> off the
> beaten
> path

Pigeon Key. There's a lot to like about this 5-acre island under the Old Seven Mile Bridge. It's reached by walking or riding a tram across a 2¼-mi section of the old bridge. Once there, tour the island on your own with a brochure or join a guided tour. The tour explores the buildings that formed the early 20th-century work camp for the Overseas Railroad, which linked the mainland to Key West. Later, their uses changed as the island became a fish camp, then a park, and then government administration headquarters. Today, the focus is on Florida Keys culture, environmental education, and marine research. Exhibits in a museum and a video recall the history of the railroad, the Keys, and railroad baron Henry M. Flagler. Pick up the shuttle at the depot on Knight's Key (MM 47, OS). ✉ *MM 45, OS ✆ Box 500130, Pigeon Key 33050* ☎ *305/289–0025 general information; 305/743–5999 tickets* ⊕ *www.pigeonkey.org* 🎟 *$8.50* ⊙ *Daily 9–5.*

Where to Stay & Eat

$$–$$$$
Fodor'sChoice
★
✕ **Barracuda Grill.** If you pigeonhole Keys food as grilled fish, Barracuda Grill will be a revelation. The sophisticated, eclectic menu capitalizes on local fish but is equally represented by tender, aged Angus beef; rack of lamb; and even braised pork shank. Innovation is in everything but not at the expense of good, solid cooking. Local favorites include Francesca's voodoo stew with scallops, shrimp, and veggies in a spicy tomato-saffron stock or sashimi of yellowfin tuna with wasabi and tamari. Decadent desserts include a rich key lime cheesecake. The well-thought-out wine list is heavily Californian. ✉ *MM 49.5, BS* ☎ *305/743–3314* ⊟ *AE, MC, V* ⊙ *Closed Sun. No lunch.*

¢–$$
✕ **Key Colony Inn.** The inviting aroma of an Italian kitchen pervades this popular family-owned restaurant. The menu has well-prepared chicken, steak, pasta, and veal dishes, and the service is friendly and attentive. For lunch there are fish and steak entrées served with fries, salad, and bread. At dinner you can't miss with traditional Continental dishes like veal Oscar and New York strip or such Italian specialties as seafood Italiano, a light dish of scallops and shrimp sautéed in garlic butter over a bed of linguine with a hint of marinara sauce. ✉ *MM 54, OS, 700 W. Ocean Dr., Key Colony Beach* ☎ *305/743–0100* ⊟ *AE, MC, V.*

¢–$
✕ **Fish Tales Market and Eatery.** Fans of the Island City Fishmarket won't be too disappointed about its sale once they learn that the new owners are George, Jackie, Johnny, and Gary Eigner of the former Grassy Key DB Seafood Grille (which has closed). They serve some of the DB's favorite dishes, such as grilled fish with homemade wasabi ($9.95) and German snapper sandwich, fried snapper on grilled rye with slaw and melted cheese. The market section ships crabs and lobsters throughout the country. Plan to dine early, as it's only open until 6:30 PM. ✉ *MM 53, OS, 11711 Overseas Hwy.* ☎ *305/743–9196 or 888/662–4822* ⊟ *MC, V* ⊙ *Closed Sun.*

¢–$
✕ **Keys Fisheries Market and Marina.** From the parking lot the commercial warehouse with fishing boats docked alongside barely hints at a restaurant inside. Order using an alias at the window outside, pick up your food in the market, then dine at a waterfront picnic table outdoors or under a protective plastic canopy. Fresh seafood and a token hamburger are the only things on the menu. A lobster reuben ($13.95) served on thick slices of toasted bread is the signature dish. There's also a 16-flavor ice cream bar and a beer-wine bar. ✉ *MM 49, BS, end of 35th St.* ☎ *305/743–4353* ⊕ *www.keysfisheries.com* ⊟ *MC, V.*

¢–$
Fodor'sChoice
★
✕ **7 Mile Grill.** This nearly 50-year-old, weatherworn open-air restaurant easily could serve as a movie set for a 1950s-era black-and-white movie based in the tropics. At the Marathon end of the Seven Mile Bridge, it serves up friendly service that rivals the casual food at breakfast, lunch, and dinner. Favorites on the mostly seafood menu include creamy shrimp bisque, grouper, and dolphinfish grilled, broiled, or fried. Don't pass up the authentic key lime pie, which won the local paper's "Best in the Keys" award three years in a row. ✉ *MM 47, BS* ☎ *305/743–4481* ⊟ *MC, V* ⊙ *Closed Wed.; Thurs. mid-Apr.–mid-Nov.; and at owner's discretion Aug.–Sept.*

★ $$$
🏨 **Seascape Ocean Resort.** The charming lobby filled with soothing sea colors and original artwork gives way to nine pastel-color guest rooms decorated with more original artwork, hand-painted headboards, and fresh flowers and fruit. Transforming the 5-acre oceanfront property with a large, two-story bay-front house into an exclusive yet unsnobbish re-

treat was the inspiration of painter Sara Stites and her husband, Bill, a magazine photographer. Swim, kayak, or relax around the pool, at the beach, or under a shade tree. Continental breakfast and afternoon cocktails and hors d'oeuvres are complimentary. ⊠ *MM 50.5, OS, 1075 75th St., 33050* ☎ *305/743–6455 or 800/332–7327* 🖷 *305/743–8469* ⊕ *www.thefloridakeys.com/seascape* ⤳ *9 rooms* ♿ *Fans, some kitchens, cable TV, pool, beach, dock, boating, Internet; no room phones, no smoking* ▤ *AE, MC, V* ⊧ *CP.*

¢–$$$ 🏨 **Coral Lagoon.** Private sundecks with hammocks have calming views of a deep-water canal and pretty landscaping. Cheerfully painted duplex cottages have king or twin beds, sofa beds, and lots of extras not usually available at this price, including hair dryers, morning coffee, dockage, barbecues, video library ($1 rental), and lots of sports equipment. For a fee, use a private beach club and go on scuba and snorkel trips arranged through the Diving Site, a dive shop that also offers certification. ⊠ *MM 53.5, OS, 12399 Overseas Hwy., 33050* ☎ *305/289–0121* 🖷 *305/289–0195* ⊕ *www.corallagoonresort.com* ⤳ *18 units* ♿ *Grill, fans, kitchens, cable TV, in-room VCRs, tennis court, pool, dive shop, dock, snorkeling, fishing, bicycles, laundry facilities; no-smoking rooms* ▤ *AE, D, MC, V.*

Sports & the Outdoors

BIKING Tooling around on two wheels is a good way to see Marathon. There are paved paths along Aviation Boulevard on the bay side of Marathon Airport, the four-lane section of the Overseas Highway through Marathon, Sadowski Causeway to Key Colony Beach, Sombrero Beach Road to the beach, and the roads on Boot Key (across a bridge on 20th Street, OS). There's easy cycling on a 1-mi off-road path that connects to the 2 mi of the Old Seven Mile Bridge that go to Pigeon Key.

"Have bikes, will deliver" could be the motto of **Bike Marathon Bike Rentals** (☎ 305/743–3204), which gets beach cruisers to your hotel door for $10 per day, $45 per week, including a helmet. It's open Monday through Saturday 9–4 and Sunday 9–2.

Equipment Locker Sport & Cycle (⊠ MM 53, BS ☎ 305/289–1670) rents cruisers for $10 per day, $50 per week, and hybrids for $15 per day and $75 per week for adults and children (it does not supply helmets). It also rents in-line skates for $25 per day, including pads and helmet. It's open weekdays 9–6, Saturday 9–5, and Sunday 10–3.

BOATING **Fish 'n' Fun** (⊠ MM 53.5, OS ☎ 305/743–2275 ⊕ www.fishnfunrentals. com), next to the Boat House Marina, lets you get out on the water on 18- to 25-ft powerboats starting at $105 for a half day, $150–$225 for a full day. You also can pick up bait, tackle, licenses, and snorkel gear. **Florida Keys Bareboat Charters** (☎ 305/743–0090 ⊕ www.slooppagankey. com) rents a 27-ft Catalina sailboat with a 4-ft draft for $200 a day.

FISHING Morning and afternoon, fish for dolphinfish, grouper, and other deep-sea game aboard the 75-ft *Marathon Lady and Marathon Lady III* (⊠ MM 53.5, OS, at 117th St., 33050 ☎ 305/743–5580), the 75- and 65-ft party boats that depart on half-day ($30, plus $3 equipment) excursions from the Vaca Cut Bridge, north of Marathon. Captain Jim Purcell, a deep-sea specialist for ESPN's *The Outdoorsman,* provides one of the best values in fishing in the Keys. His **Sea Dog Charters** (⊠ MM 47.5, BS ☎ 305/743–8255 ⊕ www.seadogcharters.net), next to the 7 Mile Grill, has personalized half- and full-day offshore, reef and wreck, tarpon, and backcountry fishing trips as well as combination fishing and snorkeling trips on the 32-ft *Bad Dog* for up to six people. The cost is $59.99 per person for a half day, regardless of whether your group fills the boat, and includes bait, light tackle, licensing, ice, and coolers. If you prefer an all-day private charter on a 37-ft boat, he offers those, too, for $550–$600.

GOLF **Key Colony Golf & Tennis** (✉ MM 53.5, OS, 8th St., Key Colony Beach ☎ 305/289–1533), a 9-hole course near Marathon, charges $8.50 for the course, $2 per person for club rental, and $1 for a pull cart. There are no tee times and there's no rush. Play from 7:30 to dusk. A little golf shop meets basic golf needs. There are two lighted tennis courts open from 7:30 to 10. Hourly rates are $4 for singles, $6 for doubles.

SCUBA DIVING & SNORKELING   There's more to diving in the Keys than beautiful reefs. So **Hall's Diving Center and Career Institute** (✉ MM 48.5, BS, 1994 Overseas Hwy., 33050 ☎ 305/743–5929 or 800/331–4255 ⊕ www.hallsdiving.com), next to Faro Blanco Resort, runs two trips a day to Looe Key, a few other reefs, and several wrecks, including *Thunderbolt,* and the *Adolphus Busch*. It also rents offers wet submarine dives and diver propulsion vehicles.

en route   The **Seven Mile Bridge** is one of the most-photographed images in the Keys. Actually measuring 6.79 mi long, it connects the Middle and Lower Keys and is believed to be the world's longest segmental

Fodor'sChoice ★   bridge. It has 39 expansion joints separating its cement sections. Each April, runners gather in Marathon for the Seven Mile Bridge Run.

The expanse parallel to it is what remains of the **Old Seven Mile Bridge**, an engineering marvel in its day that's now on the National Register of Historic Places. It rested on a record 546 concrete piers. No cars are allowed today, but a 2.2-mi segment ending at Pigeon Key is open for biking, walking, and rollerblading.

THE LOWER KEYS

In truth, the Lower Keys include Key West, but since it's covered in its own section and is as different from the rest of the Lower Keys as peanut butter is from jelly, this section covers just the limestone keys between MM 37 and MM 9. From Bahia Honda Key south, islands are clustered, smaller, and more numerous, a result of ancient tidal waters' flowing between the Florida Straits and the gulf. Here you're likely to see more birds and mangroves than other tourists, and more refuges, beaches, and campgrounds than museums, restaurants, and hotels. The islands are made up of two types of limestone, both more dense than the highly permeable Key Largo limestone of the Upper Keys. As a result, fresh water forms pools rather than percolating, creating watering holes that support Key deer, alligators, fish, snakes, Lower Keys rabbits, raccoons, migratory ducks, Key cotton and silver rice rats, pines, saw palmettos, silver palms, grasses, and ferns. (Many of these animals and plants can be seen in the National Key Deer Refuge on Big Pine Key.) Nature was generous with her beauty in the Lower Keys, which have both Looe Key Reef, arguably the Keys' most beautiful coral reef tract, and Bahia Honda State Park, considered one of the best beaches in the world for its fine sand dunes, clear warm waters, and panoramic vista of bridges, hammocks, and azure sky and sea.

Bahia Honda Key

❾ *MM 38–36.*

Fodor'sChoice ★   The 524-acre sun-soaked, state-owned **Bahia Honda State Park** sprawls across both sides of the highway, giving it 2½ mi of beautiful sandy beaches—the best in the Keys—on both the Atlantic Ocean and the Gulf of Mexico. Although swimming, kayaking, fishing, and boating are the main reasons to come, there are many other activities, including walks on the Silver Palm Trail, with rare West Indian plants and several species found nowhere else in the Keys. Seasonal ranger-led nature programs might include illustrated talks on the history of the Overseas Railroad. There are 3½ mi of flat park roads for biking, rental cabins, a campground, a snack bar, gift shop, 19-slip marina, and a concessionaire for snorkeling. Get a panoramic view of the island from what's left of the railroad—the Bahia Honda Bridge. ⊠ *MM 37, OS, 36850 Overseas Hwy., 33043* ☎ *305/872-2353* ⊕ *www.dep.state.fl.us/parks* ⊠ *$2.50 for 1 person, $5 per vehicle for 2 people, plus 50¢ per each additional person; $1.50 per pedestrian or bicyclist* ⊙ *Daily 8–sunset.*

Where to Stay

$$ ⊞ **Bahia Honda State Park.** You usually have to pay big bucks for the caliber of water views from the cabins here. Each cabin is completely furnished (although there's no television, radio, or phone); has two bedrooms, full kitchen, and bath; and sleeps six. The park also has popular campsites ($19–$21 per night), suitable for motor homes and tents. Cabins and campsites usually book up early, so reserve up to 11 months before your planned visit. ⊠ *MM 37, OS, 36850 Overseas Hwy., 33043* ☎ *305/872-2353 or 800/326-3521* ⊕ *www.reserveamerica.com* ⇝ *80 campsites, 48 RV sites, 32 tent sites; 3 duplex cabins* ⚭ *Grill, picnic area, kitchens, beach, dive shop, dock, snorkeling, boating, marina, fishing, bicycles, shop; no room phones, no room TVs* ▭ *AE, D, MC, V.*

The Outdoors

Bahia Honda Dive Shop (⊠ MM 37, OS ☎ 305/872–3210 ⊕ www.bahiahondapark.com), the concessionaire at Bahia Honda State Park, manages a 19-slip marina; rents wet suits, snorkel equipment, and corrective masks; and operates twice-a-day offshore-reef snorkel trips ($26 plus $5 for equipment) that run almost three hours (with 90 minutes on the reef). Park visitors looking for other fun can rent kayaks ($10 per hour single, $18 double), bicycles, fishing rods, and beach chairs.

Big Pine Key

⑩ *MM 32–30.*

In the Florida Keys, more than 20 animals and plants are endangered or threatened. Among them is the Key deer, which stands about 30 inches at the shoulders and is a subspecies of the Virginia white-tailed deer. The 8,542-acre **National Key Deer Refuge** was established in 1957 to protect the dwindling population of Key deer. These deer once ranged throughout the Lower and Middle Keys, but hunting, habitat destruction, and a growing human population had caused their numbers to decline to fewer than 50. However, under the refuge's aegis the deer have made a comeback, more than doubling their numbers to around 800. The best place to see Key deer in the refuge is at the end of Key Deer Boulevard (Route 940), off U.S. 1, and on No Name Key, a sparsely populated island just east of Big Pine Key. Deer may turn up along the road at any time of day, so drive slowly. Feeding them is against the law and puts them in danger. The refuge also has 22 listed endangered and threatened species of plants and animals, including 5 that are found nowhere else in the world. The **Blue Hole**, a quarry left over from railroad days, is the largest body of fresh water in the Keys. From the observation platform and nearby walking trail, you might see alligators, birds, turtles, Key deer, and other wildlife. There are two well-marked trails: the Jack Watson Nature Trail (⅔ mi), named after an environmentalist and the refuge's first warden; and the Fred Mannillo Nature Trail, one of the most wheelchair-accessible places to see an unspoiled pine rockland forest. The visitor center has exhibits on Keys biology and ecology. The refuge also provides information on the Key West National Wildlife Refuge and the Great White Heron National Wildlife Refuge. Both, accessible only by water, are popular with kayak outfitters. ☒ *Visitor Center/ Headquarters, Big Pine Shopping Center, 28950 Watson Blvd., MM 30.5, BS* ☎ *305/872–0774* ⊕ *nationalkeydeer.fws.gov* ☒ *Free* ☉ *Daily sunrise–sunset; headquarters weekdays 8–5.*

Where to Stay & Eat

¢–$ ✕ **No Name Pub.** If you don't like change you'll be delighted by this ramshackle American-casual establishment, in existence since 1936. Locals come for the cold beer, excellent pizza (from $6.25), and sometimes questionable companionship. The owners have conceded to the times by introducing a full menu, adding "city food" like pasta, seafood baskets ($10.95), and chicken wings. The lighting is poor, the furnishings are rough, and the jukebox doesn't play Ricky Martin. It's hard to find but worth the search if you want to experience the Keys as old-timers say they once were. ☒ *MM 30, BS, N. Watson Blvd., turn north at Big Pine Key traffic light, right at the fork, left at the 4-way stop, and then over a humpback bridge; pub is on left, before the No Name Bridge* ☎ *305/872–9115* ⊕ *www.nonamepub.com* ▭ *D, MC, V.*

★ $$ ▦ **Casa Grande.** On a beautiful white-sand beach abutting a rocky shoreline, this adults-only B&B offers a gracious island stay under the proprietorship of Kathleen Threlkeld. Her warm personality pervades the Mediterranean-style house with a massive Spanish door, mainly contemporary furnishings, and high open-beam ceilings. There are a screened porch and rich Berber carpeting in the spacious guest rooms. A screened, second-story waterfront atrium provides you the opportunity to gaze out across the soothing sea. Then on cool nights, cozy up to the sitting-room fireplace or watch TV. ☒ *MM 33, OS, 1619 Long Beach Dr.* ☝ *Box 430378, 33043* ☎ *305/872–2878* ⊕ *www.floridakeys. net/casagrande* �káз *3 rooms* ♿ *Grill, picnic area, fans, refrigerators, hot tub, beach, dock, snorkeling, windsurfing, boating, bicycles; no kids, no room TVs, no smoking* ▭ *No credit cards* ❄❄ *BP.*

$$ ▦ **Deer Run.** Enjoy Florida wildlife up-close at this 2-acre beachfront B&B. A herd of Key deer regularly forages along the beach a few feet from the back door. Innkeeper Sue Abbott also keeps cats and caged tropical birds. She is caring and informed, well settled and hospitable. Two large oceanfront rooms are furnished with whitewashed wicker and king-size beds. An upstairs unit looks out on the sea through trees. Guests share a living room, 52-ft veranda cooled by paddle fans, hammocks, a barbecue grill, and water toys. ☒ *MM 33, OS, 1985 Long Beach Dr.* ☝ *Box 430431, 33043* ☎ *305/872–2015* ☒ *305/872–2842* ⊕ *floridakeys.net/deer* ➚ *3 room* ♿ *Fans, cable TV, outdoor hot tub, beach, boating, bicycles; no kids, no smoking* ▭ *No credit cards* ❄❄ *BP.*

★ $–$$ ▦ **The Barnacle.** With very little air pollution in the area, the star-flecked moonlit nights seen from this B&B's atrium are as romantic as the sunny days spent lazing on the beach. Owners Tim and Jane Marquis offer two second-floor rooms in the main house; one in a cottage with a kitchen; another, below the house, that opens to the beach; and a smaller fifth room with skylights on the roof. Guest rooms are large. The former owners of a diving business, Tim and Jane offer personalized snorkel and dive charters and fishing excursions. ☒ *MM 33, OS, 1557 Long Beach Dr., 33043* ☎ *305/872–3298 or 800/465–9100* ☒ *305/872– 3863* ⊕ *www.thebarnacle.net* ➚ *5 rooms* ♿ *Fans, some kitchens, refrigerators, cable TV, outdoor hot tub, beach, dive shop, snorkeling, boating, bicycles; no kids under 16, no smoking* ▭ *D, MC, V* ❄❄ *BP.*

¢–$ ⌧ **Big Pine Key Fishing Lodge.** It's a family affair at this 30-year-old
Fodor'sChoice combination lodge and campground. Rooms and RV and tent sites
★ ($30–$37 per site) are attractively priced and have tile floors, wicker
furniture, doors that allow sea breezes to blow through, queen-size
beds, a second-bedroom loft, and vaulted ceilings. A skywalk joins
them with a pool and deck. Immaculately clean tile lines the spacious
bathhouse for campers. Separate game and recreation rooms house
TVs, organized family-oriented activities, and other amusements, and
there is dockage along a 735-ft canal. A three-day minimum is required.
Discounts are available for weekly and monthly stays. ⊠ *MM 33, OS*
⌂ *Box 430513, 33043* ☎ *305/872–2351* 🖨 *305/872–3868* ↝ *16
rooms; 158 campsites, 101 with full hookups, 57 without hookups*
⚴ *Picnic area, some kitchens, cable TV, pool, dock, boating, billiards,
Ping-Pong, shuffleboard, recreation room, Internet* ⊟ *D, MC, V.*

The Outdoors

BIKING A good 10 mi of paved and unpaved roads run from MM 30.3, BS, along
Wilder Road, across the bridge to No Name Key, and along Key Deer
Boulevard into the National Key Deer Refuge. You might see some Key
deer. Stay off the trails that lead into wetlands, where fat tires can do
damage to the environment.

Marty Baird, owner of **Big Pine Bicycle Center** (⊠ MM 30.9, BS ☎ 305/
872–0130), is an avid rider and enjoys sharing his knowledge of great
places to ride. He's also skilled at selecting the right bike for customers
to rent or purchase, and he knows his repairs, too. His old-fashioned
single-speed, fat-tire cruisers for adults rent for $6 per half day, $9 for
a full day, and $34 a week, second week $17; children for $5, $7, $26,
and $13. Helmets, baskets, and locks are included. Although the shop
is closed on Sunday, join him there Sunday mornings at 8 in winter for
a free off-road fun ride.

FISHING Fish with pros year-round in air-conditioned comfort with **Strike Zone
Charters** (⊠ MM 29.6, BS, 29675 Overseas Hwy., 33043 ☎ 305/872–
9863 or 800/654–9560 ⊕ www.strikezonecharter.com). Deep-sea charter rates are $425 for a half day, $550 for a full day. It also offers flats
fishing in the Gulf of Mexico.

SCUBA DIVING & **Strike Zone Charters.** (⊠ MM 29.6, BS, 29675 Overseas Hwy., 33043
SNORKELING ☎ 305/872–9863 or 800/654–9560 ⊕ www.strikezonecharter.com)
leads dive excursions to the wreck of the 210-ft *Adolphus Busch* ($50)
and scuba ($40) and snorkel ($25) trips to Looe Key Reef.

WATER SPORTS **Big Pine Kayak Adventures** (⊠ Old Wooden Bridge Fishing Camp, MM
30, BS, turn right at traffic light, continue on Wilder Rd. toward No
Name Key, ☎ 305/872–7474 ⊕ www.keyskayaktours.com) has a complete rental fleet and makes it very convenient to rent kayaks. Along with
bringing kayaks to your lodging or put-in point anywhere between
Seven Mile Bridge to Stock Island, the group will rent you a kayak and
then ferry you to remote islands with explicit instructions on how to
paddle back on your own. Rentals are by the half day or full day. There
are also myriad tours and fishing and sailing charters.

Little Torch Key

⑪ *MM 28–29.*

With a few exceptions, this key and its neighbor islands are more jump-
ing-off points for divers headed for Looe Key Reef, a few miles offshore,
than destinations themselves.

need a break?

The intoxicating aroma of rich, roasting coffee beans at **Baby's Coffee** (✉ MM 15, OS, Saddlebunch Keys ☎ 305/744–9866 or 800/523–2326) arrests you at the door of "the Southernmost Coffee Roaster." Buy it by the pound or by the cup along with fresh-baked goods. While sipping your warm joe, browse through the prints of Olga Manosalvas, whose work appears in tony galleries from Key West to the Hamptons.

5

The undeveloped backcountry is at your door, making this an ideal location for fishing and kayaking, too. Nearby **Ramrod Key,** which also caters to divers bound for Looe Key, derives its name from a ship that wrecked on nearby reefs in the early 1800s.

Where to Stay & Eat

★ $$$$ ✕ **Little Palm Restaurant.** The waterfront dining room at the exclusive Little Palm Island resort is one of the most romantic spots in the Keys. Chef Adam Votaw has crafted the contemporary menu to reflect a mix of Caribbean, French, and Asian tastes with dishes such as Gruyère soufflé, barbecued salmon, lobster croissants, and mojo seared chicken breast. The dining room is open to nonguests on a reservations-only basis. The tropical Sunday brunch buffet is the most popular time to come. *✉ MM 28.5, OS, 28500 Overseas Hwy., 33042 ☎ 305/872–2551 Reservations essential ▭ AE, D, DC, MC, V.*

$$$$ Fodor'sChoice ★ **Little Palm Island.** *Haute tropicale* best describes this luxury retreat on a 5-acre palm-fringed island 3 mi offshore. The 28 oceanfront one-bedroom, thatch-roof bungalow suites have Mexican-tile baths, mosquito netting–draped king beds, and wicker and rattan furniture. Other comforts include an indoor and outdoor shower, private veranda, a separate living room, and robes and slippers. Two Island Grand Suites are twice the size of the others and offer his-and-her bathrooms, an outdoor hot tub, and uncompromising ocean views. Cellular phones are *verboten* in public areas. *✉ MM 28.5, OS, 28500 Overseas Hwy., 33042 ☎ 305/872–2524 or 800/343–8567 ⎙ 305/872–4843 ⊕ www.littlepalmisland.com ⇨ 30 suites ♁ Restaurant, fans, in-room data ports, in-room safes, some in-room hot tubs, minibars, pool, hair salon, health club, massage, sauna, spa, beach, dive shop, dock, snorkeling, windsurfing, boating, marina, fishing, bar, library, shops, concierge, airport shuttle; no kids under 16, no room phones, no room TVs ▭ AE, D, DC, MC, V.*

¢–$ Fodor'sChoice ★ **Parmer's Place.** This is the perfect spot for a family getaway in the Lower Keys. You'll stay in family-style waterfront cottages with a deck or balcony. It's spread out on 5 landscaped acres, so the kids have room to play. And the price is right. Lots of families agree. Many are repeat guests and recommend it. The proprietors treat them all like family. For couples, the motel rooms are comfortable for two people and the best buy. There are water activities galore, 19 aviaries with more than 70 birds, and a sunny breakfast room. *✉ MM 29, BS, 565 Barry Ave., 33042 ☎ 305/872–2157 ⎙ 305/872–2014 ⊕ www.parmersplace.com ⇨ 45 units, 18 rooms, 12 efficiencies, 15 apartments ♁ Dining room, fans, some kitchens, cable TV, pool, dock, boating, bicycles, laundry facilities, Internet; no room phones, no-smoking rooms ▭ AE, D, MC, V ▯◎▯ CP.*

The Outdoors

FISHING The only thing grouchy about Captain Mark André of the **Grouch Charters** (✉ Summerland Key Cove Marina, MM 24.5, OS, Summerland Key ☎ 305/745–1172 or 305/304–0039 ⊕ www.grouchcharters.com) is his boat's name, derived from his father's nickname. This knowledgeable captain takes up to six passengers on deep-sea fishing trips ($450 for a half day, $625 for a full day). He also has oceanfront vacation rentals for $725–$850 a week and can package accommodations, fishing, snorkeling, and sightseeing for better deals.

SCUBA DIVING & SNORKELING
In 1744 the HMS *Looe,* a British warship, ran aground and sank on one of the most beautiful and diverse coral reefs in the Keys. Today, **Looe Key Reef** owes its name to the ill-fated ship. The 5.3-square-nautical-mi reef, part of the **Florida Keys National Marine Sanctuary** (⊠ MM 27.5, OS, 216 Ann St., Key West 33040 ☎ 305/292–0311), has stands of elk-horn coral on its eastern margin, purple sea fans, and abundant sponges and sea urchins. On its seaward side, it drops almost vertically 50–90 ft. Snorkelers and divers will find the sanctuary a quiet place to observe reef life, except in July, when the annual Underwater Music Festival pays homage to Looe Key's beauty and promotes reef awareness with six hours of music broadcast via underwater speakers. Dive shops and private char-ters transport hundreds of divers to hear the spectacle, which includes Caribbean, classical, jazz, New Age, and, of course, Jimmy Buffett.

Rather than the customary morning and afternoon two-tank, two-lo-cation trips offered by most dive shops, **Looe Key Reef Resort Dive Cen-ter** (⊠ MM 27.5, OS ⬦ Box 509, Ramrod Key 33042 ☎ 305/872–2215 Ext. 2 or 800/942–5397 ⊕ www.diveflakeys.com), the closest dive shop to Looe Key Reef, runs a single three-tank, three-location dive from 10 AM to 3 PM. The maximum depth is 30 ft, so snorkelers and divers go on the same boat. On Saturday and Wednesday, they run a 3/3 dive on wrecks and reefs in the area. It's part of the full-service Looe Key Reef Resort, which, not surprisingly, caters to divers. The dive boat, a 45-ft Corinthian catamaran, is docked outside the hotel, whose guests get a 15% discount on tanks, weights, and snorkeling equipment.

en route
The huge object that looks like a white whale floating over Cudjoe Key (MM 23–21) is not a figment of your imagination. It's Fat Albert, a radar balloon that monitors local air and water traffic.

KEY WEST

MM 4–0.

Situated 150 mi from Miami and just 90 mi from Havana, this tropi-cal island city has always maintained a strong sense of detachment, even after it was connected to the rest of the United States—by the railroad in 1912 and by the Overseas Highway in 1938. The U.S. government acquired Key West from Spain in 1821 along with the rest of Florida. The Spanish had named the island Cayo Hueso (Bone Key) after the Na-tive American skeletons they found on its shores. In 1823 Uncle Sam sent Commodore David S. Porter to chase pirates away. For three decades, the primary industry in Key West was wrecking—rescuing people and salvaging cargo from ships that foundered on the nearby reefs. According to some reports, when pickings were lean, the wreckers hung out lights to lure ships aground. Their business declined after 1849, when the federal government began building lighthouses.

In 1845 the army started construction of Fort Taylor, which held Key West for the Union during the Civil War. After the war, an influx of Cuban dissidents unhappy with Spain's rule brought the cigar industry here. Fishing, shrimping, and sponge-gathering became important industries, and a pineapple-canning factory opened. Major military installations were established during the Spanish-American War and World War I. Through much of the 19th century and into the second decade of the

20th, Key West was Florida's wealthiest city in per-capita terms. But in 1929 the local economy began to unravel. Modern ships no longer needed to provision in Key West, cigar making moved to Tampa, Hawaii dominated the pineapple industry, and the sponges succumbed to a blight. Then the Depression hit, and the military moved out. By 1934 half the population was on relief. The city defaulted on its bond payments, and the Federal Emergency Relief Administration took over the city and county governments.

By promoting Key West as a tourist destination, federal officials attracted 40,000 visitors during the 1934–35 winter season, but when the 1935 Labor Day hurricane struck the Middle Keys, it wiped out the railroad and the tourist trade. An important naval center during World War II and the Korean conflict, the island remains a strategic listening post on the doorstep of Fidel Castro's Cuba. It was during the 1960s that the fringes of society began moving here and in the mid-'70s that gay guest houses began opening in rapid succession. In April 1982 the U.S. Border Patrol threw a roadblock across the Overseas Highway just south of Florida City to catch drug runners and illegal aliens. Traffic backed up for miles as Border Patrol agents searched vehicles and demanded that the occupants prove U.S. citizenship. City officials in Key West, outraged at being treated like foreigners by the federal government, staged a mock secession and formed their own "nation," the so-called Conch Republic. They hoisted a flag and distributed mock border passes, visas, and Conch currency. The embarrassed Border Patrol dismantled its roadblock, and now an annual festival recalls the secessionists' victory.

Key West reflects a diverse population: native "Conchs" (white Key Westers, many of whom trace their ancestry to the Bahamas), fresh-water Conchs (longtime residents who migrated from somewhere else years ago), black Bahamians (descendants of those who worked the railroads and burned charcoal), Hispanics (primarily Cuban immigrants), recent refugees from the urban sprawl of mainland Florida, navy and air force personnel, and an assortment of vagabonds, drifters, and dropouts in search of refuge. The island is decidedly gay-friendly—gays make up at least 20% of Key West's citizenry. It's not unusual to see gay couples holding hands or to see advertisements aimed at gay customers. While gay men and lesbians will feel welcome in almost all establishments, there are numerous accommodations, restaurants, clubs, businesses, and visitor information services that cater exclusively to a gay clientele.

Although the rest of the Keys are more oriented to nature and the outdoors, Key West has more of a city feel. Few open spaces remain, as promoters continue to churn out restaurants, galleries, shops, and museums to interpret the city's intriguing past. As a tourist destination, Key West has a lot to sell—an average temperature of 79°F, quaint 19th-century architecture, and a laid-back lifestyle. There's also a growing calendar of festivals and artistic and cultural events—including the Conch Republic Celebration in April and a Halloween Fantasy Fest. Few cities of its size—a mere 2 mi by 4 mi—offer the joie de vivre of this one. Yet, as elsewhere, when preservation has successfully revived once-tired towns, next have come those unmindful of style and eager for a buck. Duval Street can look like a strip mall of T-shirt shops and tour shills. Mass marketers directing the town's tourism have attracted cruise ships, which dwarf the town's skyline, and Duval Street floods with day-trippers who gawk at the earringed hippies with dogs in their bike baskets, gay couples walking down the street holding hands, and the oddball lot of locals.

Old Town

The heart of Key West, this historic area runs from White Street west to the waterfront. Beginning in 1822, wharves, warehouses, chandleries, ship-repair facilities, and eventually in 1891 the U.S. Custom House sprang up around the deep harbor to accommodate the navy's large ships and other sailing vessels. Wealthy wreckers, merchants, and sea captains built lavish houses near the bustling waterfront. A remarkable number of these fine Victorian and pre-Victorian structures have been restored to their original grandeur and now serve as homes, guest houses, and museums. These, along with the dwellings of famous writers, artists, and politicians who've come to Key West over the past 175 years, are among the area's approximately 3,000 historic structures. Old Town also has the city's finest restaurants and hotels, lively street life, and popular nightspots.

a good tour

To cover a lot of sights, take the Old Town Trolley, which lets you get off and reboard a later trolley, or the Conch Tour Train. Old Town is also very manageable on foot, bicycle, or moped, but be warned that the tour below covers a lot of ground. You'll want either to pick and choose from it or break it into two days. Start on Whitehead Street at the **Hemingway House** ⑫ ▶, the author's former home, and then cross the street and climb to the top of the **Lighthouse Museum** ⑬ for a spectacular view. Exit through the museum's parking lot and cross Truman Avenue to the **Lofton B. Sands African-Bahamian Museum** ⑭ to learn about nearly two centuries of black history in Key West. Return to Whitehead Street and follow it north to Angela Street; then turn right. At Margaret Street, the **City Cemetery** ⑮ has above-ground vaults and unusual headstone inscriptions. Head north on Margaret to Southard Street, turn left, then right onto Simonton Street. Halfway up the block, Free School Lane is occupied by **Nancy Forrester's Secret Garden** ⑯. After touring it, return west on Southard to Duval Street, turn right, and look at the lovely tiles and woodwork in the **San Carlos Institute** ⑰. Return again to Southard Street, turn right, and follow it through Truman Annex to **Fort Zachary Taylor State Historic Site** ⑱; after viewing the fort, take a dip at the beach.

Go back to Simonton Street, walk north, and then turn left on Caroline Street; climb to the widow's walk on top of **Curry Mansion** ⑲. A left on Duval Street puts you in front of the **Duval Street Wreckers Museum** ⑳, Key West's oldest house. Continue west into Truman Annex to see the **Harry S Truman Little White House Museum** ㉑, President Truman's vacation residence. Return east on Caroline and turn left on Whitehead to visit the **Audubon House and Gardens** ㉒, honoring the artist-naturalist. Follow Whitehead north to Greene Street and turn left to see the salvaged sea treasures of the **Mel Fisher Maritime Heritage Society Museum** ㉓. At Whitehead's north end are the **Key West Aquarium** ㉔ and the **Key West Museum of Art and History** ㉕, the former historic U.S. Custom House. By late afternoon you should be ready to cool off with a dip or catch a few rays at the beach. (Heed signs about the water's condition.) From the aquarium, head east two blocks to the end of Simonton Street, where you'll find the appropriately named **Simonton Street Beach** ㉖. On the Atlantic side of Old Town is **South Beach** ㉗, named for its location at the southern end of Duval Street. If you've brought your pet, stroll a few blocks east to **Dog Beach** ㉘, at the corner of Vernon and Waddell streets. A little farther east is **Higgs Beach–Astro Park** ㉙, on Atlantic Boulevard between White and Reynolds streets. As the sun starts to sink, return to the north end of Old Town and follow the crowds to Mallory Square, behind the aquarium, to watch Key West's nightly sunset spectacle. For dinner, head east on Caroline Street to **Historic Seaport at Key West Bight** ㉚ (formerly known simply as Key West Bight), a renovated area where there are numerous restaurants and bars.

TIMING Allow two full days to see all the Old Town museums and homes, especially with a little shopping thrown in. For a narrated trip on the tour train or trolley, budget 1½ hours to ride the loop without getting off, an entire day if you plan to get off and on at some of the sights and restaurants.

What to See

㉒ **Audubon House and Gardens.** If you've ever seen an engraving by ornithologist John James Audubon, you'll understand why his name is synonymous with birds. See his work in this three-story house, which was built in the 1840s for Captain John Geiger but now commemorates Audubon's 1832 stop in Key West while he was traveling through Florida to study birds. Several rooms of period antiques and a children's room are also of interest. Admission includes an audiotape (in English, French, German, or Spanish) for a self-guided tour of the house and tropical gardens, complemented by an informational booklet and signs that identify the rare indigenous plants and trees. ⊠ *205 Whitehead St.* ☎ *305/294–2116* ⊕ *www.audubonhouse.com* ⊠ *$9* ⊙ *Daily 9:30–5.*

need a break? For a partying kind of town, Key West restaurants are oddly unaccommodating for those looking for breakfast at noon, or dinner at midnight. If your appetite is out of sync with most serving schedules, **Iguana Cafe** (⊠ 425C Greene St. ☎ 305/296–6420) will come to the rescue 24 hours a day. Just off Duval Street, the simple shacklike dive puts out tasty recipes from around the globe.

★ ⑮ **City Cemetery.** You can learn almost as much about a town's history through its cemetery as through its historic houses. Key West's celebrated 20-acre burial place is no exception. Among the interesting plots are a memorial to the sailors killed in the sinking of the battleship U.S.S. *Maine*, carved angels and lambs marking graves of children, and grand aboveground crypts. There are separate plots for Catholics, Jews, and martyrs of Cuba. You're free to walk around the cemetery on your own, but the best way to see it is on a 60-minute tour given by the staff and volunteers of the Historic Florida Keys Foundation. Tours leave from the main gate, and reservations are required. ⊠ *Margaret and Angela Sts.* ☎ *305/292–6718* ⊠ *$10* ⊙ *Daily, sunrise–6 PM, tours Tues. and Thurs. at 9:30 (call for additional times).*

⑲ **Curry Mansion.** See the opulence enjoyed by Key West's 19th-century millionaires in this well-preserved 22-room house. Construction was begun by William Curry, a ship salvager and Key West's first millionaire, and completed in 1899 by his son, Milton Curry. The owners have restored most of the house and turned it into a B&B. Take an unhurried self-guided tour; a brochure describes the home's history and contents. ⊠ *511 Caroline St.* ☎ *305/294–5349* ⊕ *currymansion.com* ⊠ *$5* ⊙ *Daily 9–5.*

㉘ **Dog Beach.** Next to Louie's Backyard, this small beach—the only one in Key West where dogs are allowed—has a shore that's a mix of sand and rocks. ⊠ *Vernon and Waddell Sts.* ☎ *No phone* ⊠ *Free* ⊙ *Daily sunrise–sunset.*

⑳ **Duval Street Wreckers Museum.** Most of Key West's early wealthy residents made their fortunes from the sea. Among them was Francis Watlington, a sea captain and wrecker, who in 1829 built this house, alleged to be the oldest house in South Florida. Six rooms are open, fur-

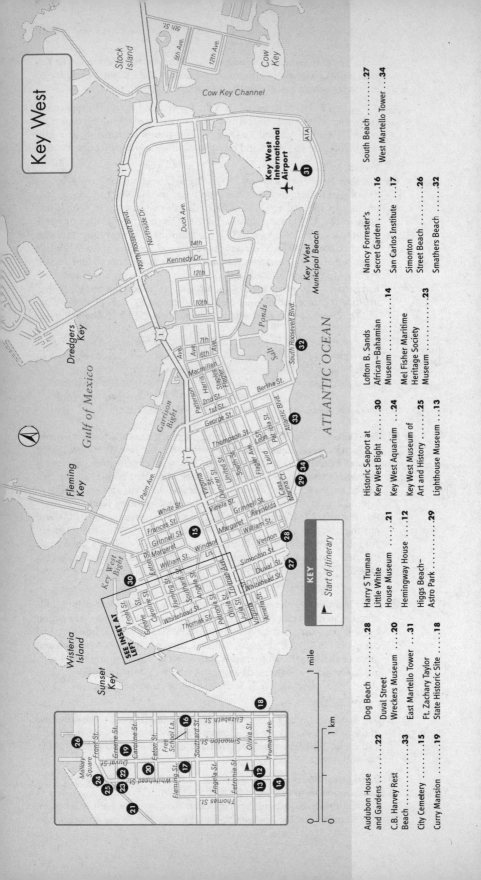

Key West

Stock Island

Cow Key

Cow Key Channel

Key West International Airport ▲ 31

A1A

ATLANTIC OCEAN

Key West Municipal Beach

Gulf of Mexico

Dredgers Key

Fleming Key

Wisteria Island

Sunset Key

Garrison Bight

Key West Bight

SEE INSET AT LEFT

KEY
▲ Start of itinerary

Mallory Square

nished with 18th- and 19th-century antiques and providing exhibits on the island's wrecking industry of the 1800s, which made Key West one of the most affluent towns in the country. ⊠ *322 Duval St.* ☎ *305/294– 9502* ⊠ *$5* ⊙ *Daily 10–4.*

★ ⑱ **Fort Zachary Taylor State Historic Site.** Construction of the fort began in 1845, and in 1861, even though Florida seceded from the Union during the Civil War, Yankee forces used the fort as a base to block Confederate shipping (more than 1,500 Confederate vessels were detained in Key West's harbor). The fort, finally completed in 1866, was also used in the Spanish-American War. Take a 30-minute guided tour of this National Historic Landmark at noon and 2 PM. On the first weekend in March, a celebration called Civil War Days includes costumed reenactments and demonstrations. Its uncrowded beach is the best in Key West. There is an adjoining picnic area with barbecue grills and shade trees. ⊠ *End of Southard St., through Truman Annex* ☎ *305/292– 6713* ⊕ *www.forttaylor.com* ⊠ *$2.50 for 1 person, $5 per vehicle for 2 people, plus 50¢ per each additional person; $1.50 per pedestrian or bicyclist* ⊙ Daily 8–sunset, tours noon and 2.

㉑ **Harry S Truman Little White House Museum.** In a letter to his wife during one of his visits, President Harry S Truman wrote, "Dear Bess, you should see the house. The place is all redecorated, new furniture and everything." If he visited today, he'd write something similar. There is a photographic review of visiting dignitaries and permanent audiovisual and artifact exhibits on the Florida Keys as a presidential retreat; Ulysses S. Grant, John F. Kennedy, and Jimmy Carter are among the chief executives who passed through here. Tours lasting 45 minutes begin every 15 minutes. On the grounds of **Truman Annex**, a 103-acre former military parade grounds and barracks, the home served as a winter White House for presidents Truman, Eisenhower, and Kennedy. The two-bedroom Presidential Suite with a veranda and sundeck is available for a novelty overnight stay. ⊠ *111 Front St.* ☎ *305/294–9911* ⊕ *www.trumanlittlewhitehouse.com* ⊠ *$10* ⊙ *Daily 9–5, grounds 8–sunset.*

★ ▶ ⑫ **Hemingway Home and Museum.** Guided tours of Ernest Hemingway's home are full of anecdotes about the author's life in the community and his household quarrels with wife Pauline. While living here between 1931 and 1942, Hemingway wrote about 70% of his life's work, including *For Whom the Bell Tolls.* Few of the family's belongings remain, but photographs help illustrate his life, and scores of descendants of Hemingway's cats have free reign of the property. Literary buffs should be aware that there are no curated exhibits from which to gain much insight into Hemingway's writing career. Tours begin every 10 minutes and take 25–30 minutes; then you're free to explore on your own. ⊠ *907 Whitehead St.* ☎ *305/294–1136* ⊕ *www.hemingwayhome.com* ⊠ *$10* ⊙ *Daily 9–5.*

☺ ㉙ **Higgs Beach–Astro Park.** This Monroe County park is a popular sunbathing spot. A nearby grove of Australian pines provides shade, and the West Martello Tower provides shelter should a storm suddenly sweep in. Across the street, **Astro Park** is a popular children's playground. The beach also has a marker commemorating the gravesite of 295 enslaved Africans who died after being rescued from three South America–bound slave ships in 1860. Archaeologists uncovered several of the forgotten graves and the site was consecrated in 2002. ⊠ *Atlantic Blvd. between White and Reynolds Sts.* ☎ *No phone* ⊠ *Free* ⊙ *Daily 6 AM–11 PM.*

㉚ **Historic Seaport at Key West Bight.** What used to be a funky—in some places even seedy—part of town is now an 8½-acre historic restoration

CloseUp

HEMINGWAY WAS HERE

N A TOWN WHERE Pulitzer Prize–winning writers are almost as common as coconuts, Ernest Hemingway stands out. Bars and restaurants around the island claim that he ate or drank there, and though he may not have been at all of them, like all legends, his larger-than-life image continues to grow.

Hemingway came to Key West in 1928 at the urging of writer John dos Passos and rented a house with wife number two, Pauline Pfeiffer. They spent winters in the Keys and summers in Europe and Wyoming, occasionally taking African safaris. Along the way they had two sons, Patrick and Gregory. In 1931 Pauline's wealthy uncle Gus gave the couple the house at 907 Whitehead Street, now known as Hemingway House and Key West's number one tourist attraction. They renovated the palatial home, added a swimming pool, and put in a tropical garden with peacocks.

In 1935, when the visitor bureau included the house in a tourist brochure, Hemingway promptly built the high brick wall that surrounds it today. He wrote of the visitor bureau's offense in a 1935 essay for Esquire, stating, "The house at present occupied by your correspondent is listed as number eighteen in a compilation of the forty-eight things for a tourist to see in Key West. So there will be no difficulty in a tourist finding it or any other of the sights of the city, a map has been prepared by the local F.E.R.A. authorities to be presented to each arriving visitor . . . This is all very flattering to the easily bloated ego of your correspondent but very hard on production."

During his time in Key West, Hemingway penned some of his most important works, including A Farewell to Arms, To Have and Have Not, Green Hills of Africa, and Death in the Afternoon. His rigorous schedule consisted of writing almost every morning in his second-story studio above the pool, then promptly descending the stairs at midday. By afternoon and evening he was ready for drinking, fishing, swimming, boxing, and hanging around with the boys.

One close friend was Joe Russell, a craggy fisherman and owner of the rugged bar Sloppy Joe's, originally at 428 Greene Street but now at 201 Duval Street. Russell was the only one in town who would cash Hemingway's $1,000 royalty check. Russell and Charles Thompson introduced him to deep-sea fishing, which became fodder for his writing. Another of Hemingway's loves was boxing. He set up a ring in his yard and paid local fighters to box with him, and he refereed matches at Blue Heaven, then a saloon but now a restaurant, at 729 Thomas Street.

Feeling at home among Key West's characters, Hemingway honed his macho image dressed in cutoffs and old shirts and took on the name Papa. In turn, he gave his friends new names and used them as characters in his stories. Joe Russell became Freddy, captain of the Queen Conch charter boat in To Have and Have Not.

Hemingway stayed in Key West for 11 years before leaving Pauline for wife number three. A foreign correspondent, Martha Gellhorn, arrived in town and headed for Sloppy Joe's, intent on meeting him. When the always restless Hemingway packed up to cover the Spanish civil war, so did she. Though he returned to Pauline occasionally, he finally left her and Key West to be with Martha in 1939. They married a year later and moved to Cuba, and he seldom returned to Key West after that. Pauline and the boys stayed on in the house, which sold in 1951 for $80,000, 10 times its original cost.

— Diane Marshall

project of 100 businesses, including waterfront restaurants, open-air peo-
ple- and dog-friendly bars, museums, clothing stores, bait shops, docks,
a marina, a wedding chapel, the Waterfront Market, the Key West Row-
ing Club, and dive shops. It's all linked by the 2-mi waterfront **Har-
borwalk,** which runs between Front and Grinnell streets, passing big ships,
schooners, sunset cruises, fishing charters, and glass-bottom boats. Additional construction continues on outlying projects.

24 **Key West Aquarium.** Explore the fascinating underwater realm of the Keys
without getting wet at this kid-friendly aquarium. Hundreds of brightly
colored tropical fish and sea creatures live here. A touch tank enables
you to handle starfish, sea cucumbers, horseshoe and hermit crabs,
even horse and queen conchs—living totems of the Conch Republic. Built
in 1934 by the Works Progress Administration as the world's first open-
air aquarium, most of the building has been enclosed for all-weather
viewing. Guided tours include shark feedings. ⊠ *1 Whitehead St.* ☎ *305/
296–2051* ⊕ *www.keywestaquarium.com* ⊠ *$9* ⊙ *Daily 9–6; tours at
11, 1, 3, and 4:30.*

25 **Key West Museum of Art and History.** When Key West was designated a
Fodor'sChoice U.S. port of entry in the early 1820s, a custom house was established.
★ Salvaged cargoes from ships wrecked on the reefs could legally enter here,
thus setting the stage for Key West to become the richest city in Florida.
Following a $9 million restoration, the imposing redbrick and terra-cotta
Richardsonian Romanesque–style U.S. Custom House reopened as a museum. Its main gallery displays major rotating exhibits. Smaller galleries
have long-term and changing exhibits about the history of Key West,
such as *Remember the Maine.* ⊠ *281 Front St.* ☎ *305/295–6616*
⊕ *www.kwahs.com* ⊠ *$6* ⊙ *Daily 9–5.*

13 **Lighthouse Museum.** For the best view in town and a history lesson at
the same time, climb the 88 steps to the top of this 92-ft lighthouse. It
was built in 1847. About 15 years later, a Fresnel lens was installed at
a cost of $1 million. The keeper lived in the adjacent 1887 clapboard
house, which now exhibits vintage photographs, ship models, nautical
charts, and lighthouse artifacts from all along the Key reefs. ⊠ *938 Whitehead St.* ☎ *305/294–0012* ⊠ *$8* ⊙ *Daily 9:30–5 (last admission at 4:30).*

14 **Lofton B. Sands African-Bahamian Museum.** Vintage photographs and
memorabilia chronicle the nearly 200-year history of Key West's black
community in this modest 1928 house on the edge of Bahama Village.
The house was built by the namesake owner, a master electrician, in the
mid-1920s in what was then called Black Town or Africa Town. There
are photographs of graduations and dances at the segregated high
school, photos of funeral parades, candids of people at social clubs and
balls, and posed wedding pictures. Crafts and demonstrations of traditional Afro-Caribbean arts are scheduled periodically. ⊠ *324 Truman
Ave.* ☎ *305/295–7337 or 305/293–9692* ⊠ *Free* ⊙ *Daily 10–6; tours
by appointment.*

23 **Mel Fisher Maritime Heritage Society Museum.** In 1622 two Spanish galleons
loaded with riches from South America foundered in a hurricane 40 mi
west of the Keys. In 1985 Mel Fisher recovered the treasures from the
lost ships, the *Nuestra Señora de Atocha* and the *Santa Margarita.* In
this museum, see, touch, and learn about some of the artifacts, including a gold bar weighing 6.3 troy pounds and a 77.76-carat natural emerald crystal worth almost $250,000. Exhibits on the second floor rotate
and might cover slave ships, including the excavated 17th-century *Hen-
rietta Marie,* or the evolution of Florida maritime history. ⊠ *200 Greene
St.* ☎ *305/294–2633* ⊕ *www.melfisher.org* ⊠ *$9* ⊙ *Daily 9:30–5.*

⑯ Nancy Forrester's Secret Garden. It's hard to believe that this green escape exists in the middle of Old Town Key West. Despite damage by hurricanes and pressures from developers, Nancy Forrester has maintained her naturalized garden for more than 30 years. Growing in harmony are rare palms and cycads, ferns, bromeliads, bright gingers and heliconias, gumbo-limbos strewn with orchids and vines, and a few surprises. The gardens are popular for weddings. An art gallery has botanical prints and environmental art. One-hour private tours cost $15 per person, four-person minimum. ⊠ *1 Free School La.* ☎ *305/294–0015* ⊕ *www.nfsgarden.org* ⬚ *$6* ⊙ *Daily 10–5.*

⑰ San Carlos Institute. South Florida's Cuban connection began long before Fidel Castro was born. The institute was founded in 1871 by Cuban immigrants. Now it contains a research library and museum rich with the history of Key West and 19th- and 20th-century Cuban exiles. Cuban patriot Jose Martí delivered speeches from the balcony of the auditorium, and opera star Enrico Caruso sang in the Opera House, which reportedly has exceptional acoustics. It's frequently used for concerts, lectures, films, and exhibits. ⊠ *516 Duval St.* ☎ *305/294–3887* ⬚ *$3* ⊙ *Tues.–Fri. 11–5, Sat. 11–9, Sun. 11–4.*

㉖ Simonton Street Beach. This small beach facing the gulf is a great place to watch boat traffic in the harbor. Parking, however, is difficult. There are rest rooms and a boat ramp. ⊠ *North end of Simonton St.* ☎ *No phone* ⬚ *Free* ⊙ *Daily 7 AM–11 PM.*

㉗ South Beach. On the Atlantic, this stretch of sand, also known as City Beach, is popular with travelers staying at nearby motels. It has limited parking and a nearby buffet-type restaurant, the South Beach Seafood and Raw Bar. ⊠ *Foot of Duval St.* ☎ *No phone* ⬚ *Free* ⊙ *Daily 7 AM–11 PM.*

New Town

The Overseas Highway splits as it enters Key West, the two forks rejoining to encircle New Town, the area east of White Street to Cow Key Channel. The southern fork runs along the shore as South Roosevelt Boulevard (Route A1A), past municipal beaches, salt ponds, and Key West International Airport. Along the north shore, North Roosevelt Boulevard (U.S. 1) passes the Key West Welcome Center, shopping centers, chain hotels, and fast-food eateries. Part of New Town was created with dredged fill. The island would have continued growing this way had the Army Corps of Engineers not determined in the early 1970s that it was detrimental to the nearby reef.

a good tour

Attractions are few in New Town. The best way to take in the sights is by car or moped. Take South Roosevelt Boulevard from the island's entrance to the historical museum exhibits at **East Martello Tower** ㉛ ►, near the airport. Continue past the Riggs Wildlife Refuge salt ponds and stop at **Smathers Beach** ㉜ for a dip, or continue west onto Atlantic Boulevard to **C. B. Harvey Rest Beach** ㉝. A little farther along, at the end of White Street, is the **West Martello Tower** ㉞ with its lovely tropical gardens.

TIMING   Allow one to two hours for brief stops at each attraction. If your interests lie in art, gardens, or Civil War history, you'll need three or four hours. Throw in time at the beach and make it a half-day affair.

What to See

㉝ C. B. Harvey Rest Beach. This beach and park were named after former Key West mayor and commissioner Cornelius Bradford Harvey. It has half a dozen picnic areas, dunes, and a wheelchair and bike path. ⊠ *Atlantic Blvd., east side of White Street Pier* ☎ *No phone* ⊠ *Free* ☉ *Daily 7 AM–11 PM.*

★ ▶ ③ **East Martello Tower.** As a Civil War citadel this spot never saw any action. Today, however, it serves as a museum with historical exhibits of the 19th to 20th century. Among the latter are relics of the U.S.S. *Maine*, a Cuban refugee raft, and books by famous writers—including seven Pulitzer Prize winners—who have lived in Key West. The tower, operated by the Key West Art and Historical Society, also has a collection of Stanley Papio's "junk art" sculptures and Cuban folk artist Mario Sanchez's chiseled and painted wooden carvings of historic Key West street scenes. Hours sometimes fluctuate; call in advance. ⊠ *3501 S. Roosevelt Blvd.* ☎ *305/296–3913* ⊠ *$6* ☉ *Weekends 9:30–5 (last admission at 4).*

③ **Smathers Beach.** This beach has nearly 2 mi of sand, rest rooms, picnic areas, and volleyball courts, all of which make it popular with the spring-break crowd. Trucks along the road rent rafts, Windsurfers, and other beach "toys." ⊠ *S. Roosevelt Blvd.* ☎ *No phone* ⊠ *Free* ☉ *Daily 7 AM–11 PM.*

③ **West Martello Tower.** Within the ruins of this Civil War–era fort is the Key West Garden Club, which maintains lovely gardens of native and tropical plants. It also holds art, orchid, and flower shows in March and November and leads private garden tours in March. ⊠ *Atlantic Blvd. and White St.* ☎ *305/294–3210* ⊠ *Donation welcome* ☉ *Tues.–Sat. 9:30–3.*

Where to Eat

American

$–$$$ ✕ **Michael's Restaurant.** White tablecloths, subdued lighting, oil paintings, and light music give Michael's the feel of a favorite restaurant in a comfortable urban neighborhood. Garden seating gives it that Key West touch. Try the *filet al forno* (tenderloin of beef rubbed with roasted garlic and Roquefort) or grouper Oscar, a fillet stuffed with jumbo lump crab. Chocolate lovers shouldn't miss the Volcano, a hot Ghirardelli chocolate cake with a molten center that erupts when the cake is broken open. ⊠ *532 Margaret St.* ☎ *305/295–1300* ☱ *AE, D, DC, MC, V* ☉ *No lunch.*

¢–$$$ ✕ **The Deli Restaurant.** Nostalgia is part of the appeal in this fourth-generation family-run 1950s-style eatery with huge desserts in glass display cases, a deli counter, friendly service, and a smoky kitchen. Roast pork and roast beef dinners, Papa's Fish Cakes (stuffed with fish and potatoes), and baked chicken with stuffing and cranberries are among the comfort foods. Most dishes cost $7–$11 and include a choice of two veggies and a biscuit or corn-bread muffin. The key lime pie is a bit sweet, but the bumbleberry pie, a mix of berries, is sweet, tart, and luscious enough to take another piece home. It's open for breakfast, lunch, and dinner. ⊠ *531 Truman Ave.* ☎ *305/294–1464* ☱ *D, MC, V.*

$–$$ ✕ **Pepe's Café and Steak House.** Pepe's is a Key West institution. It was established downtown in 1909 (making it the oldest eating house in the Keys) and moved here in 1962. With few exceptions, it's been serving three squares a day with the same nightly specials for years, such as meat loaf on Monday, seafood on Tuesday, and traditional Thanksgiving every Thursday. Dine indoors or on the garden patio under the trees. The walls are plastered with local color. Service is fast and friendly. ⊠ *806 Caroline St.* ☎ *305/294–7192* ☱ *D, MC, V.*

¢–$ ✕ **PT's Late Night Bar and Grill.** Locals like the dimly lighted homeyness (booths, TVs, pool tables), low prices (most entrées are $9.95), and late hours (open until 4 AM). There's lots of turkey in the potpie and lots of onions on the smothered pork chops. Fajitas are a specialty, with a choice of steak, chicken, shrimp, veggies, or a combo. ⊠ *920 Caroline St.* 🕾 *305/ 296–4245* 🖃 *AE, D, MC, V.*

Contemporary

$$$–$$$$
Fodor'sChoice
★

✕ **Café Marquesa.** The hospitality machine is well oiled at this refined 50-seat restaurant adjoining the intimate Marquesa Hotel. Chef Susan Ferry, who trained with Norman Van Aken (of Norman's restaurant in Coral Gables), presents 10 or so entrées each night. Although every dish she makes is memorable, frequent guests favor the peppercorn-dusted seared yellowfin tuna. Some low-fat options such as grilled meats are often highlighted, but fresh-baked breads and desserts are quite the dietary contrary. There is also a fine selection of wines and a choice of microbrewery beers. Dinner is served until 11 PM. ⊠ *600 Fleming St.* 🕾 *305/292–1244* 🖃 *AE, DC, MC, V* ☻ *No lunch.*

$$–$$$$
✕ **Louie's Backyard.** Feast your eyes on a steal-your-breath-away view and beautifully presented dishes prepared by executive chef Doug Shook. The winter menu might include grilled catch of the day with ginger butter, tomato chutney, and five-spice fried onions. Louie's key lime pie has a pistachio crust and is served with a raspberry coulis. Come for lunch if you're on a budget; the menu is less expensive and the view is just as fantastic. For night owls, the Afterdeck Bar serves cocktails on the water until the wee hours. ⊠ *700 Waddell Ave.* 🕾 *305/294–1061* 🖃 *AE, DC, MC, V.*

★ **$–$$$**
✕ **Alice's at LaTeDa.** Chef-owner Alice Weingarten, a popular local chef, serves breakfast, brunch, lunch, and dinner poolside with live evening entertainment. Dine right in the middle of LaTeDa Hotel, an in-vogue, very gay-friendly hotel-bar complex. Her talent shows in her exemplary selection of wines that complement the creative mix of seafood, game, beef, pork, and poultry dishes. She's as confident serving Aunt Alice's magic meat loaf as she is whipping up an aromatic pan-roasted Mediterranean chicken served over baby wild greens, kalamata olives, and feta cheese. The bar is as popular as the dining room. ⊠ *1125 Duval St.* 🕾 *305/ 296–6706* 🖃 *AE, D, MC, V* ☻ *No lunch Mon.*

$–$$$
✕ **Rick's Blue Heaven.** There's much to like about this historic restaurant where Hemingway once refereed boxing matches and customers watched cockfights. Fresh eats are served in the house and the big leafy yard. Nightly specials include blackened grouper or lobster with citrus beurre blanc and vegetarian options and Caribbean foods. Desserts and breads are baked on-site. There's a shop and bar, the latter named after the water tower hauled here in the 1920s. Expect a line—everybody knows how good this is. ⊠ *305 Petronia St.* 🕾 *305/296–8666* ♨ *Reservations not accepted* 🖃 *D, MC, V.*

Caribbean

$–$$
✕ **Bahama Mama's Kitchen.** At this colorful indoor-outdoor restaurant in the heart of Bahama Village, Cory Sweeting, a fourth-generation Conch from the Bahamas, prepares traditional island foods, from simple, flavorful conch fritters to complex curries. Choose from chicken—curried, gingered, or spiced and jerked—and seafood, including shrimp, red snapper, and grouper, any way you like them. Traditional sides include salads, hush puppies, collard greens, pigeon peas with rice, plantains, cheese grits, and crab with rice. Try the shrimp hashcakes if you go for breakfast. ⊠ *324 Petronia St.* 🕾 *305/294–3355* 🖃 *MC, V.*

Cuban

¢–$
✕ **El Siboney.** Dining at this sprawling three-room, family-style restaurant is like going to Mom's for Sunday dinner—that is, if your mother

is Cuban. It's noisy—everyone talks as though they're at home—and the food is traditional Cubano. There's a well-seasoned black-bean soup; local fish grilled, stuffed, and breaded; and a memorable special paella Valencia for two ($16.95). Dishes come with plantains, bread, and two sides. ⊠ *900 Catherine St.* ☎ *305/296–4184* 🖃 *No credit cards* ☉ *Closed 2 wks in June.*

French
★ **$$–$$$** ✕ **Café Solé.** This little piece of France is concealed behind a high wall and a gate in a residential neighborhood. Inside, chef John Correa shows his considerable culinary talents. Marrying his French training with local foods and produce, he creates some delicious takes on classics like half rack of lamb rubbed with *herbes de Provence* and some of the best bouillabaisse that you'll find outside of Marseilles. From the land, there is filet mignon casa nova with a wild mushroom demiglace with foie gras. His salads are lightly kissed with balsamic vinegar. ⊠ *1029 Southard St.* ☎ *305/294–0230* 🖃 *D, MC, V* ☉ *No lunch.*

Irish
¢–**$$$** ✕ **Finnegan's Wake Irish Pub and Eatery.** From friendly, heavily accented waitresses to pictures of Beckett, Shaw, Yeats, and Wilde to creaky wood floors, this restaurant exudes Irish country warmth. The certified Angus beef is pricey, except for the thick burgers ($7), and most other dishes are bargains. Traditional fare includes Dublin chicken potpie with chunks of chicken and vegetables in a creamy broth, and *colcannon*— rich mashed potatoes with scallions, sauerkraut, and melted aged white cheddar cheese. The strawberry rhubarb tart and Irish cream chocolate mousse are phenomenal. There's live music on weekends, two happy hours, and a boast of the "world's largest selection on tap." ⊠ *320 Grinnell St.* ☎ *305/293–0222* 🖃 *MC, V.*

Italian
★ **$–$$$** ✕ **Salute Ristorante Sul Mare.** This funky wooden indoor and open-air restaurant is on Higgs Beach, giving it one of the island's best lunch views (and a bit of sand and salt spray on a windy day). The dinner menu is a medley of Italian pastas, antipasto, soups, and delicious dishes such as lobster ravioli with sweet sage butter and baby greens and grilled black grouper with curry butter and basmati rice. At lunch there are bruschetta, panini, and mussels and calamari marinara, as well as a fresh local fish sandwich. The wine list shows a knowledgeable palate. ⊠ *1000 Atlantic Blvd., Higgs Beach* ☎ *305/292–1117* 🖃 *AE, MC, V* ☉ *No lunch Sun.*

★ ¢–**$$** ✕ **Mangia Mangia.** Elliot and Naomi Baron, ex-Chicago restaurateurs, serve large portions of homemade pastas that can be matched with one of the homemade sauces. Tables are arranged in a twinkly brick garden with specimen palms and in a nicely dressed-up old-house dining room. It's one of the best restaurants in Key West—and one of the best values. Everything that comes out of the open kitchen is outstanding, including the Mississippi mud pie and key lime pie. The wine list, with more than 350 offerings, the largest in Monroe County, has a good selection under $20. ⊠ *900 Southard St.* ☎ *305/294–2469* 🖃 *AE, MC, V* ☉ *No lunch.*

Japanese
¢–**$$** ✕ **Origami.** A wooden bar, artsy ceramic fish on white walls, original art, and black and white tile floors decorate this restaurant's dining room that's the size of an average bedroom. Fortunately, there's outdoor seating on a large courtyard that joins several other restaurants. Along with sushi and sashimi, there's a chicken, seafood, rice, salad, and fruit platter for kids and traditional Japanese entrées like teriyaki, tempura and

katsu. ⊠ *1075 Duval St.* ☎ *305/294–0092* ⊟ *AE, D, MC, V* ☺ *No lunch July–Dec.*

Steak/Seafood

★ $$$–$$$$ ✗ **Pisces.** Don't be dismayed when you see the sign for Pisces on the Café des Artistes building. Chef Andrew Berman and staff are still there. They've changed the name, updated the menu, and gone contemporary with a granite bar and sparkling mirrors. Some old favorites remain on the menu, such as Lobster Tango Mango, lobster flambéed in cognac and served with a saffron basil butter sauce and sliced mangoes. Other dishes include broiled Hawaiian blue prawns and pan-roasted halibut. Menu names sounded better when they were in French, but the taste lost nothing in the translation. ⊠ *1007 Simonton St.* ☎ *305/294–7100* ⊟ *AE, MC, V* ☺ *No lunch.*

★ $–$$$ ✗ **Seven Fish.** A local favorite, this small, intimate spot is good for an eclectic mix of dishes such as yellowtail snapper in a Thai curry sauce, penne with crawfish and scallops or sashimi and smoked scallop California roll. Filling out the menu are chicken, vegetable dishes, and even a meat loaf with real mashed potatoes. ⊠ *632 Olivia St.* ☎ *305/296–2777* ⊟ *AE, MC, V* ☺ *Closed Tues.*

¢–$ ✗ **Crabby Bill's.** The scene is a warehouse-size room with beer flags, a concrete floor, old surfboards, and a large bar, but what Bill lacks in decorating skills he makes up for in cooking seafood, lots of it—there are nine popular Crabby Bill's in Florida. It's priced right, from $5 for three grilled or blackened tuna skewers with a tangy cucumber-wasabi sauce to $15 for Maryland-style crabcakes. Bring the kids; there's lots of space, a pinball machine, free soda refills, and a few dishes just for the 12-and-under set. ⊠ *511 Greene St.* ☎ *305/292–0802* ⊟ *AE, D, DC, MC, V* ☺ *No lunch.*

Where to Stay

Historic cottages, restored turn-of-the-last-century Conch houses, and large resorts are among the offerings in Key West, with a few properties as low as $75 but the majority from $100 to $300 a night. Most places raise prices during October's Fantasy Fest week and other events. Many guest houses and inns do not welcome children under 16, and some do not permit smoking indoors but provide ashtrays outside. Most include an expanded Continental breakfast and, often, afternoon wine or snack.

Guest Houses

★ $$$$ 🏠 **Paradise Inn.** "Gloriously chic" best describes this romantic palm-shaded inn. Renovated cigar makers' cottages and authentically reproduced Bahamian-style houses with sundecks and balconies stand amid lush gardens with a heated pool, lily pond, and whirlpool, light-years in feeling from the hubbub of Key West. Suites are stylish, spacious, and filled with gracious touches such as French doors, sensuous fabrics, whirlpools in marble bathrooms, plush robes, and polished oak floors. Suite 205 and the Royal Poinciana Cottage are gilded lilies. ⊠ *819 Simonton St., 33040* ☎ *305/293–8007 or 800/888–9648* ☐ *305/293–0807* ⊕ *www.theparadiseinn.com* ⌨ *3 cottages, 15 suites* ⚘ *Fans, in-room data ports, in-room safes, some in-room hot tubs, minibars, refrigerators, cable TV, pool, outdoor hot tub, laundry service, concierge, business services, free parking; no kids under 12, no-smoking rooms* ⊟ *AE, D, DC, MC, V* ⦿ *CP.*

★ $$$–$$$$ 🏠 **Heron House.** A high coral fence, brilliantly splashed with spotlights at night, surrounds the compound of four Key West–style buildings with wood siding, railed porches, peaked roofs, and columns centered on a pool. Most units have a complete wall of exquisitely laid wood, entries with French doors, and bathrooms of polished granite. Some have floor-to-ceiling panels of mirrored glass and/or an oversize whirlpool. Complimenting the superb interior detailing are daily newspapers, bathrobes, and free breakfast and wine and cheese. ⊠ *512 Simonton St., 33040* ☎ *305/294–9227* 🖷 *305/294–5692 or 888/861–9066* ⊕ *www. heronhouse.com* ⌨ *23 rooms* ⌂ *Fans, in-room data ports, in-room safes, some in-room hot tubs, some minibars, some refrigerators, cable TV with movies, pool, concierge, parking (fee); no kids under 16, no smoking* ⊟ *AE, DC, MC, V* ⎺⦾⎺ *CP.*

★ **$–$$$$** 🏨 **Popular House/Key West Bed & Breakfast.** Local art—large splashy canvases, a mural in the style of Gauguin—hangs on the walls, and tropical gardens and music set the mood here. Owner Jody Carlson offers both inexpensive rooms with shared bath and luxury rooms, reasoning that budget travelers deserve the same good style (and lavish Continental breakfast) as the rich. Less-expensive rooms burst with colors; the hand-painted dressers will make you laugh. Spacious third-floor rooms are best (and most expensive), decorated with a paler palette and original furniture. Two friendly dogs live here, too. ⊠ *415 William St., 33040* ☎ *305/296–7274 or 800/438–6155* 🖷 *305/293–0306* ⊕ *www. keywestbandb.com* ⌨ *8 rooms, 4 with bath* ⌂ *Fans, outdoor hot tub, sauna; no room phones, no room TVs* ⊟ *AE, D, DC, MC, V* ⎺⦾⎺ *CP.*

★ **$$$** 🏨 **Ambrosia House.** If you desire personal attention and a casual mood with a dollop of style, stay at these twin inns with pool-view rooms, suites, town houses, and cottages spread out on nearly 2 acres. Ambrosia is more intimate. Ambrosia Too is a delightful art-filled hideaway. Rooms have original artwork by Keys artists, wicker or wood furniture, and spacious bathrooms. They all have a private entrance and deck, patio, or porch. Poolside Continental breakfast is included, and children are welcome. ⊠ *615, 618, 622 Fleming St., 33040* ☎ *305/296–9838 or 800/ 535–9838* 🖷 *305/296–2425* ⊕ *www.ambrosiakeywest.com* ⌨ *22 rooms, 3 town houses, 1 cottage, 6 suites* ⌂ *Fans, in-room data ports, some in-room hot tubs, some kitchens, refrigerators, cable TV, some in-room VCRs, 3 pools, outdoor hot tub, bicycles, concierge, some pets allowed; no smoking* ⊟ *AE, D, MC, V* ⎺⦾⎺ *BP.*

$$$ 🏨 **Center Court Historic Inn & Cottages.** Noisy Duval Street is half a block away, but when you're here, you're enveloped in quiet and calm. Units range from spacious rooms with a queen bed to efficiency cottages (sleeping two to eight) with a deck and spa to studios and fully equipped three-bedroom, two-bath house-size cottages (they sleep six). There's even a two-bedroom, two-bath house with its own pool. All units are decorated in relaxed tropical style, and both a full breakfast and happy-hour beverages are included. The heated pools are surrounded by lush foliage, whirlpools, and sundeck. ⊠ *915 Center St., 33040* ☎ *305/ 296–9292 or 800/797–8787* 🖷 *305/294–4104* ⊕ *www.centercourtkw. com* ⌨ *4 rooms, 9 suites, 4 efficiencies, 10 cottages, 8 houses* ⌂ *Grill, fans, in-room data ports, in-room safes, some in-room hot tubs, some kitchens, some microwaves, some refrigerators, cable TV, some in-room VCRs, 2 pools, exercise equipment, outdoor hot tub, business services, some pets allowed (fee); no smoking* ⊟ *AE, D, MC, V* ⎺⦾⎺ *BP.*

★ **$$$** 🏨 **Fleur de Key Guesthouse.** You could easily fill a little notebook with design ideas to take home from this charming guest house, which caters exclusively to a gay clientele. Conch-style architecture harks back to the property's origins as a boarding house and cigar makers' cottages. Standard rooms in the main house are smallish, so opt for a superior room, which is slightly more expensive but much larger. Rooms have antiques and reproductions and are tastefully decorated in whites and tropical colors. Enjoy robes, CDs, and CD players (in suites), and complimentary breakfast and evening cocktails. ⊠ *412 Frances St., 33040* ☎ *305/ 296–4719 or 800/932–9119* ⊕ *www.fleurdekey.com* ↝ *14 suites, 2 rooms* ⚬ *Fans, in-room data ports, some kitchens, refrigerators, cable TV, in-room VCRs, pool, outdoor hot tub; no kids under 16, no-smoking rooms* ▤ *AE, D, MC, V* ❀ *CP.*

$$$ ▣ **Island City House.** There's a real sense of conviviality at this three-building guest house, each with a unique style (and price). The vintage-1880s Island City House has a widow's walk, antiques, and pine floors. Arch House, a former carriage house, has a dramatic entry that opens into a lush courtyard. Although all suites front on busy Eaton Street, only Nos. 5 and 6 face it. A reconstructed cigar factory has become the Cigar House, with porches, decks, and plantation-style teak and wicker furnishings. Guests share a private tropical garden. Children are welcome—a rarity in Old Town guest houses. ⊠ *411 William St., 33040* ☎ *305/294–5702 or 800/634–8230* 🖷 *305/294–1289* ⊕ *www.islandcityhouse.com* ↝ *24 suites* ⚬ *Grill, fans, in-room data ports, some kitchens, cable TV with movies, in-room VCRs, pool, hot tub, bicycles, concierge; no smoking* ▤ *AE, D, DC, MC, V* ❀ *CP.*

★ $$$ ▣ **Mermaid & the Alligator.** Rooms in this 1904 Victorian house have a colonial Caribbean style, and wall colors are so luscious that guests frequently request paint chips. Wooden floors, furniture, and trim as well as French doors complement the colors. Some downstairs rooms open onto the deck, pool, and gardens designed by one of the resident owners, a landscape designer. Upstairs room balconies overlook the gardens. The Caribbean Queen suite has a large soaking tub, tiny shower, four-poster queen bed, and wraparound veranda, but its street-side location makes it noisy. A full breakfast is served poolside. The owners and their two retrievers make this a delightful place. ⊠ *729 Truman Ave., 33040* ☎ *305/294–1894 or 800/773–1894* 🖷 *305/295–9925* ⊕ *www. kwmermaid.com* ↝ *6 rooms* ⚬ *Fans, pool; no kids under 16, no room phones, no room TVs, no smoking* ▤ *AE, MC, V* ❀ *BP.*

$$–$$$ ▣ **Eden House.** This 1920s art deco guest house has is a terrific value. Two levels of accommodations surround a garden courtyard with a pool bordered by lounges and umbrella-shaded tables. Rooms range from small, simple spaces with a double or two twin beds and a squeaky-clean bathroom shared by two rooms to large spaces with a queen bed, kitchenette, and private porch. They all have pleasant furnishings and tropical colors. Spacious suites come in two sizes and have paler decors. The helpful, friendly staff sets up a daily complimentary happy hour. ⊠ *1015 Fleming St., 33040* ☎ *305/296–6868 or 800/533–5397* 🖷 *305/294–1221* ⊕ *www.edenhouse.com* ↝ *4 rooms with shared bath, 17 rooms, 9 suites, 1 2-bedroom unit* ⚬ *Restaurant, fans, some kitchens, some microwaves, some refrigerators, pool, outdoor hot tub, bicycles, library, shop, laundry facilities, concierge, free parking; no smoking, no TV in some rooms* ▤ *AE, MC, V.*

★ $$–$$$ ▣ **Key Lime Inn.** This inn, an 1854 Grand Bahama–style house on the National Register of Historic Places with adjacent cottages and cabanas, succeeds by offering amiable service, good value, and pretty, light-filled rooms with natural wood and white furniture. The tropical ambience comes from gardens shaded by fruit and palm trees, tin-roof buildings with clapboard siding, classic white picket fences, and breezy porches. The least expensive Cabana rooms, some with patios, surround the pool. The Garden Cottages have one room; some include a porch. All rooms in the historic Maloney House have a porch or patio. ⊠ *725 Truman Ave., 33040* ☎ *305/294–5229 or 800/549–4430* 🖷 *305/294–9623* ⊕ *www.keylimeinn.com* ↝ *30 rooms, 7 cottages* ⚬ *Fans, in-room data ports, in-room safes, some refrigerators, cable TV, some in-room VCRs, pool, concierge; no smoking* ▤ *AE, D, MC, V.*

★ **$$–$$$** ⊡ **Merlinn Inn.** Key West guest houses don't usually welcome families, but this inn is an exception. Brick walkways connect colorful rooms, suites, and cottages. A courtyard and tropical plantings further accent the grounds. Rooms in the 1930s Simonton House are most suitable for couples. They have four-poster beds and porches. Suites have wooden floors, French doors, rugs, four-poster beds, sundecks or porches, and sofa beds. Bright, roomy cottages are equally well appointed. There is no parking lot—a drawback, since it's a block off Duval Street. ☒ *811 Simonton St., 33040* ☎ *305/296–3336 or 800/642–4753* 🖶 *305/296–3524* ⊕ *www.merlinnkeywest.com* 🔊 *10 rooms, 6 suites, 4 cottages* ⚘ *Fans, in-room safes, some kitchens, some refrigerators, cable TV, pool, Internet; no room phones, no smoking* ⊟ *AE, D, MC, V* ⊡❘ *CP.*

$–$$$ ⊡ **Pearl's Rainbow.** Originally a cigar factory and cigar makers' cottages, Pearl's is now a guest house for lesbian and lesbian-friendly straight women. It's designed to promote camaraderie; guests sun themselves on lounge chairs around the pools, relax on private and shared balconies, and hang out at Pearl's Patio, a poolside bar that serves a deluxe Continental breakfast as well as burgers, sandwiches, salads, and drinks throughout the day. Service, from the housekeepers to the reception staff, is friendly and enthusiastic. Flowery furnishings, French doors, and lush gardens give it a tropical feel. ☒ *525 United St., 33040* ☎ *305/292–1450 or 800/ 749–6696* 🖶 *305/292–8511* ⊕ *www.pearlsrainbow.com* 🔊 *38 units* ⚘ *Snack bar, fans, some kitchens, some kitchenettes, cable TV, 2 pools, 2 hot tubs, laundry service, concierge; no kids* ⊟ *AE, D, MC, V.*

$–$$$ ⊡ **Speakeasy Inn.** During Prohibition, Raul Vasquez smuggled liquor from Cuba and taxi drivers stopped in here to fill suitcases with the bootleg. Today, the Speakeasy survives as an attractively priced inn. Spacious studios, suites, and two-bedroom units have bright white walls offset by bursts of color in rugs, pillows, and seat cushions; queen-size beds and tables made from salvaged pine; Saltillo tiles in the bathrooms; oak floors; and some claw-foot bathtubs. Maid and concierge service are available. Casa 325 Suites, an upscale all-suites property at the opposite end of Duval, is under the same ownership. ☒ *1117 Duval St., 33040* ☎ *305/ 296–2680 or 800/217–4884* 🖶 *305/296–2680* ⊕ *www.keywestcigar. com* 🔊 *4 suites, 4 studios, 2 2-bedroom units* ⚘ *Fans, some kitchenettes, cable TV, lobby lounge, concierge; no room phones, no smoking* ⊟ *AE, D, MC, V.*

¢–$$$ ⊡ **Angelina Guest House.** Two blocks off Duval Street, in the heart of Old Town Key West, this gambling hall and bordello turned guest house could command top dollar for its rooms. Instead, it offers simple, clean, attractively priced accommodations. There's a bed, chair, pretty curtains, and shared baths in the hallway included with the plainest rooms, a bed, sleeper sofa, refrigerator, and microwave in others. Built in the 1920s, this charming rambling, white wooden building has second-floor porches, gabled roofs, and a white picket fence. A pool, fountain, and old bricks accent a lovely garden. Breakfast of homemade baked goods is included. ☒ *302 Angela St., 33040* ☎ *305/294–4480* ⊕ *www.angelinaguesthouse. com* 🔊 *14 rooms* ⚘ *Fans, some microwaves, some refrigerators, pool; no room phones, no room TVs* ⊟ *D, MC, V* ⊡❘ *CP.*

$–$$ ⊡ **Eaton Manor.** Delaine and Jim Lowry, serious divers, fell in love with the Keys during their underwater wedding. A few years later they returned and bought Eaton Manor. Guests don't have to be divers, but it helps, because the Lowrys'enthusiasm for diving is incorporated into every aspect of the guest house, from the 125-gallon aquarium in the office to the sea-life mural to the room linens, pictures, and furnishings with fish motifs. ☒ *1024 Eaton St., 33040* ☎ *305/294–9870 or 800/305– 9870* ⊕ *www.keywest.com/eatmanor.html* 🔊 *23 units* ⚘ *Fans, refrigerators, cable TV, pool, bicycles* ⊟ *AE, D, MC, V.*

¢ ⊡ **Olivia By Duval.** This compound of clapboard buildings and mural art contains efficiencies and one- and two-bedroom apartments with wood and carpeted floors, immaculate bathrooms, and private outside sitting areas. A high white picket fence gives privacy to a pool surrounded by a wooden deck outfitted with lounge chairs. The friendly staff is especially accommodating to families and spring breakers (throughout March). ⊠ *511 Olivia St., 33040* ☎ *305/296–5169 or 800/413–1978* 🖶 *305/ 296–5590* ⊕ *www.oliviabyduval.com* ☞ *10 units* ♂ *Grill, fans, some kitchens, some kitchenettes, cable TV, pool, concierge* ⊟ *D, MC, V.*

Hostel

¢ ⊡ **Hostelling International–Key West.** A refuge in a sea of expensive hotels, this spot gets high marks for location, comfort, friendliness, and amenities. It's two blocks from the beach in Old Town yet costs only $19.50 for members of Hostelling International–American Youth Hostels, $22.50 for nonmembers. There's a communal kitchen. When you're not snorkeling ($28) or scuba diving ($55, gear included), rent bicycles, write letters in the outdoor courtyard, or enjoy a barbecue. ⊠ *718 South St., 33040* ☎ *305/296–5719* 🖶 *305/296–0672* ⊕ *www. keywesthostel.com* ☞ *96 beds in dorm-style rooms with shared bath, 10 private rooms, 1 suite* ♂ *Picnic area, fans, some in-room hot tubs, some kitchenettes, dive shop, snorkeling, bicycles, billiards, library, recreation room, laundry facilities, free parking* ⊟ *MC, V.*

Hotels

$$$$ ⊡ **Marquesa Hotel.** In a town that prides itself on its laid-back luxe, this
Fodor'sChoice restored 1884 house stands out. Guests—typically shoeless in Mar-
★ quesa robes—relax among richly landscaped pools and gardens against a backdrop of steps rising to the villalike suites. Elegant rooms have antique and reproduction furnishings, botanical-print fabrics, and marble baths. The lobby resembles a Victorian parlor, with antiques, Audubon prints, flowers, and photos of early Key West. The clientele is mostly straight, but the hotel is very gay-friendly. ⊠ *600 Fleming St., 33040* ☎ *305/292–1919 or 800/869–4631* 🖶 *305/294–2121* ⊕ *www.marquesa. com* ☞ *27 rooms* ♂ *Restaurant, room service, fans, in-room data ports, in-room safes, minibars, cable TV with movies, 2 pools, spa, bicycles, laundry service, concierge, business services* ⊟ *AE, DC, MC, V.*

★ **$$$$** ⊡ **Ocean Key Resort.** A pool and open-air bar and grill make their home on the Sunset Pier here, which provides the perfect view come sundown. Toast the day's end from private balconies that extend from brightly colored rooms that are both stylish and homey. Bring slippers for the white-tile flooring and CDs for the CD-alarm clock. High ceilings, hand-painted furnishings, a wicker sleigh bed, plaid couch, and a wooden chest for a coffee table create a personally designed look. Jet Skis can be rented at the marina, and the early evening hubbub of Mallory Square is right behind the hotel. ⊠ *Zero Duval St., 33040* ☎ *305/ 296–7701 or 800/328–9815* 🖶 *305/292–7685* ⊕ *www.oceankey.com* ☞ *10 rooms, 90 suites* ♂ *2 restaurants, room service, fans, in-room data ports, in-room safes, some in-room hot tubs, cable TV with movies, pool, health club, spa, dock, marina, bicycles, 2 bars, shops, dry cleaning, concierge, business services, meeting rooms; no-smoking rooms* ⊟ *AE, D, DC, MC, V.*

★ **$$$$** ⊡ **Pier House Resort & Caribbean Spa.** This convivial, sprawling pleasure complex of weathered gray buildings, including an original Conch house, has a courtyard of tall coconut palms and hibiscus blossoms. Rooms are light filled, cozy, and colorful and have a water, pool, or garden view. Most rooms are smaller than in newer hotels, except in the more expensive Caribbean Spa section, which has hardwood floors, two-poster plantation beds, and CD players. The best lodgings are in the Harbor

Front, each with a private balcony. Sunset on the Havana Docks is a special event. Rooms nearest the public areas can be noisy. ⊠ *1 Duval St., 33040* ☎ *305/296–4600 or 800/327–8340* 📠 *305/296–9085* ⊕ *www.pierhouse.com* ⇗ *126 rooms, 16 suites* ♦ *3 restaurants, room service, fans, in-room data ports, some in-room hot tubs, some in-room VCRs, pool, health club, spa, beach, 4 bars, shop, laundry service; no-smoking rooms* ☐ *AE, D, DC, MC, V.*

★ **$$$$** 🏨 **Sunset Key Guest Cottages at Hilton Key West Resort.** Check in at the Hilton Key West Resort; then board a 10-minute launch to their two- and three-bedroom cottages on Sunset Key. Sandy beaches, swaying palms, flowering gardens, a delicious sense of privacy—it's all here. The creature comforts are first-class. Shuttle between the island and Key West around the clock at no extra charge, or remain at Sunset Key to dine, play, and relax at the very civilized beach, complete with attendants and cabanas. ⊠ *245 Front St., 33040* ☎ *305/292–5300* 📠 *305/292–5395* ⊕ *www.hilton.com* ⇗ *37 cottages* ♦ *Restaurant, café, snack bar, room service, fans, in-room data ports, in-room safes, kitchens, cable TV with movies, in-room VCRs, putting green, 2 tennis courts, pool, gym, spa, beach, jet skiing, marina, fishing, basketball, billiards, bar, lounge, library, shops, baby-sitting, laundry service, concierge, Internet, business services, meeting rooms; no-smoking rooms* ☐ *AE, D, DC, MC, V.*

$$$$ 🏨 **Wyndham's Casa Marina Resort.** At any moment, you expect the landed gentry to walk across the manicured, oceanfront lawn, just as they did in the 1920s when this 13-acre resort was built. It has the same rich lobby with a beamed ceiling, polished pine floor, and art. Guest rooms are stylishly decorated. Armoires and wicker chairs with thick cushions add warmth. Fluffy bathrobes and luxurious designer toiletries make it feel like home. Two-bedroom loft suites with balconies face the ocean. The main building's ground-floor lanai rooms open onto the lawn. ⊠ *1500 Reynolds St., 33040* ☎ *305/296–3535 or 800/626–0777* 📠 *305/296–9960* ⊕ *www.casamarinakeywest.com* ⇗ *311 rooms, 63 suites* ♦ *2 restaurants, room service, in-room data ports, in-room safes, minibars, cable TV with movies and video games, 3 tennis courts, 2 pools, gym, hair salon, outdoor hot tub, massage, sauna, beach, dive shop, snorkeling, windsurfing, boating, jet skiing, fishing, bicycles, volleyball, 2 bars, shop, baby-sitting, children's programs (ages 4–12), laundry service, concierge, business services, meeting rooms, airport shuttle; no-smoking rooms* ☐ *AE, D, DC, MC, V.*

★ **$$$–$$$$** 🏨 **Best Western Key Ambassador Inn.** Every room in this well-maintained 7-acre property has a screened balcony, most with a view of the ocean or pool. Accommodations are roomy and cheerful, with Caribbean-style light-color furniture and linens in coordinated tropical colors. A deck-rimmed, palm-shaded pool that looks over the Atlantic and a covered picnic area with barbecue grills encourage socializing. The outdoor bar serves lunch, drinks, and light dishes. A complimentary Continental breakfast and free weekday newspaper are included. ⊠ *3755 S. Roosevelt Blvd., New Town 33040* ☎ *305/296–3500 or 800/432–4315* 📠 *305/296–9961* ⊕ *www.keyambassador.com* ⇗ *100 rooms* ♦ *Café, picnic area, fans, in-room data ports, refrigerators, cable TV with movies, pool, exercise equipment, shuffleboard, bar, laundry facilities, concierge, business services, airport shuttle, free parking; no-smoking rooms.* ☐ *AE, D, DC, MC, V* 🍴 *CP.*

Motels

$$ 🏨 **Harborside Motel & Marina.** This simple little motel neatly packages three appealing characteristics—affordability, safety, and a pleasant location between a quiet street and Garrison Bight (the charter-boat harbor), at the border of Old Town and New Town. Units are boxy, clean, and basic, with little patios, ceramic-tile floors, phones, and lots of peace and quiet. Four stationary houseboats each sleep four. Barbecue grills are available for cookouts. Spring breakers need not apply: the motel likes to maintain a relative calm. ✉ *903 Eisenhower Dr., 33040* ☎ *305/294–2780 or 800/501–7823* 🖷 *305/292–1473* ⊕ *www.keywestharborside.com* ➷ *14 efficiencies* 🕭 *Grill, fans, kitchens, cable TV, pool, dock, marina, laundry facilities* ▭ *AE, D, DC, MC, V.*

$$ 🖵 **Southwind Motel.** If you're looking for a practical, affordable place to stay that's just a short walk from Old Town, consider this friendly lodging run by the same folks who operate Harborside Motel & Marina. The pastel 1940s-style motel has mature tropical plantings, all nicely set back from the street a block from the beach. Rooms are superclean and have tile floors and basic furnishings. It's as good as you'll find at the price, and although rates have gone up, they drop if demand gets slack. ✉ *1321 Simonton St., 33040* ☎ *305/296–2215 or 800/501–7826* ⊕ *www. keywestsouthwind.com* ➷ *13 rooms, 5 efficiencies* 🕭 *Fans, some kitchens, cable TV, pool, laundry facilities* ▭ *AE, D, DC, MC, V.*

Nightlife & the Arts

The Arts

Catch the classics and the latest art, independent, and foreign films ($8) shown by the **Key West Film Society,** now daily in its new theater (✉ 416 Eaton St. ☎ 305/294–5857 ⊕ www.keywestfilm.org). In a wickedly indulgent style that is so Key West, **Cinema Shores** (✉ 510 South St. ☎ 305/296–2491 ⊕ www.atlanticshoresresort.com), at Atlantic Shores Resort, an adult alternative resort, shows classic, foreign, and new films ($5) on a large outdoor screen while viewers enjoy free popcorn and cocktail service as they stretch out on their lounge chairs on the lawn, on Thursday evenings. Sebrina Alfonso directs the **Key West Symphony** (✉ Florida Keys Community College, 5901 College Rd. ☎ 305/292–1774 ⊕ www.keywestsymphony.com), during the winter season. Watch for free pre-concert lectures at libraries and other venues. With more than 20 years' experience, the **Red Barn Theatre** (✉ 319 Duval St. [rear] ☎ 305/296–9911 ⊕ www.redbarntheatre.com), a professional small theater, performs dramas, comedies, and musicals, including works by new playwrights. The **Tennessee Williams Fine Arts Center** (✉ Florida Keys Community College, 5901 College Rd. ☎ 305/296–9081 Ext. 5 ⊕ www. keywesttheater.org), on Stock Island, presents chamber music, dance, jazz concerts, and dramatic and musical plays with major stars, as well as other performing arts events, December–April. The **Waterfront Playhouse** (✉ Mallory Sq. ☎ 305/294–5015 ⊕ www.waterfrontplayhouse. com), in its 64th season, is a mid-1850s wrecker's warehouse that was converted into a 180-seat, non-Equity regional theater presenting comedy and drama December–June.

Nightlife

BARS & LOUNGES   Pick your entertainment at the **Bourbon Street Complex** (✉ 724–801 Duval St. ☎ 305/296–1992), a gay-oriented club with five bars and two restaurants. There's a nightly drag show in the 801 Bourbon Bar and 10 video screens along with male dancers grooving to the latest music spun by DJs at the Bourbon Street Pub. In its earliest incarnation, back in 1851, **Capt. Tony's Saloon** (✉ 428 Greene St. ☎ 305/294–1838) was a morgue and icehouse, then Key West's first telegraph station. It became the original Sloppy Joe's in the mid-1930s, when Hemingway was a regular. Later, a young Jimmy Buffett sang here. Live bands play nightly. Pause for a libation at the open-air **Green Parrot Bar** (✉ 601 Whitehead St., at Southard St. ☎ 305/294–6133). Built in 1890, the bar is said to be Key West's oldest, a sometimes-rowdy saloon where locals outnumber out-of-towners, especially on weekends when bands play. It opened a smokehouse, Meteor, behind it that serves up smoked shrimp, pork, chicken, and beef. **LaTeDa Hotel and Bar** (✉ 1125 Duval St. ☎ 305/296–6706) hosts a riotously funny cabaret show nightly in the Crystal Room Cabaret Lounge. There's also live entertainment by popular local singer Lenore Troia in the Terrace Garden Bar. A youngish crowd sprinkled with aging Parrot Heads frequents **Margaritaville Café** (✉ 500 Duval St. ☎ 305/292–1435), owned by former Key West resident and recording star Jimmy Buffett, who has been known to perform here. The drink of choice is, of course, a margarita. There's live music nightly, as well as lunch and dinner.

Nightlife at the **Pier House** (✉ 1 Duval St. ☎ 305/296–4600) begins with a steel drum band (weekends) to celebrate the sunset on the beach, then moves indoors to the piano bar for live jazz (Thursday to Sunday). The **Schooner Wharf Bar** (✉ 202 William St. ☎ 305/292–9520), an open-air waterfront bar and grill in the historic seaport district, retains its funky Key West charm. There's live music all day, plus happy hour, and special events. There's more history and good times at **Sloppy Joe's** (✉ 201 Duval St. ☎ 305/294–5717), the successor to a famous 1937 speakeasy named for its founder, Captain Joe Russell. Ernest Hemingway came here to gamble and tell stories. Decorated with Hemingway memorabilia and marine flags, the bar is popular with travelers and is full and noisy all the time. Live entertainment plays daily noon–2 AM. The **Top Lounge** (✉ 430 Duval St. ☎ 305/296–2991) is on the seventh floor of the La Concha Holiday Inn and is one of the best places to view the sunset and enjoy live entertainment on Friday and Saturday. In the best traditions of a 1950s cocktail lounge, **Virgilio's** (✉ Applerouth Lane ☎ 305/296–8118) serves up chilled martinis to the soothing tempo of live jazz and blues nightly. It's part of the La Trattoria restaurant complex.

Sports & the Outdoors

Biking

Key West is a cycling town, but ride carefully: narrow and one-way streets along with car traffic result in several bike accidents a year. Some hotels rent or loan bikes to guests; others will refer you to a nearby shop and reserve a bike for you.

Keys Moped & Scooter (✉ 523 Truman Ave. ☎ 305/294–0399) rents beach cruisers with large baskets as well as scooters. Rates start at $15 for three hours. Look for the huge American flag on the roof. **Moped Hospital** (✉ 601 Truman Ave. ☎ 305/296–3344) supplies balloon-tire bikes with yellow safety baskets for adults and kids, as well as mopeds and double-seater scooters for adults.

Fishing

Captain Steven Impallomeni works as a flats-fishing guide, specializing in ultralight and fly-fishing for tarpon, permit, and bonefish, as well as near-shore and light-tackle fishing. Charters on the *Gallopin' Ghost* leave from **Murray's Marina** (✉ MM 5, Stock Island ☎ 305/292–9837). **Key West Bait and Tackle** (✉ 241 Margaret St. ☎ 305/292–1961) carries live bait, frozen rigged and unrigged bait, and fishing and rigging equipment. It also has the Live Bait Lounge; unwind and sip ice-cold beer while telling tall tales after fishing. Be sure to ask why the marlin on the roof is red.

Golf

Key West Resort Golf Course (✉ 6450 E. College Rd. ☎ 305/294–5232) is an 18-hole course on the bay side of Stock Island. Nonresident fees are $140 for 18 holes (cart included) in season, $80 off-season.

Scuba Diving & Snorkeling

Adventure Charters & Tours (✉ 6810 Front St., 33040 ☎ 305/296–0362 or 888/817–0841) has sail-and-snorkel coral reef adventure tours ($30) aboard the 42-ft trimaran sailboat *Fantasea,* with a maximum of 16 people. There are two daily departures and sometimes one at sunset. **Captain's Corner** (✉ 125 Ann St., 33040 ☎ 305/296–8865), a PADI five-star shop, has dive classes in several languages and twice-daily snorkel and dive trips to reefs and wrecks aboard the 60-ft dive boat *Sea Eagle.*

Shopping

Key West has dozens of characterless T-shirt shops, as well as art galleries and curiosity shops with lots worth toting home.

Bahama Village is an enclave of new and spruced-up shops, restaurants, and vendors leading the way in the restoration of the historic district where black Bahamians settled in the 19th century. The village lies roughly between Whitehead and Fort streets, and Angela and Catherine streets. Hemingway frequented the bars, restaurants, and boxing rings in the village.

Arts & Crafts

The **Gallery on Greene** (✉ 606 Greene St. ☎ 305/294–1669) showcases politically incorrect art by Jeff McNally and three-dimensional paintings by local artist Mario Sanchez, among others, in the largest gallery exhibition space in Key West. The oldest private art gallery in Key West, **Gingerbread Square Gallery** (✉ 1207 Duval St. ☎ 305/296–8900), represents mainly Keys artists who have attained national and international prominence, including Sal Salinero and John Kiraly, in media ranging from graphics to art glass. **Haitian Art Co.** (✉ 600 Frances St. ☎ 305/296–8932), with 4,000 paintings and spirit flags, claims the largest collection of Haitian art outside Haiti, representing artists working in wood, stone, metal, and papier-mâché. **Lucky Street Gallery** (✉ 1120 White St. ☎ 305/294–3973) sells high-end contemporary paintings, watercolors, and jewelry by internationally recognized Key West–based artists. **Pelican Poop** (✉ 314 Simonton St. ☎ 305/296–3887) sells Caribbean art around a lush, tropical courtyard garden with a fountain and pool. The owners buy direct from Caribbean artisans every year, so prices are very attractive. (Hemingway wrote *A Farewell to Arms* while living in the complex's apartment.) Potters Charles Pearson and Timothy Roeder *are* **Whitehead St. Pottery** (✉ 322 Julia St. ☎ 305/294–5067), where they display their porcelain stoneware and raku-fired vessels. They also have a photo gallery where they exhibit Polaroid image transfers and black-and-white photos. In the not-to-be-missed category is the **Woodenhead Gallery** (✉ 907 Caroline St. ☎ 305/294–3935), where the artists-owners create avant-garde works from recycled materials and *objets* found in and around Key West. Their coffee bar is a favorite meeting spot for artists, friends, and clients.

Books

Flaming Maggie's (✉ 830 Fleming St. ☎ 305/294–3931) specializes in books, cards, and magazines for and about gays and lesbians and also carries books—and artwork—by or about local authors. It has a popular coffee bar, too. The **Key West Island Bookstore** (✉ 513 Fleming St. ☎ 305/294–2904), is the literary bookstore of the large Key West writers' community. It carries new, used, and rare titles and specializes in Hemingway, Tennessee Williams, and South Florida mystery writers.

Clothes & Fabrics

Since 1964, **Key West Hand Print Fashions and Fabrics** (⊠ 201 Simonton St. ☎ 305/294–9535 or 800/866–0333) has been noted for its vibrant tropical prints, yard goods, and resort wear for men and women. It's in the Curry Warehouse, a brick building erected in 1878 to store tobacco. **Tikal Trading Co.** (⊠ 129 Duval St. ⊠ 910 Duval St. ☎ 305/296–4463) sells its own line of women's and little girl's clothing of hand-woven Guatemalan cotton and knit tropical prints.

Food & Drink

The **Blond Giraffe** (⊠ 629 Duval St. and 1209 Truman Ave. ☎ 305/293–6667) turned an old family recipe for key lime pie into a commercial success story. Its two stores often have a line for the pie, with delicate pastry, sweet-tart custard filling, and thick meringue topping. The key lime rum cake is the best-selling product for shipping home. On a hot summer day, nothing quenches the heat like a Pie-Pop, a slice of frozen key lime pie dipped in dark chocolate and sold on a stick. The air outside **Cole'z Peace Artisan Breads** (⊠ 930A Eaton St. ☎ 305/292–6511) is deliciously redolent of warm breads. Each loaf of hand-kneaded unbleached, unbromated flour, organic flour, or organic grain bread is hand-shaped, then baked in a hearth stone oven. The crusts are hard and thick, the insides light and flavorful. **Fausto's Food Palace** (⊠ 522 Fleming St. ☎ 305/296–5663 ⊠ 1105 White St. ☎ 305/294–5221) may be under a roof, but it's a market in the traditional town-square sense. Since 1926, Fausto's has been the spot to catch up on the week's gossip and to chill out in summer—it has groceries, organic foods, marvelous wines, a sushi chef on duty from 8 AM to 6 PM, and box lunches to go. You'll spend the first five minutes at the **Waterfront Market** (⊠ 201 William St. ☎ 305/296–0778) wondering how to franchise one of these great markets in your hometown. It sells savory deli items from around the world, health food, produce, salads, espresso, cold beer, and wine. Don't miss the fish market, bakery, deli, or juice bar; sushi from the Origami Restaurant; vegan dishes from Linda's Vegan Delights; or breads from Cole'z Peace. The market's open until 8 PM on Friday.

Gifts & Souvenirs

Like a parody of Duval Street T-shirt shops, the hole-in-the-wall **Art Attack** (⊠ 606 Duval St. ☎ 305/294–7131) throws in every icon and trinket anyone nostalgic for the days of peace and love might fancy: beads, necklaces, harmony bells, and, of course, psychedelic T-shirts. Best-sellers are photographic postcards of Key West by Tony Gregory. It's open until 11 PM daily. **Fast Buck Freddie's** (⊠ 500 Duval St. ☎ 305/294–2007) sells a classy, hip selection of crystal, furniture, tropical clothing, and every flamingo item imaginable. It also carries such imaginative items as a noise-activated rat in a trap and a raccoon tail in a bag. **Half Buck Freddie's** (⊠ 726 Caroline St. ☎ 305/294–2007) is the discount-outlet store for Fast Buck's. It's closed Tuesday–Wednesday.

The ambience in **Kindred Spirit** (⊠ 1204 Simonton St. ☎ 305/296–1515) is very New Age, but in addition to aromatherapy candles, inspirational music, and scented soaps there are delicate picture frames and artwork and jewelry made by Keys artists. Tea is a specialty. Buy tea leaves, tea bags, and tea cups and enjoy formal tea—complete with freshly baked scones, fruit bread, and cake and confections—on comfy overstuffed chairs inside or outside in a tropical garden. In a town with a gazillion T-shirt shops, **Last Flight Out** (⊠ 503 Greene St. ☎ 305/294–8008) stands out for its selection of classic namesake Ts, specialty clothing, and gifts that appeal to aviation types and others who reach for the stars.

Health & Beauty

Key West Aloe (✉ 524 Front St. ☎ 305/294–5592 or 800/445–2563) was founded in a garage in 1971; today it produces some 300 perfume, sunscreen, and skin-care products for men and women. Also visit the factory store at Greene and Simonton Streets.

Side Trip

Dry Tortugas National Park

This sanctuary for thousands of birds, 70 mi off the shores of Key West, consists of seven small islands. Its main facility is the long-deactivated Fort Jefferson, where Dr. Samuel Mudd was imprisoned for his alleged role in Lincoln's assassination. Tour the fort; then lay out your blanket on the sunny beach for a picnic before you head out to snorkel on the protected reef. Many people like to camp here, but note that there's no fresh-water supply and you must carry off whatever you bring onto the island. For information and a list of authorized charter boats and water taxis, contact **Everglades National Park** (✉ 40001 Rte. 9336, Homestead 33034-6733 ☎ 305/242–7700).

The fast, sleek 100-ft catamaran, the *Yankee Freedom II,* of the **Yankee Fleet Dry Tortugas National Park Ferry,** cuts the travel time to the Dry Tortugas to 2¼ hours. The time passes quickly on the roomy vessel equipped with three rest rooms, two fresh-water showers, and two bars. Stretch out on two decks; one an air-conditioned salon with cushioned seating, the other an open sundeck with sunny and shaded seating. Breakfast and lunch are included. On arrival, a naturalist leads a 45-minute guided tour, followed by lunch and a free afternoon for swimming, snorkeling (gear included), and exploring. ✉ *Lands End Marina, 240 Margaret St., Key West 33040 ☎ 305/294–7009 or 800/634–0939 ⊕ www.yankeefreedom.com* ✍ *$119* ☉ *Trips daily at 8 AM.*

THE FLORIDA KEYS A TO Z

To research prices, get advice from other travelers, and book travel arrangements, visit www.fodors.com.

AIR TRAVEL

Service between Key West International Airport and Miami, Fort Lauderdale/Hollywood, Atlanta, Naples, Orlando, St. Petersburg, and Tampa is provided by American Eagle, Cape Air, Comair/Delta Connection, Gulfstream/Continental Connection, and US Airways/US Airways Express. The Airporter operates scheduled van and bus pickup service from all Miami International Airport (MIA) baggage areas to wherever you want to go in Key Largo ($35) and Islamorada ($38). A group discount is given for three or more passengers. Reservations are required. Keys Shuttle runs scheduled service five times a day in 15-passenger vans (seven passengers maximum) between Miami Airport and Key West with stops throughout the Keys $50–$70. Add $10 to Fort Lauderdale Airport. The Super Shuttle charges $80 per passenger ($190 for entire van) for trips to the Upper Keys. To go farther into the Keys, you must book an entire van (up to 11 passengers), which costs $250 to Marathon, $350 to Key West. Super Shuttle requests 24-hour advance notice for transportation back to the airport.

CARRIERS 🛪 Airlines & Contacts **American Eagle** ☎ 800/433–7300. **Cape Air** ☎ 800/352–0714. **Comair/Delta Connection** ☎ 800/354–9822. **Gulfstream/Continental Connection** ☎ 800/525–0280. **US Airways/US Airways Express** ☎ 800/428–4322.

🔝 Airport Information **Key West International Airport** ✉ S. Roosevelt Blvd., Key West ☎ 305/296-5439. **Miami International Airport** ☎ 305/876-7000. **Airporter** ☎ 305/852-3413 or 800/830-3413. **Keys Shuttle** ☎ 305/289-9997 or 888/765-9997. **Super Shuttle** ☎ 305/871-2000.

BOAT & FERRY TRAVEL

Boaters can travel to and along the Keys either along the Intracoastal Waterway (5-ft draft limitation) through Card, Barnes, and Blackwater sounds and into Florida Bay or along the deeper Atlantic Ocean route through Hawk Channel, a buoyed passage. Refer to NOAA Nautical Charts Numbers 11451, 11445, and 11441. The Keys are full of marinas that welcome transient visitors, but they don't have enough slips for everyone. Make reservations in advance and ask about channel and dockage depth—many marinas are quite shallow. For nonemergency information contact Coast Guard Group Key West; VHF-FM Channel 16. Safety and weather information is broadcast at 7 AM and 5 PM Eastern Standard Time on VHF-FM Channels 16 and 22A. There are stations in Islamorada and Marathon. Key West Shuttle operates a ferry between Key West and Marco Island and Fort Myers, on the mainland's southwest coast. The trip takes four to five hours each way, respectively. Tickets start at $70 one-way, $119 round-trip. Key West Ferry has similar service from Fort Myers Beach on a 116-ft vessel. Rates—$80 one-way, $129 round-trip—include Continental breakfast. A current, legal photo ID is required for each passenger. All bags are subject to search. Advance reservations are recommended. Chambers of commerce, marinas, and dive shops offer Teall's Guides, land and nautical charts that pinpoint popular fishing and diving areas. Prices vary.

🔝 Boat & Ferry Information **Coast Guard Group for the Florida Keys** ✉ Key West ☎ 305/292-8779 ✉ Islamorada ☎ 306/664-8077 for information; 305/664-4404 emergencies ✉ Marathon ☎ 305/743-6778 information; 305/743-6388 emergencies. **Key West Ferry** ☎ 800/273-4496 ⊕ www.keywestferry.com. **Key West Shuttle** ☎ 888/539-2628 ⊕ www.keywestshuttle.com. **Teall's Guides** ✉ Box 522409, Marathon Shores 33052-2409 ☎ 305/872-3123 🖷 305/872-3702.

BUS TRAVEL

Greyhound Lines runs a special Keys shuttle three or four times a day (depending on the day of the week) between MIA (departing from Concourse E, lower level) and stops throughout the Keys. Fares run from about $13–$25 one-way–round-trip for Key Largo (Howard Johnson, MM 102) to around $30–$58 for Key West (3535 S. Roosevelt, Key West Airport). City of Key West Department of Transportation has four color-coded bus routes covering the island from 6:30 AM to 11:30 PM. Stops have signs with the international symbol for bus. Schedules are available on buses and at hotels, visitor centers, and shops. The fare is 75¢ (exact change) or $3 for an all-day pass that you purchase onboard. Bone Island Shuttle circles the island from 9 AM to 11 PM, stopping at attractions, hotels, and restaurants. Passengers pay $7 per day or $15 per three days for unlimited riding. Purchase at hotels and the Key West Welcome. Park at the city's Park 'n' Ride 24-hour garage at the corner of Caroline and Grinnell streets and catch a city bus to Old Town at no extra cost. Parking costs $1.25 an hour or $8 a day. The Dade–Monroe Express provides daily bus service from MM 50 in Marathon to the Florida City Wal-Mart Supercenter on the Mainland. The bus stops at major shopping centers as well as on-demand anywhere along the route for daily round-trips on the hour from 6 AM to 9:55 PM. The cost is $1.50 each way.

🔝 Bus Information **Bone Island Shuttle** ☎ 305/293-8710. **City of Key West Department of Transportation** ☎ 305/292-8160. **Dade–Monroe Express** ☎ 305/770-3131.

Greyhound Lines ☎ 800/410-5397 or 800/231-2222. **Park 'n' Ride** ⊠ 300 Grinnell St. ☎ 305/293-6426.

CAR RENTAL

Two- and four-passenger open-air electric cars that travel about 25 mph are an environmentally friendly way to get around the island. Rent them from Key West Cruisers for $89–$129 a half day for the two- or four-seater, or $119–$169 a day. Avis, Budget, and Enterprise serve Marathon Airport. Key West's airport has booths for Alamo, Avis, Budget, Dollar, and Hertz. Tropical Rent-A-Car is based in the city center. Enterprise Rent-A-Car has offices in Key Largo, Marathon, and Key West. Thrifty Car Rental has an office in Tavernier.

CUTTING COSTS Avoid flying into Key West and driving back to Miami; there are substantial drop-off charges for leaving a Key West car in Miami.

🚗 **Local Agencies Alamo** ☎ 305/294-6675 or 800/327-9633. **Avis** ⊠ Key West Airport ☎ 305/294-4846 ⊠ Marathon Airport ☎ 305/743-5428 or 800/831-2847. **Budget** ⊠ Key West Airport ☎ 305/294-8868 ⊠ Marathon Airport ☎ 305/743-3998 or 800/ 527-0700. **Dollar** ☎ 305/296-9921 or 800/800-4000. **Enterprise Rent-A-Car** ☎ 800/ 325-8007. **Hertz** ☎ 305/294-1039 or 800/654-3131. **Key West Cruisers** ⊠ 500 Truman Ave. at Duval St. ☎ 305/294-4724. **Thrifty Car Rental** ⊠ MM 91.8, OS, Tavernier ☎ 305/ 852-6088. **Tropical Rent-A-Car** ⊠ 1300 Duval St., Key West ☎ 305/294-8136.

CAR TRAVEL

From MIA follow signs to Coral Gables and Key West, which put you on Lejeune Road, then Route 836 west. Take the Homestead Extension of Florida's Turnpike south (toll road), which ends at Florida City and connects to U.S. 1. Tolls from the airport run approximately $1.50. The alternative from Florida City is Card Sound Road (Route 905A), which has a bridge toll of $1. Continue to the only stop sign and turn right on Route 905, which rejoins U.S. 1 31 mi south of Florida City. Avoid flying into Key West and driving back to Miami; there are substantial drop-off charges for leaving a Key West car in Miami. In Key West's Old Town, parking is scarce and costly ($2 per hour at Mallory Square). It's better to take a taxi, rent a bicycle or moped, walk, or take a shuttle to get around. Elsewhere in the Keys, a car is crucial. Gas costs more than on the mainland, so fill your tank in Miami and top it off in Florida City. Most of the Overseas Highway is narrow and crowded (especially weekends and in high season). Expect delays behind RVs, trucks, cars towing boats, and rubbernecking tourists. The best Keys road map, published by the Homestead–Florida City Chamber of Commerce, can be obtained for $5.50 from the Tropical Everglades Visitor Center.

🚗 **Tropical Everglades Visitor Center** ⊠ 160 U.S. 1, Florida City 33034 ☎ 305/245-9180 or 800/388-9669.

EMERGENCIES

Dial 911 for police, fire, or ambulance. Keys Hotline provides information and emergency assistance in six languages. Florida Marine Patrol maintains a 24-hour telephone service to handle reports of boating emergencies and natural-resource violations. Coast Guard Group Key West responds to local marine emergencies and reports of navigation hazards. The Keys have no 24-hour pharmacies. Hospital pharmacists will help with emergencies after regular retail business hours. The following hospitals have 24-hour emergency rooms: Fishermen's Hospital, Lower Florida Keys Health System, and Mariners Hospital.

🚑 **Coast Guard Group Key West** ☎ 305/292-8727. **Fishermen's Hospital** ⊠ MM 48.7, OS, Marathon ☎ 305/743-5533. **Florida Marine Patrol** ⊠ MM 48, BS, 2796 Overseas Hwy., Suite 100, State Regional Service Center, Marathon 33050 ☎ 305/289-2320; 800/342-5367 after 5 PM. **Keys Hotline** ☎ 800/771-5397. **Lower Florida Keys Health**

System ✉ MM 5, BS, 5900 College Rd., Stock Island ☎ 305/294–5531. **Mariners Hospital** ✉ MM 91.5, BS, Tavernier ☎ 305/852–4418.

ENGLISH-LANGUAGE MEDIA

NEWSPAPERS & MAGAZINES The best of the publications covering Key West are the weekly *Solares Hill* and the daily *Key West Citizen.* For the Upper and Middle Keys, turn to the semiweekly *Keynoter.* The *Free Press, Reporter,* and *Upper Keys Independent* cover the same area once a week. The *Miami Herald* publishes a Keys edition with good daily listings of local events. The weekly *Celebrate Key West* and the monthly *Southern Exposure* are good sources of entertainment and information for gay and lesbian travelers.

TELEVISION & RADIO WLRN (National Public Radio) is 91.3, 92.1, and 93.5, depending on where you are in the Keys. Try WKLG 102.1 bilingual (English and Spanish) for adult contemporary; WCTH 100.3 for country; WFKZ 103.1 for classic rock; WKEZ 96.9 for easy listening; WFFG AM 1300 Keys for talk radio, sports, and news; and WKYZ 101.3 classic rock.

LODGING

Brenda Donnelly's friendly, efficient family-run company represents more than 60 guest houses, B&Bs, inns, and small hotels in prices ranging from $60 to $545 a night through Inn Touch in Key West. Key West Vacation Rentals lists historic cottages, homes, and condominiums for rent. Although it prefers to handle reservations for all types of accommodations in advance, the Key West Welcome Center gets a lot of walk-in business because of its location on U.S. 1 at the entrance to Key West. Property Management of Key West, Inc. has lease and rental service for condominiums, town houses, and private homes. Rent Key West Vacations specializes in renting vacation homes and condos for a week or longer. Vacation Key West lists all kinds of properties throughout Key West.

APARTMENT & VILLA RENTALS 🏠 **Local Agents Inn Touch in Key West** ✉ 1421 Catherine St., Key West 33040 ☎ 305/296–2953 or 877/526–7775 📠 305/292–1621 ⊕ www.inntouchinkeywest.com. **Vacation Rentals Key West** ✉ 525 Simonton St., Key West 33040 ☎ 305/292–7997 or 800/621–9405 ⊕ www.oldeisland.com 📠 305/294–7501. **Key West Welcome Center** ✉ 3840 N. Roosevelt Blvd., Key West 33040 ☎ 305/296–4444 or 800/284–4482 ⊕ www.keywestwelcomecenter.com. **Rent Key West Vacations** ✉ 1107 Truman Ave., Key West 33040 ☎ 305/294–0990 or 800/833–7368 ⊕ www.rentkeywest.com. **Vacation Key West** ✉ 513 Fleming St., Suite 3, Key West 33040 ☎ 305/295–9500 or 800/595–5397 ⊕ www.vacationkw.com.

TAXIS

Serving the Keys from Ocean Reef to Key West, Luxury Limousine has luxury sedans and limos that seat up to eight passengers, as well as vans and buses. It'll pick up from any airport in Florida. In the Upper Keys (MM 94–74), Village Taxi charges $2.25 per mi for vans that hold six. It also makes airport runs. Florida Keys Taxi Dispatch operates around the clock in Key West. The fare for two or more from the Key West airport to New Town is $5 per person with a cap of $15; to Old Town it's $7 and $30, respectively. Otherwise meters register $2.25 to start, 50¢ for each ⅕ mi, and 50¢ for every 50 seconds of waiting time.

🚕 **Taxi Information Florida Keys Taxi Dispatch** ☎ 305/296–6666 or 305/296–1800. **Luxury Limousine** ☎ 305/367–2329 or 800/664–0124. **Village Taxi** ☎ 305/664–8181.

TOURS

Island Aeroplane Tours flies up to two passengers in a 1941 Waco, an open-cockpit biplane. Tours range from a quick 6- to 8-minute overview of Key West ($60 for two) to a 50-minute look at the offshore reefs ($300 for two). Seaplanes of Key West has half- and full-day trips to the Dry Tortugas; explore Fort Jefferson, built in 1846, and snorkel on the beautiful protected reef. A cooler of soft drinks and snorkel equipment is included in the $179 half-day, $305 full-day per person fee. Key West Nature Bike Tour, led by a 30-year Key West veteran, explores the natural, noncommercial side of Key West at a leisurely pace, stopping on back streets and in backyards of private homes to sample native fruits and view indigenous plants and trees, City Cemetery, and the Medicine Garden, a private meditation garden. The tours run 90–120 minutes and cost $20, plus $3 for a bike. Coral Reef Park Co. runs sailing trips on a 38-ft catamaran as well as glass-bottom boat tours. Captain Sterling's Everglades Eco-Tours operates Everglades and Florida Bay ecology tours ($39 per person), sunset cruises ($29 per person), a private-charter evening crocodile tour ($299 for up to six passengers), and a new tour, Flamingo Express, a five-hour boat tour from Key Largo to Flamingo, in mainland Everglades National Park.

Key Largo Princess offers two-hour glass-bottom boat trips ($18) and sunset cruises on a luxury 70-ft motor yacht with a 280-square-ft glass viewing area, departing from the Holiday Inn docks three times a day. M/V *Discovery* and the 65-ft *Pride of Key West* are glass-bottom boats ($30). Strike Zone Charters has glass-bottom boat excursions into the backcountry and Atlantic Ocean. The five-hour Island Excursion ($49) emphasizes nature and Keys history. Besides close encounters with birds, sea life, and vegetation, there's a fish cookout on an island. Snorkel and fishing equipment, food, and drinks are included. This is one of the few nature outings in the Keys with wheelchair access. Victoria Impallomeni, noted wilderness guide and authority on the ecology of Florida Bay, invites nature lovers—and especially children—aboard the *Imp II,* a 24-ft Aquasport, for four-hour half-day ($400) and seven-hour full-day ($600) ecotours that frequently include encounters with wild dolphins. While island-hopping, you visit underwater gardens, natural shoreline, and mangrove habitats. Tours also include Dancing Water Spirits retreats, a self-transformational retreat, with healing therapies; and optional live-aboard accommodations on a 36-ft sailboat. All equipment is supplied. Tours leave from Murray's Marina.

The Conch Tour Train is a 90-minute narrated tour of Key West, traveling 14 mi through Old Town and around the island. Board at Mallory Square and Flagler Station (901 Caroline St.) every half hour (9–4:30 from Mallory Square, later at other stops). The cost is $20. Old Town Trolley operates trackless trolley-style buses, departing from the Mallory Square and Roosevelt Boulevard depots every 30 minutes (9:15–4:30 from Mallory Square, later at other stops), for 90-minute narrated tours of Key West. The smaller trolleys go places the train won't fit. You may disembark at any of nine stops and reboard a later trolley. The cost is $20. Key West Business Guild's 75-minute Gay and Lesbian Historic Trolley Tours highlight the contributions gay and lesbian writers, artists, politicians, designers and celebrities have made to Key West's past. Tours, which cost $20, depart Saturdays at 11 AM from 512 South Street. Look for the rainbow flags. Adventure Charters & Tours loads kayaks onto the 42-ft catamaran *Island Fantasea* in Key West and heads out to the Great White Heron National Wildlife Refuge for guided kayak nature tours with a maximum of 14 passengers. Half-day trips ($35) last three hours and depart at 10 and 2. Full-day trips ($100) depart at 9:30 and include snorkeling, fishing, a grilled lunch, drinks, and a sunset. Mosquito Coast Island Outfitters and Kayak Guides runs full-day guided sea-kayak natural-history tours around the mangrove islands just east of Key West. The $55-a-day charge covers transportation, bottled water, a snack, and supplies, including snorkeling gear. Bill Keogh (naturalist, educator, and photographer) operates Big Pine Kayak Adventures, which takes visitors into remote areas of two national wildlife refuges in the Lower Keys to explore mangrove hammocks, islands, creeks, and sponge and grass flats on kayak nature tours, shallow-water skiff ecotours, backcountry catamaran sailing cruises, and shallow-water fishing expeditions. Prices start at $50 per person for a half day.

The folks at Florida Bay Outfitters know Upper Keys and Everglades waters well. Take a full-moon paddle one- to seven-day canoe or kayak tour to the Everglades or Lignumvitae or Indian Key. Trips run $50–$750. In addition to publishing several good guides on Key West, the Historic Florida Keys Foundation conducts tours of the City Cemetery Tuesday and Thursday at 9:30. As the former state historian in Key West and the current owner of a historic-preservation consulting firm, Sharon Wells of Island City Strolls knows plenty about Key West. She's authored many works, including the "The Walking and Biking Guide to Historic Key West," which has 10 self-guided tours of the historic district. It's available free at guest houses, hotels, and Key West bookstores. If that whets your appetite, sign on for one of her walking tours, including Architectural Strolls, Literary Landmarks, and Historic 1847 Cemetery Stroll, which cost $20–$25. "Pelican Path" is a free walking guide to Key West published by the Old Island Restoration Foundation. The tour discusses the history and architecture of 43 structures along 25 blocks of 12 Old Town streets. Pick up a copy at the chamber of commerce.

Tours Information **Adventure Charters & Tours** ⊠ 6810 Front St., Stock Island 33040 ☎ 305/296-0362 ⊕ www.keywestadventures.com. **Big Pine Kayak Adventures** ⊅ Box 431311, Big Pine Key 33043 ☎ 305/872-7474 ⊕ www.keyskayaktours.com. **Conch Tour Train** ☎ 305/294-5161. **Coral Reef Park Co.** ⊠ John Pennekamp Coral Reef State Park, MM 102.5, OS, Key Largo 33037 ☎ 305/451-1621. **Everglades Eco-Tours** ⊠ Dolphin's Cove, MM 102, BS, Key Largo 33037 ☎ 305/853-5161 or 888/224-6044 ⊕ www.captsterling.com. **Florida Bay Outfitters** ⊠ MM 104, BS, 104050 Overseas Hwy., Key Largo 33037 ☎ 305/451-3018 ⊕ www.kayakfloridakeys.com. **Historic Florida Keys Foundation** ⊠ 510 Greene St., Old City Hall, Key West 33040 ☎ 305/292-6718. **Island Aeroplane Tours** ⊠ Key West Airport, 3469 S. Roosevelt Blvd. ☎ 305/294-8687 ⊕ www.islandaeroplanetours.com. **Island City Strolls** ☎ 305/294-8380 ⊕ www.seekeywest.com. *Key Largo Princess* ⊠ MM 99.7, OS, 99701 Overseas Hwy., Key Largo 33037 ☎ 305/451-4655. **Key West Nature Bike Tour** ⊠ Truman Ave. and Simonton St., Key West ☎ 305/294-1882. **Mosquito Coast Island Outfitters and Kayak Guides** ⊠ 310 Duval St., Key West 33040 ☎ 305/294-7178 ⊕ www.mosquitocoast.net. **Murray's Marina** ⊠ MM 5, Stock Island. **M/V** *Discovery* ⊠ Land's End Marina, 251 Margaret St., Key West 33040 ☎ 305/293-0099. **Old Town Trolley** ⊠ 6631 Maloney Ave., Key West ☎ 305/296-6688. *Pride of Key West* ⊠ 2 Duval St., Key West 33040 ☎ 305/296-6293. **Seaplanes of Key West** ⊠ Key West Airport, 3471 S. Roosevelt Blvd. ☎ 305/294-0709 ⊕ www.seaplanesofkeywest.com. **Strike Zone Charters** ⊠ MM 29.6, BS, 29675 Overseas Hwy., Big Pine Key 33043 ☎ 305/872-9863 or 800/654-9560 ⊕ www.strikezonecharter.com. **Victoria Impallomeni** ⊠ 5710 U.S. 1, Key West 33040 ☎ 305/294-9731 or 888/822-7366 ⊕ www.captvictoria.com.

VISITOR INFORMATION

Tourist Information **Big Pine and the Lower Keys Chamber of Commerce** ⊠ MM 31, OS ⊅ Box 430511, Big Pine Key 33043 ☎ 305/872-2411 or 800/872-3722 ⊕ www.lowerkeyschamber.com 🖷 305/872-0752. **Florida Keys & Key West Visitors Bureau** ⊠ 402 Wall St., Box 1146, Key West 33041 ☎ 800/352-5397 ⊕ www.fla-keys.com. **Florida Keys Council of the Arts** ⊠ 1100 Simonton St., Key West 33040 ☎ 305/295-4369 ⊕ www.keysarts.org. **Gay and Lesbian Community Center of Key West** ⊠ 1075 Duval St., Suite C-14, Key West 33040 ☎ 305/292-3223 🖷 305/292-3237 ⊕ www.glcckeywest.org.

Greater Key West Chamber of Commerce (mainstream) ✉ 402 Wall St., Key West 33040 ☎ 305/294-2587 or 800/527-8539 🖷 305/294-7806. **Greater Marathon Chamber of Commerce & Visitor Center** ✉ MM 53.5, BS, 12222 Overseas Hwy., Marathon 33050 ☎ 305/743-5417 or 800/262-7284 ⊕ www.floridakeysmarathon.com. **Islamorada Chamber of Commerce** ✉ MM 82.5, BS ⬤ Box 915, Islamorada 33036 ☎ 305/664-4503 or 800/322-5397. **Key Largo Chamber of Commerce** ✉ MM 106, BS, 106000 Overseas Hwy., Key Largo 33037 ☎ 305/451-1414 or 800/822-1088 ⊕ www.keylargo.org 🖷 305/451-4726. **Key West Business Guild (gay)** ✉ 728 Duval St. ⬤ Box 1208, Key West 33041 ☎ 305/294-4603 or 800/535-7797 ⊕ www.gaykeywestfl.com. **Reef Relief Environmental Center & Store** ✉ 201 William St., Key West 33041 ☎ 305/294-3100.

WALT DISNEY WORLD® & THE ORLANDO AREA

FODOR'S CHOICE

Amazing Adventures of Spider-Man, Universal Orlando
Animal Planet Live!, Universal Orlando
Buzz Lightyear's Space Ranger Spin, Magic Kingdom
Cirque du Soleil, Downtown Disney
Disney's Wide World of Sports, Walt Disney World
Dueling Dragons, Universal Orlando
Eighth Voyage of Sindbad, Universal Orlando
Grand Cypress Equestrian Center, Lake Buena Vista
House of Blues, Walt Disney World Resort
Kilimanjaro Safaris, Disney's Animal Kingdom
The Magic of Disney Animation, Disney–MGM Studios
The Orlando Magic, basketball club
Osprey Ridge, golf course, Walt Disney World
Sea Lion & Otter Stadium, SeaWorld
SeaWorld Theater
Shamu Stadium, SeaWorld
Test Track, Epcot
Twilight Zone Tower of Terror, Disney–MGM Studios
Universal Horror Make-Up Show, Universal Orlando
Winter Summerland Miniature Golf Course, Orlando

HIGHLY RECOMMENDED

WHAT TO SEE Bok Tower Gardens, Lake Wales
Orlando Science Center, Orlando
Scenic Boat Tour, Winter Park
Splendid China, Kissimmee
WonderWorks, Orlando

*So many wonderful hotels and restaurants can be found in this area
that there's not enough space to list them all on this page. To see what
Fodor's editors and contributors highly recommend, please look for the
black stars as you leaf through this chapter.*

Updated by
Jennie Hess

LONG BEFORE "IT'S A SMALL WORLD" echoed through the palmetto scrub, other theme parks tempted visitors away from the beaches into the scruffy interior of Central Florida. Interstate 4 hadn't even been built when Dick and Julie Pope created Cypress Gardens, which holds the record as the region's oldest continuously running attraction—it's now more than 65 years old. But when the Walt Disney World (WDW) Resort opened with the Magic Kingdom as its centerpiece on October 1, 1971, and was immediately successful, the Central Florida theme-park scene became big business. Now there are Epcot, Disney–MGM, Disney's Animal Kingdom, SeaWorld and Discovery Cove, and Universal Studios and Islands of Adventure theme parks. Minor attractions such as the Orlando Science Center and WonderWorks, among others, also bid for your business.

The problem if you have tight schedules or slim wallets is that each park is worth a visit. The Magic Kingdom, Epcot, Disney's Animal Kingdom, and SeaWorld are not to be missed. Of the two movie parks, Universal Orlando and Disney–MGM Studios, the former is larger and rooted more in contemporary film; the latter projects the ambience of Hollywood in its heyday while incorporating modern movie themes. Islands of Adventure has more thrills for big kids and adults and will bring out the child in everyone. Two dining, shopping, and entertainment centers stand out: CityWalk at Universal and Downtown Disney at Walt Disney World Resort. If there's time, you shouldn't miss a chance to see Cirque du Soleil's acrobats, theatrics, and stunning choreography of "La Nouba," a show created for Cirque's Downtown Disney theater. DisneyQuest at Downtown Disney is an indoor theme park with several hours' worth of virtual-reality attractions. At CityWalk, Motown, Jimmy Buffet, and sports themes lend lots of dining fun to its eateries. Your best bet is to poll family or group members on their theme-park wishes, then develop a strategy to enjoy the top picks.

It is easy to forget that this ever-expanding fantasy world grew up around a sleepy farming town founded as a military outpost, Fort Gatlin, in 1838. Although not on any major waterway, Orlando was surrounded by small spring-fed lakes, and transplanted northerners planted sprawling oak trees to vary the landscape of palmetto scrub and citrus groves. Most development is in southwest Orlando, along the Interstate 4 corridor south of Florida's Turnpike. Orlando itself has become a center of international business, and north of downtown are several handsome, prosperous suburbs, most notably Winter Park, which retains its white-gloves-at-tea southern charm.

EXPLORING WALT DISNEY WORLD® & THE ORLANDO AREA

No doubt about it, the Disney parks have a special magic. You probably know lots about the Magic Kingdom, Epcot, Disney–MGM Studios, and Disney's Animal Kingdom. But there are also two wonderful water parks, Typhoon Lagoon and Blizzard Beach, as well as the indoor excitement at DisneyQuest. Before venturing into one of the big four, study the park's guidemap to note FASTPASS attractions. With your park ticket, make a free appointment to return to these locations later to gain quick admission and avoid long lines. One hitch: you usually can't make appointments for more than one FASTPASS attraction at a time. If you ask the attraction host, however, he or she can help you navigate in the system. Everyone leaves the theme parks with a different opin-

Most people spend the majority of their time at the theme parks, but Orlando and its upscale neighbor to the north, Winter Park, contain some natural and cultural attractions it would be a shame to miss.

Numbers in the text correspond to numbers in the margin and on the Orlando Area map.

6

If you have 4 days

No stay in the area would be complete without visiting the **Magic Kingdom ❶ ⌐**. The next day, take your pick between the more sophisticated **Epcot ❷** and state-of-the-art **Universal Islands of Adventure ❿**. On day three, see **Universal Studios ❾** or the smaller and more manageable **Disney–MGM Studios ❸**. On your fourth day go for **Disney's Animal Kingdom ❹** or **SeaWorld Orlando ❼**. Be sure to catch fireworks one night and one of the local dinner-show extravaganzas on another.

If you have 6 days

Spend the first four days exploring in this order: **Magic Kingdom ❶ ⌐**, **Universal Islands of Adventure ❿**, **Epcot ❷**, and **Disney's Animal Kingdom ❹** or **Universal Studios ❾**. At night make sure you get to some fireworks, sample at least one of the now-ubiquitous themed dining experiences, and visit Pleasure Island, Downtown Disney, or CityWalk at Universal. After all that theme park-ing, you'll need a rest. Depending on your interests and the ages of your children, use day five to relax and play at a Disney water park like Typhoon Lagoon, or venture into Winter Park. Take a leisurely boat tour and visit the **Charles Hosmer Morse Museum of American Art ㉑** or the **Orlando Science Center ⓳** for its great interactive activities before relaxing at your hotel. The sixth day should be for **SeaWorld Orlando ❼** or the more intimate **Discovery Cove ❽**. On your last evening take in a dinner show, perhaps SeaWorld's luau, Disney's Hoop-Dee-Doo Revue, or Kissimmee's Arabian Nights show.

If you have 10 days

You'll have time to see *all* the theme parks, but pacing is key. So that go-go Orlando tourism scene doesn't wear you down, intersperse theme-park outings with some low-key sightseeing or shopping. Start with the **Magic Kingdom ❶ ⌐**, staying late the first night for the fireworks. The second day, tackle **Epcot ❷** and hit Pleasure Island that evening. Set aside the third day for a visit to slower-paced **SeaWorld Orlando ❼**, making luau reservations when you enter the park; or, make reservations before your trip to visit **Discovery Cove ❽** to swim with dolphins and other sea creatures. On your fourth day it's back to the theme parks—either **Disney–MGM Studios ❸** or **Universal Studios ❾** or to **Blizzard Beach ❺** or **Typhoon Lagoon ❻** for some slower-paced fun. On your fifth and sixth days take in **Disney's Animal Kingdom ❹** and **Universal Islands of Adventure ❿**. Have dinner at a restaurant that suits your fancy. If it rains on one of these days, substitute the indoor adventures of DisneyQuest. On day seven, a day of (relative) rest, enjoy a boat tour through Winter Park and visit the **Orlando Science Center ⓳**. In late afternoon, stroll along downtown's Lake Eola, paddle a swan boat, and grab dinner on the porch of the Lake Eola Yacht Club or at Panera Bread. On your eighth day drive out to **Bok Tower Gardens** or one of the area's great state parks; then catch a dinner show or a Cirque du Soleil performance at Downtown Disney in the evening. Reserve day nine for one of the activities that you haven't hit yet: perhaps a water park or DisneyQuest. Your last day can be spent hitting a mall or outlet stores for some last-minute shopping or for revisiting your favorite theme park. Leave time to clean up back at the hotel, and, to ease your return to real life, have a bon voyage dinner at a restaurant outside of the resorts such as Le Coq au Vin, Memories of India, or Bahama Breeze.

---

ion about what was "the best." Some attractions get raves from all vis- itors, while others are enjoyed most by young children or older travel- ers. To take this into account, our descriptions rate each attraction with ★, ★★, or ★★★, depending on the strength of its appeal to the vis- itor group noted by the italics preceding the stars. "Young children" refers to kids ages five to seven; "very young children" are those (ages four and under) who probably won't meet the height requirements of most thrill rides anyway (for safety reasons). However, since youngsters come in different heights and confidence levels, exercise your parental judg- ment when it comes to the scarier rides.

Timing

If you're traveling without youngsters, avoid school-holiday periods. If you have preschoolers, follow the same course; crowds can overwhelm small fry. With school children, it's nice to avoid prime break times, but it's not always possible. Since the parks staff up in peak season, bigger crowds don't always mean longer lines, and busy periods bring longer hours and added entertainment and parades. Nevertheless, to steer clear of crowds, avoid Christmas, late March, the Easter weeks, and mid- June–mid-August, especially July 4 (it's too hot, anyway). Try to vaca- tion in late May or early June, as soon as the school year ends; in late August; or at Thanksgiving, or the first two weeks of December, which are not as busy as other holidays.

Magic Kingdom

▶ ❶ *Take the Magic Kingdom–U.S. 192 exit (Exit 64) off I–4; from there it's 4 mi along Disney's main entrance road and another mile to the park- ing lot; be prepared for serious traffic.*

The Magic Kingdom is the heart and soul of the Disney empire. Com- parable to California's Disneyland, it was the first Disney outpost in Florida when it opened in 1971, and it is the park that traveled, with modifications, to France and Japan. For a park that wields such world- wide influence, the Magic Kingdom is surprisingly small: at barely 98 acres, it is the tiniest of Walt Disney World Resort's big four. However, the unofficial theme song—"It's a Small World After All"—doesn't hold true when it comes to the Magic Kingdom attractions. Packed into seven different "lands" are nearly 50 major crowd pleasers, and that's not counting all the ancillary shops, eateries, live entertainment, roam- ing cartoon characters, fireworks, parades, and, of course, the sheer plea- sure of strolling through the beautifully landscaped and manicured grounds. The park is laid out on a north–south axis, with Cinderella Castle at the epicenter and the various lands surrounding it in a broad circle. Upon passing through the entrance gates, you immediately dis- cover yourself in **Town Square,** a central connection point that directly segues into **Main Street, U.S.A.,** a boulevard filled with Victorian-style stores and dining spots. Main Street runs due north and ends at the Hub, a large tree-lined circle, known as Central Plaza, in front of Cinderella

Castle. Rope Drop, the ceremonial stampede that kicks off each day, occurs at various points along Main Street and the Hub.

As you move clockwise from the Hub, the Magic Kingdom's various lands begin with **Adventureland, Frontierland,** and **Liberty Square.** Next, **Fantasyland** is directly behind Cinderella Castle—in the castle's courtyard, as it were. **Mickey's Toontown Fair** is set off the upper right-hand corner—that's northeast, for geography buffs—of Fantasyland. And **Tomorrowland,** directly to the right of the Hub, rounds out the circle.

Main Street, U.S.A.

With its pastel Victorian-style buildings filled with charming shops, Main Street is more than a mere conduit to the other enchantments of the Magic Kingdom. It is where the spell is first cast.

Walt Disney World Railroad. Step right up to the elevated platform above the Magic Kingdom's entrance for a ride into living history. The 1½-mi track runs along the perimeter of the Magic Kingdom, with much of the trip through the woods. You'll pass Tom Sawyer Island and other attractions; stops are in Frontierland and Mickey's Toontown Fair. Although the ride provides a good introduction to the layout of the park, it's best for parents with small children or as relief for tired feet and dragging legs later in the day. ☞ *Audience: All ages. Rating:* ★★

Adventureland

From the scrubbed brick, manicured lawns, and meticulously pruned trees of the Central Plaza, an artfully dilapidated wooden bridge leads to Adventureland, Disney's jungle homage.

Enchanted Tiki Room Under New Management. In its original incarnation as the Enchanted Tiki Birds, this was Disney's first Audio-Animatronics attraction. The updated version includes avian stars of two popular Disney animated films: Zazu from *The Lion King* and *Aladdin*'s Iago. ☞ *Audience: All ages. Rating:* ★★
Jungle Cruise. Cruise through three continents and along four rivers—the Congo, the Nile, the Mekong, and the Amazon—past all manner of animals from bathing elephants to slinky pythons. The guide's spiel is surprisingly funny, with just the right blend of cornball humor and gentle snideness. ☞ *Audience: All ages. Rating:* ★★★
The Magic Carpets of Aladdin. In this jewel-toned "carpet" ride around a giant genie's bottle, you control your own four-passenger, state-of-the-art carpet with a front-seat lever that moves it up and down and a rear-seat button that pitches it forward or backward. Part of the fun is trying to dodge the right-on aim of a water-spewing "camel." Though short, the ride is a big hit with kids, who are also dazzled by the colorful gems implanted in the pavement around the attraction. ☞ *Audience: All ages; parents must ride with toddlers. Rating:* ★★★
Pirates of the Caribbean. Classic Disney, this boat ride has memorable vignettes, incredible detail, a gripping story, and catchy music whose relentless yo-ho-ing can only be eradicated by "It's a Small World." Emerging from a pitch-black time tunnel, you're in the middle of a furious battle. A pirate ship, cannons blazing, is attacking a stone fortress. Cannonballs splash into the water just off your bows, and Audio-Animatronics pirates hoist the Jolly Roger. ☞ *Audience: All but young children. Rating:* ★★★
Swiss Family Treehouse. Based on the classic novel by Johann Wyss about the adventures of the Robinson family, who were shipwrecked on the way to America, the tree house shows what you can do with a big banyan and a lot of imagination. The rooms are furnished with patchwork

quilts and mahogany furniture, and great Disney detail abounds. ☞ *Audience: All ages; toddlers unsteady on their feet may have trouble with the stairs. Rating:* ★★

Frontierland

Frontierland, in the northwest quadrant of the Magic Kingdom, invokes the American frontier. Banjo and fiddle music twang from tree to tree, and guests walk around munching on the biggest turkey drumsticks you've ever seen.

Big Thunder Mountain Railroad. As any true roller-coaster lover can tell you, this three-minute ride is relatively tame. The thrills are there, however, thanks to the intricate details and stunning scenery along every inch of the 2,780-ft-long wooden track. Set in gold-rush days, the runaway train rushes and rattles past Animatronic donkeys, chickens, a goat, and a grizzled old miner surprised in his bathtub. ☞ *Audience: All but young children. No pregnant women or guests with back, neck, or leg braces; minimum height: 40".* Rating: ★★★

Country Bear Jamboree. Wisecracking, corn-pone Audio-Animatronics bears joke, sing, and play country music and 1950s rock-and-roll in this stage show. ☞ *Audience: All ages.* Rating: ★★★

Diamond Horseshoe Saloon Revue. "Knock, knock." "Who's there?" "Ya." "Ya who?" "Yaaahooo!" And they're off, with another rip-roaring, raucous, corny, nonstop, high-kicking, elbow-jabbing, song-and-dance-and-fiddling show staged in a re-creation of an Old West saloon. ☞ *Audience: All ages. Rating:* ★★

Splash Mountain. Based on the animated sequences in Disney's 1946 film *Song of the South,* this incredibly popular log-flume ride highlights a menagerie of Brer beasts (including Brer Rabbit, Brer Bear, and Brer Fox). You get one heart-stopping pause at the top, and then plummet. ☞ *Audience: All but very young children. No pregnant women or guests with back, neck, or leg braces; minimum height: 40". Rating:* ★★★

Tom Sawyer Island. The island—actually two islands connected by an old-fashioned swing bridge—is a natural playground, all hills and trees and rocks and shrubs. Check out the caves, Harper's Mill, and the rustic playground. ☞ *Audience: All ages. Rating:* ★★

Liberty Square

The weathered siding gives way to neat clapboard and solid brick, the mesquite and cactus are replaced by stately oaks, and the rough-and-tumble western frontier gently slides into Colonial America in Liberty Square.

Hall of Presidents. This multimedia tribute to the Constitution starts with a film, narrated by writer Maya Angelou, that discusses the Constitution as the codification of the spirit that founded America, then goes on to a roll call of all U.S. presidents (Animatronic robots, the first to be introduced at the park). The detail is lifelike, right down to the brace on Franklin Delano Roosevelt's leg. ☞ *Audience: Older children and adults. Rating:* ★★

Haunted Mansion. Part walk-through, part ride on a "doom buggy," this eight-minute ride is scary but not terrifying, and the special effects are a howl. Catch the glowing bats' eyes on the wallpaper, the wacky inscriptions on the tombstones, and the dancing ghosts. ☞ *Audience: All but young children. Rating:* ★★★

Liberty Belle Riverboat. A real old-fashioned steamboat takes you on a trip that is slow and not exactly thrilling, but it's a relaxing break for all concerned. ☞ *Audience: All ages. Rating:* ★

Boating

The Orlando area has one of the highest concentrations of lakes—both large and small—of anywhere in the continental United States, many of them right on WDW property. The lakes and the St. Johns River east of town provide popular vacation spots for recreational houseboaters.

Orlando Dining: A Ride in Itself

6

If they batter it, fry it, microwave it, torture it under a heat lamp until it's ready to sign a confession, and serve it with a side of fries, it's in Central Florida. On the other hand, renowned chefs such as Emeril Lagasse and Wolfgang Puck have places here, several Disney fine-dining restaurants have earned critical raves, and even the less lofty restaurant names try to put their best foot forward in Orlando, where food is consumed by millions of globally diverse visitors. The McDonald's on International Drive, for example, is the largest in the nation. This fiercely competitive dining market even brings out the best from the hometown eateries that predate Disney. The result is that dining choices in Orlando are like entertainment choices. There are simply more than you can sample on any one trip.

Golf

Professional golfers have been coming to Orlando for decades. Some of the greats, like Arnold Palmer, have established winter homes in the city. Not surprisingly, the city offers some of the best golfing anywhere, including courses designed by PGA pros and by the elite of professional golf-course designers such as Pete Dye, Tom Fazio, and Robert Trent Jones.

Shopping

It's only fitting that the world's number one tourist destination should offer excellent shopping. Every year, it seems, a new mall opens and the current hot ticket is the chichi Mall at Millenia east of Universal Studios. Disney and Universal have their own shopping "theme parks"—Downtown Disney and CityWalk, respectively. If you prefer shopping with a more eclectic feel, the tony shops and bistros of Winter Park's Park Avenue are a must.

Fantasyland

Many of the rides here are for children, and the lines move slowly. If you're traveling without young kids, skip this area, with the possible exception of Cinderella's Golden Carrousel, it's a small world, and one classic FASTPASS attraction: Peter Pan's Flight.

Cinderella Castle. At 180 ft, this castle is more than 100 ft taller than Disneyland's Sleeping Beauty Castle and, with its elongated towers and lacy fretwork, immeasurably more graceful.

Cinderella's Golden Carrousel. The whirling, musical heart of Fantasyland, this antique merry-go-round has 90 prancing horses, each one completely different. The band organ plays favorite Disney tunes. ☞ *Audience: All ages. Rating:* ★★

Dumbo the Flying Elephant. Jolly Dumbos fly around a central column, each pachyderm packing a couple of kids and a parent. It's one of Fantasyland's most popular rides. Alas, the ears do not flap. ☞ *Audience: Young children and the young at heart. Rating:* ★★

it's a small world. Visiting the Magic Kingdom and not stopping here— why, the idea is practically un-American. Barges inch through several brightly colored rooms, each representing a continent and each crammed

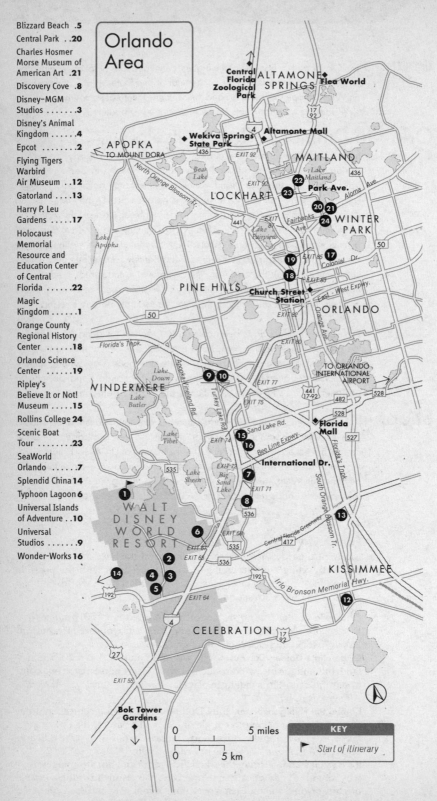

Orlando
Area

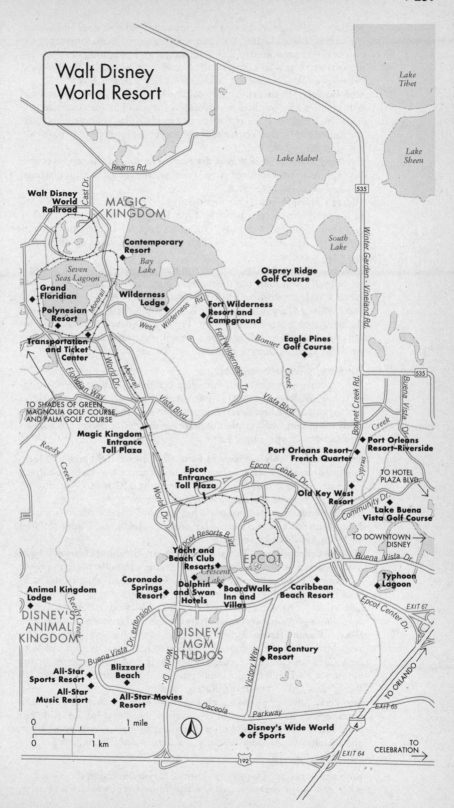

Walt Disney World Resort

Lake Tibet

Lake Sheen

Reams Rd.

Cast Dr.

Lake Mabel

535

Winter Garden - Vineland Rd.

Walt Disney World Railroad

MAGIC KINGDOM

Contemporary Resort

Bay Lake

South Lake

Osprey Ridge Golf Course

Seven Seas Lagoon

Grand Floridian

Wilderness Lodge

West Wilderness Rd.

Fort Wilderness Resort and Campground

Polynesian Resort

Monorail

Bonnet Creek

Eagle Pines Golf Course

Fort Wilderness Tr.

Transportation and Ticket Center

World Dr.

Monorail

Floridian Way

Vista Blvd.

Vista Blvd.

Bonnet Creek Rd.

535

Buena Vista Dr.

TO SHADES OF GREEN MAGNOLIA GOLF COURSE AND PALM GOLF COURSE

Reedy Creek

Magic Kingdom Entrance Toll Plaza

Creek

Port Orleans Resort–French Quarter

Cypress

Port Orleans Resort–Riverside

TO HOTEL PLAZA BLVD.

Epcot Entrance Toll Plaza

Epcot Center Dr.

Old Key West Resort

World Dr.

Community Dr.

Lake Buena Vista Golf Course

TO DOWNTOWN DISNEY

Epcot Resorts Blvd.

EPCOT

Buena Vista Dr.

Yacht and Beach Club Resorts

Crescent Lake

Typhoon Lagoon

Coronado Springs Resort

Dolphin and Swan Hotels

BoardWalk Inn and Villas

Caribbean Beach Resort

Epcot Center Dr.

EXIT 67

Animal Kingdom Lodge

Reedy Creek

DISNEY'S ANIMAL KINGDOM

Buena Vista Dr. extension

DISNEY-MGM STUDIOS

World Dr.

Victory Way

Pop Century Resort

TO ORLANDO

All-Star Sports Resort

Blizzard Beach

All-Star Music Resort

All-Star Movies Resort

Osceola Parkway

EXIT 65

0   1 mile

0   1 km

Disney's Wide World of Sports

4

TO CELEBRATION

192

EXIT 64

with musical moppets dressed in various national costumes and singing "It's a Small World After All." But somehow by the time you reach the end of the 11-minute trip, you're grinning and humming, too—as has almost everyone who's gone on the ride since it debuted at the 1964–65 New York World's Fair. ☞ *Audience: All ages. Rating:* ★★

Mad Tea Party. In this ride based on the 1951 Disney film about a girl named Alice who tumbles into Wonderland, you hop into oversize pastel teacups and whirl for two minutes around a giant platter. Check out the soused mouse that pops out of the teapot centerpiece. ☞ *Audience: All ages. Rating:* ★

The Many Adventures of Winnie the Pooh. The famous honey lover and his exploits in the Hundred Acre Wood are the theme for this charmer. ☞ *Audience: All ages.* ★★★

Mickey's PhilharMagic. This just-opened 3-D and special-effects film, at the renovated Legends of the Lion King theater, includes Mickey and Donald on an adventure with other popular Disney movie characters. ☞ *Audience: All ages. This attraction was not open for preview at press time.*

Peter Pan's Flight. Aboard two-person magic sailing ships with brightly striped sails, you soar into the moonlit skies above London en route to Never Land. ☞ *Audience: All ages. Rating:* ★★★

Snow White's Scary Adventures. This three-minute trip is complete with the evil queen, but there are also the Prince and Snow White and an honest-to-goodness kiss followed by a happily ever-after ending. ☞ *Audience: All ages; toddlers may be scared. Rating:* ★

Mickey's Toontown Fair

For a company that owes its fame to a certain endearing, big-eared little fellow, Walt Disney World Resort is astonishingly mouse-free. Until, that is, you arrive here: everything is child size. Pastel houses are positively lilliputian, with miniature driveways, toy-size picket fences, and signs scribbled with finger paint.

Barnstormer at Goofy's Wiseacres Farm. Traditional red barns and farm buildings form the backdrop here. The real attraction is the Barnstormer, a kid-size roller coaster with cars resembling 1920s crop-dusting biplanes. ☞ *Audience: Young children. Rating:* ★★★

Donald's Boat. A cross between a tugboat and a leaky ocean liner, the *Miss Daisy* is actually a water-play area. ☞ *Audience: Young children and their families. Rating:* ★★

Mickey's Country House. This slightly goofy architectural creation is right in the heart of Toontown Fairgrounds. Inside, a radio in the living room is "tooned" to scores from Mickey's favorite football team, from Duckburg University, while his clothes are neatly arranged in his bedroom beside Mickey's baby pictures and a photo of Minnie. ☞ *Audience: All ages, although teens may be put off by the terminal cuteness. Rating:* ★★

Minnie's Country House. A peek inside this baby-blue and pink house reveals Minnie's lively lifestyle. In addition to her duties as editor of *Minnie's Cartoon Country Living* magazine, the Martha Stewart of the mouse set also quilts, paints, and gardens. ☞ *Audience: All ages, although teens may be put off. Rating:* ★★

Toon Park. Another play area, this spongy green meadow is filled with foam topiary in the shapes of goats, cows, pigs, and horses. Kids can jump and hop on interactive lily pads to hear animal topiaries moo, bleat, and whinny. ☞ *Audience: Young children, mainly. Rating:* ★

Tomorrowland

Rather than predict a tomorrow destined for obsolescence, the focus here is on "the future that never was"—the future envisioned by sci-fi writers and moviemakers in the 1920s and '30s, when space flight, laser beams, and home computers belonged in the world of fiction, not fact.

Astro-Orbiter. The superstructure of revolving planets has come to symbolize the new Tomorrowland as much as Dumbo represents Fantasyland. The ride is a sort of Dumbo for grown-ups, but with Buck Rogers–style vehicles rather than elephants. You can control the altitude if not the velocity. ☞ *Audience: All ages. Rating:* ★★

Fodor'sChoice **Buzz Lightyear's Space Ranger Spin.** Based on the wildly popular *Toy Story,* this ride gives you a toy's perspective as it pits you and Buzz against the world. You're seated in a fast-moving vehicle equipped with a laser gun with which you shoot at targets to help Disney's macho spaceman save the universe. As Buzz likes to say, "To infinity—and beyond!" ☞ *Audience: Kids 3–100. Rating:* ★★★

Carousel of Progress. This 20-minute show in a revolving theater, first seen at the 1964–65 World's Fair, traces the impact of technological progress from the turn of the 20th century into the near future. In each decade an Audio-Animatronics family sings the praises of the new gadgets that technology has wrought. Carousel is only open during peak park times. ☞ *Audience: All ages. Rating:* ★

ExtraTERRORestrial Alien Encounter. This is the single scariest attraction in all of WDW, engendering start-to-finish screams among teens and ashen faces and tears among younger children who brave a very close encounter with an "extraTERRORestrial" creature, complete with realistic sound effects, smoke, and several seconds of complete darkness. ☞ *Audience: All but young children. Rating:* ★★★

Space Mountain. The 180-ft-high, gleaming white-concrete cone is a Magic Kingdom icon. Inside is a roller coaster that may well be the world's most imaginative. The ride only lasts two minutes and 38 seconds and attains a top speed of a mere 28 mph, but the devious twists and drops and the fact that it's all in the dark make it seem twice as long and four times as thrilling. ☞ *Audience: All but young children. No pregnant women or guests with back, neck, or leg braces; minimum height: 44".* *Rating:* ★★★

Timekeeper. This time-traveling adventure uses the voice of Robin Williams, who introduces you to famous inventors and visionaries of the machine age, such as Jules Verne and H. G. Wells. ☞ *Audience: All ages. Rating:* ★★

Tomorrowland Speedway. Be prepared for instant addiction among kids: brightly colored Mark VII model gasoline-powered cars swerve around the four 2,260-ft tracks with much vroom-vroom-vroom-ing. ☞ *Audience: Older children; minimum height: 52" to drive (be sure to check your youngster's height before lining up). Rating:* ★

Tomorrowland Transit Authority—TTA. All aboard for a nice, leisurely ride around the perimeter of Tomorrowland, circling the Astro-Orbiter and eventually gliding through the middle of Space Mountain. ☞ *Audience: All ages. Rating:* ★★

Entertainment

Beginning at 3 every day, the 15-minute-long **Share a Dream Come True** parade proceeds through Frontierland and down Main Street; there are floats, cartoon characters, dancers, singers, and much waving and cheering. The magic truly comes out at night (during busier times of the year)

Fodor'sChoice when **SpectroMagic** rolls down Main Street, U.S.A. in a splendidly choreographed surge of electro-luminescent, fiber-optic, and prismatic light-

Fodor'sChoice ing effects. **Fantasy in the Sky** is the Magic Kingdom fireworks display. It's a great show and well worth waiting around for (starting times for evening shows vary according to what time the sun sets).

Epcot

❷ *Take the Epcot–Downtown Disney exit (Exit 67) off I–4.*

Walt Disney World was created because of Walt Disney's dream of EPCOT, the Experimental Prototype Community of Tomorrow, which would reap the miraculous harvest of technological achievement. The permanent community that he envisioned has not yet come to be. Instead, there's Epcot—which opened in 1982, 16 years after Disney's death—a showcase, ostensibly, for the concepts that would be incorporated into the real-life Epcots of the future. Epcot is that rare paradox—an educational theme park—and a very successful one, too. In recent years, thrill rides have been added to provide a much-needed adrenaline rush. Bottom line: Epcot is best for school-age children and adults, and prime times to visit are during the spring International Flower and Garden Show or the fall International Food and Wine Festival. The two parts of Epcot are separated by the 40-acre World Showcase Lagoon. The northern half, **Future World,** is where the monorail drops you off and is the official entrance. The southern half, **World Showcase,** is accessible from the park's International Gateway entrance between the France and U.K. pavilions. Walk or take a launch from the Dolphin and Swan hotels and Disney's Yacht and Beach Club and BoardWalk resorts.

Future World

Future World is made up of two concentric circles of pavilions. The inner core is composed of the Spaceship Earth geosphere and, just beyond it, the large, computer-animated Fountain of Nations, bracketed by the crescent-shape Innoventions East and West. The outer ring comprises seven pavilions. On the east side they are, in order, the Universe of Energy, Wonders of Life, Test Track, and the new Mission: SPACE. With the exception of the Wonders of Life, the pavilions present a single, self-contained ride and an occasional post-ride showcase; a visit rarely takes more than 30 minutes, but it depends on how long you spend in the post-ride area. On the west side there are the Living Seas, the Land, and Imagination! Like the Wonders of Life, these blockbuster exhibits contain both rides and interactive displays; count on spending at least 1½ hours per pavilion—and wanting to stay longer.

Imagination! Have a sensory adventure through sound, illusion, gravity, dimensions, and color, along with a behind-the-scenes tour of what you see in the *Honey, I Shrunk the Audience* film.

Honey, I Shrunk the Audience is one of the most popular attractions in Epcot. This 3-D adventure utilizes the futuristic "shrinking" techniques demonstrated in the films that starred Rick Moranis. Be prepared to laugh and scream your head off, courtesy of the special in-theater effects, moving seats, and 3-D film technology. Don't miss this one. ☞ *Audience: All but very young children. Rating:* ★★★

The pavilion's **Image Works** is an electronic fun house with interactive games and wizardry. ☞ *Audience: All ages. Rating:* ★★★

Innoventions. In this two-building, 100,000-square-ft attraction, continually updated to reflect the latest technology, are live stage demonstrations, hands-on displays, and exhibits that highlight gadgets that affect daily living. Each major exhibition area is presented by a leading manufacturer. ☞ *Audience: All ages. Rating:* ★★★

The Land. Shaped like an intergalactic greenhouse, the enormous skylighted The Land pavilion dedicates 6 acres and a host of attractions to a popular topic: food.

Circle of Life is a film featuring three stars of *The Lion King*—Simba the lion, Timon the meerkat, and Pumbaa the waddling warthog—in an enlightening and powerful message about protecting the world's environment for all living things. ☞ *Audience: All ages, although some toddlers may nap. Rating:* ★★

Food Rocks is a rowdy concert in which recognizable rock-and-roll performers in the shape of favorite foods (the Peach Boys, Chubby Cheddar, and Neil Moussaka, to name a few) sing about the joys of nutrition. ☞ *Audience: Children and their parents. Rating:* ★

The main event is a boat ride called **Living with the Land,** piloted by an informative, overalls-clad guide. You cruise through three biomes—rain forest, desert, and prairie ecological communities—and into an experimental greenhouse that demonstrates how food sources may be grown in the future, not only on this planet but also in outer space. ☞ *Audience: All but very young children. Rating:* ★★★

Living Seas. On Epcot's western outer ring is the first satellite pavilion, Living Seas, a favorite among children. Time and technology have caught up with the 5.7-million-gallon aquarium at the pavilion's core, so what was once revolutionary has now been equaled by top aquariums around the country.

The two-level **Sea Base Alpha,** a typical Epcot playground, contains six modules, each dedicated to a specific subject: the history of robotics, ocean exploration, ocean ecosystems, dolphins, porpoises, and sea lions. ☞ *Audience: All but young children. Rating:* ★★

The three-minute **Caribbean Coral Reef Ride,** an underwater shuttle to Sea Base Alpha, is simply too short. In addition to watching the aquarium's full-time denizens, you may catch sight of a diver, testing out the latest scuba equipment, surrounded by a cloud of parrot fish. Afterward you may want to circumnavigate the tank at your own speed on an upper level, pointing out barracudas, stingrays, sea turtles, and even sharks. ☞ *Audience: All. Rating:* ★★

Spaceship Earth. Balanced like a giant golf ball waiting for some celestial being to tee off, the multifaceted silver geosphere of Spaceship Earth is to Epcot what the Cinderella Castle is to the Magic Kingdom.

The **Spaceship Earth ride** explores human progress and the continuing search for better forms of communication. Scripted by Ray Bradbury and narrated by Jeremy Irons, the journey begins in the darkest tunnels of time. It proceeds through history and ends poised on the edge of the future. ☞ *Audience: All ages, but persons who experience anxiety in dark, narrow, or enclosed spaces should not ride. Rating:* ★★

Fodor'sChoice **Test Track.** This small-scale version of a General Motors test track is billed as "the longest and fastest ride in Walt Disney World history." The heart-pounding trip takes you through seven different tests and reaches speeds near 65 mph at the end, when your vehicle bursts from the building to an outdoor finale. ☞ *Audience: All but young children. No pregnant women or guests with back, neck, or leg braces; minimum height: 40″. Rating:* ★★★

Universe of Energy. The first of the pavilions on the left, or east, side of Future World is in a large, lopsided pyramid sheathed in thousands of mirrors—solar collectors that power the attraction within.

One of the most technologically complex shows at Epcot, **Ellen's Energy Adventure** stars comedian Ellen DeGeneres as a woman who dreams she's a contestant on *Jeopardy!*, only to discover that all the categories are about a subject she knows nothing about—energy. With help from Bill Nye the Science Guy, she (and you) gets a crash course in Energy 101. The exhibit combines a ride, three films, the largest Audio-Animatronics animals ever built, 250 prehistoric trees, and enough cold, damp fog to make you think you've been transported into a defrosting refrigerator. ☞ *Audience: All ages. Rating:* ★★★

Wonders of Life. A towering statue of a DNA double helix stands outside the gold-crowned dome of one of the most popular wonders of Epcot. The attraction takes an amusing but serious and educational look at health, fitness, and modern lifestyles.

The flight simulator—**Body Wars**—takes you on a bumpy platelet-to-platelet ride through the human circulatory system. ☞ *Audience: All but young children. No pregnant women or guests with heart, back, or neck problems or motion sickness; minimum height: 40″. Rating:* ★★★

The engaging **Cranium Command** shows how the cranium manages to make the heart, the uptight left brain, the laid-back right brain, the stomach, and an ever-alert adrenal gland all work together as their host, a 12-year-old boy, suffers the slings and arrows of a typical day. ☞ *Audience: All ages. Rating:* ★★★

The **Fitness Fairground**, an educational playground that teaches both adults and children about good health, takes up much of Wonders of Life. There are games in which you can pedal around the world on a stationary bicycle and guess your stress level. ☞ *Audience: All ages. Rating:* ★★

Starring Martin Short, *The Making of Me* is a valuable film on human conception and childbearing, using both animation and actual footage from a live birth to explain where babies come from. Some scenes are explicit, but all the topics are handled with gentle humor and great delicacy. ☞ *Audience: All but very young children. Rating:* ★★★

World Showcase

The 40-acre World Showcase Lagoon is 1⅓ mi around, but in that space you circumnavigate the globe, or at least explore it, in pavilions representing 11 countries in Europe, Asia, North Africa, and the Americas. In each pavilion native food, entertainment, art and handicrafts, and usually a multimedia presentation showcase the particular culture and people; architecture and landscaping re-create well-known landmarks.

Mexico. In a spectacular Maya pyramid surrounded by a tangle of tropical vegetation, Mexico has an exhibit of pre-Columbian art, a restaurant, and, of course, a shopping plaza. The cool, dark insides of the pyramid provide a welcome respite from a hot Orlando day. True to its name, the **El Río del Tiempo** boat ride takes you on a ho-hum trip down the river of time. ☞ *Audience: All ages. Rating:* ★

Norway. Here rough-hewn timbers and sharply pitched roofs are brightened by bloom-stuffed window boxes. The pavilion complex contains a 14th-century stone fortress that mimics Oslo's Akershus, cobbled streets, rocky waterfalls, and a wood-stave church, modeled after one built in 1250, with wooden dragons glaring from the eaves. The church has an exhibit that tells the story of two early 20th-century polar expeditions by using vintage artifacts, and the pavilion's shops sell wood carvings, glass, and beautifully embroidered woolen sweaters. Norway also has a dandy boat ride: **Maelstrom,** in which dragon-headed longboats take a voyage through time that, despite its scary name and encounters with evil trolls, is actually more interesting than frightening. Let the kids frolic on the Age of the Vikings playground area, which replicates an old ship. ☞ *Audience: All ages. Rating:* ★★

China. A shimmering red-and gold three-tier replica of Beijing's Temple of Heaven towers over a serene Chinese garden, an art gallery displaying treasures from the People's Republic, a spacious emporium devoted to Chinese goods, and two restaurants. The *Wonders of China,* a sensational panorama of the land and people, is dramatically portrayed on a 360-degree CircleVision screen. ☞ *Audience: All ages, although no strollers permitted and small children have to be held aloft to see. Rating:* ★★★

Germany. In this jovial make-believe village you'll hear the hourly chimes from the glockenspiel on the clock tower, musical toots and tweets from multitudinous cuckoo clocks, and the satisfied grunts of hungry visitors chowing down on hearty German cooking. The oompah-band show in the Biergarten restaurant is also scheduled at times in the courtyard. Germany has the most shops of any pavilion. ☞ *Audience: Adults and older children. Rating:* ★★

Italy. The star here is the Piazza San Marco, complete with a re-creation of Venice's Doge's Palace that's accurate right down to the gold leaf on the ringlets of the angel perched 100 ft atop the campanile, gondolas tethered to a seawall stained with age, and Romanesque columns, Byzantine mosaics, Gothic arches, and stone walls that have all been carefully antiqued to look historic. ☞ *Audience: Adults and older children. Rating:* ★★

American Adventure. The pavilion's superlative attraction is a 100-yard dash through history called the **American Adventure.** To the music of a piece called "The Golden Dream," it combines evocative sets, one of the world's largest rear-projection screens (72 ft wide), enormous movable stages, and 35 lifelike Audio-Animatronics players. ☞ *Audience: All ages. Rating:* ★★★

Japan. A brilliant vermilion torii gate, derived from the design of Hiroshima Bay's much-photographed Itsukushima Shrine, epitomizes the striking yet serene mood here. Disney horticulturists deserve a hand for their achievement in constructing out of all-American plants and boulders a very Japanese landscape, complete with rocks, pebbled streams, pools, and hills. The peace is occasionally disturbed by performances of traditional Japanese drumming. ☞ *Audience: Adults and older children. Rating:* ★★★

Morocco. You don't need a magic carpet to be instantaneously transported into an exotic culture—just walk through the pointed arches of the Bab Boujouloud gate. Koutoubia Minaret, a replica of the prayer tower in Marrakesh, acts as Morocco's landmark. Traditional winding alleyways, each corner bursting with carpets, brasses, leather work, and other North African craftsmanship, lead to a beautifully tiled fountain and lush gardens. ☞ *Audience: Adults and older children. Rating:* ★★

France. The scaled-down model of the Eiffel Tower ought to clue you in to the fact that you've arrived in France, specifically Paris, but if that doesn't set the scene for you, poignant accordion music wafts out of concealed speakers and delicious aromas waft from the Boulangerie Pâtisserie bakeshop. The intimate Palais du Cinéma screens the film *Impressions de France,* a homage to the glories of the country: the vineyards at harvesttime, Paris on Bastille Day, the Alps, Versailles, Normandy's Mont-St-Michel, and the stunning châteaux of the Loire Valley. ☞ *Audience: Adults. Rating:* ★★★

United Kingdom. A pastiche of "There will always be an England" architecture, the United Kingdom rambles between the elegant mansions lining a London square to the bustling, half-timbered shops of a village High Street to the thatched-roof cottages of the countryside. The pavilion has no single major attraction. Instead, wander through shops selling tea and tea accessories, Welsh handicrafts, Royal Doulton figurines, and woolens and tartans. Check the entertainment schedule for performances of the British Invasion, a four-man band with a sound so like the Beatles that you'll feel the '60s all over again. ☞ *Audience: Adults and older children. Rating:* ★★★

Canada. "Oh, it's just our Canadian outdoors," said a typically modest native guide upon being asked the model for the striking rocky chasm and tumbling waterfall that represent just one of the high points of Canada. The top attraction is the CircleVision film *O Canada!* And that's just what you'll say after the stunning opening shot of the Royal Canadian Mounted Police literally surrounding you as they circle the screen. ☞ *Audience: All ages, although no strollers permitted and toddlers have to be held aloft to see. Rating:* ★★★

Entertainment

Most pavilions have entertainment; schedules are in the Times Guide that accompanies your park map. Above the lagoon every night, about a half hour before closing, don't miss the spectacular **IllumiNations** sound-and-light show, with fireworks, lasers, and lots of special effects to the accompaniment of a terrific score.

Disney–MGM Studios

❸ *Take the Disney–MGM Studios exit (Exit 64) off I–4.*

Inspired by Walt Disney's roots in show business and animated film, Disney–MGM Studios blends theme park with fully functioning movie and television production center, breathtaking rides with instructional tours, nostalgia with high-tech wonders. The park is suited for young and old, with more mature visitors appreciating cinematic references that hark back to the 1920s and '30s, while the youngsters hone in on popular film and TV of today. Surprisingly, the entire park is rather small—only 110 acres, a quarter the size of Universal Studios—with about 20 major attractions. When the lines are minimal, the park can be easily covered in a day with time for repeat rides.

Hollywood Boulevard

With its palm trees, pastel buildings, and flashy neon, Hollywood Boulevard paints a rosy picture of Tinseltown in the 1930s. The sense of having walked right onto a movie set is enhanced by the art deco–style storefronts, strolling brass bands, and roving actors dressed in costume and playing everything from would-be starlets to nefarious agents. The set is marred only by the Sorcerer Mickey hat icon that blocks a once-nostalgic view of the park's magnificent Chinese Theater reproduction. Both Hollywood and Sunset boulevards have souvenir shops and memorabilia collections galore.

Great Movie Ride. In a fire-engine-red pagoda replica of Grauman's Chinese Theater, this 22-minute tour full of Disney Magic captures great moments in film—from Gene Kelly clutching that familiar lamppost as he sings the title song from *Singin' in the Rain* to the Munchkins of Oz and some of the slimier characters from *Alien.* ☞ *Audience: All but young children, for whom it may be too intense. Rating:* ★★★

Sunset Boulevard

This avenue pays tribute to famous Hollywood monuments.

Beauty and the Beast—Live on Stage. This very popular stage show takes place in the Theater of the Stars, a re-creation of the famed Hollywood Bowl. The long-running production is a lively, colorful, and well-done condensation of the animated film. As you arrive or depart, it's fun to check out set-in-cement handprints and footprints of the television

celebrities who've visited Disney–MGM Studios. ☞ *Audience: All ages.*
Rating: ★★★

Rock 'n' Roller Coaster Starring Aerosmith. On WDW's wildest roller
coaster, the twists and turns are accentuated by a synchronized rock
sound track that resonates from speakers mounted in each vehicle.
☞ *Audience: Older children and adults. No pregnant women or guests*
with heart, back, or neck problems or motion sickness; minimum
height: 44". Rating: ★★★

Fodor'sChoice **Twilight Zone Tower of Terror.** Ominously overlooking Sunset Boulevard
is a 13-story structure that's reputedly the now-deserted Hollywood Tower
Hotel. You take an eerie stroll through the dimly lighted lobby and de-
caying library to the boiler room before boarding the hotel's giant elevator. As you head upward past seemingly deserted hallways, ghostly
former residents appear around you, until suddenly—faster than you
can say "Where's Rod Serling?"—the creaking vehicle abruptly plunges
downward in a terrifying 130-ft free-fall drop, only to repeat with several stomach-churning ups and downs. ☞ *Audience: Older children and*
adults. No pregnant women or guests with heart, back, or neck prob-
lems; minimum height: 40". Rating: ★★★

Animation Courtyard

Fodor'sChoice **The Magic of Disney Animation.** This self-guided tour through the Disney
animation process is one of the funniest and most engaging attractions
at the park. More than any other backstage tour, more than any other
revelation of stunt secrets, this tour truly takes you inside the magic as
you follow the many steps of animation from concept to charisma.
After a hilarious eight-minute film in which Walter Cronkite and Robin
Williams explain animation basics, you follow walkways with windows overlooking the working animation studios, where salaried Disney artists are at their drafting tables doing everything you just learned
about. Their desks are strewn with finished drawings of Simba, Mulan,
Aladdin, and other famous characters, and you can peer over their
shoulders at soon-to-be-famous characters. This is better than magic—
this is real. ☞ *Audience: All but toddlers. Rating:* ★★★

Playhouse Disney—Live on Stage! The former Soundstage Restaurant
now has one of the best shows for children anywhere at Walt Disney
World. There's a perky host on a larger-than-life "storybook stage" that
presents stars of several popular Disney Channel shows. Preschoolers
and even toddlers can sing and dance in the aisles as the Bear in the Big
Blue House, Rolie Polie Olie, Pooh, and Stanley cha-cha-cha their way
through positive life lessons. ☞ *Audience: Toddlers and preschoolers.*
Rating: ★★★

Voyage of the Little Mermaid. A boxy building on Mickey Avenue invites
you to join Ariel, Sebastian, and the rest of the underwater gang in this
stage show, which condenses the movie into a marathon presentation
of the greatest hits. ☞ *Audience: All ages. Rating:* ★★

Walt Disney: One Man's Dream. This photo, film, and audio tour leads
you through Walt's life in the old Walt Disney Theater. If you qualify
as a baby boomer, it's a real nostalgia trip to see Walt resurrected on
film as his "Wonderful World of Color" intro splashes across the screen.
And if you're into artifacts, there's plenty of Walt memorabilia to view
as you absorb the remarkable history of this entertainment legend.
☞ *Audience: Ages 10 and up. Rating:* ★★

Mickey Avenue

Disney–MGM Studios Backlot Tour. This combination tram ride and walking tour is a 60-minute exploration of the back-lot building blocks of
movies: set design, costumes, props, lighting, and special effects. At Catas-
trophe Canyon, the tram bounces up and down in a simulated earth-

quake, an oil tanker explodes in gobs of smoke and flame, and a water tower crashes to the ground, touching off a flash flood. ☞ *Audience: All but young children. Rating:* ★★★

Who Wants to Be a Millionaire—Play It! The syndicated TV show is now also a live stage show on Soundstages 2 and 3, where you'll have your own fastest-finger buttons and a chance at the hot seat next to the show's celebrity "Regis." You don't vie for $1 million, but you do build points to get a shot at some parting prizes. ☞ *Audience: Ages 5 and up. Rating:* ★★★

New York Street

Honey, I Shrunk the Kids **Movie Set Adventure.** Let the kids run free in this state-of-the-art playground based on the movie about lilliputian kids in a larger-than-life world. They can slide down a gigantic blade of grass, crawl through caves, and climb a mushroom mountain. ☞ *Audience: Children and those who love them. Rating:* ★★★

Jim Henson's MuppetVision 3-D. You don't have to be a Miss Piggy–phile to get a kick out of this combination 3-D movie and musical revue. The theater was constructed especially for this show, with special effects built into the walls and ceilings. ☞ *Audience: All ages. Rating:* ★★★

Echo Lake

In the center of this idealized California is cool, calm Echo Lake, an oasis fringed with trees and benches and ringed with landmarks: pink-and-aqua restaurants trimmed in chrome; Min and Bill's Dockside Diner with fast snacks; and Gertie, a Sinclair gas station dinosaur that dispenses ice cream, Disney souvenirs, and the occasional puff of smoke in true magic-dragon fashion.

Indiana Jones Epic Stunt Spectacular! Don't leave Disney–MGM Studios without seeing this 30-minute show with the stunt choreography of veteran coordinator Glenn Randall (*Raiders of the Lost Ark, Indiana Jones and the Temple of Doom, E. T.,* and *Jewel of the Nile* are among his credits). ☞ *Audience: All but young children. Rating:* ★★★

Sounds Dangerous Starring Drew Carey. This show is a delightful, multifaceted demonstration of the use of movie sound effects. It stars Drew Carey in a hilarious movie that lets you play detective. Once the theater turns pitch black, you'll hear sounds that create the effects that are used on the screen. Don't see the show if you're afraid of the dark. ☞ *Audience: All but very young children. Rating:* ★★

Star Tours. Although the flight-simulator technology used for this ride was long ago surpassed by other thrill rides, most notably Universal Studios' *Back to the Future . . . The Ride,* this *Star Wars* takeoff is still a pretty good trip. ☞ *Audience: Older children and adults. No pregnant women or guests with heart, back, or neck problems or motion sickness. Children must be 40", and those under 7 must be accompanied by an adult. Rating:* ★★★

Entertainment

The live *Beauty and the Beast* stage show is a winner. And don't miss the **Disney Stars and Motor Cars** parade, which wends its way up Hollywood Boulevard. The after-dark fireworks show **Fantasmic!** is the perfect finale to the day, with its cast of Disney characters, fountains, lasers, and dramatic musical score.

Fodor'sChoice

Disney's Animal Kingdom

❹ *Take the Disney's Animal Kingdom exit (Exit 65) off I–4.*

Humankind's enduring love for animals is the inspiration for Disney's fourth theme park in Orlando, which explores the story of all animals—real, imaginary, and extinct—in a true Disney fashion via carefully re-created and dramatic landscapes, rides, peppy musical shows, shops, and eateries.

The park is laid out very much like the Magic Kingdom; its focal point is the spectacular **Tree of Life**, in **Discovery Island**. From there, all the other "lands" are laid out like the spokes of a wheel. At the entrance is the **Oasis**, with guest relations, and to its right is **DinoLand U.S.A.** In the northeast corner is **Asia**, and **Africa** is on the northwest side. South of Discovery Island, immediately west of the Oasis, is **Camp Minnie-Mickey**, a character-greeting and show area. Make sure you arrive early, when the animals are at their liveliest, or you may miss out on some of the best reasons to go.

Discovery Island

Primarily the site of the Tree of Life and "It's Tough to Be a Bug!" inside the Tree of Life Theater, this land also has two eateries, several gift shops, and some visitor services, such as the baby-care center and lost and found.

Tree of Life. The imposing park centerpiece is 14 stories high and 50 ft. wide, and its roots, trunk, and branches are covered with 325 intricate carvings of animal forms. More than 100,000 fabric leaves in several shades of green form its realistic canopy. Once inside the Tree of Life Theater within its mammoth trunk, you'll be serenaded by crickets and get a bug's-eye view of life in the whimsical *It's Tough to Be a Bug!*, complete with in-theater special effects. ☞ *Audience: All but very young children, who might be frightened of the dark and some bug effects. Rating:* ★★★

DinoLand U.S.A.

Just as it sounds, this is the place to come in contact with creatures prehistoric.

Boneyard. Youngsters can slide, bounce, and slither around this archaeological dig site–cum–playground and even unearth a wooly mammoth in the area's huge sandbox. ☞ *Audience: Young children and their families. Rating:* ★★★

Cretaceous Trail. Walk through a re-creation of a primeval forest containing some of the plant survivors of the dinosaur age such as monkey puzzles and angiosperms. ☞ *Audience: All ages. Rating:* ★

DINOSAUR. When your car rouses a cantankerous Carnotaurus from his Cretaceous slumber, it's show time on this thrill ride. Travel back 65 million years on a twisting start-stop adventure and try to save the last living iguanodon as a massive asteroid hurtles toward Earth. ☞ *Audience: All ages who don't mind scary creatures in the dark and are tall enough to meet the minimum height requirement of 40". No pregnant women or guests with heart, back, or neck problems. Rating:* ★★★

Primeval Whirl. In this free-spinning, four-passenger outdoor "time machine" your vehicle heads on a brief journey back in time, twisting and turning along a compact track, and even venturing into the jaws of a dinosaur "skeleton." The more weight there is in the vehicle, the more you spin. ☞ *Audience: All but very young children. Minimum height: 48". Rating:* ★★★

TriceraTop Spin. Until now, there wasn't a true "kiddie ride" anywhere at Disney's Animal Kingdom. TriceraTop Spin is designed for playful little dinophiles who'll get a kick out of whirling around this ride's giant spinning toy top in their dino-mobiles. ☞ *Audience: Toddlers, school-age children and their families. Rating:* ★★

Asia

This is a typical rural village and an exotic rain forest where trees grow from a crumbling tiger shrine and two massive towers, one representing Thailand, the other Nepal.

Flights of Wonder. An outdoor show on the *Caravan Stage*, it highlights spectacular demonstrations of skill by falcons, hawks, and other rare and fascinating birds that swoop down over the audience. ☞ *Audience: All but those who might be frightened by the low-flying birds. Rating:* ★★

Kali River Rapids. Run the Chakranadi River through a huge bamboo tunnel and a series of sharp twists, turns, and one steep, very wet drop while passing rain forests, burning woodlands, and temple ruins. ☞ *Audience: Older children and adults. No guests with heart, back, or neck problems or motion sickness; minimum height: 42". Rating:* ★★★

Maharajah Jungle Trek. Get a wonderful up-close view of jungle animals, including magnificent tigers, a Komodo dragon, and fascinating fruit bats, along this trail. At the end, you walk through an aviary set with a lotus pool. ☞ *Audience: Older children and adults. Rating:* ★★

Africa

Predominately an enclave for wildlife from the continent, this is all forests and grasslands; the focus is on live animals. **Harambe,** on the northern banks of Discovery River, is Africa's starting point. Inspired by the small town of Lamu, Kenya, this coastal "village" spotlights Swahili architecture, food, and shopping with African themes.

Fodor'sChoice **Kilimanjaro Safaris.** A re-created African safari may not be a new idea, but this one goes a step beyond merely observing zebras and lions. Open-sided safari vehicles take you over some 100 acres of savanna, forest, rivers, and rocky hills to see herds of African animals including elephants, rhinos, giraffes, hippos, and even cheetahs in extremely authentic settings. There's even a wee bit of Disney's famous Audio-Animatronics animal action near the end that links the ride to its "let's-get-the-poachers" story line. Do this early in the day when animals are friskiest, and use FASTPASS if the wait is more than 30 minutes. ☞ *Audience: All ages. Parents can hold small tykes and explain the ride's poacher theme. Rating:* ★★★

Pangani Forest Exploration Trail. Take a nature walk among streams and waterfalls to see a family and a bachelor group of lowland gorillas, hippos (viewed from under the water), meerkats, exotic birds, and even naked mole rats. This is one of the best experiences in the park if the weather is cool enough for the animals to be active. ☞ *Audience: All ages. Rating:* ★★★

Rafiki's Planet Watch. Take the Wildlife Express steam train to this unique center of ecoawareness. At Habitat Habit!, cotton-top tamarins play while you learn how to live with all Earth's animals. At Conservation Station, there are animal experts, interactive exhibits, and information on worldwide efforts to protect endangered species and their habitats and about the park's behind-the-scenes operations. At Affection Section, children can get face-to-face with goats and other small critters. ☞ *Audience: All ages. Rating:* ★★

Camp Minnie-Mickey

This Adirondack-style land is a meet-and-greet area where Disney characters gather for picture-taking and autographs. Very small children may be wary around the larger-than-life renditions of Mickey Mouse, Goofy, and other characters, but everyone else will have a blast. Live performances are also staged here.

Festival of the Lion King. If you think you've seen enough Lion King to last a lifetime, you're wrong, unless you've seen this show. In an open-air theater-in-the-round, it's a delightful tribal celebration of song, dance, acrobatics, and other surprising performances on huge moving stages and with giant moving floats. ☞ *Audience: All ages. Rating:* ★★★
Pocahontas and Her Forest Friends. This show based on the Disney film stars live animals in a lesson on nature and how to preserve endangered species. Pocahontas is your official hostess, talking on the subject and breaking out in song including "Colors of the Wind." ☞ *Note: May not be scheduled daily during slower season—check entertainment guidemap. Audience: All ages. Rating:* ★★

The Disney Water Parks

Visit the water parks first thing in the morning or late in the afternoon to avoid crowds, or when the weather clears up after a thundershower. (Typically, rainstorms drive away the crowds, and lots of people simply don't come back.) If you plan to make a whole day of it, avoid weekends—Typhoon Lagoon and Blizzard Beach are big among locals as well as visitors.

Blizzard Beach

5 Blizzard Beach promises the seemingly impossible—a seaside playground with an alpine theme. The Disney Imagineers have gone all out to create a ski resort in the midst of a tropical lagoon. The snow-in-Florida motif provides lots of puns and sight gags. The park centers on **Mt. Gushmore,** a "snowcapped" mountain with all sorts of ways, such as toboggan and sled runs, to get down. At the base of the mountain, there is a sandy beach featuring the obligatory wave pool, a lazy river, and play areas for both young children and preteens. Mt. Gushmore's big gun is **Summit Plummet,** which Disney bills as "the world's tallest, fastest free-fall speed slide." From the top it's a wild 55-mph plunge straight down to a splash landing at the base of the mountain. **Teamboat Springs** is a "white-water raft ride" in which six-passenger rafts zip along a twisting series of rushing waterfalls. Of course, no water park would be complete without a flume ride—here there are three.

Typhoon Lagoon

6 Typhoon Lagoon will whirl and wow you for the better part of a day: bobbing in 4-ft waves in a surf lagoon the size of two football fields, speeding down arrow-straight water slides and around twisty storm slides, and bumping through white-water rapids. The park is popular; in fact, in summer and on weekends it often reaches capacity (7,200) by mid-morning. Try snorkeling in **Shark Reef,** a 360,000-gallon tank with an artificial coral reef and 4,000 real tropical fish. Or grab an inner tube and float along 2,100-ft **Castaway Creek,** which circles the entire park. It takes about 30 minutes to do the circuit; stop as you please along the way. If you want to get scared out of your wits in three seconds flat, slide down **Humunga Kowabunga,** with a drop of more than 50 ft. A children's area, **Ketchakiddie Creek,** replicates adult rides on a smaller scale.

Tips for Making the Most of Your Visit

- Arrive at the theme parks early—30–45 minutes before opening—so you can check belongings into lockers and rent strollers.
- See the three-star attractions first thing in the morning, at the end of the day, or during a parade, using FASTPASS whenever possible.

- Eat in a restaurant that takes reservations, bring your own food discreetly (a big time *and* money saver), or have meals before or after mealtime rush hours (from 11 AM to 2 PM and again from 6 to 8 PM).

- If a meal with the characters is in your plans, save it for the end of your trip, when your youngsters will have become accustomed to these large, looming figures.

- Familiarize yourself with all age and height restrictions to avoid having younger children get excited about rides they're too short or too young to experience.

- Call ahead to check on operating hours and parade times, which vary greatly throughout the year.

Walt Disney World Resort A to Z

ADMISSION FEES

Visiting Walt Disney World Resort is not cheap, especially if you have a child or two along. Everyone 10 and older pays adult prices; reductions are available for children ages 3 through 9. Children under three get in free. No discounted family tickets are available.

TICKETS & PASSES In Disneyspeak, "ticket" refers to a single day's admission to the Magic Kingdom, Epcot, Disney–MGM Studios, or Disney's Animal Kingdom. If you want to spend two or three days at WDW, you have to buy a separate ticket each day unless you're staying at a Disney-owned resort, where ticket options are greater. A ticket is good in the park for which you buy it only on the day you buy it. If you want to spend more than three days, you have several options. A **Park Hopper** pass allows unlimited visits to the four major parks on any four days, with any combination of parks on a day. The five-, six-, or seven-day **Park Hopper Plus** pass includes unlimited visits to the four main theme parks on any five, six, or seven days, plus two, three, or four days of admission—dated from first entry to WDW—to WDW's minor attractions, including Blizzard Beach, Disney's Wide World of Sports, Pleasure Island, and Typhoon Lagoon (but only one of these minor parks per day).

Although passes don't represent a tremendous savings over the one-day tickets, depending on the parks you plan to see and the number of days you have, they can save you some money as well as time spent in line. Be warned that it's not easy to "do" more than one park in a day, but if you want to take in the attractions of, say, the Magic Kingdom and then nip over for dinner at Epcot's World Showcase, park hopability may be attractive. Another way to save time is with **FASTPASS**, a free system that allows you to get a timed ticket to popular attractions and then return at an appointed time instead of waiting in line. Guests at Disney resorts can also purchase an **Ultimate Park Hopper,** which is good from the time of arrival until midnight of the departure day. Prices are based on the number of room nights. The pass is good for all four theme parks, as well as the two water parks, DisneyQuest, and Pleasure Island.

Tickets and passes to all Walt Disney World Resort parks can be purchased at park entrances, at admission booths at the Transportation and Ticket Center (TTC), in all on-site resorts (if you're a registered guest), and at the Walt Disney World kiosk at Orlando International Airport (second floor, main terminal). American Express, Visa, and MasterCard are accepted, as are cash, personal checks (with I.D.), and traveler's checks. Many offices of the American Automobile Association (AAA) sell discounted tickets. Check with your local office. Tickets are also available in local Disney stores, so you may want to purchase them at home before you leave. Some tickets, especially multiday passes, are available at hotels and stores off WDW property. Although these outlets may not save you much, if any, money, they could very well save time waiting in line at the park. You can also purchase your tickets before-hand at www. disneyworld.com. Save 5%–7% discount for each ticket, which can add up to $50 or more depending on the number of people in your family and the package you buy.

PRICES   WDW changes its prices at least once a year and without much notice. At press time rates (including 6% tax) were as follows:

☑ One-day ticket $53 adults, $42.40 children.

☑ Park Hopper Four days: $210.94 adults, $168.54 children; five days: $242.74 adults, $195.04 children.

☑ Park Hopper Plus Five days: $274.56 adults, $220.49 children; six days: $306.37 adults, $245.95 children; seven days: $338.17 adults, $271.38 children.

☑ Blizzard Beach & Typhoon Lagoon $32.86 adults, $26.50 children.

☑ Cirque du Soleil $76.32 and $86.92 adults, $46.64 and $51.94 children.

☑ DisneyQuest $32.86 adults, $26.30 children.

☑ Disney's Wide World of Sports (does not include events) $10 adults, $7.50 children.

☑ Pleasure Island $21.15.

GETTING AROUND

Walt Disney World Resort has its own transportation system, with boats, buses, and monorails to get you wherever you want to go. It's fairly simple and your best bet is just to ask the nearest Disney staffer when it's time for you to go somewhere. In general, allow 45 minutes to an hour to get from one point to your destination. Monorails, launches, buses, and trams all operate from early in the morning until at least midnight. (Hours are shorter when the park closes earlier.)

OPENING & CLOSING TIMES

Operating hours for the Magic Kingdom, Epcot, Disney–MGM Studios, and Disney's Animal Kingdom vary widely throughout the year. In general, the longest days are in summer and over the year-end holidays, when the Magic Kingdom is open until 10 or 11 (later on New Year's Eve), Epcot is open until 9 or 9:30 PM, and Disney–MGM Studios is open until 7 PM. There are so many variations, it pays to call ahead or check the parks' Web site calendar. The Magic Kingdom, Epcot's Future World, and Disney–MGM officially open at 9. Disney's Animal Kingdom opens at 9 AM and closes at 5 PM, though hours expand from 8 AM to 6 or 7 PM during peak times. The World Showcase at Epcot opens at 11 AM. Parking lots open at least an hour earlier. Arrive at the Magic Kingdom turnstiles before the official opening time; breakfast in a restaurant on Main Street, which opens before the rest of the park; and be ready to dash to one of the popular attractions in other areas as soon as officially possible. Arriving in Epcot, Disney–MGM Studios, or Disney's Animal Kingdom, make dinner reservations before the crowds arrive— in fact, try to reserve tables even before you arrive, utilizing Disney's central reservations number (⇨ Visitor Information). Try to take in some of the attractions and pavilions well before the major crowds descend later in the morning.

PARKING

Every theme park has a parking lot—and all are huge. Always write down exactly where you parked your car and take the note with you. Parking-area trams deliver you to the park entrance. For each lot the cost is $7 for cars and $8 for RVs and campers (free to WDW resort guests with I.D.). At Typhoon Lagoon and Blizzard Beach, parking is free.

VISITOR INFORMATION

For general information for Walt Disney World call either the information number or the switchboard. For all accommodations and shows call the central reservations number. There is a single number for all dining reservations. To inquire about resort facilities, call the individual property. For child-care information call KinderCare. One of the easiest ways to get information is via the Web site, www.disneyworld.com.

🔝 **Walt Disney World Information** ☎ 407/824-4321. **WDW switchboard** ☎ 407/824-2222. **WDW Central Reservations** ☎ 407/934-7639. **WDW Dining Reservations** ☎ 407/939-3463.

Disney-MGM Studios TV-show tapings ☎ 407/560-4651. **Kid's Nite Out** ☎ 407/827-5444 for in-room; Kindercare at 407/827-5437 for drop-off. **Pleasure Island** ☎ 407/934-7781. **Water Parks** ☎ 407/824-4321.

UNIVERSAL ORLANDO

The "umbrella" that is Universal Orlando contains Universal Studios (the original movie theme park), Islands of Adventure (the second theme park), and CityWalk (the dining-shopping-nightclub complex). Although it's bordered by residential neighborhoods and thickly trafficked International Drive, Universal Orlando is surprisingly expansive, intimate, and accessible with two massive parking complexes, easy walks to all attractions, and a motor launch that cruises to the hotels. While Universal Orlando emphasizes "two parks, two days, one great adventure," you may find the presentation, creativity, and cutting-edge technology bringing you back for more.

Universal Studios

❾ *Near the intersection of I–4 and Florida's Turnpike. Heading eastbound on I–4, take Exit 75A. Heading west on I–4, take Exit 74B and follow the signs.*

Universal Studios is a theme park with attitude. It's saucy, sassy, and hip, geared to those who like their rides loud and scary. If you want to calm down, there are quiet, shaded parks and a children's area where adults can enjoy a respite while the kids are ripping through assorted playlands at 100 mph. There are some, however, who miss the sort of connection that Disney forges with the public through its carefully developed history of singable songs and cuddly characters. The park's 444 acres are a bewildering conglomeration of stage sets, shops, reproductions of New York and San Francisco, and anonymous soundstages with theme attractions, as well as genuine moviemaking paraphernalia. On a map it looks easy. On foot, a quick run through the park to hit the top rides first is difficult, since it involves a few long detours and some backtracking. Attractions here are geared more to teenagers and adults than to the stroller set.

PRODUCTION
CENTRAL
Composed of six huge warehouses with working soundstages, this area also has added new attractions that should prove popular with kids. Follow Nickelodeon Way left from the Plaza of the Stars.

Nickelodeon Studios. Much of the cable network's production has picked up and moved out west, although one show, *Slimetime Live,* is shot here for a few months each year. If you're here when the televised show is being taped, you have a chance to be selected as a contestant—provided that a mysterious scout happens to find you and the family and that you pass the audition. This long shot is made even longer by the mystery of Nick's production scheduling. ☞ *Duration: 20 mins. Crowds: Steady, long lines. Strategy: Skip it on a first-time visit or if no shows are taping. Audience: All ages, but especially grade-schoolers. Rating:* ★★

NEW YORK Here the Big Apple is rendered with surprising detail, right down to the cracked concrete and slightly stained cobblestones.

TWISTER . . . Ride It Out. Here's your chance to see a tornado up close and personal, in the form of an ominous five-story-high funnel cloud that circulates some 2 million cubic ft of air around the theater and creates a terrifying freight-train sound. ☞ *Audience: All but young children. Rating:* ★★★

SAN FRANCISCO/ AMITY This area combines two sets. One part is the wharves and warehouses of San Francisco's Embarcadero and Fisherman's Wharf districts, with cable-car tracks and the distinctive redbrick Ghirardelli chocolate factory; the other is the New England fishing village terrorized by the shark in *Jaws.*

Beetlejuice's Graveyard Revue. A Transylvanian castle is the backdrop for Beetlejuice, who takes the stage and warms up the audience with his snappy lines and sarcastic attitude. Frankenstein's monster and his bride, the Werewolf, and Dracula soon appear, doffing their traditional costumes in favor of glitzy threads and singing the greatest hits of such diverse artists as Ricky Martin, Santana, Gloria Gaynor, and the Village People. Be prepared for some serious weirdness. ☞ *Duration: 25 mins. Crowds: Steady, but high capacity of amphitheater means no waiting. Strategy: Use Universal Express here; otherwise go when ride lines are at capacity or after dark on hot days. Audience: Older children and adults. Rating:* ★

Earthquake—The Big One. This is another headliner in Universal's "adrenaline alley." The preshow reproduces choice scenes from the movie *Earthquake,* then takes you onto San Francisco Bay Area Rapid Transit subway cars to ride out an 8.3 Richter-scale tremor and its consequences: fire, flood, blackouts. Stay away from this one if you are claustrophobic or have a fear of loud noises. ☞ *Audience: All but young children. No pregnant women or guests with heart, back, or neck problems or motion sickness; minimum height: 40" to ride alone. Rating:* ★★★

Jaws. Stagger out of San Francisco into Amity, and stand in line for this terror-filled boat trip with explosions, noise, shaking, and gnashing of sharp shark teeth. The special effects shine, especially the heat and fire from electrical explosions that could singe the eyebrows off Andy Rooney. Try it after dark for an extra thrill, then cancel the following day's trip to the beach. ☞ *Audience: All but young children. No pregnant women or guests with heart, back, or neck problems or motion sickness. Rating:* ★★★

Wild, Wild, Wild West Stunt Show. This live show is filled with trapdoors, fistfights, bullwhips, bad gags, explosions, and shootouts, but the quality of the stunts isn't always up to par. This is a good one if you don't want to waste time standing in line; there are plenty of seats, and you should be able to walk right in after the majority of the crowd has entered. ☞ *Audience: All ages. Rating:* ★★

WORLD EXPO The southeastern corner of the park has some very exciting attractions.

Back to the Future . . . The Ride. Universal's flight-simulator ride involves a one-of-a-kind seven-story Omnimax screen surrounding your DeLorean-shape simulator. Having no sense of perspective (or seat belts) makes this the rocking, rolling, pitching equivalent of a hyperactive paint mixer. It is perpetually scary, jarring, and jolting. If you like your rides shaken, not stirred, this one'll be worth the wait—and the queasy feeling that'll follow you around afterward. ☞ *Audience: Older children and adults. No pregnant women or guests with heart, back, or neck problems or motion sickness; minimum height: 40". Rating:* ★★★

Men in Black—Alien Attack. This star attraction is billed as the world's first "ride-through video game." With your on-board laser gun, you set off on a trip through New York streets, firing at aliens to rack up points. Keep in mind they can fire back at you and send your car spinning out of control. Depending on your score, the ride concludes with one of 35 endings, ranging from a hero's welcome to a loser's farewell. *Audience: Older children and adults. Rating:* ★★★

WOODY
WOODPECKER'S
KID ZONE

This area was opened so that toddler and elementary-school kids could have something to shout about.

A Day in the Park with Barney. The beloved TV playmate and Baby Bop dance and sing though the clap-along, sing-along monster classics, including "If You're Happy and You Know It" and (of course) "I Love You." After the show, a fairly elaborate play area with hands-on activities—a water harp, wood-pipe xylophone, and musical rocks—propels the already excited preschoolers to even greater heights. ☞ *Audience: Young children. Rating:* ★★

AT&T at the Movies. You can usually tell what an attraction sponsored by a corporation will be like: a boring commercial disguised as a supposedly fascinating presentation. In a few rooms of old microphones and recording devices and several computers, superimpose disguises on a picture of your face or hear your voice as it would sound on a Victrola. ☞ *Audience: All ages. Rating:* ★

Fodor'sChoice **Animal Planet Live!** An ark of animals is the star here: a raccoon opens the show, Lassie makes a brief appearance, there's a dog decathlon, and you'll also see Gizmo, the parrot from *Ace Ventura: Pet Detective*. Grand-finale highlights include impressions by Bailey the orangutan of, among others, Ricky Martin, then an overpoweringly adorable chimpanzee, and finally a sneak peek at a boa constrictor. It's a fun show that shouldn't be missed. ☞ *Audience: All ages. Rating:* ★★★

Curious George Goes to Town. The celebrated simian visits the Man with the Yellow Hat in a no-line, no-waiting interactive aqua play area that attracts kids like fish to water. Yes, there's water, water everywhere, especially atop the clock tower, which periodically dumps a 500 gallons down a roof and straight onto a screaming passel of preschoolers. Kids love the levers, valves, pumps, and hoses that gush at the rate of 200 gallons per minute. At the head of the square, footprints lead to a popular dry-play area, with a rope climb and a ball cage where youngsters can frolic among thousands of foam balls. *Audience: Water-babies of all ages. Rating:* ★★★

E. T. Adventure. This trip aboard bicycles mounted on a movable platform takes you through fantastic forests and across the moon in an attempt to help the endearing extraterrestrial find his way back to his home planet. ☞ *Audience: All ages. No guests with heart, back, or neck problems or motion sickness. Rating:* ★★★

Fievel's Playland. Based on the adventures of Steven Spielberg's mighty mini mouse, this gigantic playground incorporates a four-story net climb, tunnel slides, water-play areas, ball crawls, a 200-ft water slide, and a harmonica slide that plays music when you slide along the openings. ☞ *Audience: Young children and their families. Rating:* ★★

Woody Woodpecker's Nuthouse Coaster. This low-speed, mild thrill version roller-coaster (top speed 22 mph) makes it a safe bet for younger kids and action-phobic adults. ☞ *Audience: Young children and their parents. Rating:* ★★★

HOLLYWOOD

Angling off to the right of Plaza of the Stars, Rodeo Drive forms the backbone of Hollywood.

Lucy: A Tribute. This walk-through collection of Lucille Ball's costumes and other memorabilia plus trivia quizzes and short spots from the series is best for real fans of the ditsy redhead. ☞ *Audience: Adults. Rating:* ★

Terminator 2 3-D. Arnold said he'd be back, and he is in this exciting 3-D adventure that's among the theme-park world's most technologically advanced, with a mix of live action and film. ☞ *Audience: All but young children. Rating:* ★★★

Fodor'sChoice **Universal Horror Make-up Show.** On display in the fairly entertaining preshow area are exhibits showing the methods early filmmakers used to create special-effect makeup. The real fun kicks off in the theater when a host brings out a "special-effects expert" to describe what goes into (and what oozes out of) some of the creepiest movie effects (corn syrup and food coloring makes for a dandy blood substitute). The actors add their own jokes for an entertaining mix of movie secrets and comedy club timing. ☞ *Audience: Preteens to adults. Rating:* ★★★

Entertainment

Don't miss Universal's seasonal evening parties—most notably Mardi Gras (late February through early March), Fiesta Caliente (May), Rock the Universe (Christian music, September), the popular Halloween Horror Nights (October) and Grinchmas (November/December). Except for "Halloween" and "Rock the Universe," these festivals are included with park admission.

Universal Islands of Adventure

10 *Near the intersection of I–4 and Florida's Turnpike. Heading east on I-4, take Exit 75A; heading west, take Exit 74B.*

The creators of Islands of Adventure elevated theme-park attractions to a new level. From Marvel Super Hero Island and Toon Lagoon to Seuss Landing, Jurassic Park, and the Lost Continent, every section of the park—from the architecture to the landscaping to the technology of the rides—is truly impressive; they may have out-Disneyed Disney. A few drawbacks are a layout that's not easy to grasp and some rides and venues that are still shuttered or empty or lack a rousing ending.

SEUSS LANDING This whimsical 10-acre island is the only place in the world where the books of Dr. Seuss come to life. Make this a mandatory stop, since this is the most visually stunning piece of real estate in America.

Caro-Seuss-el. The centerpiece of Seuss Landing looks like it came straight from the pages of a Dr. Seuss book. Merry-go-round mounts are strange, bespotted, bewhiskered, and wonderfully colorful. Take a dog-alope or a cowfish for a spin. ☞ *Audience: All ages. Rating:* ★★★

The Cat in the Hat. Take a cleverly chaotic journey aboard a whirling, spinning "couch" through the pages of Dr. Seuss's most famous book about the topsy-turvy day that the Cat came to play. ☞ *Audience: All ages. Rating:* ★★★

If I Ran the Zoo. In this maze of a playground, children can climb, jump, push buttons, get splashed in interactive fountains, and work with each other to animate strange and wonderful Seussian animals. ☞ *Audience: Young children. Rating:* ★★★

One Fish, Two Fish, Red Fish, Blue Fish. It's a long wait for this ride, where you steer a rising and falling Seussian-style fish to a Jamaican-style song. Ignore the song's hints and you'll be splashed by a squirting post. ☞ *Audience: Young children. Rating:* ★★

LOST CONTINENT Ancient myths from around the world inspired this land. A visit transports you through time, past a crumbling statue of Poseidon, the Greek god of the sea, toward a revered city buzzing with humanity.

Fodor'sChoice   **Dueling Dragons.** After enduring a ½-mi-long line, you board "Ice Coaster" or "Fire Coaster" to whiz past the trees of a medieval forest, over Dragon Lake, and past oncoming cars during five inversions, three near misses, and top speeds of 55–60 mph. Cars are suspended from the track, your feet dangle freely, and your legs swing off toward the wild blue yonder. ☞ *Audience: Older children, teens, and adults. No pregnant women or guests with heart, back, or neck problems. Rating:* ★★★

Fodor'sChoice   **Eighth Voyage of Sindbad.** Seven voyages were not enough for Sindbad. So he strikes out again on his continuing search for enormous riches, encountering life-threatening perils along the way. Staged in a 1,700-seat theater, this edge-of-your-seat stunt show has water explosions, flames, and pyrotechnic effects. ☞ *Audience: Older children and adults. Rating:* ★★

Flying Unicorn. Following a walk through a wizard's workshop, the low-key children's ride places kids on the back of a unicorn for a very, very brief ride through a mythical forest. ☞ *Audience: Younger children. Minimum height: 36". Rating:* ★★★

Poseidon's Fury: Escape from the Lost City. The multimedia presentation here is an exciting battle between Poseidon (water) and his archenemy, Zeus (fire), and their "weapons" consist of more than 350,000 gallons of water and 200 flame effects, including scorching fireballs that erupt all around you. Although the first 15 minutes don't offer much, the finale is loud, powerful, and hyperactive. The show is part theater, part walk-through. One warning: if you stand near the front, you'll probably get drenched. ☞ *Audience: Older children and adults. Rating:* ★★

JURASSIC PARK   As you venture through the junglelike vegetation here and find yourself surrounded by the high-tension wires and warning signs, you'll get the feeling you've stepped into the Jurassic Park of Steven Spielberg's blockbuster movie.

Camp Jurassic. This clever park-within-a-park is loads of fun. You—or your hyperactive kids—will race along footpaths through the forests, slither down slides, clamber over swinging bridges and across boiling streams, scramble up net climbs and rock formations, and explore mysterious caves full of faux lava. ☞ *Audience: All. Rating:* ★★

Jurassic Park Discovery Center. Get close to skeletal remains of a massive T. rex and laboratories where biochemists develop the technology to bring these prehistoric creatures to life. One of the many demonstration areas shows a realistic-looking raptor being hatched. ☞ *Audience: All. Rating:* ★★

Jurassic Park River Adventure. The climax of this ride is an 85-ft plunge straight down the longest, fastest, steepest water descent ever built. Before that, however, you'll meander through a three-dimensional Jurassic Park that's scarily similar to the cinematic version—where you discover that you've become the prey of a terrifying Tyrannosaurus rex. ☞ *Audience: All but young children. No pregnant women or guests with heart, back, or neck problems. Rating:* ★★★

Pteranodon Flyers. The intent was good, but the prehistoric bird's-eye view of the Jurassic Park compound is a slow and time-consuming distraction. Go for it only if there's no one in line. ☞ *Audience: All ages. Rating:* ★

Triceratops Discovery Trail. An opportunity to pet a "living" dinosaur is offered at the feed and control stations of the resident 24-ft-long, 10-ft-high triceratops. Trainers fill you in on the family history, emotional state, and feeding habits of the creature. It's a surreal experience. ☞ *Audience: All ages. Rating:* ★

TOON LAGOON Here's your chance to leap into the Sunday funnies and romp around the animated universe with some pretty famous characters—more than 150 in all—in an environment that melts the boundaries between imagination and reality.

Dudley Do-Right's Ripsaw Falls. Based on the popular 1960s cartoon, this flume ride will take you on a wet and wild ride as you try to help Dudley rescue Nell from Snidely Whiplash. ☞ *Audience: All but young children. No pregnant women or guests with heart, back, or neck problems. Rating:* ★★★

Me Ship, the Olive. This is a huge, interactive playground-boat where you and your kids can wander through, stopping occasionally to fire water cannons at passengers in the Bilge-Rat Barges. Here's your chance to get even. ☞ *Audience: Young children. Rating:* ★★

Popeye & Bluto's Bilge-Rat Barges. A churning, turning white-water raft ride spins and drops you into whirlpools and eddies and then a fully operational boat wash. You will get wet—and so will your possessions. There are lockers at the boarding area for anything you'd prefer to keep dry. ☞ *Audience: All but young children. No pregnant women or guests with heart, back, or neck problems or motion sickness. Rating:* ★★★

MARVEL SUPER HERO ISLAND This island puts you smack in the middle of scenes straight from the pages of Marvel comics' greatest adventures.

Fodor'sChoice **Amazing Adventures of Spider-Man.** The thrill of this ride will validate any time you've spent standing on line. Unlike any other ride at any theme park anywhere, it combines moving vehicles, 3-D film, simulator technology, and special effects. No matter how many times you visit this attraction, you'll cringe when Doc Oc breaks through a brick wall, raises your car to the top of a skyscraper, and then releases you for a 400-ft sensory free fall to the pavement below. ☞ *Audience: All but young children. No pregnant women or guests with heart, back, or neck problems. Rating:* ★★★

Dr. Doom's Fearfall. It looks scary, but it's a letdown when you're elevated and dropped a few hundred feet and . . . well, that's it. Skip it if the line is too long. ☞ *Audience: Older children and adults. No pregnant women or guests with heart, back, or neck problems or motion sickness. Rating:* ★

Incredible Hulk Coaster. One of Islands' two blockbuster coasters dominates the lagoonside scenery with its spaghetti of tracks in a neon shade of green that recalls the skin of mild-mannered Bruce Banner turned Hulk. Racing along the track, you spin through seven rollovers and plunge into two deep, foggy subterranean enclosures. Afterward, the Hulk's not the only one who's green. ☞ *Audience: Older children and adults. No pregnant women or guests with heart, back, or neck problems. Rating:* ★★★

Storm Force Accelatron. This whirling indoor ride is supposed to demonstrate the power of nature. Strip away the veneer, however, and what you've got is a mirror image of Disney World's popular twirling teacups. ☞ *Audience: Older children and adults. No pregnant women or guests with heart, back, or neck problems. Minimum height: 54″. Rating:* ★★

Tips for Making the Most of Your Visit

- Universal Express is available to all park guests at all attractions. You check in at the ride entrance, are assigned a time, and then return later to bypass the line and ride within minutes.

- If you're staying at a Universal resort, use your room key as your Express ticket to bypass the line at almost all Universal attractions.

- In peak seasons, resort hotel guests are admitted to Universal parks an hour before regular park goers.

- Call a day or two before your visit to get official park hours, and arrive in the parking lot 45 minutes early. See the biggest attractions first.

- Be sure to write down your parking location.

- Have a filling snack around 10:30, lunch after 2, and dinner at 8 or later. Or lunch on the early side at a place that takes reservations; then have dinner at 5. Be sure to make your reservations ahead of time or, at the very least, when you enter the park.

Universal Orlando A to Z

ADMISSION FEES
One-day one-park tickets for Universal Studios or Islands of Adventure cost $52.95 for adults and $43.41 for children three to nine, including tax. Multiday **Escape Passes** sell for $100.65 for adults and $86.87 for children for two days, but with this ticket an ongoing program offers a third day free. Multiday passes give you early admission to the parks and the privilege of going from park to park at your leisure. Tickets do not have to be used on consecutive days. Get tickets in advance by mail through **Ticketmaster** (☎ 800/745–5000) or by contacting **Universal Studios Vacations** (☎ 888/322–5537).

DISCOUNTS   If you buy tickets at the **Orlando/Orange County Convention & Visitors Bureau** (✉ 8723 International Dr. ☎ 407/363–5871), you'll save about $3 per adult ticket ($2.20 on children's prices). American Automobile Association members get 10% off, sometimes more, at AAA offices. The **Orlando FlexTicket,** which covers the Universal parks (US, IOA, and Wet 'n Wild) as well as SeaWorld and Busch Gardens, matches Walt Disney World's pass system. The four-park version gets you into Universal Studios, Islands of Adventure, Wet 'n Wild, and SeaWorld—all for $180.15 for adults and $143.05 children ages three to nine. The five-park version ($215.46 and $175.12) buys unlimited admission to all of the above plus a safari through Busch Gardens. Both the four-park and five-park FlexTickets are good for 14 days.

PARKING
Universal's single parking-garage complex, which serves both theme parks and CityWalk, is one of the world's largest car parks. Because your vehicle is covered, it's not so sweltering at the end of the day even when it's hot. The cost is $8 for cars, $10 for campers. Valet parking is available for $14.

VISITOR INFORMATION
Universal Orlando (✉ 1000 Universal Studios Plaza, Orlando 32819-7610 ☎ 407/363–8000 or 888/331–9108 ⊕ www.universalorlando.com).

OTHER THEME PARKS

Theme parks grow so well in the sandy Central Florida soil that you might almost imagine a handful of seeds scattered across the fertile Interstate 4 belt, waiting for the right combination of money and vision to nurture them into the next Walt Disney World.

SeaWorld Orlando

❼ *Near the intersection of I–4 and the Beeline Expressway; take I–4 to Exit 71 or 72 and follow signs.*

There's a whole lot more to SeaWorld than Shamu, its mammoth killer-whale mascot. Sure, you can be splashed by Shamu, stroke a stingray, see manatees face-to-snout, learn to love an eel, and be spat upon by a walrus, but far from incidental is that this is also the world's largest marine adventure park. Every attraction at SeaWorld is devoted to demonstrating the ways that humans can protect the mammals, birds, fish, and reptiles that live in the ocean and its tributaries. The presentations are gentle reminders of our responsibility to safeguard the environment, and you'll find that SeaWorld's use of humor plays a major role in this education. First-timers may be slightly confused by the lack of distinct "lands" here—SeaWorld's performance venues, attractions, and activities surround a 17-acre lake, and the artful landscaping and curving paths sometimes lead to wrong turns. But armed with a map that lists show times, you can plan a chronological approach that flows easily from one attraction to the next.

Dolphin Nursery. In a large pool, dolphin moms and babies (with birth dates posted on signs) play and leap and splash. You can't get close enough to pet or feed them, so you'll have to be content peering from several feet away and asking the host questions during a regular Q and A session. Here's a popular answer: No, you can't take one home. ☞ *Audience: All ages. Rating:* ★★

Journey to Atlantis. Combining elements of a high-speed water ride and roller coaster with LCD technology, lasers, and holographic illusions, this thriller plunges you into the world of Greek mythology and down two of the fastest, steepest drops anywhere. You will get soaked, so bring a change of clothes (including underwear). ☞ *Audience: Older children and adults. Not recommended for pregnant women or guests with heart problems or a fear of dark, enclosed spaces; minimum height: 42".* *Rating:* ★★★

Key West at SeaWorld. In this laid-back area, feed nearly two dozen Atlantic bottle-nosed dolphins with fish purchased nearby, and at the nightly sunset celebration kids can get their faces painted and have their pictures taken with a larger-than-human-size Shamu or Dolly Dolphin. A 20-minute whale and dolphin show, *Key West Dolphin Fest,* spotlights dolphins and false killer whales who leap, do back flips, and flip a trainer into the air. ☞ *Audience: All ages. Rating:* ★★★

Kraken. Big draws for coaster enthusiasts on this high-intensity ride are the seven inversions and moments of weightlessness, courtesy of zero-G rolls. Folks around these parts claim this is the tallest (149 ft) and fastest (up to 65 mph) and only floorless coaster in Florida. ☞ *Audience: Older children and adults. Minimum height: 54". Rating:* ★★★

Manatees: The Last Generation? The lumbering, whiskered manatees look like a cross between walruses and air bags, and this display devoted to them is striking. After a short film, watch the gentle giants swim placidly alongside native fish in their 300,000-gallon tank. Keep an eye out for mamas and their calves. ☞ *Audience: All ages. Rating:* ★★★

Nautilus Theater—*Cirque de la Mer (Circus of the Sea).* This silent 30-minute live performance of fire juggling, gymnastics, and mime is alternately highly energetic, softly ethereal, mostly unbelievable, and very funny. Don't miss it. ☞ *Audience: All ages. Rating:* ★★★

Pacific Point Preserve. A nonstop chorus of "aarrrps" and "yawps" leads, no, not to a frat-house keg party but to fun-loving California sea lions and harbor and fur seals on a 2½-acre rocky promontory. Just call it Bark Avenue. ☞ *Audience: All ages. Rating:* ★★★

Penguin Encounter. A refrigerated re-creation of Antarctica, the exhibit has 17 species of penguins; a Plexiglas wall on your side of the tank lets you see that the penguins are cute as can be, waddling across icy promon-

tories and plopping into frigid waters to display their aquatic skills. A
similar viewing area for puffins and murres (a kind of seabird) is just
as entertaining. ☞ *Audience: All ages. Rating:* ★★

Fodor'sChoice **Sea Lion & Otter Stadium.** A wildly inventive, multilevel pirate ship
forms the set for *Clyde and Seamore Take Pirate Island.* SeaWorld's
celebrated sea lions, otters, and walruses prevail over pirate treachery
in this swashbuckler of a saga. Arrive early to catch the preshow—the
mime is definitely one of the best you'll ever see. ☞ *Audience: All ages.
Rating:* ★★★

SeaWorld Theater. Between Penguin Encounter and the central lagoon
roam about a dozen dogs, 18 cats, ducks, doves, parrots, and a pig (nearly
Fodor'sChoice all rescued from the local animal shelter), all stars of the lively **Pets on
Stage.** The show builds to a funny, furry finale. ☞ *Audience: All ages.
Rating:* ★★★

Shamu: Close Up! For unprecedented underwater viewing of the breeding and nursery area, this is the place to be. Follow the signs around to
the underground viewing stations for a unique glimpse of favorite whale
pastimes: tummy-rubbing and back-scratching. ☞ *Audience: All ages.
Rating:* ★★★

Shamu Stadium. The home of SeaWorld's orca mascot, the stadium is
hands down the most popular attraction in the park. Several of *The Shamu
Adventure* shows daily showcase the whales' acrobatic, spectator-drench-
Fodor'sChoice ing antics. In the slightly funkier nighttime *Shamu Rocks America,* the
famous orca jumps to the beat of "God Bless the USA." Take the splash
zone seriously, and bring a change of clothes, just in case. ☞ *Audience:
All ages. Rating:* ★★★

Shamu's Happy Harbor. If you want to take a break while your kids ex-
haust the last ounce of energy that their little bodies possess, bring them
here. This 3-acre outdoor play area has crawlable, climbable, explorable,
bounceable, and get-wet activities. ☞ *Audience: Toddlers through
grade-schoolers. Rating:* ★★★

Sky Tower. The focal point of the park is this 400-ft-tall tower, which is
the main mast for a revolving double-decker platform. During the six-
minute rotating round-trip, you'll get the inside scoop on the park.
There's a separate $3 admission. ☞ *Audience: All ages. Rating:* ★★

Stingray Lagoon. Buy a batch of smelts to feed the rays and stroke their
velvety skin. Don't worry about getting stung—these slippery swimmers
just want food. ☞ *Audience: All ages. Rating:* ★★★

Terrors of the Deep. Videos and walk-through Plexiglas tunnels let you
get acquainted with menacing eels, barracuda, and sharks. ☞ *Audience:
All ages. Rating:* ★★★

Tropical Reef. In this soothing indoor attraction, more than 30 separate
aquariums are aswim with tropical fish from around the world. ☞ *Audience: All ages. Rating:* ★★

Wild Arctic. This pseudo–ice station combines a bumpy simulated helicopter ride with educational exhibits about some of the Arctic's most
deceptively cuddly predators. At above- and below-water viewing stations take your time watching beluga whales blowing bubble rings,
polar bears cavorting with their toys, and walruses hoisting themselves
onto the ice with a groan. There's a nonmoving option for those too
small for or not interested in the jostling ride. ☞ *Audience: All ages.
Minimum height: 42" for motion option. Rating:* ★★★

SeaWorld Orlando Information
✉ *7007 Sea Harbor Dr., International Drive Area, Orlando 32821*
☎ *407/351–3600 or 800/327–2424* ⊕ *www.seaworld.com* ✄ *$55.33
adults, $45.74 children 3–9; 10% discount for on-line purchase; with
"2d Day Fun" promotion receive a complimentary pass; use it to re-*

turn within 7 days ⊙ *Daily 9–6 or 7, until as late as 11 summer and holidays; educational programs daily, some beginning as early as 6:30* AM ☎ *800/432–1178 Ext. 5.*

Discovery Cove

8 *Near the intersection of I–4 and the Beeline Expressway; take I–4 to Exit 71 or 72 and follow signs.*

Making a quantum leap from the traditional theme park, SeaWorld took a chance on opening Discovery Cove, a 32-acre limited-admission park where a maximum of 1,000 people each day enter an extraordinary environment—a re-creation of the Caribbean with coral reefs, sandy beach, margaritas, and dolphins. After walking through a huge thatched-roof tiki building, you register and are given a time to swim with the dolphins, the highlight of your Discovery Cove day. Your photo I.D. allows you to charge drinks during the day, and that's all you need to worry about. With your admission, everything else is included so you're not running to your locker (free) to get cash to buy suntan lotion (free), a towel (free), lunch (free), or a mask and fins (also free). Even if you're aware of the neighboring interstate highway, you can't help feeling that you've entered a tropical oasis. Once inside, you are awash in rocky lagoons surrounded by lush landscaping, intricate coral reefs, and underwater ruins. A resort-style pool has cascading waterfalls, and white beaches are fringed with thatched huts, cabanas, and hammocks. Exciting encounters of animal species from the Bahamas, Tahiti, and Micronesia are part of the experience, including snorkeling with stingrays and exotic fish and visiting a free-flight aviary accessed by swimming beneath a waterfall. Although $219 per person may seem steep, if you skip the dolphin swim it's only $119 in summer and as low as $109 in fall. Then when you consider that a dolphin swim in the Florida Keys runs approximately $125, and SeaWorld throws in a complimentary seven-day admission to its park (usually $52.95 a day), plus extras that include a free meal, it starts looking like a bargain. The earlier you make your reservations, the more latitude you have in selecting the time you want to swim (or interact) with the dolphins.

Discovery Cove Information
☎ *877/434–7268 reservations line (daily 9–8)* ⊕ *www.discoverycove. com* ⊙ *Daily 9–5:30.*

ELSEWHERE IN THE AREA

Once you've exhausted the theme parks, or have been exhausted by them, turn your attention to a wealth of other area offerings. Although you'll find plenty of other recreational activities of interest to kids, there are also museums and parks and gardens galore, highlighting the cultural and natural heritage of this part of the South.

Kissimmee

10 mi east of Walt Disney World Resort; take I–4 Exit 64A.

Although Kissimmee is primarily known as the gateway to Walt Disney World, its non-WDW attractions just might tickle your fancy.

12 Old war birds never die—they just become attractions. **Flying Tigers Warbird Air Museum,** a working aircraft restoration facility, is nicknamed Bombertown USA because most planes here are bombers. Once they are

CloseUp

20 ROMANTIC THINGS TO DO AT WALT DISNEY WORLD

NOT EVERYTHING AT DISNEY WORLD *involves children. Get a baby-sitter (available for a fee through WDWR) and enjoy some private time, just the two of you.*

1. Have dinner at the very grand Victoria and Albert's restaurant in the Grand Floridian.

2. Have dinner at the California Grill and watch the Magic Kingdom fireworks.

3. Rent a boat to take a cruise on the Seven Seas Lagoon or the waterways leading to it. Bring champagne and glasses.

4. Take a nighttime whirl on Cinderella's Golden Carrousel in Fantasyland. Sparkling lights make it magical.

5. Have your picture taken and grab a kiss in the heart-shape gazebo in the back of Minnie's Country House.

6. Sit on the beach at the Grand Floridian at sunrise or at dusk—a special time.

7. Have a massage day at the Grand Floridian Spa.

8. Buy a faux diamond ring at the Emporium on Main Street in the Magic Kingdom. Propose to your sweetheart at your favorite spot in the World.

9. Have a caricature drawn of the two of you at the Marketplace.

10. Sit by the fountain in front of Epcot's France pavilion and have some wine or a pastry and coffee.

11. Have a drink at the cozy Yachtsman's Crew bar in the Yacht Club hotel.

12. After dinner at Narcoosee's in the Grand Floridian, watch the Electrical Water Pageant outside.

13. Take a walk on the BoardWalk. Watch IllumiNations from the bridge to the Yacht and Beach Club. Then boogie at Atlantic Dance.

14. Tie the knot all over again at the Wedding Pavilion. Invite Mickey and Minnie to the reception.

15. Rent a hot-air balloon for a magical tour of Walt Disney World.

16. Every night is New Year's Eve at Pleasure Island. Declare your love amid confetti and fireworks.

17. Enjoy a British lager outside at Epcot's Rose & Crown Pub—a perfect IllumiNations viewing spot. Book ahead and ask for a table with a view.

18. Have your picture taken with Mickey at Toontown Fair.

19. Have dinner at Alfredo's in Epcot, right after IllumiNations—request an 8:55 reservation. After dinner, since the park is officially closed, it's incredibly lovely.

20. Have dinner at the Brown Derby in Disney–MGM Studios and book ahead for priority Fantasmic! seating.

---

operational, they are usually flown away by private collectors, but the museum also houses a permanent collection of about 30 vintage planes in its hangar, with a few big ones out on the Tarmac. ✉ *231 N. Hoagland Blvd.* ☎ *407/933–1942* ⊕ *www.warbirdmuseum.com* ✎ *$9 adults, $8 children 8–12* ⊙ *Mon.–Sat. 9–5:30, Sun. 9–5.*

⑬ Long before Walt Disney World, there was campy **Gatorland**, which has endured since 1949 without much change, despite major competition. Through the monstrous aqua gator-jaw doorway—a definite photo op—lie thrills and chills in the form of thousands of alligators and crocodiles, swimming and basking in the Florida sun. There's a Gator Wrestling Cracker-style show, and although there's no doubt who's going to win the match, it's still fun to see the handlers take on those tough guys with the beady eyes. In the educational Snakes of Florida Show, high drama is provided by the 30–40 rattlesnakes that fill the pit around the speaker. ⊠ *14501 S. Orange Blossom Trail, between Orlando and Kissimmee* ☎ *407/855–5496 or 800/393–5297* ⊕ *www.gatorland.com* ⊡ *$17.93 adults, $8.48 children 3–12* ☉ *Daily 9–6.*

★ ⑭ West of Interstate 4 and Walt Disney World is **Splendid China**, more an open-air museum than a theme park. Stroll among painstakingly re-created versions of China's greatest landmarks—such as the Dalai Lama's **Potala Palace,** the **Great Wall,** and the Forbidden City's **Imperial Palace**—and watch artisans demonstrate traditional Chinese woodworking, weaving, and other crafts while tinkling meditative music plays in the background. It took $100 million and 120 Chinese craftspeople working for two years and using, whenever possible, historically accurate building materials and techniques to create the 60-plus replicas. Both man-made structures and natural phenomena are represented—some life-size, others greatly reduced in scale (the bricks in the Great Wall, for example, are only 2 inches long). To appeal to theme-park savvy Western visitors, live entertainment and a playground are also on the grounds, and the shops and restaurants of the Chinatown section are a cut above those at typical theme parks. The park is at its most magical at night. ⊠ *3000 Splendid China Blvd.* ☎ *407/397–8800 recording; 407/396–7111 voice; 800/244–6226* ⊕ *www.floridasplendidchina.com* ⊡ *$28.88 adults, $18.88 children 5–12; parking and Chinatown free* ☉ *Daily 9:30–7, later in peak season; Chinatown shops and restaurants until 9.*

off the beaten path

★ **Bok Tower Gardens.** Perfect for a quick back-to-nature fix is this appealing but often overlooked sanctuary of plants, flowers, trees, and wildlife. Shady paths meander through a peaceful world of pine forests, silvery moats, mockingbirds and swans, blooming thickets, and hidden sundials. The majestic 200-ft Bok Tower is constructed of coquina (from seashells) and pink, white, and gray marble and has a carillon with 57 bronze bells that ring every half hour after 10 AM. Each day at 3 there is a 45-minute recital, which may include Early American folk songs, Appalachian tunes, Irish ballads, or Latin hymns. There are also moonlight recitals. To reach the gardens, take Interstate 4 Exit 55 and head south along U.S. 27, away from the congestion of Orlando and past quite a few of Central Florida's citrus groves. ⊠ *1151 Tower Blvd., Lake Wales* ☎ *863/676–1408* ⊡ *$6 adults, $2 children 5–12; Pinewood House $5 suggested donation* ☉ *Daily 8–6; Pinewood House tours mid-Sept.–mid-May, Tues. and Thurs. at 12:30 and 2, Sun. at 2.*

International Drive Area, Orlando

7 mi northeast of Walt Disney World Resort; take I–4 Exit 72 or 74A, unless otherwise noted.

Between WDW and downtown Orlando are several attractions that kids adore. Unfortunately they may put some wear and tear on parents.

A 10-ft-square section of the Berlin Wall, a pain and torture chamber, a Rolls-Royce constructed entirely of matchsticks—these and almost 200 ⑮ other oddities speak for themselves at **Ripley's Believe It or Not! Museum,** in the heart of tourist territory. It is said that the fruits of Robert Ripley's explorations are to reality what Walt Disney World is to fantasy. ✉ *8201 International Dr., International Drive Area* ☎ *407/363–4418 or 800/998–4418* ☑ *$15.95 adults, $10.95 children 4–12* ◷ *Daily 9* AM–1 AM.

★ ⓰ A playground of 75 entertaining and educational interactive experiences awaits at **WonderWorks.** Find yourself in the middle of an earthquake or a hurricane, swim with sharks, play laser tag in the largest laser-tag arena in the world, design and ride your own awesome roller coaster, or even play basketball with a 7-ft opponent. ✉ *9067 International Dr., International Drive Area* ☎ *407/352–8655* ☑ *$16.95 adults, $12.95 children 4–12. Packages include laser tag and Magical Dinner Show.* ◷ *Daily 9* AM–*midnight.*

Downtown Orlando

15 mi northeast of Walt Disney World Resort; take I–4 Exit 83B if you're heading westbound, Exit 83A if eastbound, or Exit 85 for Loch Haven Park sights.

Downtown Orlando is a dynamic community that's constantly growing and changing. Numerous parks, many of which surround lakes, provide pleasant relief from the tall office buildings. One such is Lake Eola, which has a delightful playground at one end and a walkway around its circumference that invites strolling. Just a few steps from downtown are delightful residential neighborhoods with brick-paved streets and live oaks dripping with Spanish moss.

⓱ The former estate of citrus entrepreneur Harry P. Leu, **Harry P. Leu Gardens** provides a quiet respite. On the grounds' 50 acres is a collection of historical blooms, many varieties of which were established before 1900. ✉ *1920 N. Forest Ave., Downtown Orlando* ☎ *407/246–2620* ☑ *$4 adults, $1 children 6–16* ◷ *Garden daily 9–6, guided house tours daily 10–3:30.*

⓲ Journey back in time at the **Orange County Regional History Center** to discover how Florida's Paleo-Indians hunted and fished the land; what the Sunshine State was like when Spaniards first arrived in the New World; and how life in Florida was different when citrus was king. ✉ *65 E. Central Blvd.* ☎ *407/836–8500 or 800/965–2030* ⊕ *www.thehistorycenter. org* ☑ *$7 adults, $3.50 children 3–12* ◷ *Mon.–Sat. 10–5, Sun. noon–5.*

★ ⓳ With all the high-tech glitz and imagined worlds of the theme parks, which are closer to where most stay, is it worth visiting the **Orlando Science Center,** a reality-based science museum in Orlando proper? Absolutely. The 10 themed display halls have exciting hands-on exhibits covering mechanics, electricity and magnetism, math, health and fitness, nature, the solar system, and light, lasers, and optics. Walk through an enormous open mouth (literally) and take a journey through the human body (figuratively). The **CineDome,** a movie theater with a giant eight-story screen, offers large-format Iwerks films, planetarium programs, and, on weekends, laser-light shows. The center also has its own performance troupe, the Einstein Players. ✉ *777 E. Princeton St.* ☎ *407/ 514–2000* ☑ *Exhibits $10 adults, $7.50 children 3–11; CineDome films $7 adults, $5 children; both $12 adults, $9.50 children; exhibits plus 2 CineDome experiences $16 adults, $13.50 children; parking $3.50* ◷ *Tues.–Thurs. 9–5, Fri.–Sat. 9–9, Sun. noon–5. Open Mon. 9–5 from Memorial Day through mid-Aug. and school holidays.*

Winter Park

20 mi northeast of WDW; take I–4 Exit 87 and head east 3 mi on Fairbanks Ave.

Spend a pleasant day in this upscale town shopping at chic boutiques, eating at a cozy café, visiting museums, and taking in the scenery along Park Avenue, with its hidden alleyways that lead to peaceful nooks and crannies. Away from the avenue, moss-covered trees form a canopy over brick streets, and old estates surround canal-linked lakes.

⓴ Lovely, shady, and green, **Central Park,** with a stage and gazebo, is Winter Park's gathering place, often the scene of concerts. ⊠ *Park Ave.*

㉑ Many works of Louis Comfort Tiffany, including immense stained-glass windows, lamps, watercolors, and desk sets, are at the **Charles Hosmer Morse Museum of American Art.** The 8,000-square-ft Tiffany Chapel was originally built for the 1893 World's Fair. ⊠ *445 N. Park Ave.* ☎ *407/ 645–5311* ☞ *$3 adults, $1 students* ☉ *Tues.–Sat. 9:30–4, Sun. 1–4; Fri. hrs extended to 8 PM Sept.–May.*

㉒ Exhibits at the **Holocaust Memorial Resource and Education Center of Central Florida** are arranged in chronological order and include a large number of photographs and audiovisual presentations. ⊠ *851 N. Maitland Ave., Maitland* ☎ *407/628–0555* ☞ *Free* ☉ *Mon.–Thurs. 9–4, Fri. 9–1.*

★ ㉓ From the dock at the end of Morse Avenue, depart for the **Scenic Boat Tour,** a Winter Park tradition that's been in continuous operation for more than 60 years. The one-hour pontoon boat tour, narrated by your captain, leaves hourly and cruises along 12 mi of Winter Park's opulent lakeside estates, through canals and across three lakes. ⊠ *312 E. Morse Blvd.* ☎ *407/644–4056* ⊕ *www.scenicboattours.com* ☞ *$8 adults, $4 children 2–11* ☉ *Daily 10–4.*

㉔ A private liberal arts school, **Rollins College** was once the late Mister (Fred) Rogers's neighborhood—yes, he was an alumnus. You'll see the **Knowles Memorial Chapel,** built in 1932, and the **Annie Russell Theatre,** a 1931 building often used for local theatrical productions. The **Cornell Fine Arts Museum** has interesting 19th- and 20th-century American and European paintings, decorative arts, and sculpture. ⊠ *End of Holt Ave.* ☎ *407/646–2526* ☞ *Museum free* ☉ *Museum Tues.–Fri. 10–5, weekends 1–5.*

| off the beaten path | **Wekiwa Springs State Park.** Where the tannin-stained Wekiva River meets the crystal-clear Wekiwaheadspring, you'll find this 6,400-acre park good for camping, hiking, picnicking, swimming, canoeing, fishing, and watching for alligators, egrets, and deer. Although it can be crowded on weekends, on weekdays it's Walden Pond, Florida style. Take Interstate 4 Exit 94 and turn left on Route 434 and right on Wekiwa Springs Road. ⊠ *1800 Wekiva Circle, Apopka* ☎ *407/884–2009* ☞ *$4 per vehicle* ☉ *Daily 8–sunset.* |

Celebration

10 mi southeast of WDW; take I–4 to Exit 64A and follow the Celebration signs.

This Disney-created community reminds some locals of something out of the 1970s film *The Stepford Wives.* But Celebration, which draws on vernacular architecture from all over the United States and was based on ideas from some of America's top architects and planners, can be a great retreat from the theme parks and from the garish reality of the U.S. 192 tourist strip just 1 mi to the east. The town is so perfect it could be a movie set, and it's a delightful place to spend a morning or afternoon. Sidewalks are built for strolling, restaurants have outdoor seating with lake views, and inviting shops beckon. After a walk around the lake, take your youngsters over to the huge interactive fountain, and have fun getting wet. Starting after Thanksgiving and continuing on through the new year, honest-to-goodness snow sprinkles softly over Main Street each evening, to the delight of children of all ages.

Mount Dora

35 mi northwest of Orlando and 50 mi north of WDW; take U.S. 441 (Orange Blossom Trail in Orlando) north or take I-4 to Exit 92, then take Rte. 436 west to U.S. 441, and follow the signs.

Built around the unspoiled Lake Harris chain of lakes, the quaint valley community of Mount Dora has a slow and easy pace, a rich history, New England–style charm, and excellent antiquing. Although the population is under 8,000, there's plenty of excitement here. The first weekend in February is the annual Mount Dora Art Festival. Attracting more than 200,000 people over a three-day period, it is one of Central Florida's major outdoor events. During the year there's a sailing regatta, a bicycle festival, and a crafts fair, or take in the historic buildings along Donnelly Street or 5th Avenue any time of year.

WHERE TO EAT

Because tourism is king here, casual dress is the rule, and few restaurants require fancy attire. Reservations are always a good idea; otherwise the entire Ecuadoran soccer team or the Platt City High School senior class may arrive moments before you and keep you waiting a long, long time. Save that experience for the theme parks. For restaurants within Walt Disney World Resort, reservations are especially easy to make, thanks to its **central reservations line** (☎ 407/939–3463 or 407/560–7277). Universal Orlando, which has become a major player in the culinary wars, also has its own reservations line (☎ 407/224–9255). Orlando is not big, but getting to places is frequently complicated, so always call for directions.

WHAT IT COSTS				
$$$$	**$$$**	**$$**	**$**	**¢**
RESTAURANTS over $30	$20–$30	$15–$20	$10–$15	under $10

Restaurant prices are per person for a main course at dinner.

Epcot

Canadian

$$–$$$ ✕ **Le Cellier Steakhouse.** A good selection of Canadian beer joins the best Canadian wine cellar in the state at this charming eatery. Aged beef is king, although many steaks appear only on the dinner menu. Carnivores should home in on the herb-crusted prime rib, while seafood lovers might sample the popular maple-ginger glazed Canadian salmon. Canadian fruit cobbler is the best sweet; the Canadian Club chocolate cake is a close second. ⊠ *Canada* ⊟ *AE, MC, V.*

English

¢–$$ ✕ **Rose & Crown.** If you're an Anglophile and you love a good, thick beer, this is the place to soak up both the suds and the British street culture.

"Wenches" serve up traditional English fare—fish-and-chips, meat pies, Yorkshire pudding, and the ever-popular bangers and mash, English sausage over mashed potatoes. Also sample cottage pie—ground beef and carrots topped with mashed potatoes and cheddar cheese. For dessert, try the chocolate mousse parfait. The terrace has a splendid view of IllumiNations. ⊠ *United Kingdom* ⊟ *AE, MC, V.*

French

★ $$$$ ✕ **Bistro de Paris.** The great secret in the France pavilion—and, indeed, in all of Epcot—is the Bistro de Paris, upstairs from Les Chefs de France. Dishes include lobster fricassee and roast duck with cherry brandy sauce. Come late, ask for a window seat, and plan to linger to watch the nightly Epcot light show. Moderately priced French wines are available by the glass. ⊠ *France* ⊟ *AE, MC, V.*

$$–$$$$ ✕ **Les Chefs de France.** What some consider the best restaurant at Disney
Fodor'sChoice was created by three of France's most famous chefs: Paul Bocuse, Gaston Lenôtre, and Roger Vergé. Classic escargots, a good starter, are prepared in a casserole with garlic butter; you might follow up with *marmite du pecheur parfumée au safran* (traditional Mediterranean seafood casserole of grouper, scallops, and shrimp flavored with saffron, served with garlic sauce); and end with crepes *au chocolat.* ⊠ *France* ⊟ *AE, MC, V.*

German

¢–$$ ✕ **Biergarten.** Oktoberfest runs 365 days a year here. The cheerful, sometimes raucous crowds are what you would expect in a place with an oompah band. Waitresses in Bavarian garb serve *breseln,* fresh, hot German pretzels. Other classic German fare in the one-price all-you-can-eat buffet are sauerbraten, bratwurst, and chicken schnitzel, as well as a good apple strudel and Black Forest cake. Patrons pound pitchers of beer and wine on the long communal tables—even when the yodelers, singers, and dancers aren't egging them on. ⊠ *Germany* ⊟ *AE, MC, V.*

Italian

★ $$–$$$$ ✕ **L'Originale Alfredo di Roma Ristorante.** This is the most popular restaurant at Epcot, and its namesake dish is one of the principal reasons— fettuccine sauced with cream, butter, and loads of freshly grated, imported Parmesan cheese. But the true secret to the dish here is the butter—flown in from Italy. During dinner the Italian waiters walk around singing Italian songs and bellowing arias, a show in itself. ⊠ *Italy* ⊟ *AE, MC, V.*

Japanese

$$–$$$$ ✕ **Mitsukoshi.** Three restaurants are enclosed in this complex, which overlooks tranquil gardens. Yakitori House, a gussied-up fast-food stand in a small pavilion, is modeled after a tea house in Kyoto's Katsura Summer Palace. At the Tempura Kiku, diners watch the chefs prepare sushi, sashimi, and tempura. In the five Teppanyaki dining rooms, chefs frenetically chop vegetables, meat, and fish and stir-fry them at the grills set into the communal tables. The Matsu No Ma Lounge, more serene than the restaurants, has a great view of the World Showcase Lagoon. ⊠ *Japan* ⊟ *AE, MC, V.*

Mexican

$$–$$$ ✕ **San Angel Inn.** In the dark, grottolike main dining room, a deep purple, dimly lit mural of a night scene in Central Mexico seems to envelop the diners. San Angel is a popular respite for the weary, especially when the humidity outside makes Central Florida feel like equatorial Africa. At dinner, guitar and marimba music fills the air. Try the authentic *mole poblano* (chicken simmered in a rich sauce of chiles, green tomatoes, ground tortillas, cocoa, cumin, and 11 other spices). ⊠ *Mexico* ⊟ *AE, MC, V.*

Moroccan

$$–$$$ ✕ **Marrakesh.** Chef Abrache Lahcen of Morocco presents the best cooking of his homeland in this ornate eatery. Try the couscous, served with vegetables, or *bastilla* (an appetizer made with layers of chicken or lamb in a thin pastry redolent of almonds, saffron, and cinnamon). A good way to try a bit of everything is the Marrakesh Feast ($27.75 per person), which includes chicken bastilla and beef *brewat* (minced beef in a layered pastry dusted with cinnamon and powered sugar), plus vegetable couscous and assorted Moroccan pastries. ⊠ *Morocco* ⊟ *AE, MC, V.*

Scandinavian

$$ ✕ **Restaurant Akershus.** The Norwegian buffet at this restaurant is as ex-
Fodor$Choice tensive as you'll find on this side of the Atlantic. Appetizers usually include herring and cold seafood, including *gravlax* (cured salmon served with mustard sauce) or *fiskepudding* (a seafood mousse with herb dressing). Next, pick up cold salads and meats, and on your last foray, fill up on hot lamb, veal, or venison. Try some *lefse*, a wonderful flatbread made from potatoes and wheat. The à la carte desserts include cloudberries, a delicate tundra fruit that tastes like a raspberry. ⊠ *Norway* ⊟ *AE, MC, V.*

Seafood

$$–$$$$ ✕ **Coral Reef Restaurant.** Part of the attraction here is the view of the giant Living Seas aquarium. Edible attractions include pan-seared salmon fillet with garlic pesto mash, and Caribbean lobster roasted with sautéed zucchini and shallots, braised potato, garlic, and butter (admittedly, a shade on the pricey side at $42). If you want to be able to tell the folks back home you tried alligator, the lunch menu includes grilled alligator sausage in a creole vinaigrette. ⊠ *The Living Seas* ⊟ *AE, MC, V.*

Elsewhere in Walt Disney World Resort

American/Casual

¢–$$ ✕ **ESPN Sports Club.** Watch sports on a big-screen TV and, periodically, catch ESPN sports-radio talk shows being taped here and be part of the audience. Food ranges from an outstanding half-pound burger to a 10-ounce sirloin to grilled chicken and shrimp in penne pasta, topped with marinara sauce. For dessert, how about a Superbowl Sundae? It sets you back $15, but it's easily enough for two people. This place is open quite late by Disney standards—until 2 AM on Friday and Saturday. ⊠ *Disney's BoardWalk* ☎ *407/939–5100* ⊟ *AE, MC, V.*

¢–$$ ✕ **Official All-Star Cafe.** You can't go wrong with cuisine created by renowned gastronomic experts Shaquille O'Neill, Monica Seles, Joe Montana, Tiger Woods, Andre Agassi, Wayne Gretzky, and Ken Griffey Jr. And there's nothing better than 16 big-screen TVs playing sports clips nonstop as loud rock music blares and spotlights roam around the room and across the tables. If you agree, you're going to love this place. The food, ranging from burgers to steaks to pasta, is nothing special. ⊠ *690 S. Victory Way* ☎ *407/827–8326* ⊟ *AE, MC, V.*

★ ¢–$$ ✕ **Rainforest Café.** This popular family eatery has locations at Downtown Disney Marketplace and Disney's Animal Kingdom. The lunch and dinner lines are often long, so go early or late if you can. Choices include Eyes of the Ocelot, a hearty meat loaf topped with sautéed mushrooms; and Mojo Bones, tender ribs with barbecue sauce. The coconut bread pudding with apricot filling and whipped cream is great. Breakfast is served only at the Animal Kingdom location, beginning at 7:30. ⊠ *Downtown Disney Marketplace or Disney's Animal Kingdom* ☎ *D.D.M. 407/827–8500 or D.A.K. 407/938–9100 or 407/939–3463* ⊕ *www.rainforestcafe.com* ⊟ *AE, D, DC, MC, V.*

Cajun/Creole

¢–$$$ ✕ **House of Blues.** From the outside, House of Blues resembles an old factory; the inside looks like an old church, complete with angelic frescoes. In any case, the southern-cooking is truly righteous. Best bets are catfish, Cajun meat loaf, and Louisiana crawfish and shrimp étouffée, as well as the Elwood sandwich—blackened chicken with chili-garlic mayonnaise and sour cream. The place gets noisy when live music plays (11 PM–2 AM); lunch can be almost serene. The Sunday Gospel Brunch ($30 adults, $15 children 4–12) is a feast worth its price tag. ⊠ *Downtown Disney West Side* ☎ *407/934–2583* ☰ *AE, D, MC, V.*

Contemporary

$$$$ ✕ **Victoria and Albert's.** At this Disney fantasy, the servers work in man-woman pairs, reciting specials in tandem. It's one of the plushest fine-dining experiences in Florida: a regal meal in a lavish, Victorian-style room. The seven-course, prix-fixe menu ($85; wine is an additional $42) changes daily. Appetizers might include veal sweetbreads or artichokes in a mushroom-based sauce; entrées may be grilled beef fillet with a Vidalia onion risotto. There are two seatings, at 5:45 and 9. In July and August, there's usually just one seating—at 6:30. The chef's-table dinner event is $115–$162 (with wine pairing) per person. ⊠ *Grand Floridian* ☎ *407/939–3463* ⌂ *Reservations essential* ⌂ *Jacket required* ☰ *AE, MC, V* ☺ *No lunch.*

FodorśChoice

$$$–$$$$ ✕ **Cítricos.** Although the name implies that you might be eating lots of local citrus-flavored specialties, you won't find them here, aside from drinks like a Citropolitan martini, infused with lemon and lime liqueur, and an orange chocolate mousse for dessert. Standout entrées include paprika and honey-marinated pork tenderloin with smoked eggplant dip and roasted duck breast with sweet-and-sour pomegranate glaze. The wine list, one of Disney's most extensive, includes vintages from around the world. Many are available by the glass. ⊠ *Grand Floridian* ☎ *407/939–3463* ☰ *AE, MC, V.*

★ $$–$$$$ ✕ **California Grill.** The view of the surrounding Disney parks from this rooftop restaurant is as stunning as the food; watch the nightly Magic Kingdom fireworks from the patio. Start with the brick-oven flatbread with grilled duck sausage or the *unagi* (eel) sushi. Try the pan-seared golden tilefish with wild mushroom risotto and red wine reduction for a main course. Good desserts include the orange crepes with Grand Marnier custard, raspberries and blackberry coulis, and the warm apple tart with caramel ice cream and Myer's Rum caramel sauce. ⊠ *Contemporary Resort* ☎ *407/939–3463* ☰ *AE, MC, V.*

★ $$–$$$$ ✕ **Wolfgang Puck Café.** There are lots of choices here, from wood-oven pizza at the informal Puck Express to five-course meals at the upstairs, formal dining room, where there's also a sushi bar and an informal café. Must-tries at Express include the pizzas, with toppings such as grilled chicken or salmon, and various inspired pastas, which have sauces sublimely laced with chunks of lobster, salmon, or chicken. The dining room always offers a worthy fresh ravioli and a Puck trademark—Wiener schnitzel. Special five-course prix-fixe dinners ($100 with wine and $65 without) require 24 hours' notice. ⊠ *Downtown Disney West Side* ☎ *407/938–9653* ⊕ *www.wolfgangpuck.com* ☰ *AE, MC, V.*

$$$ ✕ **Artist Point.** If you're not a guest at the Wilderness Lodge, a meal here is worth it just to see the giant totem poles and huge rock fireplace in the lobby. Cedar-plank salmon is the specialty here, and there are always some unusual offerings on the menu like grilled buffalo sirloin with sweet potato–hazelnut gratin and sweet onion jam. For dessert, try the wild berry cobbler or an apple-rhubarb tartlet with vanilla ice cream.

FodorśChoice

There's a good northwestern U.S. wine list. ☒ *Wilderness Lodge* ☏ *407/ 939–3463* ♿ *Reservations essential* ☰ *AE, MC, V.*

Continental

$$$–$$$$ ✕ **Arthur's 27.** The haute cuisine here comes with a world-class view from the 27th floor of the Wyndham Palace Resort, overlooking all of Disney World. Entrées include an excellent grilled veal loin and a consistently well prepared tenderloin of beef. There are also more exotic choices, such as roasted rack of elk or loin of rabbit. Best dessert is the stellar Grand Marnier soufflé. There are also prix-fixe options: $68 for five courses, $62 for four. ☒ *Wyndham Palace Resort & Spa, 1900 Buena Vista Dr. (I–4 Exit 68), Lake Buena Vista* ☏ *407/827–3450* ⊕ *www. wyndham.com/hotels/MCOPV/main.wnt* ♿ *Reservations essential* ☰ *AE, D, DC, MC, V.*

Cuban

$$–$$$ ✕ **Bongos Cuban Café.** Singer Gloria Estefan's Cuban eatery is inside a two-story building shaped like a pineapple. Hot-pressed Cuban sandwiches, black bean soup, deep-fried plantain chips, and beans and rice are mainstays on the menu for the lunch crowd. One of the best entrées is La Habana: lobster, shrimp, scallops, calamari, clams, and mussels in a piquant creole sauce. There's live Latin music on Friday and Saturday. ☒ *Downtown Disney West Side* ☏ *407/828–0999* ⊕ *www.bongoscubancafe. com* ♿ *Reservations not accepted* ☰ *AE, D, DC, MC, V.*

Italian

$$$–$$$$ ✕ **Portobello Yacht Club.** The northern Italian cuisine here is uniformly good. The spaghettini *alla Portobello* (with scallops, clams, and Alaskan king crab) is outstanding; other fine pasta options include the linguine with Manila clams in a white wine sauce and the rigatoni *alla Calabrese* (with sausage, mushrooms, tomatoes, and black olives). There's always a fresh-catch special, as well as tasty wood-oven pizza. ☒ *Pleasure Island* ☏ *407/934–8888* ☰ *AE, MC, V.*

Mediterranean

$$–$$$ ✕ **Spoodles.** The international tapas-style menu here draws on the best
FodorsChoice foods of the Mediterranean, from tuna with sun-dried-tomato couscous to Italian fettuccine with rich Parmesan cream sauce. Oak-fired flatbreads with toppings like roasted peppers make stellar appetizers. Best desserts include Marco Polo cake—a moist chocolate-filled layer cake—and pumpkin coconut flan. Can't decide? The dessert sampler lets you taste everything on the dessert cart. The children's menu includes macaroni and cheese and pepperoni pizza. There's a walk-up pizza window, if you prefer to stroll the boardwalk and snack. Omelets, pancakes, and other savories lead an excellent breakfast menu. ☒ *Disney's BoardWalk* ☏ *407/939–3463* ☰ *AE, MC, V.*

Seafood

$$$–$$$$ ✕ **Fulton's Crab House.** Set in a faux riverboat docked in a lagoon between Pleasure Island and the Marketplace, this fish house offers fine, if expensive, dining. The signature seafood is flown in daily. Dungeness crab from the Atlantic banks, Alaskan king crab, Florida stone crab: it's all fresh. For a real crustacean feast, try the crab and lobster for two, which includes 3 pounds of Alaskan king crab and snow crab, plus a 1¼-pound lobster, for $31.95 a head. The sublime cappuccino ice cream cake is $13, but one order is easily enough for two. ☒ *Downtown Disney Marketplace* ☏ *407/934–2628* ☰ *AE, MC, V.*

$$–$$$ ✕ **Flying Fish.** One of Disney's better restaurants, this fish house has dishes that include potato-wrapped Florida red snapper served with leek-fennel fondue and handmade triple-cheese ravioli with sweet red pepper

sauce. The Peeky Toe crab cakes with ancho-chile rémoulade is an appetizer that never leaves the frequently changing menu—try it and you will see why. Save room for the Lava Cake, chocolate cake served warm with a liquid chocolate center and topped with pomegranate ice cream. ⊠ *Disney's BoardWalk* ☎ *407/939–2359* ⊟ *AE, MC, V.*

$–$$$ ✕ **Landry's Seafood House.** Set in a fake warehouse building—popular architecture in Central Florida—this branch of a nationwide chain delivers good seafood at reasonable prices. The food is first-rate, especially Cajun dishes like the fresh-caught fish Pontchartrain, a broiled fish with slightly spicy seasoning and a creamy white-wine sauce that's topped with a lump of crabmeat. Good appetizers include bacon-wrapped shrimp en brochette with seafood stuffing, jack cheese, and jalapeño peppers, as well as excellent jumbo lump crab cakes. A $15 seafood platter lets you sample crab fingers, fried oysters, and shrimp. ⊠ *8800 Vineland Ave., Rte. 535, Lake Buena Vista* ☎ *407/827–6466* ⊕ *www.landrysseafood.com* ⊟ *AE, D, DC, MC, V.*

Steak

$$$–$$$$ ✕ **Shula's Steak House.** The hardwood floors, dark-wood paneling, and pictures of former Miami Dolphins coach Don Shula make this restaurant resemble an annex of the NFL Hall of Fame. Among the best selections are the porterhouse and prime rib. Finish the 48-ounce porterhouse and you get a football with your picture on it, but it's not an easy task to eat 3 pounds of red meat at one sitting unless you're a polar bear. If you're not a carnivore, go for the Norwegian salmon, the Florida snapper, or the huge (up to 4 pounds) Maine lobster. Save room for the seven-layer chocolate cake. ⊠ *Walt Disney World Dolphin* ☎ *407/934–1362* ⊟ *AE, D, DC, MC, V* ☉ *No lunch.*

$$–$$$$ ✕ **Yachtsman Steakhouse.** Aged beef, the attraction at this steak house in the ultra-polished Yacht and Beach Club, can be seen mellowing in the glassed-in butcher shop near the entryway. The slow-roasted prime rib is superb, as are the barbecued baby-back ribs, so tender you can eat them with just a fork. The tasty surf and turf is an 8-ounce filet mignon and a 6-ounce lobster tail. For dessert, try the tasty Jack Daniels cake: chocolate mousse flavored with the Tennessee whiskey. ⊠ *Yacht and Beach Club* ☎ *407/939–3463* ⊟ *AE, MC, V* ☉ *No lunch.*

$–$$$ ✕ **Concourse Steak House.** If you've always liked that trademark monorail that runs from the Magic Kingdom into the Contemporary Resort, you might want to have a meal here, set as it is one story below the train (the tracks run above). The place isn't as noisy as it might seem. Steaks include a succulent prime rib. Among the other entrées are mango-glazed barbecued pork ribs, oak wood–roasted chicken, herb-crusted salmon with red potatoes, and pan-seared tuna. For dessert, try the crème brûlée or the marbled cheesecake. ⊠ *Contemporary Resort* ☎ *407/939–3463* ⊟ *AE, MC, V.*

Universal's CityWalk

Take I–4 Exit 74B if you're heading westbound, 75A if eastbound.

American/Casual

★ **$$$–$$$$**   ✕ **Emeril's.** The popular eatery is a culinary shrine to celebrity chef Emeril Lagasse, who occasionally appears here. Count on such New Orleans treats as andouille, shrimp, and red beans appearing in some form. Entrées may include rack of lamb with a creole mustard crust and citrus-glazed duck with walnut-pear chutney. The wood-baked pizza, topped with exotic mushrooms, is stellar. Desserts, including bread pudding and a chocolate Grand Marnier soufflé (which must be ordered 30 minutes in advance), are also notable. ⊠ *6000 Universal Blvd., at*

Universal Orlando's CityWalk ☎ 407/224–2424 ⊕ www.emerils.com
⌂ Reservations essential ▤ AE, D, MC, V.

¢–$$ ✕ **Hard Rock Cafe Orlando.** Built to resemble Rome's Coliseum, this 800-seat restaurant is the largest of the 100-odd Hard Rocks in the world, but getting a seat at lunch can still require a long wait. The music is always loud and the walls are filled with rock memorabilia. Appetizers range from spring rolls to boneless chicken tenders. The most popular menu item is still the $8.49 burger, with the baby-back ribs and the home-made-style meat loaf both strong contenders. The best dessert is the $5 chocolate chip cookie (it's big), covered with ice cream. ✉ 6000 Universal Blvd., at Universal Orlando's CityWalk ☎ 407/224–3663 or 407/351–7625 ⊕ www.hardrockcafe.com ⌂ Reservations not accepted ▤ AE, D, DC, MC, V.

¢–$$ ✕ **Jimmy Buffett's Margaritaville.** Parrot-heads can probably name the top two menu items before they even walk in the door. You've got your cheeseburger, from the song "Cheeseburger in Paradise," and the Ultimate Margarita, from "Margaritaville." The rest of the menu is an eclectic mix of quesadillas, chowder, and crab cakes, a tasty fried fish platter, stone crab claws, and a pretty decent steak. Worthy dessert choices include the Last Mango in Paradise cheesecake, the key lime pie, and a tasty chocolate bread pudding. ✉ Universal Studios Plaza, Universal Orlando ☎ 407/224–9255 ⌂ Reservations not accepted ▤ AE, D, DC, MC, V.

¢–$$ ✕ **NASCAR Café Orlando.** If you are a racing fanatic, this is your place. If the memorabilia on the walls is not enough for you, a couple of actual race cars hang from the ceiling. The food is better than you might expect: highlights include a good chicken mushroom soup (with grilled chicken and shiitake mushrooms); the remarkably ungreasy popcorn shrimp; the Thunder Road burger, with melted pimiento cheese and sautéed onions; and a decent chicken potpie. Aside from the white chocolate cheesecake, desserts are largely forgettable. ✉ 6000 Universal Blvd., at Universal Orlando's CityWalk ☎ 407/224–3663 ⊕ www.nascarcafe.com ▤ AE, D, MC, V.

¢–$$ ✕ **NBA City.** The NBA memorabilia and video games are great, but the food is actually the real draw here. Best choices include the barbecued chicken quesadilla and a 12-ounce pork chop glazed with maple-mustard sauce. The brick-oven pizzas include an unusual BLT variety. And the milk shake is worth every bit of its $5 price tag. The big-screen TVs, which naturally broadcast nonstop basketball action, probably won't surprise you, but the relatively quiet bar upstairs, with elegant blond-wood furniture, probably will. ✉ 6000 Universal Blvd., at Universal Orlando's CityWalk ☎ 407/363–5919 ⊕ www.nbacity.com ▤ AE, D, MC, V.

¢–$ ✕ **Pat O'Brien's Orlando.** Head to this clone of the famous New Orleans bar to sip its famous (and supersweet, and fairly strong) drink, the hurricane, and munch on bayou-inspired snacks like crawfish nachos, Cajun shrimp, and alligator bites. Try the po'boys, French-bread sandwiches filled with tangy shrimp and sausage, or the *muffeletta* sandwiches, made with salami, ham, provolone, and olives. Pat's also has a good jambalaya, the spicy stew of sausage and chicken. There's live music nightly ($2 cover charge). ✉ 6000 Universal Blvd., at Universal Orlando's CityWalk ☎ 407/224–9255 ▤ AE, D, MC, V.

Universal Islands of Adventure

Take I–4 Exit 74B if you're heading westbound, 75A if eastbound.

American/Casual

¢ ✕ **Green Eggs and Ham Cafe.** This Dr. Seuss–inspired spot is the only place in Orlando where the eggs are intentionally green. The eggs (tinted with food coloring) are in an egg-and-ham sandwich, the most popular item at this walk-up, outdoor eatery, which looks like a hallucinatory McDonald's. There's also a fairly tasty "green" garden salad, as well as some other conventional fare, including a normal cheeseburger, fries, and "frings," a type of onion ring. ⊠ *6000 Universal Blvd., Seuss Landing section at Universal Studios Islands of Adventure* ☎ *407/224–9255* ▱ *AE, D, MC, V.*

American/Contemporary

$–$$$ ✕ **Confisco Grille.** You could walk right past this Mediterranean eatery, but if you want a good meal and sit-down service, don't pass by too quickly. The menu changes often, but typical entrées include pan-seared pork medallions with roasted garlic and red peppers, baked cod with spinach and mashed potatoes, and Thai noodles with chicken, shrimp, tofu, and bean sprouts. Save room for desserts like chocolate-banana bread pudding or crème brûlée. ⊠ *6000 Universal Blvd., Port of Entry section at Universal Studios Islands of Adventure* ☎ *407/224–9255* ▱ *AE, D, MC, V* ⊘ *No lunch.*

$–$$$ ✕ **Mythos.** The name sounds Greek, but the dishes are eclectic. The menu usually includes standouts like meat loaf, roast pork tenderloin, and wood-fired pizzas. Among the desserts is a fine pumpkin cheesecake. But the building itself is a draw: it resembles a giant rock formation from the outside and a huge cave (albeit one with plush upholstered seating) inside. Mythos also has a waterfront view of the big lagoon in the center of the theme park. ⊠ *6000 Universal Blvd., Lost Continent at Universal Studios Islands of Adventure* ☎ *407/224–9255* ▱ *AE, D, MC, V.*

Portofino Bay Hotel

Italian

★ $$–$$$$ ✕ **Delfino Riviera.** This lavish restaurant, a stunning copy of one in Portofino, Italy, has high-beam ceilings, stone columns, and marble floors. The cuisine is equally awe-inspiring. One of the best dishes is risotto *al frutti di mare* with cararoli rice, shrimp, squid, clams and mussels, mixed with white wine, garlic, and tomatoes. A strong second is the *filetto col vegetali*, grilled aged prime beef tenderloin, Italian eggplant, oven-dried tomatoes, and roasted garlic with red wine and rosemary oil. For dessert try the chef's spin on a cannoli, which is stuffed with apples and pine nuts in a sweet ricotta base. ⊠ *5601 Universal Blvd.* ☎ *407/503–1000* ▱ *AE, D, DC, MC, V* ⊘ *No lunch.*

$$–$$$ ✕ **Mama Della's.** The premise here is that Mama Della is a middle-age Italian housewife who has opened up her home as a restaurant. "Mama" is always on hand (there are several of them, working in shifts), strolling among the tables and making small talk. The food, served family style, is excellent. The menu has Italian traditions like chicken cacciatore and spaghetti with sirloin meatballs or bolognese sauce, and all of the pastas are made in-house. The quality of the food experience starts with hot garlic bread and continues through the dessert course; the tiramisu and the Italian chocolate torte both make sure bets. ⊠ *5601 Universal Blvd.* ☎ *407/503–1000* ▱ *AE, D, DC, MC, V* ⊘ *Closed Mon. No lunch.*

Hard Rock Hotel

Steak

$–$$$$ ✕ **The Palm.** With its dark-wood interior and hundreds of framed celebrity caricatures, this restaurant resembles its famed New York City namesake. Steaks are the reason to dine here, but most are available only at dinner. The steak fillet cooked on a hot stone is a specialty, as is the Double Steak, a 36-ounce New York strip for two (or one extreme carnivore). There are several veal dishes on the menu, along with a 3-pound

Nova Scotia lobster, broiled crab cakes, and a good linguine with white clam sauce. ⊠ *1000 Universal Studios Plaza* ☎ *407/503–7256* ⊕ *www. thepalm.com* ☰ *AE, D, DC, MC, V* ☯ *No lunch weekends.*

International Drive, Orlando

Take I–4 Exit 72 or 74A.

American/Casual

\$–\$\$\$ ✕ **B-Line Diner.** As you might expect from its hotel location, this slick, 1950s-style diner with red vinyl counter seats is not exactly cheap, but the salads, sandwiches, and griddle foods are tops. The greatest combo ever, a thick, juicy burger served with fries and a wonderful milk shake, is done beautifully. It's open 24 hours. ⊠ *Peabody Orlando, 9801 International Dr., I–Drive Area* ☎ *407/352–4000* ⊕ *www.peabodyorlando. com* ☰ *AE, D, DC, MC, V.*

¢–\$\$\$ ✕ **Dan Marino's Town Tavern.** Part of a Florida sports-bar chain begun by the Miami Dolphins quarterback, the Tavern mixes burgers and steaks with some sophisticated surprises, including seared tuna. ⊠ *Pointe*Orlando, 9101 International Dr., I–Drive Area* ☎ *407/363–1013* ⊕ *www.danmarinostowntavern.com* ☰ *AE, MC.*

Caribbean

\$–\$\$\$ ✕ **Bahama Breeze.** Even though the lineage is corporate, the menu here is creative and tasty. The casual fun and the Caribbean cooking draw a crowd, so be prepared for a wait. Meanwhile, sip piña coladas and other West Indian delights on a big wooden porch. The food is worth the wait. Start with *tostones con pollo* (plantain chips topped with chicken and cheese), followed by coconut curry chicken or paella. ⊠ *8849 International Dr., I–Drive Area* ☎ *407/248–2499* ⊠ *8735 Vineland Ave. (I–4 Exit 68), I–Drive Area* ☎ *407/938–9010* ⊕ *www.bahamabreeze.com* ⚐ *Reservations not accepted* ☰ *AE, D, DC, MC.*

Chinese

\$–\$\$\$\$ ✕ **Ming Court.** A walled courtyard and serene pond make you forget you're on International Drive. The extensive menu includes simple chicken Szechuan, plum-blossom boneless duck, and aged filet mignon grilled in a spicy Szechuan sauce. The flourless chocolate cake, certainly not Asian, has been a popular standard for years. Ming Court is within walking distance of the Orange County Convention Center and can be quite busy at lunchtime. ⊠ *9188 International Dr., I–Drive Area* ☎ *407/351–9988* ⊕ *www.ming-court.com* ☰ *AE, D, DC, MC, V.*

Contemporary

¢ ✕ **Café Tu Tu Tango.** The food here resembles tapas—everything is appetizer-size. The eclectic menu is fitting for a restaurant on International Drive. Try the Cajun chicken egg rolls with blackened chicken, Greek goat cheese, creole mustard, and tomato salsa, if you want a compendium of cuisines at one go. The restaurant goes for a whimsical artist's loft feel; artists paint at easels while diners sip drinks like Matisse Margaritas. Although no one dish costs more than \$8, it's not hard to spend \$50 for lunch for two. ⊠ *8625 International Dr., I–Drive Area* ☎ *407/ 248–2222* ⊕ *www.cafetututango.com* ⚐ *Reservations not accepted* ☰ *AE, D, DC, MC, V.*

Seafood

\$\$\$–\$\$\$\$ ✕ **Atlantis.** A harpist plays in this dining room, which is outfitted with frescoes, dark-wood paneling, and plush green carpet. The waiters even bring forth the entrées on silver-dome trays. Go for one of the various lobster dishes or the grilled fish, such as yellowfin tuna and salmon. There are also worthy red-meat dishes, including roast loin of lamb, and the

sunglasses you left in Miami Beach café: $75
golf glove you lost in Naples: $8
camera you forgot in the Everglades: $310

replacing your card anywhere:
priceless

For everything from card replacement to cash advances
to locating the nearest ATM, call 1-800-MasterCard.

there are some things money can't buy.
for everything else there's MasterCard.

Find America *with a Compass*

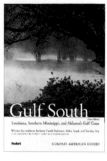

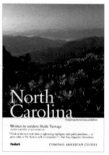

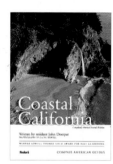

Written by local authors and illustrated throughout with spectacular color images, Compass American Guides reveal the character and culture of more than 40 of America's most fascinating destinations. Perfect for residents who want to explore their own backyards and for visitors who want an insider's perspective on the history, heritage, and all there is to see and do.

Fodor's COMPASS AMERICAN GUIDES

At bookstores everywhere.

obligatory surf-and-turf combo—in this case a sirloin served with lobster and pesto sauce. Desserts include some fine soufflés, which must be ordered 30 minutes in advance. ⊠ *Renaissance Orlando Resort, 6677 Sea Harbor Dr., I–Drive Area* ☎ *407/351–5555* ⊕ *www. atlantisorlando.com* ⊟ *AE, MC, V* ⊘ *No lunch.*

$$–$$$$ ✕ **Charlie's Lobster House.** The seafood here often takes a long plane ride before it arrives in the kitchen (lobster from New England and the Caribbean; oysters from the Pacific Northwest); the prices reflect those trips. But this is the place to dine on a good version of lobster thermidor ($37) or the 22-ounce New York strip steak ($40). It's one of Orlando's few semiformal restaurants, with white linen tablecloths and dark-wood paneling, but dine in a tank top and flip-flop sandals if you wish. ⊠ *Mercado shopping center, 8445 International Dr., I–Drive Area* ☎ *407/352–6929* ⊕ *www.charlieslobsterhouse.com* ⊟ *AE, D, DC, MC, V* ⊘ *No lunch.*

Steak

★ **$–$$$$** ✕ **Vito's Chop House.** There's a reason they keep the blinds closed most of the time: it's for the wines' sake. The dining room doubles as the cellar, with hundreds of bottles stacked in every nook and cranny. The steaks and the wood-grilled pork chops di Vito are superb. If you don't mind laying out $94.95 for Vito's Ultimate Surf 'n' Turf, you'll feast on a 50-ounce porterhouse and a 1½-pound lobster (which feeds at least two people). Worthwhile desserts include Grilled Peach di Vito, an excellent key lime pie, and Italian wedding cake. Finish your meal by enjoying a fine cigar along with a glass of aged cognac, Armagnac, or grappa in the lounge. ⊠ *8633 International Dr., I–Drive Area* ☎ *407/354–2467* ⊕ *www.vitoschophouse.com* ⟡ *Reservations essential* ⊟ *AE, D, DC, MC, V* ⊘ *No lunch.*

Thai

$–$$ ✕ **Siam Orchid.** One of Orlando's more elegant Asian restaurants is in a gorgeous structure a bit off International Drive. Waitresses, who wear costumes from Thailand, serve authentic fare such as Siam wings, chicken wings stuffed to look like drumsticks, and *pla rad prikm,* a whole, deep-fried fish with a sauce flavored with red chiles, bell peppers, and garlic. Pad thai can be ordered with beef, pork, seafood, or just vegetables. If you like your food spicy, remember to say "Thai hot"—but be sure you mean it. ⊠ *7575 Universal Blvd., I–Drive Area* ☎ *407/351–0821* ⊟ *AE, DC, MC, V.*

Downtown Orlando

Take I–4 Exit 83B if you're heading westbound, Exit 83A if eastbound, unless otherwise noted.

Contemporary

★ **$$$–$$$$** ✕ **Manuel's on the 28th.** Restaurants with great views don't always have much more than that to offer, but this lofty spot on the 28th floor is also a culinary landmark. The menu changes regularly, but there's always a representative sampling of fish, Angus beef, pork, and duck. Dinner offerings may include sea scallops covered in macadamia nuts, Black Angus filet mignon, and even wild boar loin marinated in coconut milk. For dessert, try the baked apples wrapped in pastry, beggar's-purse style, which come with caramel sauce. ⊠ *Bank of America building, 390 N. Orange Ave., Suite 2800, Downtown Orlando* ☎ *407/246–6580* ⊕ *www.manuelsonthe28th.com* ⊟ *AE, D, DC, MC, V* ⊘ *Closed Sun.–Mon. No lunch.*

$$–$$$$ ✕ **The Boheme Restaurant.** The company that operates Manuel's on the 28th also runs the Boheme. No panorama here, but the food is as adventurous. On offer are dishes like fennel-seared Atlantic salmon with artichoke and wild mushroom *barigoule* (stewed vegetables), and noisettes of Parmesan-crusted veal. Corn-fed Angus beef is always on the menu: try the pepper steak. At breakfast, the French toast with a triple sec–strawberry glaze is an excellent way to awaken your palate. The Sunday brunch is a worthwhile experience, with prime rib and sushi as well as omelets. ⊠ *Westin Grand Bohemian, 325 S. Orange Ave., Downtown Orlando* ☎ *407/313–9000* ⊕ *www.grandbohemianhotel. com* ⊟ *AE, D, DC, MC, V* ⌂ *Reservations essential for dinner.*

$–$$$ ✕ **Concha Me Crazy.** If the name of this sparkling downtown eatery makes you think that it should be contained within Disney property, it's because the place is a product of Johnny Rivers, a former head chef at Disney, who clearly believes Orlando restaurants need silly names. The food is serious business, however. Sure, there's great conch chowder and black bean soup, but other good offerings include peanut-crusted grouper with ginger soy sauce, fire-roasted chicken with cinnamon sweet potatoes, and a great filet mignon with brandy mushroom sauce. There's a big aquarium indoors; outside there's a fine sidewalk seating area. ⊠ *Embassy Suites Hotel, 191 E. Pine St., Downtown Orlando* ☎ *407/ 246–0011* ⊟ *AE, D, DC, MC, V.*

¢–$$ ✕ **Harvey's Bistro.** A loyal business crowd peoples this clubby café at lunch. It also attracts a nighttime following by staying open until 11 on weekends. On the upscale menu, which has a mix of bistro and comfort foods, escargots are the top starter. Pasta favorites include chicken stroganoff, duck and shrimp in Asian peanut sauce on linguine, and salmon with lobster Alfredo sauce. If you're a red-meat fan, rejoice. Harvey's has pot roast, a pan-seared tenderloin, and meat loaf baked in parchment. ⊠ *Bank of America building, 390 N. Orange Ave., Downtown Orlando* ☎ *407/246–6560* ⊕ *www.culinaryconceptsinc.com* ⊟ *AE, D, DC, MC, V* ⊘ *Closed Sun. No lunch Sat.*

French

$$–$$$$ ✕ **Le Provence Bistro Français.** This charming, two-story restaurant in the heart of downtown does a fine imitation of an out-of-the-way bistro on Paris's Left Bank—as long as you don't spot the palm trees out the window. For lunch try the salade niçoise, made with fresh grilled tuna, French string beans, and hard-boiled eggs; or the cassoulet *toulousain,* a hearty mixture of white beans, lamb, pork, and sausage. At dinner choose from a six-course prix-fixe menu, a less pricey four-course version, or à la carte options. The bistro doesn't always answer the phone during dinner. ⊠ *50 E. Pine St., Downtown Orlando* ☎ *407/843–1320* ⊟ *AE, DC, MC, V* ⊘ *Closed Sun. No lunch Sat.*

Elsewhere in Orlando

American/Casual

★ ¢–$$ ✕ **White Wolf Café.** A perfect fit for Orlando's small but vibrant antiques and art-gallery district, this urbane bistro offers a fine menu and sidewalk café area. A great appetizer is the *lavosh* (Mediterranean-style cracker bread) topped with artichoke hearts, sun-dried tomatoes, and mozzarella. Entrées usually include a deep-dish lasagna; there's also an excellent lasagna variation that's made with French bread rather than with pasta. For dessert, try the chocolate hazelnut torte or a chocolate-chip truffle cookie. There's live music on Friday and Saturday nights. ⊠ *1829 N. Orange Ave., Central Orlando* ☎ *407/895–5590* ⊕ *www. whitewolfcafe.com* ⊟ *AE, MC, V.*

¢–$ ✕ **Wildfires Bar n' Grill.** Inside a former auto repair shop and gas station, Wildfires is the latest addition to the trendy dining district growing in Thornton Park, just east of downtown and near Lake Eola. St. Louis ribs, rubbed with spices and slowly roasted, are the specialty here. The ribs are both spicy and tender; a half-rack with a couple sides, like pasta salad and barbecued beans, is $10. Another good choice is the chicken, rib, and pork sampler plate ($14). If you're not a red-meat person, try the wood-grilled salmon with cilantro lime vinaigrette. ⊠ *700 E. Washington St., Thornton Park* ☎ *407/872–8665* ⊟ *MC, V.*

Contemporary

★ $$$-$$$$ ✕ **Chatham's Place.** In Florida, grouper is about as ubiquitous as Coca-Cola, but to discover its full potential, try the rendition here: it's sautéed in pecan butter and flavored with cayenne. It's one of the best dishes in Orlando. A close second is the pan-roasted rack of lamb flavored with rosemary. The most popular appetizer is the Maryland-style crab cakes, but the New Orleans–style shrimp brochette is also noteworthy. The chef does wonders with desserts like pecan–macadamia nut pie. ⊠ *7575 Dr. Phillips Blvd. (I–4 Exit 74A), Southwest Orlando* ☎ *407/345–2992* ⊕ *www.chathamsplace.com* ⊟ *AE, D, DC, MC, V.*

$-$$$ ✕ **HUE.** On the ground floor of a condo high-rise on the edge of Lake Eola, this place takes its name from a self-created acronym: Hip Urban Environment. While it may not be quite as cool as its press clippings, the food is both good and eclectic, with such offerings as succulent fried oysters, tasty crab cakes, and filet mignon served with Portobello polenta. Unfortunately, the large outdoor dining area overlooks the street and not the lake. ⊠ *629 E. Central Blvd., Thornton Park* ☎ *407/849–1800* ⊟ *407/872–3348* ⌘ *Reservations not accepted.* ⊟ *AE, D, DC, MC, V.*

Cuban

★ $-$$$ ✕ **Numero Uno.** To the followers of this long-popular Latin restaurant, the name is accurate. Downtowners have been filling the place up at lunch for years. It bills itself as "the home of paella," and that's probably the best choice. If you have a good appetite and you either called to order ahead or can spare the 75-minute wait, then try the paella Valenciana, made with yellow rice, sausage, chicken, fish, and Spanish spices and served with a side order of plantains. Otherwise, go for traditional Cuban fare like shredded flank steak or arroz con pollo. Take I–4 Exit 81A or 81B. ⊠ *2499 S. Orange Ave., Central Orlando* ☎ *407/841–3840* ⊟ *AE, D, DC, MC, V.*

French

$$-$$$$ ✕ **Le Coq au Vin.** Chef-owner Louis Perrotte is something of a culinary
Fodor'sChoice god in Orlando, but he doesn't let it go to his head. He operates a modest little kitchen in a small house in south Orlando. Perrotte's homey eatery is usually filled with locals who appreciate the lovely traditional French fare: homemade chicken liver pâté, fresh trout with champagne sauce, and Long Island duck with green peppercorns. The menu changes seasonally to ensure the freshest ingredients for house specialties. But the house namesake dish is always available and always excellent. For dessert, try the Grand Mariner soufflé. ⊠ *4800 S. Orange Ave., Central Orlando* ☎ *407/851–6980* ⊟ *AE, DC, MC, V* ⊙ *Closed Mon.*

Italian

$$$-$$$$ ✕ **Christini's.** Locals, visitors, and Disney execs gladly pay the price at Christini's, one of the city's best places for northern Italian. Owner Chris Christini is on hand nightly to make sure that everything is perfect. Try the pasta with lobster, shrimp, and clams or the huge veal chops, seasoned with fresh sage. The multicourse dinner often takes a couple of hours or more, but if you like Italian minstrels at your table, this place should please you. Take I–4 Exit 74A. ⊠ *7600 Dr. Phillips Blvd., Dr. Phillips Marketplace, Sand Lake Road Area* ☎ *407/345–8770* ⊕ *www. christinis.com* ⊟ *AE, D, DC, MC, V.*

$–$$$ ✕ **Gargi's Italian Restaurant.** In the area just north of downtown filled with antiques shops and overlooking Lake Ivanhoe is a great mom-and-pop Italian restaurant with fine pasta. If you crave old-fashioned spaghetti and meatballs, lasagna, or manicotti made with sauces that have been simmering all day, this storefront hole-in-the-wall is the place. If you want more than basic pasta, try the veal marsala or the tasty linguine with shrimp, peppers, and marinara. Beer and wine are available. Take I–4 Exit 84. ✉ *1421 N. Orange Ave., Central Orlando* ☎ *407/894–7907* ▤ *AE, MC, V* ⊘ *Closed Sun.*

$–$$ ✕ **La Fontanella Da Nino.** A courtyard seating area with a lovely foun-
Fodor'sChoice tain makes a great spot to enjoy a glass of pinot grigio or chardonnay, along with what the menu calls *stuzzichini*, a Neapolitan phrase that means "something to nibble on." The *peperoni saltati* (roasted peppers sautéed with garlic, black olives, and capers) is a good choice, as is the *melenzane all griglia* (grilled marinated eggplant). A standout entrée is *pollo Scarpariello* (pasta with chicken, grilled sausage, and mushrooms in a cream sauce). ✉ *900 E. Washington St., Thornton Park* ☎ *407/425–0033* ▤ *AE, MC, V* ⊘ *No lunch Sun.*

¢–$ ✕ **Alfonso's Pizza & More.** This is a strong contender for the best pizza
Fodor'sChoice in Orlando (in the non–wood-fired-oven division). Since it's just across the street from a high school, things get frenzied at lunch. The hand-tossed pizza's toppings range from pepperoni to pineapple—but the calzones and some of the pasta dishes, like fettuccine Alfredo, are quite worthy as well. There are also subs and salads for lighter fare. The secret to the superior pizza is simple: the dough and all the sauces are made from scratch daily. Take I–4 Exit 84 to the College Park neighborhood area. ✉ *3231 Edgewater Dr., College Park* ☎ *407/872–7324* ▤ *MC, V.*

Steak

$$$–$$$$ ✕ **Del Frisco.** Locals like this quiet, uncomplicated steak house. Del Frisco delivers carefully prepared, corn-fed beef and attentive service. When your steak arrives, the waiter asks you to cut into it and check that it was cooked as you ordered it. The simple menu includes T-bones, porterhouses, filets mignons, Maine lobster, Alaskan crab, and lobster bisque. Bread is baked daily at the restaurant, and the bread pudding, with a Jack Daniels sauce, is worth a try. There's a piano bar next to the dining room. ✉ *729 Lee Rd., Central Orlando* ☎ *407/645–4443* ▤ *AE, D, DC, MC, V* ⊘ *Closed Sun. No lunch.*

$$–$$$ ✕ **Linda's La Cantina.** Beef is serious business here. As the menu says, management "cannot be responsible for steaks cooked medium-well and well done." Despite that stuffy-sounding caveat, this down-home steak house has been a favorite among locals since the Eisenhower administration. The menu is short and to the point, including about a dozen steaks and just enough ancillary items to fill up a page. Among the best cuts is the La Cantina large T-bone—more beef than most can handle, for $22. With every entrée you get a heaping order of spaghetti (which isn't particularly noteworthy) or a baked potato. ✉ *4721 E. Colonial Dr., Central Orlando* ☎ *407/894–4491* ⊕ *www.lindaslacantina.com* ▤ *AE, D, MC, V.*

Vietnamese

¢ ✕ **Little Saigon.** This local favorite represents one of the best of Orlando's
Fodor'sChoice ethnic restaurants. Sample the summer rolls (spring-roll filling in a soft wrapper) with peanut sauce, or excellent Vietnamese crepes, filled with shredded pork and noodles. Then move on to the grilled pork and egg, served atop rice noodles, or the traditional soup, filled with noodles, rice, vegetables, and your choice of either chicken or seafood; ask to have extra meat in the soup if you're hungry, and be sure they bring you the mint and bean sprouts to sprinkle in. Beer and wine are available. ✉ *1106*

E. Colonial Dr., Central Orlando ☎ *407/423–8539* ▣ *MC, V* ☞ *Beer and wine only.*

Outlying Towns

Contemporary

¢–$ ✕**Dexter's.** The good wine list and imaginative menu tend to attract quite a crowd of locals. Dexter's has its own wine label and publishes a monthly newsletter for those who appreciate a good varietal. The best entrées include chicken tortilla pie, a stack of cheese-laden tortillas that looks like a spaceship, and Cajun-spiced shrimp served with garlic bucatini. There's often live music on Thursday night. The East Washington location is in gentrified Thornton Park, just east of downtown Orlando; you may be the only out-of-towner here. ✉ *558 W. New England Ave., Winter Park* ☎ *407/629–1150* ✉ *808 E. Washington St., Orlando* ☎ *407/648–2777* ⊕ *www.dexwine.com* ⌒ *Reservations not accepted* ▣ *AE, D, DC, MC, V.*

Continental

$$$$ ✕**Chalet Suzanne.** If you are on your way south, or are visiting Bok Tower Gardens, consider making time for a good meal at this family-owned country inn. Many devotees come for the traditional dinner—all lunch and dinner meals are prix-fixe affairs—or for a sophisticated breakfast of eggs Benedict or Swedish pancakes with lingonberries. The best meal, if your are on a budget, is lunch. The house signature chicken Suzanne (baked and carefully basted) is tender and worth the dinner price of $59, but it's just as tasty at lunch for $32. ✉ *3800 Chalet Suzanne Dr. (I–4 Exit 55), Lake Wales* ☎ *863/676–6011* ⊕ *www.chaletsuzanne.com* ▣ *AE, DC, MC, V* ⊘ *Closed Mon. June–Aug.*

Italian

$–$$$$ ✕**Antonio's La Fiamma.** The wood-burning grill and oven do more than give the place a delightful smell. They're used to turn out great grilled fish dishes, delicious pizzas, and homemade bread. Try the *zuppa di pesce,* a soup made with plenty of shrimp, scallops, and langostino, and well worth its $23 price tag, or the equally compelling *pollo all'aglio e rosmarin,* which is chicken basted with fresh rosemary, garlic, and olive oil, and then roasted over a wood-burning rotisserie. For a quick bite, the deli-style version downstairs has many of the same menu items. ✉ *611 S. Orlando Ave., U.S. 17–92, Maitland* ☎ *407/645–5523* ⊕ *www. antoniosonline.com* ▣ *AE, MC, V* ⊘ *Closed Sun.*

★ $$–$$$ ✕**Enzo's on the Lake.** This is one of Orlando foodies' favorite restaurants, even though it's on a tacky stretch of highway filled with used-car lots. Enzo Perlini, the Roman charmer who owns the place, has turned a rather ordinary lakefront house into an Italian villa. It's worth the trip, about 45 minutes from WDW, to sample the antipasti. Mussels in the shell with a broth of tomatoes, olive oil, and garlic make a great appetizer. The *bucatini à la Enzo* (sautéed bacon, mushrooms, and peas served over long, hollow noodles) is very popular. ✉ *1130 S. U.S. 17–92, Longwood* ☎ *407/834–9872* ⊕ *www.enzos.com* ▣ *AE, DC, MC, V* ⊘ *Closed Sun.*

Seafood

$$–$$$$ ✕**Black Fin.** Representative offerings at this fish-focused restaurant include Canadian halibut with a Parmesan crust, oak-grilled yellowfin tuna, and Ponce Inlet mahimahi. In addition to the rotating seafood selections, there are standards like broiled Caribbean lobster, Alaskan king crab, and a lobster and filet mignon combo. Don't overlook the large selection of fresh oyster appetizers prepared on the half shell including flo-

rentine, broussard, or spicy hot. Save room for the carrot cake. The interior feels like an old mansion, even though Black Fin is inside a modern shopping complex. ⊠ *460 N. Orlando Ave., Winter Park* ☎ *407/ 691–4653* ⊕ *www.blackfinseafood.com* ⊟ *AE, D, DC, MC, V.*

WHERE TO STAY

Your basic options come down to properties that are (1) owned and operated by Disney on WDW grounds, (2) not owned or operated by Disney but on Disney property, and (3) not on WDW property. There are advantages to each. If you are coming to Orlando for only a few days and are interested solely in the Magic Kingdom, Epcot, and the other Disney attractions, the resorts on Disney property—whether or not they're owned by Disney—are the most convenient. But if you plan to spend time sightseeing in and around Orlando, it makes sense to look into the alternatives. On-site hotels are generally more expensive, although there are some moderately priced establishments on Disney property. But Orlando is not huge, and even apparently distant properties are only a half hour's drive from Disney entrance gates. Some good but inexpensive hotels can also be found in Kissimmee, 10 minutes from Disney World. As a rule, the greater the distance from Walt Disney World Resort, the lower the room rates. Reservations should be made several months in advance—as much as a year in advance for the best rooms during high season. Many hotels and attractions offer discounts up to 40% from September to mid-December. Orlando lodging prices tend to be a little higher than elsewhere in Florida, but in all but the smallest motels there is little or no charge for children under 18 who share a room with an adult.

WHAT IT COSTS				
	$$$$	**$$$**	**$$**	**$**	**¢**
HOTELS	over $220	$140–$220	$100–$140	$80–$100	under $80

Hotel prices are for a standard double room, excluding 6% sales tax (more in some counties) and 1%–4% tourist tax.

In WDW: Disney-Owned Properties

All on-site accommodations that are owned by Disney may be booked through the **Walt Disney World Central Reservations Office** (⊕ Box 10100, Suite 300, Lake Buena Vista 32830 ☎ 407/934–7639 ⊕ www. disneyworld.com). People with disabilities can call **WDW Special Request Reservations** (☎ 407/939–7807) to get information or book rooms at any of the on-site Disney properties.

Magic Kingdom Resort Area
Take I–4 Exit 62, 64B, or 65.

$$$$ ⚇ **Contemporary Resort.** Looking like an intergalactic docking bay, this 15-story, flat-topped pyramid bustles from dawn to after midnight. Upper floors of the main tower (where rooms are more expensive) offer a great view of all the day and night activities in and around the Magic Kingdom. Rooms have a modern look, with lamps that look like they might have come from the Sharper Image, and those facing the Magic Kingdom have a great view of the evening fireworks show. Restaurants include the character-meal palace Chef Mickey's, the laid-back Concourse Steak House, and the top-floor and top-rated California Grill. ☎ *407/ 824–1000* 🖷 *407/824–3539* ⤴ *1,008 rooms, 36 suites* ♿ *3 restaurants, snack bar, room service, in-room data ports, in-room safes, some re-*

frigerators, cable TV, golf privileges, 3 pools, wading pool, 6 tennis courts, health club, hair salon, indoor and outdoor hot tubs, massage, beach, boating, marina, waterskiing, shuffleboard, volleyball, 2 lobby lounges, shops, baby-sitting, children's programs (ages 4–12), playground, laundry facilities, laundry service, concierge, concierge floor, business services, convention center, meeting rooms; no-smoking rooms ☐ *AE, D, DC, MC, V.*

$$$$
Fodor'sChoice

▦ **Grand Floridian Resort & Spa.** This Victorian-style property on the shores of the Seven Seas Lagoon has a red gabled roof, delicate gingerbread, rambling verandas, and brick chimneys. Rooms have ornate hardwood furniture and fancy-print carpeting. Add a dinner or two at Victoria and Albert's, or Cítricos, and you'll probably spend more in a weekend here than on an average mortgage payment, but you'll have the memory of the best Disney offers. The Grand Floridian is what Disney considers its flagship resort—no other has better amenities, or a higher room rate. ☎ 407/824–3000 ☒ 407/824–3186 ↗ *900 rooms, 90 suites* ⚐ *5 restaurants, snack bar, room service, in-room data ports, in-room safes, cable TV, golf privileges, 2 tennis courts, 3 pools, hair salon, health club, massage, spa, beach, boating, marina, croquet, shuffleboard, volleyball, wading pool, waterskiing, 4 lounges, video game room, baby-sitting, children's programs (ages 4–12), playground, laundry facilities, laundry service, concierge, concierge floor, business services, convention center, meeting rooms; no-smoking rooms* ☐ *AE, D, DC, MC, V.*

$$$$

▦ **Polynesian Resort.** If it weren't for the kids in Mickey Mouse caps, you might think you were in Fiji. A three-story tropical atrium fills the lobby. Orchids bloom alongside coconut palms and banana trees, and water cascades from volcanic rock fountains. A mainstay here is the evening luau (Wednesday–Sunday), in which Polynesian dancers perform before a feast with Hawaiian-style roast pork. Rooms sleep five. Lagoonview rooms—which overlook the Electrical Water Pageant—are the most peaceful and the priciest. Most rooms have a balcony or patio. ☎ 407/824–2000 ☒ 407/824–3174 ↗ *853 rooms, 5 suites* ⚐ *3 restaurants, snack bar, room service, in-room data ports, in-room safes, cable TV, golf privileges, 2 pools, wading pool, health club, hair salon, massage, beach, boating, shuffleboard, volleyball, bar, lobby lounge, video game room, baby-sitting, children's programs (ages 4–12), playground, laundry facilities, laundry service, concierge, concierge floors, business services.* ☐ *AE, D, DC, MC, V.*

★ **$$$–$$$$**

▦ **Wilderness Lodge.** The architects outdid themselves with this sevenstory hotel, modeled after the turn-of-the-20th-century lodges out west, such as those in Glacier National Park. Supported by towering tree trunks, the five-story lobby has an 82-ft-high, three-sided fireplace made of rocks from the Grand Canyon and lit by enormous tepee-shape chandeliers. Two 55-ft-tall hand-carved totem poles complete the illusion. Rooms have leather chairs, patchwork quilts, and cowboy art. Each has a balcony or a patio. The hotel's showstopper is its Fire Rock Geyser, a faux Old Faithful, near the large pool, which begins as a hot spring in the lobby. ☎ 407/824–3200 ☒ 407/824–3232 ↗ *728 rooms, 31 suites* ⚐ *2 restaurants, room service, in-room data ports, cable TV with movies, pool, wading pool, beach, boating, bicycles, 2 lobby lounges, baby-sitting, children's programs (ages 4–12), laundry facilities, laundry service, concierge, concierge floor; no-smoking rooms.* ☐ *AE, D, DC, MC, V.*

★ **¢–$$$$**

🛖 **Fort Wilderness Resort and Campground.** For a calm spot amid the themepark storm, go no farther than the 700 acres of scrubby pine and tiny streams known as Fort Wilderness, on Bay Lake and about a mile from the Wilderness Lodge. Bringing a tent or RV is one of the cheapest ways to stay on WDW property, especially since sites, with outdoor grills and picnic tables, accommodate up to 10. Comfortable Wilderness Cabins put the relaxed friendliness of Fort Wilderness within reach of families who haven't brought their own RV and don't want to camp out. They can accommodate four grown-ups and two children. ⚹ *Laundry facilities, grocery, cafeteria, snack bar, playground, 2 tennis courts, 2 pools, beach, boating, bicycles, basketball, horseback riding, shuffleboard, volleyball* ⚹ *397 campsites, 386 trailer sites, 408 cabins* ☎ *407/824–2900* ⊟ *AE, MC, V.*

Epcot Resort Area
Take I–4 Exit 64B, 65 or 67.

★ $$$$ ▦ **BoardWalk Inn and Villas.** A beautiful re-creation of Victorian-era Atlantic City, WDW's smallest deluxe hotel is the crowning jewel of the BoardWalk complex. WDW's architectural master, Robert A. M. Stern, designed this inn to mimic 19th-century New England building style. A 200-ft water slide in the form of a classic wooden roller coaster cascades into the pool area. The proximity to the BoardWalk dining and entertainment area is no small benefit: it's where you'll find the popular ESPN Sports Club and some of Disney's better restaurants. ☎ *407/939–5100 inn; 407/939–6200 villas* 🖷 *407/939–5150* ⚹ *370 rooms, 19 suites, 526 villas* ⚹ *3 restaurants, room service, in-room data ports, in-room safes, tennis court, pool, gym, croquet, lobby lounge, nightclub, video game room, baby-sitting, children's programs (ages 4–12), laundry service, concierge, business services, convention center* ⊟ *AE, D, DC, MC, V.*

★ $$$$ ▦ **Yacht and Beach Club Resorts.** Straight out of a Cape Cod summer, these properties on Seven Seas Lagoon are coastal-style inns on a grand Disney scale. The five-story Yacht Club has hardwood floors, a lobby full of gleaming brass and polished leather, an oyster-gray clapboard facade, and evergreen landscaping; there's even a lighthouse on its pier. Rooms have white-and-blue naval flags on the bedspreads and a small ship's wheel on the headboard. At the Beach Club, a croquet lawn and cabana-dotted, white-sand beach set the scene. Stormalong Bay, a 3-acre water park with water slides and whirlpools, is part of this Club. ☎ *407/934–8000 Beach Club; 407/934–7000 Yacht Club* 🖷 *407/934–3850 Beach Club; 407/934–3450 Yacht Club* ⚹ *1,213 rooms, 112 suites* ⚹ *4 restaurants, snack bar, room service, 2 tennis courts, 3 pools, hair salon, health club, massage, sauna, beach, boating, croquet, volleyball, 3 lobby lounges, video game room, baby-sitting, laundry service, concierge, business services, convention center* ⊟ *AE, D, DC, MC, V.*

★ $$$ ▦ **Caribbean Beach Resort.** Awash in dizzying Caribbean colors, this hotel complex was the first of Disney's moderately priced accommodations. Six palm-studded "villages" share 45-acre Barefoot Bay, which is actually a lake, and its white-sand beach. A promenade circles the lake, and bridges over it connect to a 1-acre path-crossed play area called Parrot Cay. The Old Port Royale complex, decorated with pirates' cannons and statues, has a food court and table-service dining. There's a pool with waterfalls and a big water slide. ☎ *407/934–3400* 🖷 *407/934–3288* ⚹ *2,112 rooms* ⚹ *Restaurant, food court, cable TV with movies, golf privileges, 7 pools, wading pool, hot tub, beach, boating, bicycles, lobby lounge, baby-sitting, playground, video game room, laundry facilities, laundry service* ⊟ *AE, D, DC, MC, V.*

★ $$$ ▦ **Coronado Springs Resort.** This moderately priced hotel on yet another Disney-made lake serves two constituencies. Because of its on-property convention center, it's popular with business groups. But family vacationers come for its casual southwestern architecture; its wonderful, lively, Mexican-style Pepper Market food court; and its elaborate swimming pool complex, which has a Maya pyramid with a big water slide. There's a full-service health club, but if you like jogging, walking, or biking you're in the right place—a sidewalk circles the property's 15-acre lake. ☎ *407/*

939–1000 🖨 407/939–1001 🖘 1,967 rooms ♧ 2 restaurants, food court, room service, cable TV with movies, golf privileges, 4 pools, hair salon, health club, boating, bicycles, bar, video game room, baby-sitting, laundry service, convention center. ☰ AE, D, DC, MC, V.

Disney's Animal Kingdom Area
Take I–4 Exit 64B or 65.

★ $$$$ 🖳 **Animal Kingdom Lodge.** Giraffes, zebras, and other African wildlife roam three 11-acre savannas separated by wings of this grand hotel. The atrium lobby exudes African style, from the inlaid carvings on the hardwood floors to the massive faux-thatched roof almost 100 ft above. Cultural ambassadors from Africa give talks about their homelands, the animals, and the artwork on display; in the evening, they tell folk stories around the fire circle on the Arusha Rock terrace. All of the somewhat tentlike rooms (with drapes descending from the ceiling) have a bit of African art, including carved headboards and African prints. Most rooms have balconies. ☎ 407/934–7639 🖨 407/934–7629 🖘 1,293 rooms ♧ 3 restaurants, cable TV with movies, golf privileges, 2 pools, health club, spa, bar, lobby lounge, baby-sitting, children's programs (ages 4–12), playground, laundry facilities, laundry service ☰ AE, D, DC, MC, V.

Downtown Disney/Lake Buena Vista/WDW Resort Area
Take I–4 Exit 67 or 68.

$$$$ 🖳 **Old Key West Resort.** A red-and-white lighthouse helps you find your way through this marina-style resort. Freestanding villas resemble turn-of-the-20th-century Key West houses, with white clapboard siding and private balconies that overlook the waterways winding through the grounds. The one-, two-, or three-bedroom houses have whirlpools in the master bedrooms, full-size kitchens, full-size washers and dryers, and outdoor patios. The 2,265-square-ft three-bedroom grand villas accommodate up to 12 adults. ☎ 407/827–7700 🖨 407/827–7710 🖘 704 units ♧ Restaurant, cable TV with movies, snack bar, golf privileges, 3 tennis courts, 4 pools, health club, spa, boating, bicycles, basketball, shuffleboard, lobby lounge, video game room, baby-sitting, playground, laundry facilities, laundry service ☰ AE, D, DC, MC, V.

$$$ 🖳 **Port Orleans Resort–French Quarter.** This vision of New Orleans has ornate row houses with vine-covered balconies, clustered around squares planted with magnolias. Lamp-lighted sidewalks are named for French Quarter thoroughfares. The rooms themselves are fairly standard. The food court serves such Crescent City specialties as jambalaya and beignets. Doubloon Lagoon, one of Disney's most exotic pools, includes a clever "sea serpent" water slide that swallows swimmers and then spits them into the water. ☎ 407/934–5000 🖨 407/934–5353 🖘 1,008 rooms ♧ Restaurant, food court, cable TV with video games, golf privileges, pool, wading pool, hot tub, boating, bicycles, croquet, baby-sitting, laundry facilities, laundry service ☰ AE, D, DC, MC, V.

$$$ 🖳 **Port Orleans Resort–Riverside.** Disney's Imagineers drew inspiration from the Old South for this sprawling resort. Buildings look like plantation-style mansions and rustic bayou dwellings. Rooms accommodate up to four in two double beds. Elegantly decorated, they have wooden armoires and gleaming brass faucets; a few rooms have king-size beds. The 3½-acre old-fashioned swimming-hole complex has a pool with slides, rope swings, and a nearby play area. ☎ 407/934–6000 🖨 407/934–5777 🖘 2,048 rooms ♧ Restaurant, 3 tennis courts, 4 pools, health club, spa, boating, bicycles, basketball, shuffleboard, lobby lounge, video game room, baby-sitting, playground, laundry facilities, laundry service ☰ AE, D, DC, MC, V.

All-Star Village
Take I–4 Exit 64B.

$$ 🖭 **All-Star Sports, All-Star Music, and All-Star Movies Resorts.** These Disney economy resorts depict five sports themes, five music themes, and movie themes from *Fantasia, Toy Story, 101 Dalmatians,* and *The Mighty Ducks* to *The Love Bug.* Stairwells shaped like giant bongos frame Calypso, whereas at Sports, 30-ft tennis rackets strike balls the size of small cars, and in Movies, giant icons like *Toy Story*'s Buzz Lightyear frame each building. Each room has two double beds. The food courts sell standard fast food. 🕾 *407/939–5000 Sports; 407/939–6000 Music; 407/939–7000 Movies* 🖳 *407/939–7333 Sports; 407/939–7222 Music; 407/939–7111 Movies* ✎ *1,920 rooms at each* ♿ *3 food courts, 6 pools, cable TV with movies, 3 bars, video game rooms, baby-sitting, playground, laundry facilities, laundry service* ▤ *AE, D, DC, MC, V.*

In WDW: Other Hotels

Epcot Resort Area hotels are also noted on the Walt Disney World Resort map.

Epcot Resort Area
Take I–4 Exit 67.

★ $$$$ 🖭 **Walt Disney World Dolphin.** Architect Michael Graves is the master behind the Dolphin, where a pair of 56-ft-tall sea creatures bookend the 25-story glass pyramid of a building. The fabric-draped lobby inside resembles a giant sultan's tent. All rooms have two queen beds or one king and beach-inspired bedspreads and drapes. Extensive children's programs include Camp Dolphin summer camp and the five-hour Dolphin Dinner Club. Grotto Pool has a big water slide. ✉ *1500 Epcot Resorts Blvd., Lake Buena Vista 32830-2653* 🕾 *407/934–4000 or 800/227–1500* 🖳 *407/934–4884* ⊕ *www.swandolphin.com* ✎ *1,509 rooms, 136 suites* ♿ *9 restaurants, room service, cable TV with movies and video games, 4 tennis courts, 5 pools, wading pool, gym, massage, spa, beach, boating, 3 lobby lounges, video game room, baby-sitting, children's programs (ages 4– 12), convention center* ▤ *AE, D, MC, V.*

$$$$ 🖭 **Walt Disney World Swan.** Facing the Dolphin across Crescent Lake, the Swan is another example of the postmodern "Learning from Las Vegas" school of entertainment architecture characteristic of Michael Graves. Two 46-ft swans grace the rooftop of this coral-and-aquamarine hotel, connected to the Dolphin by a covered causeway. Guest rooms are quirkily decorated with floral and geometric patterns, pineapples painted on furniture, and exotic bird-shape lamps. Rooms have two queen beds or one king. ✉ *1200 Epcot Resorts Blvd., Lake Buena Vista 32830* 🕾 *407/934–3000 or 800/248–7926* 🖳 *407/934–4499* ⊕ *www.swandolphin.com* ✎ *750 rooms, 55 suites* ♿ *6 restaurants, room service, cable TV with movies and video games, 4 outdoor tennis courts, 5 pools, wading pool, gym, massage, spa, beach, boating, 2 lobby lounges, video game room, baby-sitting, children's programs (ages 4–12), concierge, convention center* ▤ *AE, DC, MC, V.*

Downtown Disney Resort Area
Take I–4 Exit 68.

$$–$$$ 🖭 **DoubleTree Guest Suites in the WDW Resort.** Comfortable one- and two-bedroom suites are done in tasteful hues, with gray carpeting and blond-wood furniture. Each bedroom has either a king bed or two doubles. Units come with a TV in each room plus another (black-and-white) in the bathroom, and a wet bar and coffeemaker. ✉ *2305 Hotel Plaza Blvd.,*

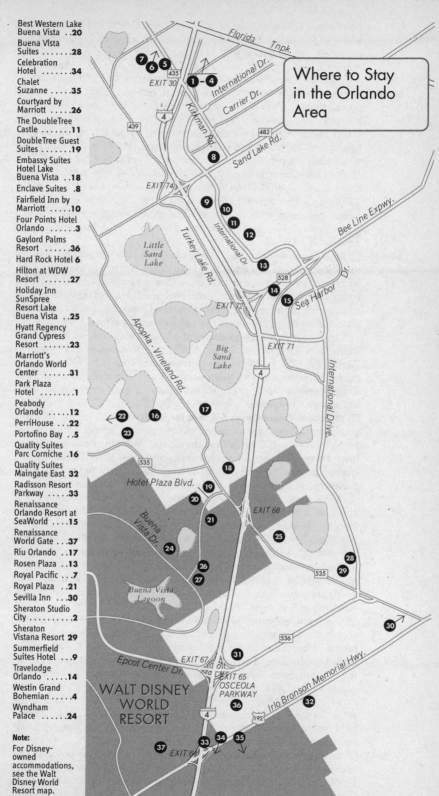

Best Western Lake Buena Vista ..**20**
Buena Vista Suites **28**
Celebration Hotel **34**
Chalet Suzanne **35**
Courtyard by Marriott **26**
The DoubleTree Castle **11**
DoubleTree Guest Suites **19**
Embassy Suites Hotel Lake Buena Vista ..**18**
Enclave Suites .**8**
Fairfield Inn by Marriott **10**
Four Points Hotel Orlando **3**
Gaylord Palms Resort **36**
Hard Rock Hotel **6**
Hilton at WDW Resort **27**
Holiday Inn SunSpree Resort Lake Buena Vista ..**25**
Hyatt Regency Grand Cypress Resort **23**
Marriott's Orlando World Center **31**
Park Plaza Hotel **1**
Peabody Orlando **12**
PerriHouse ...**22**
Portofino Bay ..**5**
Quality Suites Parc Corniche .**16**
Quality Suites Maingate East **32**
Radisson Resort Parkway **33**
Renaissance Orlando Resort at SeaWorld **15**
Renaissance World Gate ...**37**
Riu Orlando ..**17**
Rosen Plaza ..**13**
Royal Pacific ...**7**
Royal Plaza ..**21**
Sevilla Inn ...**30**
Sheraton Studio City **2**
Sheraton Vistana Resort **29**
Summerfield Suites Hotel ...**9**
Travelodge Orlando **14**
Westin Grand Bohemian **4**
Wyndham Palace **24**

Note:
For Disney-owned accommodations, see the Walt Disney World Resort map.

Where to Stay in the Orlando Area

Downtown Disney, 32830 ☎ *407/934–1000 or 800/222–8733* 🖶 *407/ 934–1015* ⊕ *www.doubletree.com* 🖙 *229 units* ☽ *Restaurant, microwaves, refrigerators, golf privileges, room service, cable TV with movies, 2 tennis courts, pool, wading pool, gym, hot tub, 2 bars, laundry facilities, laundry service, business services* ☰ *AE, DC, MC, V.*

$$–$$$ 🏨 **Hilton at WDW Resort.** It's not palatial, but this Hilton is still a fine, upscale hotel that's only a five-minute walk from Downtown Disney Marketplace. An ingeniously designed waterfall tumbles off the covered entrance and into a stone fountain surrounded by palm trees. Rooms are upbeat and cozy. The evening seafood-tasting buffet in the lobby will tempt you to step into the on-site restaurant, Finn's. ✉ *1751 Hotel Plaza Blvd., Downtown Disney, 32830* ☎ *407/827–4000; 800/782–4414 reservations* 🖶 *407/827–6369* ⊕ *www.hilton-wdwv.com* 🖙 *814 rooms, 27 suites* ☽ *6 restaurants, room service, cable TV with movies, 3 pools, health club, outdoor hot tub, lobby lounge, baby-sitting, children's programs (ages 3–12), laundry facilities, laundry service, business services* ☰ *AE, DC, MC, V.*

$$–$$$ 🏨 **Royal Plaza.** Built in the '70s, the casual and lively Royal Plaza keeps its look up-to-date and attractive. Each earth-tone room, though not extravagant, has a terrace or balcony, and some have hot tubs. Ask for a room overlooking the pool. Families like the Royal Plaza because of its moderate rates and proximity to Downtown Disney, and golfers appreciate the advance reservation privileges at five nearby courses. Children 12 and under eat free with parents at the hotel restaurant. ✉ *1905 Hotel Plaza Blvd., Downtown Disney, 32830* ☎ *407/828–2828 or 800/248– 7890* 🖶 *407/828–8046* ⊕ *www.royalplaza.com* 🖙 *394 rooms, 21 suites* ☽ *Restaurant, grill, room service, cable TV with movies, golf privileges, 4 tennis courts, pool, hot tub, sauna, 2 bars, baby-sitting, laundry service, convention center* ☰ *AE, D, DC, MC, V.*

★ $$$ 🏨 **Wyndham Palace Resort & Spa in the WDW Resort.** This luxury hotel gets kudos as much for its on-site charms (such as a huge health spa) as for its location—100 yards from the nearest Wolfgang Puck's, in Downtown Disney. All rooms have balconies or patios, as well as high-speed Internet access. At the Top of the Palace, the club-bar on the 27th floor, guests receive a free glass of champagne at sunset to accompany the wonderful view of the sun sinking into the Disney complex. Book early if you want a meal at the rooftop restaurant, Arthur's 27. ✉ *1900 Buena Vista Dr., Downtown Disney, 32830* ☎ *407/827–2727 or 800/327–2990* 🖶 *407/827–6034* ⊕ *www.wyndham.com/PalaceResort* 🖙 *1,014 rooms, 209 suites* ☽ *4 restaurants, patisserie, snack bar, room service, cable TV with movies, tennis courts, 2 pools, wading pool, health club, hot tub, spa, volleyball, 4 lobby lounges, video game room, baby-sitting, children's programs (ages 4–12), playground, laundry facilities, laundry service, convention center* ☰ *AE, D, DC, MC, V.*

$–$$ 🏨 **Courtyard by Marriott at WDW Resort.** In the tranquil 14-story atrium, accented with gazebos, white-tile trim, and tropical gardens, enjoy a well-prepared breakfast under white umbrellas. By evening, activity has shifted to the Tipsy Parrot, the hotel's welcoming bar. Rooms are attractive with green carpets, rose-color couches, and floral-print bedspreads. ✉ *1805 Hotel Plaza Blvd., Downtown Disney, 32830* ☎ *407/828–8888 or 800/223–9930* 🖶 *407/827–4623* ⊕ *www.courtyardorlando.com* 🖙 *323 rooms* ☽ *Restaurant, cable TV with movies, 2 pools, wading pool, gym, outdoor hot tub, lobby lounge, playground, laundry facilities, laundry service, business service* ☰ *AE, DC, MC, V.*

$–$$ 🏨 **Best Western Lake Buena Vista Resort Hotel.** This 18-story property was completely renovated and redecorated in spring 2002 with murals of Florida wildlife and landscapes, plus a view of a junglelike wetland out the windows of the atrium restaurant. Most rooms have private balconies with spectacular views of nightly Disney firework shows. Disney shuttles are available, but the walk to Downtown Disney is easy. ✉ *2000 Hotel Plaza Blvd., Downtown Disney, 32830* ☎ *407/828–2424 or 800/ 348–3765* 🖷 *407/828–8933* ⊕ *www.orlandoresorthotel.com* ➔ *325 rooms* ♦ *Restaurant, room service, cable TV with movies, snack bar, pool, wading pool, lobby lounge, playground, laundry facilities, laundry service, business services* ⊟ *AE, D, DC, MC, V.*

Universal Orlando

Take I–4 Exit 74B if you're heading westbound, 75A if eastbound.

$$$$ 🖭 **Portofino Bay Hotel.** Built to resemble the Italian Riviera town of Portofino, this hotel complex holds monthly Italian wine tastings and even has a boccie ball court. Other touches include gelato machines around the pool, a wood-fired pizzeria, and two great Italian restaurants. The massive pool has a Roman aqueductlike water slide. ✉ *5601 Universal Blvd., Universal Studios, 32819* ☎ *407/503–1000 or 888/322–5541* ⊕ *www.loewshotels.com* ➔ *699 rooms, 51 suites* ♦ *3 restaurants, pizzeria, room service, cable TV with movies and VCRs, 3 pools, health club, massage, spa, boccie, bar, baby-sitting, children's programs (ages 4–14), playground, laundry service, convention center* ⊟ *AE, D, DC, MC, V.*

$$$–$$$$ 🖭 **Royal Pacific Resort.** The hotel entrance—a footbridge across a trop-
FodorsChoice ical stream—sets the tone for the South Pacific theme of this hotel. The resort's focal point is a 12,000-square-ft, lagoon-style swimming pool (Orlando's largest) with its own sand beach. Emeril Lagasse's newest Orlando restaurant, Tchoup Chop, brings in crowds. ✉ *6300 Hollywood Way, Universal Studios, 32819* ☎ *407/503–3000* 🖷 *407/503–3010* ⊕ *www.loewshotels.com* ➔ *1,000 rooms, 113 suites* ♦ *3 restaurants, room service, in-room VCRs, putting green, pool, wading pool, exercise equipment, health club, hot tub, massage, sauna, steam room, 2 bars, lobby lounge, children's programs (ages 4–14), laundry facilities, laundry service, convention center* ⊟ *AE, DC, MC, V.*

$$$ 🖭 **Hard Rock Hotel.** It's not quite as plush as Portofino Bay, but then, the price tag isn't quite as high. Inside the California mission–style building, you'll find lots of rock-music memorabilia, including the slip Madonna wore in her "Like a Prayer" video. Rooms have white walls and black-and-white photos of pop icons. The pool is surrounded by a sand beach and has an underwater sound system pumping music into the water. ✉ *1000 Universal Studios Plaza, Universal Studios, 32819* ☎ *407/503–7625 or 800/232–7827* 🖷 *407/503–7655* ⊕ *www. loewshotels.com* ➔ *621 rooms, 29 suites* ♦ *3 restaurants, room service, cable TV with movies, in-room VCRs, refrigerators, 2 pools, health club, 3 bars, video game room, baby-sitting, children's programs (ages 4–14), laundry service, business services* ⊟ *AE, D, DC, MC, V.*

Orlando

International Drive

Take I–4 Exit 28 or 29.

If you plan to visit other attractions besides Walt Disney World, the sprawl of newish hotels, restaurants, and shopping malls known as International Drive—"I–Drive" to locals and "Florida Center" in formal parlance—makes a convenient base. Parallel to Interstate 4, it's just a few minutes south of downtown Orlando. It's also near SeaWorld and Universal Orlando as well as several popular dinner theaters.

★ $$$$ 🖭 **Peabody Orlando.** At 11 AM the celebrated Peabody ducks exit a private elevator and waddle across the lobby to the marble fountain where they pass the day, basking in their fame. At 5 they repeat the ritual in reverse. Built by the owners of the landmark Peabody Hotel in Memphis, this 27-story structure has an impressive interior, with gilt and marble halls. Some of the oversize upper-floor rooms have panoramic views of WDW. ⊠ *9801 International Dr., I–Drive Area, 32819* ☎ *407/352–4000 or 800/732–2639* 🖷 *407/351–9177* 🌐 *www.peabodyorlando. com* 🖵 *891 rooms* ♻ *3 restaurants, room service, cable TV with movies, golf privileges, 4 tennis courts, pool, wading pool, health club, hot tub, massage, spa, 2 lobby lounges, baby-sitting, concierge, convention center* 🖃 *AE, D, DC, MC, V.*

$$–$$$ 🖽 **Renaissance Orlando Resort at SeaWorld.** The hotel's 10-story atrium is full of waterfalls, goldfish ponds, and palm trees; as you shoot skyward in sleek, glass elevators, look for exotic birds—on loan from SeaWorld across the street—twittering in the hand-carved, gilded Venetian aviary. Rooms have more floor space than the average Central Florida hotel, plus nice touches like high-speed Internet connections, speakers, and two-line phones. Atlantis, the formal restaurant, is something of an undiscovered gem, with Mediterranean cuisine. ⊠ *6677 Sea Harbor Dr., I–Drive Area, 32821* ☎ *407/351–5555 or 800/468–3571* 🖷 *407/351–4618* 🌐 *www.renaissancehotels.com* 🖵 *778 rooms* ♻ *5 restaurants, room service, cable TV with movies, golf privileges, 4 tennis courts, pool, wading pool, hair salon, health club, hot tub, massage, sauna, volleyball, 3 lounges, baby-sitting, laundry service, convention center* 🖃 *AE, D, DC, MC, V.*

$$–$$$ 🖽 **Summerfield Suites Hotel.** Parents can use that trump-card disciplinary option "Go to your room!" at this hotel. Sleeping from four to eight people, the one- and two-bedroom units at the all-suites Summerfield are a great option for families. Two-bedroom units, the most popular, have fully equipped kitchens, plus a living room with TV and VCR, and another TV in one bedroom. Plush landscaping makes the place seem secluded. ⊠ *8480 International Dr. (I–4 Exit 74A), I–Drive Area, 32819* ☎ *407/352–2400 or 800/830–4964* 🖷 *407/352–4631* 🌐 *www. summerfield-orlando.com* 🖵 *146 suites* ♻ *Grocery, kitchens, microwaves, refrigerators, cable TV with movies, pool, wading pool, gym, hot tub, lobby lounge, laundry facilities, laundry service, video game room, meeting rooms* 🖃 *AE, D, DC, MC, V.*

$–$$$ 🖽 **Enclave Suites at Orlando.** With three 10-story buildings surrounding an office, restaurant, and recreation area, this all-suites lodging is less a hotel than a condominium complex. Here, what you would spend for a normal room in a fancy hotel gets you a complete apartment, with more space than you find in many all-suites hotels. All units have full kitchens, living rooms, two bedrooms, and small terraces with a view of a nearby lake. There's free transportation to SeaWorld, Wet 'n Wild, and Universal Orlando, but Wet 'n Wild is an easy walk. ⊠ *6165 Carrier Dr., I–Drive Area, 32819* ☎ *407/351–1155 or 800/457–0077* 🖷 *407/351–2001* 🌐 *www.enclavesuites.com* 🖵 *352 suites* ♻ *Grocery, tennis court, 3 pools (1 indoor), 2 wading pools, gym, hot tub, playground, laundry facilities, laundry service, business services, meeting rooms* 🖃 *AE, D, DC, MC, V.*

$$ 🖽 **Buena Vista Suites.** In this suites-only property, you get two rooms (a bedroom and a living room with a fold-out sofa bed), a small kitchen area, two TVs, and two phones. King suites have a king bed and a whirlpool bath. The hotel serves a complimentary breakfast buffet and provides shuttle transportation to the Walt Disney World theme parks. ⊠ *8203 World Center Dr., Southwestern Orlando, 32821* ☎ *407/239–8588 or 800/537–7737* 🖷 *407/239–1401* 🌐 *www.buenavistasuites. com* 🖵 *280 suites* ♻ *Restaurant, room service, cable TV with movies, microwaves, refrigerators, room service, outdoor pool, wading pool, hot* *tub, 2 lighted tennis courts, gym, laundry facilities* ▤ *AE, D, DC, MC, V* ☯ *BP.*

$–$$ ⊡ **The DoubleTree Castle.** You won't really think you're in a castle at this mid-price hotel, although the tall gold-and-silver-color spires, medieval-style mosaics, and arched doorways may make you feel like reading Harry Potter. Take your book to either the rooftop terrace or the inviting courtyard, which has a big, round swimming pool. Café Tu Tu Tango, one of the better restaurants in this part of Orlando, has a zesty, small-dish multicultural menu. ⊠ *8629 International Dr., I–Drive Area, 32819* ☏ *407/345–1511 or 800/952–2785* ▤ *407/248–8181* ⊕ *www. doubletreecastle.com* ⤳ *216 rooms* ♨ *2 restaurants, room service, cable TV with movies, minibars, refrigerators, pool, gym, hot tub, lobby lounge, video game room, laundry service* ▤ *AE, D, DC, MC, V.*

$–$$ ⊡ **Quality Suites Parc Corniche Resort.** A good bet for golf enthusiasts, the suites-only resort is framed by a Joe Lee–designed course. Each of the one- and two-bedroom suites has a kitchen complete with dishes and a dishwasher, plus a patio or balcony with golf-course views. The largest accommodations, with two bedrooms and two baths, can sleep up to six. A complimentary full buffet breakfast is served daily, and SeaWorld is only a few blocks away. ⊠ *6300 Parc Corniche Dr., I–Drive Area, 32821* ☏ *407/239–7100 or 800/446–2721* ▤ *407/239–8501* ⊕ *www. parccorniche.com* ⤳ *210 suites* ♨ *Restaurant, room service, baby-sitting, playground, laundry facilities, laundry service, business services* ▤ *AE, D, DC, MC, V* ☯ *BP.*

$–$$ ⊡ **Rosen Plaza Hotel.** Harris Rosen, the largest independent hotel owner in the Orlando market, loves to offer bargains, and you'll find one here. This is essentially a convention hotel, although leisure travelers like the prime location and the long list of amenities. Rooms are simple but large, with two queen-size beds. Two upscale restaurants, Jack's Place and Café Matisse, offer great steaks and a fine buffet, respectively, but the best food option is the pizza at Rossini's. ⊠ *9700 International Dr., I–Drive Area, 32819* ☏ *407/352–9700 or 800/627–8258* ▤ *407/352–9710* ⊕ *www.rosenplaza.com* ⤳ *810 rooms* ♨ *2 restaurants, coffee shop, ice cream parlor, pizzeria, room service, cable TV, pool, hot tub, bar, lobby lounge, nightclub, baby-sitting, video game room, laundry facilities, laundry service, meeting rooms* ▤ *AE, D, DC, MC, V.*

¢–$$ ⊡ **Sheraton Studio City.** Atop this Sheraton is a giant silver globe suitable for Times Square on New Year's Eve. But the interior has a Hollywood theme, with movie posters and black-and-white art-deco touches throughout the public spaces and rooms, most of which have two queen beds. The 20th floor has plush luxury suites ($300) for those ready to spring for a good view of Universal Studios (directly across I–4). Free shuttles go to the major theme parks and shopping malls. ⊠ *5905 International Dr., I–Drive Area, 32819* ☏ *407/351–2100 or 800/327–1366* ▤ *407/345–5249* ⊕ *www.grandthemehotels.com* ⤳ *302 rooms* ♨ *Restaurant, room service, cable TV with movies and video games, pool, wading pool, hair salon, hot tub, bar, lobby lounge, video game room, laundry service, business services* ▤ *AE, D, DC, MC, V.*

¢–$ ⊡ **Fairfield Inn by Marriott, Orlando International Drive.** This understated, few-frills, three-story hotel—the Marriott corporation's answer to the Motel 6 chain—is a natural for single travelers or small families on a tight budget. While it doesn't have the amenities of top-of-the-line Marriott properties, there are perks such as complimentary coffee and tea and free local phone calls. ⊠ *8342 Jamaican Ct., I–Drive Area, 32819* ☏☏ *407/363–1944* ☏ *800/228–2800* ⊕ *www.fairfieldinn.com* ⤳ *134 rooms* ♨ *Room TVs with movies, pool, business services* ▤ *AE, D, DC, MC, V.*

¢–$ 🖭 **Travelodge Orlando Convention Center.** If you don't want a room with
Fodor'sChoice just the bare essentials yet don't have the budget for luxury, this three-story motel is a find. The rooms are comfy if not spectacular; all have two double beds. Children 17 and under stay free in their parents' room (maximum of four people per room). The hotel is ¼ mi from SeaWorld. Free transportation is provided to theme parks. ⊠ *6263 Westwood Blvd., I–Drive Area, 32821* ☎ *407/345–8000 or 800/346–1551* 🖷 *407/345–1508* ⊕ *www.travelodge.com* ➫ *144 rooms* ⟐ *Restaurant, room TVs with movies, 2 pools, exercise equipment, bar, video game room, laundry facilities, laundry service, business services* ▤ *AE, DC, MC, V.*

Downtown Disney/Lake Buena Vista Area
Take I–4 Exit 68.

In addition to the Disney-owned and non-Disney-owned resorts clustered on Disney property not far from Downtown Disney, there are a number of nearby hotels unaffiliated with Walt Disney World Resort. Just outside the park's northernmost entrance, they tend to be sprawling, high-quality resorts catering to WDW vacationers.

★ $$$$ 🖭 **Hyatt Regency Grand Cypress Resort.** This spectacular resort offers every amenity imaginable, including a 45-acre nature preserve. Golf facilities, among them a high-tech golf school, are first-class. The 800,000-gallon pool resembles an enormous grotto fed by 12 waterfalls. There's even a small lake, with a white-sand beach. A striking 18-story atrium is filled with tropical plants, ancient Chinese sculptures, and tropical birds. Accommodations are divided between the Hyatt Regency Grand Cypress and the Villas of Grand Cypress. ⊠ *1 Grand Cypress Blvd., Lake Buena Vista Area, 32836* ☎ *407/239–1234 or 800/233–1234* 🖷 *407/239–3800* ⊕ *www.hyattgrandcypress.com* ➫ *750 rooms* ⟐ *5 restaurants, room service, cable TV with movies, two 18-hole and one 9-hole golf courses, 12 tennis courts, 2 pools, health club, 4 hot tubs, massage, spa, boating, bicycles, croquet, horseback riding, 4 lobby lounges, baby-sitting, children's programs (ages 5–12), laundry service, convention center* ▤ *AE, D, DC, MC, V.*

$$$ 🖭 **Sheraton Vistana Resort.** Consider this peaceful resort if you're interested in tennis. Enjoy free use of clay and all-weather courts; lessons are available for a fee. Spread over 135 landscaped acres, the spacious, tastefully decorated villas and town houses come in one- and two-bedroom versions with living room, a full kitchen, and washer and dryer. ⊠ *8800 Vistana Center Dr., Lake Buena Vista 32821* ☎ *407/239–3100 or 800/208–0003* 🖷 *407/239–3111* ⊕ *www.vistana.com/resorts/vistana* ➫ *1,700 units* ⟐ *2 restaurants, grocery, microwaves, cable TV with movies, miniature golf, 13 tennis courts, 7 pools, 5 wading pools, health club, 7 hot tubs, basketball, shuffleboard, lobby lounge, baby-sitting, children's programs (ages 4–12), meeting rooms* ▤ *AE, D, DC, MC, V.*

$$–$$$ 🖭 **Embassy Suites Hotel Lake Buena Vista.** Some locals are shocked by the wild turquoise, pink, and peach facade, but the Embassy Suites resort is an attractive option for other reasons. It's 1 mi from Walt Disney World, 3 mi from SeaWorld, and 7 mi from Universal Orlando. Each suite has a living room and two TVs. The central atrium lobby, soothed by the sounds of a rushing fountain, is a great place to enjoy the complimentary full breakfast and evening cocktails. ⊠ *8100 Lake Ave., Lake Buena Vista 32836* ☎ *407/239–1144, 800/257–8483, or 800/362–2779* 🖷 *407/239–1718* ⊕ *www.embassysuitesorlando.com* ➫ *330 suites* ⟐ *Restaurant, room service, cable TV with movies, tennis court, indoor-outdoor pool, wading pool, gym, hot tub, basketball, shuffleboard, volleyball, lobby lounge, baby-sitting, children's programs (ages 4–12), playground, meeting room* ▤ *AE, D, DC, MC, V* ⦿ *BP.*

$–$$$ ☷ **Holiday Inn SunSpree Resort Lake Buena Vista.** This place is as kid-oriented as it gets. The little ones have their own registration desk, and there's usually a costumed clown to hand out balloons and other treats. Off the lobby you'll find the CyberArcade; Camp Holiday, a free, supervised activity program; a small theater where clowns perform weekends at 7 PM; and a buffet restaurant where kids accompanied by adults eat free at their own little picnic tables. Families love the Kidsuites, playhouse-style rooms within a larger room. ⊠ *13351 Rte. 535, Lake Buena Vista 32821* ☎ *407/239–4500 or 800/366–6299* 🖷 *407/239–7713* ⊕ *www. kidsuites.com* ⇆ *507 rooms* ♻ *Restaurant, grocery, cable TV with movies and video games, microwaves, refrigerators, pool, wading pool, gym, 2 hot tubs, basketball, Ping-Pong, bar, lobby lounge, theater, video game room, children's programs (ages 4–12), playground, laundry facilities, laundry service, business services* ⊟ *AE, D, DC, MC, V.*

$–$$$ ☷ **Riu Orlando Hotel.** After traipsing through theme parks and malls, what you may want most is to lounge around a living room just the way you do at home. The rooms in this six-story complex let you do just that, with big, comfy fold-out couches and big-screen TVs. Rooms also have coffeemakers, hair dryers, irons, and ironing boards. ⊠ *8688 Palm Pkwy., Lake Buena Vista Area, 32836* ☎ *407/239–8500 or 888/222– 9963* 🖷 *407/239–8591* ⊕ *www.riu.com* ⇆ *167 rooms* ♻ *Restaurant, room service, room TVs with video games, pool, hot tub, lobby lounge, meeting rooms* ⊟ *AE, D, DC, MC, V.*

★ $–$$ ☷ **PerriHouse Bed & Breakfast Inn.** An eight-room bed-and-breakfast inside a serene bird sanctuary offers you a chance to split your time between sightseeing and spending quiet moments bird-watching. The 13-acre sanctuary has observation paths, a pond, a feeding station, and a small birdhouse museum. Lush plantings make it attractive to bobwhites, downy woodpeckers, red-tail hawks, and the occasional bald eagle. Some rooms have four-poster beds and fireplaces. ⊠ *10417 Vista Oak Ct., Lake Buena Vista 32836* ☎ *407/876–4830 or 800/780–4830* 🖷 *407/876–0241* ⊕ *www.perrihouse.com* ⇆ *8 rooms* ♻ *Cable TV, golf privileges, pool, hot tub* ⊟ *AE, D, DC, MC, V* ⭘ *CP.*

Downtown Orlando

Downtown Orlando, north of Walt Disney World and slightly north of the International Drive area, is a thriving business district with a tourist fringe in the form of Church Street Station. To get there take Exit 83 off Interstate 4 if you're heading west, Exit 82C if eastbound.

$$$–$$$$ ☷ **Westin Grand Bohemian.** This European-style property is downtown Orlando's only luxury hotel. Opposite city hall, the Grand Bohemian showcases more than 100 pieces of art—including a Bösendorfer piano, one of only two in the world, which sits in a posh ground-floor lounge. Rooms are more sedate despite red and purple curtains. All rooms have three phones and interactive television, and the suites have a fax machine–computer printer as well. Off the main lobby are a Starbucks and an art gallery. ⊠ *325 S. Orange Ave., Downtown Orlando, 32801* ☎ *407/313–9000 or 888/472–6312* 🖷 *407/313–9001* ⊕ *www. grandbohemianhotel.com* ⇆ *250 rooms, 36 suites* ♻ *Restaurant, bar, room service, cable TV with movies, pool, gym, concierge, meeting rooms, parking (fee)* ⊟ *AE, D, MC, V.*

★ $$–$$$ ☷ **Four Points Hotel Orlando Downtown by Sheraton.** Across the street from Lake Eola, this downtown oasis is a pleasant place to get away from the tourism district's mayhem, and it's an easy walk to a lot of good eateries. The exterior's gold-leaf domes give it a distinctive European look. Many of the suites have splendid lake views. ⊠ *151 Washington*

Ave., Downtown, 33801 ☎ *407/841–3220 or 800/325–3535* 🖷 *407/ 648–4758* ⊕ *www.fourpoints.com* ➪ *203 rooms, 48 suites* ዼ *Restaurant, room service, some minibars, some refrigerators, cable TV with movies, pool, health club, 2 bars, laundry service, meeting rooms* ☰ *AE, D, MC, V.*

Kissimmee

Take I–4 Exit 64A, unless otherwise noted.

$$$$ 🏨 **Marriott's Orlando World Center.** At 2,000 rooms, this is one of the largest hotels in Orlando, and one very popular with conventions. Rooms have patios or balconies. One of the pools here is the largest in Florida. Upscale villas are available for daily and weekly rentals. The hotel's Hawk's Landing Steakhouse and Grille is among the better beef-centric restaurants in the Disney area. ⊠ *8701 World Center Dr. (I–4 Exit 67), Kissimmee 32821* ☎ *407/239–4200 or 800/228–9290* 🖷 *407/238–8777* ⊕ *www. marriotthotels.com* ➪ *2,000 rooms, 98 suites, 259 villas* ዼ *6 restaurants, ice cream parlor, room service, cable TV with movies, 4 pools (1 indoor), wading pool, hair salon, health club, 4 hot tubs, 2 lobby lounges, babysitting, children's programs (ages 4–12), laundry facilities, laundry service, convention center* ☰ *AE, D, DC, MC, V.*

$$$–$$$$ 🏨 **Gaylord Palms Resort.** With a huge atrium that re-creates such Florida
Fodor'sChoice locales as the Everglades, Key West, and old St. Augustine under a 4-acre glass roof, this massive property, 5 mi from WDW, is arguably Orlando's most elaborate hotel. The five dramatic atrium restaurants include Sunset Sam's Fish Camp, set on a 60-ft fishing boat docked on the hotel's indoor ocean, and the Old Hickory Steak House in an old warehouse overlooking the alligator-ridden Everglades. Rooms carry on the Florida themes, and children's programs are extensive. ⊠ *6000 Osceola Pkwy. (I–4 Exit 65), Kissimmee 34746* ☎ *407/586–0000* 🖷 *407/586–1999* ⊕ *www.gaylordpalms.com* ➪ *1,406 rooms, 86 suites* ዼ *6 restaurants, cable TV with movies, golf privileges, 2 pools, gym, hot tub, massage, spa, 2 bars, lobby lounge, children's programs (ages 4–12), laundry service, convention center, meeting rooms* ☰ *AE, D, DC, MC, V.*

★ $$$ 🏨 **Celebration Hotel.** Like everything in the fantasy-driven, Disney-created town of Celebration, this 115-room hotel borrows from the best of several centuries. The lobby resembles that of the grand Victorian-era hotels, with hardwood floors and decorative millwork on the walls and ceilings. Room may look as if they date from the early 1900s, but each has a 25-inch TV, two phone lines, high-speed Internet access port, and a six-channel stereo sound system. Though it's less than 1 mi south of the U.S. 192 tourist strip in Kissimmee, the hotel's surroundings are serene. ⊠ *700 Bloom St., Celebration 34747* ☎ *407/566–6000 or 888/ 472–6312* 🖷 *407/566–1844* ⊕ *www.celebrationhotel.com* ➪ *115 rooms* ዼ *2 restaurants, cable TV with movies, in-room data ports, golf privileges, pool, health club, hot tub, lobby lounge, laundry service* ☰ *AE, D, DC, MC, V.*

$$–$$$ 🏨 **Quality Suites Maingate East.** Here's an excellent option for a large family or group of friends. The spacious suites come with one or two bedrooms (two double beds in each) and a living room with a pull-out couch. All suites have a dishwasher, microwave, and refrigerator. In addition to the complimentary Continental breakfast, free beer and wine are served afternoons at the poolside bar. A free shuttle takes you to theme parks. ⊠ *5876 W. Irlo Bronson Memorial Hwy., Kissimmee 34746* ☎ *407/ 396–8040 or 800/848–4148* 🖷 *407/396–6766* ⊕ *www.qualitysuites.com* ➪ *225 suites* ዼ *Restaurant, in-room cable TV, pool, wading pool, hot* tub, bar, lobby lounge, playground, laundry service, business services ▤ *AE, D, DC, MC, V* ⦿ *CP.*

$$–$$$ ⊞ **Renaissance World Gate.** A few minutes from WDW's front door, this sleek, seven-story modern hotel has cheerful guest rooms, large bathrooms, and plenty of extras for the price. It's not fancy, but it's perfectly adequate. The best rooms are those with a view of the pool. ✉ *3011 Maingate La., Kissimmee 34747* ☏ *407/396–1400 or 800/239–6478* 🖶 *407/396–0660* ⊕ *www.doubletree.com* ↩ *577 rooms, 6 suites* ♿ *Restaurant, room service, cable TV, 2 tennis courts, 2 pools, gym, hot tub, basketball, lobby lounge, baby-sitting, laundry facilities, laundry service, meeting rooms* ▤ *AE, D, DC, MC, V.*

★ $$ ⊞ **Radisson Resort Parkway.** Bright and spacious, this Radisson may offer the best deal in the neighborhood: an attractive location amid 1½ acres of lush tropical foliage, good facilities, and competitive prices. Its delicatessen comes in handy when you want to assemble a picnic, and there's an on-site Pizza Hut. Rooms with the best view and light face the pool, which has a 40-ft water slide. Off the lobby is a lively sports bar. ✉ *2900 Parkway Blvd., Kissimmee 34746* ☏ *407/396–7000 or 800/ 634–4774* 🖶 *407/396–6792* ⊕ *www.radissonparkway.com* ↩ *712 rooms, 8 suites* ♿ *Restaurant, snack bar, cable TV with movies, 2 tennis courts, 2 pools, wading pool, gym, 2 hot tubs, sauna, volleyball, lobby lounge, sports bar, laundry facilities, laundry service, meeting rooms* ▤*AE, D, DC, MC, V.*

¢ ⊞ **Sevilla Inn.** Stucco and wood on the outside, the three-story building has plain rooms with basic amenities, such as small, wall-mounted TVs. If you need a place just to drop your bags and get some rest between theme parks, this is a good bet. The pool area is encircled by palm trees and tropical shrubs. ✉ *4640 W. Irlo Bronson Memorial Hwy., Kissimmee 34746* ☏ *407/396–4135 or 800/367–1363* 🖶 *407/396–4942* ⊕ *www.sevillainn.com* ↩ *50 rooms* ♿ *Cable TV, pool, laundry facilities* ▤ *AE, D, MC, V.*

Orlando Suburbs

Travel farther afield and find more comforts and facilities for the money, and maybe even some genuine Orlando charm—of the warm, cozy, one-of-a-kind country inn variety.

$$$–$$$$ ⊞ **Chalet Suzanne.** A world away from the world of Disney, this quiet, family-owned country inn was originally constructed in the 1930s, and subsequent updates have not taken away its original architectural charm. Although painted tropical pink and aqua, the buildings otherwise resemble a Swiss village. Some of the lovely antiques-dotted guest rooms have original tile baths, whereas others have whirlpools. The best overlook a lake or garden. Perhaps the biggest treat is a meal in the inn's elegant restaurant, where a six-course dinner is the house specialty. Take I–4 Exit 55 and U.S. 27 south. ✉ *3800 Chalet Suzanne Dr., 33859* ☏ *863/ 676–6011 or 800/433–6011* 🖶 *863/676–1814* ⊕ *www.chaletsuzanne. com* ↩ *30 rooms* ♿ *Restaurant, cable TV, pool, lake, badminton, croquet, volleyball, bar* ▤ *AE, D, DC, MC, V* ⦿ *BP.*

$$–$$$ ⊞ **Park Plaza Hotel.** Small and intimate, this 1922 establishment feels almost like a private home. Best accommodations are front garden suites with a living room, which opens onto a long balcony usually abloom with impatiens and bougainvillea. There's not much for kids here, but for adults, a half-dozen sidewalk cafés are within a block, and the Charles Hosmer Morse Museum of Art is within two blocks. Take I–4 Exit 87. ✉ *307 Park Ave. S, 32789* ☏ *407/647–1072 or 800/228–7220* 🖶 *407/647–4081* ⊕ *www.parkplazahotel.com* ↩ *27 rooms* ♿ *Restau-*

*rant, room service, cable TV, lobby lounge, laundry service; no kids under
5 ⊟ AE, DC, MC, V.*

NIGHTLIFE & THE ARTS

A fair number of the millions who pour through Orlando each year are
adults traveling without children. After years of denial, Disney heeded
the command of the profits and built Pleasure Island and later West Side
to create the Downtown Disney entertainment complex. In response,
Universal Orlando opened CityWalk to siphon off from Disney what
Disney had siphoned off from downtown Orlando, which is now struggling to find its footing amid the increased competition. If you're here
for at least two nights and don't mind losing some sleep, reserve one
evening for Downtown Disney and the next for CityWalk.

The Arts

When the fantasy starts wearing thin, check out the Orlando arts scene
in the *Orlando Weekly* (⊕ www.orlandoweekly.com), a free local entertainment and opinion newspaper that accurately tracks Orlando culture, lifestyles, and nightlife. Perhaps your best source of up-to-the-week
information is in Friday's *Orlando Sentinel* (⊕ www.orlandosentinel.com).
The handy Calendar section carries reviews of plays, nightclubs, live music
venues, restaurants, and attractions and also contains a few tourist-ori-
ented coupons.

The area has a fairly active agenda of dance, classical music, opera, and
theater, much of which takes place at the **Carr Performing Arts Centre** (⊠ 401
W. Livingston St., Orlando ☎ 407/849–2577 ⊕ www.orlandocentroplex.
com). The **Broadway Series** (☎ 407/839–3900 Ticketmaster) has top-
notch touring shows such as *Beauty and the Beast, Fame,* and *Fosse.*

The downtown Orlando Arena was given a name change thanks to a
large check from a major corporation; the clunkily named **TD Waterhouse
Centre** (⊠ 600 W. Amelia St., Orlando ☎ 407/849–2020 ⊕ www.
orlandocentroplex.com) plays host to many big-name performers and
sports events.

During the school year, the Bach Festival organization at **Rollins College** (⊠ Winter Park ☎ 407/646–2233) has a three-part concert series
that is open to the public and is usually free. The choral series is held
at Rollins's Knowles Memorial Chapel. The second part, the visiting-
artists series at the Annie Russell Theater, showcases internationally celebrated artists who have performed at venues such as Carnegie Hall.
The last week in February, internationally recognized artists appear at
the **Bach Music Festival** (☎ 407/646–2182 ⊕ www.bachfestivalflorida.
org), a Winter Park tradition since 1936 and the last in the trilogy. The
festival is held at the Annie Russell Theater and the Knowles Memorial Chapel and culminates on Sunday afternoon with "Highlights,"
which includes short performances by several of the artists who appeared
during the week.

Nightlife

Bars, Lounges & Nightclubs

WALT DISNEY   When you enter the fiefdom known as Walt Disney World, you're
WORLD RESORT   likely to see as many watering holes as cartoon characters. Nightlife
awaits at various Disney shopping and entertainment complexes—
everywhere you look, jazz trios and bluesmen, DJs, and rockers are tun-
ing up and turning on their amps after dinner's done. Plus, two

long-running dinner shows provide an evening of song, dance, and dining, all for a single price. Get information on WDW nightlife from the Walt Disney World information hot line (☎ 407/824–4321 or 407/824–4500) or check on-line at www.disney.com. Disney nightspots accept American Express, MasterCard, and Visa, and you can charge your bill to your room if you're staying at a Disney-owned property. The **Laughing Kookaburra** (⊠ Wyndham Palace, Lake Buena Vista ☎ 407/827–3722) has been a longtime favorite for locals, with standard-issue Ladies' Nights and live music.

Disney's BoardWalk (☎ 407/939–3492 entertainment hot line), across Crescent Lake from the Yacht and Beach Club Resorts, recalls an Atlantic City–style turn-of-the-last-century amusement complex by the shore, complete with restaurants, clubs, souvenir sellers, surreys, saltwater taffy vendors, and shops. When the lights go on after sunset, take a nostalgic, romantic stroll. In true Disney fashion, the sports motif at the **ESPN Club** (☎ 407/939–1177) is carried into every nook and many of the crannies. The vibe is rugged and boisterous at **Jellyrolls** (☎ 407/560–8770), which has comedians at dueling grand pianos and a sing-along piano bar made interesting by all the conventioneers. Wander the promenade and you'll also come across **Atlantic Dance** (☎ 407/939–2444) for funk and **Big River Grille & Brewing Works** (☎ 407/560–0253). Cover charges vary depending on the day of the week. For information on all BoardWalk events call the entertainment hot line.

Many Disney clubs are at **Pleasure Island**, a 6-acre after-dark entertainment complex connected to the rest of Downtown Disney by footbridges. Despite its location on Disney property, the entertainment has real grit and life, even against the backdrop of the facility's gimmicky underlying concept: every night is New Year's Eve, complete with a nightly countdown to midnight and fireworks. In addition to eight clubs, you'll find a few restaurants and shops. A pay-one-price admission gets you into all the clubs and shows. Children accompanied by an adult are admitted to all clubs except BET SoundStage and Mannequins.

Adventurer's Club re-creates a private club of the 1930s. Much of the entertainment is found in looking at exotic accent pieces that clutter the walls; the rest is in watching actors lead sing-alongs and share tall tales from their adventures. **BET SoundStage Club** is backed by Black Entertainment Television and pays tribute to all genres of black music through videos and live performances. The blend has attracted legions of locals who proclaim this the funkiest nightspot in Central Florida (and perhaps also the loudest). The gifted comedians at the **Comedy Warehouse** perform various improv games, sing improvised songs, and create off-the-cuff sketches based largely on suggestions from the audience. At **8TRAX**, groove to the recorded music of Donna Summer or the Village People while the disco balls spin. You'll either love or tolerate **Mannequins'** high-tech style, complete with Top 40 hits; a revolving dance floor; elaborate lighting; suggestive, over-the-top Disney dancers; and such special effects as bubbles and snow. **Motion** plays dance music from Zoot Suit Riot to the latest techno junk. The two-story warehouse look is stark, with the emphasis put on the dance floor and the club's twirling lights and thumping sound system. With a feeling reminiscent of a 1930s speakeasy, the **Pleasure Island Jazz Company** presents nightly performances by accomplished soloists or small combos. The tapas bar is well stocked; get assorted wines by the glass. The **Rock & Roll Beach Club** throbs with live rock music from the '60s to the '90s. ⊠ *Off Buena Vista Dr., Downtown Disney* ☎ 407/934–7781 or 407/824–2222

Fodor'sChoice

🎫 *Pay-one-price admission $21, shops and restaurants free 10:30–7*
🕐 *Clubs daily 7 PM–2 AM; shops and restaurants daily 10:30 AM–2 AM.*

Downtown Disney West Side is a pleasingly hip outdoor complex of shopping, dining, and entertainment. A 24-screen AMC cinema shows the same movies you could see at home. For something a little different, drop by for a beer and a *baba-lu* at Gloria Estefan's **Bongos Cuban Café** (☎ 407/828–0999). **Cirque du Soleil** (☎ 407/939–7600) starts at 100 mph and accelerates from there. It's 90 minutes of extraordinary acrobatics, avant-garde stagings, costumes, choreography, and a grand finale that'll make you double-check Newton's laws of motion. Shows featuring 72 performers are scheduled twice daily, five days a week (call for current performance schedule). Adjacent to the **House of Blues** (HOB; ☎ 407/934–2583) restaurant, which itself showcases cool blues starting at 11, HOB's up-close-and-personal concert venue brings local and nationally known artists playing everything from reggae to rock to R&B. ✉ *Off Buena Vista Dr., Downtown Disney* ☎ 407/824–4321 or 407/824–2222.

Fodor's Choice

Fodor's Choice

UNIVERSAL **Universal's CityWalk** meets the Downtown Disney challenge with its
ORLANDO open and airy gathering place, which includes clubs ranging from quiet jazz retreats to over-the-top discotheques. **Bob Marley—A Tribute to Freedom** is a loud reggae club–restaurant with more than a touch of Jamaica. **CityJazz** is a quiet, cool, sophisticated place to chill out. A beautiful, tiered room where soft lighting and rich woods are great for live jazz and a quiet martini, **the groove** has wild lighting, visual effects, disco chrome, and funk music that will have you shakin' your groove thang all night long. The world's largest **Hard Rock Cafe** adjoins the chain's first dedicated live concert venue, **Hard Rock Live**. **The Latin Quarter** is crowded and pulsing and feels like a 21st-century version of Ricky Ricardo's Tropicana with food and entertainment from 21 Latin American countries. The 20-screen **Loew's Universal Cineplex** (☎ 407/354–5998 tickets; 407/354–3374 box office) can offer an escape from the crowds. **Jimmy Buffett's Margaritaville** has proven itself popular with Parrotheads and margarita drinkers. Expect long lines at the **Motown Cafe**, where tribute groups perform floor shows emulating the Miracles, Supremes, Four Tops, et al. Race fans will want to check out the **NASCAR Café**, the only NASCAR-sanctioned specialty restaurant featuring full-size stock cars and racing memorabilia. Having teamed up with the Hard Rock Cafe, the NBA and WNBA see a demand for the basketball-theme **NBA restaurant.** An exact duplicate of the New Orleans favorite, **Pat O'Brien's** blows into Orlando with its signature drink, the hurricane, as well as dueling pianos and a "flaming fountain" patio. Clubs charge individual covers; you can invest $12.72 for a Party Pass that grants admission to all the clubs for one evening and tosses in a free movie at the Cineplex to boot. ☎ 407/363–8000 *Universal main line; 888/331–9108; 407/224–2683; 407/224–2600 CityWalk guest services* ● *www.uescape.com.*

ORLANDO For several years, downtown Orlando clubs had a monopoly on nighttime entertainment—which came to a close when Disney and Universal muscled their way in. Nightspots still attract office workers after hours, but the once-popular Church Street Station entertainment complex has closed. Down Orange Avenue, cool clubs are now sitting beside grungy tattoo and piercing parlors that are making the downtown area look tired and seedy. Despite this, there are some gems in the surrounding neighborhoods and clubs that are worth a visit—if you're willing to seek them out.

Howl at the Moon (✉ Church St. Marketplace, 55 W. Church St., 2nd fl., Downtown Orlando ☎ 407/841–4695 or 407/841–9118) encourages its patrons to warble along to pop classics of yesteryear and campy favorites. Piano players keep the music rolling in the evening, and even though no food is served, management encourages you to bring your own or order out; several nearby restaurants deliver. There's a cover charge of $2–$5 Wednesday–Saturday; Sunday it's free. **Mulvaney's** (✉ 27 W. Church St., Downtown Orlando ☎ 407/872–3296) is downtown's most-frequented Irish pub. Seven nights a week the wood-paneled bar is packed with pub crawlers fond of simple fare, imported ales, and authentic Irish folk music. Two big pluses are no cover and live entertainment every night.

The Parliament House (✉ 410 N. Orange Blossom Trail, Downtown Orlando ☎ 407/425–7571) is the largest gay complex in Florida, with half a dozen bars and clubs and a hotel resort. Weekend female impersonator revues are a highlight of the property's perpetual entertainment scene.

Refreshingly free of stand-up comedians, lively **Sak Comedy Lab** (✉ 380 W. Amelia Ave., Downtown Orlando ☎ 407/648–0001) is where you'll find Orlando's premier comedy troupe. Duel of Fools is the regular cast; the Sak Comedy Lab Rats are apprentices with potential. Wayne Brady, star of *Whose Line Is It Anyway?*, got his start here. They play to sold-out audiences Tuesday–Saturday.

:08 (✉ 100 W. Livingston St., Downtown Orlando ☎ 407/839–4800) is a country-theme nightclub with rather unusual attractions. In addition to presenting country artists, the club sponsors Buck and Bull Night on Saturday, when professional cowboys entertain the crowd by ridin' real live snortin' bulls. The club is open Friday and Saturday nights.

Dinner Shows

For a single price, these hybrid eatery-entertainment complexes deliver a theatrical production and a multicourse dinner. Performances might include jousting or jamboree tunes, and meals tend to be better than average. Unlimited beer, wine, and soda are usually included, but mixed drinks (often *any* drinks before dinner) will cost you extra. What the shows lack in substance and depth they make up for in grandeur and enthusiasm; children often love them. Seatings are usually sometime between 7 and 9:30, but an extra show may be added during peak tourist periods. Always call and make reservations in advance, especially for weekends and shows at Walt Disney World Resort.

WALT DISNEY WORLD RESORT   Staged at rustic Pioneer Hall, the **Hoop-Dee-Doo Revue** may be corny, but it is also the liveliest show in Walt Disney World. A troupe of jokers called the Pioneer Hall Players stomp their feet, wisecrack, sing, and dance while the audience chows down on barbecued ribs, fried chicken, corn on the cob, strawberry shortcake, and all the fixin's. Shows during busy seasons sell out months in advance. ✉ *Fort Wilderness Resort, Walt Disney World* ☎ *407/939–3463 in advance; 407/824–2803 day of show* 🎟 *$49.01 adults, $24.81 children 3–11, includes tax and gratuities* ⊘ *Daily at 5, 7:15, and 9:30* ☞ *No smoking.*

At the outdoor barbecue that is the **Polynesian Luau,** the entertainment is in keeping with the colorful South Pacific look. Fire jugglers and hula-drum dancers are entertaining for the whole family, if never quite as endearing as the napkin twirlers at the Hoop-Dee-Doo Revue (although the hula dancers' navel maneuvers are something to see). There are two shows nightly. ✉ *Polynesian Resort, Walt Disney World* ☎ *407/939–3463 in advance; 407/824–1593 day of show* 🎟 *$49.01 adults, $24.81 children 3–11, including tax and gratuities* ⊘ *Daily 5:15 and 8 PM* ☞ *No smoking.*

An elaborate palace outside, **Arabian Nights** is more like an arena within, with seating for more than 1,200. The show includes eerie fog, an Arabian princess, and a buffoonish genie, but the real stars are the 60 fabulous horses that perform in acts representing horse-loving cultures from around the world. The three-course dinners of prime rib or vegetarian lasagna are functional but not very flavorful. ⊠ *6225 W. Irlo Bronson Memorial Hwy., Kissimmee* ☎ *407/239–9223 or 800/553–6116; 800/533–3615 in Canada* ⊠ *$44 adults, $27 children 3–11, plus tax* ⊙ *Shows nightly; times vary* ☰ *AE, D, MC, V.*

Capone's Dinner and Show returns to the gangland Chicago of 1931, when mobsters and their dames represented the height of underworld society. The evening begins in an old-fashioned ice cream parlor, but say the secret password and you are ushered inside Al Capone's private Underworld Cabaret and Speakeasy. Dinner is an unlimited Italian buffet that's heavy on pasta. ⊠ *4740 W. Irlo Bronson Memorial Hwy.* ☎ *407/397–2378* ⊠ *$39.95 adults, $23.95 children 4–12* ⊙ *Daily at 7:30* ☰ *AE, D, MC, V.*

In **Medieval Times,** no fewer than 30 charging horses and a cast of 75 knights, nobles, and maidens perform in a huge, ersatz-medieval manor house. The two-hour tournament includes sword fights, jousting matches, and other games, and the bill of fare is heavy on meat and potatoes. ⊠ *4510 W. Irlo Bronson Memorial Hwy., Kissimmee* ☎ *407/239–0214 or 800/229–8300* ⊠ *$45.95 adults, $29.95 children 3–11* ⊙ *Performances usually daily at 8 but call ahead to check* ☰ *AE, D, MC, V.*

At **Sleuths Mystery Dinner Show,** your four-course meal is served up with a healthy dose of conspiracy. If you haven't got a Clue, then stop here and question the characters in an attempt to solve the mystery. ⊠ *7508 Universal Blvd.* ☎ *407/363–1985 or 800/393–1985* ⊠ *$41.95 adults, $23.95 children 3–11* ⊙ *Weekdays 7:30 (and sometimes 8:30); Sat. 6, 7:30, and 9; Sun. 7:30* ☰ *AE, D, MC, V.*

Movies
If you didn't come to Orlando just to see a "regular" movie at one of the megaplexes, check out the impressive **Muvico Pointe 21.** It not only has 21 screens and stadium seating but also a large-format screen for special films (⊠ Pointe*Orlando, 9101 International Dr., I–Drive Area ☎ 407/903–0555 ⊠ $10 adults, $7.50 children for large-format films; $7.75 after 6 PM; matinees $5.75).

SPORTS & THE OUTDOORS

Orlando is the place to visit if you want to be outside. You'll find just about every outdoor sport here—unless it involves a ski lift—that you'll find anywhere else in the country. The city also holds a hot ticket as a professional-sports town. In addition to hosting the NBA Magic, Orlando lays claim to the Walt Disney Speedway. **Disney's Wide World of Sports** (☎ 407/828–3267) has tournament-type events in more than 30 individual and team sports; serves as the spring-training home of the Atlanta Braves; and offers participatory sports for guests, including basketball, football, baseball, and soccer, as part of its Multi Sport Experience.

FodorsChoice

Auto Racing
The **Richard Petty Driving Experience** allows you to ride in or even drive a NASCAR-style stock car on a real racetrack. Depending on what you're willing to spend—prices range from $95 to $1,270—do everything

from being a passenger for three laps on the 1-mi track to taking 1½ days of lessons, culminating in your very own solo behind the wheel. The Richard Petty organization has a second Central Florida location at the Daytona International Speedway, but it involves riding in the car with an experienced race-car driver rather than driving a car yourself. ⊠ *Walt Disney Speedway* ☎ *800/237–3889* ⊕ *www.1800bepetty.com.*

Basketball

Fodor'sChoice The **Orlando Magic** has driven the city to new heights of hoop fanaticism. Tickets, which run $10–$150, are next to impossible to get—your best bet for seeing a game is probably a sports bar. ⊠ *TD Waterhouse Centre, 600 W. Amelia St., Orlando, 2 blocks west of I–4 Exit 41* ☎ *407/839–3900 Ticketmaster; 407/896–2442 season tickets* ⊕ *www. nba.com/magic.*

Biking

The most scenic bike riding in Orlando is on Walt Disney World Resort property, along roads that take you past forests, lakes, golf courses, and Disney's wooded resort villas and campgrounds. Bikes are available for rent from 10 to 5 daily at the **Barefoot Bay Marina** (☎ 407/934–2850) for $7.55 per hour. Rentals at Disney's **Coronado Springs Resort** (☎ 407/939–1000) are $8 per hour and $22 per day. At **Fort Wilderness Bike Barn** (☎ 407/824–2742), bicycles rent for about $8 per hour and $21 per day. At the **BoardWalk Resort** (☎ 407/939–6486; 407/560–8754 surrey bikes) surrey bikes cost $18–23 per half hour. Orlando has two good bike trails that have been created from former railroad lines. The **West Orange Trail** runs some 22 mi through western Orlando and the neighboring towns of Winter Garden and Apopka. The best place to access the trail is at **Clarcona Horseman's Park** (⊠ 3535 Damon Rd., Apopka ☎ 407/654–5144).

Fishing

Central Florida is covered with fresh-water lakes and rivers teeming with all kinds of fish, especially largemouth black bass but also perch, catfish, sunfish, and pike. To fish in most Florida waters—but not at Walt Disney World Resort—anglers over 16 need a fishing license, available at bait-and-tackle shops, fishing camps, and sporting-goods stores.

WALT DISNEY WORLD RESORT Fishing without a guide is permitted in the canals around the Dixie Landings and Port Orleans resorts and at Fort Wilderness Resort and Campground. **Bay Lake Fishing Trips** (☎ 407/939–7529) takes two-hour fishing excursions on regularly stocked Bay Lake and Seven Seas Lagoon.

AROUND ORLANDO Top fishing waters include Lake Kissimmee, the Butler and Conway chains of lakes, and Lake Tohopekaliga (also known as Lake Toho). Arrange for a guide through one of the excellent area fishing camps. **East Lake Fish Camp** (⊠ 3705 Big Bass Rd., Kissimmee ☎ 407/348–2040) is on East Lake Tohopekaliga. **Lake Toho Resort** (⊠ 4715 Kissimmee Park Rd., St. Cloud ☎ 407/892–8795) is on West Lake Tohopekaliga. **Richardson's Fish Camp** (⊠ 1550 Scotty's Rd., Kissimmee ☎ 407/846–6540) is also on West Lake Tohopekaliga.

Golf

Golf is extremely popular in Central Florida. Be sure to reserve tee times well in advance.

Golfpac (⊠ Box 162366, Altamonte Springs 32701 ☎ 407/260–2288 or 800/327–0878) packages golf vacations and prearranges tee times at more than 60 courses around Orlando. Rates vary based on hotel and course.

CloseUp

FLORIDA SPRING TRAINING: PLAY BALL!

ALTHOUGH THE MAJORITY of Americans are addicted to baseball for only a few days each October, there are some whose passion for this pastime burns year-round. The scant months when the "Boys of Summer" aren't actually on the field is far too long for those who head south to watch the "Boys of Spring" get back to business at Florida's many spring training camps.

If you're cruising the state in March, you can join them at any of the 20 major-league spring-training camps spread across Central and South Florida. While the action on the field won't have any bearing on the outcome of the World Series, the atmosphere brings baseball back to it roots. When you're watching from wooden stands or stretched out on the lawn, the simplicity of the sport is in sharp focus. Here, there are no massive stadiums backed by software companies or financial institutions. The millionaires on the field are back on the sandlots where they learned to play. And since managers want to give every player a shot, chances are you'll see the entire roster playing a few innings at least—and you'll usually have a shot at getting a player's autograph before the game begins.

So while you're roaming around Central Florida and find yourself near a spring-training stadium, drop into one of these fields of dreams. Armed with a carton of popcorn, a soft drink, and a hot dog, you'll be able to savor the American pastime without the pretense.

Atlanta Braves. At the Wide World of Sports Complex, the Atlanta Braves play in a sparkling new stadium complete with towering archways and ballroom-style common areas. These luxuries aside, the sloping lawns that run along side the first- and third-base lines are perfect for stretching out a blanket and watching the game. ✉ Disney Baseball Stadium, 710 S. Victory Way, Kissimmee ☎ 407/939-1500 ✇ $11.50–$19.

Cleveland Indians. Upgraded seats aside, the feel in this stadium still has traces of the past (poles erected in the middle of the seating sections). The Indians were ready to leave Arizona and head to Homestead, but Hurricane Andrew forced them to go north. This is a good bet for fans who want to watch the game in a bucolic Florida town. ✉ Chain of Lakes Park, Cypress Gardens Blvd., Winter Haven ☎ 941/293-3900; 866/488-7423 for phone sales ✇ $5–$13.

Detroit Tigers. If you thought Florida was discovered by Walt Disney, consider this: the Detroit Tigers have been training in the Sunshine State each spring since 1934 (the mouse didn't come to stay until 1971). Named after the city's parks director, this slow-paced stadium is in a laid-back southern city where you can settle in and watch the game minus the taint of corporate money. ✉ Joker Marchant Stadium, 2125 N. Lake Ave., Lakeland ☎ 863/686-8075 ✇ $5–$11.

Kansas City Royals. In what was once an amusement park (Circus World) and then another amusement park (Boardwalk and Baseball) are the spring training grounds of the American League's KC Royals. Since there are just 6,000 seats, you'll have a great view of the action—even in February, when you're admitted free to watch the players limber up and practice for the following month's games. ✉ Baseball City Stadium, 300 Stadium Way, Davenport (15 mins west of Walt Disney World) ☎ 941/424-2500 ✇ $7–$11.

— Gary McKechnie

WALT DISNEY
WORLD RESORT

Fodor'sChoice

Walt Disney World has five championship 18-hole courses—all on the PGA Tour route: **Eagle Pines** (⊠ Bonnet Creek Golf Club, Walt Disney World), **Lake Buena Vista** (⊠ Lake Buena Vista Dr., Walt Disney World), **Magnolia** (⊠ Shades of Green, Walt Disney World), **Osprey Ridge** (⊠ Bonnet Creek Golf Club, Walt Disney World), and the **Palm** (⊠ Shades of Green, Walt Disney World). Except for **Oak Trail** (⊠ Shades of Green, Walt Disney World), a 9-hole layout for novice and preteen golfers, these courses are among the busiest and most expensive ($60–$179) in the region.

The three original Disney courses—Lake Buena Vista, Magnolia, and the Palm—have the same fees and discount policies regardless of season and are slightly less expensive than Eagle Pines and Osprey Ridge, whose fees change during the year. All offer a twilight discount rate, $22–$80, which goes into effect at anywhere from 2 to 3, depending on the season.

AROUND
ORLANDO

Greens fees at most non-Disney courses fluctuate with the season. A twilight discount applies after 2 in busy seasons and after 3 during the rest of the year; the discount is usually half off the normal rate.

You can only play at **Arnold Palmer's Bay Hill Club** (⊠ 9000 Bay Hill Rd. ☎ 407/876–2429 or 888/422–9445) if you're invited by a member or stay at the club's on-property hotel, but room rates that include a round of golf run as low as $189 per person. The course at the **Celebration Golf Club** (⊠ 701 Golf Park Dr., Celebration ☎ 407/566–4653) was designed by Robert Trent Jones Jr. and Sr. and is just 1 mi off the U.S. 192 strip. **Cypress Creek Country Club** (⊠ 5353 Vineland Rd. ☎ 407/351–2187) is a demanding course with 16 water holes and lots of trees. The **Falcon's Fire Golf Club** (⊠ 3200 Seralago Blvd., Kissimmee ☎ 407/239–5445) course was designed by Rees Jones. **Grand Cypress Resort** (⊠ 1 N. Jacaranda Dr. ☎ 407/239–1909 or 800/297–7377) has 45 holes of golf. **Hawk's Landing Golf Course** (⊠ Marriott's Orlando World Center, 8701 World Center Dr. ☎ 407/238–8660) includes 16 water holes, lots of sand, and exotic landscaping. **Mission Inn Resort** (⊠ 10400 Rte. 48, Howey-in-the-Hills ☎ 352/324–3885 or 800/874–9053) includes two courses. Overlooking Lake Minneola, **Palisades Country Club** (⊠ 16510 Palisades Blvd., Clermont ☎ 352/394–0085) has a Joe Lee–designed course. The exceptionally long course at **Southern Dunes Golf Club** (⊠ 2888 Southern Dunes Blvd., Haines City ☎ 941/421–4653 or 800/632–6400) is great for low handicappers. **Timacuan Golf & Country Club** (⊠ 550 Timacuan Blvd., Lake Mary ☎ 407/321–0010) has a two-part course designed by Ron Garl—an open front nine with lots of sand and a heavily wooded back nine. The low-key 9-hole **Winter Park Municipal Golf Club** (⊠ 761 Old England Ave., Winter Park ☎ 407/623–3339) is incredibly inexpensive; greens fees are $10.

Horseback Riding

Fort Wilderness Resort and Campground (⊠ Fort Wilderness Resort ☎ 407/824–2832) offers tame trail rides through backwoods. Children must be at least nine to ride, and adults must weigh less than 250 pounds. Trail rides are $32 for 45 minutes, and hours of operation vary by season. You must check in 30 minutes prior to your ride, and reservations are essential. Both horseback riding and camping are open to nonguests.

Fodor'sChoice

Grand Cypress Equestrian Center (⊠ Hyatt Regency Grand Cypress Resort, 1 Equestrian Dr., Orlando ☎ 407/239–4608) gives private lessons in hunt seat, jumping, combined training, dressage, and western. Supervised novice and advanced group trail rides are available daily between 8:30 and 5. Trail rides are $45 per hour for novice, $100 per hour

for advanced. Private lessons are $55 per ½ hour and $100 per hour.
Call at least a week ahead for reservations in winter and spring.

Basic and longer, more advanced nature-trail tours along beautifully
wooded trails near Kissimmee are available at **Horse World Riding Stables** (✉ 3705 S. Poinciana Blvd., Kissimmee ☎ 407/847–4343), open
daily between 9 and 5. Pony rides are also available, and the stables area
has picnic tables, farm animals you can pet, and a pond to fish in. Trail
rides are $34 for basic, $39 for intermediate, and $49 for advanced. Pony
rides for children under six are $6. Reservations a day in advance are
recommended for the advanced trails.

Miniature Golf

The **Fantasia Gardens Miniature Golf Course** (☎ 407/560–4870) is heavily themed in imagery from Disney's *Fantasia*. It is adjacent to the Swan
and Dolphin resort complex and is near the Disney–MGM Studios. Games
are $9.76 for adults, $7.78 for children ages three through nine, and
there's a 50% discount for the second consecutive round played, which
is also valid at the Winter Summerland course. With everything from
sand castles to snow banks, the **Winter Summerland Miniature Golf Course**
(☎ 407/560–7161) is allegedly where Santa and his elves spend their summer vacation. The course is adjacent to Blizzard Beach and is close to
the Coronado Springs and All-Star Resorts. Adults play for $10.35, and
children ages three to nine play for $8.50. A 50% discount on the sec-
ond consecutive round played can be used here or at Fantasia Gardens.

Fodor'sChoice

Rock Climbing

The **Aiguille Rock Climbing Center,** in the Orlando suburb of Longwood,
has all the cliffs you can handle. Climbers reach a height of 45 ft on
6,500 square ft of rock-studded walls. ✉ *999 Charles St., Longwood*
☎ *407/332–1430* ✑ *Day passes $15 adults, $10 children under 12;
equipment rental $6, including proper shoes and harness; rock-climb-
ing instruction $30 per hr, reservation required* ☉ *Weekdays 10–10, Sat.
10 AM–midnight, Sun. 10–7.*

Water Sports

Marinas at the Caribbean Beach Resort, Contemporary Resort, Dixie Land-
ings Resort, Downtown Disney Marketplace, Fort Wilderness Resort and
Campground, Grand Floridian, Polynesian Resort, Port Orleans Resort,
Wilderness Lodge, and Yacht and Beach clubs rent Sunfish, catamarans,
motor-powered pontoon boats, pedal boats, and tiny two-passenger Water
Sprites—a hit with kids—for use on their nearby waters: Bay Lake, Seven
Seas Lagoon, Lake Buena Vista, Club Lake, or Buena Vista Lagoon. The
Polynesian Resort marina also rents outrigger canoes, and Fort Wilderness rents canoes for paddling along the placid canals in the area. To sail
or water-ski on Bay Lake or the Seven Seas Lagoon, stop at the Fort Wilderness, Contemporary, Polynesian, or Grand Floridian marina.

SHOPPING

Factory Outlets

The International Drive area is filled with outlet stores. At the northern tip of I–Drive, **Belz Factory Outlet World** (✉ 5401 W. Oak Ridge Rd.,
Orlando ☎ 407/354–0126 or 407/352–9611 ☉ Mon.–Sat. 10–9, Sun.
10–6) is the area's largest collection of outlets—more than 170—in two
malls and four nearby annexes. **Orlando Premium Outlet** (✉ 8200 Vineland
Rd. ☎ 407/238–7787 ⊕ www.orlandopremiumoutlets.com ☉ Mon.–Sat.
10–10, Sun. 10–9), with its collection of 127 upscale shops in an open
air layout, is capitalizing on its proximity to Disney (it's at the conflu-

ence of I–4, Highway 535, and International Drive). It can be tricky to reach—you have to turn off Highway 535 and find the very subtle entrance to Little Lake Bryan Road (*hint*: it parallels I–4).

Flea Markets

Flea World (✉ 3 mi east of I–4 Exit 98 on Lake Mary Blvd., then 1 mi south on U.S. 17–92, Sanford ☎ 407/321–1792) claims to be America's largest flea market under one roof. It sells predominately merchandise—everything from car tires and pet tarantulas to coffee, leather lingerie, and beaded evening gowns. It's open Friday–Sunday 9–6. Kids love **Fun World,** next door, which offers miniature golf, arcade games, go-carts, bumper cars, bumper boats, kiddie rides, and batting cages.

On weekends, **Renninger's Twin Markets** (✉ U.S. 441, Mount Dora ☎ 352/383–8393) hosts hundreds of dealers. At the top of the hill, 400 flea-market dealers sell household items, garage-sale surplus, produce, baked goods, and pets. At the bottom of the hill, 200 antiques dealers sell ephemera, old phonographs, deco fixtures, and antique furniture. Both markets are open every weekend, but on certain weekends, the antiques market has Antique Fairs, attracting about 500 dealers. The really big shows, however, are the three-day Extravaganzas, which draw 1,400 dealers. Depending on the day of the week, entrance to Extravaganzas costs $3–$10, but the other markets are free. Hours are weekends 9 to 5.

Shopping Areas, Malls & Department Stores

WALT DISNEY WORLD RESORT Shopping is an integral part of the Disney experience, going far beyond the surfeit of Disney trinkets found in every park. The area known as Downtown Disney contains two shopping-entertainment areas with plenty of just about everything. If you're staying at a Disney property, a nice perk awaits: if you buy anything from a store inside any Disney park, you can ask the salesperson to have it delivered to your room so you don't have to lug it around all day long. The service is free, and your purchase will be waiting for you on your bed when you return to your room. **Downtown Disney Marketplace,** a pleasant complex of shops, includes the **World of Disney** (☎ 407/828–1451), the Disney superstore to end all Disney superstores, and the **LEGO Imagination Center** (☎ 407/ 828–0065), with an impressive backdrop of elaborate Lego sculptures. Among the standouts over at **Downtown Disney West Side** are **Guitar Gallery** (☎ 407/827–0118), which sells videos, music books, accessories, and guitars, guitars, and more guitars; and the enormous **Virgin Megastore** (☎ 407/828–0222), with a music, video, and book selection as large as its prices.

UNIVERSAL ORLANDO **Universal's CityWalk** (☎ 407/363–8000) brings themed shopping experiences along with its cornucopia of restaurants, clubs, bars, and cafés. Retailers include **Endangered Species** (☎ 407/224–2310), with products representing endangered animals, ecosystems, and cultures worldwide; **Cigarz** (☎ 407/370–2999), for hand-rolled cigars; **All Star Collectibles** (☎ 407/224–2380), for sports junkies with its one-of-a-kind items and paraphernalia; and **Universal Studios Store** (☎ 407/224–2207), for a slew of official merchandise.

ORLANDO The necessities, such as a 24-hour grocery and pharmacy, post office, bank, and cleaners, are all at **Crossroads of Lake Buena Vista** (✉ Rte. 535 and I–4, Lake Buena Vista), across from Downtown Disney Marketplace. **Florida Mall** (✉ 8001 S. Orange Blossom Trail, Downtown Orlando), 4½ mi east of Interstate 4 and International Drive, is the largest mall in Central Florida, with 1.6 million square ft of shopping action with big-name chain stores, 200 specialty shops, seven theaters, and one of the better food courts around. **Mall at Millenia**(✉ 4200 S. Conway Rd. ☎ 407/363–3555 ⊘ Mon.–Sat. 10–9:30, Sun. 11–7), at 1.2 million square ft, is the biggest arrival in Orlando's retail wars. A few minutes northwest of Universal Orlando, it has several stores exclusive to the area, including Neiman-Marcus, Bloomingdale's, and Macy's, and several good restaurants. The retro-nouveau design of the mall's furnishings incorporates 250-million-year-old fossilized tile as well as a dozen LED screens suspended in the mall rotunda broadcasting entertainment and fashion shows. A currency exchange counter is handy for international guests (who make up a third of the mall's shoppers). It's easy to reach; take Exit 78 off I–4. At **Mercado** (✉ 8445 International Dr., I–Drive Area), there are more than 60 specialty shops and a large food court.

Orlando Fashion Square (✉ 3201 E. Colonial Dr.), 3 mi east of Interstate 4 Exit 83B, has 165 shops, including Burdines, JCPenney, Sears Roebuck, Camelot Music, the Disney Store, and Lerner. **Pointe*Orlando** (✉ 9101 International Dr., I–Drive Area) is across from the Orange County Convention Center and has 70 specialty shops, including A/X Armani Exchange, Abercrombie & Fitch, and a mighty impressive F.A.O. Schwarz.

In a sparkling 150,000-square-ft western-style lodge, **Outdoor World** (✉ 5156 International Dr. ☎ 407/563–5200) packs in countless fishing boats, RVs, tents, rifles, deep-sea fishing gear, fresh-water fishing tackle, scuba equipment, fly-tying materials (classes are offered, too), a pro shop, outdoor clothing, Uncle Buck's Cabin (a restaurant and snack bar), and a shooting gallery. If you're an outdoor enthusiast, this is a must-see. The huge, multilevel **Sports Dominator** (✉ 6464 International Dr. ☎ 407/354–2100) could probably equip all the players of Major League Baseball and the NFL, NBA, and NHL combined. Each sport receives its own section, crowding the floor with soccer balls, golf clubs, catcher's mitts, jerseys, bows, and a few thousand more sports items.

ORLANDO SUBURBS
The New England–style village of **Mount Dora** is recognized as the Antiques Capital of Florida. Trendy and swank **Park Avenue** (✉ Winter Park) has a collection of chic boutiques and bistros and is the perfect place for a romantic evening stroll.

WALT DISNEY WORLD® & THE ORLANDO AREA A TO Z

To research prices, get advice from other travelers, and book travel arrangements, visit www.fodors.com.

AIR TRAVEL

CARRIERS More than 20 scheduled airlines and more than 30 charter firms operate into and out of Orlando International Airport, providing direct service to more than 100 cities in the United States and overseas.
🛪 Major Airlines **Air Tran** ☎ 800/247-8726. **America West** ☎ 800/235-9292. **American** ☎ 800/433-7300. **Continental** ☎ 800/523-3273. **Delta** ☎ 800/221-1212. **Northwest/KLM** ☎ 800/225-2525. **United Airlines** ☎ 800/241-6522. **US Airways** ☎ 800/428-4322.
🛪 Smaller Airlines **Frontier** ☎ 800/432-1359. **GM Spirit** ☎ 800/772-7117. **Midwest Express** ☎ 800/452-2022. **Southwest** ☎ 800/435-9792.

AIRPORTS

The Orlando airport (MCO on your baggage tag) is ultramodern, huge, and growing all the time. However, it is relatively easy to navigate. Just follow the excellent signs. Monorails shuttle you from gate areas to the core area, where you'll find baggage claim. The complex is south of Orlando and northeast of Walt Disney World.

⚑ Airport Information **Orlando International Airport (MCO)** ☎ 407/825–2001.

AIRPORT
TRANSFERS

Find out in advance whether your hotel offers a free airport shuttle; if not, ask for a recommendation. Lynx operates public buses between the airport and the main terminal downtown. Although the cost is very low, other options are preferable, since the terminal is far from most hotels used by theme-park vacationers. Mears Transportation Group meets you at the gate, helps you with your luggage, and whisks you away, either in an 11-passenger van, a town car, or a limo. Vans run to and along U.S. 192 every 30 minutes; prices range from $16 one-way for adults ($12 for children 4–11) to $28 round-trip for adults ($20 children 4–11). Limo rates run around $44–$60 for a town car that accommodates three or four and $90 for a stretch limo that seats six. Town & Country charges $35–$55 one-way for up to seven, depending on the hotel. Taxis take only a half hour to get from the airport to most hotels used by WDW visitors. They charge about $25 to the International Drive area, about $10 more to the U.S. 192 area.

⚑ Buses & Limos **Lynx** ✉ 1200 W. South St., Orlando ☎ 407/841–8240 or 800/344–5969 ⊕ www.golynx.com. **Mears Transportation Group** ☎ 407/423–5566 ⊕ www.mearstransportation.com. **Town & Country Transportation** ☎ 407/828–3035.

BUS TRAVEL

Greyhound Lines buses stop in Orlando. If you are staying along International Drive, in Kissimmee, or in Orlando proper, ride public buses to get around the immediate area. To find out which bus to take, ask your hotel clerk or call Lynx. Scheduled service and charters linking just about every hotel and major attraction in the area are available from Gray Line of Orlando and Mears Transportation Group. In addition, many hotels run their own shuttles especially for guests; to arrange a ride, ask your hotel concierge, inquire at the front desk, or phone the company directly. One-way fares are usually $8–$10 per adult, a couple of dollars less for children ages 4–11, between major hotel areas and the WDW parks.

⚑ Bus Information **Gray Line of Orlando** ☎ 407/422–0744. **Greyhound Lines** ☎ 800/231–2222 ✉ 555 N. John Young Pkwy., Orlando ☎ 407/292–3422. **Lynx** ☎ 407/841–8240. **Mears Transportation Group** ☎ 407/423–5566.

CAR TRAVEL

The Beeline Expressway (State Road 528) is the best way to get from Orlando International Airport to area attractions; however, it is a toll road, so expect to pay about $1.25 in tolls to get from the airport to I–4. Depending on the location of your hotel, follow the expressway west to International Drive, and either exit at SeaWorld for the International Drive area or stay on the Beeline to I–4, and head either west for Walt Disney World and U.S. 192/Kissimmee or east for Universal Studios and downtown Orlando. Call your hotel for the best route. Interstate 4 is the main artery in Central Florida, linking the Gulf Coast in Tampa to the Atlantic coast in Daytona Beach. While I–4 is an east–west highway, it actually follows a north–south track through the Orlando area, so traveling north on I–4 through Orlando would actually be heading east toward Daytona, and traveling south would actually be traveling west toward Tampa. So **think north when I–4 signs say east and think south when the signs say west.** In January of 2002 the Florida Department of Transportation began changing exit numbers so they would match mile markers. The new signs have both the old exit number and the new exit number, something to keep in mind when reading maps. Two other main roads you're likely to use are International Drive, also known as I–Drive, and U.S. 192, sometimes called the Spacecoast Parkway or Irlo Bronson Memorial Highway. Get onto International Drive from I–4 Exits 72 (formerly Exit 28), 74A (formerly Exit 29), and 75B (formerly Exit 30B). U.S. 192 cuts across I–4 at Exits 64A (formerly 25A) and 64B (formerly 25B).

DISCOUNTS & DEALS

There are plenty of ways to save money while you're in the Orlando area. Coupon books, such as those available from Entertainment Travel Editions for around $30, can be good sources for discounts on rental cars, admission to attractions, meals, and other typical purchases. Be a smart shopper and **compare all your options** before making decisions. A plane ticket bought with a promotional coupon from travel clubs, coupon books, and direct-mail offers or on the Internet may not be cheaper than the least-expensive fare from a discount ticket agency. And always keep in mind that what you get is just as important as what you save.

1. Shop around carefully for theme-park tickets. Discounted theme-park tickets are widely available. Be sure to **look into combination tickets** and second-day free tickets that get you admission to multiple theme parks or two days' admission for the price of one to a single park. The Orlando FlexTicket is just one example of the various combination tickets available. Also visit the Orlando/Orange County Convention and Visitors Bureau on International Drive (➪ Visitor Information) or stop in one of the many ticket booths around town, including the Tourism Bureau of Orlando, Know Before You Go, and the Tourist Information Center of Orlando. Do watch out for extra-cheap tickets (they may be expired) and discounts that require you to take time-share tours—unless you're interested in a time-share, that is.

If you're a member of the American Automobile Association, be sure to ask at your local club about getting discounted tickets. Find out if your employer belongs to the Universal Fan Club or the Magic Kingdom Club, which offer discount schemes to members' employees. Take advantage of next-day free offers on tickets, which are often available. You'll get into a theme park a second day for the price of a one-day ticket. At Busch Gardens, go for the Twilight Tickets, available after 3 PM.

2. Buy your tickets as soon as you know you're going. Prices typically go up two or three times a year, so you might beat a price hike—and save a little money.

3. Stay at hotels on U.S. 192 around Kissimmee and on International Drive that offer free transportation to and from the park. Getting to and from the parks may take a little extra time, but you won't have to pay to rent a car—or to park it.

4. In deciding whether to rent a car, do the math. Weigh the cost of renting against what it will cost to get your entire party to and from the airport and the theme parks and any other places you want to go. If you are traveling with a group of more than four, renting a car may be cheaper than other options.

5. Choose accommodations with a kitchen. Stock up on breakfast items in a nearby supermarket, and save time—and money—by eating your morning meal in your hotel room.

6. Watch your shopping carefully. Theme-park merchandisers are excellent at displaying the goods so that you (or your children) can't re-

sist them. You may find that some of the items for sale are also available at home—for quite a bit less. One way to cope is to give every member of your family a souvenir budget—adults and children alike.

7. Shop around for vacation packages. But when you do, buy a package that gives you exactly the features you want. Don't go for one that includes admission to parks or other sites you don't care about.

8. Avoid holidays and school vacation times or go off-season. You'll see more in less time, and lodging rates are lower.

9. If you fly to Orlando, check around for the lowest airline prices and buy cheaper, nonrefundable tickets if you are sure of the dates you want.

10. If you plan to eat in a full-service restaurant, have a large, late breakfast, and then eat lunch late in the day in lieu of dinner. Lunchtime prices are almost always lower than dinnertime prices. Also look for "early-bird" menus, which offer dinner entrées at reduced prices during late afternoon and early evening hours.

EMERGENCIES

Dial 911 for police or ambulance. All the area's major theme parks (and some of the minor ones) have first-aid centers. The most accessible hospital in the International Drive area is the Orlando Regional Medical Center–Sand Lake Hospital.

🛈 Police or ambulance ☎ 911.

🛈 Doctors & Dentists Dental Emergency Service ☎ 407/331-2526.

🛈 Hospitals & Clinics Centra Care ✉ 4320 W. Vine St., Orlando ☎ 407/390-1888. Centra Care ✉ 12500 S. Apopka Vineland Rd., Lake Buena Vista ☎ 407/934-2273. Florida Hospital Celebration Health is near downtown Celebration. ☎ 407/764-4000 Main Street Physicians ✉ 8324 International Drive, Orlando ☎ (407/370-4881. Orlando Regional Medical Center/Sand Lake Hospital ☎ 407/351-8500, near International Drive.
🛈 Walgreens has two 24-hour pharmacies in the area, 5501 S. Kirkman Road, near Universal Studios (407/248-0315) and 7650 W. Sand Lake Road (407/238-0400).

MEDIA

NEWSPAPERS & MAGAZINES The *Orlando Sentinel* is the area outlet for news; *Orlando Magazine* is a monthly publication. Both are mainstream and mundane. The *Orlando Weekly* is the alternative newspaper for the city, covering and criticizing local politics and recommending bars and clubs favored by college students, beatniks, and bohemians. The free weekly is found in distinctive red racks throughout the city.

RADIO **WSHE** (100.3 FM) is an oldies station. You'll find country music at **WPCV** (97.5 FM) and **WWKA** (92 FM). **WMFE** (90.7 FM) is the local National Public Radio affiliate. **WDBO** (580 AM) is an excellent source of news and traffic; **WFLA** (540 AM) has a weak news offering but carries Rush Limbaugh.

TAXIS

Taxi fares start at $2 for the first mile and cost $1.50 for each mile thereafter. Sample fares: to WDW's Magic Kingdom, about $22 from International Drive, $12–$16 from U.S. 192. To Universal Studios, $7–$12 from International Drive, $25–$32 from U.S. 192. To Church Street Station, downtown, $20–$26 from International Drive, $34–$42 from U. S. 192. For information on getting to or from the airport by taxi, *see* Airports and Transfers.
🛈 Taxi Companies A-1 Taxi ☎ 407/328-4555. Checker Cab Company ☎ 407/699-9999. Star Taxi ☎ 407/857-9999.

TRAIN TRAVEL

If you want to have your car in Florida without driving it there, consider a 900-mi shortcut with Amtrak's **Auto Train**, which departs for Florida from Lorton, Virginia, near Washington, D.C. Its southern terminus—Sanford, Florida—is 23 mi north of Orlando.

FARES &
SCHEDULES

The Auto Train runs daily with one departure at 4 PM (car boarding ends one hour earlier). You'll arrive in Sanford around 8:30 the next morning. Fares vary depending on class of service and time of year, but expect to pay between $229 and $445 for a basic sleeper seat and car passage each way. For a group of four and one car, the cost is about $520 total, or $130 per person. Note: you must be traveling with an automobile to purchase a ticket on the Auto Train.

🚩 Train Information **Auto Train** ☎ 407/321-3873 or 877/754-7495.

VISITOR INFORMATION

🚩 Tourist Information **Kissimmee/St. Cloud Convention and Visitors Bureau** ✉ 1925 Irlo Bronson Memorial Hwy., Kissimmee, FL 34744 ☎ 407/847-5000 or 800/327-9159. **Orlando/Orange County Convention & Visitors Bureau** ✉ 8723 International Dr., Orlando, FL 32819 ☎ 407/363-5871. **Winter Park Chamber of Commerce** ✉ Box 280, Winter Park, FL 32790 ☎ 407/644-8281.

THE TAMPA BAY AREA

7

FODOR'S CHOICE

Bern's Steak House, Tampa

Backwaters, Weeki Wachee

Busch Gardens, Central Tampa

Caladesi Island and Honeymoon Island State Parks, Dunedin

Clearwater Beach, Clearwater

Don CeSar Beach Resort, St. Pete Beach

Leo's Pizza, Palm Harbor

Renaissance Vinoy Resort, St. Petersburg

Sunshine Skyway, bay bridge, St. Petersburg

Ted Peters Famous Smoked Fish, St. Petersburg

Ybor City, Cuban enclave, East Tampa

HIGHLY RECOMMENDED

WHAT TO SEE BayWalk, St. Petersburg

De Soto National Memorial, Bradenton

Florida Aquarium, Tampa

Museum of Science and Industry (MOSI), Northeast Tampa

Myakka River State Park, Sarasota

Ringling Center for the Cultural Arts, Sarasota

Salvador Dalí Museum, St. Petersburg

Siesta Beach, Siesta Key

*Many other great hotels and restaurants enliven this area. For other fa-
vorites, look for the black stars as you read this chapter.*

Updated by
Chelle Koster
Walton

ALTHOUGH GLITZY MIAMI seems to hold the trendiness trump card and Orlando is the place your kids want to go annually until they hit middle school, the Tampa Bay area has that elusive quality that many attribute to the "real Florida." The state's second-largest metro area is less fast-lane than its biggest (Miami), or even Orlando, but its strengths are just as varied. Florida's third-busiest airport, a vibrant business community, world-class beaches, and superior hotels and resorts make this an excellent place to spend a week or a lifetime. Native Americans were the sole inhabitants of the region for many years. (Tampa is a Native American word meaning "sticks of fire.") Spanish explorers Juan Ponce de León, Pánfilo de Narváez, and Hernando de Soto passed through in the mid-1500s, and the U.S. Army and civilian settlers arrived in 1824. The Spanish-American War was very good to Tampa, enabling industrialist Henry Plant to create an economic momentum that was sustained through the entire 20th century. A military presence remains in Tampa at MacDill Air Force Base, the U.S. Operations Command.

Today the region offers astounding diversity. Terrain ranges from the pine-dotted northern reaches to the coast's white-sand beaches and barrier islands. Tampa is a full-fledged city with a high-rise skyline and highways jammed with traffic. Across the bay lies the peninsula that contains Clearwater and St. Petersburg. The compact St. Petersburg downtown, which has interesting restaurants, shops, and museums, is on the southeast side of the peninsula, facing Tampa. Inland is largely classic American suburbia. If it weren't for the palm trees, you could be on the outskirts of Kansas City. The peninsula's western periphery is rimmed by barrier islands with beaches, quiet parks, and little, laid-back beach towns. To the north are communities that celebrate their ethnic heritage—such as Tarpon Springs, settled by Greek sponge-divers—and, farther north, mostly undeveloped land dotted with crystal-clear rivers, springs, and nature preserves. To the south lie resort towns, including Sarasota, which fills up in winter with snowbirds escaping the cold.

Exploring the Tampa Bay Area

Whether you feel like walking on white-sand beaches, watching sponge divers, or wandering through upscale shopping districts, you'll find something to your liking in the diverse Tampa Bay area. Bright, modern Tampa is the area's commercial center. Peninsular St. Petersburg lies across the bay. Tarpon Springs, to the northwest, is still Greek in flavor. The Manatee Coast, to the north, is quite rural, with extensive nature preserves. To the south are Bradenton, which has several museums and beaches; Sarasota, a sophisticated resort town; and small, canal-crossed Venice.

About the Restaurants

Fresh seafood is plentiful, and raw bars serving oysters, clams, and mussels are everywhere. Tampa's many Cuban and Spanish restaurants serve fresh seafood, perhaps in a spicy paella, along with black beans and rice. Tarpon Springs adds hearty helpings of classic Greek specialties. In Sarasota the emphasis is on fine dining. Many restaurants offer extra-cheap early-bird menus for seatings before 6 PM.

About the Hotels

Many convention hotels in the Tampa Bay area double as family-friendly resorts—taking advantage of nearby beaches, marinas, spas, tennis courts, and golf links. However, unlike Orlando and some other areas of Florida, the area has been bustling for more than a century, and its accommodations often reflect a sense of its history. You'll find a turn-of-the-20th-century beachfront resort where Zelda and F. Scott Fitzger-

Numbers in the text correspond to numbers in the margin and on the Tampa/
St. Petersburg and Bradenton/Sarasota maps.

If you have 3 days

Florida Aquarium ❶ ⌐ and **Busch Gardens ❻**, 8 mi northeast of 🖼 **Tampa ❶–❾**, are probably the two most popular attractions in the area. You need a half day for the aquarium and a full day for Busch Gardens. Then it's on to 🖼 **Sarasota ㊹–㉛** and highlights such as the **Ringling Center for the Cultural Arts ㊹** and **Mote Marine Aquarium,** a research facility with tanks full of sharks, manatees, loggerhead turtles, and other marine creatures ㊽.

7

If you have 4 days

Start in 🖼 **Tampa ❶** ⌐–❾ with a half day at the **Florida Aquarium ❶**. Then it's just a short drive to **Ybor City ❷**. Rest your feet over lunch before an hour or two of strolling through the shops. **Busch Gardens ❻** takes your whole second day; experience thrilling rides or see animals in their natural settings. Start your third day in downtown St. Petersburg to see the world's largest display of John F. Kennedy memorabilia, at the **Florida International Museum ⓯**. Catch lunch at one of the trendy eateries in the **BayWalk ⓮** dining and entertainment complex just across the street. A few blocks east is the **Florida Holocaust Museum ⓬**. On the fourth day, choose between the beach or the streets of Sarasota. One of the best spots for a day at the beach is pristine **Fort De Soto Park ⓴**, a perfect place to picnic or watch the sun set over the Gulf of Mexico. Art lovers, circus buffs, and ecotravelers can spend their last day in **Sarasota ㊹–㉛**, traipsing through the museums at the **Ringling Center for the Cultural Arts ㊹** and at **Mote Marine Aquarium ㊽**.

If you have 10 days

With this much time, linger three days in 🖼 **St. Petersburg ❿** ⌐–㉓. While you're here, catch a meal or two and do some shopping at **BayWalk ⓮**, which is across the street from the **Florida International Museum ⓯**, in turn a short walk from the **Florida Holocaust Museum ⓬** and a five-minute drive from the **Salvador Dalí Museum ⓱**. You could easily spend a full day in downtown **Tampa ❶–❾**. Start the morning with the spectacular **Florida Aquarium ❶**. Then head to **Ybor City ❷** for a bit of touring, shopping, and lunch. End the day with the **Tampa Museum of Art ❸** and the **Channelside** dining and entertainment district for dinner. The next three attractions, clustered northeast of Tampa, can be reached by car in 45–60 minutes from St. Petersburg. Spend a day at **Busch Gardens ❻**, getting there early if you plan to see it all. If you are into water slides, set aside another day for **Adventure Island ❼**, Busch Gardens' water-park cousin. If you opt to skip Adventure Island, try the **Museum of Science and Industry (MOSI) ❽** or one of downtown Tampa's museums. Spend a day around **Tarpon Springs ㉚–㉞**, a quaint Greek village and the self-described Sponge Capital of the World. Caladesi Island State Park and nearby Honeymoon Island State Park, outside **Dunedin ㉙** are excellent choices for a day at the beach.

🖼 **Sarasota ㊹–㉛** is a convenient base for the second part of your stay. Drive up to **Bradenton ㊵–㊸** to take in its sights and beaches for a day. In Sarasota allow about four hours to cover the museums at the **Ringling Estates ㊹** and **Sarasota Jungle Gardens ㊻**. In the afternoon you might drive to St. Armands Circle on Lido Key to see shops and **Mote Marine Aquarium** ㊽. On another day explore the **Marie Selby Botanical Gardens** ㊼, quieter than Jungle Gardens, but still tropical, and give yourself a couple of hours to explore downtown Sarasota's shops and cafes. **Venice** 52 makes an enjoyable half- or full-day trip, and, of course, sprinkle in some time on the beach.

ald stayed, a massive all-wood building from the 1920s, plenty of art deco, and, of course, throwbacks to the Spanish-style villas of yore. But one thing they all have in common is a certain Gulf Coast charm.

WHAT IT COSTS				
	$$$$	**$$$**	**$$**	**$**	**¢**
RESTAURANTS	over $30	$20–$30	$15–$20	$10–$15	under $10
HOTELS	over $220	$140–$220	$100–$140	$80–$100	under $80

Restaurant prices are per person for a main course at dinner. Hotel prices are for a standard double room, excluding 6% sales tax (more in some counties) and 1%–4% tourist tax.

Timing
Winter and spring are high season, and the level of activity is double what it is in the off-season. In summer there are huge afternoon thunderstorms, and temperatures hover around 90°F during the day. Luckily the mercury drops to the mid-70s at night, and beach towns have a consistent on-shore breeze that starts just before sundown, which enabled civilization to survive here before air-conditioning was invented.

NORTH & WEST AROUND TAMPA BAY

The core of the northern bay comprises the cities of Tampa, St. Petersburg, and Clearwater. A semitropical climate and access to the gulf make Tampa an ideal port for the cruise industry. The waters around Clearwater and St. Petersburg are often filled with pleasure and commercial craft, including dozens of boats offering various types of day trips, and night trips with what the purveyors euphemistically call "Las Vegas action": gambling in international waters. It's fitting that an area with a thriving international port should also be populated by a wealth of nationalities. The center of the Cuban community is the east Tampa enclave of Ybor City, while north of Clearwater, in Dunedin, the heritage is Scottish. North of Dunedin, Tarpon Springs has supported a large Greek population for decades and is the largest producer of natural sponges in the world. Inland, to the east of Tampa, it's all suburban sprawl, freeways, shopping malls, and—the main draw—Busch Gardens.

Tampa

84 mi southwest of Orlando.

The west coast's crown jewel as well as its business and commercial hub, Tampa has numerous high-rises and heavy traffic. Amid the bustle is a concentration of restaurants, nightlife, stores, and cultural events.

★ ☺ ╒ ❶ The $84 million **Florida Aquarium** is no overpriced fishbowl. It's a dazzling architectural landmark with an 83-ft-high multitier glass dome. It has more than 4,800 specimens of fish, other animals, and plants, representing 550 species native to Florida. Five major exhibit areas reflect the diversity of Florida's natural habitats—wetlands, bays, beaches, and coral reefs. Creature-specific exhibits are the No Bone Zone (lovable invertebrates) and Sea Hunt, with predators ranging from sharks to exotic lion fish. The most impressive single exhibit is the living coral reef, in a 500,000-gallon tank ringed with viewing windows, including an awesome 43-ft-wide panoramic opening. Part of the tank is a walkable tunnel, almost giving the illusion of venturing into underwater depths. There you see a thicket of elk-horn coral teeming with tropical fish. A dark cave reveals sea life you would normally see only on night dives, and shark-feeding shows include divers chumming from the safety of a cage. If you have three hours, try the DolphinQuest Eco-Tour, which takes up to 50 passengers onto Tampa's bays in a 64-ft catamaran for an up-close look at bottlenose dolphins and other native wildlife. ⊠ *701 Channelside Dr., Downtown* ☎ *813/273–4000* ⊕ *www.flaquarium. net* ⊠ *Aquarium $15, DolphinQuest $18* ⊙ *Daily 9:30–5.*

Downtown Tampa's **Riverwalk** connects waterside entities such as the Marriott Waterside, the Channelside shopping and entertainment complex, and the Florida Aquarium. New Fort Brooke Park will include a wall of bronze plaques telling the story of Tampa's Seminole War fort from the Seminole perspective. The landscaped walkway extends 4 mi along the cruise-ship channel and along the Hillsborough River in the downtown area.

②
Fodor's Choice
★

One of only three National Historic Landmark districts in Florida, lively **Ybor City,** Tampa's Cuban enclave, has antique-brick streets and wrought-iron balconies. Cubans brought their cigar-making industry to Ybor (pronounced *ee*-bore) City in 1866, and the smell of cigars—hand-rolled by Cuban immigrants—still wafts through the heart of this east Tampa area, along with the strong aroma of roasting coffee. These days the neighborhood is emerging as Tampa's hot spot as empty cigar factories and historic social clubs are transformed into trendy boutiques, art galleries, restaurants, and nightclubs that rival those on Miami's sizzling South Beach. Take a stroll past the ornately tiled **Columbia** restaurant and the stores lining 7th Avenue. Guided walking tours of the area ($5) enable you to see artisans hand-roll cigars following time-honored methods. Step back into the past at **Centennial Park** (⊠ 8th Ave. and 18th St.), which re-creates a period streetscape and hosts a fresh market every Saturday. Ybor City's destination within a destination is the dining and entertainment palace **Centro Ybor** (⊠ 1600 E. 7th Ave.). It has shops, trendy bars and restaurants, a 20-screen movie theater, and GameWorks, an interactive playground developed by Steven Spielberg. The **Ybor City State Museum** provides a look at the history of the cigar industry. Admission includes a tour of La Casita, one of the "shot-gun" houses occupied by cigar workers and their families in the late 1890s. ⊠ *1818 9th Ave., between Nuccio Pkwy. and 22nd St., from 7th to 9th Ave.* ☎ *813/247–6323* ⊕ *www.ybormuseum.org* ⊠ *$2* ⊙ *Tues.–Sat. 9–5; tours Sat. at 10:30.*

❸ The 35,000-square-ft **Tampa Museum of Art** has an impressive permanent collection of Greek and Roman antiquities, along with five galleries that host traveling exhibits. A 124,000-square-ft space, designed by internationally renowned architect Rafael Viñoly, will be under construction until about 2005; until then, the museum will remain open at its current location next to the new building. It will close for a short time when exhibits are moved. ⊠ *600 N. Ashley Dr., Downtown* ☎ *813/274–8130* ⊕ *www.tampamuseum.com* ⊠ *$5* ⊙ *Tues.–Wed. and Fri.–Sat. 10–5, Thurs. 10–8, Sun. 11–5.*

❹ The **Henry B. Plant Museum** is one part architectural time capsule and one part magic carpet ride to gilded-era America. Originally a luxury hotel built by railroad magnate Henry B. Plant in 1891, the building has classic furnishings that date to when Colonel Theodore Roosevelt made it his U.S. headquarters during the Spanish-American War. The museum displays the finer things of life from the 1890s, including 19th-century artwork and furniture brought from Europe when the hotel opened. On Sunday afternoons get a live glimpse into the time period through "Upstairs/Downstairs," in which actors play the parts of hotel staff and guests. At periodic Saturday antique appraisals, bring up to three personal treasures for an expert evaluation. ⊠ *401 W. Kennedy Blvd., off I–275 Exit 44, Downtown* ☎ *813/254–1891* ⊕ *www. plantmuseum.com* ⊠ *$5* ⊙ *Tues.–Sat. 10–4, Sun. noon–4.*

🖐 ❺ In the 24-acre **Lowry Park Zoo,** exotic creatures from four continents live in their natural habitats. Check out the Asian Domain and its various primates, from chimpanzees to woolly monkeys. Spot some fancy flying in the free-flight bird aviary, and come face to face with alligators, panthers, bears, and red wolves at the Florida Wildlife Center. Gentle animals such as sheep and goats are the primary residents of the children's petting zoo; and get a look at another gentle creature that is quintessentially part of Florida at the Manatee Amphitheater. This zoo is particularly attuned to night events: parties range from food and beer tastings for the adults to chaperoned sleepovers for children ages 6–14. Adjacent to the zoo, the Fun Forest at Lowry Park has rides and an arcade. ⊠ *7530 North Blvd., Central Tampa* ☎ *813/935–8552* ⊕ *www. lowryparkzoo.com* ⊠ *$9.50* ⊙ *Daily 9:30–5.*

🖐 ❻ More than 2,700 animals are just part of the attraction at **Busch Gardens,** a sprawling, carefully manicured site. Themed sections attempt to capture the spirit of 19th-century Africa, and the Skyride simulates an African safari—taking in free-roaming zebras, giraffes, rhinos, lions, and other exotic animals. The 335-acre park also has live entertainment, animal exhibits, shops, restaurants, games, and thrill rides, including six roller coasters. The pulse-pumping lineup includes **Kumba** and **Montu,** both reaching speeds of more than 60 mph; **Gwazi,** a 7,000-ft-long wooden coaster; and **Python** and **Scorpion,** 360 degree–loop coasters with 60-ft drops. Passenger vans take you on a Serengeti safari in **Rhino Rally,** where you view Asian elephants, rhinos, and zebras. At one point, a bridge breaks away and passengers spend a few minutes on a rapids ride. Allow from six to eight hours to do Busch Gardens. There are a few kid-oriented attractions, such as **Land of the Dragons,** a cool playground, and children's ride area, but most of the park is geared toward teens or adults; to wit, try a beer-tasting class—after all, Anheuser-Busch owns the park. ⊠ *3000 E. Busch Blvd., 8 mi northeast of downtown Tampa and 2 mi east of I–275 Exit 50, Central Tampa* ☎ *813/ 987–5082* ⊕ *www.buschgardens.com* ⊠ *Ages 10–adult $50; ages 3–9 $41; under 3 free* ⊙ *Daily 9–6; later in summer.*

Fodor'sChoice
★

🖐 ❼ Water slides, pools, and artificial-wave pools create a 30-acre water wonderland at **Adventure Island,** a corporate cousin of Busch Gardens. Rides such as the Key West Rapids and Tampa Typhoon are creative, if geographically incorrect. (There are no rapids in Key West and *typhoon* is a term used only in Pacific regions—Tampa Hurricane just wouldn't have had the same alliterative allure.) Planners of this water park took the younger kids into account, with offerings such as Fabian's Funport, which has a scaled-down wave pool and interactive water gym. Along with a championship volleyball complex and a surf pool, you'll find cafés, snack bars, changing rooms, and video games. ⊠ *10001 Malcolm McKinley*

Beaches Every barrier island from Clearwater to Venice has excellent swimming beaches facing out on the Gulf of Mexico. Waters are calmer here than on the Atlantic Coast, a boon to families but a disappointment to surfers. Don't swim in Tampa Bay, Sarasota Bay, or the inland waterway, all of which have been polluted by boaters, marinas, and industry.

7

Biking The 34-mi-long Pinellas Trail, a paved route that follows the path of a former railroad, makes it possible to bike all the way from Tarpon Springs, at the north end of Pinellas County, to a spot not far north of the Sunshine Skyway Bridge, at the south end of the county. When completed somewhere around 2006, it will cover 47 mi. Opened in 2001, Suncoast Trail runs north from Tampa's outskirts for nearly 30 mi to Brooksville. The paved surface will eventually connect to the Pinellas Trail and extend another 10 mi.

Canoeing Several inland rivers offer superb canoeing, and outfits at different points along their shores rent equipment and lead guided tours. Skulling teams from the University of Tampa and colleges nationwide train in downtown's Hillsborough River.

Fishing Anglers flock to southwest Florida's coastal waters to catch tarpon, kingfish, speckled trout, snapper, grouper, sea trout, snook, sheepshead, and shark. Charter a fishing boat or join a group on a party boat for full- or half-day outings. Avoid fishing in polluted Tampa Bay.

Dr., less than 1 mi north of Busch Gardens, Central Tampa ☎ *813/987–5660* ⊕ *www.adventureisland.com* ✉ *Ages 10–adult $28; ages 3–9 $26; under 3 free* ☾ *Mid-Mar.–late Oct., daily 10–5.*

★ ❽ The **Museum of Science and Industry (MOSI)** is a fun and stimulating scientific playground where you learn about Florida weather, anatomy, flight, and space by seeing *and* by doing. At the Gulf Coast Hurricane Exhibit, experience what a hurricane and its 74-mph winds feel like (and live to write home about it). The Bank of America BioWorks Butterfly Garden is a 6,400-square-ft engineered ecosystem project that demonstrates how wetlands can clean water plus serves as a home for free-flying butterflies. The 100-seat Saunders Planetarium—Tampa Bay's only planetarium—has afternoon and evening shows, one of them a trek through the universe. For adventurous spirits, there's a high-wire bicycle ride 30 ft above the floor. There's also an impressive IMAX theater, where films are projected on a hemispherical 82-ft dome. ✉ *4801 E. Fowler Ave., 1 mi north of Busch Gardens, Northeast Tampa* ☎ *813/987–6300 or 800/995–6674* ⊕ *www.mosi.org* ✉ *$14* ☾ *Weekdays 9–5, weekends 9–7.*

❾ If you've brought your body to Tampa but your heart's in Vegas, satisfy that urge to hang around a poker table at 4 AM at the **Seminole Indian Casino.** The casino has poker tables, high-stakes bingo, and gaming machines. Coffee and doughnuts are free for gamblers, and the casino lounge serves drinks until 2:15 AM. ✉ *5223 N. Orient Rd., Northeast Tampa* ☎ *813/621–1302 or 800/282–7016* ⊕ *www.casino-tampa.com* ✉ *Free* ☾ *Daily.*

Where to Stay & Eat

★ $$–$$$$ ✕ **Armani's.** This northern Italian rooftop restaurant has good service, a great view of the bay and city, and one of the best sunset views along the gulf. Excellent pastas include black pepper pappardelle with scallops, shrimp, and creamy lemon pepper sauce. Another front-runner is the signature veal scallopini Armani (with wild mushrooms, cognac, and truffle sauce). The roast rack of lamb is a house specialty. ✉ *Hyatt Regency Westshore, 6200 Courtney Campbell Causeway, Airport Area* ☎ *813/207–6800* ♨ *Jacket required* ☰ *AE, D, DC, MC, V.*

$$–$$$$ ✕ **Bern's Steak House.** Fine mahogany paneling and ornate chandeliers
Fodor'sChoice define the elegance at legendary Bern's, which many feel is Tampa's best
★ restaurant. Chef-owner Bern Lexer ages his own beef, grows his own organic vegetables, roasts his own coffee, and maintains his own saltwater fish tanks. Cuts of topmost beef are sold by weight and thickness. The wine list includes some 7,000 selections (with 1,800 dessert wines). After dinner, take a tour of the kitchen and wine cellar before having dessert upstairs in a cozy booth. ✉ *1208 S. Howard Ave., Hyde Park* ☎ *813/251–2421; 800/282–1547 in Florida* ⊕ *www.bernsteakhouse. com* ☰ *AE, DC, MC, V* ☾ *No lunch.*

$$–$$$$ ✕ **Big City Tavern.** The name makes the place sound like it's merely a bar, but it's far more than that. In the ballroom of the historic Cuban social club with an ornate tin ceiling and dark wood furniture, this classy dining room serves many well-prepared dishes, ranging from veal saltimbocca with potato lasagna to a tasty panfried Carolina trout. A great starter is the homemade lobster-and-carrot soup. There's a good selection of wines by the glass and imported beers from Ireland to Australia and in between. The tavern is relatively quiet and removed from the frenzied crowds at street level. ✉ *Centro Ybor, 1600 E. 8th Ave., 2nd fl., Ybor City* ☎ *813/247–3000* ☰ *AE, D, MC, V* ☾ *No lunch weekends.*

$–$$$$ ✕ **Castaway.** The specialty of this mid-price casual restaurant with bay views is fresh local seafood—grilled, broiled, or blackened—but the menu also includes grilled steaks, such as a good New York strip, and several pasta dishes. The menu changes frequently, but past favorites have included shrimp in garlic-chardonnay sauce and coconut shrimp with orange horseradish sauce. Dine inside or on the expansive deck, particularly popular for lunch and at sunset. Don't worry, the jets dipping down over the bay on their final approach are just far enough away to avoid a noise problem. Brunch is the only meal served on Sundays. ✉ *7720 Courtney Campbell Causeway (east side), 1 mi west of Tampa International Airport, Airport Area* ☎ *813/281–0770* ☰ *DC, MC, V.*

★ $$–$$$ ✕ **Columbia.** A fixture since 1905, this magnificent structure with spacious dining rooms and a sunny courtyard takes up an entire city block. The paella is possibly the best in Florida, and the Columbia 1905 salad—with ham, olives, cheese, and garlic—is legendary. The menu has Cuban classics such as *ropa vieja* and *arroz con pollo*. There's flamenco dancing most nights. Buy and smoke hand-rolled cigars in the bar. ✉ *2117 E. 7th Ave., Ybor City* ☎ *813/248–4961* ⊕ *www. columbiarestaurant.com* ☰ *AE, D, DC, MC, V.*

★ $$–$$$ ✕ **Mise en Place.** The menu at one of Tampa's most celebrated restaurants is replete with Floribbean dishes, including creative takes on grouper. The chef's forte is combining seemingly incompatible ingredients to make a masterpiece, such as veal scallopini with goat cheese spaetzle, carrot parsnip sauté, and apple-cider Riesling sauce. ✉ *442 W. Kennedy Blvd., entrance off Hyde Park Ave., Central Tampa* ☎ *813/ 254–5373* ⊕ *www.miseonline.com* ☰ *AE, D, DC, MC, V* ☾ *Closed Sun.–Mon. No lunch Sat.*

$$–$$$ ✕ **Roy's.** Tampa Bay has a taste for trendy national restaurant names, so it's no surprise that Roy's, the Hawaiian fusion-style restaurant that

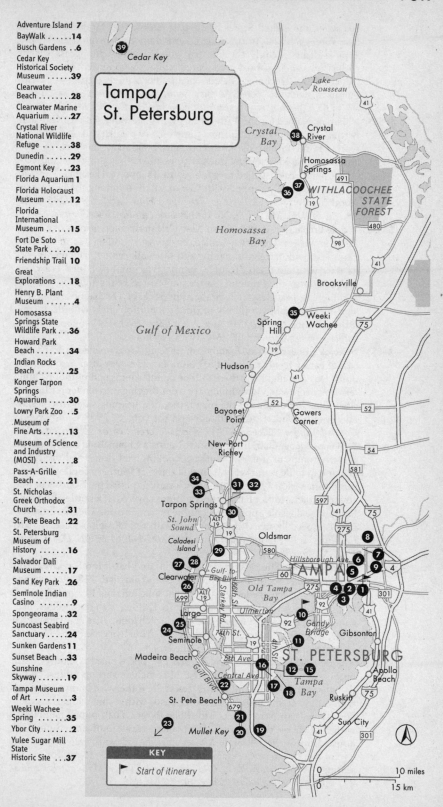

Tampa/ St. Petersburg

KEY

▶ *Start of itinerary*

has swept the United States in the past decade, has landed here. Chef Roy Yamaguchi flies in fresh ingredients daily from around the Pacific. Typical dishes include the likes of wood-roasted lemongrass shrimp with risotto and mustard-seed seared scallops with apricot–poppy seed reduction. Dessert choices include banana chocolate cheesecake and crispy pumpkin wontons. ✉ *4342 Boy Scout Blvd., Airport Area* ☎ *813/ 873–7697* ⊕ *www.roysrestaurant.com* ▤ *AE, D, DC, MC, V.*

$–$$$ ✕ **Bernini.** Named for the 17th-century Italian baroque sculptor Giovanni Bernini, this trendy restaurant is something of a gallery for copies of his works. In the former Bank of Ybor City building, it has a classy look and daring fare like crispy duck with raspberry-pepper glaze and goat cheese potato cake, grilled oregano swordfish, and veal lasagna. The Caesar pizza (basically topped with Caesar salad) is among the best of the wood-fired pizzas. ✉ *1702 E. 7th Ave., Ybor City* ☎ *813/248–0099* ▤ *AE, D, DC, MC, V* ☉ *No dinner Sun., no lunch weekends.*

$–$$$ ✕ **Café Creole.** The café looks so New Orleans it could be part of a Vieux Carré movie set. The brick-walled century-old building has an enclosed patio lush with ferns and palms, and sidewalk dining. The menu does its part with crawfish étouffée, jambalaya, gumbo, boiled crawfish, and, of course, the French Quarter staple—red beans and rice with andouille. The best dessert is praline cheesecake. The bayou pedigree is legit—it's owned by a family of third-generation chefs with deep New Orleans roots. ✉ *1330 9th Ave., Ybor City* ☎ *813/247–6283* ⊕ *www. cafecreoleybor.com* ▤ *AE, MC, V* ☉ *No lunch.*

$–$$$ ✕ **Kojak's House of Ribs.** Family-run since its doors opened in 1978, this casual eatery has been voted a Tampa favorite year after year in local polls. Day and night the three indoor dining rooms and outdoor dining terrace are crowded with hungry patrons digging into tender barbecued ribs. There's chicken on the menu, too, and heaping sides of coleslaw and potato salad, along with corn on the cob. ✉ *2808 Gandy Blvd., Central Tampa* ☎ *813/837–3774* ▤ *No credit cards* ☉ *Closed Mon.*

$–$$ ✕ **Stumps Supper Club.** In downtown Tampa's Channelside entertainment center, Stumps promises "Southern cooking and deep-fried dancing." Decorated in flea-market chic, it pokes fun at southern food while taking it quite seriously. From Brunswick stew to pulled pork barbecue and country-fried steak, it has all the traditions covered. If a bottle of Boone's Farm wine doesn't appeal, look at the martini menu. The key lime version is especially tasty and goes well with the music on stage. ✉ *615 Channelside Dr., Downtown Area* ☎ *813/226–2261* ▤ *AE, D, DC, MC, V* ☉ *No lunch.*

¢–$$ ✕ **GameWorks.** The restaurant (Jax Grill) and bar (Hop Scotch) at this fun factory are secondary attractions to the massive, 128-game arcade designed by Steven Speilberg. Jax Grill has solid offerings like grilled swordfish, baby-back ribs, and a tasty meat loaf, along with quesadillas, fish-and-chips, pizza, and burgers. The Hop Scotch lounge has many imported beers. ✉ *1600 E. 8th Ave., Unit A147, Ybor City* ☎ *813/241–9675* ⌂ *Reservations not accepted* ▤ *AE, D, DC, MC, V.*

¢–$ ✕ **Cactus Club Southwestern Grill and Bar.** The food is billed as southwestern, but it's served with a Florida twist. Hits include shrimp fajitas, chipotle barbecue chicken, and a tasty Texas Pie (otherwise known as pizza) with a thin, crispy crust—try the El Paso, with a spinach-garlic pesto. For devoted carnivores, there's the Blues Burger, a half-pound hamburger with blue cheese dressing and fried onion straws. Not surprisingly, the house drink is the Ultimate Margarita. The sidewalk café is lovely in winter and spring but brutal in summer, when it's best to opt for indoor seating. ✉ *1601 Snow Ave., Old Hyde Park Village, Hyde Park* ☎ *813/ 251–4089* ⊕ *www.cactusclub.com,* ▤ *AE, MC, V.*

¢–$ ✕ **dish.** At its two hot locations—Centro Ybor in Tampa and St. Petersburg's BayWalk—this restaurant with a bright red-and-yellow color scheme has become instantly popular. Plan on standing in line most any evening. Once inside, you get an empty dish, which you fill at various stations before ending up at a big teppanyaki station. Here a chef stir-fries your chicken, pork, beef, fish, and veggies while you watch. The price depends on how many trips to the grill station you take. Most sauces are soy-based, giving the cuisine a contemporary Asian touch. ✉ *1600 E. 8th Ave., Ybor City* ☎ *813/241–8300* ✉ *196 2nd Ave. N, St. Petersburg* ☎ *727/894–5700* ⊕ *www.diningatdish.com* ⌸ *Reservations not accepted* ▤ *AE, D, MC, V.*

¢–$ ✕ **Estela's Mexican Restaurant.** In the tiny business district of Davis Island, a sidewalk café gives this otherwise nondescript storefront a spark of vibrancy. It's the perfect place to munch on nachos and drink imported Mexican beer on a spring afternoon. The standard Tex-Mex cuisine is nothing special, so go for roasted poblano peppers stuffed with cheese, the chicken soup (with a nice touch of cilantro), or chile Colorado steak (strip steak roasted in spicy peppers). The restaurant adds a nice Florida touch: fresh squeezed fruit juices. ✉ *209 E. Davis Blvd., 1½ mi across bridge from downtown Tampa, Davis Island* ☎ *813/251–0558* ⊕ *www. estelas.com* ▤ *AE, MC, V.*

¢–$ ✕ **Newk's Lighthouse Cafe.** A popular choice with the downtown work crowd, Newk's has the feel of a neighborhood bar, though a sea-and-sky mural gives the illusion of waterfront dining. Choose from fish-house fare, pasta, and burgers. Grouper sandwiches come five different ways; notable are the crunchy version, with a corn-flake and almond coating, and a spicy buffalo style. The café has both indoor and outdoor seating. ✉ *514 Channelside Dr., Downtown Area,* ☎ *813/307–6395* ⊕ *www.newk.com* ▤ *AE, D, MC, V* ☾ *No dinner Sun.–Mon.*

¢–$ ✕ **Ovo Cafe.** The eclectic menu here pleases just about any palate. Of the excellent soups, a shrimp bisque and a Mexican corn soup with roasted pimientos are successes. A house specialty is stuffed pasta pillows (similar to ravioli, but larger), with fillings from steak Stroganoff to chicken-fennel sausage. An unusual twist is a selection of waffles as a main dish or a dessert. One of the best is the Ybor Republic, topped with chocolate ice cream and a splash of coffee liqueur. The café has about a dozen martinis, including a tasty version with Godiva white chocolate liqueur and crème de menthe. ✉ *1901 E. 7th Ave., Ybor City* ☎ *813/248–6979* ⊕ *www.ovocafe.com* ▤ *AE, D, DC, MC, V* ☾ *Closed Sun.*

$$$$ ▥ **Hyatt Regency Westshore.** As its name implies, this large 14-story luxury hotel sits on the west shore of Tampa Bay. It's convenient to Tampa International and downtown Tampa. It has a marble-accented lobby and a scattering of Spanish-style villas with private terraces. In addition to its bay views, the hotel also has a spectacular perch above a grassy, protected salt marsh and bird sanctuary. Considered one of Tampa's best business hotels, the Hyatt has the amenities and, of course, views to attract vacationers as well. ✉ *6200 Courtney Campbell Causeway, Airport Area, 33607* ☎ *813/874–1234* ⊟ *813/207–6790* ⊕ *www. hyattwestshore.com* ⇥ *422 rooms, 23 suites* ⌂ *3 restaurants, in-room data ports, some kitchenettes, minibars, some refrigerators, 2 tennis courts, 2 pools, gym, massage, boating, fishing, 3 bars, shop, baby-sitting, dry cleaning, laundry service, concierge floor, business services, meeting rooms, airport shuttle* ▤ *AE, D, DC, MC, V.*

★ $$$$ ▥ **Saddlebrook Resort Tampa.** This is arguably one of Florida's premier resorts of its type, largely because it has so many things in one spot—lots of golf, tennis, and conference space. The Arnold Palmer Golf Academy and sophisticated spa are especially popular. The heavily wooded grounds sprawl over 480 acres just 15 mi north of Tampa. Varied accommodations include one- and two-bedroom suites; breakfast and dinner are included in the rates. ⊠ *5700 Saddlebrook Way, Wesley Chapel 33543* ☎ *813/973–1111 or 800/729–8383* 📠 *813/773–4504* ⊕ *www.saddlebrookresort.com* ⟿ *660 rooms, 140 suites* ♿ *4 restaurants, room service, in-room data ports, some kitchens, some minibars, some in-room VCRs, driving range, two 18-hole golf courses, 45 tennis courts, pro shop, pool, wading pool, health club, spa, fishing, bicycles, 2 bars, baby-sitting, children's programs (ages 4–12), laundry service, concierge, business services, convention center, meeting rooms* ⊟ *AE, D, DC, MC, V* ❧ *MAP.*

$$$–$$$$ 🏨 **Tampa Marriott Waterside.** Across from the Tampa Convention Center, this downtown hotel was built for conventioneers but is also convenient to popular tourist spots such as the Florida Aquarium, the St. Pete Times Forum hockey arena, and shopping and entertainment districts Channelside, Hyde Park, and Ybor City. At least half of the rooms and most of the suites overlook the channel to Tampa Bay; the bay itself is visible from the higher floors of the 27-story resort. The lobby coffee bar overlooks the water. Il Terrazzo is the hotel's formal, Italian dining room. The three golf courses at which the hotel offers privileges are about 20 minutes away. ⊠ *700 S. Florida Ave., Downtown, 33602* ☎ *813/221–4900* 📠 *813/221–0923* ⊕ *www.tampawaterside.com* ⟿ *681 rooms, 36 suites* ♿ *3 restaurants, grill, room service, in-room data ports, in-room safes, golf privileges, pool, gym, hair salon, spa, boating, marina, bar, lobby lounge, baby-sitting, laundry facilities, laundry service, business services, car rental* ⊟ *AE, D, DC, MC, V.*

$$$ 🏨 **Wyndham Harbour Island Hotel.** Even though this 12-story hotel is on a 177-acre island in Tampa Bay, it's just an eight-minute walk and short drive from downtown Tampa. Many units have terrific views of the water or the downtown skyline. Service is attentive. There's a marina, and you may use the extensive health and fitness center and 20 tennis courts at the Harbour Island Athletic Club, next door, for a fee. This is a good choice for those who want to be downtown without actually being in the midst of the action. ⊠ *725 S. Harbour Island Blvd., Harbour Island, 33602* ☎ *813/229–5000* 📠 *813/229–5322* ⊕ *www.wyndham.com* ⟿ *279 rooms, 20 suites* ♿ *Restaurant, room service, in-room data ports, minibars, pool, dock, boating, fishing, bar, lobby lounge, laundry service* ⊟ *AE, DC, MC, V.*

★ $$–$$$ 🏨 **Don Vicente de Ybor Historic Inn.** This boutique hotel is in a carefully restored building originally constructed in 1895 by Vicente Martinez Ybor, the founder of Ybor City. From the pink stucco exterior to the white marble staircase in the main lobby, the hotel is an architectural tour de force. Rooms have antique furnishings, Persian rugs, and four-poster canopied beds. Most rooms have wrought-iron balconies. The clubs and shops of Ybor City are within a short walk. ⊠ *1915 Republica de Cuba, Ybor City, 33605* ☎ *813/241–4545* 📠 *813/241–6104* ⊕ *www.donvicenteinn.com* ⟿ *16 suites* ♿ *Restaurant, in-room data ports, bar, dry cleaning, laundry service* ⊟ *AE, D, DC, MC, V.*

$$–$$$ 🏨 **Hilton Garden Inn Tampa Ybor Historic District.** Architecturally, this property pales when compared to the century-old classic structures around it in Ybor City, but it is convenient: just across the street from the Centro Ybor complex, 2 mi from downtown Tampa, and 5 mi from Tampa International Airport. The hotel restaurant has a full breakfast buffet and doesn't try to compete with the culinary heavyweights in a six-block radius. Rooms are business traveler–friendly, with dual phone lines and a large desk with ergonomic chair. ⊠ *1700 E. 9th Ave., Ybor City, 33605* ☎ *813/769–9267* 📠 *813/769–3299* ⊕ *www.tampayborhistoricdistrict.gardeninn.com* ⟿ *84 rooms, 11 suites*

 ⚹ *Restaurant, in-room data ports, microwaves, refrigerators, pool, exercise equipment, laundry facilities, laundry service, business services* ▤ *AE, D, DC, MC, V.*

$–$$$ ▦ **Tahitian Inn.** Comfortable rooms and moderate prices are the draws at this two-story family-run motel, which underwent total reconstruction for a new classic look in 2003. It's 5 minutes from Tampa Stadium and 20 minutes from Busch Gardens. If you're looking for a chain alternative, the motel bills itself as the last independently owned and operated property in Tampa. ⊠ *601 S. Dale Mabry Hwy., Central Tampa, 33609* ☎ *813/877–6721 or 800/876–1397* 🖷 *813/877–6218* ⊕ *www. tahitianinn.com* ⋑ *99 rooms, 24 suites* ⚹ *Coffee shop, in-room data ports, minibars, microwaves, refrigerators, pool, gym, massage, sauna, spa, meeting rooms* ▤ *AE, D, DC, MC, V.*

¢–$ ▦ **Holiday Inn Busch Gardens.** Well maintained and family-oriented, this motor inn is a mile west of Busch Gardens (shuttle provided) and across the street from University Square Mall, one of Tampa's largest. Rooms are nice, but not spectacular, with contemporary furniture and two double beds. The seven KidSuites have separate bunk-bed cubby rooms decorated and equipped for the preteen set. The kids will also like the pirate-theme children's pool, complete with a ship of slides, water cannons, and fountains. ⊠ *2701 E. Fowler Ave., Central Tampa, 33612* ☎ *813/971–4710 or 800/206–2747* 🖷 *813/977–0155* ⊕ *www.holiday-inn.com* ⋑ *375 rooms, 25 suites* ⚹ *Restaurant, in-room data ports, some kitchenettes, room TVs with video games, 2 pools, exercise equipment, bar, dry cleaning, laundry service, business services, meeting room, car rental* ▤ *AE, D, DC, MC, V.*

Nightlife & the Arts

THE ARTS Occupying 9 acres along the Hillsborough River, the 290,000-square-ft **Tampa Bay Performing Arts Center** (⊠ 1010 W. C. MacInnes Pl., Downtown ☎ 813/229–7827 or 800/955–1045 ⊕ www.tbpac.org) is one of the largest such complexes south of the Kennedy Center in Washington, D.C. Among the facilities are the 2,500-seat Carol Morsani Theater, a 900-seat playhouse, a 300-seat cabaret theater, and 120-seat black box theater. Opera, concerts, drama, and ballet performances are presented here. The **Tampa Convention Center** (⊠ 333 S. Franklin St., Downtown ☎ 813/274–8511) hosts concerts throughout the year. In a restored 1926 movie palace, the **Tampa Theater** (⊠ 711 N. Franklin St., Downtown ☎ 813/274–8981 ⊕ www.tampatheatre.org) mounts shows, musical performances, and films.

NIGHTLIFE The biggest concentration of nightclubs, as well as the widest variety, is found along 7th Avenue in Ybor City. It becomes a little like Bourbon Street in New Orleans after the sun goes down. Popular **Adobe Gilas** (⊠ 1600 E. 8th Ave., Ybor City ☎ 813/241–8558) has live music on weekends, karaoke on Wednesday, and a balcony overlooking the crowds on 7th Avenue. There's a large selection of margaritas and 65 brands of tequila. Crowds tend to wear black leather at the **Castle** (⊠ 16th St. at 9th Ave., Ybor City ☎ 813/247–7547 ⊕ www.castle-ybor. com). It's no fetish club or biker bar, just a cavernous dance club with a medieval castle–style interior. Considered something of a dive—but a lovable dive—by a loyal local following that ranges from esteemed jurists to nose ring–wearing night owls, the **Hub** (⊠ 719 N. Franklin St., Downtown ☎ 813/229–1553) is known for one of Tampa's best martinis and one of its most eclectic juke boxes. **Improv Comedy Theater** (⊠ Centro Ybor, 1600 E. 8th Ave., Ybor City ☎ 813/864–4000 ⊕ www. tampaimprov.com) stars top comedians in performances Wednesday–Saturday. **Metropolis** (⊠ 3447 W. Kennedy Blvd., Central Tampa ☎ 813/871–2410 ⊕ www.metrotampa.com), near the University of

Tampa, has DJs, male strippers, and occasional appearances by big-names like Cher. At the **Pleasure Dome** (⊠ 1430 E. 7th Ave., Ybor City ☎ 813/247–2711), men onstage wear women's clothes and sing Streisand songs. The big dance club is actually predominately hetero—DJs crank out techno, dance, and hip-hop music until the female-impersonator show begins at 12:30 AM. **Pop City** (⊠ 615 Channelside Dr., Downtown ☎ 813/223–4250 ⊕ www.popcitytampa.com) has a live DJ blasting tunes and a game room with extreme-video games, billiards, and a rock-climbing wall. Catch live comedy Tuesday through Sunday nights at **Side Splitters** (⊠ 12938 N. Dale Mabry Hwy., Central Tampa ☎ 813/960–1197). **Skippers Smokehouse** (⊠ 910 Skipper Rd., Northeast Tampa ☎ 813/971–0666 ⊕ www.skipperssmokehouse.com), a junkyard-style restaurant and oyster bar, has live reggae Wednesday, blues usually Thursday through Sunday, and great smoked ribs every night. **Stumps Supper Club** (⊠ 615 Channelside Dr., Downtown ☎ 813/226–2261) serves southern food and lively dance music. The bar at the **Wyndham Harbour Island Hotel** (⊠ 725 S. Harbour Island Blvd., Harbour Island ☎ 813/229–5000) has a great bay view, and a big-screen TV.

Sports & the Outdoors

BASEBALL Locals and tourists flock each March to see the **New York Yankees** (⊠ Legends Field, 1 Steinbrenner Rd., near corner of Dale Mabry Hwy. and Martin Luther King Jr. Blvd., off I–275 Exit 41, Central Tampa ☎ 813/879–2244 or 813/875–7753 ⊕ www.legendsfieldtampa.com) play 17 spring training games against their big-league rivals at this 10,000-seat stadium. Season ticket holders typically grab up all the seats. From April through September, the stadium belongs to a Yankee farm team, the **Tampa Yankees**, who play 70 games against the likes of the Daytona Cubs and the Sarasota Red Sox.

CANOEING In northeast Tampa, **Canoe Escape** (⊠ east of I–75 on Fowler Ave., Thonotosassa ☎ 813/986–2067 ⊕ www.canoeescape.com) arranges trips from two hours' to all-day duration on the upper Hillsborough River, abounding with alligators, ibises, and hawks.

DOG RACING **Tampa Greyhound Track** (⊠ 8300 N. Nebraska Ave., Sulphur Springs ☎ 813/932–4313) holds dog races from July to December.

FISHING Capt. Jim Lemke of **Light Tackle Adventures** (⊠ 11408 Waveland Way, Central Tampa ☎ 813/968–4285 or 813/917–4989 ⊕ www.lighttackleadventures.com) is an outfitter who arranges bay, backwater, and flats fishing trips for everything from snook to tarpon.

FOOTBALL Seeing the NFL's **Tampa Bay Buccaneers** (⊠ Raymond James Stadium, 4201 N. Dale Mabry Hwy., Central Tampa ☎ 813/870–2700 or 800/282–0683 ⊕ www.buccaneers.com) play isn't easy without connections, since the entire stadium is booked by season ticket holders years in advance. The Arena Football League team **Tampa Bay Storm** (⊠ St. Pete Times Forum, 401 Channelside Dr., Downtown ☎ 813/301–6900 ⊕ www.tampabaystorm.com) plays about 16 games in its January to May season. The Storm is a perennial contender in the Arena League and has a hot rivalry with the Orlando Predators.

GOLF **Babe Zaharias Golf Course** (⊠ 11412 Forest Hills Dr., Northeast Tampa ☎ 813/631–4374) is a challenging 18-hole public course with water hazards on 8 holes. A pro is on hand to give lessons. **Bloomingdale Golfers Club** (⊠ 4113 Great Golfers Pl., Southeast Tampa ☎ 813/685–4105) has 18 holes, a two tiered driving range, a 1-acre putting green, and a restaurant. The **Saddlebrook Resort Tampa** (⊠ 5700 Saddlebrook Way, Wesley Chapel ☎ 913/973–1111 ⊕ www.saddlebrookresort.com) has two 18-hole Arnold Palmer–designed golf courses, a driving range, a golf shop, an on-site pro, and a resort spa. The **University of South Florida Course** (⊠ 13801 N. 46th St., Central Tampa ☎ 813/632–6893) is known locally as "The Claw" because of its many dog-legged fairways. It is scenic and wooded, with low greens fees.

HORSE RACING **Tampa Bay Downs** (⊠ Race Track Rd., off Rte. 580, Oldsmar ☎ 813/855–4401 ⊕ www.tampabaydowns.com) holds Thoroughbred races from December to May, plus satellite TV broadcasts of other Thoroughbred races at tracks around the nation.

ICE HOCKEY The NHL's **Tampa Bay Lightning** (⊠ St. Pete Times Forum, 401 Channelside Dr., Downtown ☎ 813/301–6600 ⊕ www.tampabaylightning. com) play at the 21,500-seat St. Pete Times Forum (formerly the Ice Palace), a classy, $153 million downtown waterfront arena. It's near the Florida Aquarium and Channelside and close enough to both Ybor City and Hyde Park to venture to either spot to eat before the game.

TENNIS & The **City of Tampa Tennis Complex** (⊠ 3901 W. Tampa Bay Blvd., Cen-
RACQUETBALL tral Tampa ☎ 813/223–8602), across from Raymond James Stadium and immediately north of Tampa International Airport, has 12 clay courts and 16 hard courts. Four are lighted. The complex also has four racquetball courts.

Shopping

For bargains stop at the **Big Top** (⊠ 9250 Fowler Ave., Northeast Tampa), open weekends 8–5, where vendors hawk new and used items at 1,000-plus booths. The new **Channelside** shopping and entertainment complex (⊠ 615 Channelside Dr., Downtown) offers movie theaters, shops, restaurants, clubs, and Pop City, a glorified games arcade. If you want to grab something at Neiman-Marcus on your way to the airport, the upscale **International Plaza** (⊠ 2223 N. Westshore Blvd., Airport Area) mall is immediately south of the airport. **Old Hyde Park Village** (⊠ Swan Ave. near Bayshore Blvd., Hyde Park) is a gentrified shopping district like the ones you find in every major American city. Williams-Sonoma and Brooks Brothers are mixed in with bistros and sidewalk cafés. More than 120 shops, department stores, and eateries are found in one of the area's biggest market complexes, **Westfield Shopping Town at Brandon** (⊠ Grand Regency and Rte. 60, Brandon), an attractively landscaped complex near Interstate 75, about 20 minutes from downtown by car. If you are shopping for hand-rolled cigars, head for 7th Avenue in **Ybor City**, where a few hand-rollers practice their craft in small shops.

St. Petersburg

21 mi west of Tampa.

St. Petersburg and the Pinellas Coast form the thumb of the hand that juts out of Florida's west coast and grasps Tampa Bay. There are two distinct parts of St. Petersburg—the downtown and cultural area, centered on the bay, and the beach area, a string of barrier islands that faces the gulf and includes St. Pete Beach, Treasure Island, and Madeira Beach. Causeways link beach communities to the mainland peninsula.

▶ ⑩ If you can't decide whether to go in-line skating or saltwater fishing, do both at once (depending on your level of athleticism) on Tampa Bay's car-free **Friendship Trail**, formerly the Gandy Bay Bridge (U.S. Hwy. 92), which connects Tampa and St. Petersburg. The trail runs parallel to the newer Gandy Bridge and can be accessed from either Tampa or St. Petersburg. The 2½-mi bridge connects to another 10 mi worth of trails to make it the world's longest over-the-water recreational trail. It has no facilities except for portable potties that have been placed mercifully every ¾ mi along the length of the two-lane concrete span. The pier is longer than any you'll encounter in Florida—the experience is like going to sea on foot. Long wooden decks on each side of the bridge (open 24 hours) are reserved for anglers, and the former traffic lanes of the bridge are open to runners, walkers, and in-line skaters. ✉ *13000 W. Gandy Blvd. (St. Petersburg side); 5200 W. Gandy Blvd. (Tampa side)* ☎ *727/ 549–6099* ⊕ *www.friendshiptrail.org.*

⑪ **Sunken Gardens** is one of Florida's most colorful attractions. Walk through an aviary full of tropical birds; stroll among more than 50,000 exotic flowers and other plants 15 ft below street level; be sure to peek into the butterfly garden. ✉ *1825 4th St. N* ☎ *727/551–3100* ⊕ *www. stpete.org/sunken.htm* ✍ *$7* ◷ *Wed.–Sun. 10–4.*

☾ ⑱ At **Great Explorations** you'll never hear "Don't touch." The museum, which moved to its new Sunken Gardens location in April 2003, is hands-on through and through, with a Robot Lab, Climb Wall, Lie Detector, and other interactive play areas. ✉ *1925 4th St. N.* ☎ *727/821–8885* ⊕ *www.greatexplorations.org* ✍ *$10* ◷ *Daily.*

⑮ In a wonderful conversion of a downtown department store, the **Florida International Museum** has become a major focal point of the central business district. John F. Kennedy, the Exhibition is the largest display of John F. Kennedy memorabilia in the world, with more than 500 personal items and a full-size copy of the Oval Office, complete with Kennedy's desk and the crayons he kept inside for his small children. There's also a replica of the Rose Garden and a depiction of the Dallas motorcade with a presidential limousine. The museum also hosts a permanent Cuban Missile Crisis exhibit and traveling exhibitions. ✉ *100 2nd St. N, off I–275 Exit 23A* ☎ *727/804–6477 or 800/777–9882* ⊕ *www.floridamuseum.org* ✍ *$12* ◷ *Mon.–Sat. 10–5, Sun. noon–5.*

★ ⑭ Downtown St. Petersburg got a massive infusion of vibrancy with the opening of **BayWalk,** a shopping, dining, and entertainment mall in a two-square-block complex incorporating California mission–style design and courtyard areas lined with trendy eateries, bars, shops, and a 20-screen movie theater. Among the restaurants at 2nd Avenue North and 2nd Street (off I–275 Exit 23A) are dish (⇨ Where to Stay & Eat *in* Tampa); Johnny Rockets, of national hamburger-chain fame; and Wet Willies, a see-and-be-seen bar. ✉ *Bordered by 2nd Ave. N, 4th Ave. N, 1st St. NE, and 2nd St. NE.*

⑫ The largest collection of Holocaust memorabilia outside the United States Holocaust Memorial Museum in Washington, D.C., is at the downtown **Florida Holocaust Museum.** The prisoner-transport rail-car exhibit is haunting, as is the extensive collection of photographs and artifacts. A popular section of the museum displays portraits and biographies of Holocaust survivors. The museum was originally conceived as a learning center for children, so many of the exhibits avoid overly graphic content; parents are warned prior to entering a gallery if any of the subject matter is potentially too intense for younger kids. ✉ *55 5th St. S* ☎ *727/820–0100* ⊕ *www.flholocaustmuseum.org* ✍ *$6* ◷ *Weekdays 10–5, weekends noon–5.*

⑬ Outstanding examples of European, American, pre-Columbian, and Far Eastern art are at the **Museum of Fine Arts.** There are also photographic exhibits. Staff members give narrated gallery tours two to five times a day. ✉ *255 Beach Dr. NE* ☎ *727/896–2667* ⊕ *www.fine-arts.org* ✍ *$6* ◷ *Tues.–Sat. 10–5, Sun. 1–5. Tours Tues.–Fri. at 10, 11, 1, 2, and 3; Sat. at 11, 1, 2, and 3; Sun. at 1 and 2.*

⑯ Learn about the region from prehistory to the present at the **St. Petersburg Museum of History.** Exhibits depict primitive shell tools, European settlement, the railroad era and Victorian Florida, commercial aviation, the growth of tourism, the Great Depression, and the renewal of tourism since the 1940s. ⊠ *335 2nd Ave. NE* ☎ *727/894–1052* ⊕ *www.museumofhistoryonline.org* ⊠ *$5* ☉ *Mon.–Sat. 10–5, Sun. 1–5.*

★ ⑰ The world's most extensive collection of originals by Spanish surrealist Salvador Dalí is found at the **Salvador Dalí Museum.** Valued at more than $125 million, the collection includes 94 oils, more than 100 watercolors and drawings, and 1,300 graphics, sculptures, photographs, and objets d'art, including floor-to-ceiling murals. Frequent tours are led by well-informed docents. How did the collection end up here? A rich northern industrialist and friend of Dalí, Ohio magnate A. Reynolds Morse, was looking for a museum site after his huge personal Dalí collection began to overflow his mansion. The people of St. Petersburg vied admirably for the collection, and the museum was established here as a result. ⊠ *1000 3rd St. S* ☎ *727/823–3767 or 800/442–3254* ⊕ *www.salvadordalimuseum.org* ⊠ *$10* ☉ *Mon.–Wed. and Fri.–Sat. 9:30–5:30, Thurs. 9:30–8, Sun. noon–5:30.*

⑲ **Sunshine Skyway,** a 4-mi-long bridge on a section of Interstate 275, con-
Fodor's Choice nects Pinellas and Manatee counties. The roadway is 183 ft above
★ Tampa Bay at its highest point, and the view out over the bay is spectacular. See the several small islands that dot the bay if you're heading southeast, St. Pete Beach if you're going northwest. Exits off the bridge lead to the old bridge, now known as "the world's longest fishing pier."

⑳ Actually spread over six small islands, or keys, 900-acre **Fort De Soto Park** lies at the mouth of Tampa Bay. It has 7 mi of beaches, two fishing piers, picnic and camping grounds, and a historic fort. The fort for which it's named was built on the southern end of Mullet Key to protect sea lanes in the gulf during the Spanish-American War. Roam the fort or wander the beaches of any of the islands within the park. ⊠ *3500 Pinellas Bayway S, Tierra Verde* ☎ *727/866–2484* ⊠ *Free* ☉ *Daily 7–sunset.*

㉑ **Pass-A-Grille Beach,** at the southern end of St. Pete Beach, has parking meters, a snack bar, rest rooms, and showers. ⊠ *Off Gulf Blvd. (Rte. 699), St. Pete Beach.*

㉒ **St. Pete Beach** (⊠ *11260 Gulf Blvd.* ☎ *727/549–6165*) is a free beach on Treasure Island. There are dressing rooms, metered parking, and a snack bar.

㉓ In the middle of the mouth of Tampa Bay lies a small and largely unspoiled island, **Egmont Key.** On the island are the ruins of Fort De Soto's sister fortification, **Fort Dade,** a military installation also built during the Spanish-American War. The primary inhabitant of the 2-mi-long island is the threatened gopher tortoise. Shelling and nature-viewing are rewarding. The only way to get here, however, is by boat. **Dolphin Landing Tours** (☎ *727/360–7411*) does a four-hour excursion, or rent a runabout, readily available throughout the Tampa Bay area. A note of caution: in addition to the tortoises, there are some huge rattlesnakes on the island. Do *not* venture off the trails.

Where to Stay & Eat

$$$ ✕ **Chateau France.** Downtown St. Petersburg has grown up around this 1910 Victorian house, which today provides a most legitimate Gallic dining experience. Have traditional French dishes such as coq au vin and Dover sole meunière. Filet mignon is a specialty; it comes in five variations nightly. Chocolate soufflé and flaming crepes suzette prepared tableside are a mainstay. There's a cigar room stocked with fine brandy and cigars hand-rolled in Tampa. ✉ *136 4th Ave. NE* ☎ *727/894–7163* ⊕ *www.chateaufrancecuisine.com* ⌖ *Reservations essential* ⊟ *AE, D, DC, MC, V* ✆ *No lunch.*

$$–$$$ ✕ **Grand Finalé.** The eclectic, urbane, ever-changing menu gives this place a big-city vibe. Crab cakes with wasabi herb vinaigrette are among the worthy appetizers. The best entrées come from the sea. Selections might include slow-roasted salmon and seared sashimi tuna. Red meat is a good bet as well, particularly the filet mignon with foie gras. ✉ *1101 1st Ave. N* ☎ *727/823–9921* ⊟ *AE, MC, V* ✆ *Closed Sun. No lunch.*

$–$$$ ✕ **Gratzzi.** This warm northern Italian eatery hits local critics' short lists of best restaurants, with tasty classics such as veal saltimbocca and osso buco with pan-seared polenta. While the *zuppa de pesce* (fish soup) is a pricey dish at $16.50 a bowl, it's also one of the best, with expertly prepared mussels, clams, shrimp, scallops, and whitefish in a red sauce on pasta. Other dishes on the extensive menu are more affordable and include rotisserie-cooked meat and seafood. ✉ *199 2nd Ave. N, Bay-Walk* ☎ *727/822–7769* ⊟ *AE, D, DC, MC, V* ✆ *No lunch.*

★ $–$$$ ✕ **Marchand's Grill.** Once the Pompeii Room in the former Vinoy Hotel, opened in 1925, this wonderful eatery has frescoed ceilings and a spectacular view of Tampa Bay and the nearby boat docks. The food is impressive as well. The imaginative, changing menu lists temptations such as asparagus ravioli, roasted eggplant soup, browned gnocchi with wild mushrooms and pinot grigio broth, and seafood bouillabaisse. The wine list is extensive, including a number of by-the-glass selections. There is live music Tuesday through Saturday nights. ✉ *Renaissance Vinoy Resort, 501 5th Ave. NE* ☎ *727/894–1000* ⊟ *AE, DC, MC, V.*

$–$$$ ✕ **Spoto's Steak Joint.** The formula is quite simple here: aged Angus beef, expertly prepared. The restaurant serves about every cut one can imagine, from a huge porterhouse to a petit fillet. And if steak is not your thing, smoked baby-back ribs is another specialty, plus you'll find chicken, duck, and seafood. Dishes are served family-style with hot bread and fresh vegetables. ✉ *4871 Park St.* ☎ *727/545–9481* ✉ *1280 Main St., Dunedin* ☎ *727/734–0008* ⊟ *AE, D, MC, V* ✆ *No lunch.*

$–$$ ✕ **Bonefish Grill.** Live jazz and a great sampling of local seafood are trademarks of this urbane eatery near downtown. Rock shrimp fettuccine diablo and wood-grilled grouper are local offerings. Mussels sautéed with tomatoes, garlic, basil, and lemon wine sauce is a must-try appetizer. If you don't care for fish, you're not totally lost—pork tenderloin Portobello piccata is stellar. You won't find the namesake fish on the menu, incidentally. Bonefish is popular for sportfishing in the Keys, but it's far too bony to eat. ✉ *5901 4th St. N* ☎ *727/521–3434* ⊕ *www.bonefishgrill. com* ⊟ *AE, D, MC, V* ✆ *No lunch.*

$–$$ ✕ **Captain Al's Waterfront Restaurant.** At the end of the St. Petersburg Pier, this cheerful and casual all-yellow café looks out at the bay and competently offers up the region's seafood; the indecisive will enjoy Captain Al's Platter, with shrimp, oysters, crab cake, and conch fritters—all fried. For something lighter and more creative, try cashew crumb tilapia, a mild fish farmed in these parts. ✉ *800 2nd Ave. NE* ☎ *727/898–5800* ⊕ *www.captainalsrestaurant.com* ⊟ *AE, MC, V.*

$–$$ ✕ **Hurricane Seafood Restaurant.** On historic Pass-A-Grille Beach, this seafood joint has been a popular hangout for locals for decades. A steady crowd of tourists now joins regulars for the catch-of-the-day prepared however you like, which could include fried, grilled, blackened, jerk, or almondine-style. Check out the Keys Club, adjacent to the dining room, for terrific live piano and specialty martinis. Crowds head up to the rooftop sundeck to view the gorgeous sunsets. At Stormy's at the

Hurricane, a disco next door, a DJ plays music every Friday and Sunday. ⊠ *807 Gulf Way* ☎ *727/360–9558* ▤ *MC, V.*

¢–$ ✕ **Ted Peters Famous Smoked Fish.** A Pinellas County beach-culture institution, this place is a favorite with flip-flop–wearing anglers who sit on the picnic benches, soak up a beer or three, and devour the wonderful smoked fish. The menu is limited to mackerel, mullet, and salmon, but all are smoked and seasoned to perfection and served with heaping helpings of German potato salad. The popular smoked fish spread is also available to go. There's also indoor seating. This place closes at 7:30 PM. ⊠ *1350 Pasadena Ave. S, Pasadena* ☎ *727/381–7931* ⌑ *Reservations not accepted* ▤ *No credit cards* ⊗ *Closed Tues.*

Fodor'sChoice ★

¢–$ ✕ **Too Jay's.** Knishes and roast brisket with potato pancakes are the mainstays at this kosher-style deli with a busy dining room at lunch and dinner. Other selections include salmon cakes, shepherd's pie, and shrimp pesto. Don't miss the éclair, a house specialty. The restaurant is nothing fancy, but it's bright and friendly, and management seems obsessed about making sure you're waited on promptly. A take-out section includes many of the menu's offerings. ⊠ *141 2nd Ave. N, St. Petersburg* ☎ *727/823–3354* ⌑ *Reservations not accepted* ▤ *AE, D, DC, MC, V.*

¢–$ ✕ **Woody's Waterfront Outdoor Restaurant.** Hang out with the locals in this off-the-beaten-path surfboard-theme institution. Burgers and beer star on the simple menu, but you can also order such dinner entrées as buffalo grouper, stuffed mahi, and chicken Alfredo. ⊠ *7308 Sunset Way, St. Pete Beach* ☎ *727/360–9165* ▤ *MC, V.*

¢ ✕ **Adobo Grill.** The made-to-order Mexican fast food here is light-years beyond that of any nationwide chain. A house specialty is the beef chipotle burrito. Also notable are roast pork burritos and grilled mahi tacos. Save room for the excellent guava turnovers. Service is over-the-counter, and there's seating indoors and under umbrellas on the patio. ⊠ *167 2nd Ave. N, BayWalk* ☎ *727/823–8226* ⌑ *Reservations not accepted* ▤ *No credit cards.*

$$$$ ▥ **Don CeSar Beach Resort.** Once a favorite of Scott and Zelda Fitzgerald, this sprawling, sybaritic beachfront "Pink Palace" has long been a Gulf Coast landmark because of its remarkable architecture. Steeped in turn-of-the-last-century elegance, the hotel claims a rich history, complete with a resident ghost. The restaurant, Maritana Grille, specializes in Florida seafood and is lined with huge fish tanks. The more casual Don CeSar Beach House, less than ½ mi from the main building, has one-bedroom condos and a great little beach bar. ⊠ *3400 Gulf Blvd., St. Pete Beach 33706* ☎ *727/360–1881 or 800/282–1116* ▤ *727/367–3609* ⊕ *www.doncesar.com* ⊃ *Resort: 234 rooms, 43 suites; Beach House: 70 condos* ⌑ *3 restaurants, ice cream parlor, room service, in-room data ports, some kitchens, 2 pools, health club, hair salon, spa, beach, boating, jet skiing, parasailing, volleyball, 2 bars, lobby lounge, shops, baby-sitting, children's programs (ages 5–12), dry cleaning, laundry service, concierge, business services, meeting room, airport shuttle* ▤ *AE, DC, MC, V.*

FodorsChoice ★

$$$$ ▥ **Renaissance Vinoy Resort.** Rooms in the original 1925 hotel building, listed on the National Register of Historic Places, have more character than others at the property, but all of the spacious units are comfortable and stylish. They come with three phones, two TVs, and bathrobes. The resort overlooks Tampa Bay, and a tiny bayside beach several blocks away is good for strolling (though is unswimmable). Transportation is provided to gulf beaches 20 minutes away. Other offerings include a Ron Garl–designed golf course with a stunning clubhouse, a big marina, and pool attendants who spritz you with cool water and deliver drinks. The hotel is convenient to downtown museums, the Pier,

FodorsChoice ★

or BayWalk. ⊠ *501 5th Ave. NE, 33701* ☎ *727/894–1000* ⊜ *727/822–2785* ⊕ *www.renaissancehotels.com* ⇋ *340 rooms, 20 suites* ♿ *5 restaurants, room service, in-room data ports, minibars, 18-hole golf course, 12 tennis courts, 2 pools, hair salon, health club, outdoor hot tub, massage, dock, boating, marina, croquet, 2 bars, lobby lounge, shop, baby-sitting, laundry facilities, laundry service, concierge, business services, car rental; no-smoking rooms* ⊟ *AE, DC, MC, V.*

$$$–$$$$ ⌧ **Tradewinds Resort.** Most rooms have a view of the beach at this sprawling gulf-front property, which is actually three resorts in one. The resort has some of the showmanship of an Orlando hotel, with a huge man-made lagoon inside the complex, complete with gondolas on its labyrinthine waterways. The resort's own kids character, Beaker the Toucan, makes appearances at kids' programs and can even tuck your child into bed at night for a fee. There are on-site swimming lessons for kids and adults. ⊠ *5500 Gulf Blvd., St. Pete Beach 33706* ☎ *727/562–1212 or 800/237–0707* ⊜ *727/562–1214* ⊕ *www.tradewindsresort.com* ⇋ *644 rooms, 473 suites (Island Grand: 378 rooms, 200 suites; Sandpiper: 56 rooms, 103 suites; Sirata Beach: 210 rooms, 170 suites)* ♿ *11 restaurants, ice cream parlor, pizzeria, in-room data ports, in-room safes, some kitchenettes, some minibars, refrigerators, some in-room VCRs, putting green, 4 tennis courts, 10 pools, outdoor hot tubs, health club, spa, beach, boating, jet skiing, volleyball, 4 bars, sports bar, video game room, shops, children's programs (ages 4–11), laundry facilities, laundry service, Internet, business services, meeting rooms* ⊟ *AE, D, DC, MC, V.*

$$–$$$$ ⌧ **Inn at the Bay.** In a three-story 1910 Victorian home, this charmer has four-poster beds and antique furniture in the guest rooms and suites. The Sailboat Suite has a fireplace and whirlpool bath. A nicely appointed tea room is the spot for afternoon tea with scones and finger sandwiches. The B&B is near downtown, a short distance from the museums and the Pier. ⊠ *126 4th Ave. NE, 33701* ☎ *727/822–1700 or 888/873–2122* ⊜ *727/896–7411* ⊕ *www.innatthebay.com* ⇋ *12 rooms* ♿ *Dining room, in-room data ports, in-room hot tubs, laundry facilities; no kids under 9* ⊟ *AE, D, DC, MC, V* ⦿ *BP.*

$–$$$ ⌧ **Island's End Resort.** These simply decorated one- and three-bedroom cottages have water views. Outdoors, attractive wooden walkways lead to latticework sitting areas and peaceful gazebos. The grounds are nicely landscaped; walk to the beach, restaurants, and shops. Grills are available if you want to barbecue. The small resort makes a great place for families who want to enjoy the beach life. ⊠ *1 Pass-A-Grille Way, St. Pete Beach 33706* ☎ *727/360–5023* ⊜ *727/367–7890* ⊕ *www.islandsend.com* ⇋ *6 cottages* ♿ *Kitchens, in-room VCRs, pool, fishing, laundry facilities* ⊟ *MC, V.*

$–$$$ ⌧ **Mansion House.** Built at the end of the 19th century, this charming wood-frame house is rumored to have been the home of the first mayor of St. Petersburg. The first and second floors of the bed-and-breakfast have five inviting, individually decorated rooms; the most appealing might be the Carriage Room, which has a cathedral ceiling and an old-fashioned four-poster bed. A pleasant 15-minute walk from the Pier, this B&B is also within walking distance of restaurants, shops, and art galleries. ⊠ *105 5th Ave., 33701* ☎ *727/821–9391* ⊜ *727/821–6906* ⊕ *www.mansionbandb.com* ⇋ *12 rooms* ♿ *Dining room, in-room data ports, library, meeting rooms* ⊟ *AE, MC, V* ⦿ *BP.*

¢–$ ⌧ **Beach Park Motel.** For downtown convenience, here's your place. Near the bay front and all its attractions, this humble motel is friendly and accommodating. A free shuttle runs to Tampa Bay Devil Ray home baseball games. ⊠ *300 Beach Dr. NE, 33701* ☎ *727/898–6325 or 800/657–7687* ⊜ *727/894–4226* ⊕ *www.florida-beach-motel.com*

🛏 *26 rooms* ♿ *Microwaves, refrigerators* ▭ *AE, DC, MC, V.*

Nightlife & the Arts

THE ARTS **American Stage** (✉ 211 3rd St. S ☎ 727/823–7529) performs in an intimate 130-setting theater. In April, it presents outdoor Shakespeare.

NIGHTLIFE **Carlie's** (✉ 7020 49th St. N ☎ 727/527–5214) is hopping practically every night, with plenty of dancing to live local bands. At the **Cha Cha Coconuts** (✉ The Pier ☎ 727/822–6655), crowds drop in to catch live contemporary music every night. **Coliseum Ballroom** (✉ 535 4th Ave. N ☎ 727/892–5202) has ballroom dancing and group lessons on some Wednesday afternoons and Saturday nights. Call ahead. Weekend crowds pack the noisy, boisterous **Joyland Country Music Night Club** (✉ 11225 U.S. 19 ☎ 727/573–1919). **Stormy's at the Hurricane** (✉ 807 Gulf Way, Pass-A-Grille Beach ☎ 727/360–9558) is a nice place to watch the sunset and then dance to music played by a DJ every Friday and Sunday.

Sports & the Outdoors

BASEBALL Hometown favorites, the **Tampa Bay Devil Rays** (✉ Tropicana Field, 1 Tropicana Dr., off I–275 ☎ 727/3250 or 888/326–7297 ⊕ www.devilrays.com) play under the air-conditioned dome. They hold their spring training at **Al Lang Stadium** (✉ 230 First St. S ☎ 727/898–7297).

DOG RACING Dog races are held January through June at **Derby Lane** (✉ 10490 Gandy Blvd. ☎ 727/812–3339 ⊕ www.derbylane.com).

GOLF Play 18 holes at **Mainlands Golf Course** (✉ 9445 Mainlands Blvd. W ☎ 727/577–4847). **Mangrove Bay Golf Course** (✉ 875 62nd Ave. NE ☎ 727/893–7800) has 18 holes and a driving range.

Shopping

One of the states's more notable bookstores is **Haslam's** (✉ 2025 Central Ave. ☎ 727/822–8616), a family-owned emporium that's been doing business just west of downtown St. Petersburg for almost 70 years. The store carries more than 300,000 volumes, from cutting-edge best-sellers to ancient tomes. If you value a good book or simply like to browse, you could easily spend an afternoon here. Designer boutiques, movie theaters, and trendy restaurants can be found at the downtown shopping plaza **BayWalk** (✉ 153 2nd Ave. N). **John's Pass Village and Boardwalk** (✉ 12901 Gulf Blvd., Madeira Beach) is a collection of shops and restaurants in an old-style fishing village, where you can pass the time watching pelicans cavorting and dive-bombing for food. A five-story structure on the bay front, the **Pier** (✉ 800 2nd Ave. NE), near the Museum of Fine Arts, looks like an inverted pyramid. Inside are numerous shops and eating spots. On weekends between 8 and 4, some 1,500 vendors set up a flea market on 125 acres at the **Wagonwheel** (✉ 7801 Park Blvd., Pinellas Park).

Clearwater

12 mi north of St. Petersburg.

This sprawling town has many residential areas and small shopping plazas. There's a semi-quaint downtown area on the mainland, but the draw is the beaches along the barrier islands offshore.

㉔ When pelicans become entangled in fishing lines, locals sometimes carry them to the nonprofit **Suncoast Seabird Sanctuary,** which is dedicated to the rescue, repair, recuperation, and release of sick and injured birds. At times there are between 500 and 600 land and sea birds in residence, including pelicans, egrets, herons, gulls, terns, sandhill cranes, hawks, owls, and cormorants. Many are kept in open-air pens while they recover. The sanctuary backs up to the Indian Rocks Beach. ✉ *18328 Gulf*

Blvd., Indian Shores ☎ 727/391–6211 ✍ *Donation welcome* ☉ *Daily 9–sunset; tours Wed. and Sun. at 2.*

㉕ **Indian Rocks Beach** (⊠ off Rte. 8, south of Clearwater Beach) tends to be a bit quieter and less crowded than Clearwater Beach.

㉖ South of Clearwater Beach, on Sand Key at Clearwater Pass, **Sand Key Park** (⊠ 1060 Gulf Blvd. ☎ 727/588–4852) has a lovely beach, plenty of green space, a playground, and picnic area.

㉗ The **Clearwater Marine Aquarium** is more than just a place to see exotic fish in a big glass tank—it's an opportunity to participate in the work of saving and caring for endangered marine species. Many of the sea turtles, dolphins, and other animals living at the aquarium were brought there to be rehabilitated from an injury or saved from danger. The aquarium conducts tours of the bays and islands around Clearwater, including a daily dolphin-watching jaunt on a pontoon boat and kayak tours of Clearwater Harbor and St. Joseph Sound. You can also sign on for a two- and four-day adventure to work with the staff on marine research programs. ⊠ *249 Windward Passage* ☎ 727/441–1790 ⊕ *www. cmaquarium.org* ✍ *$8.75* ☉ *Weekdays 9–5, Sat. 9–4, Sun. 11–4.*

㉘ Connected to downtown Clearwater by Memorial Causeway, **Clearwa-**
Fodor$Choice **ter Beach** (⊠ western end of State Rd. 60, 2 mi west of downtown Clear-
★ water) is on a narrow island between Clearwater Harbor and the gulf.
It's a popular hangout for teens and college students and has a widespread reputation for beach volleyball. There are lifeguards here as well as a marina, concessions, showers, and rest rooms. Around Pier 60 there's a big, modern playground. This is the site for a nightly sunset celebration complete with musicians and artisans. While one of the area's nicest and busiest beaches, it's also one of the costliest in terms of parking fees.

off the
beaten
path

Pinewood Cultural Park. Three out-of-the-way but worthwhile attractions grace this space. Florida Botanical Gardens (⊠ *12175 125th St. N, Largo* ☎ 727/582–2200 ⊕ *www.flbg.org* ✍ *Free* ☉ *Daily 7–6.*) welcomes you to 150 acres of native and exotic ornamental plants. Demonstrations teach environmentally friendly gardening techniques. More than 20 historic local structures gather at Heritage Village (⊠ *11909 125th St. N, Largo* ☎ 727/582–2123 ✍ *Free* ☉ *Tues.–Wed. and Fri.–Sat. 10–4, Thurs. 10–8, Sun. noon–4.*), including a log cabin and Victorian-era home. On the grounds, the Pinellas County Historical Museum traces local history back to prehistoric cultures. Gulf Coast Museum of Art (⊠ *12211 Walsingham Rd. Largo* ☎ 727/518–6833 ✍ *Free* ☉ *Tues.–Sat. 10–4, Sun. noon–4*) completes the complex with permanent showings of Florida artists and visiting exhibits.

Where to Stay & Eat

$$–$$$$ ✕ **The Lobster Pot.** The building is a little bit of faux Florida, built to look like an ancient mariner's shack. But the food is the real thing, and as the name implies, the specialty is lobster. There's Maine lobster, South African lobster tails, stuffed lobster, lobster thermidor . . . you get the idea. Other seafood delicacies complement the namesake crustacean, from local grouper to Alaskan king crab. ⊠ *17814 Gulf Blvd., Redington Shores* ☎ 727/391–8592 ⊟ *AE, DC, MC, V* ☉ *No lunch.*

$$–$$$ ✕ **The Grill at Feather Sound.** The clientele at this trendy eatery leans toward the upscale, but if you're a tourist in resort-casual dress you won't feel out of place. Eclectic menu offerings include seared tuna au poivre, house-smoked pork tenderloin with peach chutney, and chicken potpie with cream-cheese crust. Despite the name, the restaurant is not on an idyl-

lic estuary but a well-traveled commercial thoroughfare. ✉ *2325 Ulmerton Rd.* ☎ *727/571–3400* 🖃 *AE, D, DC, MC, V* 🕒 *Closed Sun.*

$$–$$$ ✕ **Kaiko Japanese Restaurant.** Step up to the counter or grab a table and settle down for some terrific Japanese food. Traditionally prepared sushi and *makimono* (rolled sushi) are specialties here, and the large appetizer menu gives you a chance to try lots of items, for instance, fried tofu, vegetable sushi, and sashimi. Entrées include teriyaki-grilled seafood, beef, and chicken and are accompanied by miso soup, a small salad, and rice. Try the fried ice cream for dessert. ✉ *7245 McMullen Booth Rd.* ☎ *727/791–6640* 🖃 *AE, MC, V* 🕒 *No lunch weekends.*

¢–$$$ ✕ **PJ's Oyster Bar.** Follow the crowds to this back-alley long-timer where rolls of paper towels spin overhead on wire hangers and beer flows freely. Seafood selections range from fried catfish to more elegant choices such as orange-glazed sushi-grade tuna. The all-day menu balances seafood with sandwiches and pastas. ✉ *500 1st St., Indian Rocks Beach* ☎ *727/ 596–5898* 🖃 *AE, MC, V.*

$$$–$$$$ 🏨 **Safety Harbor Resort & Spa.** The focus here is the 50,000-square-ft spa, with all the latest in therapies and treatments. The pleasant hamlet of Safety Harbor is also a point of interest with charming shops along the nearby main street. The resort originally was built over hot springs on Tampa Bay in 1926, but little of the original architecture remains. The springs still function, however, feeding into pools, the spa, and water coolers. The property has on-site golf and tennis academies, though golf courses are 5 mi away. ✉ *105. N Bayshore Dr., Safety Harbor 34695* ☎ *727/726–1161 or 800/237–8772* 🖷 *727/724–8772* ⊕ *www. safetyharborspa.com* 🛏 *189 rooms, 4 suites* ♤ *2 restaurants, in-room data ports, golf privileges, 9 tennis courts, 3 pools (1 indoor), aerobics, gym, spa, laundry facilities, laundry service, business services, meeting room* 🖃 *AE, D, DC, MC, V.*

$$$ 🏨 **Sheraton Sand Key Resort.** This is a supreme spot for those searching for sun, sand, and surf. On 10 well-manicured acres, the nine-story, T-shape resort has many rooms with excellent gulf views and others that look out over an adjacent park. All rooms have balconies or patios. Considered one of the top corporate meeting and convention hotels in the Clearwater area, it has amenities—such as a beautiful private beach—that make it ideal for leisure travelers, too. ✉ *1160 Gulf Blvd., Clearwater Beach 33767* ☎ *727/595–1611* 🖷 *727/596–8488* ⊕ *www. beachsand.com* 🛏 *375 rooms, 15 suites* ♤ *Restaurant, room service, some in-room data ports, some microwaves, some refrigerators, room TVs with video games, 3 tennis courts, pool, wading pool, health club, beach, windsurfing, boating, bar, playground* 🖃 *AE, DC, MC, V.*

★ $$–$$$ 🏨 **Belleview Biltmore Resort & Spa.** Built by railroad magnate Henry Plant, this huge 1896 Victorian resort looks like a *Great Gatsby* movie set. It is one of the world's largest wooden structures and is on the National Register of Historic Places. Units range from cozy little rooms to spacious suites that lie off long creaky corridors. The 21 acres overlook a narrow part of Clearwater Bay. The spa matches the Victorian opulence of the rest of the hotel, with the convenience of modern facilities. The hotel staff conducts daily historical tours. ✉ *25 Belleview Blvd., 33756* ☎ *727/373–3000 or 800/237–8947* 🖷 *727/441–4173* ⊕ *www. belleviewbiltmore.com* 🛏 *211 rooms, 33 suites* ♤ *3 restaurants, in-room data ports, 18-hole golf course, 4 tennis courts, 2 pools (1 indoor), health club, massage, spa, boating, bicycles, 2 bars, playground, business services, meeting rooms* 🖃 *AE, D, DC, MC, V.*

¢–$$$ 🏨 **Best Western Sea Wake Inn.** This white, concrete six-story hotel won't win any architectural awards, but it's right on the beach. Rooms are nicely decorated, and many have excellent views of the gulf. ✉ *691 S. Gulfview Blvd., 33967* ☎ *727/443–7652 or 888/329–8910* 🖷 *727/*

461–2836 ⊕ *www.seawake.com* ⇆ *110 rooms* ⌂ *Restaurant, room ser-vice, in-room data ports, in-room safes, microwaves, refrigerators, pool, beach, fishing, bar, lounge, playground, dry cleaning, laundry service, business services, meeting room, airport shuttle* ⊟ *AE, DC, MC, V.*

The Arts

Ruth Eckerd Hall (⊠ 1111 McMullen Booth Rd. ☎ 727/791–7400 ⊕ www.rutheckerdhall.com) hosts many national performers of ballet, opera, and pop, classical, or jazz music.

Sports & the Outdoors

BASEBALL The **Philadelphia Phillies** (⊠ Jack Russell Memorial Stadium, Seminole St. and Greenwood Ave. ☎ 727/441–8638) get ready for the season with spring training here. The stadium also hosts the Phillies' farm team, the Clearwater Phillies.

BIKING **Lou's Bicycle Center** (⊠ 8990 Seminole Blvd., Largo ☎ 727/398–2453) rents bikes, does quick repairs, and sells new bikes. There is an access point to the Pinellas Trail a couple of blocks west of Lou's on 8th Avenue Southwest.

The **Pinellas Trail** (⊕ www.co.pinellas.fl.us) is a 34-mi paved route that spans Pinellas County. Once a railway, the trail runs adjacent to major thoroughfares, no more than 10 ft from the roadway, so you can access the trail from almost any point. When completed around 2006, it will run 47 mi. You get the flavor of neighborhoods and an amalgam of sub-urbs along the way. The trail, also popular with in-line skaters, has spawned trailside businesses such as repair shops and health-food cafés. There are also many lovely rural areas to bike through and plenty of places to rent bikes. Be wary of traffic in downtown Clearwater and on the congested areas of the Pinellas Trail, which still needs more bridges for crossing over busy streets. To start riding from the south end of the trail, park at Trailhead Park (37th Street South at 8th Avenue South) in St. Petersburg. To ride south from the north end, park your car in downtown Tarpon Springs (East Tarpon Avenue at North Stafford Av-enue). The 2½-mi car-free **Friendship Trail** is part of the Pinellas Trail system. It's accessible from either Tampa or St. Petersburg, immediately adjacent to the Gandy Bridge.

GOLF **Clearwater Executive Golf Park** (⊠ 1875 Airport Dr. ☎ 727/447–5272) has 18 holes and a driving range. **Largo Municipal Golf Course** (⊠ 12500 131st St. N, Largo ☎ 727/518–3024) is an 18-hole course.

MINIATURE GOLF The live alligators advertised on the roadside sign for **Congo River Golf & Exploration Co.** (⊠ 20060 U.S. 19 N, Clearwater ☎ 727/797–4222) are not in the water traps, just in a small, fenced-off lagoon adjacent to the course. The reptiles do, however, add a Florida touch to this highly landscaped course tucked into a small parcel of land adjacent to Clear-water's busiest north–south thoroughfare.

TENNIS **Shipwatch Yacht & Tennis Club** (⊠ 11800 Shipwatch Dr., Largo ☎ 727/596–6862) has 11 clay courts, 2 of which are lighted for night play, and 2 hard courts.

Dunedin

🟢 *3 mi north of Clearwater.*

If the sound of bagpipes and the sight of men in kilts appeals to you, head to this town, named by two Scots in the 1880s. In March and April the Highland Games and in November the Celtic Festival pay tribute to the town's heritage. Dunedin also has a nicely restored historic down-town area—only about five blocks long—that has become a one-stop shopping area for antiques hunters and is also lined with gift shops and good, nonchain eateries.

Where to Eat

$–$$ ✕ **Bon Appetit.** Known for its creative fare, this restaurant has views of the Intracoastal Waterway and the gulf. European-trained chef-owners Peter Kreuziger and Karl Heinz Riedl change specials twice a month and offer salads and light entrées as well as such selections as broiled rack of lamb in herbal pecan crust and seafood mixed grill with vegetable rémoulade sauce. This is an excellent place to catch a sunset. ⊠ *148 Marina Plaza* ☎ *727/733–2151* ▭ *AE, MC, V.*

★ **$–$$** ✕ **Casa Tina.** The focus here is on vegetarian Mexican dishes. Try Casa Tina's versions of enchiladas (with veggies or chicken) or chiles rellenos, roasted cheese-stuffed peppers. Cactus salad is a dish to tell the folks about back home. It won't prick your tongue, but the tantalizing flavor created by tender pieces of cactus, cilantro, tomatoes, onions, lime, and *queso fresco* (a mild white cheese) might prick your taste buds. The place is often crowded, and service can be slow, but it's worth it. ⊠ *369 Main St.* ☎ *727/734–9226* ▭ *AE, D, DC, MC, V* ⊙ *Closed Mon.*

$–$$ ✕ **Sea Sea Riders.** In a pleasant old bungalow with a breezy patio that's enclosed and air-conditioned in summer, this seafood eatery has an eclectic menu that includes pasta dishes and homemade chili. Cornmeal-fried catfish and grouper cheek paella are among the best entrées. The homemade cheesecake is worthy as well. Sunday brunch includes great omelets and fresh seafood. ⊠ *221 Main St.* ☎ *727/734–1445* ▭ *AE, MC, V.*

off the beaten path

Caladesi Island and Honeymoon Island State Parks. Sharing an entrance and a parking lot, these two parks are just a few hundred yards from one another. However, whereas Honeymoon Island is right where you park, Caladesi Island is off the coast across Hurricane Pass and is accessible only by boat. One of Florida's few undeveloped barrier islands, 600-acre Caladesi Island has a beach on the gulf side, mangroves on the bay side, and a self-guided nature trail winding through the island's interior. Because it is so popular with locals, most of whom have their own boats, don't expect it to feel secluded on weekends. Park rangers are available to answer questions. A good spot for swimming, fishing, shelling, boating, and studying nature, the park has boardwalks, picnic shelters, bathhouses, and a concession stand. If you want to skip the ferry ride to Caladesi Island stay at Honeymoon Island, also an excellent state park but with a less spectacular beach. It has the same elements as Caladesi, but a bridge connects it to the mainland. The park has the only section of beach north of Venice where it's okay to bring your pets—on a leash. ⊠ *Dunedin Causeway to Honeymoon Island, then board ferry* ☎ *727/734–5263 for ferry information; 727/469–5918 for parks information* ▤ *Honeymoon $4 per car, ferry $7* ⊙ *Daily 8–sunset; ferry hourly 10–5 in fair weather.*

Sports & the Outdoors

BASEBALL The **Toronto Blue Jays** (⊠ Grant Field, 373 Douglas Ave., north of Rte. 88 ☎ 727/733–9302) hold about 18 spring training games here in March.

GOLF **Dunedin Country Club** (⊠ 1050 Palm Blvd. ☎ 727/733–7836) has 18 holes, a driving range, and a pro shop.

Tarpon Springs

10 mi north of Dunedin.

Tucked into a little harbor at the mouth of the Anclote River, this growing town was settled by Greek immigrants at the end of the 19th century. They came to practice their generations-old craft of sponge diving. Although bacterial and market forces seriously hurt the industry in the '40s, today sponging has returned, but mostly as a focal point for tourism. The docks along Dodecanese Boulevard, the main waterfront street, are filled with quaint old buildings with shops and eateries. Tarpon Springs' other key street is Tarpon Avenue, about a mile south of Dodecanese. This old central business district has become a hub for antiques hunters. The influence of the Greek culture is omnipresent; the community's biggest celebration is the annual Greek Orthodox Epiphany Celebration in January, in which teenage boys dive for a golden cross in Spring Bayou, a few blocks from Tarpon Avenue, during a ceremony followed by a street festival in the town's central business district.

㉛ Don't miss **St. Nicholas Greek Orthodox Church,** which is a replica of St. Sophia's in Istanbul and an excellent example of New Byzantine architecture. ✉ *36 N. Pinellas Ave.* ☎ *727/937–3540* ✎ *Donation suggested* ☉ *Daily 9–5.*

㉜ **Spongeorama** is a museum and cultural center that reveals more than you ever imagined about how a lowly sea creature, the sponge, created the industry that built this quaint little sponging village. See a film about these much-sought-after creatures from the phylum *porifera* and how they helped the town to prosper at the turn of the last century. There's also a free dive show. You'll come away converted to (and loaded up with) natural sponges and loofahs. ✉ *510 Dodecanese Blvd., off Rte. 19* ☎ *727/943–9498* ✎ *Free* ☉ *Mon.–Sat. 10:30–6, Sun. 11:30–6.*

㉚ The **Konger Tarpon Springs Aquarium** is a privately owned attraction not nearly as extensive as the big aquariums in Tampa or Clearwater, but it's got some good exhibits, including a 120,000-gallon shark tank with a living coral reef inside. Divers feed the sharks in a show performed several times a day. There's also a baby shark and stingray feeding tank, in which you can feed them yourself—without going in the water, of course. The fresh-water tank has some aggressive little fish you won't find in any Florida river or stream—piranha from the Amazon. ✉ *850 Dodecanese Blvd.* ☎ *727/938–5378* ✎ *$4.75* ☉ *Daily 10–5.*

㉝ **Sunset Beach** (✉ Gulf Rd.) is a small public beach with rest rooms, picnic tables, grills, and a boat ramp.

㉞ **Howard Park Beach** (✉ Sunset Dr.) comes in two parts: a shady mainland picnicking area and white-sand beach island. The causeway is a popular hangout for windsurfers. The park has rest rooms, picnic tables, and grills.

Where to Stay & Eat

$–$$$ ✗ **Louis Pappas' Riverside Restaurant.** Though a bit institutional, this waterside restaurant allows a great view of the Anclote River and docks. Well-prepared dishes include moussaka, chicken *spanakopita* (grilled chicken over feta and spinach with marinara sauce), and *dolmades* (grape leaves stuffed with rice and ground lamb). Grilled octopus is a more esoteric Greek specialty. There's an excellent selection of Florida classics such as stuffed shrimp and grouper. Or go Italian with the chicken Alfredo or marsala. ✉ *10 W. Dodecanese Blvd.* ☎ *727/937–5101* ⊕ *www.louispappas.com* ⊟ *AE, DC, MC, V* ☉ *No lunch Sun.*

$–$$ ✗ **Bridie Gannon's Pub & Eatery.** In a town known for its Greek food, you might think it's a mistake to go to an Irish pub, but as soon as the hot, fresh Irish soda bread gets to your table, you know you've made a good choice. The menu includes classic Irish dishes such as bangers and mash, corned beef and cabbage, and shepherd's pie but also satisfies seafood cravings with grouper piccata and grilled mahi with jalapeño pineapple sauce. There's Guinness on tap, and live Irish music on week-

BOBBING FOR SPONGES

ANIMALS THAT SWIM *or slither their way through Florida's semitropical waters have a vaunted place in state folklore. Several have been chosen as team mascots—the Miami Dolphins, Florida Marlins, and the University of Florida Gators, to name a few—a sign of the impact these animals have had on the state. But no aquatic creature has had a greater impact on the Tampa Bay area than the sponge.*

Unlike the reputedly intelligent dolphin, the sponge is no genius. It's hard to be smart when you consist of only one cell. The sponge that divers retrieve from the seabed, or perhaps the one you reach for in the shower, is actually a colony of millions of the one-cell organisms bound together in an organic matrix that makes up a soft, flexible lump.

As you learn if you check out Tarpon Springs' aging and modest Spongeorama, sponge diving predates the birth of Christ, and the first Greek sponge seekers actually worshiped the god Poseidon. For the past millennium or so, most spongers have been devoutly Greek Orthodox, and today many sponge boats carry a small shrine to St. Nicholas, the patron saint of mariners. The divers' deep devotion to their religion—and to Greek culture— resulted in the development of Tampa Bay's own little Greek village.

Sponge gathering actually began in the Florida Keys circa 1850, but it gained momentum around Tampa Bay after 1905, when George Cocoris brought to Florida the first mechanical diving apparatus, complete with a brass-helmeted diving suit and pump system that enabled divers to stay in 75–100 ft of water for two hours at a time. Cocoris and those who worked with him soon discovered a particularly marketable type of sponge: the Rock Island wool sponge, so named because it resembles fine wool and is found in abundance around Rock Island, off Florida's west coast. When word of Cocoris's success got back to Greece, more sponge-diving families headed west, and within a decade or so, several thousand of his fellow Greeks had settled

around Tarpon Springs to share in its prosperity.

By the 1930s, Tarpon Springs was the largest U.S. sponging port, but in the late '40s and early '50s a sponge blight and the growing popularity of synthetic sponges nearly wiped out the local industry. Still, the hardy Greeks held on. They discovered that tourists were drawn more by the town's Hellenic culture than by the sponges sold in the dockside markets. In the ensuing 40 years Tarpon Springs' waterfront area has been turned into a delightful tourist district filled with Greek restaurants, Greek pastry shops, and Greek art galleries. And should you choose to see divers pull sponges from the seabed, you can book passage on one of the glass-bottom boats that leave hourly from the town docks.

And so the town owes its success to the humble sponge. Yet although you'll find bronze statues of sponge divers, with the exception of Spongeorama there is no tribute to the monocellular creature itself. Perhaps a future Florida sports team will choose the "Fightin' Sponges" as its mascot.

— Rowland Stiteler

end nights. ⊠ *200 Tarpon Springs Ave., Palm Harbor* ☎ *727/942–3011* ⊕ *www.bridiegannons.com* ▭ *AE, MC, V* ⊘ *Closed Mon.*

$
Fodor'sChoice
★
✕ **Leo's Pizza.** Because of its unspectacular name, it's easy to walk right past Leo's. That would be a mistake. It's a slice of New York City transplanted to Florida. The pizza is wonderful, but entrées like the chicken cacciatore and sausage-and-peppers parmigiana are nothing short of incredible. The best dish might be the grouper *française,* battered and sautéed with lemon butter and white wine and served over linguine. Finish with an exquisite Italian cheesecake. ⊠ *2900 Alt. U.S. 19, Palm Harbor* ☎ *727/ 781–3456* ▭ *AE, MC, V.*

★ $$$$
⊞ **Westin Innisbrook Resort.** A massive pool complex with a 15-ft water slide and sand beach are highlights of this sprawling, 1,100-acre resort. Grounds are beautifully maintained, and guest suites are in 28 two-story lodges tucked in the trees between golf courses. Some of the roomy junior, one- and two-bedroom suites have balconies or patios. Once fairly remote, the Innisbrook has built in enough restaurants and lounges to make it self-contained, though today the area around it offers plenty of competition. The children's program is excellent. ⊠ *36750 U.S. 19 N, Palm Harbor 34684* ☎ *727/942–2000 or 877/752–1480* 🖨 *727/942– 5576* ⊕ *www.westin-innisbrook.com* ⟿ *600 suites* ⚲ *4 restaurants, in-room data ports, in-room safes, some kitchenettes, minibars, driving range, 4 18-hole golf courses, miniature golf, putting green, 11 tennis courts, pro shop, 6 pools, outdoor hot tub, health club, beach, bicycles, massage, racquetball, 5 bars, nightclub, children's programs (ages 3–12), playground, dry cleaning, laundry service, concierge, business services, meeting rooms, airport shuttle, car rental* ▭ *AE, DC, MC, V.*

¢
⊞ **Tarpon Inn.** On the grounds of a historic inn by the same name, this newer incarnation has only that in common with its namesake. Its location within steps of Spring Bayou and the downtown historic district and its affordability are its greatest assets. ⊠ *110 W. Tarpon Ave., Tarpon Springs 34689* ☎ *727/937–6121* 🖨 *727/942–2569* ⟿ *23 rooms, 23 efficiencies* ⚲ *Some kitchenettes, pool, laundry facilities, laundry service* ▭ *AE, MC, V.*

Sports & the Outdoors

Westin Innisbrook Resort (⊠ U.S. 19 ☎ 727/942–2000) has 72 holes of golf, driving ranges, and putting greens; it will also arrange off-property sports like deep-sea fishing. If all four courses are full, the resort can make arrangements for you at an affiliated property.

THE MANATEE COAST

The coastal area north of Tampa is sometimes called the Manatee Coast, and aptly so. Of these gentle vegetarian water mammals, distantly related to elephants, only 2,600 are alive today, and they are threatened by development and speeding motorboats. In fact, many manatees that survive today have massive scars on their backs from run-ins with boat propellers. Extensive nature preserves and parks have been created to protect them and other wildlife indigenous to the area, and these are among the best spots to view manatees in the wild. Although they are far from mythical beauties, it is believed that manatees inspired ancient mariners' tales of mermaids. U.S. 19 is the prime route through rural manatee country, and traffic flows freely once you've left the congestion of St. Petersburg, Clearwater, and Port Richey. If you are planning a day trip from the bay area, pack a picnic lunch before leaving, since most of the sights are outdoors.

Weeki Wachee

27 mi north of Tarpon Springs.

35 **Weeki Wachee Spring** flows at the remarkable rate of 170 million gallons a day with a constant temperature of 74°F. The spring has long been famous for its live "mermaids," clearly not the work of Mother Nature, as they wear bright costumes and put on an Esther Williams–like underwater choreography show that's been virtually unchanged in the more than 50 years the park has been open. Snorkel tours and canoe trips are available in the river, and a wilderness boat ride gives an up-close look at raccoons, otters, egrets, and the other semi-tropical Florida wetlands wildlife. There's also a petting zoo and an exotic-birds-of-prey show. In summer, Buccaneer Bay water park opens for swimming, beaching, and riding its thrilling slides and flumes. ✉ *U.S. 19 and Rte. 50* ☎ *352/596–2062 or 877/469–3354* ⊕ *www.weekiwachee.com* ✎ *$16.95 Mar.–Oct., $12.95 Nov.–Feb.* ☉ *Daily 10–5 in summer (water park stays open until 6); shorter hrs in fall and winter.*

Where to Eat

¢–$ ✕**Backwaters.** For a bite to eat after seeing Weeki Wachi, head west on
Fodor'sChoice Route 50 and discover a path to Old Florida and tasty seafood. This
★ whimsically painted restaurant stretches far beyond its tableau of grouper and shrimp specialties with extensive pasta, chicken, meat, and sandwich offerings. Grouper prepared any of 10 ways, all of them exceedingly fresh, is a good bet. ✉ *6024 Cortez Blvd.* ☎ *352/597–5457* ▭ *AE, D, DC, MC, V.*

Sports & the Outdoors

The 47 holes at **World Woods Golf Club** (✉ 17590 Ponce de León Blvd., Brooksville ☎ 352/796–5500 ⊕ www.worldwoods.com) are some of the best in Florida. The club also has a 22-acre practice area with a four-sided driving range and a 2-acre putting course.

Homosassa Springs

20 mi north of Weeki Wachee.

36 At the **Homosassa Springs State Wildlife Park** see many manatees and species of fish through a floating glass observatory known as the Fish Bowl—except in this case the fish are outside the bowl and the people inside it. A walk along the park's paths leads you to excellent manatee, alligator, and other animal shows. Among the species are bobcats, western cougars, white-tailed deer, black bears, pelicans, herons, snowy egrets, river otters, and even a hippopotamus, a keepsake from the park's former days as an exotic-animal park. Boat cruises on the Homosassa River (which takes its name from a Creek Indian word meaning "place of many peppers") are available across Fish Bowl Drive from the entrance. There's a restaurant in the main reception building. ✉ *Fish Bowl Dr., 1 mi west of U.S. 19* ☎ *352/628–2311* ⊕ *www.citruscounty-fl.com/statepark1.cfm* ✎ *$7.95* ☉ *Daily 9–5:30.*

37 On the **Yulee Sugar Mill State Historic Site** are the ruined remains of a 150-year-old sugar mill and other buildings that were part of a 5,100-acre sugar plantation owned by Florida's first U.S. senator, David Levy Yulee. It makes for pleasant picnicking. ✉ *Rte. 490A* ☎ *352/795–3817* ✎ *Free* ☉ *Daily dawn–dusk.*

Where to Stay & Eat

$–$$$ ✕**Charlie Brown's Crab House** There's no secret what the specialty is here; buy blue crabs by the bucketful at this Old Florida eatery on the river.

Cajun crawfish, mussels, catfish, shrimp, pasta, and prime rib fill the bill. Breakfast is southern-style. From the windows, watch the monkeys—escapees from the wildlife park—swinging around their own private island. ⊠ *Homosassa Riverside Resort, 5297 S. Cherokee Way* ☎ *352/ 628–2474* ⊕ *www.riversideresorts.com* ⊟ *AE, D, MC, V.*

$ 🖵 **Park Inn Homosassa.** Immediately adjacent to the Homosassa Springs State Wildlife Park, this simple motor inn has king-size beds in most rooms. ⊠ *4076 Hwy. 19, 34446* ☎ *352/628–4311* 🖶 *352/628–0650* 🖘 *104 rooms* ⟂ *Restaurant, 4 tennis courts, pool, bar, comedy club, playground, some pets allowed (fee)* ⊟ *AE, D, DC, MC, V* 🍴 *CP.*

¢–$ 🖵 **Homosassa Riverside Resort.** Five villas with multiple guest rooms fill this big (by Homosassa standards) complex. There's a marina with boat and scuba-equipment rentals, a restaurant and bar that overlook the river, and an island where monkeys cavort in the trees. Resort grounds cover 9 acres of semitropical forest along the riverfront. ⊠ *5279 Cherokee Way, 34448* ☎ *352/628–2474 or 800/442–2040* 🖶 *352/ 628–5208* ⊕ *www.riversideresorts.com* 🖘 *75 rooms* ⟂ *Some kitchens, some microwaves, some refrigerators, boating, marina, bar, laundry facilities* ⊟ *AE, D, MC, V.*

¢ 🖵 **Homosassa River Retreat.** On the bank of the Homosassa River, with two docks and nearby boat and pontoon rentals, this resort of one- and two-bedroom cottages is not much to look at but well situated for outdoor adventuring. Minimum stay sometimes is required. ⊠ *10605 Hall's River Rd., 34446* ☎ *352/628–7072* 🖘 *9 cottages* ⟂ *Kitchens, dock, laundry facilities* ⊟ *DC, MC, V.*

¢ 🖵 **MacRae's.** Fishing aficionados pick this fixture in the Homosassa lodge scene. Simple rooms occupy one-story structures built to look like log cabins. Efficiencies contain full kitchens. The focus is the riverside marina, complete with boat rentals, bait shop, and fishing charters. ⊠ *5300 Cherokee Way, 34487* ☎ *352/628–2602* 🖘 *12 rooms, 10 efficiencies* ⟂ *Restaurant, some kitchens, some microwaves, boating, marina, bar, laundry facilities* ⊟ *AE, D, MC, V.*

Crystal River

7 mi north of Homosassa Springs.

❸❽ The **Crystal River National Wildlife Refuge** is a U.S. Fish and Wildlife Service sanctuary for the endangered manatee. The main spring, around which manatees congregate in winter (generally from November to March), feeds crystal-clear water into the river at 72°F year-round. This is one of the best sure-bet places to see manatees in winter, since more than 100 typically congregate at this 40-acre refuge, which includes the spring that forms the headwaters of the Crystal River. The small visitor center has displays that inform about the manatee and other refuge inhabitants. In warmer months, when manatees scatter, the main spring is fun for a swim. Manatees are totally harmless, but touching them violates state law and you could get a ticket for doing so. Though accessible only by boat, the refuge provides neither tours nor boat rentals. For these, contact marinas in the town of Crystal River, such as the **American Pro Diving Center** (☎ 352/563–0041 or 800/291–3483 ⊕ www. americanprodiving.com) or the **Crystal Lodge Dive Center** (☎ 352/ 795–6798 ⊕ www.manatee-central.com). ⊠ *1502 S. Kings Bay Dr.* ☎ *352/563–2088* 🎫 *Free* ⊙ *Weekdays 9–4.*

Where to Stay & Eat

¢–$ ✕ **Charlie's Fish House Restaurant.** This popular, bright, and modern seafood place on the water serves fish caught locally, plus oysters, stone crab claws (in season), and shrimp. It's accessible by boat. ⊠ *224 U.S. 19 N* ☎ *352/795–3949* ⊟ *AE, MC, V.*

$–$$$ 🏨 **Plantation Inn & Golf Resort.** On the shore of Kings Bay, this two-story plantation-style resort is on 232 acres near several nature preserves and rivers. Although the exterior of the resort looks like a huge southern mansion, the rooms are more comfortable than palatial, with blond-wood furniture and wall-to-wall carpeting. Some rooms have patios. Condos and villas have views of the golf course. ⊠ *9301 W. Fort Island Trail, 34429* ☎ *352/795–4211 or 800/632–6262* ⊞ *352/795–1368* ⊕ *www. plantationinn.com* ⬎ *126 rooms, 2 suites, 5 condos, 12 villas* ⬧ *Dining room, grill, in-room data ports, some kitchens, refrigerators, driving range, 27-hole golf course, putting green, 2 tennis courts, pool, sauna, dive shop, boating, marina, fishing, croquet, horseshoes, shuffleboard, volleyball, bar, shop, business services* ⊟ *AE, DC, MC, V.*

¢–$ 🏨 **Best Western Crystal River Resort.** Divers favor this cinder-block roadside motel close to Kings Bay and its manatee population. Dive boats depart for scuba and snorkeling excursions from the marina. Rooms are nestled under large oak trees that make the place feel like the Old South. ⊠ *614 N.W. U.S. 19, 34428* ☎ *352/795–3171 or 800/435–4409* ⊞ *352/ 795–3179* ⊕ *www.seawake.com* ⬎ *114 rooms, 18 efficiencies* ⬧ *Restaurant, some kitchenettes, pool, outdoor hot tub, dive shop, dock, snorkeling, boating, bar, shops, laundry service, meeting room, airport shuttle* ⊟ *AE, DC, MC, V.*

Sports & the Outdoors

GOLF The **Plantation Inn & Golf Resort** (⊠ 9301 W. Fort Island Trail ☎ 352/ 795–7211), open to the public, has 27 holes, a lighted driving range, and a putting green.

Cedar Key

57 mi northwest of Crystal River; from U.S. 19, follow Rte. 24 southwest to the end.

Up in the area known as the Big Bend, Florida's long, curving coastline north of Tampa, you won't find many beaches. You will find an idyllic collection of small cays and a little island village tucked in among the marshes and scenic streams feeding the Gulf of Mexico. Once a strategic port for the Confederate States of America, remote Cedar Key is today a commercial fishing and clamming center. Change is in the air, however. Though the town used to be a well-kept secret with sparse tourism, it's becoming increasingly popular as a getaway, thanks in part to the spring arts festival and fall seafood festival, which take over the streets of the rustic downtown area. Today there are no fewer than a dozen commercial galleries, a sign that Cedar Key is now attracting travelers who carry platinum credit cards. It's also become a favorite of the college crowd, as it's only an hour from the main campus of the University of Florida in Gainesville. The upside of this popularity is that creative bars and restaurants keep popping up; several are on a Cannery Row–style pier a block from downtown.

③⑨ The **Cedar Key Historical Society Museum,** in an 1871 home, displays photographs dating back to 1850, Native American artifacts, and exhibits that focus on the area's development. ⊠ *Rte. 24 and 2nd St.* ☎ *352/ 543–5549* 🎫 *$1* ⊙ *Daily 11–4 (hrs vary with seasons).*

Where to Stay & Eat

$–$$$ ✕ **Island Room.** Like virtually every other downtown restaurant, this place in a waterfront condo complex has a good gulf view and focuses on seafood. Excellent upscale cuisine includes such treats as grouper *pic-*

cata (cooked in white wine and lemon juice), linguine *alla vongole* (with fresh herbs, garlic, and local clams sautéed in oil), and a very worthy crab bisque. Saturday, the restaurant opens at 2 and offers a luncheon special in addition to the regular menu; Sunday mornings, it serves brunch. ⊠ *Cedar Cove Beach and Yacht Club, 10 E. 2nd St.* ☎ *352/543–6520* ⊟ *AE, D, MC, V.*

$ ✕ **Captain's Table.** If you're looking for a good old-fashioned fish house, head to this salty spot on the dock with a view of the gulf waters that produced its menu. Have your mullet, grouper, shrimp, and oysters fried or broiled, or try one of the house seafood specialties such as pasta and clams or scallop bake in a rich cream sauce with mushrooms. ⊠ *On the dock* ☎ *352/543–5441* ⊟ *MC, V* ⊘ *Closed Tues.*

$–$$ 🏨 **Island Hotel.** Having enjoyed its heyday during the Confederacy, this 140-year-old property is now on the National Register of Historic Places and has been carefully restored to reflect what it was like a century ago. Rooms have antique furnishings and claw-foot bathtubs. The cooked-to-order breakfast includes a hot specialty item and toasted poppy-seed bread. The small restaurant, which fills up quickly at dinner, serves dishes made from local seafood. Management prohibits children during holiday and festival weekends. ⊠ *373 2nd St., 32625* ☎ *352/543–5111 or 800/432–4640* 🖷 *352/543–6949* ⊕ *www.islandhotel-cedarkey.com* ⇌ *13 rooms* ⚭ *Restaurant, bar, piano; no room phones, no room TV in some rooms, no smoking* ⊟ *MC, V* ⦿ *BP.*

$–$$ 🏨 **Island Place.** Gulf views are the big attraction at this waterfront condo-style hotel, and all the guest rooms have them. The suites, which have either one bedroom and one bath or two bedrooms and two baths, are set up for those who might want to stay in this lovely town a while. They come with dining-room areas; the kitchens have dishwashers. ⊠ *1st and C Sts., 32625* ☎ *352/543–5307 or 800/780–6522* ⊕ *www.islandplace-ck.com* ⇌ *30 suites* ⚭ *Kitchens, refrigerators, pool, outdoor hot tub, sauna, laundry facilities* ⊟ *MC, V.*

¢ 🏨 **Faraway Inn.** Cheery stucco cottages, efficiencies, and motel rooms accommodate at this typical Old Cedar Key establishment on the gulf. It's made for escaping and fishing. ⊠ *3rd and G Sts., 32625* ☎ *352/543–5330 or 888/543–5330* 🖷 *352/543–5523* ⊕ *www.farawayinn.com* ⇌ *5 rooms, 2 efficiencies, 5 cottages* ⚭ *Some kitchens, some microwaves, some refrigerators, beach, boating, bicycles, some pets allowed (fee)* ⊟ *MC, V.*

SOUTH OF TAMPA BAY

Bradenton and Sarasota anchor the southern end of Tampa Bay. A string of barrier islands borders the two cities with fine beaches. Sarasota County has 35 mi of gulf beaches, as well as two state parks, 22 municipal parks, and more than 30 golf courses, many open to the public. Sarasota has a thriving cultural scene, thanks mostly to circus magnate John Ringling, who chose this area for the winter home of his circus and his family. Bradenton, to the north, maintains a lower profile, while Venice, a few miles south on the Gulf Coast, claims beaches known for their prehistoric sharks' teeth.

Bradenton

49 mi south of Tampa.

This city on the Manatee River has some 20 mi of beaches and is well situated for access to fishing, both fresh- and saltwater. It also has its share of golf courses and historic sites dating to the mid-1800s.

40 The **Manatee Village Historical Park** is the real thing. It consists of an 1860 courthouse, 1887 church, 1903 general store and museum, and 1912 settler's home. The Old Manatee Cemetery, which dates to 1850, has graves of early Manatee County settlers. An appointment is necessary for a cemetery tour. ⊠ *Rte. 64 at 15th St. E* ☎ *941/749–7165* 📠 *Free* ☉ *Weekdays 9–4:30, Sun. 1:30–4:30.*

41 Florida history showcased at the **South Florida Museum and Parker Manatee Aquarium** includes state-of-the-art Native American culture displays, prehistoric artifacts and casts, and a collection of vignettes depicting eras past in South Florida. Snooty, the oldest living manatee in captivity, lives here. He shakes hands and performs other behaviors at feeding time in his 60,000-gallon home. ⊠ *201 10th St.* ☎ *941/746–4132* ⊕ *www.sfmbp.com* 📠 *$9.50* ☉ *Jan.–Apr. and July, daily 10–5; May–June and Aug.–Dec., Tues.–Sat. 10–5, Sun. noon–5.*

Hernando de Soto, one of the first Spanish explorers, set foot in Florida in 1539 near what is now Bradenton; that feat is commemorated at the ★ **42 De Soto National Memorial.** In the high season (late December–early April) park employees dressed in 16th-century costumes demonstrate period weapons and show how European explorers prepared and preserved food for their journeys over the untamed land. A film, exhibits, and a short nature trail into the mangroves and along the shoreline are contained on the grounds. ⊠ *75th St. NW* ☎ *941/792–0458* 📠 *Free* ☉ *Visitor center daily 9–5, grounds daily dawn–dusk.*

43 **Anna Maria Island,** Bradenton's barrier island to the west, has a number of worthwhile beaches. Manatee Avenue connects the mainland to the island via the **Palma Sola Causeway,** adjacent to which is a long, sandy beach fronting Palma Sola Bay. There are boat ramps, a dock, and picnic tables. **Anna Maria Bayfront Park** (⊠ N. Bay Blvd., adjacent to a municipal pier) is a secluded beach fronting both the Intracoastal Waterway and the Gulf of Mexico. Facilities include picnic grounds, a playground, rest rooms, showers, and lifeguards. In the middle of the island, **Manatee County Beach** (⊠ Gulf Dr. at 44th St., Holmes Beach) is popular with all ages. It has picnic facilities, a snack bar, showers, rest rooms, and lifeguards. **Cortez Beach** (⊠ Gulf Blvd., Bradenton Beach) is popular with those who like their beaches without facilities—nothing but sand, water, and trees. Singles and families flock to **Coquina Beach,** at the southern end of the island. There are lifeguards here, as well as a picnic area, boat ramp, playground, refreshment stand, rest rooms, and showers. Just across the inlet on the northern tip of Longboat Key, **Greer Island Beach** is accessible by boat or via North Shore Boulevard. The secluded peninsula has a wide beach and excellent shelling but no facilities.

> **off the beaten path**
>
> **Gamble Plantation Historical State Park.** Built in 1850, this, the only pre–Civil War plantation house in South Florida, still displays some of the original furnishings. The Confederate secretary of state took refuge here when the Confederacy fell to Union forces. ⊠ *3708 Patten Ave., Ellenton* ☎ *941/723–4536* 📠 *$4* ☉ *Thurs.–Mon. 8–5; tours at 9:30, 10:30, 1, 2, 3, and 4.*

Where to Stay & Eat

★ ¢–$$$ ✕ **Crab Trap and Crab Trap II.** Rustic furnishings, ultrafresh seafood, gator tail, and wild pig are among the trademarks of this casual two-house chain. Crab cakes and three-crab soup are excellent choices. The extensive menu also sways to the exotic with ostrich, octopus, kangaroo, and African rock lobster. ⊠ *U.S. 19 at Terra Ceia Bridge, Palmetto*

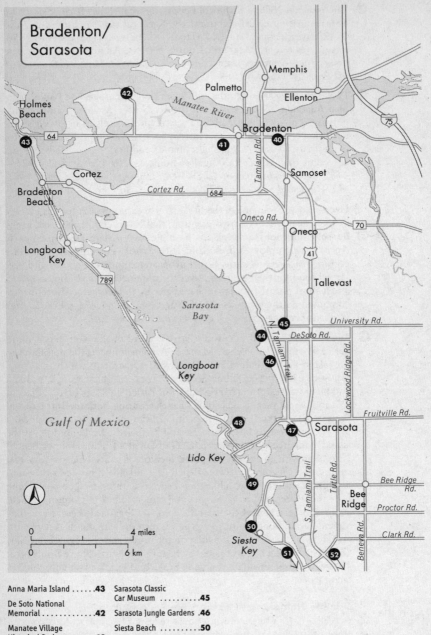

Bradenton/ Sarasota

Memphis

Palmetto

Ellenton

Manatee River

75

Holmes Beach

42

64

43

41

Bradenton

40

Samoset

Cortez

Cortez Rd.

684

Tamiami Rd.

Bradenton Beach

Oneco Rd.

Oneco

70

41

Longboat Key

789

Tallevast

Sarasota Bay

University Rd.

45

DeSoto Rd.

44

Tamiami Trail

46

Longboat Key

Lockwood Ridge Rd.

Fruitville Rd.

Gulf of Mexico

48

47

Sarasota

Lido Key

S. Tamiami Trail

49

Turtle Rd.

Bee Ridge

Bee Ridge Rd.

0   4 miles
0   6 km

50

Siesta Key

51

52

Proctor Rd.

Clark Rd.

Beneva Rd.

☎ *941/722–6255* ✉ *4815 17th St. E, Ellenton* ☎ *941/729–7777* 🖋 *No reservations* ▤ *D, MC, V.*

¢–$ ✕ **Gulf Drive Café.** Especially popular for breakfast (served all day), this unassuming landmark squats on the beach and serves cheap sit-down eats: mostly sandwiches, but also a sampling of entrées after 4 PM. ✉ *900 Gulf Dr., Bradenton Beach* ☎ *941/778–1919* ▤ *D, MC, V.*

★ $$$–$$$$ 🏨 **BridgeWalk.** An all-in-one beachfront resort on Bradenton Beach's historic street, the BridgeWalk sits across the road from the beach. It has one- and two-bedroom suites (it calls them "apartos"), with whirlpool baths, granite countertops, and terra-cotta tile floors, and town houses with electric fireplaces. The suites range in size from 750 to 1,650 square ft. The handsome tin-roof multicolored resort is within walking distance of a pier that's popular for fishing and strolling, as well as restaurants and shops, including some on-property. Minimum stays may be required during high season (February through April). ✉ *100 Bridge St., Bradenton Beach 34217* ☎ *941/779–2545 or 866/779–2545* 🖨 *941/779–0828* ⊕ *www.silverresorts.com* ➥ *28 suites* ♨ *Restaurant, room service, in-room data ports, some kitchenettes, some kitchens, pool, massage, spa, bar, shops, dry cleaning, laundry facilities, laundry service, meeting rooms* ▤ *AE, DC, MC, V.*

$$ 🏨 **Silver Surf Gulf Beach Resort.** It's hard to beat the location of this terra-cotta–color two-story hotel. The beach and heated pool are right out front, and many restaurants are nearby. Rooms are comfortable, and many have great ocean views. ✉ *1301 Gulf Dr., Bradenton Beach 34217* ☎ *941/778–6626* 🖨 *941/778–4308,* ⊕ *www.silverresorts.com* ➥ *49 rooms, 36 suites* ♨ *Picnic area, some kitchens, minibars, some microwaves, some refrigerators, pool, beach, bicycles, shuffleboard, volleyball, laundry facilities* ▤ *AE, MC, V.*

$–$$ 🏨 **Holiday Inn Riverfront.** Near the Manatee River, this Spanish Mediterranean–style motor inn is easily accessible from I–75 and U.S. 41. Every room has its own balcony, many overlooking the river. ✉ *100 Riverfront Dr. W, 34205* ☎ *941/747–3727* 🖨 *941/746–4289* ➥ *96 rooms, 57 suites* ♨ *Restaurant, grill, room service, in-room data ports, some minibars, some refrigerators, pool, gym, bar, dry cleaning, laundry service, business services* ▤ *AE, DC, MC, V.*

¢–$ 🏨 **Super 8 Motel–Bradenton.** On a commercial strip convenient to the airport and budget-priced, this 47-unit motor inn is well run and attractive. ✉ *6516 14th St. W, 34207* ☎ *941/756–6656 or 800/800–8000* 🖨 *941/758–3847* ➥ *47 rooms* ♨ *Pool, laundry facilities* ▤ *AE, D, MC, V* ⦿ *CP.*

Sports & the Outdoors

BASEBALL The **Pittsburgh Pirates** (✉ McKechnie Field, 17th Ave. W and 9th St. ☎ 941/748–4610) have spring training in March.

BIKING **Ringling Bicycles** (✉ 3606 Manatee Ave. W ☎ 941/749–1442) rents racing bicycles starting at $10 a day, $30 a week.

GOLF The excellent county-owned 18-hole **Buffalo Creek Golf Course** (✉ 8100 Erie Rd., Palmetto ☎ 941/776–2611), designed by Ron Garl, resembles a Scottish links course. **Manatee County Golf Course** (✉ 6415 53rd Ave. W ☎ 941/792–6773) has a driving range and 18 holes of golf. **Peridia Golf & Country Club** (✉ 4950 Peridia Blvd. ☎ 941/753–9097), an executive course, has 18 holes and a driving range.

Shopping

Find discount factory-outlet bargains at **Ellenton Prime Outlets** (✉ 5461 Factory Shops Blvd., off I–75 Exit 224 ☎ 888/260–7608), with more than 135 name-brand and other stores. The **Red Barn** (✉ 1707 1st St. E, ☎ 941/747–3794 or 800/274–3532) is a flea market in the requisite

big red barn. A few vendors do business during the week (Tuesday
through Sunday 9–4), but on Wednesdays and weekends the number of
vendors skyrockets to more than 600, and many open as early as 8.

Sarasota

16 mi south of Bradenton.

A sophisticated resort town, Sarasota is traditionally the home of some
ultra-affluent residents, dating back to John Ringling of circus fame. Cultural events are scheduled year-round, and there is a higher concentration of upscale shops, restaurants, and hotels than in much of the rest
of the Tampa Bay area. Across the water from Sarasota lie the barrier
islands of **Siesta Key, Longboat Key,** and **Lido Key,** with myriad beaches,
shops, hotels, condominiums, and houses.

Decades ago, circus tycoon John Ringling found this area an ideal spot
for his clowns and performers to recuperate from their months of travel
while preparing for their next journey. Along Sarasota Bay, Ringling built
himself a grand home called *Cà d'Zan* ("House of John," in Venetian
dialect), patterned after the Palace of the Doges in Venice, Italy. Today
★ ☉ **44** this winter home is part of the **Ringling Center for the Cultural Arts,** along
with the **Museum of the Circus** and the **John and Mable Ringling Museum of Art,** which has a world-renowned collection of Rubens paintings and tapestries. ⊠ *U.S. 41, ½ mi south of Sarasota-Bradenton
Airport* ☎ *941/359–5700* ⊕ *www.ringling.org* 🎫 *$15* ☉ *Daily 10–5:30.*

45 On display at the **Sarasota Classic Car Museum** are 100 restored antique
automobiles—including Rolls-Royces, Pierce Arrows, and Auburns.
The collection includes not only rare cars but cars that once belonged
to famous people such as John Lennon and John Ringling. ⊠ *5500 N.
Tamiami Trail* ☎ *941/355–6228* ⊕ *www.sarasotacarmuseum.org*
🎫 *$8.50* ☉ *Daily 9:30–6.*

☉ **46** It takes a couple of hours to stroll through the 10-acre spread of tropical plants at the **Sarasota Jungle Gardens.** The lush gardens, created in
1936, are filled not with just native species but exotic plants from
around the world, such as the rare Australian nut tree and the Peruvian
apple cactus. Also on-site are a petting zoo and playground, a shell and
butterfly museum, and reptile and bird shows. ⊠ *3701 Bayshore Rd.*
☎ *941/355–5305* ⊕ *www.sarasotajunglegardens.com* 🎫 *$10* ☉ *Daily
9–5; shows at 10, noon, 2, and 4.*

47 At the 9-acre **Marie Selby Botanical Gardens,** stroll through a world-class
display of orchids, see air plants and colorful bromeliads, and wander
through 14 garden areas along Sarasota Bay. There's also a small museum of botany and art in a gracious restored mansion. During the annual plant fair in March, experts give free advice on what types of
plants to grow at home. ⊠ *811 S. Palm Ave.* ☎ *941/366–5730* ⊕ *www.
selby.org* 🎫 *$10* ☉ *Daily 10–5.*

☉ **48** The 135,000-gallon shark tank at **Mote Marine Aquarium** lets you view
its inhabitants from above and below the water's surface. Additional
tanks show off sharks, rays, and other marine creatures native to the
area. Handle rays, guitar fish, horseshoe crabs, and sea urchins in the
touch tanks. Many opt for the two-hour boat trip onto Sarasota Bay,
conducted by **Sarasota Bay Adventures** (☎ *941/388–4200,* ⊕ www.
sarasotabayexplorers.com). On the trip, the crew brings marine life on
board in a net, explains what it is, and throws it back to swim away.
You are almost guaranteed to see bottlenose dolphins. Reservations are
required for the boat trip. ⊠ *1600 City Island Park, Lido Key* ☎ *941/*

388–4441 ⊕ www.mote.org. 🎫 Aquarium $12, boat excursion $24, combined ticket $30 ⏲ Daily 10–5.

㊾ **South Lido Park,** at the southern tip of the island, has one of the best beaches in the region. The sugar-sand beach offers little for shell collectors, but try your luck at fishing, take a dip in the gulf, roam the 100-acre park, or picnic as the sun sets through the Australian pines into the water. Facilities include nature trails, a canoe trail, volleyball court, playground, horseshoe pits, rest rooms, and picnic grounds. ✉ *Ben Franklin Dr., Lido Key.*

★ ㊿ **Siesta Beach** and its 40-acre park have nature trails, a concession stand, fields for soccer and softball, picnic facilities, a playground, rest rooms, a fitness trail, and tennis and volleyball courts. In 1987 this beach was recognized internationally as having the whitest and finest sand in the world, a powdery, quartz-based compound that is soft as down. ✉ *600 Beach Way, Siesta Key.*

(51) Only 14 acres, **Turtle Beach** is a beach-park that's popular with families. It doesn't have the soft, white sand of Siesta Beach, but it does have boat ramps, horseshoe pits, picnic and play facilities, a recreation building, rest rooms, and a volleyball court. ✉ *Turtle Beach Rd., off Midnight Pass Rd., Siesta Key.*

off the beaten path

★ **Myakka River State Park.** With 28,900 acres, this outstanding wildlife preserve is absolutely lovely and is great for bird-watching and gator sighting. Tram tours explore hammocks, airboat tours whiz over the lake, and there are hiking trails and bike rentals. A 100-ft-long canopy walkway gives you a bird's-eye view at 25 ft above ground. If you care to stay a while, the park rents cabins that have kitchens, fireplaces, and air-conditioning. There's also a campground. Reservations are essential for the cabins. ✉ *Rte. 72, 7 mi southeast of Sarasota ☎ 941/365–0100 or 941/361–6511; 800/326–3521 for cabin reservations ⊕ www.myakkariver.org 🎫 $2, $4 per vehicle (up to 8 people); tours $8 adults, $4 children; cabins $55 per night ⏲ Daily 8 AM–dusk.*

Where to Stay & Eat

★ **$$–$$$$** ✕ **Michael's on East.** Dine in trendy elegance at this downtown Sarasota favorite. The fare ranges from Maine-lobster bow-tie pasta to rack of lamb to grilled duck breast to pan-seared Chilean sea bass. Desserts, such as the house specialty strawberry soufflé, are standouts here. A light menu is served in the intimate bar, where there's always piano music or jazz in the evening. The lunch menu includes unusual sandwiches—grilled Portobello mushrooms with smoked Gouda, for example. ✉ *1212 East Ave. S ☎ 941/366–0007 ✍ Reservations essential ⏲ No lunch weekends 💳 AE, MC, V.*

$$$ ✕ **Ophelia's on the Bay.** The menu changes nightly at this intimate waterfront spot. Favorites include grouper with coconut and cashew crust with papaya jam and habañero mashed potatoes; Portobello moussaka; grilled bison rib eye with morel mushroom and roasted leek demi-glace; and roast duck. ✉ *9105 Midnight Pass Rd., Siesta Key ☎ 941/349–2212 💳 AE, D, DC, MC, V ⏲ No lunch.*

★ **$$–$$$** ✕ **Alley Cat Cafe.** Tucked away in the alley its name promises, this mostly outdoor eatery has a reputation for the creative and off-mainstream. It evokes a Florida garden with its tin-roof bar and overhead lattice arbor. The menu changes with the fish and fashion of the day. Worthy are the pecan-crusted catfish with sweet corn pudding and ginger-soy-marinated grilled ahi tuna. Try the eccentric little bar for an after-dinner libation. ⊠ *1558 4th St., in alley between 4th St. and Fruitville Rd., Sarasota* 🕾 *941/954–1228* ⊘ *No dinner Sun., Mon* ⊟ *AE, DC, MC, V.*

★ $$–$$$ ✕ **Bijou Cafe.** Wood, brass, lace, and sumptuous carpeting surround diners in this 1920 gas station turned restaurant. Specialties on the regularly changing menu could include superb crab cakes with rémoulade, a wonderfully spicy shrimp dish inspired in Mozambique, crispy roast duckling with orange-cognac sauce or port-wine cherry sauce, pepper steak, and crème brûlée for dessert. An extensive international wine list includes vintages ranging from an Australian cabernet–shiraz blend to a South African merlot and, of course, numerous selections from France and California. ⊠ *1287 1st St.* 🕾 *941/366–8111* ⊟ *AE, DC, MC, V.*

$$–$$$ ✕ **Columbia.** On trendy St. Armands Circle, this classic has most of the culinary elements of its 95-year-old mother landmark restaurant in Ybor City. The menu reflects Spanish and Cuban cooking, and includes three versions of Spanish paella and a superb black-bean soup. A house specialty is pompano papillote (pompano with shrimp, crabmeat, and artichoke in a white wine sauce, baked in parchment). There's nightly entertainment and dancing in the patio area. ⊠ *411 St. Armands Circle, Lido Key* 🕾 *941/388–3987* ⊟ *AE, DC, MC, V.*

$$–$$$ ✕ **Marina Jack.** Fresh seafood prevails at this restaurant, whose two-floor long-window dining room and outdoor patio seating overlook Sarasota Bay on three sides. Lunch specialties include crab cakes, eggs Benedict, and fried chicken livers with a mushroom demi-glace. Dinner brings ahi tuna wasabi, lobster tails, red snapper almondine, steaks, and pasta. ⊠ *2 Marina Plaza* 🕾 *941/365–4232* ⊟ *AE, MC, V.*

¢–$$$ ✕ **Patrick's.** A longtime favorite among locals, this upscale sports bar attracts crowds that belly up to the bar after work and end up staying for steak sandwiches, juicy cheeseburgers, meat loaf, pizza, pasta, and char-grilled steaks. Weekends are also busy. ⊠ *1400 Main St.* 🕾 *941/952–1170* ⊟ *AE, MC, V.*

¢–$ ✕ **Old Salty Dog.** A view of New Pass between Longboat and Lido keys and affordable eats make this a popular stop, especially for visitors to Mote Marine Aquarium. It's open-air but nonetheless comfortable even in summer, thanks to a pleasant breeze. Quarter-pound hot dogs, fish-and-chips, wings, and burgers set the menu's tone. Locals hang out at the beer bar, shaped from the hull of an old boat. ⊠ *601 Ken Thompson Pkwy., City Island* 🕾 *941/388–4311* ⚠ *Reservations not accepted* ⊟ *MC, V.*

¢–$ ✕ **Yoder's.** At this Amish family restaurant in the heart of Sarasota's Amish community, you find great homey cooking. Dinners, served family style, typically include liver and onions, turkey and dressing, a wonderful goulash, and other hearty dishes. Breakfasts are fit for an Amish lumberjack, with big stacks of pancakes and excellent waffles. The desserts might be the best part of the meal, particularly the pies. The place gets crowded around noon and early evening. ⊠ *3434 Bahia Vista Dr.* 🕾 *941/955–7771* ⊕ *www.yodersrestaurant.com* ⚠ *Reservations not accepted* ⊟ *No credit cards* ⊘ *Closed Sun.*

★ $$$$ 🏨 **Colony Beach and Tennis Resort.** If tennis is your game, this is the place to stay—such tennis greats as Björn Borg have made the Colony their home court, and for good reason. Ten courts are clay hydrosurfaced (the others are hard), and the pros are all USPTA-certified. They run clinics and camps at all levels, do video analyses of your game, and play with you when no one else is available. There are even rackets and lessons for children, plus excellent free kids' programs. The Colony dining room has a local reputation for excellence and fine wine. Suites sleep up to eight. Among the suites are a two-story penthouse as well as three private beach houses that open onto sand and sea. ⊠ *1620 Gulf of Mex-*

ico Dr., Longboat Key 34228 ☎ *941/383–6464 or 800/282–1138* 🖷 *941/383–7549* ⊕ *www.colonybeachresort.com* ⮡ *235 suites* ⚒ *2 restaurants, grocery, room service, in-room safes, some kitchens, golf privileges, 21 tennis courts, pool, health club, spa, beach, snorkeling, windsurfing, boating, bicycles, volleyball, 2 bars, wine shop, baby-sitting, children's programs (ages 3–12), playground, laundry service, meeting rooms* ▤ *AE, D, MC, V.*

$$$$ 🏨 **Resort at Longboat Key Club.** This beautifully landscaped 410-acre property is one of *the* places to golf in the state and one of the top tennis resorts in the country. Water is the test on both golf courses, which have excellent pro shops, lessons, and clinics. Tennis courts are Har-Tru–surfaced. Hobie Cats, kayaks, Sunfish, deep-sea charters, and ecology trips are also available. Suites for four or six have huge private balconies overlooking a golf course, beach, or private lagoon where manatees and bottlenose dolphins are occasionally seen. The golf and dining facilities are for resort guests or club members only. ✉ *301 Gulf of Mexico Dr., Longboat Key 34228* ☎ *941/383–8821 or 888/237–5545* 🖷 *941/383–0359* ⊕ *www.longboatkeyclub.com* ⮡ *24 rooms, 208 suites* ⚒ *5 restaurants, room service, in-room data ports, some kitchens, minibars, refrigerators, driving range, 18-hole golf course, 3 9-hole golf courses, putting greens, 38 tennis courts, pro shop, pool, gym, outdoor hot tub, massage, beach, boating, bicycles, library, baby-sitting, children's programs (ages 5–12), Internet, meeting room* ▤ *AE, DC, MC, V.*

★ $$$$ 🏨 **Ritz-Carlton Sarasota.** Developers like to say that this hotel is circus magnate John Ringling's realized dream, and it certainly has a style Ringling would have coveted. Verona, a Mediterranean restaurant, overlooks yachts in the marina. Fine artwork and fresh-cut flowers decorate marble-floored hallways. Rooms have marble bathrooms, high-speed Internet access, and private balconies. A European-style spa and guests-only beach facility on Lido Beach, about a mile away, make this city resort full-service. ✉ *1111 Ritz-Carlton Dr., 34236* ☎ *941/309–2000* 🖷 *941/309–2100* ⊕ *www.ritz-carlton.com* ⮡ *235 rooms, 31 suites* ⚒ *2 restaurants, room service, in-room data ports, in-room safes, minibars, pool, golf privileges, 3 tennis courts, health club, spa, bar, lobby lounge, shops, baby-sitting, children's programs (ages 5–12), laundry service, concierge, concierge floor, meeting rooms* ▤ *AE, DC, MC, V.*

$$$–$$$$ 🏨 **Radisson Lido Beach Resort.** Superb gulf views can be found at this classy beachfront resort. Beachfront minisuites, at the western end of the building, have balconies. A large rectangular pool is right on the beach. ✉ *700 Ben Franklin Dr., Lido Beach 34236* ☎ *941/388–2161 or 800/441–2113* 🖷 *941/388–3175* ⊕ *www.radisson.com* ⮡ *122 rooms, 120 suites* ⚒ *2 restaurants, in-room data ports, some kitchens, some microwaves, some refrigerators, pool, beach, jet skiing, bar, business services, meeting room* ▤ *AE, D, DC, MC, V.*

$$$–$$$$ 🏨 **Hyatt Sarasota.** The Hyatt is contemporary in design and is in the heart of the city, across from the Van Wezel Performing Arts Hall. All the spacious rooms overlook Sarasota Bay or the marina. ✉ *1000 Blvd. of the Arts, 34236* ☎ *941/953–1234* 🖷 *941/952–1987* ⊕ *www.sarasota.hyatt.com* ⮡ *294 rooms, 12 suites* ⚒ *2 restaurants, room service, in-room data ports, pool, health club, sauna, boating, marina, fishing, bicycles, bar, shop, baby-sitting, dry cleaning, meeting room* ▤ *AE, DC, MC, V.*

$$ 🏨 **Best Western Midtown.** This two-story motel is comfortable and very affordable during its off-season, from mid-April through early February. Set back from U.S. 41 and somewhat removed from traffic noise, it is within walking distance of a shopping center and several restaurants—including the popular Michael's on East—and is central to area attractions and downtown. Rooms have seating areas. ✉ *1425 S. Tami-*

ami Trail, 34239 ☎ *941/955–9841 or 800/722–8227* 🖷 *941/954–8948* ⊕ *www.bwmidtown.com* ⤵ *100 rooms* ⚲ *In-room safes, pool, laundry service, meeting room* ⊟ *AE, D, DC, MC, V* |◯| *CP.*

¢–$ 🖵 **Knights Inn.** Basically a motor inn convenient to the airport and Ringling Center, this property is tidy and appealing, its rooms benefiting from friendly decorative touches. ⊠ *5340 N. Tamiami Trail, 34234* ☎ *941/355–8867 or 800/843–5644* 🖷 *941/351–7718* ⤵ *48 rooms* ⚲ *Some in-room data ports, some kitchenettes, pool, laundry facilities,* ⊟ *AE, D, DC, MC, V* |◯| *CP.*

Nightlife & the Arts

THE ARTS Among the many theaters in Sarasota, the $10 million **FSU/Asolo Center for the Performing Arts** (⊠ 5555 N. Tamiami Trail ☎ 941/351–8000 or 800/361–8388) mounts productions November through May. The small, professional **Florida Studio Theatre** (⊠ 1241 N. Palm Ave. ☎ 941/366–9000) presents contemporary dramas, comedies, and musicals and has acting classes for both adults and children on main stage and cabaret-style October to June. Area music groups that perform at the **Florida West Coast Symphony Center** (⊠ 709 N. Tamiami Trail ☎ 941/953–4252 ⊕ www.fwcs.org) include the Florida West Coast Symphony, Florida String Quartet, Florida Brass Quintet, Florida Wind Quintet, and New Artists String Quartet. **Golden Apple Dinner Theatre** (⊠ 25 N. Pineapple Ave. ☎ 941/366–5454) serves up a standard buffet along with musicals and comedies. A long-established community theater, the **Players of Sarasota** (⊠ U.S. 41 and 9th St. ☎ 941/365–2494) has launched such performers as Montgomery Clift and Paul Reubens. The troupe performs comedies, thrillers, and musicals. The **Sarasota Concert Band** (⊠ 1345 Main St. ☎ 941/364–2263) has 50 players, many of them full-time musicians. **Theatre Works** (⊠ 1247 1st St. ☎ 941/952–9170) presents professional non-Equity productions at the Palm Tree Playhouse. The **Van Wezel Performing Arts Hall** (⊠ 777 N. Tamiami Trail ☎ 941/953–3366 ⊕ www.vanwezel.org) is easy to find—just look for the purple shell rising along the bay front. It hosts some 200 performances each year, including Broadway plays, ballet, jazz, rock concerts, symphonies, children's shows, and ice-skating.

The **Sarasota Film Society** (⊠ Burns Court Cinema, 506 Burns La. ☎ 941/364–8662; 941/955–3456 for theater ⊕ www.filmsociety.org) shows foreign and art films daily. Call the theater for film titles and show times and see the society's Web site for detailed descriptions of films.

Celebrating its 45th season in 2004, the **Sarasota Opera** (⊠ The Edwards Theater, 61 N. Pineapple Ave. ☎ 941/366–8450 ⊕ www.sarasotaopera. org) performs from February through March in a 1,033-seat, historic theater downtown. Internationally known artists sing the principal roles, supported by a professional chorus of 24 young apprentices.

NIGHTLIFE The **Gator Club** (⊠ 1490 Main St. ☎ 941/366–5969), in a classy, historic building downtown, has live music and dancing 365 days a year.

Sports & the Outdoors

BASEBALL The **Cincinnati Reds** (⊠ Ed Smith Stadium, 2700 12th St. ☎ 941/954–4101) have spring training here in March.

BIKING **CB's Saltwater Outfitters** (⊠ 1249 Stickney Point Rd. ☎ 941/349–4400) rents boats, fishing gear, and bikes by the hour or by the day.

CANOEING At **Myakka Outpost** (⊠ Myakka River State Park, Rte. 72, 17 mi southeast of Sarasota ☎ 941/923–1120), rent canoes, kayaks, paddles, and life vests.

DOG RACING   The greyhounds run from late December through April at the **Sarasota Kennel Club** (⊠ 5400 Bradenton Rd. ☎ 941/355–7744).

FISHING   **Flying Fish at Marina Jack's** (⊠ U.S. 41, on the bay front ☎ 941/366–3373 ⊕ www.flyingfishfleet.com) has several boats that can be chartered for deep-sea fishing and has daily group trips on its "party" fishing boat.

GOLF   **Bobby Jones Golf Course** (⊠ 1000 Circus Blvd. ☎ 941/955–8097) has 45 holes and a driving range. **Forest Lakes Golf Club** (⊠ 2401 Beneva Rd. ☎ 941/922–1312) has a practice range and 18 holes.

TENNIS   If you love tennis and aren't staying at one of the tennis resorts, you might want to play at the **Forest Lakes Golf Club** (⊠ 2401 Beneva Rd. ☎ 941/922–1312), which has four lighted, hard courts.

Shopping
St. Armands Circle (⊠ John Ringling Blvd. [Rte. 789] at Ave. of the Presidents) is a cluster of oh-so-exclusive shops and restaurants just east of Lido Beach.

Venice

🟢 *18 mi south of Sarasota.*

This small town is crisscrossed with canals like the city for which it was named. Venice beaches are good for shell collecting, but they're best known for their wealth of sharks' teeth and fossils, washed up from the ancient shark burial grounds just offshore.

Nokomis Beach (⊠ Albee Rd., Casey Key) is one of two notable beaches in the area, on the island just to the north of Venice Beach, across the pass near North Jetty Park. It has rest rooms, a concession stand, picnic equipment, play areas, two boat ramps, a volleyball court, and fishing. **North Jetty Park** (⊠ Albee Rd., Casey Key), at the south end of Casey Key, is a favorite for family outings and fishermen. Facilities include rest rooms, a concession stand, play and picnic equipment, horseshoes, and a volleyball court. **Caspersen Beach** (⊠ Beach Dr., South Venice) is the county's largest park and known for its fossil finds. It has a nature trail, fishing, picnicking, rest rooms, and lots of beach for those who prefer space to a wealth of amenities. **Manasota Beach** (⊠ Manasota Beach Rd., Manasota Key) has a boat ramp, picnic area, and rest rooms. Reach it by foot from Caspersen Beach. By road, it's a lot less direct. At **Blind Pass Beach** (⊠ Manasota Beach Rd., Manasota Key), fish, swim, and hike the nature trail. There are rest rooms and showers. **Englewood Beach** (⊠ Off Rte. 776, near the Charlotte–Sarasota county line) is popular with teenagers, although beachgoers of all ages frequent it. There are barbecue grills, picnic facilities, boat ramps, a fishing pier, a playground, and showers. There's a charge for parking.

Where to Stay & Eat
$–$$ ✕ **Sharky's on the Pier.** Gaze out on the beach and sparkling waters while dining on grilled seafood at this very casual eatery. You choose whether the catches of the day are broiled, blackened, grilled, or fried. Specialties include macadamia grouper, sea pasta, and a filet mignon–shrimp combination. There's an outdoor veranda and tables indoors as well and entertainment five nights a week. ⊠ 1600 S. Harbor Dr. ☎ 941/488–1456 ⊟ AE, MC, V ⊘ Closed Mon. in summer.

$$$ ▨ **Inn at the Beach.** Across from the beach, this little one- and two-story resort is popular with families. Some of the one- and two-bedroom suites, which have spacious living rooms, have views of the gulf. Others look out on tropical gardens. ⊠ 725 Venice Ave., 34285 ☎ 941/484–8471

🖨 941/484–8471 or 800/255–8471 ⊕ *www.inn-at-the-beach.com* ⤳ *49 rooms, 12 suites* ⅄ *Fans, in-room data ports, in-room safes, some kitchens, microwaves, refrigerators, pool, outdoor hot tub, shuffleboard, laundry facilities* ⊟ *AE, DC, MC, V.*

$ 🖥 **Days Inn Venice Resort.** Only 10 minutes from the beach, this simple but well-kept motel is on the main business route through town. Rooms are comfortable. ✉ *1710 S. Tamiami Trail, 34293* ☎ *941/493–4558* 🖨 *941/493–1593* ⊕ *www.daysinn.com* ⤳ *72 rooms* ⅄ *Restaurant, room service, in-room data ports, pool, bar, laundry facilities, laundry service, meeting rooms, some pets allowed (fee)* ⊟ *AE, D, DC, MC, V.*

The Arts

Venice Little Theatre (✉ 140 W. Tampa Ave. ☎ 941/488–1115 ⊕ www. venicestage.com) is a community theater showing comedies, musicals, dramas, and contemporary works on two stages during its October–May season.

Sports & the Outdoors

BIKING **Bicycles International** (✉ 1744 Tamiami Trail S ☎ 941/497–1590) rents some of its varied stock weekly as well as hourly and daily.

FISHING At **Florida Deep Sea Fishing Charters** (✉ 1709 Keyway Rd., Englewood ☎ 941/473–4603 ⊕ www.charter-boatfishing.com), Capt. Dave Pinkham offers half-day and full-day deep-sea fishing trips for tarpon, shark, amberjack, and other fighting fish.

GOLF **Bird Bay Executive Golf Course** (✉ 602 Bird Bay Dr. W ☎ 941/485–9333) has 18 holes. **Plantation Golf & Country Club** (✉ 500 Rockley Blvd. ☎ 941/493–2000) has 36 holes and a driving range.

WATER SPORTS **Don and Mike's Boat and Jet Ski Rental** (✉ 482 Blackburn Point Rd. ☎ 941/966–4000) rents water skis, Jet Skis, and pontoon boats and has instruction for all activities.

Shopping

If you like flea markets, check out the **Dome** (✉ Rte. 775, west of U.S. 41), where dozens of sheltered stalls sell new and recycled wares. It's open October through August, Friday through Sunday 9–4.

THE TAMPA BAY AREA A TO Z

To research prices, get advice from other travelers, and book travel arrangements, visit www.fodors.com.

AIR TRAVEL

CARRIERS Many carriers serve Tampa International Airport. Sarasota's airport is served by major carriers (⇨ Smart Travel Tips A to Z). Scheduled service to St. Petersburg–Clearwater International is limited, and from many areas of the country, you have to supply your own plane. However, American TransAir, Discover Air, Southeast, and Pan American Airlines connect to U.S. cities, and Air Transat flies from Toronto.

🚩 Airlines & Contacts **Air Transat** ☎ 877/872-6728 ⊕ www.airtransat.com. **America West Airlines** ☎ 800/235-9292 ⊕ www.americawest.com. **American TransAir** ☎ 800/435-9282 ⊕ www.ata.com. **Cayman Airways** ☎ 800/422-9626 ⊕ www.caymanairways.com. **Condor** ☎ 800/524-6975 ⊕ www.condoramericas.com. **Discover Air** ☎ 866/359-3247 ⊕ www.discoverair.com. **Gulfstream International** ☎ 800/525-0280 ⊕ www.gulfstreamair.com. **Pan American Airlines** ☎ 800/359-7262 ⊕ www.flypanam.com. **Southeast** ☎ 800/383-7807 ⊕ www.flyseal.com.

AIRPORTS & TRANSFERS

Airport Information Tampa International Airport ⊠ 5507 Spruce St., 6 mi from downtown Tampa 813/870-8700 ⊕ www.tampaairport.com. **St. Petersburg-Clearwater International** ⊠ off Rte. 686, 9 mi from downtown St. Petersburg 727/535-7600 ⊕ www.fly2pie.com. **Sarasota-Bradenton International Airport** ⊠ off U.S. 41, just north of Sarasota 941/359-5200 ⊕ www.srq-airport.com.

AIRPORT
TRANSFERS
Central Florida Limousine provides Tampa International Airport service to and from Hillsborough and Polk counties, and Super Shuttle serves Pinellas County. Expect taxi fares to be about $12–$25 for most of Hillsborough County and about twice that for Pinellas County. Transportation to and from Sarasota–Bradenton Airport is provided by West Coast Executive Sedan. The average cab fare between the airport and downtown is $16–$25.

Taxis & Shuttles Central Florida Limousine 813/396-3730. **Super Shuttle** 727/572-1111 or 800/282-6817 ⊕ www.supershuttle.com. **West Coast Executive Sedan** 941/359-8600.

BUS TRAVEL

Service to and throughout the state is provided by Greyhound Lines. Around Tampa, the Hillsborough Area Regional Transit serves the county, plus the new TECO Line Streetcars replicate the city's first electric streetcars, transporting cruise-ship passengers to Ybor City. Around St. Petersburg, Pinellas Suncoast Transit Authority serves Pinellas County. The Looper trolley operates to downtown area attractions. In Sarasota the public transit company is Sarasota County Area Transit. Fares for local bus service range from 50¢ to $2.50 (for an all-day pass), and exact change is required.

FARES &
SCHEDULES
Bus Information Greyhound Lines 800/231-2222 ⊕ www.greyhound. com. **Greyhound Sarasota** ⊠ 575 N. Washington Blvd., Sarasota 941/955-5735. **Greyhound Clearwater** ⊠ 2811 Gulf-to-Bay Blvd., Clearwater 727/796-7315. **Greyhound St. Petersburg** ⊠ 180 9th St. N, St. Petersburg 727/822-1497. **Greyhound Tampa** ⊠ 610 E. Polk St., Tampa 813/229-2174. **Hillsborough Area Regional Transit (HART)** 813/254-4278 ⊕ www.hartline.org. **Pinellas Suncoast Transit Authority (PSTA)** 727/530-9911 ⊕ www.psta.net. **Sarasota County Area Transit (SCAT)** 941/316-1234 ⊕ www.co.sarasota.fl.us/public_works_scat. **TECO Line Street Cars** 813/274-8543.

CAR TRAVEL

Interstate 75 spans the region from north to south. Once you cross the Florida border from Georgia, it should take about three hours to reach Tampa and another hour to reach Sarasota. Interstate exits are numbered according to mileage from their southern terminus, rather than sequentially. Coming from Orlando, you're likely to drive west into Tampa on Interstate 4. Along with Interstate 75, U.S. 41 (which runs concurrently with the Tamiami Trail for much of the way) stretches the length of the region. U.S. 41 links the business districts of many communities, so it's best to avoid it and all bridges during rush hours (7–9 AM and 4–6 PM). U.S. 19 is St. Petersburg's major north–south artery; traffic can be heavy, and there are many lights, so use a different route when possible. Interstate 275 heads west from Tampa across Tampa Bay to St. Petersburg, swings south, and crosses the bay again on its way to Terra Ceia, near Bradenton. Along this last leg—the Sunshine Skyway and its stunning suspension bridge—you'll get a bird's-eye view of bustling Tampa Bay. The Gandy Bridge (Highway 92) also yields a spectacular view of Tampa Bay, and Route 679 takes you along two of St. Petersburg's most pristine islands, Cabbage and Mullet keys. Route 64 connects Interstate 75 to Bradenton and Anna Maria Island. Route 789 runs over several slender barrier islands, past miles of blue-green gulf waters, beaches, and waterfront homes. The road does not connect all the islands, however; it runs from the village of Anna Maria off the Bradenton coast south to Lido Key, then begins again on Siesta Key and again on Casey Key south of Osprey, and runs south to Nokomis Beach.

EMERGENCIES
Dial 911 for police, ambulance, and fire. There are 24-hour emergency rooms at Bayfront Medical Center, Manatee Memorial Hospital, Sarasota Memorial Hospital, and University Community Hospital.

🏥 Hospitals **Bayfront Medical Center** ✉ 701 6th St. S, St. Petersburg ☎ 727/893-6100. **Manatee Memorial Hospital** ✉ 206 2nd St. E, Bradenton ☎ 941/745-7466. **Sarasota Memorial Hospital** ✉ 1700 S. Tamiami Trail, Sarasota ☎ 941/917-9000. **University Community Hospital** ✉ 3100 E. Fletcher Ave., Tampa ☎ 813/ 971-6000.

🏥 24-Hour Pharmacies **Eckerd Drug** ✉ 6607 N. Dale Mabry St., Tampa ☎ 813/873-0472 ✉ 30387 U.S. 19 N, Clearwater ☎ 727/781-2955.

ENGLISH-LANGUAGE MEDIA

NEWSPAPERS & MAGAZINES
Daily newspapers in the area are the *Bradenton Herald, Sarasota Herald–Tribune, St. Petersburg Times,* and *Tampa Tribune.* The *Cedar Key Beacon, Longboat Observer,* and *Tampa Bay Business Journal* are weekly newspapers. *Tampa Bay Life* is a monthly magazine.

RADIO
Local AM stations include WFLA 970 (news and talk radio); WDAE 1250 (ESPN radio, sports talk, and Tampa Bay Lightning broadcasts); WQBN 1300 (all-Spanish); WWMI 1380 (Radio Disney); and WPSO 1500 (Greek-language).

Local FM stations include WJIS 88.1 (Christian music); WMNF 88.5 (alternative and eclectic); WUSF 89.7 (National Public Radio); WYUU 92.5 (oldies); WFLZ 93.3 (Top 40); WQYK 99.5 (country music and Tampa Bay Buccaneers football broadcasts); WHPT 102.5 (classic rock); WBBY 107.3 (soft rock); and WGUL 106.3 (big band).

TOURS
Tours of the bay area and the Gulf Coast, given by Helicopter Charter & Transport Co., leave from Tampa International. West Florida Helicopters gives bay-area tours. The latest vessels for day tours of Tampa and St. Petersburg are exotic. They include the WWII vintage amphibious "ducks" (part bus, part boat) operated by Duck Tours of Tampa Bay in both cities, and a daily hovercraft tour from St. Petersburg, operated by Hover USA. The *American Victory* Mariners Memorial & Museum Ship offers weekend day trips aboard the restored WW II–era merchant marine vessel with historical reenactments of life aboard during its service in WWII, Korea, and Vietnam. Hovercraft tours depart from multiple points around St. Petersburg and to Egmont Key, and private charters are available. Gourmet meals and a stunning view of the Tampa skyline are available aboard StarShip Cruises, which has both lunch and dinner cruises aboard its namesake *StarShip,* which seats up to 350 people in the dining room.

On Captain Memo's Pirate Cruise, crew members dressed as pirates take you on sightseeing and sunset cruises in a replica of a 19th-century sailing ship. Dolphin Landing Tours has daily, four-hour cruises to unspoiled Egmont Key at the mouth of Tampa Bay. Myakka Wildlife Tours runs four-hour-long tours daily of the wildlife sanctuary aboard the *Gator Gal,* a large airboat, and also has tram tours through Myakka River State Park. Aboard the glass-bottom boats of St. Nicholas Boat Line, you take a sightseeing cruise of Tarpon Springs' historic sponge docks and see an actual diver at work. The *Starlite Princess,* an old-fashioned paddle wheeler, and *Starlite Majestic,* a sleek yacht-style vessel, make sightseeing and dinner cruises.

🔁 Tour Operators *American Victory* Mariners Memorial & Museum Ship ⊠ 705 Channelside Dr., Berth 271, behind Florida Aquarium, Tampa ☎ 813/228-866 ⊕ www. americanvictory.org. **Captain Memo's Pirate Cruise** ⊠ Clearwater Beach Marina, Clearwater Beach ☎ 727/446-2587. **Dolphin Landing Tours** ⊠ 4737 Gulf Blvd., St. Pete Beach ☎ 727/360-7411. **Duck Tours of Tampa Bay** ⊠ Newk's Cafe, 514 Channelside Dr., Tampa ☎ 813/310-3825 ⊠ The Pier, 800 2nd Ave. NE, St. Petersburg ☎ 727/432-3825 ⊕ www.ducktoursoftampabay.com. **Helicopter Charter & Transport Co.** ⊠ 9000 18th St., Tampa ☎ 813/933-2686. **Hover-USA** ☎ 866/359-4683 ⊕ www.hover-usa.com. **Myakka Wildlife Tours** ⊠ Myakka River State Park, Rte. 72 southeast of Sarasota ☎ 941/365-0100. **St. Nicholas Boat Line** ⊠ 693 Dodecanese Blvd., Tarpon Springs ☎ 727/942-6425. *Starlite Princess* and *Starlite Majesty* ⊠ Clearwater Beach Marina, at the end of Rte. 60, Clearwater Beach ⊠ Corey Causeway, 3400 S. Pasadena, St. Pete Beach ☎ 727/462-2628 ⊕ www.starlitecruises.com. **StarShip Cruises** ⊠ 603 Channelside Dr., Tampa ☎ 813/223-7999 or 877-744-7999. **West Florida Helicopters** ⊠ Albert Whitted Airport, 107 8th Ave. SE, St. Petersburg ☎ 727/823-5200.

TRAIN TRAVEL

Amtrak trains run from the Northeast, Midwest, and much of the South to the Tampa station.

🔁 Train Information **Amtrak** ⊠ Tampa Union Station, 601 N. Nebraska Ave., Tampa ☎ 800/872-7245 or 813/221-7600 ⊕ www.amtrak.com.

VISITOR INFORMATION

🔁 Tourist Information **Bradenton Area Convention & Visitors Bureau Tourist Information Center** ⊠ 5030 Hwy. 301 N, at I-75 Exit 224, Ellenton 34222 ☎ 941/729-7040 ⊕ www.flagulfislands.com. **Cedar Key Chamber of Commerce** ⓓ Box 610, Cedar Key 32625 ☎ 352/543-5600 ⊕ www.cedarkey.org. **Clearwater Regional Chamber of Commerce** ⊠ 1130 Cleveland St., Clearwater 33755 ☎ 727/461-0011 ⊕ www. clearwaterflorida.org. **Greater Dunedin Chamber of Commerce** ⊠ 301 Main St., Dunedin 34698 ☎ 727/733-3197 ⊕ www.dunedin-fl.com. **Greater Tampa Chamber of Commerce** ⓓ Box 420, Tampa 33601 ☎ 813/228-7777; 813/223-1111 Ext. 44 for Visitors Information Department ⊕ www.tampachamber.com. **Sarasota Convention and Visitors Bureau** ⊠ 655 N. Tamiami Trail, Sarasota 34236 ☎ 941/957-1877 or 800/800-3906 ⊕ www.sarasotafl.org. **St. Petersburg Area Chamber of Commerce** ⊠ 100 2nd Ave. N, St. Petersburg 33701 ☎ 727/821-4715 ⊕ www.stpete.com. **St. Petersburg/Clearwater Area Convention & Visitors Bureau** ⊠ 14450 46th St. N, Suite 108, St. Petersburg 33762 ☎ 727/464-7200 or 877/352-3224 ⊕ www.floridasbeach.com. **Tampa Bay Beaches Chamber of Commerce** ⊠ 6990 Gulf Blvd., St. Pete Beach 33706 ☎ 727/360-6957 or 800/944-1847 ⊕ www.tampabaybeaches.com. **Tampa Bay Convention and Visitors Bureau** ⊠ 400 N. Tampa St., Suite 2800, Tampa 33602 ☎ 800/368-2672 or 813/223-1111 ⊕ www.visittampabay.com. **Tarpon Springs Chamber of Commerce** ⊠ 11 E. Orange St., Tarpon Springs 34689 ☎ 727/937-6109 ⊕ www.tarponsprings.com.

SOUTHWEST FLORIDA

8

FODOR'S CHOICE
Bowman's Beach, Sanibel
Corkscrew Swamp Sanctuary, Naples area
Delnor-Wiggins Pass State Recreation Area, Naples
Hotel Escalante, Naples
LaPlaya Beach & Golf Resort, Naples
Mel's Diner, Fort Myers
Sign of the Vine, Naples
Thomas A. Edison's Winter Home, Fort Myers
Twilight Cafe, Sanibel

HIGHLY RECOMMENDED

RESTAURANTS   Bha! Bha!, Naples
Bistro 41, Fort Myers
Michel & Michelle's, North Fort Myers
Old Marco Island Inn, Marco Island
Sale e Pepe, Marco Island
Tide Restaurant, Marco Island
Traders Store & Cafe, Sanibel

HOTELS   Hyatt Coconut Point Resort & Spa, Bonita Springs
Marriott's Marco Island Resort and Golf Club, Marco Island
Registry Resort, Naples
Ritz-Carlton, Naples
Sanibel Harbour Resort & Spa, Fort Myers
South Seas Resort and Yacht Harbour, Captiva

WHAT TO SEE   Bailey-Matthews Shell Museum, Sanibel
Imaginarium, Fort Myers
J. N. "Ding" Darling National Wildlife Refuge, Sanibel
Naples Museum of Art
Sanibel Historical Village and Museum, Sanibel

Updated by
Chelle Koster
Wulton

WITH ITS SUBTROPICAL CLIMATE and beckoning family-friendly beaches, Southwest Florida is a favorite vacation spot of Florida residents as well as visitors. Compact though it is, there's lots to do in addition to the sun and surf scene throughout its several distinctly different travel destinations. Small and pretty Fort Myers rises inland along the Caloosahatchee River. It got its nickname, the City of Palms, from the hundreds of towering royal palms that inventor Thomas Edison planted between 1900 and 1917 along McGregor Boulevard, the main residential street and site of his winter estate. Edison's idea caught on, and more than 2,000 royal palms now line McGregor Boulevard alone. Museums and educational attractions are the draw here. Off the coast west of Fort Myers are more than 100 coastal islands in all shapes and sizes—among them Sanibel and Captiva, two thoughtfully developed resort islands. Connected to the mainland by a 3-mi causeway, Sanibel is known for its world-class shelling, fine fishing, beachfront resorts, and wildlife refuge. Here and on Captiva, to which it is connected by a causeway, most houses hide behind behind thick vegetation, but the gulf beaches are readily accessible. Just southwest of Fort Myers is Estero Island, home of busy Fort Myers Beach, and farther south, Lovers Key State Park and the growing area north of Naples, Bonita Springs.

Down the coast still farther lies Naples, once a small fishing village and now a thriving and sophisticated town—a smaller, more understated version of Palm Beach with fine restaurants, chichi shopping areas, and—locals will tell you—more golf courses per capita than anywhere else recorded in the world. A lovely small art museum has moved into the town's 1,200-seat performing-arts center, and the town is the west-coast home of the Miami City Ballet. The beaches are soft and white, and access is relatively easy. East of Naples stretches the Big Cypress National Preserve, and a half hour south basks Marco Island; see tight clusters of tiny pristine miniature mangrove islands by airboat. Although high-rises line much of the island's waterfront, natural areas have been preserved, including the tiny fishing village of Goodland, an outpost of Old Florida. Everglades City, to the southeast, serves as the western gateway to Everglades National Park.

Exploring Southwest Florida

In this region vacationers tend to spend most of their time outdoors—swimming, sunning, shelling, fishing, boating, and playing tennis or golf. Fort Myers is the only major inland destination; it has several interesting museums and parks. The barrier islands vary from tiny and undeveloped to sprawling and chockablock with hotels and restaurants.

About the Restaurants

In this part of Florida fresh seafood reigns supreme. Succulent native stone crab claws, a particular treat, in season from mid-October through mid-May, are usually served with drawn butter or tangy mustard sauce. Fortunately, supplies should remain plentiful, since these crabs are not killed to harvest their claws and their limbs regenerate in time for the next season. In Naples's handful of excellent restaurants, mingle with locals, winter visitors, and other travelers and catch up on the latest culinary trends. Throughout the region, early-bird discounts go to those who sit down before 6 PM.

About the Hotels

Lodging in Fort Myers and Naples can be pricey, but you'll find affordable properties even during the busy winter season. Beachfront properties tend to be more expensive; to spend less, look for properties away from the water. In high season—Christmas through Easter—always reserve ahead

for the top properties. Fall is the slowest season: rates are low and
availability is high, but this is also the prime time for hurricanes.

	$$$$	$$$	$$	$	¢
WHAT IT COSTS					
RESTAURANTS	over $30	$20–$30	$15–$20	$10–$15	under $10
HOTELS	over $220	$140–$220	$100–$140	$80–$100	under $80

Restaurant prices are per person for a main course at dinner. Hotel prices are for a
standard double room, excluding 6% sales tax (more in some counties) and
1%–4% tourist tax.

Timing

In winter this is one of the warmest areas of the United States, although
occasionally temperatures drop below freezing in December or January. From January through April you may find it next to impossible
to find a hotel room. Fewer people visit off season, but there really is
no bad time to come. Discounted room rates make summer attractive,
and there's plenty of water for keeping cool.

FORT MYERS AREA

In Fort Myers, old southern mansions peek out from behind rows of
stately palms, and views over the broad, flat Caloosahatchee River,
which borders the city's small but businesslike cluster of office buildings downtown, soften the look of the area. These days, it's showing
the effects of age and urban sprawl, but renowned planner Andres
Duany, father of "new urbanism," has been engaged to help revive it.
North of Fort Myers are small fishing communities and new retirement
towns, including Boca Grande on Gasparilla Island; Port Charlotte, north
of the Peace River; and Punta Gorda, at the convergence of the Peace
River and Charlotte Harbor.

Fort Myers

▶ ❶ *90 mi southeast of Sarasota, 140 mi west of Palm Beach.*

This small, inviting city lies inland along the banks of the Caloosahatchee
River, a half hour from the nearest beach. The town is best known as
the winter home of inventors Thomas A. Edison and Henry Ford.

Majestic palms, some planted by Thomas Edison, line **McGregor Boulevard**, one of the city's most scenic streets. It runs from downtown to
Summerlin Road, which takes you to the barrier islands.

Fodor'sChoice **Thomas A. Edison's Winter Home,** Fort Myers's premier attraction, pays
★ homage to the prolific inventor who gave the world the stock ticker, the
incandescent lamp, and the phonograph, among other inventions. Donated to the city by Edison's widow, the 14-acre estate is a remarkable
place, with a laboratory, botanical gardens, and a museum. The laboratory is just as Edison left it when he died in 1931. Edison traveled south
from New Jersey and devoted his time to inventing things (there are 1,093
patents to his name), experimenting with rubber for friend and frequent
visitor Harvey Firestone and planting some 600 species of plants col-
lected around the world. Next door is **Henry Ford's Winter Residence,**
the more modest seasonal home of Edison's fellow inventor, automaker,
and longtime friend. It is said that the V-8 engine in essence was designed
on the back porch. One admission covers both homes. ⊠ *2350 McGregor
Blvd.* ☎ *239/334–3614* ⊕ *www.edison-ford-estate.com* ☎ *$13* ⊙ *Tours
Mon.–Sat. 9–4, Sun. noon–4.*

Numbers in the text correspond to numbers in the margin and on the Southwest Florida map.

If you have 2 days

🏨 **Fort Myers** ❶ ► is a good base for a short visit. It's not directly on the beach, but its central location makes day trips easy. On the morning of your first day, visit **Thomas A. Edison's Winter Home,** in downtown Fort Myers, and then take McGregor Boulevard to 🏨 **Sanibel Island** ❼. There, stop by the **Bailey-Matthews Shell Museum** and the **J. N. "Ding" Darling National Wildlife Refuge** before heading to **Bowman's Beach** for shelling, swimming, and its famous sunset. The next day drive down Interstate 75 to 🏨 **Naples** ⓫–⓳. Check out the subtropical plants and exotic animals at **Caribbean Gardens: The Zoo in Naples** ⓯. If you have a soft spot for stuffed toys, stop by the **Teddy Bear Museum** ⓮ before hitting Old Naples for some shopping and relaxing on the nearby beach.

If you have 4 days

Stay near the water on 🏨 **Sanibel Island** ❼ ►. Spend your first day shelling and swimming, taking a break from the beach for a stop at the **Bailey-Matthews Shell Museum.** On day two, head into **Fort Myers** ❶ to **Thomas Edison's Winter Home** and **Henry Ford's Winter Residence** and, if you have kids, the hands-on **Imaginarium** nearby. Spend your third day back on Sanibel, dividing your time between the beach and the **J. N. "Ding" Darling National Wildlife Refuge;** go kayaking or try bird-watching in the early morning or evening. On day four, drive south to 🏨 **Naples** ⓫–⓳ and the sights mentioned in the two-day itinerary, or for even more wildlife, head to the **Corkscrew Swamp Sanctuary,** a nature preserve east of **Bonita Springs** ❿.

If you have 10 days

An extended stay enables you to move your base and explore several areas in more depth. With two days in the area around **Fort Myers** ❶ ►, add the **Eden Vineyards Winery and Park, Babcock Wilderness Adventures,** and the **Calusa Nature Center and Planetarium** to the sights on the four-day itinerary. An extra day on 🏨 **Sanibel Island** ❼ allows you to visit by boat an isolated island such as **Cabbage Key** ❺ or the little town of **Boca Grande,** on **Gasparilla Island** ❹. For the second half of your trip, relocate to 🏨 **Naples** ⓫–⓳, stopping en route at **Lovers Key State Park** for some sensational shelling along its 2½ mi of white-sand beach. Once in Naples, divide your time between the beach and the galleries and shops. The **Caribbean Gardens: The Zoo in Naples** ⓯ and the **Corkscrew Swamp Sanctuary** are good bets for kids; to try your hand at paddling, rent a canoe or kayak at the **Naples Nature Center** ⓰. Or get your dose of culture at the impressive **Naples Museum of Art** ⓬. As a diversion, head to **Marco Island** ⓴ or Everglades City for a day of fishing or a wildlife-viewing boat trip in the Everglades.

In a restored railroad depot, the **Fort Myers Historical Museum** showcases the area's history dating to 800 BC. Displays include prehistoric Calusa artifacts, a reconstructed *chickee* hut, canoes, clothing and photos from Seminole settlements, the Ethel Cooper collection of decorative glass, and a replicated Florida Crackerhouse. A favorite attraction is the *Esperanza,* a private rail car from the 1930s. ⊠ *2300 Peck St.* ☎ *239/332–5955* ⊠ *$6* ☉ *Tues.–Sat. 9–4.*

☺ ★ Kids can't wait to get their hands on the wonderful interactive exhibits at the **Imaginarium**, a lively museum-aquarium combo that explores the environment, physics, anatomy, weather, and other science topics. Check out the marine life in the aquariums, the touch pool, the living-reef tank, and the outdoor lagoon; be sure to see what's doing in the 3-D theater and in the butterfly garden; then prepare to get blown away in the Hurricane Experience. ⊠ *2000 Cranford Ave.* ☎ *239/337–3332* ☜ *$7* ⊗ *Mon.–Sat. 10–5, Sun. noon–5.*

For a look at exhibits on wildlife, fossils, and Florida's native animals and habitats, head to the **Calusa Nature Center and Planetarium.** Rustic boardwalks lead through subtropical wetlands, a birds of prey aviary, and a Seminole Indian village. There are snake, alligator, and other live animal demonstrations several times daily. The 90-seat planetarium has astronomy shows daily. ⊠ *3450 Ortiz Ave.* ☎ *239/275–3435* ⊕ *www. calusanature.com* ☜ *Nature center and planetarium $7* ⊗ *Nature center Mon.–Sat. 9–5, Sun. 11–5; planetarium shows daily at 1:30 and 3.*

At **Manatee Park** you may glimpse Florida's most famous marine mammal. When gulf waters are cold—usually from November to March—the gentle sea cows congregate in these waters, which are warmed by the outflow of a nearby power plant. Pause at any of the three observation decks and watch for bubbles. Periodically one of the mammoth creatures will surface. They are huge—mature adults weigh hundreds of pounds. The park rents kayaks on weekends, and kayaking clinics and free guided walks are available. ⊠ *1½ mi east of I–75 at 10901 Rte. 80* ☎ *239/694–3537 viewing update; 239/432–2038 office* ☜ *Parking 75¢ per hr to maximum of $3 per day* ⊗ *Apr.–Sept., daily 8–8; Oct.–Mar., daily 8–5. Gates lock automatically and promptly at closing time.*

Where to Stay & Eat

$$–$$$ ✕ **The Veranda.** A favorite of business and government bigwigs, this spot serves up imaginative Continental fare with a trace of a southern accent. Notable are tournedos with smoky sour-mash whiskey sauce, rack of lamb with rosemary merlot sauce, grilled grouper with blue crab hash, and a southern-grilled seafood sampler. The restaurant is a combination of two turn-of-the-20th-century homes, with sconces and antique oil paintings on its pale yellow walls. Meals are also served in the courtyard. ⊠ *2122 2nd St.* ☎ *239/332–2065* ⊟ *AE, MC, V* ⊗ *Closed Sun. No lunch Sat.*

★ $–$$$ ✕ **Bistro 41.** In this brightly painted bistro the menu roams from chicken potpie and Yucatan pork to seafood paella, rotisserie chicken, and meat loaf. To experience the kitchen at its imaginative best, peruse the night's specials, which often include daringly done seafood. ⊠ *13499 S. Cleveland Ave.* ☎ *239/466–4141* ⊟ *AE, MC, V* ⊗ *No lunch Sun.*

$–$$$ ✕ **La Brasserie.** Chef-owner Gerard Pinault is tried-and-true in these parts, known for his inimitable French flair. Here he does it affordably and casually, offering traditional daily brasserie specials such as beef bourguignon, bouillabaisse, and Basque chicken. More elegant, creative fare builds on local and imported seafood and butcher cuts—grilled scallops, blackened tuna, and filet mignon, for instance. Leave room and time to savor dessert. ⊠ *15660 San Carlos Blvd.* ☎ *239/415–4375* ⊟ *AE, D, MC, V* ⊗ *No lunch Sat.*

$–$$ ✕ **University Grill.** Although seafood is the boss at this clubby, dark-paneled place—specials might include horseradish-crusted grouper and sesame tuna—the menu covers many bases, including burgers, steaks, and pasta (the pasta Maria, with tomato sauce, mascarpone, and smoked mozzarella, is divine). Eat inside, or out on the porch, overlooking a foun-

8

Beaches Gorgeous, long white-sand beaches fringe Southwest Florida's coastline and barrier islands. Many strands, most notably those on Sanibel and Captiva, are celebrated for their shelling. Find tiny coquina shells, bright conch shells, whelks, augurs, scallops, cockles, and much more. Waters are usually calm and friendly to both swimmers and saltwater anglers.

Canoeing A network of narrow waterways makes Sanibel Island's J. N. "Ding" Darling National Wildlife Refuge a favorite destination for canoeing. Sea kayakers hit bay waters, where the annual Captiva Sea Kayak Classic races take place. Also, canoe inland in the less developed areas of the region; several outfits offer half- and full-day as well as overnight trips.

Golf Often referred to as the Golf Capital of the World, Naples is a golfer's delight, with nearly perfect weather most of the year and many beautifully situated courses. There are more than 50 courses in the area, with new ones opening all the time.

Shopping As one of the world's premier shelling grounds, Sanibel Island has numerous shops seriously selling shells (try to say that three times fast). Shells come plain, in all shapes and sizes. But a coterie of crustacean crafters also turn them into everything from picture frames and lamps to jewelry and dozens of supremely kitschy creations (a cowrie turtle, anyone?). Elsewhere on Sanibel appealing boutiques showcase sea-life jewelry along with fashionable resort wear. Naples shops, unique but often pricey, stock lovely antiques, clothing, shoes, linens, and lingerie. Especially noteworthy are the art galleries and the secondhand shops, where, for a fraction of the original price, you can pick up high-end designer clothing discarded—barely worn—by wintering millionaires from all over the United States.

---

tained pond with cavorting turtles and fish. ⊠ 7790 Cypress Lake Dr. ☎ 239/437–4377 ▤ AE, MC, V ◷ No lunch weekends.

¢–$ ✕ **La Casita.** When you spot the charming purple houselike structure in the Kmart parking lot, authentic Mexican food may not spring to mind, but it's in here and done more imaginatively than in other Mexican restaurants. The menu is inspired by Mexico's Guanajuato region; try the potato tamales, basil chicken, or shrimp a la diabla. It's equally bright and cheery inside and opens for breakfast on weekends. ⊠ 15185 McGregor Blvd. ☎ 239/415–1050 ▤ AE, D, MC, V.

¢–$ ✕ **Mel's Diner.** During peak hours you'll wait a while for a seat at this 1950s-
Fodor'sChoice style diner, infused with neon and memorabilia. But it's worth the wait.
★ The booths are comfortable, and the daily blue-plate specials—pot roast, chicken potpie, honey-glazed ham, and such—come with real mashed potatoes. Or try the Windy City Chili, a burger, ribs, or an omelet. For dessert, the popular mile-high pies hit the spot. ☎ 4820 S. Cleveland Ave. ☎ 239/275–7850 ⊕ www.melsdiner.com ▤ AE, DC, MC, V.

¢–$ ✕ **Philly Junction.** From the bread to the beer, it comes from Philadelphia here. Not only are the Philly cheese steaks delicious and authentic, but the burgers and other sandwiches are excellent—and the prices

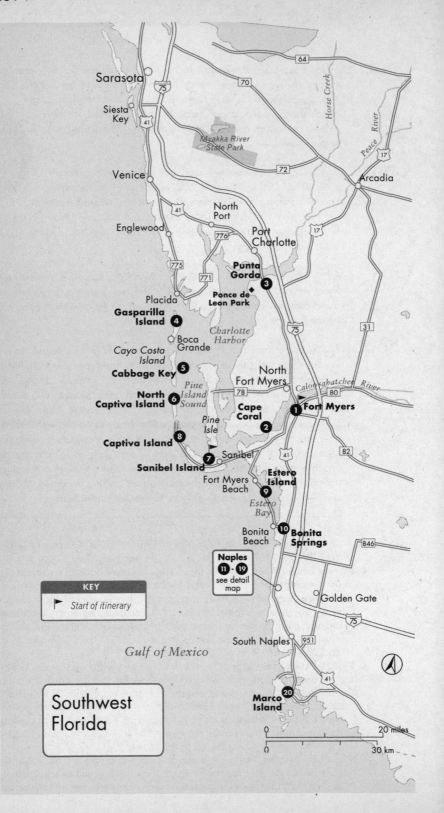

Sarasota

Siesta
Key

Venice

Englewood

North
Port

Port
Charlotte

Arcadia

Myakka River
State Park

Horse Creek

Peace River

Punta
Gorda **3**

Ponce de
Leon Park

Placida

Gasparilla
Island **4**

Boca
Grande

Cayo Costa
Island

Cabbage Key **5**

Charlotte
Harbor

North
Fort Myers

Caloosahatchee River

Pine
Island
Sound

North
Captiva Island **6**

Cape
Coral **2**

1 Fort Myers

Pine
Isle

Captiva Island **8**

Sanibel Island

Sanibel

7

Fort Myers
Beach

Estero
Island

9

Estero
Bay

Bonita
Beach

10 Bonita
Springs

Naples
11 - **19**
see detail
map

Golden Gate

South Naples

Gulf of Mexico

Marco
Island **20**

KEY

▶ Start of itinerary

Southwest
Florida

0   20 miles
0   30 km

are among the lowest around. Stay for an old-fashioned sundae from the fountain, or join the Philly natives for pork roll and scrapple at breakfast time. ✉ *4600 Summerlin Rd.* ☎ *239/936–6622* ☰ *MC, V* ☾ *No dinner Sun.*

$$–$$$ 🖾 **Holiday Inn Riverwalk.** Riverside and close to downtown, this find is known for its lively tiki bar. The elegant coral rock lobby and lush pool courtyard let you know you're in Florida. Rooms and suites are more lavish than you might expect, and some have whirlpools. The hotel underwent complete renovation in 2003, including the remake of its waterfront restaurant into two eateries: the casual Toucan Charlie's in the open-air tiki bar and more formal dining with seating indoors and out. ✉ *2220 W. 1st St., 33901* ☎ *239/334–3434 or 800/644–7775* 🖷 *239/ 334–3844* ⌨ *133 rooms, 13 suites* ⌕ *2 restaurants, pool, exercise equipment, bar, playground, meeting rooms* ☰ *AE, D, DC, MC, V.*

$$ 🖾 **Hilton Garden Inn.** Near Fort Myers' cultural and commercial areas is this compact, prettily landscaped low-rise. Rooms, done in dark green, are spacious and have high-speed Internet access and free HBO. A huge aquarium in the lobby adds a nice Florida touch. ✉ *12601 University Dr., 33907* ☎ *239/790–3500* 🖷 *239/790–3501* ⊕ *www.fortmyers. gardeninn.com* ⌨ *109 rooms, 17 suites* ⌕ *Restaurant, in-room data ports, microwaves, some kitchens, refrigerators, pool, exercise equipment, outdoor hot tub, bar, shop, laundry facilities, laundry service, Internet, business services* ☰ *AE, DC, MC, V.*

$$ 🖾 **Ramada Inn & Suites at Amtel Marina.** Rising tall above the river and yacht basin, this modern 25-story tower commands respect in the downtown skyline. Well-furnished rooms have expansive views of the water or the city. The downtown historic district and the Harborside Convention Center are within walking distance, and Thomas Edison's home is about 1 mi away. ✉ *2500 Edwards Dr., 33901* ☎ *239/337–0300 or 800/833– 1620* 🖷 *239/337–1530* ⊕ *www.amtelmarinahotel.com* ⌨ *247 rooms, 170 suites* ⌕ *Restaurant, tennis court, 2 pools, gym, hot tub, dock, basketball, bar, meeting rooms, airport shuttle* ☰ *AE, D, DC, MC, V.*

Nightlife & the Arts

THE ARTS The **Barbara B. Mann Performing Arts Hall** (✉ 8099 College Pkwy. SW ☎ 239/481–4849) presents plays, concerts, musicals, and dance programs. The **Broadway Palm Dinner Theater** (✉ 1380 Colonial Blvd. ☎ 239/278–4422 ⊕ www.broadwaypalm.com) serves up buffet dinners along with some of Broadway's best comedies and musicals. There's also a cabaret in a smaller 90-seat theater.

NIGHTLIFE Lively most every night, **Bahama Breeze** (✉ 14701 Tamiami Trail ☎ 239/ 454–9234) sways tropical with calypso, soca, and other island sounds. **Indigo Room** (✉ 2219 Main St. ☎ 239/332–0014), downtown, serves up live rock and blues on weekends. **Laugh In Comedy Café** (✉ College Plaza, 8595 College Pkwy. ☎ 239/479–5233), south of downtown, has comedians Thursday, Friday, and Saturday. **Stevie Tomato's Sports Page** (✉ 11491 S. Cleveland Ave. ☎ 239/939–7211) has big-screen TVs.

Sports & the Outdoors

BASEBALL The **Boston Red Sox** (✉ 2201 Edison Ave. ☎ 239/334–4700) train in Fort Myers every spring. The **Minnesota Twins** (✉ Lee County Sports Complex, 1410 Six Mile Cypress Pkwy. ☎ 239/768–4270) play exhibition games in town during March and April.

BIKING The best bike path in Fort Myers is along Summerlin Road. It passes through commercial areas, and close to Sanibel's wide open spaces that are nonetheless quickly dwindling. Linear Park, which runs parallel to Metro Parkway, offers more natural, less congested views. For a good selection of rentals try the **Bike Route** (✉ 14530 Hwy. 41 S ☎ 239/481–3376).

FISHING — Anglers typically head for the gulf, its bays, and estuaries for saltwater fishing—snapper, sheepshead, mackerel, and other species. The Caloosahatchee River, Orange River, canals, and small lakes offer fresh-water alternatives. For local fishing charters, contact **Lee County Professional Guides Association** (☎ 239/337–1118). These guides can take you to whatever kind of fish you prefer.

GOLF — A driving range and 18-hole course are at the **Eastwood Golf Club** (⊠ 4600 Bruce Herd La. ☎ 239/275–4848). The **Fort Myers Country Club** (⊠ 3591 McGregor Blvd. ☎ 239/936–2457) offers lessons and an 18-hole course. Head to the **Shell Point Golf Club** (⊠ 15000 Shell Point Blvd. ☎ 239/433–9790) for an 18-hole course and a driving range.

ICE SKATING — Recreational ice skating, in-line skating, ice-hockey programs, and figure skating plus skate rentals are offered at downtown's **Fort Myers Skatium** (⊠ 2250 Broadway Ave., Fort Myers ☎ 239/461–3145).

SAILING — **Southwest Florida Yachts** (⊠ 3444 Marinatown La. NW ☎ 239/656–1339 or 800/262–7939) charters sailboats and offers lessons.

Shopping

The **Bell Tower Shops** (⊠ U.S. 41 and Daniels Pkwy., South Fort Myers), an open-air shopping center, has about 50 stylish boutiques and specialty shops, a Saks Fifth Avenue, and 20 movie screens. **Edison Mall** (⊠ Colonial Blvd. at U.S. 41) is the largest mall in Southwest Florida, with several major department stores and more than 150 specialty shops. Many unique shops, along with a number of charming restaurants, have taken over the circa-1920 buildings downtown on **1st Street** and its side streets, and sometimes street musicians and artists are on hand to entertain. **Sanibel Tanger Factory Outlets** (⊠ McGregor Blvd. and Summerlin Rd. ☎ 888/471–3939) has outlets for Dexter, Van Heusen, Maidenform, Coach, Jones New York, and Corning–Revere, among others. The **Miromar Outlets complex** (⊠ Corkscrew Rd. at I–75 Exit 123 in Estero, near Teco Arena ☎ 941/948–3766) includes Adidas, Nike, Nautica, and Calvin Klein.

Just east of Fort Myers, more than 800 vendors sell new and used goods at **Fleamasters Fleamarket** (⊠ 1 mi west of I–75 Exit 138 on Rte. 82), Friday through Sunday between 8 and 4.

Cape Coral & North Fort Myers

❷ *13 mi from downtown Fort Myers via North Fort Myers, just across the river (1 mi) from south Fort Myers.*

Four bridges cross from Fort Myers to Cape Coral and its eastern neighbor, North Fort Myers. Families especially find fun in these residential communities and their rural backyards, including undiscovered Pine Island to Cape Coral's west.

Nature walks, bubble bins, Xeriscape displays, an iguana garden, whisper dishes, mazes, telescopes, optical tricks, mind-benders, and brain twisters keep things lively at the **Children's Science Center.** ⊠ *2915 N.E. Pine Island Rd.* ☎ *239/997–0012* ⊕ *www.cyberstreet.com/csc* ⊠ *$5* ◷ *Weekdays 9:30–4:30, weekends noon–5.*

Sun Splash Family Waterpark has more than two dozen wet and dry attractions, including three large water slides; the Lilypad Walk, where you step from one floating "lily pad" to another; an arcade; Squirtworks, a special play area for very young children; and Cape Fear, a lightning-fast tube slide. ⊠ *400 Santa Barbara Blvd.* ☎ *239/574–0558* ⊕ *www. sunsplashwaterpark.com* ⊠ *$9.95* ◷ *Mar.–Sept., hrs vary; call ahead.*

off the beaten path

ECHO. Educational Concerns for Hunger Organization is a small Christian ministry group striving to end world hunger via creative farming. The gardens have Florida's largest collection of tropical food plants. Walk through a simulated rain forest and up a two-story, man-made mountain, and look at farm animals and crops such as sesame and rice grown without soil. ✉ *17391 Durrance Rd., North Fort Myers* ☎ *239/543–3246* ⊕ *www.echonet.org* 🎟 *Free* ☾ *Tours Tues. and Fri.–Sat. at 10 or by appointment.*

Where to Stay & Eat

★ **$–$$$** ✗ **Michel & Michelle's.** Tucked away in an unassuming strip mall, this little corner of France serves authentic cuisine at reasonable prices. In addition to classics such as chicken Marsala and Dover sole *meunière*, the menu holds surprises such as ostrich au poivre and rack of lamb with Roquefort cheese. ✉ *1515 S.E. 47th Terr.* ☎ *239/541–1255* ▤ *D, MC, V.*

$–$$ ✗ **Siam Hut.** Thai music pings and twangs in the background while servers bring forth lively renditions of *pad thai* (a mixture of rice noodles, crushed peanuts, chicken, shrimp, egg, bean sprouts, and scallions) and crispy Siam rolls (spring rolls stuffed with ground chicken, bean thread, and vegetables). Get your food fiery hot or extra mild. ✉ *4521 Del Prado Blvd.* ☎ *239/945–4247* ▤ *MC, V* ☾ *Closed Sun. No lunch Sat.*

¢–$ ✗ **Bert's Bar & Grill.** Looking to hang out with the locals on Pine Island? You get that, cheap eats, and a water view to boot at Bert's. Speaking of boots, you're likely to see much of the clientele wearing white rubber fishing boots, known here as Pine Island Reeboks. Order pizza, a burger, fried oysters, or Cajun grouper from the no-nonsense menu. ✉ *4271 Pine Island Rd., Matlacha* ☎ *239/282–3232* ⊕ *www.bertsbar. com* ▤ *MC, V.*

$$$ 🛏 **Tarpon Lodge Sportsman Inn.** If you're looking for no-frills escape and fishing, this aptly named lodge, built in 1926 on a sweep of green lawn with magnificent views out to sea, may do the trick. Rooms are small and simple, and the sunny restaurant dishes up creative surprises. It's in the fishing village of Pineland, on the edge of Pine Island Sound, settled in the 16th century by Calusa Indians and stocked with charming Cracker fishing shacks in the 1920s. ✉ *13771 Waterfront Dr., Pineland, Pine Island 33945* ⎙ *239/283–3999* ⊕ *www.tarponlodge.com* ⤳ *20 rooms, 1 suite* ♿ *Restaurant, pool, dock, fishing, bar, shops* ▤ *AE, MC, V.*

¢–$ 🛏 **Casa Loma Motel.** At this pretty little motel, 15 minutes from Fort Myers at the end of the Croton Canal, all units are efficiencies with a porch or balcony overlooking the canal. ✉ *3608 Del Prado Blvd., 33904* ☎ *239/549–6000 or 877/227–2566* ⎙ *239/549–4877* ⤳ *49 efficiencies* ♿ *Kitchenettes, pool, dock, fishing, recreation room, laundry facilities* ▤ *AE, D, MC, V.*

Sports & the Outdoors

GOLF The **Golf Club** (✉ 4003 Palm Tree Blvd. ☎ 239/542–7879) has an 18-hole course, a driving range, and a putting green. **Coral Oaks Golf Course** (✉ 1800 N.W. 28th Ave. ☎ 239/573–3100) has an 18-hole layout and a practice range.

TENNIS **Cape Coral Yacht Club Community Park** (✉ 5819 Driftwood Pkwy. ☎ 239/574–0808) has five lighted Har-Tru courts. **Judd Park** (✉ 1297 Driftwood Dr., North Fort Myers ☎ 239/656–5138) has tennis courts.

Shopping

The vast **Shell Factory** (✉ 2787 N. Tamiami Trail, North Fort Myers ☎ 239/995–2141 or 800/282–5805 ⊕ www.shellfactory.com) claims to have the world's largest display of seashells, coral, sponges, and fossils. But this is as much entertainment complex as store, so you'll find bumper boats, a glass factory ($3), a petting zoo, and a display of lions, monkeys, birds, tigers, and snakes called the Octagon Animal Showcase, which you must pay to experience. (This small zoo, open 10–7 daily, will set you back $8 per adult.)

Punta Gorda

❸ *23 mi north of Cape Coral and Fort Myers.*

In this small, old town on the mouth of the Peace River, where it empties into Charlotte Harbor, street art, water views, and some 20 murals enliven the compact, downtown historic district. Although there is plenty of waterfront in the area, between this town and sprawling adjacent Port Charlotte there is only a single beach—and it's man-made and on the river rather than on the gulf. This is a place to come for fishing, canoeing, walking in the woods, and, most of all, escaping the crowds.

The **Ponce de León Historical Park and Peace River Wildlife Center** is named for the famous *conquistador* who, according to local lore, took a fatal arrow here. A humble shrine pays homage, but the park's best features are the fishing, wildlife, and view at the mouth of the Peace River. The rehabilitation facility that shares the point of land conducts tours. ☒ *3400 W. Marion Ave.* ☎ *941/637–3830* ☒ *By donation* ☉ *Wildlife center Wed.–Mon. 11–3; park daily sunrise–sunset.*

off the beaten path

Ⓒ **Babcock Wilderness Adventures.** To see what Florida looked like centuries ago, visit 90,000-acre Babcock Crescent B Ranch, southeast of Punta Gorda and northeast of Fort Myers. During the 90-minute swamp-buggy excursion you ride in a converted school bus through several ecosystems, including the unusual and fascinating Telegraph Cypress Swamp. Along the way an informative and amusing guide describes the area's social and natural history while you keep an eye peeled for alligators, wild pigs, all sorts of birds, and other denizens of the wild. The tour also takes in the ranch's bison herd, resident cattle, and Florida panthers in captivity. There's also a three-hour bike tour, with bikes and helmets provided. Reserve ahead for both tours. ☒ *8000 Rte. 31* ☎ *941/637–4611 or 800/500–5583* ⊕ *www.babcockwilderness.com* ☒ *Bus tour $17.95, bike tour $35* ☉ *Tours daily, with varying schedules, weather permitting.*

Where to Stay & Eat

$$–$$$ ✕ **Amimoto Japanese Restaurant.** Sit at the sushi bar or a table in the small dining room decorated simply with Japanese art prints and scrolls. Most popular for lunch, it offers a nice selection of *obentos*, Japanese box lunches, which might include pork loin, tempura shrimp or squid, or scallops sautéed with lime. The extensive sushi and appetizer menus give you many grazing options. ☒ *Towles Plaza, 2705 S. Tamiami Trail* ☎ *941/505–1515* ⊟ *AE, D, DC, MC, V* ☉ *No lunch weekends.*

$$ ☶ **Fishermen's Village Villas.** Go for a shopping spree or jump onto a boat without ever leaving the premises when you stay at this complex of affordable, nicely decorated two-bedroom time-share units. Sleeping up to six, they're above Punta Gorda's lively shopping center, on the site of an old crab-packing plant. ☒ *1200 W. Retta Esplanade, No. 58, 33950* ☎ *941/639–8721 or 800/639–0020* 🖶 *941/637–1054* ⊕ *www.fishville. com* ⊲ *47 suites* ♨ *7 restaurants, tennis court, pool, massage, docks, boating, marina, bars, shops* ⊟ *AE, DC, MC.*

$ ☶ **Harbour Inn Motel & Antique Mall.** Antiques shoppers will feel at home in this motel on the northeast side of the bridge over the Peace River.

Some 50 dealers sell their wares daily and hold an antiques fair the second Saturday of each month. More than half of the rooms make up for their plainness with stunning views of the Peace River. The tearoom is a classy amenity. ⑤ *5000 Tamiami Trail, Charlotte Harbour 33980* ☎ *941/625–6126 or 800/646–6037* 🖷 *941/743–8774* ⊕ *www. theharbourinn.com* ⟿ *45 rooms* ⚭ *Tea shop, pool, fishing, boating, shopping* ⊟ *AE, D, MC, V.*

Sports & the Outdoors

BIKING   Bicycles can be rented by the hour or by the day at **Ralph's Bicycle Shop** (⊠ 258 W. Marion Ave. ☎ 941/639–3029). For information on the local bike trails, which range from bike lanes through local neighborhoods to recreational trails such as the Cape Haze Pioneer Trail and the rails-to-trails Boca Grande Trail, request a copy of the brochure "Charlotte County Bikeways" from the Charlotte County Chamber of Commerce.

CANOEING Kayaking and canoeing in Charlotte Harbor and along the Peace River are a good reason to visit this area. Up the Peace River, about 25 mi from Punta Gorda, **Canoe Outpost** (⊠ 2816 N.W. Rte. 661, Arcadia ☎ 863/ 494–1215 or 800/268–0083) conducts all-day and overnight canoe trips, camping equipment included. On this part of the river, the tannin-tinted water runs narrow. Tall cypress trees, birds, and alligators are plentiful; the last pose no threat to canoeists in their vessels.

FISHING   For half- and full-day fishing trips in the bay or the ocean, call **King Fisher Charter** (⊠ Fishermen's Village ☎ 941/639–0969 ⊕ www.kingfisherfleet. com).

GOLF   Play 18 holes at affordable and semi-private **Punta Gorda Country Club** (⊠ 6100 Duncan Rd. ☎ 941/639–1494). There are 18 holes to play at the **Deep Creek Golf Club** (⊠ 1260 San Cristobal Ave., Port Charlotte ☎ 941/625–6911).

TENNIS   **Port Charlotte Tennis Club** (⊠ 22400 Gleneagles Terr., Port Charlotte ☎ 941/625–7222) has four lighted hard courts.

THE COASTAL ISLANDS

A maze of islands in various stages of habitation fronts the mainland from Charlotte County to Fort Myers, separated by the Intracoastal Waterway. Some are accessible via a causeway; to reach others, you may need a boat. If you cut through Pine Island Sound, you have a good chance of being escorted by bottle-nosed dolphins. Mostly birds and other wild creatures inhabit some islands, which are given over to state parks. Traveler-pampering hotels on Sanibel, Captiva, and Fort Myers Beach give way to rustic cottages, old inns, and cabins on quiet Cabbage Key and Pine Island, which have no beaches because they lie between the barrier islands and mainland. Still more are devoted to resorts for the Robinson Crusoe in you. When exploring island beaches, keep one eye on the sand; shelling is a major pursuit in these parts.

Gasparilla Island (Boca Grande)

❹ *43 mi northwest of Fort Myers, 23 mi southwest of Punta Gorda.*

Before roads to Southwest Florida were even talked about, wealthy northerners came by train to spend the winter at the **Gasparilla Inn**, built in 1912 in Boca Grande on Gasparilla Island. Although condominiums and modern sprawl creep up on the rest of Gasparilla, much of the town of Boca Grande looks like another era. The mood is set by the Old Florida homes and tree-framed roadways. The island's calm is disrupted in the spring when anglers descend with a vengeance on Boca Grande Pass, considered among the best tarpon-fishing spots in the world.

Where to Stay

$$$$ 🖾 **Gasparilla Inn.** Social-register members such as the Vanderbilts and DuPonts still winter at the gracious, pale-yellow wooden hotel built by shipping industrialists in the early 1900s. The lodge rooms are not lavishly decorated by today's standards. The cottage rooms are more modern and less spartan. The inn takes up most of the town of Boca Grande with its rich-blooded amenities—sprawling lawns, golf course, beach club, and restaurants. In summer the main lodge closes and cottage rates include breakfast and dinner only. ⌂ *500 Palm Ave., Boca Grande 33921* ☎ *941/964–2201* 🖷 *941/283–1384* 💬 *140 rooms* ⚐ *Restaurant, dining room, 18-hole golf course, 7 tennis courts, 2 pools, gym, hair salon, beach, croquet* ⊟ *No credit cards* ¶◎⫿ *FAP.*

Cabbage Key

⑤ *5 mi south of Boca Grande.*

You'll have to take a boat from Bokeelia, on Pine Island, or from Captiva Island, to get to this island, which sits at Mile Marker 60 on the Intracoastal Waterway.

Where to Stay

$ 🖾 **Cabbage Key Inn.** Atop an ancient Calusa Indian shell mound is the friendly inn built by novelist and playwright Mary Roberts Rinehart in 1938. It's surrounded by 100 acres of tropical vegetation. In addition to the historic inn rooms, there are guest cottages scattered throughout the property, some of which have kitchens. There's a full-service marina and a restaurant whose dining room is papered with thousands of dollar bills. One of the many perks of staying here is access to the remote and pristine beach of Cayo Casto, a short boat trip from Cabbage Key. The resort is also accessible only by boat. ⌂ *Box 200, Pineland 33945* ☎ *239/283–2278* 🖷 *239/283–1384* ⊕ *www.cabbagekey.com* 💬 *6 rooms, 7 cottages* ⚐ *Restaurant, marina, fishing, bar, shop* ⊟ *MC, V.*

North Captiva Island

⑥ *3 mi south of Cabbage Key.*

No bridges lead to this 750-acre island, and most visitors arrive by prearranged water taxi from Pine Island. They come for the isolation and complete absence of "civilization." Some of the scattering of private houses and condos can be rented by the week through the 35-acre **Safety Harbor Club** (☎ 239/472–1056 ⊕ www.safetyharborclub.com). The complex has a pool and tennis courts, which you're free to use; it's a good idea to bring your own groceries, as there's only one small store, and it's stocked mainly with utilitarian items.

Sanibel & Captiva Islands

23 mi southwest of downtown Fort Myers.

▶ **⑦** **Sanibel Island,** accessible from the mainland via the Sanibel Causeway (toll $3 round-trip), is famous as one of the world's best shelling grounds, a function of the unusual east–west orientation of the island's south end. Just as the tide is going out and just after storms, the pickings can be superb, and shell seekers with the telltale "Sanibel stoop" patrol every beach laden with bags of conchs, whelks, coquinas, and other bivalves and gastropods. (Remember, if you join them, that it's unlawful to pick up live shells.) Away from the beach, flowery vegetation decorates small shopping complexes, pleasant resorts and condo complexes, mom-and-pop motels, and casual restaurants. But much of the narrow highway down the spine of the island is bordered by nature reserves that have made Sanibel as well known among bird-watchers as it is among seashell collectors.

8 **Captiva Island,** connected to the northern end of Sanibel by a bridge, is quirky and engaging. Australian pines and jungled vegetation canopy the twisting main road; you'll barely see the palatial houses on either side for their dense fringe of greenery. A sense of seclusion prevails.

At Sanibel's southern tip, the frequently photographed **Sanibel Lighthouse,** built in 1884, before the island was settled, guards **Lighthouse Beach.** Although the lighthouse is not open to the public, the area around it has been a wildlife refuge since 1950. A fishing pier, nature trail, and rest rooms are available. ⊠ *Periwinkle Way, Sanibel* ☎ *239/472–6477* 🚗 *Parking $2 per hr.*

★ The charming **Sanibel Historical Village and Museum** shows off buildings from the island's past—a 1927 post office, a garage housing a Model T Ford, the Old Bailey general store, a tea house, a 1925 winter vacation cottage, and the 1913 Rutland House Museum, with old documents and photographs and a Calusa Indian exhibit. ⊠ *950 Dunlop Rd., Sanibel* ☎ *239/472–4648* 🚗 *$3* 🕙 *Nov.–June, Wed.–Sat. 10–4; June–mid-Aug., 10–1.*

The beach in **Gulfside Park** is lesser-known and quiet, good for solitude and shells. There are rest rooms and picnic tables. ⊠ *Algiers La. off Casa Ybel Rd., Sanibel* ☎ *239/472–6477* 🚗 *Parking $2 per hr.*

Tarpon Bay Beach is centrally located and safer for swimming than beaches at the passes, where waters move swiftly. Sometimes in season there's a mobile concession stand. ⊠ *Tarpon Bay Rd. off Sanibel–Captiva Rd., Sanibel* ☎ *239/472–6477* 🚗 *Parking $2 per hr.*

☾ ★ To help you identify your Sanibel Island beach finds, stop at the **Bailey-Matthews Shell Museum,** which displays more than a million shells from around the world. A shell-finder display identifies specimens from local waters, each shown in sizes ranging from tiny to huge; handle these and sea creatures in the kids' area. A 6-ft revolving globe at the center of the museum rotunda highlights where the museum's shells were found. ⊠ *3075 Sanibel–Captiva Rd., Sanibel* ☎ *239/395–2233 or 888/679–6450* ⊕ *www.shellmuseum.org* 🚗 *$5* 🕙 *Tues.–Sun. 10–4.*

★ More than half of Sanibel is occupied by the subtly beautiful **J. N. "Ding" Darling National Wildlife Refuge,** 6,300 acres of wetlands and lush, jungly mangrove forests named after a conservation-minded Pulitzer Prize–winning political cartoonist, who became the first director of the government body that later became the U.S. Fish & Wildlife Service. The masses of roseate spoonbills and ibis and the winter flock of white pelicans here make for a good show even if you're not a diehard bird-watcher. Experts can count some 230 species, including herons, ospreys, and the timid mangrove cuckoo. Raccoons, otters, alligators, and one lone American crocodile also can be spotted. The 4½-mi Wildlife Drive is the main way to explore the preserve; drive, walk, or bicycle along it, or ride a specially designed open-air tram with a naturalist on board. There are also a couple of short walking trails, including one to a Calusa shell mound. Or explore from the water via canoe or kayak (guided tours are available). The best time for bird-watching is in the early morning about an hour before or after low tide, and the observation tower along the road offers prime viewing. Interactive exhibits in the Education

Center, at the entrance to the refuge, demonstrate the refuge's various ecosystems and explain its status as a rest stop along a major bird migration route. Because Wildlife Drive is closed to vehicular traffic on Friday, try to time your visit for another day. Alternatively, rent a bike for the trip or allow enough time to walk. ⊠ *1 Wildlife Dr., Sanibel* ☎ *239/ 472–1100; 239/395–0900 tram* ✆ *$5 per car, $1 for pedestrians and bicyclists; tram $10; Education Center free* ⊙ *Education Center Nov.–Apr., daily 9–5; May–Oct., daily 9–4.*

For a good look at snowy egrets, great blue herons, alligators, and other inhabitants of Florida's wetlands, follow one of the 10 short walking trails at the 1,800-acre wetlands managed by the **Sanibel/ Captiva Conservation Foundation.** See island research projects and nature displays, visit a butterfly house, and touch sea creatures. Guided walks are available. ⊠ *3333 Sanibel–Captiva Rd., Sanibel* ☎ *239/472–2329* ✆ *$3* ⊙ *Dec.–mid-Apr., weekdays 8:30–4, Sat. 10–2; mid-Apr.–Dec., weekdays 8:30–3.*

Fodor'sChoice
★ Long, wide **Bowman's Beach,** on Sanibel's northwest end, is the island's most secluded strand. Walk the length of it and leave humanity behind, finding some of the greatest concentrations of shells along the way. And the sunsets at the north end are spectacular—try to spot the green flash said to occur just as the sun sinks below the horizon. ⊠ *Bowman Beach Rd., Sanibel* ☎ *239/472–6477* ✆ *Parking 75¢ per hr; maximum $3 a day.*

Turner Beach is the sunset-watching spot on the southern tip of Captiva. Strong currents through the pass make swimming tricky, and parking is limited. ⊠ *Captiva Dr., Captiva* ☎ *239/472–6477* ✆ *Parking 75¢ per hr.*

Captiva Beach fronts many private homes. The parking lot is small, so arrive early. ⊠ *Captiva Dr., Captiva* ☎ *239/472–6477* ✆ *Parking 75¢ per hr.*

Where to Stay & Eat

$$$–$$$$ ✕ **Sunshine Café.** The food is terrific in this busy, efficient eatery, a good bet when you feel like a lighter meal. Sit out on the porch and order a sesame-crusted yellowfin tuna salad for lunch or Colorado lamb chops with lamb shank reduction and roasted garlic for dinner. The mixed berry cobbler is the indulgence of choice for dessert. ⊠ *Captiva Village Square, Captiva Dr., Captiva* ☎ *239/472–6200* ▤ *AE, MC, V.*

$–$$$$ ✕ **The Porter House.** A steak-house craze has hit the islands, and this faux New York chophouse is one of the more exclusive. The signature porterhouse weighs in at 20 ounces and $46, and there are other prime, aged cuts from which to choose, as well as a few seafood dishes. The cognac selection is impressive. ⊠ *South Seas Resort, 5400 Captiva Dr., Captiva* ☎ *239/472–7535* ▤ *AE, D, DC, MC, V* ⊙ *No lunch.*

★ $$$ ✕ **Traders Store & Cafe.** Artifacts from Africa and other exotic locales accent this bistro, a favorite of locals, in a corner of a warehouse-size import store. The marvelous seared tuna appetizer with Asian slaw and wasabi vinaigrette exemplifies the creative fare. Or go for the barbecued baby back ribs or any of the day's finely crafted specials. ⊠ *1551 Periwinkle Way, Sanibel* ☎ *239/472–7242* ▤ *AE, D, MC, V.*

$$$ ✕ **Twilight Cafe.** Crawfish mashed potatoes are a tasty specialty at this
Fodor'sChoice tiny, artistic nook in Gallery Place. The menu changes daily but often
★ includes such artistic daredevils as grilled scallops over homemade tangerine linguine or pan-seared blackened filet on a bed of braised fennel with mango salsa. ⊠ *751 Tarpon Bay Rd., Sanibel* ☎ *239/472–8818* ▤ *AE, MC, V* ⊙ *Closed Sun. off-season.*

$$-$$$ ✕ **Bubble Room.** At this lively, kitschy favorite, servers wear scout uniforms and funny headgear. Electric trains circle overhead, glossies of 1940s Hollywood stars fill walls, and tabletops showcase old-time toys. After grazing your basket of cheesy Bubble Bread and sweet, yeasty sticky buns, go for aged prime rib or the poached grouper steamed in a paper bag. Have a hefty slice of one of the homemade triple-layer cakes; the red velvet cake is legendary. Be prepared to wait for a table. ⊠ *15001 Captiva Dr., Captiva* ☎ *239/472–5558* ⚐ *Reservations not accepted* ▤ *AE, D, DC, MC, V.*

$-$$$ ✕ **Green Flash.** Good food and terrific views of quiet waters edged by mangroves keep people coming back to this casual café. Seafood is the specialty, but there's a bit of everything on the menu, from shrimp in beer batter and grilled swordfish to pork tenderloin Wellington. For lunch, try the Green Flash sandwich (smoked turkey or vegetables and cheese on grilled foccacia). ⊠ *15183 Captiva Dr., Captiva* ☎ *239/472–3337* ▤ *AE, D, DC, MC, V.*

$$ ✕ **McT's Shrimphouse and Tavern.** In this informal Sanibel landmark, the menu spotlights fresh seafood. Look for oyster and mussel appetizers and the all-you-can-eat shrimp and crab, although ribs, prime rib, and blackened chicken are also available. There's always a dessert du jour, but few can resist the Sanibel mud pie, a delicious concoction heavy on the Oreos. ⊠ *1523 Periwinkle Way, Sanibel* ☎ *239/472–3161* ⚐ *Reservations not accepted* ▤ *AE, D, MC, V.*

¢–$$ ✕ **Lighthouse Café.** Although Sanibel's oldest restaurant looks pretty much like a plain old coffee shop, it consistently wins the local nod for serving best breakfast on the island. Whole-wheat pancakes, muffins, frittatas, and mimosas bring people in the morning and beyond—breakfast is served until 3 PM. At lunch and dinner order hamburgers, seafood, and salads. ⊠ *362 Periwinkle Way, Sanibel* ☎ *239/472–0303* ⚐ *Reservations not accepted* ▤ *MC, V* ☺ *No dinner Apr.–Dec.*

$$$$ ▦ **Casa Ybel Resort.** The Victorian ornamentation of this time-share reflects the history of the property, which dates from the early 20th century. Palms, ponds, a footbridge, and gazebos set the mood on the 23 acres of gulf-facing grounds. Inside, the one- and two-bedroom apartments are contemporary, with full kitchens, a scattering of bright tropical prints, and big screened-in porches that look out to the beach. The respected Thistle Lodge restaurant resides in a re-created Victorian home with a beach view. ⊠ *2255 W. Gulf Dr., Sanibel 33957* ☎ *239/472–3145 or 800/276–4753* ▣ *239/472–2109* ⊕ *www.casaybelresort.com* ➬ *40 1-bedroom units, 74 2-bedroom units* ♨ *2 restaurants, kitchens, 6 tennis courts, pool, beach, windsurfing, boating, bicycles, shuffleboard, bar, baby-sitting, children's programs (ages 4–11), playground* ▤ *AE, D, DC, MC, V.*

★ **$$$$** ▦ **Sanibel Harbour Resort & Spa.** This high-rise resort complex is not on Sanibel proper but instead towers over the bay at the last mainland exit before the causeway. Laid-back, beachy Sanibel style is not the draw; instead, people come for the sweeping views of island-studded San Carlos Bay as well as the racquet club, the exceptional spa, and the large free-form pool, among other facilities and activities. Rent a kayak, take a wildlife-viewing cruise, or go fishing. Transportation to Sanibel is free. ⊠ *17260 Harbour Pointe Dr., Fort Myers 33908* ☎ *239/466–4000 or 800/767–7777* ▣ *239/466–6050* ⊕ *www.sanibel-resort.com* ➬ *281 rooms, 66 suites, 60 condominiums* ♨ *3 restaurants, snack bar, 8 tennis courts, 5 pools (1 indoor), hair salon, health club, 14 hot tubs, spa, beach, dock, boating, fishing, basketball, racquetball, 3 bars, children's programs (ages 5–12)* ▤ *AE, D, DC, MC, V.*

$$$$ ⊞ **Sanibel's Seaside Inn.** Tucked among the subtropical greenery, right on the beach, this quiet inn, a part of South Seas Resorts properties, is a pleasant alternative to the area's larger resorts. Bright tropical prints and rattan furniture fill the guest quarters, which are studios, one- to three-bedroom units, and individual cottages. Continental breakfast is complimentary, and videos are on hand to borrow. Transportation is free to other Sundial Beach Resort and other South Seas facilities. ⊠ *541 E. Gulf Dr., Sanibel 33957* ☎ *239/472–1400 or 800/831–7384* 🖷 *239/481–4947* ⊕ *www.seasideinn.com* ⋑ *12 rooms, 20 suites* ᐘ *Picnic area, some kitchens, microwaves, refrigerators, in-room VCRs, pool, beach, bicycles, shuffleboard, library, laundry facilities* ▤ *AE, D, DC, MC, V* ⧀ *CP.*

$$$$ ⊞ **Shalimar Motel.** Well-maintained grounds and an inviting beach are the appeal of this small property. Units occupy small two-story cottages set back from the beach amid subtropical greenery. The small pool is in the courtyard, and there are barbecue grills. ⊠ *2823 W. Gulf Dr., Sanibel 33957* ☎ *239/472–1353 or 800/995–1242* 🖷 *239/472–6430* ⊕ *www.shalimar.com* ⋑ *20 efficiencies, 11 1-bedroom units, 2 2-bedroom units* ᐘ *Kitchens, pool, beach, basketball, shuffleboard, laundry facilities* ▤ *DC, MC, V.*

★ **$$$$** ⊞ **South Seas Resort and Yacht Harbour.** Like a bustling town, this polished Captiva resort packs a lot into 330 acres, yet the natural world remains. Manatees and pelicans patrol the marina at the property's north end, with osprey and gulls overhead; dunes fringe a pristine 2½-mi beach; and mangroves edge the single main road. Stylish, low-rise hotel rooms, villas, and houses are all over the property but are concentrated at either end, near the marina and, to the south near the entry gate and the small shopping complex. The windswept golf course has dazzling water views. ⊠ *5400 Plantation Rd., Box 194, Captiva 33924* ☎ *239/472–5111 or 800/965–7772* 🖷 *239/481–4947* ⊕ *www.south-seas-resort.com* ⋑ *138 units, 482 suites* ᐘ *5 restaurants, snack bar, room service, kitchens, cable TV with movies, 9-hole golf course, putting green, 21 tennis courts, 18 pools, gym, hair salon, hot tub, massage, beach, dock, windsurfing, boating, jet skiing, parasailing, waterskiing, fishing, bicycles, shuffleboard, 3 bars, children's programs (ages 3–18), meeting rooms* ▤ *AE, D, DC, MC, V.*

$$–$$$ ⊞ **Waterside Inn.** Palm trees and white sand set the scene at this quiet beachside vacation spot made up of white one- and two-story buildings. Rooms and efficiencies are modestly furnished but have balconies or patios and at least a partial view of the gulf. ⊠ *3033 W. Gulf Dr., Sanibel 33957* ☎ *239/472–1345 or 800/741–6166* 🖷 *239/472–2148* ⊕ *www.watersideinnonthebeach.com* ⋑ *4 rooms, 10 efficiencies, 8 cottages* ᐘ *Some kitchens, microwaves, refrigerators, pool, beach, bicycles, shuffleboard, laundry facilities, meeting rooms, some pets allowed* ▤ *AE, D, MC, V.*

Sports & the Outdoors

BIKING Everyone bikes around flatter-than-a-pancake Sanibel and Captiva—on bikeways that edge the main highway in places, on the road through the wildlife refuge, and along side streets. Free maps are available at bicycle liveries. On Sanibel, rent by the hour or the day at **Bike Route** (⊠ 2330 Palm Ridge Rd., Sanibel ☎ 239/472–1955). On Captiva, bikes are available at **Jim's Rentals** (⊠ 11534 Andy Rosse La., Captiva ☎ 239/472–1296).

BOATING **Boat House of Sanibel** (⊠ Sanibel Marina, 634 N. Yachtsman Dr., Sanibel ☎ 239/472–2531) rents powerboats. **Sweet Water Boat Rental** ('Tween Waters Marina, ⊠ 15951 Captiva Dr., Captiva ☎ 239/472–6336) can set you up with a 19-ft center console boat.

CANOEING &
KAYAKING
Scout out the wildlife refuge in a canoe or kayak from **Tarpon Bay Explorers** (✉ 900 Tarpon Bay Rd., Sanibel ☎ 239/472–8900). Guided tours are also available.

FISHING
Local anglers head out to catch mackerel, pompano, grouper, reds, snook, bluefish, and shark. To find a charter captain on Sanibel, ask around at its main public marina, **Sanibel Marina** (✉ 634 N. Yachtsman Dr., Sanibel ☎ 239/472–2723). On Captiva, the place to look for guides is **'Tween Waters Marina** (✉ 15951 Captiva Dr., Captiva ☎ 239/472–5161).

GOLF
Rent clubs and take lessons as well as test your skills against the water hazards on the 18-hole course at the **Dunes Golf & Tennis Club** (✉ 949 Sandcastle Rd., Sanibel ☎ 239/472–2535).

TENNIS
At the **Dunes Golf & Tennis Club** (✉ 949 Sandcastle Rd., Sanibel ☎ 239/472–3522), there are seven clay courts and two pros who give lessons.

Shopping

Sanibel is known for its art galleries, shell shops, and one-of-a-kind boutiques; the several small open-air shopping complexes are inviting, with their tropical flowers and shady ficus trees. The largest cluster of shops is **Periwinkle Place** (✉ 2075 Periwinkle Way, Sanibel), with 55 shops. **Aboriginals** (✉ 2340 Periwinkle Way, Sanibel ☎ 239/395–2200) sells museum-quality textiles, baskets, pottery, sculptures, and jewelry made by Native Americans, Australians, and Africans. At **She Sells Sea Shells** (✉ 1157 Periwinkle Way, Sanibel ☎ 239/472–6991 ✉ 2422 Periwinkle Way, Sanibel ☎ 239/472–8080), everything imaginable is made from shells, from decorative mirrors and lamps to Christmas ornaments.

Estero Island (Fort Myers Beach)

⑨ *18 mi southwest of Fort Myers.*

Crammed with motels, hotels, and restaurants, this island is one of Fort Myers's more frenetic gulf playgrounds. Dolphins are frequently spotted in Estero Bay, a protected arm of the gulf, and marinas provide a starting point for boating adventures, including sunset cruises, sightseeing cruises, and deep-sea fishing. At the southern tip, a bridge leads to Lovers Key State Park.

At the 17-acre **Lynn Hall Memorial Park,** in the commercial northern part of Estero Island, the shore slopes gradually into the usually tranquil and warm gulf waters, providing safe swimming for children. And since houses, condominiums, and hotels line most of the beach, you're never far from civilization. There are picnic tables, barbecue grills, playground equipment, and a free fishing pier, and a bathhouse with rest rooms, a pedestrian mall, and a number of restaurants are nearby. Parking is metered. ✉ *Estero Blvd.* ☎ *239/463–1116* ☉ *Daily 7 AM–10 PM.*

off the
beaten
path
Lovers Key State Park. This out-of-the-way park encompasses 700 acres on two islands and several uninhabited islets. Bike, hike, or walk the park's trails; go shelling on its 2½ mi of white-sand beach; rent a canoe or a kayak; or spend the night at a campsite. Watch for osprey, bald eagles, herons, ibis, pelicans, and roseate spoonbills, or sign up for an excursion to observe manatees, dolphins, and loggerhead turtles. Weddings often take place at the romantic gazebo on the beach. There are also rest rooms, picnic tables, a snack bar, and showers. ✉ *8700 Estero Blvd.* ☎ *239/463–4588* ✇ *$4 2–8 people in one vehicle, $1 one person in one vehicle, $1 per person pedestrians and bicyclists* ☉ *Daily 8–sunset.*

CloseUp

WEST INDIAN MANATEE

SO THEY WON'T WIN *any beauty contests. Florida's West Indian manatees, also known as sea cows, are enormous aquatic mammals.* The average adult male is about 10 ft long and weighs in at around a thousand pounds, so it should come as no surprise that their closest relative is the elephant. (What may surprise you, however, is the speculation that early sailor sightings of "mermaids" were actually manatees.) Yet despite their mass, these creatures somehow manage a sweet appeal. Their big lump of a body has wrinkly gray-brown skin, a tiny paddle-shape tail, two little flippers, and a stubby, pug-nose face that is at once whiskery and winsome.

In spite of their giant size, sea cows are entirely harmless. In fact, they are extremely docile. Moving very slowly, they sometimes submerge and rest, coming up for a breath of fresh air every three to five minutes. These completely herbivorous animals spend the day grazing along the floor and surface of a body of water in search of aquatic greenery. Consummate munchers, the gentle giants can eat close to 15% of their body weight in plants each day.

Male manatees take about nine years to reach adulthood, while females take only five. Baby manatees stay with their mothers for as long as two years.

Although sea cows have no natural enemies and can live to be 60 years old, only about 3,000 are left in all of the United States. As an endangered species, they are protected under U.S. federal law by the 1973 act of the same name as well as by the Marine Mammal Protection Act of 1972 and the Florida Manatee Sanctuary Act of 1978. Florida waterways have manatee zones with restricted, no-wake speed limits, yet each year too many manatees are still wounded and killed by watercraft and their propellers. Others die from eating fishing line, plastic, or fishhooks and from natural causes; development continues to swallow up the manatees' natural habitats.

Manatees live in shallow, slow-moving waters, such as quiet rivers, peaceful saltwater bays, and calm coastal canals. To see them, look in both coasts' Intracoastal Waterway from spring to fall. In the winter, the creatures search for warmer waters, heading to inland springs or even to the heated outflow of a power plant. Spotting them can be tricky. Since manatees usually travel together in a long line with their bodies mostly submerged, look for something resembling drifting coconuts. Also look for concentric circles in the water, a signal that manatees are about to surface.

Several organizations are intent on helping manatees. The Save the Manatee Club, which operates under the auspices of the U.S. Fish and Wildlife Service, welcomes new members. If you choose to "adopt" a sea cow, you'll receive a picture of "your" manatee, a little history about him or her, a handbook about manatees, and a certificate of adoption. A newsletter includes periodic updates about your adoptee. For more information contact the **Save the Manatee Club and Adopt a Manatee** (✉ 500 N. Maitland Ave., Maitland 32751 ☎ 800/432-5646 ⊕ www.savethemanatee.org).

— Pam Acheson

Where to Stay & Eat

$–$$$$ ✕ **Chloës.** One of Fort Myers Beach's most elegant restaurants, Chloës has sweeping gulf views and a mostly seafood menu with some pasta and prime beef dishes. Start with the crab chowder or mini–beef Wellington; then go on to panko-crusted Parmesan salmon stuffed with spinach and mascarpone, coconut-crusted grouper, or the twin tenderloins of beef. Breakfast is also served. ✉ *DiamondHead Resort, 2000 Estero Blvd.* ☎*239/765–0595* ⚭*Reservations essential* ☐*AE, D, MC, V* ☯*No lunch.*

$–$$ ✕ **Snug Harbor.** Watch boats coming and going whether you sit inside or out at this casual restaurant, which moved into a new building next door to the old in 2003. The secret of its success is absolutely fresh seafood, which comes from the restaurant's own fishing fleet. The grouper Popeye (on spinach) is a signature dish. ✉ *Old San Carlos Blvd. and 1st St.* ☎ *239/463–4343* ⊕ *www.snugharborrestaurant.com* ☐ *AE, D, MC, V.*

¢–$ ✕ **Plaka.** A casual long-timer and a favorite for quick breakfast, lunch breaks, and sunset dinners, Plaka—Greek for "beach"—has such typical Greek fare as moussaka, pastitso, gyros, and roast lamb, as well as burgers, hot dogs, sandwiches, and strip steak. There's indoor dining, but grab a seat on the porch. ✉ *1001 Estero Blvd.* ☎ *239/463–4707* ☐ *AE, MC, V.*

$$$$ ▦ **Best Western Pink Shell Beach Resort.** The 12 acres of this established property on the northern end of the island extend between Estero Bay, in the gulf, on one side, and Matanzas Bay on the other; a county park borders part of the grounds. It's fun to take a picnic there or to the beach. Or spend your days hanging out by the pool, which has a great view of the Gulf. For better, and for worse, the quaint old stilted cottages that once added a measure of barefoot charm to the place have been replaced by stylish new beachfront villas containing 92 one- and two-bedroom condos. ✉ *275 Estero Blvd., 33931* ☎ *239/463–6181 or 888/847–8939* ⎙ *239/463–1229* ⊕ *www.pinkshell.com* ⇰ *60 rooms, 150 suites* ⚭ *2 restaurants, kitchens, 2 tennis courts, 4 pools, beach, dock, boating, jet skiing, parasailing, fishing, shuffleboard, volleyball, bar, children's programs (ages 3–11)* ☐ *AE, D, MC, V.*

$$$$ ▦ **DiamondHead.** This 12-story, all-suite resort sits on the beach, and many rooms, especially those on higher floors, have stunning views. Units are done in bright pastels, and each has a living room with sleeper sofa, a separate bedroom, and a kitchen. The well-organized children's programs include everything from crafts to scavenger hunts to sand golf. ✉ *2000 Estero Blvd., 33931* ☎ *239/765–7654 or 888/765–5002* ⎙ *239/765–1694* ⊕ *www.diamondheadfl.com* ⇰ *124 suites* ⚭ *2 restaurants, kitchens, pool, gym, hot tub, beach, boating, bar, video game room, children's programs (ages 4–14), laundry facilities* ☐ *AE, D, MC, V.*

$$–$$$ ▦ **Grand View.** Views can be stupendous from upper floors in this 15-story beachfront resort just north of Lovers Key State Park. The gulf seems to stretch forever, and sunsets are quite a show. Other units look out on bay or gardens. All have a living room with sleeper sofa, a separate bedroom, kitchen, and balcony. ✉ *8701 Estero Blvd., 33931* ☎ *239/765–4422 or 800/723–4944* ⎙ *239/765–4499* ⊕ *www.grandviewfl.com* ⇰ *51 suites* ⚭ *Kitchens, pool, hot tub, beach, boating, bicycles* ☐ *AE, D, MC, V.*

$$–$$$ ▦ **Outrigger Beach Resort.** On a wide gulf beach, this casual resort has rooms and efficiencies with configurations to suit different families and budgets. You'll also find a broad sundeck, tiki cabanas, sailboats, and a beachfront pool with a popular tiki bar. ✉ *6200 Estero Blvd., 33931* ☎ *239/463–3131 or 800/749–3131* ⎙ *239/463–6577* ⊕ *www.outriggerfmb.com* ⇰ *112 rooms, 32 suites* ⚭ *Restaurant, putting green,* *pool, beach, jet skiing, bicycles, shuffleboard, volleyball, bar* ⊟ *AE, D, MC, V.*

¢–$$$ ☒ **Days Inn Island Beach Resort.** In the thick of things at Fort Myers Beach's so-called Times Square, this property is among the prettier in the chain, with gingerbread trim. It's one of the most affordable options on the beach. ⊠ *1130 Estero Blvd., 33931* ☎ *239/463–9759 or 800/544–4592* 🖷 *239/765–4240* ⊕ *www.daysinnftmyers.com* ⇩ *33 rooms* ⚘ *In-room data ports, refrigerators, pool, beach, jet skiing, parasailing, bar* ⊟ *AE, D, MC, V.*

Sports & the Outdoors

BIKING Fort Myers Beach has no designated trails, so most people pedal along the road. **Fun Rentals** (⊠ 1901 Estero Blvd. ☎ 239/463–8844) rents bicycles and Rollerblades by the half or full day or for the week.

FISHING **Getaway Deep Sea Fishing** (⊠ 18400 San Carlos Blvd. ☎ 239/466–3600) rents fishing equipment, sells bait, and can arrange half- and full-day charters. Party-boat and private fishing charters can be arranged at **Deebold's Marina** (⊠ 18500 San Carlos Blvd. ☎ 239/466–3525).

GOLF The **Bay Beach Golf Club** (⊠ 7401 Estero Blvd. ☎ 239/463–2064) has 18 holes and a practice range.

NAPLES AREA

As you head south from Fort Myers on U.S. 41, you soon come to Bonita Springs, followed by the Naples and Marco Island areas, which are sandwiched between Big Cypress Swamp and the Gulf of Mexico. East of Naples the land is largely undeveloped and mostly wetlands, all the way to Fort Lauderdale. Here, along the northern border of the Florida Everglades, there are stunning nature preserves and parks. Tours and charters out of Everglades City explore the mazelike Ten Thousand Islands. These waters are full of fish and wildlife. Between Naples and Everglades City, acres of breeze-swept swamp grass stretch off to the horizon. Keep your eye peeled, and you may even spot alligators in the waterways alongside the road. Naples itself is a major vacation destination, an Old Florida town that has sprouted pricey high-rise condominiums and a spate of restaurants and shops to match. A similar but not as thorough evolution has occurred on Marco Island, once a quiet fishing community.

Estero/Bonita Springs

⑩ *10 mi south of Fort Myers.*

Towns below Fort Myers have started to flow seamlessly into one another since the opening of Florida Gulf Coast University in San Carlos Park and as a result of the growth of Estero and Bonita Springs, agricultural communities until not long ago. Bonita Beach, the closest beach to Interstate 75, has evolved from a fishing community to a repository of upscale golfing developments. Beach homes and a few resorts line its laid-back strip of white sand.

Tour one of Florida's quirkier chapters from the past at **Koreshan State Historic Site.** Named for a religious cult that was active at the turn of the 20th century, Koreshan preserves a dozen structures where the group practiced arts, worshiped a male-female divinity, and created its own branch of science called cosmogony. The cult floundered when leader Cyrus Reed Teed died in 1908, and in 1961, the four remaining members deeded the property to the state. Rangers lead tours, and the grounds, planted with exotic gardens, are lovely for picnicking. Canoeists paddle the woods-fringed Estero River, and there's camping. ⊠ *Tami-*

ami Trail, Estero ☎ 239/992–0311 🖃 $3.25 per vehicle with up to 8 passengers; $1 per cyclist, pedestrian, or extra passenger ⊙ Daily 8 AM–sunset.

Opened in 1936 and one of the first attractions of its kind in the state, the **Everglades Wonder Gardens** captures the beauty of untamed Florida. The old-fashioned zoological gardens house Florida panthers, black bears, crocodiles and alligators, tame Florida deer, flamingos, and trained otters and birds. There's also a funky natural-history museum. Tours, which include an otter show and alligator feedings, run continuously. The swinging bridge over the alligator pit is a real thrill. ⊠ Old U.S. 41 ☎ 239/992–2591 🖃 $12 ⊙ Daily 9–5.

Bonita Springs Public Beach, at the south end of Bonita Beach, has picnic tables and a restaurant next door. ⊠ Hickory Blvd. at Bonita Beach Rd. ☎ 239/495–5811 🖃 Parking 75¢ per hr.

The 342-acre **Barefoot Beach Preserve** is a quiet place, accessible via a road around the corner from the buzzing public beach. It has picnic tables, a nature trail and learning center, a butterfly garden, and refreshment stands. ⊠ Lely Beach Rd. ☎ 239/353–0404 🖃 $3.

off the beaten path

Fodor'sChoice
★

Corkscrew Swamp Sanctuary. To get a feel for what this part of Florida was like before civil engineers began draining the swamps, drive 13 mi east of Bonita Springs (30 mi northeast of Naples) to these 11,000 acres of pine flatwood and cypress, grass-and-sedge "wet prairie," saw-grass marshland, and lakes and sloughs filled with water lettuce. Managed by the National Audubon Society, the sanctuary protects North America's largest remaining stand of ancient bald cypress, 600-year-old trees as tall as 130 ft, as well as endangered birds, such as wood storks, which often nest here. This is a favorite destination for serious birders. If you spend a couple of hours to take the 2¼-mi self-guided tour along the boardwalk, you will spot ferns, orchids, and air plants as well as wading birds and possibly alligators and otters. A nature center educates you about this precious, unusual habitat with a dramatic re-creation of the preserve and its creatures in the Swamp Theater. ⊠ 16 mi east of I–75 on Rte. 846 ☎ 239/348–9151 ⊕ www.audubon.org 🖃 $8 ⊙ In season daily 7–5:30, off-season daily 7–7:30.

Where to Stay & Eat

$–$$$ ✕ **South Bay Bistro.** A retro, space-age design sets the scene for stylish cuisine such as blackened tuna with coconut curry sauce, grilled pork porterhouse with ragout of wild mushrooms, and grilled honey horseradish salmon. Outdoor seating is available. ⊠ The Promenade at Bonita Bay, 26821 South Bay Dr., Bonita Springs ☎ 239/949–6030 ▤ AE, D, MC, V ⊙ No lunch in summer.

$–$$ ✕ **Toucan Grille.** Spinning lazily from high ceilings, rattan paddle fans swirl cool air and hot reggae around this sandy-hued place, which is done in rattan, wicker, and bamboo and splashed with bright Caribbean colors. With its offerings of coconut shrimp, jerk chicken, and tuna with mango salsa, the menu, too, makes an island statement. ⊠ 4480 Bonita Beach Rd., Bonita Springs ☎ 239/495–9464 ▤ AE, D, MC, V.

¢–$ ✕ **Doc's Beach House.** Right next door to the public access, Doc's has fed hungry beachers for decades. Come barefoot and grab a quick libation or meal downstairs, or escape the heat in the air-conditioned second floor with a great view of beach action. Simple fare ranges from a popular Angus burger to pizza and seafood plates and baskets. ⊠ 27908

Hickory Blvd., Bonita Springs 📞 *239/992–6444* ⊕ *www.docsbeachhouse. com* ⊟ *No credit cards.*

★ **$$$$** 🏨 **Hyatt Coconut Point Resort & Spa.** This secluded luxury Hyatt, with its marble-and-mahogany lobby and 18 floors, stands in stark contrast to the pristine estuary environment that surrounds it. Man-made water features include a slide pool, lap pool, and fountain-waterfall pool. For nature-made water features, catch a ferry to the hotel's private island beach. Handsomely appointed rooms overlook the gulf or the golf course. The kids' program educates about Calusa Indian heritage and the environment, and an interpretative center showcases natural and pre-historic history. ⊠ *5001 Coconut Rd., Bonita Springs 34134* 📞 *239/ 444–1234 or 800/554–9288* 🖷 *239/390–4277* ⊕ *www.coconutpoint. hyatt.com* ⌨ *426 rooms, 30 suites* ♻ *3 restaurants, coffee shop, room service, in-room data ports, refrigerators, 27-hole golf course, 2 tennis courts, 3 pools, outdoor hot tubs, health club, spa, beach, boating, 2 bars, shops, children's programs (ages 3–12), concierge, concierge floor, business services, meeting room, car rentals* ⊟ *AE, D, DC, MC, V.*

$$$ 🏨 **Trianon Bonita.** Convenient to Bonita Springs' best shopping and dining, this branch of a downtown Naples favorite feels European in its peaceful, sophisticated way. Rooms are oversize, and a fireplace dominates the lobby, with its vaulted ceiling and marble columns; cocktails and complimentary breakfasts are served in the library. ⊠ *3401 Bay Commons Dr., Bonita Springs 34134* 📞 *239/948–4400 or 800/859–3939* 🖷 *239/948–4401* ⊕ *www.trianon.com* ⌨ *100 rooms* ♻ *Pool* ⊟ *AE, D, DC, MC, V* ⎮◎⎮ *CP.*

Sports & the Outdoors

BIKING Rent bicycles by the day or by the week at **Bonita Beach Bike** (⊠ 4892 Bonita Beach Rd. 📞 239/947–6377).

BOATING **Bonita Beach Resort Motel** (⊠ 26395 Hickory Blvd. 📞 239/992–2137) rents pontoon boats by the hour or day.

CANOEING The meandering Estero River is pleasant for canoeing as it passes through Koreshan State Historic Site to the bay. **Estero River Tackle and Canoe Outfitters** (⊠ 20991 Tamiami Trail S, Estero 📞 239/992–4050) provides rental canoes, kayaks, and equipment.

DOG RACING Greyhounds race year-round at the **Naples/Fort Myers Greyhound Track** (⊠ 10601 Bonita Beach Rd. 📞 239/992–2411).

FISHING **Estero Bay Boat Tours** (⊠ 5231 Mamie St., Estero 📞 239/992–2200) can set you up with a fishing guide or take you out on shelling, nature, and archaeological tours.

GOLF Swamp and thick vegetation border the 36-hole **Pelican's Nest Golf Course** (⊠ 4450 Pelican's Nest Dr. 📞 239/947–4600).

ICE HOCKEY Fort Myers's minor-league hockey team, the **Florida Everblades** (⊠ TECO Arena, 11000 Everblades Pkwy., Estero 📞 239/948–7825), battle their opponents from October through March.

ICE SKATING Skaters can head to the **TECO Arena** (⊠ 11000 Everblades Pkwy., Estero 📞 239/948–7825) for ice, in-line, and figure skating.

Shopping

The **Promenade at Bonita Bay** (⊠ South Bay Dr. 📞 239/430–1670) in the Bonita Bay subdivision is Bonita Springs' chic shopping venue, with an upscale collection of shops and some of the town's best restaurants.

Shop for imported furniture, objets d'art, and home decorative items, and then grab a bite to eat, at **Traders Store & Café** (⊠ 26501 S. Tamiami Trail 📞 239/949–0202).

Naples

⓫–⓳ *21 mi south of Bonita Springs.*

Thirty years ago, Naples was a sleepy relic of Old Florida, a cluster of bungalows, a beach, and a brace of tile-roofed stucco buildings painted in pastel hues. Nowadays, Naples is west-coast Florida's Palm Beach, though it's far less brazen about showing off its money. Much of the north shore is lined with 20-story condominiums; their residents crowd the town's many pricey, sophisticated restaurants and run their errands in chichi shopping areas such as tree-lined 5th Avenue South, 3rd Street South, the Waterside Shops, and the Village on Venetian Bay. The beach is stunning, the tennis abundant, and the golf stellar. No wonder it's tough to snag a table—or a room—at the last minute in winter.

⓫ The well-maintained 100-acre **Delnor-Wiggins Pass State Recreation Area** has guarded beaches, barbecue grills, picnic tables, a boat ramp, an observation tower, rest rooms with wheelchair access, bathhouses, showers, and lots of parking. Fishing is best in Wiggins Pass, at the north end of the park. Rangers conduct sea-turtle walks in summer. ⊠ *11100 Gulf Shore Dr. N, at Rte. 846* ☎ *239/597–6196* ⌨ *$4 per vehicle with up to 8 people, $2 for single driver, $1 for pedestrians and bicyclists* ☉ *Daily 8–sunset.*

Fodor'sChoice
★

★ ⓬ The cool, contemporary **Naples Museum of Art,** around the corner from the Waterside Shops in the Naples Philharmonic Center for the Arts, has provocative, innovative pieces, including American miniatures, antique walking sticks, ancient Asian art, and traveling exhibits. Dazzling installations by glass artist Dale Chihuly include a fiery cascade of a chandelier and an illuminated ceiling layered with many-hued glass bubbles, glass corkscrews, and other shapes that suggest the sea; alone, this warrants a visit. ⊠ *5833 Pelican Bay Blvd.* ☎ *239/597–1900 or 800/597–1900* ⊕ *www.naplesphilcenter.org* ⌨ *$6* ☉ *Tues.–Sat. 10–4, Sun. noon–4.*

⓭ Kayak through the mangroves or into the surf at **Clam Pass Recreation Area.** A 3,000-ft boardwalk winds through the mangrove area to the beach. Tram service is available. ⊠ *Seagate Dr.* ☎ *239/353–0404* ⌨ *Parking $4* ☉ *Daily 8–sunset.*

☾ ⓮ A life-size Three Bears House and a "libeary" stocked solely with books about bears keep company with the nearly 4,000 bears from 28 countries on display at the $2 million **Teddy Bear Museum of Naples.** Oil heiress Frances Pew Hayes, an area resident, had the log structure built when she ran out of room to keep the bears in her home. Some are just an inch high, while others are as tall as a basketball player; some are handmade, while others were crafted by well-known manufacturers such as Gund. The stuffed bruins by Stieff are superb, and the collection of Herrmann Teddy Originals is the largest anywhere. ⊠ *2511 Pine Ridge Rd.* ☎ *239/598–2711 or 866/365–2327* ⊕ *www.teddymuseum. com* ⌨ *$8* ☉ *Tues.–Sat. 10–5.*

☾ ⓯ The lush and entertaining 52-acre **Caribbean Gardens: The Zoo in Naples,** established in the 1900s as a botanical garden, today draws visitors curious to see African lions, kinkajou, Bengal tigers, lemurs, antelope, and monkeys. But it's the tours and shows that keep you rushing from one corner of the property to the next. The Primate Expedition Cruise takes you through islands of monkeys and apes. The Safari Canyon show mixes live animals and videos of the creatures in their natural habitat. Youngsters get to play in their own special Young Explorers Playground Forest, and there are meet-the-keeper times and alligator feedings as well.

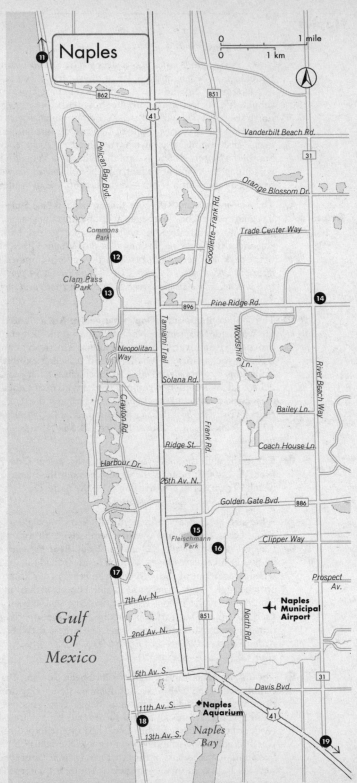

✉ *1590 Goodlette Rd.* ☎ *239/262–5409* ⊕ *www.napleszoo.com* ⧓ *$14.95* ☉ *Daily 9:30–5:30 (gates close at 4:30).*

⑯ On 14 acres bordering a tidal lagoon teeming with wildlife, the **Naples Nature Center** includes an aviary, a wildlife rehabilitation clinic, a natural-history museum with a serpentarium, and a 3,000-gallon sea-turtle aquarium. Short trails are dotted with interpretive signs, and there are free guided walks and boat tours on the mangrove-bordered Gordon River several times daily. Canoes and kayaks are available for rent as well. ✉ *1450 Merrihue Dr.* ☎ *239/262–0304* ⊕ *www.conservancy. org* ⧓ *$7.50* ☉ *Mon.–Sat. 9–4:30.*

⑰ Stretching along Gulf Shore Boulevard, **Lowdermilk Park** has more than 1,000 ft of beach as well as volleyball courts, a playground, rest rooms, showers, vending machines, and picnic tables. ✉ *Gulf Shore Blvd. at Banyan Blvd.* ☎ *239/213–3029* ⧓ *Parking 75¢ per hr* ☉ *Daily 7–sunset.*

⑱ Houses in 19th-century South Florida were often built of a cementlike material made of sand and seashells. For a fine example of such tabby construction, stop by **Palm Cottage,** built in 1895 and one of Southwest Florida's only tabby homes. The historically accurate interior contains the simple furnishings of the period. ✉ *137 12th Ave. S* ☎ *239/261–8164* ⧓ *$6* ☉ *Sept.–July, weekdays 1–4.*

⑲ To get a feel for local history, stop by the **Collier County Museum,** where a Seminole chickee hut, native plant garden, swamp buggy, reconstructed 19th-century trading post, steam logging locomotive, and other historical exhibits capture important developments from prehistoric times to the World War II era. ✉ *Airport Rd. at U.S. 41* ☎ *239/774–8476* ⊕ *www.colliermuseum.com* ⧓ *Free* ☉ *Weekdays 9–5.*

Where to Stay & Eat

$$$–$$$$ ✗ **Chardonnay.** A bastion of the Naples culinary scene for decades, this classic serves French cuisine with a Florida twist. Look for rack of lamb with herbs, veal sweetbreads, rabbit with champagne sauce, blackened mahimahi, and lobster and scallops St. Jacques. The elegant dining room looks out onto a lush garden with pools. ✉ *2331 N. Tamiami Trail* ☎ *239/261–1744* ⚐ *Reservations essential* ▭ *AE, MC, V* ☉ *No lunch.*

$$$–$$$$
Fodor'sChoice
★ ✗ **Sign of the Vine.** The menu is presented as a framed work of art at this romantic spot in an out-of-the-way cottage complete with fireplace and candlelight. Roasted bourbon and peach duckling, tenderloin with cognac cream sauce, and lobster hash are signature dishes. Between courses come delightful surprises—salad, condiment tray, a popover with citrus butter or grilled fruit, perhaps; after dessert, a plate of homemade fudge and sugared walnuts materializes. ✉ *980 Solano Rd.* ☎ *239/261–6745* ⚐ *Reservations essential* ▭ *AE* ☉ *Closed Mon. and some summer months. No lunch.*

$$–$$$$ ✗ **Chops City Grill.** This 5th Avenue darling, ultrasophisticated while let-your-hair-down casual, has become so popular it spawned a spin-off in Bonita Springs. Its name reflects a personality split between chopstick cuisine and fine cuts of meat. Sushi and Pacific Rim inspirations such as beef satay and honey-teriyaki-glazed chicken breast represent the former; lamb chops, dry-aged beef, Roquefort-and-ricotta crusted grilled veal chop, and peppercorn-crusted strip steak with blackberry-cabernet sauce, the latter. The settings are just as creative as the food. ✉ *837 5th Ave. S* ☎ *239/262–4677* ⧓ *Hwy. 41 at Brooks Grand Plaza, Bonita Springs* ☎ *239/992–4677* ▭ *AE, DC, MC, V* ☉ *No lunch.*

$–$$$ ✗ **Aqua Grill.** This new-wave bistro in the chic Waterside Shops mall is decorated with wave motifs. Traditional dishes such as meat loaf, steak au poivre, seafood paella, and rosemary-lemon chicken anchor the menu, while nightly specials showcase the kitchen's prowess: to wit, the blue-crab stuffed yellowtail snapper with jalapeño and white cheddar mashed potatoes. ⊠ *5555 Tamiami Trail* ☎ *239/254–1234* ⊟ *AE, MC, V.*

$–$$$ ✕ **Tommy Bahama's Tropical Café.** When you're in the mood to be ultra-casual in Naples, this faux-Caribbean spot is the place to be. On the deck outside, in the spacious dining room inside, and in the bar, everybody's munching sandwiches, salads, ribs, and grilled seafood with a tropical flair and sampling Tommy's famous Bungalow Brew. ⊠ *1220 3rd St. S* ☎ *239/643–6889* ⊟ *AE, MC, V.*

★ $$ ✕ **Bha! Bha!** Ochre walls and the stuffed ottomans and exotic tapestries around the room explain the "Persian bistro" on this restaurant's sign. Classic and fusion Middle Eastern cooking fill the menu. Specialties include cumin-braised lamb, garlic eggplant chicken, spicy marinated charbroiled fish, and spicy beef. Sunday brings on a massive brunch buffet. ⊠ *847 Vanderbilt Rd.* ☎ *239/594–5557* ⊟ *AE, MC, V.*

¢–$$ ✕ **Old Naples Pub.** Tucked away from shopping traffic at 3rd Street Plaza, this comfortable pub stays open until late at night. Taste some 20 kinds of beer and order from pub menu with fish-and-chips, burgers, bratwurst, pizza, and chicken Caesar salad, and nachos, as well as such not-so-traditional pub snacks as tamales and fried gator tail. There's musical entertainment between Wednesday and Saturday. ⊠ *255 13th Ave. S* ☎ *239/649–8200* ⊟ *AE, MC, V.*

¢–$ ✕ **Aurelio's Is Pizza.** Transplanted from Chicago, the pizza here is steeped in tradition and flavor. The selections are typical with a few show-offs such as taco, barbecue, and stuffed pizza. For non-pizza appetites, there's pasta with homemade sauces, spinach Calabrese, and chicken Parmesan or Alfredo. Situated in a strip mall, the spot is accented with red-and-white tablecloths and old license plates. ⊠ *590 N. Tamiami Trail* ☎ *239/403–8882* ⊕ *www.aureliospizza.com* ⊟ *AE, MC, V* ☺ *Closed Mon.*

$$$$ ▦ **Edgewater Beach Hotel.** This compact waterfront high-rise anchors the north end of fashionable Gulf Shore Boulevard. The one- and two-bedroom suites are brightly decorated and have patios or balconies, many with exquisite gulf views. Have meals by the pool or in the elegant penthouse restaurant, or stop by the lounge for piano music during happy hour. Some units are time-shares. ⊠ *1901 Gulf Shore Blvd. N, 34102* ☎ *239/403–2000 or 800/821–0196; 800/282–3766 in Florida* ☐ *239/ 403–2100* ⊕ *www.edgewaternaples.com* ⇆ *98 1-bedroom suites, 26 2-bedroom suites* ♿ *Restaurant, café, microwaves, refrigerators, pool, gym, beach, bicycles, bar* ⊟ *AE, DC, MC, V.*

$$$$
FodorsChoice
★ ▦ **LaPlaya Beach & Golf Resort.** LaPlaya has renovated and redesigned for posh and panache down to the smallest detail–custom-designed shorebird duvet covers, for instance. When reopened in 2002, the boutique resort debuted a Thai-style spa, rock-waterfalls pools, a tony Miami-style beachfront restaurant, and guest rooms remade for luxury and comfort. Of its 189 units, 141 are beachfront with private balconies. Some have jetted soak tubs with a view of the gulf. ⊠ *9891 Gulf Shore Dr., 34108* ☎ *239/597–3123 or 800/237–6883* ☐ *239/567–6278* ⊕ *www.laplayaresort.com* ⇆ *180 rooms, 9 suites* ♿ *Restaurant, golf privileges, 3 pools, gym, spa, parasailing, volleyball, 2 bars, concierge, meeting rooms* ⊟ *AE, D, MC, V.*

$$$$ ▦ **Naples Beach Hotel and Golf Club.** Family-owned and -managed for more than 50 years, this beach resort is a piece of Naples history. On a prime stretch of powdery sand, it stands out for its par-72, 18-hole championship golf course, the first resort course in the state. Rooms, decorated in light colors, are in six high- and mid-rise pink buildings, and good packages make an extended stay affordable. ✉ *851 Gulf Shore Blvd. N, 34102* ☎ *239/261–2222 or 800/237–7600* 🖷 *239/261–7380* ⊕ *www.naplesbeachhotel.com* ⤳ *255 rooms, 41 suites, 22 efficiencies* ⚑ *4 restaurants, 18-hole golf course, putting green, 6 tennis courts, pro shop, pool, health club, spa, beach, 2 bars, children's programs (ages 5–12), meeting rooms* ▤ *AE, D, DC, MC, V.*

★ **$$$$** 🏨 **Registry Resort.** Rooms are spacious and comfortable at this high-rise hotel with a polished lobby full of marble and crystal. One of the glories of the property—at least for families—is the immense freeform family swimming pool with a 100-ft waterslide. The hotel sits behind dusky, twisted mangrove forests; to get to the 3 mi of powdery white sand, it's a short walk or tram ride. Indigenous cypress and pines frame the Naples Grande Golf Club, the hotel's 18-hole Rees Jones layout. ✉*475 Seagate Dr., 34103* ☎ *239/597–3232* 🖷 *239/566–7919* ⊕ *www. registryresort.com* ⤳ *395 rooms, 78 suites* ⚑ *5 restaurants, coffee shop, 18-hole golf course, 15 tennis courts, 5 pools, health club, hair salon, spa, beach, windsurfing, boating, bicycles, 2 bars, lobby lounge, dance club, shops, children's programs (ages 4–12), business services, meeting rooms* ▤ *AE, DC, MC, V.*

$$$$ 🏨 **Ritz-Carlton Golf Resort.** Ardent golfers with a yen for luxury will find their dream vacation at Naples's most elegant golf resort. Ritz style prevails all the way; rooms are regal but with a touch of Florida, and all rooms have balconies with links views. The golf academy can help you polish your skills, and you have access to the spa, kids' program, and other amenities of the beachside Ritz-Carlton, which is nearby. Dining at Tuscan-style Lemonia is divine. ✉ *2600 Tiburón Dr., 34109* ☎ *239/ 593–2000 or 800/241–3333* 🖷 *239/593–2010* ⊕ *www.ritzcarlton.com* ⤳ *257 rooms, 38 suites* ⚑ *2 restaurants, coffee shop, room service, in-room data ports, 27-hole golf course, 4 tennis courts, pro shop, pool, billiards, 3 bars, laundry service, concierge, concierge floors, Internet* ▤ *AE, D, DC, MC, V.*

★ **$$$$** 🏨 **Ritz-Carlton, Naples.** This is a classic Ritz-Carlton, awash in marble, antiques, and 19th-century European oil paintings. In the rooms, the comforts of home prevail—assuming your home is a palace. Outside, steps away, the beach is soft, white, and dense with seashells. Given the graciousness of the staff, you quickly get over the incongruity of traipsing through the regal lobby in flip-flops, aromatic with sun cream, clutching a plastic bag of beach finds. It doesn't hurt that the kitchen is a wonder as well, making meals in the tropical Dining Room and the oh-so-clubby Grill, and even dessert in the lobby, just a little bit special. ✉*280 Vanderbilt Beach Rd., 34108* ☎*239/598–3300 or 800/241–3333* 🖷 *239/598–6691* ⊕ *www.ritzcarlton.com* ⤳ *435 rooms, 28 suites* ⚑ *7 restaurants, room service, golf privileges, 4 tennis courts, pool, health club, spa, beach, windsurfing, boating, 2 bars, children's programs (ages 5–12), baby-sitting, laundry service, concierge, concierge floors, Internet* ▤ *AE, D, DC, MC, V.*

$$$–$$$$ 🏨 **Hotel Escalante.** On 4½ landscaped tropical acres at the edge of down-
Fodor'sChoice town, this is a truly lovely boutique property. The bright, airy guest rooms,
★ replete with mahogany, have a certain plantation style, and Frette linens add that touch of luxury. The beach is a block away, and the hotel delivers everything from umbrellas to coolers of drinks to your beach chair. The spa is poolside. ✉ *290 5th Ave. S, 34102* ☎ *239/659–3466 or 877/ 485–3466* 🖷 *239/262–8748* ⊕ *www.hotelescalante.com* ⤳ *58 rooms, 13 suites* ⚑ *Pool, outdoor hot tub, gym, spa, library* ▤ *AE, D, MC, V* ⦿❖ *CP.*

$$$ 🏨 **Trianon Old Naples.** A residential area in the heart of Old Naples is the site of this three-story pink stucco European-style boutique hotel. It's within walking distance of shops and restaurants. Wrought-iron balconies and manicured lawns set the stage outside; inside, the elegant lobby has high ceilings, a working fireplace, antique furnishings, and glittering chandeliers. Rooms are large and lavishly furnished, with heavy draperies. ⊠ *955 7th Ave. S, 34102* ☎ *239/435–9600 or 877/482–5228* 🖷 *239/261–0025* ⊕ *www.trianon.com* ⤶ *55 rooms, 3 suites* ♨ *Pool* ⊟ *AE, D, DC, MC, V* ⦿❘ *CP.*

$$–$$$ ⊡ **Cove Inn.** For the best deal in lodging on the water, check in to this boaters' favorite on the edge of Naples Bay, around the corner from restaurants and shops. Rooms and efficiencies, which are individually owned and decorated, have a view of the boats at the city dock. Older and more casual than most other guest quarters in town, this place revolves around fishing and nautical pastimes. ⊠ *900 Broad Ave. S, 34102* ☎ *239/ 262–7161 or 800/255–4365* 🖷 *239/261–6905* ⤶ *52 rooms, 32 efficiencies* ♨ *3 restaurants, pool* ⊟ *AE, D, DC, MC, V.*

$$–$$$ ⊡ **Holiday Inn.** Although this two-story motel is on a major highway, it's set back from the road and the rooms are quiet because they're behind the restaurant and pool. Decorated in florals and rattan, they're also clean and comfortable. Landscaping is well maintained and the location convenient if you plan to sightsee. The bar is popular at happy hour. ⊠ *1100 9th St. N, 34102* ☎ *239/263–3434 or 800/465–4329* 🖷 *239/261–3809* ⊕ *www.hinaples.com* ⤶ *137 rooms* ♨ *Restaurant, pool, bar* ⊟ *AE, D, DC, MC, V.*

¢ ⊡ **Tamiami Motel.** South of Naples, this strip of motel rooms is less than 10 minutes from downtown's shopping and beaches. The rooms are small but tidy and equipped with all the basics, including a small refrigerator. ⊠ *2164 E. Tamiami Trail, 34112* ☎ *239/774–4626* ⤶ *14 rooms* ♨ *Refrigerators* ⊟ *AE, MC, V.*

Nightlife & the Arts

THE ARTS Naples is the cultural capital of this stretch of coast. The **Naples Philharmonic Center for the Arts** (⊠ 5833 Pelican Bay Blvd. ☎ 239/597–1900 or 800/598–1900 ⊕ www.naplesphilcenter.com) has a 1,222-seat performance center with plays, concerts, and exhibits year-round. It's home to the 71-piece Naples Philharmonic, which presents both classical and pop concerts; the Miami Ballet Company also performs here during its winter season. The **Naples Players** (⊠ Sugden Community Theatre, 701 5th Ave. S ☎ 239/263–7990 ⊕ www.naplesplayers.org), on 5th Avenue, performs musicals and dramas between October and May; winter shows often sell out well in advance.

NIGHTLIFE **Club Zanzibar** (⊠ 475 Seagate Dr. ☎ 239/514–3777), at the Registry Resort, is a light and airy multilevel nightclub where DJs pump out Top 40 hits from 9 PM until 2 AM Thursday, Friday, and Saturday. It's packed on weekends. Downtown's 5th Avenue South is the scene of lively nightclubs and sidewalk cafés. **McCabe's Irish Pub** (⊠ 699 5th Ave. S ☎ 239/ 403–7170) hosts Irish bands most weekends and some weeknights. Audiences often participate in the lusty lyrics. The **Club at the Ritz-Carlton** (⊠ 280 Vanderbilt Beach Rd. ☎ 239/598–3300) gets lively with contemporary bands on stage Thursday, Friday, and Saturday.

Sports & the Outdoors

BIKING Try the **Bicycle Shoppe of Naples** (⊠ 8789 Tamiami Trail N ☎ 239/566–3646) for rentals by the day, week, or month. Free maps detail the bike trails in the area.

BOATING **Naples Watersports at Port-O-Call Marina** (⊠ 550 Port-O-Call Way ☎ 239/ 774–0479) rents 21-ft deck boats.

FISHING The *Lady Brett* (⊠ Tin City ☎ 239/263–4949) makes fishing and sightseeing trips twice daily. Take a guided boat and learn to cast and tie flies at **Mangrove Outfitters** (⊠ 4111 E. Tamiami Trail ☎ 239/793–3370).

GOLF The **Ironwood Golf Club** (✉ 4710 Lakewood Blvd. ☎ 239/775–2584) is an 18-hole, all-par-3 public course with a putting green and rentals. At **Lely Flamingo Island Club** (✉ 8004 Lely Resort Blvd. ☎ 239/793–2223 or 800/388–4653), there are 18 holes and a golf school. **Naples Beach Hotel & Golf Club** (✉ 851 Gulf Shore Blvd. N ☎ 239/434–7007) has 18 holes, a golf pro, and a putting green. **Naples Golf Center** (✉ 7700 E. Davis Blvd. ☎ 239/775–3337) has a 300-yard driving range and offers private and group lessons by a PGA teaching staff; it even has computerized swing analysis. At **Riviera Golf Club** (✉ 48 Marseille Dr. ☎ 239/774–1081), you'll find 18 holes.

TENNIS **Cambier Park Tennis Courts** (✉ 735 8th St. S ☎ 239/213–3060) offers clinics and play on 12 lighted clay courts.

Shopping

Old Naples encompasses two distinct shopping areas marked by historic buildings and flowery landscaping: 5th Avenue South and 3rd Street South. Both are known for their abundance of fine art galleries. Near 5th Avenue South, **Old Marine Market Place at Tin City** (✉ 1200 5th Ave. S), in a collection of tin-roof former boat docks along Naples Bay, has more than 40 boutiques, eateries, and souvenir shops with everything from scrimshaw to T-shirts and seafood. At the classy **Village on Venetian Bay** (✉ 4200 Gulf Shore Blvd.), more than 60 shops and restaurants have been built over the water. Only in South Florida can you find something like **Waterside Shops** (✉ Seagate Dr. and U.S. 41), with four dozen plus boutiques and eating places wrapped around a series of waterfalls, waterways, and shaded but open-air promenades. Saks Fifth Avenue is one of the anchors.

Gattle's (✉ 1250 3rd St. S ☎ 239/262–4791 or 800/344–4552) stocks pricey, beautifully made linens. **Marissa Collections** (✉ 1167 3rd St. S ☎ 239/263–4333) showcases designer women's wear, including Donna Karan. At the **Mole Hole** (✉ 1201 3rd St. S ☎ 239/262–5115), gift items large and small, from glassware to paperweights to knickknacks, cover every surface. **Kirsten's Boutique** (✉ Waterside Shops, 5415 Tamiami Trail N ☎ 239/598–3233) is filled with African-inspired clothing, jewelry, and decorative art. Naples's ladies-who-lunch-often donate their year-old Armani castoffs to a spate of terrific thrift shops such as **Options** (✉ 968 2nd Ave. N ☎ 239/434–7115). The most upscale clothes sometimes go to consignment shops such as **New to You** (✉ 933 Creech Rd. ☎ 239/262–6869). Pawing through wealthy folks' high-end designer castoffs is a favorite Naples activity for penny-pinching vacationers and residents alike at **Lynne's Consignment** (✉ 13560 Tamiami Trail ☎ 239/514–1410). **Clothes by Consignment** (✉ 4596 N. Tamiami Trail ☎ 239/261–8630) yields many a treasure thanks to its automatic markdown policy.

Marco Island

20 *20 mi south of Naples.*

High-rises line part of the shore of Marco Island, which is connected to the mainland by causeway. Yet it retains an isolated feeling much appreciated by those who love this corner of the world. Many natural areas have been preserved, and the down-home fishing village of Goodland is resisting change. Fishing, sunning, swimming, and tennis are the primary activities.

Tigertail Beach is on the southwest side of the island, with a view of both developed and undeveloped areas. You'll find parking, a concession stand, a picnic area, sailboat rentals, volleyball, rest rooms, and showers. ✉ *480 Hernando Ct.* ☎ *239/642–0818* 🚗 *Parking $4* ☉ *Daily 8–sunset.*

In the midst of 12,000-acre Rookery Bay Estuarine Reserve, **Briggs Nature Center** interprets the Everglades environment with live animal exhibits, a touch table, a butterfly-native plant garden, and boardwalk trails through mangrove, hammock, marsh, and other plant communities. In 2003, the Department of Environmental Protection opened a hands-on Environmental Learning Center in the reserve. ✉ *401 Shell Island Rd.* ☎ *239/775–8569* 🚗 *Nature Center $4* ☉ *Mon.–Sat. 9–4:30.*

Where to Stay & Eat

$–$$$$ ✕ **Old Marco Lodge Crab House.** Built in 1869, this waterfront restaurant is Marco's oldest landmark, and boaters often cruise in and tie up dockside to sit on the veranda and dine on local seafood and pasta entrées. Start with a wholesome bowl of vegetable crab soup. The blue crabs in garlic butter is a specialty, but the menu does flex beyond crab to all manner of shellfish, pasta, grouper, and steak. Save room for the authentic key lime pie. ✉ *1 Papaya St., Goodland* ☎ *239/642–7227* ▭ *AE, DC, MC, V* ☉ *Closed Mon.*

$$–$$$ ✕ **Café de Marco.** This cozy little bistro serves some of the best food on the island. The kitchen matches up fresh local fish with original preparations, and there are always good daily specials. Or try the stuffed Florida lobster. Steaks, chicken, and pasta are also available. ✉ *244 Palm St.* ☎ *239/394–6262* ▭ *AE, MC, V* ☉ *No lunch.*

★ $$–$$$ ✕ **Old Marco Island Inn.** Dating from the turn of the 20th century, this inn lends grace and patina to intimate meals. The menu covers a cross section of global and creative cuisines such as orange rotisserie duckling, macadamia-crusted salmon, sesame tuna, and grouper Oscar. The inn serves all meals, plus a Sunday brunch. A piano player entertains nightly. ✉ *100 Palm St.* ☎ *239/394–3131 or 977/475–3466* ▭ *AE, D, MC, V.*

★ $$–$$$ ✕ **Sale e Pepe.** The name means "salt and pepper," an indication that this palatial restaurant with patio seating overlooking the beach adheres to the basics of home Italian cuisine. Pasta, sausage, and sinful pastries are made right here in the kitchen. Simple dishes, such as veal ravioli, tomato-based fish stew, roasted halibut, grilled lamb chops, and veal chops, explode with home-cooked, long-cooked flavors. ✉ *Marco Beach Ocean Resort, 480 S. Collier Blvd.* ☎ *239/393–1600* ▭ *AE, D, MC, V.*

$$–$$$ ✕ **Verdi's.** Prints and plants add warmth to this spare American bistro, whose reputation is built on friendly, professional service and creative American and fusion cuisine. You might start with steamed littleneck clams or shrimp egg roll, then move on to entrées such as grilled swordfish, seared Chilean sea bass, or tilapia piccata. Cuban coffee crème brûlée and bananas Foster are among the tempting desserts. ✉ *241 N. Collier Blvd.* ☎ *239/394–5533* ▭ *AE, D, DC, MC, V* ☉ *Closed Sun. No lunch.*

¢–$$ ✕ **The Crazy Flamingo.** Burgers, seafood, and finger foods like conch fritters and chicken wings are the draw at this neighborhood bar. Or go for a seafood steamer pot, oysters, or a grouper sandwich. ✉ *Marco Island Town Center, 1049 N. Collier Blvd.* ☎ *239/642–9600* 🍽 *Reservations not accepted* ▭ *No credit cards.*

★ ¢–$$ ✕ **Tide Restaurant.** Head to this local favorite for the best casual dining with a view of the beach and a menu of ribs, thick sandwiches, burgers, chicken-finger and shrimp baskets, and pastas. The lively bar scene adds to the fun indoors; a porch accommodates al fresco diners. ✉ *Apollo Condominiums, 900 S. Collier Blvd.* ☎ *239/393–8433* ▭ *AE, D, MC, V.*

$$$$ 🏨 **Marco Beach Ocean Resort.** One of the area's first condo hotels, this 12-story class act has one- and two-bedroom suites, done in royal blues and golds. All rooms face the gulf and the property's crescent-shaped rooftop pool (on the fifth floor). The bathrooms are full of marble. Golf and tennis are nearby. ⊠ 480 S. Collier Blvd., 34145 ☏ 239/393–1400 or 800/260–5089 🖷 239/393–1401 ⊕ www.marcoresort.com ⌁ 87 1- and 16 2-bedroom suites ♨ Restaurant, in-room data ports, kitchens, golf privileges, 4 tennis courts, pool, outdoor hot tub, health club, spa, beach, boating, 2 bars, shops, children's programs (ages 3–12), playground, concierge, business services, meeting rooms ⊟ AE, D, DC, MC, V.

$$$$ 🏨 **Marco Island Hilton Beach Resort.** This 11-story beachfront hotel is smaller than other big-name local resorts, and it seems less crowded. All rooms are spacious and have private balconies with unobstructed gulf views, a sitting area, a wet bar, and a refrigerator. ⊠ 560 S. Collier Blvd., 34145 ☏ 239/394–5000 or 800/443–4550 🖷 239/394–8410 ⊕ www.marcoisland.hilton.com ⌁ 271 rooms, 26 suites ♨ 3 restaurants, snack bar, minibars, refrigerators, 3 tennis courts, pool, outdoor hot tub, health club, beach, windsurfing, boating, parasailing, waterskiing, bar ⊟ AE, D, DC, MC, V.

★ $$$$ 🏨 **Marriott's Marco Island Resort and Golf Club.** A circular drive and manicured grounds front this beachfront resort made up of two 11-story towers. It's delightfully beachy outside, yet the interior is elegant, with many shops and restaurants and large, plush rooms with good to exceptional water views. A recent makeover yielded a new spa and restaurant plus a waterfalls pool with slides. The hotel's golf course is 10 minutes away by tram. ⊠ 400 S. Collier Blvd., 34145 ☏ 239/394–2511 or 800/438–4373 🖷 239/642–2672 ⊕ www.marcomarriottresort.com ⌁ 727 rooms, 54 suites ♨ 6 restaurants, refrigerators, 18-hole golf course, 4 tennis courts, 3 pools, wading pool, health club, spa, beach, windsurfing, boating, waterskiing, bicycles, 3 bars, shops, children's programs (ages 3–12), playground ⊟ AE, DC, MC, V.

$$$$ 🏨 **Old Marco Island Inn & Suites.** This Victorian with tin roofs and royal blue shutters and awnings used to be the only place to stay on the island. Although it's away from the beach, it's in the heart of Old Marco, and the large one- and two-bedroom tiled suites with screened lanais are ideal for families. ⊠ 100 Palm St., 34145 ☏ 239/394–3131 or 877/475–3466 🖷 239/394–4485 ⊕ www.oldmarco.com ⌁ 52 suites ♨ 2 restaurants, coffee shop, in-room data ports, kitchenettes, pool, gym, spa, bar, shops, meeting rooms ⊟ AE, D, DC, MC, V.

$$$$ 🏨 **Radisson Suite Beach Resort.** At this 12-story beachfront property designed for families, all units are tastefully decorated. The rooms are a bit tight, but the one- and two-bedroom suites are spacious. ⊠ 600 S. Collier Blvd., 34145 ☏ 239/394–4100 or 800/333–3333 🖷 239/394–0419 ⊕ www.marcobeachresort.com ⌁ 55 rooms, 214 suites ♨ 3 restaurants, kitchens, microwaves, refrigerators, pool, gym, beach, parasailing, bicycles, 2 bars, children's programs (ages 3–12) ⊟ AE, D, DC, MC, V.

$$–$$$ 🏨 **Boat House Motel.** For a great location at a good price, check into this two-story motel. Modest but appealing with its white facade and turquoise trim, it's at the north end of Marco Island, on a canal close to the gulf. Units are light and bright and furnished with natural wicker and pastel print fabrics. All have a balcony or terrace, and some have great water views. Fish from the motel's own dock. ⊠ 1180 Edington Pl., 34145 ☏ 239/642–2400 or 800/528–6345 🖷 239/642–2435 ⊕ www.theboathousemotel.com ⌁ 20 rooms ♨ Pool, dock, fishing ⊟ MC, V.

The Outdoors

BIKING Rentals are available at **Scootertown** (⊠ 845 Bald Eagle Dr. ☎ 239/394–8400) for use on the island's bike path along beachfront condos and resorts.

FISHING **Sunshine Tours** (⊠ Marco River Marina, 951 Bald Eagle Dr. ☎ 239/642–5415 ⊕ www.sunshinetoursmarcoisland.com) operates deep-sea and back-country fishing charters.

SAILING **Kahuna Sea Excursions** (⊠ Marco River Marina, 951 Bald Eagle Dr. ☎ 239/642–7704 ⊕ www.sail-kahuna.com) can help you sail into the sunset or take you out in search of dolphins and shells.

SOUTHWEST FLORIDA A TO Z

To research prices, get advice from other travelers, and book travel arrangements, visit www.fodors.com.

AIR TRAVEL

CARRIERS Southwest Florida International Airport is served by Air Canada, AirTran Airways, American/American Eagle, American TransAir, America West, Cape Air, Continental, Delta, Frontier, JetBlue, Northwest, Spirit, TWA, United, USA 3000, and US Airways. The Naples Municipal Airport is served by Cape Air, Delta ComAir, and US Airways.

🛪 Airlines & Contacts Air Canada ☎ 888/247-2262. AirTran Airways ☎ 800/247-8726. America West ☎ 800/235-9292. American Eagle ☎ 800/433-7300. American TransAir ☎ 800/435-9282. Cape Air ☎ 800/352-0714. Continental ☎ 800/523-3273. Delta ☎ 800/221-1212. Frontier Airlines ☎ 800/432-1359. Midwest Express ☎ 800/452-2022. Northwest ☎ 800/225-2525. Spirit ☎ 800/772-7117. TWA ☎ 800/221-2000. United ☎ 800/241-6522. USA 3000 Airlines ☎ 877/872-3000. US Airways ☎ 800/428-4322.

AIRPORTS

The area's main airport is Southwest Florida International Airport, about 12 mi southwest of Fort Myers, 25 mi north of Naples. A taxi to Fort Myers, Sanibel, or Captiva costs about $8–$60; it's about $50–$60 to Naples. Transportation companies include AAA Airport Transportation, Boca Grande Limo, Charlotte Limousine Service, and Sanibel Island Taxi. The Naples Municipal Airport is a small facility east of downtown. Shuttle service to Naples is generally $15–$25 per person. Once you have arrived, call Naples Taxi.

🛪 Airport Information Naples Municipal Airport ☎ 239/643-0733. Southwest Florida International Airport ☎ 239/768-1000. AAA Airport Transportation ☎ 800/872-2711. Aaron Airport Transportation and Best Value Taxi ☎ 239/768-1898 or 800/998-1898. Boca Grande Limo ☎ 941/964-0455 or 800/771-7433. Charlotte Limousine Service ☎ 941/627-4494. Naples Taxi ☎ 239/643-2148 Sanibel Taxi ☎ 239/472-4160.

BOAT & FERRY TRAVEL

From Thanksgiving through May, Key West Shuttle operates a ferry from Marco Island and Fort Myers Beach to Key West. The cost for the round-trip (four hours each way) from Marco Island is $119. The almost five-hour trip from Fort Myers Beach costs $129 round-trip.

🛪 Boat & Ferry Information Key West Shuttle ☎ 239/394-9700 or 888/539-2628 ⊕ www.keywestshuttle.com.

BUS TRAVEL

Greyhound Lines has service to Fort Myers and Naples. LeeTran serves most of the Fort Myers area.

🛪 Bus Information Greyhound Lines ☎ 800/231-2222 ⊠ 2275 Cleveland Ave., Fort Myers ☎ 239/334-1011 ⊠ 2669 Davis Blvd., Naples ☎ 239/774-5660. LeeTran ☎ 239/275-8726 ⊕ www.rideleetran.com.

CAR TRAVEL

I–75 spans the region from north to south. Once you cross the border into Florida, it's about six hours to Fort Myers and another half hour to Naples. Alligator Alley, a section of Interstate 75, is a two-lane toll road ($1.50 to enter) that runs from Fort Lauderdale through the Everglades to Naples. The trip takes about two hours. U.S. 41 also runs the length of the region. Also known as the Tamiami Trail, U.S. 41 goes through downtown Fort Myers and Naples and is also called Cleveland Avenue in the former and 9th Street in the latter. McGregor Boulevard (Route 867) and Summerlin Road (Route 869), Fort Myers's main north–south city streets, head toward Sanibel and Captiva Islands. San Carlos Boulevard runs southwest from Summerlin Road to Fort Myers Beach, and Pine Island–Bayshore Road (Route 78) leads from North Fort Myers through northern Cape Coral onto Pine Island.

EMERGENCIES

Dial 911 for police or ambulance.
🚹 Late-Night Pharmacies **Walgreens Drug Store** ⊠ 15601 San Carlos Blvd., Fort Myers ☎ 239/489–3400 ✉ 2170 Del Prado Blvd. S, Cape Coral ☎ 239/574–1928.

MEDIA

NEWSPAPERS & MAGAZINES
The local rags are the *Naples Daily News* and the Fort Myers *News Press*.

RADIO
Tune in WARO 94.5 FM for classic rock; WRXK 96 FM for rock; WAVV 101.1 FM for easy listening; and WCKT 107 FM for country.

TOURS

Boca Grande Seaplane Service operates sightseeing tours in the Charlotte Harbor area. One way to see the cluster of small, undeveloped, protected islands known as the Ten Thousand Islands is on an airboat tour run by Airboat Experience of the Everglades. You'll probably see many birds, including pelicans, egrets, ibises, and hawks, as well as alligators swimming alongside the boat. Everglades National Park also runs a boat tour into the deepest wildlife lair, and this one is less noisy than airboats, so not as likely to scare birds away. Estero Bay Boat Tours takes you on guided tours of waterways once inhabited by the Calusa Indians. You'll see birds and other wildlife and may even spot some manatees or dolphins. At the South Seas Resort marina, Captiva Cruises runs sailboat charters and shelling, nature, luncheon, beach, and sunset cruises to and around the out islands of Cabbage Key, Useppa Island, Cayo Costa, and Gasparilla Island. For a luxury sailing tour of the upper islands and beyond, charter Sanibel Island Adventure's *Adventure Cat.*

J. C.'s Cruises explores the Caloosahatchee and Orange rivers of Lee County. In summer, the *Capt. J. P.,* a stern paddle wheeler, does jungle cruises. In winter, lunch and dinner cruises are available. For manatee-sighting tours, hook up with Fort Myers Manatee World or Manatee Sightseeing Adventure at Marco Island. In Punta Gorda, King Fisher Cruise Lines has half-day sightseeing, full-day island, and sunset cruises in Charlotte Harbor, the Peace River, and the Intracoastal Waterway. One of the best ways to see the J. N. "Ding" Darling National Wildlife Refuge is by taking a canoe or kayak tour with Tarpon Bay Explorers. The knowledgeable naturalist guides can help you see so much more of what's there among the mangroves and under the water's surface. Take a narrated sightseeing, dinner, or murder-mystery excursion aboard the old-fashioned Seminole Gulf Railway. Daytime trips, which run Wednesday, Saturday, and Sunday, travel north for a scenic Caloosahatchee bridge crossing in season. Naples Trolley Tours offers five narrated tours daily, covering more than 100 points of interest. Pick it up at 25 places around town, including the Coastland Mall. The tour ($17) lasts about 1¾ hours, but you can get off and reboard at no extra cost.

🚹 Tours Information **Airboat Experience of the Everglades** ⊠ 3200 San Marco Rd., Marco Island ☎ 239/642-3141. **Boca Grande Seaplane Service** ⊠ 375 Park Ave., Boca Grande ☎ 941/964-0234 or 800/940-0234. **Captiva Cruises** ⊠ South Seas Resort, Captiva ☎ 239/472-5300. **Sanibel Island Adventures** ⊠ Port Sanibel, Fort Myers ☎ 239/826-7566 ⊕ www.sanibeladventures.com. **Estero Bay Boat Tours** ⊠ 5231 Mamie St., Bonita Springs ☎ 239/992-2200. **J. C.'s Cruises** ⊠ Fort Myers Yacht Basin, 2313 Edwards Dr., Fort Myers ☎ 239/334-7474. **Fort Myers Manatee World** ⊠ Coastal Marine Mart, Rte. 80, Fort Myers ☎ 239/693-1434. **King Fisher Cruise Lines** ⊠ Fishermen's Village, 1200 W. Retta Esplanade, Punta Gorda ☎ 239/639-0969. **Manatee Sightseeing Adventure** ☎ 800/379-7440). **Naples Trolley Tours** ☎ 239/262-7300. **Seminole Gulf Railway** ⊠ Colonial Station, Fort Myers ☎ 239/275-8487 or 800/736-4853. **Tarpon Bay Explorers** ⊠ 900 Tarpon Bay Rd., Sanibel ☎ 239/472-8900.

VISITOR INFORMATION

The following are open weekdays 9–5: Charlotte County Chamber of Commerce, Lee County Visitor and Convention Bureau, Naples Area Chamber of Commerce, and Marco Island Chamber of Commerce. The Sanibel & Captiva Chamber of Commerce stays open Monday to Saturday 9–7 and Sunday 10–5.

🚹 Tourist Information **Charlotte County Chamber of Commerce** ⊠ 2702 Tamiami Trail, Port Charlotte 33952 ☎ 941/627-2222 ⊠ 326 Marion Ave., Suite 112, Punta Gorda 33950 ☎ 941/639-2222. **Lee County Visitor and Convention Bureau** ⊠ 2180 W. 1st St., Suite 100, Fort Myers 33901 ☎ 239/338-3500 or 800/237-6444. **Naples Chamber of Commerce** ⊠ 895 5th Ave. S, Naples 34102 ☎ 239/262-6141. **Marco Island Area Chamber of Commerce** ⊠ 1102 N. Collier Blvd., Marco Island 34145 ☎ 239/394-7549 or 800/788-6272. **Sanibel-Captiva Chamber of Commerce** ⊠ 1159 Causeway Rd., Sanibel 33957 ☎ 239/472-1080.

THE PANHANDLE

9

FODOR'S CHOICE

Cafe Thirty-A, Seagrove Beach

Grayton Beach State Park, Grayton Beach

Marriott's Bay Point Resort Village, Panama City Beach

Sandestin Golf and Beach Resort, Destin

St. Andrews State Park, Panama City Beach

St. George Island State Park, St. George Island

Tamara's Cafe Floridita, Apalachicola

HIGHLY RECOMMENDED

RESTAURANTS Andrew's 2nd Act, Tallahassee

Magnolia Grill, Apalachicola

Marina Café, Destin

Pandora's Steakhouse and Lounge, Fort Walton Beach

HOTELS Bluewater Bay Golf & Tennis Resort, Destin

Edgewater Beach Resort, Panama City Beach

Governors Inn, Tallahassee

New World Inn, Pensacola

Seaside Cottage Rental Agency, Seaside

WHAT TO SEE Air Force Armament Museum, Fort Walton Beach

New Capitol, Tallahassee

Old Capitol, Tallahassee

Wakulla Springs State Park, Wakulla Springs

Updated by
David
Downing

FLORIDA'S THIN, GREEN NORTHWEST CORNER snuggles up between the Gulf of Mexico and the Alabama and Georgia state lines. Known as the Panhandle, it's sometimes called "the other Florida," since in addition to palm trees what thrives here are the magnolias, live oaks, and loblolly pines common in the rest of the Deep South. As South Florida's season is winding down in May, action in the northwest is just picking up. The area is even in a different time zone: the Apalachicola River marks the dividing line between eastern and central times. Until World War II, when activity at the Panhandle air bases took off, this section of the state was little known and seldom visited. But by the mid-1950s, the 100-mi stretch along the coast between Pensacola and Panama City was dubbed the Miracle Strip because of a dramatic rise in property values. In the 1940s this beachfront land sold for less than $100 an acre; today that same acre can fetch tens of thousands of dollars. To convey the richness of the region, with its white sands and sparkling green waters, swamps, bayous, and flora, public-relations pros ditched the Redneck Riviera moniker that locals had created and coined the phrase Emerald Coast.

It's a land of superlatives: it has the biggest military installation in the Western Hemisphere (Eglin Air Force Base), many of Florida's most beautiful beaches, and the most productive fishing waters in the world (off Destin). It has glitzy resorts, campgrounds where possums invite themselves to lunch, and every kind of lodging in between. Students of the past can wander the many historic districts or visit archaeological digs. For sports enthusiasts there's a different golf course or tennis court for each day of the week, and for nature lovers there's a world of hunting, canoeing, biking, and hiking. And most anything that happens on water happens here, including scuba diving and plenty of fishing, both from deep-sea charter boats or the end of a pier.

Exploring the Panhandle

There are sights in the Panhandle, but sightseeing is not the principal activity here. The area is better known for its ample fishing and diving spots, and for being a spot to simply relax.

Although it's Florida's westernmost city, Pensacola, with its antebellum homes and historic landmarks, is a good place to start your trek through northwest Florida. After exploring the museums and preservation districts, head out to Pensacola Beach and drive east on Santa Rosa Island to the small town of Navarre Beach, where a bridge connects back to U.S. 98 on the mainland. Proceed east to Fort Walton Beach, the Emerald Coast's largest city, and on to neighboring Destin, where sportfishing is king. Continuing along the coast, you'll find the quiet family-friendly beaches of South Walton, where there is a beautiful and stunning contrast between the sugar-white, quartz-crystal sands and emerald-green waters. The next resort center along the coast is Panama City Beach, while to the far southeast is Apalachicola, an important oyster-fishing town. Just south of Apalachicola, St. George Island is a 28-mi-long barrier island bordered by the gulf and Apalachicola Bay. Inland, a number of interesting towns and state parks lie along Interstate 10 on the long eastward drive to the state capital, Tallahassee.

About the Restaurants

A staggering quantity and variety of seafood is harvested from the Panhandle's coastal waters each day, and much of it appears within hours at restaurants throughout the region. You'll find oysters, crab, shrimp, scallops, and fish served fresh and simply prepared at casual beachside cafés as well as fresh and fancy at upscale resort dining rooms. Don't overlook small-town seafood shacks, where you can dine "Florida Cracker"–style on deep-fried mullet, cheese grits, cole slaw, and hush puppies. Some restaurants in resort areas and beach communities close or modify their hours during low season, so call first if visiting during winter months.

About the Hotels

You'll find chain hotels and motels along the major highways and in all but the smallest towns here if you've come to the area for just a day or two. Most visitors, however, come to stay and play for a week or more, so long-term lodging is definitely the most popular and plentiful option. Beach communities all along the coast offer long-term rentals tailored to fit every lifestyle, from the simplest to the most lavish. Do your own housekeeping and explore the area on your own, or opt to stay at one of the inclusive resorts where everything you might need or wish to do is available on-site.

WHAT IT COSTS				
$$$$	**$$$**	**$$**	**$**	**¢**
RESTAURANTS over $30	$20–$30	$15–$20	$10–$15	under $10
HOTELS over $220	$140–$220	$100–$140	$80–$100	under $80

Restaurant prices are per person for a main course at dinner. Hotel prices are for a standard double room, excluding 6% sales tax (more in some counties) and 1%–4% tourist tax.

Timing

North Florida enjoys as much sunshine as the southern part of the state, but the climate here is more temperate than tropical. Unlike in the rest of Florida, the Panhandle's high season falls roughly between Memorial Day and Labor Day, when hordes of tourists and vacationing families from neighboring states head south for the summer. Lodging prices in the region are usually based on a four-season system: spring break and summer rates are highest, winter lowest, and fall and spring are between the two extremes. If you prefer your beach less crowded, plan to visit in the autumn—October can be the loveliest month of the year here —when warm, sunny days alternate with cool, rainy spells and there's relatively little humidity. Winter days can be both brilliant and bitterly cold, perfect for fishing or walking along miles of deserted beach.

AROUND PENSACOLA BAY

In the years since its founding, Pensacola has come under the control of five nations, earning this fine, old southern city its nickname, the City of Five Flags. Spanish conquistadors, under the command of Don Tristan de Luna, landed on the shores of Pensacola Bay in 1559, but discouraged by a succession of destructive tropical storms and dissension in the ranks, de Luna abandoned the settlement two years after its founding. In 1698 the Spanish once again established a fort at the site, and during the early 18th century control jockeyed back and forth among the Spanish, the French, and the British. Finally, in 1821 Pensacola passed into U.S. hands, although during the Civil War it was governed by the Confederate States of America and flew yet another flag. The city itself has many historic sights, while across the bay lies Pensacola Beach on Santa Rosa Island, where pristine coastline provides delightful beaches for recreational activities.

Pensacola

▶ **①** *59 mi east of Mobile, Alabama.*

Historic Pensacola consists of three distinct districts—Seville, Palafox, and North Hill—though they are easy to explore as a unit. Stroll down streets mapped out by the British and renamed by the Spanish, such as Cervantes, Palafox, Intendencia, and Tarragona. A recent influx of restaurants and bars is bringing new nightlife to the historic districts, but one-way streets can make navigating the area a bit tricky, especially at night.

The best way to orient yourself is to stop at the **Pensacola Visitor Information Center,** at the foot of the Pensacola Bay Bridge. Pick up maps here of the self-guided historic-district tours. ⊠ *1401 E. Gregory St.* ☎ *850/ 434–1234 or 800/874–1234* ⊕ *www.visitpensacola.com.*

The **Seville Square Historic District** is the site of Pensacola's first permanent Spanish colonial settlement. Its center is Seville Square, a live oak–shaded park bounded by Alcaniz, Adams, Zaragoza, and Government streets. Roam these brick streets past honeymoon cottages and bayfront homes. Many of the buildings have been converted into restaurants, commercial offices, and shops.

Within the Seville district is the **Historic Pensacola Village,** a complex of several museums, whose indoor and outdoor exhibits trace the area's history back 450 years. The Museum of Industry (200 E. Zaragoza St.), in a late 19th-century warehouse, hosts permanent exhibits dedicated to the lumber, maritime, and shipping industries—once mainstays of Pensacola's economy. A reproduction of a 19th-century streetscape is displayed in the Museum of Commerce (201 E. Zaragoza St.). Also in the village are the Julee Cottage (210 E. Zaragoza St.), Dorr House (311 S. Adams St.), Lavalle House (205 E. Church St.), and Quina House (204 S. Alcaniz St.). Strolling through the area gives you a good look at many architectural styles, but to enter the museums you must purchase an all-inclusive ticket at the T. T. Wentworth Jr. Florida State Museum (included in the admission price) or the Village gift shop in the Tivoli House. *Tivoli House* ⊠ *205 E. Zaragoza St.* ☎ *850/595–5985* ⊕ *www.historicpensacola. org* ⊠ *$6, including Wentworth Museum* ⊙ *Tues.–Sat. 10–4.*

⟳ A former City Hall dating to 1908 now houses the **T. T. Wentworth Jr. Florida State Museum.** It has an eclectic mixture of exhibits that children find especially intriguing—particularly the shrunken heads and Discovery, a hands-on exhibit on the third floor. ⊠ *330 S. Jefferson St.* ☎ *850/ 595–5990* ⊠ *$6, including Historic Pensacola Village* ⊙ *Mon.–Sat. 10–4.*

Palafox Street is the main stem of the **Palafox Historic District,** which was the commercial and government hub of Old Pensacola. Note the Spanish Renaissance–style **Saenger Theater,** Pensacola's old movie palace, and the **Bear Block,** a former wholesale grocery with wrought-iron balconies that are a legacy from Pensacola's Creole past. On Palafox between Government and Zaragoza streets is a **statue of Andrew Jackson** that commemorates the formal transfer of Florida from Spain to the United States in 1821. While in the area, stop by the **Wall South,** in Veterans Memorial Park, just off Bayfront Parkway near 9th Avenue. The ¾-scale replica of the Vietnam Memorial in Washington, D.C., honors the more than 58,000 men and women who lost their lives in the Vietnam War.

Pensacola's city jail once occupied the 1906 Spanish-revival style building that is now the **Pensacola Museum of Art.** It provides a secure home for the museum's permanent collections of Oriental porcelain and works

Numbers in the text correspond to numbers in the margin and on the Panhandle map.

If you have
3 days

History and nature are the two biggest calling cards of this part of the Sunshine State. Visit 🏛 **Fort Walton Beach** ❸ 🏳 or Eglin Air Force Base, depending on whether your heart lies on the seas or in the skies. Kids might enjoy a stop at the Indian Temple Mound and Museum. On day two drive to the capital, 🏛 **Tallahassee** ⑬, and soak up some of Florida's past. On day three, make a trip to nearby **Wakulla Springs State Park** ⑮, where you'll find one of the world's deepest springs—perfect for sightseeing and swimming.

9

If you have
5 days

Start with a visit to the Palafox Historic District in 🏛 **Pensacola** ❶ 🏳 and spend the day enjoying a glimpse of Old Florida, as well as visiting the National Museum of Naval Aviation. Next move on to 🏛 **Fort Walton Beach** ❸ and stop by Eglin Air Force Base and the antebellum mansion at the Eden Gardens State Park, set amid moss-draped live oaks. Be sure to spend an afternoon at the Grayton Beach State Park, one of the most scenic spots along the Gulf Coast. Moving inland, explore the caves at the **Florida Caverns State Park** ⑫ before heading to 🏛 **Tallahassee** ⑬. From there make day trips to **Wakulla Springs State Park** ⑮ and **St. Marks National Wildlife Refuge and Lighthouse** ⑯, to hike, swim, or have a leisurely picnic.

If you have
7 days

From a base in 🏛 **Pensacola** ❶ 🏳, take a couple of side trips: to the Gulf Islands National Seashore, paying special attention to Fort Pickens and to the zoo in Gulf Breeze. Swing north to the Blackwater River and spend two days taking an Adventures Unlimited canoe trip and roughing it in an outdoor cabin. Proceed to 🏛 **DeFuniak Springs** ⑩, where must-sees are the quaint Walton DeFuniak Public Library and the Chautauqua Winery. Head south to 🏛 **Destin** ❹ for a day of deep-sea fishing or a shopping spree at Silver Sands. Wind up your expedition through the other Florida at the beaches and amusement parks of 🏛 **Panama City Beach** ❼, after an afternoon's stopover at the planned community of **Seaside** ❻.

---

on paper by 20th-century artists; traveling exhibits range from photography to Dutch masters to works from local artists. ⊠ *407 S. Jefferson St.* ☎ *850/432–6247* ⊕ *www.pensacolamuseumofart.org* ▧ *$2; free Tues.* ⊗ *Tues.–Fri. 10–5, Sat. 10–4.*

The collections of the **Civil War Soldiers Museum** hold a large number of items pertaining to Civil War medicine as well as an equally impressive collection of Civil War books. ⊠ *108 S. Palafox Pl.* ☎ *850/469–1900* ⊕ *www.cwmuseum.org* ▧ *$5* ⊗ *Tues.–Sat. 10–4:30.*

Pensacola's affluent families, many made rich in the turn-of-the-20th-century timber boom, built their homes in the **North Hill Preservation District,** where British and Spanish fortresses once stood. Residents still occasionally unearth cannonballs in their gardens. North Hill occupies 50 blocks, with more than 500 homes in Queen Anne, neoclassical, Tudor revival, and Mediterranean styles. Take a drive through this community, but remember these are private residences. Places of general interest include the 1902 Spanish mission–style **Christ Episcopal Church;** **Lee Square,** where a 50-ft obelisk stands as a tribute to the Confederacy; and **Fort George,** an undeveloped parcel at the site of the largest of three forts built by the British in 1778.

The **Pensacola Naval Air Station,** established in 1914, is the nation's oldest such facility. On display in the **National Museum of Naval Aviation** (☎ 850/452–3604 ⊕ www.naval-air.org) are more than 200 aircraft that played an important role in aviation history. Among them are the NC-4, which in 1919 became the first plane to cross the Atlantic; the famous World War II fighter the F6 *Hellcat*; and the Skylab Command Module. Other attractions include a 14-seat flight simulator and an IMAX theater playing *The Magic of Flight* and *Straight Up: Helicopters in Flight* ✉ *1750 Radford Blvd.* ☎ *850/452–3604; 850/453–2024 for IMAX theater* ☞ *Free, IMAX film $6.25* ☺ *Daily 9–5.*

Dating from the Civil War, **Fort Barrancas** has picnic areas and a ½-mi woodland nature trail on its grounds. The fort is part of the Gulf Islands National Seashore, maintained by the National Park Service. ✉ *Navy Blvd.* ☎ *850/455–5167* ☞ *Free* ☺ *Dec.–Jan., Wed.–Sun. 10:30–4; Feb.–Nov., daily 9:30–5.*

off the beaten path

The Zoo. The local zoo, near Gulf Breeze, has more than 700 animals, including many endangered species. Kids especially enjoy the tiger cubs, baby zebras, and a tall platform where they can have face-to-face meetings with giraffes—and a glimpse of cute-as-a-button baby giraffes as well. ✉ *5701 Gulf Breeze Pkwy., Gulf Breeze* ☎ *850/932–2229* ☞ *$9.95* ☺ *Daily 9–5.*

Where to Stay & Eat

$$–$$$ ✕ **Dharma Blue.** On Seville Square, this trendy restaurant is a popular destination for both lunch and dinner. A collection of southern folk art lends sly wit and exuberant color to the walls. A full sushi bar, cocktail bar, and both inside and outside dining guarantee a pleasant wait for chef Andrea O'Bannon's creations. Daily specials vary with the season, but the regular luncheon menu includes choices like a grilled fresh salmon burger or a fried-green-tomato club sandwich. For dinner try sesame-crusted grouper with tempura-fried zucchini and sweet potatoes, cranberry glaze, and basmati rice. ✉ *300 S. Alcaniz St.* ☎ *850/433–1275* ⊟ *AE, MC, V* ☺ *No lunch Sun.*

$$–$$$ ✕ **Lou Michael's.** This downtown restaurant has an uptown ambience that makes it a local favorite for special romantic dinners. The imaginative menu and extensive wine selection ensure a memorable meal, and the restaurant's art gallery and live music make it a feast for all your senses. Chef Frank Taylor's creations vary daily according to the availability of fresh seafood, meats, and seasonal produce; breads and desserts are also prepared fresh each day. ✉ *25 S. Palafox Pl.* ☎ *850/470–9191* ⊟ *AE, D, DC, MC, V* ☺ *Closed Sun.–Mon.*

$–$$$ ✕ **Mesquite Charlie's.** Saddle up and head on over to this Wild West saloon, with brick walls, arched doorways, mounted game, and a second-floor balcony overlooking the lobby. All that's missing are the swinging doors. The 32-ounce porterhouse is large enough to satisfy a posse of cowboys, but there are also smaller selections for dainty appetites. All are charbroiled with 100% mesquite charcoal and seasoned with natural spices. ✉ *5901 N. W St.* ☎ *850/434–0498* ⊟ *AE, D, MC, V.*

¢–$$ ✕ **McGuire's Irish Pub.** Spend anywhere from $10 to $100 for a hamburger here, depending on whether you want it topped with cheddar or served with caviar and champagne. Beer is brewed on the premises, and

9

Beaches
Thanks to restrictions against commercial development imposed by Eglin Air Force Base (AFB) and the Gulf Islands National Seashore, the Emerald Coast has been able to maintain several hundred miles of unspoiled beaches. Dr. Stephen Leatherman of Florida International University, a.k.a. Dr. Beach, consistently ranks Panhandle beaches among the top 20 in the world in the book *America's Best Beaches*.

Biking
Some of the nation's best bike paths run through northwest Florida's woods and dunelands, particularly on Santa Rosa Island, where you can pedal for nearly 20 mi and never lose sight of the water. Eglin AFB Reservation presents cyclists with tortuous wooded trails.

Boating
With major shipping ports located at Pensacola and Panama City, and fleets of commercial and charter boats based all along the Gulf Coast, the Panhandle's waters are heavily traveled year-round. When recreational boaters add their numbers during the summer months, the region's coastal waterways can be as crowded as its coastal highways. Those arriving by boat to cruise the Intracoastal Waterway will find an abundance of full-service marinas along the way. Rentals are available for nearly every type of watercraft, but you should be familiar with state regulations and safety procedures if you want to operate a boat here; penalties are severe for those caught boating recklessly or under the influence of alcohol or drugs.

Canoeing
The Panhandle is often referred to as the Canoe Capital of Florida, and both beginners and veterans enjoy canoeing the area's abundant waterways. The shoals and rapids of the Blackwater River in the Blackwater River State Forest, 40 mi northeast of Pensacola, challenge even seasoned canoeists, while the gentler currents of sheltered marshes and inlets are less intimidating.

Fishing
Options range from fishing for pompano, snapper, marlin, and grouper in the saltwater of the gulf to angling for bass, catfish, and bluegill in freshwater. Deep-sea fishing is immensely popular on the Emerald Coast, so there are boat charters aplenty. A day costs about $575, a half day about $350.

---

the wine cellar has more than 8,000 bottles. Menu items range from Irish-style corned beef and cabbage to a hickory-smoked rib roast. In an old firehouse, the pub is replete with antiques, moose heads, Tiffany-style lamps, and Erin-go-bragh memorabilia. More than 250,000 dollar bills signed and dated by the pub's patrons flutter from the ceiling. ⊠ *600 E. Gregory St.* ☎ *850/433–6789* ⊟ *AE, D, DC, MC, V.*

$$–$$$ 🏨 **Residence Inn by Marriott.** In the downtown bay-front area, this all-suites hotel is perfect for extended stays, whether for business or pleasure. The location is ideal for exploring Pensacola's historic streets on foot, and families will especially appreciate the fully equipped kitchens and free grocery delivery. Breakfast and evening social hour are complimentary. ⊠ *601 E. Chase St., 32501* ☎ *850/432–0202* 🖨 *850/438–7965* ⥅ *78 suites* ⚭ *Kitchens, some microwaves, some refrigerators, cable TV, tennis court, pool, gym, some pets allowed (fee)* ⊟ *AE, D, DC, MC, V.*

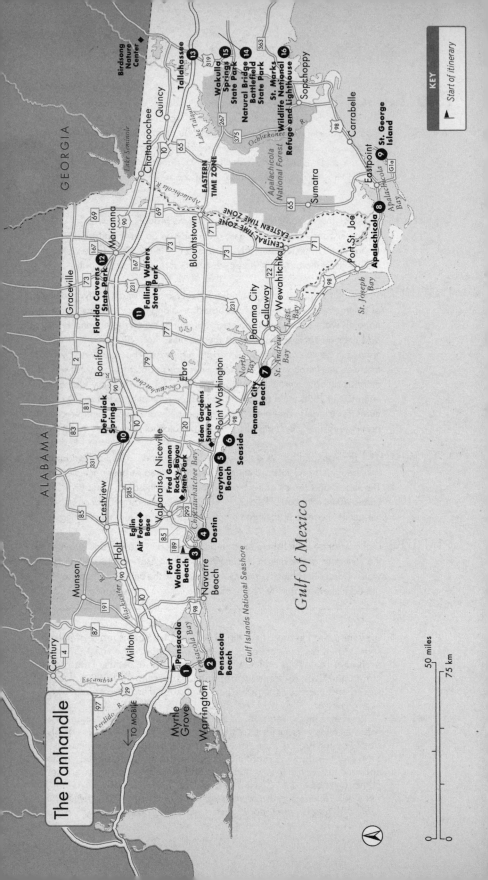

The Panhandle

★ ¢–$$$ ⊞ **New World Inn.** If a small, warm, and cozy inn sounds appealing, this is the place for you. In the downtown historic area two blocks from Pensacola Bay, it contains furnishings that reflect the five periods of Pensacola's past: French and Spanish provincial, Early American, antebellum, and Queen Anne. Exquisite baths are handsomely appointed. ⊠ *600 S. Palafox St., 32501* ☎ *850/432–4111* 🖷 *850/432–6836* ⊕ *www.newworldlanding.com* ⇆ *14 rooms, 1 suite* ⌂ *Meeting rooms* ▤ *AE, MC, V* ⦿ *CP.*

$–$$ ⊞ **Crowne Plaza–Pensacola Grand Hotel.** The lobby of the former 1912 Louisville & Nashville train depot still has intact ticket and baggage counters, and old railroad signs remind you of the days when steam locomotives chugged up to these doors. A canopied two-story galleria leads to a 15-story tower—one of the tallest structures in town—where you leave the past behind and enjoy all the amenities of deluxe accommodations. Bi-level penthouse suites have snazzy wet bars and whirlpool baths. The hotel's proximity to downtown dining and nightlife, along with its amenities, makes it a good choice for business travelers. ⊠ *200 E. Gregory St., 32501* ☎ *850/433–3336 or 800/348–3336* 🖷 *850/432–7572* ⊕ *www.pensacolagrandhotel.com* ⇆ *212 rooms, 8 suites* ⌂ *Restaurant, some in-room hot tubs, some minibars, cable TV, pool, gym, bar, library, business services, airport shuttle* ▤ *AE, D, DC, MC, V.*

Nightlife & the Arts

THE ARTS   The **Pensacola Little Theatre** (⊠ 400 S. Jefferson St. ☎ 850/432–2042) presents plays and musicals year-round. **Pensacola's Symphony Orchestra** (☎ 850/435–2533) offers 11 concerts each season at the Saenger Theatre. Productions at the restored 1926 **Saenger Theatre** (⊠ 118 S. Palafox St. ☎ 850/444–7686) include touring Broadway shows and three locally staged operas a year.

NIGHTLIFE   **Emerald City** (⊠ 406 E. Wright St. ☎ 850/433–9491) is a straight-friendly gay dance bar across from the Crowne Plaza hotel downtown. Nightly drink specials, karaoke nights, and drag performances keep the party going Wednesday through Monday. After dark, **McGuire's Irish Pub** (⊠ 600 E. Gregory St. ☎ 850/433–6789) welcomes those of Irish descent or anyone else who enjoys cold ale, beer, or lager. If you don't like crowds, stay away from McGuire's on Friday night and when Notre Dame games are televised. **Mesquite Charlie's** (⊠ 5901 N. W St. ☎ 850/434–0498) offers country music and all the western trappings. The **Seville Quarter** (⊠ 130 E. Government St. ☎ 850/434–6211) has seven fabulous bars playing music from disco to Dixieland; it's Pensacola's equivalent of the New Orleans French Quarter.

Sports & the Outdoors

CANOEING &   **Adventures Unlimited** (⊠ Rte. 87, 12 mi north of Milton ☎ 850/623–6197
KAYAKING   or 800/239–6864), on Coldwater Creek, rents light watercraft as well as campsites. Canoe season lasts roughly from March through mid-November. Canoe and kayak rentals for exploring the Blackwater River—the state's only sand-bottom river, and one of only three in the world—are available from **Blackwater Canoe Rental** (⊠ 6974 Deaton Bridge Rd., Milton ☎ 850/623–0235 or 800/967–6789), northeast of Pensacola off I–10 Exit 10.

FISHING   In a pinch you can drop a line from Old Pensacola Bay Bridge. Call **Rod and Reel Marina** (⊠ 10045 Sinton Dr. ☎ 850/492–0100), a mile west of Blue Angel Parkway off Gulf Beach Highway, to schedule a half- or full-day fishing charter. Bring your own food; the marina will supply everything else.

GOLF There are several outstanding golf courses in and around Pensacola. The **Moors** (✉ 3220 Avalon Blvd., Milton ☎ 850/994–2744), an 18-hole, par-70, Scottish links–style course, was designed by John LaFoy and is well known as the home of the Senior PGA Tour Emerald Coast Classic. The **Sportsman of Perdido** (✉ 1 Doug Ford Dr. ☎ 850/492–1223) has a well-kept 18-hole course. **Tiger Point Golf & Country Club** (✉ 1255 Country Club Rd., Gulf Breeze ☎ 850/932–1330) is a semiprivate 36-hole club.

TENNIS There are find public tennis courts in more than 30 locations in the Pensacola area. The **Pensacola Racquet Club** (✉ 3450 Wimbledon Dr. ☎ 850/434–2434) has 10 clay and 2 hard courts, plus a pool and restaurant.

Shopping

Cordova Mall (✉ 5100 N. 9th Ave., ☎ 850/477–5563), anchored by four department stores, has specialty shops and a food court. **Harbourtown Shopping Village** (✉ 913 Gulf Breeze Pkwy., Gulf Breeze) has trendy shops and the look of a wharfside New England village.

Pensacola Beach

❷ *5 mi south of Pensacola via U.S. 98 to Rte. 399 (Bob Sikes) Bridge.*

The skinny barrier island of Santa Rosa has beaches, natural areas, and the tourist town of Pensacola Beach. Truth be told, most of the culture—as well as most of the good restaurants—in the greater Pensacola area is found on the mainland, so you're better off heading to the beaches for gorgeous seascapes, myriad water sports, miles of cycling trails, and prime bird-watching (more than 280 species of birds have been spotted here). Two caveats for visitors: "Leave nothing behind but your foot-prints" and—enforced by mighty big fines—"Don't pick the sea oats," the natural grasses that help keep the dunes intact. You should also mind the speed limit when passing through the town of Gulf Breeze on the way to the beach—the police there are famous for handing out unwelcome souvenirs of their own.

Dotting the 150-mi stretch between Destin and Gulfport, Mississippi, is **Gulf Islands National Seashore** (☎ 850/934–2600 ⊕ www.nps.gov/guis), managed by the National Park Service. Many good beach and recreational spots are part of the national seashore along this beautiful stretch of island coast. While the park is open year-round, there are seasonal restrictions, so call ahead. At **Opal Beach Day Use Area** (✉ Rte. 399, 5 mi east of Pensacola Beach) you'll find pristine coastline, barbecue areas, covered picnic facilities, and rest rooms. At the western tip of the island and part of the Gulf Islands National Seashore, **Fort Pickens** dates to 1834. Constructed of more than 21 million locally made bricks, the fort once served as the prison of Apache chief Geronimo. A National Park Service plaque describes the complex as a "confusing jumble of fortifications," but the real attractions here are the beach, nature exhibits, a large campground, an excellent gift shop, and breathtaking views of Pensacola Bay and the lighthouse across the inlet. It's the perfect place for a picnic lunch and a bit of history, too. ✉ *Ft. Pickens Rd.* ☎ *850/934–2635* ✐ *$6 per car* ☉ *Daily 7–sunset.*

The 1,471-ft-long **Pensacola Beach Gulf Pier** bills itself as the longest pier on the Gulf of Mexico. Serious anglers will find everything they'll need—from pole rentals to bait—to land that big one, but those looking to catch only a beautiful sunset are welcome, too. Check the pier's Web site for the latest fishing reports on what's biting. ✉ *41 Ft. Pickens Rd.* ☎ *850/934–7200* ⊕ *www.fishpensacolabeachpier* ✐ *Observers $1, fishing $6.50.*

Where to Stay & Eat

¢–$$$ ✕ **Flounder's Chowder and Ale House.** Combine a gulf-front view at this casual restaurant with a fruity tropical libation, and you're all set for a night of "floundering" at its best. An eclectic collection of antiques and objets d'art contributes to the overall funkiness. The house specialty is seafood charbroiled over a hardwood fire, but the extensive menu offers several choices for those who don't love fish. After dinner, dance beneath the stars at the Key West–style beach bar. ✉ *800 Quietwater Beach Blvd.* ☎ *850/932–2003* ▤ *AE, D, DC, MC, V.*

$$–$$$ ⌂ **Hampton Inn Pensacola Beach.** The exterior's pink-and-green color scheme is reminiscent of Miami Beach's art deco buildings, and the easygoing Florida style continues inside. Directly on the gulf and centrally located, this lodging is within walking distance of several popular restaurants and shops. Most rooms have a gulf view, and all are oversized. Gulf-front rooms have private balconies. There's an evening cocktail hour, and an expansive Continental breakfast buffet is served. ✉ *2 Via de Luna, Pensacola Beach 32561* ☎ *850/932–6800 or 800/320–8108* ☏ *850/932–6833* ⊕ *www.hamptonbeachresort.com* ⇌ *181 rooms* ♢ *Microwaves, refrigerators, cable TV with movies, 2 pools, gym, beach, bar* ▤ *AE, D, DC, MC, V* ⦿l *CP.*

$–$$$ ⌂ **Perdido Sun.** This high-rise is the perfect expression of gulfside resort living. One-, two-, and three-bedroom decorator-furnished condos all have seaside balconies with spectacular water views. Choose to make this your home away from home—accommodations include fully equipped kitchens—or pamper yourself with daily maid service. ✉ *13753 Perdido Key Dr., Perdido Key 32507* ☎ *850/492–2390 or 800/227–2390* ☏ *850/492–4125* ⊕ *www.perdidosun.com* ⇌ *93 condos* ♢ *Cable TV with movies, 2 pools, gym, beach* ▤ *AE, D, MC, V.*

¢–$$ ⌂ **Comfort Inn Pensacola Beach.** One of the best deals on the beach, this well-kept chain motel sits on the bay side overlooking Little Sabine Bay, but the upper floors have views of the gulf just across the street. Breezy, floral-print fabrics and rattan furnishings lend a cheeriness to the guest rooms, and complimentary Continental breakfast and free local phone calls seal the deal. Restaurants and shops are within walking distance. ✉ *40 Fort Pickens Rd., 32561* ☎ *850/934–5400 or 800/934–5470* ☏ *850/932–7210* ⊕ *www.comfortinn.com* ⇌ *99 rooms* ♢ *Picnic area, microwaves, refrigerators, cable TV, pool, volleyball, meeting rooms* ▤ *AE, D, DC, MC, V* ⦿l *CP.*

Sports & the Outdoors

FISHING For a full- or half-day deep-sea charter (from $450 to $1,000 per day), try the **Beach Marina** (✉ 655 Pensacola Beach Blvd. ☎ 850/932–8466), which represents several charters.

GOLF The **Club at Hidden Creek** (✉ 3070 PGA Blvd., Navarre ☎ 850/939–4604) is a semiprivate 18-hole course.

WATER SPORTS When you rent a sailboat, Jet Ski, or catamaran from **Bonifay Water Sports** (✉ 460 Pensacola Beach Blvd. ☎ 850/932–0633), you'll also receive safety and sailing instructions. There is also a 24-ft pontoon boat—perfect for a picnic cruise down the Intracoastal—for rent here.

THE GULF COAST

On U.S. 98, several towns, each with its own personality, are strung along the shoreline from Pensacola southeast to St. George Island. The twin cities of Destin and Fort Walton Beach seemingly merge into one sprawling destination and continue to spread as more condominiums, resort developments, shopping centers, and restaurants crowd the skyline each year. The view changes drastically farther along the coast as you enter the quiet stretch known as the Beaches of South Walton. Here building restrictions prohibit high-rise developments, and the majority of dwellings are privately owned homes, most of which are available to vacationers. A total of 19 beach communities cluster along this quiet strip off U.S. 98. Many are little more than a wide spot in the road, and all are among the least-known and least-developed in the entire Gulf Coast area, even though the University of Maryland's Laboratory for Coastal Research has ranked Grayton Beach among the country's top 20 beaches for years. Seaside, a town less than 20 years old, is a thriving planned community with old-fashioned Victorian architecture, brick streets, and a quaint shopping village. Continuing southeast on U.S. 98, you'll find Panama City Beach, its "Miracle Strip" crammed with every teenager's dream—from the carnival-like amusement parks to junk-food vendors to T-shirt shops by the dozens. Farther east, past the behemoth paper mills of Port St. Joe and the shoulder-to-shoulder condos that line Mexico Beach, you'll come to the quiet blue-collar town of Apalachicola, Florida's main oyster fishery. Watch local oystermen ply their trade, using long-handled tongs to bring in their catch. Cross the Apalachicola Bay via the Bryant Patton Bridge to St. George Island. This unspoiled 28-mi-long barrier island offers some of America's most scenic beaches, including St. George Island State Park, which has the longest beachfront of any state park in Florida.

Fort Walton Beach

▶ ❸ *46 mi east of Pensacola.*

This coastal town dates from the Civil War but had to wait more than 75 years to come into its own. Patriots loyal to the Confederate cause organized Walton's Guard (named in honor of Colonel George Walton, onetime acting Territorial governor of West Florida) and camped at a site on Santa Rosa Sound, later known as Camp Walton. In 1940 fewer than 90 people lived in Fort Walton Beach, but within a decade the city became a boomtown, thanks to New Deal money for roads and bridges and the development of Eglin Field during World War II. The military is now Fort Walton Beach's main source of income, but tourism runs a close second.

Encompassing 724 square mi of land, **Eglin Air Force Base** includes 10 auxiliary fields and a total of 21 runways. Jimmie Doolittle's Tokyo Raiders trained here, as did the Son Tay Raiders, a group that made a daring attempt to rescue American POWs from a North Vietnamese prison camp in 1970. Off-limits to civilians, there are private tours for ROTC and military reunion groups. ⊠ *Rte. 85* ☎ *850/882–3931* ⊕ *www. eglin.af.mil.*

★   The collection at the **Air Force Armament Museum,** just outside the Eglin Air Force Base's main gate, contains more than 5,000 air force armaments from World Wars I and II and the Korean and Vietnam wars. Included are uniforms, engines, weapons, aircraft, and flight simulators; larger craft such as transport planes are exhibited on the grounds outside. A 32-minute movie about Eglin's history and its role in the development of armaments plays continuously. ⊠ *Rte. 85, Eglin Air Force Base* ☎ *850/882–4062* ▨ *Free* ◷ *Daily 9:30–4:30.*

John C. Beasley Wayside Park is Fort Walton Beach's seaside playground on Okaloosa Island. A boardwalk leads to the beach, where you'll find covered picnic tables, changing rooms, and freshwater showers. Lifeguards are on duty in summer. ⊠ *Okaloosa Island* ☎ *850/830–5505.*

🐣 Kids especially enjoy the **Indian Temple Mound and Museum,** where they can learn all about the prehistoric peoples who inhabited northwest Florida up to 10,000 years ago. It's a small museum, but the prehistoric Native American artifacts and weaponry on display are particularly fascinating, as are the few hands-on exhibits. The museum is adjacent to the 600-year-old **National Historic Landmark Temple Mound,** a large earthwork built near saltwater. ✉ *139 Miracle Strip Pkwy. (U.S. 98)* ☎ *850/833–9595* 🎟 *$2* ⊗ *Weekdays 11–4, Sat. 9–4.*

🐣 When the weather drives you off the beach, the **Gulfarium** is a great place to spend your time. Its main attraction is the Living Sea, a 60,000-gallon tank that simulates conditions on the ocean floor. See cheesy performances by trained porpoises, sea-lion shows, and marine-life exhibits. Don't overlook the old-fashioned Dolphin Reef gift shop, where you can buy anything from conch shells to beach toys. There's also a dolphin interaction program, but you don't swim with them. Instead, you sit in a pool as spotted dolphins swim up to your lap. ✉ *U.S. 98 E* ☎ *850/243–9046 or 800/247–8575* ⊕ *www.gulfarium.com* 🎟 *$16, dolphin interaction $100* ⊗ *Daily 9–6.*

Where to Stay & Eat

★ **$$–$$$** ✗ **Pandora's Steakhouse and Lounge.** On the Emerald Coast the name Pandora's is synonymous with prime rib. The weather-beaten exterior gives way to a warm and cozy interior with alcoves and tables for four that lend an air of intimacy. Steaks are cooked over a wood-burning grill, and you can order your prime rib regular or extra-cut; fish aficionados should try the char-grilled yellowfin tuna, bacon-wrapped and topped with Jamaican jerk sauce. The mood turns a bit more gregarious in the lounge, where there is live entertainment Wednesday through Saturday. ✉ *1120 Santa Rosa Blvd.* ☎ *850/244–8669* ⊟ *AE, D, DC, MC, V* ⊗ *Closed Mon.*

$$–$$$ ✗ **Staff's.** Sip a Tropical Depression or a rum-laced Squall Line while you peruse a menu tucked into the centerfold of a tabloid-size newspaper filled with snippets of local history, early photographs, and family memorabilia. Since 1931 folks have been coming to this garage turned eatery for steaks and seafood dishes like freshly caught Florida lobster and char-grilled amberjack. The grand finale is a trip to the delectable dessert bar; try a generous wedge of cherry cheesecake. ✉ *24 Miracle Strip Pkwy. SE* ☎ *850/243–3482* ⊟ *AE, D, MC, V.*

$$$ 🏨 **Radisson Beach Resort.** This U-shape hotel consists of a six-story tower flanked by three-story wings. Rooms have a pastel green-and-peach color schemes and face either the gulf or one of the pools, although even poolside rooms have a bit of a sea view. ✉ *1110 Santa Rosa Blvd., 32548* ☎ *850/243–9181* 🖨 *850/664–7652* ⊕ *www.radissonresort.com* ⇆ *287 rooms* ⚮ *Restaurant, cable TV, 2 tennis courts, 3 pools, gym, beach, bar, Internet* ⊟ *AE, D, DC, MC, V.*

$$–$$$ 🏨 **Ramada Plaza Beach Resort.** Activity here revolves around a heated pool with a grotto and swim-through waterfall; there's also an 800-ft private beach. All rooms have refrigerators, but the twin double beds are the only sleeping option. ✉ *1500 Miracle Strip Pkwy. SE, 32548* ☎ *850/243–9161 or 800/874–8962* 🖨 *850/243–2391* ⊕ *www.ramadafwb.com* ⇆ *309 rooms, 26 suites* ⚮ *2 restaurants, refrigerators, cable TV with movies and video games, 2 pools, gym, beach, 3 bars, Internet* ⊟ *AE, D, DC, MC, V.*

Nightlife & the Arts

THE ARTS Based in Fort Walton Beach, the **Northwest Florida Ballet** (☎ *850/664–7787*) has presented classical and contemporary dance performances to audiences along the Gulf Coast for more than 30 years. Call for season schedule and ticket information as well as their current performance venue.

NIGHTLIFE   Dueling pianos and a beachfront bar fuel the furious sing-alongs that make **Howl at the Moon** (✉ 1450 Miracle Strip Pkwy. ☎ 850/301–0111), at the Boardwalk on Okaloosa Island, one of Fort Walton's most popular evening entertainment spots. The place rocks every night until 2 AM but can go as late as 4 AM in season.

Sports & the Outdoors

BIKING   **Eglin Air Force Base Reservation** is the size of Rhode Island—724 square mi, 463,448 acres—and has 810 mi of creeks and plenty of challenging, twisting wooded trails. Biking here requires a $5 permit, which can be obtained from the **Jackson Guard** (✉ 107 Rte. 85 N, Niceville ☎ 850/882–4164). Rentals are available from **Bob's Bicycle Center** (✉ 431 Bryn Athen Blvd., Mary Esther ☎ 850/243–5856).

FISHING   **Harbor Walk Marina** (✉ 66 U.S. 98 E, Destin 32541 ☎ 850/337–8250) is a rustic-looking waterfront complex where you can get bait, gas, tackle, food, and anything else you might need for a day of fishing. Party fishing boat excursions cost as little as $40, a cheaper alternative to chartering or renting your own boat.

GOLF   The **Fort Walton Beach Golf Club** (✉ Rte. 189 ☎ 850/833–9529) is a 36-hole municipal course whose links (Oaks and Pines) lie about 1,000 yards from each other. The two courses are considered by many to be one of Florida's best public layouts. **Shalimar Pointe Golf & Country Club** (✉ 302 Country Club Dr., Shalimar ☎ 850/651–1416) has 18 holes with a pleasing mix of water and bunkers.

SCUBA DIVING   Take diving lessons, arrange excursions, and rent all the necessary equipment at the **Scuba Shop** (✉ 348 Miracle Strip Pkwy. ☎ 850/243–1600). Don't expect clear Caribbean waters in the gulf: visibility is about 20–50 ft, and diving depths range between 50 ft and 90 ft—not great, but not too bad.

TENNIS   Play tennis on seven Rubico and two hard courts at the **Fort Walton Racquet Club** (✉ 1819 Hurlburt Rd. ☎ 850/862–2023). The **Municipal Tennis Center** (✉ 45 W. Audrey Dr. ☎ 850/833–9588) has 12 lighted hard courts, four racquetball courts, and four practice walls.

Shopping

Stores in the **Manufacturer's Outlet Center** (✉ 255 Miracle Strip Pkwy.) offer well-known brands of clothing and housewares at a substantial discount. There are four department stores in the **Santa Rosa Mall** (✉ 300 Mary Esther Cutoff, Mary Esther, ☎ 850/244–2172), as well as 118 other shops, 15 bistro-style eateries, and a 10-screen movie theater.

Destin

❹ *8 mi east of Fort Walton Beach.*

Fort Walton Beach's neighbor lies on the other side of the strait that connects Choctawhatchee Bay with the Gulf of Mexico. Destin takes its name from its founder, Leonard A. Destin, a Connecticut sea captain who settled his family here sometime in the 1830s. For the next 100 years Destin remained a sleepy little fishing village until the strait, or East Pass, was bridged in 1935. Then recreational anglers discovered its white sands, blue-green waters, and abundance of some of the most sought-after sport fish in the world. More billfish are hauled in around Destin each year than from all other gulf fishing ports combined, giving credence to its nickname, the World's Luckiest Fishing Village. But you don't have to be the rod-and-reel type to love Destin. There's plenty to entertain the sand-pail set as well as senior citizens, and there are many nice restaurants, which you'll have an easier time finding if you remember that the main drag through town is referred to as both U.S. 98 and Emerald Coast Parkway. The name makes sense, but part of what makes the Gulf look so emerald in these parts is the contrasting whiteness of the sand on the beach. Actually, it's not sand—it's pure, powder-soft Appalachian quartz that was dropped off by a glacier a few thousand years back. Since quartz doesn't compress (and crews clean and rake the beach each evening), your tootsies get the sole-satisfying benefit of soft, sugary "sand."

In addition to a seasonal water park, **Big Kahuna's Lost Paradise** has year-round family attractions, including 54 holes of miniature golf, two go-cart tracks, an arcade, thrill rides for kids of all ages, and an amphitheater. ⊠ *U.S. 98 E* ☎ *850/837–4061* ⊕ *www.bigkahunas.com* ⊡ *Grounds free, water park $29.95, miniature golf $6.50, go-carts $6* ⊙ *Mid-Sept.–May, Fri.–Sat. 10 AM–midnight; June–mid-Sept., daily 10 AM–midnight* ⊙ *Water park closed mid-Sept.–Apr.*

> off the beaten path

Fred Gannon Rocky Bayou State Park. North of Destin is a quiet park offering picnic areas, nature trails, boat ramps, and 42 uncrowded campsites with electrical and water hook-ups. It's secluded yet easy to find. ⊠ *4281 Rte. 20, Niceville* ☎ *850/833–9144* ⊡ *Day use $2 per vehicle; campsites $8.48, $10.48 with electricity* ⊙ *Daily 8–sunset.*

Where to Stay & Eat

$$$–$$$$ ✕ **Elephant Walk.** Never mind that the name comes from an old Elizabeth Taylor movie—here, the food is the star, and the setting's worthy of a movie of its own. Ask for a seat near the large picture windows overlooking the dunes, and then order the lobster spring roll appetizer. For dinner, try either the coconut-crusted gulf prawns or the sesame-seared ahi tuna. Duck, pork, and steak entrées round out the menu, but stick to seafood and you won't be disappointed. The cozy Governor's Attic upstairs is the perfect spot for a sunset cocktail or an after-dinner drink. ⊠ *Sandestin Resort, 9300 U.S. 98* ☎ *850/267–4800* ⚑ *Reservations essential* ⊟ *AE, D, DC, MC, V.*

$$–$$$$ ✕ **Flamingo Café.** Indoors, you'll find freshly starched white linen and refined elegance; outdoors, the patio is Florida casual all the way. Either way there's a panoramic view of Destin Harbor from every seat in the house, and boaters are welcome to tie up at the dock. The food is Floribbean—a mixture of Caribbean and Floridian elements. The chef is known for his special snapper and grouper dishes; try the delicious snapper en croûte—an oven-roasted snapper fillet layered in phyllo pastry with crabmeat and braised spinach in a cream sauce. ⊠ *414 U.S. 98 E* ☎ *850/837–0961* ⊟ *AE, D, MC, V* ⊙ *No lunch.*

★ **$$–$$$** ✕ **Marina Café.** A harbor view, impeccable service, and sophisticated fare create one of the finest dining experiences on the Emerald Coast. The ocean motif is expressed in shades of aqua, green, and sand accented with marine tapestries and sea sculptures. The chef calls his creations contemporary Continental, offering diners a choice of classic creole, Mediterranean, or Pacific Rim dishes. One regional specialty is the popular black pepper–crusted yellowfin tuna with braised spinach and spicy soy sauce. The menu changes daily, and the wine list is extensive. ⊠ *404 U.S. 98 E* ☎ *850/837–7960* ⊟ *AE, D, DC, MC, V* ⊙ *No lunch.*

$–$$$ ✕ **Louisiana Lagniappe.** In Louisiana when you say *lagniappe*, it means you're getting a little something extra—here it's the extra zing fresh local seafood gets when transformed into Cajun-style cuisine. You can't go wrong ordering Cajun standards like shrimp creole, crab bisque, and crawfish étouffée. Locals love the chef's innovations such as grouper cocodrie, sautéed and topped with fried crawfish, artichoke hearts, and a rich béarnaise sauce. There's outside dining overlooking Destin Harbor and delicious sunset views, whether you're dining inside or out. ⊠ 775 *Gulf Shore Dr., at Sandpiper Cove* ☏ *850/837–0881* ⊟ *AE, D, DC, MC, V* ⊗ *No lunch.*

$$$–$$$$ 🏨 **Henderson Park Inn.** Tucked discreetly away at the end of a quiet road bordering Henderson Beach State Park, this B&B has become Destin's premier getaway for couples seeking elegance and pampering. A green mansard roof and shingle siding are reminiscent of Queen Anne–era architecture and complement the inn's Victorian-era furnishings. Each romantic room is furnished with a four-poster, canopied, or iron bed draped with fine linen. You'll find plush robes and refrigerators with ice makers in all rooms, as well as balconies, perfect for admiring the gulf's smashing sunsets. ⊠ *2700 Scenic U.S. 98 E, 32541* ☏ *850/654–0400 or 800/336–4853* 🖷 *850/654–0405* ⊕ *www.hendersonparkinn. com* ⮑ *35 suites* ⚫ *Restaurant, microwaves, refrigerators, pool, beach; no kids* ⊟ *AE, D, MC, V.*

$$$ 🏨 **Holiday Inn Destin.** Lounge on sugar-white sands, get to several golf courses with ease, and walk to some of Destin's amusement parks. Common areas jazzed up with skylights and greenery are spacious and eye-pleasing. The standard rooms are uniformly bright and well kept; prices vary depending on the view. ⊠ *1020 U.S. 98 E, 32541* ☏ *850/837–6181* 🖷 *850/837–1523* ⊕ *www.hidestin.com* ⮑ *233 rooms* ⚫ *Restaurant, 3 pools, beach, bar* ⊟ *AE, D, DC, MC, V.*

$$$ 🏨 **Sandestin Golf and Beach Resort.** Newlyweds, conventioneers, and fam-
Fodor'sChoice ilies all fit in at this 2,400-acre resort with villas, cottages, condominiums,
★ boat slips, and an inn. A recent addition is Baytowne Wharf, a "festival marketplace" of shops and restaurants; the Lagoons, a 7-acre family-friendly water park, is expected to open in 2005. All rooms have a view, either of the gulf, Choctawhatchee Bay, a golf course, a lagoon, or a natural wildlife preserve. This resort accommodates an assortment of tastes, from the simple to the extravagant, but the gigantic suites at the Westwinds are a cut above the rest. ⊠ *9300 U.S. 98 W, 32550* ☏ *850/267–8000 or 800/277–0800* 🖷 *850/267–8222* ⊕ *www.sandestin.com* ⮑ *175 rooms, 250 condos, 275 villas* ⚫ *4 restaurants, some kitchens, some microwaves, some refrigerators, 81-hole golf course, 16 tennis courts, pro shop, 11 pools, health club, beach, dock, 3 bars* ⊟ *AE, D, DC, MC, V.*

★ **$–$$$** 🏨 **Bluewater Bay Golf & Tennis Resort.** Popular for its 36 holes of championship golf (on courses designed by Jerry Pate and Tom Fazio), this upscale resort is 12 mi north of Destin via the Mid-Bay Bridge on the shores of Choctawhatchee Bay. It offers vacation rentals ranging from motel rooms to villas to patio homes. ⊠ *1950 Bluewater Blvd., Niceville 32578* ☏ *850/897–3613 or 800/874–2128* 🖷 *850/897–2424* ⊕ *www. bwbresort.com* ⮑ *85 units* ⚫ *Restaurant, cable TV, 36-hole golf course, 19 tennis courts, 4 pools, bar, playground* ⊟ *AE, D, DC, MC, V.*

Nightlife

Folks come by boat and car to **AJ's Club Bimini** (⊠ 116 U.S. 98 E ☏ 850/837–1913), a supercasual bar and restaurant overlooking a marina. Live music on weekends means young, lively crowds packing the dance floor. **Harbor Docks** (⊠ 538 U.S. 98 E ☏ 850/837–2506) is another favorite with the local sea-faring set. It's famous for live music and, oddly enough, high-quality sushi. The **Hog's Breath Saloon** (⊠ 541 E. U.S. 98 E ☏ 850/837–5991), a chain hot spot with other locations in Key West, Fort Walton Beach, and Cozumel, presents live music on weekends. The food—steaks, burgers, salads—isn't bad, either. Café Grazie's **Sky Bar** (⊠ 1771 U.S. 98 E ☏ 850/837–7475) draws a more mature crowd for dancing, cocktails, and live music.

Sports & the Outdoors

FISHING Pier-fish from the 3,000-ft-long Destin Catwalk, along the East Pass Bridge. **Adventure Charters** (⊠ East Pass Marina, 288 U.S. 98 E ☎ 850/654–4070) offers deep-sea, bay-bottom, and light-tackle fishing excursions. **East Pass Bait and Tackle** (⊠ East Pass Marina, 288 U.S. 98 E ☎ 850/837–2622) sells bait, tackle, and most anything else you'd need for a day of fishing.

GOLF **Bluewater Bay Resort** (⊠ 1950 Bluewater Blvd., Niceville ☎ 850/897–3241 or 800/874–2128), 6 mi east of Niceville via Route 20 East, has 36 holes of championship golf on courses designed by Jerry Pate and Tom Fazio. The **Indian Bayou Golf & Country Club** (⊠ Airport Rd., off U. S. 98 ☎ 850/837–6192) has a 27-hole course. The 18-hole, Fred Couples–designed **Kelly Plantation Golf Club** (⊠ 34851 Emerald Coast Pkwy. ☎ 850/650–7600) is a semiprivate course that runs along Choctawhatchee Bay. For sheer number of holes, the **Sandestin Golf and Beach Resort** (⊠ 9300 U.S. 98 W ☎ 850/267–8211) tops the list, with 81.

SCUBA DIVING Scuba-diving and snorkeling instruction and outings are available through **Emerald Coast Scuba** (⊠ 110 Melvin St. ☎ 850/837–0955 or 800/222–0955).

TENNIS The **Destin Racquet & Fitness Center** (⊠ 995 Airport Rd. ☎ 850/837–7300) has six Rubico courts. **Sandestin Golf and Beach Resort** (⊠ 9300 U.S. 98 W ☎ 850/267–7110), one of the nation's five-star tennis resorts, has 116 courts with grass, hard, and Rubico surfaces.

Shopping

The **Market at Sandestin** (⊠ 9375 U.S. 98 W ☎ 850/267–8092) has 33 upscale shops that peddle such goods as expensive chocolates and designer clothes in an elegant mini-mall with boardwalks. It also has the area's only Starbucks Coffee franchise. **Silver Sands Factory Stores** (⊠ 10562 Emerald Coast Pkwy. ☎ 850/654–9771) is one of the Southeast's largest retail outlets. More than 100 shops sell top-name merchandise that ranges from gifts to kids' clothes to menswear.

Grayton Beach

❺ *18 mi east of Destin.*

The 26-mi stretch of coastline between Destin and Panama City Beach is referred to as the Beaches of South Walton. Add to the sun and fun at these amazing beaches enough good restaurants to make selecting a dinner spot the day's most challenging decision. Accommodations consist primarily of private-home rentals, the majority of which are managed by local real estate firms. Also scattered along Route 30A are a few small artistic boutiques, with unique hand-painted furniture, jewelry, and contemporary gifts and clothing. Inland, thick pine forests and hardwoods surround the area's 14 lakes, giving anglers ample spots to drop a line. Grayton Beach, the oldest community in this area, has reached its 100-year mark. You can still see some of the old weathered cypress homes scattered along sandy streets. The town has made some minor concessions to growth in the way of a small market and a couple of restaurants in its single-road "downtown" district. Don't expect much more. Stringent building restrictions, designed to protect the pristine beaches, ensure that Grayton maintains its small-town feel and look.

Fodor'sChoice The 2,133-acre **Grayton Beach State Park** is one of the most scenic spots
★ along the Gulf Coast. Composed primarily of untouched Florida woodlands, it also has salt marshes, rolling dunes covered with sea oats, crystal-white sand, and contrasting blue-green waters. The park offers

facilities for swimming, fishing, snorkeling, and camping. Even if you are just passing by, the beach here is worth the stop. Thirty new cabins are now available for rent (*see* Where to Stay & Eat, *below*). ⊠ *357 Main Park Rd.* ☎ *850/231–4210* ⊠ *$3.25 per vehicle (up to 8 people)* ⊙ *Daily 8–sunset.*

> **off the beaten path**

Eden Gardens State Park. Scarlett O'Hara might be at home here on the lawn of an antebellum mansion amid an arcade of moss-draped live oaks. Furnishings in the spacious rooms date as far back as the 17th century. The surrounding gardens are beautiful year-round, but they're nothing short of spectacular in mid-March, when the azaleas and dogwoods are in full bloom. ⊠ *Rte. 395, Point Washington* ☎ *850/231–4214* ⊠ *Gardens $2, mansion tour $1.50* ⊙ *Daily 8–sunset, mansion tours hourly Thurs.–Mon. 10–3.*

Where to Stay & Eat

$$–$$$$ ✕ **Criollas.** Inventive, contemporary, and constantly changing fare continues to win local raves for this spot. You might choose to experience Island Hopping—a three-course dinner focusing on a particular Caribbean region. The region varies from month to month, so returning diners can sample a different cuisine each visit. ⊠ *170 E. Rte. 30A* ☎ *850/267–1267* ⊟ *AE, D, MC, V* ⊙ *Closed Sun–Mon. Nov.–Jan. No lunch.*

$–$$ ✕ **Picolo Restaurant & Red Bar.** You could spend weeks here just taking in all the eclectic memorabilia—from Marilyn Monroe posters to flags to dolls—dangling from the ceiling and tacked to every available square inch of wall. The equally contemporary menu is small, changes daily, and is very Floridian. A baked eggplant dish stuffed with shrimp, scallops, and grilled vegetables is a popular entrée. Live blues and jazz can be heard nightly. ⊠ *70 Hotz Ave.* ☎ *850/231–1008* ⊟ *No credit cards.*

$ 🏠 **Cabins at Grayton Beach State Park.** Back-to-nature enthusiasts and families like these basic yet stylish accommodations set among the sand pines and scrub oaks of this pristine state park. The two-bedroom, tin-roof accommodations, which have white trim and tropical wooden window louvers, come with air-conditioning and full-size kitchens complete with pots and pans. There is no daily maid service—fresh linens are provided, however—and no room phones, but gas fireplaces, barbecue grills, and screen porches add a homey touch. ⊠ *357 Main Park Rd.* ☎ *800/326–3521 for reservations* ⊕ *www.reserveamerica.com* ↬ *30 cabins* ♦ *Full kitchens; no room phones, no room TVs* ⊟ *AE, MC, V.*

Nightlife

The **Red Bar** (⊠ 70 Hotz Ave. ☎ 850/231–1008), the local watering hole, is elbow to elbow on Friday and Saturday nights, when red-hot bands serve up blues and jazz.

The Outdoors

The **Santa Rosa Golf & Beach Club** (⊠ Rte. 30A, Santa Rosa Beach ☎ 850/267–2229) is a semiprivate 18-hole course that, thankfully, has little residential development beside the fairways.

Shopping

Gaffrey Art Gallery (⊠ 21 Blue Gulf Dr., 3 mi west of Grayton Beach, Santa Rosa Beach ☎ 850/267–0228) sells hand-painted furniture and furniture handmade by the Gaffrey family. Under the shade trees of Grayton Beach, **Magnolia House** (⊠ 2 Magnolia St. ☎ 850/231–5859) sells gift items, bath products, and accessories for the home. The **Shops of Grayton** (⊠ Rte. 283 [Grayton Rd.], 2 mi south of U.S. 98 ☎ No phone) is a colorful complex of eight Cracker-style cottages where you'll find gifts, artwork, and antiques. **Wild Women Art Gallery** (✉ 39 Blue Gulf Dr., 3 mi west of Grayton Beach on Rte. 30A ☎ 850/653–4099), which sells "art for the wild at heart," carries adorable hand-painted children's furniture, prints, artwork, and glass.

Seaside

❻ *2 mi east of Grayton Beach.*

This community of Victorian-style homes is so reminiscent of a story-book town that producers chose it for the set of the 1998 film *The Truman Show,* starring Jim Carrey. The brainchild of Robert Davis, the town was designed to promote a neighborly, old-fashioned lifestyle, and there's much to be said for an attractive, billboard-free village where you can park your car and walk everywhere you need to go. Pastel-color homes with white picket fences, front-porch rockers, and captain's walks are set amid redbrick streets, and all are within walking distance of the town center and its unusual cafés and shops. Seaside's popularity continues to soar, and the summer months can be crowded. If you're seeking a little solitude, you might prefer visiting during the off-season—between Labor Day and Memorial Day.

Where to Stay & Eat

$$–$$$ ✕ **Bud & Alley's.** This down-to-earth beachside bistro has been a local favorite since 1986. Indoors are hardwood floors, ceiling fans, and 6-ft windows looking onto an herb garden; the roof-top Tarpon Club bar makes a great perch for a sunset toast. A porch provides the perfect spot for admiring the orange sunsets common in the fall. Daily salad specials are tangy introductions to such entrées as sesame-seared rare tuna on wild greens with a rice-wine vinaigrette and a soy dipping sauce. ✉ *Rte. 30A* ☎ *850/231–5900* ▤ *MC, V* ☉ *Closed Tues. and Oct.–Dec.*

$$–$$$ ✕ **Cafe Thirty-A.** In a beautiful Florida-style home with high ceilings and
Fodor'sChoice a wide veranda, this restaurant has an elegant look—bolstered by white
★ linen tablecloths—and impeccable service. The menu changes nightly and includes such entrées as lemon-marinated salmon, oven-roasted black grouper, and braised Arizona rabbit. Even if you're not a southerner, you should try the appetizer of grilled Georgia quail with creamy grits and sage fritters. With nearly 20 creative varieties, the martini menu alone is worth the trip. ✉ *3899 E. Scenic Rte. 30A, Seagrove Beach* ☎ *850/ 231–2166* ▤ *AE, D, DC, MC, V* ☉ *No lunch.*

$$$–$$$$ ▦ **Josephine's French Country Inn.** The charming rooms in this grand, Georgian-style accommodation have gulf views, four-poster beds, fireplaces, and claw-foot tubs, bringing a bit of elegance to a modern seaside spot. The daily country-style breakfast is delicious, and dinners are garnished with fresh herbs and flowers from the owners' garden. ✉ *38 Seaside Ave., 32459* ☎ *850/231–1940 or 800/848–1840* ▥ *850/231–2446* ⊕ *www.josephinesinn.com* ⇨ *7 rooms, 2 suites* ⌂ *Microwaves, in-room VCRs* ▤ *AE, D, MC, V.*

$$$–$$$$ ▦ **WaterColor Inn.** Nature meets seaside chic at this new botique property, the crown jewel of the area's latest—and largest—planned community. Rooms are done in seashell tones with vibrant, sea-blue comforters and accents; stylish armoires and desks look as natural and unfinished as driftwood. Dune level bungalows have private courtyards with outdoor showers, while upper rooms have huge balconies and walk-in showers with windows overlooking the Gulf. Standard rooms come with a king-size bed and a queen sleeper-sofa, but consider one of the three Rotunda rooms for something larger and more spectacular. ✉ *34 Goldenrod Circle 32459* ☎ *850/534–5000* ▥ *850/534–5001* ⊕ *www. watercolorinn.com* ⇨ *42* ⌂ *Restaurant, fans, in room-dataports, in-*

room safes, minibars, cable TV, golf privileges, pool, massage, outdoor hot tub, beach, library, Internet, airport shuttle, no-smoking rooms.

★ $$$–$$$$ 🏨 **Seaside Cottage Rental Agency.** When residents aren't using their homes, they rent out their one- to six-bedroom, porticoed, faux-Victorian cottages furnished with fully equipped kitchens, TV/VCRs, and vacuum cleaners—a perfect option for a family vacation or a large group. Gulf breezes blowing off the water remind you of the unspoiled sugar-white beaches a short stroll away. ✉ *Rte. 30A* 📮 *Box 4730, 32459* ☎ *850/231–1320 or 800/277–8696* 🖷 *850/231–2373* ⊕ *www.seasidefl. com* ⇆ *270 units* ♿ *Kitchens, 6 tennis courts, 3 pools, bicycles, badminton, croquet* 🟰 *AE, D, MC, V.*

The Outdoors

An 8-ft-wide pathway covering 18 mi of scenic Route 30A winds past freshwater lakes, woodlands, and beaches. **Butterfly Rentals** (✉ 3657 E. Rte. 30A ☎ 855/231–2826) rents bikes and kayaks and has free delivery and pickup. In Seaside, consult the **Cabana Man** (☎ 850/231–5046) for beach chairs, umbrellas, rafts, kayaks, and anything else you might need for a day at the beach. If there's no answer, just head to the beach and you'll find him there.

Shopping

Seaside's central square and open-air market, along Route 30A, offer a number of unique and whimsical boutiques carrying clothing, jewelry, and arts and crafts. **Perspicasity** (✉ 178 Market St. ☎ 850/231–5829), an open-air market in Sant Rosa Beach, sells simply designed women's clothing and accessories perfect for easy, carefree beach-town casualness. At **Ruskin Place Artist Colony,** in the heart of Seaside, a collection of small shops and artists' galleries has everything from toys and pottery to fine works of art.

Panama City Beach

❼ *21 mi southeast of Seaside.*

In spite of the shoulder-to-shoulder condominiums, motels, and amusement parks that make it seem like one big carnival ground, this coastal resort has a natural beauty that, in some areas at least, manages to excuse its gross overcommercialization. Public beaches along the Miracle Strip combine with a plethora of video-game arcades, miniature golf courses, sidewalk cafés, souvenir shops, and shopping centers to lure people. The incredible white sands, navigable waterways, and plentiful marine life that attracted Spanish conquistadors bring family vacationers today. Beware of holiday weekends, however, when everyone and his or her cousin descends from Alabama and Georgia.

⟳ Enjoy dozens of rides at **Miracle Strip Amusement Park,** from a traditional Ferris wheel to a roller coaster with a 65-ft drop. ✉ *12000 Front Beach Rd.* ☎ *850/234–5810* ⊕ *www.miraclestrippark.com* 🎟 *$17* ⊘ *Apr.–May, Fri.–Sat. 6 PM–11 PM; June–early Sept., Sun.–Fri. 6 PM–11 PM, Sat. 2 PM–11:15 PM.*

⟳ The Miracle Strip Amusement Park also operates **Shipwreck Island,** a 6-acre water park offering everything from speedy slides and tubes to the slow-moving Lazy River. ✉ *12000 Front Beach Rd.* ☎ *850/234–0368* ⊕ *www.shipwreckisland.com* 🎟 *$22.50* ⊘ *Mid-Apr.–May, weekends 10:30–5; June–early Sept., daily 10:30–5.*

⟳ At the unique **Museum of Man in the Sea,** see rare examples of breathing apparatus and diving equipment, some dating as far back as the 1600s, in addition to exhibits on Florida's historic shipwrecks. There are also treasures recovered from famous wrecks, including artifacts from the Spanish galleon *Atocha*, and live creatures found in the area's coastal waters. ✉ *17314 Panama City Beach Pkwy.* ☎ *850/235–4101* 💲 *$5* 🕙 *Daily 9–5.*

🐚 **Gulf World** is the resident marine park, with a tropical garden, tropical bird theater, and alligator and otter exhibits. The shark-feeding and scuba demonstrations are popular with the kids, but the old favorites—performing sea lions, otters, and bottle-nosed dolphins—still hold their own. ✉ *15412 Front Beach Rd.* ☎ *850/234–5271* 🌐 *www.gulfworldmarinepark.com* 💲 *$19.42 plus tax* 🕙 *Late May–early Sept., daily 9 AM–4 PM; call for hrs at other times of year.*

🐚 At the eastern tip of Panama City Beach, the **St. Andrews State Park** includes 1,260 acres of beaches, pinewoods, and marshes. There are complete camping facilities here, as well as places to swim, pier-fish, or hike the dunes along clearly marked nature trails. Board a ferry to **Shell Island**—a barrier island in the Gulf of Mexico with some of the best shelling north of Sanibel Island. An artificial reef creates a calm, shallow play area that is perfect for young children. Come to this spectacular park for a peek at what the entire beach area looked like before developers got ahold of it. ✉ *4607 State Park La.* ☎ *850/233–5140* 💲 *$4 per vehicle (up to 8 people)* 🕙 *Daily 8–sunset.*

FodorsChoice ★

Where to Stay & Eat

$–$$$$ ✕ **Capt. Anderson's.** Come early to watch the boats unload the catch of the day on the docks, and be among the first to line up to eat in this noted restaurant. A nautical theme is reinforced by tables made of hatch covers, and in the attached bar, which attracts long-time locals. The Greek specialties aren't limited to feta cheese and shriveled olives; charcoal-broiled fish and steaks have a prominent place on the menu as well. If you're visiting in the off-season, call to make sure they are adhering to the posted hours before venturing out. ✉ *5551 N. Lagoon Dr.* ☎ *850/234–2225* 🍴 *Reservations not accepted* ▭ *AE, D, DC, MC, V* 🕙 *Closed Nov.–Feb. and Sun. No lunch.*

$–$$$ ✕ **Boar's Head.** An exterior that looks like an oversize thatch-roof cottage sets the mood for dining in this ersatz-rustic restaurant and tavern. Prime rib has been the number one people-pleaser since the house opened in 1978, but blackened seafood and broiled shrimp with crab-meat stuffing are popular, too. ✉ *17290 Front Beach Rd.* ☎ *850/234–6628* ▭ *AE, D, DC, MC, V* 🕙 *No lunch.*

¢–$$ ✕ **Billy's Steamed Seafood Restaurant, Oyster Bar, and Crab House.** Roll up your sleeves and dig into some of the gulf's finest blue crabs and shrimp seasoned to perfection with Billy's special recipe. Homemade gumbo, crawfish, and the day's catch as well as sandwiches and burgers round out the menu. The taste here is in the food, not the surroundings, but you can eat on an outdoor patio in the cooler months. ✉ *3000 Thomas Dr.* ☎ *850/235–2349* ▭ *AE, D, MC, V.*

¢–$$ ✕ **Schooner's.** Billing itself as the "last local beach club," this beachfront spot is the perfect place for a casual family lunch or early dinner: kids can have burgers and play on the beach while Mom and Dad enjoy grown-up drinks and more substantial fare such as homemade gumbo, steak, or simply prepared seafood. Late-night crowds pile in for live music and dancing. ✉ *5121 Gulf Dr.* ☎ *850/235–3555* ▭ *AE, D, DC, MC, V.*

★ **$$$–$$$$** ⊞ **Edgewater Beach Resort.** Luxurious one-, two-, and three-bedroom apartments in beachside towers and golf-course villas are elegantly furnished with wicker and rattan. The resort centerpiece is a Polynesian-style lagoon pool with waterfalls, reflecting ponds, footbridges, and more than 20,000 species of tropical plants. This resort is a good option for longer stays or family vacations. ✉ *11212 Front Beach Rd., 32407* ☎ *850/235–4044 or 800/874–8686* 🖷 *850/233–7529* ⊕ *www.edgewaterbeachresort.com* ➾ *520 apartments* ♨ *2 restaurants, 9-hole golf course, 11 tennis courts, hair salon, spa, beach, 2 bars, recreation room* ⊟ *D, DC, MC, V.*

$$$　🏨 **Marriott's Bay Point Resort Village.** Across the Grand Lagoon from St.
Fodor's Choice　Andrews State Park, this expansive property exudes sheer elegance. The
★　tropical-chic feel starts in the light-filled lobby, with its polished marble floors, glowing chandeliers, potted palms, and colorful floral paintings. Quiet guest rooms continue the theme with light wood furnishings and armoires, floral-print fabrics, and private balconies or patios overlooking the lush grounds and peaceful bay. Rooms on the upper floors of the main building have expansive views of the bay and the gulf beyond, and kitchen-equipped villas are a mere tee-shot away from the hotel. A meandering boardwalk (which doubles as a jogging trail) leads to a private bayside beach where an open-air bar and water sports await. ✉ *4200 Marriott Dr., 32408* ☎ *850/236–6000 or 800/874–7105* 🖷 *850/233–1308* ⊕ *www.marriottbaypoint.com* ➾ *278 rooms, 78 suites* ♨ *5 restaurants, some kitchens, cable TV, 2 golf courses, 4 tennis courts, 6 pools, health club, marina, 2 bars, airport shuttle* ⊟ *AE, D, MC, V.*

$$–$$$　🏨 **Boardwalk Beach Resort.** Four family-oriented hotels—the Howard Johnson, Convention Center Hotel, Gulfwalk, and Beachwalk inns—have staked out this mile of beachfront. While this resort is not as glitzy as some of its neighbors, its reasonable prices are hard to beat. All share the long beach, and group parties are given regularly by all four hotels. Each has its own pool. Refrigerators and microwaves are available in some rooms. ✉ *9450 S. Thomas Dr., 32408* ☎ *850/234–3484 or 800/224–4853* 🖷 *850/233–4369* ⊕ *www.boardwalkbeachresort.com* ➾ *625 units* ♨ *5 restaurants, 3 grills, some microwaves, some refrigerators, 4 pools, beach, video game room, playground, some pets allowed* ⊟ *AE, D, DC, MC, V.*

Nightlife & the Arts

THE ARTS　Broadway touring shows, top-name entertainers, and concert artists are booked into the **Marina Civic Center** (✉ 8 Harrison Ave., Panama City ☎ 850/769–1217 or 850/763–4696).

NIGHTLIFE　**Club La Vela** (✉ 8813 Thomas Dr. ☎ 850/235–1061) might also be known as the club that MTV built. The spring-break crowd has 48 bar stations, 14 dance floors, and three band stages to choose from in season, but there's something going on year-round. **Pineapple Willy's** (✉ 9875 S. Thomas Dr. ☎ 850/235–0928) is an eatery and bar geared toward families and tourists—as well as sports fans. **Schooner's** (✉ 5121 Gulf Dr. ☎ 850/235–3555), a beachfront bar and restaurant, draws huge crowds of mostly locals for live music and late-night dancing on weekends.

Sports & the Outdoors

CANOEING　Rentals for a trip down Econofina Creek, "Florida's most beautiful canoe trail," are supplied by **Econofina Creek Canoe Livery** (✉ Strickland Rd., north of Rte. 20, Youngstown ☎ 850/722–9032).

DOG RACING　Find pari-mutuel betting year-round and live greyhound racing five nights and two afternoons a week at the **Ebro Greyhound Park.** Simulcasts of Thoroughbred racing from the Miami area are also shown throughout the year. Schedules change periodically, so call for details. ✉ *Rte. 79, Ebro* ☎ *850/234–3943* 🎟 *General $2, clubhouse $1 additional.*

GOLF　The **Hombre Golf Club** (✉ 120 Coyote Pass ☎ 850/234–3673) has a 27-hole course that occasionally hosts professional tours. **Marriott's Bay Point Resort** (✉ 4200 Marriott Dr. ☎ 850/235–6937 or 800/874–7105) has a country club that has 36 holes open to the public.

TENNIS The tennis center at **Marriott's Bay Point Resort** (⊠ 4200 Marriott Dr. ☎ 850/235–6910) has 10 Har-Tru tennis courts.

Shopping

Stores in the **Manufacturer's Outlet Center** (⊠ 105 W. 23rd St., Panama City) offer well-known brands at a substantial discount. The **Panama City Mall** (⊠ 2150 Martin Luther King, Jr. Blvd., Panama City ☎ 850/785–9587) has a mix of more than 100 franchise shops and national chain stores.

Apalachicola

❽ *65 mi southeast of Panama City Beach.*

Meaning "land of the friendly people" in the language of its original Native American inhabitants, Apalachicola—known in these parts as simply Apalach—lies on the Panhandle's southernmost bulge. Settlers began arriving in 1821, and by 1847 the southern terminus of the Apalachicola River steamboat route was a bustling port town. Although the town is now known as the Oyster Capital of the World, oystering became king only after the local cotton industry flagged—the city's extrawide streets, built to accommodate bales of cotton awaiting transport, are a remnant of that trade—and the sponge industry moved down the coast after depleting local sponge colonies. But the newest industry here is tourism, and visitors have begun discovering the Forgotten Coast, as the area is known, flocking to its intimate hotels and B&Bs, dining at excellent restaurants, and browsing through unique shops selling everything from handmade furniture to brass fixtures recovered from nearby shipwrecks. If you like oysters or you want to go back in time to the Old South of Gothic churches and spooky graveyards, Apalachicola is a good place to start.

Drive by the **Raney House,** circa 1850, and **Trinity Episcopal Church,** built from prefabricated parts in 1838. The town is at a developmental turning point of late, pulled in one direction by well-intentioned locals who want to preserve Apalachicola's port-town roots and in the other by long-time business owners who fear preservation will inhibit commercial growth. For now, however, the city exudes a refreshing authenticity—think Key West in the early 1960s—that many others in the Sunshine State lost long ago, one that might be lost to Panama City Beach–style overdevelopment unless local government institutes an official historic preservation committee.

Stop in at the **John Gorrie Museum State Park,** which honors the physician credited with inventing ice making and, almost, air-conditioning. Although he was hampered by technology, later air-conditioning patents utilized Gorrie's discoveries. Exhibits of Apalachicola history are displayed here as well. ⊠ *Ave. D and 6th St.* ☎ *850/653–9347* ⚐ *$1* ☉ *Thurs.–Mon. 9–5.*

Where to Stay & Eat

★ **$$–$$$** ✕ **Magnolia Grill.** Chef-owner Eddie Cass has earned local and regional acclaim from major food critics who have discovered the culinary pearl in this small oyster town. Such dishes as Magnolia Grill Surf and Turf, which weds oak-grilled pork tenderloin with béarnaise sauce to jumbo shrimp with New England crabmeat stuffing and lobster sauce, pleasingly unite the flavors of Eddie's native New England and the coastal South. Dinners here tend to be leisurely events, and the stellar desserts—anything chocolate will wow you—deserve an hour of their own. Because the restaurant is small, reservations are recommended. ⊠ *99 11th St.* ☎ *850/653–8000* ▤ *MC, V* ☉ *Closed Sun. No lunch.*

$$–$$$ ✕ **Nola's Grill.** Hobnob with Apalachicola aristocracy as you eat in a serene, Edwardian-style dining room at the town's traditional hotel. The place is a bit formal—crisp, creased linen tablecloths and atmospheric lighting—and the food's impeccable. The menu changes seasonally, but count on fresh seafood, namely oyster, shrimp, and grouper preparations. Even if you've eaten dinner elsewhere, make sure to stop by the cozy wooden bar for an after-dinner drink and a taste of Apalachicola of yesteryear. ⊠ *51 Ave. C.* ☎ *850/653–2191* 🖃 *AE, MC, V.*

$$–$$$ ✕ **Tamara's Cafe Floridita.** Tamara, a native Venezuelan, brings the food
Fodor'sChoice and warmth of her homeland to this colorful bistro, which mixes Florida
★ flavors with South American flair. For starters, try the creamy black bean soup or the pleasantly spicy oyster stew; for dinner choose from grouper paella, proscuitto-wrapped salmon with mango-cilantro sauce, or margarita chicken and scallops with a tequila-lime glaze. All entrées come with black beans and rice, fresh vegetables, and focaccia bread, but if you still have room for dessert try the fried banana split or the *tres leches,* a South American favorite. The chef, who keeps watch over the dining room from an open kitchen, is happy to accommodate most any whim. ⊠ *17 Ave. E* ☎ *850/653–4111* 🖃 *AE, MC, V.*

$–$$$ ✕ **Boss Oyster.** Eat your oysters fried, Rockefeller-style, or on the half shell at this laid-back eatery overlooking the Apalachicola River. Eat 'em alfresco at picnic tables or inside in the busy, rustic dining room, but don't let the modest surroundings fool you—oysters aren't cheap here or anywhere in Apalach. If you're allergic to seafood, don't worry. The menu also includes such staples as steak and pizza. ⊠ *123 Water St.* ☎ *850/653–9364* 🖃 *AE, D, DC, MC, V.*

¢–$ ✕ **Owl Café.** This old-fashioned, charming lunch and dinner spot pleases modern palates, both in the white-linen elegance of the dining room and in the colorful garden terrace. The food is an artful blend of old and new as well: Grandma's chicken sandwich with potato salad seems as much at home on the lunch menu as the crab and shrimp quesadillas. Dinner seafood specials are carefully prepared, but special requests are sometimes met with resistance from the kitchen. Fine wines for adults and special menu selections for children make this a family-friendly place. ⊠ *15 Ave. D* ☎ *850/653–9888* 🖃 *AE, MC, V* ☻ *Closed Sun.*

$$$–$$$$ 🖬 **The Consulate.** These four elegant suites, on the second story of the former offices of the local French Consul, range in size from 600 to 1,600 square ft and combine a 19th-century feel with 21st-century luxury. Exposed wooden beams and brick walls, 13-ft ceilings, hardwood floors, and antique appointments add more than a hint of charm, while custom-built kitchens, full-size washers and dryers, and cordless room phones make living easy. The two front units share an expansive balcony, where you can take in the constant parade of fishing vessels headed out the Intracoastal. The homelike amenities make this a popular spot for families, larger groups, and even wedding parties, and discounts are given for stays longer than two nights. The Grady Market, a locally owned art and clothing boutique, occupies the building's first floor. ⊠ *76 Water St. 32320* ☎ *850/653–1515 or 877/239–1159* ⊕ *www.consulatesuites.com* ➳ *4 suites* ♢ *Kitchens, cable TV with VCRs* 🖃 *AE, MC, V.*

$–$$$$ 🖬 **Coombs House Inn.** Nine fireplaces and an ornate oak staircase with lead-glass windows on the landing lend authenticity to this restored 1905 mansion. No two guest rooms are alike, but all are appointed with Victorian-era settees, four-poster or sleigh beds, English chintz curtains, and Asian rugs on polished hardwood floors. A full breakfast is served in the dining room. Eighty steps away is Coombs House East, and, beyond that, a renovated carriage house. Popular for weddings and receptions, these may be the most elegant homes in Apalachicola. Free tours are offered in the afternoon if the accommodations are not in use. ⊠ 80 6th St., 32320 ☎ 850/653–9199 🖹 850/653–2785 ⊕ www.coombshouseinn. com ⟿ 18 rooms ⚭ Dining room, cable TV, bicycles ▤ D, MC, V.

$–$$ 🏨 **Gibson Inn.** One of a few inns on the National Register of Historic Places still operating as a full-service facility, this turn-of-the-20th-century hostelry in the heart of downtown is easily identified by its wraparound porches, fretwork, and captain's watch. Rooms are furnished with period pieces, such as four-poster beds, antique armoires, and pedestal lavatories, which have wide basins and porcelain fixtures. ⊠ 57 Market St., 32320 ☎ 850/653–2191 🖹 850/653–3521 ⊕ www. gibsoninn.com ⟿ 30 rooms, 2 suites ⚭ Restaurant, bar, some pets allowed ▤ AE, MC, V.

¢–$ 🏨 **Rancho Inn.** This mom-and-pop operation—the owners live on-site—prides itself on its homeyness and personalized service. Rooms are spotless, if a little dated in their beige-and-brown color schemes, but 25″ color TVs (complete with HBO and other premium channels) and in-room coffee makers, refrigerators, and microwaves make it a hard to beat option for those on a budget. ⊠ 240 U.S. 98 W 32320 ☎ 850/653–9435 🖹 850/653–9180 ⊕ http://209.238.155.43 ⟿ 32 rooms, 1 suite ⚭ Microwaves, refrigerators, cable TV, pool ▤ AE, D, DC, MC, V.

¢ 🏨 **Best Western Apalach Inn.** Basic but impeccably kept, this modern property situated 1 mi from the downtown waterfront area has everything you need for a safe overnight. Standard guest rooms are done in earth tones with wicker headboards and burgundy-print curtains and bedspreads. A large swimming pool, free local calls, and a complimentary Continental breakfast are unexpected bonuses. ⊠ 249 U.S. 98 W, 32320 ☎ 850/653–9131 🖹 850/653–9136 ⊕ www.bwapalachinn.com ⟿ 42 rooms ⚭ In-room data ports, pool ▤ AE, D, MC, V ⦿ CP.

Shopping
The **Tin Shed** (⊠ 170 Water St., Apalachicola ☎ 850/653–3635) has an impressive collection of antiques and knickknacks, from antique brass luggage tags to 1940s-era nautical charts to sponge-diver wetsuits to hand-glazed tiles and architectural elements salvaged from demolished buildings. The **Grady Market** (⊠ 76 Water St., Apalachicola ☎ 850/653–4099) is a collection of more than a dozen boutiques, including several antiques dealers and the gallery of Richard Bickel, known for his stunning black-and-white photographs of local residents. **Avenue E** (⊠ 15 Ave. E, Apalachicola ☎ 850/653–1411) is a stylish store specializing in reasonably priced antique and reproduction pieces, including furniture, lamps, artwork, and interior accessories.

St. George Island
❾ *8 mi southeast of Apalachicola.*

Pristine St. George Island sits 5 mi out into the Gulf of Mexico just south of Apalachicola. Accessed via the Bryant Patton Bridge off U.S. 98, the island is bordered by both Apalachicola Bay and the gulf, offering vacationers the best of both. The rich bay is an angler's dream, while the snowy-white beaches and clear gulf waters satisfy even the most finicky beachgoer. Indulge in bicycling, hiking, canoeing, and snorkeling or find a secluded spot for reading, gathering shells, or bird-watching. Accommodations mostly take the form of privately owned, fully furnished condos and single-family homes, which allow for plenty of privacy.

FodorśChoice **St. George Island State Park** gives you Old Florida at its undisturbed best.
★ On the east end of the island are 9 mi of undeveloped beaches and dunes—

the longest beachfront of any state park in Florida. Sandy coves, salt marshes, oak forests, and pines provide shelter for many species, including such birds as bald eagles and ospreys. Spotless rest rooms and plentiful parking make a day at this park a joy. ☎ 850/927–2111 ⌦ $4 per vehicle (up to 8 people) ☉ Daily 8–sunset.

off the beaten path

Carrabelle. Where, exactly, is Carrabelle? Why, it's between Sopchoppy and Wewahitchka, of course. Known locally as "a quaint drinking village with a fishing problem," one of the last true fishing ports on the Gulf Coast is most famous for having the World's Smallest Police Station, a former phone booth off U.S. 98 (you can buy the postcard at the nearby general store). Talk a walk around the docks and watch the gulls compete for handouts above the rusted shrimp boats. But do it soon: there's talk of a major condo development in the works that will likely put this sleepy port on the snowbird map. ✉ 15 mi east of St. George Island on U.S. 98.

Where to Stay & Eat

$$–$$$ ✕ **Oyster Cove Seafood Bar & Grill.** Tucked in among trees, this blue-and-white cottage yields scenic views of Apalachicola Bay through its large windows. Mediterranean grouper and shrimp Dijon are two favored seafood dishes, but the house specialty is East Bay steak, a tender rib eye grilled with oysters and Spanish onions. Some years the restaurant closes from mid-November to mid-February; it's best to call ahead to check at that time of year. ✉ E. Pine and E. 2nd Sts. ☎ 850/927–2600 ▤ AE, MC, V.

$–$$ ✕ **Blue Parrot.** You'll feel like you're sneaking in the back door as you climb the side stairs leading to an outdoor deck overlooking the gulf. Or if you can, grab a table indoors. During special-event weekends, the place is packed, and service may be a little slow. The food is hard to beat if you're not looking for anything fancy. Baskets of shrimp, oysters, and crab cakes—fried or char-grilled and served with fries—are more than one person can handle. Daily specials are on the blackboard. ✉ 68 W. Gorrie Dr. ☎ 850/927–2987 ▤ AE, D, MC, V.

¢ ✕ **Carrabelle Junction.** Stop by this eclectic spot for a cup of gourmet coffee—no small feat in these parts—and freshly made classic sandwiches ranging from tuna salad to BLTs. Or get a scoop of ice cream, grab a table out front, and enjoy the music that Ron, the proprietor, spins on a real record player. Locally produced artwork and knickknacks are sold here, too. ✉ 88 Tallahassee St., Carrabelle ☎ 850/697–9550 ▤ No credit cards ☉ No dinner.

$$–$$$ ▥ **The St. George Inn.** A little piece of Key West smack in the middle of the Panhandle, this cozy inn has tin roofs, hardwood floors, wraparound porches—even a widow's walk. Personal touches like private porches and in-room coffeemakers keep things homey. Both beach and bay are within view, and several restaurants and a convenience store are within walking distance. Two larger suites have full kitchens, and the pool is heated for year-round swimming. Specials are posted on the inn's Web site during off-season, when prices can drop by more than half. ✉ 135 Franklin Blvd., 32320 ☎ 850/927–2903 or 800/332–5196 ⊕ www. stgeorgeinn.com ➥ 15 rooms, 2 suites ♤ Some kitchens, refrigerators, cable TV, pool ▤ MC, V.

The Outdoors

BOATING For a **boat tour** (✉ Box 696, Carrabelle 32322 ☎ 850/697–3989) of St. George Sound and Apalachicola Bay, call charter captain A. P. Whaley. He's famous in these parts for his uncanny ability to attract dolphin to the stern of his boat, the Gat V.

INLAND ACROSS THE PANHANDLE

Farther inland, where the northern reaches of the Panhandle butt up against the back porches of Alabama and Georgia, you'll find a part of Florida that goes a long way toward explaining why the state song is "Suwannee River" (and why its parenthetical title is "Old Folks at Home"). Stephen Foster's musical genius notwithstanding, the inland Panhandle area is definitely more Dixie than Sunshine State, with few lodging options other than the chain motels that flank the I–10 exits and a decidedly slower pace of life than on the tourist-heavy Gulf Coast. But the area's natural attractions—hills and farmlands, untouched small towns, pristine state parks—make for great day trips from the coast should the sky turn gray or the skin red. Explore underground caverns where eons-old rock formations create bizarre scenes, visit one of Florida's up-and-coming wineries, or poke around small-town America in DeFuniak Springs.

DeFuniak Springs

⑩ *28 mi east of Crestview.*

This scenic spot has a rather unusual claim to fame: at its center lies a nearly perfectly symmetrical spring-fed lake, one of only two such naturally circular bodies of water in the world (the other is in Switzerland). In 1848, the Knox Hill Academy was founded here, and for more than half a century it was the only institution of higher learning in northwestern Florida. In 1885 the town was chosen as the location for the New York Chautauqua educational society's winter assembly. The Chautauqua programs were discontinued in 1922, but DeFuniak Springs attempts to revive them, in spirit at least, by sponsoring a county-wide Chautauqua Festival in April.

By all accounts, the 16-ft by 24-ft **Walton-DeFuniak Public Library** is Florida's oldest library continuously operating in its original building. Opened in 1887, the original space has been added to over the years and it now contains nearly 30,000 volumes, including some rare books, many older than the structure itself. The collection also includes antique musical instruments and impressive European armor. ✉ *3 Circle Dr.* ☎ *850/892-3624* ⊙ *Mon. and Wed.–Fri. 9–5, Sat. 9–3, Tues. 9–8.*

The **Chautauqua Winery** (✉ I–10 and U.S. 331 ☎ 850/892–5887) opened in 1989, and its vintages have earned raves from oenophiles nationwide. Take a free tour to see how ancient art blends with modern technology; then retreat to the tasting room and gift shop.

Some of the finest examples of Victorian architecture in the state can be seen on a walking tour of **Circle Drive.** In addition to the Walton-DeFuniak Public Library, the Dream Cottage and the Pansy Cottage are beautiful Victorian specimens. Most of the other notable structures are private residences, but you can still admire them from the street.

Falling Waters State Park

⑪ *35 mi east of DeFuniak Springs.*

This site of a Civil War–era whiskey distillery and, later, an exotic plant nursery—some imported species still thrive in the wild—is best known for being the site of one of Florida's most notable geological features—the Falling Waters Sink. The 100-ft-deep cylindrical pit provides the background for a waterfall, and there's an observation deck for viewing this natural phenomenon. The water free-falls 67 ft to the bottom of the sink, but where it goes after that is a mystery. ⊠ *Rte. 77A, Chipley* ☏ *850/ 638–6130* ⊕ *www.dep.state.fl.us/parks* 🖃 *$3.25 per vehicle (up to 8 people)* ☉ *Daily 8–sunset.*

Florida Caverns State Park

⑫ *13 mi northeast of Falling Waters off I–10 on U.S. 231.*

Take a ranger-led cave tour to see stalactites, stalagmites, and "waterfalls" of solid rock at this expansive park. Some of the caverns are off-limits to the public or open for scientific study only with a permit, but you'll still see enough to fill a half day or more. Between Memorial Day and Labor Day, rangers offer guided lantern tours on Friday and Saturday nights. There are also hiking trails, campsites, and areas for swimming and canoeing on the Chipola River. ⊠ *Rte. 166, Marianna* ☏ *850/482–9598; 850/482–1228 for camping reservations* 🖃 *Park $3.25 per vehicle (up to 8 people); caverns $4* ☉ *Daily 8–sunset; cavern tours daily 9:30–4.*

TALLAHASSEE

⑬ *61 mi southeast of Florida Caverns.*

Interstate 10 rolls east over the timid beginnings of the Appalachian foothills and through thick pines into the state capital, with its canopies of ancient oaks and spring bowers of azaleas. Along with Florida State University, the perennial Seminoles football champions, and FAMU's fabled "Marching 100" band, the city also has more than a touch of the Old South. Tallahassee maintains a tranquillity quite different from the sun-and-surf hedonism of the major coastal towns. Acknowledging the cosmopolitan pace of other Florida cities, residents claim their hometown is "Florida with a southern accent." Vestiges of the city's colorful past are found throughout; for example, in the capitol complex, the turn-of-the-20th-century Old Capitol building is strikingly paired with the New Capitol skyscraper. Tallahassee's tree-lined streets are particularly memorable—among the best canopied roads are St. Augustine, Miccosukee, Meridian, Old Bainbridge, and Centerville, all dotted with country stores and antebellum plantation houses.

Downtown

The downtown area is compact enough so that most sights can be seen on foot, although it's also served by a free, continuous shuttle trolley. Start at the capitol complex, which contains the **Old Capitol** ▶ and its counterpoint, the **New Capitol.** Across the street from the older structure is the restored **Union Bank Building,** and two blocks west of the new statehouse you'll find the **Museum of Florida History,** with exhibits on many eras of the state's history and prehistory. If you really want to get a feel for Old Tallahassee, walk the **Downtown Tallahassee Historic Trail** as it wends its way from the capitol complex through several of the city's historic districts.

TIMING   You can't do justice to the capitol complex and downtown area in less than two hours. Allow four hours to walk the 8-mi stretch of the historic trail. If you visit between March and April, you'll find flowers in bloom and the Springtime Tallahassee festival in full swing.

What to See

Downtown Tallahassee Historic Trail. A route originally mapped and documented by an eager Eagle Scout as part of a merit-badge project, this trail has become a Tallahassee sightseeing staple. The starting point is the New Capitol, at whose visitor center you can pick up maps and descriptive brochures. You'll walk through the **Park Avenue and Calhoun Street historic districts,** which will take you back to Territorial days and the era of postwar reconstruction. The trail is dotted with landmark churches and cemeteries, along with outstanding examples of Greek revival, Italianate, and Prairie-style architecture. Some houses are open to the public. The **Brokaw-McDougall House** (⊠ 329 N. Meridian St. ⊙ Weekdays 9–3 ⊠ Free) is a superb example of the Greek revival and Italianate styles. The **Meginnis-Monroe House** (⊠ 125 N. Gadsden St. ⊙ Tues.–Sat. 10–5, Sun. 2–5 ⊠ Free) served as a field hospital during the Civil War and is now an art gallery.

Museum of Florida History. If you thought Florida was founded by Walt Disney, stop here. Covering 12,000 years, the displays explain Florida's past by highlighting the unique geological and historical events that have shaped the state. Exhibits include a mammoth armadillo grazing in a savannah, the remains of a giant mastodon found in nearby Wakulla Springs, and a dugout canoe that once carried Indians into Florida's backwaters. ⊠ *500 S. Bronough St.* ☎ *850/245–6400* ⊕ *dhr.dos.state.fl.us/ museum* ⊠ *Free* ⊙ *Weekdays 9–4:30, Sat. 10–4:30, Sun. noon–4:30.*

★ **New Capitol.** This modern skyscraper looms up 22 stories directly behind the low-rise Old Capitol. From the fabulous 22nd-floor observation deck, on a clear day, catch a panoramic view of Tallahassee and the surrounding countryside—all the way into Georgia. Also on this floor is the Florida Artists Hall of Fame, a tribute to Floridians such as Ray Charles, Burt Reynolds, Tennessee Williams, Ernest Hemingway, and Marjorie Kinnan Rawlings. To pick up information about the area, stop at the Florida Visitors Center, on the plaza level. ⊠ *400 S. Monroe St.* ☎ *850/488–6167* ⊠ *Free* ⊙ *Visitor center weekdays 8–5, self-guided or guided tours weekdays 8–5.*

★ ⌐ **Old Capitol.** The centerpiece of the capitol complex, this pre–Civil War structure has been added to and subtracted from several times. Having been restored, the jaunty red-and-white stripe awnings and combination gas-electric lights make it look much as it did in 1902. Inside, historically accurate legislative chambers and exhibits offer a very interesting peek into the past. ⊠ *S. Monroe St. at Apalachee Pkwy.* ☎ *850/487– 1902* ⊠ *Free* ⊙ *Self-guided or guided tours weekdays 9–4:30, Sat. 10–4:30, Sun. noon–4:30.*

Union Bank Building. Chartered in 1833, this is Florida's oldest bank building. Since it closed in 1843, it has played many roles, from ballet school to bakery. It has been restored to what is thought to be its original appearance and currently houses Florida A&M's Black Archives Extension, which depicts black history in Florida. Call ahead for hours, which are subject to change, and directions. ⊠ *Calhoun St. at Apalachee Pkwy.* ☎ *850/487–3803* ⊠ *Free* ⊙ *Weekdays 9–4.*

Away from Downtown

What to See

Alfred Maclay Gardens State Park. Starting in December the grounds are afire with azaleas, dogwood, and other showy or rare plants. Allow half a day to wander past the reflecting pool into the tiny walled garden, and around the lakes and woodlands. The Maclay residence, furnished as it was in the 1920s; picnic areas; and swimming and boating facilities are open to the public. The gardens are both peaceful and perfect. ⊠ *3540 Thomasville Rd.* ☎ *850/487–4556* ⊠ *Jan.–Apr. $6.25 per vehicle (up to 8 people); May–Dec. $3.25* ⊙ *Daily 8–sunset.*

Lake Jackson Mounds Archaeological State Park. Here are waters to make bass fishermen weep. For sightseers, Indian mounds and the ruins of an early 19th-century plantation built by Colonel Robert Butler, adjutant to General Andrew Jackson during the siege of New Orleans, are found along the shores of the lake. ☒ *3600 Indian Mounds Rd.* ☏ *850/562–0042* ☒ *$2* ☉ *Daily 8–sunset.*

San Luis Archaeological and Historic Site. This museum focuses on the archaeology of 17th-century Spanish mission and Apalachee Indian town sites. In its heyday, in 1675, the Apalachee village here had a population of at least 1,400. Threatened by Creek Indians and British forces in 1704, the locals burned the village and fled. Take self-guided tours and watch scientists conducting digs daily (usually). The museum's popular "Living History" program is held on the third Saturday of the month (10 AM–2 PM). ☒ *2020 W. Mission Rd.* ☏ *850/487–3711* ☒ *Free* ☉ *Tues.–Sun 10–4.*

☙ **Tallahassee Museum of History and Natural Science.** It could have been dull, but this bucolic park showcases a peaceful and intriguing look at Old Florida. A working 1880s pioneer farm offers daily hands-on activities for children, such as soap making and blacksmithing. A boardwalk meanders through the 52 acres of natural habitat that make up the zoo, which has such varied animals as panthers, bobcats, white-tailed deer, and black bears. Also on site are nature trails, a one-room schoolhouse dating from 1897, and an 1840s southern plantation manor, where you can usually find someone cooking on the weekends. ☒ *3945 Museum Dr.* ☏ *850/576–1636* ☒ *$6.50* ☉ *Mon.–Sat. 9–5, Sun. 12:30–5.*

off the beaten path

Birdsong Nature Center. This 500-acre preserve's 12 mi of nature trails, with lakes, woodlands, deer—and a skittish Florida bobcat or two—provide a taste of what all of North Florida and southern Georgia used to look like. Visitors come here for the exact opposite reason they go to Disney—to bask in the natural environment, learn about natural history and preservation, and get away from it all. The Evening Sky program, a nighttime study of stars and constellations, is especially popular, and the 20-minute drive north on Meridian Road out of Tallahassee, beneath canopies of oaks whose beards of Spanish moss hang from above like soft, green stalactites, is an adventure in itself. ☒ *2106 Meridian Rd. Thomasville GA 31792* ☏ *229/377–4408* ⊕ *tfn.net/birdsong* ☒ *$5* ☉ *Wed., Fri, and Sat. 9–5; Sun. 1–5.*

Where to Stay & Eat

★ **$$–$$$** ✕ **Andrew's 2nd Act.** Part of a smart complex in the heart of the political district, this place serves up classic food: elegant and understated. For dinner, the tournedos St. Laurent and the peppered New York strip are both flawless. Seafood lovers can feast on the day's fresh catch. ☒ *228 S. Adams St.* ☏ *850/222–3444* ▭ *AE, D, MC, V.*

$–$$$ ✕ **Chez Pierre.** You'll feel as if you've entered a great-aunt's old plantation home in this restored 1920s house set back from the road in historic Lafayette Park. Since 1876, its warm, cozy rooms, gleaming hardwood floors, and large French doors separating dining areas have created an intimate place to go for authentic French cuisine. Try the tournedos of beef or one of the special lamb dishes. ☒ *1215 Thomasville Rd.* ☏ *850/222–0936* ▭ *AE, D, DC, MC, V.*

$ ✕ **Nicholson's Farmhouse.** The name says a lot about this friendly, informal country place with an outside kitchen and grill. A few miles out in the Tallahassee countryside, the steak house is a retreat from the already calming capital city. A farm, gift shop, mule-drawn wagon rides, and a folk guitarist named Hoot Gibson (not the astronaut) create a rural re-treat where you can enjoy hand-cut steaks, chops, and seafood. ⊠ *From U.S. 27 follow Rte. 12 toward Quincy and look for signs* ☎ *850/539–5931* ▤ *AE, D, MC, V* ⛾ *BYOB* ☻ *Closed Sun.–Mon. No lunch.*

¢–$ ✕ **Rice-Bowl Oriental.** Bamboo woodwork and thatched-roof booths lend an air of authenticity to this Asian-hybrid spot tucked away in a Tallahassee strip mall. Chinese, Japanese, Thai, and Vietnamese favorites are all represented here, from General Tso's Chicken to fresh sushi to green curry and rice noodle dishes. The all-you-can-eat Saturday-night buffet, complete with entrées, salads, soups, and fresh sushi, just might be one of the best deals in town. ⊠ *3813 N. Monroe St.* ☎ *850/514–3632* ▤ *AE, D, DC, MC, V.*

¢ ✕ **Hopkins' Eatery.** Locals in the know flock here for superb salads, homemade soups, and sandwiches—expect a short wait at lunchtime—via simple counter service. Kids will like the traditional PBJ sandwich (offered with bananas and sprouts, if they dare); adults might opt for a chunky chicken melt, smothered beef, or garden vegetarian sub. The orange and spearmint iced tea is a must-have, as is a slice of freshly baked chocolate cake. A second location on North Monroe Street serves lunch only. ⊠ *1415 Market St.* ☎ *850/668–0311* ⊠ *1840 N. Monroe St.* ☎ *850/ 386–1809* ▤ *AE, D, DC, MC, V* ☻ *Closed Sun. No dinner Sat.*

★ $$–$$$$ ▥ **Governors Inn.** Only a block from the capitol, this plushly restored historic warehouse is abuzz during the week with politicians, press, and lobbyists. It's a perfect location for business travelers and on weekends for tourists who want to visit downtown sites. Rooms are a rich blend of mahogany, brass, and classic prints. The VIP treatment includes cocktails, robes, shoe shine, and a daily paper. ⊠ *209 S. Adams St., 32301* ☎ *850/681–6855; 800/342–7717 in Florida* 🖷 *850/222–3105* ⇆ *28 rooms, 12 suites* ↻ *Cable TV, laundry service, parking (fee)* ▤ *AE, D, DC, MC, V* �OⅠ *CP.*

$$–$$$ ▥ **DoubleTree Hotel Tallahassee.** This hotel a mere two blocks from the capitol hosts heavy hitters from the worlds of politics and media. Since it's also an easy walk from the Florida State University campus, it welcomes plenty of FSU fans during football season. Rooms are basic and have two full-size beds—these are pushed together to create a "king" bed. ⊠ *101 S. Adams St., 32301* ☎ *850/224–5000* 🖷 *850/513–9516* ⇆ *243 rooms* ↻ *Restaurant, pool, gym, bar* ▤ *AE, D, DC, MC, V.*

¢ ▥ **Shoney's Inn.** The quiet courtyard with its own pool and the darkly welcoming cantina (where a complimentary Continental breakfast is served) convey the look of Old Spain. Rooms are furnished in heavy Mediterranean style—but only have double beds. Rates jump $30 on game weekends. ⊠ *2801 N. Monroe St., 32303* ☎ *850/386–8286* 🖷 *850/422–1074* ⊕ *www.shoneysinn.com* ⇆ *113 rooms, 27 suites* ↻ *Pool* ▤ *AE, D, DC, MC, V.*

Nightlife & the Arts

The Arts

Florida State University (☎ 050/644–4774 School of Music, 850/644–6500 School of Theatre ⊕ www.music.fsu.edu) annually hosts more than 400 concerts and recitals given year-round by its School of Music, and many productions by its School of Theatre. The **Monticello Opera House** (⊠ 185 W. Washington [U.S. 90 E], Monticello ☎ 850/997–4242) presents concerts and plays in a restored 1890s gaslight-era opera house. The **Tallahassee Little Theatre** (⊠ 1861 Thomasville Rd. ☎ 850/224–8474 ⊕ www.tallytown.com/tlt) has a five-production season that runs from September through May. The season of the **Tallahassee Symphony Orchestra** (☎ 850/224–0461 ⊕ www.tsolive.org) runs from October through April; performances are usually held at Florida State University's Ruby Diamond Auditorium.

Nightlife

Waterworks (⊠ 1133 Thomasville Rd. ☎ 850/224–1887), with its retro-chic Tiki-bar fittings, attracts jazz fans and hipsters of all ages for live music and cocktails. Call for the latest on who's playing. **Floyd's Music Store** (⊠ 666-1 W. Tennessee St. ☎ 850/222–3506) hosts some of the hottest local and touring acts around. Other performers, from dueling pianos to Dave Matthews cover bands to assorted DJs, round out the schedule. Don't let the name fool you: the **Late Night Library** (⊠ 809 Gay St. ☎ 850/224–2429) is the quintessential college-town party bar. Think dancing, drinking, and you'll get the picture.

Side Trips

South to the Gulf

South of the capital and east of the Ochlockanee River are several fascinating natural and historic sites. Since they're near one another, string several together on an excursion from Tallahassee.

⑭ **Natural Bridge Battlefield State Park** marks the spot where in 1865 Confederate soldiers stood firm against a Yankee advance on St. Marks. The Rebs held, saving Tallahassee—the only southern capital east of the Mississippi that never fell to the Union. Ten miles southeast of Tallahassee, the site is a good place for a hike and a picnic. Visit the first week in March to see a reenactment of the battle. ⊠ *Natural Bridge Rd., off Rte. 363, Woodville* ☎ *850/922–6007* ⊡ *Free* ⊙ *Daily 8–sunset.*

★ ⑮ Known for having one of the deepest springs in the world, **Wakulla Springs State Park** remains relatively untouched, retaining the wild and exotic look it had in the 1930s, when Tarzan movies were made here. Take a glass-bottom boat deep into the lush, jungle-lined waterways to catch glimpses of alligators, snakes, nesting limpkins, and other waterfowl. An underground river flows into a pool so clear that you can see the bottom more than 100 ft below. The park is 15 mi south of Tallahassee on Route 61. If you can't pull yourself away from this idyllic spot, rest the evening in the 1930s lodge. ⊠ *550 Wakulla Park Dr., Wakulla Springs* ☎ *850/922–3632* ⊡ *$3.25 per vehicle (up to 8 people), boat tour $4.50* ⊙ *Daily 8–sunset, boat tours hourly 9:15–4:30.*

⑯ As its name suggests, **St. Marks National Wildlife Refuge and Lighthouse** is of both natural and historical interest. The once-powerful Fort San Marcos de Apalache was built nearby in 1639, and stones salvaged from the fort were used in the lighthouse, which is still in operation. In winter the refuge is the resting place for thousands of migratory birds, but the alligators seem to like it year-round. The visitor center has information on more than 75 mi of marked trails, some of which wend through landscapes with foliage more reminiscent of North Carolina than Florida. Twenty-five miles south of Tallahassee, the refuge can be reached via Route 363. ⊠ *1255 Lighthouse Rd., St. Marks* ☎ *850/925–6424* ⊡ *$4 per vehicle* ⊙ *Refuge daily sunrise–sunset; visitor center weekdays 8–4, weekends 10–5.*

Spreading north of Apalachicola and west of Tallahassee and U.S. 319 is the **Apalachicola National Forest,** with campsites, hiking trails, picnic areas, and plentiful lakes for old-fashioned swimmin'. Honor-system fees range from $3 admission to $8 camping. ☎ *850/643–2282.*

CANOEING **TNT Hideaway** (⊠ U.S. 98 at the Wakulla River, St. Marks ☎ 850/925–6412), 18 mi south of Tallahassee, arranges canoe trips on the spring-fed Wakulla River. An average trek takes about three hours, and a four-hour canoe rental for two costs $20.

WHERE TO STAY & EAT ¢–$ ✕⊞ **Wakulla Springs Lodge and Conference Center.** Built in 1937, this is a preserved piece of Florida history on the grounds of Wakulla Springs State Park. There is a huge fireplace in the lobby; broad, painted Moorish-style beams across the ceiling; and cozy, if spartan, rooms. Activities are at a minimum, so if you put relaxation at a premium, this might be your place. The facility serves three meals a day in a sunny, simple room that seems little changed from the 1930s. Schedule lunch here to sample the famous bean soup, home-baked muffins, and a slab of pie. In the soda shop, order a "ginger yip" (ice cream, whipped cream, and ginger ale) or buy a wind-up toy alligator as a memento of your stay. ⊠ *550 Wakulla Park Dr., Wakulla Springs* ☎ *850/224–5950* 🖷 *850/561–7251* 🖙 *27 rooms* ⚭ *Restaurant, beach* 🖃 *AE, D, MC, V.*

THE PANHANDLE A TO Z

To research prices, get advice from other travelers, and book travel arrangements, visit www.fodors.com.

AIR TRAVEL

CARRIERS Pensacola Regional Airport is served by Air Tran, Continental, Delta, and US Airways. Okaloosa County Regional Airport is served by Atlantic Southeast, Delta, Northwest, and US Airways Express. Panama City–Bay County International Airport is served by Delta Connection, Northwest Airlink, and US Airways Express. Tallahassee Regional Airport is served by AirTran, Atlantic Southeast/Delta, Delta, Delta Connection, Skywest, and US Airways Express.

🚹 Airlines & Contacts **AirTran** ☎ 800/247-8726. **Continental** ☎ 800/523-3273. **Delta** ☎ 800/221-1212. **Northwest** ☎ 800/225-2525. **Northwest Airlink** ☎ 800/225-2525. **US Airways/US Airways Express** ☎ 800/428-4322.

AIRPORTS

AIRPORT TRANSFERS A trip from Pensacola Regional Airport via Yellow Cab costs about $13 to downtown and $22 to Pensacola Beach. A ride from the Okaloosa County Regional Airport via Checker Cab costs $18 to Fort Walton Beach and $24 to Destin. Bluewater Car Service charges $15 to Fort Walton Beach and $24 to Destin. Yellow Cab charges about $15–$27 from Panama City–Bay County International Airport to the beach area, depending on the location of your hotel. DeLuxe Coach Limo Service provides van service to downtown Panama City and to Panama City Beach for $1.25 per mile. Yellow Cab travels from Tallahassee Regional Airport to downtown for $12–$15. Some Tallahassee hotels provide free shuttle service.

🚹 Airport Information **Okaloosa County Regional Airport** ☎ 850/651-7160 ⊕ www.co.okaloosa.fl.us. **Panama City-Bay County International Airport** ☎ 850/763-6751 ⊕ www.pcairport.com. **Pensacola Regional Airport** ☎ 850/436-5005 ⊕ www.flypensacola.com/airlines.asp. **Tallahassee Regional Airport** ☎ 850/891-7800 ⊕ www.ci.tallahassee.fl.us/citytlh/aviation.

🚹 Airport Transportation Contacts **American Cab** ☎ 850/244-4491. **Bluewater Car Service** ☎ 850/837-9141. **DeLuxe Coach Limo Service** ☎ 850/763-0211. **Yellow Cab** ☎ 850/763-4691 or 850/222-3070 in Pensacola; 850/763-4691 or 850/222-3070 in Panama City; 850/763-4691 or 850/222-3070 in Tallahassee.

BUS TRAVEL

Greyhound has stations in Crestview, DeFuniak Springs, Fort Walton Beach, Panama City, Pensacola, and Tallahassee. The Baytown Trolley serves Bay County including downtown Panama City (50¢) and the beaches ($1). The Old Town Trolley in Tallahassee offers free downtown transportation from the Visitor Information Center at 106 East Jefferson Street. In Pensacola, Escambia County Area Transit (ECAT) provides regular city-wide bus service ($1), downtown trolley routes, tours through the historic district (25¢), and from Memorial Day to Labor Day free trolley service on Friday, Saturday, and Sunday.

🚌 Bus Information Baytown Trolley ☎ 850/769-0557. **Escambia County Area Transit** ☎ 850/595-3228. **Greyhound Lines** ☎ 800/231-2222; 850/682-6922 in Crestview; 850/892-5566 in DeFuniak Springs; 850/243-1940 in Fort Walton Beach; 850/785-7861 in Panama City; 850/785-6111 in Panama City; 850/476-4800 in Pensacola; 850/222-4240 in Tallahassee. **Old Town Trolley** ☎ 850/891-5200.

CAR RENTAL

🚗 Alamo ☎ 800/462-5266. **Avis** ☎ 800/331-1212. **Budget** ☎ 800/527-7000. **Hertz** ☎ 800/654-3131. **National** ☎ 800/227-7368.

CAR TRAVEL

The main east–west arteries across the top of the state are I–10 and U. S. 90. Pensacola is about an hour's drive east of Mobile. Tallahassee is 3½ hours west of Jacksonville. It takes about four hours from Pensacola to Tallahassee. Driving along I–10 can be monotonous, but U.S. 90 piques your interest by routing you along the main streets of several county seats. U.S. 98 snakes eastward along the coast, splitting into 98 and 98A at Inlet Beach before rejoining at Panama City and continuing down to Port St. Joe and Apalachicola. The view of the gulf from U.S. 98 can be breathtaking, especially at sunset, but ongoing construction projects, frequent 35 mph speed limits, and growing congestion make it slow going most of the time. If you need to get from one end of the Panhandle to the other in a timely manner, you're better off driving inland to I–10, where the speed limit runs as high as 70 mph in places. Even with the extra time it takes to drive inland, you'll wind up getting where you need to go much more quickly. Route 399 between Pensacola Beach and Navarre Beach takes you down Santa Rosa Island, a spit of duneland that juts out into the turquoise and jade waters of the Gulf of Mexico. It's a scenic drive if the day is clear; otherwise, it's a study in gray. Major north–south highways that weave through the Panhandle are (from east to west) U.S. 231, U.S. 331, Route 85, and U.S. 29. From U.S. 331, which runs over a causeway at the east end of Choctawhatchee Bay between Route 20 and U.S. 98, the panorama of barge traffic and cabin cruisers on the twinkling waters of the Intracoastal Waterway will get your attention.

EMERGENCIES

🚑 Ambulance or Police Emergencies ☎ 911.

🚑 24-Hour Medical Care Destin Urgent Care and Diagnostic Center ✉ 996 Airport Rd., Destin ☎ 850/837-9194. **Fort Walton Beach Medical Center** ✉ 1000 Mar-Walt Dr., Fort Walton Beach ☎ 850/862-1111. **Gulf Coast Medical Center** ✉ 449 W. 23rd St., Panama City ☎ 850/769-8341. **Tallahassee Memorial Hospital** ✉ Magnolia Dr. and Miccosukee Rd., Tallahassee ☎ 850/431-1155. **West Florida Regional Medical Center** ✉ 8383 N. Davis Hwy., Pensacola ☎ 850/494-4000.

MEDIA

NEWSPAPERS & MAGAZINES Check *The Weekender,* the weekly entertainment magazine of the *Pensacola News Journal,* or the *Pensacola Downtown Crowd* to find out what's happening around the region and in the historic district. For the latest information in the Destin and Fort Walton areas, look for the *Emerald Coast's Insider Magazine. Chuck Spicer's Coast Line* (⊕ www. ForgottenCoastLine.com) offers an informative and offbeat perspective on Florida's "Forgotten Coast" between Mexico Beach in Bay County and St. Marks in Wakulla County. In Tallahasse, the entertainment section of the *Tallahassee Democrat* is the most comprehensive local arts and entertainment guide.

TELEVISION & RADIO
Try WMEZ 94.1 for soft rock, WWRO 100.7 for classic rock, WXBM 102 for country, and WUWF 88.1 public radio for opera, classical, jazz, and NPR.

TRAIN TRAVEL
Amtrak connects the Panhandle to the east and west coasts via the transcontinental *Sunset Limited* route, with station stops in Pensacola, Crestview, and Tallahassee.
🚆 Train Information **Amtrak** ☎ 800/872-7245.

VISITOR INFORMATION
The Apalachicola Bay Chamber of Commerce is open weekdays 9:30–4. The Beaches of South Walton Visitor Information Center is open daily 8–5:30. The Destin Chamber of Commerce and the Walton County Chamber of Commerce are open weekdays from 8 or 9 to 4 or 5. The Emerald Coast Convention & Visitors Bureau, Panama City Beach Convention & Visitor Bureau, and Pensacola Visitor Information Center are open daily from 8 or 9 to 4 or 5. The Tallahassee Area Convention and Visitors Bureau is open weekdays 8–5 and Saturday 9–noon. The Panhandle is blessed with many beautiful areas that are being preserved as parks by the state of Florida. Check out the Florida Department of Environmental Protection's excellent parks Web site for hours and admission fees, as well as photos and brief histories of the parks.
🚆 Tourist Information **Apalachicola Bay Chamber of Commerce** ✉ 99 Market St., Apalachicola 32320 ☎ 850/653-9419 ⊕ www.apalachicolabay.org. **Beaches of South Walton Visitor Information Center** ✉ U.S. 331 and U.S. 98, Santa Rosa Beach 32459 ☎ 850/267-1216 or 800/822-6877 ⊕ www.beachesofsouthwalton.com. **DeFuniak Springs Visitors Bureau** ✉ 1162 Circle Dr., DeFuniak Springs 32433 ☎ 850/892-3191. **Destin Chamber of Commerce** ✉ 1021 U.S. 98 E, Destin 32541 ☎ 850/837-6241 or 850/837-2711 ⊕ www.destinchamber.com. **Emerald Coast Convention & Visitors Bureau** ✉ 1540 Miracle Strip Pkwy. SE, Fort Walton Beach 32548 ☎ 850/651-7122 or 800/322-3319 ⊕ www.destin-fwb.com. **Florida Department of Environmental Protection–Parks Division** ☎ 850/488-9872 Help Line ⊕ www.dep.state.fl.us/parks. **Panama City Beach Convention & Visitor Bureau** ✉ 17001 Panama City Beach Pkwy., Panama City Beach 32413 ☎ 850/233-6503 or 800/722-3224 ⊕ www.800pcbeach.com. **Pensacola Visitor Information Center** ✉ 1401 E. Gregory St., Pensacola 32501 ☎ 850/434-1234 or 800/874-1234 ⊕ www.visitpensacola.com. **Tallahassee Area Convention and Visitors Bureau** ✉ 106 E. Jefferson St., Tallahassee 32301 ☎ 850/413-9200 or 800/628-2866 ⊕ www.seetallahassee.com. **Walton County Chamber of Commerce** ✉ 95 Circle Dr., DeFuniak Springs 32433 ☎ 850/892-3191 ⊕ www.waltoncountychamber.com.

WHERE TO STAY
In the Beaches of South Walton, two of the larger vacation-rental management companies that handle furnished rentals and offer free vacation guides are Abbott Resorts and Rivard of South Walton. On St. George Island, fully furnished homes can be rented through Coldwell Banker Suncoast Realty and Prudential Resort Realty.

APARTMENT & VILLA RENTALS
🚆 Local Agents **Abbott Resorts** ☎ 800/336-4853 ⊕ www.abbott-resorts.com. **Coldwell Banker Suncoast Realty** ☎ 800/341-2021 ⊕ www.uncommonflorida.com. **Prudential Resort Realty** ☎ 800/332-5196 ⊕ www.stgeorgeisland.com. **Rivard of South Walton** ☎ 800/423-3215 ⊕ www.rivardnet.com.

NORTHEAST FLORIDA

10

FODOR'S CHOICE

The Grill, Amelia Island

The Lodge & Club, Ponte Vedra Beach

Ponte Vedra Inn & Club, Ponte Vedra Beach

The Ritz-Carlton Amelia Island

Toni and Joe's, New Smyrna Beach

HIGHLY RECOMMENDED

WHAT TO SEE   Amelia Island Historic District

Castillo de San Marcos National Monument, St. Augustine

Fort Clinch State Park, Fernandina Beach

Kennedy Space Center Visitor Complex, Cocoa Beach

Lightner Museum, St. Augustine

Paynes Prairie State Preserve, Micanopy

Talbot Island State Parks, Talbot Island

*Many other great hotels and restaurants enliven this area. For other fa-
vorites, look for the black stars as you read this chapter.*

Updated by
Nancy Orr
Athnos

SOME OF THE OLDEST SETTLEMENTS in the state—indeed in all of the United States—are in northeastern Florida, although the region didn't get much attention until the Union army came through during the Civil War. The soldiers' rapturous accounts of the mild climate, pristine beaches, and lush vegetation captured the imagination of folks up north. First came the speculators and the curiosity seekers. Then the advent of the railroads brought more permanent settlers and the first wave of winter vacationers. Finally, the automobile transported the full rush of snowbirds, seasonal residents escaping from harsh northern winters. They still come, to sop up sun on the beach, to tee up year-round, to bass-fish and bird-watch in forests and parks, and to party in the clubs and bars of Daytona, a popular spring-break destination. The region is remarkably diverse. Tortured, towering live oaks; plantations; and antebellum-style architecture recollect the Old South. The mossy marshes of Silver Springs and the St. Johns River look as untouched and junglelike today as they did generations ago. Horse farms around Ocala resemble Kentucky's bluegrass country or the hunt clubs of Virginia. St. Augustine is a showcase of early U.S. history, and Jacksonville is a young but sophisticated metropolis. Yet these are all but light diversions from northeastern Florida's primary draw—absolutely sensational beaches. Hugging the coast are long, slender barrier islands whose entire eastern sides make up a broad band of spectacular sand. Except in the most populated areas, development has been modest, and beaches are lined with funky, appealing little towns.

Exploring Northeast Florida

The region defies any single description. Much of its tourist territory lies along the Atlantic coast, both on the mainland and on the barrier islands just offshore. A1A (mostly called Atlantic Avenue) is the main road on all the barrier islands, and it's here that you find the best beaches. Both Jacksonville, the region's only real high-rise city, and the relatively remote Amelia Island, just south of the Georgia border, are in the far northeast. St. Augustine, about a 45-minute drive south of Jacksonville on I–95, is the historic capital of this part of Florida. Farther south along the coast, the diversity continues among neighbors like Daytona Beach, where annual events are geared toward spring-breakers, auto racers, and bikers; New Smyrna Beach, which offers quiet appeal; and Cocoa Beach, the ultimate boogie-board beach town. Inland are charming small towns, the sprawling Ocala National Forest, and bustling Gainesville, home of the University of Florida.

About the Restaurants

The ocean, the Intracoastal Waterway, and numerous lakes and rivers are teeming with fish, and so, naturally, seafood dominates local menus. In coastal towns, catches are often from the restaurant's own fleet. Shrimp, snapper, swordfish, and grouper are especially popular.

About the Hotels

In the busy seasons—during the summer around Jacksonville, and during holiday weekends in summer all over Florida—always reserve ahead for the top properties. Fall is the slowest season: rates are low and availability is high, but this is also the prime time for hurricanes. St. Augustine stays busy all year because of its historic character.

WHAT IT COSTS					
	$$$$	**$$$**	**$$**	**$**	**¢**
RESTAURANTS	over $30	$20–$30	$15–$20	$10–$15	under $10
HOTELS	over $220	$140–$220	$100–$140	$80–$100	under $80

Restaurant prices are per person for a main course at dinner. Hotel prices are for a standard double room, excluding 6% sales tax (more in some counties) and 1%–4% tourist tax.

Timing

The fair weather is one of the many factors drawing residents to the area. The temperature dips slightly below 60 in winter and hovers around 80 in summer. February is the height of the auto-racing season in Daytona. The ocean warms up by March, when college kids on spring break often pack the beaches—but this is also the best month to see the azalea gardens in bloom. Midsummer is breezy and hot as long as you stick to the beaches; inland, the summer heat and humidity can be stifling.

JACKSONVILLE TO AMELIA ISLAND

The northeasternmost corner of Florida is a land of tall pine trees, red earth reminiscent of neighboring Georgia, and coastal marshes. It can be 20 degrees colder than Miami in winter, and the "season" here (and the most expensive room rates) runs from April to September. Jacksonville is the hub of this area; the communities to the east serve as its beaches. To the north is Amelia Island and its old seaport town, Fernandina Beach.

Jacksonville

①–⑥ *399 mi north of Miami.*

One of Florida's oldest cities and, in terms of square mi (730), the largest U.S. city, Jacksonville makes for an underrated vacation spot. It offers appealing downtown riverside areas, handsome residential neighborhoods, the region's only skyscrapers, a thriving arts scene, and, for football fans, the NFL Jaguars. (The city has been chosen to host the 2005 Super Bowl.) Remnants of the Old South flavor the city, as does the sense of subtropical paradise for which Florida is famous.

Exploring Jacksonville

Because Jacksonville was settled along both sides of the twisting St. Johns River, many attractions are on or near a riverbank. Both sides of the river, which is spanned by myriad bridges, have downtown areas and waterfront complexes of shops, restaurants, parks, and museums; some attractions can be reached by water taxi, a handy alternative to driving back and forth across the bridges, but a car is generally necessary.

Numbers in the text correspond to numbers in the margin and on the Jacksonville map.

③ Boehm, Royal Copenhagen, and Bing and Grondahlporcelains are among the collections at the **Alexander Brest Museum**, at Jacksonville University. Also on display are cloisonné pieces, pre-Columbian artifacts, and one of the finest collections of ivory from the early 17th to the late 19th century. The home of composer Frederick Delius, moved to the campus years ago, has tours on request. ⊠ *Jacksonville University, Phillips Fine Arts Bldg., 2800 University Blvd.* ☎ *904/744-3950 Ext. 3371* ☜ *Free* ☉ *Weekdays 9–4:30, Sat. noon–5.*

④ The **Jacksonville Museum of Modern Art** showcases a permanent collection of 20th-century art as well as traveling exhibitions in its loftlike

Numbers in the text correspond to numbers in the margin and on the Northeast Florida and St. Augustine maps.

If you have
3 days

Spend your first night in ⊞ **Jacksonville** ❶ ⌐–❻, using it as a base to explore the **Jacksonville Museum of Modern Art** ❹ or the **Cummer Museum of Art and Gardens** ❻, as well as Fort Clinch State Park on **Amelia Island** ❾, which has one of the best-preserved brick forts in the United States. Take Interstate 95 south to **St. Augustine** ❿–㉙ and see the restored **Spanish Quarter Village** ⑭ and the **Castillo de San Marcos National Monument** ⑮ before continuing down the coast. Enjoy Canaveral National Seashore—accessible from either ⊞ **New Smyrna Beach** ㉜ or ⊞ **Cocoa Beach** ㉝— and don't miss the Kennedy Space Center Visitor Complex.

If you have
5 days

Before leaving **Jacksonville** ❶ ⌐–❻ try to visit the three largest museums, the **Museum of Modern Art** ❹, the **Cummer Museum** ❻, and the **Museum of Science and History** ❺. Then focus your sightseeing on **Amelia Island** ❾, including its historic district and Fort Clinch State Park. Going south on Interstate 95, stop in **St. Augustine** ❿–㉙. Follow the Old City Walking Tour suggested by the **Visitor Information and Preview Center** ⑪ and stroll through the restored **Spanish Quarter Village** ⑭. Consider taking the slightly longer but more scenic Route A1A to **Daytona Beach** ㉛; visit the Museum of Arts and Sciences and the famous beaches. For your last night, stay in ⊞ **New Smyrna Beach** ㉜ or ⊞ **Cocoa Beach** ㉝, both within reach of Canaveral National Seashore and Kennedy Space Center.

If you have
10 days

As in the previous two itineraries, start in ⊞ **Jacksonville** ❶ ⌐–❻ and visit the attractions mentioned above; by staying three nights, however, you'll have time to make the drive north to Kingsley Plantation, Florida's oldest remaining plantation, on Fort George Island, and hike or picnic in Fort Clinch State Park on **Amelia Island** ❾. Next, head to ⊞ **St. Augustine** ❿–㉙. Three days here enables you to conduct a more leisurely exploration of the extensive historic district and to take in the **Lightner Museum** ⑱, in what was originally one of Henry Flagler's fancy hotels. Another three-day stay, this time based at ⊞ **Daytona Beach** ㉛, ⊞ **New Smyrna Beach** ㉜, or ⊞ **Cocoa Beach** ㉝, allows you to cover Daytona's Museum of Arts and Sciences, drive along the shoreline, spend some time at the beach, and see Canaveral National Seashore and the Kennedy Space Center Visitor Complex. Then head inland for a day in **Ocala National Forest** ㊱, a beautiful wilderness area.

---

building, which is the former headquarters of the Western Union Telegraph Company. The museum also has special exhibits, film and lecture series, and workshops. ⊠ *Hemming Plaza, 333 N. Laura St.* ☎ *904/366–6911* ⊕ *www.jmoma.org* ⊠ *$6* ☉ *Tues.–Wed. and Fri.–Sat. 10–6, Thurs. 10–9, Sun. noon–4 (subject to change).*

🐾 ❺ Permanent exhibits at the **Museum of Science and History** range from those on pre-Columbian history and the ecology and history of the St. Johns River to the Maple Leaf Civil War Collection, the hands-on Kidspace section, and a display on whales, dolphins, and manatees. A fascinating exhibit chronicles 12,000 years of northeast Florida history. The ever-changing special exhibits are usually excellent. Physical-science shows are held weekends in the science theater. The Alexander Brest Planetarium has a popular 3-D laser show and many starry presentations throughout the year. ⊠ *1025 Museum Circle* ☎ *904/396–6674* ⊕ *www.themosh. org.* ☒ *$7.50* ⊙ *Weekdays 10–5, Sat. 10–6, Sun. 1–6.*

❻ The world-famous Wark Collection of early 18th-century Meissen porcelain is just one reason to see the **Cummer Museum of Art and Gardens.** This former baron's estate includes 12 permanent galleries, with more than 2,000 items spanning over 4,000 years; an interactive teaching gallery for children and adults; and 3 acres of gardens. ⊠ *829 Riverside Ave.* ☎ *904/356–6857* ⊕ *www.cummer.org* ☒ *$6, free Tues. 4–9* ⊙ *Tues. and Thurs. 10–9, Wed. and Fri.–Sat. 10–5.*

▶ ❶ If you're a beer connoisseur, don't miss a guided or self-guided tour of the **Anheuser–Busch Jacksonville Brewery,** which takes you through the entire brewing and bottling process. There are free beer tastings and logo-filled gift shops. ⊠ *111 Busch Dr.* ☎ *904/696–8373* ⊕ *www. budweisertours.com* ☒ *Free* ⊙ *Mon.–Sat. 9–4:30; guided tours Mon.–Sat. 10–3 on the hr; self-guided tours Mon.–Sat. 9–4.*

☝ ❷ Among the **Jacksonville Zoo**'s outstanding exhibits is its collection of rare waterfowl and the Serona Overlook, which showcases some of the world's most venomous snakes. The Florida Wetlands is a 2½-acre area with black bears, bald eagles, white-tailed deer, and other animals native to Florida. The African Veldt has alligators, elephants, and white rhinos, among other species of African birds and mammals. Kids get a kick out of the petting zoo, and everyone goes bananas over Great Apes of the World. Private, "behind the scenes" one-hour walking tours let you see the buffalo, rhino, and elephant barns; the fee is $20 and two weeks' advance notice is required. ⊠ *8605 Zoo Rd., off Heckscher Dr. E* ☎ *904/757–4463* ⊕ *www.jaxzoo.org.* ☒ *$9.50* ⊙ *Daily 9–5.*

> **off the beaten path**

Fort Caroline National Memorial. Spread over 130 acres along the St. Johns River 13 mi northeast of downtown Jacksonville (via Route 113), this place holds both historical and recreational interest. The original fort was built in the 1560s by French Huguenots, who were later slaughtered by the Spanish in the first major clash between European powers for control of what would become the United States. An oak-wooded pathway leads to a replica of the original fort—a great, sunny place to picnic (bring your own food and drink), stretch your legs, and explore a small museum. There is also a 1-mi self-guided trail with signs describing natural and cultural history. ⊠ *12713 Fort Caroline Rd.* ☎ *904/641–7155* ⊕ *www.nps.gov/foca* ☒ *Free* ⊙ *Museum daily 9–5.*

Where to Stay & Eat

$$$–$$$$ ✕ **Wilfried's 24 Miramar.** Hidden in a small shopping center on the south side of the river is this long, narrow restaurant, stylish in minimalist black and white. Nightly specials dominate the menu and may include pork tenderloin basted with Caribbean spices and dark rum. The hallmark dish is Seafood Beggar's Purse, a medley of lobster, scallops, shrimp, salmon, and shiitake mushrooms wrapped in phyllo pastry with a brandied lobster cream sauce. For dessert try the poached apple, stuffed with walnuts and chocolate and baked in a puffed pastry. ⊠ *Miramar Shopping Center, 4446 Hendricks Ave., San Marco* ☎ *904/448–2424* ☐ *AE, DC, MC, V* ⊙ *Closed Sun. No lunch.*

$$–$$$$ ✕ **River City Brewing Company.** Take one of the free daily brewery tours (by appointment only) at this popular brewpub overlooking the river

10

Beaches

The northeast has luxuriously long beaches. Some are hard-packed white sand, while others have slightly reddish sand with a coarse, grainy texture. Waves are normally gentle, and many areas are safe for swimming. However, take care when the surf is up and obey lifeguard instructions. The very fragile dunes, held in place by sea grasses, are responsible for protecting the shore from the sea; Florida law mandates that you neither pick the sea oats nor walk on or play in the dunes. A single afternoon of careless roughhousing can destroy a dune forever. The area's most densely developed beaches, with rows of high-rise condominiums and hotels, are in Daytona and Cocoa Beach. Elsewhere, coastal towns are still mostly small and laid-back, and beaches are crowded only on summer weekends.

Bird-Watching

Florida's diverse habitat is a bird-watcher's haven. The wetlands, marshes, and warm weather attract hundreds of migratory birds, many of which are rare and seldom seen. The Great Florida Birding Trail (www.floridabirdingtrail.com), a program of the Florida Fish and Wildlife Conservation Commission, maps out Northeast Florida's best birding locations. What you can see through your binoculars depends on the season, location, and time of day.

Canoeing

Canoeing is excellent here. Inland, especially in Ocala National Forest, sparkling-clear spring "runs" may be mere tunnels through tangled jungle growth. Grassy marshes near the coast and the maze of shallow inlets along the inland waterway side of Canaveral National Seashore are other favored canoeing spots.

Fishing

From cane-pole fishing in a roadside canal to throwing a line off a pier to deep-sea fishing from a luxury charter boat, options abound. There's no charge (or a nominal one) to fish from many causeways, beaches, and piers. Deep-sea fishing charters are available up and down the coast.

Skydiving

DeLand is the skydiving capital of the world. Spectators can watch high-flying competitions, while those interested in swooping down from an airplane from thousands of feet up can try solo or tandem jumping.

---

and then sample the day's brew. Lunch leans toward sandwiches and salads; dinner selections include shrimp, fresh fish, grilled steaks, and seafood jambalaya. A DJ spins tunes Friday and Saturday nights. Sunday brunch is a scrumptious event. If you miss brunch, catch the Sunday-night seafood buffet. ⊠ *835 Museum Circle Dr., Southbank Riverwalk* ☎ *904/398–2299* ⊟ *AE, D, DC, MC, V.*

$$–$$$ ✕ **Bistro Aix.** Locals head for the patio for a delightful candlelight dinner when the weather is nice; indoors, there are romantic velvet drapes and exposed brick walls. Try the grilled salmon or filet mignon. Crispy thin-crust pizzas, baked in the wood-burning oven, pastas, and salads are among the lighter choices. Belgian chocolate cake, served warm and topped with vanilla whipped cream, caps a perfect evening. ⊠ *1440 San Marco Blvd., San Marco* ☎ *904/398–1949* ⊟ *AE, D, DC, MC, V* ⊘ *No lunch weekends.*

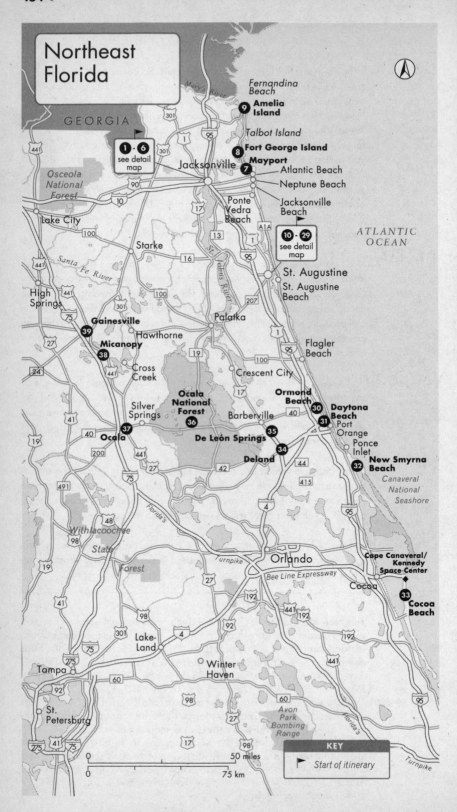

★ **$$–$$$** ✗ **Matthew's.** Chef-owner Matthew Medure creates masterpieces in one of Jacksonville's trendiest neighborhoods. The dramatically spare decor—stainless steel, polished bronze, and terrazzo flooring—is a perfect foil for his dazzling food. The menu changes nightly but might include lemon-roasted Amish chicken with honey-truffle spaghetti squash or herb-roasted rack of lamb with mustard pistachio crust. Try one of the baked warm soufflés for dessert. ⊠ *2107 Hendricks Ave., San Marco* ☎ *904/ 396–9922* ⊟ *AE, D, DC, MC, V* ⊘ *Closed Sun. No lunch.*

$$–$$$ ✗ **Wine Cellar.** Tables are well spaced in cozy dining areas on several levels and on an outdoor patio in this elegant candlelit spot with exposed brick walls. Diners return for such dishes as filet mignon served over a potato-leek and Asiago tart, topped with wild mushroom demi-glace. Chocolate truffle torte, key lime pie, and cheesecake du jour are dessert highlights. The wine list includes more than 225 choices. ⊠ *1314 Prudential Dr., San Marco* ☎ *904/398–8989* ⊟ *AE, DC, MC, V* ⊘ *Closed Sun. No lunch Sat.*

$–$$ ✗ **Biscottis.** The local artwork on the redbrick walls is a mild distraction from the jovial crowds jockeying for tables in this midsize restaurant. Elbows almost touch, but no one seems to mind. The menu offers such unexpected combinations as wild-mushroom ravioli with a broth of corn, leek, and dried apricot; or seared fillet of beef with red-onion marmalade and caramelized pear–and–English Stilton bread pudding. Look for the daily specials, which are equally creative. ⊠ *3556 St. Johns Ave., Avondale* ☎ *904/387–2060* ⊟ *AE, MC, V* ⊘ *No dinner Sun.*

$$$ ▦ **Embassy Suites Hotel.** The Baymeadows location puts this six-story, all-suites hotel near some "in" restaurants, clubs, and shops. All units overlook the atrium. Each has a separate living room with sleep sofa, a refrigerator, and a microwave. Rates are a real value and include a cooked-to-order breakfast and a two-hour cocktail reception on weekdays. ⊠ *9300 Baymeadows Rd., Southside, 32256* ☎ *904/731–3555 or 800/362–2779* 🖷 *904/731–4972* ⊕ *www.embassysuitesjax.com* ⇰ *277 suites ⚗ Restaurant, room service, in-room data ports, kitchenettes, microwaves, refrigerators, cable TV with movies, indoor pool, fitness room, hot tub, sauna, bar, lounge, dry cleaning, laundry facilities, laundry service, business services, meeting rooms, free parking; no-smoking rooms* ⊟ *AE, DC, MC, V* ¶⊙ *BP.*

★ **$$–$$$** ▦ **Hilton Jacksonville Riverfront.** Sitting on the water, this handsome eight-story hotel has a commanding presence. Its location on the south side of the St. Johns River puts it within easy walking distance of museums, restaurants, and the water taxi; Ruth's Chris Steak House is one of the on-site restaurants. Rooms are spacious, and many have outstanding river views and balconies. Celebrate a special occasion aboard the hotel's private yacht, the *Jacksonville Princess.* ⊠ *1201 Riverplace Blvd., 32207* ☎ *904/398–8800* 🖷 *904/398–9170* ⊕ *www. jacksonvillehilton.com* ⇰ *292 rooms ⚗ 2 restaurants, room service, in-room data ports, cable TV with movies and video games, pool, gym, outdoor hot tub, 2 bars, shop, dry cleaning, laundry service, Internet, business services, meeting rooms, parking (fee); no-smoking rooms* ⊟ *AE, D, MC, V.*

$$–$$$ ▦ **Radisson Riverwalk Hotel.** The Riverwalk complex connects to this bustling five-story hotel. Rooms are done in blond wood with pastel striped fabrics and have either a king-size or two double beds. Four restaurants, a museum, and the water taxi to Jacksonville Landing are within walking distance. Units overlooking the St. Johns River command the highest prices. ⊠ *1515 Prudential Dr., 32207* ☎ *904/396–5100 or 800/333– 3333* 🖷 *904/396–7154* ⊕ *www.radisson.com/jacksonvillefl* ⇰ *322 rooms, 13 suites ⚗ Restaurant, in-room data ports, cable TV, tennis court,*

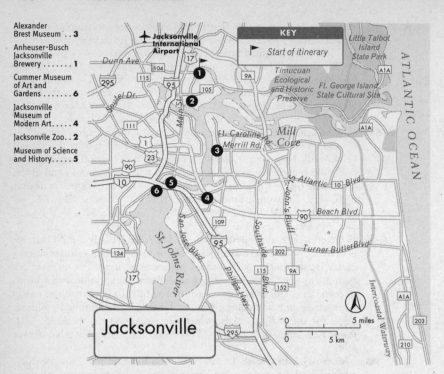

Jacksonville

pool, fitness room, gym, bar, Internet, business services, meeting rooms, free parking; no-smoking rooms ☰ *AE, DC, MC, V.*

★ **$–$$$** ⌂ **Omni Jacksonville Hotel.** The 16-story ultramodern facility is in the heart of downtown. The splashy marble-floor lobby leads to the reception area, an upscale bar and lounge, and a restaurant with cozy banquettes and tables that look up to a soaring atrium; Sunday brunch is popular here. Many of the stylish, extra-large rooms have views of the St. Johns River. ✉ *245 Water St., 32202* ☎ *904/355–6664 or 800/843–6664* 🖷 *904/791–4809* ⊕ *www.omnijacksonville.com* ➥ *354 rooms, 4 suites* ᕫ *Restaurant, room service, in-room data ports, minibars, cable TV with movies and video games, pool, exercise equipment, gym, bar, shop, children's programs (ages 3–10), dry cleaning, laundry service, concierge, Internet, meeting rooms, parking (fee), some pets allowed (fee); no-smoking rooms* ☰ *AE, D, DC, MC, V.*

$$ ⌂ **House on Cherry Street.** Pewter, Oriental rugs, antique canopy beds, and other remnants of a rich past furnish this early 20th-century treasure. Afternoon tea doesn't come any fresher. Select your favorite blend from owner Victoria Freeman's own tea garden and have it brewed right on the spot. Fresh flowers in rooms are a nice touch. The parks and gardens of the chic Avondale district are a walk away. ✉ *1844 Cherry St., 32205* ☎ *904/384–1999* 🖷 *904/387–4007* ⊕ *www.1bbweb.com/cherry* ➥ *4 rooms, 1 suite* ᕫ *Dining room, fans, some refrigerators, bicycles, croquet, horseshoes, laundry facilities, Internet, meeting rooms, business services, free parking; no kids under 10, no room phones, no smoking, no TV in some rooms* ☰ *AE, MC, V* ⊙ *CP.*

¢ ⌂ **Fairfield Inn Jacksonville.** The convenient Baymeadows location is within easy access to the interstates, making it well liked by business travelers. It's also close to several major thoroughfares and some popular restaurants. Guests receive discounted greens fees. ✉ *8050 Baymeadows Circle W, 32256* ☎ *904/739–0739 or 800/228–2800* 🖷 *904/739–3080* ➥ *102 rooms, 13 suites* ᕫ *In-room data ports, cable TV, 18-hole*

golf course, pool, gym, meeting rooms, free parking; no-smoking rooms.
▭ *AE, D, MC, V.*

Nightlife & the Arts

THE ARTS The **Alhambra Dinner Theater** (✉ 12000 Beach Blvd. ☎ 904/641–1212)
serves up professional theater along with a menu that's often altered with
each new play. Broadway touring shows, top-name entertainers, and other
major events are booked at the **Florida Theater Performing Arts Center**
(✉ 128 E. Forsyth St. ☎ 904/355–5661). The **Jacksonville Symphony Orchestra** (☎ 904/354–5547) performs at the Jacoby Music Hall in the
Times–Union Center for the Performing Arts and gives outdoor concerts
at downtown's Metro Park. The oldest continuously operating community
theater in the United States, **Theatre Jacksonville** (✉ 2032 San Marco Blvd.
☎ 904/396–4425) presents outstanding productions ranging from
Shakespeare to programs for children. The **Times–Union Center for the
Performing Arts** (✉ 300 W. Water St. ☎ 904/630–0701) draws rock
bands, musicals, and children's shows.

NIGHTLIFE Crowds head to **Dave & Buster's** (✉ 7025 Salisbury Rd. ☎ 904/296–1525)
for its huge video-game room and for a part in the "whodunit" at the
mystery theater Saturday night. **57 Heaven** (✉ 8136 Atlantic Blvd.
☎ 904/721–5757) draws a crowd in their forties and fifties with its selection of oldies Wednesday through Saturday nights beginning at 7 PM.
At the **Marquee** (✉ 1028 Park Ave. ☎ 904/355–1119), couples move
to the nightly sounds of alternative high-energy techno and disco music.
River City Brewing Company (✉ 835 Museum Circle Dr., Southbank
Riverwalk ☎ 904/398–2299) showcases live local bands or DJs Thursday through Saturday nights.

Sports & the Outdoors

BASEBALL For some family fun take in a ball game. The **Jacksonville Suns** (✉ Ran-
dolph Blvd. at Adams St. ☎ 904/358–2846), the AA minor-league affiliate of the Los Angeles Dodgers, is in its new $25 million ballpark,
part of the downtown sports complex.

DOG RACING Race seasons are split among two tracks. In town, the **Jacksonville Kennel Club** (✉ 1440 N. McDuff Ave. ☎ 904/646–0001) runs greyhound
races late May through early September. At the **Orange Park Kennel Club**
(✉ ½ mi south of I–295 on U.S. 17 ☎ 904/646–0001), the dogs hit the
track early September through late May.

FOOTBALL The region's blockbuster event is the **Gator Bowl** (✉ Alltell Stadium, One
Stadium Pl. ☎ 904/396–1800), on New Year's Day, during which the
best two college football teams of the season square off. The NFL **Jacksonville Jaguars** (✉ Alltell Stadium, One Stadium Pl. ☎ 904/633–6000;
904/633–2000 for tickets) are incredibly popular locally, but you'll
often be able to find some tickets available outside the stadium right
before game time.

GOLF The **Eagle Harbor Golf Club** (✉ 2217 Eagle Harbor Pkwy., Orange Park
☎ 904/269–9300) has an 18-hole, par-72 course designed by Clyde John-
ston and offers a driving range, club rentals, and discount packages. The
18-hole, 71-par **Golf Club of Jacksonville** (✉ 1440 Tournament La. ☎ 904/
779–0800), 15 mi west of downtown, has a driving range and offers
club rentals. **Windsor Parke Golf Club** (✉ 4747 Hodges Blvd. ☎ 904/223–
4972) offers 18 holes (par 72) on tree-lined fairways and amid natural
marshlands. A driving range, discount packages, and club rentals are
available.

Shopping

Jacksonville Landing (✉ 2 Independent Dr., at Main Street Bridge ☎ 904/
353–1188), on the north side of the river, has unique specialty shops,

as well as some chain branches, and several restaurants with outdoor seating. The **Riverside–Avondale Shopping Center,** in the heart of historic Avondale, is a quiet two-block area bordered by St. Johns Avenue and Highway 17. Here you'll find a number of restaurants, art galleries, and specialty boutiques. At the **San Marco Square Shopping Center** (⊠ 25 San Marco Blvd.), you'll find dozens of interesting stores and restaurants in 1920s Mediterranean revival–style buildings.

Jacksonville Beaches

20 mi east of Jacksonville on U.S. 90 (Beach Blvd.).

Jacksonville's main beaches run along the barrier island that includes the popular, laid-back towns of Jacksonville Beach and Atlantic Beach and the area around Ponte Vedra Beach. The large number of private homes along Ponte Vedra's beaches makes access difficult, however. A favored surfing area is Atlantic Beach; catamaran rentals and instruction are available around the popular Sea Turtle Inn. Five areas have lifeguards on duty in the summer daily 10–6. Neptune Beach, south of Atlantic Beach, is more residential and offers easy access to quieter beaches. Surfers consider it and Atlantic the area's two best surfing sites. Jacksonville Beach is the liveliest; young people flock here for beach volleyball, bicycling, in-line skating, shopping, and bar-hopping.

Where to Stay & Eat

$$–$$$$ ✕ **Gio's Café.** Several levels of dining create intimacy at this art deco–style spot done in black and white. The menu ranges from handmade pasta creations to salmon baked in phyllo; veal piccata (sautéed with white wine, lemon, and capers); and Maine lobster. The signature dish is filet mignon stuffed with roasted garlic and pepper and served with a Portobello cap, port sauce, and blue-cheese butter. ⊠ *900 Sawgrass Village, Ponte Vedra Beach* ☎ *904/273–0101* ⊟ *AE, MC, V* ☉ *No lunch.*

$–$$ ✕ **Lighthouse Grille.** Char-grilled New York strip, filet mignon, giant porterhouse steak, tender prime rib—it's the high-quality beef that draws the dinner crowds to this snappy-looking spot. The dining room has a marble-topped bar and polished hardwood floors; an open-air deck looks out to the Intracoastal Waterway. Local fish and shrimp are on the menu, too, and the sensational house salad, with crumbled bacon, chopped eggs, and almonds, is large enough to be a meal. ⊠ *2600 Beach Blvd., Atlantic Beach* ☎ *904/242–8899* ⊟ *AE, D, DC, MC, V.*

★ **$–$$** ✕ **Ragtime Tavern.** A New Orleans theme prevails at this loud spot popular with a sophisticated young bunch in their twenties and thirties. Bayou bouillabaisse (lobster, shrimp, scallops, fish, crab, clams, and crawfish in a creole court bouillon) and Ragtime Shrimp (deep-fried fresh shrimp rolled in coconut) are the true specialties here. If you aren't into creole and Cajun, try a po'boy sandwich or fish sizzled on the grill. ⊠ *207 Atlantic Blvd., Atlantic Beach* ☎ *904/241–7877* ⊟ *AE, DC, MC, V.*

¢–$$ ✕ **Homestead.** A two-story log cabin built in 1934, this down-home place serving classic southern cooking is always busy. The specialty is skillet-fried chicken with rice and gravy, but newer, regional fare now includes such offerings as crispy Parmesan-crusted rainbow trout, pan-fried Georgia quail, Memphis-style barbecued duck, and low-country braised lamb shank. Sunday brunch is also popular. ⊠ *1712 Beach Blvd., Jacksonville Beach* ☎ *904/249–9660* ⊟ *AE, D, MC, V* ☉ *No lunch.*

$$$$ 🖼 **The Lodge & Club.** The Spanish roof tiles and white-stucco exterior
Fodor's Choice yield a look that's Mediterranean-villa grand luxe at this spot, a sister
★ property of the Ponte Vedra Inn & Club. Rooms are classy and elegant and have cozy window seats, appealing artwork, and private balconies overlooking the Atlantic; some units include a whirlpool tub and gas fireplace. The restaurant, the bar, and the heated pools offer more ocean

views. ✉ 607 *Ponte Vedra Blvd., Ponte Vedra Beach 32080* ☎ *904/273–9500 or 800/243–4304* 🖷 *904/273–0210* ⊕ *www.pvresorts.com* 📲 *42 rooms, 24 suites ⚒ 1 restaurant, fans, in-room data ports, in-room safes, some in-room hot tubs, some kitchenettes, minibars, some refrigerators, cable TV, golf privileges, 4 pools, fitness classes, gym, health club, hot tub, spa, beach, boating, fishing, bicycles, bar, lounge, shops, children's programs (ages 4–12), playground, laundry service, meeting rooms, free parking; no-smoking rooms* ▭ *AE, D, DC, MC, V.*

$$$$
Fodor'sChoice
★

🏨 **Ponte Vedra Inn & Club.** Accommodations at this 1928 landmark country-club resort are in a series of white-stucco Spanish-style buildings lining the beach; rooms are extra-large, and most have ocean views. The main house holds the registration area and some common spaces, including a big living room with fireplace. ✉ *200 Ponte Vedra Blvd., Ponte Vedra Beach 32082* ☎ *904/285–1111 or 800/234–7842,* 🖷 *904/285–2111,* ⊕ *www.pvresorts.com* 📲 *194 rooms, 27 suites ⚒ 3 restaurants, 3 snack bars, fans, in-room data ports, in-room safes, some in-room hot tubs, some kitchenettes, minibars, some microwaves, some refrigerators, cable TV, 2 18-hole golf courses, putting green, 15 tennis courts, pro shop, 4 pools, fitness classes, health club, spa, beach, boating, fishing, bicycles, volleyball, 3 bars, lounge, shops, children's programs (ages 4–12), laundry service, business services, convention center, meeting rooms, free parking; no-smoking rooms* ▭ *AE, D, DC, MC, V.*

$$$–$$$$
🏨 **Sawgrass Marriott Resort and Beach Club.** The main building and lobby areas feel more like a business hotel than like a plush resort—the property does include a 46,000-square-ft high-tech business center—but the grounds are beautiful and the rooms are spacious, with deep-color carpets and drapes, wood furniture, and roomy bathrooms. Also the international headquarters of the Association of Tennis Professionals (the governing body of the men's professional tennis circuit), this is truly a full-service resort, whether you've come to laze about or spend some time on the courts yourself. ✉ *1000 PGA Tour Blvd., Ponte Vedra Beach 32082* ☎ *904/285–7777 or 800/457–4653* 🖷 *904/285–0259* ⊕ *www. marriotthotels.com/jaxsw* 📲 *508 rooms, 24 suites ⚒ 6 restaurants, room service, in-room data ports, some kitchens, minibars, some microwaves, some refrigerators, cable TV with movies and video games, golf privileges, 17 tennis courts, pro shop, 3 pools, wading pool, health club, hot tub, sauna, beach, boating, bicycles, 4 bars, lounge, shop, children's programs (ages 3–12), playground, laundry facilities, laundry service, concierge, Internet, business services, meeting rooms, some pets allowed (fee), free parking; no-smoking rooms* ▭ *AE, D, DC, MC, V.*

$–$$$$
🏨 **Sea Turtle Inn.** Some of the rooms at this popular eight-story hotel overlooking the Atlantic have full oceanfront views and private balconies; all rooms are spacious and have "turtle windows," made of light-deflective glass designed to prevent sea turtles and their hatchlings from mistaking indoor lighting for natural light (which would disorient them in their journey from beach to sea). This is a great spot for families because of its homelike amenities and convenient location. ✉ *One Ocean Blvd., Jacksonville Beach 32233* ☎ *904/249–7402 or 800/874–6000* 🖷 *904/249–1119* ⊕ *www.seaturtle.com* 📲 *193 rooms, 3 suites ⚒ Restaurant, in-room data ports, refrigerators, cable TV with movies, pool, beach, bar, dry cleaning, laundry service, Internet, meeting rooms; no-smoking rooms* ▭ *AE, D, MC, V.*

$$–$$$
🏨 **Comfort Inn Oceanfront.** The Atlantic is the front yard of this seven-story hotel, which offers water views from the private balconies of each of its pastel-color rooms. Families enjoy the four waterfalls that cascade into a giant, heated free-form pool. ✉ *1515 N. 1st St., Jacksonville Beach 32250* ☎ *904/241–2311 or 800/654–8776* 🖷 *904/249–3830* ⊕ *www. comfortinnjaxbeach.com* 📲 *177 rooms, 15 suites ⚒ Restaurant, in-room*

data ports, in-room safes, some microwaves, some kitchenettes, some refrigerators, cable TV with movies and video games, pool, exercise equipment, outdoor hot tub, beach, bicycles, volleyball, bar, shop, dry cleaning, laundry facilities, laundry service, meeting rooms, free parking; no-smoking floors ⊟ *AE, D, DC, MC, V* ⦿ *CP.*

Nightlife

On Friday and Saturday nights the **Ragtime Tavern** (✉ 207 Atlantic Blvd., Atlantic Beach ☏ 904/241–7877) resonates with live music, from jazz to blues to progressive to good old rock and roll. The entertainment at the **Sun Dog Steak & Seafood** (✉ 207 Atlantic Blvd., Neptune Beach ☏ 904/241–8221) often includes acoustical guitarists.

Sports & the Outdoors

BIKING   **Ponte Vedra Bicycles** (✉ 250 Salana Rd., Ponte Vedra Beach ☏ 904/ 273–0199) includes free bike maps with a rental.

FISHING   **North Florida Fishing Charters** (✉ 2221 Larchmont Rd., Jacksonville ☏ 904/346–3868) specializes in in-shore light tackle fishing from St. Augustine to Amelia Island.

GOLF   Ponte Vedra Beach is home of the PGA Tour. The **Ponte Vedra Inn & Club** (✉ 200 Ponte Vedra Blvd., Ponte Vedra Beach ☏ 904/285–1111 or 800/234–7842) has two 18-hole courses, the par-72 Ocean Course and the par-70 Lagoon Course. **Ravines Inn & Golf Club** (✉ 2932 Ravines Rd., Middleburg ☏ 904/282–7888) has 18 holes (par 72) and a putting course. The **Tournament Players Club at Sawgrass** (✉ 110 Tournament Dr., Ponte Vedra Beach ☏ 904/273–3235) hosts the Tournament Players Championship in March. The club has two 18-hole, par-72 courses.

TENNIS   Ponte Vedra Beach is the headquarters of the Association of Tennis Professionals (ATP). The **Sawgrass Marriott Resort** (✉ 1000 PGA Blvd., Ponte Vedra Beach ☏ 904/285–7777 or 800/457–4653) has four green clay courts. A shuttle service provides transportation to ATP headquarters and its four grass, four red clay, and five cushioned hard courts. The **Ponte Vedra Inn & Club** (✉ 200 Ponte Vedra Blvd., Ponte Vedra Beach ☏ 904/285–1111) has 15 Har-Tru courts.

Mayport

❼ *20 mi northeast of Jacksonville.*

Dating back more than 300 years, this is one of the oldest fishing communities in the United States. Today it has several excellent and very casual seafood restaurants and a large commercial shrimp-boat fleet. It's also the Navy's fourth-largest home port.

Kathryn Abbey Hanna Park (✉ 500 Wonderwood Dr., Mayport ☏ 904/ 249–4700 ⊕ www.coj.net), the area's showplace park, has beaches, bike trails, campsites, showers, and snack bars that operate April through Labor Day. Admission is $1 per person and the park is open from 8 AM to sunset.

> **en route**   Take your car on the **St. Johns River ferry** between Mayport and Fort George Island. ☏ *904/241–9969* ⊕ *www.stjohnsferry.com* ✉ *$2.75 per vehicle, pedestrians 50¢* ⊙ *Daily 6:20 AM–10 PM every ½ hr.*

Fort George Island

❽ *25 mi northeast of Jacksonville.*

One of the oldest inhabited areas of Florida, Fort George Island is lush with foliage, natural vegetation, and wildlife. A 4-mi nature and bike trail meanders through the island, revealing shell mounds dating as far back as 6,000 years.

Built in 1792 by Zephaniah Kingsley, an eccentric slave trader, the **Kingsley Plantation** is the oldest remaining cotton plantation in the state. The ruins of 23 tabby (a cementlike mixture of sand and crushed shells) slave houses, a barn, and the modest Kingsley home are open to the public and reachable by ferry or bridge. ⊠ *Rte. A1A, Fort George Island* ☎ *904/251-3537* ⊠ *Free* ⊙ *Daily 9–5; ranger talks weekdays at 1, weekends at 1 and 3.*

off the beaten path

★ **Talbot Island State Parks.** The Talbot Island State Parks, including Big and Little Talbot islands, have 17 mi of gorgeous beaches, sand dunes, and golden marshes that hum with birds and native waterfowl. Come to picnic, fish, swim, snorkel, or camp. Little Talbot Island, one of the few remaining undeveloped barrier islands in Florida, has river otters, marsh rabbits, raccoons, bobcats, possums, and gopher tortoises. A 4-mi nature trail winds across Little Talbot, and there are several smaller trails on Big Talbot. ⊠ *12157 Heckscher Dr., Talbot Island* ☎ *904/251-2320* ⊕ *www.funandsun. com/parks/LittleTalbot/littletalbot.html* ⊠ *$3.25 per vehicle (up to 8 people)* ⊙ *Daily 8–sunset.*

Amelia Island (Fernandina Beach)

⑨ *35 mi northeast of Jacksonville.*

At the northeasternmost reach of Florida, Amelia Island has beautiful beaches with enormous sand dunes along its eastern flank, a state park with a Civil War fort, sophisticated restaurants, interesting shops, and accommodations that range from B&Bs to luxury resorts. The quaint town of Fernandina Beach is on the island's northern end; a century ago casinos and brothels thrived here, but those are gone, and today there's little reminder of the town's wild days.

★ The **Amelia Island Historic District,** in Fernandina Beach, has more than 50 blocks of buildings listed on the National Register of Historic Places; 450 ornate structures built prior to 1927 offer some of the nation's finest examples of Queen Anne, Victorian, and Italianate homes. Many date to the haven's mid-19th-century glory days. Pick up a self-guided tour map at the chamber of commerce, in the old railroad depot—once a stopping point on the first cross-state railroad.

Founded in 1859, **St. Peter's Episcopal Church** (⊠ 801 Atlantic Ave., Fernandina Beach ☎ 904/261-4293) is a Gothic revival structure with Tiffany glass–style memorials and an original, turn-of-the-20th-century L. C. Harrison organ with magnificent hand-painted pipes.

One of the country's best-preserved and most complete brick forts is at ★ **Fort Clinch State Park.** Fort Clinch was built to discourage further British intrusion after the War of 1812 and was occupied in 1863 by the Confederacy; a year later it was retaken by the North. During the Spanish-American War it was reactivated for a brief time but for the most part wasn't used. Today, the 1,086-acre park has camping, nature trails, carriage rides, a swimming beach, and surf and pier fishing. Wander through restored buildings, including furnished barracks, a kitchen, and a repair shop. Scheduled periodically are living-history reenactments of life in the garrison at the time of the Civil War. ⊠ *2601 Atlantic Ave., Fernandina Beach* ☎ *904/277-7274* ⊕ *www.funandsun.com/parks/ FortClinch/fortclinch.html* ⊠ *$3.25 per vehicle (up to 8 people)* ⊙ *Daily 8–sunset.*

Amelia Island's eastern shore, which includes **Main Beach,** is a 13-mi stretch of white-sand beach edged with dunes, some 40 ft high. It's one of the few beaches in Florida where horseback riding is allowed.

Where to Stay & Eat

$$$$
Fodor'sChoice
★

✕ **The Grill.** The Ritz-Carlton's signature restaurant is quietly elegant and truly outstanding, with dishes such as seared bison tenderloin with grilled vegetables and salmon escallop with angel-hair pasta in tomato-basil oil. Choose the "blind tasting" menu to have the chef personalize a multicourse dinner. ✉ *Ritz-Carlton, Amelia Island, 4750 Amelia Island Pkwy., Fernandina Beach* ☎ *904/277–1100* ⌕ *Reservations essential* ⌂ *Jacket required* ▤ *AE, DC, MC, V* ☉ *No lunch.*

★ $$$–$$$$

✕ **Beech Street Grill.** Hardwood floors, high ceilings, and marble fireplaces adorn many rooms on two floors to create a pleasant environment in this 1889 sea captain's house. An extensive menu includes such house favorites as roasted lamb with mint and apple salsa, Parmesan-crusted red snapper with mustard-basil cream sauce, and crab-stuffed local shrimp with *tasso* (a smoked Cajun ham) gravy. A blackboard lists four or five fresh fish specials nightly. The outstanding wine list includes some coveted Californians. ✉ *801 Beech St., Fernandina Beach* ☎ *904/277–3662* ⌕ *Reservations essential* ▤ *AE, D, DC, MC, V* ☉ *No lunch.*

$–$$

✕ **Down Under.** Fresh local fish is the specialty of this casual place nestled beneath the overpass of the A1A bridge. Enjoy the glorious views of the tranquil Intracoastal Waterway and order baskets of fried shrimp or fried oysters; dine on stuffed tuna, shrimp scampi, or grilled tuna; or go for the seafood platter. For landlubbers, chicken and steak are available. ✉ *Intracoastal Waterway, under the Rte. A1A Bridge, Fernandina Beach* ☎ *904/261–1001* ▤ *AE, DC, MC, V* ☉ *Closed Mon. No lunch.*

$–$$

✕ **O'Kane's Irish Pub.** The authentic Irish fare here includes shepherd's pie, steak and Guinness pie, and fish-and-chips. Also on the menu are sandwiches, ribs, pasta, and soup served in a bowl of sourdough bread (you eat the whole thing). The quiet dining room in back has an old-fashioned tin ceiling and upholstered chairs. This is one of the few bars where the Irish coffee is prepared as it is in Ireland—with very cold, barely whipped, heavy cream floating on top. ✉ *318 Centre St., Fernandina Beach* ☎ *904/261–1000* ▤ *AE, MC, V.*

$$$$
Fodor'sChoice
★

▥ **The Ritz-Carlton, Amelia Island.** The elegance, superb comfort, excellent service, and exquisite beach are enough to make you swoon. All accommodations in the eight-story building have balconies and ocean views; suites and rooms are spacious and luxurious and are furnished in classic Ritz-Carlton style, with heavy print draperies, plush carpet, framed prints on the walls, and comfortable upholstered chairs. Public areas are exquisitely maintained, and fine cuisine can be had at a choice of restaurants, including the accoladed Grill. ✉ *4750 Amelia Island Pkwy., 32034* ☎ *904/277–1100* ⎙ *904/261–9064* ⊕ *www.ritzcarlton.com* ⇨ *449 rooms, 61 suites* ⌕ *3 restaurants, room service, in-room data ports, in-room safes, minibars, cable TV with movies and video games, 18-hole golf course, putting green, 9 tennis courts, 2 pools (1 indoor), wading pool, fitness roomhealth club, hair salon, spa, beach, boating, bicycles, billiards, horseback riding, 3 bars, shop, baby-sitting, children's programs (ages 5–12), video game room, playground, dry cleaning, laundry service, concierge, Internet, business services, meeting rooms, some pets allowed (fee); no-smoking floors* ▤ *AE, D, DC, MC, V.*

★ $$$–$$$$

▥ **Elizabeth Pointe Lodge.** The inn, built to resemble a (supersize) Nantucket shingle-style house, is set just behind the dunes. Oceanside units have great water views, albeit through disappointingly small windows. A chair-lined porch offers everyone a chance to rock in ocean breezes, and on cold nights guests can cluster around the living-room fireplace.

Two adjacent cottages have additional rooms and a suite. The restaurant is open for lunch only. ⊠ *98 S. Fletcher Ave., 32034* ☎ *904/277–4851 or 800/772–3359* 🖷 *904/277–6500* ⊕ *www.elizabethpointelodge. com* 🛏 *24 rooms, 1 suite, 1 2-bedroom cottage* ⚘ *Restaurant, some in-room hot tubs, cable TV, beach, laundry facilities, laundry service, Internet, business services, meeting rooms, free parking; no smoking* ⊟ *AE, MC, V* ⦿ *BP.*

$$–$$$$ 🏨 **Amelia Island Plantation.** The first-rate golf, tennis, and spa facilities are big draws at this sprawling, family-oriented resort where accommodations include full-service hotel rooms as well as home and condo (or "villa") rentals. The hotel rooms tend to be large, with comfortable seating areas, balconies, and true ocean views. Much of the hotel lobby is devoted to a popular piano bar, which stays busy late into the evening. With its ancient oaks, marshes, and lagoons, the resort is also a worthy destination for hiking, biking, and bird-watching. Good dining and shopping options mean you don't have to leave the property. ⊠ *6800 First Coast Hwy., 32034* ☎ *904/261–6161 or 800/874–6878* 🖷 *904/277–5945* ⊕ *www.aipfl.com* 🛏 *249 rooms; 418 1-, 2-, and 3-bedroom villas* ⚘ *7 restaurants, 2 grills, grocery, room service, in-room data ports, in-room safes, some microwaves, some kitchenettes, refrigerators, cable TV with movies and video games, 3 18-hole golf courses, 23 tennis courts, pro shop, 23 pools (1 indoor), health club, spa, beach, fishing, bicycles, hiking, horseback riding, racquetball, volleyball, 3 bars, shops, baby-sitting, children's programs (ages 3–10), playground, dry cleaning, laundry service, Internet, business services, meeting rooms, airport shuttle; no-smoking rooms* ⊟ *AE, D, MC, V.*

$$–$$$ 🏨 **Ash Street Inn.** A white picket fence frames the yard of this appealing inn a block from the heart of downtown Fernandina Beach. Rooms are spacious and have decorator window treatments and armoires, as well as some antique pieces; some have claw-foot tubs, others have whirlpools, and one has a working fireplace. As part of the full breakfast included in the rate, you might be served banana pancakes or a cheese soufflé, either in the bright dining room or out on the porch. ⊠ *102 S. 7th St., Fernandina Beach 32034* ☎ *904/277–6660 or 800/277–6660* 🖷 *904/277–4646* ⊕ *www.ashstinn.com* 🛏 *10 rooms* ⚘ *Some fans, some in-room hot tubs, some refrigerators, cable TV, some in-room VCRs, golf privileges, pool, massage, bicycles, meeting rooms, free parking; no kids under 12, no smoking* ⊟ *AE, MC, V* ⦿ *BP.*

$$–$$$ 🏨 **Florida House Inn.** The rambling two-story clapboard inn, more than 100 years old, is definitely of another era, with creaking floors and small doors. Rooms have handmade quilts and hooked rugs but also include such modern amenities as king-size beds and whirlpool tubs. Some even have fireplaces. Guests can relax in the cozy parlor and often dine in the popular restaurant, which serves heaping quantities at family-style breakfasts, lunches, and dinners. ⊠ *20 S. 3rd St., 32034* ☎ *904/261–3300 or 800/258–3301* 🖷 *904/277–3831* ⊕ *www.floridahouseinn.com* 🛏 *15 rooms, 1 suite* ⚘ *Restaurant, fans, cable TV, some in-room hot tubs, bicycles, laundry facilities, meeting rooms, some pets allowed (fee), free parking; no smoking* ⊟ *AE, MC, V.*

$$–$$$ 🏨 **Hoyt House Bed & Breakfast.** A redbrick walkway leads to this fine example of Queen Anne Victorian architecture (built in 1905). Relax in one of the rockers on the wide veranda. Shade trees keep the B&B's yard cool. Inside, inviting rooms show off antique and reproduction furniture, down quilts, and walls painted in rich hues. All rooms have private baths, and one has a whirlpool. In the late afternoon guests congregate in the parlor for complimentary wine and cheese. The house is in the historic district, at the edge of Fernandina Beach. ⊠ *804 Atlantic Ave., 32034* ☎ *904/277–4300 or 800/432–2085* 🖷 *904/277–9626*

⊕ *www.hoythouse.com,* ⇔ *10 rooms* ⅃ *Some in-room hot tubs, cable TV, pool, business services, meeting rooms, some pets (fee), free parking; no children under 10, no smoking* ⊟ *AE, MC, V.*

Sports & the Outdoors

GOLF **Amelia Island Plantation** (⊠ 6800 First Coast Hwy. ☎ 904/261–6161 or 800/874–6878) offers three courses: the 18-hole, 72-par Oak Marsh, designed by Pete Dye; the par-70, Bobby Weed–designed Ocean Links, where several of the 18 holes are oceanfront; and Tom Fazio's 18-hole, par-72 Long Point. At the **Ritz-Carlton, Amelia Island** (⊠ 4750 Amelia Island Pkwy. ☎ 904/277–1100), live oaks, palm trees, and sand dunes frame 18 holes.

HORSEBACK **Country Day Stables** (⊠ 2940 Jane La., Fernandina Beach ☎ 904/879–
RIDING 9383) offers individual and group rides, including private picnic outings, on its 40-acre ranch.

TENNIS **Amelia Island Plantation** (⊠ 6800 First Coast Hwy., Amelia Island ☎ 904/277–5145 or 800/486–8366) has 23 clay courts and is the site of the nationally televised, top-rated Women's Tennis Championships in April and the Men's All-American Tennis Championship in September. The **Ritz-Carlton, Amelia Island** (⊠ 4750 Amelia Island Pkwy., Amelia Island ☎ 904/277–1100) has nine Har-Tru tennis courts.

Shopping

Within the Amelia Island Historic District are numerous shops, art galleries, and boutiques, many of which are clustered along cobblestone Centre Street. The **Island Art Association Co-op Gallery** (⊠ 205 Centre St., Fernandina Beach ☎ 904/261–7020) displays and sells paintings, prints, and other artwork by local artists.

ST. AUGUSTINE

35 mi south of Jacksonville.

Founded in 1565 by Spanish explorers, St. Augustine is the nation's oldest city and has a wealth of historic buildings and attractions. In addition to the historic sites on the mainland, however, the city has 43 mi of beaches on two barrier islands to the east, both reachable by causeways. Several times a year St. Augustine holds historic reenactments, such as December's Grand Christmas Illumination, which marks the town's British occupation.

Exploring St. Augustine

The core of any visit is a tour of the historic district, a showcase for more than 60 historic sites and attractions, plus 144 blocks of historic houses listed on the National Register of Historic Places. You could probably spend several weeks exploring these treasures, but don't neglect other, generally newer, attractions found elsewhere in town.

Numbers in the text correspond to numbers in the margin and on the St. Augustine map.

a good
walk

A good place to start is the **Visitor Information and Preview Center** ⑪ ▶; pick up maps, brochures, and information. It's on San Marco Avenue between Castillo Drive and Orange Street. From there cross Orange Street to reach the **City Gate** ⑫, the entrance to the city's popular restored area. Walk south on St. George Street to the **Oldest Wooden Schoolhouse** ⑬. Directly across from it is the **Spanish Quarter Village** ⑭, a state-operated living-history village. Go out Fort Alley and cross San Marco Avenue to the impressive **Castillo de San Marcos National Monument** ⑮, a won-

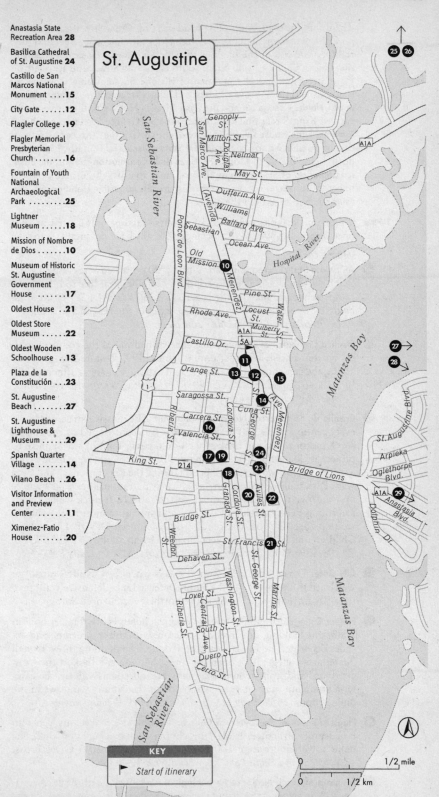

St. Augustine

KEY

▶ *Start of itinerary*

0 ____ 1/2 mile

0 ____ 1/2 km

derful fort for exploring. Now head west on Cuna Street and turn left
on Cordova Street. Walk south three blocks to Valencia Street and turn
right. At the end of the block is the splendid **Flagler Memorial Presbyterian Church** ⑯. Head one block south on Sevilla Street and turn left on
King Street to find the **Museum of Historic St. Augustine Government
House** ⑰ and three more of Henry Flagler's legacies: the **Lightner Museum** ⑱, **Flagler College** ⑲, and the Casa Monica Hotel. Continue two blocks
east on King Street and turn right onto St. George Street to reach the
Ximenez-Fatio House ⑳. For a taste of the turn of the 20th century, head
east on Artillery Lane to the **Oldest Store Museum** ㉒. Finally, head back
north to the Bridge of Lions, the **Plaza de la Constitución** ㉓, and the **Basilica Cathedral of St. Augustine** ㉔. You have to cross the Bridge of Lions
to get to Anastasia Island and the historic **St. Augustine Lighthouse & Museum** ㉙, but it's worth the effort.

TIMING   Though most sights keep the same hours (daytime only), a few are not
open on Sunday. Weekday mornings generally have the smallest crowds.

What to See

㉘ **Anastasia State Recreation Area.** With 1,700 protected acres of bird sanctuary, this Anastasia Island park draws families that like to hike, bike,
camp, swim, and play on the beach. ✉ *1340 Rte. A1A S, Anastasia Island* ☎ *904/461–2033* ⊕ *www.dep.state.fl.us/parks* 🖃 *$3.25 per ve-
hicle (up to 8 people)* ☉ *Daily sunrise–sunset.*

㉔ **Basilica Cathedral of St. Augustine.** The cathedral has the country's oldest written parish records, dating from 1594. Restored in the mid-
1960s, the current structure (1797) had extensive changes after an 1887
fire. ✉ *40 Cathedral Pl.* ☎ *904/824–2806* 🖃 *Donation welcome*
☉ *Weekdays 7–5, weekends 7–7.*

★ ⑮ **Castillo de San Marcos National Monument.** The massive structure looks
every century of its 300 years. The fort was constructed of coquina, a
soft limestone made of broken shells and coral. Built by the Spanish to
protect St. Augustine from British raids (English pirates were handy with
a torch), the fort was used as a prison during the Revolutionary and Civil
wars. Park rangers provide an introductory narration, after which you're
on your own to explore the moat, turrets, and 16-ft-thick walls. Garrison rooms depict the life of the era, and special cannon-firing demonstrations are held on weekends from Memorial Day to Labor Day.
Children under 17 must be accompanied by an adult. ✉ *1 Castillo Dr.*
☎ *904/829–6506* ⊕ *www.oldcity.com/fort* 🖃 *$5* ☉ *Daily 8:45–4:45.*

⑫ **City Gate.** The gate is a relic from the days when the Castillo's moat ran
westward to the river, and the Cubo Defense Line (defensive wall) protected against approaches from the north. ✉ *St. George St.*

⑲ **Flagler College.** Originally one of two posh hotels Henry Flagler built in
1888, this building is a riveting structure with towers, turrets, and arcades decorated by Louis Comfort Tiffany. The building, now a small
liberal-arts college, isn't open for tours, but you can look at the front
courtyard and walk around the lobby area. If you ask nicely, the cafeteria attendant may let you take a look at the Tiffany windows in the
dining room. ✉ *78 King St.* ☎ *904/829–6481* ⊕ *www.flagler.edu.*

⑯ **Flagler Memorial Presbyterian Church.** To look at a marvelous Venetian
Renaissance structure, head to this church, built by Flagler in 1889. The
dome towers more than 100 ft and is topped by a 20-ft Greek cross.
✉ *Valencia and Sevilla Sts.* ☉ *Weekdays 8:30–4:30.*

㉕ **Fountain of Youth National Archeological Park.** Well north of St. Augustine's main sights is this tribute to explorer Ponce de León, marking the

HENRY FLAGLER'S
ST. AUGUSTINE LEGACY

HENRY MORRISON FLAGLER, who, with John D. Rockefeller, founded the Standard Oil Company, first visited the tiny town of St. Augustine in 1885 while honeymooning with his second wife. His choice proved to be very fortunate for the city. It was during this trip that Flagler decided to make St. Augustine "the Newport of the South": a winter resort for wealthy northern industrialists. And to get his select clientele to Florida, he built a luxurious railroad—the Florida East Coast Railway—which eventually would stretch from New York all the way to the Florida Keys.

To incorporate the city's Spanish heritage, Flagler chose Spanish Renaissance revival as his architectural theme. He created the St. Augustine Golf Club and the St. Augustine Yacht Club so there would be leisure activities to enjoy in the warm

climate. He also built the city's hospital, churches, the city hall, and winter residences. The most visible manifestations of Flagler's dream were the spectacular hotels with castlelike towers, turrets, and red-tile roofs. His most opulent hotel resort, the Ponce de León, is now a private four-year liberal-arts college that bears his name; another flagship resort, the Alcazar, has been turned into the Lightner Museum; the Casa Monica Hotel is again functioning as a luxury resort, more than a century after Flagler created it; and despite the wrath of multiple hurricanes, most of the railroad routes Flagler built and developed are still in use today.

location of the legendary spring that flowed through folklore as the Fountain of Youth. In the complex is a springhouse, an explorer's globe, a planetarium, a Native American village, and exhibits about early Timucuan Indian inhabitants. The spring has been here for more than 4,000 years and is rich in iron and sulfur. Since León's discovery, people have made pilgrimages here to sip from the waters. Taste it if you must, but be prepared—there's a reason sulfur-flavored beverages have never been marketed. ⊠ *11 Magnolia Ave.* ☎ *904/829–3168 or 800/356–8222* ⊕ *www.fountainofyouthflorida.com* ⊑ *$6* ☉ *Daily 9–5.*

★ ⑱ **Lightner Museum.** In his quest to turn Florida into an American Riviera, Henry Flagler built two fancy hotels in 1888—the Ponce de León, which became Flagler College, and the Alcazar, which now houses this museum. The building showcases three floors of furnishings, costumes, and Victorian art glass, plus ornate antique music boxes (demonstrations daily at 11 and 2). The Lightner Antiques Mall perches on three levels of what was the hotel's indoor pool. ⊠ *75 King St.* ☎ *904/824–2874* ⊕ *www. lightnermuseum.org* ⊑ *$6* ☉ *Museum daily 9–5.*

⑩ **Mission of Nombre de Dios.** The site, north of the historic district, commemorates where America's first Christian mass was celebrated. A 208-ft stainless-steel cross marks the spot where the mission's first cross was planted. ⊠ *San Marco Ave. and Old Mission Rd.* ☎ *904/824–2809* ⊑ *Donation requested* ☉ *Weekdays 8–5:30, weekends 9–5.*

⑰ **Museum of Historic St. Augustine Government House.** Featuring a collection of more than 300 artifacts from both archaeological digs and Spanish shipwrecks off the Florida coast, this museum reflects five centuries of history. ⊠ *48 King St.* ☎ *904/825–5033* ⊑ *$2.50* ☉ *Daily 10–4.*

㉑ **Oldest House.** Known as the Gonzalez-Alvarez House, the Oldest House is a National Historic Landmark. The current site dates from the early 1700s, but a structure has been on this site since the early 1600s. Much of the city's history is seen in the building's changes and additions, from the coquina blocks—which came into use to replace wood soon after the town burned in 1702—to the house's enlargement during the British occupation. ⊠ *14 St. Francis St.* ☏ *904/824–2872* ⊕ *www.oldcity. com/oldhouse* ⊡ *$5* ⊙ *Daily 9–5.*

㉒ **Oldest Store Museum.** High-button shoes, lace-up corsets, patent drugs, and confectionery specialties are part of the display at this re-creation of a turn-of-the-20th-century general store. ⊠ *4 Artillery La.* ☏ *904/829– 9729* ⊕*www.oldcity.com/oldstore* ⊡*$5* ⊙ *Mon.–Sat. 10–4, Sun. noon–4.*

⑬ **Oldest Wooden Schoolhouse.** Automated mannequins of a teacher and students relate the school's history. The tiny 18th-century building of cypress and cedar is thought to be one of the nation's oldest schoolhouses. Because it was the closest structure to the city gate, it served as a guardhouse and sentry shelter during the Seminole Wars. ⊠ *14 St. George St.* ☏ *904/824–0192* ⊕ *www.oldestschoolhouse.com* ⊡ *$3* ⊙ *Daily 9–5.*

㉓ **Plaza de la Constitución.** The central area of the original settlement was laid out in 1598 by decree of King Philip II, and little has changed since. At its center is a monument to the Spanish constitution of 1812, while at the east end is a public market dating from Early American days. Just beyond is a statue of Juan Ponce de León, who "discovered" Florida in 1513. ⊠ *St. George St. and Cathedral Pl.*

㉗ **St. Augustine Beach.** This very popular strand is the closest beach to downtown. It's on the northern end of Anastasia Island, directly east of town. ⊠ *1200 Rte. A1A S* ☏ *No phone* ⊡ *Free.*

㉙ **St. Augustine Lighthouse & Museum.** Its beacon no longer guides ships to St. Augustine's shores, but the historic lighthouse continues to draw thousands of visitors each year. The 1874 structure replaced an earlier lighthouse built by the Spanish when the city was founded in 1565. The visitor center has an exhibit gallery and a store. ⊠ *81 Lighthouse Ave.* ☏ *904/ 829–0745* ⊕ *www.staugustinelighthouse.com* ⊡ *$6.95* ⊙ *Daily 9–6.*

⑭ **Spanish Quarter Village.** Wander through the narrow streets at your own pace in this village with eight sites. Along your way you may see a blacksmith building his shop (a historic reconstruction) or artisans busy at candle-dipping, spinning, weaving, or cabinetmaking. They are all making reproductions for use within the restored area. **Triay House** (⊠ 29 St. George St.) has period artifacts and an orientation center. Buy your tickets at the Museum Store. ⊠ *33 St. George St.* ☏ *904/825–6830* ⊕ *www.oldcity.com/spanishquarter* ⊡ *$6.50* ⊙ *Daily 9–5:30.*

㉖ **Vilano Beach.** The once-quiet Vilano Beach, just north of St. Augustine, is slowly blossoming into a bustling community with a town center, cozy restaurants and outdoor cafés, condos, and hotels. ⊠*3400 Coastal Hwy., across the St. Augustine Inlet* ☏ *No phone* ⊡ *Free.*

⛳ ⑪ **Visitor Information and Preview Center.** An entertaining film on the founding of St. Augustine, *Struggling to Survive* is shown hourly 9–4. ⊠ *10 Castillo Dr.* ☏ *904/825–1000* ⊡ *$1* ⊙ *Daily 9–4.*

off the beaten path

World Golf Hall of Fame. This stunning tribute to the game of golf is the centerpiece of World Golf Village, an extraordinary complex that includes 36 holes of golf, a golf academy, two resorts, and a convention center. The Hall of Fame has an IMAX theater as well as more than 70 separate exhibits combining historical artifacts with the latest in interactive technology. Stand up to the pressures of the TV camera and crowd noise as you try to sink a final putt or have your swing computer-analyzed. ⊠ *21 World Golf Pl.* ☎ *904/940–4123* ⊕ *www.wgv.com* ⊠ *$12, IMAX film $10, combined ticket $17* ☉ *Mon.–Thurs. 10–5, Fri.–Sat. 10–8, Sun. noon–7.*

⑳ Ximenez-Fatio House. Originally built as a merchant's house and store in 1797, the place became a tourist boardinghouse in the 1800s. It's been restored to look like it did during its inn days. ⊠ *20 Aviles St.* ☎ *904/ 829–3575* ⊕ *www.oldcity.com/ximenez* ⊠ *Donation welcome* ☉ *Oct.–Aug., Thurs.–Sat. and Mon. 11–4, Sun. 1–4.*

Where to Stay & Eat

★ **$$–$$$$** ✕ **95 Cordova.** Find twists on traditional southwestern, Florida, and Asian food in the dining room of the historic Casa Monica Hotel. Appetizers include chicken–and–white bean gumbo and seafood-and-broccoli crepes. For entrées, shrimp and andouille combine with penne; apple, walnut, sausage, and rum gravy accompany pork tenderloin; and a maple-mustard-tarragon sauce dresses the blackened chicken. Save room for the St. Johns mud cake with fresh berry sauce. Brunch brings 'em in on Sunday. ⊠ *115 Cordova St.* ☎ *904/810–6810* ▤ *AE, MC, V.*

$$–$$$ ✕ **Columbia.** Arroz con pollo, fillet *salteado* (with a spicy sauce), and a fragrant seafood paella: this heir to the original Columbia, founded in Tampa in 1905 and still going strong, serves the same time-honored Cuban and Spanish dishes. Sunday's Fiesta Brunch has everything from cheeses and cold meats to Belgian waffles. ⊠ *98 St. George St.* ☎ *904/824–3341; 800/227–1905 in Florida* ▤ *AE, D, DC, MC, V.*

★ **$$–$$$** ✕ **La Parisienne.** Attentive and enthusiastic in its approach to honest bistro cuisine, this tiny place in a white stucco building with a little flower-filled courtyard is a true find (which, unfortunately, everyone seems to have found). Try the grilled rack of lamb, the roasted duck, or the seafood chowder with pompano, clams, mussels, and oysters, and be sure to save room for the pastries. Brunch is available on weekends. ⊠ *60 Hypolita St.* ☎ *904/829–0055* ⟡ *Reservations essential* ▤ *AE, D, MC, V* ☉ *No lunch weekdays.*

$–$$$ ✕ **Fiddler's Green.** Spectacular views of the Atlantic and St. Augustine Inlet complement the open-flame-grilled seafood and steaks. Coconut shrimp come with citrus-mustard salsa, while the Italian-seasoned crab cakes are made with fresh blue crabs and served with a mustard sauce. Beef lovers will want to try the New York strip or filet mignon. ⊠ *2750 Anahama Dr., Vilano Beach* ☎ *904/824–8897* ▤ *AE, D, DC, MC, V* ☉ *Closed Mon. No lunch.*

$–$$$ ✕ **Harry's Seafood Bar and Grill.** Although this casual eatery calls itself a seafood bar and grill, you might think you're on Bourbon Street when you step inside and get a whiff of the spicy cooking. Red beans with rice and sausage, shrimp and crab étouffée, and jambalaya are house specialties, but the menu also includes lobster and seafood pasta, catfish Pontchartrain, and tasty desserts such as bayou brownies and bananas Foster. Tables are in several small rooms and are almost always full. ⊠ *46 Avenida Menendez* ☎ *904/824–7765* ▤ *AE, D, MC, V.*

★ **$–$$$** ✕ **Salt Water Cowboys.** Rustic handmade twig furniture and 100-year-old hardwood floors are reminders that this spot hidden in the salt marshes flanking the Intracoastal Waterway began its life as a secluded fish camp. Clam chowder, oyster stew, barbecue ribs, and crispy fried chicken are standard fare along with blackened and broiled seafood, steamed oysters, and steak. For more adventuresome palates, the menu includes frogs' legs, alligator, and cooter (fried soft-shell turtle rolled in seasoned bread crumbs). ⊠ *299 Dondanville Rd.* ☎ *904/471–2332* ⚲ *Reservations essential* ⊟ *AE, D, DC, MC, V* ✆ *Closed Mon. No lunch.*

$–$$ ✕ **O.C. White's Seafood& Spirits.** Waterfront views add to the charm of dining at this popular bay-front eatery, which makes its home in the General Worth house, circa 1791. Local favorites include coconut shrimp, blue crab cakes, Caribbean jerk chicken and Alaskan snow crab clusters. Beef lovers may want to try the 20-ounce porterhouse or the 12-ounce New York strip. Ask for an upstairs table to admire the marina. ⊠ *118 Avenida Menendez, 32084* ☎ *904/824–0808* ⊟ *AE, D, MC, V.*

★ **¢–$$** ✕ **Florida Cracker Cafe.** Works by local artists adorn the walls of this well-liked café in the heart of the historic district. Dine inside or out on the shaded patio and enjoy fresh local seafood, pastas, salads, and hamburgers. Daily specials might include fried shrimp stuffed with crab or seafood pasta salad. Key lime pie is the dessert of choice here. ⊠ *81 St. George St.* ☎ *904/829–0397* ⊟ *D, DC, MC, V* ✆ *No dinner Mon.–Thurs.*

¢ ✕ **El Gallinero.** Home-style meals, homemade soups, and Cuban sandwiches as well as wonderful pastries and scrumptious desserts are what draw visitors and locals to this small, popular bakery and café. Try one of the homemade potpies or the vegetable soup. ⊠ *17 Hypolita St., 32084* ☎ *904/810–6852* ⊟ *No credit cards* ✆ *No dinner.*

★ **$$$$** ▦ **World Golf Village Renaissance Resort.** When you want to be within walking distance of all World Golf Village has to offer, this full-service resort is an excellent choice. The 10-story building dwarfs the surrounding palm trees and overlooks a peaceful lake. Rooms and suites surround a soaring atrium, at the bottom of which is a restaurant set amid tropical foliage and cool streams. Units are oversized and are furnished in muted pastels. The hotel has an IMAX movie theater, adjoins a convention center, is adjacent to the World Golf Hall of Fame, and borders the championship golf course. ⊠ *500 S. Legacy Trail, 32092* ☎ *904/940–8000 or 888/740–7020* 🖷 *904/940–8008* ⊕ *www.worldgolfrenaissance.com* ⌨ *273 rooms, 28 suites* ⚬ *Restaurant, in-room data ports, some in-room safes, some in-room hot tubs, some kitchenettes, minibars, refrigerators, cable TV with movies and video games, golf privileges, putting green, pool, fitness room, outdoor hot tub, fishing, billiards, bar, video game room, cinema, shops, baby-sitting, playground, dry cleaning, laundry facilities, concierge, Internet, business services, convention center, meeting rooms, free parking; no-smoking rooms* ⊟ *AE, D, DC, MC, V.*

★ **$$$–$$$$** ▦ **Casa Monica Hotel.** Hand-stenciled Moorish columns and arches, hand-crafted chandeliers, and gilded iron tables decorate the lobby of this late-1800s Flagler-era masterpiece. A retreat for the nation's wealthiest until the Great Depression put it out of business, it has returned to its perch as St. Augustine's grande dame. The turrets, towers, and wrought-iron balconies offer a hint of what's inside. Rooms—dressed in blues, greens, and whites—include wrought-iron two- and four-poster beds and mahogany writing desks and nightstands. The downtown location is within walking distance of many attractions. ⊠ *95 Cordova St., 32084* ☎ *904/819–6087 or 800/648–1888* 🖷 *904/827–0426* ⊕ *www.casamonica.com* ⌨ *138 rooms, 12 suites* ⚬ *Restaurant, in-room data ports, in-room safes, some in-room hot tubs, some kitchenettes, some minibars, some microwaves, some refrigerators, cable TV with movies and video games, pool, gym, outdoor hot tub, bar, shops, dry cleaning, laundry service, concierge, Internet, business services, meeting rooms, parking (fee); no-smoking floors* ⊟ *AE, DC, MC, V.*

$$$–$$$$ ▦ **Centennial House Bed & Breakfast.** Wide steps lead up to the entrance of this charming B&B in a fully restored 19th-century frame house in the heart of downtown St. Augustine. Each room is different, but all are painted in deep hues and have 10-ft-high ceilings and a mix of antiques and reproduction furniture. Some rooms have gas fireplaces and some have whirlpools. A brick courtyard is a peaceful outdoor oasis. ✉ *26 Cordova St., 32084* ☎ *904/810–2218 or 800/611–2880* 🖷 *904/810–1930* ⊕ *www.centennialhouse.com* ➫ *8 rooms* ♨ *Dining room, some in-room hot tubs, cable TV, in-room VCRs, Internet, business services, free parking; no kids under 10, no smoking* ▤ *MC, V* ⑩ *BP.*

★ **$–$$$$** 🏨 **Casablanca Inn Bed & Breakfast on the Bay.** Breakfast comes with scenic views of the Matanzas Bay at this restored 1914 Mediterranean revival stucco-and-stone house, just north of the historic Bridge of Lions. Rooms vary in size and shape; some have separate sitting rooms, some have views of the bay, and some have whirlpool tubs, but all are decorated with period and reproduction furniture. If not dining on the patio, you'll breakfast in the sunny dining room. Sip a glass of complimentary sherry in the cozy parlor. ✉ *24 Avenida Menendez, 32084* ☎ *904/829–0928* 🖷 *904/826–1892 or 800/826–2626* ⊕ *www.casablancainn.com* ➫ *10 rooms, 10 suites* ♨ *Dining room, some in-room hot tubs, bicycles, free parking; no kids under 12, no room phones in some rooms, no smoking, no TV in some rooms* ▤ *AE, D, DC, MC, V* ⑩ *BP.*

★ **$$–$$$** 🏨 **Sheraton's Vistana Resort at World Golf Village.** Watch the action at the 17th and 18th holes from many rooms at this golfer's haven. One- and two-bedroom units are in three six-story pink-and-green buildings that overlook a golf course and lakes in World Golf Village. Rooms are richly appointed, painted deep shades of green or ocher, and decorated with framed prints and earth-tone fabrics. All units have a separate living room, a full kitchen, a washer and dryer, and a balcony. Nongolfers can spend their time relaxing by the pool or on the tennis courts. ✉ *100 Front Nine Dr., 32092* ☎ *904/940–2000 or 800/477–3340* 🖷 *904/940–2092* ⊕ *www.sheraton.com* ➫ *134 villas* ♨ *In-room safes, some in-room hot tubs, kitchens, kitchenettes, microwaves, refrigerators, cable TV, in-room VCRs, golf privileges, 2 tennis courts, pool, wading pool, gym, outdoor hot tub, basketball, volleyball, library, baby-sitting, playground, dry cleaning, laundry facilities, concierge, Internet, business services, convention center, meeting rooms, free parking* ▤ *AE, D, DC, MC, V.*

$–$$$ 🏨 **Carriage Way Bed and Breakfast.** The grandly restored Victorian mansion is within walking distance of the old town. Innkeepers Bill Johnson and his son Larry see to such welcoming touches as fresh flowers, home-baked breads, and evening cordials. Special-occasion breakfasts, flowers, picnic lunches, romantic dinners, or a simple family supper can be arranged with advance notice. ✉ *70 Cuna St., 32084* ☎ *904/829–2467 or 800/908–9832* 🖷 *904/826–1461* ⊕ *www.carriageway.com* ➫ *11 rooms* ♨ *Some in-room hot tubs, some kitchenettes, cable TV, bicycles, laundry facilities, Internet, business services, meeting rooms, free parking; no kids under 8, no smoking, no TV in some rooms* ▤ *D, MC, V* ⑩ *BP.*

$–$$$ 🏨 **Kenwood Inn.** For more than a century, this stately Victorian inn has welcomed wayfarers, and the Constant family continues the tradition. In the heart of the historic district, the inn is near restaurants and sightseeing. A Continental buffet breakfast of home-baked cakes and breads is included. ✉ *38 Marine St., 32084* ☎ *904/824–2116 or 800/824–8151* 🖷 *904/824–1689* ⊕ *www.thekenwoodinn.com* ➫ *14 rooms, 7 suites* ♨ *Cable TV, pool, bicycles, Internet, free parking; no kids under 8, no room phones, no smoking* ▤ *D, MC, V* ⑩ *CP.*

$–$$$ 🏨 **Old City House Inn and Restaurant.** It's hardly noticeable amid the palatial Flagler-era architecture of the historic district, but this small two-story inn is certainly worth a visit. Paris, Venice, and India are just a few of the surprises you find within its coquina walls, where innkeepers Ilse and James Philcox, both avid travelers, have decorated the rooms to reflect different international cities or themes. Although it's downtown and near busy attractions, the property's tall brick walls and lush foliage offer ample privacy. Each room has its own entrance, and a second-floor deck is perfect for taking in the magnificent sunsets. ⊠ *115 Cordova St., 32084* ☎ *904/826–0113* ⊕ *www.oldcityhouse.com* ⇆ *7 rooms* ⚭ *Restaurant, cable TV, some in-room VCRs, bicycles, free parking; no kids under 10, no smoking* ⊟ *AE, MC, V.*

$–$$$ 🛏 **St. Francis Inn Bed & Breakfast.** If the walls could whisper, this late-18th-century house in the historic district would tell tales of slave up-risings, buried doubloons, and Confederate spies. The inn, a guest house since 1845, offers rooms, suites, a room in the former carriage house, and a five-room cottage. Furnishings are a mix of antiques and just plain old. ⊠ *279 St. George St., 32084* ☎ *904/824–6068 or 800/824–6062* 🖶 *904/810–5525* ⊕ *www.stfrancisinn.com* ⇆ *13 rooms, 4 suites, 1 2-bedroom cottage* ⚭ *Dining room, in-room data ports, some in-room hot tubs, some kitchenettes, some microwaves, some refrigerators, cable TV, pool, bicycles, free parking; no kids under 12 in main house, no smoking* ⊟ *MC, V* ⚭ *BP.*

¢–$ 🛏 **Monterey Inn.** Location—right across from the Castillo de San Mar-cos National Monument and across the street from Matanzas Bay—is the draw of this modest two-story motel. Rooms are on the plain side. It's within walking distance of many restaurants and sights. ⊠ *16 Avenida Menendez, 32084* ☎ *904/824–4482* 🖶 *904/829–8854* ⊕ *www. themontereyinn.com* ⇆ *59 rooms* ⚭ *Café, in-room data ports, some kitchenettes, some microwaves, some refrigerators, cable TV, pool, busi-ness services, free parking; no-smoking rooms* ⊟ *AE, D, DC, MC, V.*

Nightlife

The **Mill Top Tavern** (⊠ 19½ St. George St. ☎ 904/829–2329) is one of the city's hottest night spots. If you're staying on Anastasia Island, the **Oasis Deck and Restaurant** (⊠ 4000 Rte. A1A, at Ocean Trace Rd., Anas-tasia Island ☎ 904/471–3424) is your best bet for nightly entertainment, offering 24 draft beers and beach access. Something is always happen-ing at **Scarlett O'Hara's** (⊠ 70 Hypolita St. ☎ 904/824–6535). Some nights it's live blues or jazz bands; on others it might be disco, Top 40, or karaoke; and many nights the early and late-night entertainment are completely different. **Trade Winds** (⊠ 124 Charlotte St. ☎ 904/829–9336) showcases live bands every night, from country and western to rock.

Sports & the Outdoors

Biking
Rent bikes to ride on the beach or in the bike lanes along A1A at **Bike America** (⊠ 3936 Rte. A1A S, St. Augustine ☎ 904/461–5557).

Fishing
K-2 Fishing Charters (⊠ U.S. 1 and Rte. 207 ☎ 904/824–9499 or 800/608–8195) offers half- or full-day charters in addition to overnight and extended-stay trips. Charter the *Sea Love II* (⊠ 250 Vilano Rd. ☎ 904/824–3328), or sign up to join a half- or full-day fishing trip.

Golf
Find 72 holes at the **Sheraton Palm Coast** (⊠ 300 Clubhouse Dr., Palm Coast ☎ 904/445–3000). As part of its complex, **World Golf Village** (⊠ 21 World Golf Pl. ☎ 904/940–4000) has two 18-hole layouts named for and partially designed by golf legends Sam Snead, Gene Sarazen, Arnold Palmer, and Jack Nicklaus.

Tennis

Ron Parker Memorial Field (⊠ 901 Pope Rd.) has two lighted tennis courts and four paddle-ball courts.

Public courts are available at **Treaty Park** (⊠ 1595 Wildwood Dr.). It has six lighted tennis courts, eight paddle-ball and eight racquetball courts, and a skate park with ramps and jumps.

Water Sports

Rent surfboards and sailboards at the **Surf Station** (⊠ 1002 Anastasia Blvd. ☎ 904/471–9463).

Shopping

Just north of St. Augustine, at Exit 95 on Interstate 95, is the **St. Augustine Outlet Center** (⊠ 2700 State Rd. 16, St. Augustine ☎ 904/825–1555 ⊕ www.staugustineoutlets.com), with 95 designer and brand-name outlets. In town, be sure to walk along car-free **St. George Street** (⊠ between Cathedral Pl. and Orange St.) to check out the art galleries and one-of-a-kind shops with candles, home accents, handmade jewelry, aromatherapy products, pottery, books, and clothing.

Side Trips from St. Augustine

Marineland
☁ *18 mi south of St. Augustine.*

Constructed in 1938, Marineland has earned a spot on the National Register of Historic Places, and though it may be showing its age, it's still worth a visit. Watch divers put dolphins through daily training routines, view underwater feedings, and participate in several interactive programs, including diving, snorkeling, and a touch-and-feel dolphin encounter (additional fee). You'll can also get up close and personal with an African penguin (additional fee). ⊠ *Rte. A1A, St. Augustine* ☎ *904/460–1275 or 888/279–9194* ⊕ *www.marineland.net* ☑ *$14* ☉ *Wed.–Mon. 9:30–4:30.*

Ravine State Gardens
35 mi southwest of St. Augustine.

For a great picnic spot, make your way to one of the state's wonderful azalea gardens, which began during the Depression as a WPA project. The ravines are atypical of flat Florida. They're steep and deep, threaded with brooks and rocky outcroppings, and floored with flatlands. Although any month is a good time to hike the shaded glens here, for a truly stunning scene, head here in February and March when the azaleas are in full bloom. ⊠ *Off Twig St. from U.S. 17 S, Palatka* ☎ *904/329–3721* ☑ *$3.25 per vehicle (up to 8 people)* ☉ *Daily 8–sunset.*

ALONG THE COAST
DAYTONA TO NEW SMYRNA BEACH TO COCOA BEACH

This section of coast covers only 75 mi, yet it includes three separate barrier islands. At the northern end are the small city of Ormond Beach and its neighbor to the south, Daytona Beach. Daytona is primarily associated with auto racing and spring break, and its beach, which is at the southern end of the same barrier island that includes St. Augustine Beach, is fronted with a mixture of tall condos and apartments, hotels, and low-rise motels. Farther south is the small town of New Smyrna

Beach. Its beach, which is lined with private houses, some empty land, and an occasional taller condominium, is the only developed section of the island. The rest of the island is devoted to the Canaveral National Seashore and, farther south, the northern and inaccessible boundaries of the John F. Kennedy Space Center. As a result, this island is unusually unpopulated. The towns of Cape Canaveral, Cocoa, and Cocoa Beach are still farther south and include the northern end of a third barrier island. Cocoa Beach is a laid-back beach town, but it gets crowded on weekends all year, as it's the closest beach to Orlando.

Ormond Beach

30 *60 mi south of St. Augustine.*

The town got its reputation as the birthplace of speed because early car enthusiasts such as Alexander Winton, R. E. Olds, and Barney Oldfield raced their autos on the sands here. The Birthplace of Speed Antique Car Show and Swap Meet is held every Thanksgiving, attracting enthusiasts from across the nation. Ormond Beach borders the north side of Daytona Beach on both the mainland and the barrier island; nowadays you can't tell you've crossed from one to the other unless you notice the sign.

The scenic **Tomoka State Park,** 3 mi north of Ormond Beach, is perfect for fishing, camping, hiking, and boating. It is the site of a Timucuan Indian settlement discovered in 1605 by Spanish explorer Alvaro Mexia. Wooded campsites, bicycle and walking paths, and guided canoe tours on the Tomoka and Halifax rivers are the main attractions. ⊠ *2099 N. Beach St.* ☎ *386/676–4050; 800/326–3521 Reserve America for camping reservations* ☏ *386/676–4060* ⊕ *www.dep.state.fl.us/parks/district3/ tomoka* ⊠ *$3.25 per vehicle (up to 8 people); campsites $10 per day May–Oct., $15 per day Nov.–Apr.; additional $2 for electric campsite* ☉ *Daily 8–sunset.*

Listed on the National Register of Historic Places, the **Casements,** the restored winter retreat of John D. Rockefeller, is now a cultural center and museum. Take a tour through the period Rockefeller Room, with some of the family's memorabilia. The estate and its formal gardens host an annual lineup of events and exhibits; there's also a permanent exhibit of Hungarian folk art and musical instruments. ⊠ *25 Riverside Dr.* ☎ *386/676–3216* ⊕ *www.echotourism.com/cultural/casements. htm* ⊠ *Donation welcome* ☉ *Weekdays 9–5, Sat. 9–noon.*

Take a walk through 4 acres of lush tropical gardens, past fish ponds and fountains, at the **Ormond Memorial Art Museum and Gardens.** The museum has historical displays, symbolic religious paintings by Malcolm Fraser, and special exhibits by Florida artists. ⊠ *78 E. Granada Blvd.* ☎ *386/676–3347* ⊠ *$2* ☉ *Weekdays 10–4, weekends noon–4.*

Where to Stay & Eat

★ **$$$–$$$$** ✕**La Crepe en Haut.** Outside stairs lead up to this quiet and elegant French restaurant with several dining rooms and many window tables. Consider starting with the onion soup; then try the fillet of beef with burgundy sauce or the roasted duck with berries. Leave room for a sweet fruit tart or a slice of creamy cheesecake. The wine list includes excellent French labels. If you're in search of lighter fare, stop by the Bistro, next door but with the same kitchen. ⊠ *142 E. Granada Blvd.* ☎ *386/ 673–1999* ▤ *AE, DC, MC, V* ☉ *Closed Mon. No lunch Sat.*

$$–$$$ ▥ **Surfside Resort and Suites.** The reasonable rates and large number of efficiencies at this former Quality Inn make it a popular spot for families. Rooms are ample and festive. ⊠ *251 S. Atlantic Ave., 32176*

☎ 386/672–8510 or 800/227–7220 🖷 386/672–7221 ⊕ *www. daytonasurfsideresortandsuites.com* ⇨ *148 rooms, 30 suites ♠ 2 restaurants, in-room data ports, some in-room hot tubs, some kitchenettes, some microwaves, cable TV with movies, golf privileges, 3 pools (1 indoor), wading pool, outdoor hot tub, beach, volleyball, bar, video game room, laundry facilities, laundry service, business services, meeting rooms, some pets (fee); no-smoking rooms ☰ AE, MC, V.*

$–$$$ 🏨 **Best Western Mainsail Inn & Suites.** The rooms and suites (they have two bedrooms) are basic but comfortably furnished; rates are very reasonable; and management is caring. Plus, the three-story, U-shape building is right on the beach. ⊠ *281 S. Atlantic Ave., 32176* ☎ *386/677–2131 or 800/843–5142* 🖷 *386/676–0323* ⊕ *www.bestwesternmainsail. com* ⇨ *44 rooms, 10 suites ♠ In-room safes, some in-room hot tubs, some kitchenettes, cable TV, pool, wading pool, beach, dry cleaning, laundry service, business services, free parking; no-smoking rooms ☰ AE, D, DC, MC, V* ¶◎¶ *CP.*

Daytona Beach

③¹ *65 mi south of St. Augustine.*

Best known for the Daytona 500, Daytona has been the center of automobile racing since cars were first raced along the beach here in 1902. February is the biggest month for race enthusiasts, and there are weekly events at the International Speedway. During race weeks, bike weeks, the spring-break periods, and summer holidays, expect extremely heavy traffic along the strip as well as on the beach itself, since driving on the sand is allowed; areas marked "no car zones" are less frenetic and more family friendly. On the mainland, near the Inland Waterway, several blocks of Beach Street have been "street-scaped," and shops and restaurants open onto an inviting, broad brick sidewalk.

Memorabilia from the early days of beach automobile racing are on display at the **Halifax Historical Society Museum,** as are historic photographs, Native American artifacts, a postcard exhibit, and a video that details city history. There's a shop for gifts and antiques, too. ⊠ *252 S. Beach St.* ☎ *386/255–6976* ⊕ *www.halifaxhistorical.org* 🖃 *$3, free Sat.* ⊙ *Tues.–Sat. 10–4.*

The interactive motor-sports attraction at **Daytona USA** lets you experience the thrill of a race from the driver's seat with its Dreamlaps motion simulator. For the truly brave, Accelerator Alley puts the pedal to the medal with speeds reaching 200 mph. Participate in a pit stop on a NASCAR Winston Cup stock car or computer-design your own race car. There's also an exhibit of the history of auto racing. Several cars are on display, including the late Dale Earnhardt's Number 3 Chevrolet Monte Carlo, which he drove to victory in the 1998 Daytona 500, and Sir Malcolm Campbell's fully restored Bluebird V, which reached 276 mph in the 1935 Daytona race, when races were still held on the beach. ⊠ *1801 W. International Speedway Dr.* ☎ *386/947–6800* ⊕ *www.daytonausa. com* 🖃 *$20* ⊙ *Daily 9–7.*

One of only a dozen photography museums in the country, the **Southeast Museum of Photography,** at Daytona Beach Community College, has changing historical and contemporary exhibits. ⊠ *1200 W. International Speedway Blvd.* ☎ *386/254–4475* ⊕ *www.smponline.org* 🖃 *Donation welcome* ⊙ *Mon. and Wed.–Fri. 10–4, Tues. 11–7, weekends noon–5.*

Klassix Auto Attraction has dozens of exhibits and more than 120 vehicles, from vintage cycles to rare collector cars and including the Munster's Drag–ula, the Flintstone's Carriage, and the Batmobile. Stop here for a true time capsule of automotive history. In between ogling cars order yourself a double scoop at the 1950s-style ice-cream parlor. ⊠ *2909 W. International Speedway Dr.* ☎ *386/252–3802 or 800/881–8975* ⊕ *www. klassixauto.com* 🎟 *$12* ⊙ *Mon.–Fri. 10–4, Sat.–Sun. 9:30–5:30.*

The humanities section of the **Museum of Arts and Sciences,** one of the largest museums in Florida, includes displays of Chinese art and glass, silver, gold, and porcelain examples of decorative arts. The museum also has pre-Castro Cuban art, Florida Native American items, pre-Columbian art, Indian and Persian miniature paintings, and an eye-popping complete skeleton of a giant sloth that is 13 ft long and 130,000 years old. ⊠ *1040 Museum Blvd.* ☎ *386/255–0285* ⊕ *www.moas.org* 🎟 *$7* ⊙ *Tues.–Fri. 9–4, weekends noon–5.*

Ⓒ **Adventure Landing** is both a wet and dry park. On the water-park side, kids of all ages float on tubes in the Lazy River, careen down 15 water slides, and get doused in the playhouse, where a 1,000-gallon bucket dumps water on them every eight minutes. On the dry side, race one- and two-seat go-carts on a ¼-mi, multilevel track; play miniature golf on three different courses that thread through ominous caves and raging waterfalls; or try your hand at any of 130 state-of-the-art video games and realistic simulators. ⊠ *601 Earl St.* ☎ *386/258–0071* ⊕ *www. adventurelanding.com* 🎟 *Water park $19.99; miniature golf $6 per course; single-seat go-carts $6, double-seat $7.99* ⊙ *Mar.–Oct., Mon.–Thurs. noon–10, Fri.–Sat. 10 AM–midnight, Sun. 10–10.*

Daytona Beach, which bills itself as the World's Most Famous Beach, permits you to drive your car right up to your beach site, spread out a blanket, and have all your belongings at hand; this is especially convenient for beachgoers who are elderly or have disabilities. However, heavy traffic during summer and holidays makes it dangerous for children, and families should be extra careful or stay in the designated car-free zones. The speed limit is 10 mph. To get your car on the beach, look for signs on Route A1A indicating beach access via beach ramps. Sand traps are not limited to the golf course, though—cars can get stuck.

off the beaten path

Ponce Inlet. At the southern tip of the barrier island that includes Daytona Beach is this sleepy town with a small marina, a few bars, and informal restaurants specializing in very fresh fish. Boardwalks traverse delicate dunes and provide easy access to the beach, although storms have caused serious erosion. Marking this prime spot is the bright-red, century-old Ponce de León Lighthouse, a historic monument and museum. It's one of the few in the country in which all the original buildings are still standing. Climb to the top of the lighthouse tower for a bird's-eye view of Ponce Inlet. ⊠ *4931 S. Peninsula Ave.* ☎ *386/ 761–1821* ⊕ *www.ponceinlet.org* 🎟 *$5* ⊙ *Early Sept.–mid-May, daily 10–5; mid-May–early Sept., daily 10–9.*

Where to Stay & Eat

★ **$–$$$** ✕ **Gene's Steak House.** Quiet and intimate, this family-operated restaurant, a bit west of town, has long upheld its reputation as *the* place for steaks in the area. Signature entrées include filet mignons, sirloins, and porterhouses. Seafood is also available. The wine list is one of the state's largest. ⊠ *3674 W. International Speedway Blvd. (U.S. 92)* ☎ *386/255–2059* ▤ *AE, DC, MC, V* ⊙ *Closed Sun.–Mon. No lunch.*

★ **$–$$$** ✕ **Rosario Ristorante.** Excellent northern Italian fare drives this busy place, nestled in the Live Oak Inn. Worthy are the tender veal marsala and fresh local grouper poached in white wine, but the menu also has a full page of pastas, including tortellini *alla Rosario* (stuffed with ricotta cheese, prosciutto, and mushrooms in a creamy cheese sauce) and spaghetti *puttanesca* (with sun-dried tomatoes, olives, capers, and anchovies). Save room for the sweet cannoli. ⊠ *448 S. Beach St.* ☎ *386/258–6066* ☰ *MC, V* ⊘ *Closed Sun.–Mon. No lunch.*

$–$$ ✕ **Anna's Italian Trattoria.** White table linens and flowers complement delightful Italian fare at this cozy spot. Choose from a long list of delicious pastas, such as the spaghetti with Italian sausage and onions, angel-hair pasta with fresh chopped tomatoes and garlic, or spinach-stuffed ravioli. Try one of the many classic Italian desserts here. ⊠ *304 Seabreeze Blvd.* ☎ *386/239–9624* ☰ *AE, D, DC, MC, V* ⊘ *No lunch.*

$–$$ ✕ **Aunt Catfish's on the River.** Hot cinnamon rolls and hush puppies come with any entrée, one of the lures of this spot popular with locals and visitors. Other draws are a terrific salad bar, southern-style fried chicken, and seafood (fried shrimp, fried catfish, and crab cakes are specialties). It's on the west bank of the Intracoastal Waterway (off U.S. 1, before crossing the Port Orange Causeway), just south of Daytona. ⊠ *4009 Halifax Dr., Port Orange* ☎ *386/767–4768* ☰ *AE, MC, V.*

¢–$$ ✕ **McK's Dublin Station.** Crowds fill up the bar, the tables in the bar, and the cozy booths in this lively tavern. The fare is simple but hearty and portions are large; cheeseburgers are thick and juicy, the chili is extra-spicy, and a big slice of homemade meat loaf comes with mashed potatoes. There's a long list of stuffed sandwiches. Onion rings are a house specialty. ⊠ *218 S. Beach St.* ☎ *386/238–3321* ☰ *AE, MC, V* ⊘ *Closed Sun.*

$$–$$$$ ⊞ **Hilton Daytona Beach Oceanfront Resort.** Right on the beach, this 11-story hotel is a favorite with families. The pastel-color rooms are on the large side, and most have balconies; some have a kitchenette, patio, or terrace. Convenient touches include a hair dryer, a makeup mirror with lights, and a bar with refrigerator. The rooftop restaurant has excellent views and is a popular stop for Sunday brunch. ⊠ *2637 S. Atlantic Ave., 32118* ☎ *386/767–7350 or 800/525–7350* ☐ *386/760–3651* ⊕ *www.daytonabeach.hilton.com* ↝ *214 rooms, 2 suites* ♧ *Restaurant, room service, in-room data ports, in-room safes, some kitchenettes, some microwaves, refrigerators, cable TV with movies, pool, wading pool, fitness room, hair salon, hot tub, sauna, beach, billiards, bar, video game room, playground, dry cleaning, laundry facilities, laundry service, Internet, business services, meeting rooms, free parking; no-smoking rooms* ☰ *AE, D, DC, MC, V.*

★ $–$$$$ ⊞ **Adam's Mark Resort.** Daytona's most luxurious high-rise hotel has two towers that sit on a traffic-free beach. Every room has a great ocean view and is comfortably furnished in pleasing pastels and blond oak. Spacious sun decks and pools are perfect for those not into the beach. Dine in the resort's food court or live it up in an elegant restaurant. ⊠ *100 N. Atlantic Ave., 32118* ☎ *386/254–8200 or 800/444–2326* ☐ *386/253–8841* ⊕ *www.adamsmark.com* ↝ *746 rooms, 19 suites, 23 cabanas* ♧ *3 restaurants, food court, room service, in-room data ports, some minibars, cable TV with movies and video games, indoor-outdoor pool, outdoor pool, wading pool, 2 health clubs, massage, beach, volleyball, 3 bars, video game room, playground, laundry facilities, laundry service, concierge, Internet, business services, meeting rooms, free parking; no-smoking floors* ☰ *AE, DC, MC, V.*

$$–$$$ ⊞ **Beach Quarters Resort.** Freshly baked free goodies and coffee, served in the home-style Galley overlooking the ocean, is one of the extra personal touches at this all-suites inn. The one- and two-bedroom units are done in bright yellows with teal or red and blue accents and have coordinating window treatments and oak furnishings. Each unit has a private balcony and full kitchen. Penthouse suites have electric fireplaces.

⊠ *3711 S. Atlantic Ave., Daytona Beach Shores 32127* ☎ *386/767–3119 or 800/332–3119* 🖷 *386/767–0883* ⊕ *www.thebeachquarters.com* 🛏 *26 suites* ⚱ *Restaurant, some in-room hot tubs, kitchens, cable TV, in-room VCRs, pool, massage, beach, laundry facilities, Internet, business services, free parking* 🖃 *AE, D, MC, V.*

$–$$$ 🏨 **Perry's Ocean-Edge.** Long regarded as a family resort, Perry's is known for its free homemade doughnuts and coffee—a breakfast ritual served in the lush solarium. Units are in one two-story building and two six-story buildings that face the beach. Most of the rooms have kitchens and great ocean views. There are several pools, a wide beach, and a putting green. ⊠ *2209 S. Atlantic Ave., 32118* ☎ *386/255–0581 or 800/447–0002* 🖷 *386/258–7315* ⊕ *www.perrysoceanedge.com* 🛏 *163 rooms, 42 suites* ⚱ *Café, in-room data ports, some kitchens, cable TV, putting green, 3 pools (1 indoor), fitness classes, gym, spa, beach, horseshoes, shuffleboard, volleyball, children's programs (ages 4–12), playground, laundry facilities, laundry service, Internet, free parking; no-smoking rooms* 🖃 *AE, D, DC, MC, V.*

★ $–$$ 🏨 **Live Oak Inn.** Two restored homes next door to each other, both listed on the National Register of Historic Places, make up this lovely B&B. Each room is different, but all are beautifully furnished with antiques. Some have long enclosed porches and look out over the marina or onto gardens. Three have whirlpools. The first floor of one of the homes contains the fine Rosario restaurant as well as a small lounge and reception area. Downstairs in the other house is the breakfast room. ⊠ *448 S. Beach St., 32114* ☎ *386/252–4667 or 800/881–4667* 🖷 *386/239–0068* 🛏 *14 rooms* ⚱ *Restaurant, dining room, some in-room hot tubs, fishing, bar, free parking; no smoking* 🖃 *AE, MC, V* ⍻ *CP.*

Nightlife & the Arts

THE ARTS Touring Broadway shows, symphony orchestras, international ballet companies, and popular entertainers appear at the **Ocean Center** (⊠ 101 N. Atlantic Ave. ☎ 386/254–4545; 800/858–6444 in Florida). **Peabody Auditorium** (⊠ 600 Auditorium Blvd. ☎ 386/671–3461) is used for concerts and programs year-round. **Seaside Music Theater** (⊠ 176 N. Beach St. ☎ 386/252–6200 or 800/854–5592) presents musicals in two venues January through February and June through August.

NIGHTLIFE Popular **La Playa Penthouse Cocktail Lounge** (⊠ 2500 N. Atlantic Ave. ☎ 386/672–0990), on the top floor of the Best Western La Playa Resort, has a dance floor and live entertainment some nights. Acts range from contemporary musicians in their twenties to the original Platters, from the 1950s. At **Razzles** (⊠ 611 Seabreeze Blvd. ☎ 386/257–6236), DJs play high-energy dance music from 8 PM to 3 AM.

Sports & the Outdoors

AUTO RACING The massive **Daytona International Speedway** (⊠ 1801 W. International Speedway Blvd. ☎ 386/254–2700), on Daytona's major east–west artery, has year-round auto and motorcycle racing, including the Daytona 500 in February and the Pepsi 400 in July. When races aren't on, you can take a 20-minute tour (daily 9–5).

DOG RACING Bet on the dogs every night but Sunday year-round at the **Daytona Beach Kennel Club** (⊠ U.S. 92 near International Speedway ☎ 386/252–6484).

FISHING Contact **Critter Fleet Marina** (⊠ 4950 S. Peninsula Dr. ☎ 386/767–7676) for full- or half-day deep-sea party trips. **Half-n-Half Charters** (⊠ 79 E. Dunlawton Ave. ☎ 386/767–0583) offers 5-, 8-, 10-, and 12-hour fishing excursions.

GOLF **Indigo Lakes Golf Club** (⊠ 312 Indigo Dr. ☎ 386/254–3607) has 18 holes of golf. **Pelican Bay South Country Club** (⊠ 550 Sea Duck Dr. ☎ 386/

788–6496) rents clubs and has a pro shop and a restaurant, in addition to 18 holes. There's an 18-hole course at **Spruce Creek Golf & Country Club** (⊠ 1900 Country Club Dr. ☎ 386/756–6114), along with practice and driving ranges, rental clubs, a pro shop, and a restaurant.

WATER SPORTS Rent surfboards or boogie boards at any **Salty Dog** (⊠ 700 E. International Speedway Blvd. ☎ 386/258–0457 ⊠ 100 S. Atlantic Ave. ☎ 386/253–2755 ⊠ Bellair Plaza, 2429 N. Atlantic Ave. ☎ 386/673–5277).

Shopping

Daytona Flea & Farmer's Market (⊠ I–4 at U.S. 92 ☎ 386/253–3330 ⊕ www.daytonafleamarket.net) is one of the largest in the South. The **Volusia Mall** (⊠ 1700 W. International Speedway Blvd. ☎ 386/253–6783) has more than 100 stores, including Burdines and Dillards.

New Smyrna Beach

③ *19 mi south of Daytona Beach.*

The long, dune-lined beach of this small town abuts the Canaveral National Seashore. Behind the dunes sit beach houses, small motels, and an occasional high-rise (except at the extreme northern tip, none are higher than seven stories). Canal Street, on the mainland, and Flagler Avenue, with many beachside shops and restaurants, have both been "streetscaped" with wide brick sidewalks and stately palm trees. The town is also known for its internationally recognized artists' workshop.

Changing every two months, the **Atlantic Center for the Arts** has works of internationally known artists. Media include sculpture, mixed materials, video, drawings, prints, and paintings. Intensive three-week workshops are periodically run by visual, literary, and performing master artists such as Edward Albee, James Dickey, and Beverly Pepper. ⊠ *1414 Art Center Ave.* ☎ *386/427–6975* ⊕ *www.atlanticcenterforthearts.org* ⊠ *Free* ⊙ *Weekdays 9–5, Sat. 10–2.*

In a warehouse that has been converted into a stunning high-ceiling art gallery, **Arts on Douglas** has a new exhibit of works by a Florida artist every month. Representing more than 60 artists, some of the gallery's previous exhibits include handmade jewelry by Mary Schimpff Webb and landscape and still-life oils by Barbara Tiffany. The gallery also hosts an open reception every first Saturday of the month from 4 to 7 PM. ⊠ *123 Douglas St.* ☎ *386/428–1133* ⊠ *Free* ⊙ *Tues.–Fri. 11–6, Sat. 10–2, and by appointment.*

Smyrna Dunes Park is on the northern tip of its barrier island. Here 1½ mi of boardwalks crisscross sand dunes and delicate dune vegetation to lead to beaches and a fishing jetty. Botanical signs identify the flora, and there are picnic tables and an information center. ⊠ *N. Peninsula Ave.* ☎ *386/424–2935* ⊠ *$3.50* ⊙ *Daily 6 AM–sunset.*

New Smyrna Beach's public beach extends 7 mi from the northernmost part of the barrier island south to the Canaveral National Seashore. It is mostly hard-packed white sand and at low tide can be stunningly wide. The beach is lined with heaps of sandy dunes, but because they're endangered, it's against the law to walk on or play in them or to pick the sea grass, which helps to stabilize the dunes. Note that from sunrise to sunset cars are allowed on certain sections of the beach (speed limit: 10 mph). In season, there is a nominal beach access fee for cars.

★ Miles of grassy, windswept dunes and a virtually empty beach await you at **Canaveral National Seashore,** a remarkable 57,000-acre park with 24 mi of undeveloped coastline. Stop at any of the six parking areas and

follow the wooden walkways to the beach. Ranger-led weekly programs range from canoe trips to sea-turtle talks. ⊠ *7611 S. Atlantic Ave.*
☎ *386/428–3384* ⊕ *www.nps.gov/cana* ⊠ *$5 per vehicle* ☉ *Nov.–Mar.
6–6, Apr.–Oct. 6 AM–8 PM; call for Playalinda Beach hrs.*

Where to Stay & Eat

$$–$$$ ✕ **New Smyrna Steakhouse.** Superb steaks and ribs bring locals and vis-
itors to this dark, busy spot. Booths are lit by individual, low-hanging
lamps that provide intimacy but enough light to read the menu. Try the
12-ounce New York strip or sirloin, the 22-ounce porterhouse, the 8-
ounce filet mignon, or a rack of tender ribs. Other good choices are the
Cajun pizza, shrimp Caesar salad, and mesquite chicken. ⊠ *723 E. 3rd
Ave.* ☎ *386/424–9696* ⊟ *AE, D, MC, V.*

★ **$–$$$** ✕ **Victor's Backstreet Cuisine.** A blue neon sign lights the way to this tiny
restaurant. Although the interior is humble—specials scrawled on a
blackboard, tightly arranged wooden tables, and a small, open kitchen—
the fare here is definitely bold. Spicy barbecue ribs, herb-seasoned tuna
or chicken on a dense berry sauce, and sirloin with datil-pepper salsa
are just some of the many choices. Specials could be filet mignon or os-
trich prepared with a twist. You'll see Victor in the kitchen, working
his culinary magic, and in the photos on the walls, accepting accolades.
On weekends reservations are a must. ⊠ *103 S. Pine St.* ☎ *386/426–
5000* ⊟ *No credit cards* ☉ *Closed Mon.–Tues. No lunch.*

$–$$ ✕ **Captain J. B.'s Famous Fishing Camp and Seafood Restaurant.** Better known
simply as J. B.'s, this local landmark is on the eastern shore of the In-
dian River. Crowds gather around the picnic-style tables inside and out
or belly up to the bar to dine on mounds of spicy seafood, fresh crabs,
Cajun alligator, or crab cakes. It's a great place to catch the sunset, and
there's live music Saturday and Sunday afternoons. ⊠ *859 Pompano
Ave.* ☎ *386/427–5747* ⊟ *AE, D, MC, V.*

$–$$ ✕ **Chase's on the Beach.** Eat on the deck beneath the stars—gazing at ei-
ther the ocean or the pool—or dine indoors. Barefooted beachgoers wander up for beverages, hamburgers, and salads during the day (shoes
required inside), whereas the evening crowd comes for fried shrimp,
grouper sandwiches, and weekend entertainment. ⊠ *3401 S. Atlantic
Ave.* ☎ *386/423–8787* ⊟ *AE, D, MC, V.*

$–$$ ✕ **Norwood's Seafood Restaurant.** Fresh local fish and shrimp are the spe-
cialties at this casual New Smyrna Beach landmark, open since 1945.
Also order steak, blackened chicken breast, or pasta. Prices are incredibly low, and more than 1,200 bottles of wine are on hand. ⊠ *400 E.
2nd Ave.* ☎ *386/428–4621* ⊟ *AE, D, DC, MC, V.*

$–$$ ✕ **Spanish River Grill.** Michelle and Henry Salgado own this first-rate restau-
rant, which many consider the best in New Smyrna Beach. Henry com-
bines his Cuban grandmother's recipes with local ingredients for knockout
results. Start with fried green plantains or clams tossed with garlic and
avocado. For the main course, try some seafood, the incredible paella,
or a tender rib-eye steak stuffed with chorizo. Be sure to save room for
one of Michelle's desserts. ⊠ *737 E. 3rd Ave.* ☎ *386/424–6991* ⊟ *AE,
MC, V* ☉ *Closed Mon. No lunch weekends.*

¢–$ ✕ **Toni and Joe's.** This longtime ultracasual favorite opens onto the
Fodor'sChoice beach and has a large terrace perfect for people-watching. Step in here
★ (no shoes required) for the famous hoagies: long rolls of fresh bread stuffed
with slices of steak, cheese, sweet peppers, and onions and heated until
the cheese is perfectly melted. ⊠ *309 Buenos Aires* ☎ *386/427–6850*
⊟ *No credit cards* ☉ *Closed Mon. No dinner.*

$$–$$$$ ▦ **Holiday Inn Hotel& Suites.** Families tend to like these comfortable
suites, which sleep four, six, or eight people. Bedrooms are raised and
set behind the living room, which opens out to a balcony and a spec-

tacular view of the ocean. ✉ *1401 S. Atlantic Ave., 32169* ☎ *386/426–0020 or 800/232–2414* 🖷 *386/423–3977* ⊕ *www.sixcontinentshotels.com* ⇱ *102 suites* ᲊ *Restaurant, in-room data ports, microwaves, refrigerators, cable TV with movies, pool, beach, fitness room, dry cleaning, laundry facilities, laundry service, Internet, business services, car rental, free parking; no-smoking rooms* ⊟ *AE, MC, V.*

★ **$$–$$$** 🖭 **Riverview Hotel and Restaurant.** A landmark since 1886, this former bridge tender's home is set back from the Intracoastal Waterway at the edge of the North Causeway, which to this day has an operating drawbridge. Rooms open out to plant-filled verandas and balconies, and views look either through trees to the Intracoastal or onto the private courtyard and pretty pool. Each room is furnished differently with charming antique touches, such as an old washbasin, a quilt, or a rocking chair. Continental breakfast is served in your room. The inn has an excellent gift shop and is near interesting art galleries and stores. ✉ *103 Flagler Ave., 32169* ☎ *386/428–5858 or 800/945–7416* 🖷 *386/423–8927* ⊕ *www.riverviewhotel.com* ⇱ *16 rooms, 2 suites* ᲊ *Restaurant, fans, in-room data ports, in-room safes, cable TV, pool, bicycles, bar, laundry facilities, laundry services, Internet, meeting rooms, business services, free parking* ⊟ *AE, D, DC, MC, V* ⦿ *CP.*

$–$$$ 🖭 **Coastal Waters Inn.** Popular with families, this three-story blue-and-white beachfront hotel has one- and two-bedroom suites with kitchens as well as standard rooms. Some units have excellent ocean views, and many have balconies or patios. Furnishings are spare but comfortable. The beach is steps away. ✉ *3509 S. Atlantic Ave., 32169* ☎ *386/428–3800 or 800/321–7882* 🖷 *396/423–5002* ⊕ *www.volusia.com/horizonresorts* ⇱ *8 rooms, 32 suites* ᲊ *Some kitchenettes, some microwaves, cable TV, pool, wading pool, beach, laundry facilities, Internet, free parking* ⊟ *AE, D, DC, MC, V.*

$–$$$ 🖭 **Little River Inn Bed & Breakfast.** A formal driveway leads to this charming B&B in an Old Florida home built in 1883. The house, set on a slight rise, is surrounded by nearly 2 acres of oak trees and is across the road from the peaceful marshes of the Indian River. One guest room is on the first floor, three are on the second, and two are on the third. All have views of the river. Two of the rooms share a bathroom. Relax on the wide terrace, or settle in a corner of the living room with a good book. Guests gather for breakfast in the sunny dining area. Room televisions must be requested ahead of time. ✉ *532 N. Riverside Dr., 32168* ☎ *386/424–0100* ⊕ *www.little-river-inn.com* ⇱ *6 rooms, 4 with bath* ᲊ *Dining room, tennis court, bicycles, piano, free parking; no kids under 12, no smoking* ⊟ *AE, MC, V* ⦿ *BP.*

The Arts

The **Little Theater of New Smyrna Beach** (✉ 726 3rd Ave. ☎ 386/423–1246) has been offering productions for more than half a century. The six productions a season vary from comedy to mystery to drama.

The Outdoors

BOATING **Florida Coastal Cruises, Inc.** (✉ Seaharvest Marina ☎ 386/428–0201 or 800/881–2628) is a relaxed and wonderful way to experience some of the natural beauty of the New Smyrna Beach area. The good ship *Manatee* and its skipper offer lunch, sunset, and dinner cruises. Kids who help steer the boat receive a Captain's Certificate.

Shopping

Flagler Avenue (North Causeway) is the major entranceway to the beach, and art galleries, gift shops, and surf shops line the street. **Arts on Douglas** (✉ 123 Douglas St. ☎ 386/428–1133) displays works by 60 artists plus a solo exhibit, which changes monthly.

Cocoa & Cocoa Beach

50 mi south of New Smyrna Beach.

The town of Cocoa, on the mainland, includes the quaint shopping area known as Olde Cocoa Village. Cocoa's neighbor on the barrier island ❸ is **Cocoa Beach,** a popular year-round escape for folks who live in Central Florida. Motels and inexpensive restaurants line the beach, and Kennedy Space Center is just 10 minutes away.

North of Cocoa, **Playalinda Beach,** part of the **Canaveral National Seashore,** is the longest stretch of undeveloped coast on Florida's Atlantic seaboard. Hundreds of giant sea turtles come ashore here between May and August to lay their eggs, and the extreme northern area is favored by nude sun worshipers. There are no lifeguards, but park rangers patrol. Take Exit 80 from Interstate 95 and follow Route 406 east across the Indian River, then Route 402 east for another 12 mi. ⊠ *Rte. 402, Titusville* ☎ *321/267–1110* 🖾 *$5 per vehicle* ⊘ *Daily 6–6.*

Examine wildlife and rivers of grass at the 140,000-acre **Merritt Island National Wildlife Refuge,** adjacent to the Canaveral National Seashore. Wander along nature trails at this habitat for wintering migratory waterfowl, and take a self-guided, 7-mi driving tour along Black Point Wildlife Drive. On the Oak Hammock Foot Trail, learn about the plants of a hammock community. ⊠ *Rte. 402, across Titusville causeway* ☎ *321/ 861–0667* 🖾 *Free* ⊘ *Daily sunrise–sunset; visitor center daily 8–4:30* ⊘ *Sun., Apr.–Oct.*

★ ⊙ At the **Kennedy Space Center Visitor Complex,** exhibits include **Astronaut Encounter,** where you can question a real astronaut, and **Exploration in the New Millennium,** a journey through time from the early Vikings' discoveries of Greenland and Iceland to 1976, when the first U.S. probe landed on Mars. You have an opportunity to touch a piece of Mars and to sign up for a future space flight. **Robot Scouts** is a walk-through exhibit of unmanned planetary probes; **Early Space Exploration** highlights the Mercury and Gemini programs; and the **Rocket Garden** contains a collection of authentic rockets. **The Apollo Saturn V Center** has multimedia shows as well as the 363-ft Saturn V rocket, and the **International Space Station Center** displays a detailed re-creation of a space-station module. Twin 5½-story-tall IMAX theaters with awesome sound systems can make you think you're at a launch (note that the center closes for certain actual launch dates). There are two IMAX movies: *The Dream Is Alive,* narrated by Walter Cronkite, takes you through astronaut training and into the cabins where the astronauts live while in space; *Space Station,* narrated by Tom Cruise, leads you on an awesome journey to the International Space Station, some 220 mi above Earth. The 3-D technology lets you experience a space walk and navigate the Space Station much in the same way an astronaut does. You must purchase tickets for all exhibits and areas of the space complex. ⊠ *Rte. 405, Kennedy Space Center* ☎ *321/449–4444 or 800/572–4636* ⊕ *www. kennedyspacecenter.com* 🖾 *$26 all-inclusive* ⊘ *Daily 9–5:30 (last tour at 2:45); call ahead for closures on launch dates.*

At the entrance to the Kennedy Space Center Visitor Complex, the **United States Astronaut Hall of Fame** focuses not only on the milestones of the space program but also on the personal stories of the astronauts. Highlights of the interactive **Astronaut Adventure** include a mock liftoff with a take-your-breath-away g-force simulator, a hair-raising re-creation jet-aircraft dogfight complete with 360-degree barrel rolls. For a quiet interlude, view videotapes of historic moments in the space program.

The **First on the Moon** exhibit focuses on the crew selection for *Apollo 11* and the Soviet Union's role in the space race. Also here is U.S. Space Camp, with budding astronauts in a hands-on learning environment. ⊠ *6225 Vectorspace Blvd., off Rte. 405, Kennedy Space Center, Titusville* ☎ *321/269–6100* ⊕ *www.astronauts.org* ⊠ *$13.95* ☉ *Sept.–May, daily 9–5; June–Aug., daily 9–6.*

The **Astronaut Memorial Planetarium and Observatory,** one of the largest public-access observatories in Florida, has a 24-inch telescope through which you can view objects in the solar system and deep space. The planetarium also has two theaters. One shows such films as *Deep Space Frontiers, Hubble Vision* and *Planet Safari*. The other showcases a number of planetarium and laser-light shows. The Science Quest Hall has an exhibit of scales calibrated to other planets. Travel 2½ mi east of Interstate 95 Exit 201 on Route 520, and take Route 501 north for 1¾ mi. ⊠ *1519 Clearlake Rd., Cocoa* ☎ *321/634–3732* ⊕ *www.brevard.cc. fl.us* ⊠ *Observatory and exhibit hall free; film or planetarium show $6, both $10; laser show $6; Triple Combination (planetarium, movie, laser show) $14* ☉ *Wed. 1:30–4:30, Fri.–Sat. 6:30–10:30; call for current shows and schedules.*

Don't overlook the hands-on discovery rooms and the Taylor Collection of Victorian memorabilia at the **Brevard Museum of History and Natural Science.** Its nature center has 22 acres of trails encompassing three distinct ecosystems—sand pine hills, lake lands, and marshlands. ⊠ *2201 Michigan Ave., Cocoa* ☎ *321/632–1830* ⊕ *www.brevardmuseum.com* ⊠ *$5* ☉ *Tues.–Sat. 10–4, Sun. 1–4.*

Sydney Fisher Park at Cocoa Beach (⊠ 2100 block of Rte. A1A) has showers, playgrounds, changing areas, picnic areas with grills, snack shops, and plenty of well-maintained, inexpensive surfside parking lots. Beach vendors carry necessities for sunning and swimming. The parking fee is $3 for cars and $5 for RVs.

Exhibits of contemporary art; presentations of decorative arts, ethnographic works, photography, and experimental art forms; and hands-on activities for children are the draws at the **Brevard Museum of Art and Science.** ⊠ *1463 Highland Ave., Melbourne* ☎ *321/242–0737* ⊕ *www. artandscience.org* ⊠ *$5* ☉ *Tues.–Sat. 10–5, Sun. 1–5.*

Where to Stay & Eat

$$–$$$$ ✕ **Mango Tree Restaurant.** Dine in elegance at tables discretely spaced amid orchid gardens, with piano music playing in the background. House favorites include fresh grouper with shrimp and scallops glazed in hollandaise sauce, Indian River crab cakes, coq au vin, and veal Chandlier (scallopini seared with scallops and cognac). ⊠ *118 N. Atlantic Ave., Cocoa Beach* ☎ *321/799–0513* ⊟ *AE, MC, V* ☉ *Closed Mon. No lunch.*

★ **$$–$$$** ✕ **Black Tulip.** Two cozy, intimate rooms yield some of Cocoa Village's finest food. Starters include island conch fritters served with a spicy mango dipping sauce or a three-cheese, baked French onion soup. The chef's signature dish is roast duckling served with a sauce made of apples, cashews, and red wine. Or, try the filet mignon medallions with a tangy mustard and artichoke sauce, or the baked mahimahi topped with sliced bananas and served with a lemon dill sauce. Lunch selections are lighter and include sandwiches and salads. ⊠ *207 Brevard Ave., Cocoa* ☎ *321/ 631–1133* ⊟ *AE, DC, MC, V* ☉ *Closed Sun.*

$$–$$$ ✕ **Cafe Margaux.** Choose a table outside in a charming courtyard or indoors in a cozy, flower-decorated dining room at this intimate Cocoa Village spot. If wild game suits your palate, try the pan-seared pheasant breast or the Long Island duckling. Seafood lovers may want to try the phyllo-encased Norwegian salmon medallions stuffed with French goat cheese or the sesame-seared ahi tuna over Japanese cucumbers. ⊠ *220 Brevard Ave., Cocoa* ☎ *321/639–8343* ☰ *AE, D, DC, MC, V* ⊗ *Closed Sun. and Tues.*

$–$$$ ✕ **Dixie Crossroads.** Crowds hungry for snow crabs, St. Louis–style barbecue ribs, rock shrimp, shrimp, scallop, and Maine lobster dishes head for this large family-style eatery nestled beneath 100-year-old live oaks. Local artists' works decorate the walls, and Dixie's own house band is often on deck Saturday afternoon. ⊠ *1475 Garden St., Titusville* ☎ *321/ 268–5000* ☰ *AE, D, DC, MC, V.*

¢–$ ✕ **Lone Cabbage Fish Camp.** The natural habitat of wildlife and local characters, this one-of-a-kind spot sits on the St. Johns River, 9 mi north of the Cocoa city limits and 4 mi west of Interstate 95. Catfish, country ham, and fried turtle and alligator make the drive worthwhile. Also fish from a dock here or take an airboat ride. Check out the gator souvenirs behind the bar and the Swamp Monster, stuffed and mounted on the wall; it was "caught" by one of the owners, Charlie Jones. ⊠ *8199 Rte. 520, Cocoa* ☎ *321/632–4199* ☰ *AE, MC, V.*

★ $$–$$$$ ▦ **Inn at Cocoa Beach.** The finest accommodations in Cocoa Beach are in this charming oceanfront inn. Each spacious room is decorated differently, but all have some combination of reproduction 18th- and 19th-century armoires, four-poster beds, and comfortably upholstered chairs and sofas. There are several suites, some with whirlpool baths. All units have balconies or patios and views of the ocean. Included in the rate are an evening spread of wine and cheese and a sumptuous Continental breakfast with delicious homemade muffins and breads, served in the sunny breakfast room. ⊠ *4300 Ocean Beach Blvd., Cocoa Beach 32931* ☎ *321/799–3460; 800/343–5307 outside Florida* ☐ *321/784– 8632* ⊕ *www.theinnatcocoabeach.com* ↩ *50 rooms* ♿ *In-room safes, some in-room hot tubs, cable TV, pool, fitness room, beach, bicycles, shuffleboard, bar, dry cleaning, meeting rooms, free parking; no kids under 12* ☰ *AE, D, MC, V* ⦿ *CP.*

$$–$$$ ▦ **Cocoa Beach Hilton Oceanfront.** It's easy to pass by the Hilton, as its sign is sometimes hidden by the dense natural foliage that grows right out to the edge of Route A1A. Once you turn into the parking lot, however, it's impossible to miss. At seven stories, it's one of the tallest buildings in Cocoa Beach. Just a small strip of sand dunes separates this resort from a wide stretch of excellent beach. Most rooms have ocean views, but for true drama get a room on the east end directly facing the water. The floor-to-ceiling windows really show off the scenery. ⊠ *1550 N. Atlantic Ave., Cocoa Beach 32931* ☎ *321/799–0003 or 800/526–2609* ☐ *321/799–0344* ⊕ *www.cocoabeachhilton.com* ↩ *296 rooms, 11 suites* ♿ *2 restaurants, room service, in-room data ports, cable TV with movies, pool, fitness room, beach, volleyball, bars, video game room, dry cleaning, laundry facilities, Internet, convention center, meeting rooms, free parking; no-smoking rooms* ☰ *AE, D, DC, MC, V.*

$–$$$ ▦ **Wakulla Resort.** There's nothing fancy about these two-bedroom suites. They attract families because they're clean and comfortable, are just two blocks from the beach, and are convenient to NASA's attractions as well as those in Orlando. The five-room suites, designed to sleep six, include two bedrooms, a living room, dining room, and fully equipped kitchen. Outdoor grills are available. ⊠ *3550 N. Atlantic Ave., Cocoa Beach 32931* ☎ *321/783–2230 or 800/992–5852* ☐ *321/ 783–0980* ⊕ *www.wakulla-suites.com* ↩ *116 suites* ♿ *Kitchens, cable TV with movies and video games, pool, shuffleboard, dry cleaning, laundry facilities, business services, free parking; no-smoking rooms* ☰ *AE, D, DC, MC, V.*

The Outdoors

BIKING Rent a beach cruiser bike from **Ten Speed Drive** (✉ 166 N. Atlantic Ave. ☎ 321/783–1196) and ride like the wind up and down the beach.

FISHING **Cape Marina** (✉ 800 Scallop Dr., Port Canaveral ☎ 321/783–8410) has 8, 10, and 16-hour charter-fishing trips.

Shopping

In downtown Cocoa, cobblestone walkways wend through **Olde Cocoa Village,** a cluster of restored turn-of-the-20th-century buildings now occupied by restaurants and specialty shops purveying crafts, fine art, and clothing. **Ron Jon Surf Shop** (✉4151 N. Atlantic Ave., Cocoa Beach ☎321/799–8888) is an attraction in its own right—a castle that's purple, pink, and glittery as an amusement park, plunked down in the middle of the beach community. The multilevel store is packed with swimwear and surfboards and is open around the clock. It's worth a stop just to see what all those billboards are about.

INLAND TOWNS

Inland, peaceful little towns are separated by miles of two-lane roads running through acres of dense forest and flat pastureland and skirting one lake after another. There's not much else to see but cattle, though you may catch a glimpse of the few hills found in the state. Gentle and rolling, they're hardly worth noting to folks from true hill country, but they're significant enough in Florida for much of this area to be called the "hill and lake region."

DeLand

34 *21 mi southwest of Daytona Beach.*

The quiet college town is home to Stetson University, established in 1886 by hat magnate John Stetson. Several inviting state parks are nearby; as for activities, there's great manatee watching during the winter as well as skydiving for both spectators and participants.

Soaring ceilings and neoclassical furnishings provide the backdrop at the **Duncan Gallery of Art,** on the Stetson University campus. The gallery hosts exhibits by southwestern and national artists and Stetson students. ✉ *Stetson University, Sampson Hall, Michigan and Amelia Aves.* ☎ *386/822-7266* ⌨ *Donation welcome* ☉ *Tues.–Sat. 10–4, Sun. 1–4.*

The **DeLand Museum of Art,** in the Cultural Arts Center across from Stetson University, has nationally recognized exhibits of painting, photography, sculpture, and fine crafts. ✉ *600 N. Woodland Blvd.* ☎ *386/734-4371* ⌨ *$2 (can be more for some exhibits)* ☉ *Tues.–Sat. 10–4, Sun. 1–4.*

One of the largest private collections of gems and minerals in the world can be found in the **Gillespie Museum of Minerals,** on the Stetson University campus. ✉ *Stetson University, Michigan and Amelia Aves.* ☎ *386/822-7330* ⌨ *Donation welcome* ☉ *Tues.–Fri. 10–4.*

February is the top month for sighting manatees, but they begin to head here in November, as soon as the water gets cold enough (below 68°F). **Blue Spring State Park,** once a river port where paddle wheelers stopped to take on cargoes of oranges, also contains a historic homestead that is open to the public. Hike, camp, or picnic here. Your best bet for spotting a manatee is to walk along the boardwalk. ✉ *2100 W. French Ave., Orange City* ☎ *386/775-3663* ⊕ *www.dep.state.fl.us/parks/district3/bluespring* ⌨ *$4 per vehicle (up to 8 people)* ☉ *Daily 8–sunset.*

Where to Stay & Eat

$–$$$ ✕ **Pondo's.** You step back in time about 70 years when you enter what was once a romantic hideaway for young pilots who trained in DeLand during the war. The owner-chef's specialty is Pondo's beef with pasta, but you'll also find duck, rack of lamb, veal, fish, and chicken on the menu. The old-fashioned bar recalls *Cheers,* and a pianist entertains most Friday and Saturday evenings. ⊠ *1915 Old New York Ave.* ☎ *386/734–1995* ⊟ *AE, MC, V* ☾ *Closed Sun. No lunch.*

¢ ✕ **Dublin Station.** The large, dimly lighted bar and restaurant has dark wood walls, a wooden floor, and a thoroughly Irish streak. In addition to lagers and ales, meat pies, and fish-and-chips, there are chops, steaks, burgers, and salads. Seating is at a long bar, at tables in a lounge and dining room, in comfortable booths, or outside along the sidewalk. But whether it's day or night, the place is always busy. ⊠ *105 W. Indiana Ave.* ☎ *386/740–7720* ⊟ *AE, MC, V* ☾ *Closed Sun.–Mon.*

¢ ✕ **Original Holiday House.** The original location of what has become a small chain of buffet restaurants is enormously popular with senior citizens, families, and especially with college students (it's across from the Stetson University campus). Choose from three categories: salads only, salads and vegetables only, or the full buffet. The lunch buffet is only $7.10, and dinner is $8.10. ⊠ *704 N. Woodland Blvd.* ☎ *386/734–6319* ⊟ *DC, MC, V.*

$–$$$ ▦ **Holiday Inn DeLand.** Picture a snazzy big-city hotel run by friendly, small-town folks with city savvy. An enormous painting by nationally known local artist Fred Messersmith dominates the plush lobby. Rooms are done in subdued colors and styles; prestige suites have housed the likes of Tom Cruise. Tennis and golf privileges at the DeLand Country Club are offered. ⊠ *350 E. International Speedway Blvd. (U.S. 92), 32724* ☎ *386/738–5200 or 800/826–3233* 🖷 *386/943–9091* ⊕ *www.holiday-inn.com* ⤸ *148 rooms, 8 suites* ⚭ *Restaurant, in-room data ports, some refrigerators, cable TV, pool, gym, hot tub, billiards, bar, dry cleaning, laundry facilities, laundry service, Internet, business services, some pets allowed (fee); no-smoking rooms* ⊟ *AE, D, DC, MC, V.*

¢–$$$ ▦ **University Inn.** For years this has been the choice of business travelers and visitors to Stetson University. The inn is on campus and next door to the Original Holiday House restaurant. ⊠ *644 N. Woodland Blvd., 32720* ☎ *386/734–5711 or 800/345–8991* 🖷 *386/734–5716* ⤸ *60 rooms* ⚭ *In-room data ports, some kitchenettes, microwaves, refrigerators, pool, fitness room, business services, meeting rooms, free parking, some pets allowed (fee); no smoking* ⊟ *AE, D, DC, MC, V* ⦿◎ *CP.*

The Outdoors

BOATING Pontoon boats, houseboats, and bass boats for the St. Johns River are available from **Hontoon Landing Marina** (⊠ 2317 River Ridge Rd. ☎ 386/734–2474 or 800/248–2474).

FISHING **Hontoon Landing Marina** (⊠ 2317 River Ridge Rd. ☎ 386/734–2474 or 800/248–2474) rents bass boats and offers fishing-guide service. One of the savviest guides to St. Johns River bass fishing is Bob Stonewater of **Stonewater's Guide Service** (☎ 386/736–7120). He'll tow his boat to the launch to meet clients for the day's fishing.

SKYDIVING In addition to hosting competitions, DeLand has tandem jumping; you are attached at the hip—literally—to an experienced instructor-diver, which means that even novices are able to take their maiden voyage after one day. **Skydive DeLand** (⊠ 1600 Flightline Blvd. ☎ 386/738–3539), open daily 8 AM–sunset, offers lessons.

De León Springs

㉟ *7 mi northwest of DeLand, 26 mi southwest of Daytona Beach.*

The town (population 1,500) is a small spot on the map just outside the eastern edge of the Ocala National Forest.

Near the end of the 19th century, **De León Springs State Recreation Area** was promoted as a fountain of youth to winter guests. Today visitors are attracted to the year-round 72°F springs for swimming, fishing, canoeing, and kayaking. Nature trails draw hikers and outdoor enthusiasts. Explore an abandoned sugar mill at **Lake Woodruff National Wildlife Refuge**—accessible through DeLeón Springs—which also has plenty of lakes, creeks, and marshes for scuba diving, canoeing, and hiking. ⊠ *Ponce de León Blvd. at Burt Parks Rd., east off U.S. 17* ☎ *386/ 985–4212* ⊕ *www.dep.state.fl.us/parks/district3/deleonsprings* ⊠ *$4 per vehicle (up to 8 people)* ⊗ *Daily 8–sunset.*

Where to Eat

$–$$ ✕ **Karlings Inn.** A sort of Bavarian Brigadoon, set beside a forgotten highway, this restaurant is decorated like a Black Forest inn inside and out. Karl Caeners oversees the preparation of the sauerbraten, red cabbage, and succulent roast duckling, as well as charcoal-grilled steaks, seafood, and fresh veal. The menu has Swiss, German, French, and Italian selections, and house specialties include blue-crab cakes with spicy apricot sauce, seafood sausages (a blend of scallops, shrimp, and fish) served with a smoked chorizo–and–toasted garlic sauce, and roasted duck with Montmorency sauce. Ask to see the dessert tray. ⊠ *4640 N. U.S. Hwy. 17* ☎ *386/985–5535* ⊟ *MC, V* ⊗ *Closed Sun.–Mon. No lunch.*

¢ ✕ **The Old Spanish Sugar Mill Grill and Griddle House.** You may enjoy poking around the old sugar mill, but there's a lot more fun inside: pitchers of homemade batter arrive at your table, where you do the pouring and flipping. Top them off with blueberries, bananas, pecans, or whatever else is available. Side items include sausage, ham, bacon, eggs, and homemade breads. Although breakfast fare is available until 4 PM (the place closes at 5), salads and sandwiches are also on the menu during lunch hours. You have to pay the $4 admission to the park to eat at the restaurant. ⊠ *De León Springs State Recreation Area, Ponce de León Blvd. at Burt Parks Rd., east off U.S. 17* ☎ *386/985–5644* ⚒ *Reservations not accepted* ⊗ *No dinner.*

Ocala National Forest

★ **㊱** *Eastern entrance 40 mi west of Daytona Beach, northern entrance 52 mi south of Jacksonville.*

This delightful 366,000-acre wilderness with lakes, springs, rivers, hiking trails, campgrounds, and historic sites has three major recreational areas (listed here from east to west): **Alexander Springs** (⊠ off Rte. 40 via Rte. 445 S) has a swimming lake and a campground; **Salt Springs** (⊠ Off Rte. 40 via Rte. 19 N) has a natural saltwater spring where Atlantic blue crabs come to spawn each summer; **Juniper Springs** (⊠ Off Rte. 40) includes a picturesque stone waterwheel house, a campground, a natural-spring swimming pool, and hiking and canoe trails. Close to 30 campsites ($) are sprinkled throughout the park and range from bare sites to those with electric hookups, showers, and bathrooms. Note that credit cards aren't accepted. ⊠ *Visitor center, 10863 E. Rte. 40, Silver Springs* ☎ *352/625–7470; 352/625–2520 for campsite locations* ⊕ *www. r8.web.com/florida/forests/ocala.htm* ⊠ *Free.*

The Outdoors

CANOEING The 7-mi **Juniper Springs run** is a narrow, twisting, and winding canoe ride, which, although exhilarating, is not for the novice. You must arrange with the canoe-rental concession at **Juniper Wayside Park** (✉ Rte. 40 ☎ 352/625–2808) for rehaul—getting picked up and brought back to where you started—but it's included in the rental price.

FISHING **Captain Tom's Custom Charters** (✉ Rte. 40, Silver Springs ☎ 352/546–4823) allows you to charter fishing trips ranging from three hours to a full day.

HORSEBACK RIDING The stable closest to Ocala that's open to the public, **Fiddler's Green Ranch** (✉ Demko Rd., Altoona ☎ 352/669–7111 or 800/947–2624) organizes trail rides into the national forest.

Ocala

③⑦ *78 mi west of Daytona Beach, 123 mi southwest of Jacksonville.*

This is horse country. Here at the forest's western edge are dozens of horse farms with grassy paddocks and white wooden fences. Hills and sweeping fields of bluegrass make the area feel more like Kentucky than Florida, which is entirely appropriate. The peaceful town is considered a center for Thoroughbred breeding and training, and Kentucky Derby winners have been raised in the region's training centers. Sometimes the farms are open to the public.

The **Appleton Museum of Art,** a three-building cultural complex, is a marble-and-granite tour de force with a serene esplanade and reflecting pool. The collection lives up to its surroundings, thanks to more than 6,000 pre-Columbian, Asian, and African artifacts and 19th-century objets d'art. ✉ *4333 N.E. Silver Springs Blvd.* ☎ *352/236–7100* ⊕ *www. appletonmuseum.org* ☞ *$6* ☉ *Daily 10–6.*

Retired drag racer Don Garlit pays tribute to the cars and the drivers of that sport at **Garlit's Museum of Drag Racing.** Among his extensive collection is the only car in history to run more than 290 mph in the quarter mile, the 1963 Pontiac Firebird Jet. ✉ *13700 S.W. 16th Ave.* ☎ *877/ 271–3278* ⊕ *www.garlits.com* ☞ *$12* ☉ *Daily 9–5.*

> off the beaten path

Silver Springs. The 350-acre natural theme park outside Ocala at the western edge of the Ocala National Forest has the world's largest collection of artesian springs. The state's first tourist attraction, it was established in 1890 and is listed on the National Register of Historic Landmarks. Today the park presents wild-animal displays, glass-bottom boat tours in the Silver River, a jungle cruise on the Fort King Waterway, a Jeep safari through 35 acres of wilderness, and walks through natural habitats. Exhibits include the Panther Prowl, which enables visitors to watch and photograph the endangered Florida panther, and the Big Gator Lagoon, a ½-acre swamp featuring alligators. A great place to cool off, Silver Springs Wild Waters (☎ 352/236–2121 ⊕ www.wildwaterspark.com) has a giant wave pool and seven water-flume rides. The water park is open March through September 10–5 (call for operating schedule); admission is $23.99. ✉ *Rte. 40, Exit 352 east off I–75 or Exit 268 west off I–95* ☎ *352/236–2121* ⊕ *www.silversprings.com* ☞ *$32.99, $34.99 including Wild Waters* ☉ *Daily 10–5.*

Where to Stay & Eat

$$–$$$ ✕ **Arthur's.** Don't pass up this elegant restaurant, set in an open area at the back of the lobby in the Ocala Silver Springs Hilton. Filet mignon

with port sauce and chicken breast stuffed with spinach and sun-dried tomatoes are favorites. The Sunday brunch is a must. ⊠ *3600 S.W. 36th Ave.* ☎ *352/854–1400* ▤ *AE, D, DC, MC, V* ۞ *No lunch Sat.*

$–$$$ ✕**Petite Jardin.** In this cozy bistro, tables line the windows and walls, potted plants hang from the ceiling, and much of the menu is truly French. Start, for instance, with escargots or French onion soup. Then try the steak Diane flambé, the pecan-encrusted tuna, or the boneless breast of duck with Caribbean jerk spices. Dessert here is definitely worth the calories, but choosing between the chocolate truffle mousse pie and the bananas Foster flambé may be difficult. ⊠ *2209 E. Silver Springs Blvd.* ☎*352/351–4140* ⚖ *Reservations essential* ▤ *AE, DC, MC, V* ۞ *Closed Sun.–Tues. No lunch.*

★ **$$–$$$$** ⊞ **Seven Sisters Inn.** A pair of showplace Queen Anne mansions functions as a B&B. Each room has been lovingly furnished with period antiques and has its own bath. Some have a fireplace, some a canopy bed. A loft furnished with wicker sleeps four. Rates include a delicious breakfast and afternoon tea. ⊠ *820 S.E. Fort King St., 32671* ☎ *352/867–1170 or 800/250–3496* 🖷 *352/867–5266* ⊕ *www.7sistersinn.com* ➟ *13 rooms* ⚬ *Dining room, in-room data ports, bicycles, library, free parking; no kids under 12, no smoking* ▤ *AE, MC, V* ⏇ *BP.*

$–$$$ ⊞ **Ocala Silver Springs Hilton.** A winding, tree-lined boulevard leads to this nine-story pink tower nestled in a forested patch of countryside just off Interstate 75 and a bit removed from downtown. The marble-floor lobby has a piano bar. Your spacious guest room is decorated in deeply colored contemporary prints. ⊠ *3600 S.W. 36th Ave., 34474* ☎ *352/854–1400 or 877/602–4023* 🖷 *352/854–4010* ⊕ *www.hiltonocala. com* ➟ *185 rooms, 12 suites* ⚬ *Restaurant, room service, in-room data ports, cable TV with movies, putting green, 2 tennis courts, pool, wading pool, fitness room, hot tub, croquet, horseshoes, volleyball, bar, dry cleaning, laundry service, Internet, business services, meeting rooms; no-smoking rooms* ▤ *AE, D, DC, MC, V.*

$–$$ ⊞ **The Refuge at Ocklawaha.** This ecofriendly getaway sits amid 6,000 acres of forest and wetlands adjacent to the Ocala National Forest. Cracker-style one- and two-bedroom cottages are basic but do have fully furnished kitchens. The main lodge is a handsome stone-and-wood building on the banks of the quiet Ocklawaha River. Numerous walking and biking trails lead out into the forest. Arrange for a guided boat or canoe tour, or rent your own canoe or kayak. ⊠ *14835 S.E. 85th St., 32179* ☎ *352/288–2233* 🖷 *352/288–6369* ⊕ *www.floridarefuge. org/refuge* ➟ *25 cottages* ⚬ *Restaurant, kitchens, pool, boating, bicycles, horseback riding, playground; no room TVs* ▤ *MC, V* ⏇ *CP.*

¢ ⊞ **Best Western Ocala Park Centre.** This four-story motor inn is one of the best you'll find in the area for the price. It also has a superb location, near shopping, and it's just 3 mi from Silver Springs theme park. A free Continental breakfast further sweetens the deal. ⊠ *3701 S.W. 38th Ave., 34474* ☎ *352/237–4848 or 800/704–0849* 🖷 *352/237–2281* ➟ *139 rooms* ⚬ *In-room data ports, pool, outdoor hot tub, laundry facilities, laundry service, business services, meeting rooms, free parking; no smoking* ▤ *AE, D, DC, MC, V* ⏇ *CP.*

Sports & the Outdoors

GOLF Many of the 18 holes at the **Golden Ocala Golf Club** (⊠ *7340 N. U.S. Hwy. 27* ☎ *352/629–6229 or 800/251–7674*) replicate the famous designs found at Augusta National and the Old Course at St. Andrews.

JAI ALAI One of the speediest of sports, jai alai is played year-round at **Ocala Jai–Alai** (⊠ *4601 N.W. Hwy. 318, Orange Lake* ☎ *352/591–2345*).

Micanopy

38 *36 mi north of Ocala.*

Though this was the state's oldest inland town, site of both a Timucuan Indian settlement and a Spanish mission, there are few traces left from before white settlement, which began in 1821. Micanopy (pronounced micka-*no*-pea) does still draw those interested in the past, however. The main street of this beautiful little town, its streets lined with live oaks, has quite a few antiques shops, and in fall roughly 200 antiques dealers descend on the town for the annual Harvest Fall Festival.

★ A 20,000-acre wildlife preserve with ponds, lakes, trails, and a visitor center with a museum, **Paynes Prairie State Preserve** is a wintering area for many migratory birds where alligators and a wild herd of American bison also roam. There was once a vast lake here, but a century ago it drained so abruptly that thousands of beached fish died in the mud. The remains of a ferry stranded in the 1880s can still be seen. Swimming, boating, picnicking, and camping are permitted. ⊠ *Off U.S. 441 1 mi north of Micanopy* ☎ *352/466-3397* ⊕ *www.dep.state.fl.us/parks/district2/ paynesprairie* ⊠ *$3.25 per vehicle (up to 8 people)* ☉ *Daily 8–sunset.*

off the beaten path

Marjorie Kinnan Rawlings State Historic Site. The presence of Rawlings, whose works include *The Yearling* and *Cross Creek,* permeates this home where the typewriter rusts on the ramshackle porch, the closet where she hid her booze during Prohibition yawns open, and clippings from her scrapbook reveal her legal battles and marital problems. Bring lunch and picnic in the shade of one of Rawlings' trees. Then visit her grave a few miles away at peaceful Island Grove. ⊠ *Rte. 325, Hawthorne* ☎ *352/466-3672* ⊕ *www. dep.state.fl.us/parks/district2/marjoriekinnan* ⊠ *Grounds free, tours $3* ☉ *Thurs.–Sun. 10–4; tours Oct.–July, hourly 10–11 and 1–4.*

Where to Stay

$$–$$$ ▥ **Herlong Mansion.** Spanish moss clings to the stately oak trees surrounding this beautifully restored southern mansion built in the early 1900s. The imposing Greek revival–style B&B has Corinthian columns and wide verandas perfect for relaxing in a rocker. Rooms and suites have period furniture, Oriental rugs, and armoires. Some units have working fireplaces, lead-glass windows, claw-foot tubs, or whirlpools. A full breakfast, which is included in the rate, is an event here and includes many courses and much innkeeper humor. ⊠ *402 N.E. Cholokka Blvd., 32667* ☎ *352/466-3322 or 800/437-5664* ⊕ *www.herlong.com* ☞ *5 rooms, 4 suites, 2 cottages* ☼ *Dining room, some in-room hot tubs, some kitchenettes, piano, free parking; no kids under 12, no room phones, no room TVs, no smoking* ⊟ *AE, MC, V.*

Gainesville

39 *11 mi north of Micanopy on U.S. 441.*

The University of Florida anchors this sprawling town. Visitors are mostly Gator football fans and parents with kids enrolled at the university, so the styles and costs of accommodations are primarily aimed at budget-minded travelers rather than luxury-seeking vacationers. The surrounding area encompasses several state parks and interesting gardens and geologic sites.

☾ On the campus of the University of Florida, the **Florida Museum of Natural History** has several interesting replicas, including a Maya palace, a typical Timucuan household, and a full-size replica of a Florida cave. The collections from throughout Florida's history warrant at least half a day. ⊠ *University of Florida, S.W. 34th St. at Hull Rd.* ☎ *352/846–2000* ⊕ *www.flmnh.ufl.edu* ☜ *Free* ☉ *Mon.–Sat. 10–5, Sun. 1–5.*

About 10,000 years ago an underground cavern collapsed and created a geological treat. Today at **Devil's Millhopper State Geological Site,** see the botanical wonderland of exotic subtropical ferns and trees growing in the 500-ft-wide, 120-ft-deep sinkhole. You pass a dozen small waterfalls as you head down 232 steps to the bottom. ⊠ *4732 Millhopper Rd., off U.S. 441* ☎ *386/462–7905* ☜ *$2.00 per vehicle (up to 8 people)* ☉ *Daily 8–sunset.*

Where to Stay & Eat

★ **$$–$$$** ✕**Sovereign.** Crystal, candlelight, and a jazz pianist set a tone of restrained elegance in this 1878 carriage house. An iron gate and a narrow walkway lead back to the elegant dining room. Veal specialties are notable, particularly the *saltimbocca*, braised in white wine, flavored with sage, and topped with ham. Duckling and rack of baby lamb are dependable choices, too. ⊠ *12 S.E. 2nd Ave.* ☎ *352/378–6307* ☍ *Reservations essential* ⊟ *AE, D, DC, MC, V* ☉ *Closed Sun. No lunch.*

$–$$$ ✕**Emiliano's Cafe.** Linen tablecloths and art deco–ish artwork create a casual, elegant feel here. Dine indoors or beneath the stars on the sidewalk café. Start with the Gallician stew (a family recipe) or the black bean soup, and then move on to one of the chef's signature dishes—Spanish saffron rice with shrimp, clams, mussels, fresh fish, chicken, artichoke hearts, peas, asparagus, and pimientos. Also worthy is the beef tenderloin encrusted with crushed coriander seed and black peppercorns and served over julienned yuca fries topped with a mango cabernet sauce. ⊠ *7 S.E. 1st Ave.* ☎ *352/375–7381* ⊟ *AE, D, MC, V* ☉ *Closed Sun.–Mon. No lunch Tues.–Thurs.*

$–$$$ ✕**Paramount Grill.** You may be rubbing elbows with your neighbor, but the meal is definitely worth the inconvenience. Try one of the five house salads and such entrées as the pan-roasted pork tenderloin with a creamy blue-cheese polenta and an apple-cider lemon-thyme reduction sauce or the Asian spiced tuna served over wasabi pancakes with grilled green tomatoes, served with sweet sesame vinaigrette and a gingered spinach salad. If you miss doing dinner here, try the Sunday brunch. ⊠ *12 S. W. 1st Ave.* ☎ *352/378–3398* ⊟ *AE, D, MC, V* ☉ *No lunch Sat.*

$–$$ ✕**Melting Pot.** Eating is a group activity at this fondue spot; sit downstairs or upstairs in the cozy loft. Dip slivers of fish or steak in sizzling hot oil, or cubes of crusty French bread in pots of melted cheese. Save room for dessert—more fondue, naturally—bits of fruit you dip into rich melted chocolate. ⊠ *418 E. University Ave.* ☎ *352/372–5623* ⊟ *AE, MC, V* ☉ *No lunch.*

$ ✕**Bistro 1245.** Get high-quality meals at bargain-basement prices. The butternut-squash bisque and the seared-tuna club sandwich served with bacon, lettuce, and tomato are popular menu items. For a lighter meal, and a lighter price, order off the lunch menu in the evening. ⊠ *1245 W. University Ave.* ☎ *352/376–0000* ⊟ *AE, MC, V* ☉ *Closed Sun.*

$ ✕**Market Street Pub.** The large, British-style pub brews its own beer and also serves up homemade sausage, fish-and-chips, salads, and hearty sandwiches. Dine indoors or outdoors at the sidewalk café. The pub has live music on weekends and a DJ some weeknights. ⊠ *120 S.W. 1st Ave.* ☎ *352/377–2927* ⊟ *AE, MC, V* ☉ *Closed Sun.–Mon. No lunch.*

$$–$$$ ▥**Residence Inn by Marriott.** One- and two-bedroom suites with a kitchen and fireplace make a cozy pied-à-terre. Cocktails are part of the hospitality. The central location is convenient for the university or business traveler. ⊠ *4001 S.W. 13th St., at U.S. 441 and Rte. 331, 32608* ☎ *352/*

*371–2101 or 800/331–3131 ▧ 352/377–2247 ⊕ www.marriott.com
↩ 80 suites ♿ In-room data ports, kitchens, cable TV, pool, fitness room,
hair salon, hot tub, basketball, volleyball, dry cleaning, laundry service,
Internet, meeting rooms, free parking, some pets allowed (fee); no-
smoking rooms ▤ AE, D, DC, MC, V ℍ CP.*

$–$$ ▥ **The Magnolia Plantation Bed and Breakfast Inn.** You'll be within min-
utes of historic downtown and the University of Florida, and owners
Joe and Cindy Montalto will welcome you like old friends, whether you
stay in the main house or in one of the adorable cottages. The inn's unique
French Second Empire architecture is one of only a handful found in
the southeastern United States. The lush gardens and gazebos offer
quiet, shady spots to relax. All rooms have a gas fireplace and private
bath with claw-foot tub (except for the whirlpool tub). A full breakfast
is standard fare and is served in the formal dining room or in the privacy of your cottage. ⊠ 309 S.E. 7th St., 32601 ☎ 352/375–6653 or
800/201–2379 ▧ 352/338–0303 ⊕ www.magnoliabnb.com ↩ 5 rooms,
6 cottages ♿ Some in-room data ports, some in-room hot tubs, some
kitchenettes, some microwaves, some refrigerators, laundry facilities, business services, meeting rooms, free parking; no phones in some rooms,
no smoking, no TV in some rooms ▤ AE, D, MC, V.*

$–$$ ▥ **Sweetwater Branch Inn Bed & Breakfast.** You'll find such modern con-
veniences as data ports, hair dryers, and business services mixed with
southern charm and hospitality all wrapped up in two grand Victorian
homes surrounded by lush tropical gardens. Gleaming hardwood floors
and antique furnishings lend a European flair to nicely appointed rooms.
The Sweetwater is in historic downtown, adjacent to the University of
Florida, and within walking distance of many of the area's better restaurants and entertainment venues. ⊠ 625 E. University Ave., 32601
☎ 352/373–6760 or 800/595–7760 ▧ 352/371–3771 ⊕ www.
sweetwaterinn.com ↩ 13 rooms, 3 suites ♿ In-room data ports, some
kitchenettes, some microwaves, some refrigerators, some in-room hot
tubs, business services, meeting rooms; no smoking ▤ AE, MC, V.*

¢   ▥ **LaQuinta Inn.** If you're visiting someone at the university, you might
appreciate that this property is both an economical choice and a mere
five minutes from campus. It's also within walking distance of many downtown restaurants and nightspots. ⊠ 920 N.W. 69th Terr., 32606 ☎ 352/
332–6466 ▧ 352/332–7074 ↩ 135 rooms ♿ In-room data ports,
cable TV with movies, some microwaves, some refrigerators, business
services, meeting rooms, free parking, some pets allowed; no smoking
▤ AE, D, MC, V ℍ CP.*

Nightlife

Alligator Rocks (⊠ 108 S. Main St. ☎ 352/377–1619) is Gainesville's popular entertainment dance complex; it's always hopping. Gainesville's oldest bar, **Lillian's Music Store** (⊠ 112 S.E. 1st St. ☎ 352/372–1010) has
rock and Top 40 music, live bands, and karaoke.

Sports & the Outdoors

AUTO RACING   Hot-rod auto racing goes on at the **Gatornationals** (⊠ Gainesville Raceway, 1121 N. County Rd. 225 ☎ 352/377–0046; 626/914–4761 for Na-
tional Hot Rod Association), the championship competitions of the
National Hot Rod Association. They're held each year in late winter at
the Gainesville Raceway.

FOOTBALL   The games of the **University of Florida Gators** (⊠ Ben Hill Griffin Stadium,
111 North South Hwy. ☎ 352/375–4683) are extremely popular, and
tickets are very difficult to get.

NORTHEAST FLORIDA A TO Z

To research prices, get advice from other travelers, and book arrangements, visit www.fodors.com.

AIR TRAVEL

The main airport for the region is Jacksonville International (JAX). It is served by American and American Eagle, Comair, Continental, Delta, TWA, United, and US Airways. Delta and Gulfstream serve Daytona Beach International Airport (DAB). Gainesville Regional Airport (GNV) is served by ASA–The Delta Connection, Piedmont, and US Airways. Although Orlando isn't part of the area, visitors to northeastern Florida often choose to arrive at Orlando International Airport (MCO) because of the huge number of convenient flights. Driving east on the Beeline Expressway brings you to Cocoa Beach in about an hour. Reach Daytona, about a two-hour drive, by taking the Beeline Expressway to Interstate 95 and driving north.

CARRIER ▪ Airlines & Contacts **American** ☎ 800/433–7300. **American Eagle** ☎ 800/433–7300. **ASA-The Delta Connection** ☎ 800/282–3424. **Comair** ☎ 800/354–9822. **Continental** ☎ 800/523–3273. **Delta** ☎ 800/221–1212. **Gulfstream** ☎ 800/525–0280. **United** ☎ 800/241–6522. **US Airways** ☎ 800/428–4322.

AIRPORTS

▪ Airport Information **Daytona Beach International Airport** (DAB) ☎ 386/248-8069 ⊕ www.flydaytonafirst.com. **Gainesville Regional Airport** (GNV) ☎ 352/373-0249 ⊕ www.gra-gnv.com. **Jacksonville International** (JAX) ☎ 904/741-4902 ⊕ www.jaxairports.org. **Orlando International Airport** (MCO) ☎ 407/825-2001 ⊕ www.orlandoairports.net.

TRANSFERS At Jacksonville International, free shuttles run from the terminal to all parking lots (except the garage) around the clock. Vans from the airport to area hotels cost $18 per person. Taxi fare is about $25 to downtown, $48 to the beaches and Amelia Island. Limousine services must be booked in advance; East Coast Transportation, one of these services, charges $28 for one to four people going downtown ($10 for each additional person) and $50 for one to four people going to the Jacksonville beaches or Amelia Island. From Daytona Beach International Airport, taxi fare to beach hotels runs about $13–$18; taxi companies include Yellow Cab, Checker Cab, and A&A Cab. DOTS Transit Service has scheduled service connecting the Daytona Beach and Orlando International airports, the Sheraton Palm Coast area, DeLand (including its train station), New Smyrna Beach, Sanford, and Deltona; fares are $27 one-way and $46 round-trip between the Daytona and Orlando airports, $20 one-way and $36 round-trip from the Orlando airport to DeLand or Deltona. From the Gainesville Regional Airport, taxi fare to the center of Gainesville is about $12; some hotels provide free airport pickup.

▪ **A&A Cab** ☎ 386/677-7777. **Carey Jacksonville** ☎ 904/246-3741. **Checker Cab** ☎ 800/566-4222. **DOTS Transit Service** ☎ 386/257-5411 or 800/231-1965. **Yellow Cab** ☎ 904/260-1111 or 888/442-8294.

BOAT & FERRY TRAVEL

Connecting the banks of the St. Johns River, in Jacksonville, the S.S. Marine Taxi runs between several locations, including Riverwalk and Jacksonville Landing. The one-way trip takes about five minutes. The ferry runs 1–10 daily (except during rainy or other bad weather). Round-trip fare is $3; one-way fare is $5.

▪ Boat & Ferry Information **S.S. Marine Taxi** ☎ 904/733-7782.

BUS TRAVEL

Greyhound Lines serves the region, with stations in Jacksonville, St. Augustine, Gainesville, Daytona Beach, and DeLand. Daytona Beach has an excellent bus network, Votran, which serves the beach area, airport, shopping malls, and major arteries. Exact fare ($1), in bills or change, is required for Votran.

🚍 Bus Information **Greyhound Lines** ☎ 800/231-2222; 904/255-7076 in Daytona Beach; 386/734-2747 in DeLand; 352/376-5252 in Gainesville; 904/356-9976 in Jacksonville; 904/829-6401 in St. Augustine. **Votran** ☎ 386/756-7496.

CAR TRAVEL

East–west traffic travels the northern part of the state on Interstate 10, a cross-country highway stretching from Los Angeles to Jacksonville. Farther south, Interstate 4 connects Florida's west and east coasts. Signs on Interstate 4 designate it an east–west route, but actually the road rambles northeast from Tampa to Orlando, then heads north-northeast to Daytona. Two interstates head north–south on Florida's peninsula: Interstate 95 on the east coast (from Miami to Houlton, Maine) and Interstate 75 on the west. If you want to drive as close to the Atlantic as possible and are not in a hurry, stick with A1A. It runs along the barrier islands, changing its name several times along the way. Where there are no bridges between islands, cars must return to the mainland via causeways; some are low, with drawbridges that open for boat traffic on the inland waterway, and there can be unexpected delays. The Buccaneer Trail, which overlaps part of Route A1A, goes from St. Augustine north to Mayport (where a ferry is part of the state highway system), through marshlands and beaches, to the 300-year-old seaport town of Fernandina Beach, and then finally into Fort Clinch State Park. Route 13, also known as the William Bartram Trail, runs from Jacksonville to East Palatka along the east side of the St. Johns River through tiny hamlets. It's one of the most scenic drives in North Florida—a two laner lined with huge oaks that hug the riverbanks—very "Old Florida." U.S. 17 travels the west side of the river, passing through Green Cove Springs and Palatka. Route 40 runs east–west through the Ocala National Forest, giving a nonstop view of stately pines and bold wildlife; short side roads lead to parks, springs, picnic areas, and campgrounds.

EMERGENCIES

Alachua General, Fish Medical Center, Halifax Medical Center, Munroe Regional Medical Center, and St. Luke's Hospital all have 24-hour emergency rooms.

🚑 Emergency Services ☎ 911.

🏥 Hospitals **Shands at Alachua General** ✉ 801 S.W. 2nd Ave., Gainesville ☎ 352/372-4321. **Bert Fish Medical Center** ✉ 401 Palmetto St., New Smyrna Beach ☎ 386/424-5000. **Halifax Medical Center** ✉ 303 N. Clyde Morris Blvd., Daytona ☎ 386/254-4100. **Munroe Regional Medical Center** ✉ 131 S.W. 15th St., Ocala ☎ 352/351-7200. **St. Luke's Hospital** ✉ 4201 Belfort Rd., Jacksonville ☎ 904/296-3700.

🏥 24-Hour Pharmacies **Eckerd Drug** ✉ 4397 Roosevelt Blvd., Jacksonville ☎ 904/389-0314. **Walgreens** ✉ 4150 N. Atlantic Ave., Cocoa ☎ 321/799-9112 ✉ 1500 Beville Rd., Daytona ☎ 386/257-5773.

MEDIA

NEWSPAPERS & MAGAZINES Local daily papers include the *Daytona Beach News-Journal,* Jacksonville's *Florida Times-Union Ocala Star-Banner, Gainesville Daily Register,* and the *Gainesville Sun.* Among the periodicals are the *Jacksonville Business Journal* and *Jacksonville Magazine.*

RADIO   The Jacksonville dial has a servicable smattering of stations: WFSJ 97.9 FM plays top 40; WKQL 96.9 FM, oldies; WQIK 99.9, country; WAPE 95.1, contemporary rock; and WOKV 690 AM, talk radio.

TOURS

La CRUISE offers day and evening cruises from Mayport, with live bands, dancing, and gambling. In Jacksonville, River Cruises has dinner and dancing cruises on five different boats; schedules vary with the season. A Tiny Cruise Line leaves from the Daytona Public Marina and explores the Intracoastal Waterway. Tour Time Inc. has bus tours of the area; prior arrangement is necessary. The Jacksonville Historical Society arranges tours only for groups of 20 or more.

Jacksonville Historical Society Tours ☎ 904/665-0064. **La CRUISE** ☎ 904/241-7200 or 800/752-1778 ⊕ www.lacruise.com. **River Cruises** ☎ 904/396-2333 ⊕ www.rivercruise.com. **A Tiny Cruise Line** ☎ 386/226-2343. **Tour Time Inc.** ☎ 904/282-8500 or 800/822-4278 ⊕ www.tourtimeinc.com.

TRAIN TRAVEL

Amtrak schedules stops in Jacksonville, DeLand, Waldo (near Gainesville), Ocala, and Palatka. The Auto Train carries cars between Sanford and Lorton, Virginia (just south of Washington, D.C.). Schedules vary depending on the season.

Train Line Amtrak ☎ 800/872-7245 ⊕ www.amtrak.com.

VISITOR INFORMATION

Most visitor-information offices are open weekdays from 8 or 9 to 5. The St. Augustine Visitor Information Center is open daily 8:30–5:30.

Tourist Information Amelia Island-Fernandina Beach Chamber of Commerce ✉102 Centre St., Amelia Island 32034 ☎ 904/261-3248 or 800/226-3542. **Cocoa Beach Area Chamber of Commerce** ✉ 400 Fortenberry Rd., Merritt Island 32952 ☎ 321/459-2200 ⊕ www.cocoabeachchamber.com. **Daytona Convention and Visitors Bureau** ✉ 126 E. Orange Ave., Daytona 32120 ☎ 800/854-1234 ⊕ www.daytonabeach.com. **Gainesville Visitors and Convention Bureau** ✉ 30 E. University Ave., Gainesville 32601 ☎ 352/374-5231 ⊕ www.visitgainesville.net. **Jacksonville and Its Beaches Convention & Visitors Bureau** ✉ 6 E. Bay St., Suite 200, Jacksonville 32202 ☎ 904/798-9111 ⊕ www.jaxcvb.com. **Ocala-Marion County Chamber of Commerce** ✉ 110 E. Silver Springs Blvd., Ocala 34470 ☎ 352/629-8051 ⊕ www.ocalacc.com. **St. Augustine, Ponte Vedra & The Beaches Visitors & Convention Bureau** ✉ 10 Castillo Dr., St. Augustine 32084 ☎ 800/653-2489 ⊕ www.visitoldcity.com.

UNDERSTANDING FLORIDA

PORTRAITS OF FLORIDA

BOOKS & MOVIES

THE SUNSHINE STATE

I F THE NICKNAME THE OCEAN STATE weren't being used by Rhode Island, Florida could easily adopt it. Jutting into warm waters at the southeastern corner of the United States, this largely flat, finger-shape peninsula is rimmed by more than 1,200 mi of coastline, attracting beachgoers, water-sports enthusiasts, scenery gazers, and nature lovers.

Luckily, its real nickname—the Sunshine State—is every bit as accurate. While much of the rest of the country endures Old Man Winter, most of Florida maintains a pleasant, subtropical climate. The net result is that for more than a century, warm weather (and the bounty that flows from it) has drawn—and continues to draw—hordes of vacationers, snowbirds (winter residents), retirees, immigrants, and other new permanent denizens. Among those who have at one time or another been seduced by its charms (and in some cases seduced others to come to the state) are developers Henry Morrison Flagler and Henry Plant, circus tycoon John Ringling, writers Ernest Hemingway and Marjorie Kinnan Rawlings, singers Jimmy Buffett and Gloria Estefan, and inventors Thomas Edison and Henry Ford.

Fly into any Florida airport during the Christmas season or spring break, and you'll have little doubt as to the economic importance of tourism. Examine the contents of travelers' suitcases—swimsuits, sunscreen, golf clubs, tennis rackets, credit cards—and there's even less doubt about their reasons for visiting: relaxation and recreation.

Of course, the most popular activities center on all that coastline. Florida has a surprising variety of beaches: from the wave-lapped strands along the Atlantic Ocean (east coast) to the sugar-sand, sunset-hung beaches of the Gulf of Mexico (west coast and Panhandle), from people-watcher beaches to family beaches to secluded beaches. For those with sand aversion, there are the largely sandless, coral-reef-lined shore of Florida's Keys and the mangrove-studded margins in places like the Ten Thousand Islands and Biscayne National Park.

Florida's largest and most cosmopolitan city, Miami, hugs the state's southeastern coast. Whereas Miami Beach has its share of sun and sand, the metropolitan area is equally known for its international trade and international (most notably, Latin) flavor, as well as glitz and celebrity. It seems fitting in this varied state that just a stone's throw away from Miami is one of Florida's other distinctive treasures: the Everglades. This national park—comprising a quiet, slow-flowing river of grass—is home to unusual wildlife, including that quintessential Florida creature, the alligator.

In case you think that Florida action is only on the coasts, travel inland; agriculture flourishes here—unfortunately, however, sometimes at the expense of the natural environment. Citrus fruits like oranges and grapefruit are as synonymous with Florida as pineapples are with Hawaii, but Florida farms and ranches also produce sugarcane and cattle. In one formerly sleepy farming town, the soil seems particularly fertile for growing world-famous amusement parks. In just over a quarter century, Orlando has sprouted eight major theme parks, five water parks, and countless—in fact, uncountable—other attractions, entertainment options, hotels, restaurants, and shops.

So how did the phenomenon that's Florida come about? Almost from its beginnings as a flat, swampy plateau emerging from the ocean, Florida has been home to all sorts of animals disinclined to the cold (at that time, glaciated) weather up north. It wasn't until 12,000–10,000 BC that humans (probably hunter-gatherers) arrived. These original Floridians began to farm and develop societies, and their descendants would become Florida's Timucuan (central and north), Apalachee (eastern Panhandle), Seminole (south-central to southwest), Calusa (southwest coast), Miccosukee (south), and Tequesta (southeast) tribes.

As in much of the Americas, the sovereignty of Florida's native peoples did not last. By the 16th century, a succession of Spanish explorers, including Pánfilo de Narváez, Hernando de Soto, Tristán de

Luna y Arellano, and Pedro Menéndez de Avilés had arrived with visions of wealth. Though they found little gold and often didn't stay long, they still managed to ravage, enslave, and spread disease among the native population. In 1565 the first permanent settlement was founded at St. Augustine, and in the years that followed, the Spanish, French, and British all tried to establish Florida footholds. Pensacola, in fact, got the nickname the City of Five Flags because at one time or another it was under the rule of Spain, France, England, the Confederacy, and the United States.

Eventually Florida became a U.S. territory and state, but that didn't end the struggles. An influx of whites from the North, eager to farm and ranch, created friction with Native Americans, and a series of three wars, known as the Seminole Wars, ensued. Led by then General (later president) Andrew Jackson, the Anglos ultimately drove many Native Americans off their lands and out.

Conflict returned during the Civil War, though to a lesser degree than in the states to the north. In fact, Tallahassee was the only Confederate capital east of the Mississippi not to fall to Union forces. When the South lost the war, however, Florida rejoined the United States.

By the late 19th century, a group of aggressive developers had begun to see Florida's potential as a tourist destination. Henry Plant built a railroad to the west coast as well as the big Tampa Bay Hotel. Henry Morrison Flagler had even grander plans, extending his Florida East Coast Railway to places like St. Augustine, Palm Beach, Fort Lauderdale, Miami, and eventually Key West. Flagler also built opulent hotels that attracted Vanderbilts, DuPonts, Rockefellers, and their confrères. Other developers created their own legacies—Addison Mizner in Palm Beach and Boca Raton, Carl Fisher in Miami Beach, George Merrick in Coral Gables. These names live on today, in everything from island and street names to museums and shopping malls. Unfortunately, their and others' ideas of progress often meant draining swampland, paving or building over animal habitats, and straightening, damming, dredging, or building new waterways, thereby altering the natural environment forever.

The 20th century saw a succession of land booms and busts as tourists repeatedly rediscovered the appeal of Florida and its climate. The late '20s and early '30s Depression hit tourism hard, as did a 1935 hurricane that cut off Key West from the mainland (except by boat). The '20s and '30s brought art deco to Miami Beach, whereas the '50s brought grand hotels, like Morris Lapidus's Fountainebleau and Eden Roc. But by the '70s and early '80s, Miami Beach and many other Florida towns had become rundown geriatric centers (sometimes pejoratively referred to as "God's waiting room"); Fort Lauderdale was primarily known as a center for spring-break debauchery; and family tourism headed in greater and greater numbers to the new theme parks sprouting up around Orlando.

By the late '80s, however, towns and cities were beginning to renew themselves. By the '90s, Miami Beach, its art deco jewels preserved and restored, became hot again. Miami, with its ever-growing Latin population and flavor, finally began to embrace and even tout its multiculturalism. Fort Lauderdale and West Palm Beach spruced up and added new arts and entertainment attractions. Towns and resorts on both east and west coasts grew, attracting visitors and residents alike. And today, Florida is once again basking in the sunshine.

FLORIDA, MY FLORIDA

HOWDY, KIDS. Looks like you'll be coming to Florida. Personally, I couldn't think of a better place to visit (except that I live here already). And why not? The folks at the tourist board say that Florida is sun-sational! And they're right. Without Florida there would be no space program, no Disney empire, no tropical deco, no pink lawn flamingos. And you know the way Florida sticks down into the Caribbean? If Florida weren't the United States' East Coast counterweight, our nation would just flip right over into the Pacific Ocean—and that's a geological fact.

Florida is *different*. It has almost as many millionaires as migrant workers and an equal number of rednecks and rocket scientists. It houses muck farms and million-dollar condos, and its churches welcome straitlaced Baptists and pious practitioners of Santeria, a mixture of Haitian voodoo, African tribal religions, and Christianity. Florida is where you can spend your vacation clapping happily as a robot bear sings Patsy Cline or screaming in terror as a real live alligator devours a senior citizen's toy poodle. This state may not be schizophrenic, but it does display multiple personalities.

Are you familiar with the saying attributed to Harvey Korman or somebody else that America is the melting pot of the world? Well, Florida is the melting pot of America. In 1990 a U.S. Census Bureau report revealed that fewer than a third of Florida's population are natives and only 13% were born in other states south of the Mason-Dixon line. You'll notice this when you visit, because Florida is the only state in the Deep South where you'll see the Union and Confederacy living side by side. Ironically, down here northerners live in the south and southerners live in the north. No one knows why this is; it just is.

If you're wondering if you'll receive a warm welcome, don't worry. The land of sunshine accommodates just about everybody. In 1950 this was the 20th-most-populous state; now we're number 4. During the Mariel Boatlift of 1980, 125,000 Cuban defectors showed up, and we didn't even call out the National Guard—we only did that when a similar number of New Yorkers arrived for the opening of the new Miami Bloomingdale's.

This influx of outsiders is nothing new. In 1513 Ponce de León decided to land in Florida to avoid the traffic around Newark. That did it. By 1565 Ponce's foothold became the oldest permanent settlement in what would become the United States. Check your history books, and you'll see this was a half century before the English arrived in Jamestown and the Pilgrims knocked on Plymouth Rock. It seemed everybody wanted to be in Florida. While the French, English, and Spanish spent 250 years battling for possession of the territory, Caribbean pirates sailing the Gulf Stream were making withdrawals from the explorers' ships and using Florida's hidden bays and swamps as safe-deposit boxes. Eventually, the pirates and foreign pioneers cleared out, and in 1821 the United States paid Spain $5 million for 59,000 square mi of marshes, mosquitoes, and alligators.

Later, Virginians and Carolinians began moving south to create Panhandle communities like Quincy, Madison, and Monticello. Then in the late 1880s, Henry M. Flagler started building a hotel and railroad empire that started in St. Augustine, arrived in Miami by 1896, and reached the end of the line in Key West in 1912. Thanks to Flagler's promotional and engineering abilities, northern tourists started heading south and have been arriving ever since.

Although it rarely makes the evening news anymore, people are still battling over Florida. Retirees, dropouts, drug runners, natives, multinational companies, and foreign tourists all want to claim Florida for their own. So what's all the fuss about?

The answer, my friend, is blowing in the warm Atlantic winds that comfort us in the middle of January, in the primeval pleasures of paddling a canoe down the Wekiva River, and in the 3,000-plus varieties of indigenous plants and flowers that color our landscape, and in the fire, smoke, and thunder of the space shuttle as it blazes into the clear blue sky above the Indian River. You'll find it in more than 400 species of birds, ranging from cardinals, ospreys, and bald eagles to wading egrets, herons, and pink flamingos. It is felt in the 220 days of sunshine we savor each year and the approximately 1 inch of snow a century that we don't.

* * *

THESE ARE THE TYPES OF THINGS you may not know about the Shoeshine State. That is why my editors looked at my birth certificate and tan lines to confirm that I was a native and then asked me to share with you the many-splendored things that make up this paradoxical paradise. Even with my more than 35 years of memories and hundreds of thousands of miles spent trekking, biking, motorcycling, and stumbling across my favorite subtropical peninsula, this is a difficult task. Relating all that Florida represents is an impossibility because the typical Floridian could be grunting for worms in Sopchoppy, rounding up cattle in Kissimmee, or posing for the cover of a European fashion magazine in Miami.

And it's not only Americans who come to Florida. Hit Palm Beach during polo season, and you'll find that even Prince Charles is an occasional Floridian. If you stay awhile (and you simply *must*), you'll find yourself eavesdropping on conversations spoken in a Berlitz blitz of mother tongues: Haitian, Chinese, Serbo-Croatian, Portuguese, Yiddish, Italian, Greek, Spanish, Jamaican, Russian, French, Esperanto . . . E Pluribus Unum, y'all. Only California (a relatively insignificant state somewhere out west) challenges Florida in terms of its social, cultural, and environmental diversity. You may have heard its residents claim that in one day they can breakfast on the beach, lunch in the desert, and enjoy dinner in the mountains. So? With a full tank of gas and a fast car (my cousin Chick's got a cherry '74 Pacer), Floridians can leave Pensacola in the western panhandle, drive beside the crystal blue gulf on U.S. 98, head north to Tallahassee to tell the governor not to stay the execution, cruise over to St. Augustine for a carriage ride, and drop down to Daytona Beach to hoist a brew with some bikers.

Then it's lunchtime.

Afterward, they'd head to Disney for a quick twirl in a teacup, race over to Tampa's Ybor City to snag a stogie, fill up the tank, and head south to dine at one of Miami's oceanfront cafés before meeting Jimmy Buffett in Key West to slam a pitcher of margaritas.

There's a whole lotta shakin' goin' on, that's for sure, but there is one thing missing from Florida: Old Florida. October 1, 1971, was the day that Disney drove old Dixie down. Over the last 30 years a new state has emerged, reflecting a not-so-perfect union. It is one of sprawling theme parks that provide a big bang for the buck. It is a place where part-time tourists become full-time residents, and corridors of condos, generic housing developments, strip malls, and highways are built to appease them. The changing nature of Key West is a prime example. A generation ago this was a laid-back island paradise filled with eclectic lodgings and quixotic characters. Then it was popularized in song and literature and through word of mouth until the buzz reached executive boardrooms. Today the island's individuality is endangered by a homogenized mass of Hôtels Banal and rich refugees who are turning the once casual hideaway into the places they left behind.

Keep in mind this is the opinion of someone who knew Florida B. D. (Before Disney). When Disney opened, I was a perceptive nine-year-old who had filed away the singular offerings of this endangered lifestyle. The essence of Florida was in the air as my mom and I drove past thick groves of plump oranges and savored the sweet smell of the delicate blossoms. At night the air was perfumed with Central Florida's omnipresent gardenias, night-blooming jasmine, honeysuckle, and pine. Back then Orlando was so quiet that at night I could hear the lonesome train whistles from 6 mi away.

For entertainment I swam in a creek called Snake Run and took field trips to orange-juice factories. Our family would visit roadside attractions where we could SEE! Walking Catfish! And SEE! Big Sam, the World's Largest Bull! We'd travel to places like Bok Tower, in Lake Wales, and tranquil Tarpon Springs, the Sponge Capital of America. (It's not your fault you were unaware that America had a sponge capital; you didn't own this book yet.)

As a friend, let me give you a tip: when you come to Florida, keep this book with you wherever you go—even in the bath. It will help you find traces of Old Florida in small towns like Micanopy and Mount Dora. You'll find it at Florida's old faithful attractions: Weeki Wachee, Cypress Gardens, Silver Springs, and Monkey Jungle. You'll experience it at Florida's wealth of botanical gardens and at rare winters-only resorts.

* * *

FLORIDIANS LEAP FROM PLANES at 15,000 ft and plunge into blue waters to explore real reefs and artificial ones built upon the hulls of sunken 727s. We motorcycle, ski, sail, paddle, soar, float, climb, cruise, race, run, trek, and, on rare occasions, spelunk. And if you don't like physical activity, what the hell? When you're through sipping margaritas from a coconut shell, sit in the stands and watch pro teams in Miami, Orlando, St. Pete, Tampa, Sunrise, and Jacksonville beat up on visiting players in football, baseball, roller hockey, arena football, ice hockey, and basketball.

Many of our activities are in the great outdoors. We love nature, and we treasure our manatees, sea turtles, and bald eagles. Although it's true that developers and engineers have drained, dredged, and destroyed a million-plus acres of Everglades and other environmentally sensitive land, we're trying to fix things up real nice for your arrival. Stiff fines are handed out to anyone who plucks the sea oats that hold the sandy shoreline in place, and we've set aside hundreds of thousands of acres for wildlife refuges, nature preserves, and state and national parks. Florida, I'll have you know, was the first state to establish a national forest and national bird sanctuary.

Measures such as these have led to fringe benefits. This environmental Valhalla cannot help but foster artistic pursuits. JFK wrote *Profiles in Courage* in Palm Beach, Ernest Hemingway spent 12 years in Key West getting drunk and writing books, and the *National Enquirer* is based in Lantana. Ray Charles attended the Florida School of the Deaf and Blind, in St. Augustine; the Beatles made their second *Ed Sullivan Show* appearance from Miami; and the Rolling Stones wrote "(I Can't Get No) Satisfaction" at (but not as a reflection on) a Clearwater hotel. Artist Robert Rauschenburg lives on Captiva and . . . oh, you get the idea.

If this book doesn't convince you that Florida is the most perfect state in the union, when you get here, ask for me. I'll fill up the DeSoto with some high-test ethyl, put the top down, and we'll take off to see some of Florida's 4,300 square mi of wonderful waterways, where we can swim with manatees or snorkel, scuba, or paddle to our heart's content. I'll take you to a happening diner in Orlando and a great bookstore in St. Pete. If there's time, we'll go tubing down the Ichetucknee and then hook up with some of my hepcat friends down in Coconut Grove.

Now stop reading and get down here.

— Gary McKechnie

BOOKS & MOVIES

Books

Suspense novels that are rich in details about Florida include Pulitzer Prize–winner Edna Buchanan's *Miami, It's Murder* and *Contents Under Pressure*; Les Standiford's *Done Deal*, about violence in the Miami construction business; former prosecuting attorney Barbara Parker's *Suspicion of Innocence*; Clifford Irving's *Final Argument*; Elmore Leonard's *La Brava*; John D. MacDonald's *The Empty Copper Sea*; Joan Higgins's *A Little Death Music*; and Charles Willeford's *Miami Blues*. James W. Hall features Florida in many of his big sellers, such as *Mean High Tide*, the chilling *Bones of Coral*, and *Hard Aground*.

Marjorie Kinnan Rawlings's classic *The Yearling* poignantly portrays life in the brush country, and her *Cross Creek* re-creates the memorable people she knew there. Peter Matthiessen's *Killing Mister Watson* re-creates turn-of-the-last-century lower southwest Florida. A more recent look at Florida's past is in Bill Belleville's *River of Lakes: A Journey on Florida's St. Johns River*, which shows there are still traces of wilderness here.

Look for *Princess of the Everglades*, a novel about the 1926 hurricane, by Charles Mink, and *Snow White and Rose Red* and *Jack and the Beanstalk*, Ed McBain's novels about a gulf city attorney. Miami's Carl Hiaasen has turned out lots of Florida-based books, including *Double Whammy*, *Lucky You*, and, most recently, *Sick Puppy*.

Other recommended titles include Roxanne Pulitzer's *Facade*, set against a backdrop of Palm Beach; Pat Booth's *Miami*; Sam Harrison's *Bones of Blue Coral* and *Birdsong Ascending*; T. D. Allman's *Miami*; Joan Didion's *Miami*; David Rieff's *Going to Miami*; Alice Hoffman's *Turtle Moon*; *Scavenger Reef* and *Florida Straits*, by Laurence Shames; *To Have and Have Not*, by Ernest Hemingway; *The Day of the Dolphin*, by Robert Merle; and *Their Eyes Were Watching God*, by Zora Neale Hurston.

Among recommended nonfiction books are *The Commodore's Story*, by Ralph Munroe and Vincent Gilpin, a luminous reminiscence about the golden years (pre-railroad) of Coconut Grove; *Key West Writers and Their Homes*, by Lynn Kaufelt; *The Everglades: River of Grass*, by Marjory S. Douglas; *The Other Florida*, by Gloria Jahoda; and *Florida's Sandy Beaches*, University Press of Florida. Mark Derr's *Some Kind of Paradise* is an excellent review of the state's environmental follies; John Rothchild's *Up for Grabs: A Trip Through Time and Space in the Sunshine State*, equally good, is about Florida's commercial lunacy. For a great overview on the politics and behind-the-scenes genius that went behind Florida's most popular theme park, look for *Since the World Began: Walt Disney World, the First 25 Years*, by Jeff Kurtti. Good anthologies include *The Florida Reader: Visions of Paradise* (Maurice O'Sullivan and Jack Lane, editors), *The Rivers of Florida* (Del and Marty Marth, editors), and *Subtropical Speculations: An Anthology of Florida Science Fiction* (Richard Mathews and Rick Wilber, editors).

A good companion to this guide, Fodor's *Compass American Guides: Florida* has handsome photos and historical, cultural, and topical essays.

Books that are also available on audiotape include Peter Dexter's *The Paperboy*, as well as several by Carl Hiaasen: *Native Tongue*, *Skin Tight*, *Stormy Weather*, *Strip Tease*, *Basket Case*, and *Tourist Season*, his immensely funny declaration of war against the state's environment-despoiling hordes. For more on Miami's questionable politics and weird culture, pick up *Kick Ass*, a collection of Hiaasen's newspaper columns.

Movies

There's a great misconception that California is the center of the motion picture industry. Never heard of it. Florida is the *true* film capital, and we have the recount to prove it. Well, at least we have more than a century of movie footage that began in 1898 with the spectacular "U.S. Calvary Supplies Unloading at Tampa." Then consider that Oliver Hardy got his start making movie shorts in Jacksonville, which, between 1910 and 1917, was a film factory town for more than 30 studios and 1,000 actors and extras. That lasted until folks started heading west when a conservative electorate booted the film-friendly mayor from office.

Despite the rocky beginning, the Sunshine State has maintained a high profile on the Silver Screen. Don't think so? Then what about Johnny Weismuller's Tarzan movies that were shot at Wakulla Springs? Or Esther Williams's movies made at Cypress Gardens? Where do you think Elvis Followed That Dream? Near Ocala! And then there were classics such as *The Creature from the Black Lagoon* and *Where the Boys Are*. Shot right here!

So take a break and run to the video store and check out some more Florida films that you know and love: *Parenthood; There's Something about Mary; Rosewood; Ace Ventura: Pet Detective; Edward Scissorhands; The Birdcage; My Girl; True Lies; Doc Hollywood; Caddyshack; Passenger 57; Cocoon; Matinee; Contact; Yulee's Gold; Speed 2; GI Jane; Body Heat; Instinct; Sunshine State;* and Tom Hanks's $50 million series, *From the Earth to the Moon.*

Still think that fancy-schmancy Hollywood has anything over Florida? Didn't think you did.

For an in-depth study on Florida's role in the movies, check out *Hollywood East* (1992), by James Ponti.

— Gary McKechnie

GOLF IN THE SUNSHINE STATE

GOLF DIGEST'S PICKS FOR GOLFING
THROUGHOUT THE STATE

With more courses than any other state, Florida is a golfer's paradise. The warm climate makes for year-round play on hundreds of courses, from which *Golf Digest* has chosen the best from all corners of the state.

How could golfers feel under par in the Sunshine State? One out of every 10 rounds of golf played in the United States is played here, and golfers visit Florida more than any other state. One of the reasons may be that there is plenty of green to go around. Florida has more golf courses than any other state, and it's always among the top five in the number of courses either newly opened or under construction each year. According to National Golf Foundation figures, the current count is more than 1,200 places at which to tee up.

A big part of the appeal of Florida golf is its year-round availability. Although a few courses might close for a day or two in fall to reseed greens and a few in northern Florida might delay morning tee times in winter when there's frost, it's still fair to say you can find a fairway here 365 days a year. That's why a large number of touring professionals—including Jack Nicklaus, Tiger Woods, and Mark O'Meara—have homes here.

What sort of play can you expect? It's no state secret that Florida is flat. With its highest elevation at 345 ft, it can't claim many naturally rolling courses. The world's leading golf-course designers, including Tom Fazio, Jack Nicklaus, and Ed Seay, have added the rolls and undulations that nature omitted. No designer, however, has been more notable in this regard than Pete Dye, pioneer of stadium-style courses, which are designed for large tournament audiences.

Deep rough is unusual as a penalizing element in Florida play, short rough is especially prevalent during winter, and water and sand are common. Often, lakes and canals have to be carved out to make fairways. Although Florida fairways are characteristically wide, greens tend to be heavily bunkered or protected by water. A diabolically popular invention of Florida course builders is the island green surrounded by water. Sand is also a natural part of the Florida environment, although a special fine-grain sand is sometimes imported; it isn't unusual to come across a hole in Florida with 10 or more traps, and several courses have more than 100 traps each. On the other hand, because the sandy soil drains well, the playing surface is more forgiving of iron shots than denser clay-rich soil. What this adds up to is a premium on accuracy when it comes to approach shots.

Wind also comes into play in Florida, particularly at courses near the state's 3,000 mi of coastline. Inland, it swirls and becomes unpredictable as it moves through tall pine and palm trees.

Finally, keep in mind that for most of the year, Florida greens are seeded with Bermuda grass. If you're familiar with putting on the bent-grass greens found in other parts of the country, you may find that the speed (on the slow side) and grain of Bermuda greens take getting used to.

Golf Digest: **The Basics**

To help you find your perfect course out of the more than 1,200 available for play in Florida, we're happy to bring you a list of the top golf courses in the Sunshine State according to *Fodor's Golf Digest's Places to Play, Fifth Edition.* To compile the information for *Places to Play,* the editors at *Golf Digest* had more than 20,000 of their readers to fill out course ballots sharing their opinions and experiences on more than 6,500 courses in the United States, Canada, Mexico, and the Caribbean. Then a team of savvy *Golf Digest* editors spent countless hours editing the comments for each individual course and all 6,500-plus courses were contacted for their latest, up-to-date information, such as their address, phone number, green fee, and directions. The courses were then rated from one to five stars and presented in the comprehensive *Fodor's Golf Digest's Places to Play, Fifth Edition* guide. For *Fodor's Florida 2004*, we've gone one step further, and culled the *Golf Digest* findings down to the very best that's available—the 5-star, 4½-star, and 4-star rated courses for the state.

Here are basic explanations for some of the information in the course listings:

Yards: The yardage from the back/front tees.

Par: The figures shown represent the par from the back/front tees.

Course Rating: The USGA course rating from the back/front tees.

Slope: The USGA slope rating from the back/front tees.

Green Fee: Listed from lowest to highest, for one 18-hole round of golf.

Walkability: Rated on a 1 to 5 scale, with 1 being flat and 5 being extremely hilly.

Season: The months of the year when the course is open for play.

High: When the course is likely to be busiest and the rates typically higher.

BF: Beginner-friendly.

FF: Female-friendly.

PU: Public course.

R: Resort course.

SP: Semi-private course.

Note that 27-hole courses are shown in combinations (18 combo).

Published fees are subject to change.

For an all-inclusive list of *Golf Digest's* Florida picks, as well as information on *Golf Digest's* course picks for the rest of the country, pick up a copy of *Fodor's Golf Digest's Places to Play, Fifth Edition* available at bookstores everywhere or by calling 800/262–1556. Happy golfing!

Golf Digest's Places to Play

Amelia Island Plantation. Facility Holes: 54. Cart Fee: Included in greens fee. Opened: 1987. Architect: Tom Fazio. Season: Year-round. To obtain tee times: Call golf shop. Miscellaneous: Reduced fees (guests, twilight, juniors), range (grass), lodging (249 rooms), credit cards (AE, D, MC, V, resort charge card). R. ⊠ *6800 1st Coast Hwy., Amelia Island, 32035, Nassau County, 35 mi from Jacksonville,* ☎ *904/277–5907 or 800/874–6878,* ⊕ *www.aipfl.com.*

Long Point Golf Club. Holes: 18. Yards: 6,775/4,927. Par: 72/72. Course Rating: 72.9/69.1. Slope: 129/121. Greens Fee: $140/$160. Walkability: 2. High: Oct.–Nov. Rating: ★★★★½

Oak Marsh. Holes: 18. Yards: 6,108/4,341. Par: 70/70. Course Rating: 70.3/66.4. Slope: 134/115. Greens Fee: $120/$140. High: Mar.–May. Rating: ★★★★

Ocean Links. Holes: 18. Yards: 6,592/4,983. Par: 72/72. Course Rating: 71.7/66.4. Slope: 130/115. Greens Fee: $120/$140. Walkability: 1. High: Oct.–Nov. Rating: ★★★★

Arnold Palmer's Bay Hill Club & Lodge. Facility Holes: 27. Greens Fee: $205. Cart Fee: Included in greens fee. Walkability: 2. Architect: Dick Wilson/ Arnold Palmer/Ed Seay. Season: Year-round. To obtain tee times: Call golf shop. Miscellaneous: Reduced fees (guests, juniors), range (grass), caddies, lodging (65 rooms), credit cards (AE, MC, V). R. ⊠ *9000 Bay Hill Blvd., Orlando, 32819, Orange County, 15 mi from Orlando,* ☎ *407/876–2429 Ext. 630,* ⊕ *www.bayhill.com.*

Challenger/Champion. Holes: 18. Yards: 7,207/5,235. Par: 72/72. Course Rating: 75.1/72.7. Slope: 139/130. Walking Policy: Walking with Caddie. Opened: 1961. Miscellaneous: BF, FF. Notes: Ranked 97th in 1997–98 America's 100 Greatest; 8th in 2001 Best in State; 25th in 1996 America's Top 75 Upscale Courses. Rating: ★★★★½

Baytree National Golf Links. Holes: 18. Yards: 7,043/4,803. Par: 72/72. Course Rating: 74.4/67.5. Slope: 138/118. Greens Fee: $34/$85. Cart Fee: Included in greens fee. Walking Policy: Mandatory carts. Walkability: 2. Opened: 1994. Architect: Gary Player. Season: Year-round. High: Jan.–Apr. To obtain tee times: Call golf shop. Miscellaneous: Reduced fees (guests, twilight), range (grass), credit cards (AE, MC, V), BF, FF. PU. ⊠ *8207 National Dr., Melbourne, 32940, Brevard County, 50 mi from Orlando,* ☎ *321/259–9060 or 888/955–1234,* ⊕ *www.golfbaytree.com.* Rating: ★★★★

Bobcat Trail Golf & Country Club. Holes: 18. Yards: 6,748/4,741. Par: 71/71. Course Rating: 72.9/68.7. Slope: 129/115. Greens Fee: $24/$60. Cart Fee: $15/person. Walking Policy: Mandatory carts. Walkability: 3. Opened: 1998. Architect: Lee Singletary, Bob Tway. Season: Year-round. High: Oct.–Apr. To obtain tee times: Call up to 7 days in advance. Miscellaneous: Reduced fees (twilight), range (grass), credit cards (AE, D, MC, V), BF, FF. PU. ⊠ *1350 Bobcat Tr., North Port, 34286, Sarasota County, 35 mi from Sarasota,* ☎ *941/429–0500,* ⊕ *bobcattrail.com.* Rating: ★★★★½

Boca Raton Resort & Club. Facility Holes: 36. Cart Fee: $25/person. Season: Year-round. High: Oct.–May. To obtain tee times: Call golf shop. Miscellaneous: Reduced fees (twilight), range (grass), lodging (965 rooms), credit cards (AE, D, DC, MC, V). R. ⊠ *17751 Boca Club Blvd., Boca Raton, 33487, Palm Beach County, 17 mi from West Palm Beach,* ☎ *561/997–8205 or 800/327–0101,* ⊕ *www.bocaresort.com.*

Country Club Course. Holes: 18. Yards: 6,513/5,365. Par: 72/72. Course Rating: 71.8/72.1. Slope: 131/128. Greens Fee: $50/$150. Walkability: 2. Opened: 1984. Architect: Joe Lee. Rating: ★★★★

Celebration Golf Club Service. Holes: 18. Yards: 6,786/5,724. Par: 72/72. Course Rating: 73.0/68.1. Slope: 135/122. Greens Fee: $75/$130. Cart Fee: Included in greens fee. Walking Policy: Walking at certain times. Walkability: 3. Opened: 1996. Architect: Robert Trent Jones/Robert Trent Jones Jr. Season: Year-round. High: Jan.–Apr. To obtain tee times: Call up to 30 days in advance. Miscellaneous: Reduced fees (twilight, juniors), range (grass), credit cards (AE, D, DC, MC, V), BF, FF. PU. ⊠ *701 Golf Park Dr., Celebration, 34747, Osceola County, 15 mi from Orlando,* ☎ *407/566–4653 or 888/275–2918,* ⊕ *www.celebrationgolf.com.* Rating: ★★★★

The Club at Eaglebrooke. Holes: 18. Yards: 7,005/4,981. Par: 72/72. Course Rating: 74.0/69.0. Slope: 136/115. Greens Fee: $20/$70. Cart Fee: $19/person. Walking Policy: Mandatory carts. Walkability: 3. Opened: 1997. Architect: Ron Garl. Season: Year-round. High: Jan.–May. To obtain tee times: Call golf shop. Miscellaneous: Reduced fees (weekdays, twilight, juniors), range (grass), credit cards (AE, D, MC, V), BF, FF. SP. ⊠*1300 Eaglebrooke Blvd., Lakeland, 33813, Polk County, 30 mi from Tampa,* ☎ *863/701–0101,* ⊕ *www.eaglebrooke.com.* Rating:★★★★½

The Club at Hidden Creek. Holes: 18. Yards: 6,862/5,213. Par: 72/72. Course Rating: 73.2/70.1. Slope: 139/124. Greens Fee: $25/$55. Cart Fee: Included in greens fee. Walking Policy: Mandatory carts. Walkability: 2. Opened: 1988. Architect: Ron Garl. Season: Year-round. To obtain tee times: Call up to 7 days in advance. Miscellaneous: Reduced fees (weekdays, twilight, juniors), range (grass), credit cards (MC, V), BF, FF. SP. ⊠ *3070 PGA Blvd., Navarre, 32566, Santa Rosa County, 20 mi from Pensacola,* ☎*850/939–4604,* ⊕*www.hiddengolf.com.* Rating:★★★★½

Colony West Country Club. Facility Holes: 36. Cart Fee: Included in greens fee. Walkability: 1. Opened: 1970. Architect: Bruce Devlin/Robert von Hagge. Season: Year-round. High: Dec.–Apr. To obtain tee times: Call golf shop. Miscellaneous: Reduced fees (weekdays, twilight), credit cards (AE, MC, V). PU. ⊠ *6800 N.W. 88th Ave., Tamarac, 33321, Broward County, 10 mi from Fort Lauderdale,* ☎ *954/726–8430,* ⊕ *www.colonywestcc.com.*

Championship Course. Holes: 18. Yards: 7,312/4,415. Par: 71/71. Course Rating: 75.5. Slope: 146. Greens Fee: $58/$90. Walking Policy: Mandatory carts. Rating:★★★★

DeBary Golf & Country Club. Holes: 18. Yards: 6,776/5,060. Par: 72/72. Course Rating: 72.3/68.8. Slope: 128/122. Greens Fee: $24/$40. Cart Fee: Included in greens fee. Walking Policy: Mandatory carts. Walkability: 3. Opened: 1990. Architect: Lloyd Clifton. Season: Year-round. To obtain tee times: Call golf shop. Miscellaneous: Reduced fees (twilight, juniors), range (grass), credit cards (AE, MC, V), BF, FF. SP. ⊠ *300 Plantation Dr., DeBary, 32713, Volusia County, 15 mi from Orlando,* ☎ *407/668–1709,* ⊕ *www.debary-cc.com.* Rating:★★★★

Deer Island Golf & Lake Club. Holes: 18. Yards: 6,676/5,139. Par: 72/72. Course Rating: 73.1/70.4. Slope: 137/118. Greens Fee: $25/$59. Cart Fee: Included in greens fee. Walking Policy: Mandatory carts. Walkability: 2. Opened: 1994. Architect: Joe Lee. Season: Year-round. High: Jan.–Apr. To obtain tee times: Call up to 7 days in advance. Miscellaneous: Reduced fees (weekdays, twilight, seniors), range (grass), credit cards (AE, D, MC, V), BF, FF. SP. ⊠ *18000 Eagles Way, Tavares, 32778, Lake County, 30 mi from Orlando,* ☎ *352/343–7550 or 800/269–0006,* ⊕ *www.deerislandgolf.com.* Rating:★★★★

Diamondback Golf Club. Holes: 18. Yards: 6,805/5,061. Par: 72/72. Course Rating: 73.3/70.3. Slope: 138/122. Greens Fee: $30/$75. Cart Fee: Included in greens fee. Walking Policy: Mandatory carts. Walkability: 5. Opened: 1995. Architect: Joe Lee. Season: Year-round. High: Jan.–Apr. To obtain tee times: Call up to 7 days in advance. Miscellaneous: Reduced fees (weekdays, twilight, juniors), range (grass), credit cards (MC, V, AE), BF, FF. SP. ⊠ *6501 State Rd. 544 E, Haines City, 33844, Polk County, 25 mi from Orlando,* ☎ *863/421–0437 or 800/222–5629,* ⊕ *www.diamondbackgc.com.* Rating:★★★★

Doral Golf Resort & Spa. Facility Holes: 90. Walkability: 1. Season: Year-round. Misc: Lodging (693 rooms), credit cards (AE, D, DC, MC, V),

BF, FF. R. ✉ *4400 N.W. 87th Ave., Miami, 33178, Dade County,* ☎ *305/592–2000 Ext. 2105 or 800/713–6725,* ● *www.doralresort.com.*

Blue Course. Holes: 18. Yards: 7,125/5,392. Par: 72/72. Course Rating: 74.5/73.0. Slope: 130/124. Greens Fee: $175/$275. Cart Fee: Included in greens fee. Walking Policy: Walking at certain times. Opened: 1961. Architect: Dick Wilson. High: Dec.–Apr. To obtain tee times: Call golf shop. Miscellaneous: Reduced fees (weekdays, guests, twilight), range (grass/mats), caddies. Notes: Ranked 20th in 2001 Best in State; 42nd in 1996 America's Top 75 Upscale Courses. Rating: ★★★★

El Diablo Golf & Country Club. Holes: 18. Yards: 7,045/5,144. Par: 72/72. Course Rating: 75.3/69.8. Slope: 147/117. Greens Fee: $25/$49. Walking Policy: Unrestricted walking. Walkability: 4. Opened: 1998. Architect: Jim Fazio. Season: Year-round. To obtain tee times: Call golf shop. Miscellaneous: Reduced fees (twilight), range (grass), credit cards (AE, MC, V), BF, FF. Notes: Ranked 12th in 2001 Best in State; 1st in 1999 Best New Affordable Public. PU. ✉ *10405 N. Sherman Dr., Citrus Springs, 34434, Citrus County, 20 mi from Ocala,* ☎ *352/465–0986 or 877/353–4225,* ● *www.eldiablo.cc.* Rating: ★★★★½

Emerald Dunes Golf Course. Holes: 18. Yards: 7,006/4,676. Par: 72/72. Course Rating: 73.8/67.1. Slope: 133/115. Greens Fee: $65/$150. Cart Fee: Included in greens fee. Walking Policy: Unrestricted walking. Walkability: 3. Opened: 1990. Architect: Tom Fazio. Season: Year-round. High: Dec.–Apr. To obtain tee times: Call up to 60 days in advance. Miscellaneous: Reduced fees (weekdays, twilight), range (grass), credit cards (AE, D, DC, MC, V), BF, FF. PU. ✉ *2100 Emerald Dunes Dr., West Palm Beach, 33411, Palm Beach County, 3 mi from West Palm Beach,* ☎ *561/684–4653 or 888/650–4653,* ● *www.emeralddunes.com.* Rating: ★★★★½

Falcon's Fire Golf Club. Holes: 18. Yards: 6,901/5,417. Par: 72/72. Course Rating: 72.5/70.4. Slope: 125/118. Greens Fee: $45/$130. Cart Fee: Included in greens fee. Walking Policy: Mandatory carts. Walkability: 1. Opened: 1993. Architect: Rees Jones. Season: Year-round. High: Jan.–Mar. To obtain tee times: Call golf shop. Miscellaneous: Reduced fees (twilight, juniors), metal spikes, range (grass), credit cards (AE, D, MC, V), BF, FF. PU. ✉ *3200 Seralago Blvd., Kissimmee, 34746, Osceola County, 3 mi from Orlando,* ☎ *407/239–5445,* ● *www.falconsfire.com.* Rating: ★★★★

Gateway Golf & Country Club. Holes: 18. Yards: 6,974/5,323. Par: 72/72. Course Rating: 74.1/70.1. Slope: 129/121. Greens Fee: $40/$80. Cart Fee: Included in greens fee. Walkability: 1. Opened: 1989. Architect: Tom Fazio. Season: Year-round. High: Jan.-Mar. To obtain tee times: Call golf shop. Miscellaneous: Reduced fees (twilight), range (grass), credit cards (AE, MC, V). SP. ✉ *11360 Championship Dr., Fort Myers, 33913, Lee County,* ☎ *239/561–1010.* Rating: ★★★★

The Golden Bear Club at Keene's Pointe. Holes: 18. Yards: 7,173/5,071. Par: 72/72. Course Rating: 74.8/69.1. Slope: 136/118. Cart Fee: Included in greens fee. Walking Policy: Mandatory carts. Walkability: 2. Opened: 1999. Architect: Jack Nicklaus/Bruce Borland. Season: Year-round. High: Jan.–Apr. To obtain tee times: Call up to 7 days in advance. Miscellaneous: Reduced fees (twilight, juniors), range (grass), credit cards (MC, V), BF, FF. SP. ✉ *6300 Jack Nicklaus Pkwy., Windermere, 34786, Orange County, 10 mi from Orlando,* ☎ *407/876–1461.* Rating: ★★★★

Grand Cypress Golf Club. Facility Holes: 45. Greens Fee: $115/$175. Cart Fee: Included in greens fee. Walkability: 2. Architect: Jack Nicklaus. Season: Year-round. To obtain tee times: Call golf shop. Miscellaneous: Reduced fees (twilight, juniors), range (grass), caddies, lodging (896 rooms), credit cards (AE, D, DC, MC, V, Carte Blanche), BF, FF. R. ✉ *One N. Jacaranda, Orlando, 32836, Orange County,* ☎ *407/239–1904 or 800/ 835–7377,* ⊕ *www.grandcypress.com.*

New Course. Holes: 18. Yards: 6,773/5,314. Par: 72/72. Course Rating: 72.2/69.8. Slope: 122/115. Walking Policy: Unrestricted walking. Opened: 1988. Rating: ★★★★½

North/East. Holes: 18 combo. Yards: 6,955/5,056. Par: 72/72. Course Rating: 75.0/69.5. Slope: 139/118. Walking Policy: Mandatory carts. Opened: 1984. **North/South.** Holes: 18 combo. Yards: 6,993/5,328. Par: 72/72. Course Rating: 75.1/71.6. Slope: 137/121. **South/East** Holes: 18 combo. Yards: 6,906/5,126. Par: 72/72. Course Rating: 74.7/70.3. Slope: 138/121. Rating: ★★★★½

Grand Haven Golf Club. Holes: 18. Yards: 7,069/4,985. Par: 72/72. Course Rating: 74.9/70.4. Slope: 135/123. Greens Fee: $53/$73. Cart Fee: Included in greens fee. Walkability: 3. Opened: 1998. Architect: Jack Nicklaus. Season: Year-round. High: Jan.–Apr. To obtain tee times: Call golf shop. Miscellaneous: Reduced fees (guests, juniors), range (grass), lodging (150 rooms), credit cards (AE, MC, V). Notes: 1999 U.S. Open Qualifier; 1999 U.S. Junior Amateur Qualifier. SP. ✉ *2001 Waterside Pkwy., Palm Coast, 32137, Flagler County, 30 mi from Daytona Beach,* ☎ *386/445–2327 or 888/522–5642,* ⊕ *www.grandhavenfla.com.* Rating: ★★★★

Harbor Hills Country Club. Holes: 18. Yards: 6,910/5,363. Par: 72/72. Course Rating: 72.8/70.3. Slope: 128/115. Greens Fee: $28/$49. Cart Fee: Included in greens fee. To obtain tee times: Call golf shop. SP. ✉ *6538 Lake Griffin Rd., Lady Lake, 32159, Lake County,* ☎ *352/ 753–7711.* Rating: ★★★★

Heron Creek Golf & Country Club. Holes: 18. Yards: 6,869/4,787. Par: 72/ 72. Course Rating: 73.1/69.9. Slope: 140/124. Greens Fee: $25/$75. Cart Fee: Included in greens fee. Walking Policy: Walking at certain times. Walkability: 2. Opened: 2000. Architect: Arthur Hills/Brian Yoder. Season: Year-round. High: Jan.–Apr. To obtain tee times: Call up to 4 days in advance. Miscellaneous: Reduced fees (twilight), range (grass), credit cards (AE, MC, V), BF, FF. PU. ✉ *5303 Heron Creek Blvd., North Port, 34287, Sarasota County, 15 mi from Sarasota,* ☎ *941/423–6955 or 800/ 877–1433,* ⊕ *www.heron-creek.com.* Rating: ★★★★

Kelly Plantation Golf Club Service. Holes: 18. Yards: 7,099/5,170. Par: 72/ 72. Course Rating: 74.2/70.9. Slope: 146/124. Greens Fee: $75/$125. Cart Fee: Included in greens fee. Walking Policy: Unrestricted walking. Walkability: 2. Opened: 1998. Architect: Fred Couples/Gene Bates. Season: Year-round. To obtain tee times: Call up to 30 days in advance. Miscellaneous: Reduced fees (twilight, juniors), range (grass), lodging (100 rooms), credit cards (AE, D, MC, V), BF, FF. SP. ✉ *307 Kelly Plantation Dr., Destin, 32541, Okaloosa County, 3 mi from Destin,* ☎ *850/ 650–7600 or 800/811–6757,* ⊕ *www.kellyplantation.com.* Rating: ★★★★½

Lake Jovita Golf & Country Club. Holes: 18. Yards: 7,151/5,091. Par: 72/ 72. Course Rating: 74.4/68.4. Slope: 140/136. Greens Fee: $85/$115. Cart Fee: Included in greens fee. Walking Policy: Unrestricted walking. Walkability: 3. Opened: 1999. Architect: Kurt Sandness/Tom Lehman. Season: Year-round. High: Jan.–May. To obtain tee times: Call golf shop. Miscellaneous: Range (grass), credit cards (AE, MC, V), BF, FF.

Notes: Ranked 11th in 2001 Best in State; 9th in 2000 Best New Up-scale Courses. SP. ✉ *12900 Lake Jovita Blvd., Dade City, 33525, Pasco County, 20 mi from Tampa,* ☎ *352/588–9200 or 877/481–2652,* ⊕ *www.lakejovita.com.* Rating: ★★★★½

The Legacy Club at Alaqua Lakes. Holes: 18. Yards: 7,160/5,383. Par: 72/72. Course Rating: 74.5/70.7. Slope: 132/119. Greens Fee: $59/$109. Cart Fee: Included in greens fee. Walking Policy: Walking at certain times. Walkability: 3. Opened: 1998. Architect: Tom Fazio. Season: Year-round. High: Jan.–May. To obtain tee times: Call up to 3 days in advance. Miscellaneous: Reduced fees (weekdays, guests, twilight), range (grass), credit cards (MC, V), BF, FF. SP. ✉ *1700 Alaqua Lakes Blvd., Longwood, 32779, Seminole County, 10 mi from Orlando,* ☎ *407/444–9995,* ⊕ *www.legacyclubgolf.com.* Rating: ★★★★½

The Legacy Golf Course at Lakewood Ranch. Holes: 18. Yards: 7,067/4,886. Par: 72/72. Course Rating: 73.7/68.2. Slope: 143/125. Greens Fee: $45/$95. Cart Fee: Included in greens fee. Walkability: 3. Opened: 1997. Architect: Arnold Palmer/Ed Seay/Vici Martz. Season: Year-round. High: Jan.–Apr. To obtain tee times: Call golf shop. Miscellaneous: Reduced fees (weekdays, twilight), metal spikes, range (grass), credit cards (AE, MC, V). PU. ✉ *8255 Legacy Blvd., Bradenton, 34202, Manatee County, 30 mi from Tampa,* ☎ *941/907–7067.* Rating: ★★★★

Lely Resort Golf & Country Club. Facility Holes: 36. Greens Fee: $35/$129. Cart Fee: Included in greens fee. Walking Policy: Mandatory carts. Season: Year-round. High: Nov.–Apr. To obtain tee times: Call up to 3 days in advance. Miscellaneous: Reduced fees (twilight), range (grass), credit cards (AE, D, DC, MC, V). R. ✉ *8004 Lely Resort Blvd., Naples, 34113, Collier County, 30 mi from Fort Myers,* ☎ *239/793–2223 or 800/388–4653.*

Lely Flamingo Island Club. Holes: 18. Yards: 7,171/5,377. Par: 72/72. Course Rating: 73.9/70.6. Slope: 135/126. Opened: 1990. Architect: Robert Trent Jones. Miscellaneous: BF, FF. Rating: ★★★★

Lely Mustang Golf Club. Holes: 18. Yards: 7,217/5,197. Par: 72/72. Course Rating: 75.2/70.5. Slope: 141/120. Opened: 1996. Architect: Lee Trevino. Rating: ★★★★½

LPGA International. Facility Holes: 36. Greens Fee: $30/$95. Cart Fee: Included in greens fee. Walking Policy: Mandatory carts. Season: Year-round. High: Jan.–Apr. To obtain tee times: Call up to 7 days in advance. Miscellaneous: Reduced fees (twilight, juniors), range (grass), credit cards (AE, MC, V), BF, FF. PU. ✉ *1000 Champions Dr., Daytona Beach, 32124, Volusia County, 50 mi from Orlando,* ☎ *386/523–2001,* ⊕ *www.lpgainternational.com.*

Champions. Holes: 18. Yards: 7,088/5,131. Par: 72/72. Course Rating: 74.0/68.9. Slope: 134/122. Walkability: 2. Opened: 1994. Architect: Rees Jones. Rating: ★★★★

Legends. Holes: 18. Yards: 6,984/5,131. Par: 72/72. Course Rating: 74.5/70.2. Slope: 138/123. Walkability: 3. Opened: 1998. Architect: Arthur Hills. Rating: ★★★★

Marriott's Bay Point Resort. Facility Holes: 36. Cart Fee: Included in greens fee. Walking Policy: Mandatory carts. Season: Year-round. To obtain tee times: Call up to 60 days in advance. Miscellaneous: Reduced fees (guests, twilight, juniors), range (grass), lodging (356 rooms), credit cards (AE, D, MC, V), BF, FF. R. ✉ *Box 27880, Panama City Beach,*

32411, Bay County, 90 mi from Pensacola, ☎ *850/235–6950,* ⊕ *www.baypointgolf.com.*

Lagoon Legend. Holes: 18. Yards: 6,921/4,942. Par: 72/72. Course Rating: 75.3/69.8. Slope: 152/127. Greens Fee: $60/$90. Walkability: 2. Opened: 1986. Architect: Bruce Devlin/Robert von Hagge. High: Feb.–May. Rating: ★★★★

Marsh Landing Country Club. Holes: 18. Yards: 6,821/5,097. Par: 72/72. Slope: 135/124. Greens Fee: $115/$185. Cart Fee: $30/person. Walking Policy: Walking at certain times. Opened: 1986. Architect: Ed Seay. Season: Year-round. To obtain tee times: Call golf shop. Miscellaneous: Range (grass), credit cards (MC, V), BF, FF. Special Notes: Limited access available to guests staying at Marriott at Sawgrass. R. ✉ *25655 Marsh Landing Pkwy., Ponte Vedra Beach, 32082, St. Johns County, 15 mi from Jacksonville,* ☎ *904/285–6459 or 800/457–4653.* Rating: ★★★★

MetroWest Country Club. Holes: 18. Yards: 7,051/5,325. Par: 72/72. Course Rating: 74.1/70.3. Slope: 132/122. Greens Fee: $49/$115. Cart Fee: Included in greens fee. Walking Policy: Mandatory carts. Walkability: 4. Opened: 1987. Architect: Robert Trent Jones. Season: Year-round. High: Dec.–Apr. To obtain tee times: Call golf shop. Miscellaneous: Reduced fees (twilight, juniors), metal spikes, range (grass), credit cards (AE, MC, V), BF, FF. SP. ✉ *2100 S. Hiawassee Rd., Orlando, 32835, Orange County, 5 mi from Orlando,* ☎ *407/299–1099,* ⊕ *www.metrowestorlando.com.* Rating: ★★★★

Mission Inn Golf & Tennis Resort. Facility Holes: 36. Cart Fee: Included in greens fee. Walking Policy: Mandatory carts. Season: Year-round. High: Nov.–Apr. To obtain tee times: Call up to 7 days in advance. Miscellaneous: Range (grass), lodging (187 rooms), BF, FF. R. ✉ *10400 County Rd. 48, Howey in the Hills, 34737, Lake County, 30 mi from Orlando,* ☎ *352/324–3885 or 800/874–9053,* ⊕ *www.missioninnresort.com.*

El Campeon Course. Holes: 18. Yards: 6,923/4,811. Par: 72/73. Course Rating: 73.6/67.3. Slope: 133/118. Greens Fee: $60/$125. Walkability: 3. Opened: 1926. Architect: Charles Clark. Miscellaneous: Credit cards (AE, D, MC, V). Rating: ★★★★

The Moors Golf Club. Holes: 18. Yards: 6,828/5,259. Par: 70/70. Course Rating: 72.9/70.3. Slope: 126/117. Greens Fee: $33/$47. Cart Fee: $12/person. Walking Policy: Walking at certain times. Walkability: 2. Opened: 1993. Architect: John B. LaFoy. Season: Year-round. High: Feb.–May. To obtain tee times: Call up to 7 days in advance. Miscellaneous: Reduced fees (weekdays, guests), range (grass/mats), lodging (8 rooms), credit cards (AE, D, MC, V), BF, FF. PU. ✉ *3220 Avalon Blvd., Milton, 32583, Santa Rosa County, 6 mi from Pensacola,* ☎ *850/995–4653 or 800/727–1010,* ⊕ *www.moors.com.* Rating: ★★★★½

Naples Grande Golf Club. Holes: 18. Yards: 7,078/5,209. Par: 72/72. Course Rating: 75.1/70.5. Slope: 143/119. Greens Fee: $70/$170. Cart Fee: Included in greens fee. Walking Policy: Unrestricted walking. Walkability: 3. Opened: 2000. Architect: Rees Jones. Season: Year-round. High: Jan.–Apr. To obtain tee times: Call golf shop. Miscellaneous: Reduced fees (twilight), range (grass), credit cards (AE, D, MC, V), BF, FF. R. ✉ *7760 Golden Gate Pkwy., Naples, 34105, Collier County,* ☎ *239/659–3710,* ⊕ *www.naplesgrande.com.* Rating: ★★★★½

Orange County National Golf Center & Lodge. Facility Holes: 36. Cart Fee: Included in greens fee. Walking Policy: Mandatory carts. Walkability:

5. Architect: Phil Ritson/David Harman/Isao Aoki. Season: Year-round. To obtain tee times: Call golf shop. Miscellaneous: Reduced fees (weekdays, guests, twilight, juniors), range (grass), lodging (46 rooms), credit cards (AE, DC, MC, V), BF, FF. PU. ✉ *16301 Phil Ritson Way, Winter Garden, 34787, Orange County, 5 mi from Orlando,* ☎ 407/656–2626 or 888/727–3672, ⊕ *www.ocngolf.com.*

Crooked Cat Course. Holes: 18. Yards: 7,277/5,262. Par: 72/72. Course Rating: 75.4/70.3. Slope: 140/120. Greens Fee: $19/$65. Opened: 1999. Rating: ★★★★½

Panther Lake Course. Holes: 18. Yards: 7,295/5,073. Par: 72/72. Course Rating: 75.7/71.5. Slope: 137/125. Greens Fee: $19/$75. Opened: 1997. Rating: ★★★★½

Orange Lake Country Club. Facility Holes: 54. Cart Fee: Included in greens fee. Season: Year-round. High: Jan.–Apr. To obtain tee times: Call golf shop. Miscellaneous: Reduced fees (weekdays, guests, twilight, juniors), range (grass/mats), credit cards (AE, MC, V). R. ✉ *8505 W. Irlo Bronson Mem. Hwy., Kissimmee, 34747, Osceola County, 15 mi from Orlando,* ☎ 407/239–1050.

The Legends at Orange Lake. Holes: 18. Yards: 7,072/5,188. Par: 72/72. Course Rating: 74.3/69.6. Slope: 132/120. Greens Fee: $40/$125. Opened: 1982. Architect: Arnold Palmer. Rating: ★★★★

Palisades Golf Course. Holes: 18. Yards: 7,004/5,528. Par: 72/72. Course Rating: 73.8/72.1. Slope: 127/122. Greens Fee: $30/$55. Cart Fee: Included in greens fee. Walking Policy: Mandatory carts. Walkability: 5. Opened: 1991. Architect: Joe Lee. Season: Year-round. High: Jan.-Mar. To obtain tee times: Call golf shop. Miscellaneous: Reduced fees (weekdays, twilight, seniors), range (grass), credit cards (AE, D, MC, V), BF, FF. SP. ✉ *16510 Palisades Blvd., Clermont, 34711, Lake County, 20 mi from Orlando,* ☎ *352/394–0085,* ⊕ *www.golfpalisades.com.* Rating: ★★★★

Palm Coast Golf Resort. Facility Holes: 90. Cart Fee: Included in greens fee. Walkability: 2. Season: Year-round. High: Jan.–Apr. To obtain tee times: Call up to 6 days in advance. Miscellaneous: Reduced fees (guests, juniors), range (grass), credit cards (AE, D, MC, V), BF, FF. R. ✉ *53 Easthampton Blvd., Palm Coast, 32164, Flagler County, 25 mi from Daytona Beach,* ☎ *386/445–6330 or 800/654–6538,* ⊕ *www.palmcoastgolfresort.com.*

Matanzas Woods Golf Club. Holes: 18. Yards: 6,929/5,236. Par: 72/72. Course Rating: 74.9/71.0. Slope: 141/121. Greens Fee: $55/$80. Walking Policy: Mandatory carts. Opened: 1986. Architect: Arnold Palmer/Ed Seay. Rating: ★★★★

Pine Lakes Country Club. Holes: 18. Yards: 7,074/5,166. Par: 72/72. Course Rating: 73.5/71.4. Slope: 126/124. Greens Fee: $55/$80. Walking Policy: Mandatory carts. Opened: 1981. Architect: Arnold Palmer/Ed Seay. Rating: ★★★★

PGA National Resort & Spa. Facility Holes: 90. Cart Fee: $35/person. Walking Policy: Mandatory carts. Walkability: 1. Season: Year-round. High: Nov.–Apr. To obtain tee times: Call golf shop. Miscellaneous: Metal spikes, range (grass/mats), lodging (300 rooms), credit cards (AE, D, MC, V), BF, FF. R. ✉ *1000 Ave. of the Champions, Palm Beach Gardens, 33418, Palm Beach County, 15 mi from West Palm Beach,* ☎ *561/627–1800 or 800/633–9150,* ⊕ *www.pga-resorts.com.*

Champion Course. Holes: 18. Yards: 7,022/5,377. Par: 72/72. Course Rating: 74.7/71.1. Slope: 142/123. Greens Fee: $109/$280. Opened: 1981. Architect: Tom Fazio/Jack Nicklaus. Rating: ★★★★

General Course. Holes: 18. Yards: 6,768/5,324. Par: 72/72. Course Rating: 73.0/71.0. Slope: 130/122. Greens Fee: $109/$180. Opened: 1984. Architect: Arnold Palmer. Rating: ★★★★

Squire Course. Holes: 18. Yards: 6,478/4,982. Par: 72/72. Course Rating: 71.3/69.8. Slope: 127/123. Greens Fee: $109/$180. Opened: 1981. Architect: Tom Fazio. Rating: ★★★★

Regatta Bay Golf & Country Club. Holes: 18. Yards: 6,864/5,092. Par: 72/72. Course Rating: 73.8/70.8. Slope: 148/119. Greens Fee: $59/$114. Cart Fee: $15/person. Walking Policy: Mandatory carts. Walkability: 3. Opened: 1998. Architect: Bob Walker. Season: Year-round. To obtain tee times: Call golf shop. Miscellaneous: Reduced fees (twilight, juniors), range (grass), credit cards (AE, MC, V), BF, FF. SP. ⊠ *465 Regatta Bay Blvd., Destin, 32541, Okaloosa County,* ☎ *850/650–7800 or 800/648–0123,* ⊕ *www.regattabay.com.* Rating: ★★★★

Riverwood Golf Club. Holes: 18. Yards: 6,938/4,695. Par: 72/72. Course Rating: 73.8/68.0. Slope: 133/114. Greens Fee: $50/$90. Cart Fee: Included in greens fee. Walking Policy: Mandatory carts. Walkability: 2. Opened: 1993. Architect: Gene Bates. Season: Year-round. To obtain tee times: Call golf shop. Miscellaneous: Reduced fees (guests, twilight, juniors), range (grass), credit cards (MC, V), BF, FF. SP. ⊠ *4100 Riverwood Dr., Port Charlotte, 33953, Charlotte County, 45 mi from Sarasota,* ☎ *941/764–6661.* Rating: ★★★★½

Saddlebrook Resort. Facility Holes: 36. Greens Fee: $45/$120. Cart Fee: $25/person. Walking Policy: Mandatory carts. Season: Year-round. To obtain tee times: Call golf shop. Miscellaneous: Reduced fees (guests), range (grass), credit cards (AE, D, MC, V), BF, FF. R. ⊠ *5700 Saddlebrook Way, Wesley Chapel, 33543, Pasco County, 20 mi from Tampa,* ☎ *813/973–1111 or 800/729–8383,* ⊕ *www.saddlebrookresort.com.*

Palmer Course. Holes: 18. Yards: 6,469/5,187. Par: 71/71. Course Rating: 71.9/71.0. Slope: 134/127. Opened: 1986. Architect: Arnold Palmer/Ed Seay. Rating: ★★★★

Saddlebrook Course. Holes: 18. Yards: 6,564/4,941. Par: 70/70. Course Rating: 72.0/70.6. Slope: 127/126. Opened: 1976. Architect: Dean Refram. Rating: ★★★★

Sandestin Resort. Facility Holes: 73. Cart Fee: Included in greens fee. Walkability: 2. Season: Year-round. Miscellaneous: Range (grass), lodging (740 rooms), credit cards (AE, D, DC, MC, V), BF, FF. R. ⊠ *9300 Hwy. 98 W, Destin, 32541, Walton County, 20 mi from Fort Walton Beach,* ☎ *850/267–8155 or 800/277–0800,* ⊕ *www.sandestin.com.*

Baytowne Golf Club at Sandestin. Holes: 18. Yards: 6,890/4,862. Par: 72/72. Course Rating: 73.4/68.5. Slope: 127/114. Greens Fee: $65/$109. Walking Policy: Mandatory carts. Opened: 1985. Architect: Tom Jackson. High: Feb.–May. To obtain tee times: Call up to 14 days in advance. Miscellaneous: Reduced fees (guests, twilight, juniors). Rating: ★★★★½

Burnt Pines Course. Holes: 18. Yards: 7,046/5,950. Par: 72/72. Course Rating: 74.1/68.7. Slope: 135/124. Greens Fee: $85/$149. Walking Policy: Unrestricted walking. Opened: 1994. Architect: Rees Jones. To obtain tee times: Call up to 14 days in advance. Miscellaneous: Reduced fees (guests, juniors). Notes: Ranked 29th in 1999 Best in State; 64th in 1996 America's Top 75 Upscale Courses; 3rd in 1995 Best New Resort Courses. Rating: ★★★★

Links Course. Holes: 18. Yards: 6,710/4,969. Par: 72/72. Course Rating: 72.8/69.2. Slope: 124/115. Greens Fee: $65/$109. Walking Policy: Unrestricted walking. Opened: 1977. Architect: Tom Jackson. To obtain tee times: Call golf shop. Miscellaneous: Reduced fees (guests, twilight, juniors). Rating: ★★★★

The Raven Golf Club. Holes: 19. Yards: 6,910/5,065. Par: 71/71. Course Rating: 73.8/70.6. Slope: 138/126. Greens Fee: $79/$129. Walking Policy: Unrestricted walking. Opened: 2000. Architect: Robert Trent Jones, Jr. High: Feb.–Aug. To obtain tee times: Call up to 14 days in advance. Miscellaneous: Reduced fees (guests, twilight, juniors). Special Notes: 16th hole has twin par 3s played on alternate days. Rating: ★★★★

Sandridge Golf Club. Facility Holes: 36. Greens Fee: $16/$42. Cart Fee: Included in greens fee. Walking Policy: Walking at certain times. Architect: Ron Garl. Season: Year-round. High: Jan.–Apr. To obtain tee times: Call up to 2 days in advance. Miscellaneous: Reduced fees (weekdays, twilight, juniors), range (grass), credit cards (D, MC, V), BF, FF. PU. ✉ *5300 73rd St., Vero Beach, 32967, Indian River County, 70 mi from West Palm Beach,* ☎ *772/770–5000.*

Lakes Course. Holes: 18. Yards: 6,200/4,625. Par: 72/72. Course Rating: 70.1/67.1. Slope: 128/112. Walkability: 2. Opened: 1992. Rating: ★★★★

Southern Dunes Golf & Country Club. Holes: 18. Yards: 7,727/5,200. Par: 72/72. Course Rating: 74.7/72.4. Slope: 135/126. Greens Fee: $35/$110. Cart Fee: Included in greens fee. Walking Policy: Mandatory carts. Walkability: 3. Opened: 1993. Architect: Steve Smyers. Season: Year-round. High: Jan.–Apr. To obtain tee times: Call up to 30 days in advance. Miscellaneous: Reduced fees (weekdays, guests, twilight, juniors), range (grass/mats), credit cards (AE, D, MC, V), BF, FF. PU. ✉ *2888 Southern Dunes Blvd., Haines City, 33844, Polk County, 20 mi from Orlando,* ☎ *863/421–4653 or 800/632–6400,* ⊕ *www.southerndunes. com.* Rating: ★★★★½

Tiburon Golf Club. Facility Holes: 27. Greens Fee: $60/$165. Cart Fee: Included in greens fee. Walking Policy: Mandatory carts. Walkability: 2. Opened: 1998. Architect: Greg Norman. Season: Year-round. High: Jan.–Apr. To obtain tee times: Call up to 60 days in advance. Miscellaneous: Reduced fees (guests, twilight, juniors), range (grass), lodging (257 rooms), credit cards (AE, MC, V), BF, FF. R. **North/South.** Holes: 18 combo. Yards: 7,170/5,140. Par: 72/72. Course Rating: 74.5/70.6. Slope: 137/124. **North/West.** Holes: 18 combo. Yards: 7,193/5,148. Par: 72/72. Course Rating: 74.5/69.6. Slope: 135/122. **West/South.** Holes: 18 combo. Yards: 6,977/4,988. Par: 72/72. Course Rating: 73.4/70.4. Slope: 131/123. ✉ *2620 Tiburon Dr., Naples, 34109,* ☎ *239/594–2040 or 888/387–8417,* ⊕ *www.wcigolf.com.* Rating: ★★★★½

Tournament Players Club at Heron Bay. Holes: 18. Yards: 7,268/4,961. Par: 72/72. Course Rating: 74.9/68.7. Slope: 133/113. Greens Fee: $41/$140. Cart Fee: Included in greens fee. Walking Policy: Unrestricted walking. Walkability: 3. Opened: 1996. Architect: Mark McCumber/Mike Beebe. Season: Year-round. High: Dec.–Apr. To obtain tee times: Call golf shop. Miscellaneous: Reduced fees (weekdays, twilight, juniors), metal spikes, range (grass), lodging (224 rooms), credit cards (AE, DC, MC, V). PU. ✉ *11801 Heron Bay Blvd., Coral Springs, 33076, Broward*

County, 20 mi from Fort Lauderdale, ☎ *954/796–2000 or 800/511–6616,* ⊕ *www.pgatour.com.* Rating: ★★★★

Tournament Players Club at Sawgrass. Facility Holes: 36. Cart Fee: $31/person. Walking Policy: Walking with Caddie. Season: Year-round. High: Feb.–May. To obtain tee times: Call golf shop. Miscellaneous: Reduced fees (juniors), range (grass), lodging (515 rooms), credit cards (AE, DC, MC, V, resort charge card). R. ⊠ *110 TPC Blvd., Ponte Vedra Beach, 32082, St. Johns County, 15 mi from Jacksonville,* ☎ *904/273–3235,* ⊕ *www.pgatour.com.*

Stadium Course. Holes: 18. Yards: 6,937/5,000. Par: 72/72. Course Rating: 73.3/64.9. Slope: 138/120. Greens Fee: $115/$280. Walkability: 3. Opened: 1980. Architect: Pete Dye. Notes: Ranked 63rd in 2001–2002 America's 100 Greatest; 2nd in 2001 Best in State. Rating: ★★★★½

Valley Course. Holes: 18. Yards: 6,864/5,126. Par: 72/72. Course Rating: 72.8/68.7. Slope: 130/120. Greens Fee: $85/$145. Walkability: 4. Opened: 1987. Architect: Pete Dye/Bobby Weed. Rating: ★★★★

Tournament Players Club of Tampa Bay. Holes: 18. Yards: 6,898/5,036. Par: 71/71. Course Rating: 73.4/69.1. Slope: 130/119. Greens Fee: $71/$136. Cart Fee: Included in greens fee. Walking Policy: Mandatory carts. Walkability: 3. Opened: 1991. Architect: Bobby Weed/Chi Chi Rodriguez. Season: Year-round. High: Jan.-Mar. To obtain tee times: Call golf shop. Miscellaneous: Reduced fees (weekdays, twilight, juniors), range (grass), credit cards (AE, DC, MC, V), BF, FF. PU. ⊠ *5300 W. Lutz Lake Fern Rd., Lutz, 33549, Hillsborough County, 15 mi from Tampa,* ☎ *813/949–0090,* ⊕ *www.playatpc.com.* Rating: ★★★★

Turnberry Isle Resort & Club. Facility Holes: 36. Greens Fee: $75/$125. Cart Fee: $24/person. Walking Policy: Mandatory carts. Walkability: 2. Opened: 1971. Architect: Robert Trent Jones. Season: Year-round. To obtain tee times: Call up to 60 days in advance. Miscellaneous: Reduced fees (twilight), range (grass/mats), lodging (395 rooms), credit cards (AE, MC, V), BF, FF. R. ⊠ *19999 W. Country Club Dr., Aventura, 33180, Dade County, 10 mi from Fort Lauderdale,* ☎ *305/933–6929 or 800/327–7028,* ⊕ *www.turnberryisle.com.*

North Course. Holes: 18. Yards: 6,348/4,991. Par: 70/70. Course Rating: 70.3/67.9. Slope: 127/107. Rating: ★★★★

South Course. Holes: 18. Yards: 7,003/5,581. Par: 72/72. Course Rating: 73.7/71.3. Slope: 136/116. Rating: ★★★★½

University Park Country Club. Facility Holes: 27. Greens Fee: $50/$100. Cart Fee: Included in greens fee. Walking Policy: Walking at certain times. Walkability: 1. Opened: 1991. Architect: Ron Garl. Season: Year-round. High: Nov.–Apr. To obtain tee times: Call up to 3 days in advance. Miscellaneous: Reduced fees (weekdays, twilight), range (grass/mats), credit cards (D, MC, V), BF, FF. SP. **Course 1 & 19.** Holes: 18 combo. Yards: 7,247/5,576. Par: 72/72. Course Rating: 74.4/71.8. Slope: 132/122. **Course 10 & 1.** Holes: 18 combo. Yards: 7,001/5,511. Par: 72/72. Course Rating: 73.6/71.6. Slope: 138/126. **Course 19 & 10.** Holes: 18 combo. Yards: 7,152/5,695. Par: 72/72. Course Rating: 74.0/72.4. Slope: 134/124. ⊠ *7671 Park Blvd., University Park, 34201, Manatee County, 1 mi from Sarasota,* ☎ *941/359–9999.* Rating: ★★★★

Viera East Golf Club. Holes: 18. Yards: 6,720/5,428. Par: 72/72. Course Rating: 72.1/71.0. Slope: 129/122. Greens Fee: $29/$59. Cart Fee: Included in greens fee. Walking Policy: Walking at certain times. Walkability: 1. Opened: 1994. Architect: Joe Lee. Season: Year-round. High:

Jan.–Apr. To obtain tee times: Call up to 7 days in advance. Miscellaneous: Reduced fees (guests, twilight, juniors), range (grass), credit cards (AE, D, MC, V), BF, FF. PU. ✉ *2300 Clubhouse Dr., Viera, 32955, Brevard County, 5 mi from Melbourne,* ☎ *321/639–6500 or 888/ 843–7232,* ⊕ *www.vieragolf.com.* Rating: ★★★★

Walt Disney World Resort. Facility Holes: 99. Season: Year-round. High: Jan.–Apr. To obtain tee times: Call golf shop. Miscellaneous: Reduced fees (guests, twilight), metal spikes, range (grass/mats), credit cards (AE, D, DC, MC, V, Disney Card). R. ✉ *3451 Golf View Dr., Lake Buena Vista, 32830, Orange County, 20 mi from Orlando Airport,* ☎ *407/ 939–4653,* ⊕ *www.disney.go.com/disneyworld.*

Eagle Pines Golf Course. Holes: 18. Yards: 6,772/4,838. Par: 72/72. Course Rating: 72.3/68.0. Slope: 131/111. Greens Fee: $104/$154. Cart Fee: Included in greens fee. Opened: 1992. Architect: Pete Dye. Rating: ★★★★½

Lake Buena Vista Golf Course. Holes: 18. Yards: 6,819/5,194. Par: 72/ 73. Course Rating: 72.7/69.4. Slope: 128/120. Greens Fee: $94/$140. Cart Fee: Included in greens fee. Walking Policy: Walking at certain times. Walkability: 1. Opened: 1972. Architect: Joe Lee. Rating: ★★★★

Magnolia Golf Course. Holes: 18. Yards: 7,190/5,232. Par: 72/72. Course Rating: 73.9/70.5. Slope: 133/123. Greens Fee: $94/$145. Cart Fee: Included in greens fee. Walkability: 1. Opened: 1971. Architect: Joe Lee. Rating: ★★★★

Osprey Ridge Golf Course. Holes: 18. Yards: 7,101/5,402. Par: 72/72. Course Rating: 73.9/70.5. Slope: 135/122. Greens Fee: $114/$179. Cart Fee: Included in greens fee. Walkability: 4. Opened: 1992. Architect: Tom Fazio. Rating: ★★★★½

Palm Golf Course. Holes: 18. Yards: 6,957/5,311. Par: 72/72. Course Rating: 73.0/70.4. Slope: 133/124. Greens Fee: $94/$140. Cart Fee: Included in greens fee. Opened: 1971. Architect: Joe Lee. Rating: ★★★★

Waterlefe Golf & River Club. Holes: 18. Yards: 6,908/4,770. Par: 72/72. Course Rating: 73.8/68.0. Slope: 141/119. Greens Fee: $30/$85. Cart Fee: Included in greens fee. Walking Policy: Walking at certain times. Walkability: 2. Opened: 2000. Architect: Ted McAnlis. Season: Year-round. High: Jan.–May. To obtain tee times: Call up to 7 days in advance. Miscellaneous: Reduced fees (weekdays), range (grass), credit cards (AE, MC, V), BF, FF. PU. ✉ *1022 Fish Hook Cove, Bradenton, 34202, Manatee County, 40 mi from Tampa,* ☎ *941/744–9771,* ⊕ *www. wcigolf.com.* Rating: ★★★★

The Westin Innisbrook Resort. Facility Holes: 72. Cart Fee: Included in greens fee. Walking Policy: Mandatory carts. Walkability: 3. Season: Year-round. High: Nov.–Mar. To obtain tee times: Call golf shop. Miscellaneous: Reduced fees (guests, juniors), range (grass/mats), lodging (1000 rooms), credit cards (AE, D, MC, V), BF, FF. R. ✉ *36750 Hwy. 19 N., Palm Harbor, 34684, Pinellas County, 25 mi from Tampa,* ☎ *727/ 942–2000,* ⊕ *www.westin-innisbrook.com.*

Copperhead Course. Holes: 18. Yards: 7,291/5,537. Par: 71/71. Course Rating: 74.4/72.0. Slope: 140/128. Greens Fee: $120/$220. Opened: 1972. Architect: Lawrence Packard/Roger Packard. Notes: Ranked 25th in 2001 Best in State. Rating: ★★★★

Island Course. Holes: 18. Yards: 6,999/5,578. Par: 72/72. Course Rating: 74.1/73.0. Slope: 132/129. Greens Fee: $100/$180. Opened: 1970. Architect: Lawrence Packard. Rating: ★★★★½

Windsor Parke Golf Club. Holes: 18. Yards: 6,740/5,206. Par: 72/72. Course Rating: 71.9/69.4. Slope: 133/123. Greens Fee: $50/$70. Cart Fee: Included in greens fee. Walking Policy: Walking at certain times. Walkability: 1. Opened: 1991. Architect: Arthur Hills. Season: Year-round. High: Feb.–Apr. To obtain tee times: Call up to 14 days in advance. Miscellaneous: Reduced fees (weekdays, twilight, seniors, juniors), range (grass), credit cards (AE, D, MC, V), BF, FF. SP. ⊠ *13823 Sutton Park Dr. N., Jacksonville, 32224, Duval County, 12 mi from Jacksonville,* ☎ *904/223–4653,* ⊕ *www.windsorparke.com.* Rating: ★★★★

World Golf Village. Facility Holes: 36. Cart Fee: Included in greens fee. Walking Policy: Unrestricted walking. Walkability: 2. Season: Year-round. High: Mar.-Apr. To obtain tee times: Call up to 30 days in advance. Miscellaneous: Reduced fees (guests, twilight, juniors), metal spikes, range (grass), lodging (600 rooms), credit cards (AE, D, MC, V), BF, FF. R. ⊠ *1 King and Bear Dr., St. Augustine, 32092, St. Johns County, 5 mi from St. Augustine,* ☎ *904/940–6200,* ⊕ *www.kingandbeargolf.com.*

Slammer & Squire. Holes: 18. Yards: 6,940/5,001. Par: 72/72. Course Rating: 73.8/69.1. Slope: 135/116. Greens Fee: $50/$120. Opened: 1998. Architect: Bobby Weed. Rating: ★★★★

World Woods Golf Club. Facility Holes: 45. Greens Fee: $50/$85. Cart Fee: Included in greens fee. Walking Policy: Unrestricted walking. Walkability: 4. Opened: 1993. Architect: Tom Fazio. Season: Year-round. To obtain tee times: Call golf shop. Miscellaneous: Reduced fees (weekdays, twilight), range (grass), credit cards (AE, D, DC, MC, V), BF, FF. R. ⊠ *17590 Ponce De Leon Blvd., Brooksville, 34614, Hernando County, 60 mi from Tampa,* ☎ *352/796–5500,* ⊕ *www.worldwoods.com.*

Pine Barrens Course. Holes: 18. Yards: 6,902/5,301. Par: 71/71. Course Rating: 73.7/70.9. Slope: 140/132. Notes: Ranked 97th in 2000–2001 America's 100 Greatest; 5th in 2001 Best in State; 9th in 1996 America's Top 75 Upscale Courses. Rating: ★★★★½

Rolling Oaks Course. Holes: 18. Yards: 6,985/5,245. Par: 72/72. Course Rating: 73.5/70.7. Slope: 136/128. Notes: Ranked 24th in 2001 Best in State; 73rd in 1996 America's Top 75 Upscale Courses. Special Notes: Also has 9-hole executive course. Rating: ★★★★½

INDEX

NOTES

NOTES

NOTES

NOTES

NOTES

NOTES

NOTES

NOTES

NOTES

FODOR'S KEY TO THE GUIDES

America's guidebook leader publishes guides for every kind of traveler.
Check out our many series and find your perfect match.

FODOR'S GOLD GUIDES
America's favorite travel-guide series
offers the most detailed insider reviews
of hotels, restaurants, and attractions
in all price ranges, plus great background information, smart tips, and
useful maps.

COMPASS AMERICAN GUIDES
Stunning guides from top local writers
and photographers, with gorgeous
photos, literary excerpts, and colorful
anecdotes. A must-have for culture
mavens, history buffs, and new
residents.

FODOR'S CITYPACKS
Concise city coverage in a guide plus a
foldout map. The right choice for urban
travelers who want everything under
one cover.

FODOR'S EXPLORING GUIDES
Hundreds of color photos bring your
destination to life. Lively stories lend
insight into the culture, history, and
people.

FODOR'S TRAVEL HISTORIC AMERICA
For travelers who want to experience
history firsthand, this series gives in-
depth coverage of historic sights, plus
nearby restaurants and hotels. Themes
include the Thirteen Colonies, the Old
West, and the Lewis and Clark Trail.

FODOR'S POCKET GUIDES
For travelers who need only the
essentials. The best of Fodor's in
pocket-size packages for just $9.95.

FODOR'S FLASHMAPS
Every resident's map guide, with 60
easy-to-follow maps of public transit,
parks, museums, zip codes, and more.

FODOR'S CITYGUIDES
Sourcebooks for living in the city:
thousands of in-the-know listings for
restaurants, shops, sports, nightlife,
and other city resources.

FODOR'S AROUND THE CITY WITH KIDS
Up to 68 great ideas for family days,
recommended by resident parents.
Perfect for exploring in your own
backyard or on the road.

FODOR'S HOW TO GUIDES
Get tips from the pros on planning the
perfect trip. Learn how to pack, fly
hassle-free, plan a honeymoon or cruise,
stay healthy on the road, and travel
with your baby.

FODOR'S LANGUAGES FOR TRAVELERS
Practice the local language before you
hit the road. Available in phrase books,
cassette sets, and CD sets.

KAREN BROWN'S GUIDES
Engaging guides—many with easy-to-
follow inn-to-inn itineraries—to the
most charming inns and B&Bs in the
U.S.A. and Europe.

BAEDEKER'S GUIDES
Comprehensive guides, trusted since
1829, packed with A–Z reviews and
star ratings.

OTHER GREAT TITLES FROM FODOR'S
Baseball Vacations, The Complete
Guide to the National Parks, Family
Vacations, Golf Digest's Places to Play,
Great American Drives of the East,
Great American Drives of the West,
Great American Vacations, Healthy
Escapes, National Parks of the West,
Skiing USA.